Transforming Learning. Transforming Lives.

CENTERING ON
Value

CENTERING ON
Choice

CENTERING ON
Engagement

WADSWORTH
CENGAGE Learning

is committed to vailable, with the support ormat you choose.

Learning Solutions – Training & Support

We're your partner in the classroom – online and off.

CengageCourse delivers dynamic, interactive ways to teach and learn using relevant, engaging content with an accent on flexibility and reliability. When you select the **CengageCourse** solution that matches your needs, you'll discover ease and efficiency in teaching and course management.

CourseCare is a revolutionary program providing you with exceptional services and support to integrate your Cengage Learning Digital Solution into your course. Our dedicated team of digital solutions experts will partner with you to design and implement a program built around your course needs. We offer in-depth, one-on-one professional training of our programs and access to a 24/7 Technical Support website. **CourseCare** provides one-on-one service every step of the way—from finding the right solution for your course to training to ongoing support—helping you to drive student engagement.

For more than a decade, **TeamUP Faculty Programs** have helped faculty reach and engage students through peer-to-peer consultations, workshops, and professional development conferences. Our team of **Faculty Programs Consultants and Faculty Advisors** provide implementation training and professional development opportunities customized to your needs.

Access, Rent, Save, and Engage.
Save up to 60%

CENGAGE brain.com

At CengageBrain.com students will be able **to save up to 60%** on their course materials through our full spectrum of options. Students will have the option to **Rent** their textbooks, purchase print **textbooks, eTextbooks,** or individual **eChapters** and **Audio Books** all for substantial savings over average retail prices.

CengageBrain.com also includes single sign-on access to Cengage Learning's broad range of homework and study tools, and features a selection of free content.

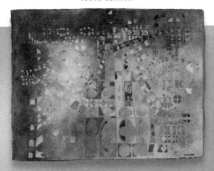

David Sue

Derald Wing Sue

Stanley Sue

Diane M. Sue

Understanding Abnormal Behavior, 10th Edition

ISBN 13: 978-1-111-83459-3
Copyright 2013
reflects **our commitment** to you and your students:

CENTERING ON
Value

BBC Motion Gallery, ABC® videos, PowerLecture™ for easy lecture preparation, and other teaching and learning supplements are available to enhance your course.

CENTERING ON
Choice

Choose the format that best suits the needs of you and your students:

- Cengage Learning Advantage Edition (loose-leaf format)

- Cengage Learning eBook

- Chapter-by-chapter purchase

- Textbook rental

CENTERING ON
Engagement

Innovative, interactive media resources such as **CengageNOW™** and **CourseMate** engage students in the excitement of psychology.

WADSWORTH
CENGAGE Learning™

Content Accessibility
Get the content you value in the format you want.
Save up to 60%

In addition to casebound or paperbound format, many titles are offered in alternate, money-saving formats **(30-60% off),** such as:

- Rental

- Loose-Leaf

- Compact Editions

- Black-and-white

- eTextbooks

- eChapters

- Audiobooks

Custom Solutions
Tailor content to fit your course.

It's now **simpler** than ever to create your perfect customized learning **solution** drawing from Cengage Learning's breadth of content and depth of **services** providing **sophisticated results** for you, your students and your course.

Enrichment Modules: Consider adding enrichment content to your text or digital solution to expand coverage on special topics. Some popular module options are Career and Study Skills.

Presets: Our Preset options provide alternate print and digital variations of traditional titles and are created based upon popular custom options that typically include a supplement or enrichment content bound into the book or included in the digital solution.

Gather > Build > Publish: With **CengageCompose** you can build your own text to meet specific course learning objectives. Gather what you need from our vast library of market-leading course books and other enrichment content. Build your book the way you want it organized, personalized to your students. Publish the title using easy to use tools that guarantee you will get what you have designed.

www.cengage.com/cengagecompose

Understanding
Abnormal Behavior

Tenth Edition

David Sue

Department of Psychology
Western Washington University

Derald Wing Sue

Department of Counseling and Clinical Psychology
Teachers College, Columbia University

Diane Sue

Private Practice

Stanley Sue

Professor of Psychology
Palo Alto University

WADSWORTH
CENGAGE Learning

Australia • Brazil • Japan • Korea • Mexico • Singapore • Spain • United Kingdom • United States

Understanding Abnormal Behavior,
Tenth Edition
David Sue, Derald Wing Sue, Diane Sue,
and Stanley Sue

Publisher: Jon-David Hague

Psychology Editor: Jaime Perkins

Developmental Editor: Tangelique Williams

Freelance Development Editor: Thomas Finn

Assistant Editor: Paige Leeds

Editorial Assistant: Jessica Alderman

Media Editor: Lauren Keyes

Marketing Manager: Christine Sosa

Marketing Assistant: Janay Pryor

Marketing Communications Manager: Laura
Localio

Content Project Manager: Charlene
M. Carpentier

Design Director: Rob Hugel

Art Director: Vernon Boes

Print Buyer: Karen Hunt

Rights Acquisitions Specialist: Tom
McDonough

Production Service: Graphic World Inc.

Text Designer: Cheryl Carrington

Photo Researcher: Bill Smith Group

Text Researcher: Karyn Morrison

Copy Editor: Graphic World Inc.

Illustrator: Graphic World Inc.

Cover Designer: Cheryl Carrington

Cover Image: Geoffrey Clements/Corbis

Compositor: Graphic World Inc.

For product information and technology assistance, contact us at
Cengage Learning Customer & Sales Support, 1-800-354-9706.

For permission to use material from this text or product,
submit all requests online at **www.cengage.com/permissions.**
Further permissions questions can be e-mailed to
permissionrequest@cengage.com.

Library of Congress Control Number: 2011939377

Student Edition:

ISBN-10: 1-111-83459-8

ISBN-13: 978-1-111-83459-3

Loose-leaf Edition:

ISBN-10: 1-111-83839-9

ISBN-13: 978-1-111-83839-3

Wadsworth
20 Davis Drive
Belmont, CA 94002-3098
USA

Cengage Learning is a leading provider of customized learning solutions with office locations around the globe, including Singapore, the United Kingdom, Australia, Mexico, Brazil, and Japan. Locate your local office at **www.cengage.com/global.**

Cengage Learning products are represented in Canada by Nelson Education, Ltd.

To learn more about Wadsworth, visit **www.cengage.com/Wadsworth**

Purchase any of our products at your local college store or at our preferred online store **www.CengageBrain.com.**

Printed in Canada
1 2 3 4 5 6 7 15 14 13 12 11

Brief Contents

Contents

3 Assessment and Classification of Abnormal Behavior   71

4 The Scientific Method in Abnormal Psychology   97

5 Anxiety and Obsessive-Compulsive and Related Disorders   121

6 Trauma and Stress-Related Disorders   157

7 Somatic Symptom and Dissociative Disorders   185

8 Depressive and Bipolar Disorders   213

13 Neurocognitive Disorders 381

14 Sexual Dysfunction and Gender Dysphoria 407

17 Legal and Ethical Issues in Abnormal Psychology 517

Features

Preface

The 10th edition of *Understanding Abnormal Behavior* has been completely revised to accommodate updated research and changes in the classification and diagnosis of mental disorders, including proposed changes in the American Psychiatric Association's *Diagnostic and Statistical Manual* (DSM-5). We have incorporated the latest information from the committee involved in the restructured organization of DSM-5 and the thirteen DSM-5 work groups (multi-disciplinary groups of professionals who have extensively reviewed scientific research on various mental health conditions) to guide our discussion of disorders throughout the text, including controversies and trends in the field. Many chapters have been significantly rewritten and reorganized. More than 1,600 new references have been added. The inclusion of an additional author, Diane M. Sue, with an academic background in neuropsychology and extensive practical experience working with children, adolescents, and families from a variety of socioeconomic, racial, ethnic, and linguistic backgrounds has strengthened our coverage of gender issues, disorders of childhood and adolescence, neurocognitive disorders, substance-use disorders, and depressive and bipolar disorders.

We continue to use and have expanded our discussion of the multipath model introduced in the previous edition. Thus, we once again emphasize the importance of considering biological, psychological, social, and sociocultural factors and their interactions in the etiology of mental disorders. Also, throughout the text, there is continued emphasis on the importance of multicultural issues in abnormal psychology, a topic that is increasingly salient given the growing diversity of the population. Topics of interest and relevance to college students (e.g., eating disorders, traumatic brain injuries in sports, suicide, and substance use in college populations) as well as contemporary issues in abnormal psychology, such as the influence of pharmaceutical companies in the treatment of mental disorders, are presented. This edition of our book provides current information on a variety of topics in the field of abnormal psychology, as illustrated by the new information added to each chapter.

New and Updated Coverage of the Tenth Edition

Our foremost objective in preparing this edition was to thoroughly update the content of the text and present the latest trends in research and clinical thinking, with a particular emphasis on the DSM revision. This has led to updated coverage of dozens of topics throughout the text, including the following:

Chapter 1—Abnormal Behavior

- Discussion of the proposed DSM-5 definition of mental disorders and its implications.
- New statistics on the incidence and prevalence of mental disorders.
- Revised section on the contextual, sociopolitical, and cultural limitations involved in defining mental disorders.
- Extension of cultural relativism and cultural universality with respect to the conceptualization of mental disorders.

- Discussion of new topics, including the role of spirituality and religion in mental health care, positive psychology and optimal psychological health, and trends in the use of psychopharmacology.

Chapter 2—Models of Abnormal Behavior

- Expanded multipath model coverage, including a focus on epigenetics and cultural neuroscience.
- Expanded coverage of the inadequacy of single etiological models.
- Updated discussion of the social and sociocultural etiological dimensions.
- New discussion of Shamanism and the role ancient healers played in defining and treating abnormal behaviors.
- Discussions of implicit bias, the relationship between brain function and aggression, and cultural neuroscience.

Chapter 3—Assessment and Classification of Abnormal Behavior

- Updated material on assessment, differential diagnosis, and classification of abnormal behavior.
- New discussion of mental status exams and their use, illustrated with a case study.
- Discussion of DSM-5 and controversies regarding the new classification system.
- Expanded coverage on the assessment of ethnic minorities.

Chapter 4—The Scientific Method in Abnormal Psychology

- Updated sections on scientific evidence, the scientific method, and research design.
- New discussions about autism and vaccines, cannabis use and psychoses, the use of identical twins in research, and ethical considerations in research.

Chapter 5—Anxiety and Obsessive-Compulsive and Related Disorders

- Complete reorganization to incorporate proposed DSM-5 changes.
- Discussion of obsessive-compulsive and related disorders, including obsessive-compulsive disorder, body dysmorphic disorder, hair-pulling disorder (trichotillomania), and skin-picking disorders.
- New discussion of hoarding disorder.
- Expanded multipath discussion regarding biological, psychological, social, and sociocultural factors involved in these disorders.

Chapter 6—Trauma and Stress-Related Disorders

- Expanded discussion about the physiological and psychological effects of stress.
- New discussion of trauma, post-traumatic stress disorder, and acute stress disorders.
- Expanded discussion of biological factors contributing to stress disorders.
- Updated section on psychophysiological disorders, including a focus on the relationship between stress and cancer.

Chapter 7—Somatic Symptom and Dissociative Disorders

- Complete reorganization of somatic disorders based on proposed DSM-5 changes.

- Discussion of complex symptom disorders, including functional neurological symptom disorder, factitious disorder, and factitious disorder imposed on another.
- Expanded coverage on the validity of dissociative disorders.

Chapter 8—Depressive and Bipolar Disorders

- Substantially revised and reorganized chapter incorporating a clear division between depressive and bipolar disorders, new diagnostic categories, and significantly updated research on etiological factors and treatment approaches.
- Discussion of new topics, including premenstrual dysphoric disorder, seasonal affective disorder, and mixed anxiety/depression.
- Expanded coverage of the biological underpinnings of depressive and bipolar disorders and gender differences in depression.
- New discussion of the overlap between bipolar disorders and schizophrenia.
- New discussion regarding the use of computer-assisted technology in the treatment of depression and controversy over the use of antidepressant medications.

Chapter 9—Suicide

- Updated statistics on suicide and sociodemographic correlates of suicide risk.
- New focus on suicide on college campuses.
- New discussion of suicide among youth and children.
- Updated presentation regarding individual rights regarding suicide and legal implications.
- Expanded multipath analysis of suicide.

Chapter 10—Eating Disorders

- Up-to-date information on eating disorders, including obesity.
- New critical analysis of the use of underweight models and digitally "enhanced" photos in advertising.
- Increased coverage of muscle dysphoria.
- Updated discussion of the Web presence of groups promoting anorexia and bulimia.

Chapter 11—Substance-Use Disorders

- Chapter completely rewritten and reorganized, with substantial new research on a variety of topics.
- Inclusion of many new statistics and charts illustrating the prevalence of substance use and abuse, with a particular focus on alcohol.
- Significantly expanded discussion regarding the abuse of illicit and prescription drugs.
- Expanded discussion of drug and alcohol use among college students.
- New focus on relapse prevention and the efficacy of treatment for the most commonly abused substances.
- Coverage of new topics, including dissociative anesthetics, inhalants, energy drinks, and caffeinated alcoholic beverages.
- New critical discussions about cognitive-enhancing drugs and alcohol prevention programs.

Chapter 12—Schizophrenia and Other Psychotic Disorders

- Updated research on schizophrenia and explanations of new diagnostic categories.

- New discussion of attenuated psychosis syndrome and psychotic disorder not otherwise specified.
- Updated discussion of the controversy regarding Morgellons disease.
- New critical discussion about the marketing of atypical antipsychotic medications.

Chapter 13—Neurocognitive Disorders

- Completely rewritten and reorganized chapter, including new research and incorporation of changes in diagnostic categories.
- Discussion of new diagnostic categories (including mild neurocognitive disorder and major neurocognitive disorder) and disorders such as Lewy Body Dementia.
- Continued focus on neurocognitive disorders across the lifespan, with a strong emphasis on lifestyle changes that can help prevent the development of degenerative disorders such as dementia.
- Expanded section on traumatic brain injury.
- New discussions about sports concussions, brain injuries sustained in combat, and genetic testing for neurocognitive disorders.

Chapter 14—Sexual Dysfunction and Gender Dysphoria

- New statistics and data on the sexual behavior of men and women in the United States.
- Discussion of "hypersexual disorder."
- Updated terminology related to sexual disorders, gender incongruence, and paraphilias.
- New discussion of the controversy "Are transgendered people suffering from a mental disorder?"
- Updated application of multipath model to sexual disorders.

Chapter 15—Personality Psychopathology

- Chapter completely revised to incorporate the significant changes proposed in the DSM revision.
- Revised definition of personality disorders with emphasis on assessing impairment of self and interpersonal functioning.
- Discussion of six personality types (antisocial, avoidant, borderline, narcissistic, obsessive-compulsive, and schizotypal) and five personality trait domains that form the basis of diagnosing a personality disorder.
- Providing the rationale for diagnostic changes in personality psychopathology.
- Discussion of the DSM-5 change of focus from a categorical to a hybrid dimensional-categorical model of personality assessment.
- New and detailed use of the multipath model to explain the antisocial personality type.
- Application of personality traits to a case vignette.

Chapter 16—Disorders of Childhood and Adolescence

- Substantial reorganization of the chapter to reflect a more developmental perspective.
- Multiple case descriptions illustrating various disorders.
- New topics in the chapter include neurodevelopmental disorders, childhood anxiety, depressive and bipolar disorders, childhood post-traumatic stress disorder, reactive attachment disorder, and tics and Tourette's syndrome.

- Discussion of new diagnostic categories, including non-suicidal self-injury, disruptive mood dysregulation disorder, disinhibited social engagement disorder, and the callous and unemotional subtype of conduct disorder.

Chapter 17—Legal and Ethical Issues in Abnormal Psychology

- New cases illustrating dilemmas posed by the interaction of psychology and the law.
- New focus on the therapeutic and legal implications of disclosure by clients in regard to violent behaviors and/or child abuse.
- New findings on therapists predicting dangerousness in clients.
- Updated profiles of mass murderers and serial killers.

In writing and revising this book, we have sought to engage students in the exciting process of understanding abnormal behavior and the ways that mental health professionals study and attempt to treat various disorders. In pursuing this goal, we have been guided by three major objectives:

- to provide students with scholarship of the highest quality,
- to offer an evenhanded treatment of abnormal psychology as both a scientific and a clinical endeavor, giving students the opportunity to explore topics thoroughly and responsibly, and
- to make our book inviting and stimulating to a wide range of students by focusing on topics such as eating disorders, traumatic head injury in sports, and the abuse of alcohol and other substances frequently encountered by college populations.

Our Approach

We take an eclectic, evidence and research-based, multicultural approach to understanding abnormal behavior, drawing on important contributions from various disciplines and theoretical perspectives. The text covers the major categories of disorders proposed for the updated *Diagnostic and Statistical Manual of Mental Disorders* (DSM-5), but it is not a mechanistic reiteration of the DSM. We believe that different combinations of life experiences and constitutional factors influence mental disorders, and we project this view throughout the text. This combination of factors is demonstrated in our multipath model, which was introduced in our 9th edition. There are several elements to our multipath model. First, possible contributors to mental disorders are divided into four dimensions: biological, psychological, social, and sociocultural. Second, factors in the four dimensions can interact and influence each other in any direction. Third, different combinations and interactions within the four dimensions can cause abnormal behaviors. Fourth, many disorders appear to be heterogeneous in nature; therefore, there may be different versions of a disorder (a spectrum of the disorder). Finally, distinctly different disorders (such as anxiety and depression) can be caused by similar factors.

Sociocultural factors, including cultural norms, values, and expectations, are given special attention in our multipath model. We are convinced that cross-cultural comparisons of abnormal behavior and treatment methods can greatly enhance our understanding of disorders; cultural and gender influences are emphasized throughout the text. *Understanding Abnormal Behavior* was the first textbook on abnormal psychology to integrate and emphasize the role of multicultural factors. Although many texts have since followed our lead, the 10th edition continues to provide the most extensive coverage and integration of multicultural models, explanations, and concepts available. Not only do we discuss how changing demographics increase the importance of multicultural psychology, we also introduce multicultural models of psychopathology in the opening chapters and address multicultural issues throughout the text whenever research findings and theoretical formulations allow. Such an approach adds richness to students' understanding of mental disorders. As psychologists (and professors), we know that learning is enhanced whenever material is presented in a lively and engaging manner. We therefore provide case vignettes and clients' descriptions of their experiences to complement and illustrate symptoms of various disorders and research-based explanations. Our goal is to encourage students to think critically rather than to merely assimilate a collection of facts and theories. As a result, we hope that students will develop an appreciation of the study of abnormal behavior.

Special Features

The 10th edition includes a number of new features as well as features that were popularized in earlier editions and that, in some cases, have been revised and enhanced. These features are aimed at aiding students in organizing and integrating the material in each chapter.

As previously noted, our multipath model provides a framework through which students can understand the origins of mental disorders. The model is introduced in Chapter 2 and applied throughout the book, with multiple figures highlighting how biological, psychological, social, and sociocultural factors contribute to the development of various disorders.

Critical Thinking boxes provide factual evidence and thought-provoking questions that raise key issues in research, examine widely held assumptions about abnormal behavior, or challenge the student's own understanding of the text material.

Controversy boxes deal with controversial issues, particularly those with wide implications for our society. These boxes stimulate critical thinking, evoke alternative views, provoke discussion, and allow students to better explore the wider meaning of abnormal behavior in our society.

Myth versus Reality discussions challenge the many myths and false beliefs that have surrounded the field of abnormal behavior and help students realize that beliefs, some of which may appear to be "common sense," must be checked against scientific facts and knowledge.

Did You Know? boxes found throughout the book provide fascinating, at-a-glance research-based tidbits for students.

Chapter Outlines and Focus Questions, appearing in the first pages of every chapter, provide a framework and stimulate active learning.

Integrated Chapter Summaries keyed to the Focus Questions provide students with a concise recap of the chapter's most important concepts via brief answers to the chapter's opening Focus Questions.

New and updated case studies and examples allow issues of mental health and mental disorders to "come to life" for students and instructors. Many cases are taken from journal articles and actual clinical files.

Streamlined disorder charts provide snapshots of disorders in an easy-to-read format.

Key terms are highlighted in the text and appear in the margins.

Ancillaries

This text is supported by a rich set of supplementary materials designed to enhance the teaching and learning experience. Several new components make use of new instructional technologies.

For Instructors

- *Instructor's Resource Ma*nual: The *Instructor's Resource Manual* includes an extended chapter outline, learning objectives, discussion topics, classroom exercises, handouts, and lists of supplementary readings and multimedia resources. *The Instructor's Resource Manual* is available on the instructor Web site, www.cengage.com/psychology/sue, and is also available in print. Please consult your sales representative for further details.

- *Test Bank*: The *Test Bank* is a static test bank in Word that contains 100 multiple-choice and 3 essay questions (with sample answers) per chapter. Each question is labeled with the corresponding text page reference as well as the type of question being asked for easier test creation. *The Test Bank* is available on the *Diploma Testing CD-ROM* and in print. Please consult your sales representative for further details.

- *Psychology CourseMate. Understanding Abnormal Behavior* includes *Psychology CourseMate*, a complement to your textbook. *Psychology CourseMate* includes:
  - an interactive eBook
  - interactive teaching and learning tools including:
    - Quizzes
    - Flashcards
    - Videos
    - and more
  - Engagement Tracker, a first-of-its-kind tool that monitors student engagement in the course

  Go to login.cengage.com to access these resources, and look for this icon 🖥 which denotes a resource available within *CourseMate*.

- *PowerLecture* with *JoinIn*™ for *Understanding Abnormal Behavior*, 10/e: The fastest, easiest way to build powerful, customized, media-rich lectures, *PowerLecture* provides a collection of book-specific PowerPoint® lecture and class tools to enhance the educational experience.

- *CengageNOW. CengageNOW* offers all of your teaching and learning resources in one intuitive program organized around the essential activities you perform for class—lecturing, creating assignments, grading, quizzing, and tracking student progress and performance. *CengageNOW's* intuitive "tabbed" design allows you to navigate to all key functions with a single click and a unique homepage tells you just what needs to be done and when. *CengageNOW*, in most cases, provides students access to an integrated eBook, interactive tutorials, videos, animations, games, and other multimedia tools that help them get the most out of your course.

- WebTutor™ on Blackboard and WebCT: Jump-start your course with customizable, rich, text-specific content within your Course Management System. Whether you want to Web-enable your class or put an entire course online, WebTutor delivers. WebTutor offers a wide array of resources, including media assets, quizzing, weblinks, and more! Visit webtutor.cengage.com to learn more.

- *ABC Video: Abnormal Psychology*
  Vol 1 978-0-495-59639-4
  Vol 2 978-0-495-60494-5

For Students

- *Study Guide*: The *Study Guide,* available on the student Web site and in print, provides a complete review of each chapter with chapter outlines, learning objectives, fill-in-the-blank review of key terms, and multiple-choice questions. Answers to test questions include an explanation for both the correct answer and incorrect answers.

- *Case Studies in Abnormal Psychology*: *Case Studies in Abnormal Psychology* by Clark Clipson, California School of Professional Psychology, and Jocelyn Steer, San Diego Family Institute, contains 16 studies and can be shrink-wrapped with the text at a discounted package price. Each case represents a major psychological disorder. After a detailed history of each case, critical-thinking questions prompt students to formulate hypotheses and interpretations based on the client's symptoms, family and medical background, and relevant information. The case proceeds with sections on assessment, case conceptualization, diagnosis, and treatment outlook, and is concluded by a final set of discussion questions.

- *Abnormal Psychology in Context: Voices and Perspectives*: *Abnormal Psychology in Context: Voices and Perspectives* is a supplementary text written by David Sattler, College of Charleston; Virginia Shabatay, Palomar College; and Geoffrey Kramer, Grand Valley State University, that features 40 cases and can be shrink-wrapped with the text at a discounted package price. This unique collection contains first-person accounts and narratives written by individuals who live with a psychological disorder and by therapists, relatives, and others who have direct experience with someone suffering from a disorder. These vivid and engaging narratives are accompanied by critical-thinking questions and a psychological concept guide that indicates which key terms and concepts are covered in each reading.

Acknowledgments

We continue to appreciate the critical feedback received from reviewers and colleagues. The following individuals helped us prepare the 10th edition by sharing valuable insights, opinions, and recommendations.

    Sandra K. Arntz, Northern Illinois University

    Jay Brown, Texas Wesleyan University

    Jeffrey D. Burke, University of Pittsburgh

    Catherine Chambliss, Ursinus College

    Alice L. Godbey, Daytona State College

    Deborah Huerta, The University of Texas at Brownsville

    Arlene Lacombe, St. Joseph's University

    Vicki Lucey, Las Positas College

    Polly McMahon, Spokane Falls Community College

    Jeffrey J. Pedroza, Santa Ana College

    Jessica L. Yokley, University of Pittsburgh

We also thank the reviewers of the previous editions of *Understanding Abnormal Behavior.*

    Julia C. Babcock, University of Houston

    Betty Clark, University of Mary-Hardin

    Irvin Cohen, Hawaii Pacific University & Kapiolani Community College

Lorry Cology, Owens Community College
Bonnie J. Ekstrom, Bemidji State University
Greg A. R. Febbraro, Drake University
Kate Flory, University of South Carolina
David M. Fresco, Kent State University
Jerry L. Fryrear, University of Houston, Clear Lake
Michele Galietta, John Jay College of Criminal Justice
Christina Gordon, Fox Valley Technical College
Robert Hoff, Mercyhurst College
George-Harold Jennings, Drew University
Kim L. Krinsky, Georgia Perimeter College
Brian E. Lozano, Virginia Polytechnic Institute and State University
Jan Mohlman, Rutgers University
Sherry Davis Molock, George Washington University
Rebecca L. Motley, University of Toledo
Gilbert R. Parra, University of Memphis
Kimberly Renk, University of Central Florida
Mark Richardson, Boston University
Alan Roberts, Indiana University
Daniel L. Segal, University of Colorado at Colorado Springs
Tom Schoeneman, Lewis & Clark College
Michael D. Spiegler, Providence College
Ma. Teresa G. Tuason, University of North Florida
Theresa A. Wadkins, University of Nebraska, Kearney
Susan Brooks Watson, Hawaii Pacific University
Fred Whitford, Montana State University

We also wish to acknowledge the support, and high quality of work done by Tom Finn and Tangelique Williams, Development Editors; Jaime Perkins, Executive Editor; Charlene Carpentier, Content Project Manager; Jessica Alderman, Editorial Assistant; Paige Leeds, Assistant Editor; and Vernon Boes, Art Director. We also thank text designer Cheryl Carrington, text researcher Karyn Morrison, and photo researcher Sarah Bonner. We are particularly grateful for the patience, efficiency, and creativity shown by production editor Kate Mannix.

D. S.

D. W. S.

D. M. S.

S. S.

About the Authors

David Sue is Professor Emeritus of Psychology at Western Washington University, where he is an associate of the Center for Cross-Cultural Research. He has served as the director of both the Psychology Counseling Clinic and the Mental Health Counseling Program. He and his wife co-authored the book *Counseling and Psychotherapy in a Diverse Society* and he is co-author of *Counseling the Culturally Diverse: Theory and Practice*. He received his Ph.D. in Clinical Psychology from Washington State University. His research interests revolve around multicultural issues in individual and group counseling. He enjoys hiking, snowshoeing, traveling, and spending time with his family.

Derald Wing Sue is Professor of Psychology and Education in the Department of Counseling and Clinical Psychology at Teachers College, Columbia University. He has written extensively in the field of counseling psychology and multicultural counseling/therapy and is author of a best-selling book *Counseling the Culturally Diverse: Theory and Practice*. Dr. Sue has served as president of the Society of Counseling Psychology and the Society for the Psychological Study of Ethnic Minority Issues and has received numerous awards for teaching and service. He received his doctorate from the University of Oregon and is married and the father of two children. Friends describe him as addicted to exercise and the Internet.

Diane M. Sue received her Ed.S. in School Psychology and her Ph.D. in Educational Psychology from the University of Michigan, Ann Arbor. She has worked as a school psychologist and counselor, and with adults needing specialized care for mental illness and neurocognitive disorders. She has taught courses at Western Washington University as an adjunct faculty member. She received the Washington State School Psychologist of the Year Award, the Western Washington University College of Education Professional Excellence Award, and has co-authored the book *Counseling and Psychotherapy in a Diverse Society*. Her areas of expertise include child and adolescent psychology, neuropsychology, and interventions with ethnic minority children and adolescents. She enjoys travel and spending time with friends and family.

Stanley Sue is Professor of Psychology and Director of the Center for Excellence in Diversity at Palo Alto University. From 1971 to 1981, he was Assistant and Associate Professor of Psychology at the University of Washington; Professor of Psychology at University of California, Los Angeles (1981–1996); and Professor of Psychology at University of California–Davis (1996–2010) and now Emeritus Distinguished Professor. He recently served as president of the Western Psychological Association and has received the Award for Distinguished Contributions to Diversity in Clinical Psychology from the American Psychological Association. His hobbies include working on computers and swimming.

1

Abnormal Behavior

I n 2007, college student Seung Hui Cho used two semiautomatic hand-guns on the Virginia Tech campus to kill twenty-seven students and five faculty members, wound twenty-five others, and commit suicide with a shot to his head. The incident was the deadliest mass shooting in modern U.S. history and left many grief-stricken, horrified, and baffled at Cho's actions. The Virginia Tech rampage began in the early morning hours, when Cho shot a female student and male resident assistant in a dormitory. Approximately two hours later, he entered a building where classes were in session, chaining the doors to prevent easy escape. There he fired some 174 rounds, killing and wounding many students and professors as he moved from classroom to classroom. Chaos ensued as students fled for their lives (summarized from the Virginia Tech Review Panel, August 2007).

I n an attempt to make sense out of an apparently "senseless" act, many questions were asked. What could have motivated Cho to carry out such a heinous deed and take so many innocent lives? Why did he commit suicide? Was he deranged, a psychopathic killer, or high on drugs? Were there warning signs that he was homicidal or suicidal? Did he suffer from a mental disorder? Would therapy or medication have helped him? Did his race, culture, and immigration status play any role in his actions?

These questions are extremely difficult to answer for a number of reasons. First, we do not know enough about the causes of abnormal behavior and mental disorders to arrive at a definitive answer. Psychopathology, or abnormal behavior, is not the result of any singular cause but an interaction of many factors. Most mental disorders have multiple contributors, a fact that we discuss in the next chapter.

Second, Cho did not survive the incident, so it was impossible to assess his state of mind. As a result, we must rely on secondary sources such as health or school records; observations by peers, family, and acquaintances; and any other available data (suicide notes, essays, pictures, and media communications) to construct a portrait of his state of mind. Sadly, the Virginia Tech massacre illustrates how complex the study of abnormal psychology is in real life.

In a sense, the purpose of this book, *Understanding Abnormal Behavior,* is to help you answer such questions. To do so, however, requires us to first examine some basic aspects of the study of abnormal behavior, including some of its history and emerging changes in the

1

© HO/Reuters/Corbis

Seung Hui Cho Photo Sent to NBC on Day of the Massacre

Was Cho mentally disturbed? At college he became known as the "question mark kid" because he would only put down a question mark for his name. He would not respond when greeted, sat for hours in his dorm room staring out the window, and referred to an imaginary girlfriend by the name of "Jelly," a supermodel who lived in outer space. At one time, he informed a roommate that he was vacationing with Vladimir Putin, the president of Russia.

field. Periodically, throughout this chapter, we use the Cho case to illustrate complex issues in the mental health field.

The Concerns of Abnormal Psychology

Abnormal psychology is an area of scientific study that attempts to describe, explain, predict, and modify behaviors that are considered strange or unusual. Its subject matter ranges from the bizarre and spectacular to the more commonplace—from the violent homicides, suicides, and "perverted" sexual acts that are widely reported by the news media to unsensational (but more prevalent) concerns such as depression, sleep disturbances, and anxiety.

Describing Abnormal Behavior

Understanding a particular case of abnormal behavior begins with systematic observations by an attentive professional. These observations, usually paired with the results of the person's psychological history, become the raw material for a psychodiagnosis, an attempt to describe, assess, and systematically draw inferences about an individual's psychological disorder.

For example, several years before the massacre, Cho received a psychiatric evaluation at a mental health clinic in Virginia. Because we have limited access to these records, the precise nature of the therapist's observations is tentative. Usually, however, mental status exams are conducted by mental health professionals to ascertain the degree to which clients are in contact with reality, whether they suffer from hallucinations or delusions, and whether they are potentially dangerous. Based on clinical observations, analysis of Cho's history, and possibly psychological testing, the therapist concluded that Cho was of "imminent danger to self or others," "mentally ill," and in need of hospitalization. The precise psychiatric diagnosis is unknown because of confidentiality laws. Instead of

psychopathology a term clinical psychologists use as a synonym for *abnormal behavior*

abnormal psychology the scientific study whose objectives are to describe, explain, predict, and modify behaviors that are considered strange or unusual

psychodiagnosis an attempt to describe, assess, and systematically draw inferences about an individual's psychological disorder

2

commitment to a mental institution, a court magistrate ordered only outpatient treatment. Cho, however, never complied with the order to seek therapy.

Explaining Abnormal Behavior

To explain abnormal behavior, the psychologist first identifies possible causes for the described behavior. This information, in turn, bears heavily on the program of treatment chosen. One popular explanation of Cho's behavior was that he was high on drugs. An autopsy, however, revealed no evidence of alcohol or drugs present in his system. Nevertheless, Cho's background suggests many other possible causes for his rampage:

Did You Know?

Some have speculated that cultural factors may have played a significant role in Cho's intense anger toward others. Few are aware that his younger sister attended Princeton; as the oldest son, he attended "only" a state school. In traditional Korean families, many parents expect their children, especially an older son, to be admitted to a top-notch institution, to achieve, and to do well, bringing pride and honor to the family name. To do otherwise would be a source of unimaginable shame and disgrace. As a result, Cho may have harbored resentment toward Virginia Tech and fellow students because it was a constant reminder of his failure.

- As a child, Cho was described by family members as mute, cold, and shy. His mother speculated that he was autistic, a condition associated with social isolation, delayed speech, and repetitive behavior that is believed to have a strong constitutional component. Some relatives say that he was different from birth and suggest that his problem was biological in nature.
- Cho was often the subject of teasing and cruel taunts by classmates, probably because of his unusual behaviors. He was often bullied, called names, mocked, and told to "go back to China." Although he seldom showed anger, rumors abounded that he kept a "hit list" of students he wanted to kill.
- Cho was a twenty-three-year-old South Korean citizen with U.S. permanent resident status in Virginia. He immigrated to this country at age eight with his parents and sister. Some believe he never adequately adjusted to his new life in the United States and encountered culture conflicts. He felt isolated, alone, and alienated from others. Unable or unwilling to make connections with people, Cho had difficulty distinguishing between fantasy and reality.
- Cho grew up in poverty. His father was a self-employed secondhand bookstore owner who made little money and moved his family to the United States to improve their financial state. Cho appeared very self-conscious about being poor and resented "rich kids," materialism, and hedonism. His writings and video recordings sent to NBC News contained extremely hostile statements toward those "with money."

From these snippets of Cho's life, many explanations for his rampage can be offered. There was something biologically wrong with him from birth; he could not tolerate the merciless teasing and bullying; his alienation from a new culture created social isolation and resentment; and his poverty made him envious and angry toward more affluent students. Depending on your viewpoint, some explanations may appear more valid than others. As we will see in the next chapter, no one explanation is sufficient to explain the complexity of the human condition; normal and abnormal behaviors result from a combination of factors.

Predicting Abnormal Behavior

If a therapist can correctly identify the source of a client's difficulty, he or she should be able to predict the kinds of problems the client will face during therapy and the symptoms the client will display. Many believe that there was sufficient evidence to predict that Cho was likely to take the lives of others and his own based on a number of reported events:

- Cho was involved in three stalking incidents on the Virginia Tech campus. All three involved female students in whom he developed brief but intense interest. His contacts were made through instant messaging on his computer. He sent them annoying messages, made an uninvited appearance at one student's dorm room, and left graffiti on her bulletin board. Cho was warned by campus police to cease his unwanted contacts with them. He apparently acceded to their warnings.

- Several professors reported that Cho was menacing and had a mean streak and that his writings were often intimidating, obscene, and violent. His writings, they contend, "dripped with anger," were graphic and disturbing, and possessed macabre violence. One professor became so fearful for her own safety and that of others that she reported Cho to the student affairs office, the dean's office, and campus police. Each unit responded that nothing could be done if Cho made no overt threats against others.

In light of these reports, why was Cho allowed to stay on campus? Why was he allowed to purchase firearms despite having a diagnosed mental condition? Why did mental health professionals not intervene more quickly? There appear to be several reasons. First, civil commitment, or involuntary confinement, represents an extreme decision that has major implications for an individual's civil liberties. Our legal system operates under the assumption that people are innocent until proven guilty. Locking someone up before he or she commits a dangerous act potentially violates that person's civil rights. Second, although the therapist who assessed Cho proved to be correct in declaring Cho dangerous, a judge concluded outpatient therapy was sufficient. In addition, even if Cho had cooperated and sought treatment, his therapy would have been confidential unless the therapist became aware of a clear and present danger to others.

Modifying Abnormal Behavior

Abnormal behavior may be modified through therapy, which is a program of systematic intervention designed to improve a client's behavioral, affective (emotional), and/or cognitive state. For example, many therapists believe Cho could have been helped and the mass killings prevented if he had received treatment. Allowing Cho an opportunity to

David Harry Stewart/Stone/Getty Images

Intervening Through Therapy

therapy a program of systematic intervention whose purpose is to improve a client's behavioral, affective (emotional), and/or cognitive state

Group therapy is a widely used form of treatment for many problems, especially those involving interpersonal relationships. In this group session, participants are learning to develop new and adaptive social skills in coping with social problems rather than relying on alcohol or drugs to escape the stresses of life.

get in touch with and to vent his anger may have reduced his chances of doing harm to others. Some mental health professionals might also recommend family therapy or social skills training. Those who see Cho's condition as caused by a chemical imbalance might prescribe medication, such as antipsychotic drugs. Many, like the psychiatrist who assessed him, might have recommended hospitalization to allow for additional assessment and comprehensive treatment.

As we shall see shortly, psychologists focus first on understanding the cause of abnormal behavior and from there plan treatment. Just as there are many ways to explain abnormal behaviors, there are many possible ways to conduct therapy and many professional helpers offering their services. Along with the demand for mental health treatment, the numbers and types of qualified helping professionals have grown. In the past, mental health services were offered primarily by psychiatrists, psychologists, and psychiatric social workers. The list of service providers has expanded rapidly. Table 1.1 lists the

TABLE 1.1   The Mental Health Professions

Clinical psychologists	• Must hold a Ph.D. or a Psy.D. (doctor of psychology) degree, a more practitioner-oriented degree. • Undergo training includes course work in psychopathology, personality, diagnosis, psychological testing, psychotherapy, and human physiology. • Work in a variety of settings, including academic settings, but most commonly provide therapy to clients in hospitals and clinics and in private practice.
Counseling psychologists	• Have academic and internship requirements that are similar to those for clinical psychologists, but the emphasis differs. • Are more immediately concerned with the study of life problems in relatively normal people. • Are more likely to be found in educational settings than in hospitals and clinics.
Forensic psychologists	• Are concerned with the interface of psychology and the legal system. • Provide psychological services that are both clinical and legal in nature. • Are similar to clinical psychologists but have formed a distinct specialty in their own right.
Health psychologists	• Are concerned with understanding how biology, behavior, and social context influence health and illness. • Work with other medical professionals in clinical, public health, and community health settings.
Marriage and family counselors and therapists	• Are specialists with their own professional organization, journals, and state licensing requirements. • Undergo training that usually includes a master's degree in counseling or therapy and many hours of supervised clinical experience.
Mental health counselors	• Work in a variety of settings. • Receive intensive training in personal, emotional, vocational, and human development. • Have their own professional association. • Must meet many hours of supervised clinical experience and possess a master's degree.
Psychiatrists	• Hold M.D. degrees. • Undergo the four years of medical school required for an M.D., along with an additional three or four years of training in psychiatry. • Until recently, were the only mental health professionals who could prescribe medication.
Psychoanalysts	• Usually hold either M.D. or Ph.D. degrees. • Receive intensive training in the theory and practice of psychoanalysis at an institute devoted to the field. • Undergo their own analysis by an experienced analyst as part of their training.
Psychiatric social workers	• Are trained in a school of social work, usually in a two-year graduate program leading to a master's degree. • Work in family counseling services or community agencies, where they specialize in intake (assessment and screening of clients), take psychiatric histories, and deal with other agencies.
School psychologists	• Are concerned with the cognitive and emotional development of students in educational settings. • Focus on the processes of learning and on human development as it applies to the educational process. • May hold a master's or a doctoral degree. • Are often employed by school districts to assess and intervene with emotional and learning difficulties.

qualifications, training, and workplace settings of various mental health professionals. As you can see, students desiring to enter practice can choose from a variety of professional careers.

Determining Abnormality

Implicit in our discussion is the one overriding concern of abnormal psychology: abnormal behavior itself. But what exactly is abnormal behavior, and how do psychologists define a mental disorder? The *Diagnostic and Statistical Manual of Mental Disorders* (DSM), the most widely used classification system of mental disorders, defines abnormal behavior as

> a behavioral or psychological syndrome or pattern that reflects an underlying psychobiological dysfunction, that is associated with distress (e.g., a painful symptom) or disability (i.e., impairment in one or more important areas of functioning) and is not merely an expectable response to common stressors or losses. (www.dsm5.org)

This definition is quite broad and raises many questions. First, when is a syndrome or pattern of behavior significant enough to have meaning? From early descriptions of Cho in elementary school, his behavioral patterns were noticed but apparently were not considered significant (that is, not associated with pathology). He was a good student in math and English, quiet in class, and not disliked or feared by classmates. Some teachers even viewed him as a model example of compliant and appropriate classroom behavior. It was only much later that Cho's withdrawn behaviors became pronounced.

Second, what constitutes "present distress" and "painful symptoms"? We have limited access to psychiatric records, but there is little evidence suggesting Cho felt distressed or was looking for psychological help. Some say that because he took his own life, he must have been depressed. However, as we will see in Chapter 9, the relationship of suicide to depression is complex. Certainly, however, we can speculate that his intense anger might have been distressful. Is it possible to have a mental disorder without any feelings of distress or discomfort? For example, those who commit antisocial acts such as rape, murder, or robbery may not feel remorseful; rather, they may be quite contented with their acts.

Third, what criteria do we use in ascertaining an underlying psychobiological dysfunction and not merely an expectable response to common stressors? Again, it is obvious to us that Cho met this criterion due to his long history of atypical behavior and because he killed himself and others. But Cho's action was an extreme one, far outside normative standards. Despite problems in defining abnormal behavior, practitioners tend to agree that it represents behavior that departs from some norm and that harms the affected individual or others. Nearly all definitions of abnormal behavior use some form of statistical average to gauge deviations from normative standards. Four major means of judging psychopathology include *distress, deviance* (bizarreness), *dysfunction* (inefficiency in behavioral, affective, and/or cognitive domains), and *dangerousness.*

Distress

Most people who seek the help of therapists are suffering psychological distress that may show up physically and/or psychologically. We know that many physical conditions have a strong psychological component; among them are disorders such as asthma and hypertension, as well as physical symptoms such as fatigue, pain, and heart palpitations. In the psychological realm, distress is also manifested in extreme or prolonged emotional reactions such as anxiety and depression. Of course, it is normal for a person to feel depressed after suffering a loss or a disappointment. But if the reaction is so intense, exaggerated, and

abnormal behavior a behavioral or psychological syndrome or pattern that reflects an underlying psychobiological dysfunction, that is associated with distress or disability, and that is not merely an expectable response to common stressors or losses

prolonged that it interferes with the person's capacity to function adequately, it is likely to be considered abnormal.

Deviance

Deviance is most closely related to using a statistical average. Statistical criteria equate normality with those behaviors that occur most frequently in the population. Abnormality is therefore defined in terms of those behaviors that occur least frequently. Bizarre or unusual behavior is an abnormal deviation from an accepted standard of behavior (such as an antisocial act) or a false perception of reality (such as a hallucination or delusion). This criterion can be extremely subjective; it depends on the individual being diagnosed, on the diagnostician, and on the particular cultural context.

Certain sexual acts, criminal behavior, and homicide are examples of acts that our society considers deviant. But social norms are far from static, and behavioral standards cannot be considered absolute. Changes in our attitudes toward human sexuality provide a prime example. Many American magazines and films now openly exhibit the naked human body, and topless and bottomless nightclub entertainment is hardly newsworthy. Various sex acts are explicitly portrayed in NC-17-rated movies, and women are freer to question traditional sex roles and to act more assertively in initiating sex. Such changes in attitudes make it difficult to subscribe to absolute standards of normality.

Nevertheless, some behaviors are judged abnormal in most situations. Among these are severe disorientation, hallucinations, and delusions. *Disorientation* is confusion with regard to identity, place, or time. People who are disoriented may not know who they are, where they are, or what historical era they are living in. *Hallucinations* are false impressions—either pleasant or unpleasant—that involve the senses. People who have hallucinations may hear, feel, or see things that are not really there, such as seeing loved ones who have passed away, voices accusing them of vile deeds, insects crawling on their bodies, or monstrous apparitions. *Delusions* are false beliefs steadfastly held by the individual despite contradictory objective evidence. A *delusion of grandeur* is a belief that one is an exalted personage, such as Jesus Christ or Joan of Arc; a *delusion of persecution* is a belief that one is controlled by others or is the victim of a conspiracy.

Dysfunction

In everyday life, people are expected to fulfill various roles. Emotional problems sometimes interfere with the performance of these roles, and the resulting role dysfunction may be used as an indicator of abnormality. Thus one way to assess dysfunction is to compare an individual's performance with the requirements of a role.

Another related way to assess dysfunction is to compare an individual's performance with his or her potential. For example, concern develops when an individual with an IQ score of 150 is failing in school. Similarly, a productive worker who suddenly becomes unproductive may be experiencing emotional stress. The major weakness of this approach is that it is difficult to accurately assess potential. How do we know whether a person is performing at his or her peak? To answer such questions, psychologists, educators, and the business sector have relied heavily on testing. Tests of specific abilities and intelligence are attempts to assess potential and to predict performance in schools or jobs.

AP Images/Richmond Times-Dispatch/Dean Hoffmeyer

Societal Norms and Deviance

Societal norms often affect our definitions of normality and abnormality. When social norms begin to change, standards used to judge behaviors or roles also shift. Here we see four male nurses in an overwhelmingly female occupation. In the past, being a male nurse would have been regarded as less than masculine. Role reversals in employment, hobbies, sports, and other activities, however, are becoming more acceptable over time.

Dangerousness

Predicting the dangerousness of clients to themselves and others has become an inescapable part of clinical practice (Haggard-Grann, 2007; Scott & Resnick, 2009). Ever since the landmark California Supreme Court ruling (*Tarasoff v. Regents of the University of California,* 1976) requiring therapists to assess the dangerousness of clients (to themselves and others) and to protect any intended victim, psychologists have attempted to devise risk-assessment procedures and to ascertain what actions a therapist must take to comply with "a duty to protect." Certainly, the case of Cho is a graphic example of the need for mental health professionals to accurately assess the risk of violence. Yet, as we shall see in later chapters, this is a tall order. Despite the fear that persons suffering from a mental disorder might become violent, it is a statistical rarity (Corrigan & Watson, 2005). Furthermore, predicting dangerousness is not easy. One of the strongest risk factors, for example, is previous violent behavior. Yet, as we know, there is no evidence of violent behavior in Cho's history.

Abnormal Behavior in Context: Sociopolitical and Cultural Limitations

Nearly all criteria used to define abnormality involve a statistical deviation from some normative standard. Doing so, however, presents many problems. One problem mentioned previously is that statistical criteria are static and fail to take into account differences in place, time, and community standards. Another is that statistical criteria do not provide any basis for distinguishing between desirable and undesirable deviations from the norm. An IQ score of 100 is considered normal or average. But what constitutes an abnormal deviation from this average? More important, is abnormality defined in only one direction or in both? An IQ score of 55 is considered abnormal by most people, but should people with IQ scores of 145 or higher also be considered abnormal? How does one evaluate such personality traits as assertiveness and dependence in terms of statistical criteria? If normality is defined as whatever occurs most frequently in the population, then wouldn't common, yet undesirable traits like anxiety be considered normal? What about people who strike out in new directions—artistically, politically, or intellectually? May they not be seen as candidates for psychotherapy simply because they do not conform to normative behavior? What about unpopular political positions? This latter fear has been expressed by psychiatrist Thomas Szasz who claims that mental illness is both a myth and a political construction.

Mental Illness as a Sociopolitical Construction

> In my opinion, mental illness is a myth. People we label "mentally ill" are not sick, and involuntary mental hospitalization is not treatment. It is punishment. . . . The fact that mental illness designates a deviation from an ethical rule of conduct, and that such rules vary widely, explains why upper-middle-class psychiatrists can so easily find evidence of "mental illness" in lower-class individuals; and why so many prominent persons in the past fifty years or so have been diagnosed by their enemies as suffering from some types of insanity. Barry Goldwater was called a paranoid schizophrenic . . . Woodrow Wilson a neurotic . . . Jesus Christ, according to two psychiatrists . . . was a born degenerate with a fixed delusion system. (Szasz, 1970, pp. 167–168)

Thomas Szasz's (1987) assertions that mental illness is a myth, a fictional creation by society used to control and change people, are a radical departure from conventional beliefs. According to Szasz, people may suffer from "problems in living," not from "mental illness." His argument stems from three beliefs: (1) that abnormal behavior is so labeled because it is different, not necessarily because it is a reflection of "illness"; (2) that unusual belief systems are not necessarily wrong; and (3) that abnormal behavior is frequently a reflection of something wrong with society rather than with the individual.

According to Szasz, individuals are labeled "mentally ill" because their behaviors violate the social order and their beliefs challenge the prevailing wisdom of the times. Szasz finds the concept of mental illness to be dangerous and a form of social control used by those in power. Hitler branded Jews as abnormal. Political dissidents in many countries, including both China and the former Soviet Union, have often been cast as mentally ill. And the history of slavery indicates that African Americans who tried to escape their white masters were often labeled as suffering from *drapetomania,* defined as a sickness that makes the person desire freedom.

Few mental health professionals would take the extreme position advocated by Szasz, but his arguments highlight an important area of concern. Those who diagnose behavior as abnormal must be sensitive to individual value systems, societal norms and values, and potential sociopolitical ramifications.

Multicultural Limitations in Determining Abnormality

Perhaps one of the strongest criticisms of abnormality definitions comes from the multicultural perspective. If deviations from the majority are considered abnormal, then many ethnic and racial minorities who show strong cultural differences from the majority could be classified as abnormal. When we use a statistical definition, the dominant or most influential group generally determines what constitutes normality and abnormality. Multiculturalists contend that all behaviors, whether normal or abnormal, originate from a cultural context. Psychologists are increasingly recognizing that this is an inescapable conclusion and that culture plays a major role in our understanding of human behavior.

AP Images/James A. Finley

Determining What's Abnormal

By most people's standards, the full-body tattoos of these three men would probably be considered unusual at best and bizarre at worst. Yet despite the way their bodies appear, these three openly and proudly display them at the National Tattoo Convention. Such individuals may be very "normal" and functional in their work and personal lives. This leads to the an important question: What constitutes abnormal behavior, and how do we recognize it?

But what is culture? There are many definitions of "culture." For our purposes, *culture* is the configuration of shared learned behavior that is transmitted from one generation to another by members of a particular group; the components of culture include the values, beliefs, and attitudes embedded in a group's worldview and symbolized by artifacts, roles, expectations, and institutions (Sue & Sue, 2008a). Three important points should be emphasized:

1. Culture is not synonymous with *race* or *ethnic group*. Jewish, Polish, Irish, and Italian Americans represent diverse ethnic groups whose individual members may share a common racial classification. Yet their cultural contexts may differ substantially from one another. Likewise, an Irish American and an Italian American, despite their different ethnic heritages, may share the same cultural context.

2. Every society or group that shares and transmits behaviors to its members possesses a culture. European Americans, African Americans, Latino/Hispanic Americans, Asian Americans/Pacific Islanders, Native Americans, and other social groups within the United States have cultures. A strong argument can be made that people with hearing impairments also possess a culture (Cheyne, 2010) and "signing" represents a language. Others go further by indicating that people with disabilities are the largest minority group in the United States and that they share and transmit learned behaviors and thus have their own culture (Artman & Daniels, 2010).

3. Culture is a powerful determinant of worldviews (Sue & Sue, 2008a). It affects how normal and abnormal behaviors are defined and how disorders encountered by members of that culture are treated.

These three points give rise to a major problem: one group's definition of mental illness may not be shared by another. This contradicts the traditional view of abnormal psychology, which is based on cultural universality—the assumption that there exists a fixed set of mental disorders whose obvious manifestations cut across cultures (Eshun & Gurung, 2009; McGoldrick, Giordano, & Garcia-Preto, 2005). This psychiatric tradition dates back to Emil Kraepelin (discussed later in this chapter), who believed that depression, sociopathic behavior, and especially schizophrenia were universal disorders that appeared in all cultures and societies. From this flowed the belief that a disorder such as depression is similar in origin, process, and manifestation in all societies and, therefore, no modifications in diagnosis and treatment need be made; Western concepts of normality and abnormality can be considered universal and equally applicable across cultures.

In contrast to the traditional view of cultural universality, the principle of cultural relativism emphasizes that lifestyles, cultural values, and worldviews affect the expression and determination of behavior, thus underscoring the importance of culture and diversity in the manifestation of abnormal symptoms. For example, a body of research supports the conclusion that acting-out behaviors (aggressive acts, antisocial behaviors, and so forth) associated with mental disorders are much higher in the United States than in Asia and that even Asian Americans in the United States are less likely to express symptoms via acting out (Sue & Sue, 2008a; Yang & WonPat-Borja, 2007). Researchers have proposed that Asian cultural values (restraint of feelings, emphasis on self-control, and need for subtlety in approaching problems) all contribute to this restraint. Proponents of cultural relativism also point out that cultures vary in what they consider to be normal or abnormal behavior. In some societies and cultural groups, hallucinating (having false sensory impressions) is considered normal in specific situations. In the United States, hallucinating is generally perceived to be a manifestation of a disorder.

Which view is correct? Should the criteria used to determine normality and abnormality be based on cultural universality or cultural relativism? Few mental health professionals today embrace the extreme of either position, although most gravitate toward one or the other. Proponents of cultural universality focus on the specifics of a disorder

cultural universality the assumption that a fixed set of mental disorders exists whose obvious manifestations cut across cultures

cultural relativism the belief that lifestyles, cultural values, and worldviews affect the expression and determination of behavior

Cultural Relativism

Cultural differences often lead to misunderstandings and misinterpretations. In a society that values technological conveniences and clothing that comes from the runways of modern fashion, the lifestyles and cultural values of others may be perceived as strange. The Amish, for example, continue to rely on traditional modes of transportation (horse and buggy). And women in both the Amish and Islamic cultures wear simple, concealing clothing; in their circumstances, dressing in any other way would be considered deviant. Revealing clothes are not allowed in sunbathing or swimming.

and minimize cultural factors. Proponents of cultural relativism focus on the culture and on how the disorder is manifested given the cultural context. Both views have validity. Clearly, some disorders manifest similarly across cultures. Similarly, it is clear that cultural values and characteristics of a society affect how mental disorders manifest.

A more fruitful approach to studying multicultural criteria of abnormality is to explore two questions:

- What is universal in human behavior that is also relevant to understanding psychopathology?
- What is the relationship between cultural norms, values, and attitudes and the incidence and manifestation of psychological disorders?

These are important questions that we hope you will ask as we continue our journey into the field of abnormal psychology. In Chapter 2, we address these questions by presenting a multipath model that takes into consideration biological, psychological, social, and sociocultural dimensions in understanding the complexity of the human condition.

The Frequency and Burden of Mental Disorders

A student once asked one of the authors, "How crazy is this nation?" This question, put in somewhat more scientific terms, has occupied psychologists for some time. Psychiatric epidemiology, the study of the prevalence of mental illness in a society, provides insights into factors that contribute to the occurrence of specific mental disorders. To address this question, some terms need to be clarified. The prevalence of a disorder indicates the percentage of people in a population who suffer from a disorder at a given point in time; lifetime prevalence refers to the percentage of people in the population who have had a disorder at some point in their life. Incidence refers to the onset or occurrence of a given disorder over some period of time. From this information, we can find out how frequently or infrequently various disturbances occur in the population. We can also consider how the prevalence of disorders varies by ethnicity, gender, and age and whether current mental health practices are effective. See Figure 1.1 for the statistical breakdown of one-year prevalence rates.

psychiatric epidemiology the study of the prevalence of mental illness in a society

prevalence the percentage of people in a population who suffer from a disorder at a given point in time

lifetime prevalence the percentage of people in the population who have had a disorder at some point in their life

incidence the onset or occurrence of a given disorder over some period of time

Figure 1.1

One year prevalence of mental disorders in adult Americans and lifetime prevalence of mental disorders in American adolescents.

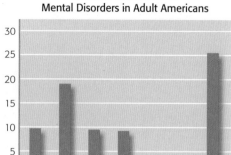

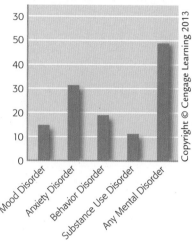

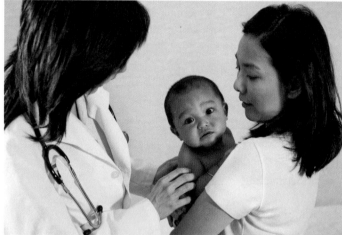

Mental disorders are believed to begin early in life. Well baby visits are important to monitor developmental milestones. Identifying possible biological, psychological, and social abnormalities is important to preventing the development of mental disorders in later life.

Did You Know?

About 15 percent of Canadians and 20 percent of U.S. Americans stated they would probably not seek care for mental health problems even if they suffered from a severe disorder! What accounts for these attitudes? It has been found that negative attitudes toward help-seeking behavior are most associated with socioeconomically challenged young, single, lesser-educated men (Jagdeo, Cox, Stein, & Sareen, 2009). Substance use and antisocial personalities were also associated with greater negative attitudes. Aversion to seek therapy may be associated with social stigma.

Mental disorders begin early in life. In a study investigating the lifetime prevalence of mental disorders in American youth (Merikangas et al., 2010), data from a face-to-face survey of more than 10,000 youth between the ages of 13 and 18 years revealed the following: nearly half of the youth met the criteria for at least one psychological disorder, and of this group, 40 percent met the criteria for an additional disorder. Anxiety disorder was the most common (31.9 percent), followed by behavior disorders (19.1 percent), mood disorders (14.3 percent), and substance use disorder (11.4 percent). Severe impairment or distress was reported by 22.2 percent of those found to have a mental disorder. Figure 1.1 summarizes prevalence data from these studies. What might account for the higher prevalence rates seen in the youth sample?

The cost and burden of mental disorders to our society are indeed a major source of concern. Not only do 25 percent of adults suffer from a diagnosable mental health condition in a given year, many more people suffer from "mental health problems" that do not meet the criteria for a mental disorder. These problems may be equally debilitating unless adequately treated.

These epidemiological findings are troubling, to say the least. Clearly, mental disturbances are widespread, and many persons are currently suffering from them. What is more troubling is that two-thirds of all people suffering from diagnosable mental disorders are not receiving or seeking mental health services (President's New Freedom Commission on Mental Health, 2003). In addition, spending on mental health services continues to decline.

Stereotypes about the Mentally Disturbed

Americans tend to be suspicious of people with mental disorders. Are those suffering from mental illness really maniacs who at any moment may be seized by uncontrollable urges to murder, rape, or maim? Such portrayals seem to emerge from the news media and the entertainment industry, but they are rarely accurate. Indeed, the Virginia

Tech incident must be seen in the context of realistic facts; Cho's actions are a statistical anomaly. Violence in people suffering from a mental disorder is a rarity (Corrigan & Watson, 2005; Grann & Langstrom, 2007). People with mental disturbances are subject to rampant stereotyping and popular misconceptions. It is worthwhile at this point to dispel the most common of these misconceptions or myths.

MYTH: Mentally disturbed people can always be recognized by their abnormal behavior.

REALITY: Mentally disturbed people are not always distinguishable from others on the basis of consistently unusual behavior. Even in an outpatient clinic or a psychiatric ward, distinguishing patients from staff on the basis of behavior alone is often difficult. There are two main reasons for this difficulty. First, as already noted, no sharp dividing line usually exists between normal and abnormal behavior. Second, even when people are suffering from some form of emotional disturbance, their difficulties may not always be detectable in their behavior.

MYTH: The mentally disturbed have inherited their disorders. If one member of a family has an emotional breakdown, other members will probably suffer a similar fate.

REALITY: The belief that insanity runs in certain families has caused misery and undue anxiety for many people. Heredity does play a role in some mental disorders, such as schizophrenia and mood disorders. However, evidence suggests that even though heredity may predispose an individual to certain disorders, environmental factors are also extremely important. This has led many mental health professionals to posit a biopsychosocial model of mental disorders in which disorders are the result of an interaction of biological, psychological, and social factors.

MYTH: Mentally disturbed people can never be cured and will never be able to function normally or hold jobs in the community.

REALITY: This erroneous belief has caused great distress to many people who have at some time been labeled mentally ill. Some have endured social discrimination and have been denied employment because of the public perception that "once insane, always insane." Unfortunately, this myth may discourage those experiencing emotional problems from seeking help. Nearly three-fourths of clients who are hospitalized with severe disorders will improve and go on to lead productive lives.

MYTH: People become mentally disturbed because they are weak willed. To avoid emotional disorders or cure oneself of them, one need only exercise will power.

REALITY: These statements show a lack of understanding regarding the nature of mental disorders. Needing help to resolve difficulties does not indicate a lack of will power. In fact, recognizing one's own need for help is a sign of strength rather than a sign of weakness. Many problems stem from situations not under the individual's control, such as the death of a loved one or loss of a job. Other problems stem from lifelong patterns of faulty learning; it is naive to expect that a simple exercise of will can override years of experience.

MYTH: Mental illness is always a deficit, and the person suffering from it can never contribute anything of worth until cured.

REALITY: Many persons who suffered from mental illness were never "cured," but they nevertheless made great contributions to humanity. Ernest Hemingway, one of the great writers of the twentieth century and winner of a Nobel Prize for Literature, suffered from lifelong depression, alcoholism, and frequent hospitalizations. The famous Dutch painter Vincent van Gogh produced great works of art despite the fact that he was severely disturbed. Not only did he lead an unhappy and tortured life, he also frequently heard voices and once cut off a piece of his left ear as a gift to a prostitute. Others, such as Pablo Picasso and Edgar Allan Poe, contributed major artistic and literary works while seriously disturbed. The point of these examples is not to illustrate that madness and genius go hand in hand but that individuals with mental illness can lead productive and worthwhile lives.

MYTH: Mentally disturbed people are unstable and potentially dangerous.

REALITY: This misconception has been perpetuated by the mass media. Many murderers featured on television are labeled "psychopathic," and the news media concentrate on the occasional mental patient who kills. However, the vast majority of individuals who are mentally ill do not commit crimes, do not harm others, and do not get into trouble with the law—and therefore are not news. According to epidemiologic surveys (Elbogen & Johnson, 2009), there is a small elevation of risk of violence, especially among individuals with a dual diagnosis (suffering from a mental disorder and substance abuse), but the risk is minimal (Eronen, Angermeyer, & Schulze, 1998; Swanson, 1994). Unfortunately, the myth persists.

MYTH VS. REALITY

© 20th Century Fox/Courtesy Everett Collection

Popular movie portrayals of mental disorders often perpetuate stereotypes and myths by showing the extremes in abnormality. In *Me, Myself, and Irene*, nice-guy cop Jim Carrey plays a person suffering from dissociative identity disorder.

biopsychosocial model a model in which mental disorders are the result of an interaction of biological, psychological, and social factors

Historical Perspectives on Abnormal Behavior

In this section and the next, we briefly review the historical development of Western thought concerning abnormal behavior. We must be aware, however, that our journey is necessarily culture-bound and that other civilizations have histories of their own.

It is clear that many current attitudes toward abnormal behavior, as well as modern ideas about its causes and treatment, have been influenced by early beliefs. In fact, some psychologists contend that modern societies have, in essence, adopted more sophisticated versions of earlier concepts. For example, the use of electroconvulsive therapy to treat depression is in some ways similar to ancient practices of exorcism in which the body was physically assaulted. The Greek physician Hippocrates believed 2,500 years ago that many abnormal behaviors were caused by imbalances and disorders in the brain and the body, a belief shared by many contemporary psychologists.

Most ideas about abnormal behavior are firmly rooted in the system of beliefs that operate in a given society at a given time. Abnormal psychology evolved from a humanistic and scientific explanation of abnormal behavior. It remains to be seen whether such an explanation will still be thought valid in decades to come. (Much of this history section is based on discussions of deviant behavior by Alexander & Selesnick, 1966; Hunter & Macalpine, 1963; Neugebauer, 1979; Spanos, 1978; and Zilboorg & Henry, 1941.)

Prehistoric and Ancient Beliefs

Prehistoric societies some half a million years ago did not distinguish sharply between mental and physical disorders. Abnormal behaviors, from simple headaches to convulsive attacks, were attributed to evil spirits that inhabited or controlled the afflicted person's body. According to historians, these ancient peoples attributed many forms of illness to demonic possession, sorcery, or the behest of an offended ancestral spirit. Within this system of belief, called *demonology,* the victim was usually held at least partly responsible for the misfortune.

It has been suggested that Stone Age cave dwellers may have treated behavior disorders with a surgical method called trephining, in which part of the skull was chipped away to provide an opening through which the evil spirit could escape. People may have believed that when the evil spirit left, the person would return to his or her normal state. Surprisingly, some trephined skulls have been found to have healed over, indicating that some patients survived this extremely crude operation. Some historians, however, do not believe trephining was a therapeutic intervention. Rather, they believe it was used to remove bone splinters and blood clots from combat blows to the head (Maher & Maher, 1985). This is consistent with findings that most trephined skulls were those of men, that the skulls possess fractures (suggesting a blow), and that the holes are usually on the left (resulting from a right-handed assailant).

Another treatment method used by the early Greeks, Chinese, Hebrews, and Egyptians was exorcism. In an exorcism, elaborate prayers, noises, emetics (drugs that induce vomiting), and extreme measures such as flogging and starvation were used to cast evil spirits out of an afflicted person's body.

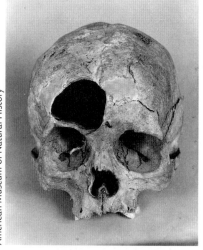

Trephining: Evidence of Therapy?

Anthropologists speculate that this human skull was evidence of trephining, the centuries-old manner of treating mentally disturbed individuals by chipping a hole in the skull to release the evil spirit causing the bizarre behaviors.

trephining a surgical method from the Stone Age in which part of the skull was chipped away to provide an opening through which an evil spirit could escape

exorcism treatment method used by the early Greeks, Chinese, Hebrews, and Egyptians in which prayers, noises, emetics, flogging, and starvation were used to cast evil spirits out of an afflicted person's body

Naturalistic Explanations (Greco-Roman Thought)

With the flowering of Greek civilization and its continuation into the era of Roman rule (500 B.C.–A.D. 500), naturalistic explanations gradually became distinct from supernatural ones. Early thinkers, such as Hippocrates (460–370 B.C.), a physician who is often called the father of medicine, actively questioned prevailing superstitious beliefs and proposed much more rational and scientific explanations for mental disorders.

Naturalistic explanations relied heavily on observations—the foundation of the scientific method. These explanations negated the intervention of demons in the development of abnormality and instead stressed organic causes. Fortunately, the treatment they prescribed for mental disorders tended to be more humane than previous treatments.

Hippocrates believed that, because the brain was the central organ of intellectual activity, deviant behavior was caused by brain pathology—that is, a dysfunction or disease of the brain. He also considered heredity and environment important factors in psychopathology. He classified mental illnesses into three categories—mania, melancholia, and phrenitis (brain fever)—and for each category, he gave detailed clinical descriptions of disorders such as paranoia, alcoholic delirium, and epilepsy. Many of his descriptions of symptoms are still used today, eloquent testimony to his keen powers of observation.

To treat melancholia, Hippocrates recommended tranquility, moderate exercise, a careful diet, abstinence from sexual activity, and, if necessary, bloodletting. His belief in environmental influences on behavior sometimes led him to separate disturbed patients from their families. He seems to have gained insight into a theory popular among psychologists today: that the family constellation often fosters deviant behavior in its own members.

Other thinkers who contributed to the organic explanation of behavior were the philosopher Plato and the Greek physician Galen, who practiced in Rome. Plato (429–347 B.C.) carried on the thinking of Hippocrates; he insisted that the mentally disturbed were the responsibility of the family and should not be punished for their behavior. Galen (A.D. 129–199) made major contributions through his scientific examination of the nervous system and his explanation of the role of the brain and central nervous system in mental functioning. His greatest contribution may have been his codification of all European medical knowledge from Hippocrates' time to his own.

Reversion to Supernatural Explanations (the Middle Ages)

With the collapse of the Roman Empire and the rise of Christianity, rational and scientific thought gave way to a reemphasis on the supernatural. Religious dogma included the beliefs that nature was a reflection of divine will and beyond human reason and that earthly life was a prelude to the "true" life (after death). Scientific inquiry—attempts to understand, classify, explain, and control nature—was less important than accepting nature as a manifestation of God's will.

The Dark Ages (Fifth through Tenth Centuries)

Early Christianity did little to promote science and in many ways actively discouraged it. The church demanded uncompromising adherence to its tenets. Christian fervor brought with it the concepts of heresy and punishment; certain truths were deemed sacred, and those who challenged them were denounced as heretics. Scientific thought that was in conflict with church doctrine was not tolerated. Because of this atmosphere, rationalism and scholarly scientific works went underground for many years, preserved mainly by Arab scholars and European monks. Natural and supernatural explanations of illness were fused.

People came to believe that many illnesses were the result of supernatural forces, although they had natural causes. In many cases, the mentally ill were treated gently and with compassion in monasteries and at shrines, where they were prayed over and allowed to rest. In other cases, treatment could be quite brutal, especially if illnesses were believed to be God's wrath. Because illness was then perceived to be punishment for sin, the sick person was assumed to be guilty of wrongdoing, and relief could come only through atonement or repentance.

During this period, treatment of the mentally ill sometimes consisted of torturous exorcistic procedures seen as appropriate to combat Satan and eject him from the possessed person's body. Prayers, curses, obscene epithets, and the sprinkling of holy water— as well as such drastic and painful "therapy" as flogging, starving, and immersion in

brain pathology a dysfunction or disease of the brain

Casting out the Cause of Abnormality

During the Middle Ages, people suffering from mental disorders were often perceived as being victims of a demonic possession. The most prevalent form of treatment was exorcism, usually conducted by religious leaders who used prayers, incantations, and sometimes torturous physical techniques to cast the evil spirit from the bodies of the afflicted.

hot water—were used to drive out the devil. The humane treatments that Hippocrates had advocated centuries earlier were challenged severely. A time of trouble for everyone, the Dark Ages were especially bleak for the mentally ill.

Mass Madness (Thirteenth Century)

Belief in the power of the supernatural became so prevalent and intense that it frequently affected whole populations. Beginning in Italy early in the thirteenth century, large numbers of people were affected by various forms of mass madness, or group hysteria, in which a great many people exhibit similar symptoms that have no apparent physical cause. One of the better known manifestations of this disorder was *tarantism,* a dance mania characterized by wild raving, jumping, dancing, and convulsions. The hysteria was most prevalent during the height of the summer and was attributed to the sting of a tarantula. A victim would leap up and run out into the street or marketplace, jumping and raving, to be joined by others who believed that they had also been bitten. The mania soon spread throughout the rest of Europe, where it became known as Saint Vitus' Dance.

Another form of mass madness was *lycanthropy,* a mental disorder in which victims imagine themselves to be wolves and imitate wolves' actions. (Motion pictures about werewolves—people who assume the physical characteristics of wolves during the full moon—are modern reflections of this delusion.)

How can these phenomena be explained? Stress and fear are often associated with outbreaks of mass hysteria. During the thirteenth century, for example, there was

mass madness   group hysteria in which a great many people exhibit similar symptoms that have no apparent physical cause

enormous social unrest. The bubonic plague had destroyed one-third of the population of Europe. War, famine, and pestilence were rampant, and the social order of the times was crumbling.

Witchcraft (Fifteenth through Seventeenth Centuries)

During the fifteenth and sixteenth centuries, the authority of the church was increasingly challenged by social and religious reformers. Reformers such as Martin Luther attacked the corruption and abuses of the clergy, precipitating the Protestant Reformation of the sixteenth century. Church officials viewed such protests as insurrections that threatened their power. According to the church, Satan himself fostered these attacks. By doing battle with Satan and with people supposedly influenced or possessed by Satan, the church actively endorsed an already popular belief in demonic possession and witches.

To counter the threat, Pope Innocent VIII issued a papal bull (decree) in 1484 calling on the clergy to identify and exterminate witches. This resulted in the 1486 publication of the extremely influential *Malleus Maleficarum* (The Witch's Hammer). The mere existence of this document acted to confirm the existence of witches, and it also outlined means to detect them. For example, red spots on the skin (birthmarks) were supposedly made by the claw of the devil in sealing a blood pact and thus were damning evidence of a contract with Satan. Such birth defects as clubfoot and cleft palate also aroused suspicion. The church initially recognized two forms of demonic possession: unwilling and willing. God let the devil seize an unwilling victim as punishment for a sinful life. A willing person, who made a blood pact with the devil in exchange for supernatural powers, was able to assume animal form and cause disasters such as floods, pestilence, storms, crop failures, and sexual impotence. Although unwilling victims of possession at first received more sympathetic treatment than that given those who willingly conspired with the devil, this distinction soon evaporated.

People whose actions were interpreted as peculiar were often suspected of witchcraft. It was acceptable to use torture to obtain confessions from suspected witches, and many victims confessed because they preferred death to prolonged agony. Thousands of innocent men, women, and even children were beheaded, burned alive, or mutilated.

Witch hunts occurred in both colonial America and in Europe. It has been estimated that some 20,000 people (mainly women) were killed as witches in Scotland alone and that more than 100,000 throughout Europe were executed as witches from the middle of the fifteenth to the end of the seventeenth century. The witchcraft trials of 1692 in Salem, Massachusetts, are infamous. Several hundred people were accused, many were imprisoned and tortured, and twenty were killed. It would seem reasonable to assume that the mentally ill would be especially prone to being perceived as witches. Indeed, psychiatric historians argue that mental disorders were at the roots of witchcraft persecutions (Alexander & Selesnick, 1966; Deutsch, 1949; Zilboorg & Henry, 1941).

The Rise of Humanism (the Renaissance)

A resurgence of rational and scientific inquiry during the Renaissance (fourteenth through sixteenth centuries) led to great advances in science and humanism, a philosophical movement that emphasizes human welfare and the worth and uniqueness of the individual. Until this time, most asylums were at best custodial centers in which the mentally disturbed were chained, caged, starved, whipped, and even exhibited to the public for a small fee, much like animals in a zoo. But the new way of thinking held that if people were "mentally ill" and not possessed, then they should be treated as though they were sick. A number of new methods for treating the mentally ill reflected this humanistic spirit.

In 1563, Johann Weyer (1515–1588), a German physician, published a revolutionary book that challenged the foundation of ideas about witchcraft. Weyer asserted that many

humanism a philosophical movement that emphasizes human welfare and the worth and uniqueness of the individual

What Role Should Spirituality and Religion Play in Mental Health Care?

The role of demons, witches, and possessions in explaining abnormal behavior has been part and parcel of past religious teachings. Religion's role in the historic persecution of individuals and groups who voiced beliefs at odds with church teachings and/or who behaved in strange and peculiar ways is well documented. The contribution to our understanding of abnormal behavior has, at best, been less than enlightening and, at worst, contributed to falsehoods and mistaken beliefs of the mentally disturbed (Engh, 2006). Psychology's reluctance to incorporate religion into the profession may be understandable in light of the historical role played by the church in the oppression of the mentally ill. Furthermore, psychology as a science stresses objectivity and naturalistic explanations of human behavior; this approach is at odds with religion as belief system with supernatural overtones (Sue & Sue, 2008a).

Until recently, the mental health profession has been largely silent about the influence or importance of spirituality and religion in mental health. Thus, during therapy or work with clients, therapists have generally avoided discussing such topics (Sanders, Miller, & Bright, 2010). It has been found, for example, that many therapists (1) do not feel comfortable nor competent in discussing spiritual or religious issues with their clients, (2) are concerned they will appear proselytizing or judgmental if they touch on such topics, (3) believe they may usurp the role of the clergy, and (4) may feel inauthentic addressing client concerns, especially if they are atheists or agnostics (Gonsiorek, Richards, Pargament, & McMinn, 2009; Knox, et al, 2005; Sanders et al., 2010; Sue & Sue, 2008a).

Yet, it has been found that more than 80 percent of Americans say that religion is important in their lives; that in both medical and mental health care, patients express a strong desire for providers to discuss spiritual and faith issues with them; and that racial/ethnic minorities believe that spiritual issues are intimately linked to their cultural identities (Gallop

Organization, 2009; Sanders et al., 2010; Sue & Sue, 2008a). More compelling are findings that reveal a positive association between spirituality/religion and optimal health outcomes, longevity, and lower levels of anxiety, depression, suicide, and substance abuse (Cornah, 2006). In a meta-analysis of 200 published studies on the relationship of spirituality and health, it was found that higher levels of spirituality were associated with lower disease risk, fewer physical health problems, and higher psychosocial functioning (Thoresen, 1998). On a therapeutic level, these findings provide a strong rationale for psychologists to incorporate spirituality into their research and practice.

Surveys support the inescapable conclusion that many in the United States are experiencing a "spiritual hunger" or a strong need to reintegrate spiritual or religious themes into their lives (Hage, 2004). Many mental health professionals are becoming increasingly open to the potential benefits of spirituality in the treatment of clients. As part of that process, psychologists are making distinctions between spirituality and religion. Spirituality is an animating life force that is inclusive of religion and speaks to the thoughts, feelings, and behaviors related to a transcendent state. Religion is narrower, involving a specific doctrine and particular system of beliefs. Spirituality can be pursued outside a specific religion because it is transpersonal and includes one's capacity for creativity, growth, and love (Cornish & Wade, 2010). Mental health professionals are increasingly recognizing that people are thinking, feeling, behaving, social, cultural *and* spiritual beings and that the human condition is broad, complex, and holistic.

What thoughts do you have about the role of spirituality and religion in psychology and mental health? Should therapists avoid discussing these matters with clients and leave it to the clergy? What are the possible positive and negative outcomes of doing so? If you were in therapy, how important would it be to discuss your religious or spiritual beliefs?

---

people who were tortured, imprisoned, and burned as witches were mentally disturbed, not possessed by demons. The emotional agonies he was made to endure for committing this heresy are well documented. His book was severely criticized and banned by both church and state, but it proved to be a forerunner of the humanitarian perspective on mental illness. Others eventually followed his lead.

The Reform Movement (Eighteenth and Nineteenth Centuries)

In France, Philippe Pinel (1745–1826), a physician, was put in charge of La Bicêtre, a hospital for insane men in Paris. Pinel instituted what came to be known as the **moral treatment movement**—a shift to more humane treatment of the mentally disturbed. He ordered that inmates' chains be removed, replaced dungeons with sunny rooms, encouraged exercise outdoors on hospital grounds, and treated patients with kindness and reason. Surprising many disbelievers, the freed patients did not become violent; instead, this humane treatment seemed to foster recovery and improve behavior. Pinel later instituted similar, equally successful reforms at La Salpêtrière, a large mental hospital for women in Paris.

In England, William Tuke (1732–1822), a prominent Quaker tea merchant, established a retreat at York for the "moral treatment" of mental patients. At this pleasant

spirituality the animating life force or energy of the human condition that is broader than but inclusive of religion

moral treatment movement movement instituted by Philippe Pinel that resulted in a shift to more humane treatment of the mentally disturbed

country estate, the patients worked, prayed, rested, and talked out their problems—all in an atmosphere of kindness quite unlike that of the lunatic asylums of the time.

In the United States, three individuals—Benjamin Rush, Dorothea Dix, and Clifford Beers—made important contributions to the moral treatment movement. Benjamin Rush (1745–1813), widely acclaimed as the father of U.S. psychiatry, attempted to train physicians to treat mental patients and to introduce more humane treatment policies into mental hospitals. He insisted that patients be accorded respect and dignity and that they be gainfully employed while hospitalized, an idea that anticipated the modern concept of work therapy. Yet Rush was not unaffected by the established practices and beliefs of his times: his theories were influenced by astrology, and his remedies included bloodletting and purgatives.

Dorothea Dix (1802–1887), a New England schoolteacher, was the preeminent American social reformer of the nineteenth century. While teaching Sunday school to female prisoners, she became familiar with the deplorable conditions in which jailed mental patients were forced to live. (Prisons and poorhouses were commonly used to incarcerate these patients.) For the next forty years, Dix worked tirelessly for the mentally ill. She campaigned for reform legislation and funds to establish suitable mental hospitals and asylums. She raised millions of dollars, established more than thirty modern mental hospitals, and greatly improved conditions in countless others. But the struggle for reform was far from over. Although the large hospitals that replaced jails and poorhouses had better physical facilities, the humanistic, personal concern of the moral treatment movement was lacking.

That movement was given further impetus in 1908 with the publication of *A Mind That Found Itself,* a book by Clifford Beers (1876–1943) about his own mental collapse. His book describes the terrible treatment he and other patients experienced in three mental institutions, where they were beaten, choked, spat on, and restrained with straitjackets. His vivid account aroused great public sympathy and attracted the interest and support of the psychiatric establishment, including such eminent figures as psychologist-philosopher William James. Beers founded the National Committee for Mental Hygiene (forerunner of the National Mental Health Association, now known as Mental Health America), an organization dedicated to educating the public about mental illness and about the need to treat the mentally ill rather than punish them for their unusual behaviors.

It would be naive to believe that these reforms totally eliminated inhumane treatment of the mentally disturbed. Books such as Mary Jane Ward's *The Snake Pit* (1946) and films such as Frederick Wiseman's *Titicut Follies* (1967) were historically important in documenting the harsh treatment of mental patients. Even the severest critic of the mental health system, however, would have to admit that conditions and treatment for the mentally ill have improved over the past century.

Dorothea Dix (1802–1887)

During a time when women were discouraged from political participation, Dorothea Dix, a New England schoolteacher, worked tirelessly as a social reformer to improve the deplorable conditions in which the mentally ill were forced to live.

Archives of the History of American Psychology—The University of Akron

■ Causes: Early Viewpoints

Paralleling the rise of humanism in the treatment of mental illness was an inquiry into its causes. Two schools of thought emerged. The *biological,* or *organic, viewpoint* holds that mental disorders are the result of physiological damage or disease; the *psychological viewpoint* stresses an emotional basis for mental illness. It is important to note that most people were not extreme adherents of one or the other. Rather, they tended to combine elements of both. In the next chapter, we introduce a multipath model that provides an overarching umbrella to understand the multifactorial nature of mental disorders.

The Biological Viewpoint

Hippocrates' suggestion of an organic explanation for abnormal behavior was ignored during the Middle Ages but revived after the Renaissance. Not until the nineteenth century, however, did the biological or organic view—the belief that mental disorders have

biological (organic) view the belief that mental disorders have a physical or physiological basis

a physical or physiological basis—become important. The ideas of Wilhelm Griesinger (1817–1868), a German psychiatrist who believed that all mental disorders had physiological causes, received considerable attention. Emil Kraepelin (1856–1926), a follower of Griesinger, observed that certain symptoms tend to occur regularly in clusters, called syndromes. Kraepelin believed that each cluster of symptoms represented a mental disorder with its own unique—and clearly specifiable—cause, course, and outcome. He attributed all disorders to one of four organic causes: metabolic disturbance, endocrine difficulty, brain disease, or heredity. In his *Textbook of Psychiatry* (1883/1923), Kraepelin outlined a system for classifying mental illnesses on the basis of their organic causes. That system was the original basis for the diagnostic categories in the *Diagnostic and Statistical Manual of Mental Disorders* (DSM), the classification system of the American Psychiatric Association.

The acceptance of an organic or biological cause for mental disorders was accelerated by medical breakthroughs in the study of the nervous system. The study of brain disorders led many scientists to suspect or advocate organic factors as the sole cause of all mental illness. And, as we will see in Chapter 2, the drug revolution of the 1950s made medication available for almost every disorder. Issues regarding the therapeutic effectiveness of these drugs and how they work, however, are still hotly debated today.

The biological viewpoint gained even greater strength with the discovery of the organic basis of *general paresis,* a progressively degenerative and irreversible physical and mental disorder (*paresis* is syphilis of the brain). Several breakthroughs had led scientists to suspect that the deterioration of mental and physical abilities exhibited by certain mental patients might actually be caused by an organic disease. The work of Louis Pasteur (1822–1895) established the germ theory of disease (invasion of the body by parasitic microorganisms). Then, in 1897, Richard von Krafft-Ebing (1840–1902), a German neurologist, inoculated paretic patients with pus from syphilitic sores; when the patients failed to develop the secondary symptoms of syphilis, Krafft-Ebing concluded that the patients had been previously infected by that disease. Finally, in 1905, a German zoologist, Fritz Schaudinn (1871–1906), isolated the microorganism that causes syphilis and thus paresis. These discoveries convinced many scientists that every mental disorder might eventually be linked to an organic cause.

The Psychological Viewpoint

Some scientists noted, however, that certain types of emotional disorders were not associated with any organic disease in the patient. Such observations led to the psychological view—the belief that mental disorders are caused by psychological and emotional factors rather than organic or biological ones. For example, the inability to attain personal goals and resolve interpersonal conflicts could lead to intense feelings of frustration, depression, failure, and anger, which may consequently lead to disturbed behavior.

Mesmerism and Hypnotism

The unique and exotic techniques of Friedrich Anton Mesmer (1734–1815), an Austrian physician who practiced in Paris, presented an early challenge to the biological point of view. Mesmer developed a highly controversial treatment that came to be called *mesmerism* and that was the forerunner of the modern practice of hypnotism.

Mesmer performed his most miraculous cures in the treatment of *hysteria*—the appearance of symptoms such as blindness, deafness, loss of bodily feeling, and paralysis that seemed to have no organic basis. According to Mesmer, hysteria was a manifestation of the body's need to redistribute the magnetic fluid that determined a person's mental and physical health. His techniques for curing this illness involved inducing a sleeplike state,

syndromes certain symptoms that tend to occur regularly in clusters

psychological view the belief that mental disorders are caused by psychological and emotional factors rather than organic or biological ones

during which his patients became highly susceptible to suggestion. During this state, their symptoms often disappeared. Mesmer's dramatic and theatrical techniques earned him censure, as well as fame. A committee of prominent thinkers, including U.S. ambassador to France Benjamin Franklin, investigated Mesmer and declared him a fraud. He was finally forced to leave Paris.

Although Mesmer's basic assumptions were discredited, the power of suggestion proved to be a strong therapeutic technique in the treatment of hysteria. The cures he effected stimulated scientific interest in, and much bitter debate about, the psychological view.

The Nancy School

About ten years after Mesmer died, a number of researchers began to experiment actively with hypnosis. Among them was Jean-Martin Charcot (1825–1893), a neurosurgeon at La Salpêtrière Hospital in Paris and the leading neurologist of his time. His initial experiments with hypnosis led him to abandon it in favor of more traditional methods of treating hysteria, which he claimed was caused by organic damage to the nervous system. Other experimenters had more positive results using hypnosis, however, which persuaded Charcot to try it again. His subsequent use of the technique in the study of hysteria did much to legitimize the application of hypnosis in medicine.

Charcot's conversion was most influenced by two physicians practicing in the city of Nancy, located in eastern France. First working separately and then together, Ambroise-Auguste Liébeault (1823–1904) and Hippolyte-Marie Bernheim (1840–1919) hypothesized that hysteria was a form of self-hypnosis. The results they obtained in treating patients attracted other scientists, who collectively became known as the "Nancy School." In treating hysterical patients under hypnosis, they were often able to remove symptoms of paralysis, deafness, blindness, and anesthesia. They were also able to produce these symptoms in healthy persons through hypnosis. Their work demonstrated impressively that suggestion could cause certain forms of mental illness; that is, that symptoms of mental and physical disorders could have a psychological rather than an organic explanation. This conclusion represented a major breakthrough in the conceptualization of mental disorders.

Breuer and Freud

The idea that psychological processes could produce mental and physical disturbances began to gain credence among several physicians who were using hypnosis. Among them was the Viennese doctor Josef Breuer (1842–1925), who discovered that one of his female patients was cured of her symptoms after she spoke about her past traumatic experiences while in a trance. He achieved even greater success when the patient recalled and relived the emotional aspects of previously forgotten memories. This latter technique became known as the cathartic method, a therapeutic use of verbal expression to release pent-up emotional conflicts. It foreshadowed psychoanalysis, founded by Sigmund Freud (1856–1939). Freud's theories have had a great and lasting influence in the field of abnormal psychology.

Behaviorism

Whereas psychoanalysis offered an intrapsychic explanation of abnormal behavior, another viewpoint that emerged during the latter part of this period was more firmly rooted in laboratory science: behaviorism. The behavioristic perspective stressed the importance of directly observable behaviors and the conditions or stimuli that evoked, reinforced, and extinguished them. As we will see in Chapter 2, behaviorism not only offered an alternative explanation regarding the development of both normal and abnormal behavior but also demonstrated a high degree of success in treating maladaptive behaviors.

Stock Montage

Emil Kraepelin (1856–1926)

In an 1883 publication, psychiatrist Emil Kraepelin proposed that mental disorders could be directly linked to organic brain disorders and further proposed a diagnostic classification system for all disorders.

cathartic method   a therapeutic use of verbal expression to release pent-up emotional conflicts

behaviorism   psychological perspective that stresses the importance of learning and behavior in explanations of normal and abnormal development

Anton Mesmer (1734–1815)

Mesmer's techniques for treating hysteria by inducing a sleeplike state in which his patients were highly susceptible to suggestion was a forerunner of modern hypnotism. Although highly controversial and ultimately discredited, Mesmer's efforts stimulated inquiry into psychological and emotional factors, rather than biological factors, as causes of mental disorders.

Did You Know?

How different is the other 95 percent of the world from us? Do these differences influence psychological functioning and mental disorders?

- Half the world's population lives on $2/day; 80 percent of the world's population lives on a family income of less than $6,000/year.

- In developing countries, one in five children do not complete primary school; only half enroll in secondary school.

- About 17 percent of children are malnourished, in comparison to less than 1 percent in the United States.

- Life expectancy in developing countries is fifteen years less than in the United States.

Taken from United Nations Development Programme, 2006; Kent & Haub, 2005.

multicultural psychology an approach that stresses the importance of culture, race, ethnicity, gender, age, socioeconomic class, and other similar factors in its effort to understand and treat abnormal behavior

Contemporary Trends in Abnormal Psychology

Earlier, we made the statement that our current explanations of abnormal behavior have been heavily influenced by the beliefs of the past. Much has changed, however, in our understanding and treatment of psychopathological disorders. Twentieth-century views of abnormality continue to evolve in the twenty-first century as they incorporate the effects of several major events and trends in the field: (1) the influence of multicultural psychology, (2) positive psychology and optimal human functioning, and (3) changes in the therapeutic landscape (the drug revolution, prescription privileges for psychiatrists, evidence-based treatments, and managed health care).

The Influence of Multicultural Psychology

In a hard-hitting and insightful article, Arnett (2008) argues forcefully that psychological research published in scholarly journals focus too narrowly on U.S. Americans, who comprise only 5 percent of the world's population. Can the findings and principles/ theories of psychology and mental health derived from the United States be applicable to the "neglected" 95 percent of the rest of the world? Are Western concepts of mental health and mental disorders equally applicable to Africans in Africa, Asians in Asia, and Latinos in Latin America? Are human beings similar enough that studying them in only one part of the world allows us to generalize findings to people residing in other parts of the world? Do stark differences in income, education, health, and life expectancy between developing countries and the United States affect psychological functioning? Furthermore, how important are cultural differences in determining the causes and manifestation of mental disorders?

The answers seem to indicate that American psychology is too insular, that it may not be universally applicable, and that differences in culture, standard of living, and life circumstances have major influence on psychological functioning (Arnett, 2008; Cole, 2006; Valsiner, 2007). Even the DSM recognizes the existence of "culture-bound syndrome," mental disorders unique to only certain countries. The focus on global psychology has reawakened the profession to the importance of cultural and multicultural psychology (Shweder et al., 2006).

As international and global psychology have challenged the universality of Western psychology, so have the changing demographics of the United States. We are fast becoming a multicultural, multiracial, and multilingual society (Figure 1.2). The U.S. Census Bureau reveals that within several decades, racial and ethnic minorities will become a numerical majority (Sue & Sue, 2008a). These changes have been referred to as "the diversification of the United States" or, literally, the "changing complexion of society." Much of this change is fueled by two major trends in the United States: (1) the increased immigration of visible racial and ethnic minorities and (2) the differential birthrates among the various racial and ethnic groups in our society. The "diversity index," which measures the probability of selecting two randomly chosen individuals from different parts of the nation that differ from each other in race or ethnicity, stands at 49. In other words, there is nearly a 50 percent chance that these two individuals would be of a different race or ethnicity. Nowhere is the explosive growth of minorities more noticeable than in our public schools, where students of color now make up 45 percent of those attending.

Diversity has had a major impact on the mental health profession, creating a new field of study called multicultural psychology. As noted earlier in this chapter, the multicultural

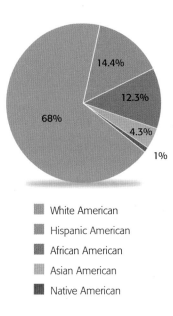

White American

Hispanic American

African American

Asian American

Native American

Figure 1.2

CENSUS 2005 RACIAL/ETHNIC COMPOSITION OF THE UNITED STATES

The rapid demographic transformation of the United States is illustrated by the fact that minorities now constitute an increasing proportion of the population. Several trends are evident. First, within several short decades, people of color will constitute a numerical majority. Second, the number of Hispanic Americans has surpassed the number of African Americans. Third, mental health providers will increasingly be coming into contact with clients who differ from them in race, ethnicity, and culture.

Source: U.S. Census Bureau, National Population Estimates, www.infoplease.com/ipa/A0762156.html.

approach stresses the importance of culture, race, ethnicity, gender, age, socioeconomic class, and other similar factors in its effort to understand and treat abnormal behavior. There is now recognition that mental health professionals need to (1) increase their cultural sensitivity, (2) acquire knowledge of the worldviews and lifestyles of a culturally diverse population, and (3) develop culturally relevant therapy approaches in working with different groups (American Psychological Association, 2003; Sue & Sue, 2008a). Although issues of race, culture, ethnicity, and gender have traditionally been ignored or distorted in the mental health literature, these forces are now increasingly recognized as powerful influences on many aspects of normal and abnormal human development. Four primary dimensions related to cultural diversity—social conditioning, cultural values and influence, sociopolitical influences, and bias in diagnosis—seem to explain how cultural forces exert their influence.

Social Conditioning

How we are raised, what values are instilled in us, and how we are expected to behave in fulfilling our roles seem to have a major effect on the type of disorder we are most likely to exhibit. In our culture men have traditionally been raised to fulfill the masculine role, to be independent, assertive, courageous, active, unsentimental, and objective. Women, in contrast, are commonly raised to be dependent, helpful, fragile, self-deprecating, conforming, empathetic, and emotional. Some mental health professionals believe that, as a result, women are more likely to internalize their conflicts (resulting in anxiety and depression), whereas men are more likely to externalize and act out (resulting in drug or alcohol abuse). Although gender roles have begun to change, their effects continue to be widely felt.

Cultural Values and Influences

Mental health professionals now recognize that types of mental disorders differ from country to country and that differences in cultural traditions among various racial and ethnic minority groups in the United States may influence susceptibility to certain emotional disorders. Among Hispanic/Latino Americans and Asian Americans, experiencing physical complaints is a common and culturally accepted means of expressing psychological and emotional stress (Santiago-Rivera, Arredondo, & Gallardo-Cooper, 2002; Yang & WonPat-Borja, 2007). People with these cultural backgrounds believe that physical problems cause emotional distress and that the emotional disturbance will disappear as soon as appropriate treatment for the physical illness is instituted. In addition, mental illness among

Did You Know?

- Racial/ethnic minorities form a majority in one-third of the most populous U.S. counties.

- More than 50 percent of California's population is composed of persons of color.

- Thirty percent of New York City residents were born in other countries.

- Seventy percent of the population of the District of Columbia is African American.

- Thirty-seven percent of the population of San Francisco is Asian American/Pacific Islander.

- Sixty-seven percent of the population of Detroit is African American.

- Sixty-seven percent of the population of Miami is Latino/Hispanic American.

Age Bias

In making diagnoses and conducting research, clinicians and researchers must be careful to avoid age bias, as well as race, gender, and social class biases. Japanese mountaineer Yuichiro Miura set a record by becoming the oldest man to climb Mount Everest. He was 70 years old and put to shame many climbers decades younger who could not complete the task.

Asians is seen as a source of shame and disgrace, although physical illness is acceptable. Asian values also emphasize restraint of strong feelings. Thus, when stress is encountered, the mental health professional is likely to hear complaints involving headaches, fatigue, restlessness, and disturbances of sleep and appetite.

Sociopolitical Influences

In response to a history of prejudice, discrimination, and racism, many minorities have adopted various behaviors (in particular, behaviors toward whites) that have proved important for their survival (Ponterotto, Utsey, & Pedersen, 2006; Sue, 2010). Mental health professionals may define these behaviors as abnormal and deviant, yet from the minority group perspective, such behaviors may function as healthy survival mechanisms. Early personality studies of African Americans concluded that, as a group, they tend to appear more "suspicious," "mistrustful," and "paranoid" than their white counterparts. But are African Americans inherently pathological, as studies suggest, or are they making healthy, adaptive responses? Members of minority groups who have been victims of discrimination and oppression in a society not yet free of racism have good reason to be suspicious and distrustful of white society. The "paranoid orientation" may reflect not only survival skills but also *accurate reality testing*. Certain behaviors and characteristics need to be evaluated not only by an absolute standard but also by the sociopolitical context in which they arise.

Bias in Diagnosis

Epidemiological studies reporting the distribution and types of mental disorders that occur in the population may be prone to bias on the part of clinicians and researchers. The mental health professional is not immune to inheriting the prejudicial attitudes, biases, and stereotypes of the larger society. Even the most enlightened and well-intentioned mental health professional may be the victim of race, gender, and social class bias. One source of bias is the tendency to overpathologize—to exaggerate the severity of disorders—among clients from particular socioeconomic, racial, or ethnic groups whose cultural values or lifestyles differ markedly from the clinician's own. The overpathologizing of disorders has been found to occur in psychological evaluations of African Americans, Hispanic Americans, and women (Lopez & Hernandez, 1987; Sue & Sue, 2008a).

It is clear that one of the most powerful emerging trends in the mental health field is the increased interest in and respect for multicultural psychology. Understanding abnormal behavior requires a realistic appraisal of the cultural context in which behavior occurs and an understanding of how culture influences the manifestations of abnormality. This recognition led the American Psychological Association to adopt "Guidelines on Multicultural Education, Training, Research, Practice, and Organizational Change for Psychologists" (APA, 2003). It states explicitly that the guidelines "reflect the continuing evolution of the study of psychology, changes in society at large, and emerging data about the different needs of particular individuals and groups historically marginalized or disenfranchised within and by psychology based on their ethnic/racial heritage and social group identity or membership" (p. 277).

Positive Psychology and Optimal Human Functioning

> Our message is to remind our field that psychology is not just the study of pathology, weakness, and damage; it is also the study of strength and virtue. (Seligman & Csikszentmihalyi, 2000)

Positive psychology, focused on optimal human functioning, has had a significant impact on psychology in recent years, and more specifically on the mental health field. The preceding quote reminds us that the other side of mental illness is *mental health* and that it is therefore important for psychologists to consider assets, strengths, and optimal human functioning (Day & Rottinghaus, 2003; Seligman 2007). By focusing on the inadequacies, problems, and limitations of people, we inadvertently see a very narrow picture of the human condition; we know more about fear than courage, selfishness than altruism, hate than love, stagnation than creativity, sadness than happiness, ignorance than wisdom, and hostility than affiliation.

Positive psychology is a branch of the profession that seeks to add balance to our view of human functioning; its purpose is to study, develop and achieve scientific understanding of positive human qualities that build thriving individuals, families, and communities (Seligman & Csikszentmihalyi, 2000). In its quest to do so, it has reinvigorated the early contributions of humanistic psychologists such as Abraham Maslow, Carl Rogers, Erik Erikson, and Marie Jahoda, all advocates of the concept of optimal human functioning.

Positive psychology and optimal human functioning can be divided into three domains (Seligman, 2007; Seligman & Csikszentmihalyi, 2000). First, subjectively, it can be measured in feelings of well-being, contentment, and satisfaction in the past; hope and optimism for the future; and flow and happiness in the present. Second, at the individual level, it is about positive traits such as capacity for love, courage, interpersonal skill, perseverance, spirituality, and wisdom. Third, at the group level, it is about civic virtues and the institutions that move us toward better citizenship and responsibility. Although the concepts of positive psychology and optimal human functioning may appear to be the domain of philosophers, they have not only validated the historical work of humanists but have impacted many aspects of mental health philosophy and practice.

- Conceptualizing client strengths have become increasingly important in therapeutic assessment and treatment (Gelson & Woodhouse, 2003). Therapists realize that clients are not just passive beings without adaptive skills, helpless to deal with life problems. Identifying strengths has been found to be a positive experience for clients. In what areas of life does the client do well? What are the client's internal assets? How adaptable is the client? What are the client's relationship strengths? What is the client's capacity for self-insight? What social supports does the client have?

- Positive psychology also focuses on prevention rather than remediation. The goal is to identify the strengths and assets of people, to arm them with adaptive coping skills, and to promote mental health. If the positive qualities of human functioning and adaptive coping can be identified, then clients are better able to meet adjustment challenges. Movement toward the study of the "healthy personality" marks such a trend (Ponterotto, Utsey, & Pedersen, 2006).

- Positive psychology has generated renewed interest in adaptive healthy coping. When one encounters a traumatic stress in life or is a target of violence, abuse, bullying, racism, or discrimination, what distinguishes those who handle adversity well as opposed to those who do not? Are these qualities or life strategies teachable? If so, can we teach people and even children how to handle life stressors so that they become inoculated to the many demanding challenges of life?

positive psychology the philosophical and scientific study of positive human functioning and the strengths and assets of individuals, families, and communities

optimal human functioning qualities such as subjective well-being, happiness, optimism, resilience, hope, courage, ability to cope with stress, self-actualization, and self-determinism

Positive psychology has reawakened the profession's need to present a more balanced picture of the human condition. Yet, it is not without critics. Some believe the movement to be a fad, think that the language used to describe optimal human functioning is unnecessarily vague, or suggest that, although inspiring, this approach belongs more to the field of philosophy. Perhaps the most problematic criticism comes from multicultural psychologists who claim that definitions and concepts of positive psychology are ethnocentric, culture-bound, and not completely applicable to racial/ethnic minorities within the United States or in different world populations (Sue & Constantine, 2003). They suggest that positive psychology and characteristics of the "good life" are intimately tied to the values of the larger society. Concepts of "happiness" and self-fulfillment arise from individualistic cultures and do not reflect fulfillment from a collectivistic perspective. Would China, Africa, and Latin America define optimal human functioning as their Western counterparts would?

Changes in the Therapeutic Landscape

Major scientific discoveries in treatment of the mentally disturbed, a movement toward accountability in clinical interventions, and the need for cost containment of health care services have literally changed the therapeutic landscape of the profession.

The Drug Revolution in Psychiatry

Many mental health professionals consider the introduction of psychiatric drugs in the 1950s as one of the great medical advances of the twentieth century (Norfleet, 2002). Although some might find such a statement excessive, it is difficult to overemphasize the impact that drug therapy has had. It started in 1949, when lithium was discovered to radically calm manic patients who had been hospitalized for years. Several years later, the discovery that the drug chlorpromazine (brand name, Thorazine) was extremely effective in treating agitated schizophrenics was received with great fanfare. Within a matter of years, drugs were developed to treat disorders such as depression, schizophrenia, phobias, obsessive-compulsive disorders, and anxiety.

These drugs were considered revolutionary because they sometimes rapidly and dramatically decreased or eliminated troublesome symptoms experienced by patients. As a result, other forms of therapy became available to the most seriously mentally ill, who were then more able to focus their attention on their therapy. Stays in mental hospitals were shortened and treatment became more cost-effective. In addition, many were able to return home while receiving treatment.

The new drug therapies were credited with the depopulation of mental hospitals, often referred to as *deinstitutionalization,* which we discuss in more detail in Chapter 17. To handle the large number of patients returning to the community, outpatient treatment became the primary mode of service for the severely disturbed. In addition to changing the way therapy was dispensed, the introduction of psychiatric drugs revived strong belief in the biological bases of mental disorders.

The Push by Psychologists for Prescription Privileges

One of the major features distinguishing psychiatrists from psychologists has been the right to prescribe medication. Should psychologists have a legal right to prescribe medication? Within the mental health field, this controversy has been extremely divisive. Psychologists have increasingly exerted pressure on state legislatures to allow them to prescribe medication in treating the mentally ill. They have argued that such a move would be cost-effective and benefit the American public by containing escalating health care costs.

Even though surveys suggest that most nonmedical mental health organizations favor prescription privileges for psychologists, and even though current statutes have never stipulated that only physicians can prescribe medication, the American Medical Association has adamantly opposed any such move. Although a good part of this stance may be due to psychiatry's fears of economic loss and the blurring of boundaries between professions, other reasons are cited as well. The medical establishment has argued that granting such privileges could endanger the public because psychologists lack medical training and the expertise to recognize medical risks and potential drug interaction effects.

Proponents of prescription privileges, on the other hand, present compelling reasons for approval (Foxhall, 2001; Gutierrez & Silk, 1998): (1) studies reveal that psychologists would be more cautious than psychiatrists in prescribing medication, (2) it is a logical extension of the psychologist's role, (3) psychologists are equally if not better trained to understand mind-body relationships than their psychiatric counterparts, and (4) psychologists wishing to prescribe would be required to master rigorous psychopharmacological training. As of this writing, Guam (a U.S. Territory), Louisiana, and New Mexico allow prescription privileges for psychologists.

The Development of Managed Health Care

Managed health care refers to the industrialization of health care, whereby large organizations in the private sector control the delivery of services. In the past, psychotherapy was carried out primarily by individuals in solo offices or in small group practices. Some clients paid for services out of their own pockets. Others had health plans that covered treatment, generally with minimal restrictions on the number of sessions the client could attend and usually with reimbursable treatment for a broad array of "psychological problems." The fees, number of sessions, and types of treatment were determined by the mental health practitioner. When mental health costs rapidly escalated in the 1980s, attempts were made to contain costs via managed health care or some form of health care reform (Cantor & Fuentes, 2008; Sammons, 2004). This industrialization of health care has brought about major changes in the mental health professions:

- Business interests are exerting increasing control over psychotherapy by determining reimbursable diagnoses, limiting the number of sessions psychologists may offer clients, and imposing other such restrictions.
- Current business practices are depressing the income of practitioners. Some organizations prefer hiring therapists with master's degrees rather than those with doctoral degrees, or they reimburse at rates below those set by the therapist.
- Psychologists are being asked to justify the use of their therapies on the basis of whether they are empirically based—that is, are they using established treatments with research support? This last point is especially important. For example, if research reveals that cognitive-behavioral forms of treatment are more successful than psychodynamic approaches for a certain form of phobia, then therapy using the latter approach might be denied by the insurance carrier.

These trends have alarmed many psychologists, who fear that decisions will be made not so much for health reasons but for business ones, that the need for doctoral-level practitioners will decrease, and that the livelihood of clinicians will be threatened. Although no one can say with certainty whether these fears will be realized, studies suggest that managed care policies are not based on scientific foundations and that patients are being deprived of adequately skilled treatment on a massive scale (Holloway, 2004; Scribner, 2001). As a result, lawsuits against major health care plans over accountability, patient access, and both patient and provider rights threaten to change the managed care landscape (Cantor & Fuentes, 2008; Holloway, 2004).

On a positive note, in 2010, mental health advocates celebrated the enactment of ground-breaking mental health and substance abuse parity legislation; health insurance organizations can no longer discriminate in the coverage offered to those with addictions or mental illness. Instead of being restricted by arbitrary limits, individuals covered by insurance can now access more comprehensive treatment.

managed health care the industrialization of health care, whereby large organizations in the private sector control the delivery of services

An Increased Appreciation for Research

Breakthroughs in neuroscience, identification of the role that neurotransmitters play in mental disorders, and increasing interest in exploring evidence-based forms of psychotherapy have produced another contemporary trend: a heightened appreciation for the role of research in the study of abnormal behavior. The success of psychopharmacology spawned renewed interest and research into brain-behavior relationships. Indeed, more and more researchers are now exploring the biological bases (chemical and structural) of abnormal behavior. Within recent years, biological factors have been associated with many psychological disorders, such as depression, suicide, schizophrenia, alcoholism, and Alzheimer's disease.

Currently, researchers are seeking insights into the most effective means of understanding and treating specific disorders through studies comparing the effectiveness of drug treatment with that of cognitive treatment and through the development of empirically based treatments (Hays, 2009; LaRoche & Christopher, 2009). The move toward empirically based treatments is one of the most visible aspects of the profession's use of research to determine the most effective forms of therapy for various disorders (Norcross, 2004; Wampold, Lichtenberg, & Waehler, 2002).

Although the move to evidence-based practice is accepted as important, it is not without controversy. Some claim that the call for empirically based treatments is biased against certain theoretical orientations. For example, studies reveal that 60 to 80 percent of those treatments identified as most effective are cognitive-behavioral treatments (Norcross, 2004). Others assert that evidence-based practice is too restrictive and does not recognize clinical intuition and the dynamic basis of therapy. Furthermore, the majority of disorders identified for treatment are those that can be easily measured and have a discrete but narrow symptom cluster, such as phobias. What about disorders that are more global and less susceptible to precise description, such as alienation in life, feelings of meaninglessness, and so on (Messer, 2001)? Lastly, as noted earlier, some fear that managed care companies will use this information to place more restrictions on types of treatments they are willing to reimburse.

CRITICAL THINKING

I Have It, Too: The Medical Student Syndrome

To be human is to encounter difficulties and problems in life. A course in abnormal psychology dwells on human problems—many of them familiar. As a result, we may be prone to the *medical student syndrome:* reading about a disorder may lead us to suspect that we have the disorder or that a friend or relative has it when indeed that is not the case. This reaction to the study of abnormal behavior is a common one, and one we must all guard against. When reading about physical disorders and listening to lecturers describe illnesses, some medical students begin to imagine that they themselves have one disorder or another. "Diarrhea? Fatigue? Trouble sleeping? That's me!" In this way, a cluster of symptoms—no matter how mild or how briefly experienced—can lead some people to suspect that they are ill.

Students who take a course that examines psychopathology may be equally prone to believe that they have a mental disorder that is described in their text. The problem is compounded by easy access to the Internet where googling a disorder like schizophrenia, bipolar disorder, or anxiety can produce a multitude of descriptors that seem to fit them.

It is possible, of course, that some do suffer from disorders and would benefit from counseling or therapy. Most, however, are merely experiencing an exaggerated sense of their susceptibility to disorders.

Two influences in particular may make us susceptible to these imagined disorders. One is the universality of the human experience. All of us have experienced misfortunes in life. We can all remember and relate to feelings of anxiety, unhappiness, guilt, lack of self-confidence, and perhaps even thoughts of suicide. In most cases, however, these feelings are normal reactions to stressful situations, not symptoms of disease. Depressed mood following the loss of a loved one or anxiety before giving a speech to a large audience may be perfectly normal and appropriate.

Another influence is our tendency to compare our own functioning with our perceptions of how other people are functioning. The outward behaviors of fellow students may lead us to conclude that they experience few difficulties in life, are self-assured and confident, and are invulnerable to mental disturbance. If we were privy to their inner thoughts and feelings, however, we might be surprised to find that they share our apprehension and insecurities.

If you see yourself anywhere in the pages of this book, we hope you will take the time to discuss your feelings with a friend or with one of your professors. You may be responding to pressures that you have not encountered before—a heavy course load, for example—and to which you have not yet adjusted. Other people can help point out these pressures to you. If your discussion supports your suspicion that you have a problem, however, then by all means consider getting help from your campus counseling center or health clinic.

Summary

1. What is abnormal psychology?

   - Abnormal psychology is the scientific study whose objectives are to describe, explain, predict, and modify behaviors that are considered strange or unusual.

2. What criteria are used to determine normal and abnormal behaviors?

   - Nearly all definitions include statistical deviation from some normative standard. The *Diagnostic and Statistical Manual of Mental Disorders* definition is used by most mental health practitioners. Abnormality is often determined by four criteria: distress, deviance, dysfunction, and dangerousness.

3. How do context, sociopolitical experiences, and cultural differences affect definitions of abnormality?

   - Criteria used to define normality or abnormality must be considered in light of community standards and changes over time. What is considered acceptable behavior in urban environments, for example, may not be considered acceptable in rural communities. With the increasing diversity in our society, we have also become very sensitive to how culture and unique group characteristics affect the definition of psychopathology as well.

4. How common are mental disorders?

   - Over the course of a year, approximately 25 percent of adults in the United States suffer from mental health problems; the human and economic costs are enormous. In addition, two-thirds of all people suffering from diagnosable mental disorders are not receiving or seeking mental health services.

5. What are some common misconceptions about the mentally disturbed?

   - Unfortunately, many myths and stereotypes have emerged regarding people who suffer from mental disorders. Beliefs that mental disorders are inherited, incurable, and the result of a weak will and that those who suffer from them will never contribute to society have caused undue worry and harm to many. The reality is that most people who have mental disorders improve, are little different from those without mental disorders, and go on to lead normal productive lives.

6. How have explanations of abnormal behavior changed over time?

- Ancient peoples believed in demonology and attributed abnormal behaviors to evil spirits that inhabited the victim's body. Treatments consisted of trephining, exorcism, and bodily assaults.

- Rational and scientific explanations of abnormality emerged during the Greco-Roman era. Especially influential was the thinking of Hippocrates, who believed that abnormal behavior was due to organic, or biological, causes, such as a dysfunction or disease of the brain. Treatment became more humane.

- With the collapse of the Roman Empire and the increased influence of the church and its emphasis on divine will and the hereafter, rationalist thought was suppressed and belief in the supernatural again flourished. During the Middle Ages, famine, pestilence, and dynastic wars caused enormous social upheaval. Forms of mass hysteria affected groups of people. In the fifteenth century, some of those killed in church-endorsed witch hunts were people we would today call mentally ill.

- The Renaissance brought a return to rational and scientific inquiry, along with a heightened interest in humanitarian methods of treating the mentally ill. The eighteenth and nineteenth centuries were a period characterized by reform movements.

7. What were early viewpoints on the causes of mental disorders?

- In the nineteenth and twentieth centuries, major medical breakthroughs fostered a belief in the biological roots of mental illness. An especially important discovery of this period was the microorganism that causes general paresis. Scientists believed that they would eventually find organic causes for all mental disorders.

- The uncovering of a relationship between hypnosis and hysteria corroborated the belief that psychological processes could produce emotional disturbances.

8. What are some contemporary trends in abnormal psychology?

- Three major contemporary developments have had or are having important influence in the mental health professions: (1) the multicultural psychology movement, (2) positive psychology and optimal human functioning, and (3) changes in the therapeutic landscape (drug revolution, prescription privileges for psychologists, managed care, and evidence-based practice).

Media Resources

Psychology CourseMate   Access an interactive eBook, chapter-specific interactive learning tools, including flash cards, quizzes, videos, and more, in your Psychology CourseMate, accessed through CengageBrain.com.

CENGAGENOW

CengageNow   CengageNOW is an easy-to-use online resource that helps you study in less time to get the grade you want—NOW. If your textbook does not include an access code card, go to CengageBrain.com to gain access.

CENGAGEbrain

CengageBrain   More than just an interactive study guide, WebTutor is an anytime, anywhere customized learning solution with an eBook, keeping you connected to your textbook, instructor, and classmates. Purchase the access chosen by your instructor at CengageBrain.com.

2

Models of Abnormal Behavior

S teve V., a twenty-one-year-old college student, had been suffering from a crippling bout of depression. Eighteen months earlier, Steve's friend, Linda, had broken off their relationship. However, Steve's long psychiatric history had begun well before he first sought help from the university's psychological services center. Steve had been in and out of psychotherapy since kindergarten and had been hospitalized twice for depression when he was in high school. His case records, nearly two inches thick, contained a number of diagnoses, including labels such as schizophrenia (paranoid type), and bipolar mood disorder. Although his present therapist did not find these labels particularly helpful, Steve's clinical history did provide some clues to the causes of his problems.

S teve V. was born in a suburb of San Francisco, the only child of an extremely wealthy couple. His father, who is of Scottish descent, was a prominent businessman who worked long hours and traveled frequently. On those rare occasions when he was home, Mr. V. was often preoccupied with business matters and held himself aloof from his son. The few interactions they had were characterized by his constant ridicule and criticism of Steve. Mr. V. was disappointed that his son seemed so timid, weak, and withdrawn. Steve was extremely bright and did well in school, but Mr. V. felt that he lacked the "toughness" needed to prosper in today's world. Once, when Steve was about ten, he came home from school with a bloody nose, crying and complaining of being picked on by his schoolmates. His father showed no sympathy; instead, he berated Steve for losing the fight. In his father's presence, Steve usually felt worthless, humiliated, and fearful of doing or saying the wrong thing.

Mrs. V. was very active in civic and social affairs, and she, too, spent relatively little time with her son. Although she treated Steve more warmly and lovingly than his father did, she seldom came to Steve's defense when Mr. V. bullied him. She generally allowed her husband to make family decisions. In reality, Mrs. V. was quite lonely. She felt abandoned by Mr. V. and harbored a deep resentment toward him, which she was frightened to express.

When Steve was a child, his mother had often allowed him to sleep in her bed when her husband was away on business trips. She usually dressed minimally on these occasions and was very demonstrative—holding, stroking, and kissing Steve. This behavior had continued until Steve was twelve, when his mother abruptly refused to let Steve into her

CHAPTER OUTLINE

focus questions

1 What models of psychopathology have been used to explain abnormal behavior?

2 What is the multipath model of mental disorders?

3 How much of mental disorder can be explained through our biological makeup?

4 What psychological models are used to explain the etiology of mental disorders?

5 What role do social factors play in psychopathology?

6 What sociocultural factors may play a role in the etiology of mental disorders?

bed. The sudden withdrawal of this privilege had confused and angered Steve, who was not certain what he had done wrong. He knew, though, that his mother had been quite upset when she awoke one night to find him masturbating next to her.

Most of the time, Steve's parents seemed to live separately from each other and from their son. Steve was raised, in effect, by a non-English-speaking maid whose idea of caring for him was to lock him in his room during the day. His birthdays were celebrated with a cake, but the only celebrants were Steve and his mother. By age ten, Steve had learned to keep himself occupied by playing "mind games," letting his imagination carry him off on flights of fantasy. He frequently imagined himself as a powerful figure—Superman or Batman. His fantasies were often extremely violent, and his foes were vanquished only after much blood had been spilled.

As Steve grew older, his fantasies and heroes became increasingly menacing and evil. When he was fifteen, he obtained a pornographic video that he watched repeatedly in his room. Often, Steve would masturbate as he watched scenes of women being sexually violated. Steve now recalls that he spent much of his spare time between the ages of fifteen and seventeen watching X-rated videos or violent movies, his favorite being *The Texas Chainsaw Massacre*, in which a madman saws and hacks women to pieces. Steve always identified with the character perpetrating the outrage; at times, he imagined his parents as the victims.

At about age sixteen, Steve became convinced that external forces were controlling his mind and behavior and were drawing him into his fantasies. He was often filled with guilt and anxiety after one of his mind games. Although he was strongly attracted to his fantasy world, he also felt that something was wrong with it and with him. After seeing the movie *The Exorcist*, he became convinced that he was possessed by the devil.

Up until this time, Steve had been quiet and withdrawn. In kindergarten the school psychologist had described his condition as "autistic-like" because Steve seldom spoke, seemed unresponsive to the environment, and was socially isolated. With the development of his interest in the occult and in demonic possession, however, he became outgoing, flamboyant, and even exhibitionistic. Steve was hospitalized twice by his parents with diagnoses of bipolar affective disorder and schizophrenia in remission. Mr. V. often suggested that Steve had inherited "bad genes" from his wife's side of the family because one of Mrs. V's brothers had suffered from a history of mental illness.

What do you make of Steve? He certainly fulfills our criteria as someone suffering from a mental disorder. Yet, how do we make sense of his bizarre behaviors, thoughts, and feelings? Where do they come from? Is Steve correct in his belief that he is possessed by evil spirits? Is his father correct in suggesting that "bad genes" caused his disorder? What role did his upbringing, isolation, and bullying from his father play in the development of his problems? These complex questions lead us into a very important aspect of abnormal psychology: the etiology, or causes, of disorders.

One-Dimensional Models of Mental Disorders

In the previous chapter, we described how the rise of humanism influenced society's attitude toward mental disorders. As rational thought replaced superstition in the eighteenth and nineteenth centuries, the mentally disturbed were increasingly regarded as unfortunate human beings who deserved humane treatment, not as monsters inhabited by the devil.

This humanistic view gave rise, in the late nineteenth and early twentieth centuries, to two different schools of thought about the causes of mental disorders. According to one group of thinkers, mental disorders are caused primarily by biological problems, and the disturbed individual is displaying symptoms of physical disease or damage. The second group of theorists believed that abnormal behavior is essentially psychosocial, rooted not in cells and tissues but in the invisible complexities of the human mind or in stressful environmental forces.

etiology causes of disorders

Today we realize that these two perspectives are overly simplistic because they (1) set up a false "either/or" dichotomy between nature and nurture, (2) fail to recognize the reciprocal influences of one on the other, and (3) mask the importance of acknowledging the biological, psychological, social, and sociocultural dimensions in the origin of mental disorders (Sue & Sue, 2008a; Zhang & Meaney, 2010). In this chapter, we propose a *multipath model* for explaining abnormal behavior that integrates these four major dimensions. Before we begin, however, let's look at how one-dimensional models have traditionally explained Steve's psychopathology.

- **Biological Explanations** Adherents to the biological perspective would say that Steve's mental disorders are caused by some form of biological malfunctioning. Steve's problems reside in a possible genetic predisposition to mental disorders; an imbalance of brain/body chemistry (neurotransmitters or hormones); or, perhaps, in structural abnormalities in his neurological makeup. The fact that he suffers from paranoid schizophrenia and a bipolar affective disorder (both disorders that have an increased probability of being present in blood relatives) seems to support such an explanation. Although biological explanations acknowledge that environmental influences are important, they are seen as secondary in the manifestation of psychopathology.

- **Psychological Explanations** From a psychological perspective, there are a variety of ways to explain Steve's behavior. *Psychodynamic explanations* would stress that Steve's problems reside in his early childhood experiences, his inability to confront his own intense feelings of hostility toward his father (fears of castration), and his unresolved sexual longing toward his mother. *Behavioral explanations* would trace the roots of Steve's problems to his behavioral repertoire. Many of the behaviors he has learned are inappropriate, and his repertoire lacks useful, productive behaviors. Other explanations might stress the development of irrational beliefs and Steve's distorted thinking that leads to his "mind games" (misinterpretations of reality).

- **Social Explanations** From a social-relational perspective, Steve's problem resides in the family system, which is therefore the primary unit of analysis. Parental neglect, rejection, and abuse may explain much of his pathological symptoms. It is obvious that the relationships between Steve and his father, between Steve and his mother, and between his father and his mother are unhealthy. The constant bullying of Steve by his father and the lack of support by his mother are the primary culprits.

- **Sociocultural Explanations** The societal and cultural context in which Steve's problems arise must be considered in understanding his dilemma. He is a white European American of Scottish descent, born to a wealthy family in the upper socioeconomic class. He is a male, raised in a cultural context that values individual achievement and competitiveness. Because Steve does not live up to his father's benchmarks of masculinity, he is considered a failure by his father. To truly understand Steve, we must recognize that multicultural variables—race, ethnicity, gender, socioeconomic class, sexual orientation, and so on—are powerful factors. As such, they influence the types of sociocultural stressors Steve is likely to experience and the ways in which he will manifest disorders.

Using Models to Describe Psychopathology

As evidenced by the preceding analysis of Steve, all four explanations seem to contain kernels of truth. But which is more accurate? Does accepting the validity of one perspective preempt the applicability of another? Is it possible that combinations of biological, psychological, social, and sociocultural factors all interact and contribute to Steve's mental disorder? To answer these questions, let's first examine how scientists use analogies to discuss a phenomenon that is difficult to describe or explain. A diagnosis such as "schizophrenia," for example, is generally inferred and made more understandable by likening the phenomenon to something more concrete. A model is an analogy that scientists often use to describe a phenomenon or process that they cannot directly observe. In using an analogy, the scientist borrows terms, concepts, or principles from one field and applies them to another, such as when a physician describes the eye as a "camera."

Psychologists have used models extensively to help conceptualize the causes of abnormal behavior, to ask probing questions, to determine relevant information, and to interpret data obtained from observations, records, and interviews. For example, when psychologists refer to people as "patients" or speak of deviant behavior as "mental illness," they are borrowing the terminology of medicine and applying a *medical model* of abnormal behavior. They may also describe certain external symptoms (such as snake phobia or motor tics) as being visible signs of deep underlying conflict. Again, the medical analogy is clear: Just as fevers, rashes, perspiration, or infections may be symptoms of a bacterial or viral invasion of the body, bizarre behavior may be a symptom of a mind "invaded" by unresolved conflicts. Psychologists use a variety of such models, each embodying a particular theoretical approach. Hence, we tend to use the terms *model, theory, viewpoint,* and *perspective* somewhat interchangeably. Most theorists realize that the models they construct will be limited and will not correspond in every respect to the phenomena they are studying (Brooks-Harris, 2008). Because of the complexity of human behavior and our relatively shallow understanding of it, psychologists do not expect to develop the definitive model. Rather, they use the models to visualize psychopathology as if it truly worked in the manner described.

Models of psychopathology, whether they are biological, psychological, social or sociocultural, enable us to organize and make sense of the complexity of data related to the disturbance being studied. Models, however, can foster a one-dimensional and linear explanation of a mental disorder that limits the ability to consider other perspectives. If, for example, we use a psychological explanation of Steve's behavior and consider his problems to be rooted in unconscious incestuous desires for his mother and ambivalent competitiveness toward his father (a psychodynamic explanation), we may unintentionally ignore all research findings pointing to powerful biological causes of certain disorders, such as schizophrenia and depression.

A Multipath Model of Mental Disorders

Nearly all texts on abnormal psychology expose students to a variety of theories that purport to explain mental disorders. For example, students may hear of how researchers have made breakthroughs in the genetics of a disorder, how the unconscious mind may influence one's behaviors, why irrational thoughts or distorted thinking lead to pathology, or how learned inappropriate behaviors may be culprits. Because psychologists may favor one model over another, textbooks have typically presented different theories as if each alone can explain a disorder or as if each has equal validity. Research shows, however, that disorders are caused by factors that cross various theories. For instance, in the case of Steve V., genetics and brain functioning (a biological perspective) may interact with ways of thinking (a cognitive perspective) in a given family environment (a social perspective) to produce abnormal behavior (Mann & Haghihgi, 2010; University of Michigan, 2010).

This line of thinking has led to the formulation of the "biopsychosocial model" that attempts to integrate biological, psychological, and social factors in explaining human behavior. Although the model represented a major step in recognizing the diversity of factors that influence the manifestation of mental disorders, some have noted failings (Ghaemi, 2010; Sue & Sue, 2008a): (a) it provides little information about how factors interact to produce illness; (b) it seems to allow practitioners to do everything, but provides no specific guidance to do anything; and (c) it fails to consider the equally powerful influence of culture.

What, then, is the "best" way to conceptualize the causes of mental disorders? We propose an integrative and interacting multipath model as a way of viewing disorders and their causes. The multipath model is not a theory but a way of looking at the variety and

model an analogy used by scientists, usually to describe or explain a phenomenon or process they cannot directly observe

multipath model a model of models that provides an organizational framework for understanding the numerous causes of mental disorders, the complexity of their interacting components, and the need to view disorders from a holistic framework

complexity of contributors to mental disorders. In some respects it is a *metamodel*, a model of models that provides an organizational framework for understanding the numerous causes of mental disorders, the complexity of their interacting components, and the need to view disorders from a holistic framework.

The multipath model operates under several assumptions: (1) No one theoretical perspective is adequate to explain the complexity of the human condition and the development of mental disorders. (2) There are multiple pathways to and causes of any single disorder. It is a statistical rarity to find a disorder due to only one cause. (3) Explanations of abnormal behavior must consider biological, psychological, social, and sociocultural elements. (4) Not all dimensions contribute equally to a disorder. The model is guided by the state of research and scientific findings as to the relative merits of a proposed cause. In some cases, greater support for a biological perspective, for example, may be present, but this may evolve as research enlightens us about the contributions of other factors. (5) The multipath model is integrative and interactive. It acknowledges that factors may combine in complex and reciprocal ways so that people exposed to the same factors may not develop the same disorder and that different individuals exposed to different factors may develop a similar mental disorder.

Let's look at how the multipath model operates under these assumptions. First, the etiology of mental disorders can be subsumed under four dimensions, as shown in Figure 2.1:

- **Dimension One: Biological Factors** This dimension includes genetics, brain anatomy, biochemical imbalances, central nervous system functioning, autonomic nervous system reactivity, and so forth.
- **Dimension Two: Psychological Factors** This dimension includes personality, cognition, emotions, learning, stress coping, self-esteem, self-efficacy, values, developmental history, and so forth.
- **Dimension Three: Social Factors** This dimension includes family, relationships, social support, belonging, love, marital status, community, and so forth.
- **Dimension Four: Sociocultural Factors** This dimension includes race, gender, sexual orientation, spirituality/religion, socioeconomic status, ethnicity, culture, and so forth.

Within each dimension, how the multiplicity of factors is organized to explain abnormal behavior depends on a particular theoretical perspective. First, let's take the psychological dimension as an example. Psychodynamic theories might emphasize the

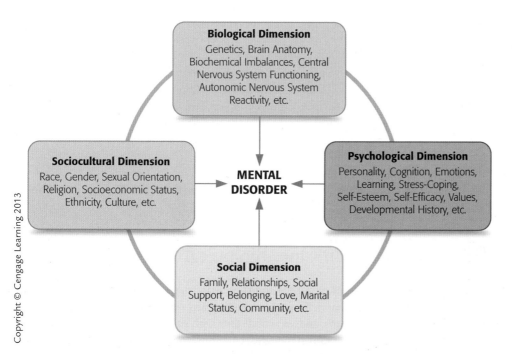

Figure 2.1

THE MULTIPATH MODEL
Each dimension of the multipath model contains factors found to be important in explaining abnormal behavior.

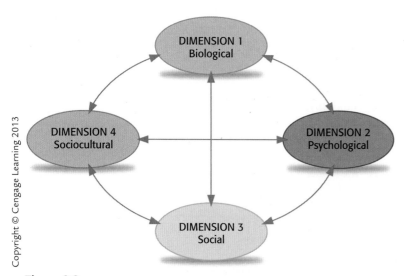

Figure 2.2

**THE FOUR DIMENSIONS AND POSSIBLE PATHWAYS OF
INFLUENCE**

Abnormal behavior can be conceptualized as arising from four possible
dimensions.

importance of childhood experiences in the formation
of abnormal behavior; learning theories would emphasize learning and personality; and cognitive theories
would emphasize cognition and thinking. Thus, it is
possible to have considerable differences even within
a categorical dimension. Likewise, we note that some
theories can be categorized in more than one dimension. Theories of stress, for example, could be seen as
falling under the psychological or the social dimension.
It is therefore best to view these four dimensions as having permeable boundaries with considerable overlap.

Second, factors in the four dimensions can interact
and influence each other in any direction. For example,
research shows that brain functioning affects behaviors.
However, research also demonstrates that engaging in
certain behaviors can affect brain functioning (Pajonk,
Wobrock, Gruber et al., 2010). We also know that
sociocultural factors can influence biological factors
(Azar, 2010). The actual situation is much more complex because the interaction of factors may involve all
four dimensions, as noted in Figure 2.2.

Third, different combinations within the four di-
mensions may cause abnormal behaviors. For instance, let's assume that a woman suffers
from severe depression. Her depression may be caused by a single factor (e.g., the death
of a loved one) or by an interaction of factors in different dimensions (e.g., child abuse
occurring in early life and stressors in adulthood). Thus, a disorder such as depression may
be caused by a single factor or by different combinations of factors, as noted in Figure 2.3.

Fourth, many disorders appear to be heterogeneous in nature. Therefore, there may
be different types or versions of a disorder (or a spectrum of the disorder). For example,
schizophrenia appears to be composed of a group of different but related disorders. Likewise, there may be different types of depression that are caused by different factors. For
example, severe cases of depression seem to have a stronger genetic basis than less severe
cases. Finally, different disorders may be caused by similar factors. For example, anxiety, as
well as depression, may be caused by child abuse and interpersonal stress. In fact, anxiety
and depression often occur concurrently in people.

It can be seen that finding causes of abnormal behavior is complex. Although a multipath model helps to conceptualize the complexities, the reality is that our research is currently insufficient to precisely link different dimensions of analysis for most disorders. By
proposing a multipath model, we do not imply that disorders can be caused by any events
or by random events. Rather, certain combinations of factors increase the likelihood of
disorders. These factors often occur in different dimensions. They account for commonalities, as well as uniqueness in disorders. That is, they can help predict the occurrence and
nonoccurrence of disorders and provide insight into means of controlling disorders. Our
task is to identify linkages in different dimensions and the meaningfulness of the linkages
in explaining and controlling abnormal behaviors.

To aid in understanding more thoroughly the contributions of each of the four
dimensions, we discuss them in the following sections.

Dimension One: Biological Factors

Modern biological explanations of normal and abnormal behavior continue to share certain
assumptions: (1) The things that make people who they are—their physical features, susceptibility to diseases, temperaments, and ways of dealing with stress—are embedded in the genetic material of their cells. (2) Human thoughts, emotions, and behaviors are associated with

neuron   nerve cell that transmits
messages throughout the body

nerve cell activities of the brain and spinal cord. (3) A change in thoughts, emotions, or behaviors will be associated with a change in activity or structure (or both) of the brain. (4) Mental disorders are highly correlated with an inherited predisposition, and/or some form of brain or other organ dysfunction. (5) Mental disorders can be treated by drugs, genetic manipulation, or somatic intervention (DeLisi & Fleischbaker, 2007; Lambert & Kingsley, 2005; Paris, 2009; Sarter, Bruno, & Parikh, 2007).

Biological models have been heavily influenced by the neurosciences, a group of subfields that focus on brain structure, function, and disorder. Understanding biological explanations of human behavior requires knowledge about the structure and function of the central nervous system (composed of the brain and spinal cord). Especially important is knowledge about how the brain is organized; how it works; and, particularly, the chemical reactions that enhance or diminish normal brain actions.

The Human Brain

The brain is composed of billions of neurons, or nerve cells that transmit messages throughout the body. The brain is responsible for three very important and highly complicated functions. It receives information from the outside world, it uses the information to decide on a course of action, and it implements decisions by commanding muscles to move and glands to secrete. Weighing approximately three pounds, this relatively small organ continues to amaze and mystify biological researchers.

The brain is separated into two hemispheres: the left hemisphere and the right hemisphere. A disturbance in either one (such as by a tumor or by electrical stimulation with electrodes) may produce specific sensory or motor effects. Each hemisphere controls the opposite side of the body. For example, paralysis on the left side of the body indicates a dysfunction in the right hemisphere. In addition, the right hemisphere is associated with visual-spatial abilities and emotional behavior. The left hemisphere controls the language functions for nearly all right-handed people and for most left-handed ones.

Viewed in cross-section, the brain has three parts: forebrain, midbrain, and hindbrain. Although each part is vital for functioning and survival, the forebrain is probably the most relevant to a discussion of abnormality.

The Forebrain

The *forebrain* probably controls all the higher mental functions associated with human consciousness, learning, speech, thought, and memory. Within the forebrain are the thalamus, hypothalamus, reticular activating system, limbic system, and cerebrum (Figure 2.4). The specific functions of these structures are still being debated, but we can discuss their more general functions with some confidence.

The *thalamus* appears to serve as a "relay station," transmitting nerve impulses from one part of the brain to another. The *hypothalamus* ("under the thalamus") regulates bodily drives, such as hunger, thirst, and sex, and body conditions, such as temperature

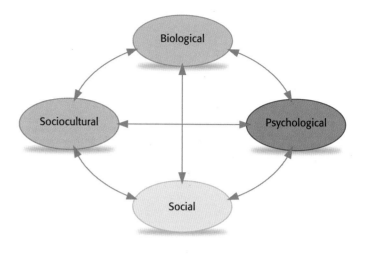

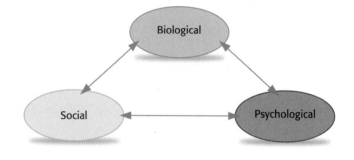

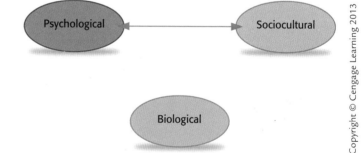

Figure 2.3

THE NUMBER OF DIMENSIONS THAT MAY LEAD TO PARTICULAR DISORDERS

The dimensions shown are examples only because any of them can serve to influence a particular disorder.

MYTH: Most mental disorders have either a biological or psychological cause. Those with the former should be treated with biological interventions, whereas the latter should be treated with psychological ones.

REALITY: Although it is important to identify biological and psychological correlates of psychopathology, this dichotomous and simplistic thinking is unfortunate and has served to hinder integrated approaches to explaining and treating mental disorders. We now realize, for example, that gene activity and changes in biology are influenced by the psychological environment and vice versa. The relationship between the biological and psychological makeup of people is complex and interrelated (Diamond, 2009).

MYTH VS. REALITY

Figure 2.4

THE INTERNAL STRUCTURE OF THE BRAIN

A cross-sectional view of the brain reveals the forebrain, midbrain, and hindbrain. Some of the important brain structures are identified within each of the divisions.

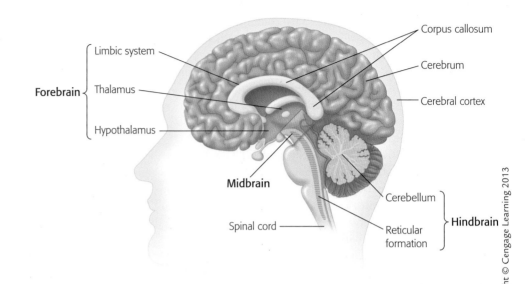

Copyright © Cengage Learning 2013

and hormone balance. The *limbic system* is involved in experiencing and expressing emotions and motivation—pleasure, fear, aggressiveness, sexual arousal, and pain. The largest structure in the brain is the *cerebrum*, with its most visible part, the *cerebral cortex*, covering the midbrain and thalamus.

The Midbrain and Hindbrain

The midbrain and hindbrain also have distinct functions:

- The *midbrain* is involved in vision and hearing and—along with the hindbrain—in the control of sleep, alertness, and pain. Mental health professionals are especially interested in the midbrain's role in manufacturing chemicals—serotonin, norepinephrine, and dopamine—that have been implicated in certain mental disorders.
- The *hindbrain* also manufactures serotonin. The hindbrain appears to control functions such as heart rate, sleep, and respiration. The *reticular formation*, a network of nerve fibers that controls bodily states such as sleep, alertness, and attention, starts in the hindbrain and threads its way into the midbrain.

Did You Know?

The size of a male brain is about 10 percent larger than a female brain; men's head size is also 2 percent bigger. Does this mean that men are smarter than women? The answer is "no." The larger muscle mass and physical stature of men may mean they require more neurons to control them. But there are other differences between male and female brains that may be associated with potential susceptibility to certain disorders such as Alzheimer's disease and other human functioning.

Because the brain controls all aspects of human functioning, it is not difficult to conclude that damage or interruption of normal brain function and activity could lead to observable mental disorders. There are, of course, many biological causes for psychological disorders. Damage to the nervous system is one: As Fritz Schaudinn demonstrated (see Chapter 1), general paresis results from brain damage caused by parasitic microorganisms. Tumors, strokes, excessive intake of alcohol or drugs, and external trauma (such as a blow to the head) have also been linked to cognitive, emotional, and behavioral disorders.

Biochemical Theories

Two specific biological sources—body chemistry and heredity—have given rise to important biological theories of psychopathology. The basic premise of biochemical theories is that chemical imbalances underlie mental disorders. This premise relies on the fact that most physiological and mental processes, from sleeping and digestion to reading and thinking, involve chemical actions within the body. Support for the biochemical theories has been found in research into anxiety disorders, mood disorders (both depression and bipolar disorder), Alzheimer's disease, autism, dyslexia, and schizophrenia (Andreasen, 2005; Lambert & Kinsley, 2005; Sarter et al., 2007). In fact, it is possible that our gene pool affects such characteristics as alienation, leadership, career choice, risk aversion, religious conviction, and pessimism. To see how biochemical imbalances in the brain can result in abnormal behavior, we need to understand how messages in the brain are transmitted from nerve cell to nerve cell.

Nerve cells (neurons) vary in function throughout the brain and may appear different, but they all share certain characteristics. Each neuron possesses a cell membrane that separates it from the outside environment and regulates the chemical contents within it. On one end of the cell body are dendrites, numerous short rootlike structures whose function is to receive signals from other neurons. At the other end is an axon, a much longer extension that sends signals to other neurons, some a considerable distance away. Under an electron microscope, dendrites can be distinguished by their many short branches (Figure 2.5).

Messages travel through the brain by electrical impulses via neurons: An incoming message is received by a neuron's dendrites and is sent down the axon to bulblike swellings called *axon terminals*, usually located near dendrites of another neuron. Note that neurons do not touch one another. A minute gap (the synapse) exists between the axon of the sending neuron and the dendrites of the receiving neuron (Figure 2.6). The electrical impulse crosses the synapse when the axon releases chemical substances called neurotransmitters. When the neurotransmitters reach the dendrites of the receiving neuron, they attach themselves to receptors and, if their "shapes" correspond, bind with them (Figure 2.7). The binding of transmitters to receptors in the neuron triggers either a synaptic excitation (encouragement to produce other nerve impulses) or synaptic inhibition (a state preventing production of nerve impulses).

The human body has many different chemical transmitters, and their effect on neurons varies (Table 2.1). An imbalance of certain neurotransmitters in the brain is believed

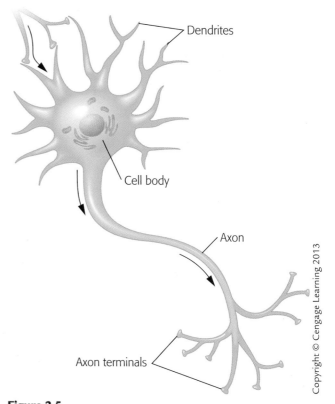

Figure 2.5

MAJOR PARTS OF A NEURON

The major parts of a neuron include dendrites, the cell body, the axon, and the axon terminals.

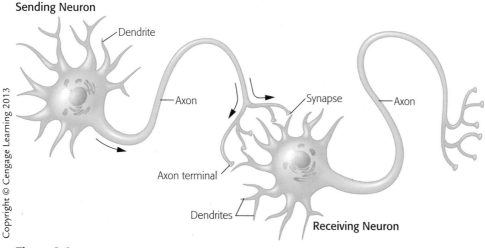

Figure 2.6

SYNAPTIC TRANSMISSION

Messages travel via electrical impulses from one neuron to another. The impulse crosses the synapse in the form of chemicals called neurotransmitters. Note that the axon terminals and the receiving dendrites do not touch.

dendrite   short rootlike structure on the cell body whose function is to receive signals from other neurons

axon   extension on the cell body that sends signals to neurons, some a considerable distance away

synapse   minute gap that exists between the axon of the sending neuron and the dendrites of the receiving neuron

neurotransmitter   chemical substance released by the axon of the sending neuron and involved in the transmission of neural impulses to the dendrite of the receiving neuron

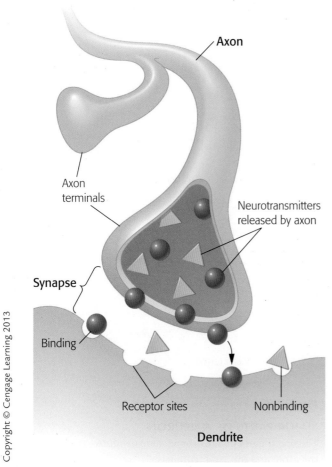

Figure 2.7

NEUROTRANSMITTER BINDING

Neurotransmitters are released into the synapse and travel to the receiving dendrite. Each transmitter has a specific shape that corresponds to a receptor site. Like a jigsaw puzzle, binding occurs if the transmitter fits into the receptor site.

to be implicated in mental disorders. As discussed in Chapter 1, the search for chemical causes and cures for mental problems accelerated tremendously in the early 1950s with the discovery of psychoactive drugs. Since that time, three convincing lines of evidence have contributed to the search for biochemical causes and cures:

1. Studies showed that antipsychotic drugs have beneficial effects on people with schizophrenia, that lithium is useful in controlling affective disorders, and that tricyclics and monoamine oxidase inhibitors alleviate symptoms of severely depressed patients.

2. These drugs seem to work by blocking or facilitating neurotransmitter activity at receptor sites. Most current psychiatric drugs seem to affect one of five different transmitters: acetylcholine, dopamine, gamma aminobutyric acid (GABA), norepinephrine, and serotonin.

3. Certain chemical imbalances appear to be disorder specific. Insufficient dopamine, for example, is a possible cause of Parkinson's disease. Ironically, an excess of dopamine has been implicated in the development of schizophrenia. Two hypotheses have been proposed: that people with schizophrenia may have too many postsynaptic dopamine receptors (a structural explanation) or that their receptors may be supersensitive to dopamine. The effect of drug therapy on receptor sites has been shown with other disorders. Drugs used to treat depression alter norepinephrine and serotonin sensitivity and receptivity at the receptor sites. Drugs used in the treatment of anxiety affect receptor reactivity to GABA.

Research into biochemical mechanisms holds great promise for our understanding and treatment of mental disorders. It appears unlikely, however, that biochemistry alone can provide completely satisfactory explanations of the biological bases of abnormal behavior. Researchers should instead expect to find hundreds—or perhaps even thousands—of pieces in the biological puzzle.

TABLE 2.1   Major Neurotransmitters and Their Effects

Neurotransmitter	Source and Function
Acetylcholine (ACH)	One of the most widespread neurotransmitters. Occurs in systems that control the muscles and in circuits related to attention and memory. Reduction in levels of acetylcholine is associated with Alzheimer's disease.
Dopamine	Concentrated in small areas of the brain, one of which is involved in the control of the muscles. In excess, dopamine can cause hallucinations. Associated with schizophrenia.
Endorphins	Found in the brain and spinal cord. Suppresses pain.
Gamma aminobutyric acid (GABA)	Widely distributed in the brain. Works against other neurotransmitters, particularly dopamine.
Norepinephrine	Occurs widely in the central nervous system. Regulates moods and may increase arousal and alertness. Often associated with mood disorders and eating disorders.
Serotonin	Occurs in the brain. Works more or less in opposition to norepinephrine, suppressing activity and causing sleep. Linked with anxiety disorders, mood disorders, and eating disorders.

Genetic Explanations

Research strongly indicates that genetic makeup plays an important role in the development of certain abnormal conditions. There is strong evidence that autonomic nervous system (ANS) reactivity is inherited in human beings; that is, a person may be born with an ANS that makes an unusually strong response to stimuli (Andreasen, 2005). Heredity has been implicated as a causal factor in alcoholism, schizophrenia, and depression. To show that a particular disorder is inherited, however, researchers must demonstrate that it could not be caused by environmental factors alone, that closer genetic relationships produce greater similarity of the disorder in human beings, and that people with these problems have similar biological and behavioral patterns.

Biological inheritance is transmitted by genes. A person's genetic makeup is called his or her genotype. Interaction between the genotype and the environment results in the person's phenotype, or observable physical and behavioral characteristics. At times, however, it is difficult to determine whether genotype or environment is exerting a stronger influence. For example, characteristics such as eye color are determined solely by our genotype—by the coding in our genes. But other physical characteristics, such as height, are determined partly by the genetic code and partly by environmental factors. Adults who were undernourished as children are shorter than the height they were genetically capable of reaching, but even the most effective nutrition would not have caused them to grow taller than their "programmed" height limit.

Perhaps the greatest breakthrough in our attempt to understand the impact of genes on human life comes from the accomplishments of the Human Genome Project (HGP). Scientists have been able to map the locations of all genes in the nucleus of a human cell, and to determine its sequencing (the order of the DNA chemical subunits in each cell). Often referred to as the "map of life" or the "total body manual," the HGP was successful in creating a basic blueprint of the entire genetic material found in each cell of the body. The human genome is composed of all the genetic material in the chromosomes of a particular organism and is the most complex instruction manual ever conceived on how the body works. Many scientists believe that the successful mapping and sequencing of the human genome will reveal life's secrets: how our physical characteristics are determined, how we age, our susceptibility to diseases, personality traits, and the proclivity to develop mental disorders, for example. The challenge is our inability to fully read the manual or to understand what it means.

However, we have begun to accumulate scientific data that suggest the potential importance of the HGP. In 1993, for example, scientists discovered the gene that determines the occurrence of Huntington's disease, which causes an irreversible degeneration of the nervous system. The genes associated with hereditary diseases such as cystic fibrosis, muscular dystrophy, neurofibromatosis, and retinoblastoma have been identified as well. Proponents of the HGP speculate that findings may offer a way of understanding the causes, prevention, and treatment for many types of sleep disorders, addictions, obesity, cancer, heart disease, and sickle cell anemia. Already, a new field called *pharmacogenomics*, the science of understanding the correlation between a patient's genetic makeup and his or her response to drug treatment, has drug manufacturers poised to develop more effective pharmacological treatments.

Biology-Based Treatment Techniques

Biological or somatic treatment techniques use physical means to alter the patient's physiological state and hence his or her psychological state (Andreasen, 2005; Kolb et al., 2003; Miller & Keller, 2000). As our understanding of human physiology and brain functioning has increased, so has our ability to provide more effective biologically based therapies for the mentally ill.

Psychopharmacology

Psychopharmacology is the study of the effects of drugs on the mind and on behavior; it is also known as *medication* or *drug therapy*. Medication is now widely used throughout the United

genotype   person's genetic makeup

phenotype   observable physical and behavioral characteristics caused by the interaction between the genotype and the environment

genome   all the genetic material in the chromosomes of a particular organism

States: More mental patients receive drug therapy than receive all other forms of therapy combined (Levinthal, 2005). The four major classes of medication are (1) *antianxiety drugs* (or *minor tranquilizers*), (2) *antipsychotic drugs* (or *major tranquilizers*), (3) *antidepressant drugs* (which relieve depression by elevating one's mood), and (4) *antimanic drugs* (such as lithium). Many of these drugs are discussed more thoroughly in the context of specific disorders in forthcoming chapters.

Antianxiety drugs (minor tranquilizers) such as *propanediols* (*meprobamate compounds*) and *benzodiazepines* are the preferred medications to calm and reduce anxiety in people. Researchers first developed *meprobamate* (the generic name of Miltown and Equanil) for use as a muscle relaxant and anxiety reducer. Within a few years, it was being prescribed for patients who complained of anxiety and nervousness or who had psychosomatic problems. Soon other drugs, such as the *benzodiazepines* (Librium and Valium), also entered the market. The benzodiazepines work by binding to specific receptor sites at the synapses and blocking transmission.

Although antianxiety medications reduce anxiety in patients, they have minimal impact on the hallucinations and distorted thinking of highly agitated patients and patients with schizophrenia. In 1950, a synthetic antipsychotic drug (major tranquilizer) was developed in France called *chlorpromazine* (the generic name of Thorazine). It had an unexpected tranquilizing effect (believed to be a biochemical effect of blocking dopamine receptors) that decreased patients' interest in the events around them and significantly reduced psychotic symptoms. Within a year of its introduction, some 2 million patients used Thorazine. Thereafter, a number of other major tranquilizers were developed, mainly for patients with schizophrenia.

Antidepressant drugs help individuals feel less depressed. Three large classes of the medication compounds have been identified: monoamine oxidase inhibitors, tricyclics, and selective serotonin reuptake inhibitors (a type of tricyclic). *Monoamine oxidase inhibitors* (*MAOIs*) are antidepressant compounds that are believed to correct the balance of neurotransmitters in the brain. They block the action of monoamine oxidase, thereby preventing the breakdown of norepinephrine and serotonin. More frequently used in cases of depression are the *tricyclics*, antidepressant compounds that relieve symptoms of depression and seem to work like the MAOIs but produce fewer of the side effects associated with prolonged drug use. The medication *imipramine*, a tricyclic, has been at least as effective as psychotherapy in relieving the symptoms of depression. Increasingly, however, *selective serotonin reuptake inhibitors* (*SSRIs*) have become the preferred choice for treating depression. They work by inhibiting the central nervous system's neuronal uptake of serotonin—a mechanism that appears to be extremely effective for treating unipolar depression. The drugs Prozac (fluoxetine hydrochloride), Paxil (paroxetine), and Zoloft (sertraline) are SSRIs.

Antimanic drugs such as *lithium* are mood-controlling medications that have been very effective in treating bipolar disorders, especially mania. About 70 to 80 percent of manic states can be controlled by lithium, and it also controls depressive episodes. How lithium works remains highly speculative. One hypothesis is that it limits the availability of serotonin and norepinephrine at the synapses and produces an effect opposite from that of antidepressants. Yet, lithium's ability to relieve depression appears to contradict this explanation. Other speculations involve electrolyte changes in the body, which alter neurotransmission in some manner.

The use of antidepressant, antianxiety, antipsychotic, and antimanic drugs has greatly changed therapy. Patients who take them report that they feel better, that symptoms decline, and that overall functioning improves. Long periods of hospitalization are no longer needed in most cases, and patients are more amenable to other forms of treatment, such as psychotherapy. Remember, however, that medications do not cure mental disorders. Some would characterize their use as "control measures," somewhat better than traditional hospitalization, "straitjackets," or "padded cells." Furthermore, medications seem to be most effective in treating "active" symptoms such as delusions, hallucinations, and aggression and much less effective with "passive" symptoms such as withdrawal, poor interpersonal relationships, and feelings of alienation. Medication does not help patients improve their living skills.

Electroconvulsive Therapy

Besides medication, *electroconvulsive therapy* (*ECT*) can be used to treat certain mental disorders. ECT is the application of electric voltage to the brain to induce convulsions. The patient lies on a padded bed or couch and is injected with a muscle relaxant to minimize the chance of self-injury during the convulsions. Evidence suggests that the treatment is particularly useful for endogenous cases of depression—those in which some internal cause can be determined (see Chapter 8). But how ECT acts to improve depression is still unclear. Despite its success, the use of ECT has declined significantly since the 1960s and 1970s because of potential permanent damage to the brain and the ethical objections raised by detractors.

Psychosurgery

During the 1940s and 1950s, *psychosurgery*—brain surgery performed for the purpose of correcting a severe mental disorder—became increasingly popular. The treatment was used most often with patients suffering from schizophrenia and severe depression, although many who had personality and anxiety disorders also underwent psychosurgery. Critics of psychosurgical procedures have raised both scientific and ethical objections.

Multipath Implications of Biological Explanations

In keeping with our multipath model, we believe that the majority of human diseases are multidimensional and multifactorial, caused by many genes interacting in a cellular environment of hormones, electrical signals, and nutrient supplies, as well as in our physical, psychological, social, and cultural environments. If the majority of mental disorders are indeed multifactorial, then any single gene or group of genes has small effects, not large ones. Our multipath model places in context our wider view of the etiology of mental disorders.

First, most biological explanations implicitly assume a correspondence between organic dysfunction and mental dysfunction, with only a minimal impact from environmental, social, or cultural influences. They are one-dimensional and linear (that is, unidirectional rather than bidirectional). Muscular dystrophy, for example, was found to be traceable to a single gene. Such a relationship is often cited as evidence not only of the power of biology but also that disorders are the result of a one-way cause-effect direction. A one-to-one correspondence such as this one, however, is a statistical rarity in behavioral genetics. Such diseases account for only 2 percent of the disease load, whereas disorders associated with the genes for bipolar disorders, cancers, and heart disease together make up 70 percent of the disease load (Strohman, 2001).

Second, mental health researchers have increasingly come to reject a simple linear explanation of genetic determinism: that bad biology leads to a mental disorder or the simple model of "one gene for one disease" (Rucker & McGuffin, 2010). Rather, disorders are seen as the result of complex interactive and oftentimes reciprocal processes (Mann & Hahghghi, 2010). Such an early formulation is the diathesis-stress theory originally proposed by Meehl (1962) and developed further by Rosenthal (1970). The diathesis-stress theory holds that it is not a particular abnormality that is inherited but rather a *predisposition to develop illness* (diathesis). Certain environmental forces, called *stressors*, may activate the predisposition, resulting in a disorder. Alternatively, in a benign and supportive environment, the abnormality may never materialize.

Third, findings in the field of epigenetics indicate that even the diathesis-stress theory of having a "predisposition" to develop a disorder may be an oversimplification (Zhang & Meaney, 2010). Epigenetics was first coined as a way to explain gene-environment interactions, especially any change in gene function not mediated by changes in DNA sequencing (Bale, Baram, Brown, Goldstein et al., 2010). Environmental events can actually modify

diathesis-stress theory theory that holds that people do not inherit a particular abnormality but rather a *predisposition to develop illness* (diathesis) and that certain environmental forces, called *stressors*, may activate the predisposition, resulting in a disorder

epigenetics reciprocal gene-environment interactions that actually modify the expression of the genome

the epigenetic state of the genome, which leads to changes in gene expression and neural functioning. This means that cellular function can only be understood as a constant and reciprocal conversation between the genome and the environment. For example, certain genes or gene combinations may actually promote an environment likely to elicit stressors that negatively affect the individual (Diamond, 2009; Plomin & McGuffin, 2003). In other words, in addition to conveying a predisposition for a disorder like depression, genes may also predispose a person to seek out situations that place them at high risk of experiencing stressors that trigger depression. Adolescent girls prone to depression, for example, may actually seek out situations that promote mood disorders (such as selecting unstable boyfriends who increase the probability of breakups).

Fourth, studies reveal that different forms of the same genes, called *alleles*, and *critical developmental periods* in the life of an individual may determine whether, when, how, and what mental disturbances develop (Bale, Baram, Brown et al., 2010). In one longitudinal study of children from age five through their mid-twenties, researchers assessed multiple variables such as abuse, stressful life events, and depression (Caspi et al., 2003). They measured a particular gene, the *serotonin transporter gene* (5-HTT), in each of the participants. They identified three groups of people: (1) those with two short alleles, (2) those with two long alleles, and (3) those with one short and one long allele. Children with the two short alleles and with one short and one long allele who had been mistreated were more likely to experience depression as adults. However, those with the same gene combinations who had not been abused as children were less likely to develop depression. Additionally, those with the long-long combination, even when mistreated, were also less likely to develop depression. A review of studies on affective and anxiety disorders is not only consistent with these findings but also suggests strongly that gene-environment interactions that occur at early critical periods can set the stage for later behavioral phenotypes (Leonardo & Hen, 2006). It is clear that simply having a specific gene and encountering environmental stressors is not enough to predict the manifestation of a mental disorder. Rather, the configuration of the gene, the specific stressors, and the times at which they occur (critical periods) play important roles.

Fifth, accumulating evidence strongly suggests that biochemical changes, brain activity, and even structural neurological circuitry often occur because of environmental influence (Foster & MacQueen, 2008; Leonardo & Hen, 2006). We know, for example, that stress-produced fear and anger cause the secretion of adrenaline and noradrenalin. Similarly, schizophrenia, rather than resulting from the presence of such chemicals as dopamine, could *cause* the secretion of excess amounts of the chemicals in persons with the disorder. Through brain imaging studies we also know that psychotherapeutic interventions have been found to "normalize" brain circuitry in people suffering from depression (Leuchter et al., 2002), obsessive-compulsive disorders (Baxter et al., 1992), phobias (Paquette et al., 2003), and tolerance of pain (Petrovic, Kalso, Peterson, & Ingvar, 2002). In conclusion, although biology influences the development of mental disorders, an equally powerful reciprocal influence on brain activity, brain circuitry, and biochemical production/inhibition is exerted by the environment as well.

Did You Know?

Over the past few years the University of Michigan, University of California Los Angeles, and Emory University have opened up cultural neuroscience centers to study how biology shapes culture, and how culture shapes biology. In one neuroimaging study, it was found that when Chinese think about honesty for themselves and honesty for a close relative, their brain activities are nearly identical for each task. When Americans think about honesty for themselves and relatives, their patterns are very different. It appears that Americans see themselves more as individuals, whereas the Chinese view themselves as part of the family. These findings are consistent with either a collectivistic or individualistic cultural perspective. In other words, culture shapes how the brain functions (Azar, 2010).

Dimension Two: Psychological Factors

Figure 2.1 lists a number of psychological factors that have been shown to be important in the etiology of mental disorders. Especially important for the psychological dimension are conflicts in the mind, emotions, learned behavior, and cognitions in personality formation. Like many biological explanations, psychological theories can also be prone to viewing normal and abnormal human development in a linear and one-dimensional fashion. They can also suffer from tunnel vision in explaining mental disorders as arising from psychological rather than biological, social, or sociocultural factors. Interestingly, psychological explanations of abnormal behavior vary considerably depending on the psychologist's theoretical orientation. For example, in our chapter-opening case, Steve's therapist might stress his client's *intrapsychic conflicts* and the need to resolve and control extreme feelings of rage and hostility toward authority figures. Other psychologists might concentrate on his *social isolation*, being cared for by a caretaker who spoke no English and who would send him to his room when he misbehaved. As a result, Steve had few role models from whom to learn appropriate social skills that would lead to successful interpersonal relationships. Other theorists might conjecture that Steve crafted a fantasy world from his violent videos (his source of reality) because of infrequent checks and balances from his primary caretaker or parents. As a result, not only is the content of his thoughts irrational, but his thinking process has also become distorted.

In this section, we briefly describe four major psychological perspectives in explaining abnormal behavior: psychodynamic, behavioral, cognitive, and existential-humanistic. We then apply a multipath analysis to these four approaches.

Psychodynamic Models

Psychodynamic models of abnormal behavior have two main distinguishing features. First, they view disorders as the result of childhood trauma or anxieties. Second, they hold that many of these childhood-based anxieties operate unconsciously; because experiences are too threatening for the adult to face, they are repressed through mental defense mechanisms—ego-protection strategies that shelter the individual from anxiety, operate unconsciously, and distort reality. As a result, people exhibit symptoms that they are unable to understand because they are manifestations of the unconscious conflicts. The early development of psychodynamic theory is credited to Sigmund Freud (1938, 1949). Freud was convinced that powerful mental processes could remain hidden from consciousness and could cause abnormal behaviors. He believed that the therapist's role was to help the patient achieve insight into these unconscious processes.

Personality Structure

Freud believed that personality is composed of three major components—the *id*, the *ego*, and the *superego*—and that all behavior is a product of their interaction. The *id* is the original component of the personality; it is present at birth, and from it the ego and superego eventually develop. The id operates from the pleasure principle—the impulsive, pleasure-seeking aspect of our being—and it seeks immediate gratification of instinctual needs, regardless of moral or realistic concerns. In contrast, the *ego* represents the realistic and rational part of the mind. It is influenced by the reality principle—an awareness of the demands of the environment and of the need to adjust behavior to meet these demands. The ego's decisions are dictated by realistic considerations rather than by moral judgments.

Moral judgments and moralistic considerations are the domain of the *superego*. The superego is composed of the *conscience*, which instills guilt feelings about engaging in immoral or unethical behavior, and the *ego ideal*, which rewards altruistic or moral behavior with feelings of pride.

The energy system from which the personality operates occurs through the interplay of *instincts*. Instincts give rise to our thoughts and actions and fuel their expression. Freud emphasized *sex* (libido) and *aggression* as the dominant human instincts because he recognized that the society in which he lived placed strong prohibitions on these drives and that, as a result, people were taught to inhibit them. A profound need to express one's instincts is often frightening and can lead a person to deny their existence. Most impulses are hidden from one's consciousness; they nonetheless determine human actions.

psychodynamic model model that views disorders as the result of childhood trauma or anxieties and that holds that many of these childhood-based anxieties operate unconsciously

defense mechanism in psychoanalytic theory, an ego-protection strategy that shelters the individual from anxiety, operates unconsciously, and distorts reality

pleasure principle the impulsive, pleasure-seeking aspect of our being from which the id operates

reality principle an awareness of the demands of the environment and of the need to adjust behavior to meet these demands from which the ego operates

Library of Congress / Woodfin Camp & Associates

Sigmund Freud (1856–1939)

Freud began his career as a neurologist. He became increasingly intrigued with the relationship between illness and mental processes and ultimately developed psychoanalysis, a therapy in which unconscious conflicts are aired so that the patient can become aware of and understand his or her problems.

psychosexual stages   in psychodynamic theory, the sequence of stages—oral, anal, phallic, latency, and genital—through which human personality develops

psychoanalysis   the goals of this therapy are to uncover repressed material, to help clients achieve insight into inner motivations and desires, and to resolve childhood conflicts that affect current relationships

free association   psychoanalytic therapeutic technique in which the patient says whatever comes to mind for the purpose of revealing his or her unconscious

resistance   during psychoanalysis, a process in which the patient unconsciously attempts to impede the analysis by preventing the exposure of repressed material

transference   process by which a patient reenacts early conflicts by applying to the analyst feelings and attitudes that the patient had toward significant others in the past

Psychosexual Stages

Human personality develops through a sequence of five psychosexual stages, each of which brings a unique challenge. If unfavorable circumstances prevail, the personality may be drastically affected. Because Freud stressed the importance of early childhood experiences, he saw the human personality as largely determined in the first five years of life—during the *oral* (first year of life), *anal* (around the second year of life), and *phallic* (beginning around the third or fourth years of life) stages. The last two psychosexual stages are the *latency* (approximately six to twelve years of age) and *genital* (beginning in puberty) stages.

The importance of each psychosexual stage for later development lies in whether fixation occurs during that stage. *Fixation* is the arresting of emotional development at a particular psychosexual stage. According to the psychodynamic model, each stage is characterized by distinct traits and, should fixation occur, by distinct conflicts.

Traditional Psychodynamic Therapy

Psychoanalytic therapy, or psychoanalysis, has three main goals: (1) uncovering repressed material, (2) helping clients achieve insight into their inner motivations and desires, and (3) resolving childhood conflicts that affect current relationships. Psychoanalysts traditionally use four methods to achieve their therapeutic goals: free association, dream analysis, analysis of resistance, and analysis of transference.

- In free association, the patient says whatever comes to mind, regardless of how illogical or embarrassing it may seem, for the purpose of revealing the contents of the patient's unconscious. Psychoanalysts believe the material that surfaces in this process is determined by the patient's psychic makeup and can provide understanding of the patient's conflicts, unconscious processes, and personality dynamics.
- *Dream analysis* is a therapeutic technique that depends on interpretation of hidden meanings in dreams. Psychoanalysts believe that when people sleep, defenses and inhibitions of the ego weaken, allowing unacceptable motives and feelings to surface. The therapist's job is to uncover the disguised symbolic meanings and let the patient achieve insight into the anxiety-provoking implications.
- Analysis of resistance—a process in which the patient unconsciously attempts to impede the analysis by preventing the exposure of repressed material—is used to interpret and uncover the repressed material. In free association, for example, the patient may suddenly change the subject, lose his or her train of thought, go blank, or become silent. The therapist can make use of properly interpreted instances of resistance to show the patient that repressed material is coming close to the surface and to suggest means of uncovering it.
- In transference the patient reenacts early conflicts by applying to the analyst feelings and attitudes that the patient had toward significant others—primarily parents—in the past. Working through transference is considered therapeutic.

Contemporary Psychodynamic Theories

Freud's psychoanalytic approach attracted many followers. Some of Freud's disciples, however, came to disagree with his insistence that the sex instinct is the major determinant of behavior. Many of his most gifted adherents broke away from him and formulated psychological models of their own. The major differences between the various post-Freudian theories and psychoanalysis lie in their greater emphasis on freedom of choice and future goals, ego autonomy, social forces, object relations (past interpersonal relations), and treatment of seriously disturbed people. Some of these major theorists and their contributions are outlined in Table 2.2. Today, very few psychodynamic therapists practice traditional psychoanalysis. Most are more active in their sessions, restrict the number of sessions they have with clients, place greater emphasis on current rather than past factors, and seem to have adopted a number of client-centered techniques in their practice (Nystul, 2003).

TABLE 2.2   Contributions of Post-Freudians and Psychoanalytic Therapists

Traditional psychoanalytic theory has changed over the years due to the work of post-Freudians and others. Although most of the individuals listed here accept many of the basic tenets of the theory, they have stressed different aspects of the human condition. Some differences are listed in the following table.

1. **Freedom of choice and future goals** People are not just mechanistic beings. They have a high degree of free choice and are motivated toward future goals.
   Alfred Adler (1870–1937) Stressed that people are not passive victims of biology, instincts, or unconscious forces. Stressed freedom of choice and goals directed by means of social drives.
   Carl Jung (1875–1965) Believed in the collective unconscious as the foundation of creative functioning. Believed that humans were goal directed and future oriented.

2. **Ego autonomy** The ego is an autonomous entity and can operate independently from the id. It is creative, forward moving, and capable of continual growth.
   Anna Freud (1895–1982) Emphasized the role, operation, and importance of the ego. Believed ego is an autonomous component of the personality and not at the mercy of the id.
   Erik Erikson (1902–1994) Perhaps the most influential of the ego theorists. Formulated stages of ego development from infancy to late adulthood—one of the first true developmental theorists. Considered personality to be flexible and capable of growth and change throughout the adult years.

3. **Social forces** Interpersonal relationships are of primary importance in our psychological development. Especially influential are our primary social relationships.
   Karen Horney (1885–1952) Often considered one of the first feminist psychologists who rejected Freud's notion of penis envy. Stressed that behavior disorders are due to disturbed interpersonal childhood relationships.
   Harry Stack Sullivan (1892–1949) Major contribution was his interpersonal theory of psychological disorders. Believed that the individual's psychological functions could be understood only in the context of his or her social relationships.

4. **Object relations** The technical term "object relations" is roughly equivalent to "past interpersonal relations." It refers to how people develop patterns of living from their early relations with significant others.
   Heinz Kohut (1913–1981) Felt it was especially important to study the mother-child relationship. Known for his work on the narcissistic personality.
   Otto Kernberg (1928–) Known for his studies of the borderline personality. Especially interested in understanding how clients seem to have difficulty in forming stable relationships because of pathological objects in their past.

5. **Treatment of the seriously disturbed** Freud believed that psychoanalysis could not be used with very seriously disturbed individuals because they were "analytically unfit." By this he meant that they did not have sufficient contact with reality to benefit from insight.
   Hyman Spotnitz (1908–) Demonstrated that modern psychoanalysis could be used with severely disturbed clients. Associated with new treatment techniques that do not require clients to be intellectually capable of understanding interpretations. Techniques provide feedback that helps clients resolve conflicts by experiencing them rather than understanding them.

Criticisms of Psychodynamic Models

Psychodynamic theory has strongly affected the field of psychology, and psychoanalysis and its variations are widely employed. Nonetheless, three major criticisms are often leveled at psychodynamic theory and treatment.

First, the empirical procedures by which Freud validated his hypotheses have grave shortcomings. His observations about human behavior were often made under uncontrolled conditions and relied heavily on case studies. He also used his own self-analysis as a basis for formulating theory. His patients, from whom he drew conclusions about universal aspects of personality dynamics and behavior, tended to represent a narrow spectrum of relatively affluent Victorian-era Austrian women.

Second, his theory of female sexuality and personality has drawn heavy criticism from feminists. Phallic-stage dynamics, penis envy, unfavorable comparisons of the clitoris to the penis, the woman's need for a male child as a penis substitute, and the belief that penetration is necessary for a woman's sexual satisfaction all rest on assumptions that are biologically questionable and that fail to consider social forces that shape women's behavior.

A third criticism of psychoanalysis is that it cannot be applied to a wide range of disturbed people. Research studies have shown that psychoanalytic therapy is best suited to well-educated people of the middle and upper socioeconomic classes who exhibit anxiety disorders rather than psychotic behavior (Corey, 2008). It is more limited in therapeutic

Ivan Pavlov (1849–1936)

A Russian physiologist, Pavlov discovered the associative learning process we know as classical conditioning while he was studying salivation in dogs. Pavlov won the Nobel Prize in physiology and medicine in 1904 for his work on the principal digestive glands.

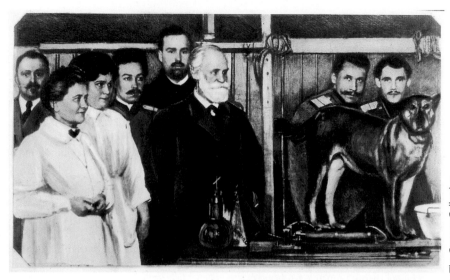

The Granger Collection

value with people of lower socioeconomic levels and with people who are less verbal, less psychologically-minded, and more severely disturbed.

Behavioral Models

The behavioral models of psychopathology are concerned with the role of learning in abnormal behavior. The differences among them lie mainly in their explanations of how learning occurs (Corey, 2008). The three learning paradigms are *classical conditioning*, *operant conditioning*, and *observational learning*.

The Classical Conditioning Paradigm

Early in the twentieth century, Ivan Pavlov (1849–1936), a Russian physiologist, discovered a process known as classical conditioning, in which responses to new stimuli are learned through association. This process involves involuntary responses (such as reflexes, emotional reactions, and sexual arousal), which are controlled by the autonomic nervous system.

Pavlov was measuring dogs' salivation as part of a study of their digestive processes when he noticed that the dogs began to salivate at the sight of an assistant carrying their food. This response puzzled Pavlov and led to his formulation of classical conditioning. He reasoned that food is an unconditioned stimulus (UCS), which, in the mouth, automatically elicits salivation; this salivation is an unlearned or unconditioned response (UCR) to the food. Pavlov then presented a previously *neutral* stimulus (one, such as the sound of a bell, that does not initially elicit salivation) to the dogs just before presenting the food. He found that, after a number of repetitions, the sound of the bell alone elicited salivation. This learning process is based on association: The neutral stimulus (the bell) acquires some of the properties of the unconditioned stimulus (the food) when they are repeatedly paired. When the bell alone can provoke the salivation, it becomes a conditioned stimulus (CS). The salivation elicited by the bell is a conditioned response (CR)—a learned response to a previously neutral stimulus. Each time the conditioned stimulus is paired with the unconditioned stimulus, the conditioned response is *reinforced*, or strengthened. Pavlov's conditioning process is illustrated in Figure 2.8.

Classical Conditioning in Psychopathology

John B. Watson (1878–1958) is credited with recognizing the importance of associative learning in the explanation of abnormal behavior. In a classic and oft-cited experiment, Watson (Watson & Rayner, 1920), using classical conditioning principles, was able to demonstrate that the acquisition of a *phobia* (an exaggerated, seemingly illogical fear of a particular object or class of objects) could be explained by classical conditioning. In fact, classical conditioning has provided explanations not only for the acquisition of phobias but also for certain

behavioral models   models of psychopathology concerned with the role of learning in abnormal behavior

classical conditioning   a process in which responses to new stimuli are learned through association

unconditioned stimulus (UCS)   in classical conditioning, the stimulus that elicits an unconditioned response

unconditioned response (UCR)   in classical conditioning, the unlearned response made to an unconditioned stimulus

conditioned stimulus (CS)   in classical conditioning, a previously neutral stimulus that has acquired some of the properties of another stimulus with which it has been paired

conditioned response (CR)   in classical conditioning, a learned response to a previously neutral stimulus that has acquired some of the properties of another stimulus with which it has been paired

| Stimulus: | UCS (food) | UCS & CS (food & bell) | CS (bell alone) |
| Response: | UCR (salivation) | UCR (salivation) | CR (conditioned salivation) |

Figure 2.8

A BASIC CLASSICAL CONDITIONING PROCESS

Dogs normally salivate when food is provided (left drawing). With his laboratory dogs, Ivan Pavlov paired the ringing of a bell with the presentation of food (middle drawing). Eventually, the dogs would salivate to the ringing of the bell alone, when no food was near (right drawing).

unusual sexual attractions and other extreme emotional reactions. Yet, the passive nature of associative learning limited its usefulness as an explanatory and treatment tool. Most human behavior, both normal and abnormal, tends to be much more active and voluntary. To explain how these behaviors are acquired or eliminated necessitates an understanding of operant conditioning.

The Operant Conditioning Paradigm

An operant behavior is a voluntary and controllable behavior, such as walking or thinking, that "operates" on an individual's environment. In an extremely warm room, for example, you would have difficulty consciously controlling your sweating—"willing" your body not to perspire. You could, however, simply walk out of the uncomfortably warm room—an operant behavior. Most human behavior is operant in nature.

Edward Thorndike (1874–1949) first formulated the concept of operant conditioning, which he called *instrumental conditioning*. This theory of learning holds that behaviors are controlled by the consequences that follow them. Some fifty years later, B. F. Skinner (1904–1990) developed Thorndike's work and made the concept of *reinforcement* central. Operant conditioning differs from classical conditioning in two primary ways. First, classical conditioning is linked to the development of involuntary behaviors, such as fear responses, whereas operant conditioning is related to voluntary behaviors. Second, behaviors based on *classical* conditioning are controlled by stimuli, or events *preceding* the response: Salivation occurs only when it is preceded by a UCS (food in the mouth) or a CS (the thought of a sizzling, juicy steak covered with mushrooms, for example). In *operant* conditioning, however, behaviors are controlled by reinforcers—consequences that influence the frequency or magnitude of the event they follow. Positive consequences increase the likelihood and frequency of a response. But when the consequences are negative, the behavior is less likely to be repeated.

Operant Conditioning in the Classroom

In operant conditioning, positive consequences increases the likelihood and frequency of a desired response. This is particularly important in teaching young children that appropriate behavior will be rewarded and inappropriate behavior will be punished. These first graders are being treated to a petting zoo for good behavior maintained in the classroom. The reward is changed on a monthly basis.

Steve Warnowski / The Image Works

Operant Conditioning in Psychopathology

Studies have demonstrated a relationship between environmental reinforcers and certain abnormal behaviors. For example, self-injurious behavior, such as head banging, is a dramatic form of psychopathology that is often reported in psychotic, autistic, and mentally retarded children. It has been hypothesized that some forms of head banging may be linked to reinforcing features in the environment, as when parents distract the child by giving him or her candy (Corey, 2008; Sommers-Flanagan & Sommers-Flanagan, 2004).

operant behavior a voluntary and controllable behavior, such as walking or thinking, that "operates" on an individual's environment

operant conditioning a theory of learning that holds that behaviors are controlled by the consequences that follow them

AP Images

B. F. Skinner (1904–1990)

Skinner was a leader in the field of behaviorism. His research and work in operant conditioning started a revolution in applying the principles of learning to the psychology of human behavior. He was also a social philosopher, and many of his ideas fueled debate about the nature of the human condition. These ideas were expressed in his books *Walden II* and *Beyond Freedom and Dignity*.

MYTH: Behavioral approaches assume that people are completely the products of their conditioning histories, that they are passive participants in the developmental process, and that they have little free will. These approaches deny the importance of "mental life" in people. They seem more focused on behaviors and seem to believe people are mechanistic and robotic in their actions.

REALITY: Whereas early behaviorism, under the influence of John B. Watson (and to some extent B. F. Skinner), saw people as primarily the products of their conditioning histories and felt that speculating about the "inner life" of a person was unscientific, such rigid concepts have given way to a more holistic and integrated interpretation of the learning process. Behaviorally oriented mental health professionals are now very much involved in understanding how the internal mental life of the person affects the acquisition and treatment of certain disorders. They now acknowledge that people are not passive beings and have increasingly moved toward using social modeling and cognitive processes to supplement the principles of both classical and operant learning models.

MYTH VS. REALITY

observational learning theory theory that suggests that an individual can acquire new behaviors by watching other people perform them

modeling process of learning by observing models (and later imitating them)

It has also been found that self-injurious behaviors, hallucinations, and delusional statements can be developed and maintained through reinforcement. Likewise, some forms of alcohol or substance abuse may be due to the initial pleasurable feelings and lowered anxieties people experience.

Although positive reinforcement can account for some forms of self-injurious or other undesirable behaviors, in some instances other variables seem more important. *Negative reinforcement* (the removal of an aversive stimulus), for example, can also strengthen and maintain unhealthy behaviors. Consider a student who has enrolled in a class in which the instructor requires oral reports. The thought of doing an oral presentation in front of a class produces anxiety, sweating, an upset stomach, and trembling in the student. Having these feelings is aversive. To stop the unpleasant reaction, the student switches to another section in which the instructor does not require oral presentations. The student's behavior is reinforced by escape from aversive feelings, and such avoidant responses to situations involving "stage fright" increase in frequency.

The Observational Learning Paradigm

The traditional behavioral theories of learning—classical conditioning and operant conditioning—require that the individual actually perform behaviors to learn them. Observational learning theory suggests that an individual can acquire new behaviors simply by watching other people perform them (Bandura, 1997). The process of learning by observing models (and later imitating them) is called *vicarious conditioning* or modeling. Direct and tangible reinforcement (such as giving praise or other rewards) for imitation of the model is not necessary, although reinforcers are necessary to maintain behaviors learned in this manner. Observational learning can involve both respondent and operant behaviors, and its discovery has had such an impact in psychology that it has been proposed as a third form of learning.

Observational Learning in Psychopathology

Models that attribute psychopathology to observational learning assume—as do those that emphasize classical and operant conditioning—that abnormal behaviors are learned in the same manner as normal behaviors. More specifically, the assumption is that exposure to disturbed models is likely to produce disturbed behaviors. For example, when monkeys watched other monkeys respond with fear to an unfamiliar object, they learned to respond in a similar manner

Criticisms of the Behavioral Models

Behavioral approaches to psychopathology have had a tremendous impact in the areas of etiology and treatment, and they are a strong force in psychology today. Opponents of the behavioral orientation, however, point out that it often neglects or places a low importance on the inner determinants of behavior. They criticize the behaviorists' extension to human beings of results obtained from animal studies. Some also charge that because of its lack of attention to human values in relation to behavior, the behaviorist perspective is mechanistic, viewing people as "empty organisms." This specific criticism is less applicable to proponents of modeling.

Cognitive Models

Cognitive models are based on the assumption that conscious thought mediates, or modifies, an individual's emotional state and/or behavior in response to a stimulus. According to these models, people actually create their own problems (and symptoms) by the ways they interpret events and situations. For example, one person who fails to be hired for a job may become depressed, blaming himself or herself for the failure. Another might become only mildly irritated, believing that failure to get the job had nothing to do with personal inadequacy. How does it happen that the event (not being hired for a job) is identical for both people but the responses are very different?

Cognitive theories argue that modifying thoughts and feelings is essential to changing behavior. How people label a situation and how they interpret events profoundly affect their emotional reactions and behaviors. How a person interprets events is a function of his or her schema—a set of underlying assumptions heavily influenced by a person's experiences, values, and perceived capabilities. Cognitive psychologists usually search for the causes of psychopathology in one of two processes: in actual irrational and maladaptive assumptions and thoughts or in distortions of the actual thought process.

Irrational and Maladaptive Assumptions and Thoughts

Almost all cognitive theorists stress that disturbed individuals have both irrational and maladaptive thoughts (Beck & Weishaar, 2010; Ellis, 2008). Aaron Beck (1921–) and Albert Ellis (1913–2007) are cognitive psychologists who explain psychological problems as being produced by irrational thought patterns that stem from the individual's belief system. Unpleasant emotional responses that lead to anger, unhappiness, depression, fear, and anxiety result from one's *thoughts* about an event rather than from the *event itself*. These irrational thoughts have been conditioned through early childhood, but we also add to the difficulty by reinstilling these false beliefs in ourselves by autosuggestion and self-repetition (Ellis, 2008). Although being accepted and loved by everyone is desirable, it is an unrealistic and irrational idea, and as such it creates dysfunctional feelings and behaviors. Consider a student who becomes depressed after an unsuccessful date. An appropriate emotional response in such an unsuccessful dating situation might be

Bob Daemmrich/Stock Boston

Learning by Observing

Observational learning is based on the theory that behavior can be learned by observing it. Although much has been made of the relationship between violence and aggression viewed on television and in movies and violent behavior in real life, observational learning can have positive benefits as well.

cognitive models   models based on the assumption that conscious thought mediates an individual's emotional state and/or behavior in response to a stimulus

schema   a set of underlying assumptions heavily influenced by a person's experiences, values, and perceived capabilities

frustration and temporary disappointment. A more severe depression develops only if the student adds irrational thoughts, such as "Because this person turned me down, I am worthless. I will never succeed with anyone of the opposite sex. I am a total failure."

Distortions of Thought Processes

The study of cognitions as a cause of psychopathology has led many therapists to concentrate on the process (as opposed to the content) of thinking that characterizes both normal and abnormal individuals. Ellis (1997; 2008) described the process by which an individual acquires irrational thoughts through interactions with significant others, and he called it the *A-B-C theory of personality. A* is an event, a fact, or the individual's behavior or attitude. *C* is the person's emotional or behavioral reaction. The activating event *A* never causes the emotional or behavioral consequence *C*. Instead, *B*, the person's beliefs about *A,* causes *C.*

Think back to the two job hunters. Job hunter 1, whose activating event *A* was being turned down for the position, may think to himself (irrational beliefs *B*), "How awful to be rejected! I must be worthless. I'm no good." Thus he may become depressed and withdraw (emotional and behavioral consequence *C*). Job hunter 2, on the other hand, reacts to the activating event *A* by saying (rational beliefs *B*), "How unfortunate to get rejected. It's frustrating and irritating. I'll have to try harder" (healthy consequence *C*). The two sets of assumptions and expectations are very different. Job hunter 1 blamed himself and was overcome with feelings of worthlessness; job hunter 2 recognized that not every person is right for every job (or vice versa) and left the situation with self-esteem intact. Job hunter 1 interprets the rejection as "awful and catastrophic" and, as a result, reacts with depression and may cease looking for a job. Job hunter 2 does not interpret the rejection personally, reacts with annoyance, and redoubles her efforts to seek employment. Figure 2.9 illustrates the A-B-C relationship and suggests a possible path for a cognitive approach to treatment.

Cognitive Approaches to Therapy

Certain commonalities characterize almost all cognitive approaches to psychotherapy. These have been summarized by Beck and Weishaar (2010):

> Cognitive therapy consists of highly specific learning experiences designed to teach patients (1) to monitor their negative, automatic thoughts (cognitions);

Figure 2.9

ELLIS'S A-B-C THEORY OF PERSONALITY

The development of emotional and behavioral problems is often linked to a dysfunctional thinking process. The cognitive psychologist is likely to attack these problematic beliefs using a rational intervention process, resulting in a change in beliefs and feelings.

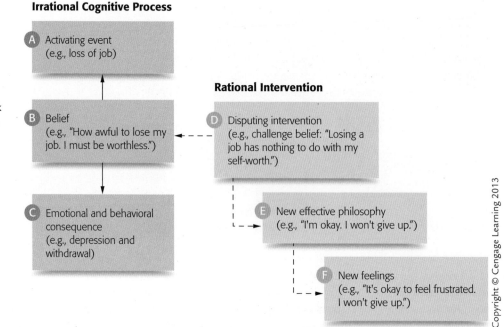

Irrational Cognitive Process

A Activating event (e.g., loss of job)

B Belief (e.g., "How awful to lose my job. I must be worthless.")

C Emotional and behavioral consequence (e.g., depression and withdrawal)

Rational Intervention

D Disputing intervention (e.g., challenge belief: "Losing a job has nothing to do with my self-worth.")

E New effective philosophy (e.g., "I'm okay. I won't give up.")

F New feelings (e.g., "It's okay to feel frustrated. I won't give up.")

(2) to recognize the connections between cognition, affect, and behavior; (3) to examine the evidence for and against distorted automatic thoughts; (4) to substitute more reality-oriented interpretations for these biased cognitions; and (5) to learn to identify and alter the beliefs that predispose them to distort their experiences. (p. 308)

Criticisms of the Cognitive Models

Some behaviorists remain quite skeptical of the cognitive schools. Just before his death, B. F. Skinner (1990) warned that cognitions are not observable phenomena and cannot form the foundations of empiricism. In this context, he echoed the historical beliefs of John B. Watson, who stated that the science of psychology was observable behaviors, not "mentalistic concepts." Although Watson's reference was to the intrapsychic dynamics of the mind postulated by Freud, Watson might have viewed cognitions in the same manner.

Cognitive theories have also been attacked by more humanistically oriented psychologists who believe that human behavior is more than thoughts and beliefs (Corey, 2008). They object to the mechanistic manner by which human beings are reduced to the sum of their cognitive parts. Do thoughts and beliefs really cause disturbances, or do the disturbances themselves distort thinking?

Criticisms have also been leveled at the therapeutic approach taken by cognitive therapists. The nature of the approach makes the therapist a teacher, expert, and authority figure. The therapist is quite direct and confrontive in identifying and attacking irrational beliefs and processes. In such interactions, clients can readily be intimidated into acquiescing to the therapist's power and authority. Thus the therapist may misidentify the client's disorder, and the client may be hesitant to challenge the therapist's beliefs.

Humanistic and Existential Models

Describing humanistic-existential approaches to the development of mental disorders is a major challenge. In many respects, humanistic approaches are philosophical in nature, deal with values, speak to the nature of the human condition, decry the use of diagnostic labels, and prefer a holistic view of the person. For example, humanists would describe Steve V. as a flesh-and-blood person, alive, organic, and moving, with thoughts, feelings, and emotions. Diagnostic labels would be objectionable and serve only to pigeonhole people and act as barriers to the development of a therapeutic relationship. According to the humanist perspective, Steve needs to realize that he is responsible for his own actions, that he cannot find his identity in others, and that his life is not predetermined.

The humanistic and existential approaches evolved as a reaction to the determinism of early models of psychopathology. For example, many psychologists were disturbed that Freudian theory did not focus on the inner world of the client but rather categorized the client according to a set of preconceived diagnoses. They described clients in terms of blocked instinctual forces and psychic complexes that made them victims of some mechanistic and deterministic personality structure. Similarly, cognitive-behavioral schools of thought described human beings as "learned responses," "automatic beings," and "deterministic creatures" who were victims of their conditioning histories.

Although the humanistic and existential perspectives represent many schools of thought, they nevertheless share a set of assumptions that distinguishes them from other approaches. The first of these assumptions is that people's realities are products of unique experiences and perceptions of the world. Moreover, a person's subjective universe—how he or she construes events—is more important than the events themselves. Hence, to understand why people behave as they do, psychologists must reconstruct the world from an individual's vantage point.

Second, humanistic-existential theorists assume that individuals have the ability to make free choices and are responsible for their own decisions. Third, they believe in the "wholeness" or integrity of the person and view as pointless all attempts to reduce human beings to a set of formulas, to explain them simply by measuring responses to certain stimuli. And fourth, they assume that people have the ability to become what they want, to fulfill their capacities, and to lead the lives best suited to them.

The Humanistic Perspective

One of the major contributions of the humanistic perspective is its positive view of the individual. Carl Rogers (1902–1987) is perhaps the best known of the humanistic psychologists. Rogers's theory of personality (1959; 1961) reflects his concern with human welfare and his deep conviction that humanity is basically "good," forward moving, and trustworthy.

The Actualizing Tendency

Instead of concentrating exclusively on behavior disorders, the humanistic approach is concerned with helping people *actualize* their potential and with bettering the state of humanity. Humanistic psychological theory is based on the idea that people are motivated not only to satisfy their biological needs (for food, warmth, and sex) but also to cultivate, maintain, and enhance the self. The *self* is one's image of oneself, the part one refers to as "I" or "me."

The quintessence of this view is the concept of self-actualization—a term popularized by Abraham Maslow (1954)—which is an inherent tendency to strive toward the realization of one's full potential. The actualizing tendency can be viewed as fulfilling a grand design or a genetic blueprint. This thrust of life that pushes people forward is manifested in such qualities as curiosity, creativity, and joy of discovery. How one views the self, how others relate to the self, and what values are attached to the self all contribute to one's self-concept—the individual's assessment of his or her own value and worth.

Development of Abnormal Behavior

Rogers believed that if people were left unencumbered by societal restrictions and were allowed to grow and develop freely, the result would be fully functioning people. In such a case, the self-concept and the actualizing tendency would be considered congruent. However, society frequently imposes *conditions of worth* on its members, standards by which people determine whether they have worth. These standards are transmitted via *conditional positive regard.* That is, significant others (such as parents, peers, friends, and spouse) in a person's life accept some but not all of that person's actions, feelings, and attitudes. The person's self-concept becomes defined as having worth only when others approve. But this reliance on others forces the individual to develop a distorted self-concept that is inconsistent with his or her self-actualizing potential, inhibiting that person from being self-actualized. A state of disharmony or *incongruence* is said to exist between the person's inherent potential and his or her self-concept (as determined by significant others). This state of incongruence forms the basis of abnormal behavior.

Rogers believed that fully functioning people have been *allowed to grow* toward their potential. The environmental condition most suitable for this growth is called *unconditional positive regard* (Rogers, 1951). In essence, people who are significant figures in someone's life value and respect that person *as a person.* Giving unconditional positive regard is valuing and loving regardless of behavior. People may disapprove of someone's actions, but they still respect, love, and care for that someone.

Person-Centered Therapy

The assumption that humans need unconditional positive regard has many implications for child rearing and psychotherapy. For parents, it means creating an open and accepting environment for the child. For the therapist, it means fostering conditions that allow clients to grow and fulfill their potential; this approach has become known as *nondirective* or *person-centered therapy.* Rogers emphasized that therapists' attitudes are more important than specific counseling techniques. The therapist needs to have a strong positive regard for the client's ability to deal constructively with all aspects of life. The more willing the therapist is to rely on the client's strengths and potential, the more likely it is that the client discovers such strengths and potential. The therapist cannot help the client by explaining

humanistic perspective the optimistic viewpoint that people are born with the ability to fulfill their potential and that abnormal behavior results from disharmony between the person's potential and his or her self-concept

self-actualization an inherent tendency to strive toward the realization of one's full potential

self-concept an individual's assessment of his or her own value and worth

the client's behavior or by prescribing actions to follow. Therapeutic techniques involve expressing and communicating respect, understanding, and acceptance.

The Existential Perspective

The existential approach is not a systematized school of thought but a set of attitudes. It shares with humanistic psychology an emphasis on individual uniqueness, a quest for meaning in life and for freedom and responsibility, a phenomenological approach (understanding the person's subjective world of experience) to understanding the person, and a belief that the individual has positive attributes that are eventually expressed unless they are distorted by the environment. The existential and humanistic approaches differ in several dimensions:

1. Existentialism is less optimistic than humanism; it focuses on the irrationality, difficulties, and suffering all humans encounter in life. Although humanism allows the clear possibility of self-fulfillment and freedom, existentialism deals with human alienation from the social and spiritual structures that no longer provide meaning in an increasingly technological and impersonal world.
2. Both approaches stress phenomenology—the attempt to understand people's subjective world of experience. Humanistic therapists attempt to reconstruct the subjective world of their clients through empathy. Existentialists believe that the individual must be viewed within the context of the human condition and that moral, philosophical, and ethical considerations are part of that context.
3. The approaches differ in their views on responsibility. Humanism stresses individual responsibility: The individual is ultimately responsible for what he or she becomes in this life. Existentialism stresses not only individual responsibility but also responsibility to others. Self-fulfillment is not enough.

Criticisms of the Humanistic and Existential Approaches

Criticisms of the humanistic and existential approaches point to their "fuzzy," ambiguous, and nebulous nature and to the small population in which these approaches can be applied. Although these phenomenological approaches have been extremely creative in describing the human condition, they have been less successful in constructing theory. Moreover, they are not suited to scientific or experimental investigation. The emphasis on subjective understanding rather than prediction and control, on intuition and empathy rather than objective investigation, and on the individual rather than the more general category all tend to hinder empirical study.

Carl Rogers has certainly expressed many of his ideas as researchable propositions, but it is difficult to verify scientifically the humanistic concept of people as rational, inherently good, and moving toward self-fulfillment. The existential perspective can be similarly criticized for its lack of scientific grounding because of its reliance on the unique subjective experiences of individuals to describe the inner world. Such data are difficult to quantify and test. Nevertheless, the existential concepts of freedom, choice, responsibility, being, and nonbeing have had a profound influence on contemporary thought beyond the field of psychology.

Another major criticism leveled at the humanistic and existential approaches is that they do not work well with severely disturbed clients. They seem to be most effective with intelligent, well-educated, and relatively "normal" individuals who may be suffering adjustment difficulties. This limitation, along with the occasional vagueness of humanistic and existential thought, has hindered broad application of these ideas to abnormal psychology.

Multipath Implications of Psychological Explanations

All the psychological theories discussed have both strengths and weaknesses; no one of them can claim to tell "the whole truth." Each model—whether psychodynamic, behavioral, cognitive, or existential-humanistic—represents different views of pathology. Each

Carl Rogers (1902–1987)

Rogers believed that people need both positive regard from others and positive self-regard. According to Rogers, when positive regard is given unconditionally, a person can develop freely and become self-actualized.

existential approach a set of attitudes that has many commonalities with humanism but is less optimistic, focusing (1) on human alienation in an increasingly technological and impersonal world, (2) on the individual in the context of the human condition, and (3) on responsibility to others, as well as to oneself

details a different perspective from which to interpret reality, the nature of people, the origin of disorders, standards used for judging normality and abnormality, and the therapeutic cure. Each model has devout supporters.

The multipath model would suggest that we best understand abnormal behavior only by evidence-based integration of the various approaches. It is possible that the models of psychopathology are describing the same phenomena but from different vantage points. Many models of psychopathology focus on one aspect of the human condition to the exclusion of others, overlooking the person as a "total package" and resulting in a distorted view. Some models emphasize the importance of *history* (psychodynamic), some of *feeling* (humanistic-existential), some of *thinking* (cognitive), and still others of *behaving* (behavioral). A truly comprehensive model of human behavior, normal and abnormal, must address the possibility that people are all of these—*biological, historical, feeling, thinking,* and *behaving* beings—and probably much more: social, cultural, spiritual, and political ones as well.

▆▆ Dimension Three: Social Factors

Almost all theories of psychopathology discussed so far focus on the individual and less so on the social environment. They have been negligent in addressing such important aspects of our lives as relationships with people and how such factors as family, social support, love, community, and belonging affect the manifestation and expression of behavior disorders. It is clear that we are social beings and that our relationships can influence the development, manifestation, and/or amelioration of mental disorders.

Social Relational Models

Studies support the conclusion that social isolation and lack of emotional support and intimacy are correlated with asthma, depression, suicide, lower stress tolerance, and low self-esteem (Collishaw, Pickles et al., 2007; Elsevier, 2010; Nagano, Kakuta, Motomura, Odajima et al., 2010; Smyke et al., 2007). On the other hand, people with rich relationships and social networks have been found to live longer, are less prone to commit suicide, are less likely to develop psychiatric disorders such as depression and alcoholism, enjoy better physical health, recover quicker after an illness, and are generally happier and more optimistic (Berman, 2006; Segrin et al., 2003; University of Michigan, 2010). Social relationships are important in places of employment, churches, neighborhoods, schools, and communities, and especially as they relate to family relationships. For example, Steve V. can be seen as a product of a dysfunctional family, a person who was never nurtured or loved by his parents. It does not take any stretch of the imagination to entertain the notion that parental neglect, abuse, separation/divorce, and inadequate parenting can contribute to mental disorders of offspring.

Social-relational explanations of abnormal behavior make several important assumptions (Johnson & Johnson, 2003): (1) healthy relationships are important for human development and functioning; (2) these relationships provide many intangible healthy benefits (social support, love, compassion, trust, faith, sense of belonging, resistance to stress, etc.); and (3) when relationships prove dysfunctional or are absent, the individual may be subject to mental disturbances. Treatment of socially produced disorders is most effective by improving interpersonal relationships of clients through a systemic approach.

Family, Couples, and Group Perspectives

In contrast to traditional psychological models, social-relational models emphasize how other people, especially significant others, influence our behavior. This viewpoint holds that all people are enmeshed in a network of interdependent roles, statuses, values, and norms. One of these, the family systems model, assumes that the behavior of one family

family systems model model that assumes that the behavior of one family member directly affects the entire family system

member directly affects the entire family system. Correspondingly, people typically behave in ways that reflect family influences (both healthy and unhealthy responding).

We can identify three distinct characteristics of the family systems approach (Corey, 2008). First, personality development is ruled largely by the attributes of the family, especially by the way parents behave toward and around their children. Second, abnormal behavior in the individual is usually a reflection or "symptom" of unhealthy family dynamics and, more specifically, of poor communication among family members. Third, the therapist must focus on the family system, not solely on the individual, and must strive to involve the entire family in therapy. As a result, the locus of disorder is seen to reside not within the individual but within the family system.

Social-Relational Treatment Approaches

The family systems model has spawned a number of treatment approaches. One group emphasizes the importance of clear and direct *communications* for healthy family system development (Satir, 1967). Virginia Satir's *conjoint family therapeutic approach* stresses the importance of teaching message-sending and message-receiving skills to family members. Like other family therapists, Satir believes that the identified patient is really a reflection of the family system gone awry. *Strategic family approaches* (Haley, 1963, 1987) deal with power struggles that occur among family members by attempting to shift the balance to a more healthy distribution. *Structural family approaches* (Minuchin, 1974) attempt to reorganize family members because they are either too involved or too little involved with one another. All of these approaches focus on communication, balancing power relationships among family members, and the need to restructure the troubled family system.

Couples therapy includes both marital relationships and intimate relationships between unmarried partners. It is a treatment aimed at helping couples understand and clarify their communications, role relationships, unfulfilled needs, and unrealistic or unmet expectations. Couples therapy has become an increasingly popular treatment for those who find that the quality of their relationship needs improvement (Nichols & Schwartz, 2005).

Another form of social-relational treatment is group therapy. Unlike couples and family therapy, members of the group are initially strangers. Group members may, however, share various characteristics. Groups may be formed to treat older clients, unemployed workers, or pregnant women; to treat clients with similar psychological disturbances; or to treat people with similar therapeutic goals. Most group therapies focus on interrelationships and the dynamics of interaction among members. Despite their wide diversity, successful groups and group approaches share several features that promote change in clients (Corey, 2008; Yalom, 2005): (1) The group experience allows each client to become involved in a social situation and to see how his or her behavior affects others. (2) The therapist can see how clients actually respond in a real-life social and interpersonal context. (3) Group members can develop new communication skills, social skills, and insights. (4) Groups often help members feel less isolated and less fearful about their problems. (5) Groups can provide members with strong social and emotional support. The feelings of intimacy, belonging, protection, and trust (which members may not be able to experience outside the group) can be a powerful motivation to confront one's problems and seek to overcome them.

Criticisms of Social-Relational Models

There is no denying that we are social creatures, and by concentrating on this aspect of human behavior, the social-relational models have added an important social dimension to our understanding of abnormal behavior. Research on the effects of family and couples therapy has been consistent in pointing to the value of therapy compared with no-treatment and alternative-treatment control groups. However, research studies have generally not been rigorous in design; they often lacked appropriate control groups, follow-up periods of outcome, or good measures of outcome. Further, considerable evidence exists that couples,

couples therapy a treatment aimed at helping couples understand and clarify their communications, role relationships, unfulfilled needs, and unrealistic or unmet expectations

group therapy a form of therapy that involves the simultaneous treatment of two or more clients and may involve more than one therapist

Family Dynamics and Positive Self-Image

Family interaction patterns can exert tremendous influence on a child's personality development, determining the child's sense of self-worth and the acquisition of appropriate social skills. This picture shows a Hispanic family preparing dinner together. Notice the attentiveness and obvious expressions of joy by the parents toward their children (communicating a sense of importance to them) and how every family member is actively involved in their respective roles (emphasizing family cohesion and belonging).

Hill Street Studios / Getty Images

marital, and family therapy operate under culture-bound definitions (Sue & Sue, 2008a). Other critics have voiced concern that family systems models may have unpleasant consequences. Too often, psychologists have pointed an accusing finger at the parents of children who suffer from certain disorders, despite an abundance of evidence that parental influence may not be a factor in those disorders. The parents are then burdened with unnecessary guilt over a situation they could not have controlled.

▬ Dimension Four: Sociocultural Factors

Sociocultural perspectives emphasize the importance of considering race, ethnicity, gender, sexual orientation, religious preference, socioeconomic status, physical disabilities, and other such factors in explaining mental disorders. Research consistently reveals that belonging to specific sociodemographic groups influences the manifestation of behavior disorders and may subject members to unique stressors not experienced by other groups (Keller & Calgay, 2010; Smith & Reddington, 2010; Sue, 2010).

The importance of the sociocultural dimension is clearly evident in *Diagnostic and Statistical Manual of Mental Disorders* (DSM) in which a number of culture-bound syndromes are listed. These are disorders generally limited to a specific society or cultural group. For example, *taijin kyofusho* is a culture-specific disorder (not seen in the United States but in Japan) in which the individual fears that his or her body parts or function are offensive to other people because of appearance, odor, or movements. *Ataque de nervios* is reported among Latinos from the Caribbean and includes symptoms of uncontrollable shouting, seizure-like episodes, trembling, and crying. It is clear that people's cultural experiences are important factors in the manifestation of mental disorders (Sue & Sue, 2008a). We briefly discuss three major sociocultural factors to illustrate their importance in understanding psychopathology: gender, socioeconomic class, and race/ethnicity.

Gender Factors

Women are consistently subjected to greater stressors than their male counterparts (Smith, 2010; Spradlin & Parsons, 2008). They carry more of the domestic burden, more responsibility for child care, and more responsibility for social and interpersonal relationships.

Multicultural Perspectives

Multicultural models of human behavior regard race, culture, and ethnicity as central to the understanding of normality and abnormality. In China, children are taught to value group harmony over individual competitiveness. In contrast, in the United States, individual efforts and privacy are valued. Note the common use of cubicles in work settings to separate people from one another.

This is true even if they are employed full time outside of the home (Sue, 2010). The National Academies (National Academy of Sciences, National Academy of Engineering, & Institute of Medicine, 2006) describe the plight of women in the United States to be: (1) predominantly employed in low-wage, traditional female occupations; (2) subjected to sexual harassment (81 percent of eighth through eleventh graders, 30 percent of undergraduates, and 40 percent of graduate students); (3) paid less than their male counterparts in similar jobs; (4) given less recognition, encouragement, and approval in classrooms than their male counterparts; (5) more likely to live in poverty; (6) faced with more barriers to their career choices; and (7) faced with greater discrimination and victimization.

While it is clear that many factors may contribute to these inequities, some believe that institutional and individual sexism explain many of the problems encountered by young girls and women in this society (Capodilupo, Nadal, Corman et al., 2010). In 2008, the Equal Employment Opportunity Commission received 11,648 charges of sexual harassment toward women in comparison to 2,219 by men. It is estimated that 60 percent of women in the United States have experienced some form of sexual harassment in the workplace. Adolescent girls often report multiple instances of being called demeaning names ("bitch" or "whore"), receiving unwanted romantic attention, and being taunted about their physical appearance (Capodilupo et al., 2010). Sexism has been linked to feelings of invalidation, loss of personal control, anger, anxiety, eating disorders, and sexual dysfunction.

The importance of gender in understanding psychopathology is also clearly seen in rates of depression among women. Up to 7 million women currently suffer from depression, which is twice the number for men (Schwartzman & Glaus, 2000). Rather than a narrow explanation (biological or psychological alone), it is highly probable that many factors contribute, including sociocultural ones. Further, women are placed in an unenviable position of fulfilling stereotyped feminine social roles defined by our society. In our chapter on eating disorders, we discuss more fully how stereotyped standards of beauty in advertisements and the mass media can affect the health and self-esteem of girls and women. Body dissatisfaction, eating disorders, and depression are all significantly related to sociocultural standards.

Socioeconomic Class

Social class and "classicism" are two frequently overlooked sociodemographic factors in psychology and mental health (Smith, 2010). Lower socioeconomic class is related to lower sense of self-control, poorer physical health, and higher incidence of depression

(Sue, 2010). Increasingly, psychologists are beginning to appreciate how poverty subjects the poor to increased stressors (Smith & Redington, 2010). The life of a person living in poverty is characterized by low wages, unemployment, underemployment, lack of savings, little property ownership, and lack of food reserves. Meeting even the most basic needs of food and shelter becomes a major challenge. In such circumstances, the poor are likely to experience feelings of hopelessness, helplessness, dependence, and inferiority.

Considerable bias against the poor is well documented in the literature (American Psychological Association Task Force on Socioeconomic Status, 2006; Smith, 2010). As a group, they are more likely to be oppressed and harmed. For example, they are more likely to be perceived unfavorably than middle- or upper-class persons, to be considered less worthy, to be stereotyped as less capable for jobs, and to be socially isolated (Smith & Redington, 2010). Low socioeconomic class is also associated with (1) exposure to stressors that undermine mental and physical health, (2) receiving less desirable forms of therapeutic treatment, and (3) clinician biases in assessment, diagnosis, and treatment that work to the detriment of those in poverty.

Race/Ethnicity: Multicultural Models of Psychopathology

Early attempts to explain differences between various minority groups and their white counterparts tended to adopt one of two models. The first, the inferiority model, contends that racial and ethnic minorities are inferior in some respect to the majority population. For example, this model attributes low academic achievement and higher unemployment rates among African Americans and Latinos to low intelligence (heredity). The second model—the deprivations or deficit model—explains differences as the result of "cultural deprivation." It implies that minority groups lacked the "right" culture. Both models have

The Universal Shamanic Tradition: Wizards, Sorcerers, and Witchdoctors

Since the beginning of human existence, all societies and cultural groups have developed their own explanations of abnormal behavior and their own culture-specific ways of dealing with human suffering and distress (Moodley, 2005). A surprising consequence of the multicultural psychology movement has been a revival of interest in nonwestern indigenous explanations of human disorders and their treatments. Much of this is due to changing demographics. Many individuals are immigrants from Asia, Latin America, and Africa who may hold nonwestern beliefs of illness, mental disorder, and treatment quite alien to Western thinking.

© Roger Bamber / Alamy

Western science defines reality as grounded in what can be observed and measured through the five senses, whereas many indigenous explanations believe that the nature of reality transcends the senses (Walsh & Shapiro, 2006). The term Universal Shamanic Tradition (UST) encompasses the belief that there are special healers who are blessed with powers to act as intermediaries or messengers between the human and spirit worlds. It refers to the centuries-old group of healers who are believed to possess unusual powers beyond the sensory and physical planes of existence. They are (a) sanctioned by their communities as extraordinary persons; (b) regarded highly, respected, and sometimes feared; (c) keepers of timeless wisdom; and (d) believed able to muster up spiritual forces to heal the sick (Lee & Armstrong, 1995; Lee, Oh, & Montcastle, 1992; Moodley, 2005).

The anthropological term "Shaman" often includes people called witches, witch doctors, wizards, medicine men/women, sorcerers, and magic men/women. When a person is afflicted by a mental or physical disorder, treatment may involve special ceremonies that include rituals, prayers, and sacred symbols all aimed at summoning spiritual forces to help in the cure. Shamans are believed to possess the power to enter altered states of consciousness, to journey to an existence beyond the physical world, and to contact and communicate with spirit(s).

People who study indigenous psychologies and UST do not make an *a priori* assumption that one particular perspective is superior to another (Lee & Armstrong, 1995; Mikulas, 2006). The Western explanation of abnormal behavior and psychotherapy, however, does consider scientific methods to be more advanced than those found in many cultures (Moodley, 2005). Universal Shamanic Tradition shares common beliefs and assumptions in its explanations of disorders and healing.

- Illness, distress, or problematic behaviors are seen as an imbalance in people relationships, a disharmony between the person and his/her group, or a lack of synchrony with internal and external forces. Mind, body, spirit, and nature are seen as a single unified entity with little separation between the realities of life, medicine, and religion. Illness is seen as a break in the hoop of life, an imbalance, or a separation between these elements. In many respects, Western values of individualism, separation, and autonomy are seen as unhealthy functioning. In nonwestern cultures, for example, the psychosocial unit of operation is not the individual but the family, group, or communal society.

- Nonwestern indigenous psychologies accept as given the existence of different planes of consciousness, experience, or existence. There is a strong belief that causes of illness or problems often reside in a plane of reality separate from the physical world of existence. Shamans or healers have an ability to enter extraordinary reality states that allow them to access an invisible world surrounding the physical one. There they can enlist the aid of spirits and/or mollify those that are displeased.

- Many cultures believe that accessing higher states of consciousness enhances perceptual sensitivity, clarity, concentration, and emotional well-being. Having clients attain a higher state of consciousness is part of mental and physical health treatments. Asian philosophies, for example, believe that attaining enlightenment and liberation can be achieved through meditation and yoga. In fact, one could make a strong argument that meditation and yoga are the most widely practiced form of therapy in the world today. They have been shown to reduce anxiety, specific phobias, substance abuse, chronic pain, and high blood pressure and enhance self-confidence, marital satisfaction, and sense of control (Sue & Sue, 2008a).

- Spirituality or a belief in an animating life force is a strong component of most nonwestern indigenous psychologies. Western science and society operate from the principle of *separation of Church and State*. One might also find the statement *separation of science and religion* equally applicable. Most nonwestern indigenous psychologies believe in the interconnectedness of spirituality, life, and the cosmos. Among Native Americans, for example, spirituality focuses on the harmony that comes from our connection with all parts of the universe, that people and things were created with a purpose, and that part of healthy living is to seek our place in the universe. Our spiritual connectedness or lack of connectedness to the universe and the human condition foretells the "good life" or a life filled with troubles. When one falls out of alignment with spirituality, he or she travels an unhealthy path (isolation, loss of meaning, selfishness, etc.) that may be characterized by substance abuse, depression, anxiety, and other psychological disorders.

For Further Consideration

1. How valid are Shamanic explanations of illness? Are Shamans therapists? In what ways do you believe they are the same? Can you identify commonalities between what therapists and Shamans do?

2. What can we learn from indigenous forms of healing? In what ways do religion and spirituality affect your life? Do you believe in altered states of consciousness or different planes of existence?

3. Are there dangers or downsides to Shamanism as a belief system or form of treatment?

---

been severely criticized as inaccurate, biased, and unsupported in the scientific literature (Ridley, 2005; Sue & Sue, 2008a).

During the late 1980s and early 1990s, a new and conceptually different model emerged in the literature. Often referred to as the multicultural model (or the *culturally diverse model*; Sue & Sue, 2008a), the new approach emphasized that being culturally different does not equal deviancy, pathology, or inferiority. The model recognizes that each culture has strengths and limitations. Behaviors are to be evaluated from the perspective of a group's value system, as well as by other standards used in determining normality and abnormality (Ivey, D'Andrea, Ivey, & Simek-Morgan, 2007).

The multicultural model makes an explicit assumption that all theories of human development arise from a particular cultural context (Ivey et al., 2007). Thus, many traditional European American models of psychopathology are culture bound, evaluating and viewing events and processes from a worldview not experienced or shared by other cultural groups. For example, individualism and autonomy are highly valued in the United States and are equated with healthy functioning. Most European American children are raised to become increasingly independent, to be able to make decisions on their own, and to "stand on their own two feet." In contrast, many traditional Asians and Asian Americans place an equally high value on "collectivity," in which the psychosocial unit of identity is the family, not the individual. Similarly, whereas European Americans fear the loss of "individuality," members of traditional Asian groups fear the loss of "belonging."

inferiority model early attempt to explain differences in minority groups that contends that racial and ethnic minorities are inferior in some respect to the majority population

deficit model early attempt to explain differences in minority groups that contends that differences are the result of "cultural deprivation"

Universal Shamanic Tradition a set of belief and practices from nonwestern indigenous psychologies that assume special healers are blessed with powers to act as intermediaries or messengers between the human and spirit worlds

multicultural model contemporary attempt to explain differences in minority groups that suggests that behaviors be evaluated from the perspective of a group's value system, as well as by other standards used in determining normality and abnormality

Did You Know?

Social psychological studies on implicit bias reveal that nearly everyone born and raised in a particular society like the United States inherits racial stereotypes, biases, and prejudices. On a conscious level most of us believe we are good, moral, and decent human beings who would never deliberately or intentionally discriminate against others. Yet, many of our stereotypes operate outside the level of conscious awareness and can be expressed in a discriminatory fashion without our knowledge (Dovidio, Kawakami, Smoak & Gaertner, 2009). Given that we are unaware of our hidden biases, how do we rid ourselves of them?

Given such different experiences and values, unenlightened mental health professionals may make biased assumptions about human behavior—assumptions that may influence their judgments of normality and abnormality among various racial and ethnic minorities. For example, a mental health professional who does not understand that Asian Americans value a collectivistic identity might see them as overly dependent, immature, and unable to make decisions on their own. Likewise, such a person might perceive "restraint of strong feelings"—a valued characteristic among some Asian groups—as evidence of being "inhibited," "unable to express emotions," or "repressed."

The multicultural model also suggests that problems in life may be due to sociocultural stressors residing in the social system rather than conflicts within the person. Racism, bias, discrimination, economic hardships, and cultural conflicts are just a few of the sociopolitical realities with which racial and ethnic minorities must contend. As a result, the role of therapist may be better served by ameliorating oppressive or detrimental social conditions than by attempting therapy aimed at changing the individual. Appropriate individual therapy may, however, be directed at teaching clients self-help skills and strategies focused on influencing their immediate social situation.

Criticisms of the Multicultural Model

In many respects, the multicultural model operates from a relativistic framework; that is, normal and abnormal behavior must be evaluated from a cultural perspective. The reasoning is that behavior considered disordered in one context—seeing a vision of a dead relative, for example—might not be considered disordered in another time or place. As indicated in DSM some religious practices and beliefs consider it normal to hear or see a deceased relative during bereavement. In addition, certain groups, including some American Indian and Hispanic/Latino groups, may perceive "hallucinations" not as disordered but actually as positive events.

Critics of the multicultural model argue that "a disorder is a disorder," regardless of the cultural context in which it is considered. For example, a person suffering from schizophrenia and actively hallucinating is evidencing a malfunctioning of the senses (seeing, hearing, or feeling things that are not there) and a lack of contact with reality. Regardless of whether *the person* judges the occurrence to be desirable or undesirable, it nevertheless represents a disorder (biological dysfunction), according to this viewpoint.

Another criticism leveled at the multicultural model is its lack of empirical validation concerning many of its concepts and assumptions. The field of multicultural counseling and therapy, for example, has been accused of not being solidly grounded in research (Ponterotto & Casas, 1991). Most of the underlying concepts of the multicultural model are based on conceptual critiques or formulations that have not been subjected to formal scientific testing. There is generally heavy reliance on case studies, ethnographic analyses, and investigations of a more qualitative type.

Multicultural psychologists respond to such criticisms by noting that they are based on a Western worldview that emphasizes precision and empirical definitions. They point out that there is more than one way to ask and answer questions about the human condition.

Applying the Models of Psychopathology

CRITICAL THINKING

A useful learning exercise to evaluate your mastery of the various models is to apply them to a case study. We invite you to try your hand at explaining the behavior of Bill, a hypothetical client. Afterward, we invite you to attempt a more integrated multipath approach to explaining Bill's problem.

Bill was born in Indiana to extremely religious parents who raised him in a strict moralistic manner. His father, a Baptist minister, often told Bill and his two sisters to "keep your mind clean, heart pure, and body in control." He forbade Bill's sisters to date while they lived at home. Bill's own social life and contacts were extremely limited, and he recalled how anxious he was around girls.

Bill's memories of his father included feelings of fear and intimidation. No one in the family dared disagree with the father openly, lest they be punished and ridiculed. The father appeared to be hardest on Bill's two sisters, especially when they expressed any interest in boys. The arguments and conflicts between father and daughters were often loud and extreme, disrupting the typical quietness of the home. Although it was never spoken of, Bill was aware that one of his sisters suffered from depression, as did his mother; his sister had twice attempted suicide.

Bill's recollections of his mother were unclear, except that she was always sick with what his father referred to as "the dark cloud," which seemed to visit her periodically. His relationships with his sisters, who were several years older, were uncomfortable. When Bill was young, they teased him mercilessly, and when he reached adolescence, they seemed to take sadistic delight in arousing his hormones by flaunting their partially exposed bodies. The result was that Bill became obsessed with having sex with one of his sisters, and he tended to masturbate compulsively. Throughout his adolescence and early adulthood he was tortured by feelings of guilt and believed himself to be, as his father put it, "an unclean and damned sinner."

By all external standards, Bill was a quiet and well-behaved child. He did well in school, attended Sunday school without fail, never argued or spoke against his parents, and seldom ventured outside of the home. Although Bill did exceptionally well in high school, some of his teachers were concerned about his introverted behavior and occasional bouts of depression. When they brought Bill's depression to the attention of his father, however, Mr. M. dismissed it as no reason to worry. Indeed, Mr. M. complimented Bill on his good grades and unobtrusive behavior, rewarding him occasionally

with small privileges, such as a larger portion of dessert or the choice of a TV program. To some degree of awareness, Bill felt that his worth as a person was dependent only on "getting good grades" and "staying out of trouble."

As a young child, Bill had exhibited excellent artistic potential, and his teachers tried to encourage him in that direction. In elementary school he had won several awards for his drawings, and teachers frequently asked him to paint murals in their classrooms or to design posters for school events. His artistic interests continued into high school, where his art instructor entered one of Bill's drawings in a state contest. His entry won first prize. Unfortunately, Mr. M. discouraged Bill from his talents and told him "God calls you in another direction." Attempting to please his father, Bill became less involved in art and concentrated more on math and science. He did very well in these subjects, obtaining nearly straight A's in high school.

When Bill entered college, his prime objective was to remain a straight-A student. Although he had originally loved the excitement of learning and mastering new knowledge, he became cautious and obsessed with "safety"; he was fearful of upsetting his father. As his string of perfect grades became longer, safety (not risking a B grade) became more important. He began to choose safe and easy topics for essays, to enroll in easy courses, and to take incompletes or withdrawals when courses appeared tough.

Toward the end of his sophomore year, Bill suffered a mental breakdown characterized by pessimism and hopelessness. He became depressed and was subsequently hospitalized after he tried to take his own life.

Table 2.3 summarizes the various models, and the following hints will help you to begin this exercise:

- Consider what each theory proposes as the basis for the development of a mental disorder.
- Consider the type of data that each perspective considers most important.
- Compare and contrast the models.
- Because there are eight models represented, you might wish to do a comparison only between selected models (psychoanalytic, humanistic, and behavioral, for example).

As you attempt to explain Bill's behavior, notice how your adoption of a particular framework influences the type of data you consider important. Is it possible that all the models hold some semblance of truth? Are their positions necessarily contradictory? Is it possible to integrate them into a unified explanation of Bill? (Again, you may wish to consult Table 2.3.)

TABLE 2.3 Comparison of the Most Influential Models of Psychopathology

	Motivation for Behavior	Basis for Assessment	Theoretical Foundation	Source of Abnormal Behavior	Treatment
Biological	State of biological integrity and health	Medical tests, self-reports, and observable behaviors	Animal and human research, case studies, and other research methods	Biological trauma, heredity, biochemical imbalances	Biological interventions (drugs, ECT, surgery, diet)
Psychodynamic	Unconscious influences	Personal history, oral self-reports	Case studies, correlational methods	Internal: early childhood experiences	Dream analysis, free association, transference; locating unconscious conflict from childhood; resolving problem and reintegrating personality
Behavioral	External influences	Observable, objective data; overt behaviors	Animal research, case studies, experimental methods	External: learning maladaptive responses or not acquiring appropriate responses	Direct modification of problem behavior; analysis of environmental factors controlling behavior and alteration of contingencies
Cognitive	Interaction of external and cognitive influences	Self-statements, alterations in overt behaviors	Human research, case studies, experimental methods	Internal: learned pattern of irrational or negative self-statements	Understanding relationship between self-statements and problem behavior; modification of internal dialogue
Humanistic	Self-actualization	Subjective data, oral self-reports	Case studies, correlational and experimental methods	Internal: incongruence between self and experiences	Nondirective reflection, no interpretation, providing unconditional positive regard, increasing congruence between self and experience
Existential	Capacity for self-awareness; freedom to decide one's fate; search for meaning	Subjective data, oral self-reports, experiential encounter	An approach to understanding the human condition rather than a firm theoretical model	Failure to actualize human potential, avoidance of choice and responsibility	Providing conditions for maximizing self-awareness and growth, to enable clients to be free and responsible
Family Systems	Interaction with significant others	Observation of family dynamics	Case studies, social psychological studies, experimental methods	External: faulty family interactions (family pathology and inconsistent communication patterns)	Therapy aimed at treating the entire family, not just the identified patient
Multicultural	Cultural values and norms	Study of group norms/behaviors, understanding of societal values and minority/dominant group relations	Study of cultural groups; data from anthropology, sociology, and political science	Culture conflicts and oppression	

Summary

1. What models of psychopathology have been used to explain abnormal behavior?

   - One-dimensional models have been traditionally used to explain disorders. They have become increasingly inadequate because mental disorders are multidimensional.

2. What is the multipath model of mental disorders?

   - The multipath model is proposed to explain the interaction of biological, psychological, social, and sociocultural contributors to mental disturbances. The model is not a theory but a way of looking at the variety and complexity of contributors to mental disorders. In some respects it is a metamodel, a model of models that provides an organizational framework for understanding the numerous causes of mental disorders, the complexity of their interacting components, and the need to view disorders from a holistic framework.

3. How much of mental disorder can be explained through our biological makeup?

   - Biological models cite various organic causes of psychopathology, including genetics, brain anatomy, biochemical imbalances, central nervous system functioning, and autonomic nervous system reactivity. A good deal of biochemical research has focused on identifying the role of neurotransmitters in abnormal behavior. Researchers have also found correlations between genetic inheritance and certain psychopathologies. Mental health research reveals that a predisposition to a disorder, not the disorder itself, may be inherited. Epigenetics provide strong evidence that gene-environment interactions are a two-way process that is reciprocal in nature.

4. What psychological models are used to explain the etiology of mental disorders?

   - Psychodynamic models emphasize childhood experiences and the role of the unconscious in determining adult behavior. The early development of psychodynamic theory is credited to Freud. Psychoanalytic therapy attempts to help the patient achieve insight into his or her unconscious.

   - Behavioral models focus on the role of learning in abnormal behavior. The traditional behavioral models of psychopathology hold that abnormal behaviors are acquired through association (classical conditioning), reinforcement (operant conditioning), or modeling. Negative emotional responses, such as anxiety, can be learned through classical conditioning: A formerly neutral stimulus evokes a negative response after it has been presented along with a stimulus that already evokes that response. Negative voluntary behaviors may be learned through operant conditioning if those behaviors are reinforced (rewarded) when they occur. In observational learning, a person learns behaviors, which can be quite complex, by observing them in other people and then imitating, or modeling, those behaviors.

   - Cognitive models are based on the assumption that conscious thought mediates, or modifies, an individual's emotional state and/or behavior in response to a stimulus. Cognitive therapeutic approaches are generally aimed at normalizing the client's perception of events.

   - The humanistic perspective actually represents many perspectives and shares many basic assumptions with the existential perspective. Both view an individual's reality as a product of personal perception and experience. Both see people as capable of making free choices and fulfilling their potential. Both emphasize the whole person and the individual's ability to fulfill his or her capacities.

5. What role do social factors play in psychopathology?

- Impairment or absence of social relationships have been found to be correlated with increased susceptibility to mental disorders. Good relationships seem to immunize people against stressors.

- From the perspective of family systems, abnormal behavior is viewed as the result of distorted or faulty communication or unbalanced structural relationships within the family. Children who receive faulty messages from parents or who are subjected to structurally abnormal family constellations may develop behavioral and emotional problems.

- Three social treatments described are family therapy, couples therapy, and group therapy.

6. What sociocultural factors may play a role in the etiology of mental disorders?

- Proponents of the sociocultural approach believe that race, culture, ethnicity, gender, sexual orientation, religious preference, socioeconomic status, physical disabilities, and other variables are powerful influences in determining how specific cultural groups manifest disorders, how mental health professionals perceive disorders, and how disorders are treated.

- Cultural differences have been perceived in three ways: (1) the inferiority model, in which differences are attributed to the interplay of undesirable elements in a person's biological makeup; (2) the deprivation or deficit model, in which differences in traits or behaviors are blamed on not having the "right culture"; and (3) the multicultural model, in which differences do not necessarily equate with deviance.

Media Resources

Psychology CourseMate   Access an interactive eBook, chapter-specific interactive learning tools, including flashcards, quizzes, videos, and more in your Psychology CourseMate, accessed through CengageBrain.com.

CENGAGENOW

CengageNow   CengageNOW is an easy-to-use online resource that helps you study in less time to get the grade you want—NOW. If your textbook does not include an access code card, go to CengageBrain.com to gain access.

CENGAGE brain.com

CengageBrain   More than just an interactive study guide, WebTutor is an anytime, anywhere customized learning solution with an eBook, keeping you connected to your textbook, instructor, and classmates. Purchase the access chosen by your instructor at CengageBrain.com.

3

Assessment and Classification of Abnormal Behavior

P olice were called when Ms. Y. became physically aggressive, breaking several windows and leaving her house in disarray. Police officers described Ms. Y.'s behavior as threatening and violent. Emergency department personnel noted that she was agitated and confused. Because Ms. Y. was not in a condition to be interviewed, her boyfriend provided background information. He reported that she had been hospitalized six months previously with auditory hallucinations and beliefs that she was God. She had also been hospitalized on one other occasion when similar symptoms developed after taking drugs. Ms. Y.'s family history includes an aunt diagnosed with schizophrenia (Lavakumar, Garlow, & Schwartz, 2011).

Different conditions can result in psychotic symptoms such as those demonstrated by Ms. Y. An extended drug screen ruled out alcohol and illicit drugs as causal factors. No infections that might produce delirium or transient psychosis were found. During questioning about the intake of other substances, Ms. Y. volunteered that she had been taking carnitine, an over-the-counter weight-loss supplement. In fact, Ms. Y. had been taking twice the recommended levels of carnitine. In addition, she had been drinking 16 ounce energy drinks that listed the main ingredients as L-carnitine and caffeine. The mental health team diagnosed her as having a psychotic reaction produced by carnitine intoxication. Fortunately, her psychotic symptoms resolved within 24 hours.

I n the mental health field, assessment is critical. Therapists collect and organize information about a person's current condition and past history. Among the assessment tools available to clinicians are observations, interviews, psychological and neurological tests, and input from relatives and friends. Once data is gathered from a variety of sources, a therapist can gain a good picture of the individual's symptoms and mental state. In the case of Ms. Y., the therapists relied on observations, laboratory tests, and interviews to arrive at their diagnosis. With any mental disorder, the first step is rule out physical or biological causes for the symptoms.

As we noted in Chapter 1, evaluation of gathered information leads to a *psychodiagnosis*, which involves describing and drawing inferences about an individual's psychological state. To arrive at a diagnosis, the therapist attempts to obtain a clear description of the client's concerns and behavioral patterns and to classify or group them based on the symptom picture that emerges. Psychodiagnosis is usually the first step in the treatment process. In this chapter, we examine assessment

focus questions

1 What kinds of standards should tests or evaluation procedures meet?

2 What kinds of tools do clinicians employ in evaluating a client's mental health?

3 How are mental health problems categorized or classified?

methods and clinicians' use of assessment tools. We also discuss the most widely employed diagnostic classification system, DSM, as well as criticism regarding labeling and the use of classification systems. We start the chapter with a discussion of reliability and validity, important considerations when evaluating assessment tools and diagnostic systems.

Reliability and Validity

To be useful, assessment tools and classification systems must demonstrate reliability and validity. Reliability is the degree to which a procedure or test—such as an evaluation tool or classification scheme—yields the same results repeatedly under the same circumstances. There are many types of reliability (Coaley, 2010; Golafshani, 2003).

Test-retest reliability determines whether a measure yields the same results when given to an individual at two different points in time. For example, if we administer a personality measure to an individual in the morning and then re-administer the measure later in the day, the measure is reliable if the results show consistency or stability (that is, if the results are the same) from one point in time to another. Another measure of reliability, *internal consistency*, requires that various parts of a measure yield similar or consistent results (Kline, 2005). For example, if responses to different items on a measure of anxiety are not related to one another, the test may be unreliable because test items may be measuring different things, not just anxiety.

Finally, *interrater reliability* determines consistency of responses when different raters administer the measure. For instance, imagine that two clinicians are trained to diagnose individuals according to a certain classification scheme. Yet one clinician presented with a set of symptoms diagnoses an anxiety disorder, whereas another considers the same symptoms and diagnoses depression. If this were to occur, there would be poor interrater reliability.

Validity is the extent to which a test or procedure actually performs the function it was designed to perform. If a measure that is intended to assess depression instead assesses anxiety, the measure is an invalid measure of depression. The most common forms of validity considered in assessment are predictive, criterion-related, construct, and content validity (Weiner & Greene, 2008).

Predictive validity refers to the ability of a test or measure to predict or foretell how a person will behave, respond, or perform. Colleges and universities often use applicants' SAT or ACT scores to predict their future college grades. If the tests have good predictive validity, they should be able to differentiate students who will perform well from those who will perform poorly in college.

Criterion-related validity determines whether a measure is related to the phenomenon in question. Assume, for example, that we devise a measure that is intended to tell us whether persons recovering from alcoholism are likely to return to drinking. If we find that those who score high on the measure start drinking again and that those who score low do not, then the measure is valid.

Determining *construct validity* involves a series of tasks with one common theme: all are designed to test whether a measure is related to certain phenomena that are empirically or theoretically related to that measure. Let's say that a researcher has developed a questionnaire to measure anxiety. To determine construct validity, the researcher needs to demonstrate that the questionnaire is correlated with other measures, such as existing tests of anxiety. Furthermore, we would have increased confidence that the questionnaire is measuring anxiety if it is related to other phenomena that appear in anxious people, such as muscle tension, sweating, tremors, or startle responses.

Finally, *content validity* refers to the degree to which a measure is representative of the phenomenon being measured. For example, we know that depression involves cognitive, emotional, behavioral, and physiological characteristics. If a self-report measure of depression contains items that assess only cognitive features, such as items indicating pessimism, then the measure has poor content validity because it fails to assess three of the four known aspects of the disorder.

reliability the degree to which a procedure or test yields the same results repeatedly under the same circumstances

validity the extent to which a test or procedure actually performs the function it was designed to perform

Let's look at the use of reliability and validity on a measure developed to assess psychotic-like experiences. Individuals with a disorder such as schizophrenia show unusual thinking patterns such as believing that innocuous stimuli have personal significance. Cicero, Kerns, and McCarthy (2010) constructed the Aberrant Salience Inventory (ASI) and wanted to determine if the instrument was a valid and reliable measure of individuals' likelihood of developing psychosis. The items for the test were constructed from descriptions of psychosis in the literature, characteristics observed during the early stage of schizophrenia, and interviews with people who had schizophrenia. Overlapping descriptions were eliminated and the final measure was comprised of 29 items. It has found to have high (0.89) internal reliability (i.e., consistency among the items). Test-retest reliability was not performed because psychotic symptoms typically fluctuate and would not be expected to be the same on two occasions. To determine if the measure actually assesses likelihood of developing psychosis, the inventory was compared to other scales that measure psychosis (criterion validity). The ASI was highly correlated to other measures of psychosis, which increased confidence in the validity of the measure. If the ASI is a measure of likelihood to develop psychosis, you would also expect that patients with psychosis would score higher on this test than nonpsychotic psychiatric patients. This was also found. Although the researchers concluded that additional research should be performed to further document reliability and validity, they believe the ASI is a useful measure of susceptibility to psychosis in clinical and nonclinical samples.

Reliability and validity are also influenced by the conditions under which a test or measure is administered. Standardization, or standard administration, requires that those who administer a test strictly follow common rules or procedures. If an examiner creates a tense and hostile environment for some individuals who are taking a test, for example, the test scores may vary simply because all examinees were not treated in a similar or standard fashion.

An additional concern is the standardization sample—the group of people who originally took the measure and whose performance is used as a standard or norm. The performance of others is subsequently interpreted against this norm. However, the standardization sample must be representative of the backgrounds of those being evaluated. For example, interpretations may not be valid if the test score of a twenty-year-old African American woman is compared with scores from a standardization sample of middle-aged white men.

◼◼◼◼ The Assessment of Abnormal Behavior

Assessment involves gathering information and drawing conclusions about the traits, skills, abilities, emotional functioning, and psychological problems of the individual; information from assessment is used in developing a diagnosis. Assessment tools allow data to be collected so that psychologists can conduct meaningful research, develop theories, and evaluate psychotherapy. Data collection involves the use of tools to systematically record the observations, behaviors, or self-reports of individuals. Four principal means of assessment are available to clinicians: observations, interviews, psychological tests and inventories, and neurological tests. Whenever possible, assessment is conducted using multiple methods in order to get a more accurate view of the client (Godoy & Haynes, 2011; Kendall, Holmbeck, & Verduin, 2004).

Observations

Case Study

[A] 9-year-old boy . . . was referred to a neurologist for treatment of "hysterical paralysis." . . . Medical tests indicated no apparent neurological damage. . . . He reported that his legs simply did not work no matter how he tried. As the child was describing

standardization the use of identical procedures in the administration of tests or the establishment of a norm or comparison group to which an individual's test performance can be compared

assessment the process of gathering information and drawing conclusions about the traits, skills, abilities, emotional functioning, and psychological problems of an individual

his difficulties, we noted that he would shift his feet and legs in his wheelchair so his legs could swing freely. . . . When we asked him to describe his paralysis, he would look at his feet and . . . his leg movements would diminish. However, when we asked him to discuss other topics (e.g., school, friends), he would look up, become engaged in the interview, and his feet would swing. (O'Brien & Carhart 2011, p. 14)

Observations of overt behavior provide the most basic method of assessing symptoms. Clinical observations can be either controlled or naturalistic. *Controlled* (or *analogue*) *observations* occur in a laboratory, clinic, or other contrived (artificial) setting (Haynes, 2001). *Naturalistic observations* are made in a natural setting—a schoolroom, an office, a hospital ward, or a home—rather than in a laboratory. Observations can be highly structured and specific. For example, an observer may count episodes of off-task behavior and the circumstances under which off-task behaviors occur. On other occasions, observations may be less formal and specific, as when a clinician simply looks for any unusual behaviors when interacting with a client. In such a situation, the observations and interpretations of the behaviors may be quite subjective in nature.

Observations of behavior are usually made in conjunction with an interview. Psychologists watch for cues that may have diagnostic significance. The client's general mode of dress (neat, sloppy, flashy), significant scars or tattoos, and even choice of jewelry may be associated with personality traits or a disorder. Similarly, expressive behaviors, such as posture, facial expression, and language and verbal patterns can provide important clues as seen in the following case.

Case Study

Margaret was a thirty-seven-year-old patient seen by one of the authors in a hospital psychiatric ward. She had recently been admitted for treatment of severe depression. It was obvious from a casual glance that Margaret had not taken care of herself for weeks. Her face, hands, and hair were dirty. Her beat-up tennis shoes were only halfway on her stockingless feet. Her disheveled appearance and stooped body posture made her appear much older than she was.

When first interviewed, Margaret sat as though she did not have the strength to straighten her body. She avoided eye contact and stared at the floor. When asked questions, she usually responded in short phrases: "Yes," "No," "I don't know," "I don't care." There were long pauses between the questions and her answers.

Interviews

The clinical interview is a time-honored means of psychological assessment. It allows the therapist to observe the client and collect data about the person's life history, current situation, and personality. Verbal and nonverbal behaviors, as well as the content and process of communications are important to analyze; therapists listen carefully to what clients are saying and whether clients are expressing anxiety, hesitation, anger or other emotions via their manner of speaking. Interviews can vary in the degree to which they are structured, the manner in which they are conducted, and the degree of freedom of response on the part of the client. The most structured interview is the formal standardized interview, which often includes a list of questions or the use of standardized rating scales. The interviewer often uses a checklist to ask a standard series of questions so that errors are minimized. Although structured interviews do not permit interviewers to probe interviewees' responses in depth, they have the advantage of allowing consistent data to be collected across interviewees and are less subject to interviewers' biases (Hill & Lambert, 2004).

A widely used interview procedure is the mental status examination. The intent of this examination is to evaluate the client's cognitive, psychological, and behavioral functioning by means of questions, observations, and tasks posed to the client (Goldberg, 2009). The clinician considers the appropriateness and quality of the client's responses (behaviors, speech, emotions, and intellectual functioning) and then attempts to render provisional evaluations of diagnosis, prognosis, client dynamics, and treatment issues (Brannon, 2011). When assessing these characteristics, it is important to consider possible cultural influences. A mental status report on Margaret (described previously in the case study) might indicate:

- Appearance—Poor self-care in grooming, clothes. Disheveled appearance, shoes halfway off her feet, stooped body posture, and avoidance of eye contact.
- Mood—Appears to be depressed, hopeless. Margaret verified that she has felt "depressed," "exhausted," and "worthless" for months.
- Affect—Margaret exhibited constricted emotions and very little affect. Her overall demeanor is suggestive of depression.
- Speech—Margaret spoke slowly, was slow in answering questions, and used short responses or "I don't know" and "I don't care."
- Thought Process—Margaret's lack of responsiveness makes the assessment of thought process difficult. There was no evidence of racing or tangential thinking.
- Thought Content—Margaret denied experiencing any hallucinations or delusions (false beliefs). She indicated that she had been thinking about suicide multiple times each day but denied having a suicide plan or thoughts of hurting someone else. She reports that she constantly worries about what others think of her, especially her coworkers.
- Memory—In obtaining Margaret's history, she seemed to have good recall of family background, past events, jobs, and educational background. However, she had difficulty with short-term memory—she was able to recall only one out of three words after a five-minute delay.
- Abstract Thought—Margaret was slow to respond but was able to explain the proverbs "a rolling stone gathers no moss" and "people in glass houses should not throw stones."
- General Knowledge—Margaret was able to name the last four presidents but gave up before determining the number of nickels in $135 explaining that she "just can't concentrate."

The mental status exam is a useful diagnostic tool that helps clinicians cover areas that are ordinarily not part of a clinical interview. However, many aspects of the exam are subjective and one's cultural background can influence the assessment. As Goldberg (2009) points out. "[T]here is a major distinction between 'different' and 'abnormal.' Proverbs, for example, are not necessarily a part of any communal experience. Thus, a 'failure' to provide a correct interpretation may in fact have nothing to do with an individual's intellectual function but rather may simply reflect a different upbringing or background. Similarly, tests of memory which require the subject to recite past U.S. presidents may not be an appropriate measuring tool depending on a person's country of origin, language skills, educational level, etc" (p. 3). Observations regarding a client's eye contact and body posture must also consider possible cultural factors. Individuals from diverse cultural backgrounds may show different patterns of eye contact, dress, and body postures during interviews (Sue & Sue, 2008a).

Psychological Tests and Inventories

Psychological tests and inventories are standardized instruments that are used to assess characteristics of the individual including personality, maladaptive behavior, social skills, intellectual abilities, vocational interests, and cognitive impairment. Tests

Naturalistic versus Controlled Observations

Naturalistic observations are made in settings that occur naturally in one's environment. Here, on the left, a female researcher is taking notes while observing children at play in a playground in Los Angeles, California. The playground is a natural setting for the children to play in. In this photo on the right, a female researcher with a laptop computer is rating the behaviors in a mother-child interaction session conducted in a clinic laboratory. What are the advantages and disadvantages of naturalistic versus controlled observations?

Did You Know?

Imaginary friends that appear and disappear are a source of comfort to many children. Children often report hearing voices from these "friends." Reports of such friends would be considered a symptom of psychosis in adults, but rarely in children.

Source: Sidhu & Kickey, (2010)

differ in form (that is, they may be oral or written and may be administered to groups or to individuals), structure, degree of objectivity, and content. We examine two general types of personality tests and measures (projective and self-report inventories) and tests of intelligence and cognitive impairment. It should be noted that two-thirds of the assessments used by clinical psychologists are evaluations of personality and intellectual achievement. Neuropsychological assessment and adaptive-functional behavior assessment are also commonly used.

Projective Personality Tests

In a projective personality test, the test taker is presented with ambiguous stimuli, such as inkblots, pictures, or incomplete sentences, and asked to respond to them in some way. The stimuli are generally novel, and the test is relatively unstructured. When responding to such stimuli, people "project" their attitudes, motives, and other personality characteristics onto the situation. The nature of the appraisal is generally well disguised: Participants are often unaware of the true nature or purpose of the test and usually do not recognize the significance of their responses. Projective tests presumably tap into the individual's unconscious needs and motivations (Meyer et al., 2003).

Swiss psychiatrist Hermann Rorschach devised the *Rorschach technique* for personality appraisal in 1921. A Rorschach test consists of ten cards that display symmetrical inkblot designs. The cards are presented one at a time to participants, who are asked (1) what they see in the blots and (2) what characteristics of the blots make them see that. Inkblots are considered appropriate stimuli because they are ambiguous, nonthreatening, and do not elicit learned responses. What people see in the blots, whether they attend to large areas or to details, whether they respond to color, and whether their perceptions suggest movement are assumed to be symbolic of inner promptings, motivations, and conflicts. Both the basic premise of the Rorschach test and the psychologist's

projective personality test testing involving responses to ambiguous stimuli, such as inkblots, pictures, or incomplete sentences

CONTROVERSY

Wikipedia and the Rorschach Test

In 2009, editors of the online encyclopedia Wikipedia decided to publish the entire set of Rorschach inkblot plates, the most common responses for each inkblot and the characteristics each inkblot are purported to measure. One of the inkblots, for example, is considered representative of a "father figure;" responses to this card are supposed to reveal one's attitude toward males and authority figures. Similar information regarding the characteristics purportedly being tapped is provided for each of the other cards.

Although there are questions regarding reliability and validity of the inkblot test, many clinicians still utilize this assessment tool. As Bruce Smith, president of the International Society of Rorschach and Projective Methods, states,

"The more test material are promulgated widely, the more possibility there is to game the test" (Cohen, 2009, p. 1). In other words, awareness of answers that are typically given to each inkblot may change the responses of individuals taking the test and invalidate the results. There is additional concern that other test materials will also be published, limiting their usefulness.

In defense of their decision to publish the inkblot information, editors at Wikipedia argue that the Rorschach test is in the public domain because intellectual property rights have expired, and it does not have copyright protection. Did Wikipedia go too far in publishing the entire Rorschach inkblot test?

interpretation of the symbolism within the client's responses rely on psychoanalytic theory. For example, seeing eyes or buttocks may imply paranoid tendencies; fierce animals may imply aggressive tendencies; blood may imply strong uncontrolled emotions; food may imply dependency needs; and masks may imply avoidance of personal exposure (Klopfer & Davidson, 1962). However, research has found that interpretation of these "signs" often reflect the bias or cultural expectation of the clinician (Chapman & Chapman, 1967).

There are actually a variety of approaches to interpreting and scoring Rorschach responses. The most extensive and recent is the comprehensive system of Exner (1983, 1990), whose scoring system is based on reviews of research findings and studies of the Rorschach technique. Exner views the Rorschach technique as a problem-solving task; test takers are presented with ambiguous stimuli that they interpret according to their preferred mode of perceptual cognitive processing. Exner's system has yielded indexes associated with specific disorders such as depression. However, researchers have called into question the validity of Exner's system due to its tendency to make "normal" individuals appear to have serious psychopathology (Garb, Wood, Lilienfield, & Nezworsky, 2005). Although many believed the Rorschach test could discriminate between psychopaths (individuals who lack empathy and have few morals) and nonpsychopaths, it was unable to do so (Wood et al., 2010).

Rorschach H. Diagnostics

The Rorschach Technique

Devised by Swiss psychiatrist Hermann Rorschach in 1921, the Rorschach technique uses a number of cards, each showing a symmetrical inkblot design similar to the one shown here. The earlier cards in the set are in black and white; the later cards are more colorful. A client's responses to the inkblots are interpreted according to assessment guidelines and can be compared with responses of individuals diagnosed with various disorders.

Although proponents of the Rorschach test argue that it is useful in clinical assessment and can tap dimensions not possible with other instruments (Society for Personality Assessment, 2005), others argue that a moratorium should be placed on many applications of the Rorschach until further research demonstrates its validity (Garb, Wood, Lilienfield, & Nezworksi, 2005).

The *Thematic Apperception Test (TAT)*, another projective personality test, was developed in 1935 (Murray & Morgan, 1938). It consists of thirty picture cards, most depicting two human figures. Their poses and actions are vague and ambiguous enough to be open to different interpretations. Some cards are designated for specific age levels or for a single gender, and some are appropriate for all groups. Like the Rorschach technique, the TAT relies on projection to tap underlying motives, drives, and personality processes. Generally, twenty TAT cards are administered, one at a time, with instructions to tell a story about each picture. Typically, the tester says, "I am going to show you some pictures. Tell me a story about what is going on in each one, what led up to it, and what its outcome will be." The entire story is recorded verbatim. There is usually no limit on time or the length of the stories. The purpose is to gain insight into the individual's conflicts and worries, as well as clues about his or her core personality structure. Woike and McAdams (2001) found that the TAT is particularly valuable in ascertaining an individual's personality and motivational traits.

Other types of projective tests include sentence-completion and draw-a-person tests. In the *sentence-completion test*, the participant is given a list of partial sentences and is asked to complete each of them. Typical partial sentences are "My ambition . . .," "My mother was always . . .," and "I can remember . . . " Clinicians try to interpret the meaning of the individual's responses. In *draw-a-person tests*, such as the Machover D-A-P (Machover, 1949), the participant is asked to draw a person. Then he or she may be asked to draw a person of the opposite sex. Finally, the participant may be instructed to make up a story about the characters that were drawn or to describe the first character's background. Many clinicians analyze these drawings for size, position, detail, and so on, assuming that the drawings provide diagnostic clues. Well-controlled studies cast doubt on such diagnostic interpretations (Anastasi, 1982; Lilienfeld, Wood, & Garb, 2000). The validity of conclusions drawn from these tests is open to question, as can be seen in the following case.

Lewis J. Merrim/Photo Researchers, Inc.

The Thematic Apperception Test

In the Thematic Apperception Test, patients tell a story about each of a series of pictures they are shown. These pictures—often depicting one, two, or three people doing something—are less ambiguous than Rorschach inkblots.

Case Study

A seven-year-old girl was asked to draw a picture of her family doing something. She drew a picture of herself and her sister with their hands up in the air with the father standing next to them and smiling. The child told the psychologist that she and her sister were "cheering at a show" (Wakefield & Underwager, 1993, p. 55).

Instead of relying on the child's explanation of the picture, the psychologist focused on the "symbolism" inherent in the picture and her belief that the girls raising their hands in the air represented a sense of helplessness. She noted that the father's hands were large and asserted that sexually abused children often draw large hands on their perpetrators (neither of these interpretations are supported by research). The psychologist believed that the father was sexually abusing the girl who had drawn the family picture, even though she denied any such acts had taken place. The psychologist argued that the girl should be protected from further abuse.

The analysis and interpretation of responses to projective tests are subject to wide variation. Clinicians given the same data frequently disagree with one another about scoring. Much of this disparity is caused by differences in clinicians' orientations, skills, and personal styles. But, as noted earlier, the demonstrably low reliability and validity of these instruments means that they should be used with caution and only in conjunction with other assessment measures. Norms for projective tests are either nonexistent or inadequate. Support for the TAT and Rorschach interpretations is very limited and even poorer for the draw-a-person test (Lilienfeld, Wood, & Garb, 2000). The cultural relevance of these tests is also called into question. These tests were developed many decades ago and have limited applicability to people living today, particularly diverse populations. For instance, the pictures on the TAT cards show clothing, hairstyles, furniture, and surroundings of the 1930s when the test was developed and none of the pictures include ethnic minorities. Can modern day individuals identify with these pictures?

Self-Report Inventories

Unlike projective tests, self-report inventories require test takers to answer specific written questions or to select specific responses from a list of alternatives—usually self-descriptive statements. Participants are asked to either agree or disagree with the statement or to indicate the extent of their agreement or disagreement. Because a predetermined score is assigned to each possible answer, subjective factors in scoring and interpretation are minimized. In addition, participants' responses and scores can be compared readily with a standardization sample.

Perhaps the most widely used self-report personality inventory is the *Minnesota Multiphasic Personality Inventory*, or *MMPI* (Hathaway & McKinley, 1943). The MMPI-2, a revision by Butcher and colleagues (see Butcher, 1990; Graham, 1990; Greene, 1991), restandardized the inventory, refined the wording of certain items, eliminated items considered outdated, and attempted to include appropriate representations of ethnic minority groups. The MMPI-2 consists of 567 statements; participants are asked to indicate whether each statement is true or false as it applies to them. There is also a "cannot say" alternative, but clients are strongly discouraged from using this category because too many such responses can invalidate the test.

The test taker's MMPI-2 results are rated on ten clinical scales and a number of validity scales. The ten clinical scales were originally constructed by analyzing the responses of diagnosed psychiatric patients (and the responses of normal participants) to the 567 test items. These analyses allowed researchers to determine what kinds of responses each of the various types of psychiatric patients usually made, in contrast to those of normal individuals. The validity scales, which assess factors such as degree of candor, confusion, or falsification on the part of the respondent, help clinicians detect potential faking or symptom exaggeration (Groth-Marnat, 2009; Tolin, Steenkamp, Marx, & Litz, 2010). Figure 3.1 shows possible responses to ten sample MMPI-2 items and the kinds of responses that contribute to a high rating on the ten MMPI clinical scales.

A basic assumption of the original version of the MMPI was that a person whose MMPI answers are similar to those of diagnosed patients is likely to behave similarly to those patients. However, such single-scale interpretations are fraught with hazards. For example, although a person with a high rating on Scale 6 may be labeled paranoid, this scale does not detect many persons with paranoia. Generally, multiple-scale interpretations (pattern analysis) and characteristics associated with the patterns are examined. Interpretation of the MMPI-2 scales can be quite complicated and requires special training. Although client responses to questions on the MMPI-2 can also be viewed as direct communication of important content, including information about the client's symptoms, attitudes, and behaviors (Butcher, 1995), the MMPI-2 should only be used by clinicians who have mastered its intricacies, who understand relevant statistical concepts, and who can accurately interpret the client's responses (Butcher, 1995; Graham, 2005).

Whereas the MMPI-2 assesses a number of different personality characteristics, some self-report inventories or questionnaires focus only on certain kinds of personality traits or emotional problems, such as depression or anxiety. For example, the *Beck Depression Inventory (BDI)* is composed of twenty-one items that measure various aspects of depression, such as mood, appetite, functioning at work, suicidal thinking, and sleeping patterns (Beck et al., 1961).

Though widely used, personality inventories have limitations (Sollman, Ranseen, & Berry, 2010). First, the fixed number of alternatives can hinder individuals from presenting an accurate picture of themselves. Being asked to answer "true" or "false" to the

SAMPLE ITEMS

TEN MMPI CLINICAL SCALES WITH SIMPLIFIED DESCRIPTIONS	I like mechanics magazines.	I have a good appetite.	I wake up fresh and rested most mornings.	I think I would like the work of a librarian.	I am easily awakened by noise.	I like to read newspaper articles on crime.	My hands and feet are usually warm enough.	My daily life is full of things that keep me interested.	I am about as able to work as I ever was.	There seems to be a lump in my throat much of the time.
1. **Hypochondriasis (Hs)**—Individuals showing excessive worry about health with reports of obscure pains.		NO	NO				NO		NO	
2. **Depression (D)**—People suffering from chronic depression, feelings of uselessness, and inability to face the future.		NO			YES			NO	NO	
3. **Hysteria (Hy)**—Individuals who react to stress by developing physical symptoms (paralysis, cramps, headaches, etc.).		NO	NO			NO	NO	NO	NO	YES
4. **Psychopathic Deviate (Pd)**—People who show irresponsibility, disregard social conventions, and lack deep emotional responses.								NO		
5. **Masculinity-Femininity (Mf)**—People tending to identify with the opposite sex rather than their own.	NO			YES						
6. **Paranoia (Pa)**—People who are suspicious, sensitive, and feel persecuted.										
7. **Psychasthenia (Pt)**—People troubled with fears (phobias) and compulsive tendencies.			NO					NO		YES
8. **Schizophrenia (Sc)**—People with bizarre and unusual thoughts or behavior.								NO		
9. **Hypomania (Ma)**—People who are physically and mentally overactive and who shift rapidly in ideas and actions.										
10. **Social Introversion (Si)**—People who tend to withdraw from social contacts and responsibilities.										

Figure 3.1

THE TEN MMPI-2 CLINICAL SCALES AND SAMPLE MMPI-2 TESTS

Shown here are the MMPI-2 clinical scales and a few of the items that appear on them. As an example, answering "no" or "false" (rather than "yes" or "true") to the item "I have a good appetite" would result in a higher scale score for hypochondriasis, depression, and hysteria.
Source: Adapted from Dahlstrom & Welsh, (1965). These items from the original MMPI remain unchanged in the MMPI-2.

statement "I am suspicious of people" does not permit an individual to qualify the item in any way. Second, a person may have a unique response style or response set (e.g., a tendency to respond to test items in a certain way regardless of content) that may distort the results. For example, many people have a need to present themselves in a favorable light, and this can cause them to give answers that are socially acceptable but inaccurate. Some individuals may fake having a disorder or try to avoid appearing deviant. Third, interpretations of responses of people from different cultural groups may be inaccurate if norms for these groups have not been developed. For example, consistent normative patterns on specific scales on the MMPI-2 have been found with African Americans (Monot, Quirk, Hoerger, & Brewer, 2009). Fourth, cultural factors may shape the way a trait or characteristic is viewed. Asian Americans tend to score higher on measures of social anxiety, but their scores may be a reflection of cultural values of modesty and self-restraint rather than a sign of psychopathology (Melka et al., 2010). African Americans also show a different pattern of responding to measures of social anxiety (Melka et al., 2010).

Despite these potential problems, personality inventories are widely used. Some, such as the MMPI-2, have been extensively researched throughout the world, and in many cases their validity has been established. Sophisticated means have also been found to control for faking. For example, although individuals can lower their psychopathology scores by trying to hide their symptoms on the MMPI (i.e., trying to fake being healthy when they are not), the MMPI has scales that can help alert clinicians to possible faking (Groth-Marnat, 2009). However, other tests are more susceptible to feigning. For example, performance on intelligence tests and tests to measure attention-deficit hyperactivity disorder has been successfully "faked" (i.e., faked without detection) (Shandera et al., 2010; Sollman, Ranseen, & Berry, 2010).

Intelligence Tests

Intelligence testing, intended to obtain an estimate of a person's current level of cognitive functioning, results in a score called the *intelligence quotient (IQ)*. An IQ score indicates an individual's level of performance relative to that of other people of the same age. As such, an IQ score is an important aid in predicting school performance or detecting intellectual disability. (Through statistical procedures, IQ test results are converted into numbers, with 100 representing the mean, or average, score. An IQ score of about 130 indicates performance exceeding that of 95 percent of all same-age peers.)

The two most widely used intelligence tests are the Wechsler scales (Wechsler, 1981) and the Stanford-Binet scales (Terman & Merrill, 1960; Thorndike, Hagen, & Sattler, 1986). The *Wechsler Adult Intelligence Scale* (the *WAIS* and its revised version, *WAIS-IV*)

CRITICAL THINKING

The Validity of a Measure of Dissociation

Dissociation involves a disruption in an individual's state of consciousness that can lead to disorders such as psychogenic amnesia and dissociative identity disorder. The validity of the Adolescent Dissociative Experiences Scale (A-DES) (Armstrong, Putnam, Carlson, Libreo, & Smith, 1997), a test developed to measure this phenomenon, has been questioned due to concerns that items in the questionnaire actually represent "normal" experiences, or are phrased in a way to produce a specific answer. Do you agree with these criticisms of items on the Dissociative Experiences Scale?

Sample statements from the Adolescent Dissociative Experience Scale (A-DES)*

A-DES: *I get so wrapped up in watching TV, reading, or playing a video game that I don't have any idea what's going on around me.*

Comment: Isn't that what any "normal" human would do if he or she has enough attention and concentration?

A-DES: *People tell me I do or say things that I don't remember doing or saying.*

I get confused about whether I have done something or only thought about doing it.

I can't figure out if things really happened or if I only dreamed or thought about them.

People tell me that I sometimes act so differently that I seem like a different person.

Comment: These items are crafted in a way to encourage false positives. First, "people tell me" does not qualify as an "experience." Second, one wonders why the scale was made up of declarative statements instead of questions. Third, "I seem like a different person" is a leading statement.

A-DES: *I am so good at lying and acting that I believe it myself.*

Comment: This should be an immediate tip-off that the reporter is unreliable.

A-DES: *I feel like my past is a puzzle and some of the pieces are missing.*

Comment: Isn't this the human condition?

*A-DES statements are italicized; comments by Dr. Gharaibeh are in plain text.
Source: Gharaibeh, (2009)

is administered to persons age sixteen and older. Two other forms are appropriate for children ages six to sixteen (the *Wechsler Intelligence Scale for Children*, or *WISC-IV*) and ages two to seven (the *Wechsler Preschool and Primary Scale of Intelligence*, or *WPPSI-III*). The WAIS-IV consists of six verbal and five performance scales, which yield verbal and performance IQ scores. These scores are combined to present a total IQ score. The WAIS consists of four factors: Verbal Comprehension, Perceptual Organization, Working Memory, and Processing Speed (Saklofske, Hildebrand, & Gorsuch, 2000). Table 3.1 shows subtest items similar to those used in the WAIS-IV.

The *Stanford-Binet Intelligence Scale,* now in its fifth edition, is used for individuals ages two to age eighty-five. Much more complicated in administration and scoring, the Stanford-Binet requires considerable skill in its use. The test procedure is designed to establish a basal age (the participant passes all subtests for that age) and a ceiling age (the participant fails all subtests for that age), from which an IQ score is calculated. In general, the WISC is preferred over the Stanford-Binet for school-age children (La Greca & Stringer, 1985). It is easier to administer and yields scores on different cognitive skills (such as verbal and performance subtests). Yet the Stanford-Binet is the standard to which other tests are compared because of its long history, careful revision, and periodic updating (Kline, 2005).

There are four major critiques of the use of IQ tests. First, some investigators believe that IQ tests have been popularized as a means of measuring innate intelligence, when in truth the tests largely reflect cultural and social factors (Sternberg, 2005). The issue of racial differences in innate intelligence has a long history of debate. Publication of *The Bell Curve* (Herrnstein & Murray, 1994) refocused attention on this issue when the book's authors proposed that racial differences in IQ scores are determined by heredity and that social and status differences between intellectually different groups are therefore difficult to overcome (Figure 3.2). More recently, Rushton and Jensen (2005) also argued that racial differences in IQ scores are determined by heredity. Critics (e.g., Nisbett, 2005; Suzuki & Aronson, 2005) have charged that the basic premises of these books are faulty and that the frequent assumption that IQ tests measure innate intelligence is false.

Second, the predictive validity of IQ tests has been criticized. That is, do IQ test scores accurately predict the future behaviors or achievements of different cultural groups? Many believe that factors such as motivation and work ethic are much better predictors of future success. Third, investigators often disagree over criterion variables (in essence, what is actually being predicted by IQ tests). For example, two investigators may be interested in the ability of IQ tests to predict future success. One may define success as grades received in school and be pleased to a find a correlation between IQ test scores and grade point average. The other investigator, believing that leadership

TABLE 3.1   Items Similar to Those for the Wechsler Adult Intelligence Scale-V

Information	1. How many pennies make a nickel? 2. What is ice made of?
Comprehension	1. Why do some people save rubber bands? 2. Why is copper often used in water pipes?
Arithmetic (all calculated "in the head")	1. Susan had three pieces of candy, and John gave her two more. How many pieces of candy did Susan have altogether? 2. Four women divided twenty pieces of candy equally among themselves. How many pieces of candy did each person receive?
Similarities	In what way are the following alike? 1. horse/zebra 2. rake/lawn mower 3. triangle/rectangle
Vocabulary	This test consists simply of asking, "What is a _____?" or "What does _____ mean?" The words cover a wide range of difficulty.

skills and the ability to work with people are indicators of success, may find only a weak correlation between IQ scores and these variables.

Fourth, some researchers have questioned whether our current conceptions of IQ tests and intelligence are adequate. A number of researchers have proposed that intelligence is a multidimensional attribute. E. H. Taylor (1990) stated that an important aspect of intelligence, and one that cannot be adequately assessed using IQ tests, is social intelligence and social competency. Social skills often affect problem solving, adaptation to life, social knowledge, and the ability to use resources effectively. Sternberg (2004) finds that intelligence can be viewed as analytical (ability to analyze and evaluate ideas, solve problems, and make decisions), creative (going beyond what is given to generate novel and interesting ideas), and practical (ability that individuals use to find the best fit between themselves and the demands of the environment), characteristics not assessed by the most commonly used tests of intelligence.

The controversies over the validity and usefulness of IQ testing may never fully subside. Some continue to claim that IQ tests demonstrate predictive validity for many important attributes, including future success (Barrett & Depinet, 1991). Others maintain that such tests are biased and are of limited utility (Helms, 1992). Reliance on IQ scores has resulted in discriminatory actions. In many states, for example, African American and Latino children have been disproportionately assigned to special education classes on the basis of IQ results. The criticisms regarding cultural biases have resulted in attempts to find more culturally appropriate tests.

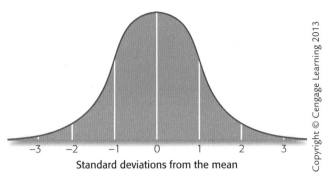

Figure 3.2

A BELL CURVE SHOWING STANDARD DEVIATIONS

The bell curve refers to the fact that the distribution of IQ scores in a population resembles the shape of a bell, with most scores hovering over the mean and fewer scores falling in the outlying areas of the distribution. IQ scores are transformed so that the mean equals 100, and deviations from the mean are expressed in terms of standard deviations. One standard deviation from the mean (about 15 IQ points above or below the mean, or IQ scores between 85 and 115) represents about 68 percent of the scores. Two standard deviations (about 30 IQ points above or below the mean, or IQs between 70 and 130) account for more than 95 percent of the scores.

Tests for Cognitive Impairment

Clinical psychologists, especially those who work in a hospital setting, are concerned with detecting and assessing cognitive impairment resulting from brain damage. Such damage can have profound effects both physically (e.g., motor behavior) and psychologically (e.g., memory, attention, thinking, emotions, etc.) (Gass, 2002; Grant & Adams, 2009). The use of individual intelligence tests such as the WAIS-IV can sometimes identify such impairments. For example, a difference of twenty points between verbal and performance scores on the WAIS-IV may indicate the possibility of brain damage. Overall, IQ scores have been significantly correlated with neuropsychological test performance (Diaz-Asper, Schretlen, & Pearlson, 2004). Certain patterns of scores on the individual subtests, such as those that measure verbal concept formation or abstract thinking, can also reveal brain damage.

One of the routine means of assessing cognitive impairment is the *Bender-Gestalt Visual-Motor Test* (Bender, 1938; Brannigan, Decker, & Madsen, 2004), shown in Figure 3.3. Nine geometric designs, each drawn in black on a piece of white cardboard, are presented one at a time to the test taker, who is asked to copy them on

Testing for Intellectual Functioning

Intelligence tests can provide valuable information about intellectual functioning and can help psychologists assess intellectual disability and intellectual deterioration. Although many of these tests have been severely criticized as being culturally biased, if used with care, they can be beneficial tools. Here, a three-year-old child is shown taking the Stanford-Binet test. The Stanford-Binet Intelligence Scale is a standardized test that assesses intelligence and cognitive abilities in children and adults ages two to eighty-five.

Figure 3.3

THE NINE BENDER DESIGNS

The figures presented to participants are shown on the left. The distorted figures drawn by an individual with suspected brain damage are shown on the right.

Source: Bender, (1938)

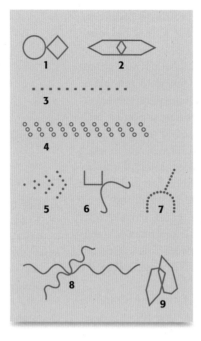
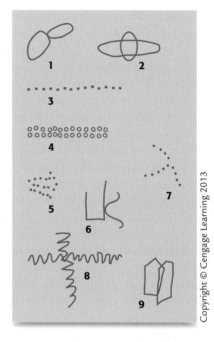

Copyright © Cengage Learning 2013

a piece of paper. Certain errors in the copies are characteristic of neurological impairment. Among these are rotation of figures, perseveration (continuation of a pattern to an exceptional degree), fragmentation, oversimplification, inability to copy angles, and reversals.

Neuropsychological tests are widely used (Camara, Nathan, & Puente, 2000; Goldstein & Beers, 2004) and are effective and valid in evaluating cognitive impairment due to brain damage. In fact, they are far more accurate in documenting cognitive deficits than are interviews or informal observations (Kubiszyn et al., 2000). The *Halstead-Reitan Neuropsychological Test Battery* successfully differentiates patients with brain damage from those without brain damage and can provide valuable information about the type and location of the damage (Goldstein & Beers, 2004; Boll, 1983). The full battery consists of eleven tests. Examinees are presented with a series of tasks that assess sensorimotor, cognitive, and perceptual functioning, including abstract concept formation, memory and attention, and auditory perception. The full battery takes more than six hours to administer, so it is an expensive and time-consuming assessment tool.

Neurological Tests

In addition to psychological tests, a variety of neurological medical procedures are available for diagnosing cognitive impairments due to brain damage or abnormal brain functioning. A widely used means of examining the brain is the *electroencephalograph (EEG)*. Electrodes attached to the skull record electrical activity (brain waves); abnormalities in the activity can provide information about the presence of tumors or other brain conditions. Additionally, x-ray studies can help detect brain tumors. A more sophisticated procedure, the *computerized axial tomography (CT) scan*, repeatedly scans different areas of the brain with beams of x-rays and, with the assistance of a computer, produces a three-dimensional, cross-sectional image of the structure of the brain. That image can provide a detailed view of brain deterioration or abnormality.

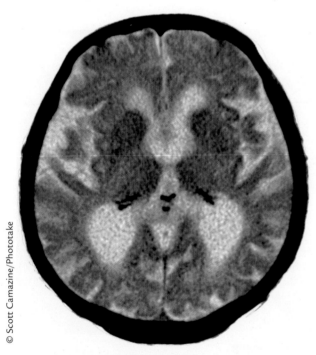

© Scott Camazine/Phototake

CT Scan Showing Brain Atrophy

Cerebral CT scans, which involve multiple, cross-sectional x-rays of the brain, are able to document a variety of brain changes associated with neurocognitive disorders. This CT scan of the brain of a 94-year-old woman shows enlarged ventricles and atrophy indicative of a loss of neurons in some regions of the brain.

In addition to the study of brain damage, CT scans have been used to study brain tissue abnormalities among patients diagnosed with a variety of disorders including schizophrenia, mood disorders, Alzheimer's disease, and alcoholism (Lin & Alavi, 2009).

The *positron emission tomography (PET) scan* enables noninvasive study of the physiological and biochemical processes of the brain, rather than the anatomical structures seen in the CT scan. In PET scans, a radioactive substance is injected into the patient's bloodstream. The scanner detects the substance as it is metabolized in the brain, yielding information about brain functioning. PET scans, like CT scans, have been used to study a variety of mental disorders and brain diseases. Characteristic metabolic patterns have been observed in many of these disorders (Lynch, 2007). PET scans can be combined with information from other scans (such as CT scans) to provide comprehensive information about the brain.

A final technique, *magnetic resonance imaging (MRI)*, creates a magnetic field around the patient and uses radio waves to detect abnormalities. MRIs can produce an amazingly clear cross-sectional "picture" of the brain and its tissues. Because of these superior pictures, which are reminiscent of postmortem brain slices, MRIs can often provide more detailed images of lesions compared to CT scans (Burghart & Finn, 2010; Morihisa et al., 1999). In functional magnetic resonance imaging, both the structures and changes in blood flow in different brain regions can be observed. This technique provides high resolution, noninvasive views of neural activity.

These neurological techniques, coupled with psychological tests, are increasing diagnostic accuracy and understanding of brain functioning and disorders. Some researchers predict that in the future such techniques will allow clinicians to make more precise diagnoses and to pinpont precise areas of the brain affected by disorders such as Alzheimer's disease and schizophrenia.

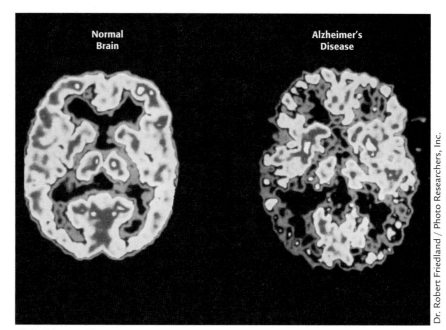

Alzheimer's Disease

As can be seen in these PET scans comparing brain activity between someone with Alzheimer's disease and a healthy control, glucose metabolism is reduced in the temporal and parietal lobes of the individual with Alzheimer's disease.

The Classification of Abnormal Behavior

The goal of having a classification system for abnormal behaviors is to provide distinct categories, indicators, and nomenclature for different patterns of behavior, thought processes, and emotional disturbances. Thus the pattern of behavior classified as *social phobia* should be clearly different from the pattern named *dissociative identity disorder* (DSM-5) as seen in the following symptom descriptions:

- Social phobia: (1) fear or anxiety involving social situations in which one is observed; (2) fear that the anxiety is evident to others, resulting in humiliation or rejection; (3) severe distress or impairment results from the anxiety.
- Dissociative identity disorder: (1) identity disruptions involving two or more personality states within an individual, (2) inability to recall important personal information, (3) this state is associated with severe distress or impairment.

At the same time, the categories should be constructed in such a way as to accommodate wide variation in these patterns. That is, the clinician should be able to categorize dissociative disorder as such, even when the client does not show the "perfect" or "textbook" symptom pattern.

Neuroimaging with MRI

Structural MRI (left) and functional MRI (right) scans reveal that some violent individuals have reduced volume and activity in the anterior cingulate cortex (blue area in front part of brain at left and corresponding yellow area in brain on the right), which is thought to be the hub of a circuit responsible for regulating impulsive aggression.

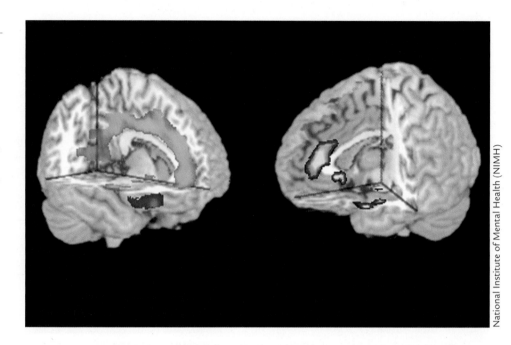

National Institute of Mental Health (NIMH)

Diagnostic and Statistical Manual of Mental Disorders (DSM)

The *Diagnostic Statistical Manual* (DSM) is widely used by mental health professionals. It lists all officially designated mental disorders and the characteristics or symptoms needed to confirm a diagnosis. What is contained in the DSM impacts the consumer, health care providers, insurance companies, and the pharmaceutical industry. The most recent revision of the diagnostic manual, DSM-5, is touted as an improvement over previous editions of the DSM. However, it is not without its own set of controversies. We begin by reviewing earlier efforts to define mental disorders, including shortcomings with these efforts, and then examine the most recent attempt to develop a reliable classification system.

The number of identified psychological "disorders" has increased dramatically over time. In 1840, the United States census had only two categories of mental disorders—idiocy or insanity (Cloud, 2010). The first DSM published by the American Psychiatric Association in 1952, identified 106 different mental disorders. The number increased to 182 disorders when DSM-II was published in 1968. Richard Spitzer, head of the task force that developed DSM-III (published in 1980), focused on increasing the reliability of the classification system. DSM-III contained 265 disorders. DSM-III was further refined, resulting in the 1987 publication of DSM-III-R with 292 diagnoses. DSM-IV with 297 diagnoses was published in 1994. DSM-IV-TR, published in 2000, included additional information on the different disorders. DSM-5, scheduled for final publication in 2013, introduces a dimensional approach to diagnosis combined with acknowledgment that most disorders involve a continuum of symptom severity (thus addressing concerns about categorical diagnostic systems). Each new edition of the DSM has attempted to correct or refine problems in previous editions and improve reliability and validity.

The reliability and validity of diagnoses using different versions of the DSM have been problematic, although they have improved with each successive edition. Early studies of the DSM found poor agreement (poor interrater reliability) between clinicians making diagnoses based on the same information, as well as weak test-retest reliability. The greatest disagreement was found in certain diagnostic categories. As a rule, reliability was higher for broad distinctions than for fine distinctions. For example, clinicians might agree that

Can We Accurately Assess the Status of Members of Different Cultural Groups?

We often have a difficult time evaluating the behaviors of people from other cultures. Cultural groups differ in many aspects, including dietary practices, type of clothing, religious rituals, and social interactions. How do we decide whether an individual from a different culture is behaving in a certain way because of a mental disorder or because of cultural practices? What signs or clues indicate that someone is truly mentally and emotionally disturbed? Can we use assessment measures standardized in the United States with people from other countries? Can assessment measures administered in English be applied to those with limited English proficiency (Kohn & Scorcia, 2007)?

These questions are only a sampling of the kinds of issues clinicians must consider when conducting assessments involving members of ethnic minority groups or individuals from different cultures. Brislin (1993) has identified several major problems, including the equivalence of concepts and scales.

First, certain concepts may not be equivalent across cultures. For instance, Americans living in the United States and the Baganda living in East Africa have different concepts of intelligent behavior. In the United States, one indicator of intelligence is quickness in mental reasoning; among the Baganda, slow, deliberate thought is considered a mark of intelligence. Obviously, tests of intelligence devised in the two cultures would differ.

Second, scores on assessment instruments may not really be equivalent in cross-cultural research. For example, many universities use the Scholastic Assessment Test (SAT), which has a verbal and a quantitative component, as a criterion for admissions. Do the test scores mean the same thing for different groups in terms of assessing academic potential, achievements, and ability to succeed? SAT scores are moderately successful predictors of subsequent university grades. However, among African American students attending primarily white institutions, the ability to deal with and understand racism and humanist attitudes were shown to be the best predictor of academic achievement (Nasim, Robert, Harrell, & Young, 2005). Garrison (2009) also argues that standardized tests like the GRE and SAT have more to do with social desirability than scholastic potential and handicap members of ethnic groups and those from lower socioeconomic backgrounds.

Third, the manner in which symptoms are expressed may vary from culture to culture, and certain cultural groups may have disturbances that are specific to those groups (Steel et al., 2009; Sue & Sue, 2008a, b).

an individual had a personality disorder, but might disagree on finer details such as the subtype of disorder. As with DSM-III and DSM-IV, the development of DSM-5 has used reliability and validity field trials. This ongoing process involves having sets of two DSM-5–trained clinicians independently review and assess the same client and formulate a diagnosis. Twenty percent of these sessions are being videotaped so that clinician diagnoses can be compared with "expert consensus" diagnoses (i.e., experts are reviewing the videotapes and providing a diagnosis) to gauge criterion validity. How the reliability and validity of DSM-5 will compare with the previous DSMs will be determined through ongoing research and continued use of the diagnostic criteria.

All the DSMs are based primarily on the classification scheme developed by Emil Kraepelin toward the end of the nineteenth century. Kraepelin believed that mental disorders were like physical disorders in that each had its own set of symptoms, course, etiology, and treatment outcome. The DSM has traditionally been a categorical system in that separate symptoms are listed for each disorder and an individual either has or does not have a particular disorder (Shorter, 2010). However, many disorders have overlapping symptoms and disorders typically cannot be distinguished from one another in terms of etiology or laboratory findings. For example, depressive and anxiety disorders share many of the same symptoms and have common neurobiological underpinnings as well as similar response to some medications (Nasrallah, 2009).

Dissatisfaction with the categorical model, led to the DSM-5 dimensional system in which most disorders are seen to lie on a continuum with "normality" appearing at one end of the continuum. From this perspective, anxiety, depression, and even psychotic-like experiences are not an "either or" phenomenon; instead, individuals might experience varying degrees of symptoms related to these disorders. Dimensional ratings are reflected in the development of a new category, "risk syndromes," which includes disorders such as attenuated psychosis syndrome and mild neurocognitive disorder that represent milder forms of well-established disorders. Also, dimensional ratings allow clinicians to rate depression, anxiety, cognitive impairment, and reality distortion for each client on a scale of "none," "slight," "mild," "moderate," or "severe" (Kraemer, Kupfer, Narrow, Clarke, & Regier,

2010). Although Pincus (2011) agrees with some of the dramatic changes initiated with DSM-5, such as using a dimensional system, he believes further research is necessary before wholesale adoption of this approach. In practical terms, the use of dimensional ratings may require mental health professionals to receive extensive training to maintain the diagnostic integrity of the new system. Although DSM-5 has received criticism, it does provide clear guidelines to assist clinicians to diagnose and categorize mental disorders and has incorporated dimensional measures. Let's look at an example of a client and a diagnostic evaluation based on the DSM-5. We then discuss concern with labeling and classification systems.

Case Study

Mark is a fifty-year-old machine operator referred for treatment by his supervisor due to concerns that Mark's performance at work has deteriorated in the past four months. Mark is frequently absent from work, has difficulty getting along with others, and frequently appears to have a strong odor of liquor on his breath after his lunch break. The supervisor knows that Mark is a heavy drinker and suspects that Mark's performance is affected by alcohol consumption. In truth, Mark cannot stay away from drinking. He consumes alcohol every day; during weekends, he averaged about sixteen ounces of Scotch per day. Although he has been a heavy drinker for thirty years, his alcohol intake increased after his wife left him six months previously. She claimed she could no longer tolerate his drinking, extreme jealousy, and unwarranted suspicions concerning her marital fidelity. Coworkers avoid Mark because he is a cold, unemotional person who distrusts others and overreacts to any perceived criticism. Mark has no close friends although he does hang out with "regulars" at a local bar.

A medical examination revealed that Mark was developing cirrhosis of the liver due to his chronic, heavy drinking. During interviews with the therapist, Mark revealed that he began drinking in his early teens. He blames others for his drinking problems: If his wife had been faithful, or if others were not out to get him, he would drink less. He eventually shared that his father is an alcoholic who goes into rages due to suspicions about his mother's marital fidelity; Mark and his siblings were often physically and verbally abused during his father's drunken rampages. Mark believes that his mother has stayed with his father only because of the family's Catholic religion.

Mark's heavy use of alcohol, which interfered with his social and occupational functioning, resulted in an alcohol use disorder diagnosis. Mark also exhibited a personality disorder with prominent paranoid personality traits involving suspiciousness, hypervigilance, and hostility toward others. This was supported by dimensional measures regarding personality functioning and the degree of match between his attitudes and behaviors and prominent personality traits (American Psychiatric Association, 2011). Mark was also given dimensional assessments regarding possible suicidality, anxiety, depression, and cognitive functioning. Mark was found to have some mild cognitive deficits (presumably resulting from his heavy alcohol consumption) and moderate depressive symptoms. Suicidality and anxiety did not emerge as areas of concern. Cirrhosis of the liver was listed as a significant medical condition. The clinician noted Mark's pending divorce, work difficulties, and poor relationships with coworkers when assessing psychosocial functioning.

In addition to making a diagnosis (or diagnoses, if multiple disorders are present) and assessing areas of psychological functioning, clinicians also identify "causal specifiers" (i.e., etiological factors associated with identified disorders) for the diagnosis. Because the same diagnosis can result from different causal factors, clarification of such factors can assist with treatment planning. Clinicians consider various etiological factors related to the diagnosis, including biological/genetic (e.g., substance use, family history of the same or similar disorders); environmental (e.g., trauma, living conditions, employment, and housing); developmental (e.g., childhood maltreatment, modeling of parental behaviors); cultural (e.g., religious, ethnic status); social (e.g., marriage, divorce, family, children), and behavioral problems (Aboraya, 2010a, b). Mark's diagnosis, then, was as follows:

- Alcohol use disorder
- Personality disorder with prominent paranoid traits
- Physical disorder: cirrhosis of the liver
- Causal specifiers
  1. *Biological/genetic*—There is a family history of alcohol abuse. The early onset of Mark's heavy drinking may be related to genetic vulnerability to alcohol abuse.
  2. *Environmental*—Mark is in jeopardy of losing his job and is facing financial stress due to his upcoming divorce.
  3. *Developmental*—Mark's father exhibited paranoia, drank heavily, and was physically and verbally abusive throughout Mark's childhood. Mark began drinking in early adolescence; this appears to have affected emotional maturation and social development.
  4. *Social*—There is limited family support. Mark's wife is seeking a divorce. Mark has very few friends other than a few "drinking buddies."
  5. *Cultural*—Mark is very concerned about family reactions to his upcoming divorce due to his Catholic upbringing.
  6. *Behavioral*—Mark tends to blame others and is often "cold and unemotional" in interactions with others. Mark has a strong tendency to be suspicious of others, a psychological factor that affects all social relationships.

DSM-5 Mental Disorders

The task of making a diagnosis of a mental disorder involves classifying individuals according to DSM criteria. It should be noted that many individuals who have one mental disorder also suffer from another. For example, an individual who is diagnosed with depression may also have a second disorder such as a substance-use disorder. Comorbidity refers to this co-occurrence of different disorders. One large-scale survey (Kessler, Chiu et al., 2005) found that the rate of comorbidity is high—60 percent of those with one disorder also had another disorder. Physical disorders are also noted during the diagnostic process. Table 3.2 lists the broad categories of mental disorders, most of which are discussed in this book.

Evaluation of the DSM Classification System

DSM-5 has taken the first step toward moving away from a categorical system and towards a dimensional system with the hopes of improving reliability, validity, and clinical utility (having a clinician-friendly classification system). A major criticism of previous versions of the DSM has been the lack of clarity regarding differential categorization of disorders. For example, research shows that for many disorders the distinction between major and less severe symptoms states is a matter of degree rather than kind (Ruscio & Ruscio, 2000). Furthermore, as mentioned earlier, many disorders are comorbid (i.e., occurring together). Additionally, symptoms of one disorder often overlap symptoms of other disorders (Clark, 2005; Widiger & Samuel, 2005). These findings have led to questions regarding whether disorders are better conceptualized as categorical or dimensional (i.e., appearing on a continuum). The move towards dimensional ratings and inclusion of milder forms of disorders in DSM-5 is an attempt to deal with this problem.

When symptoms do not clearly fit those specified by a diagnostic category, mental disorders are often recorded as "unspecified" or "Not Otherwise Specified"; findings that suggest the diagnostic criteria were difficult to use or did not fit symptoms

comorbidity co-occurrence of different disorders

TABLE 3.2   DSM-5 Disorders

Categories of Disorders	Features
Neurodevelopmental Disorders	Cognitive, learning, and language disabilities, autism spectrum disorders, attention deficit/ hyperactivity disorder, and so on
Neurocognitive Disorders	Psychological or behavioral abnormality associated with a dysfunction of the brain, including problems that arise from head injuries, ingestion of toxic/intoxicating substances, brain degeneration or disease, and so on
Mental Disorders Due to a General Medical Condition	When medical conditions cause a disorder, the patient is considered to have a mental disorder due to a general medical condition. For example, hypothyroidism can be a cause of major depressive disorder, so the diagnosis would be "major depressive disorder due to a general medical condition (hypothyroidism)"
Substance-Use and Addictive Disorders (Includes Behavioral Addictions)	Excessive use of alcohol, illicit drugs, or prescription medications that results in impaired functioning; nonsubstance addictions, including behavioral addictions such as gambling
Schizophrenia Spectrum and Other Psychotic Disorders	Disorders marked by severe impairment in thinking and perception; often involving delusions, hallucinations, and inappropriate affect
Bipolar and Related Disorders	Bipolar disorders are characterized by the occurrence of mania or hypomania, and may also include episodes of depressed mood; they include bipolar I, bipolar II, and cyclothymic disorder
Depressive Disorders	Depressive disorders involve feelings of sadness, emptiness and social withdrawal and include major depressive disorder, chronic depressive disorder, and mixed anxiety/depression
Anxiety Disorders	Disorders characterized by excessive or irrational anxiety over everyday situations, often accompanied by avoidance behaviors and fearful cognitions or worry
Obsessive-Compulsive and Related Disorders	Disorders characterized by obsessions (recurrent thoughts) and/or compulsions (repetitive behaviors)
Trauma and Stressor-Related Disorders	Disorders associated with exposure to stressors such as acute stress and post-traumatic stress disorder
Complex Somatic Symptom Disorders	Individuals complain of physical symptoms that cause distress and disability, bodily dysfunctions, and preoccupation with beliefs of having a health problem. There may be high levels of health anxiety and disproportionate concern.
Dissociative Disorders	Disturbance or alteration in memory, identity, or consciousness; individuals may not remember who they are, assume new identities, have two or more distinct personalities, or experience feelings of depersonalization
Sexual Dysfunctions	Disorders involving the disruption of any stage of a normal sexual response cycle, including desire, arousal, or orgasm
Gender Dysphoria	Clinically significant discontentment or conflict with biological sex and gender assigned at birth
Paraphilias	Recurrent, intense sexual fantasies or urges involving nonhuman objects, pain or humiliation, or children
Eating Disorders	Disorders characterized by disturbed eating patterns, such as bingeing, purging, excessive dieting, and body dissatisfaction
Sleep–Wake Disorders	Symptoms involve problems in initiating/maintaining sleep, excessive sleepiness, sleep disruptions, repeated awakening associated with nightmares and sleepwalking
Personality Disorders	Personality disorders involve stable traits that are inflexible and maladaptive and notably impair functioning or cause subjective distress
Not Otherwise Specified	These categories are intended to include disorders that do not fully meet the criteria for a particular disorder

Differential Diagnosis: The Case of Charlie Sheen

CRITICAL THINKING

During the first week of March 2011, actor Charlie Sheen appeared on numerous television and radio shows. He appeared energized and made exaggerated gestures while stating that he had "tiger blood" with "Adonis DNA." Individuals that he disagreed with were referred to as "trolls," among other terms (Gardner, 2011). Some of the statements he made on mass media included (Boudreault, 2011):

- "I am on a drug, it's called Charlie Sheen. It's not available, 'cause if you try it once, you will die. Your face will melt off and your children will weep over your exploded body."
- "I'm tired of pretending like I'm not special. I'm tired of pretending like I'm not bitchin', a total frickin' star from Mars."
- "I have cleansed myself. I closed my eyes and in a nonsecond, I cured myself. . . . The only thing I'm addicted to is winning."
- "[Regular guys] lay down with their ugly wives in front of their ugly children and just look at their loser lives and then they look at me and they say, 'I can't process it!' Well, no, and you never will . . ."

If you were to make a differential diagnosis, what condition, if any, do you believe would be associated with an individual making such statements? Is he an angry individual spouting off? Should allowances be made for his behavior because he is a celebrity? If a therapist were to conduct an assessment to determine if a mental health condition exists, it might be hypothesized that Sheen is showing symptoms of:

- A manic episode, a condition characterized by rapid speech and pressure to keep talking; restlessness; irritability; decreased need to sleep; distractibility; poor judgment; grandiosity and inflated self-esteem; reckless behavior.
- Narcissistic personality characteristics such as reacting to criticism with rage; exaggerated sense of self-importance, achievement, and talent; preoccupation with fantasies of success, power, and ideal love; unreasonable expectations of favorable treatment; need for constant attention and admiration; pursuit of selfish goals; limited empathy; and disregard for the feelings of others (PubMed, 2010).
- A delusional disorder with grandiose features that includes an inflated sense of self, power, and knowledge.
- A psychotic reaction with grandiose features produced by substance use or withdrawal.

Of course, a clinician conducting an assessment would evaluate background information, self-reports of symptom onset as well as reports from friends and family members, and medical tests (including drug screening) and would conduct observations, interviews, and consider psychological and/or neurological assessment that could shed light on the nature of the difficulties. Important considerations would include information regarding the onset of symptoms, previous experiences with similar symptoms, and patterns of previous behaviors.

---

demonstrated by many clients. DSM-5 hopes to remedy this problem and has identified clinical utility (i.e., the usefulness of the diagnostic system for practicing clinicians) as a major goal (Reed, 2010). The success of this attempt to improve clinical utility awaits future evaluation.

Another positive feature of DSM-5 is its continued emphasis on cross-cultural assessment. It has an introductory section that places diagnosis within a cultural context. It provides a description of pertinent culture, age, and gender features for each disorder and supplies guidelines for addressing the cultural background of the client and the variables to consider when evaluating clients. DSM-5 also contains an outline of culture-bound syndromes, disorders unique to particular cultural groups. Many culture-bound syndromes involve not only psychological symptoms but also bodily or somatic symptoms; this reflects the fact that the mind-body distinction prevalent in western societies is absent in many other societies (Sue & Sue, 2008a, b).

However, DSM-5 has also been subject to a variety of criticism:

1. Frances (2011), the chair of the DSM-IV task force, has expressed concern that viewing mental disorders on a continuum will have "unexpected consequences" resulting in "pushing the boundary of mental disorders deep into what has heretofore been considered normality" (p. 1). Frances's concerns may have some validity. In one study assessing regular drinkers (individuals who indicated they had used alcohol more than 12 times in the previous 12 months), use of the DSM-5 criteria for alcohol use disorder resulted in a 61.7 percent increase in prevalence of those diagnosed with an alcohol use disorder compared to the DSM-IV criteria (Mewton, Slade, McBride, Grove, & Teesson, 2011).

2. Concern has been expressed that decisions concerning the DSM-5 diagnostic categories were unduly influenced by outside pressure. Seventy percent of the DSM-5 Work Group members had direct ties to pharmaceutical

companies. This raises the possibility that subtle pressure may exist for an expansion of disorders that would result in an increased need for medication; additionally, having a "diagnosis" allows more people to receive insurance reimbursement for medications they purchase (Cosgrove, Bursztain, Kupfer, & Regier, 2009).

3. Some wonder about the new category of "behavioral addictions." Although it currently only includes gambling, other possible "addictions" (such as addiction to the Internet, video games, shopping, or eating) were also considered for inclusion. Frances (2009) believes that such diagnostic expansion amounts to medicalizing behavioral problems, a factor that might reduce personal responsibility for problems as well as complicate insurance and forensic evaluations.

4. Other controversial or proposed diagnoses include: (1) Hypersexual Disorder characterized by excessive masturbation, use of pornography, cybersex, strip clubs, and adultery; (2) Gender Dysphoria—The transgendered community does not believe that gender dysphoria belongs in DSM-5. They argue that having genitalia inconsistent with gender identity should not be considered a mental disorder (Gever, 2010; Ross, 2009); (3) Paraphilic coercive disorder (sexual arousal from forced sex) has been criticized by forensic psychiatrics who are concerned that rapists may try to use the disorder as a defense for their behavior (Franklin, 2011); (4) Premenstrual Dysphoric Disorder has been the subject of heated discussion. Critics of this category acknowledge that many women have symptoms associated with hormonal changes during menses; however, they believe that the disorder should be treated as a physiological or gynecological disorder and that labeling it as a psychiatric disorder stigmatizes women, suggests women are emotional and controlled by "raging hormones," and pathologizes a normal biological condition.

5. Although DSM-5 has strengthened cultural considerations in its diagnoses, questions remain regarding its cross-cultural applicability. Can diagnostic criteria developed by Western countries have validity for use with other countries? The prevalence of anxiety disorders, for example, differs greatly worldwide. Higher rates of panic disorder, specific phobia, and social anxiety disorder are found in the United States and Europe compared with Asian and African countries. The DSM criteria for these disorders may be less valid for cultural groups that place more emphasis on somatic rather than cognitive symptoms (Lewis-Fernandez et al., 2010). In a cross-national study, the prevalence of bipolar disorder was highest in the United States (4.4 percent) and lowest in India (0.1 percent). What accounts for this variability? It may be that some descriptions of disorders developed in Western countries do not fit other cultures. As cross-cultural psychiatrist Kleinman (1997) observed, Western bias is ironically evident in the designation of "culture-bound" syndromes—a designation which implies that the DSM diagnostic characteristics are universal.

6. The DSM-5 classification continues to rely on assessment that emphasizes deficits, creating a negative bias in the client's self-view and in the therapist's view of the client. It is important to focus not only on problems experienced by clients but also on their strengths (e.g., positive personal characteristics, accomplishments, satisfying relationships, and prior strategies for dealing with adversities and stress). Rashid and Ostermann (2009) treated a woman who had elevated depression scores on the MMPI-2 and Beck Depression Inventory. She received a DSM diagnosis of major depression. When talking about her symptoms (deficit model), she expressed feelings of hopelessness and despair. The clinicians then conducted a strength assessment by asking her to describe a life story that would show her at her best. She relayed a story

about defending a boy in school who was being laughed at by other students. As she discussed this story, her face lit up, and she described her strengths as courage and fairness. Other strengths were identified and applied to the problems she was facing. After 20 sessions, the woman no longer met the criteria for major depressive disorder. Use of strength assessments can provide a more balanced picture for both the mental health professional and client. Patterson and Seligman (2005) developed a classification system involving character strengths and virtues to complement the DSM; the system focuses on six overarching virtues (wisdom, courage, humanity, justice, temperance, and transcendence), characteristics that are important to assess and consider when working with mental disorders.

Although there are many valid criticisms of the DSM, the fact remains that it is the most frequently used diagnostic and classification system in the United States and some other countries. A classification system is necessary as a means of diagnosing disorders in those seeking mental health treatment, facilitating communication among mental health professionals, and forming a foundation for research on the etiology and treatment of mental disorders. Without the means to identify and group disorders, none of these goals can be accomplished. DSM-5 has taken some dramatic steps to improve the classification system. The debates over the usefulness of the DSM system have been valuable in suggesting new research directions, increasing the role of research in developing the system, and stimulating the examination of conceptual, methodological, philosophical, and clinical assumptions in the classification of mental disorders. Future research, particularly research that examines the construct validity of the DSM, is essential to evaluating the usefulness of the system.

Although we have focused on the DSM, another important classification system is the International Classification of Disease (ICD). This system covers all health conditions, including mental disorders. The World Health Organization oversees the system. In recent years, those revising the DSM have attempted to move towards greater comparability with the ICD section on mental disorders. (ICD-11 is scheduled for publication in 2014.) Interestingly, in a survey study of 265 psychiatrists from 66 different countries, ICD-10 was used for clinical training and diagnoses, whereas the DSM was used primarily for research purposes (Mezzich, 2002).

Objections to Classification and Labeling

Although classification schemes such as the DSM can be of immense aid in categorizing disorders, communicating information about disorders, and conducting research, they are also subject to criticism because of the negative consequences that sometimes result from classification and labeling.

1. *Labeling a person as having a mental disorder can result in overgeneralizations, stigmas, and stereotypes.* For example, former mental patients may have a difficult time finding employment because of employers' fears and stereotypes about mental disorders. Stereotypes about mental illness can lead to inaccurate generalizations about individuals that are transformed into discriminatory behavior. It then becomes more difficult for others to respond to the person's strengths and makes accurate, differentiated, and unique impressions less likely (Nelson, 2009). In one study, those hypothetically given a general mental illness label (versus a general physical illness label) were judged less humanely and perceived as more dangerous (Martinez, Piff, Mendoza-Denton, & Hinshaw, 2011).

2. *A label may lead others to treat a person differently.* A classic study by Rosenthal and Jacobson (1968) showed that responses to a label can cause differential treatment. They tested schoolchildren and then randomly assigned them to one of two groups. Teachers were told that tests of one group indicated

that they were potential intellectual "bloomers" (i.e., they demonstrated competence and maturity); the other group was not given this label. After a one-year interval, children from both groups were retested. Children who had been identified as bloomers showed dramatic gains in IQ scores. How did this occur? Many have speculated that the label led teachers to have higher expectations for the bloomers and thus to treat them differently. Even though there was no significant difference in IQ levels between the two groups to begin with, differences were present by the end of the year. Other studies have yielded similar results (Bernsburg & Krohn, 2003; Rappaport & Cleary, 1980).

3. *A label may lead those who are labeled to believe that they do indeed possess characteristics associated with the label or may cause them to behave in accordance with the label.* Labels can become self-fulfilling prophecies. In the Rosenthal and Jacobson (1968) study just cited, the label not only caused teachers to behave differently but also may have affected the children's self-perceptions. When people are constantly told that they have particular characteristics, they may come to believe such labels. It is reasonable to believe that people who ascribe certain stereotypical traits to a particular group will behave differently toward members of that group and may, in fact, cause cognitive and behavioral changes among group members. Steele and his colleagues have also shown that labels and stereotypes can influence individuals not only to act out the stereotypes but also to devalue their personal status (Davies, Spencer, & Steele, 2005). For example, labeling a child a "slow learner" may be detrimental to the child's self-esteem and sense of personal competence. Negative societal reactions can have a profound effect on a person's self-image.

4. *Although social systems often require labels, mental health labels may not provide the precise, functional information required by health care organizations.* Today, many forms of managed care organizations—such as health maintenance organizations, preferred provider organizations, and others—are responsible for efficiently providing health and mental health care. Although many of these systems rely on diagnoses for making decisions about treatment and health care reimbursement, they have a more pressing need to precisely identify current levels of functioning and the projected treatment needs of their participants. Given this trend, the assessment of functioning at work, home, school, and elsewhere may be of greater utility than a particular clinical diagnosis.

Did You Know?

D. L. Rosenhan (1973) sent eight "normal" researchers (pseudopatients) to different psychiatric hospitals. Their assignment was first to fake psychiatric symptoms to gain admission into psychiatric wards (i.e., they reported hearing the words "empty," "hollow," and "thud"); once admitted, they behaved in a normal manner. Interestingly, no hospital staff detected that the pseudopatients were normal. However, other patients did. What might account for this difference?

Summary

1. What kinds of standards must tests or evaluation procedures meet?

   - In developing assessment tools and useful classification schemes, it is important to consider reliability (the degree to which a procedure or test yields the same results repeatedly, under the same circumstances) and validity (the extent to which a test or procedure actually performs the function it was designed to perform).

2. What kinds of tools do clinicians employ in evaluating a client's mental health?

   - Clinicians primarily use four methods of assessment: observations, interviews, psychological tests and inventories, and neurological tests.

   - Observations of external signs and expressive behaviors are often made during an interview and can have diagnostic significance.

   - Interviews involve a face-to-face conversation, after which the interviewer differentially weighs and interprets verbal information obtained from the interviewee. The mental status exam is frequently used as an interview tool in clinical assessment.

   - Psychological tests and inventories provide a more formalized means of obtaining information.

   - Neurological assessment, including x-rays, CT and PET scans, EEG, and MRI, have added highly important and sophisticated means to detect brain abnormalities.

3. How are mental health problems categorized or classified?

   - The DSM contains detailed diagnostic criteria; research findings and expert judgments were used to help assess reliability and validity of diagnostic categories.

   - DSM-5 has both dimensional and categorical assessment, and has attempted to make differential diagnosis more clear-cut.

   - General objections to classification are based primarily on the problems involved in labeling and the loss of information about a person when that person is labeled or categorized.

Media Resources

Psychology CourseMate Access an interactive eBook; chapter-specific interactive learning tools, including flash cards, quizzes, videos; and more in your Psychology CourseMate, accessed through CengageBrain.com.

CENGAGENOW

CengageNow CengageNOW is an easy-to-use online resource that helps you study in less time to get the grade you want—NOW. If your textbook does not include an access code card, go to CengageBrain.com to gain access.

CENGAGEbrain.com

CengageBrain More than just an interactive study guide, WebTutor is an anytime, anywhere customized learning solution with an eBook, keeping you connected to your textbook, instructor, and classmates. Purchase the access chosen by your instructor at CengageBrain.com.

4

The Scientific Method in Abnormal Psychology

A twenty-four-year-old married Puerto Rican woman, Nayda, reported during an initial interview that she was in "utter anguish" and incapacitated by "epileptic fits." These seizures were preceded by a strong headache and involved a loss of consciousness and convulsions. A neurologist had diagnosed her as suffering from intractable (difficult-to-treat) epilepsy. However, some symptoms appeared to be atypical compared with those seen in epilepsy. First, when regaining consciousness, she would sometimes not recognize her husband or children and claim not to be Nayda. Second, during some episodes she appeared fearful and would plead to an invisible presence to have mercy and not to kill her. Third, Nayda would often hit herself during seizures and burn items in the house. Her most recent seizures included hallucinations involving blood, during which she attempted to strangle herself with a rope. These behaviors were perplexing because she said she loved her husband and children and did not know why she would try to harm herself. Because of these unusual symptoms, Martinez-Taboas (2005) entertained the possibility that the seizures were psychogenic (generated from psychological causes) and that cultural beliefs might be involved.

Psychogenic Contributors

The therapist wondered if Nayda had experienced any significant trauma. Nayda told of an event that had occurred when she was seventeen—two years before the seizures began. She tearfully related that one night at about 2 A.M., she was awakened by the smell of something burning. She was shocked to find her grandmother's house in flames (her grandmother lived in a small house in the backyard). Strangely, she decided to go back to sleep and repeatedly told herself, "Tomorrow I will tell my parents of the fire" (Martinez-Taboas, 2005, p. 8). A few minutes later, the rest of the family was awakened by the smoke. Their attempts to rescue the grandmother failed. It was later determined that the grandmother had set the fire to take her own life. When Nayda was asked about her feelings regarding the incident, she cried profusely and said that it was her fault her grandmother had died. During the next session, while talking about the incident, Nayda had a seizure and began to beg an invisible presence not to kill her. Using hypnosis to further explore these reactions, the therapist asked about the seizures; Nayda responded with terror and said,

focus questions

1 In what ways is the scientific method used to evaluate psychotherapy?

2 How does the use of an experimental design differ from other ways of investigating phenomena?

3 What are correlations, and how are they used to indicate the degree to which two variables are related?

4 What are analogue studies, and when is this type of investigation used?

5 What are field studies, and how are they used?

6 What are the various types of single-participant studies, and how are they used?

7 What are some of the advantages and shortcomings of the biological approach to understanding abnormal behavior?

8 What is epidemiological research, and how is it used to determine the extent of mental disturbance in a targeted population?

"There is blood," and began to convulse on the floor. The therapist placed his hand on Nayda's head and commanded that the seizure stop. It ended. The influence of psychogenic factors on Nayda's seizures was clear.

Cultural Formulation

From a Western perspective, Nayda's symptoms of loss of personal identity, amnesia, seizures, and hallucinations could be indicative of a serious mental disorder. The therapist wanted to investigate cultural influences as possible contributors to these symptoms. In many Latin American countries, there is a belief in *espiritismo*—that the soul is immortal and, under certain circumstances, able to inhabit or possess a living person. Auditory or visual hallucinations when experiencing *espiritismo* are not uncommon. When Nayda was asked about the seizures, she said that the spirit of her grandmother was not at peace and was causing her seizures and other problems. She believed that her failure to help her grandmother during the fire resulted in a disturbed and revenge-seeking spirit. The therapist wanted to determine whether Nayda would be open to an alternative explanation and mentioned the possibility that her symptoms were due to traumatic memories and guilt rather than possession. Nayda did not accept this perspective, and she remained convinced of her *espiritismo* beliefs.

Approach to Therapy

Although one possible therapeutic approach might be to challenge Nayda's belief that she was responsible for her grandmother's death and question the utility of her belief in spiritual possession (Castro-Blanco, 2005), the therapist decided to work within Nayda's belief system and combine it with Western strategies. In the twenty-two therapy sessions that followed, the therapist had Nayda confront the spirit of her grandmother through the empty-chair technique, a process by which a client has a dialogue with a significant other, imagined to be in the chair. Using this technique, Nayda explained to her grandmother that she loved her children and husband and that they needed her. Initially, the attempts were failures, and, in one episode, the grandmother spoke through Nayda and said that Nayda would never be free from her. In subsequent sessions, Nayda continued to confront her guilt and fear regarding her grandmother. Cognitive therapy was used to help Nayda develop alternative ways of thinking about her grandmother's suicide. The family also participated in the empty-chair technique, telling the grandmother that Nayda was not responsible for her death. After several months of therapy, the grandmother's presence became negligible and eventually disappeared completely. At a twelve-month follow-up, Nayda was no longer taking medication and had had only one brief seizure. Her depression score was within the normal range and her other symptoms had been dramatically reduced.

This case illustrates several points that are important in research and therapy. First, there is a tendency for individuals within their own fields of study to interpret events within a given paradigm. For example, the biological model assumes that every disease has a specific physical cause, and little attention is placed on psychological or environmental factors. In the case of Nayda, her neurologist, believing the seizures were due to epilepsy, prescribed an antiseizure medication to treat the condition. Conversely, psychological theories tend to view disorders only from a psychological framework, placing less emphasis on biological, sociocultural, and social explanations. A cognitive-behavioral analysis of Nayda's behaviors might focus primarily on irrational thoughts. Therapy would involve challenging these thoughts or beliefs and substituting more realistic ones. Etiological explanations from a sociocultural perspective may focus on cultural practices or beliefs.

Second, research is often conducted from a specific perspective with little attention paid to other contributing factors. For example, discovery of an obesity gene made headlines. A short time after this story was published, another article informed readers that, according to another group of researchers, perceived social ties are predictive of obesity. The reader is left with a puzzle. Is obesity caused by a gene or by specific social patterns? We now know that the majority of mental health disorders are the result of a convergence of biological, psychological, sociocultural, and social risk factors. Therefore, when you are exposed to mental health research, remember that issues are best understood when a multipath model is utilized. As with Nayda, it is important to consider all possible contributors to a problem. The symptoms experienced by Nayda could result from biological, psychological, sociocultural, or social factors or a combination of these influences. From a scientific perspective, we must investigate all possible causes and consider alternative explanations for behavior.

Scientists are often described as skeptics. Rather than accept the conclusions from a single study, scientists demand that other researchers *replicate* (repeat) the results. Replication reduces the chance that findings are due to experimenter bias, methodological flaws, or sampling errors. The following findings were initially reported as "conclusive" in the mass media. Note their current status after further investigation:

- *Childhood vaccines may cause autism.* Due to media reports, half of all parents are concerned about vaccine safety and side effects, and 11 percent of parents have refused at least one recommended vaccine (Freed, Clark, Butchart, Singer, & Davis, 2010). *Status:* Research does not support a link between vaccines and autism (Price et al., 2010; U.S. Court of Federal Claims, 2010).
- *Antidepressants raise suicide risk in children and adolescents.* In 2004, the Food and Drug Administration (FDA) required manufacturers of antidepressants to add a "black box" warning on the label. *Status:* Needs further research. Although one study linked the use of antidepressants with a two-fold increase in suicide attempts (Olfson & Marcus, 2008), others have not found any such relationship (Healy, Whitaker, Lapierre, & Slife, 2010).
- *Cannabis use leads to the development of psychoses.* Drug prevention efforts nationwide cite this concern regarding marijuana use. *Status:* A number of studies have found that use of marijuana during adolescence is related to an increased risk of adult psychosis, particularly among those with a pre-existing genetic vulnerability (McGrath et al, 2010).
- *The majority of sexually abused children exhibit signs or symptoms of trauma that can be reliably detected by experts in the field of child sexual abuse. Status:* There are no signs or symptoms that characterize the majority of abused children, and a significant number of abused children appear to be asymptomatic (Kuehnle & Connell, 2009; Hagen, 2003).

As you can see, the search for "truth" is often a long journey. Answers regarding the causes of abnormal behavior come and go. In evaluating studies, we must consider the adequacy of the research. As Hunsley (2007) observed, "not all evidence is created equal" (p. 114). Some types of studies provide stronger evidence (more accuracy, reliability, and generalizability) because of their methodological or conceptual soundness (Table 4.1).

If we were to construct an evidence hierarchy based on internal validity considerations (i.e., confidence that one thing causes another), expert opinion and case studies would be placed on the lowest level of the hierarchy. Group research designs (such as observational studies) and single participant designs generally provide stronger evidence. Randomized

TABLE 4.1   Levels of Evidence

Level 1: Randomized, controlled studies
Level 2: Observational studies and single-subject research design
Level 3: Case studies and clinical judgment or opinions

Adapted from Ghaemi (2010).

controlled designs are considered the "gold standard" and would occupy the highest level of the evidence hierarchy. Each kind of study has its own strengths and weaknesses. In general, evidence is considered to be more valid at higher levels in the hierarchy, although higher levels do not guarantee certainty without replication (Ghaemi, 2010). Understanding different research designs and their shortcomings is necessary when evaluating reported findings in abnormal psychology. In this chapter, we discuss the components of the scientific method.

The Scientific Method in Clinical Research

Case Study

A 10-year-old girl named Candace was diagnosed with a reactive attachment disorder, a condition that prevents the formation of loving relationships. In an attempt to help her bond with her adoptive mother, her therapist decided to use "rebirthing therapy." Candace was wrapped in a blanket, surrounded by four adults pressing pillows against her, in a process intended to simulate birth. During the seventy minute session, Candace complained about not being able to breathe. After being unwrapped, Candace had no pulse. The cause of death was suffocation (Kohler, 2001). Because of this case, the governor of Colorado signed a law outlawing rebirthing therapy (Associated Press, 2001).

Hundreds of different forms of psychotherapies exist. How can so many different ways of conceptualizing the cause and treatment of the same disorder be accurate? This question must be addressed if psychotherapy is to have a scientific foundation (Melchert, 2007). Do therapists use the scientific method to determine the validity or effectiveness of approaches they are using to treat mental disorders? Baker, McFall, & Shoham (2008) argue that most clinicians value their own experience and judgment over that of research in regards to the

CRITICAL THINKING

Attacks on Scientific Integrity

- *Dr. Andrew Mosholder, a medical reviewer for the FDA, stated that he had been pressured to alter and hide information on a document submitted to congressional investigators concerning the possible link between antidepressant use and suicide in children (Richwine, 2004b).*
- *An internal pharmaceutical company memo concerning a study of antidepressant medication use with children stated that it would be "commercially unacceptable" to admit that the medication did not work in children and that the company would have to "effectively manage the dissemination of these data in order to minimize any potential negative impact" (Dyer, 2004, p. 1395).*
- *The manufacturers of popular antidepressants medications did not publish nearly one-third of the studies evaluating their effectiveness, most with results not favoring the medication. In addition, some studies with negative or questionable results were published as if the drugs were effective (Turner et al., 2008).*

The scientific method requires a commitment from researchers to search for the truth and to remain objective. When personal beliefs, values, political position, or conflicts of interest are allowed to influence our interpretation of data, scientific integrity is threatened. We rely on scientists to maintain high ethical standards so we can make informed decisions based on valid research. Unfortunately, when financial considerations intersect with science, research can become the tool of the interested party rather than a mechanism to promote the welfare of society.

Part of the problem is that researchers often have a vested interest in the drug companies themselves. Research spending by pharmaceutical companies rose from $1.5 billion to $22 billion between 1980 and 2001 (Warner & Roberts, 2004) and accounted for about 60 percent of funded studies in 2002 (Kelly et al., 2006). Equally problematic is the increasing number of researchers in academic medical centers who have financial interests in or who receive funding from for-profit companies (Warner & Roberts, 2004). These ties with pharmaceutical companies can produce a conflict of interest that threatens scientific integrity. There is suspicion that many findings unfavorable to "interested parties" (the source of funding) are not being published. In some cases, the publication of data is subject to the approval of the funding source. With researchers receiving funding from or sitting on the board of directors of pharmaceutical companies, how can the interests of consumers be promoted and scientific integrity be maintained?

practice of psychotherapy. They advocate using therapies that are supported by randomized controlled research. However, this may not be possible with many disorders. Zeldow (2009) points out "many problems that clinicians encounter will invariably fall outside the purview of scientific evidence" (p. 1). Accordingly, clinical experience (Level 3 evidence) often must also be employed. What do you see as the advantages and disadvantages of requiring some type of experimental support for different therapies?

The scientific method is a method of inquiry that provides for the systematic collection of data, controlled observation, and the testing of hypotheses. A hypothesis is a conjectural statement that usually describes a relationship between two variables. Different theories may result in different hypotheses for the same phenomenon. A theory is a group of principles and hypotheses that together explain some aspect of a particular area of inquiry. For example, hypothesized reasons for eating disorders have included biological or neurochemical causes, fear of sexual maturity, societal demands for thinness in women, and pathological family relationships. Each of these hypotheses reflects a different theory.

Characteristics of Clinical Research

Clinical research can proceed only when the relationship expressed in a hypothesis is clearly and systematically stated and when the variables of concern are measurable and defined. We need to understand exactly what we are studying and make sure that the variables are measured with reliable and valid instruments. Clinical research relies on characteristics of the scientific method, including the potential for self-correction, the development of hypotheses about relationships, the use of operational definitions, consideration of reliability and validity, the acknowledgment of base rates, and the requirement that research findings be evaluated in terms of their statistical significance.

Potential for Self-Correction

One of the unique characteristics of the scientific method is the *potential for self-correction*. Under ideal conditions, data and conclusions are freely exchanged and experiments are replicable (reproducible). Discussion, testing, and verification are encouraged, resulting in data that are as free as possible from the scientists' personal beliefs, perceptions, biases, values, attitudes, and emotions. When researchers do not follow these guidelines, ethical concerns arise.

Hypothesizing Relationships

Another characteristic of the scientific method is that it attempts to identify and explain (hypothesize) the relationship between variables. Examples of hypotheses include: "Some seasonal forms of depression may be due to decreases in light," "Autism is the result of poor parenting," and "Eating disorders are the result of a chemical imbalance in the brain."

Operational Definitions

Concrete definitions of the variables being studied are called operational definitions. For example, an operational definition of depression might involve (1) a specific pattern of responses to a self-report depression inventory, (2) a rating assigned by an observer using a depression checklist, or (3) laboratory identification of specific neurochemical changes. Operational definitions are important because they force an experimenter to clearly define what he or she means by the variable. This allows others to agree or disagree with the way the variable was defined. When operational definitions of a phenomenon differ, comparing research is problematic, and conclusions can be faulty.

Child sexual abuse has been associated with a number of negative effects such as anxiety, eating disorders, depression, and substance abuse (Knapik, Martsolf, Draucker, & Strickland, 2010). Unfortunately, studies exploring this important topic define it

scientific method a method of inquiry that provides for the systematic collection of data, controlled observation, and the testing of hypotheses

hypothesis a conjectural statement that usually describes a relationship between two variables

theory a group of principles and hypotheses that together explain some aspect of a particular area of inquiry

operational definitions concrete definitions of the variables that are being studied

Associated Press/Rui Veira

Controlled Observations

Research on animals can provide clues to the development of emotions in humans. Baby orangutans show empathy, laughter, and the ability to copy facial expressions.

differently (Haugaard, 2000). Consider the following operational definitions of *child sexual abuse* used in the research literature:

- A child or adolescent under the age of 16 being involved in sexual activities she does not and cannot fully comprehend and to which she does not fully consent (Williamson, 2009, p. 3).
- Any sexual contact between a child of 13 years or younger with another person who was at least 5 years older or a family member who was at least 2 years older (Lab & Moore, 2005, p. 325).

Other definitions of child sexual abuse include "unwanted sexual experiences ranging from overt verbal advances, exposure to sexual media, unwanted touching or penetration" (Noll, Shenk, & Putnam, 2009) and being made to look at private parts using force or surprise (Finkelhor, Ormrod, Turner, & Hamby, 2005). The use of so many different definitions of child sexual abuse makes conclusions difficult when evaluating the research. Operational definitions need to be clear and precise.

Reliability and Validity of Measures and Observations

The scientific method requires that the measures we use be reliable (consistent). *Reliability* refers to the degree to which a measure or procedure yields the same results repeatedly. Consider, for example, an individual who has been diagnosed, by means of a questionnaire, as having a personality disorder. If the questionnaire is reliable, the individual should receive the same diagnosis after filling out the questionnaire again. Results must be consistent if we are to have any faith in them.

Even if consistent results are obtained, questions can arise over the *validity* of a measure. Does the testing instrument really measure what it was developed to measure? If we claim to have developed a test that identifies post-traumatic stress disorder, we must demonstrate that it can accomplish this task. The validity of many of the clinical tests used in studies has not been determined.

Base Rates

A base rate is the rate of natural occurrence of a phenomenon in the population studied. When the base rate is not known or not considered, research findings can be misinterpreted. For example, both unwanted sexual events and eating problems are reported by a high percentage of females (Conners & Morse, 1993; Fischer, Stojek, & Hartzell, 2010; Pope & Hudson, 1992). As a result, clinicians may find that the many individuals treated for eating problems report a history of sexual abuse. An investigator, not recognizing that both of these conditions occur with high frequency (have high base rates), may mistakenly conclude that one is the cause of the other.

Base rate data is helpful in interpreting phenomena such as sexual behaviors in children. Is the presence of "sexualized" behaviors a sign of sexual abuse or a normative type of behavior? Primary caregivers reported a wide range of sexual behaviors in 1,114 children between the ages of two and twelve who were not sexually abused. As the researchers state regarding sexual touching, "Simply because a five-year-old boy touches his genitals occasionally, even after a weekend visit with his noncustodial parent, it does not mean he has been sexually abused. Rather, it is a behavior that is seen in nearly two-thirds of boys at that age" (Friedrich et al., 1998, p. 8). Base rate data, however, provide only the context within which to evaluate behavior. Whether "normative" sexual behaviors are due to abuse must be determined on an individual basis.

The importance of base rates in clinical research can be seen in the responses of a control group to a psychotic-traits questionnaire. Persons with severe mental disorders often have unusual thoughts or reactions. On a psychotic-traits questionnaire, however, 28 percent of the control group surveyed reported unusual thoughts or reactions (Kendler, Gallagher,

base rate the rate of natural occurrence of a phenomenon in the population studied

Repressed Memories: Issues and Questions

Patricia Burgus claimed that during psychiatric therapy for postpartum depression, treatment that included hypnosis and hypnotic drugs, she came to believe that she had eaten human flesh, was part of a satanic cult, had been abused by numerous men, and was sexually abusing her two sons (Ewing, 1998). Burgus's memories were later determined to be the result of suggestions and techniques used by her therapists. She was awarded $10.6 million in damages.

Elizabeth Loftus argues that there is little scientific evidence that a memory, however painful, can be temporarily banned from consciousness and return years or even decades later (Loftus, Garry, & Hayne, 2008). Pope and Hudson (2007) believe that repressed memory is not a scientifically valid phenomenon but rather a condition "manufactured" after the 1800s. In fact, they offered a $1,000 reward to anyone who can produce a published case of the phenomenon in fiction or nonfiction before 1800. They argue that if "repressed memory" were genuine, it would have been the subject of writings in the past. Conversely, the Recovered Memory Project (2007) is assembling information and cases of recovered memory. As they state on their website, "The purpose of this project is to collect and disseminate information relevant to the debate over whether traumatic events can be forgotten and then remembered later in life." They want to assemble "evidence of [repressed memory] cases ignored or overlooked by self-described skeptics of various sorts."

The controversy over the existence of "repressed memory" is especially pronounced between experimental psychologists

and therapists. In one study, only 34 percent of the experimental psychologists reported that they believed in the validity of the phenomenon, compared with over 60 percent of the clinicians (Dammeyer, Nightingale, & McCoy, 1997). The study also revealed some differences among the clinicians themselves. Those with psychoanalytic, psychodynamic, or eclectic orientations believed more strongly in repressed memories than did those with cognitive orientations. Many clinicians also believe that some therapeutic techniques can lead to false memories.

Cases of repressed memory have been brought up in court. To address "junk science," the Supreme Court in 1993 set forth the Daubert Standard, under which evidence offered by expert witnesses must meet certain standards: (1) The theory or technique must be falsifiable and testable; (2) it must have been subjected to peer review and publication; (3) the reliability of procedures or potential error rate should be specified; and (4) the theory or technique must be generally accepted by the relevant scientific community (Sanders, Diamond, & Vidmar, 2002).

For Further Consideration

1. Do you believe repressed memories are real? How would you decide whether to maintain or abandon repressed memory as a genuine phenomenon? What would be the implications of your decision?
2. Why are experimental psychologists more likely than clinicians to have doubts regarding the existence of repressed memories?

Abelson, & Kessler, 1996). Using another questionnaire, Johns et al. (2004) found that 66 percent of the control group endorsed having one or more psychotic symptoms (Figure 4.1). The fact that an individual or patient reports having odd or bizarre thoughts or being bothered by the feeling of being watched may, therefore, not be indicative of a disorder. Further assessment would be necessary to make a valid determination.

Statistical versus Clinical Significance

The scientific method also requires that research findings be evaluated in terms of their *statistical significance*— the likelihood that the relationship is not due to chance alone. Even a statistically significant finding may have little practical significance in a clinical setting, however. For example, based on a study by Phillips, Van Voorhees, and Ruth (1992), various news reports have stated that women are more likely to die the week after their birthdays than in any other week of the year. This finding seemed to show that psychological factors have a powerful effect on biological processes. The study involved 2,745,149 persons, and the findings were statistically significant (that is, not due to chance). The number of deaths for the week after a birthday, however, was only 3.03 percent higher than would be expected in any other week. Thus, psychological factors associated

Percent answering yes to the questions regarding thoughts and behaviors over the past year.

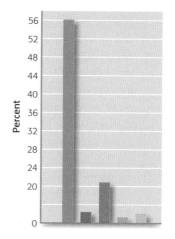

Figure 4.1

RESPONSE TO PSYCHOSIS SCREENING QUESTIONNAIRE

This figure shows the percentage of "normal" individuals endorsing items on a questionnaire use to identify psychotic thinking and beliefs.

Source: Data from Johns et al., 2004.

- Feeling very happy without a break for days on end
- Thoughts being interfered with or controlled by some outside force or person
- Felt that people were against you
- Heard voices or saw things that other people could not
- Felt like something strange was going on

with deaths and birthdays, although statistically significant, appear to play only a small role in deaths among women. When evaluating research, you must determine whether the statistical significance reported is really "clinically" significant. This problem—a finding being statistically significant but not necessarily meaningful—is most likely to occur in studies with large sample sizes.

Experiments

The experiment is perhaps the best tool for testing cause and effect relationships. In its simplest form, the experiment involves the following:

1. An experimental hypothesis, which is the prediction concerning how an independent variable will affect a dependent variable in an experiment
2. An independent variable (the possible cause), which the experimenter manipulates to determine its effect on a dependent variable
3. A dependent variable, which is expected to change as a result of changes in the independent variable

The experimenter is also concerned about controlling extraneous or *confounding* variables (factors other than the independent variable that may affect the dependent variable). For example, expectancies of both research participants and researchers may influence the outcome of a study. Participants in a study may try to "help" the researcher succeed and, in so doing, may confound the results of the study (Anderson & Strupp, 1996). If the experimenter is effective in eliminating confounding variables in a study, the study has high internal validity. That is, we can be relatively certain that changes in the dependent variable are due only to the independent variable. The experimenter is also interested in external validity. This refers to whether the findings of a particular study can be generalized to other groups or conditions. Let's clarify these concepts by examining an actual research study.

experiment a technique of scientific inquiry in which a prediction—an experimental hypothesis—is made about two variables; the independent variable is then manipulated in a controlled situation, and changes in the dependent variable are measured

experimental hypothesis a prediction concerning how an independent variable will affect a dependent variable in an experiment

independent variable a variable or condition that an experimenter manipulates to determine its effect on a dependent variable

dependent variable a variable that is expected to change when an independent variable is manipulated in a psychological experiment

internal validity the degree to which changes in the dependent variable are due solely to the effect of changes in the independent variable

external validity the degree to which findings of a particular study can be generalized to other groups or conditions

Case Study

Melinda N., a nineteen-year-old sophomore, sought help from a university psychology clinic for dental phobia. Her strong fear of dentists began when she was about twelve years old. It had been suggested to her that she might have a low pain threshold or have experienced some type of traumatic incident during dental work. Melinda had several cavities that were painful, so she decided to see if a therapist could offer some help. Because she had an appointment to see the dentist the following week, Melinda wanted something that could work quickly. The therapist had heard that antianxiety medication and psychological methods (relaxation training and changing thoughts about the procedure) were both successful in treating dental phobia. Before deciding which treatment to recommend, the therapist reviewed the research literature to determine whether studies had compared the effectiveness of these approaches.

A study by Thom, Sartory, & Johren (2000) seemed to provide some direction. In that study, fifty patients with dental phobia were assigned to either a psychological, medication, or no-treatment group. The psychological treatment took only one session and involved stress management training (relaxation exercises, visualization of dental work, and the identification and use of coping thoughts). The exercises learned in therapy were to be performed at home daily for one week. Those in the medication group received the antianxiety medication thirty minutes before the dental procedure. Those in the control condition were told that their surgeon specialized in patients with dental anxiety and would treat them carefully.

The Experimental Group

An *experimental group* is the group that is subjected to the independent variable. In their study, Thom and her colleagues created two experimental groups: One group received a single-session psychological treatment and the other received antianxiety medication. The psychological treatment included exposure to images of dental scenes and teaching of stress management, relaxation, and breathing exercises, which were then practiced daily for one week.

Because the investigators were interested in how treatment affects level of anxiety and reports of panic, the dependent variables were measured in several ways. Pre- and post-treatment measures were obtained for dental fear, as well as subjective ratings for pain during the procedure. The investigators also tabulated how many of the patients completed dental treatment with further appointments.

The Control Group

If the participants in the two experimental groups in the study by Thom and her colleagues showed a reduction in anxiety based on pretesting to post-testing measures, could the researchers conclude that the treatments were effective forms of therapy? The answer would be no, because participants may have shown less anxiety about dental procedures merely as a result of the passage of time or as a function of completing the assessment measures. The use of a control group enables researchers to eliminate such possibilities.

A *control group* is a group that is similar in every way to the experimental group except for the manipulation of the independent variable. In the study by Thom and her colleagues, the control group also took the pretest measures, received dental work, and took the post-test measures. However, those in the control group did not receive any treatment. Because of this, we can be more certain that any differences found between the control and experimental groups were due to the independent variable (i.e., the treatment received).

The findings revealed that the groups treated with either psychological intervention or antianxiety medication had significantly greater reductions on the Dental Fear Scale and Pain Scale than the control group. However, those treated with medication showed a relapse following dental surgery, whereas those who received psychological intervention showed further improvement and continued dental treatment. Of those who completed additional dental procedures, 70 percent had been in the psychological intervention group, 20 percent in the antianxiety medication group, and 10 percent in the control group.

Given these findings, the therapist might tell Melinda that both treatments can help her during her dental appointment but that psychological interventions might offer more long-term effects. The psychological intervention included relaxation, visualization, and exposure strategies, so it is unclear which component or components were responsible for the reduction in fear. If researchers wanted to further determine which of the psychological interventions (or combination of interventions) was most effective, how might they design a study to investigate this issue?

MYTH: Building more controls into an experiment always results in greater generalizability of the findings.

REALITY: Although a tightly controlled study increases internal validity, problems can occur with external validity—that is, the findings may not be generalizable to other populations because the conditions existing in an experimental setting may not resemble those found in real-life situations. Both internal and external validity have to be considered when designing a study.

MYTH VS. REALITY

The Placebo Group

You should note that the results of an experiment may also be challenged for another reason. For example, what if the participants in the treated experimental groups improved not because of the treatment, but because they had an expectancy that they would improve? Some researchers have found that if participants expect to improve from treatment, this expectancy—rather than specific treatment—is responsible for the outcome.

One method by which an expectancy can be induced without using a specific treatment is to include a placebo control group. Thom and her colleagues could have given another group a medication capsule containing an inert drug (a placebo). A plausible

Did You Know?

Many findings are based on research involving undergraduate participants. The following conclusions were reported by the Associated Press (2007c):

- Muscular men are twice as likely as less muscular men to have had more than three sex partners (based on ninety-nine University of California, Los Angeles undergraduates)

- Despite being stereotyped as "chatty," women spoke only 3 percent more per day than men (based on 400 college students)

- Younger individuals are 6 percent more likely to make jokes than those who are older (based on eighty-one college participants).

Peterson (2001) raises questions about whether samples of college students are representative of "people in general," "adults," or even "college students in general." In addition, the number of participants is certainly too low for any conclusions to be meaningful.

psychological placebo condition (one that the experimenter believes would not reduce dental fear, such as a single-session group convened to discuss nutrition) could also be utilized. If the therapy groups improved more than the placebo control group, then one could be more confident that therapy, rather than expectancy, was responsible for the results.

Additional Concerns in Clinical Research

Although researchers hope to control expectations of outcome through the use of a placebo control group, several problems can occur. First, the placebo control group may also show significant improvement. In one review of research, placebos duplicated up to 89 percent of the improvement seen with antidepressants (Antonuccio, Burns, & Danton, 2002). This finding would make it difficult to separate treatment from expectancy effects. Second, participants may "guess" correctly that they are receiving a placebo, thereby further increasing expectancy effects. Another problem associated with medication trials is that individuals who are strong responders to placebos are often eliminated from studies, ensuring a more favorable showing for medication (Sue & Sue, 2008b).

Both experimenter and participant expectations can also influence the outcome of a study. To control for experimenter expectations, the researcher may use a *blind design*, in which those helping with the study are not aware of the purpose of the research. A method to reduce the impact of both experimenter and participant expectations is the *double-blind design*. In this procedure, neither the individual working directly with the participant (such as the therapist or physician) nor the participant is aware of the experimental conditions. The effectiveness of this design is dependent on whether participants are truly "blind" to the intervention, which may not always be the case. In drug studies, over 75 percent of subjects may correctly guess their treatment assignment due to either the presence or absence of side effects or other physical symptoms (Perlis, Ostacher, Fava,

Double-Blind Design

When researching the effects of a drug, experimenters often use a double-blind design to ensure that neither participants nor experimenter are aware of the experimental conditions. Shown here is a prepared card of drugs that could be used in a research study in such a way that neither patient nor doctor actually knows whether the patient is receiving a drug or a placebo. How would you determine whether this manipulation was successful?

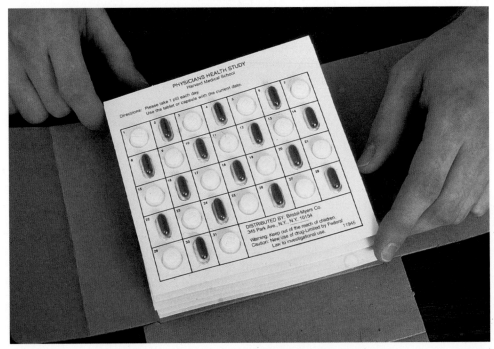

Christopher Morrow/Stock Boston

Nierenberg, Sachs, & Rosenbaum, 2010). Physicians are also able to distinguish between placebos and antidepressants or even between different types of antidepressants based on the reactions of the patients (Margraf et al., 1991). These findings indicate the need to modify experimental designs so that the degree of "blindness" is increased. Otherwise, the results may be influenced by both client and experimenter expectations.

As you can see, researchers have a difficult time controlling extraneous or confounding variables. The *external validity* of a study (the ability to generalize the results to other settings) is also very important to determine. In the study by Thom and her colleagues, we would want to know whether psychotherapy and antianxiety medication are also effective in reducing anxiety in other populations or situations. Sometimes importing a therapy from a research setting to a real-life environment is difficult. Martin Seligman (1996) points out that research designs that produce high *internal validity* (such as those that use a manual to provide therapy, prescribe only a fixed number of sessions, and involve random assignments of clients with a single disorder) may have problems with external validity. "Real" therapy often does not follow treatment manuals precisely and may not be of a fixed duration. Patients frequently have multiple problems and are not randomly assigned to therapists in clinic settings. Thus, in some cases, designing research with very high internal validity may reduce the generalizability of the findings.

Correlation

A correlation is the extent to which variations in one variable are accompanied by increases or decreases in a second variable. The variables in a correlation, unlike those in an experiment, are not manipulated. Instead, a statistical analysis is performed to determine whether there is a relationship between the variables. The relationship is expressed as a statistically derived *correlation coefficient*, symbolized by the symbol r, which has a numerical value between -1 and $+1$. In a *positive correlation*, an increase in one variable is accompanied by an increase in the other. When an increase in one variable is accompanied by a decrease in the other variable, there is a *negative correlation*. The greater the value of r, positive or negative, the stronger the relationship. See Figure 4.2 for examples of correlations.

Correlations indicate the degree to which two variables are related but not the reason for the relationship. For example, the Parents Television Council (2007) reported that during the family hour time slots (8 P.M.–9 P.M. Monday through Saturday and 7 P.M.–9 P.M. on Sunday), nearly 50 percent of TV programs contained violent content, with approximately 4.19 violent acts or images per hour. Does watching aggressive programming lead to aggressive behavior?

Johnson and colleagues (2002) assessed the relationship between the number of hours of television viewing and the number of aggressive behaviors over a seventeen-year period. A significant correlation was found. The greater the number of hours spent watching television per day, the greater the number of aggressive acts (assaults, robbery, threats to injure someone, or using a weapon to commit a crime). Of those who watched television less than one hour per day, 5.7 percent committed a violent act; 25.3 percent of those who watched more than three hours a day did so. The study controlled for possible confounding variables such as childhood neglect, low family income, unsafe neighborhoods, and psychiatric disorders. Because this was a correlational study, the authors cautioned, "It should be noted that a strong inference of causality cannot be made without conducting a controlled experiment, and we cannot rule out the possibility that some other covariates that were not controlled in the present study may have been responsible for these associations" (Johnson et al., 2002, p. 2470). Such cautions are common with correlational studies; they cannot be used to demonstrate cause and effect.

correlation the extent to which variations in one variable are accompanied by increases or decreases in a second variable

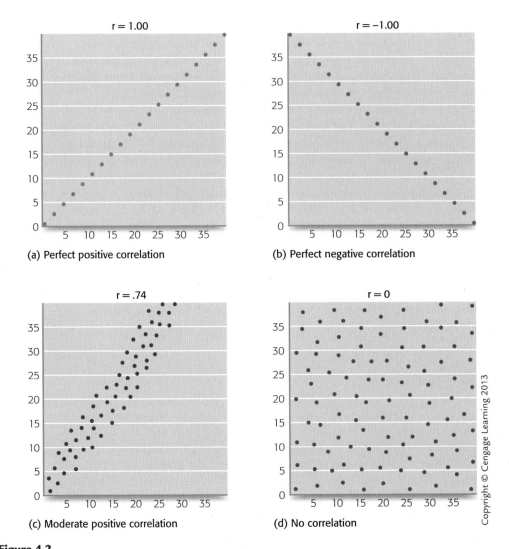

Figure 4.2

POSSIBLE CORRELATION BETWEEN TWO VARIABLES

The more closely the data points approximate a straight line, the greater the magnitude of the correlation coefficient *r*. The slope of the regression line rising from left to right in example (a) indicates a perfect positive correlation between two variables, whereas example (b) reveals a perfect negative correlation. Example (c) shows a lower positive correlation. Example (d) shows no correlation whatsoever.

There are numerous ways that a third variable might affect a correlation. Consider the following observations. What third-variable explanations can you suggest?

- There is a positive correlation between the number of churches in a city and the number of individuals living in the city who have been diagnosed with depression.
- There is a positive correlation between the number of mental health professionals working in a community and the number of violent crimes committed in the region.

In summary, a correlation indicates the degree to which two variables are related. It is a very important method of scientific inquiry because there are many variables we cannot control. Additionally, manipulating variables such as exposing a child to trauma or abuse would be completely unethical. Correlations can tell us how likely it is that two variables occur together. Even when the variables are highly related, however, we

Ethical Considerations—Risk/Benefit versus Social Value

CRITICAL THINKING

In medical research on human subjects, considerations related to the well-being of the human subject should take precedence over the interests of science and society (Declaration of Helsinki, 2004).

Investigators using research designs involving components such as placebo trials and random assignment must consider the risk/benefit ratio to the participants and the social value of the data obtained. For example, even though we might want to demonstrate a cause and effect relationship between smoking and adverse health conditions, it would be unethical to randomly assign adolescents to either a "smoking condition" or "nonsmoking condition," require them to smoke for 20 years, and then assess their health after this period of time. The risk to the participants would be considered too high even if a causal relationship between smoking and health conditions could be demonstrated. Review committees monitor research proposals involving human participants, especially when there are potential ethical dilemmas.

1. What issues need to be considered when deciding if a research design is ethical?

   Random assignment allows an investigator to have confidence that differences found in the study are due to differences in treatment rather than the individual characteristics of members of each group.

   Researchers were asked by Romanian officials to conduct a study regarding the effects of institutional care. One hundred thirty-six young children living in a Romanian institution were randomly assigned to continued institutional care or placement in foster care (Zeanah et al., 2009). Mental health assessments were made: (1) prior to the assignments and (2) after the children were 54 months of age. Noninstitutionalized Romanian children served as a comparison group. The findings revealed children assigned to foster care had fewer psychiatric problems than those who were in the continued institutionalization group. It appears that placement in foster care can ameliorate some of the effects of early institutionalization.

2. Does the study have social value? How important were the findings of the study? Were the participants put at risk? What kinds of ethical issues do you find with this study? If

you have qualms, are there suggestions you would make in conducting the research? Many studies employ random assignment. In what kinds of studies should the use of random assignment be limited?

   Placebo controlled trials—a placebo group allows the investigator to compare effects from factors such as expectations and attention with the effects of the medication or other treatment.

   Adolescents with major depressive disorder were randomly assigned to receive either an antidepressant medication, cognitive behavioral therapy (CBT), or a placebo pill. (After the experimental phase, individuals in the latter group were allowed to choose to be treated with either the antidepressant or CBT.) All participants were tracked to identify any worsening of depression in any of the conditions. The remission rate (i.e., percentage successfully treated) for the two treatment groups was 59 percent versus 48 percent for the placebo control group (Kennard et al., 2009). A strength of this study was that ongoing risk of harm was monitored, something few studies that compare the effectiveness of treatments do. In this study the participants had major depression. Is this a condition where you would approve of the use of a placebo?

   Glass (2008) believes that placebo trials put the participants at risk and that we should use a placebo group only when there is no other effective treatment that can be used for comparison. However, Streiner (2008) argues that placebo trials are a "necessary evil" and provide the best opportunity for obtaining a clear-cut research finding. He focuses on the social and research value of placebo conditions.

   In your opinion, how would you weigh the risk to the participants versus the value to society of using placebo trials? Would it be ethical to use a placebo condition for individuals with illnesses that get progressively worse (e.g., Alzheimer's, cancer, or schizophrenia)? Would the research be acceptable if you continuously monitored the participants? Would you sign up for a study if you had a progressive condition and understood that you might receive a placebo as treatment? Placebo controlled trials are highly prevalent in medication and psychotherapy research. How would you weigh the risk to the participants versus societal value?

must exercise caution in interpreting causality. The two variables can be highly correlated but not causally related. Some of the misinformation regarding immunizations mentioned earlier in the chapter developed in part because variables were correlated and assumptions were made that there was a causal link. For example, the age of onset of autism is correlated with the timing of childhood vaccines; this correlation resulted in the widespread but inaccurate conclusion that childhood vaccines cause autism. It is also important to remember that even if variables are causally related, the correlation cannot tell us the direction of causality.

Analogue Studies

As we have noted, ethical, moral, or legal standards may prevent researchers from devising certain studies. Additionally, studying real-life situations is often not feasible because it is difficult to control all possible variables. Sometimes researchers resort to an

Correlational Studies

Identical twins are often used in correlational studies to determine the influence of genetic factors. They tend to show greater behavioral similarities than do fraternal twins or siblings. This similarity is attributed to genetic factors. Could the way identical twins are treated also contribute to similarities in behaviors?

analogue study—an investigation that attempts to replicate or simulate, under controlled conditions, a situation that occurs in real life. Here are some examples of analogue studies:

1. To study the possible effects of a new treatment for anxiety disorders, the researcher experiments with students who have test anxiety rather than individuals diagnosed with anxiety disorders.

2. To test the hypothesis that human depression is caused by continual encounters with events that one cannot control, the researcher exposes rats to uncontrollable aversive stimuli and looks for an increase in depressive-like behaviors (such as lack of motivation, inability to learn, and general apathy) and changes in chemical activity in the brains of the animals.

3. To test the hypothesis that sexual sadism is influenced by watching sexually violent media, an experimenter exposes "normal" male participants to either violent or nonviolent sexual programs. The participants then complete a questionnaire assessing their attitudes and values toward women and their likelihood of engaging in violent behaviors with women.

Obviously, each example is only an approximation of real life. Students with test anxiety may not be equivalent to individuals with anxiety disorders. Findings based on rats may not be applicable to human beings. And exposure to one violent sexual film and the use of a questionnaire may not be sufficient to allow a researcher to draw the conclusion that sexual sadism is caused by long-term exposure to such films. However, analogue studies can give researchers insight into the processes that might be involved in abnormal behavior and facilitate the search for effective treatment.

■ Field Studies

analogue study an investigation that attempts to replicate or simulate, under controlled conditions, a situation that occurs in real life

field study an investigative technique in which behaviors and events are observed and recorded in their natural environment

In some cases, analogue studies would be too contrived to accurately reflect a real-life situation. Investigators may then resort to a field study, in which behaviors and events are observed and recorded in their natural environment. Field studies sometimes employ data collection techniques, such as questionnaires, interviews, and analysis of existing records, but the primary technique is observation. Observers must be highly trained and have enough self-discipline to avoid disrupting or modifying the behavioral processes they are observing and recording.

A field study may be used to examine mass behavior after events of major consequence, such as wars, floods, and earthquakes or to study personal crises, as in military combat, major surgery, terminal disease, or the loss of loved ones. Field studies using in-person interviews were conducted in New York City three to six months after the terrorist attacks on the World Trade Center on September 11, 2001. Researchers learned that although 18.5 percent of those interviewed displayed post-traumatic stress disorder (PTSD) symptoms, only 11.3 percent had received any help for the symptoms (DeLisi et al., 2003).

Although field studies offer a more realistic investigative environment than other types of research, they suffer from certain limitations. First, as with other nonexperimental research, determining the direction of causality is difficult in field studies because the data are correlational. Second, so many factors affect real-life situations that it is impossible to control—and sometimes even distinguish—all possible variables. As a result, the findings may be difficult to interpret. Third, observers can never be absolutely sure that their presence did not influence the interactions they observed.

Single-Participant Studies

Most scientists advocate the study of large numbers of people to uncover the basic principles governing behavior. This approach, called the *nomothetic orientation*, is concerned with formulating general laws or principles while de-emphasizing individual variations or differences. Experiments and correlational studies are nomothetic. Other scientists advocate the in-depth study of one person. This approach, exemplified by the single-participant study, has been called the *idiographic orientation*. There has been much debate over which method is more fruitful in studying psychopathology.

Although the idiographic method of studying a single participant has many limitations, especially lack of generalizability, it has proven very valuable in applied clinical work. Furthermore, arguing over which method is more helpful is not productive because both approaches are needed to study abnormal behavior. The nomothetic approach seems appropriate for researchers, whereas

© ROB & SAS/Corbis

Correlational Findings

Social contact and support are associated with better mental health. How would you determine the direction of the relationship? Does friendship prevent mental disturbances or do individuals with psychological problems have fewer friends? What other factors might be involved to produce the relationship between mental health and social relationships?

© James Robert Fuller/Corbis

Field Studies

The catastrophic damage wrought by the tsunami on December 26, 2004, caused nearly 100,000 fatalities in Meulaboh, Indonesia, alone. The majority of victims were women and children. Here, survivors survey the ruins. Many individuals involved in or witnessing the disaster suffered severe emotional and physical trauma. Disasters such as this provide a unique, though unwelcome, opportunity to observe events and reactions of individuals in the natural environment. Can social scientists remain detached and objective when recording a tragedy of such magnitude?

the idiographic approach seems appropriate for psychotherapists, who regularly face the challenge of providing effective treatment.

There are two types of single-participant studies: the *case study* and the *single-participant experiment*. Both techniques may be used to examine a rare or an unusual phenomenon, to demonstrate a novel diagnostic or treatment procedure, to test an assumption, to generate future hypotheses on which to base controlled research, or to collect comprehensive information to better understand an individual. Only the single-participant experiment, however, can determine cause and effect relationships.

The Case Study

Physicians have used the case study extensively in describing and treating illness. In psychology, a case study is an intensive study of one individual that relies on clinical data, such as observations, psychological tests, and historical and biographical information. A case study lacks the control and objectivity of many other methods and cannot be used to demonstrate cause and effect relationships. It can, however, serve as the primary source of data in cases in which systematic experimental procedures are not feasible. Case studies can also be helpful in determining diagnosis, characteristics, course, and outcome of a complicated disorder, as illustrated in the following example.

Case Study

Around 18 months of age, Craig's behavior around others changed. He communicated in a very unusual manner (echoing what was said to him) and no longer seemed interested in other children. He began to line up his toys rather than play with them and became highly distressed with even minor changes in his environment. His initial diagnosis was that of a speech and language delay. By the age of three he was given a provisional diagnosis of autism. At 12 years of age, Craig expressed serious concerns about his identity. He complained that he did not want to be autistic, saying he would rather have something like Down's syndrome so he could look like and fit in with other children in his special education classes. He became preoccupied with his appearance, complaining that was he was too tall, too heavy, and too "old looking." His obsession with his appearance continued during his teen years despite psychotherapy and pharmacological interventions. He complained of boredom, anxiety, and suicidal thoughts. The deepening of feelings of unhappiness resulted in an additional diagnosis of major depression. He started taking an antidepressant medication and over a period of two months his mood improved. Although he continued to have some concern about his appearance and weight, his anxiety and distress decreased significantly (Warren, Sanders, & Veenstra-VanderWeele, 2010).

This case study provides information regarding the early development of an autism spectrum disorder (impairment in socialization and communication and repetitive and restrictive behaviors). Of interest is Craig's development of additional mental disorders—body dysmorphic disorder (intense anxiety and distress over one's physical appearance) and major depression (severe, disabling depression). Initial therapies were ineffective until a medication prescribed to treat his depression also helped diminish the other concerns. A case study such as this allows therapists to better understand the development and experience of disorder, as well as gaining insight into possible treatments.

The Single-Participant Experiment

The **single-participant experiment** differs from the case study in that the former is actually an experiment in which some aspect of the person's behavior is used as a control or baseline for comparison with future behaviors. To determine the

case study an intensive study of one individual that relies on clinical data, such as observations, psychological tests, and historical and biographical information

single-participant experiment an experiment performed on a single individual in which some aspect of the person's behavior is used as a control or baseline for comparison with future behaviors

effectiveness of a treatment, for example, the experimenter determines the frequency of a behavior before intervention. The treatment is introduced, and the person's behavior is observed. Once behavior change occurs, the treatment is withdrawn. If, after the withdrawal of treatment, the person's behavior again resembles that observed during the baseline condition, we can be fairly certain that the treatment was responsible for the behavior changes observed earlier. In the final step, the treatment is reinstated.

A multiple-baseline study is a single-participant experimental design in which baselines on two or more behaviors or the same behavior in two or more settings are obtained prior to intervention. An intervention is first introduced for one behavior or setting, its effects observed, and then the intervention is applied to the next behavior or setting. If the behaviors change only with the intervention, confidence is increased that the intervention caused the changed behavior.

Bock (2007) used a multiple-baseline approach to determine the effectiveness of a training program for four children with Asperger's syndrome, a disorder characterized by the inability to develop peer relationships, understand social customs and demonstrate social or emotional reciprocity. Baselines for the children's behaviors were obtained during (1) cooperative learning activities, (2) organized sports, and (3) lunch with peers. Very few appropriate behaviors were seen in any of these conditions. The intervention program, called "SODA," provided rules and instructions to help the children attend to social cues and to develop appropriate responses. The program trained the children to use the following strategies to reflect on their own behavior, the environment, and other individuals: **S**top (What is the activity that people are engaged in?), **O**bserve (What is he/she doing or saying?), **D**eliberate (What would I like to do or say? How will others feel or act if I do or say these things?), and **A**ct (I plan to …). The SODA strategies were applied sequentially—first to the cooperative learning situation for a number of sessions, then to recess, and finally to lunch. Figure 4.3 demonstrates how one of the students, Bob, increased appropriate behaviors in each of the three conditions after the intervention. (The same effect was observed for the other three students.)

Single-participant designs are used with less frequency because researchers often rely on models that involve group comparisons or hypothesis testing. Because only one participant is used in this design, questions are raised about external validity or the generalizability of the findings.

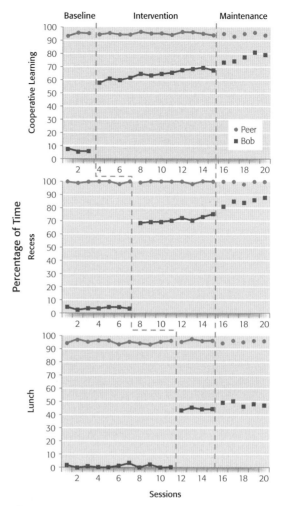

Figure 4.3

A MULTIPLE-BASELINE STUDY

The figures show the percentage of time Bob and a non-Asperger peer spent behaving appropriately during cooperative learning, recess, and lunch. During baseline, the percentage of time Bob displayed appropriate behaviors in cooperative learning, recess, and lunch was under 10 percent. With the SODA intervention, the percentage increased to about 70 percent during cooperative learning and recess and to more than 40 percent during lunch. At a five-month follow-up, it was found that the gains in appropriate behaviors were maintained.
Source: From Bock (2007, p. 92).

Biological Research Strategies

We are seeing increased reliance on biological research to determine the causes of and effective treatment for mental disorders.

Genetics and Epigenetics

Ongoing developments in the field of genetic research are contributing greatly to the field of abnormal psychology. Not only are scientists focusing on the influence of specific genes in the development of psychopathology, major advances are being made in

multiple-baseline study a single-participant experimental design in which baselines on two or more behaviors or the same behavior in two or more settings are obtained prior to intervention

the field of epigenetics. Epigenetic research is shedding light on how the environment influences or "programs" gene expression thus influencing an individual's risk of developing disorders such as depression, schizophrenia, and phobias (Bale et al., 2010). Researchers are finding that environmental stressors such as trauma, toxins, or diet have the greatest impact during certain sensitive periods in early development (Mann & Haghighi, 2010). Not only do children's experiences early in life affect their own development, certain experiences in childhood can change traits inherited by their descendants by leaving an imprint, a genetic marker, on their eggs and sperm that in effect "turns off" or "turns on" specific genetic characteristics in future generations (Weinhold, 2006).

Genetic Linkage Studies

Genetic linkage studies attempt to determine whether a disorder follows a genetic pattern. If a disorder is genetically linked, individuals closely related to the person with the disorder (who is called the *proband*) are more likely to display that disorder or a related disorder. Genetic studies of psychiatric disorders often employ the following procedure (Smoller, Shiedly, & Tsuang, 2008):

1. The proband and his or her family members are identified.
2. The proband is asked for the psychiatric history of specific family members.
3. These members are contacted and given some type of assessment such as psychological tests, brain scans, or neuropsychological examinations to determine whether they have the same or a related disorder.

This research strategy depends on the accurate diagnosis of both the proband and the relatives. Caution must be used in employing the family history method in genetic linkage studies. An individual's psychiatric status ("sick" or "well") may influence the accuracy of his or her assessment of the mental health of relatives. This bias in reporting may be reduced by using multiple informants or by assessing the family members directly. In a comprehensive study looking at psychological disorders in more than 11,000 twins, researchers increased the reliability of their findings by interviewing each twin and co-twin at least twice and at different points of time; they also relied on independent assessments to increase the accuracy of their research (Kendler & Prescot, 2006).

The Endophenotype Concept

If we know who is at greatest risk to develop a particular disorder, then it is possible to focus efforts on prevention or on rapid diagnosis and treatment if symptoms develop. In order to help predict who might develop a disorder, some researchers focus on locating biomarkers for particular disorders. Endophenotypes are measurable characteristics (neurochemical, endocrinological, neuroanatomical, cognitive, or neuropsychological) that can give clues regarding the genetic pathways involved in a disorder. All endophenotypes can be inherited, are seen even in family members who do not have the disorder, and occur more frequently in affected families than in the general population.

For example, it has been found that as many as 80 percent of individuals diagnosed with schizophrenia (a severe mental illness we will discuss in chapter 12) and 45 percent of their close relatives show irregularities in the way they track objects with their eyes. In families without schizophrenia, only 10 percent have this irregularity. This irregularity qualifies as an endophenotype: It's inherited, is seen in families with a particular disorder (schizophrenia) and occurs more often in those families than the general population. Thus this biomarker can be used to assist in predicting risk of schizophrenia. Although the majority of the asymptomatic relatives never develop the disorder, risk information can be used for prevention and early treatment efforts (Gottesman & Gould, 2003).

Despite a surge in interest in the use of endophenotypes (Walters & Owen, 2007), progress has been slow. As we learned in Chapter 2, there are many possible pathways leading

genetic linkage studies   studies that attempt to determine whether a disorder follows a genetic pattern

endophenotypes   measurable characteristics (neurochemical, endocrinological, neuroanatomical, cognitive, or neuropsychological) that can give clues regarding the specific genes involved in disorders

to the development of a disorder, not just genetics. Additionally, the symptoms and severity of symptoms for many disorders vary significantly even for those with the same diagnosis (Viding & Blakemoer, 2007) complicating the search for clear-cut indicators of risk.

Other Concepts in Biological Research

Iatrogenic effects are unintended effects of therapy—such as an unintended change in behavior resulting from a medication prescribed or a psychological technique employed by a therapist. The behavior change may be treated as a separate disorder rather than as a side effect of the medication or technique. For example, some have mistakenly diagnosed memory loss—a side effect of antidepressant medication—as Alzheimer's disease.

Psychological interventions or prevention efforts can also produce unexpected results. For example, certain group-based prevention and treatment programs have resulted in increases rather than decreases in substance use (Moos, 2005) and delinquent behaviors (Bootzin & Bailey, 2005).

Penetrance refers to the degree to which individuals carrying a specific gene or genes associated with it manifest a genetic characteristic. Complete penetrance occurs when a

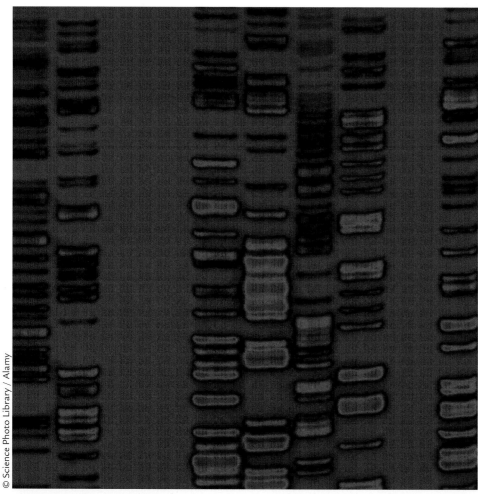

© Science Photo Library / Alamy

The Human Genome Project

This massive undertaking involved deciphering, mapping, and identifying DNA sequencing patterns and variations in approximately 30,000 genes in human DNA. Scientists hope to determine the "message" contained in the DNA patterns that may contribute to human attributes and diseases. Such research raises ethical, legal, and social concerns.

iatrogenic effects unintended effects of an intervention—such as an unintended change in behavior resulting from a medication or a psychological technique used in treatment

carrier always manifests the characteristic associated with the gene or genes. In mental disorders, incomplete penetrance is the rule. Even in cases of schizophrenia, only about half of the identical twins of a proband develop the disorder.

Biological challenge tests are often used to determine the effect of a substance on behavior. For example, to determine if a specific additive is responsible for hyperactivity in a child, behaviors after eating food with the additive (the "challenge" phase) and after eating other food without the additive are compared. If the additive and disruptive behaviors are linked, the behavior should be present during the challenge phase and absent during the other phase.

The use of *animal models*, relying on animals as surrogates for humans, is a frequent practice in genetic and epigenetic studies. Such experiments allow for considerable control over the variables studied and analysis across multiple generations and permit experimental procedures that would not be practical to use with humans. In one such study, newborn mice were exposed to frequent, unpredictable separation from their mothers; follow-up with the mice and their offspring yielded the highly important findings that this stressor affected not only the behavior, emotional development, and genetic make-up of the original mice but also of their offspring, particularly male offspring (Franklin et al., 2010). The researchers were also able to pinpoint the exact biological processes that occurred in the mice and their offspring. Advocates of such research point to the critical information gleaned from such studies, particularly with respect to understanding causality and advancing treatment.

We now examine some major techniques used in clinical research. They vary in their adherence to the scientific method.

Epidemiological and Other Forms of Research

In the field of abnormal psychology, investigators may employ experimental, correlational, case-study, or field-observation strategies in their research. The following strategies are important sources of information about disorders and their treatment.

- **Survey Research** Collecting data from all or part of a population to assess the relative prevalence, distribution, and interrelationships of different phenomena.
- **Longitudinal Research** Observing, assessing, and evaluating people's behaviors over a long period of time.
- **Historical Research** Reconstructing the past by reviewing and evaluating evidence available from historical documents.
- **Twin Studies** Focusing on identical twins as a population of interest because twins are so similar genetically. Twin studies are often used to evaluate the influence of heredity and environment.
- **Treatment Outcome Studies** Evaluating the effectiveness of treatment in alleviating mental disorders. Outcome research helps answer the question of whether treatment is effective.
- **Treatment Process Studies** Analyzing how therapists, clients, or situational factors influence one another during the course of treatment. Process research focuses on how or why treatment is effective.
- **Program Evaluation** Analyzing the effectiveness of an intervention or prevention program.

Reliance on experimental, correlational, or single-participant methods varies depending on the research strategy used. For instance, survey researchers often collect data and then correlate certain variables, such as social class and adjustment, to discover whether they are related. Researchers may also combine elements of different methods in their research. For example, an investigator conducting treatment outcome studies may use both surveys and longitudinal studies.

epidemiological research the study of the rate and distribution of mental disorders in a population

Surveys are frequently used in epidemiological research, which examines the rate and distribution of mental disorders in a population. This important type of research is used to determine both the extent of mental disturbance found in a targeted population and the factors that influence the rate of mental disturbance. Two terms, *prevalence* and *incidence*, are used to describe the rates. As noted in Chapter 1, the *prevalence rate* tells us the percentage of individuals in a targeted population who have a particular disorder during a specific period of time. For example, we might be interested in how many preschool-aged children had a spider phobia during the previous six months (six-month prevalence rate), during the previous year (one-year prevalence rate), or at any time during their lives (lifetime prevalence rate). In general, shorter time periods have lower prevalence rates. When we compare the prevalence rate of disorders cited in studies, it is important to identify the specified time periods. Determining the prevalence rate is vital for planning treatment services because mental health workers need to know the percentage of people who are likely to be afflicted with particular disorders.

The *incidence rate* tells the number of *new* cases of a disorder that appear in an identified population within a specified time period. The incidence rate is likely to be lower than the prevalence rate because incidence involves only new cases, whereas prevalence includes both new and existing. Incidence rates are important for examining hypotheses about the causes or origins of a disorder. For example, if we find that new cases of a disorder are more likely to appear in a population exposed to a particular stressor compared with another population not exposed to the stressor, we can hypothesize that the stress caused the disorder. Epidemiological research, then, is important not only in describing the distribution of disorders but also in analyzing possible causal factors.

Summary

1. In what ways is the scientific method used to evaluate psychotherapy?

   - The scientific method is a method of inquiry that provides for the systematic collection of data, controlled observation, and the testing of hypotheses.
   - Characteristics such as the potential for self-correction, the development of hypotheses, the use of operational definitions, a consideration of reliability and validity, an acknowledgment of base rates, and the requirement that research findings be evaluated in terms of their statistical significance enable us to have greater faith in our findings.

2. How does the use of an experimental design differ from other ways of investigating phenomena?

   - The experiment is the most powerful research tool we have for determining and testing cause and effect relationships. In its simplest form, an experiment involves an experimental hypothesis, an independent variable, and a dependent variable.

   - The investigator manipulates the independent variable and measures the effect on the dependent variable. The experimental group is the group subjected to the independent variable. A control group is employed that is similar in every way to the experimental group except for the manipulation of the independent variable.
   - Additional concerns include expectancy effects on the part of the participants and the investigator and the extent to which an experiment has internal and external validity.

3. What are correlations, and how are they used to indicate the degree to which two variables are related?

   - A correlation is a measure of the degree to which two variables are related, not what causes the relationship. It is expressed as a correlation coefficient, a numerical value between -1 and $+1$, symbolized by r. Correlational techniques provide less precision, control, and generality than experiments, and they cannot be taken to imply cause and effect relationships.

4. What are analogue studies, and when is this type of investigation used?

- In the study of abnormal behavior, an analogue study is used to create a situation as close to real life as possible. It permits the study of phenomena under controlled conditions when such study might otherwise be ethically, morally, legally, or practically impossible. The generalizability of the findings to clinical populations has to be evaluated and cannot be automatically assumed.

5. What are field studies, and how are they used?

- The field study relies primarily on naturalistic observations in real-life situations. As opposed to analogue studies, events are observed as they naturally occur. However, a field study cannot determine causality, and it may be difficult to sort out all the variables involved.

6. What are the various types of single-participant studies, and how are they used?

- A case study is an intensive study of one individual that relies on clinical data, such as observations, psychological tests, and historical and biographical information. The case study is especially appropriate when a phenomenon is so rare that it is impractical to try to study more than a few instances.
- Single-participant experiments differ from case studies in that cause and effect relationships can be determined. They rely on experimental procedures; some aspect of the person's behavior is taken as a control or baseline for comparison with future behaviors.
- A multiple-baseline study is another type of single-participant experimental design in which baselines on two or more behaviors or the same behavior in two or more settings are obtained prior to intervention.

7. What are some of the advantages and shortcomings of the biological approach to understanding abnormal behavior?

- Biological research strategies allow us to search for genetic and epigenetic factors involved in psychological disorders and to identify biological indicators of a disorder.

8. What is epidemiological research, and how is it used to determine the extent of mental disturbance in a targeted population?

- Epidemiological research examines the rate and distribution of mental disorders in a population. It can also provide insight into what groups are at risk for mental disturbance and what factors may influence disturbance.
- There is often confusion between prevalence and incidence rates. Prevalence rates are composed of both new and existing cases during a specified time period. Incidence rates involve only new cases.

Media Resources

Psychology CourseMate Access an interactive eBook, chapter-specific interactive learning tools, including flashcards, quizzes, videos and more in your Psychology CourseMate, accessed through CengageBrain.com.

CENGAGE**NOW**

CengageNow CengageNOW is an easy-to-use online resource that helps you study in less time to get the grade you want—NOW. If your textbook does not include an access code card, go to CengageBrain.com to gain access.

CENGAGE **brain**.com

CengageBrain More than just an interactive study guide, WebTutor is an anytime, anywhere customized learning solution with an eBook, keeping you connected to your textbook, instructor, and classmates. Purchase the access chosen by your instructor at CengageBrain.com.

5

Anxiety and Obsessive-Compulsive and Related Disorders

Emily was hiking with her dog when another dog attacked her and bit her on the wrist. She was terrified. The wound became badly infected and very painful, requiring medical treatment. On another occasion, her sister, Marian, was walking in the fields when three large, growling dogs chased her. One began tearing at her pant legs. The owner heard the commotion and intervened before she was physically injured. Marian developed a fear of dogs, but Emily, who suffered painful injuries, did not. What could account for these differences? (Mineka & Zinbarg, 2006, p. 10)

Anxiety, a feeling of uneasiness or apprehension, is a fundamental human emotion that was recognized as long as five thousand years ago. It is common to experience anxiety. In fact, many observers regard anxiety as a basic condition of modern existence. "Reasonable doses" of anxiety act as a safeguard to keep us from ignoring danger, and anxiety appears to have an adaptive function, producing bodily reactions that prepare us for "fight or flight." These physiological responses allow us to cope with potentially dangerous situations. In some cases, however, fear or anxiety occur even when no danger is present, resulting in an anxiety disorder. Fear or anxiety symptoms are considered a disorder only when they interfere with an individual's day-to-day functioning.

The terms *anxiety* and *fear* are often used interchangeably, perhaps because they both produce the same physiological responses. However, *anxiety* is anticipatory; the dreaded event or situation has not yet occurred. *Fear* is a more intense emotion experienced in response to a threatening situation. If either fear or anxiety becomes overwhelming, a panic attack can occur. Panic attacks are experienced as intense fear accompanied by symptoms such as a pounding heart, trembling, shortness of breath, or fear of losing control or dying. Not everyone who experiences a panic attack has an anxiety disorder.

Anxiety disorders are the most common mental condition in the United States and affect about 40 million adults (approximately 18 percent) in a given year (Kessler, Chiu et al., 2005) (Figure 5.1). It is estimated that nearly 29 percent of adults living in the United States are affected by an anxiety disorder sometime during their lives (Kessler, Chiu et al., 2005). In a large survey of adolescents, 31.9 percent had experienced an anxiety disorder (lifetime prevalence), with 8.3 percent suffering severe impairment (Merikangas et al., 2011). People with anxiety disorders report a lower quality of life than nonanxious individuals (Barrera & Norton, 2010). The financial cost to the United States

focus questions

1 How are biological, psychological, social, and sociocultural factors involved in the development of anxiety disorders? Why is the multipath model important?

2 What are phobias, what contributes to their development, and how are they treated?

3 What is panic disorder, what produces it, and how is it treated?

4 What is generalized anxiety disorder, what are its causes, and how is it treated?

5 What are characteristics of obsessive-compulsive and related disorders, what are their causes, and how are they treated?

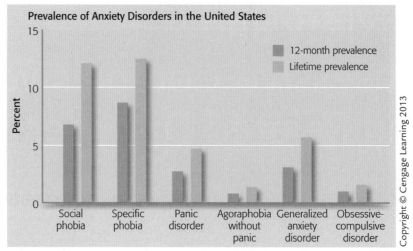

Figure 5.1

PREVALENCE OF ANXIETY DISORDERS IN THE UNITED STATES
Anxiety disorders are the most common mental condition in the United States.
Source: Kessler, Berglund, et al. (2005); Kessler, Chiu, et al. (2005).

of anxiety disorders is estimated to be more than $42 billion a year, with over half of these costs due to frequent usage of health care services (Anxiety Disorders Association of America [ADAA], 2007). Anxiety disorders are responsible for a great deal of distress and dysfunction and are often accompanied by comorbid disorders such as depression, substance abuse, or other anxiety disorders. The strong co-occurrence between depression and anxiety disorders suggests that they may involve different expressions of a common vulnerability (Brown, 2007). Substance abuse that coexists with anxiety disorders may be the result of individuals attempting to manage their anxiety symptoms by "self-medicating." In this chapter, we discuss four major groups of anxiety disorders—*phobias, panic disorder, agoraphobia,* and *generalized anxiety disorder.* (The anxiety disorders are shown in Table 5.1.) Because obsessive-compulsive and related disorders (*obsessive-compulsive disorder, hair-pulling disorder, body dysmorphic disorder, and skin-picking disorder*) have important similarities with anxiety disorders, they are also discussed in this chapter. Acute stress disorder and post-traumatic stress disorder, which are also anxiety disorders, are covered in Chapter 6. In order to give you an understanding of some of the predisposing factors that can result in an anxiety disorder, we begin our discussion with the multipath model defined in Chapter 2.

Understanding Anxiety Disorders from a Multipath Perspective

In the case at the beginning of the chapter, Emily was exposed to greater trauma when she was attacked by a dog, but it was her sister Marian who developed an anxiety disorder. All of us have faced frightening situations. What factors affect the likelihood of someone developing an anxiety disorder? In general, single etiological models, whether biological, psychological, or sociocultural, are insufficient to explain individual variations in response to fearful situations. A number of different factors may play a role in the acquisition of fears or phobias, including biological factors such as genetically based vulnerabilities and psychological factors such as personality variables, an individual's sense of mastery or control, or direct or indirect conditioning experiences (Mineka & Zinbarg, 2006). In addition, cultural rules and norms can also influence the expression of anxiety disorders. The multipath model for anxiety disorders is shown in Figure 5.2. In the next section we consider the biological underpinnings of anxiety disorders, including a discussion involving how genes exert their influence and how the environment influences the expression of genes.

anxiety a fundamental human emotion that produces bodily reactions that prepare us for "fight or flight;" anxiety is anticipatory; the dreaded event or situation has not yet occurred

anxiety disorder fear or anxiety symptoms that interfere with an individual's day-to-day functioning

panic attack intense fear accompanied by symptoms such as a pounding heart, trembling, shortness of breath, fear of losing control or dying

TABLE 5.1   Anxiety Disorders

Anxiety Disorder	Symptoms	Gender and Cultural Factors	Age of Onset
Social Phobias	• Irrational fear of being scrutinized or judged by others; extreme self-consciousness in social situations • Exposure to feared stimulus produces intense fear or panic attacks • Avoidance responses are almost always present • Anxiety dissipates when phobic situation is not being confronted	More common in females; in Asian cultures may involve fear of offending others	Mid-teens
Specific Phobias	• Irrational fear of specific objects or situations with little or no danger • Exposure produces intense fear or panic attacks	Approximately twice as common in females, although depends on type of phobia	Childhood or early adolescence (depends on type of phobia)
Agoraphobia	• Anxiety or panic-like symptoms in situations where escape might be difficult or embarrassing	Far more prevalent in females	20s to 40s
Panic Disorder	• Recurrent and unexpected panic attacks • Concern about expected future panic attacks or about losing control • Can occur with or without agoraphobia	May involve intense fear of the supernatural in some cultures; 2–3 times more common in females	Late adolescence and early adulthood
Generalized Anxiety Disorder	• Excessive anxiety and worry over life circumstances for at least 3 months • Accompanied by symptoms such as vigilance, muscle tension, restlessness, edginess, and difficulty concentrating	Up to 2 times more prevalent in females	Usually childhood or adolescence

Copyright © Cengage Learning 2013

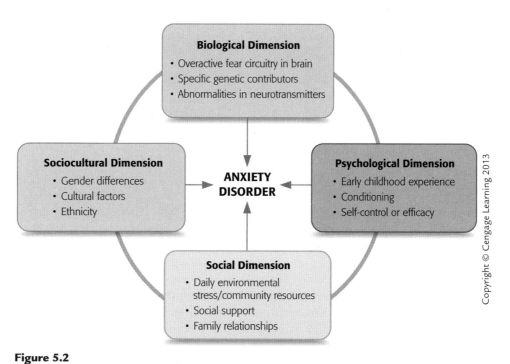

Figure 5.2

MULTIPATH MODEL OF ANXIETY DISORDERS

The dimensions interact with one another and combine in different ways to result in a specific anxiety disorder. The importance and influence of each dimension varies from individual to individual.

Biological Dimension

Two main biological factors affect anxiety disorders: *brain function* and *genetic influences*.

Brain Function

The *amygdala* (the part of the brain involved in the formation and memory of emotional events) plays a central role in anxiety disorders. In response to potential threats, signals from the amygdala alert other brain structures, such as the *hippocampus* and *prefrontal cortex*, and trigger a fear response. There are two pathways to the amygdala. In the first, a potentially dangerous sensory stimulus results in immediate activation of the amygdala. The second and slower pathway involves signals that travel first to the prefrontal cortex, allowing evaluation of the stimulus and an opportunity to override the initial fear response. For example, when passengers in an airplane encounter turbulence, they may initially feel fear. However, when the pilot gives a reassuring explanation for the turbulence, signals from the prefrontal cortex reduce anxiety by inhibiting fear responses from the amygdala (Casey et al., 2011; Fava & Morton, 2009). In some individuals, however, neural structures involved in the fear network appear to be overactive, resulting in symptoms seen in anxiety disorders. Neuroimaging techniques such as positron emission tomography (PET) scans and magnetic resonance imaging (MRI) have documented increased reactivity in the amygdala when individuals with anxiety disorders are exposed to specific emotional stimuli (Stein, Simmons, Feinstein, & Paulus, 2007; Sehlmeyer et al., 2010). In addition, differences in the metabolism of certain areas of the brain can be seen in individuals with anxiety disorders even when fearful stimuli are not present.

Did You Know?

Neuroimaging studies of a woman who was unable to experience fear or recognize dangerous situations revealed bilateral damage to her amygdala; this brain abnormality likely caused her absence of fear (Feinstein, Adolphs, Damasio, & Tranel, 2011).

Neuroimaging techniques allow us to observe the effects of both medication and psychotherapy in the treatment of anxiety disorders. Medication appears to "normalize" anxiety circuits in the brain. Interestingly, psychotherapies also produce neurobiological changes similar to those seen with medications for anxiety disorders (Kumari, 2006). The connections between the amygdala and cortex allow us to speculate about why medications and psychotherapy may both be effective in treating anxiety disorders: Each may operate on a different level of the brain. Therapy may reduce arousal by deconditioning fear at the level of the hippocampus while also strengthening the ability of the prefrontal cortex to inhibit fear responses from the amygdala. Medication may directly influence or decrease activity in the amygdala and other brain structures (Figure 5.3) (Britton, Lissek, Grillon, Norcross, & Pine, 2011; Gorman et al., 2000).

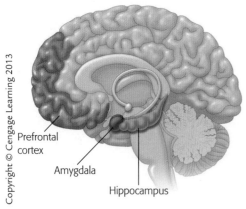

Copyright © Cengage Learning 2013

Prefrontal cortex

Amygdala

Hippocampus

Figure 5.3

NEUROANATOMICAL BASIS FOR PANIC AND OTHER ANXIETY DISORDERS

The fear network in the brain is centered in the amygdala and interacts with the hippocampus and areas of the prefrontal cortex. Antianxiety medications appear to desensitize the fear network. Some psychotherapies also affect brain functioning related to anxiety.

Genetic Influences

Genes make a modest contribution to anxiety disorders and interact with other important multipath factors (Bienvenu, Davydow, & Kendler, 2011). Currently, researchers are trying to identify how genes exert their influence. As you learned in Chapter 2, *neurotransmitters* are chemicals that help transmit messages in the brain. One specific neurotransmitter, serotonin, is implicated in mood and anxiety disorders. Consequently, a serotonin transporter gene (5-HTTLPR) has been the focus of attention. Alleles (the gene pair responsible for each trait) influence the expression of genetic characteristics. In the case of the serotonin transporter gene (5-HTTLPR), a *polymorphic variation* of this gene (a common DNA mutation) affects the length of the associated alleles; it is possible to inherit two short alleles, two long alleles, or one short and one long allele. Researchers have found that short alleles in the serotonin transporter gene are associated with (1) a reduction in serotonin activity and (2) increased fear and anxiety-related behaviors (Pezawas et al., 2005). This means that carriers of the short allele show more reactivity of the amygdala when exposed to threatening stimuli. Those with the short allele also show differences in brain structure in areas that affect mood and emotions such as anxiety and depression (Hariri,

Mattay et al., 2002; Hariri, Drabant et al., 2005), including weaker connections between the amygdala and the cingulated cortex. This may result in a reduction of the cingulated cortex's ability to regulate a "runaway" amygdala fear response (Pezawas et al., 2005).

Although this research is promising, it is probable that numerous genes affect vulnerability to anxiety disorders. Additionally, identified genes only influence *predisposition* to develop an anxiety disorder. In most cases, the presence of certain alleles increases the chances that a characteristic is expressed; however, actual expression of the gene depends on interactions between the allele and environmental influences (Klauke, Deckert, Reif, Pauli, & Domschke, 2010; Leonardo & Hen, 2006).

Complicating the search for biological causes of anxiety disorders is the finding that other neurotransmitters, such as glutamate and gamma-aminobutyric acid (GABA), are also involved in the modulation of learning and extinction of fear in the amygdala. In fact, benzodiazepines, a class of medications that are effective in treating anxiety disorders, exert their influence on GABA neurotransmitters present in the amygdala (Rauch, Shin, & Wright, 2003). Thus the search for biological factors includes identifying genes and gene interactions, understanding the relationship of the different brain systems, and determining which combinations of neurotransmitters are involved in anxiety disorders.

Biological, Psychological, and Social Interactions

Although expressed characteristics are determined by the genes and alleles that are present, environmental variables affect their expression. Researchers were initially puzzled by conflicting findings regarding carriers of the short allele of the serotonin transporter gene. Auerbach and colleagues (2001) found that infants' fear responses associated with the short allele of the 5-HTTLPR gene were greatly reduced by the time the infants were twelve months old. Researchers began to wonder whether environmental factors such as parenting styles might influence the expression of genes. Characteristics such as anxiety and fear may result from genetic and environmental influences that are encoded by neural systems in the brain during certain critical periods of development, such as infancy (Leonardo & Hen, 2006).

If the short allele of the 5-HTTLPR gene is associated with anxiety, why are only some children who are carriers of this allele behaviorally inhibited (i.e., shy)? Fox and colleagues (2005) hypothesized that environmental factors such as parental behaviors may interact with a genetic predisposition to produce behavioral inhibition. Using a longitudinal design, 153 children were observed and rated for characteristics of behavioral inhibition at age fourteen months and again at seven years. Mothers were rated in terms of nurturing behaviors and social assistance provided to their children. DNA from each child was analyzed, and children were divided into two groups: those with and those without the short allele of the 5-HTTLPR gene. Fox and colleagues (2005) found that children with short alleles only showed behavioral inhibition when they were raised in a stressful environment with low levels of maternal social support. As Fox observed, "If you have two short alleles of this serotonin gene, but your mom is not stressed, you will be no more shy than your peers as a school age child. . . . But . . . [i]f you are raised in a stressful environment, and you inherit the short form of the gene, there is a higher likelihood that you will be fearful, anxious or depressed" ("Genes and Stressed-Out Parents Lead to Shy Kids, 2007," p. 1).

Gene × environment interaction explanations have received a great deal of attention and show greater promise than single-model approaches. However, other multipath variables are also involved. Not all children who carry short alleles develop behavioral inhibition, even in stressful family environments, and some with long alleles are socially inhibited.

Psychological Dimension

Individual characteristics sometimes interact with biological predispositions to produce anxiety symptoms. Cognitive-behavioral theories emphasize the importance of cognitive processes (e.g., negative, catastrophic, or irrational thoughts) in the development and maintenance of anxiety disorders (Rinck & Becker, 2006). Those who interpret events, even ambiguous ones, as threatening are more likely to develop an anxiety disorder. A personality variable, *anxiety sensitivity* (McLaughlin & Hatzenbuehler, 2009), may also be a risk factor. Individuals who are fearful of physiological changes in their bodies (i.e., have anxiety sensitivity) and interpret such changes as signs of danger may be particularly vulnerable to developing anxiety symptoms. One's sense of control may also be a factor in the development of an anxiety disorder. Young monkeys reared in environments in which they could control access to water and food showed less fear when exposed to anxiety-provoking situations than monkeys without this control. Similarly, children who develop a sense of self-control and mastery also appear to be less vulnerable to anxiety (Chorpita & Barlow, 1998). Thus a number of psychological characteristics can affect individual vulnerability to anxiety disorders.

Social and Sociocultural Dimensions

Any etiological theory of anxiety disorders should consider the impact of social and socio-cultural factors and stresses. Daily environmental stress is a social factor that can produce anxiety, especially in individuals who have biological or psychological vulnerabilities. For example, those with lower incomes have higher rates of anxiety disorders (Kessler, Berglund et al., 2005). Living in poverty or in an unsafe environment can exacerbate both stress and anxiety. Traumatic events such as terrorist attacks, school shootings, and natural disasters also increase rates of anxiety disorders (Palmieri, Weathers, Difede, & King, 2007; Weems et al., 2007). How these stressors are viewed by an individual's social support network (family, friends, and peers) can either exacerbate or mitigate anxiety reactions (Brewin, Andrews, & Valentine, 2000; Ozer, Best, Lipsey, & Weiss, 2003). Additionally, the meaning that a community ascribes to stressful events can influence reactions of the residents. When Hurricane Katrina struck New Orleans in 2005, for example, anxiety was heightened because people of color believed that the inadequate response of the federal government was due to race and class bias (Bourne, Watts, Gordon, & Figueroa-Garcia, 2006).

Ellen B. Senisi/The Image Works

Self-Control and Mastery Decrease Anxiety

Children who develop a sense of control and mastery are less susceptible to anxiety disorders. In this case, the child is allowed to choose her dinner from an assortment of healthy foods and to serve herself. Within developmentally appropriate limits, how else can choices and independence be encouraged in young children?

Gender also plays a role in the development of anxiety disorders. Females are more likely to experience anxiety disorders than males. Is the reason biological, social, or a combination of the two? Nolen-Hoeksema (2004) argues that women are more likely to be diagnosed with emotional disorders due to their lack of power and status and stressors associated with poverty, lack of respect, and limited choices. Stress hormones produced by these social factors may make women more vulnerable to depression and anxiety. Thus interactions between psychological, social, and biological factors may help explain the overrepresentation of women with respect to anxiety disorders.

Cultural factors such as acculturation conflicts also contribute to anxiety disorders among ethnic minorities. Among Native Americans and Asian American undergraduate students, there is evidence of high levels of self-reported anxiety (De Coteau, Anderson, & Hope, 2006; Okazaki et al., 2002). Increased anxiety among some cultural groups may result from differing cultural standards regarding appropriate social interactions. Exposure to discrimination and prejudice may also increase the anxiety of ethnic minorities or other marginalized group members such as individuals with disabilities or a different sexual orientation. Culture may influence how anxiety is expressed; for example, *ataque de nervios*—symptoms similar to a panic attack combined with crying or uncontrollable shouting—can be found among Latino groups. Awareness of cultural manifestations of anxiety in different groups is essential for clinicians working with clients from diverse backgrounds.

Biological, psychological, social, and sociocultural explanations can all help answer the question, "What is the cause of this disorder?" Keep this in mind as we now turn our attention to understanding anxiety disorders, beginning with phobias. We conclude the chapter with a focus on the obsessive-compulsive and related disorders.

Phobias

The word *phobia* comes from the Greek word for fear. A phobia is a strong, persistent, and unwarranted fear of some specific object or situation. An individual with a phobia often experiences extreme anxiety or panic when he or she encounters the phobic stimulus. Attempts to avoid the object or situation can notably interfere with the individual's life. Adults with phobias realize that their fear is excessive, although children may not. Many people with phobias also have anxiety, mood, or substance-use disorders (Hofmann, Lehman, & Barlow, 1997; Nedic, Zivanovic, & Lisulov, 2011). Phobias are the most common mental disorder in the United States. Indeed, nearly anything can become the focus of intense fear. There is even a fear of phobias called *phobophobia* (Table 5.2). There are three subcategories of phobias: social phobia, specific phobia, and agoraphobia.

Social Phobias

Case Study

In any social situation, I felt fear. I would be anxious before I even left the house, and it would escalate as I got closer to a college class, a party, or whatever. When I would walk into a room full of people, I'd turn red, and it would feel like everybody's eyes were on me. I was embarrassed to stand off in a corner by myself, but I couldn't think of anything to say. . . . It was humiliating. . . . I couldn't wait to get out. (National Institute of Mental Health [NIMH], 2009a, p. 9)

TABLE 5.2 Examples of Phobias

Phobia	Object of Phobia
Acrophobia	Heights
Ailurophobia	Cats
Algophobia	Pain
Astrapophobia	Storms, thunder, lightning
Dementophobia	Insanity
Genitophobia	Genitals
Hematophobia	Blood
Microphobia	Germs
Monophobia	Being alone
Mysophobia	Contamination/germs
Nyctophobia	Dark
Pathophobia	Disease
Phobophobia	Phobias
Pyrophobia	Fire
Xenophobia	Strangers

Copyright © Cengage Learning 2013

A social phobia is an intense fear of being scrutinized or doing something embarrassing or humiliating in the presence of others (Bruch, Fallon, & Heimberg, 2003; Lipsitz, 2006). Social fears and anxieties are quite common worldwide, but social phobia is more common in developed (6.1 percent) than in developing countries (2.1 percent) (Stein et al., 2010). Individuals with social phobia are so self-conscious that they literally feel sick with fear at the prospect of activities such as eating in public or walking in a mall. Albert Ellis (1913–2007), the psychologist who developed rational emotive behavior therapy, reported that as a teenager he would wait until a movie started before going to a seat because he was fearful about being observed by other patrons. The most common social phobias involve public speaking and meeting new people (American Psychiatric Association, 2011).

Individuals with high social anxiety tend to believe that others view them negatively (Winton, Clark, & Edelmann, 1995; Wong & Moulds, 2009), engage in negative self-observation and monitoring, and remain alert to "threat" cues such as signs of disapproval or criticism (Mogg, Philippot, & Bradley, 2004; Taylor & Alden, 2010). To avoid drawing attention to themselves, they engage in "safety behaviors"

phobia a strong, persistent, and unwarranted fear of a specific object or situation

social phobia an intense fear of being scrutinized in one or more social or performance situations

such as avoiding eye contact, talking less, sitting alone, holding a glass tightly to prevent tremors, or wearing makeup to hide blushing (Moukheiber et al., 2010; Vassilopoulos, Benerjee, & Prantzalou, 2009). They show high levels of submissiveness in an effort to avoid conflicts with others (Russell et al., 2010). People with social phobias, like those with other phobias, usually realize that their behavior and fears are irrational, but this understanding does not reduce the distress they feel. Social phobias can involve high levels of anxiety in most social situations (*generalized type*), or they can be very specific (*performance type*), associated with particular activities such as playing a musical instrument, public speaking, eating in a restaurant, or using a public restroom.

Social phobia can be chronic and disabling, especially for those who develop the disorder early in life (Dalrymple & Zimmerman, 2011; Nedic, Zivanovic, & Lisulov, 2011). In a five-year naturalistic follow-up study, only 40 percent of those with the disorder recovered (Beard, Moitra, Weisberg, & Keller, 2010). Social phobia, especially the generalized type, is comorbid with (i.e., often occurs with) major depressive disorders, substance-use disorders, and suicidal ideation or attempts (El-Gabalawy, Cox, Clara, & Mackenzie, 2010). Individuals with social phobia report impairment in the quality of interpersonal relationships (Rodebaugh, 2009) and even display less emotional expression, self-disclosure, and intimacy with romantic partners (Sparrevohn & Rapee, 2009).

Social phobias affect 8.7 percent of adults in a given year. More than 48 percent, however, rate the severity of their symptoms as "mild" (Kessler, Chiu et al., 2005). Women are twice as likely as men to have this disorder; however, more men seek treatment (Kessler, Berglund et al., 2005). Having generalized social phobia appears to affect the occupational status of women, limiting career choices and resulting in underemployment (Bruch, Fallon, & Heimberg, 2003).

Phobias

Coulrophobia, a fear of clowns, may result from their painted eyes and smiles and never-changing expressions. Celebrities reported to have a fear of clowns include Johnny Depp, Daniel Radcliffe, Billy Bob Thornton, and Sean "P. Diddy" Combs. Uma Thurman is reported to have claustrophobia (fear of enclosed places). What do you believe may cause these fears?

Specific Phobias

A specific phobia is an extreme fear of a specific object (such as snakes) or situation (such as being in an enclosed place). Exposure to the stimulus nearly always produces intense anxiety or a panic attack. There are five primary types of specific phobias:

1. Animal (e.g., spiders, insects, dogs, snakes)
2. Natural environmental (e.g., heights, earthquakes, thunder, water)
3. Blood/injections or injury (e.g., needles, invasive medical procedures)
4. Situational (e.g., fear of traveling in cars, planes, tunnels, or over bridges)
5. Other (e.g., situations that may lead to choking, vomiting, contracting an illness; in children, loud sounds or costumed characters)

The following case study illustrates a common specific phobia exhibited by a twenty-six-year-old public relations executive.

Case Study

If I see a spider in my house, I get out! I start shaking, and I feel like I'm going to throw up. I get so scared, I have to bolt across the street to drag my neighbor over to get rid of the spider. Even after I know it's gone, I obsess for hours. I check between my sheets 10 times before getting in bed, and I'm so creeped out that I won't get up and go to the bathroom at night, even if my bladder feels like it's about to burst. (Kusek, 2001, p. 183)

Specific phobias are estimated to affect 19 million adults in a given year in the United States (approximately 8.7 percent of the population) and are twice as common in women as in men (Kessler, Berglund et al., 2005; NIMH, 2009). The degree to which they interfere with daily life depends on how easy it is to avoid the feared object or situation. These phobias often begin during childhood. Animal phobias tend to have the earliest onset (age seven), followed by blood phobia (age nine), dental phobia (age twelve), and claustrophobia (age twenty) (Öst, 1987, 1992). Figure 5.4 illustrates ages at which different phobias typically begin.

The most common childhood fears have traditionally included spiders, the dark, frightening movies, and being teased, whereas adolescents most frequently fear heights, animals, or speaking in class or speaking to strangers (Muris, Merckelbach, & Collaris, 1997). However, contemporary fears of students now include "being raped," "terrorist attacks," "having to fight in a war," "drive-by shootings," and "snipers at school" (Burnham, 2009). In a sample of 160 primary-school children, 17.6 percent met the criteria for a specific phobia (Muris & Merckelbach, 2000). Most early fears do remit without treatment (Broeren, Lester, Muris, & Field, 2011).

Blood phobias differ from other phobias because they are associated with a unique physiological response: fainting in the phobic situation. Fainting appears to result from an initial increase in autonomic arousal followed by a sudden drop in blood pressure and heart rate (Ayala, Meuret, & Ritz, 2009). Nearly 70 percent of those with blood phobias report a history of fainting in medical situations (Antony, Brown, & Barlow, 1997); many avoid medical examinations or are unable to care for an injured child (Hellstrom, Fellenius, & Öst, 1996). Intense inoculation anxiety was reported by 8.2 percent of travelers at a health clinic (Nir, Paz, Sabo, & Potasman, 2003), and 7.2 percent of

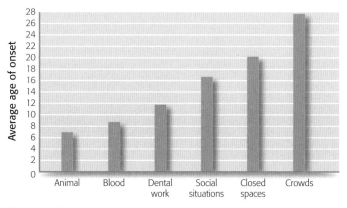

Figure 5.4

PHOBIA ONSET

This graph illustrates the average ages at which 370 people said their phobias began. Animal phobias began during childhood, whereas the onset of agoraphobia did not occur until the individuals were in their late twenties. What accounts for the differences reported in the age of onset for the types of phobias?
Source: Data from Öst, (1987, 1992)

specific phobia an extreme fear of a specific object (such as snakes) or situation (such as being in an enclosed place)

pregnant women receiving prenatal care met the criteria for blood and injection phobia (Lilliecreutz & Josefsson, 2008).

Agoraphobia

Agoraphobia is an intense fear of at least two of the following situations: (1) being outside of the home alone; (2) traveling in public transportation; (3) being in open spaces (e.g., parking lot or park); (4) being in stores or theaters; or (5) standing in line or being in a crowd. These situations are feared because escape or help may not be readily available (American Psychiatric Association, 2011). Agoraphobia arises from a fear that panic-like symptoms, such as fainting, losing control over bodily functions, or displaying excessive fear in public, will incapacitate the person or cause severe embarrassment. Anxiety over having a panic attack can prevent people from leaving their homes. Agoraphobia occurs much more frequently in females than in males. Although this phobia is relatively uncommon (less than 1 percent of U.S. adults in a given year), 41 percent of those affected rate the symptoms as serious (Kessler, Chiu et al., 2005).

Individuals who have agoraphobia may misinterpret and overreact to bodily sensations. Normal changes precipitate anxiety; anxiety reactions further increase bodily sensations (e.g., sweating or heart palpitations) resulting in a vicious cycle that can culminate in a panic attack (Rudaz, Craske, Becker, Ledermann, & Margraf, 2010). In support of this view, Reiss and colleagues (1986) found that people with agoraphobia scored high on the Anxiety Sensitivity Inventory (ASI), which measures the degree to which individuals "fear" their physiological reactions.

Etiology of Phobias

How do such strong and "irrational" fears develop? As we indicated at the beginning of the chapter, in most cases, predisposing genetic factors interact with psychological, social, and sociocultural influences. In this section, we examine the factors related to the etiology of phobias, as shown in Figure 5.5.

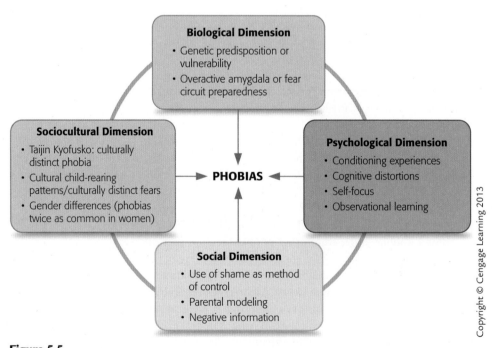

Figure 5.5

MULTIPATH MODEL OF PHOBIAS

The dimensions interact with one another and combine in different ways to result in a phobia.

agoraphobia an intense fear of being in public places where escape or help may not be readily available

Biological Dimension

Studies on male and female twin pairs have supported a moderate genetic contribution (heritability of 31 percent) for all phobia subtypes (Hettema et al., 2003; Kendler & Prescott, 2006). Individuals with phobias may have an innate tendency to be anxious and respond more strongly to emotional stimuli; thus their chances of developing an irrational fear response are increased. Exaggerated responsiveness of the amygdala and other structures in the fear network may make an individual more susceptible to developing a phobia (Sehlmeyer et al., 2010). Neuroimaging studies have confirmed that individuals with phobias show increased activation within the fear network (medial prefrontal cortex, amygdala, and thalamus) in reaction to phobic-related stimuli (Schweckendiek et al., 2011).

A different biological view of the development of fear reactions is that of *preparedness.* Proponents of this position argue that fears do not develop randomly. In particular, they believe that it is easier for humans to develop fears to which we are physiologically predisposed, such as fear of heights or snakes. Such quickly aroused (or "prepared") fears may have been necessary to the survival of pretechnological humanity. In fact, evolutionarily prepared fears (e.g., fear of fire or deep water) occur even without exposure to traumatic conditioning experiences (Forsyth, Eifert, & Thompson, 1996; Muhlberger et al., 2006; Seligman, 1971). In one study, participants were able to detect fear-relevant stimuli (spiders and snakes) more quickly than neutral stimuli (mushrooms) against a background of fruits. This may demonstrate greater innate attentional efficiency for fear-relevant stimuli (Soares, Esteves, Lindqvist, & Ohman, 2009). Macaque monkeys also appear to show an evolutionarily predisposed visual system that rapidly detects pictures of snake stimuli (Shibasaki & Kawai, 2009).

Although preparedness is an interesting theory, it is hard to believe that most phobias stem from prepared fears. Many simply do not fit into the prepared-fear model. It would be difficult, for example, to explain the survival value of social phobias such as fear of using public restrooms or of eating in public, as well as many of the other specific phobias. In addition, prepared fears are relatively easy to eliminate.

Psychological Dimension

There are multiple psychological pathways involved in the development of phobias: (1) fear conditioning, (2) observational learning or modeling, (3) negative informational effects, and (4) cognitive processes. The pathway involved often depends on the specific type of phobia. For example, modeling seems to be more important in spider phobia, whereas direct conditioning plays a major role in blood or injection phobia (Coelho & Purkis, 2009).

Did You Know?

- 3.5 percent of Americans have a severe injection phobia.

- 50 percent of individuals who use medications that require self-injections are unable to perform the injections.

- Those with an injection phobia fear pain or have unrealistic thoughts such as "the needle might break off."

Source: Mohr, Cox, & Merluzzi, (2005)

CONTROVERSY

Fear or Disgust?

Do phobias such as fears of spiders and rats result from disgust evoked rather than a threat of physical danger? Some researchers (Davey et al., 1998; de Jong, Vorage, & van den Hout, 2000; Oaten, Stevenson, & Case, 2009) point out that spiders and rats are, in general, harmless. These researchers attribute the avoidance reaction to an inherent or "prepared" fear of disease or contamination, not to a threat of physical danger. In an experiment to determine whether disgust is involved in spider phobia, Mulkens, de Jong, and Merckelbach (1996) had women with and without spider phobias indicate their willingness to eat a cookie that a "medium sized" spider (*Tegenaria atrica*) had walked across. The researchers reasoned that if disgust is a factor, those with a spider phobia should be more reluctant to eat the "contaminated" cookie. Results supported this idea: Only 25 percent of women with spider phobia eventually ate some of the cookie, compared with 70 percent of the control group participants.

For Further Consideration:

1. Other insects, such as cockroaches, maggots, and slugs, can also elicit disgust. Does the avoidance of spiders and snakes stem from fear, disgust, or both?
2. How would you design an experiment to test this question?

Classical Conditioning Perspective   The view that phobias are conditioned fear responses evolved from psychologist John Watson's classic conditioning experiment with an infant, Little Albert. Watson caused Little Albert to develop a fear of white rats by pairing a white rat with a loud sound (Watson & Rayner, 1920/2000), demonstrating that fears can result through an association process. Similarly, conditioning occurred when women undergoing chemotherapy for breast cancer were given lemon-lime Kool-Aid in a container with a bright orange lid. After repeated pairings of the drink and the chemotherapy, the women indicated emotional distress and nausea when presented with the container (Jacobsen et al., 1995). There is increasing evidence that emotional reactions can be conditioned through enhanced activation of the fear network involving the amygdala and the medial prefrontal cortex (Schweckendiek et al., 2011).

Many children with severe phobias report conditioning experiences as the cause (King, Clowes-Hollins, & Ollendick, 1997; King, Eleonora, & Ollendick, 1998). Similarly, more adults attribute their phobias to direct (classical) conditioning experiences than to any other factor (Öst, 1987; Öst & Hugdahl, 1981). Öst and Hugdahl (1981) found that the phobia most likely to be attributed to direct conditioning experiences is agoraphobia, followed by claustrophobia and dental phobia. However, a substantial number of individuals with phobias report something other than a direct conditioning experience as the "key" to their phobias.

Observational Learning, or Modeling, Perspective   Fears can develop through observational learning. Participants watched a video of a male involved in a fear conditioning experiment. The video displayed an uncomfortable shock being delivered to the man's wrist in response to a stimulus. The observers were told that they would participate in a similar experiment after viewing the video. When they were shown the same stimulus that had been associated with the shock, the participants responded with fear. Neuroimaging scans of the participants during the conditioning experiment showed activation of the amygdala when participants saw the stimulus (Olsson, Nearing, & Phelps, 2007).

Fear responses in children can result from the observation of fear displayed by others either in real life or in mass media. In a study (Burstein & Ginsburg, 2010) parents of children aged eight to twelve were trained to either act anxiously or in a relaxed manner before their child took a spelling test. Children exposed to an anxious-acting parent reported higher anxiety levels, more anxious thoughts, and a greater avoidance of the spelling test as opposed to those in the relaxed parent condition. Watching peers who showed either calm or anxious behaviors in interacting with a novel animal also influenced how much fear children displayed when asked to interact with the animal (Broeren, Lester, Muris, & Field, 2011). Thus, it appears that observational learning can play a role in the development of fear.

Negative Information Perspective   Can information cause someone to fear an object or situation? To determine this, parents were given varying descriptions regarding an unfamiliar animal (a cuscus), including negative (has long teeth, can jump at your throat, has sharp claws); ambiguous (has white teeth, can jump, likes to drink all sorts of things); or positive (has nice tiny teeth, eats tasty strawberries, likes to play with other animals) descriptors. Using this information, the parents then described to their children how the cuscus might behave in certain situations. Children whose parents received the negative description reacted with more fear to the cuscus (Muris, van Zwol, Huijding, & Mayer, 2010) than those receiving positive or ambiguous information. Similarly, toddlers who were given negative information about novel toys showed greater avoidance of the toys (Askew, Kessock-Philip, & Field, 2008). Thus, fears can be induced through negative or threatening information. Many children (73.3 percent) attributed their fears to negative information acquired from sources such as television (Muris et al., 2001). However, it is still not clear whether negative information is sufficient to produce a phobia.

Cognitive-Behavioral Perspective   Why do individuals with spider phobia react with such terror at the sight of a spider? Some researchers believe threat appraisal, cognitive distortions, and catastrophic thoughts may cause strong fears to develop (Rinck & Becker, 2006). For example, people with spider phobia believe that spiders single them out for attack and that moving spiders are coming rapidly and aggressively toward them (Riskind, Moore, & Bowley, 1995). Others report thoughts such as the spider "will attack" or "will take revenge" (Mulkens, de Jong, & Merckelbach, 1996). Similar negative thoughts, such as "I will be trapped," "I will suffocate," or "I will lose control," have been reported by individuals with claustrophobia.

Negative cognitions involving attentional bias have been found to play a role in phobias (Schmidt, Richey, Buckner, & Timpano, 2009). Individuals with social phobia believe they are being scrutinized by others and think, "Everyone in the room is watching me. I know I am going to do something stupid!" They tend to endorse negative interpretations of potentially threatening social situations. When ten- and eleven-year-old children with high social anxiety were asked questions involving ambiguous social situations such as the following, they often chose the negative interpretation.

> During arts education, you ask your fellow student for one of his/her crayons, but he/she refused. What would you think if this was happening to you?
>
> **(a)** He/she dislikes me (negative interpretation)
> **(b)** He/she needs the crayon to finish his/her drawing (benign interpretation)
>   Source: Vassilopoulos, Banerjee, & Prantzalou, (2009, p. 1086)

The tendency to endorse negative interpretations of ambiguous social events was reduced after the children were trained to reflect on how benign interpretations might be the most accurate.

Social Dimension

Family interaction patterns are also related to the development of anxiety disorders. Behavioral inhibition (shyness) and family process variables were measured in a sample of 242 boys and girls at age three and again four years later. Anxiety symptoms were predicted both by early negative family affect and family stress in middle childhood (Schmidt, Richey, Buckner, & Timpano, 2009). A punitive maternal parenting style (based on child report) has been linked with increased tendency to have fearful beliefs (Field, Ball, Kawycz, & Moore, 2007). Victimization by peers during childhood is also associated with increased social anxiety (McCabe, Miller, Laugesen, Antony & Young, 2010).

Sociocultural Dimension

Females are more likely to have a phobia, with the difference showing up as early as nine years of age. However, this difference is found mainly for repulsive animals such as snakes rather than harmless animals such as dogs. Fewer gender differences exist for fears of bodily injury, social fears, or fears of enclosed spaces. Such differences may be due to biological factors, temperamental factors, or social norms and values (McLean & Anderson, 2009). Some of the gender differences in phobias may be due to the fact that women show a stronger disgust response than men and some phobic objects produce both fear and disgust responses (Rohrmann, Hopp, & Quirin, 2008).

Social phobias appear to be more common in families who use shame as a method of control and who stress the importance of the opinions of others (Bruch & Heimberg, 1994). These are common child-rearing practices in Asian families; fear of being evaluated by others is more common in Chinese children and adolescents than in Western comparison groups (Dong, Yang, & Ollendick, 1994). Asian American undergraduate students score higher on measures of social anxiety compared with white undergraduate students (Okazaki et al., 2002). Additionally, in a study of eighty-six American Indian adolescents, self-reports of social anxiety were higher than those reported in other adolescent samples (West & Newman, 2007). It is likely that experiences with discrimination and prejudice also contribute to social anxiety.

It is important to note that social fears and other anxiety disorders may be expressed differently in other cultures. *Taijin kyofusho*, for instance, is a culturally distinctive phobia found in Japan that is similar to social phobia. However, instead of a fear involving social or performance situations, *taijin kyofusho* is a fear of offending or embarrassing others, a concept consistent with the Japanese cultural emphasis on maintaining interpersonal harmony (Okazaki, 1997; Suzuki et al., 2003). Individuals with this disorder are fearful that their appearance, facial expression, eye contact, body parts, or body odor are offensive to others. In DSM-5, fear of offending others was added to the description of social phobia for more cross-cultural relevance (DSM-5 Work Group, 2011).

Treatment of Phobias

For all anxiety disorders, it is first important to rule out possible medical or physical causes of anxiety symptoms such as hyper- or hypothyroidism, temporal-lobe epilepsy, asthma, cardiac arrhythmias, effects of stimulants (e.g., excessive intake of caffeine), or withdrawal from alcohol (Katon, 2006). Phobias have been successfully treated by both behavioral methods and medication (Kpszychi, Taljaard, Segal, & Bradwejn, 2011).

Biochemical Treatments

Biochemical treatments are predicated on the view that anxiety disorders involve neurobiological abnormalities that can be normalized with medication. The most commonly identified neurotransmitters thought to be involved in anxiety reactions are norepinephrine, serotonin, and dopamine. In treating phobias, a number of medications appear to be effective. For social phobia, both benzodiazepines (a class of antianxiety medication) and the antidepressant selective serotonin reuptake inhibitors (SSRIs) have shown evidence of efficacy, and benzodiazepines have been used with some success in treating specific phobias (Lader & Bond, 1998; Otto et al., 2010). As with most medications, side effects can occur. Benzodiazepines can produce dependence, withdrawal symptoms, and paradoxical reactions such as increased talkativeness, excessive movement, and even hostility and rage (Mancuso, Tanzi, & Gabay, 2004). In addition, symptoms often recur when the medication is discontinued (Sundel & Sundel, 1998). Although antidepressants also have side effects, they can help reduce not only the extreme fear but also the depression that often accompanies anxiety disorders.

Behavioral Treatments

Phobias have also been successfully treated with a variety of behavioral approaches. These approaches include:

- Exposure therapy: gradually introducing the individual to the feared situation or object until the fear dissipates.
- Systematic desensitization: similar to exposure but with an additional response, such as relaxation, to help combat anxiety.
- Cognitive restructuring: identifying and changing irrational or anxiety-arousing thoughts associated with the phobia.
- Modeling therapy: demonstration of another person's successful interactions with the feared object or situation.

Most behavioral treatments combine several techniques (Lipsitz, 2006).

Exposure Therapy   In exposure therapy, treatment involves gradual and increasingly difficult encounters with a feared situation. For example, when treating fear of leaving the house, a therapist may first ask the client to visualize or imagine the anxiety-evoking situation. Eventually, the client might walk outside the home with the therapist until the fear has been eliminated. Exposure therapy has been used successfully to treat social phobia (Schneier, 2006), agoraphobia (Vogele et al., 2010), speech anxiety (Hofmann et al., 2004), fear of spiders (Muris, Merckelbach, & de Jong, 1995; Carlin, Hoffman,

exposure therapy   treatment that involves gradually introducing the client to increasingly difficult encounters with a feared situation

& Weghorst, 1997), claustrophobia (Booth & Rachman, 1992), fear of flying (Rothbaum et al., 1996), and fear of heights (Meyerbroker & Emmelkamp, 2010).

A variant of exposure therapy has been developed for the treatment of the fainting and drop in blood pressure associated with blood-injection phobia. A procedure known as *applied tension* (described in the following case), combined with exposure, has proven effective (Hellstrom, Fellenius, & Öst, 1996).

Case Study

Mr. A. reported feeling faint when exposed to any stimuli involving blood, injections, injury, or surgery. Even hearing an instructor discuss the physiology of the heart caused Mr. A. to feel sweaty and faint. Mr. A. was taught to recognize the first signs of a drop in blood pressure and then to combat this autonomic response by tightening (tensing) the muscles of his arms, chest, and legs until his face felt warm. Mr. A. was then taught to stop the tension for about fifteen to twenty seconds and then to reapply the tension, repeating the procedure about five times. (The rise in blood pressure that follows this process prevents fainting, and the fear becomes extinguished.) After going through this process, Mr. A. was able to watch a video of thoracic surgery, watch blood being drawn, listen to a talk about cardiovascular disease, and read an anatomy book—stimuli that in the past would have produced fainting (Anderson, Taylor, & McLean, 1996). This muscle tension procedure is used only for phobias in which fainting may occur.

Systematic Desensitization   Systematic desensitization uses muscle relaxation to reduce the anxiety associated with phobias. Wolpe (1958, 1973), who developed the treatment, first taught clients to relax their muscles. Second, he had them visualize feared stimuli (arranged from least to most anxiety provoking) while in the relaxed state. This was continued until the clients reported little or no anxiety with the stimuli. This procedure was adapted for a man who had a fear of urinating in restrooms when others were present. He was trained in muscle relaxation and, while relaxed, learned to urinate under the following conditions: no one in the bathroom, therapist in the stall, therapist washing hands, therapist at adjacent urinal, therapist waiting behind client. These conditions were arranged in ascending difficulty. The easier items were practiced first until anxiety was sufficiently reduced (McCracken & Larkin, 1991).

Cognitive Restructuring   In cognitive restructuring, unrealistic thoughts believed to be responsible for phobias are altered (Kendall, Khanna, Edson, Cummings, & Harris, 2011). Individuals with social phobias, for example, tend to be intensely self-focused and fearful that others will see them as anxious, incompetent, or weak. Their own self-criticism is the basis for their phobia (Britton, Lissek, Grillon, Norcross, & Pine, 2011; Hofmann, 2000; Taylor & Alden, 2010). Cognitive strategies can help "normalize" social anxiety by encouraging individuals to interpret emotional and physical tension as "normal anxiety" and by helping them redirect their attention away from themselves in social situations. This approach has been successful in treating individuals with public-speaking phobia; as self-focus decreased so did speech anxiety (Woody, Chambless, & Glass, 1997). Claustrophobic individuals have also been successfully treated by identifying specific beliefs about danger and assessing their accuracy while in an enclosed chamber (Kamphuis & Telch, 2000; Öst et al., 2001).

Modeling Therapy   In modeling therapy, the individual with the phobia observes a model (either in a visual portrayal or in person) coping with, or responding appropriately

systematic desensitization exposure strategy that uses muscle relaxation to reduce the anxiety associated with specific and social phobias

cognitive restructuring cognitive strategy that attempts to alter unrealistic thoughts that are believed to be responsible for phobias

modeling therapy procedures (including filmed modeling, live modeling, and participant modeling) that are used to treat certain phobias

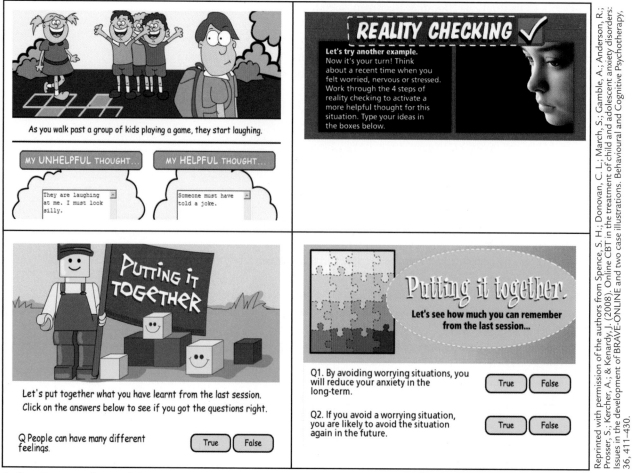

Reprinted with permission of the authors from Spence, S. H.; Donovan, C. L.; March, S.; Gamble, A.; Anderson, R.; Prosser, S.; Kercher, A.; & Kenardy, J. (2008). Online CBT in the treatment of child and adolescent anxiety disorders: Issues in the development of BRAVE-ONLINE and two case illustrations. Behavioural and Cognitive Psychotherapy, 36, 411–430.

Online Program for Social Anxiety

Pictured are sample items from a computerized treatment program dealing with social phobia in adolescents.

in, the fear-producing situation. The individual with the phobia may be asked to repeat the model's interactions with the phobic object (Kelly, Barker, Field, Wilson, & Reynolds, 2010; Ollendick et al., 2009). Ninety-seven children saw a positive or negative modeling film in which a peer interacted with an unfamiliar animal. After watching positive peer modeling, the children's fear toward the animal decreased significantly (Broeren, Lester, Muris, & Field, 2011). Some believe that modeling is a unique therapeutic approach in its own right, whereas others believe that it is a type of exposure treatment.

Panic Disorder

Case Study

For me, a panic attack is almost a violent experience. . . . My heart pounds really hard, I feel like I can't get my breath and there's an overwhelming feeling that things are crashing in on me. . . . In between attacks, there is this dread and anxiety that it's going to happen again. I'm afraid to go back to places where I've had an attack. Unless I get help, there soon won't be any place where I can go and feel safe from panic. (NIMH, 2009a, p. 3)

Jeff Greenberg/Photo Edit

Modeling

Watching a fear-producing act being performed successfully can help people overcome their fear. In this photo, a friend exposes a reluctant teen to a python. Modeling is effective in treating both specific and social phobias. Why do you think modeling works?

Earlier, we defined *panic attacks* as intense fear accompanied by symptoms such as a pounding heart, trembling, shortness of breath, or fear of losing control or dying. A diagnosis of **panic disorder** involves recurrent unexpected panic attacks in combination with (1) apprehension over having another attack or worrying about the consequences of an attack (e.g., feeling a loss of control or inability to breathe) or (2) changes in behavior or activities designed to avoid another panic attack, such as avoiding situations. These reactions must be present for a period of one month or more (American Psychiatric Association, 2011). The attacks are especially feared because they often occur unpredictably and without warning. Three types of panic attacks are recognized: (1) *situationally bound* attacks, which occur before or during exposure to a feared stimulus; (2) *situationally predisposed* attacks, which sometimes, but not always, occur when encountering the feared situation (e.g., people who have a fear of crowds may not always have a panic attack when in a group situation; (3) *unexpected* or *uncued* attacks, which occur "spontaneously" and without warning (American Psychiatric Association, 2011). An individual with panic disorder may have all of these types of panic attacks.

Panic attacks often begin in late adolescence or early adulthood (NIMH, 2009a). Although panic disorder is diagnosed in only a small percentage of individuals, panic attacks appear to be fairly common. Approximately 40 percent of the general population experience panic attack symptoms sometime in their lifetime. The twelve-month prevalence rate for panic disorder is 2.7 percent (Kessler, Chiu et al., 2005); it is twice as common in women as in men (NIMH, 2009a). Among postmenopausal women, 18 percent reported a panic attack within a six month period (Smoller et al., 2003). During the attacks, people report a variety of physical symptoms, such as breathlessness, sweating, choking, nausea, and heart palpitations. Many go to emergency departments with complaints of chest pain (Fleet et al., 2003). Those who have more recurrent panic symptoms tend to have comorbid depression, generalized anxiety, or substance abuse (Bystritsky et al., 2010). Many individuals diagnosed with a panic disorder also have agoraphobia, caused by fear of having a panic episode in a public place.

Etiology of Panic Disorder

As with the other disorders we have discussed so far, biological, psychological, social, and sociocultural factors and their interactions play a role in the etiology of panic disorder, as shown in Figure 5.6.

Scala/White Images/Art Resource, NY

***The Scream,* by Edvard Munch**

The Norwegian painter describes the scene this way: "I was walking along the road with two friends. The sun set. I felt a touch of melancholy. Suddenly the sky became a blood red. I stopped, leaned against a railing, dead tired (my friends looked at me and walked on), and I looked at the flaming clouds that hung like blood and a sword . . . over the blue-black fjord and the city. My friends walked on. I stood there trembling with fright. And I felt a loud unending scream piercing nature." (Harris, 2004, p. 15)

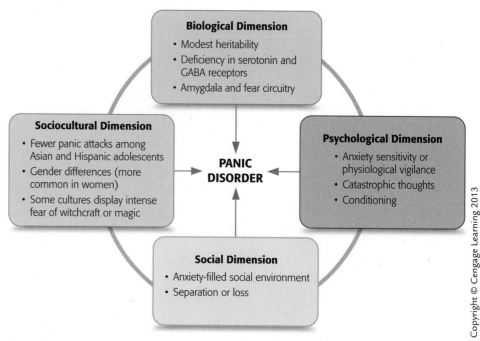

Figure 5.6

MULTIPATH MODEL FOR PANIC DISORDER

The dimensions interact with one another and combine in different ways to result in a panic disorder.

Biological Dimension

Higher concordance rates (i.e., percentages of relatives sharing the same disorder) for panic disorder have been found in monozygotic (identical) twins than in dizygotic (fraternal) twins; heritability is estimated to be about 32 percent, which is considered a modest contribution (Kendler & Prescott, 2006). Research has also been directed at identifying specific gene × environment interactions, neural structures, and a neurochemical basis for panic disorder (Klauke, Deckert, Reif, Pauli, & Domschke, 2010).

As we mentioned earlier, brain structures (such as the amygdala) are involved in anxiety disorders (including panic disorder), and neurotransmitters (such as serotonin) play an important role in emotions. Some studies have linked anxiety and fear with a reduction in GABA receptors in the hippocampus and amygdala (Roy-Byrne, Craske, & Stein, 2006). Additionally, disturbances or abnormalities in a serotonin receptor gene (5-HT1A) may contribute to panic disorder (Klauke, Deckert, Reif, Pauli, & Domschke, 2010; Nash et al., 2008). Neuroimaging has revealed that individuals with panic disorder have nearly one-third fewer serotonin 5-HT1A receptors than controls (Neumeister et al., 2004); this results in decreased availability of serotonin. It is interesting to note that SSRIs, medications designed to increase levels of serotonin in the brain, are effective in treating panic disorders, as well as other anxiety disorders. Women diagnosed with panic disorder report more severe premenstrual symptoms, so it is also possible that premenstrual hormonal fluctuations contribute to panic disorder in women (Nillni, Rohan, Bernstein, & Zvolensky, 2010).

Did You Know?

The word *panic* originates from Greek mythology. Pan was a Greek demigod who lived in isolated forests. He amused himself by making noises while following travelers who were traveling at night through the woods. He would continue to frighten them until they bolted in *panic.*

Psychological Dimension

Certain psychological characteristics have been associated with panic disorders. Individuals with panic disorder score high on anxiety sensitivity measures assessing fear responses to bodily sensations (Schmidt et al., 2010). They display *interoceptive sensitivity,* which is vigilance over changes in the physiological condition of the body such as heart rate, blood pressure, and respiration. When physical bodily changes are detected, anxiety increases, resulting in even greater physiological responses and more anxiety; this cycle often culminates in a panic attack (Domschke, Stevens, Pfleiderer, & Gerlach, 2010). It is possible that physiological sensitivity is learned by watching parents or friends express fears about physical sensations or witnessing a traumatic event such as a heart attack (Schmidt et al., 2010; Schmidt, Lerew, & Jackson, 1997).

Cognitive Behavioral Perspective   The cognitive-behavioral model attributes panic attacks to the individual's interpretation of unpleasant bodily sensations as indicators of an impending disaster. Cognitions and somatic symptoms can best be viewed as a positive feedback loop that results in increasingly higher levels of anxiety. The following pattern may lead to the development of a panic disorder (Roy-Byrne, Craske, & Stein, 2006; Rudaz, Craske, Becker, Ledermann, & Margraf, 2010):

1. A physiological change occurs, such as faster breathing or increased heart rate due to a precipitant (e.g., exercise, excitement, hypervigilance, a stressor).
2. Catastrophic thoughts develop, such as "Something is wrong," "I'm having a heart attack," or "I'm going to die."
3. These thoughts result in increased apprehension and fear and even more physiological changes in the body.
4. A circular pattern develops as the amplified bodily changes now result in even more fearful thoughts.
5. Through classical conditioning, the pairing of changes in internal bodily sensations (e.g., increases in heart rate, respiration, muscle tension) with fear results in *interoceptive conditioning*—that is, the perception of bodily changes can now automatically produce fear and lead to panic attacks.

Some research supports the cognitive hypothesis. Anxiety-producing cognitions (such as thoughts of dying, passing out, or acting foolishly) have been found to precede or accompany panic attacks (Bakker et al., 2002; Schmidt, Lerew, & Trakowski, 1997; Whittal & Goetsch, 1995). Also, a reduction in panic-related cognitions (as a result of cognitive-behavioral therapy) is associated with a subsequent reduction in panic symptoms (Hoffman et al., 2007; Teachman, Marker, & Clerkin, 2010).

Social and Sociocultural Dimensions

Many individuals with panic disorder report a stressful childhood involving separation anxiety, family conflicts, school problems, or the loss of a loved one (Klauke, Deckert, Reif, Pauli, & Domschke, 2010; Mahoney, 2000). Such environmental stressors may create a predisposition to developing anxiety reactions and subsequently a panic disorder. Some individuals with panic attacks report facing major life changes just before the attacks began (Pollard, Pollard, & Corn, 1989).

Did You Know?

Examples of Catastrophic Thoughts in Panic Disorder

Physical	Mental	Social
"I will die"	"I will go crazy"	"People will think I'm crazy or weird"
"I will have a heart attack"	"I will become hysterical"	"People will laugh at me"
"I will suffocate"	"I will uncontrollably try to escape"	"People will stare at me"
"I will pass out"		

Source: Hicks et al., (2005)

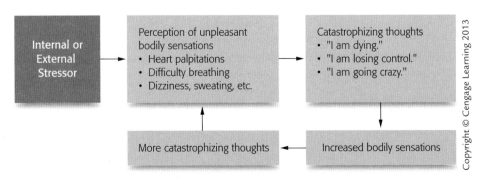

Figure 5.7

Positive feedback loop between cognitions and somatic symptoms leading to panic attacks.
Source: Roy-Byrne, Craske, & Stein, (2006, p. 1027)

Copyright © Cengage Learning 2013

Culture can also play a role in panic disorder. Asian and Hispanic adolescents reported higher anxiety sensitivity than white adolescents but were less likely to have panic attacks. This may be due to cultural differences in the way Asian and Hispanic adolescents interpret anxiety or bodily symptoms (Weems et al., 2002). Symptoms differences are also found in India, where panic attacks are associated with physiological symptoms such as tachycardia and shortness of breath more than with thoughts of losing control or of going crazy (Neerakal & Srinivasan, 2003).

Treatment of Panic Disorder

Both medication and cognitive-behavioral therapies have been effective in treating panic disorder (Hicks et al., 2005). With either therapy, it is important to give clients information about panic disorders to counteract beliefs that they have a serious physical condition or might die.

Biochemical Treatment

A number of different classes of medications have been used successfully to treat panic disorder. Benzodiazepines are sometimes used, although they are less effective with panic episodes than with other anxiety disorders (Roy-Byrne, Craske, & Stein, 2006). Panic disorder also has been treated with tricyclic antidepressants (TCAs) and SSRIs; the older antidepressants, TCAs, are effective but have more side effects than the SSRIs (Marcus et al., 2007). It usually takes four to eight weeks for the medications to become fully effective, and some individuals may initially have more panic attacks than usual during the first few weeks. Relapse rates after cessation of drug therapy appear to be quite high, especially among clients who believe that the remission of symptoms was due to the medication (Biondi et al., 2003).

Cognitive-Behavioral Treatment

Cognitive-behavioral treatments (CBT) have been successful in treating panic disorder (Barlow, Gorman, Shear, & Woods, 2000; Roy-Byrne et al., 2010). In several studies, 80 percent or more of those treated with CBT achieved and maintained panic-free status (Fava et al., 1995; Margraf et al., 1993). Along with the reduction or elimination of panic symptoms, CBT has been found to improve the quality of life of individuals with panic disorder (Marchand, Roberge, Primiano, & Germain, 2009). Cognitive-behavioral treatment involves extinction of fear associated with both internal bodily sensations (e.g., heart rate, sweating, dizziness, breathlessness) and environmental situations associated with fear, such as being in crowds or in unfamiliar areas. Catastrophic thoughts are also identified and changed with corrective information (Hoffman et al., 2007). In general, cognitive-behavioral treatment for panic disorder involves the following steps (Hicks et al., 2005; Pincus, May, Whitton, Mattis, & Barlow, 2010; Roy-Byrne, Craske, & Stein, 2006):

1. Educating the client about panic disorder and correcting misconceptions regarding the symptoms.
2. Identifying and correcting catastrophic thinking. For example, the therapist might comment, "Maybe you are overreacting to what is going on in your body," or "A panic attack will not stop your breathing."
3. Teaching the client to self-induce physiological symptoms associated with panic (such as hyperventilating or breathing through a straw) in order to extinguish panic reactions in response to bodily cues or sensations.
4. Encouraging the client to face the symptoms, both within the session and in the outside world, using statements such as, "Allow your body to have its reactions and let the reactions pass."
5. Teaching coping statements such as, "This feeling is not pleasant, but I can handle it."
6. Helping the client to identify the antecedents of the panic: "What stresses are you under?"

MYTH: Because brain activity associated with anxiety disorders can be "normalized" with medication, biological explanations and treatments provide the best alternatives for treatment.

REALITY: Psychotherapy is highly effective with anxiety disorders and may also affect brain metabolism. Medications appear to temporarily affect the fear network at the level of the amygdala, whereas cognitive-behavioral therapy leads to changes in the prefrontal cortex and hippocampus.

MYTH VS. REALITY

Panic Disorder Treatment: Should We Focus on Internal Control?

CRITICAL THINKING

Imagine standing in the middle of a busy mall when suddenly your heart starts to pound and you begin to sweat. Soon, you feel nauseated, disoriented, and can barely breathe. You fear you are going to either pass out or die. What is happening to you? What brought on this terrifying experience? Will it happen again? When you regain your composure, you think about what has just happened. You may decide to explore treatment options. If so, what treatment techniques will you choose? Consider the following studies.

Abraham Bakker and his colleagues (2002) compared outcomes of two groups of individuals with panic disorder. One group was treated with cognitive-behavioral therapy (CBT)—a therapy that encouraged clients to accept personal control over their panic reactions. The other group was treated with antidepressant medications without psychotherapy. Clients in the CBT group had lower relapse rates than those treated pharmacologically, perhaps because those in the CBT group learned to view their symptoms *and* their gains as the result of their own efforts, not as a matter of luck, therapy, or medication.

Biondi and colleagues (2003) compared medication alone with a combination of medication and CBT. The CBT strategies included sharing information about panic disorders, challenging catastrophic misinterpretations, considering alternative explanations for bodily sensations, practicing relaxation strategies, exposing clients to feared situations, and understanding the implications of having a panic disorder. Before, during, and at the end of treatment, the researchers assessed participants' beliefs concerning what accounted for their recovery. After the treatment, relapse rate was 78.1 percent for those in the medication group compared with 14.3 percent for the CBT group. Long-term outcomes were found to be significantly better for those who attributed their anxiety and recovery to internal factors compared with those who credited their improvement to medication.

A common factor in both cognitive-behavioral approaches was the enhancement of self-efficacy—a belief that both recovery and ability to manage anxiety were under personal control. Individuals who believe (or who come to believe) that success is up to them are significantly more likely to reduce anxiety symptoms than those who attribute their improvement to external factors, such as medication.

Do you attribute anxiety in your life to internal factors (e.g., "I must be making myself anxious") or to external elements (e.g., "Things like this always happen to me")? Do you believe that most individuals with panic disorder feel they are in control when it comes to understanding and dealing with anxiety-provoking events? Based on these studies, how would you structure an intervention for panic disorder?

■ Generalized Anxiety Disorder

Case Study

Lana, age 12, has worried about many things over the past year, including what will happen if her mother gets sick, if their parents cannot afford their house, or if she fails a math test. She has trouble concentrating and becomes easily fatigued. Usually, if she starts worrying about one issue, she starts thinking about others, and often seeks reassurance from her mother. (Rynn et al., 2011, p. 77)

All of us have had concerns or worries that are specific and time limited. Generalized anxiety disorder (GAD), however, is characterized by persistent, high levels of anxiety and excessive worry over many life circumstances; diagnosis requires that symptoms be present on the majority of days for at least three months and be accompanied by physical or somatic symptoms. Worry appears to be the defining characteristic of GAD, and some believe a better term for this disorder would be "pathological worry behavior" (Andrews et al., 2010). Vigilance for possible threats and future catastrophes is often present, and the worrying often shifts to different concerns depending on current life stressors (Stapinski, Abbott, & Rapee, 2010). The worry produces symptoms such as "feeling on edge," muscle tension, restlessness, sleep difficulties, poor concentration, avoidance of situations associated with the worry, and repeatedly seeking reassurance concerning the worry. GAD develops gradually, often beginning in childhood or adolescence (Rynn et al., 2011; NIMH, 2009a). Individuals with GAD report higher anxiety levels, are more sensitive to bodily changes, and exhibit greater physiological responsiveness than control participants (Hoehn-Saric et al., 2004). Interestingly, most undergraduates believe that GAD symptoms are just a reaction to life stressors and not signs of a mental disorder (Coles & Coleman, 2010).

More than two-thirds of people with GAD have comorbid (co-occurring) disorders such as depression, substance abuse, or phobia (Stein, 2001). In any given year, about 3.1 percent of the adult U.S. population has GAD (Kessler, Chiu et al., 2005); women are twice as likely to receive this diagnosis as men (Kessler, Berglund et al., 2005). In medical settings around the world, GAD is the most frequently diagnosed anxiety disorder (Goldberg, 1996; Stein, 2001). Because cultures differ in their expressions of worry and anxiety, the cultural context has to be considered when assessing anxiety symptoms (American Psychiatric Association, 2011).

Etiology of Generalized Anxiety Disorder

GAD is the result of biological factors combined with psychosocial stressors, as shown in Figure 5.8. Let's take a look at each of the factors that may contribute to the etiology of GAD.

Biological Dimension

There appears to be less support for the role of genetic factors in GAD than in panic disorder. Still, heritability appears to play a small but significant role in GAD (Gorman, 2001; Kendler & Prescott, 2006). Twin studies indicate a modest contribution of genetic influence (Ehringer et al., 2006). Genes may be expressed in terms of abnormalities with the GABA receptors, other neurotransmitter abnormalities, or overactivity of the anxiety circuit in the brain.

As mentioned earlier, the prefrontal cortex can modulate the response of the amygdala to threatening situations. GAD may involve a disruption in this system. In an MRI investigation, Monk and colleagues (2006) exposed eighteen adolescents with GAD and fifteen without GAD to angry faces. Those with GAD showed greater activation of the prefrontal cortex in response to angry faces. The researchers hypothesize that the prefrontal cortex may be attempting to regulate the anxiety aroused by the angry faces.

Did You Know?

In a two-year study of adolescents with GAD or social phobia, it was found:

- GAD (but not social phobia) was associated with increased frequency of underage drinking.

- GAD symptoms preceded alcohol and cannabis use.

- Adolescents with social phobia used less alcohol and cannabis compared to those with GAD or no anxiety disorder.

Source: Frojd, Ranta, Kaltiala-Heino, & Marttunen, (2011)

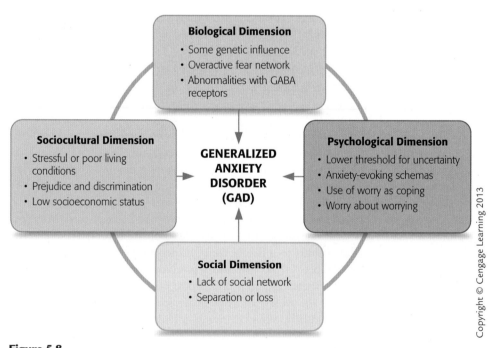

Figure 5.8

MULTIPATH MODEL FOR GENERALIZED ANXIETY DISORDER (GAD)
The dimensions interact with one another and combine in different ways to result in generalized anxiety disorder (GAD).

Psychological Dimension

Cognitive theories emphasize the importance of dysfunctional thinking and beliefs. Individuals with GAD have a lower threshold for uncertainty, which leads to worrying. They have erroneous beliefs regarding worry and assume that "worry is an effective way to deal with problems" or that it prevents some type of negative outcome from occurring (Ladouceur et al., 2000). Beck (1985) believes that anxiety disorders involve dysfunctional mental structures or schemas that result from a combination of temperament and negative early learning. Schemas may involve beliefs such as, "I am incompetent" or "The world is dangerous." The individual interprets events through the filter of the schema so that ambiguous or even positive situations are viewed with concern and apprehension.

Cognitive approaches built on the work of Beck focus on the beliefs underlying the worry experienced by those with GAD (Riskind, 2005). Wells (2005, 2009) developed a theoretical model of GAD. He believes that the roots of GAD lie in beliefs regarding the function of worrying. In the model, there are two types of worry. The first involves a belief that worry has a positive, coping function; thus, it occurs frequently. However, the stress of constantly generating solutions to "what if" scenarios eventually results in a belief that worry is uncontrollable, harmful, and dangerous. GAD develops when the second type of worry ("worrying about worry") occurs. This "worrying about worry" leads to increased anxiety and thus reinforces the view that worry has negative effects. The increased anxiety results in the avoidance of situations and thoughts associated with the worries. This avoidance, in turn, prevents the individual from determining whether the worry is accurate. Without the ability to evaluate the worry, worrying is maintained and GAD develops (Ellis & Hudson, 2010; McLaughlin, Mennin, & Farach, 2007; Wells & Carter, 2001).

Social and Sociocultural Dimensions

Stressful conditions such as poverty, poor housing, prejudice, and discrimination also contribute to GAD. The disorder is twice as prevalent among those with low income (Kessler, Chiu et al., 2005). It is also seen more frequently in individuals who are separated, divorced, or widowed and in the unemployed (Wittchen & Hoyer, 2001). GAD is more common among African Americans, especially females (Horwath & Weissman, 1997). Traumatic events can contribute to anxiety. According to Silverman and La Greca (2002) and La Greca (2006), a substantial number of children exposed to trauma develop an anxiety disorder such as GAD.

Treatment of Generalized Anxiety Disorder

Benzodiazepines have been successful in treating GAD, but because it is a chronic condition, medication dependence is a concern (Nutt, 2001), particularly if there is a history of substance abuse. Tricyclic and SSRI antidepressants have been used in treating GAD and are the medications of choice because they do not have the potential of dependence associated with the benzodiazepines (Allgulander et al., 2007; Davidson, 2001; Seidel & Walkup, 2006). A newer antianxiety medication, buspirone, is also used to treat GAD. Like antidepressants, it takes at least two weeks to achieve the antianxiety effect (NIMH, 2009a).

Cognitive-behavioral therapy (CBT) is the only consistently validated psychological treatment for GAD (Ballenger et al., 2000). In an evaluation of thirteen controlled clinical trials, cognitive-behavioral strategies were not only effective in treating GAD, but also were associated with low dropout rates and long-term improvement (Borkovec & Ruscio, 2001). CBT has also been found to be effective in treating GAD in older adults (Ayers et al., 2007).

This treatment generally involves teaching clients to (Dugas & Ladouceur, 2000; Eisen & Silverman, 1998; Stanley et al., 2003):

1. Identify worrisome thoughts
2. Discriminate between worries that are amenable to problem solving and those that are not

Did You Know?

3. Evaluate beliefs concerning worry, including evidence for and against any distorted beliefs
4. Develop self-control skills to monitor and challenge irrational thoughts and substitute more positive, coping thoughts
5. Use muscle relaxation to deal with somatic symptoms

We now discuss another set of disorders characterized by persistent troublesome thoughts: obsessive-compulsive and related disorders.

Obsessive-Compulsive and Related Disorders

Case Study

Mrs. A. is a thirty-two-year-old married mother of two who has been spending increasing amounts of time (approximately 4 hours per day) cleaning and making sure everything in her house is in its perfect place. If Mrs. A. sees or hears words pertaining to death she immediately begins to repeat the Lord's Prayer in her mind 100 times. She believes that failure to perform this ritual will lead to the untimely death of her children (Greenberg, 2010).

The obsessive-compulsive and related disorders include: obsessive-compulsive disorder (illustrated in the preceding case), body dysmorphic disorder, hair-pulling disorder (trichotillomania), and skin-picking disorder (Table 5.3). These disorders are grouped together because they have similar symptoms, such as repetitive disturbing thoughts and irresistible urges, and may share the same neurobiological causes. These disorders also have much in common with anxiety disorders (Mathews & Grados, 2011; Phillips et al., 2010a, b).

Obsessive-compulsive disorder (OCD) is characterized by obsessions (intrusive, repetitive thoughts or images that produce anxiety) or compulsions (the need to perform acts or to dwell on thoughts to reduce anxiety). Although obsessions and compulsions can occur separately, they frequently occur together; in fact, only 25 percent of those with OCD report distressing obsessions without compulsive behaviors (Foa & Kozak, 1995;

DISORDERS CHART   OBSESSIVE-COMPULSIVE SPECTRUM DISORDERS

TABLE 5.3	Obsessive-Compulsive and Related Disorders	Symptoms	Gender and Cultural Factors	Age of Onset
	Obsessive-Compulsive Disorder	• Recurrent and persistent intrusive thoughts and impulses • Attempts are made to suppress the thoughts or behaviors • Thoughts or behaviors are recognized as unreasonable	Equally common in males and females. Less prevalent among African Americans, Asian Americans, and Hispanic Americans than white Americans	Usually adolescence or early adulthood
	Body Dysmorphic Disorder	• Preoccupation with imagined defects in appearance or excessive concern with slight defects if they exist	Equally common in males and females; prevalence from 5 to 15% depending on setting	Early adolescence to 20s; onset may be sudden or gradual
	Hair-Pulling Disorder	• Recurrent pulling of hair resulting in hair loss	4 times more common in females; prevalence—up to 4%	Onset usually before 17
	Skin-Picking Disorder	• Recurrent picking resulting in lesions	75% are females	Onset childhood through adulthood

Source: American Psychiatric Association, (2011); PubMed Health, (2010); Tucker, Woods, Flessner, Franklin, & Franklin, (2011)

Markarian et al., 2010). About 21 percent to 25 percent of the general population claims to have some OCD symptoms, but without the severity required to meet the diagnostic criteria for OCD (Fullana et al., 2009).

Individuals with OCD often describe the associated thoughts and actions as being out of character and not being under voluntary control. The inability to resist or rid oneself of uncontrollable, unacceptable thoughts or to refrain from performing ritualistic acts over and over again arouses intense anxiety. The majority of those with OCD recognize that their thoughts and impulses are senseless, yet they feel unable to control them (American Psychiatric Association, 2011). Failure to engage in ritual acts often results in mounting anxiety and tension. As one individual noted, "The reason I do these kinds of rituals and obsessing is that I have a fear that someone is going to die. This is not rational thinking to me. I know I can't prevent somebody from dying by putting 5 ice cubes in a glass instead of 4" (Jenike, 2001, p. 2122).

OCD may be underdiagnosed. If it is suspected, screening questions such as these may be useful: "Do you have unpleasant thoughts you can't get rid of?" "Do you worry that you might impulsively harm someone?" "Do you count things, or check things over and over?" "Do you worry a lot about whether you performed religious rituals correctly or having been immoral?" "Do you have troubling thoughts about sexual matters?" "Do you need to have things arranged symmetrically or in a very exact order?" "Do you have trouble discarding things, so that your house is quite cluttered?" (Work Group on Obsessive-Compulsive Disorder, 2007, p. 12).

Although OCD is a single diagnostic category, it is composed of distinct subtypes, some of which show different patterns of genetic inheritance, neural activity, and response to treatment. The four types identified are (Saxena, 2007):

1. Harm-related, sexual, aggressive, and/or religious obsession with checking compulsions
2. Symmetry obsessions with compulsions to arrange things or repeat behaviors
3. Contamination obsessions with cleaning compulsions
4. Hoarding and saving compulsions

In a given year, about 1 percent of the U.S. adult population has obsessive-compulsive disorder. More than half reports the severity of the disorder as "serious." Only 15 percent consider it to be "mild" (Kessler, Chiu et al., 2005). Onset usually occurs in childhood or adolescence (Yadin & Foa, 2009). Children tend to have poor insight as to the nature of their obsessions, which frequently involve themes of harm or separation (Geller, 2006). The disorder is about equally common in males and females but is less common in African Americans and Mexican Americans (Zhang & Snowden, 1999). Possibly because of the emotional distress associated with the symptoms of OCD, many with this disorder are depressed and may abuse substances (Canavera, Ollendick, May, & Pincus, 2010). Tic disorders are also common in those with OCD (Work Group on Obsessive-Compulsive Disorder, 2007). See Figure 5.9 for some examples of obsessions and compulsions.

Obsessions

As mentioned earlier, an *obsession* is an intrusive and repetitive anxiety-arousing thought or image. Common obsessions involve contamination (e.g., dirt, germs, body wastes or secretions); making errors or uncertainty (e.g., checking locks, appliances, or paperwork; obsessing over decisions); unwanted impulses (e.g., thoughts of sexual acts or harming self or others); and orderliness (e.g., striving for perfect order or symmetry) (Yadin & Foa, 2009). Contamination fears often involve anxiety about being polluted by either direct or indirect contact with the item, place, or person that is considered to be unclean or harmful (Cisler et al., 2011). The person may realize that the thought is irrational, but he or she cannot keep it from arising over and over again. To reduce the discomfort caused by obsessions, strategies such as trying to change thoughts, focusing on something positive, listening to music, taking a walk, or reading are often used (Freeston & Ladouceur, 1997). Although most of us have experienced persistent thoughts—for instance, a song or tune that keeps running through our minds—obsessions are far stronger and more intrusive.

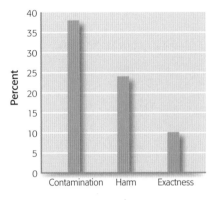

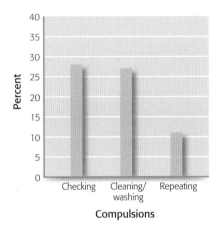

Figure 5.9

COMMON OBSESSIONS AND COMPULSIONS

About half of the clients reported both obsessions and compulsions. Twenty-five percent believed that their symptoms were reasonable. How would a therapist work with a client who believed that his or her symptoms were sensible?
Source: Data from Foa & Kozak, (1995)

obsession intrusive, repetitive thought or image that produces anxiety

compulsion the need to perform acts or to dwell on thoughts to reduce anxiety

Do "normal" people have intrusive, unacceptable thoughts and impulses? Several studies (Edwards & Dickerson, 1987; Freeston & Ladouceur, 1993; Ladouceur, Freeston et al., 2000) have found that more than 80 percent of normal samples report the existence of some unpleasant intrusive thoughts and impulses. The content of obsessions reported by those with OCD overlap considerably with thoughts reported by the general population. However, those with OCD report that their obsessions last longer, are more intense, produce more discomfort, and are more difficult to dismiss (Morillo, Belloch, & Garcia-Soriano, 2007). Intrusive thoughts may increase during times of stress. Some women with postpartum mood changes report intrusive thoughts that the baby might stop breathing or that they might scream at, slap, or drop the baby (Abramowitz et al., 2010).

Compulsions

A *compulsion* is the need to perform repetitive behaviors (e.g., handwashing, checking, ordering) or mental acts (praying, counting, repeating words silently) (American Psychiatric Association, 2011). Compulsions are often, but not always, associated with obsessions and are often performed to neutralize or counteract an obsession. Distress or anxiety occurs if the behavior is not performed or if it is not done "correctly." Mild forms include behaviors such as refusing to walk under a ladder or step on cracks in a sidewalk, throwing salt over one's shoulder, and knocking on wood. The three most common compulsions among a sample of children and adolescents (Swedo et al., 1989) involved excessive or ritualized washing, repeating rituals (such as going in and out of a door and getting up and down from a chair), and checking behaviors (doors and appliances).

Compulsions are also a common phenomenon in nonclinical populations (Muris, Merckelbach, & Clavan, 1997). A continuum appears to exist between "normal" rituals and "pathological" compulsions. In individuals with obsessive-compulsive disorder, the compulsions are more frequent and of greater intensity, and they produce more discomfort. In the severe compulsive state, the behaviors become stereotyped and rigid; if they are not performed in a certain manner or a specific number of times, the compulsive individual is flooded with anxiety. Table 5.4 contains additional examples of obsessions and compulsions.

Did You Know?

- Intrusive thoughts are common among college students.

- 50 percent of men and 42 percent of women have thoughts of hurting a family member.

- 24 percent of men and 14 percent of women have thoughts of indecently exposing themselves.

- 19 percent of men and 7 percent of women have thoughts of sex with a child or minor.

Source: Purdon & Clark, (2005)

TABLE 5.4   Clinical Examples of Obsessions and Compulsions

Client Age	Gender	Duration of Obsession in Years	Content of Obsession
21	M	6	Teeth are decaying, particles between teeth
55	F	35	Fetuses lying in the street, people buried alive
29	M	14	Shoes dirtied by dog excrement
32	F	7	Contracting AIDS

Client Age	Gender	Duration of Compulsion in Years	Content of Compulsion
42	F	17	Handwashing triggered by touching surfaces touched by other people
21	M	2	Intense fear of contamination after touching money
9	M	4	Going back and forth through doorways five hundred times

Source: Based on data from Greenberg, (2010); Jenike, (2001); Kraus & Nicholson, (1996); Rachman, Marks, & Hodgson, (1973); Zerdizinski (2008)

Body Dysmorphic Disorder

Case Study

A twenty-four-year-old Caucasian male in his senior year of college reported, "I've got a physical deformity (small hands) and it makes me very uncomfortable, especially around women with hands bigger than mine. I see my deformity as a sign of weakness; it's like I'm a cripple." He also reported being concerned that women might believe small hands are indicative of having a small penis. (Schmidt & Harrington, 1995, pp. 162–163)

Body dysmorphic disorder (BDD) involves a preoccupation with a perceived physical defect in a normal-appearing person or excessive concern over a slight physical defect that is accompanied by repetitive behaviors such as checking appearance in mirrors, applying make-up to mask "flaws," and comparing appearance to others (American Psychiatric Association, 2011). The term comes from the Greek word *dysmorphia*, which means abnormal shape. The preoccupation produces marked clinical distress and is underdiagnosed because individuals are unwilling to bring attention to their "problem" (Grant, Kim, & Crow, 2001). Individuals with this disorder often engage in compulsive behaviors such as frequent mirror checking, excessive grooming, skin-picking, or seeking constant reassurance regarding their appearance (Phillips et al., 2010a). They regard their "defect" with embarrassment and loathing and are concerned that others may be looking at or thinking about the defect. Some make frequent requests for cosmetic surgery (Fontenelle et al., 2006; Rivera & Borda, 2001). Some individuals with BDD may recognize that their beliefs are untrue, whereas others maintain strong delusional beliefs about their bodies (Mancuso, Knoesen, & Castle, 2010).

Concern commonly focuses on bodily features such as excessive hair or lack of hair and/or the size or shape of the nose, face, or eyes (Figure 5.10). Among individuals with BDD in Brazil, many had other psychiatric disorders, and three-quarters had obsessive-compulsive disorder. More than one-third had active suicidal ideation, and 30 percent had no insight into their difficulties (Fontenelle et al., 2006). BDD tends to be chronic and difficult to treat. In a one-year follow-up of 183 individuals with BDD (84 percent had received mental health treatment), only 9 percent had full remission and 21 percent had partial remission of symptoms (Phillips et al., 2006). However, another study showed a more favorable outcome with 76 percent recovered over an eight-year period (Bjornsson et al., 2011).

Muscle dysphoria, the belief that one's body is too small or insufficiently muscular, is a form of BDD. Some bodybuilders who show a pathological preoccupation with their muscularity may also suffer from BDD. Researchers identified a subgroup of bodybuilders who scored high in body dissatisfaction, had low self-esteem, and mistakenly believed they were "small" even though they were large and very muscular (Choi et al., 2002; Olivardia, Pope, & Hudson, 2000).

ASSESSMENT FOR BODY DYSMORPHIC DISORDER

1. Do you believe that there is a "defect" in a part of your body or appearance?
2. Do you spend considerable time checking this "defect"?
3. Do you attempt to hide or cover up this "defect" or remedy it by exercising, dieting, or seeking surgery?
4. Does this belief cause you significant distress, embarrassment, or torment?
5. Does the "flaw" interfere with your ability to function at school, at social events, or at work?
6. Do friends or family members tell you that there is nothing wrong or that the "defect" is minor?

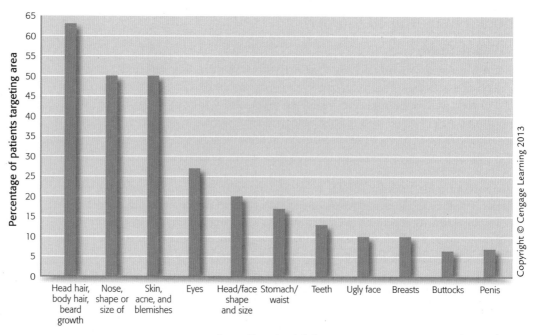

Figure 5.10

IMAGINED DEFECTS IN PATIENTS WITH BODY DYSMORPHIC DISORDER

This graph illustrates the percentage of thirty patients who targeted different areas of their body as having "defects." Many of the patients selected more than one body region.

Did You Know?

In a survey of college students:

- 74 percent were "very concerned" about the appearance of parts of their body

- 29 percent were preoccupied with a "defective" part

- 6 percent reported spending from one to over three hours a day worrying about their perceived defect

- 4 percent appeared to meet the criteria for BDD

Source: Bohne et al., (2002).

Hair-Pulling Disorder (Trichotillomania)

Trichotillomania involves recurrent and compulsive hair pulling that causes significant distress and results in hair loss. The hair pulling may occur sporadically during the day or for sustained periods of time that may last for hours (Neal-Barnett et al., 2010). Symptoms usually begin before the age of 17 and may affect up to 4 percent of the population. The prevalence is four times higher in women than men. Younger children tend to outgrow the behavior (PubMed Health, 2010).

Skin-Picking Disorder

Skin-picking disorder involves repetitive and recurrent picking of the skin and resultant skin lesions. The behavior causes significant distress. About three-quarters of individuals with this disorder are females. It is often comorbid with body dysmorphic disorder or trichotillomania. Those with this disorder spend one or more hours per day thinking about, resisting, or picking the skin. Episodes are preceded by rising tension; picking results in feelings of relief or pleasure (Tucker, Woods, Flessner, Franklin, & Franklin, 2011). As with trichotillomania, individuals with this disorder report psychosocial impairment and a lower quality of life than healthy controls (Odlaug, Kim, & Grant, 2010). CBT and SSRIs have been helpful in treating the condition (Fama, 2010).

Etiology of Obsessive-Compulsive and Related Disorders

The causes of obsessive-compulsive and related disorders remain speculative. OCD may even be a heterogeneous set of disorders with different triggers and etiology (Thorpe, Bennett, Friend, & Nottingham, 2011). In this section we examine the biological, psychological, social, and sociocultural dimensions of obsessive-compulsive and related disorders (Figure 5.11).

Does Hoarding Belong with Obsessive-Compulsive and Related Disorders?

In the past, hoarding was believed to be a form of obsessive-compulsive disorder. Some continue to argue that it is closely related to OCD (Phillips et al., 2010a, b). However, others believe that its characteristics differ from those in the OCD spectrum (Tolin & Villavicencio, 2011). Instead of the hypermetabolism in the orbitofrontal cortex, the caudate nuclei, and the thalamus that is found in OCD, individuals who hoard showed a pattern of significantly lower activation of the cingulate cortex (Saxena, 2007). Regardless of its category, we believe the disorder is of great enough significance to discuss.

Compulsive hoarding involves the inability to discard items regardless of their value. Accumulating possessions fill up and clutter the home or workplace, preventing use of the area and increasing the risk of fire, disease, or injury. Social pressure to cease hoarding is distressing to the individual because of an irrational emotional attachment to the items (Rachman, Elliott, Shafran, & Radomsky, 2009). One client collected discarded objects such as soda cans, paper bags, and newspapers, saying she "may need them sometime." Although movement around her house was impeded, she could not decide what to throw away (Samuels et al., 2007). The prevalence of hoarding disorder ranges from 2 percent to 5 percent (Lervolino et al., 2009; Mueller, 2009); up to 25 percent of individuals with anxiety disorders report significant hoarding symptoms (Tolin, Meunier, Frost, & Steketee, 2011). Cognitive-behavioral therapy can be effective with hoarding disorder, but about half of the individuals do not complete treatment due to their extreme distress at the idea of parting with their possessions (Skeketee, Frost, Tolin, Rasmussen, & Brown, 2010). In what ways does hoarding seem similar or dissimilar to OCD and related disorders?

© WR Publishing/Alamy

Hoarding

Individuals who hoard believe the items collected are "valuable" and resist having them removed, even when the possessions are worthless, unsanitary or create a fire danger.

Biological Dimensions

Biological explanations for obsessive-compulsive behaviors are based on data relating to brain structure, genetic studies, and biochemical abnormalities. First-degree relatives of individuals with OCD show impairment in decision making, planning, and mental flexibility, so these cognitive characteristics may be an endophenotype for OCD (Cavedina, Zorzi, Piccinni, Cavallini, & Bellodi, 2010). Genetic factors appear to account for about half the variance in compulsive hoarding (Lervolino et al., 2009).

Neuroimaging has revealed that some people with obsessive-compulsive disorder show increased metabolic activity in the frontal lobe of the left hemisphere. Perhaps this area of the

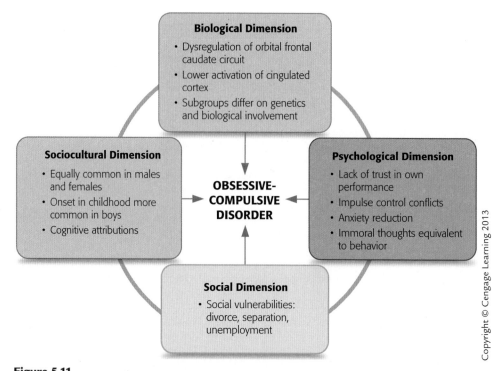

Figure 5.11

MULTIPATH MODEL FOR OBSESSIVE-COMPULSIVE DISORDER
The dimensions interact with one another and combine in different ways to result in obsessive-compulsive disorder.

brain, the orbital frontal cortex, is associated with obsessive-compulsive behaviors (Figure 5.12) (Blier et al., 2000; Freyer et al., 2011). Symptoms of obsessive-compulsive disorder suggest dysregulation involving the orbital frontal-caudate circuit. The orbital frontal cortex alerts the rest of the brain when something is wrong. When it is hyperactive, it triggers the feeling that something is not right. Connections to the caudate nucleus and gyrus (a ridge on the cerebral cortex) produce an even stronger feeling that something is "deadly wrong." This message is relayed through the thalamus to the caudate nuclei, which normally lets only powerful impulses get through. In OCD, the gate-keeping ability of the caudate nuclei is weakened, and disturbing thoughts leak through (Markarian et al., 2010; Saxena et al., 1998).

Of special interest is the fact that when individuals with OCD are given fluoxetine (a medication that increases the availability of serotonin), the cerebral blood flow to the frontal lobes is decreased to values found in individuals without the disorder and symptoms are reduced (Hoehn-Saric, Pearlson, Harris, Machlin, & Camargo, 1991). Similar neurological changes have been reported in individuals treated with cognitive-behavioral therapy (Freyer et al., 2011; Rauch et al., 2003).

Some researchers believe that OCD should be viewed as comprising a number of different subgroups rather than as a single disorder (Chamberlain et al., 2007; Mataix-Cols et al., 2004; Samuels et al., 2007). MRI imaging has found that different brain regions are activated by different OCD symptoms (Saxena et al., 2004). Instead of the hypermetabolism in the orbital frontal cortex, the caudate nuclei, and the thalamus found in other types of OCD, individuals who hoard show a pattern of significantly lower activation of the cingulate cortex (Saxena, 2007). Additional support for the view that OCD is an etiologically diverse condition is the finding that certain symptom types show different responses to treatment (Hurley, Saxena, Rauch, Hoehn-Saric, & Taber, 2002). Behavior therapy seems to be more effective for clients with checking, contamination-cleaning, and symmetry-ordering symptoms than for those with sexual-religious obsessions (Mataix-Cols et al., 2002).

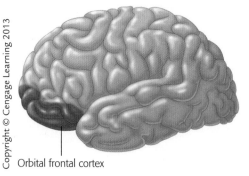

Orbital frontal cortex

Figure 5.12

ORBITAL FRONTAL CORTEX

Individuals with untreated obsessive-compulsive disorder show a high metabolism rate in this area of the brain. Certain medications reduce metabolic rates to "normal" levels and also reduce obsessive-compulsive symptoms.

Medications that increase the amount of available serotonin in the brain have been effective in treating many individuals with OCD. As a result, researchers have hypothesized that the disorder is the result of a serotonin deficiency (Greenberg, Altemus, & Murphy, 1997; Perse et al., 1987; Tollefson et al., 1994). Drugs that are effective with other anxiety disorders but that do not raise serotonin availability show limited success in the treatment of OCD (Zohar et al., 2007).

Psychological Dimension

Proponents of the behavioral perspective maintain that obsessive-compulsive behaviors develop because they reduce anxiety. That is, distracting thoughts or actions such as those seen in OCD recur because they serve the purpose of reducing anxiety. For example, many college students develop mild forms of compulsive behavior during finals week. During this anxiety-filled time, students may find themselves engaging in escape activities such as daydreaming, straightening up their rooms, or eating five or more times a day, all of which serve to shield them from thoughts of the upcoming tests. If the stress (and avoidance behaviors) last a long time, behaviorists believe that OCD may develop.

Psychologists have also studied the cognitive factors that lead to the severe doubts associated with obsessive-compulsive behavior. Individuals with OCD show certain cognitive characteristics (Clark & Beck, 2009):

1. **Threat estimation**—an exaggerated estimate regarding the probability of harm (e.g., "If the door isn't locked, I'll be killed by an intruder").
2. **Control**—"If I am not able to control my thoughts, I will be overwhelmed with anxiety."
3. **Intolerance of uncertainty**—"I have to be absolutely certain that I turned off the computer."

These patterns of thoughts can lead to compulsive rituals to reduce anxiety. Individuals with OCD believe that if they don't act in a certain way, negative consequences occur (Ghisi, Chiri, Marchetti, Sanavio, & Sica, 2010). Individuals with OCD do not trust their own memories and judgment and make futile attempts to determine whether they actually performed the behavior or performed it "correctly." Someone with a compulsive need to check things "may turn the key in the lock over and over again without being able to convince himself or herself that the door has in fact been locked, even though he or she can plainly see that the key is in the proper position, hear it engaging, and feel the lock snapping" (Dar et al., 2000, p. 673). Individuals with OCD may have a disconfirmatory bias—that is, they generate a search for evidence that undermines their confidence. The person checking the lock may develop thoughts of all the factors that may have prevented the door from staying locked.

Individuals with obsessive-compulsive disorders show two other cognitive characteristics: (1) probability bias, or the belief that having a thought, such as shouting obscenities in church, increases the chance that the action will occur; and (2) morality bias, or the view that having an immoral thought, such as throwing a child in front of a car, is as bad as the actual behavior. Research has supported the view that this manner of thinking is an important aspect of OCD and that therapy should address these cognitive biases (Rassin, Muris, Schmidt, & Merckelbach, 2000).

Social and Sociocultural Dimensions

Family variables such as a controlling, overly critical style of parenting, less parental warmth, and discouragement of autonomy are related to the development of OCD symptoms (Challacombe & Salkovskis, 2009). Individuals raised in adverse environments may develop maladaptive beliefs relating to personal responsibility; they may believe it is their responsibility to prevent harm to themselves or others and overestimate threats and feeling of responsibility (Briggs & Price, 2009). Individuals with OCD who perceive their relatives to be critical or hostile have more evere symptoms (Van Noppen & Steketee, 2009).

These reports are based on retrospective data; it is also possible that the OCD symptoms in the child resulted in admonishment or adverse reactions from parents or relatives.

OCD is more common among the young and among individuals who are divorced, separated, or unemployed (Karno & Golding, 1991). African Americans and Hispanic Americans are less likely to receive a diagnosis of OCD than are European Americans (Zhang & Snowden, 1999); ethnic minorities with OCD have been underrepresented in clinical outcome studies (Williams, Powers, Yun, & Foa, 2010). Culture may affect the how the symptoms of OCD are expressed and may not be picked up by current diagnostic systems.

Treatment of Obsessive-Compulsive and Related Disorders

The primary modes of treatment for obsessive-compulsive and related disorders are either biological or behavioral in nature. Behavioral therapies have been used successfully for many years, but treatment with medication is becoming more common.

Biological Treatments

Because obsessive-compulsive and related disorders have similarities with anxiety disorders, it might seem that benzodiazepines would be an effective treatment. However, these medications are less effective with OCD symptoms than with the anxiety disorders (Huppert et al., 2004). For severe cases of OCD, improvement has occurred with a combination of cognitive-behavioral therapy and medication (Bouvard, Milliery, & Cottraux, 2004).

SSRIs are the antidepressants recommended for the treatment of OCD because they have fewer side effects than older antidepressants and are equally as effective (American Psychiatric Association, 2007). However, only 60 to 80 percent of persons with OCD respond to these medications, and often the relief is only partial (Pigott & Murphy, 1991; Pigott & Seay, 1997). In addition, there is a rapid return of symptoms, and relapse occurs within months of stopping the medication (Jenike, 2001; Stanley & Turner, 1995). Children with OCD appear to be less responsive to treatment with antidepressants compared to adults (Ulloa et al., 2007). Nearly two-thirds of a sample of individuals with body dysmorphic disorder improved with SSRIs (Phillips et al., 2001; Phillips & Rasmussen, 2004) and hair-pulling disorder has also been successfully treated with SSRIs (PubMed Health, 2010).

Behavioral Treatments

The treatment of choice for obsessive-compulsive disorder is a combination of exposure and response prevention (Abramowitz, Foa, & Franklin, 2003; Abramowitz & Larsen, 2007; Valderhaug, Larsson, & Gotestam, 2007). In treating OCD, exposure therapy involves continued actual or imagined exposure to a fear-arousing situation; it can involve immediate presentation of the most frightening stimuli (flooding) or more gradual exposure. Response prevention involves not allowing the individual with OCD to perform the compulsive behavior. The steps in exposure therapy with response prevention generally include (Franklin et al., 2000):

1. Education about OCD and the rationale for exposure and response prevention
2. Development of an exposure hierarchy (from somewhat fearful to most-feared situations)
3. Exposure to feared situations until anxiety has diminished
4. Prevention of the performance of compulsive rituals such as handwashing

Riemann (2006) also includes cognitive restructuring to help clients identify and correct errors in thinking, such as overestimating the probability of a negative event (e.g., the chances of getting a disease from touching a doorknob) and catastrophic thinking (e.g., thinking that someone will die if a ritual is not completed a certain number of times).

flooding   a technique that involves inducing a high anxiety level through continued actual or imagined exposure to a fear-arousing situation

Summary

1. How are biological, psychological, social, and sociocultural factors involved in the development of anxiety disorders? Why is the multipath model important?

   - The multipath model stresses the importance of considering the contribution of and interaction between biological, psychological, social and sociocultural factors in the etiology of anxiety disorders; the contribution of each of the factors varies for each of the disorders.

   - Biological contributors include inherited overactivity of the fear circuitry in the brain and neurotransmitter abnormalities. However, anxiety disorders may not develop in genetically predisposed individuals living in a supportive family or social environment. The impact of stressors can also be mitigated by personality variables, such as a sense of control and mastery.

   - Sociocultural factors such as power and status, discrimination, and poverty may be responsible for the greater number of women with anxiety disorders.

2. What are phobias, what are their causes, and how are they treated?

   - Phobias are strong, irrational fears. Social phobias involve anxiety over situations in which others can observe the person. Specific phobias include all the irrational fears that are not classed as social phobias or agoraphobia. Commonly feared objects include small animals, heights, and the dark. Agoraphobia is an intense fear of being in public places where escape or help may not be possible.

   - Biological explanations are based on studies of the influence of genetic, biochemical, and neurological factors and on the idea that humans are predisposed to develop certain fears. Psychological explanations include the classical conditioning view, in which phobias are based on an association between an aversive event and a conditioned stimulus, observational learning, negative information, and cognitions that are distorted and frightening.

   - The most effective treatments for phobias seem to be biochemical (antidepressants) and cognitive-behavioral (exposure and flooding, systematic desensitization, modeling, and graduated exposure).

3. What is panic disorder, what causes it, and how is it treated?

   - Panic disorder is marked by episodes of extreme anxiety and feelings of impending doom. It is characterized by attacks that seem to occur "out of the blue."

   - The causes of panic disorder include biological factors (genetic contribution, neural structures, and neurotransmitters), psychological factors (the cognitive-behavioral view emphasizes the importance of catastrophic thoughts regarding bodily sensations), and social and sociocultural factors (such as a disturbed childhood environment and gender-related issues).

   - Treatments for panic disorder include biochemical treatments (benzodiazepines and antidepressants) and behavioral treatments (identification of catastrophic thoughts, correcting them, and substituting more realistic ones).

4. What is generalized anxiety disorder, what are its causes, and how is it treated?

   - Generalized anxiety disorder involves chronically high levels of anxiety and excessive worry that are present for three months or more.

   - There appears to be less support for the role of genetics in GAD than in other anxiety disorders, although there are some reports of abnormalities with the GABA receptors or overactivity of the anxiety circuitry in the brain. Cognitive-behavioral theorists emphasize erroneous beliefs regarding the purpose of worry or the existence of dysfunctional schemas. Social and sociocultural factors such as poverty and discrimination can also contribute to GAD.

   - Drug therapy (antidepressant medications) and behavioral therapies have been used to treat these disorders.

5. What are obsessive-compulsive and related disorders, what are their causes, and how are they treated?

- Obsessive-compulsive disorder involves thoughts or actions that are involuntary, intrusive, repetitive, and uncontrollable. Most persons with obsessive-compulsive disorder are aware that their distressing behaviors are irrational.

- Neuroimaging shows increased metabolic activity in the orbital frontal cortex in those with OCD. According to the anxiety-reduction hypothesis, obsessions and compulsions develop because they reduce anxiety. Cognitive-behavioral therapists have focused on factors such as confirmatory bias, probability bias, and morality bias. Some antidepressants have been effective in treating OCD. However, antianxiety medications are less effective with this disorder than with anxiety disorders. The treatment of choice is a combination of flooding and response prevention, sometimes combined with cognitive therapy.

- Body dysmorphic disorder involves excessive concern or preoccupation with a perceived defect in a part of the body.

- Hair-pulling disorder involves the compulsive pulling out of one's hair, resulting in noticeable hair loss.

- Skin-picking disorder involves the repetitive picking of one's skin resulting in the development of lesions.

Media Resources

Psychology CourseMate Access an interactive eBook; chapter-specific interactive learning tools, including flash cards, quizzes, videos; and more in your Psychology CourseMate, accessed through CengageBrain.com.

CENGAGENOW

CengageNow CengageNOW is an easy-to-use online resource that helps you study in less time to get the grade you want—NOW. If your textbook does not include an access code card, go to CengageBrain.com to gain access.

CENGAGEbrain.com

CengageBrain More than just an interactive study guide, WebTutor is an anytime, anywhere customized learning solution with an eBook, keeping you connected to your textbook, instructor, and classmates. Purchase the access chosen by your instructor at CengageBrain.com.

6

Trauma and Stress-Related Disorders

Caroline, a 26-year-old woman, was traumatized by the sexual abuse perpetrated by her grandfather when she was in her early teens. The grandfather was brought to trial on the abuse allegations; he was convicted but died of a heart attack after a few months. This further traumatized Caroline. She has recurrent flashbacks of seeing her grandfather's eyes when she is physically close to her boyfriend (Kramer, 2009).

Nineteen adults who appeared to have had a massive heart attack after an emotional event (e.g., car accident, news of a death, surprise birthday party, armed robbery, court appearance) were found to have 30 times the normal level of adrenalin, or epinephrine, in their bloodstream, an amount toxic to the heart and capable of producing heart failure. This reversible cardiac condition, which is precipitated by emotional stress, has been called the "broken heart" syndrome (Wittstein et al., 2005).

What is the relationship between stress, mental health, and physical disorders? Stressors are external events or situations that place a physical or psychological demand on a person. They range from chronic irritation and frustration to acute and traumatic events. Stress is an internal psychological or physiological response to a stressor. We know that extreme or traumatic stressors, such as death, serious injury, or harm, can lead to the development of acute stress disorder and post-traumatic stress disorder. These conditions will be discussed shortly.

Should we also be concerned about exposure to worrisome but less traumatic events? Some answers can be found in the "Stress in America Survey" (American Psychological Association, 2010). Of those surveyed, 44 percent indicated that their stress levels have increased over the past five years. Women in general, married women, generation X-ers, and overweight children and adults have the greatest stress levels. Symptoms such as irritability or anger (45 percent), fatigue (41 percent), feeling nervous or anxious (36 percent), headache (36 percent), feeling depressed (34 percent), and muscle tension (23 percent) were identified as by-products of stress. Thus, stress can lead to the development of both psychological and physical conditions. But how does this occur? And why are most people who are exposed to stressors, even traumatic ones, able to adjust, whereas others develop intense, long-lasting psychological or physical symptoms? As we will see, this question is best answered by examining biological, psychological, social, and sociocultural dimensions using the multipath model.

focus questions

1 What are acute and post-traumatic stress disorders, and how are they diagnosed?

2 What causes acute and post-traumatic stress disorders?

3 What are possible treatments for acute and post-traumatic stress disorders?

4 What role does stress play in physical health, and what are the psychophysiological disorders?

5 What causes psychophysiological disorders?

6 What methods have been developed to treat psychophysiological disorders?

7 What future lines of research involving stress are likely to be explored?

stressor an external event or situation that places a physical or psychological demand on a person

stress an internal psychological or physiological response to a stressor

acute stress disorder (ASD) disorder characterized by anxiety and dissociative symptoms that occur within one month after exposure to a traumatic stressor

post-traumatic stress disorder (PTSD) disorder characterized by anxiety, dissociative, and other symptoms that last for more than one month and that occur as a result of exposure to extreme trauma

Acute and Post-traumatic Stress Disorders

Case Study

I was raped when I was twenty-five years old. For a long time, I spoke about the rape as though it was something that happened to someone else. I was very aware that it had happened to me, but there was just no feeling. Then I started having flashbacks. They kind of came over me like a splash of water. I would be terrified. Suddenly I was reliving the rape. Every instant was startling. I wasn't aware of anything around me. I was in a bubble, just kind of floating. And it was scary. Having a flashback can wring you out. (NIMH, 2007f, p. 7)

Both acute stress disorder (ASD) and post-traumatic stress disorder (PTSD) begin with a normative reaction ("fight or flight") that occurs when an individual faces some type of danger. However, with these disorders, the fear response remains even though the original basis for the fear is no longer present. Individuals with ASD or PTSD remain frightened or alarmed even when the danger has passed. Indirect or secondhand exposure to trauma can also lead to ASD or PTSD. Of parents learning that their children were injured in a car accident, 18 percent of mothers suffered from probable PTSD (Alenou et al., 2011). Not everyone who faces a psychological or physical trauma develops a stress disorder. The probability of developing either ASD or PTSD depends both on the magnitude and type of stressor and risk factors specific to the individual.

Diagnosis of Acute and Post-traumatic Stress Disorders

The diagnostic criteria for acute stress disorder and post-traumatic stress disorder include (American Psychiatric Association, 2011):

1. Direct or indirect (observing, learning of the event, or repeated exposure to aversive details of an event) exposure to a traumatic stressor. This does not typically include exposure through media, television, or pictures.

2. Intrusive symptoms associated with the traumatic event, including distressing recollections of the event, distressing dreams related to the event, dissociative reactions such as flashbacks where the event is relived, and intense physiological reactivity or distress when exposed to reminders of the event. One woman who had been forced to play Russian roulette described flashbacks and nightmares of the event, "Different scenes came back, replays of exactly what happened, only the time is drawn out. . . . It seems to take forever for the gun to reach my head" (Hudson et al., 1991, p. 572).

3. Persistent evasion of stimuli associated with the trauma, such as avoiding internal recall of the event (thoughts, feelings, or physical sensations associated with the trauma) or external reminders (people, places, or objects) that arouse recollections of the event. One Iraq veteran avoided social events and cookouts: Even grilling hamburgers reminded him of the burning flesh he had been exposed to in Iraq (Keltner & Dowben, 2007).

4. Alterations in cognitions and mood associated with the traumatic event, such as inability to remember important aspects of the event; persistent negative expectations of one's self, others, or the future; persistent blame of self or others about the trauma; persistent negative mood; marked lack of interest in activities; feelings of detachment and estrangement from others; and persistent inability to experience positive emotions.

5. Heightened autonomic arousal or reactivity involving symptoms, such as irritable or aggressive behavior, reckless or self-destructive behavior, hypervigilance,

exaggerated startle response, problems with concentration, and sleep disturbance. Veterans of the Iraq war can become "unglued" at the sound of a door slamming, a nail gun being used, or the click of a camera. An Iraq veteran who almost attacked some strangers at a sports event remarked, "When friends say 'I know where you're coming from,'. , . How could they? They didn't have to deal with insects, the heat, not knowing who is the enemy, not knowing where the bullet is coming from" (Lyke, 2004, p. A8).

A diagnosis of ASD is made when eight or more of the symptoms listed are present three days to one month after the traumatic event; PTSD is diagnosed when symptoms continue for more than one month. An individual with an initial diagnosis of ASD is likely to receive a diagnosis of PTSD if the symptoms persist for more than four weeks. In both ASD and PTSD, the individual's initial, acute reactions are considered normative responses to an overwhelming and traumatic stimulus. Most individuals who have experienced trauma show a marked decrease in symptoms with time (Delahanty, 2007; Shalev et al., 1998).

What situations can result in a stress disorder? A follow-up of individuals directly affected by the terrorist attacks on September 11, 2001 (those who were in the World Trade Center complex during the attacks, experienced injury in the attacks, witnessed people falling or jumping from the towers, were caught in the dust clouds from the collapsing towers, or had friends or relatives killed in the attacks), revealed that up to 15 percent developed PTSD (DiGrande, Neria, Brackbill, Pulliam, & Galea, 2011; Marshall et al., 2007). The prevalence of PTSD is as high as 19 percent among veterans who have served in Iraq or Afghanistan (Hoge et al., 2004; Seal et al., 2007). Other situations that may lead to PTSD include being sexually assaulted or affected by violent crime or domestic violence (Curry, 2001; Zinzow et al., 2010), sexual harassment (O'Donohue et al., 2006), terrorist attacks (Baschnagel, Gudmundsdottir, Hawk, Jr., & Beck, 2009), natural disasters such as hurricanes and earthquakes (Le Greca, Silverman, Lai, & Jaccard, 2010; Lommen, Sanders, Buck & Arntz, 2009), car accidents, work related accidents, or other situations that produce a fear of severe injury or death (Buodo et al., 2011; National Institute of Mental Health [NIMH], 2007f). As many as 85 percent of undergraduate students have experienced a traumatic event sometime in their lifetime (Table 6.1); exposure to family violence and unwanted sexual attention or assault were associated with the highest levels of distress. Ethnic minority students reported the highest rates of exposure to traumatic events (Frazier, 2009).

TABLE 6.1   Undergraduates Lifetime Exposure to Traumatic Events

	Women	Men
Unexpected death	49%	41%
Another's life-threatening event	31%	25%
Witnessing family violence	25%	20%
Unwanted sexual attention	27%	5%
Severe injury (self or someone else)	18%	22%
Motor vehicle accident	17%	15%
Life threatened	11%	19%
Stalking	15%	4%
Childhood physical abuse	7%	7%
Partner violence	7%	3%
Unwanted sexual contact	8%	3%

Source: Frazier et al., 2009

Impact of Natural Catastrophes

Acute stress disorders increased dramatically in the victims of natural disasters. Here Leona Watts sits in a chair in the wreckage of her home of sixty-one years. She had returned to look for some of her belongings. Not everyone develops a stress disorder after facing a catastrophe. Why?

Did You Know?

In 2009 the Department of Defense ruled that veterans whose primary wartime injury is PTSD will not be awarded the Purple Heart, the honor given to wounded veterans. In part, this decision was made because physical wounds can be objectively identified, whereas "mental wounds" are subjective. If neuroscience is able to identify and document the brain dysfunction involved in PTSD, should military veterans affected by PTSD be given the award?

Source: Dobbs (2009)

Did You Know?

After indirect exposure to a traumatic event such as a terrorist attack or airplane crash, it is common to develop exaggerated fears of vulnerability to the event. The *real* probability of death from each of these events is:

- Auto accidents: 1 in 6,029

- Homicide: 1 in 25,123

- Hit by a car when walking: 1 in 46,960

- Terrorist attack: 1 in 97,927

- Airplane crash: 1 in 619,734,440 person trips

Source: Marshall et al. (2007)

Post-traumatic stress disorder symptoms can develop in individuals faced with repeated mild or low magnitude stressors, such as employment problems, marital distress (Astin et al., 1995; Scott & Stradling, 1994), parental separation, or relationship problems (Copeland, Keeler, Angold, & Costello, 2010); in fact, mental health professionals sometimes provide trauma-focused therapy in these circumstances (Elwood, Mott, Lohr, & Galovski, 2011). Under current diagnostic guidelines, these events, although stressful, would not be considered "traumatic"—a necessary criterion for the diagnosis of ASD or PTSD. Some psychologists believe that individuals who show symptoms of PTSD should be recognized as having, and receive treatment for, a stress disorder (Cameron, Palm, & Follette, 2010). If an individual shows the symptoms of PTSD but has not been exposed to a traumatic stressor, should a diagnosis of PTSD be given?

The lifetime prevalence of PTSD is highest among African Americans (8.7 percent), intermediate among Hispanic Americans (7 percent) and Caucasians (7.4 percent) and lowest among Asian Americans (4 percent). Asian Americans have lower exposure to trauma and are less likely to develop PTSD once exposed. In terms of traumatic incidents, African Americans and Hispanic Americans are more likely to experience childhood maltreatment and witness domestic violence (Roberts, Gilman, Breslau, Breslau, & Koenen, 2010). Women are twice as likely as men to receive the diagnosis of PTSD (Kessler, Berglund et al., 2005; NIMH, 2007f). Of the few studies available on ASD, lifetime prevalence rates ranging from 14 to 33 percent of those exposed to traumatic stress have been reported (American Psychiatric Association, 2000a). However, the prevalence of ASD may be underestimated, as those with the symptoms may not seek treatment within the thirty-day period that defines the disorder.

Etiology of Acute and Post-traumatic Stress Disorders

What are the factors associated with an increased risk of developing ASD or PTSD after exposure to trauma? Higher magnitude stressors and more severe physical injuries are associated with a greater likelihood of PTSD (Kolassa, Ertl, Onyut, & Elbert, 2010). In a study of Cambodian refugee immigrants who had experienced multiple stressors, such as the deaths of family members, torture, extreme fear, and deprivation during their escapes, 86 percent met the criteria for PTSD (Carlson & Rosser-Hogan, 1991). It is estimated that 37 percent of the survivors of the World Trade Center 9/11 attacks met the diagnostic criteria for ASD (Delahanty, 2007). Rape and sexual assault are also clearly traumatic events resulting in PTSD for over 30 percent of those exposed to this trauma (Kilpatrick, Amstadter, Resnick, & Ruggiero, 2007). Table 6.2 shows PTSD prevalence associated with specific stressors.

Not everyone exposed to a traumatic event develops one of the stress disorders. Other factors, such as individual characteristics, perceptions of the event and specific vulnerabilities moderate the impact of a traumatic event (La Greca & Silverman, 2006). In

TABLE 6.2   Lifetime Prevalence of Exposure to Stressors
by Gender and PTSD Risk

Trauma	Lifetime Prevalence (%)		PTSD Risk	
	Male	*Female*	*Male*	*Female*
Life-threatening accident	25.0	13.8	6.3	8.8
Natural disaster	18.9	15.2	3.7	5.4
Threatened with weapon	19.0	6.8	1.9	32.6
Physical attack	11.1	6.9	1.8	21.3
Rape	0.7	9.2	65.0	45.9

Some traumas are more likely to result in PTSD than others. Significant gender differences were found in reactions to "being threatened with a weapon" and "physical attack." What accounts for the differences in risk for developing PTSD among the specific traumas and for the gender differences?

Source: Ballenger et al. (2000)

this section we use the multipath model to consider the biological, psychological, social, and sociocultural dimensions of the stress disorders, as shown in Figure 6.1.

Biological Dimension

As compared with trauma-exposed individuals who do not have PTSD, those who develop the disorder have a sensitized autonomic system (Keltner & Dowben, 2007; Orr et al., 2000; Rauch, Shin, & Wright, 2003). That is, their nervous system has become highly reactive to fear and stress. PTSD is not a biologically normative stress response but one in which a number of neural and biological systems demonstrate increased reactivity, resulting in hypersensitivity to stimuli that are similar to the traumatic event; this occurs in combination with a diminished ability to inhibit or extinguish conditioned fear (Kennedy, 2002; Ressler, 2010). The normal fear response involves the amygdala, the part of the brain that is the major interface between sensory experiences such as trauma and the neurochemical and neuroanatomical circuitry of fear. The medial prefrontal cortex is involved in the extinction of fear and inhibition of emotional reactivity (Piefke et al., 2007). One's response to a fear stimulus is rapid, occurring in milliseconds. The signal to the sympathetic nervous system produces increases in heart rate and blood pressure. Additional stress responses occur from the hypothalamic-pituitary-adrenal (HPA) axis, the neuroendocrine system involved in stress reactions and regulation of body processes such as the immune system, mood, digestion, and energy. When there is a fear response, epinephrine (also known as adrenaline) and cortisol are released. These hormones prepare the body for "fight or flight" by raising blood pressure, blood sugar level, and heart rate; their purpose is to provide the speed and strength needed to react to dangerous situations. Cortisol also helps restore homeostasis (metabolic equilibrium) after the stressor is removed. Individuals with PTSD continue to demonstrate physiological stress reactions even when the stressor is no longer present (Dedovic, D'Aguiar, & Pruessner, 2009; Kendall-Tackett & Kest, 2009).

Why homeostasis is not restored is unclear. It is possible that chronic release of cortisol results in alterations of the brain structures involved in the fear response. Neuroimaging studies of those with stress disorders have shown heightened amygdala reactivity in response to fear stimuli along with reduced medial prefrontal cortex functioning. The overactive amygdala (producing an exaggerated fear response) is thus able to overcome

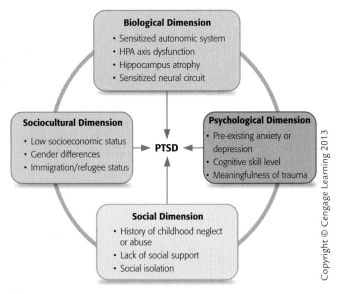

Figure 6.1

MULTIPATH MODEL FOR POST-TRAUMATIC STRESS DISORDER

The dimensions interact with one another and combine in different ways to result in post-traumatic stress disorder (PTSD).

sensitized autonomic system | when the nervous system has become highly reactive to fear and stress

the weakened inhibitory influence of inefficient medial prefrontal cortex functioning; the result is indiscriminately heightened sensitivity (Jovanovic et al., 2010). The nature of neurobiological alterations affecting PTSD is still being investigated. The changes in sensitivity seen in neural and biological systems may not be permanent, as over half of those with PTSD recover (Kolassa, Ertl, Eckart, Onyut, & Elbert, 2010; Yehuda, 2000).

About one third of the risk for PTSD is due to genetic factors. Having a short allele of the serotonin transporter gene (5-HTTLPR Ss) is associated with increased amygdala reactivity (Bryant et al., 2010). However, many of the genes affecting susceptibility to stress disorders have not been clearly identified. Genes involved with enhanced responsiveness of the glucocorticoid receptors are also being investigated. In addition, epigenetic factors could be involved; an environmental event such as childhood trauma may produce changes in biologic processes involving the serotonin transporter gene that subsequently increase vulnerability for PTSD (Yehuda et al., 2009).

It is possible that increased resting metabolic activity may represent a familial risk factor for developing PTSD (Shin et al., 2009). A twin study showed that veterans with PTSD and their co-twin had higher resting cerebral metabolic rates compared to combat-exposed veterans without PTSD and their co-twin. Thus, it appears that individuals with specific biological vulnerabilities may be predisposed to developing PTSD or other stress disorders.

Psychological Dimension

What are the psychological factors that contribute to the development of a stress disorder? Specific psychological vulnerabilities have been identified, although the precise role they play varies from individual to individual. Individuals with dysfunctional cognitions regarding oneself (e.g., "I am incompetent") or the environment (e.g., "The world is a dangerous place") have increased vulnerability to PTSD (Bennett, Beck, & Clapp, 2009). Individuals who engage in this type of cognition may interpret negative events in a catastrophic manner and exacerbate the impact of any trauma. These negative cognitions may exist before or develop as a consequence of exposure to trauma. Consistent with this cognitive model is the finding that guilt regarding abusive violence during combat is associated with PTSD in veterans (Marx, Foley, Feinstein, Wolf, Kaloupek, & Keane, 2010). Negative cognitions involving mental pollution (feelings of dirtiness without physical contact) have also been reported by sexual assault victims, a factor which may increase traumatic stress (Olatunji, Elwood, Williams, & Lohr, 2008). Among child and adolescent assault and motor vehicle accident survivors, maladaptive appraisals, such as "I will never be the same," were associated with the development and maintenance of PTSD symptoms (Meiser-Stedman, Dalgleish, Gluckman, Yule, & Smith, 2009). Negative thoughts such as these produce sustained and heightened HPA and autonomic nervous system reactivity, making the development of ASD or PTSD more likely. Instead of self-blame or a negative view of the world, positive cognitive styles such as attempting to solve or alter the problem (Baschnagel, Gudmundsdottir, Hawk, Jr., & Beck, 2009), reframing traumatic events in a more positive light (Gupta & Bonanno, 2010), believing that good things are more likely to happen than bad things (Prati & Pietrantoni, 2009), and believing in one's ability to control both actions and thoughts (Walter, Gunstad, & Hobfoll, 2010) appear to reduce risk of developing PTSD.

Pre-existing conditions such as trait anxiety and depression were found to be risk factors for the development of PTSD among youths exposed to Hurricane Katrina (Weems et al., 2007). Also, individuals who are anxiety prone and who score high on the characteristic of neuroticism (Breslau, Davis, & Andreski, 1995) are more vulnerable to PTSD. Anxious individuals may overestimate the probability that aversive events will follow and react much more strongly to a traumatic event (Engelhard, de Jong, van den Hout, & Overveld, 2009). Other psychological factors may also play a role. Disaster survivors with psychiatric histories were more likely to develop PTSD than those without previous disorders (North, Smith, & Spitznagel, 1997). Another study showed that war veterans who developed PTSD were more likely to have sustained injuries, engaged in firefights, come closer to their own deaths, and witnessed others die (Hoge et al., 2004).

Social Dimension

Poor or inadequate support during childhood and adulthood has also been identified as possibly contributing to the development of stress disorders. Pre-existing family conflict and overprotectiveness may augment the impact of stress during exposure to a traumatic event (Bokszczanin, 2008). Family of origin conflicts or maltreatment may increase an individual's anxiety, lead to negative cognitive styles, or "trigger" a genetic predisposition toward greater physiological reactivity and thus increase the risk of developing PTSD. Although social support may function as a protective factor, individuals who are socially isolated and lacking in support systems appear to be more vulnerable. Social support may act to dampen the anxiety associated with a trauma or to prevent negative cognitions from occurring. In one study, those who reported low social support in the six months prior to exposure to the 9/11 attacks were more than twice as likely as those with high levels of social support to report symptoms of PTSD (Galea et al., 2002). The lack of social support after experiencing a trauma may have stronger effects than influences of childhood abuse and family history (Brewin, Andrews, & Valentine, 2000; Ozer, Best, Lipsey, & Weiss, 2003).

What other pre-existing conditions may predispose an individual to developing a stress disorder? In a twin study, Gilbertson and colleagues (2006) compared forty-three Vietnam veterans and their twin brothers who had not been exposed to combat. All had been given tests of cognitive functioning prior to combat experience. The researchers found that the twins with higher test scores on memory, attention, and intellectual functioning were less likely to develop PTSD. In other words, above average cognitive skills act as a protective factor. Why this occurs and which cognitive processes are important in PTSD is not known.

Sociocultural Dimension

Recent immigrants and refugees from countries in which there have been civil disturbances or conflict have elevated risk of stress disorders (Sue & Sue, 2008a). Additionally, ethnic differences in response patterns were seen in a survey of 1,008 New York adult residents following the terrorist attacks of 9/11: 3.2 percent of Asian Americans, 6.5 percent of white Americans, 9.3 percent of African Americans, and 13.4 percent of Hispanic Americans

Did You Know?

PTSD was not officially recognized as a diagnosis until 1980, but its symptoms have been recorded throughout history and known by different names:

- *Soldier's heart* in the Civil War (most prevalent among soldiers ages 9–17)

- *Shell shock* in World War I

- *Battle fatigue* in World War II

- *Post-Vietnam syndrome* after the Vietnam War

Source: Pizarro, Silver, & Prause (2006)

AP Images

Post-traumatic Stress Disorder and Abuse

In this photo, Cheryl, center, consoles Catherine, twenty-four, during group therapy. Catherine is reliving the physical and emotional abuse she received during her childhood. Post-traumatic stress disorder is not isolated to combat situations. Women who have been battered or have suffered sexual assaults often report high rates of acute stress or post-traumatic stress disorder.

reported symptoms consistent with PTSD (Galea et al., 2002). Ethnic group differences may be due to pre-existing variables such as differential exposure to previous trauma, childhood environment or cultural differences in responding to stress (Triffleman & Pole, 2010). Perceived racial and sexual orientation discrimination is related to an increased risk for PTSD (Flores, Tschann, Dimas, Pasch, & de Groat, 2010). Being exposed to discrimination can lead to higher anxiety levels and the development of negative cognitions about oneself and the world. Ethnic and sexual minorities also report higher levels of childhood maltreatment and interpersonal violence, experiences that can increase risk for PTSD (Roberts, Austin, Corliss, Vandermorris, & Koenen, 2010; Roberts, Gilman, Breslau, Breslau, & Koenen, 2010).

Women are also twice as likely as men to suffer from a stress disorder (Galea et al., 2002; NIMH, 2007f). This may result from an inherent vulnerability or from greater exposure to stressors that are likely to result in PTSD. In analyzing the data from the National Violence Against Women Project, Cortina and Kubiak (2006) concluded that the greater prevalence of stress disorders in women was due to more exposure to violent interpersonal situations. In a similar fashion, Tolin and Foa (2006) performed a meta-analysis of studies to determine whether gender differences existed in terms of PTSD vulnerability. When they controlled for exposure to interpersonal violence, the difference in rates of PTSD between men and women was reduced, but not eliminated, suggesting that additional factors impact gender differences in prevalence. Interestingly, although female police officers face greater assaultive violence than civilian women, they are less likely to have symptoms of PTSD (Lilly, Pole, Best, Metzler, & Marmar, 2009) and female veterans deployed to Iraq and Afghanistan have only a moderately higher rate of PTSD compared to male veterans (Street, Vogt, & Dutra, 2009). What accounts for the difference in PTSD prevalence among civilian women and women who join the police force or military? Women in the latter group may differ biologically from civilian women, engage in emotional suppression to cope with the challenges of their work or to conform to male norms (Lilly et al., 2009). It is also possible that the threat perception of women may change when adopting the role of a soldier or a police officer.

▇ Treatment of Acute and Post-traumatic Stress Disorders

Selective serotonin reuptake inhibitor (SSRI) antidepressant medication (Zoloft, Paxil, Prozac) has been successful in the treatment of ASD and PTSD (Nacasch et al., 2007). These medications alter serotonin levels, acting at the level of the amygdala and its connections to desensitize the fear network. Depending on the specific medication, 50 to 85 percent of those taking antidepressants report significant symptom relief, although from 17 to 62 percent of those on placebos also report the same degree of improvement (Davidson, 2000). However, treatment discontinuation rates are twice as high with medication as compared with behavioral treatments (Davidson, 2000; Foa, 2000), perhaps due to side effects such as insomnia, diarrhea, nausea, and fatigue.

Psychotherapy strategies have generally focused on extinguishing the fear of trauma-related stimuli or correcting dysfunctional cognitions that are thought to perpetuate PTSD symptoms. Exposure to cues associated with the trauma appears to be effective in treating PTSD (Basoglu, Livanou, & Salcioglu, 2003; Nacasch et al., 2007; Foa, 2000; Taylor et al., 2003). The process of exposure may involve asking the person to re-create the traumatic event in his or her imagination. In one study of victims of sexual assault (Foa et al., 1999), the women were asked to repeatedly imagine and describe the assault "as if it were happening now." They verbalized the details of the assault, as well as their thoughts and emotions regarding the incident. Their descriptions were recorded, and this process was repeated for about an hour. The women were then instructed to listen to the recordings once a day and, when doing so, to "imagine that the assault is happening now." This process allowed extinction of their fear to occur. It is believed that the more accurate the imagined details, the more effective the therapy. Exposure also appears to effectively correct erroneous cognitions associated with the traumatic event. In a meta-analytic review of the therapeutic technique of prolonged exposure, those treated using this procedure fared better than 86 percent of those in control conditions (Powers, Halpern, Ferenschak, Gillihan, & Foa, 2010). For PTSD as a result of child abuse, skills training in emotional regulation appeared to augment the effects of exposure (Cloitre et al., 2010).

Because cognitive factors also affect symptoms of PTSD, some therapists teach their clients to identify and challenge dysfunctional cognitions about the traumatic event and current beliefs about oneself and others. For example, battered women with PTSD often have thoughts associated with guilt or self-blame. Cognitions such as "I could have prevented it," "I never should have . . . ,," and "I'm so stupid" maintain the symptoms of PTSD. In one study, the condition remitted in 87 percent of battered women who learned more about PTSD, the importance of developing a solution-oriented attitude and reducing negative self-talk, were then therapeutically exposed to potential fear triggers (such as photos of their partner or movies involving domestic violence), and practiced relaxation and stress management techniques (Kubany et al., 2004).

Cayton Photography/The Image Works

Post-traumatic Stress Disorder and the Military

The 2nd Brigade Combat Team from Fort Carson, Colorado, suffered heavy casualties in Iraq. Many of the soldiers in the unit suffered from post-traumatic stress disorder (PTSD). However, the Army was not always receptive to complaints related to PTSD. An investigation showed systematic abuse of soldiers with this disorder. Tyler Jennings, Corey Davis, and Alex Orum all received a diagnosis of PTSD and suffered mistreatment by the Army.

Psychological Factors Affecting Medical Conditions: Psychophysiological Disorders

Case Study

The data from 200 patients who happened to have cardiac defibrillators implanted before the World Trade Center attack on September 11, 2001, provided interesting information regarding the physiological impact of the stressful event. The defibrillators, which record and respond to serious arrhythmias, showed that the frequency of life-threatening arrhythmias increased two-fold for thirty days after 9/11 (Steinberg et al., 2004).

As we mentioned earlier, Americans are an overstressed people, with finances being a major source of concern. (See Figure 6.2 for the major causes of stress.) Stress experienced by parents is often apparent to their children. More than 90 percent of children report knowing their parents are stressed because of behavior such as arguments, yelling, and complaining (American Psychological Association, 2010). Stress results in a multitude of physiological, psychological, and social changes that influence health conditions. In this part of the chapter, we consider how these factors are involved in physical illnesses.

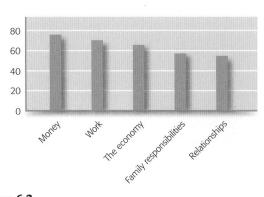

Figure 6.2

FIVE LEADING CAUSES OF STRESS IN AMERICA

The Stress in America Survey shows the toll that the economic recession has had on the well-being of American families.

Source: American Psychological Association (2010)

Most researchers acknowledge that attitudes and emotional states can have an impact on physical well-being. In the past, physical disorders such as asthma, hypertension, and headaches that are affected by stressors were referred to as *psychosomatic disorders*. The use of this term was meant to distinguish disorders affected by psychological factors from conditions considered strictly physical in nature. Mental health professionals now recognize, however, that almost any physical disorder can have a strong psychological component or basis. The term *psychosomatic disorder* has been replaced with psychophysiological disorder, which references any physical disorder that has a strong psychological basis or component.

The category "Psychological Factors Affecting Medical Conditions" includes medical conditions in which psychological or behavioral factors influence the course or treatment of the disorder, constitute an additional risk factor, or exacerbate the illness (American Psychiatric Association, 2011). Emotional states, patterns of interpersonal interaction, and coping styles are examples of psychological or behavioral influences. The criteria for this disorder are:

A. A medical condition is present

B. Psychological or behavioral factors are adversely influencing the medical condition in one of the following ways:

    1. A close temporal relationship between the development, exacerbation, or delayed recovery of the condition and psychological factors

    2. Psychological factors interfere with treatment

    3. Psychological factors cause additional health risks for the individual

    4. Psychological factors influence physiology and thus precipitate or aggravate the condition

MYTH: Psychophysiological disorders are merely psychological in nature and can be treated with only psychotherapy. Real physical problems are not present.

REALITY: Although psychophysiological disorders do have a psychological component, actual physical processes or conditions are involved. Any physical condition can be considered a psychophysiological disorder if psychological factors contribute to the development of the disorder, make the condition worse, or delay improvement. In most cases, both medical and psychological treatments are needed.

MYTH VS. REALITY

Characteristics of Psychophysiological Disorders

Psychophysiological disorders involve actual tissue damage (such as coronary heart disease), a disease process (impairment of the immune system), or physiological dysfunction (as in asthma or migraine headaches). Both medical treatment and psychotherapy are usually required. The relative contributions of physical and psychological factors to a physical disorder can vary greatly. Although psychological events are often difficult to detect, repeated association between a stressor and symptoms of the disorder increases suspicion that a psychological component is involved.

In this section we discuss several of the more prevalent psychophysiological disorders—coronary heart disease, hypertension (high blood pressure), headaches, and asthma—and then consider the topic of how stress influences immunological functioning. Research identifying biological, psychological, social, and sociocultural influences on specific psychophysiological disorders is also reviewed.

Coronary Heart Disease

psychophysiological disorder any physical disorder that has a strong psychological basis or component

coronary heart disease (CHD) the narrowing of cardiac arteries, resulting in the restriction or partial blockage of the flow of blood and oxygen to the heart

Coronary heart disease (CHD) involves the narrowing of cardiac arteries, resulting in the restriction or partial blockage of the flow of blood and oxygen to the heart as seen in Figure 6.3. When coronary arteries are narrowed or blocked, oxygen-rich blood can't reach the heart muscle. This can result in angina (chest pain) or, if blood flow to the heart is significantly blocked, a heart attack.

Approximately 17,600,000 or 7.9 percent of Americans have CHD; almost 500,000 die of this condition each year. Risk factors for CHD include high cholesterol levels;

The Hmong Sudden Death Syndrome

CRITICAL THINKING

Vang Xiong is a former Hmong (Laotian) soldier who, with his wife and child, resettled in Chicago in 1980. The change from his familiar rural surroundings and farm life to an unfamiliar urban area must have produced a severe culture shock. In addition, Vang vividly remembered seeing people killed during his escape from Laos, and he expressed feelings of guilt about having to leave his brothers and sisters behind in that country. He reported having problems almost immediately.

[He] could not sleep the first night in the apartment, nor the second, nor the third. After three nights of sleeping very little, Vang went to see his resettlement worker, a bilingual Hmong man named Moua Lee. Vang told Moua that the first night he woke suddenly, short of breath, from a dream in which a cat was sitting on his chest. The second night, the room suddenly grew darker, and a figure, like a large black dog, came to his bed and sat on his chest. He could not push the dog off, and he grew quickly and dangerously short of breath. The third night, a tall, white-skinned female spirit came into his bedroom from the kitchen and lay on top of him. Her weight made it increasingly difficult for him to breathe, and as he grew frantic and tried to call out he could manage but a whisper. He attempted to turn onto his side, but found he was pinned down. After fifteen minutes, the spirit left him, and he awoke, screaming. (Tobin & Friedman, 1983, p. 440)

These dream-state symptoms are indicative of Hmong Sudden Death Syndrome. As of 1993, 150 cases of sudden death among Southeast Asian refugees had been reported. Almost all were men, with the possible exception of one or two women; most occurred within the first two years of residence in the United States. Autopsies produced no identifiable cause for the deaths. Some cases of sudden unexplained deaths have also been reported in Asian countries (Aoki et al., 2003). Although the number of cases is declining, these deaths remain a most puzzling phenomenon (Gib Parrish, Centers for Disease Control, personal communication, 1993). All of the reports were the same: A person in apparently good health went to sleep and died in his or her sleep. Often, the victim displayed labored breathing, screams, and frantic movements just before death. Some consider the deaths to represent an extreme and very specific example of the impact of psychological stress on physical health (Figure 6.4).

Vang was one of the lucky victims of the syndrome—he survived. He went for treatment to a Hmong woman, Mrs. Thor, who is a highly respected Shaman in Chicago's Hmong community. She interpreted his problem as being caused by unhappy spirits and performed the ceremonies required to release them. After that, Vang reported he had no more problems with nightmares or with breathing during sleep.

In many non-Western cultures, physical or mental problems may be attributed to supernatural forces such as witchcraft or evil spirits (Sue & Sue, 2008a). The spiritual treatment Vang received using non-Western methods seemed to have been successful. Had he gone to a doctor who practiced Western medicine, what do you think his treatment would have consisted of? In this case, which do you think is the best course of treatment?

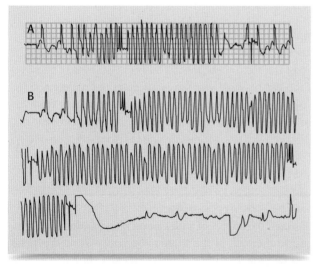

Figure 6.4

VENTRICULAR FIBRILLATION IN SUDDEN UNEXPLAINED DEATH
A Thai man fitted with a defibrillator showed ventricular episodes (rapid spikes on the graph) when asleep. **A** represents a transient episode that resolved itself. **B** depicts a sustained ventricular episode accompanied by labored breathing that set off the defibrillator, which normalized the heart rate. Is this the explanation for the sudden unexplained death syndrome?
Source: Nademanee et al. (1997)

hypertension; cigarette smoking; abdominal obesity; a lack of physical activity; and psychosocial factors, such as depression, perceived stress, and difficult life events (American Heart Association, 2010). Stress plays a role in coronary heart disease from both a biological and psychological perspective. Stress causes the release of hormones that activate the sympathetic nervous system, which can lead to changes in heart rhythm, such as *ventricular*

Figure 6.3

ATHEROSCLEROSIS

Atherosclerosis occurs when fat, cholesterol, and other substances build up in the wall of arteries and form a hard structure called *plaque*. The plaque can make the artery narrow and reduce or even stop blood flow. Pieces of plaque may also break off and block smaller blood vessels. These situations can lead to heart attacks and strokes.

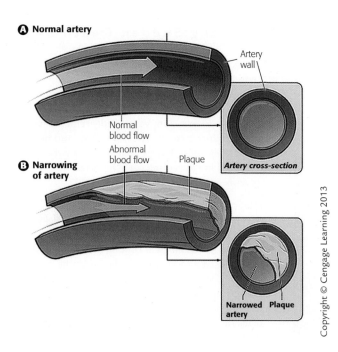

fibrillation (rapid, ineffective contractions of the heart), *bradycardia* (slowing of the heartbeat), *tachycardia* (speeding up of the heartbeat), or *arrhythmia* (irregular heartbeat). Figure 6.4 shows an example of ventricular fibrillation.

Hypertension

Case Study

Scott Cote, a 41-year-old software engineer, lost weight, cut sodium, and began exercising to control his blood pressure, all as a result of new attention being given to the condition "prehypertension" (Landro, 2010, p. 1).

Case Study

On October 19, 1987, the stock market drastically dropped 508 points. By chance, a forty-eight-year-old stockbroker was wearing a device measuring stress in the work environment on that day. The instrument measured his pulse every fifteen minutes. At the beginning of the day, his pulse was sixty-four beats per minute and his blood pressure was 132 over 87 (somewhat above the normal range). As stock prices fell dramatically, the man's physiological system surged in the other direction. His heart rate increased to eighty-four beats per minute and his blood pressure hit a dangerous 181 over 105. His pulse was "pumping adrenaline, flooding his arteries, and maybe slowly killing him in the process" (Tierney, 1988).

The stockbroker's reaction illustrates the impact of a stressor on blood pressure, the measurement of the force of blood against the walls of the arteries and veins. We all experience transient physiological responses to stressors, but some people develop a chronic condition called hypertension, a blood pressure of 140 (systolic) over 90 (diastolic) or higher. Normal blood pressure is considered to be lower than 120 over 80 while a blood pressure up to 139 over 89 is considered to be "prehypertension." Prehypertension, described in the earlier case study, is believed to be a precursor to hypertension, stroke, and heart disease and is found in 28 percent of adults (34 percent of men and 22 percent of women) (Ostchega, Yoon, Hughes, & Louis, 2008). More than 74 million Americans have high blood pressure that

hypertension a chronic condition characterized by blood pressure of 140 (systolic) over 90 (diastolic) or higher

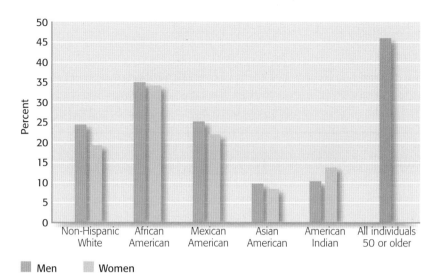

Figure 6.5

GENDER AND ETHNIC DIFFERENCES IN HYPERTENSION AMONG ADULTS IN THE UNITED STATES

The highest prevalence of chronic high blood pressure occurs among African Americans and among all individuals over the age of fifty. Women tend to score somewhat lower than other groups. Biological, psychological, social, and sociocultural factors have been implicated in the gender and ethnic differences in hypertension.

Source: Data from Burt et al. (1995); American Heart Association (2007)

needs treatment (American Heart Association, 2010). However, 30 percent are unaware of their hypertension, and more than 40 percent are not being treated (Chobanian et al., 2003). Nearly three-quarters of women and two-thirds of men over the age of seventy-five have hypertension (Centers for Disease Control, 2010). Hypertension is most prevalent in the African American population and in older adults (American Heart Association, 2010). Chronic hypertension leads to arteriosclerosis (narrowing of arteries) and to increased risk of stroke and heart attack. In 90 to 95 percent of the cases, the cause for the hypertension is not known (American Heart Association, 2010). Figure 6.5 shows some gender and ethnic comparisons of hypertension among adults.

Stress and Hypertension

On September 11, 2001, many survivors of the World Trade Center attacks recounted the terror they felt during the attack and their fight for survival. Onlookers were also horrified to see people jump to their deaths; many people barely escaped the collapsing building. The survivors and observers went through a traumatic event that produced severe physiological reactions.

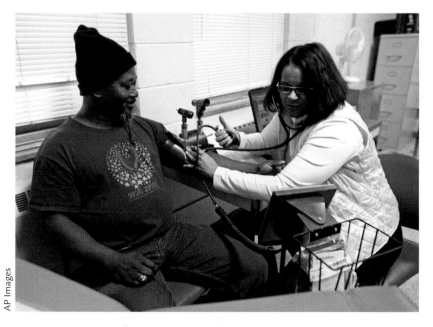

Ethnicity and Hypertension

David Thomas was buying groceries and decided to get a blood pressure check at a clinic located in the store. He found that he was a prime candidate for a stroke and received blood pressure treatment along with his bread. African Americans have much higher rates of hypertension than their white counterparts, whereas Asian Americans and American Indians have much lower rates. What factors may account for the large between-group differences?

Migraine, Tension, and Cluster Headaches

Case Study

A forty-two-year-old woman described her headaches as a throbbing that pulsed with every heartbeat. Visual effects, such as sparklers, flashing across her visual field, accompanied the pain. The symptoms would last for up to three days (Adler & Rogers, 1999).

Case Study

A patient seeking help for excruciating headaches describes the pain in the following manner: "It feels like someone walked up to me, took a screwdriver and jammed it up in my right eye and kept digging it around for 20 minutes" (Linn, 2004, p. A1).

Headaches are among the most common psychophysiological complaints. About 90 percent of males and 95 percent of females have at least one headache during a given year. More than 45 million Americans suffer from chronic, recurring headaches (Meeks, 2004). The pain of a headache can vary in intensity from dull to excruciating. Although we discuss migraine, tension, and cluster headaches separately, the same person can be susceptible to more than one type of headache. (Figure 6.6 illustrates some differences

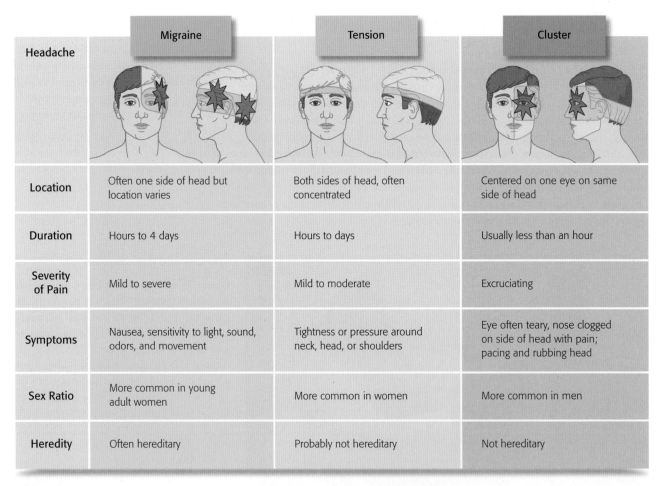

Headache	Migraine	Tension	Cluster
Location	Often one side of head but location varies	Both sides of head, often concentrated	Centered on one eye on same side of head
Duration	Hours to 4 days	Hours to days	Usually less than an hour
Severity of Pain	Mild to severe	Mild to moderate	Excruciating
Symptoms	Nausea, sensitivity to light, sound, odors, and movement	Tightness or pressure around neck, head, or shoulders	Eye often teary, nose clogged on side of head with pain; pacing and rubbing head
Sex Ratio	More common in young adult women	More common in women	More common in men
Heredity	Often hereditary	Probably not hereditary	Not hereditary

Figure 6.6

THREE TYPES OF HEADACHES

Some differences in the characteristics of migraine, tension, and cluster headaches have been reported, although similarities between them also exist.

Source: Data adapted from "Headaches" (2006); Silberstein (1998)

among the three types.) A number of biological, psychological, social, and sociocultural factors have been associated with the onset of headaches, including stress, negative emotions, sexual harassment, poor body posture, eyestrain, noise, too much or too little sleep, exposure to smoke or strong odors, the weather, hormonal factors in women, and certain foods (Martin & MacLeod, 2009; National Institute of Neurological Disorders and Stroke [NINDS], 2007a; Silberstein, 1998). Headaches have also been reported as a result of coughing, exertion, and sexual activity (Wang & Fu, 2010).

In an experiment, Martin and Seneviratne (1997) attempted to verify that food deprivation and negative emotions can precipitate headaches. For nineteen hours, they either withheld food from thirty-eight women and eighteen men who suffered from migraine or tension headaches or exposed them to a stressor that produced negative emotions (difficult-to-solve anagrams). The findings supported the view that the two conditions can induce headaches. Individuals who had been deprived of food or subjected to the anagrams reported both more headaches and headaches of greater intensity than individuals who had been allowed to eat or were not exposed to stress.

Migraine Headaches

Moderate to severe pain resulting from constriction of the cranial arteries followed by dilation of the cerebral blood vessels is the distinguishing feature of migraine headaches. Anything that affects the size of these blood vessels, which are connected to sensitive nerves, can produce a headache. Thus certain chemicals, such as sodium nitrate (found in hot dogs), monosodium glutamate (MSG) (a food additive), and tyramine (found in red wines), can produce headaches by distending blood vessels in certain people. Pain from a migraine headache may be mild, moderate, or severe. Most individuals who suffer from this form of headache report migraines once or twice a month; 10 percent have migraines weekly, 20 percent have them every two or three days, and 15 percent have them more than 15 days a month (Dodick & Gargus, 2008). Migraines may last from a few hours to several days and are often accompanied by nausea and vomiting. The one-year prevalence of migraine is 11.7 percent (17.1 percent in women and 5.6 percent in men). Prevalence peaks at middle life and is lower in adolescents and those over age 60. Migraine headaches are common not only among women but also among people with lower incomes. They are less common among African Americans than among white Americans (Lipton et al., 2007).

Tension Headaches

Tension headaches are produced by prolonged contraction of the scalp and neck muscles, resulting in vascular constriction and steady pain. They are the most common form of headache and tend to disappear once the stress producing the muscle tension is over (NINDS, 2007). About 31 percent of children report having tension headaches (Monteith & Sprenger, 2010). In one study, psychological factors were found to precipitate the headaches in up to 61 percent of the patients, most of who were women (Martin & Seneviratne, 1997). Tension headaches are generally not as severe as migraine headaches, and they can usually be relieved with aspirin or other analgesics.

Cluster Headaches

Cluster headaches involve an excruciating, stabbing or burning sensation located in the eye or cheek. Cluster headaches occur in cycles, and incapacitating attacks can occur a number of times a day (Meeks, 2004). In about 20 percent of cases, the headaches are preceded by an aura, which is a visual or physical sensation such as tingling of an extremity or seeing flashes of light (Rozen, 2010). Each attack may last from fifteen minutes to three hours before ending abruptly. Along with the headache, the individual may experience tears or a stuffy nose on the same side of the head on which the pain is felt (Silberstein, 1998). The cycles may last from several days to months, followed by pain-free periods. Only about 10 to 20 percent of cluster headaches are chronic. Cluster headaches do not appear to run in families and, in contrast to other headaches, are more common in men (Silberstein, 1998).

migraine headache   moderate to severe pain resulting from constriction of the cranial arteries followed by dilation of the cerebral blood vessels

tension headache   produced by prolonged contraction of the scalp and neck muscles, resulting in vascular constriction and steady pain

cluster headache   excruciating stabbing or burning sensations located in the eye or cheek

Figure 6.7

AN ASTHMA ATTACK

Asthma attacks and deaths have increased dramatically since the 1980s.

Source: Cowley & Underwood (1997, p. 61)

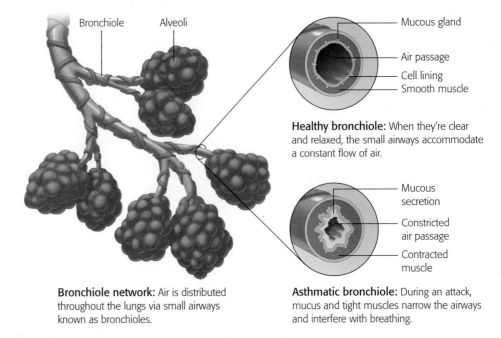

Bronchiole network: Air is distributed throughout the lungs via small airways known as bronchioles.

Healthy bronchiole: When they're clear and relaxed, the small airways accommodate a constant flow of air.

Asthmatic bronchiole: During an attack, mucus and tight muscles narrow the airways and interfere with breathing.

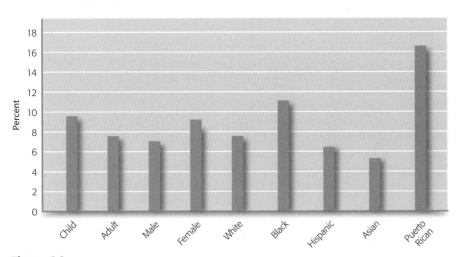

Figure 6.8

ASTHMA PREVALENCE

This figure shows the prevalence of asthma among adults and children, men and women, and members of different ethnic minorities. Of these groups, Puerto Ricans, African Americans, and children appear to be especially vulnerable.

Source: Akinbami et al. (2011)

Asthma

Asthma is a chronic inflammatory disease of the airways in the lungs. Bronchospasms, excessive mucus secretion, and edema constrict the airways, making it difficult to completely empty the lungs and thereby reducing the amount of air that can be inhaled (Figure 6.7). Symptoms range from mild and infrequent wheezing or coughing to severe respiratory distress requiring emergency care. In severe asthma attacks, respiratory failure can occur.

In the United States, asthma has increased dramatically since the 1980s. It afflicts up to 8.2 percent or about 24.6 million individuals, with a disproportionate recent increase among women (Akinbami, Moorman, & Liu, 2011; Asthma and Allergy Foundation of America, 2007). Ethnic minority children living in inner cities and African American, American Indian, and Filipino children are more vulnerable to asthma (Brim, Rudd, Funk, & Callahan, 2008; Forno & Celedon, 2009). Puerto Ricans and African Americans are more than three times more likely to die from asthma than other Americans (National Center for Health Statistics, 2007). Figure 6.8 shows asthma prevalence among different groups.

Asthma is the sixth leading cause of death in children 5–14 years of age (Katon, 2010). Many of the deaths that occur from asthma may happen because the individual or others underestimate the severity of the attack and delay seeking assistance; people with asthma seem to have a poor perception of air flow obstruction (Janssens, Verleden, De Peuter, Van Diest, & Van den Bergh, 2009). Some fail to notice when their airflow is reduced even by 50 percent (Stout, Kotses, & Creer, 1997). Asthma appears to have a diurnal variation: Symptoms often are worse during the night and early morning. For reasons that

asthma   chronic inflammatory disease of the airways in the lungs

are not clearly understood, adolescents with asthma are twice as likely to commit suicide than those without the illness (Kuo et al., 2010).

The recent increase in the number of asthma cases in the United States is puzzling. Suspicion grows that a number of different pollutants (cigarette smoke, air pollution, pet hair and dander, indoor molds, and cockroaches) may be responsible (Forno & Celedon, 2009). Rosenstreich, Eggleston, and Kattan (1997) examined 476 children with asthma who lived in inner cities. They found that 23 percent were allergic to pets, 35 percent to dust mites, and 37 percent to cockroaches. Allergy to cockroaches had the highest association with emergency room treatment, hospitalization, and school absences in these children. A program to reduce environmental allergens within the houses of children with asthma was associated with a reduction in symptoms (Morgan et al., 2004).

Stress and the Immune System

Case Study

Florida was hit by four hurricanes within a six-week period. One woman was able to deal with the first, even though it smashed her windows, flooded her carpets, and caused her to throw food away. Then a second hurricane struck, causing similar damage. She had to wait in the hot sun to get ice and was without food or water for her children. As she related, "The first one, I stayed strong. But this second one, I started crying and couldn't stop" (Barton, 2004, p. A3).

We have already suggested a relationship between stress and illness. How do emotional and psychological states influence the disease process? We know that stress is related to illness, but what is the precise relationship between the two? How does stress affect health?

Stress itself does not appear to cause infections, but it may decrease the immune system's efficiency, thereby increasing a person's susceptibility to disease. The white blood cells in the immune system help maintain health by recognizing and destroying pathogens such as bacteria, viruses, fungi, and tumors. In an intact system, more than one thousand billion white blood cells circulate through the bloodstream. Two major classes of white blood cells are lymphocytes and phagocytes. *Lymphocytes* include *B cells* (which produce antibodies against invaders), *T cells* (which organize immune response to infected or malignant cells), and *natural-killer (NK) cells* (which kill tumor or virus-infected cells). *Phagocytes* respond to infection by ingesting harmful cells (Kendall-Tackett, 2009; Kiecolt-Glaser & Glaser, 1993).

As mentioned earlier in this chapter, stress produces physiological changes in the body. Part of the stress response involves the release of neurohormones that can impair immune functioning. For example, the role of cortisol in maintaining homeostasis involves suppressing the immune system and reducing inflammation in the body. A deficient immune system may fail to detect invaders or produce antibodies. The ability to fight infection may be impaired, or white blood cells may be unable to multiply. Because of the weakening of defenses, infections and diseases are more likely to develop or worsen.

Did You Know?

Strong relationships lead to a longer life. Having strong, close relationships overcomes the influence of risk factors such as obesity or not exercising, whereas poor or limited social relationships are the equivalent of smoking 15 cigarettes a day or having more than six drinks of alcohol a day.

Source: Holt-Lundstad, Smith, & Layton (2010)

Exposure to chronic stress appears to increase vulnerability to infection and accelerate the progression of disease by decreasing immunity (Miller, Chen, & Zhou, 2007). A group of law students were evaluated five times over a period of six months. On each occasion they indicated how optimistic they were about their law school experience and were injected with an antigen designed to generate an immune response. Current level of optimism was related to the magnitude of the response. When students were more optimistic about law school, greater immune response was noted. Thus, expectations about their performance in school influenced their immunity (Segerstrom & Sephton, 2010). Similarly, Cohen and his associates (1998) had 276 volunteers complete a life stressor interview, after which they were evaluated

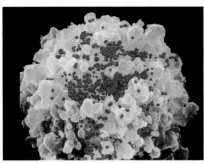

NIBSC / Photo Researchers, Inc.

Under Attack

This highly magnified photo shows the surface of a T-cell that is infected with the HIV virus. T-cells function as a part of the immune response to viruses and infections. In this case, it is being compromised. Some believe that one's attitude can influence the effectiveness of components of the immune system, such as T-cells.

to determine whether they were ill. Those who were healthy were then quarantined and given nasal drops containing cold viruses to determine whether they would develop a cold within five days. Of this group, 84 percent became infected with the virus, but only 40 percent developed cold symptoms. Participants who suffered severe stress for one or more months were much more likely to develop colds. The types of chronic stressors most closely related to colds were long-term conflicts with family or friends and unemployment or underemployment. Deterioration in immune system functioning can increase vulnerability to certain illnesses, but can immune system dysfunction influence the development of diseases such as cancer? Consider the following case:

Case Study

Anne is an unhappy, passive individual who always accedes to the wishes and demands of her husband. She has difficulty expressing strong emotions, especially anger, and often represses her feelings. She has few friends and no one to confide in. She often feels a pervasive sense of hopelessness and depression. During a routine physical exam, Anne's doctor discovers a lump in her breast. A biopsy reveals that the tumor is malignant.

Did Anne's personality or emotional state contribute to the formation or the growth of the malignant tumor? Can she now alter the course of her disease by changing her emotional state and thereby improve her immune functioning?

Several problems exist in research investigating the effects of mood and personality on the development of cancer (Honda & Goodwin, 2004). First, *cancer* is a general name for a variety of disease processes, each of which may have a varying susceptibility to emotions. Second, cancer develops over a relatively long period of time. Determining a temporal relationship between its occurrence and a specific mood or personality is not possible. Third, most studies examining the relationship between psychological variables and cancer are retrospective—that is, personality or mood states were assessed after the cancer was

---

CONTROVERSY

Can Laughter or Humor Influence the Course of a Disease?

Can humor reduce the severity of a physical illness or even be curative? Watching funny videos is associated with improved "vascular compliance" or greater blood flow through the arteries (Sugawara, Tarumi, & Tanaka, 2010) and laughter is also associated with improved heart functioning (Sakuragi, Sugiyama, & Takeuchi, 2002). Norman Cousins, who suffered from rheumatoid disease, described how he recovered his health through laughter. He claimed that ten minutes of laughter would provide two hours of pain relief (Cousins, 1979). In 1999, Patch Adams, a physician who used humor with his patients, received an award for "excellence in the field of therapeutic humor" at the American Association of Therapeutic Humor. Ohio psychologist Steve Wilson quit clinical practice in 1998 to found the World Laughter Tour and to teach classes in therapeutic laughter. He believes humor can reduce the need for pain medication, possibly boost immune functioning, and lower blood pressure ("Psychosomatic Medicine," 2004). Some research shows that exposing participants to humorous videos reduces stress and improves immune system functioning (Bennett, Zeller, Rosenberg, & McCann, 2003). However, the evidence is mixed and relatively weak (Bennett & Lengacher, 2006).

How might humor influence the disease process? Several routes are possible:

1. Humor may have a direct impact on physiological functioning.
2. Humor may influence people's beliefs about their ability to carry out health-promoting behaviors and give them greater confidence that their actions can relieve the illness.
3. Humor may serve as a buffer between exposure to stressors and the development of negative states, such as depression, which have been found to be related to the development or severity of physical conditions.
4. Humor may make an individual more likely to receive social support from friends and family.

For Further Consideration

1. How would you respond to someone arguing that laughter and humor play no role in slowing the progression of a disease such as cancer and that it is disrespectful to furnish false hope?
2. Knowing that humor produces physiological changes in the body, what might account for studies that find minimal effects of humor on the disease process?

diagnosed. The discovery that one has a life-threatening disease can produce a variety of emotions. People who receive the life-threatening diagnosis of cancer may respond with depression, anxiety, and confusion. Thus, instead of being a cause, negative emotions may be an emotional response to having a life-threatening disease.

Do stress, emotional difficulties, or personality characteristics increase the chance that a person develops cancer or increase disease severity if it does occur? Certain emotions and stressors have been associated with decreases in immune system functioning; under these conditions, cancer might be more likely to gain a foothold (Kiecolt-Glaser, 2009). Nevertheless, the connection between stress and naturally occurring cancers has yet to be demonstrated. In a critical review of the literature on the impact of psychological factors on the progression of cancer, Coyne, Stefanek, and Palmer (2007) concluded, "an adequately powered study examining effects of psychotherapy on survival after a diagnosis of cancer would require resources that are not justified by the strength of the available evidence" (p. 367).

Etiology of Psychophysiological Disorders

As we have seen, not everyone who faces stressful events develops a psychophysiological disorder or shows reduced immune functioning. Daily living involves constant exposure to stressors: work expectations at school or on the job, relationship problems, illness, marriage, and divorce to name a few. Why do only some individuals develop a physical disorder when exposed to stressors? In this section, we use the multipath model to explore some of the biological, psychological, social, and sociocultural dimensions of the disease process, as shown in Figure 6.9. Although we are discussing these dimensions separately, there are significant interactions among them.

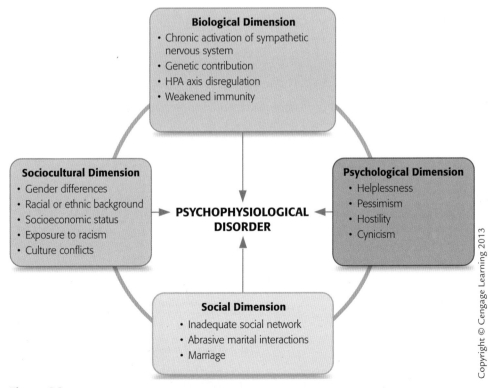

Copyright © Cengage Learning 2013

Figure 6.9

MULTIPATH MODEL FOR PSYCHOPHYSIOLOGICAL DISORDERS

The dimensions interact with one another and combine in different ways to result in a specific psychophysiological disorder.

Biological Dimension

Stressors, especially chronic ones, can dysregulate the HPA axis and the sympathetic nervous system through the release of neurohormones (epinephrine, norepinephrine, catecholamines, and cortisol). These neurohormones, along with the activation of the sympathetic nervous system, prepare the body for emergency action by increasing heart rate, respiration, alertness, and decreased vulnerability to inflammation. This preparation helps humans respond quickly to a crisis situation. However, when such activation occurs over an extended period of time, a psychophysiological disorder can develop (Kendall-Tackett, 2009; Stone et al., 2000; White & Moorey, 1997). Research supports the view that brief exposure to stressors enhances immune functioning, whereas long-lasting stress is associated with its deterioration (Segerstrom & Miller, 2004). Heightened HPA activity results in increased cortisol production: Excess cortisol has been linked with coronary artery calcification, a contributor to coronary heart disease (Hamer, O'Donnell, Lahiri, & Steptoe, 2010). Table 6.3 compares short-term adaptive responses to stress with symptoms that can result from chronic stress.

Early environmental influences such as traumatic childhood experiences may produce changes in brain structure and in the stress-responsive neurobiological systems, resulting in increased vulnerability to the development of a psychophysiological disorder (Anda et al., 2006). Additionally, genetic influences contribute to psychophysiological disorders. For example, cardiovascular stress reactivity as measured by blood pressure is more similar among monozygotic twins compared to dizygotic twins (De Geus et al., 2007). Genetic factors also appear to play a role in asthma. If one parent has asthma, a child has a one in three chance of developing asthma. If both parents have asthma, the chances increase to seven in ten (Asthma and Allergy Foundation of America, 2007). Migraine headaches may involve a biological predisposition, such as greater reactivity of the blood vessels in the brain in response to physical and psychological stressors. The precise mechanism involved, however, is not known, although recent research has pointed to the possible involvement of the brainstem (Dodick & Gargus, 2008).

Although genetics and physiological response to chronic stress play a role in physical illness, so do psychological, social, and sociocultural factors.

Psychological Dimension

Psychological and personality characteristics can also mediate the effects of exposure to stressors. Positive affect such as optimism, happiness, joy, and contentment enhance the parasympathetic modulation of heart rate, blood pressure, and other physiological stress reactions, whereas negative emotions accentuate the stress response (Davidson, Mostofsky,

TABLE 6.3   Adaptive and Maladaptive Responses to Stress

Adaptive Responses (Short-term Stress)	Maladaptive Responses (Chronic Stress)
increased glucose	hyperglycemia (diabetes)
increased blood pressure	hypertension, breakage of plaque in arteries
increased immunity	impaired immune response to illnesses
increased vigilance	hypervigilance
diminished interest in sex	global loss of interest in sex
improved cognition and memory	increased focus on traumatic events, lack of attention to current environment
faster blood clotting	increased thickness of coronary artery walls (coronary vascular disease, strokes)

Source: From Carels et al. (2003); Keltner & Dowben (2007)

& Whang, 2010). For example, a longitudinal study of employees remaining after nearly half of the workforce was laid off showed that although two-thirds developed health problems, one-third appeared to thrive. The individuals who did well had three characteristics: (1) commitment—they were involved in ongoing changes rather than giving up and feeling isolated; (2) control—they made attempts to influence decisions and refused to feel powerless; and (3) challenge—changes were viewed as opportunities (Maddi, 2002). These characteristics form the attribute of "hardiness," which appears to protect people from the harmful effect of stressors (Eshleman, Bowling, & Alarcon, 2010; Hamer, O'Donnell, Lahiri, & Steptoe, 2010).

A number of other psychological characteristics are also associated with health. Higher levels of personal control are associated with lower levels of stress (Christie & Barling, 2009). Those who have limited perception of control over life events ("I have little control over things that happen to me") show an increased risk of mortality from CHD (Surtees, Wainright, Luben, Wareham, Bingham, & Khaw, 2010). Control and the perception of control over the environment and its stressors appear to mitigate the effects of stress (Christie & Barling, 2009). In a sample of 335 older adults in Pittsburgh, Pennsylvania, diary ratings of stressful demands and levels of perceived control in daily life were obtained. Individuals who perceived greater daily stress and lower control were found to have thickening of the lining of the carotid artery, a marker of atherosclerosis (Kamarck et al., 2007). Similarly, among older adults with physical health problems, those with high levels of control behaviors, such as engaging in health-improving strategies, seeking help, and remaining motivated to address their physical problems, did not show the pattern of biological dysregulation typical of those with health issues (Wrosch et al., 2007). Women with demanding jobs involving little personal control had nearly double the chance of having a heart attack than women with more personal control over stressful jobs (Albert, Glynn, & Buring, 2010).

Research has identified positive emotions that impact the disease process. In a study of nearly 10,000 women over a 8-year follow-up period, those who scored high on optimism ("In unclear times, I usually expect the best") had a 9 percent lower risk of developing heart disease and a 14 percent lower risk of dying, whereas cynical women who had hostile thoughts about others ("I often have to take orders from someone who did not know as much as I did") were 16 percent more likely to die during the same time period (Tindle et al., 2009).

In general, negative emotional states such as depression, hostility, anxiety, and cynicism are related to elevated CHD risk (Low, Thurston, & Mattews, 2010). Depression can influence both physiological functioning and behaviors that affect health. Depressed individuals show a dysregulation of the autonomic nervous system. They have elevated levels of catecholamines (epinephrine and norepinephrine), resulting in exaggerated cardiovascular responses to stressors (Carney, Freedland, & Veith, 2005). In addition, an individual who is depressed may sleep and exercise less, eat less healthy food, and consume more caffeine, alcohol, or cigarettes. These behaviors may in turn increase the individual's susceptibility to disease or may prolong an existing illness.

The emotion of hostility has been implicated in several physiological disorders, particularly CHD (Tindle et al., 2010). Several possibilities exist that may explain the relationship between hostility and CHD. First, hostility may increase the hostile person's cardiovascular responsivity and physiology, subsequently increasing the risk of developing CHD. At least one study (Miller et al., 1998) supports this view. In that study, individuals who scored high on hostility showed exaggerated cardiovascular reactivity to a stressor (verbal harassment) compared with participants who were low on hostility. Thus, hostility may lead to damaging physiological responses. The experience of strong anger in young healthy males when they were frustrated or treated unfairly was related to elevations in serum cholesterol and low-density lipoproteins, both of which have been found to increase the risk of developing CHD (Richards et al., 2000). Hostility in children and adolescents has also been related to elevated lipids and blood pressure (Raikkonen, Matthews, & Salomon, 2003).

Social Dimension

Coronary heart disease (CHD), impaired immunological functioning, and other adverse health outcomes have been associated with a variety of social stressors (Dickerson & Kemeny, 2004; Pike et al., 1997). Childhood adversities such as physical or sexual abuse have been linked to adult onset headaches (Lee et al., 2009). Divorced or separated men tend to have more physical illness than their married counterparts (Eaker et al., 2007), and separated and divorced men who are preoccupied with thoughts of their former partners show a lower level of immune functioning (Kiecolt-Glaser et al., 1987). Abrasive marital interactions between long-married men and women are also associated with negative health changes (Kiecolt-Glaser et al., 1997). However, having a strong and positive social network is associated with positive health (Cohen & Lemay, 2007). In fact, good relationships may moderate the link between hostility and poor health. In one study, hostile individuals in high-quality relationships showed reduced physiological reactivity to stress (Guyll, Cutrona, Burzette, & Russell, 2010). Among African American and Caucasian adolescents, those who scored low on social skills and high on anger or hostility measures had increased abdominal fat and greater arterial stiffness (hardening of the arteries); these associations were stronger for African American participants (Midei & Matthews, 2009). Although our discussion has focused on the direct physiological impact of stress on health, indirect pathways must also be considered. For example, an individual with a spouse or a large social network may receive encouragement for healthy eating habits, exercise, and other health-promoting activities, thus increasing resistance to disease.

Did You Know?

Spirituality and religion have been shown to be associated with physical health. In one study of 5,300 African Americans, a group at risk for high blood pressure, those involved in religious activities had significantly lower blood pressure than those who were not. This effect was found even though religious African Americans were heavier and were less likely to take medications as prescribed.

Source: Wyatt (2006)

Sociocultural Dimension

Discrimination, cultural expectations and conflicts with societal standards can have a significant impact on health. Women are more likely to be affected by stress because of their role as caregivers for children, partners, and parents (Stambor, 2006). Women who report high job stress or who perceive their relationships with their supervisors to be poor had higher fibrinogen levels than other female employees. Fibrinogen, a blood-clotting compound, can increase risk of CHD by contributing to atherosclerosis and the formation of blood clots (Davis, Mathews, Meilahn, & Kiss, 1995). Social relationships are very important for women. In a longitudinal study of men and women, high loneliness in women (discrepancy between actual and desired social relationships) was associated with a nearly 80 percent increase in coronary heart disease; this association was not found in men (Thurston & Kuzansky, 2009).

Although genetic and other biological factors may perhaps partially explain the high rate of hypertension in African Americans, another line of research supports a sociocultural explanation. Perceived discrimination can heighten the stress response and elevate blood pressure and heart rate (Pascoe & Richman, 2009). Exposure to racism is associated with elevations in cardiovascular responses in African American men and women (Clark, 2006; Merritt et al., 2006; Pascoe & Richman, 2009). African Americans who watched videos or imagined depictions of social situations involving racism showed increases in heart rate and blood pressure (Fang & Myers, 2001; Jones et al., 1996). Elevations in cardiovascular responses were also observed among a sample of African American men who were exposed to subtle racism (Merritt et al., 2006). Thus, exposure to discrimination may function as a chronic stressor and increase the chances of hypertension (Troxel et al., 2003). This relationship may be more complicated, however, at least among African American women. Increases in blood pressure when exposed to racism were found among those who were low in seeking social support, whereas those most likely to seek social support did not show this tendency (Clark, 2006). Thus, coping ability, resources, and social support may mitigate vascular reactivity.

Cultural changes have been found to affect health in Samoa. Samoans have a culture that stresses rigid control of behaviors, including strict discipline for children, control of anger for

David Sacks / TSI / Getty Images

females, and suppression of emotions in adults. Steele and McGarvey (1997) hypothesized that the Samoan traditional pattern in which women were expected to suppress their emotions might conflict with the expanded roles expected by modern young women, resulting in increases in blood pressure. In support of their hypothesis, the investigators found an interesting contrast: Higher blood pressure was related to an inhibition of anger in young women but to an outward expression of anger in older women. The roles or behavior patterns the women were socialized to (modern or traditional) appeared to influence whether the expression of anger increased blood pressure.

Treatment of Psychophysiological Disorders

Psychotherapy has been found to be effective in treating the psychophysiological disorders. Individuals who showed "burnout" due to chronic job stress had significantly lower cortisol levels as compared with a control group. After fourteen sessions of psychotherapy, they showed an increase in morning cortisol levels (Mommersteeg et al., 2006). Although mind-body techniques may not cure illness, individuals who engage in stress-management techniques report less pain, less anxiety, improved sleep, a higher quality of life, and a sense of participation in their treatment. Stress hormones are also reduced (Tyre, 2004). Physical treatments such as drug therapy, eliminating certain foods associated with migraines, and exercise can reduce migraine symptoms. Several psychological interventions, such as relaxation, cognitive therapy, and biofeedback, have also been used to treat headaches (NINDS, 2007).

Treatment programs for psychophysiological disorders generally consist of both medical treatment for the physical symptoms and psychological therapy to eliminate stress and anxiety. This combination provides a wide array of approaches to these disorders, with mainly positive results. Two of the dominant psychological approaches are stress management and anxiety management programs, which usually include either relaxation training or biofeedback.

Relaxation Training

Relaxation training is a therapeutic technique in which a person acquires the ability to relax the muscles of the body in almost any circumstance. It is possible that this reduces the "fight or flight" reaction that may be triggered by muscle tension (Marr, 2006).

relaxation training therapeutic technique in which a person acquires the ability to relax the muscles of the body in almost any circumstance

Progressive muscle relaxation has been effective in reducing physiological arousal and the impact of stressors (Rausch, Gramling, & Auerbach, 2006; Trautmann & Kroener-Herwig, 2010). Current programs are typically modeled after Jacobson's (1938, 1967) progressive relaxation training. Imagine that you are a client who is beginning the training. You are instructed to concentrate on one set of muscles at a time—first tensing them and then relaxing them. First you clench your fists as tightly as possible for approximately ten seconds, then you release them. As you release your tightened muscles, you are asked to focus on the sensation of warmth and looseness in your hands. You practice this tightening and relaxing cycle several times before proceeding to the next muscle group, in your lower arms. After each muscle group has received individual attention in tensing and relaxing, the trainer asks you to tighten and then relax your entire body. The emphasis throughout the procedure is on the contrast between the feelings produced during tensing and those produced during relaxing. For a novice, the entire exercise lasts about thirty minutes.

A relaxation-based treatment was found to be effective in producing "clinically significant" reductions in headache activity among recurrent headache sufferers. The program was unique in that it was conducted over the Internet and through e-mail. Participants received instructions for applied relaxation and its application in stressful situations. Although dropout rates were high, a large number of participants appeared to benefit from self-help–focused intervention with minimal therapist contact (Strom, Pettersson, & Andersson, 2000; Trautmann & Kroener-Herwig, 2010).

Biofeedback

In biofeedback training, the client is taught to *voluntarily* control some physiological functions, such as heart rate or blood pressure. During training, the client receives second-by-second information (feedback) regarding the activity of the organ or function of interest. For someone attempting to lower high blood pressure, for example, the feedback might be actual blood pressure readings, which are presented visually on a screen or as some auditory signal transmitted through a set of headphones. The biofeedback device enables the patient to learn to control the targeted physiological function. Eventually the patient learns to use that method without benefit of the feedback device.

Case Study

A twenty-three-year-old male reported having a resting heart rate that varied between 95 and 120 beats when he was in high school. This variation was associated with apprehension over exams. The patient came into treatment because his high heart rate had continued and he was concerned that it might lead to a serious cardiac condition. The treatment consisted of eight sessions of biofeedback training. The patient's heart rate was monitored, and he was provided with both a visual and an auditory feedback signal. After the treatment period and one year later, his heart rate had stabilized and was within normal limits (73 beats per minute). The patient reported that he had learned to control his heart rate during stressful situations by both relaxing and concentrating on reducing the heart rate (Janssen, 1983).

biofeedback training a physiological and behavioral approach in which an individual receives information regarding particular autonomic functions and is rewarded for influencing those functions in a desired direction

Biofeedback is essentially an operant conditioning technique in which the feedback serves as reinforcement. It has been used to help people lower their heart rates and decrease their blood pressure during stressful situations (Nakao et al., 1997; Westm, 2007), treat migraine and tension headaches (Holroyd et al., 1995; Schwartz & Andrasik, 2003), decrease the need for medication in asthma (Lehrer et al., 2004), reduce muscle tension (Fogel, 2003), and redirect blood flow (Reading & Mohr, 1976). Biofeedback and verbal reinforcement were used to help children with asthma control their respiratory functioning (Kahn, Staerk, & Bonk, 1974).

Cognitive-Behavioral Interventions

Because hostility is associated with hypertension, cognitive-behavioral programs have been developed to reduce the expression of this emotion. In one study, individuals with hypertension participated in a six-week anger management program (Larkin & Zayfert, 1996). When initially exposed to confrontational role-playing situations, they experienced sharp rises in blood pressure. The participants learned to relax by using muscle relaxation techniques and to change their thoughts about confrontational situations. They also received assertiveness training to learn appropriate ways of expressing disagreements. After the various types of training, their blood pressure was significantly reduced when they again participated in confrontational role-playing scenes.

Social-cognitive processing approaches can help individuals who have been told they have a life-threatening disease attempt to adjust and find validation and meaning in the experience. This approach is helpful for those who may see the world as unfair, who are experiencing reactive depression or avoidance, or who find it difficult to process the disease experience. In a study of seventy female cancer survivors, cognitive processing opportunities were found to predict adjustment to cancer (Cordova et al., 2001). Those who were unable to cognitively process their diseases because of invalidation ("When I talk about cancer, my husband tells me I'm living in the past") or because of discomfort ("It's difficult to share with those you love, as they are scared, too"; p. 709) reported more depressive symptoms. In contrast, women who reported being able to talk about cancer were less depressed and better adjusted.

Cognitive strategies to improve coping skills and to manage stress have also been effective in improving both physiological functioning and psychological distress in individuals with chronic illness (Cruess et al., 2000). Improved immune functioning and reduced cortisol levels (associated with a reduction in stress) was found among breast cancer patients who participated in cognitive behavioral treatment, whereas patients in a control group continued to show deterioration of their immune response (Witek-Janusek, Albuquerque, Chroniak, Chroniak, Durazo-Arvizu, & Mathews, 2008). In a one-year follow-up study, prostate and breast cancer patients who learned techniques to cope with stress showed improved quality of life and altered immune and cortisol levels that are consistent with lower levels of stress (Carlson, Speca, Faris, & Patel, 2007). Patients with asthma who engaged in three sessions of writing about a trauma ("Write about the most stressful experience in your life") significantly improved lung function, as opposed to those who wrote only about time management (Stone et al., 2000). With many diseases, having the opportunity to express fears, to cognitively process beliefs, and to develop adaptive strategies appears to improve patients' feelings of well-being and physical health.

© Michael A. Kelles/CORBIS

Controlling Physiological Responses

Meditation is associated with a relaxed bodily state produced by minimizing distractions and focusing on a positive image, mantra, or word. This process has been associated with the reduction in the level of stress hormones and the development of a sense of control. It has been found to be helpful in the treatment of hypertension and headaches.

Future Directions in Research Involving Stress

As we mentioned earlier, psychologists are becoming increasingly aware that single-cause models of psychophysiological illness are inadequate. Not everyone exposed to the same set of stressors develops a psychophysiological disorder. In addition, we must be able to explain why an individual develops coronary heart disease rather than asthma. It is clear that the search for an explanation must consider biological, psychological, social, and sociocultural dimensions. We are just beginning to understand the biology of stress disorders and the specific brain structures involved, but many questions remain. For example, what does it mean that parts of the brain become "sensitized"? Have structural changes occurred, and are they reversible? Psychological characteristics also mediate the relationship between a stressor and its impact on the body. Negative emotions may amplify the event, whereas cognitive characteristics such as control, optimism, and self-efficacy may defuse its impact. Do these qualities directly affect physical health through the immune system, or is it that individuals with these qualities behave in a manner that affects health (amount of exercise, sleep, type of food)? Social networks and sociocultural factors are also related to health. Why does marriage appear to have more health benefits for men than for women? Why are there gender and racial differences in the prevalence of both the psychological and physical stress disorders? As you can see, many questions remain that can be answered only by continuing to examine the multitude of possible contributors to the stress disorders.

Summary

1. What are acute and post-traumatic stress disorders, and how are they diagnosed?

    - Acute and post-traumatic stress disorders involve exposure to a traumatic event, resulting in intrusive memories of the occurrence, attempts to forget or repress the memories, emotional withdrawal, and increased arousal.

    - Acute stress disorder (ASD) is characterized by anxiety and dissociative symptoms that occur within one month after exposure to a traumatic stressor. Post-traumatic stress disorder (PTSD) is characterized by anxiety, dissociative, and other symptoms that last for more than one month and that occur as a result of exposure to extreme trauma.

2. What causes acute and post-traumatic stress disorders?

    - Various biological, psychological, sociocultural, and social factors have been implicated in the stress disorders. Possible biological factors involve a sensitized autonomic system, involvement of stress hormones, and brain cell damage. Psychological factors include level of cognitive functioning, trait anxiety and depression, and classical conditioning. Poor or inadequate support during childhood has also been identified as possibly contributing to the development of the stress disorders, as have various sociocultural factors, such as immigration status and gender.

3. What are possible treatments for acute and post-traumatic stress disorders?

    - Antidepressant medication has been successful in the treatment of ASD and PTSD, as has exposure to cues associated with the trauma. Exposure and cognitive-based therapies such as psychoeducation have also proven effective in some cases.

4. What role does stress play in physical health, and what are the psychophysiological disorders?

    - Any external events or situations that place a physical or psychological demand on a person can serve as stressors and can affect physical health. Stressors can range from chronic irritation and frustration to acute and traumatic events.

    - A psychophysiological disorder is any physical disorder that has a strong psychological basis or component. Psychophysiological disorders involve actual tissue damage (such as coronary heart disease), a disease process (immune impairment), or physiological dysfunction (as in asthma or migraine headaches). Examples of psychophysiological disorders include coronary heart disease (CHD); hypertension; migraine, tension, and cluster headaches; and asthma.

    - Not everyone develops an illness when exposed to the same stressor or traumatic event because stress is an internal psychological or physiological response to a stressor. Individuals reacting to the same stressor may do so in very different ways.

5. What causes psychophysiological disorders?

- Various biological, psychological, sociocultural, and social factors have been implicated in the psychophysiological disorders.
- Biological explanations include (1) chronic activation of the sympathetic nervous system and continual release of neurohormones, and (2) genetic contributions.
- Psychological contributors include characteristics such as helplessness, isolation, cynicism, pessimism, and hostility, as well as feelings of depression or anxiety.
- Social contributors include having an inadequate social network; abrasive interpersonal interactions; a stressful environment; and, for men, being unmarried.
- Sociocultural factors such as gender, racial, or ethnic background are risk factors in certain physiological disorders. Stressful environments associated with poverty, prejudice, and racism, and cultural conflicts have been related to illnesses.

6. What methods have been developed to treat psychophysiological disorders?

- These disorders are treated through stress management or anxiety management programs, combined with medical treatment for physical symptoms or conditions.
- Relaxation training and biofeedback training, which help the client learn to control muscular or organic functioning, are usually a part of such programs.
- Cognitive-behavioral interventions, which involve changing anxiety-arousing thoughts, have also been useful.

7. What future lines of research involving stress are likely to be explored?

- Stress continues to be explored from a variety of perspectives, and many questions remain that can be answered only by continuing to examine the multitude of possible contributors to the stress disorders.

Media Resources

Psychology CourseMate   Access an interactive eBook, chapter-specific interactive learning tools, including flash cards, quizzes, videos, and more in your Psychology CourseMate, accessed through CengageBrain.com.

CENGAGE**NOW**

CengageNow   CengageNOW is an easy-to-use online resource that helps you study in less time to get the grade you want—NOW. If your textbook does not include an access code card, go to CengageBrain.com to gain access.

CENGAGE**brain**.com

CengageBrain   More than just an interactive study guide, WebTutor is an anytime, anywhere customized learning solution with an eBook, keeping you connected to your textbook, instructor, and classmates. Purchase the access chosen by your instructor at CengageBrain.com.

7

Maciej Laska

Somatic Symptom and Dissociative Disorders

A boy of twelve was referred for investigation of a gait disorder. He was noted to walk with a bizarre staggering gait, which on close inspection could be seen to be carefully coordinated. Systematic detailed clinical examination showed no neurological abnormality. Shortly before the onset of his illness he had moved with his peer group to a secondary school with high academic expectations of pupils. He had not been able to achieve these, and the teacher of his favorite subject had humiliated him by rejecting class work he had done and throwing his workbook on the floor. (Leary, 2003, p. 436)

Joe Beiger, a beloved husband, father, grandfather, and high school assistant athletic director, walked out of his front door one morning with his two dogs. Minutes later, his very identity was seemingly wiped from his brain's hard drive. For twenty-five days, he wandered the streets of Dallas, unable to remember his name, what he did for a living or where he lived, until finally a contractor he had been working with happened to recognize him (Associated Press, 2007b).

In this chapter, we discuss (1) somatic symptom disorders, conditions that involve physical complaints or bodily symptoms that cannot be fully explained by a medical condition, and (2) dissociative disorders, which involve alterations in memory, consciousness, or identity as reflected in the earlier cases studies. These disorders, and the genuine distress experienced by those with these conditions, are believed to occur because of underlying psychological or social factors. We discuss dissociative and somatic symptoms disorders together because they have been found to have common etiological roots. For example, in a study of 118 psychiatric patients, 30.5 percent had both somatic and dissociative symptoms (Malhotra, Singh, & Mohan, 2005). Dissociative disorders are thought to involve psychological mechanisms for coping with stress, whereas those with a somatic symptom disorder express stress through physical symptoms (Cloninger & Dokucu, 2008). We begin with a discussion of the somatic symptom disorders.

CHAPTER OUTLINE

Somatic Symptom Disorders

The somatic symptom disorders are a disparate group of disorders, including the complex somatic symptom disorders, conversion disorders, and factitious disorders. Psychological factors affecting medical

focus questions

1 When do somatic complaints represent a psychological disorder? What are the causes and treatments of these conditions?

2 What are dissociations? What forms can they take? How are they caused, and how are they treated?

conditions (psychophysiological disorders) discussed in the previous chapter are also part of this category. These conditions are grouped together primarily because they involve physical symptoms and/or anxiety over illness (DSM-5, 2011). We decided to separate the psychophysiological disorders from the other somatic symptom disorders because the former involves identifiable medical conditions, whereas the others do not. Differences between the somatic symptoms disorders are shown in Table 7.1.

Complex Somatic Symptom Disorder

The complex somatic symptom disorders (CSSD) are composed of categories previously known in the DSM-IV as somatization disorder and pain disorders. As opposed to psychophysiological disorders such as hypertension and migraine headaches, complex somatic symptoms disorders do not involve an identifiable medical condition. They are often considered to be "nuisance medical problems" because there is no "legitimate" disease (Frohm & Beehler, 2010). Patients with these disorders are often considered to be faking their symptoms (So, 2008). Although a physiological basis for the complaints cannot be identified, mental health professionals do not consider the symptoms to be under voluntary or conscious control (Parish & Yutzy, 2011).

Individuals with CSSD tend to have great anxiety regarding their health, report suffering from somatic symptoms, and often believe that they have an undiagnosed medical condition. These concerns often result in depressive symptoms (Burton, McGorm, Weller & Sharpe, 2010). Many undergo unnecessary surgical or assessment procedures. With the CSSD disorders, reassurance that there is no medical problem or that the problem is not severe is ineffective; the search for medical advice or help continues (Lahmann, Loew, Tritt, & Nicket, 2008). Because of this, some researchers believe that "health anxiety disorder" would be a more accurate description for these conditions (Abramowitz & Braddock, 2011; Kroenkek, Sharpe, & Sykes, 2007; Taylor, Jang, Stein, & Asmundson, 2008). (See Table 7.2 for types of somatic complaints reported by individual with CSSD.)

Depending on the particular primary care setting, 10 to 50 percent of all patients report excessive concerns over physical symptoms (Arnold et al., 2006; DeWaal et al., 2004; McCarron, 2006; McGorm, Burton, Weller, Murray, & Sharpe, 2010). Deciding if someone has a CSSD can be problematic. Sykes (2007) points out that it is often difficult to determine whether physical complaints are, in fact, "disproportionate" or "not fully explained." In some cases, physical or neurological factors that explain the symptoms are later discovered (Alao & Chung, 2007; Moser et al., 1998).

Diagnosis of Complex Somatic Symptom Disorder

Complex somatic symptom disorder is characterized by excessive distress over somatic symptoms that are accompanied with high levels of health related anxiety. These concerns over the symptoms have been present for six months or more (American Psychiatric Association, 2011). A diagnosis of CSSD can involve any of the following predominant features: multiple somatic complaints (somatization disorder) or predominantly pain.

complex somatic symptom disorders a group of disorders involving physical symptoms or complaints that have no physiological basis; believed to occur due to an underlying psychological conflict or need

dissociative disorders a group of disorders, including dissociative amnesia, dissociative fugue, dissociative identity disorder, and depersonalization disorder, all of which involve some sort of dissociation, or separation, of a part of the person's consciousness, memory, or identity

DISORDERS CHART   SOMATIC SYMPTOM DISORDERS

TABLE 7.1

Disorders	Identifiable Medical Condition?	Voluntarily Produced?
Psychophysiological Disorders	Yes	No
Complex Somatic Symptom Disorder	No	No
Functional Neurological Symptom Disorder	No	No
Illness Anxiety Disorder	No	No
Factitious Disorder	Self-Induced	Yes

Complex Somatic Symptom Disorder with Somatization Features

Individuals with complex somatic symptom disorder (CSSD) with somatization features, have a multiplicity of physical complains that can involve: pain symptoms in different parts of the body; gastrointestinal symptoms such as nausea, diarrhea, and bloating; sexual symptoms such as sexual indifference, irregular menses, or erectile dysfunction; and pseudoneurological symptoms such as amnesia or breathing difficulties (Yates, 2010).

The next case illustrates several of the characteristics involved in these disorders.

Case Study

Cheryl was a thirty-eight-year-old, separated Italian American woman who was raising her ten-year-old daughter, Melanie, without much support. Cheryl suffered from vertigo and had a history of neck pain and other vague somatic complaints, as well as a history of several abusive relationships and unresolved grief about the loss of her mother. Cheryl and Melanie described in rich detail an elaborate system of cues that Melanie had learned to respond to by comforting her mother, providing remedies such as back rubs and hot compresses or taking over activities such as grocery shopping if her mother felt dizzy in the store (McDaniel & Speice, 2001).

TABLE 7.2 Symptoms Reported by Patients with Complex Somatic Symptoms Disorder (CSSD)

Gastrointestinal Symptoms	Pseudoneurological Symptoms
Vomiting	Amnesia
Abdominal pain	Difficulty swallowing
Nausea	Loss of voice
Bloating and excessive gas	Difficulty walking
	Seizures

Pain Symptoms	Reproductive Organ Symptoms
Diffuse pain	Burning sensation in sex organs
Pain in extremities	Dyspareunia
Joint pain	Irregular menstrual cycles
Headaches	Excessive menstrual bleeding

Cardiopulmonary Symptoms	Other Conditions
Shortness of breath at rest	Vague food allergies
Palpitations	"Hypoglycemia"
Chest pain	Chronic Fatigue Syndrome
Dizziness	Fibromyalgia
	Chemical sensitivity

From: So (2008)

In this case, a therapist encouraged Cheryl and Melanie to identify both adaptive behaviors and "nonhelpful behaviors" that could be reinforcing the symptoms. Alternate ways of getting support were also discussed. However, in many cases the "cause" of the behavior is much more difficult to determine.

Anxiety, depression, and other psychiatric disorders often coexist with CSSD with somatization features (Allen et al., 2001; Bleichhardt, Timmer, & Reif, 2005). Although it is considered a chronic condition, in one large study, only about one-third of those diagnosed with the disorder met the criteria twelve months later (Simon & Gureje, 1999). Although physical complaints and concerns are common in the general population, CSSD with somatization features (or *hysteria*, as it was once called) is relatively rare, with an overall prevalence rate of up to 2 percent for women and less than 0.2 percent for men (Yates, 2010). The diagnosis is more prevalent in African Americans and twice as likely among those with less than a high school education or those of lower socioeconomic status (Noyes et al., 2006; Swartz et al., 1991).

Did You Know?

The expression of psychological and social distress through physical symptoms is the norm in many cultures of the world:

- Worldwide, the most common somatic symptoms are gastrointestinal complaints or abnormal skin sensations, whereas in the United States menstrual pain, abdominal pain, and chest pain are the most common somatic symptoms.

- Distinctive cultural somatic symptoms include concerns about body odor (Japan), body heat and coldness (Nigeria), losing semen while urinating (India), and kidney weakness (China).

Source: Singh (2007)

Complex Somatic Symptom Disorder with Pain Features

Complex somatic symptom disorder (CSSD) with pain features is characterized by reports of severe pain that (1) appears to have no physiological or neurological basis; (2) seems significantly greater than would be expected with an existing physical condition; or (3) lingers long after a physical injury has healed. As is the case with the other somatic symptom disorders, psychological conflicts are involved. People who have pain disorder have numerous physical complaints, make frequent visits to physicians, and may become drug or medication abusers.

Chronic pain is relatively common and affects 30 percent of the U.S. population (Hoffman, Papas, Chatkoff, & Kerns, 2007; Turk, Swanson, & Tunks, 2008). In one

complex somatic symptom disorder (CSSD) with somatization features chronic complaints of specific bodily symptoms that have no physical basis

complex somatic symptom disorder (CSSD) with pain features reports of severe or lingering pain that appears to have no physical basis

A Physical or Psychological Disorder?

CSSD with pain features is most frequently diagnosed in women, in minority group members, and among those living in poverty. How can we determine if the cause of the pain is psychological, physical, or both?

study, somatic complaints included back pain (30 percent), joint pain (25 percent), pain in the extremities (20 percent), headache (19 percent), bloating (11 percent), abdominal pain (11 percent), and chest pain (5 percent) (Walker & Furer, 2008). Higher rates of pain disorder are reported in women, those of lower socioeconomic class, African Americans and Latinos (Poleshuck et al., 2010). Unexplained physical pain involving the abdomen, head, and limbs is frequently present in young children (Furness, Glazebrook, Tay, Abbas, & Slaveska-Hollis, 2009; Hunfeld et al., 2002).

Because psychological factors can play a role in exacerbating pain, it is sometimes difficult to determine when pain is "excessive" or "lingering too long." Understandably, questioning the veracity of reports of pain results in feelings of anger and frustration from patients (Furness et al., 2009; Merten & Brunnhuber, 2004). Some researchers believe that the pain type of CSSD should be viewed as a psychophysiological disorder, indicating that both physical and psychological factors are involved (Fava & Wise, 2007).

Illness Anxiety Disorder

Case Study

A 41-year-old woman, Linda, reported having a history of concerns about cancer, especially stomach or bowel cancer. Her grandmother had bowel cancer when Linda was twenty-two. Media stories of illness, medical documentaries, or reading about people who are ill triggers her worries: "I notice a feeling of discomfort and bloating in my abdomen. I wonder if this could be an early sign of cancer. Cancer is something that can happen at my age. People can have very few symptoms and then suddenly it is there and a few months later they are gone." (Furer & Walker, 2005, p. 261)

The primary characteristic of **illness anxiety disorder** (also referred to as hypochondriasis) is high anxiety about one's health that exists in the absence of or with only mild somatic symptoms. Instead, there is a preoccupation with and oversensitivity to normal variations in bodily function or sensations. Illness anxiety disorder appears to be a cognitive disorder in which the individual misinterprets bodily sensations and variations as indications that they have a serious illness or are dying from an undetected disease (White, Craft, & Gervino, 2010). This bodily focus produces feelings of alarm when unpleasant or "unusual" symptoms are identified (Furer & Walker, 2005; Lahmann, Loew, Tritt, & Nicket, 2008; Sorensen, Birket-Smith, Wattar, Buemann, & Salkovskis, 2011).

Those with illness anxiety disorder report recurring and distressing intrusive images such as being told that they have a life-threatening illness, dying due to the illness, and the reaction of loved ones to their death (Muse, McManus, Hackman, Williams, & Williams, 2010). They engage in excessive behaviors such as checking their body for signs of illness or disease, seeking reassurances from others or on the Internet, and avoiding activities such as exercising that they believe might exacerbate their condition. The preoccupation with illness must be present for at least six months for the diagnosis (American Psychiatric Association, 2011). Approximately 4 to 6 percent of those who visit doctors have this condition (Yates, 2010).

illness anxiety disorder (hypochondriasis) persistent health anxiety and concern that one has an undetected physical illness, even in the face of physical evaluations that reveal no organic problems

In a study of twenty individuals with hypochondriasis (ten females and ten males), the most common health concerns involved undetected cancer, heart attack, and brain tumors. In contrast with individuals in a control group, the participants showed a tendency to overestimate negative outcomes with ambiguous health-related information (Haenen et al., 2000). See Table 7.3 for examples of the fears related to health seen in individuals with hypochondriasis.

Functional Neurological Symptom Disorder

Case Study

A., a thirty-four-year-old woman, described frequent attacks of sudden onset, often resembling sleep but sometimes involving violent jerking of arms and legs and arching of her back. She experienced violent outbursts. She viewed herself as disabled and needing constant care and was extremely dependent on her partner and teenage stepsons (Howlett & Reuber, 2009, p. 129). Interviews revealed that she was raped at the age of thirteen by her biological father and was very traumatized by the death of her grandparents.

TABLE 7.3   Percentage of Adults with Illness Anxiety Disorder Who Endorse Selected Fears Related to Health

Item	Much or Very Much Agree (%)
When I notice my heart beating rapidly, I worry I might have a heart attack	51
When I get aches or pains, I worry that there is something wrong with my health	75
It scares me when I feel "shaky" (trembling)	47
It scares me when I feel tingling or prickling sensations in my hands	50
When I feel a strong pain in my stomach, I worry it might be cancer	62

Source: Walker & Furer, 2008

Case Study

The boy was referred at age ten as a case of juvenile myasthenia gravis (weakening of the voluntary muscles). For five weeks he had been unable to open his eyes, and the consequent "blindness" had stopped him from attending school. On detailed physical examination, no other abnormalities were found. In the hospital ward it was noted that he did not walk into furniture. He was the local village football star and had been blamed for his team's defeat, and from that day he had been unable to open his eyes. (Leary, 2003, p. 436)

Functional neurological symptom disorder (FNSD) (also known as conversion disorder) involves motor, sensory, or seizure-like symptoms that are incongruent with any recognized neurological or medical disorder. The most common conversion symptoms seen in neurological clinics involve psychogenic movement disorders such as disturbances of stance and gait, sensory symptoms such as blindness, loss of voice, motor tics, dizziness, and psychogenic seizures (Friedman & LaFrance, 2010; Marshall, Landau, & Carroll, 2008; Rechlin, Loew, & Joraschky, 1997). Neurologists report that about 2 percent to 3 percent of new referrals involve cases of conversion disorder (Friedman & LaFrance, 2010). Individuals with this disorder are not consciously faking symptoms, as are those who are malingering (feigning illness for an external purpose such as getting out of work duties). A person with FNSD actually believes that there is a genuine physical problem.

As illustrated in the earlier case studies, the appearance of conversion symptoms is often related to traumas or even milder stressors such as the loss of employment or divorce (Marshall, Landau, & Carroll, 2008). Nearly 75 percent of respondents in one sample reported that their conversion symptoms developed after they had experienced a stressor (Singh & Lee, 1997). In a ten-year follow-up study of individuals diagnosed with FNSD, symptoms persisted in about 40 percent of the cases (Mace & Trimble, 1996). Sudden onset, shorter duration of symptoms, and a good premorbid (pre-illness) personality are associated with positive outcome (Crimlisk et al., 1998; Singh & Lee, 1997).

In general, individuals with FNSD do not incur any physical damage from the symptoms. For example, a person with hysterical paralysis of the legs rarely shows the atrophy of the lower limbs that occurs when there is an underlying biological cause. In some persistent cases, however, disuse *can* result in atrophy (Schonfeldt-Lecuona et al., 2003). Some symptoms, such as glove anesthesia (a loss of feeling in the hand, ending in a straight line at the wrist) or an inability to talk or whisper combined with the ability to cough are easily diagnosed as conversion disorders because coughing indicates an intact

functional neurological symptom disorder (conversion disorder) impairments in sensory or motor functioning controlled by the voluntary nervous system that suggest a neurological disorder but with no underlying medical cause

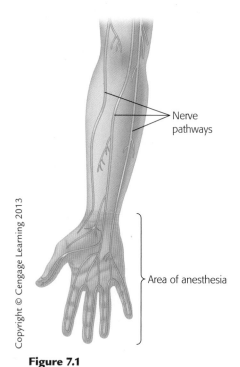

Nerve pathways

Area of anesthesia

Figure 7.1

GLOVE ANESTHESIA

In glove anesthesia, the lack of feeling covers the hand in a glove-like shape. It does not correspond to the distribution of nerve pathways. This discrepancy leads to a diagnosis of functional neurological symptom disorder.

vocal cord function and, in glove anesthesia, the area of sensory loss does not correspond to the distribution of nerves in the body (Brown, 2004) (Figure 7.1). Other symptoms may require extensive neurological and physical examinations to rule out a true medical disorder before a diagnosis of FNSD can be made. Discriminating between FNSD and actual medical conditions can be difficult when no specific tests exist to confirm the diagnosis (Friedman & LaFrance, 2010). Neurologists are reluctant to make a FNSD diagnosis unless absolutely certain (Kanaan, Armstrong, & Wesseley, 2009).

Factitious Disorder and Factitious Disorder Imposed on Another

Case Study

Mandy was not hesitant to discuss how she was diagnosed with leukemia at the age of thirty-seven, right after her husband left her. She shared how chemotherapy damaged her immune system, liver, and heart, resulting in a stroke and weeks in a coma. She posted her story and updates on a Web site and the virtual community rallied support for her as she shared her story of additional surgeries and bouts of life-threatening infections. It was later discovered that Mandy was not sick and had made up the entire story (Kleeman, 2011).

Before we discuss the factitious disorders, we should note that these disorders are completely different from malingering—faking a disorder to achieve some goal, such as an insurance settlement. With malingering, the goals are usually apparent, and the individual can "turn off" the symptoms whenever they are no longer useful. In factitious disorders, the purpose of the simulated or induced illness is much less apparent. Complex psychological variables are assumed to be involved, and the individual is usually unaware of the motivation for the behavior. Simulation of illness is often done almost compulsively. Factitious disorders are mental disorders in which the symptoms of physical or mental illnesses are deliberately induced or simulated with no apparent incentive—other than attention from medical personnel or others. Factitious disorder involves inducing or simulating illness in oneself, whereas factitious disorder imposed on another involves inducing or falsifying illness in another.

Factitious Disorder

In the past, this condition was called "hospital addiction" or professional patient syndrome. In 1951, it was given the name Munchausen syndrome after an eighteenth century German nobleman who was noted for making up fanciful stories (Bande & Garcia-Alba, 2008). Factitious disorder is characterized by the presentation of oneself to others as ill or impaired through the recurrent falsification of physical or psychological symptoms. This is done without any obvious external rewards (American Psychiatric Association, 2011).

Signs of a factitious disorder may include lingering unexplained illnesses with multiple surgical or complex treatments; "remarkable willingness" to undergo painful or dangerous treatments such as amputations and prophylactic double mastectomy; a tendency to anger if the illness is questioned; and the involvement of multiple doctors (Flaherty et al., 2001; Gregory & Jindal, 2006; Worley, Feldman, & Hamilton, 2009). Depending on the study, the prevalence rate for adults is about 1.3 percent and about 0.7 percent among adolescents (Ehrlich, Pfeiffer, Salbach, Lenz, & Lehmkuhl, 2008).

Factitious Disorder Imposed on Another Person

A hidden camera at a children's hospital captured the image of a mother suffocating the baby she had brought in for treatment of breathing problems. In another case, a child was brought in for treatment of ulcerations on his back; hospital staff discovered the mother had been rubbing oven cleaner on his skin. Another "sick" infant had been fed laxatives

factitious disorder symptoms of physical or mental illnesses are deliberately induced or simulated with no apparent external incentive

for nearly four months (Wartik, 1994). In each of these cases, no apparent motive was found other than the attention the parent received from the hospital staff caring for the child's "illness."

If an individual deliberately feigns or induces an illness in another person (or even pets) in the absence of any obvious external rewards, the diagnosis is factitious disorder imposed on another person. In the preceding cases, the mothers produced symptoms in their children to vicariously assume the sick role. Because this diagnostic category is somewhat new, little information is available on prevalence, age of onset, or familial patterns. In the vast majority of cases, the perpetrator is a mother who appears to be loving and attentive toward the child while simultaneously sabotaging the child's health (Kannai, 2009; Siegel, 2009).

However, diagnosis of this condition is difficult. In Seattle, one pediatrician has been involved in over one hundred purported cases during the past twenty-five years, some resulting in children being removed from their families. One appeals court judge wrote that the pediatrician "apparently has a penchant for diagnosing Munchausen syndrome by proxy, notwithstanding its rarity and his questioned qualification to make that diagnosis" (Smith, 2002, p. A10). What safeguards should be put in place to balance protection of the child with the possibility of a false accusation against a parent?

Etiology of Complex Somatic Symptom Disorders, Illness Anxiety Disorder, Functional Neurological Symptoms, and Factitious Disorders

Most etiological theories tend to focus on what they consider to be the "primary" cause of these disorders. However, they are unable to explain why only some individuals exposed to these "causes" develop the symptoms associated with these disorders. In the majority of cases, multiple factors contribute to the development of the disorder, as evidenced by the multipath model that includes biological (sensitivity to bodily cues), psychological (negative thoughts related to pain or bodily functioning), social (modeling by parents, relatives, or friends), and sociocultural dimensions (gender and cultural influences) (Figure 7.2).

Biological Dimensions

Research involving twin (Kato, Sullivan, Evengard, & Pedersen, 2009) and family studies (Noyes et al., 1997) suggest only a modest contribution of genetic factors to the disorders discussed in this chapter. Environmental influences appear to play a much greater role. However, biological vulnerabilities in terms of lower pain thresholds and heightened sensitivity to pain as well as greater sensitivity to somatic cues have been also hypothesized to play an important role in the development of these disorders (Kellner, 1985; Starcevic, 2005). Several researchers (Barsky and Wyshak, 1990; Taylor, Jang, Stein, & Asmundson, 2008) suggest that a biological predisposition, "hard-wired" into the central nervous system, results in: (1) hypervigilance or exaggerated focus on bodily sensation; (2) increased sensitivity to even mild bodily changes; and (3) a tendency to react to somatic sensations with alarm. The predisposition can become a fully developed disorder if an overwhelming trauma or stressor occurs.

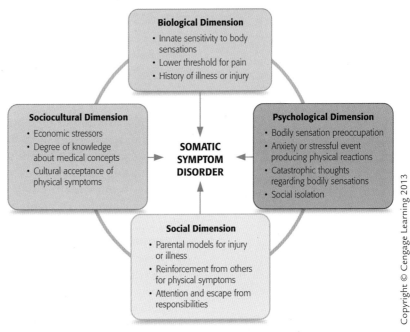

Figure 7.2

MULTIPATH MODEL FOR SOMATIC SYMPTOM DISORDERS
The dimensions interact with one another and combine in different ways to result in a specific somatic symptom disorder.

factitious disorder imposed on another person a pattern of falsification of physical or psychological symptoms in another individual

Similarly, Sauer, Burris, and Carlson (2010) believe that chronic exposure to stressors can lead to an increase in pain sensations or sensitivity of the nerves associated with pain. War veterans with combat exposure are more likely to report high levels of somatic symptoms compared to veterans without exposure to trauma (Ginzburg & Solomon, 2010). It is possible that repetitive activation of the sympathetic nervous system can lead to increased sensitivity of the neural structures associated with pain (Farrugia & Fetter, 2009; McFarlane, Ellis, Barton, Browne, & Van Hooff, 2008).

In a test involving a physical stressor (foot placed in cold water), individuals with illness anxiety disorder demonstrated greater increases in heart rate, displayed a greater drop in temperature in the immersed limb, rated the experience as more unpleasant, and terminated the task more frequently relative to a control group (Gramling, Clawson, & McDonald, 1996). Innate factors may account for greater sensitivity to pain and bodily functions (Kellner, 1985; Starcevic, 2005). People who continually report being bothered by pain and bodily sensations may have a higher-than-normal arousal level, which results in "increased perception of internal stimuli" (Hanback & Revelle, 1978, p. 523).

Psychological Dimension

Psychological theoretical explanations have included the psychodynamic and cognitive-behavioral perspectives. Certain psychological characteristics have also been associated with these disorders.

Psychodynamic perspective In psychodynamic theory, somatic symptoms are seen as a defense against the awareness of unconscious emotional issues (Dworkin, VonKorff, & LeResche, 1990). Freud believed that hysterical (somatic) reactions (biological complaints of pain, illness, or loss of physical function) were caused by the repression of some type of conflict, usually sexual in nature. To protect the individual from intense anxiety, this conflict is converted into a physical symptom (Breuer & Freud, 1895/1957). The psychodynamic view suggests that two mechanisms produce and then sustain somatic symptoms. The first provides a *primary gain* for the person by protecting him or her from the anxiety associated with the unacceptable desire or conflict; the need for protection gives rise to the physical symptoms. This focus on the body keeps the patient from an awareness of the underlying conflict (Simon & VonKorff, 1991). Then a *secondary gain* accrues when the person's dependency needs are fulfilled through attention and sympathy. In one study of twenty-five patients with complex somatic symptoms, all relied on family members and friends to complete domestic tasks and were receiving disability allowances (Allanson, Bass, & Wade, 2002).

Cognitive-behavioral perspective Cognitive-behavioral researchers point to the importance of reinforcement, modeling, cognitions, or a combination of these factors in the development of these disorders. Some contend that people with CSSD, FNSD, and factitious disorders assume the "sick role" because it is reinforcing and because it allows them to escape unpleasant circumstances or to avoid responsibilities (Schwartz, Slater, & Birchler, 1994; Turk, Swanson, & Tunks, 2008). The importance of reinforcement was shown in a study of male pain patients. Men with supportive wives (attentive to pain cues) reported significantly greater pain when their wives were present than when their wives were absent. The reverse was true of patients whose wives were nonsupportive: Reports of pain were greater when their wives were absent (Williamson, Robinson, & Melamed, 1997).

Individuals with CSSD often have had serious illness, physical injury, depression, or an anxiety disorder (Burton, McGorm, Weller, & Sharpe, 2010; Smith et al., 2000; Starcevic, 2005), all of which are risk factors for developing for CSSD (Leiknes, Finset, Moum, & Sandanger, 2008).

The most recent views of somatic disorders stress the importance of cognitive factors (Avia & Ruiz, 2005; Furer & Walker,

Did You Know?

In the second century, hysteria in women was believed to be a result of sexual deprivation. Treatment involved marriage or, for women who remained single, vaginal massage by a midwife. Later, physicians treated the condition by producing "hysterical paroxysm," or orgasm, in women. An electric vibrator was advertised in a Sears catalog in 1918 to treat hysteria.

Source: Maines (1999)

2005; Lipsitt & Starcevic, 2006; Severeijns et al., 2004). According to this perspective, somatic disorders may develop in predisposed individuals (that is, those who have somatic sensitivity, a low pain threshold, a history of illness, or have received parental attention for somatic symptoms) in the following manner (Barsky, 1991; Starcevic, 2005; Walker & Furer, 2008): (1) external triggers (traumatic or anxiety-evoking stressors) or internal triggers (anxiety-producing thoughts such as "My father died of cancer at age 47") result in an anxiety or physiologically arousing reactions; (2) the individual perceives bodily changes such as increased heart rate or respiration; (3) thoughts and worries about possible disease begin in response to these sensations; (4) bodily sensations become amplified because of the thought, causing even more bodily sensations and concern; and (5) catastrophic thoughts regarding these sensations increase, creating a circular feedback pattern.

Consistent with this perspective, individuals reporting chest pain in the absence of cardiac pathology were attuned to cardiac-related symptoms and reacted with anxiety to heart palpitations and chest discomfort (White, Craft, & Gervino, 2010). Individuals with CSSD have been shown to unrealistically interpret and overestimate the dangerousness of bodily symptoms (Haenen et al., 2000).

Social Dimension

Individuals with somatic disorders have reported being rejected or abused by family members and feeling unloved (Rivera & Borda, 2001; Tunks, Weir, & Crook, 2008). A history of sexual abuse such as rape has been associated with chronic pelvic pain and gastrointestinal disorders in women (Paras et al., 2009). Some patients may seek out contact with medical staff as a source of reinforcement because of social isolation or an inability to connect with family or friends (Stuart & Noyes, 2005). Reinforcement of illness behaviors may also be influential in determining reactions to illness. More than 50 percent of a sample of individuals with FNSD, CSSD, or illness anxiety disorder had experienced a serious physical illness in the preceding twelve months (Smith et al., 2000).

Individuals with somatic disorders often have parents or family members with chronic physical illnesses (Smith et al., 2000; Starcevic, 2005). The development of illness or injury sensitivity appears to be closely linked to parental modeling (e.g., "Did your father or mother have problems with dizziness, being short of breath, etc.") and reinforcement of sick behaviors (e.g., "Were you allowed to stay home from school when having physical symptoms, etc."). Individuals with the greatest number of physical symptoms responded affirmatively to the questions such as these (Watt, O'Connor, Stewart, Moon, & Terry, 2008).

Sociocultural Dimensions

Hysteria, now known as FNSD (conversion disorder), was originally perceived as a problem that afflicted only women; in fact, it derived its name from *hystera*, the ancient Greek word for uterus. Hippocrates believed that a shift or movement of the uterus resulted in complaints of breathing difficulties, anesthesia, and seizures. He presumed that the movement was due to the uterus "wanting a child." However, others (Satow, 1979) argued that hysteria was more prevalent in women when social mores did not provide them with appropriate channels for the expression of aggression or sexuality.

The Granger Collection

Functional Neurological Symptom Disorder or Society's Victim?

Anna O., whose real name was Bertha Pappenheim, was diagnosed as being severely disturbed, even though her later years were extremely productive. Were the paralysis and other physical disturbances she experienced products of societal restrictions on the role of women in the late 1800s or her inability to conform to that role? Or was it something totally different?

Anna O., a patient of physician Josef Breuer, was a twenty-one-year-old woman who developed a variety of symptoms, including muscle rigidity and insensitivity to feeling. Freud and Breuer both believed that these symptoms were the result of intrapsychic conflicts. They did not consider the impact of social role restrictions on abnormal behavior. According to Hollender (1980), Anna O. was highly intelligent, but her educational and intellectual opportunities were severely restricted because she was a woman. Breuer described her as "bubbling over with intellectual vitality." As Hollender pointed out, "Not only was Anna O., as a female, relegated to an inferior position in her family with future prospects limited to that of becoming a wife and mother, but at the age of twenty-one she was suddenly called on to assume the onerous chore of nursing her father" (Hollender, 1980, p. 798). It is possible that many of her symptoms were produced to relieve the guilt she felt because of her resentment of this duty—as well as to maintain her intellectually stimulating contact with Breuer. After treatment, Anna O. was supposedly cured. However, she, in fact, remained severely disturbed and received additional treatment at an institution. Later, she headed a home for orphans, was involved in social work, and became recognized as a feminist leader.

Cultural factors can influence the frequency, expression, and interpretation of somatic complaints. Risk factors associated with somatic disorders include lower educational levels, ethnicity, and immigrant status (Noyes et al., 2006). Among Asian populations, physical complaints often occur in reaction to stress (Ryder et al., 2008; Sue & Sue, 2008a). In fact, Asian Indian children who were referred for psychiatric services had three times as many complex somatic symptoms disorders as their white counterparts (Jawed, 1991). Among some African groups, somatic complaints (feelings of heat, peppery and crawling sensations, and numbness) differ from those expressed in Western cultures (Ohaeri & Odejide, 1994). Reports of pain also differ between white and Hispanic patients with current health problems. Hispanics report more pain, which might be due to the cultural acceptance of physical problems as an expression of distress (Hernandez & Sachs-Ericsson, 2006).

Differences such as those just described may reflect different cultural views of the relationship between mind and body. The dominant view in Western culture is the *psychosomatic* perspective, in which psychological conflicts are expressed in physical complaints. But many other cultures have a *somatopsychic* perspective, in which physical problems produce psychological and emotional symptoms. Although we probably believe that our psychosomatic view is the "correct" one, the somatopsychic view is the dominant perspective in most cultures. As White (1982) claimed, "It is rather the more psychological and psychosomatic mode of reasoning found in Western cultures which appears unusual among the world's popular and traditional system of belief" (p. 1520). Physical complaints expressed by persons of ethnic minorities may need to be interpreted differently from similar complaints made by members of the majority culture.

Treatment of Somatic Symptom Disorders

Although somatic symptom disorders are considered to be difficult to treat, newer biological and psychological treatments have met with greater success. There is also increasing recognition of the necessity of moving away from a mind-body distinction, understanding the client perspective regarding somatic symptom disorders, and acknowledging the relationship between stressors and their role in physical complaints as seen in the following case:

Case Study

Mr. X, a sixty-eight-year-old Chinese man, reported sleep disturbance, a loss of appetite, dizziness, and a sensation of tightness around his chest. Several episodes of chest pain led to admission and medical evaluation at the local hospital. All results, including tests for ischemic heart disease, were normal. He was referred for psychiatric consultation. Because traditional Chinese views of medicine recognize an interconnection between mind and body, the psychiatrist accepted and showed interest in the somatic symptoms, such as their onset, duration, and exacerbating and relieving factors. Medication was provided as a supportive treatment. A stressor was identified that involved arguments with his wife. Suggestions were made on how to improve communication, which led to a decrease in physical complaints. (Yeung & Deguang, 2002)

Biological Treatment

Antidepressant medications such as the selective serotonin reuptake inhibitors (SSRIs) have shown promise with complex somatic symptom disorders, primarily somatization pain disorders (Taylor, Asmundson, & Coons, 2005). For more severe pain, opioids are often prescribed, although there are concerns about addiction and the possibility of abuse (Tunks, Weir, & Crook, 2008). In addition, interventions involving an increase in physical activity have been recommended for conversion disorders (Smith et al., 2000).

Psychological Treatments

The most promising interventions for somatic symptom disorders involve the cognitive-behavioral approach. A fundamental focus involves understanding the client's view regarding his or her problem. Individuals with somatic symptom disorders are often frustrated, disappointed, and angry following years of encounters with the medical profession. They believe that treatment strategies have been ineffective and resent the implication that they are "fakers" or "problem patients" (Frohm & Beehler, 2010; Lipsitt & Starcevic, 2006). Medical personnel often do, in fact, show negative reactions when interacting with individuals with somatic symptoms disorders (Merten & Brunnhuber, 2004). Because of these reactions, patients and physicians have a difficult time establishing a positive relationship.

A newer approach has been to demonstrate empathy regarding the physical complaints and focus on helping the individual develop better coping skills, as indicated in the following statement to a patient: "I don't know exactly the cause of your problem, and I'm not certain that I can provide immediate relief. Nevertheless, I will work with you as best I can to find solutions" (Monopoli, 2005, p. 293). Eliciting the patient's conceptualization of the difficulties and providing psychoeducation regarding the relationship between somatic symptoms, emotional state, and interpersonal relationships can enhance working relationships between physicians and patients with somatic symptom disorders (Poleschuck et al., 2010).

In another approach, somatic symptom disorders are viewed within a social context—a belief that somatic complaints are a reflection of unsatisfying or inadequate social relationships. Individuals who assume a "sick role" often receive some reinforcement, such as escape from responsibility or control of others through bodily complaints. However, negative aspects can include criticism and rejection from others, which may result in increased social isolation. Therapy is therefore directed toward developing and improving the individual's social network. A therapist may say something such as: "There is treatment available that may be helpful to you, if you would like to participate. This involves learning new ways of understanding and coping with stresses, other than turning to substances or going to the nearest emergency room. Treatment will also involve learning more about yourself and finding out what gets in the way of developing more fulfilling relationships" (Gregory & Jindal, 2006, p. 34).

A randomized controlled trial was conducted (Allen et al., 2006) to compare cognitive-behavioral therapy (CBT) with standard medical care augmented by psychiatric consultation for somatization disorder. Cognitive-behavioral therapy (CBT) was based on the biopsychological model in which pain or bodily symptoms were seen to be related to the degree of stress or anxiety affecting the patient. The approach involved: (1) scheduling regular appointments rather than making appointments by patient request; (2) brief examinations by a physician regarding the physical complaints; (3) providing psychoeducation regarding the relationship between pain or bodily symptoms and stress and anxiety; (4) relaxation training to reduce physiological arousal; (5) encouraging more social contact and involvement in pleasurable and meaningful activities; and (6) identifying and modifying negative thoughts. The ten-session CBT program was significantly more effective in reducing somatization symptoms and complaints than standard medical care augmented with psychiatric consultation.

Because many patients with somatic symptom disorders appear to have cognitive distortions, such as a conviction that they are especially vulnerable to disease, cognitive-behavioral approaches focused on correcting these misinterpretations have been successful (Barsky & Ahern, 2004; Buwalda & Bouman, 2008). In one program, individuals with illness anxiety disorder (hypochondriasis) who had fears of having cancer, heart disease, or other fatal diseases were educated about the relationship between misinterpretations of bodily sensations and selective attention to illness themes. Six two-hour group sessions were held that covered topics such as: "What Is Hypochondriasis?"; "The Role of Your Thoughts"; "Attention and Illness Anxiety"; "Stress and Bodily Symptoms"; and "Your Own Vicious Cycle." As homework, participants monitored and challenged hypochondriacal thoughts. After completing these sessions, most participants showed considerable improvement or no longer met the criteria for hypochondriasis; the gains were maintained at a six-month follow-up (Hiller et al., 2002).

Because individuals with somatic disorders often show a fear of internal bodily sensations, CBT therapists have utilized *interoceptive* exposure (exposure to bodily sensations) during treatment. Clients are asked to perform activities that typically trigger anxiety such as breathing through a straw, hyperventilating, spinning, or climbing stairs until feared reactions such as light-headedness, chest discomfort, or increased heart rate occur. The activities are performed over and over again until the resultant bodily sensations no longer elicit anxiety or fear (Flink, Nicholas, Boersma, & Linton, 2009). In general, CBT is one of the more effective therapies for somatic symptom disorders. Relaxation training can also effectively reduce sympathetic nervous system activity levels (Sauer, Burris, & Carlson, 2010).

Dissociative Disorders

Case Study

A twenty-nine-year-old female who was in China for an academic trip was found unconscious in the hotel bathroom. The woman was unable to remember her identity or any information about her life. Examinations showed no neurological abnormalities or evidence of substance use. She remained in an amnesiac state for 10 months until blood on her fingers triggered memories of witnessing a murder in China and being unable to help the victim because of her fear. Once this memory surfaced, she began to remember other aspects of her life (Reinhold & Markowitsch, 2009).

The dissociative disorders—*dissociative amnesia (localized and fugue types), depersonalization/derealization disorder*, and *dissociative identity disorder (multiple personality)*—are shown in Table 7.4. Each disorder involves some sort of dissociation, or separation, of a part of the person's consciousness, memory, or identity.

The dissociative disorders are highly publicized and sensationalized; yet, except for depersonalization disorder, they are considered relatively rare. As with many of the somatic symptom disorders discussed earlier, there are no objective assessments to confirm the existence of a dissociative disorder. Thus, the possibility of feigning must be considered. Among young criminal offenders, 19 percent reported partial amnesia and 1 percent reported complete amnesia for their violent crimes (Evan, Mezey, & Ehlers, 2009). Wadlh El-Hage, charged as a conspirator with Osama bin Laden in the attacks on the U.S. embassies in Kenya and Tanzania, claimed that he suffered from a loss of memory. Court-appointed experts voiced the opinion that he was "faking the symptoms of amnesia" (Weiser, 2000). Lee Malvo, involved in multiple sniper attacks in the Washington, D.C., area, claimed to have a dissociative disorder (Jackson, 2003).

In addition to the possibility of feigning, other questions have arisen about several of the dissociative disorders. For example, some researchers are concerned about sudden increases in reports of dissociative identity disorder and dissociative amnesia. They believe that counselors and therapists (or their clients) may be inadvertently "creating" these disorders.

Questions regarding the validity of dissociative disorders have resulted in legal debate with respect to acts performed when an individual was purportedly in a dissociated state. The following examples offer a glimpse into this controversy:

- A therapist claimed that it was one of her client's twenty-four personalities who kidnapped and took sexual liberties with her and that the main personality was not responsible (Haley, 2003).
- A man was charged with the rape of a woman with multiple personalities when one of the nonconsenting personalities brought up the charge.
- A South Carolina woman going through a divorce, who had twenty-one personalities, claimed that she had not committed adultery and that she had tried to stop the responsible personality, "Rosie," from becoming involved in an extramarital affair. (In South Carolina, adultery is grounds for barring alimony payments.)

Cases such as these raise questions regarding responsibility in these disorders. Does a diagnosis of dissociative identity disorder or dissociative amnesia constitute mitigating circumstances and "diminished capacity"?

Dissociative Amnesia

Dissociative amnesia is the partial or total loss of important personal information that is not "ordinary" forgetting that sometimes occurs suddenly after a stressful or traumatic event (American Psychiatric Association, 2011). Although amnesia can also be caused by strokes, substance abuse, or other medical conditions, dissociative amnesia results from psychological factors or stressors (Schauer & Elbert, 2010; Tikhonova et al., 2003). For example, several individuals listed as missing after the September 11, 2001, attacks on the World Trade Center had apparently developed amnesia (Tucker, 2002). An affected individual may be unable to recall information such as his or her name, address, or names of relatives, yet remember the necessities of daily life—how to read, write, and drive. Individuals with this disorder often score high on tests measuring hypnotizability and are likely to report depression, anxiety, or a history of trance states (American Psychiatric Association, 2000a).

There are two primary forms of dissociative amnesia: localized amnesia involves lack of memory for a specific event or events, and dissociative fugue is a generalized amnesia for one's identity and life history that may be accompanied by bewildered wandering or purposeless travel (American Psychiatric Association, 2011). The most common type of dissociative amnesia, localized amnesia, involves failure to recall events occurring during a specific short period of time, typically after a highly painful or disturbing event (Enea & Dafinoiu, 2008). The following case is typical of localized amnesia.

Case Study

An eighteen-year-old woman who survived a dramatic fire claimed not to remember it or the death of her child and husband in the fire. She maintained her relatives were lying about the fire. However, she became extremely agitated and emotional several hours later, when her memory abruptly returned.

Localized amnesia may also involve an inability to remember certain details of an incident. For example, a man remembered having an automobile accident but could not recall that

David McNew/Getty Images

Hypnosis as Therapy

Some practitioners continue to use hypnosis to assess and treat dissociative disorders, based on the belief that these disorders may be induced by self-hypnosis. Is the trance induced by hypnosis similar to disturbances in consciousness found in the dissociative disorders?

dissociative amnesia partial or total loss of important personal information due to psychological factors; may involve failure to recall all events that occurred during the period of time involving a highly painful or disturbing event

localized amnesia lack of memory for a specific event or events

dissociative fugue confusion over personal identity, often involving complete loss of memory of one's entire life, unexpected travel to a new location, and the partial or complete assumption of a new identity

DISORDERS CHART   DISORDERS CHART DISSOCIATIVE DISORDERS

TABLE 7.4

Dissociative Disorder	Symptoms	Prevalence	Age of Onset	Course
Dissociative Amnesia, Localized Type	The sudden inability to recall information of specific events—not due to ordinary forgetting or other physical conditions	Recent increase involving forgotten early childhood trauma	Any age group	Acute forms may remit spontaneously, others are chronic; usually related to trauma or stress
Dissociative Amnesia, Fugue Type	Inability to recall personal identity and past, with: • Sudden departure to new area • Confusion about personal identity or assumption of new identity	0.2%; may increase during natural disasters or wartime	Usually adulthood	Related to stress or trauma; recovery is generally rapid
Depersonalization Disorder	Persistent symptoms involving changes in perception and being detached from one's own thoughts and body May feel that things are unreal or have a sense of being in a dreamlike state Reality testing remains intact	About 1%; 50% to 75% of adults may experience brief episodes of stress-related depersonalization	Adolescence or adulthood	May be short lived or chronic
Dissociative Identity Disorder (Multiple-Personality Disorder)	Disruption of identity by the existence of two or more distinct personality states or experience of possession Discontinuities in sense of self, memories, emotions, cognitions, and perceptions Disruption may be observed by others or reported by the patient Inability to recall important personal information	Sharp rise in recently reported cases; up to nine times more frequent in women	Childhood to adolescence, but misdiagnosis may result in late reporting	Fluctuates; tends to be chronic and recurrent

Source: Data from American Psychiatric Association (2011)

his child had died in the crash. This type of amnesia is often claimed by people accused of violent criminal offenses. Many individuals accused of murder report that they remember arguments but do not remember killing anyone (Evan, Mezey, & Ehlers, 2009; Mendlowicz et al., 2002). However, according to one estimate, about 70 percent of criminals who say they have amnesia for the crime are feigning (Merryman, 1997).

Dissociative fugue (also called *fugue state*) involves confusion over personal identity (often involving the partial or complete assumption of a new identity), accompanied by unexpected travel away from home. The following case illustrates some of the psychological events associated with dissociative fugue.

Case Study

An eighteen-year-old woman was found outside a Manhattan youth center. She claimed to have no memory of her identity, family, or home. When found, she was lying in a fetal position and said she wanted to know who she was. The authorities believe that she was on the streets for quite a while. She was identified when a photo of her aired on CNN. Her father indicated that she had previous episodes of lost identity (Moore, 2009).

Most cases of dissociative fugue involve only short periods away from home and an incomplete change of identity. Because of the complete loss of memory of the individual's entire life, law enforcement agencies or hospitals often become involved. However, there are exceptions, as shown in the following case.

Case Study

Jane Dee Williams says she remembers nothing before the day in May 1985 when she was found wandering and disoriented in an Aurora, Colorado, shopping mall, wearing a green coat and carrying a Toyota key, a copy of *Watership Down*, two green pens, and a notebook—but having no clue as to who she was. She went to Aurora police for help and ended up at the Colorado Mental Health Institute at Fort Logan with a diagnosis of psychogenic fugue. She was treated and released without recovering her memory. During the next twelve years, she remained amnesic but started a new life, marrying and giving birth to two sets of twins. In 1997, a tip to the police from someone who recognized Williams from photographs led to her discovery. Jane Dee Williams was actually Jody Roberts, who had disappeared from her home and job as a reporter in Tacoma, Washington. She still has no memory of her biological family. (Merryman, 1997, A8)

AP Images

Dissociative Fugue

Jeff Ingram was on his way to visit a terminally ill friend in Alberta and woke up four days later in Denver without any memory of his life. He was without his car or any personal identification. Although most people with dissociative amnesia recover their memories within a short period of time, Jeff has not. He now wears a necklace jump drive and bracelet that contains his personal information. What psychological processes produce dissociative fugue?

As with localized amnesia, recovery from a fugue state is often abrupt and complete, although the gradual return of bits of information may also occur. Kopelman (2002) believes that genuine cases are short lived: "Fugue states usually last only a few hours or days, if prolonged, suspicion of simulation must always arise" (p. 2171). However, some fugue states may last for months (American Psychiatric Association, 2000a).

Cases of dissociative amnesia in which the amnesia comes to light only after an individual begins to recall a repressed memory have increased in recent years. These cases are generally believed to involve exposure to trauma that is so overwhelming or threatening that the individual represses the event (McNally, 2007). For example, it was twenty years after the event that one woman recovered memories of a teacher molesting her when she was in the sixth grade. These memories were uncovered after years of psychiatric treatment. The teacher was convicted, but the case was later overturned because of the weakness of the evidence (Loftus, 2003). In a sample of psychologists who had experienced childhood abuse, 40 percent reported a period of amnesia regarding some or all of the abuse. In 56 percent of the cases, the memory returned during therapy (Feldman-Summers & Pope, 1994).

However, not all researchers believe in the validity of this phenomenon and the hypothesis that certain threatening memories can be pushed out of consciousness. Laney and Loftus (2005) point out the complexities involved in interpreting reports of repressed memories:

- Many abuse survivors with recovered memories claim that they had forgotten their abuse, but this does not necessarily mean that they repressed memories of it.
- Many abuse survivors do not mention abuse when initially asked, but this is not proof of repression.
- Memory is malleable. Details can be distorted, and wholly false memories can be planted.
- Just because a memory report is detailed, confidently expressed, and emotional does not mean that it reflects a true experience. False memories can have these same features (p. 823).

Did You Know?

Similarly, Pezdek, Blandon-Gitlin, and Gabbay (2006) believe that even implausible memories can be planted and further strengthened by information provided by parents or therapists. At this point, it is not clear how many cases of genuine "repressed memory" actually exist, or whether the phenomenon exists at all. Others argue that disorders such as dissociative amnesia are culture-bound syndromes—that is, they are not natural, neuropsychological phenomena but are, instead, socially constructed entities (Pettus, 2008; Pope et al., 2006).

Depersonalization/Derealization Disorder

Depersonalization disorder is perhaps the most common dissociative disorder. It is characterized by feelings of unreality or being detached from oneself and the environment (Brand & Lowenstein, 2010; Sierra, 2009). Questions such as "Have you ever had the feeling that things around you were unreal?" or "Have you yourself felt unreal, that you were not a person, not living in the real world?" are used to screen for this disorder (Lambert et al., 2001). One woman described her symptoms this way: "It is as if the real me is taken out and put on a shelf and stored somewhere inside of me. Whatever makes me me is not there" (Simeon et al., 1997, p. 1110). Episodes of depersonalization can be fairly intense, and they can produce great anxiety because those who suffer from them consider them unnatural, as the following case illustrates.

Case Study

Ms. A., age twenty-three, presents to our clinic complaining of feeling detached for the past four years. She feels "fuzzy all the time, like I lost touch of reality." She complains of confused thinking: "It feels like I'm watching my life on television; I don't feel any emotions." These symptoms began immediately after a college party, which the police stopped because of underage drinking. (Janjua, Rapport, & Ferrara, 2010, p. 62).

A diagnosis of depersonalization disorder is given only when the feelings of unreality and detachment cause major impairment in social or occupational functioning. The prevalence of this disorder is about 1 percent. It typically begins in teenage years and may be short lived or may last for decades, depending on individual circumstances. Fleeting experiences of depersonalization are reported in up to 70 percent of college students and 23 percent of general population. Depersonalization may be a response to extreme stressors and is often accompanied by mood and anxiety disorders (Janjua, Rapport, & Ferrara, 2010; Simeon et al., 2000).

Dissociative Identity Disorder (Multiple-Personality Disorder)

depersonalization disorder disorder characterized by feelings of unreality concerning the self and the environment

dissociative identity disorder (DID) a condition in which two or more relatively independent personality states appear to exist in one person, including experiences of possession; also known as multiple-personality disorder

Dissociative identity disorder (DID), formerly known as *multiple-personality disorder*, is a disruption of identity as evidenced by two or more distinct personality states or an experience of possession (replacement of the sense of personal identity with a new identity). Possession was added to the DID definition in DSM-5 to "provide more cross-cultural utility." Many individuals with DID also have conversion symptoms (American Psychiatric Association, 2011). In situations in which two or more personalities exist, only one personality is typically evident at any one time, and the alternation of personalities usually produces periods of amnesia in the personality that has been displaced. However, one or several personalities may be aware of the existence of the others. The personalities usually differ from one another and sometimes are direct opposites, as the following case illustrates:

Whitney Museum of American Art, New York; Purchase, with funds from the Juliana Force Purchase Award 50.23

Depersonalization Disorder

An individual may feel like an automaton—mechanical and robotlike—when suffering from depersonalization disorder. This painting, "The Subway" (ca. 1950), by George Tooker, captures this feeling.

Case Study

"Little Judy" is a young child who laughs and giggles. "Gravelly Voice" is a man who speaks with a raspy voice. The "one who walks in darkness" is blind and trips over furniture. "Big Judy" is articulate, competent, and funny. These are four of the forty-four personalities that exist within Judy Castelli. She was initially diagnosed with schizophrenia but later told that dissociative identity disorder was the appropriate diagnosis. She is a singer, a musician, an inventor, and an artist whose work appeared on the February 2000 cover of the *American Psychological Association Monitor*; she has also become a lay expert on mental health issues (Woliver, 2000).

The characteristics of DID have changed over time. Goff and Simms (1993) compared case reports from between the years 1800 and 1965 with those from the 1980s. The earlier cases involved fewer personalities (an average of three versus twelve), a later age of onset of first dissociation (age twenty as opposed to age eleven in the 1980s), a greater proportion of males, and a much lower prevalence of child abuse (Figure 7.3). Similarly, Pope and colleagues (2006) tracked publications related to dissociative disorder and dissociative amnesia over a twenty-year period. The number of articles related to these disorders was low in the 1980s, rose to a sharp peak in the mid-1990s, and then declined sharply by 2003. No other disorder showed this bubble phenomenon. The researchers concluded that both DID and dissociative amnesia "enjoyed a brief period of fashion that has now waned. . . . [T]hese diagnostic entities presently do not command widespread scientific acceptance" (p. 19).

Did You Know?

Individuals with DID often claim that information about events happening to one personality is unavailable to other personalities. Research has found that learning does in fact transfer between the different personalities (Kong, Allen, & Glisky, 2008; Huntjens et al., 2007).

Dissociative Identity Disorder

Judy Castelli stands beside her stained glass artwork. The people in the art have no faces but are connected and touching each other. She considers her artistic endeavors a creative outlet for her continuing struggle with multiple personalities.

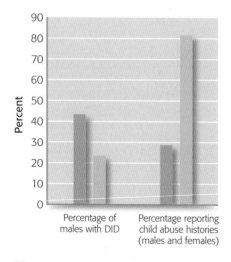

■ Between 1800 and 1965

■ 1980s

Figure 7.3

COMPARISON OF CHARACTERISTICS OF REPORTED CASES OF DISSOCIATIVE IDENTITY DISORDER (MULTIPLE PERSONALITY DISORDER)

This graph illustrates characteristics of dissociative identity disorder (DID) cases reported in the 1980s versus those reported between 1800 and 1965. What could account for these differences?

Source: Data from Goff & Simms (1993)

Diagnostic Controversy

Before the case of Sybil (a patient who appeared to have sixteen different personalities) became popularized in a movie and book in the 1970s, there had been fewer than two hundred reported cases of dissociative identity disorder worldwide. Now thousands of new cases are reported each year (Milstone, 1997). Foote and colleagues (2006) believe that the condition is relatively common but often not recognized and diagnosed. In their assessment of eighty-two admissions to an inner-city outpatient psychiatric clinic, 29 percent met the criteria for a dissociative disorder, with five patients (6 percent) receiving a diagnosis of DID, eight patients (10 percent) diagnosed with dissociative amnesia, and four patients (5 percent) having depersonalization disorder. However, other practitioners believe that DID is rare and that the increase in numbers may be due to clinician bias, the use of faulty assessment, or the use of therapeutic techniques that increase the likelihood of a DID diagnosis (Cormier & Thelen, 1998; Gharaibeh, 2009).

With the exception of the Netherlands and Turkey, DID is rarely diagnosed outside the United States and Canada (Chaturvedi, Desai, & Shaligram, 2010; Merskey, 1995; Phelps, 2000; Tutkun et al., 1998). In a study of DID in Switzerland, Modestin (1992) concluded that it is relatively rare and estimated its prevalence rate to be 0.05 percent to 0.1 percent of patients. He also found that three psychiatrists accounted for more than 50 percent of the patients given this diagnosis. Why is it that some psychiatrists or therapists report treating many patients with DID, whereas the majority does not? The psychiatrists who treated "Eve," another well-known case detailed in the classic movie "The Three Faces of Eve," received tens of thousands of referrals, but found only one genuine case of dissociative identity disorder (Thigpen & Cleckley, 1984).

After studying patients with reported DID, Merskey (1992) and Piper & Merskey (2004) conclude that the "personalities" represent differences in mood, memory, or attention and that they are developed by unwitting therapists through expectation,

Gordon M. Grant Photography

suggestion, and social reinforcement. Cases of dissociated states and multiple personalities produced through hypnosis or suggestion have, in fact, been reported (Coons, 1988; Freeland, Manchanda, Chiu, Sharma, & Merskey, 1993; McHugh, 2009; Ofshe, 1992). Dissociation symptoms such as alterations in memory, thoughts, and perceptions or a sense of depersonalization (feeling detached or numb) are not uncommon in the face of stress (Cardena & Weiner, 2004; Freinkel, Koopman, & Spiegel, 1994). Some clinicians may mistakenly interpret these symptoms of stress as indicators of dissociative disorders. Whether the increase in diagnosis of DID is the result of more accurate diagnosis, false positives, an artifact, or an actual increase in the incidence of the disorder is still being debated.

Etiology of Dissociative Disorders

The possible causes of dissociative disorders are subject to much conjecture. Because diagnosis depends heavily on patients' self-reports, as noted, feigning or faking is always a possibility. Fabricated amnesia, fugue, or DID can be produced by individuals who "are attempting to flee a situation involving legal, financial, or personal difficulties, as well as in soldiers who are attempting to avoid combat or unpleasant military duties" (American Psychiatric Association, 2000a, p. 525).

MYTH: Dissociative identity disorder is relatively easy to diagnose, and most mental health professionals accept the category.

REALITY: There are no objective measures from which a diagnosis can be made, and cases involving feigning the disorder have been reported. Those who question the category raise the possibility that symptoms of the disorder are inadvertently produced through suggestion or hypnosis.

MYTH VS. REALITY

CRITICAL THINKING

Culture and Somatic Symptom and Dissociative Disorders

A fifty-six-year-old South American man requested an evaluation and treatment. He had the firm belief that his penis was retracting and entering his abdomen, and he was reacting with a great deal of anxiety. He attempted to pull on his penis to prevent the retraction. This procedure had been effective with a previous episode that occurred when he was nineteen. An evaluation of his mental state ruled out other psychiatric diagnoses such as obsessive-compulsive disorder or schizophrenia (Hallak, Crippa, & Zuardi, 2000).

Dibuk ak Suut, a Malaysian woman, goes into a trancelike state in which she follows commands, blurts out offensive phrases, and mimics the actions of people around her. This happens when she has been suddenly frightened. She displays profuse sweating and increased heart rate, but claims to have no memory of what she did or said (Osbourne, 2001).

The symptoms of the first case fit the description of *koro*, a culture-bound syndrome that has been reported primarily in Southeast Asia, although cases have also been reported in West Africa (Dzokoto & Adams, 2005). The symptoms involve an intense fear that the penis or, in a woman, the labia, nipples, or breasts are receding into the body. Koro may be related to body dysmorphic disorder, but it differs in that koro is usually of brief duration and is responsive to positive reassurances. In the second case, the woman is displaying symptoms related to *latah*, a condition found in Malaysia and many other parts of the world that involves mimicking or following the instructions or behaviors of others and dissociation or trancelike states. Other culture-bound disorders may be related to either somatic symptom or dissociative disorders:

- *Brain fag* Found primarily in West Africa, this condition affects high school and college students who experience somatic symptoms involving a "fatigued" brain, neck or head pain, or blurring of vision due to difficult course work or classes.
- *Dhat* A term used in India to describe hypochondriacal concerns and severe anxiety over the discharge of semen. The condition produces feelings of weakness or exhaustion.
- *Ataque de nervios* Commonly found in Hispanics residing in the United States and Latin America, the symptoms can include "brain aches," stomach disturbances, anxiety symptoms, and dizziness. Patterns of symptoms can resemble somatic symptom or dissociative disorders.
- *Pibloktoq* Generally found in Inuit communities, these dissociative-like episodes accompanied by extreme excitement are sometimes followed by convulsions and coma. The individual may perform aggressive and dangerous acts and report amnesia after the episode.
- *Zar* A condition found in Middle Eastern or North African societies that involves the experience of being possessed by a spirit. Individuals in a dissociative state may engage in bizarre behaviors, including shouting or hitting their heads against a wall.

Culture-bound syndromes are interesting because they point to the existence of a pattern of symptoms that are associated primarily with specific societies or groups. These "disorders" do not fit easily into the DSM-5 classification or into many of the biological and psychological models used to explain dissociative and somatic symptom disorders. What does it mean when disorders are discovered that do not fit into Western-developed classification systems? Would we assume that the etiology and treatment would be similar to those developed for somatic symptom and dissociative disorders?

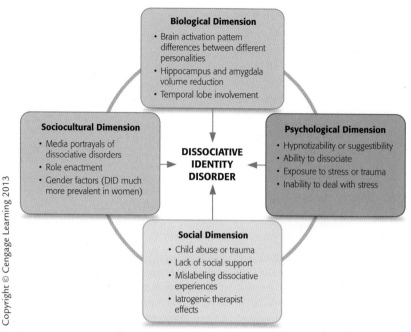

Figure 7.4

MULTIPATH MODEL FOR DISSOCIATIVE DISORDERS

The dimensions interact with one another and combine in different ways to result in a dissociative identity disorder.

However, true cases of these disorders may also result from these types of stressors. Differentiating between genuine cases of dissociative disorders and faked ones is difficult.

In this section, we consider the multipath dimensions that contribute to the dissociative disorders (Figure 7.4). Although two models—the psychologically based *posttraumatic model (PTM)* and the *sociocognitive model (SCM)*—are currently the most influential etiological perspectives, neither is sufficient to explain why only some individuals develop these disorders. It is likely that vulnerabilities in the biological, psychological, social, and sociocultural dimensions play a role.

Biological Dimension

A number of studies using PET scans and MRIs on individuals diagnosed with DID have found variations in brain activity when comparing different personalities (Reinders et al., 2003; Sheehan, Sewall, & Thurber, 2005; Tsai et al., 1999). Switching between personalities is associated with activation or inhibition of certain brain regions, particularly the hippocampus (Tsai et al., 1999), an area involved in memories and hypothesized to be involved in the generation of dissociative states and amnesia (Staniloiu & Markowitsch, 2010; Teicher et al., 2002). Differences in temporal lobe activity have also been found among different personalities within an individual. This is interesting because temporal lobe seizures sometimes involve altered states of consciousness (Sheehan et al., 2005). However, these patterns of brain activity are difficult to interpret because it is unclear what causes them and what specific role they play, if any.

Teicher and colleagues (2002) believe that permanent structural changes in the brain can occur as a result of childhood trauma through the chronic activation of a stress response. This may result in the reduction of the volume of the hippocampus and amygdala, which, in turn, may hamper the ability of the brain to encode, store, and retrieve memory, comprehend contradictory information, and integrate emotional memories (Spiegel, 2006). These alterations may play an etiological role in dissociative amnesia, DID, and depersonalization (Janjua, Rapport, & Ferrara, 2010).

Vermetten and colleagues (2006) used MRIs to compare the hippocampal and amygdalar volumes in fifteen females with DID, all of whom reported histories of childhood sexual and/or physical abuse, with imaging from twenty-three females without DID. Hippocampal and amygdalar volumes were 19.2 percent and 31.6 percent smaller, respectively, in those with DID than in those in the comparison group. However, decreased brain volume in certain structures is also found with increasing age and among other psychiatric patients. In the Vermetten and colleagues study, the mean age of DID patients was 42.7 years versus 34.6 for the control group. After controlling for age, only the amygdalar volume was found to be significantly reduced among the DID patients (Smeets, Jelicic, & Merkelbach, 2006). Conclusions are difficult to reach because of the small number of participants involved in the study, the age differences among control and DID patients, and the presence of other comorbid psychiatric disorders in the patients studied.

Psychological Dimension

The primary psychological explanations for the dissociative disorders come from psychodynamic theory, although individual vulnerabilities such as hypnotizability or suggestibility are also thought to play an important role. Psychodynamic theory views the dissociative disorders as a result of an individual's use of repression to block from consciousness unpleasant or traumatic events (Richardson, 1998). When complete repression of these impulses is not possible because of the intensity of the impulses or poor ego strength, dissociation or separation of certain mental processes may occur. In dissociative amnesia and fugue, for example, large parts of the individual's personal identity are no longer available to conscious awareness. This process protects the individual from painful memories or conflicts. Dissociation is carried to an extreme in DID. Here, the splits in mental processes become so extreme that more or less independent identities are formed, each with its unique set of memories (Baker, 2010; Gleaves, 1996).

Following this line of thinking, the contemporary psychodynamic perspective conceptualizes DID as resulting from severe childhood abuse as illustrated in their post-traumatic model (PTM). According to Kluft (1987), the four factors necessary for the development of DID are:

1. Exposure to overwhelming childhood stress, such as traumatic physical or sexual abuse
2. The capacity to dissociate
3. Encapsulating or walling off the experience
4. Developing different memory systems

If a supportive environment is not available or if the personality is not resilient, DID results from these factors (Irwin, 1998) (Figure 7.5).

Thus, according to the PTM, the split in personality develops because of traumatic early experiences combined with an inability to escape them. In the case of Sybil, for example, Sybil was severely abused by her mother. Dr. Wilbur, Sybil's psychiatrist, speculated that "by dividing into different selves [which were] defenses against an intolerable and dangerous reality, Sybil had found a [design] for survival" (Schreiber, 1973, p. 158). Consistent with this perspective, most individuals diagnosed with DID do report a history of physical or sexual abuse during childhood (Boon & Draijer, 1993; Coons, 1994; Foote et al., 2006; Sheehan et al., 2005; Vermetten et al., 2006).

To develop DID, the individual must have the capacity to dissociate—or separate—certain memories or mental processes in response to traumatic events. A person's susceptibility to hypnotism may be a characteristic of the dissociation process, and, in fact, people who have DID appear to be very susceptible to hypnotic suggestion. Some researchers believe that pathological dissociation is a result of the interaction between auto- or self-hypnosis and acute traumatic stress (Butler et al., 1996). People might escape unpleasant experiences through self-hypnosis—by entering a hypnotic state. In contrast to individuals with other psychiatric disorders, females with DID have a history of trance states and sleepwalking and report more alterations in consciousness (International Society for the Study of Dissociation, 2005; Scroppo et al., 1998).

As with most psychodynamic conceptualizations, it is difficult to formulate and test hypotheses. In addition, the PTM presupposes exposure to childhood trauma. In most studies, information on child abuse is based on patient self-reports, is not independently corroborated, and involves varying definitions of abuse (Gharaibeh, 2009; Piper & Merskey, 2004; Lilienfeld et al., 1999). Questions have also been raised regarding reports of memories retrieved from very early ages. Clients with DID have reported the emergence of alternate personalities at the age of two or earlier (Dell & Eisenhower, 1990), and in one study, 11 percent reported being abused before age one (Ross et al., 1991). Reports regarding memories of events at these ages would be highly suspect.

Social and Sociocultural Dimensions

An approach that takes both social and sociocultural factors into consideration is the sociocognitive model (SCM) of DID, developed by Spanos (1994) and further

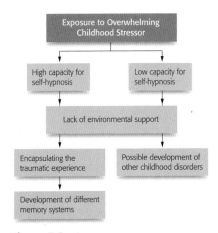

Figure 7.5

THE POST-TRAUMATIC MODEL FOR DISSOCIATIVE IDENTITY DISORDER

Note the importance of each of the factors in the development of dissociative identity disorder.

Source: Adapted from Kluft (1987); Loewenstein (1994)

elaborated by Scott Lilienfeld and his colleagues (1999). In this perspective, the disorder is conceptualized as

> a syndrome that consists of rule-governed and goal-directed experiences and displays of multiple role enactments that have been created, legitimized, and maintained by social reinforcement. Patients with DID synthesize these role enactments by drawing on a wide variety of sources of information, including the print and broadcast media, cues provided by therapists, personal experiences, and observations of individuals who have enacted multiple identities. (Lilienfeld et al., 1999, p. 507)

According to this model, patients learn about the phenomenon and its characteristics through the mass media. The behaviors of individuals with DID become well known, and, under the right circumstances, people can enact these roles. Vulnerable individuals may demonstrate these behaviors when therapists provide the appropriate cues. The "personalities" developed through this process are displayed spontaneously and *without conscious deception*. Proponents of the SCM model cite the large increase shown in DID cases after mass media portrayals of this disorder as support for this perspective. For example, after the 1973 publication of *Sybil* (whose subject had sixteen personalities), the mean number of personalities for those diagnosed rose from three to twelve (Goff & Simms, 1993).

Therapists are also influenced by exposure to mass media regarding DID and may "unconsciously" encourage reports of DID from clients. This would be referred to as an *iatrogenic disorder*—a condition unintentionally produced by a therapist through mechanisms such as selective attention, suggestion, reinforcement, and expectations that are placed on the client. Could some or even most cases of dissociative identity disorder be iatrogenic? A number of researchers and clinicians say yes. They believe that many of the "cases" of DID and dissociative amnesia have unwittingly been produced by therapists, self-help books, and the mass media (Aldridge-Morris, 1989; Chodoff, 1987; Goff & Simms, 1993; Lilienfield, Lynn, & Lohr, 2004; Loftus, Garry, & Feldman, 1994; Ofshe, 1992; Piper & Mersky, 2004; Weissberg, 1993). Clients most sensitive to these influences may have predisposing characteristics. For example, research findings indicate that

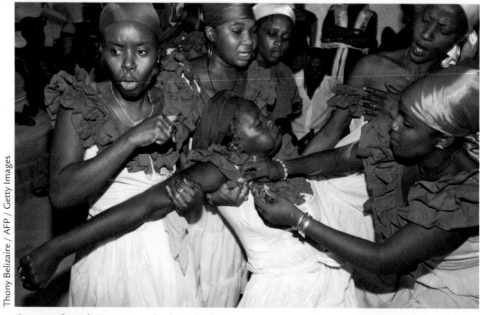

Thony Belizaire / AFP / Getty Images

Cross-cultural Factors and Dissociation

Dissociative trance states can be entered voluntarily as part of certain cultural or religious practices, as demonstrated by this Haitian woman during a voodoo ceremony. Can the study of such phenomena in another culture shed light on the process of dissociation in Western societies?

"Suspect" Techniques Used to Treat Dissociative Identity Disorder

CONTROVERSY

Bennett Braun, who founded the International Society for the Study of Dissociation and who trained many therapists to work with dissociative identity disorder, was brought up on charges by the Illinois Department of Professional Regulation. A former patient, Patricia Burgess, claimed that Braun inappropriately used hypnotic drugs, hypnosis, and leather strap restraints to stimulate "abuse" memories. Under repressed-memory therapy, Burgess became convinced that she possessed three hundred personalities, was a high priestess in a satanic cult, ate meatloaf made of human flesh, and sexually abused her children. Burgess later began to question her "memories." In November 1997, she won a $10.6 million lawsuit, alleging inappropriate treatment and emotional harm (Associated Press, 1998). Braun lost his license to practice for two years and was placed on probation for an additional five years (Bloomberg, 2000).

Another former patient, Elizabeth Gale, also won a $7 million settlement against Braun and other staff at the hospital. She became convinced she was raised as a "breeder" to produce babies who would be subjected to sexual abuse. She has since sought to re-establish relationships with family members whom she accused of being part of a cult (Dardick, 2004).

Such lawsuits create a quandary for mental health practitioners. Many feel intimidated by the threat of legal action if they attempt to treat adult survivors of childhood sexual abuse, especially cases involving recovered memories. However, discounting the memories of patients may represent further victimization. Especially worrisome is the use of techniques such as hypnosis, trance work, body memories, or age regression because they may produce inaccurate "memories" (Benedict & Donaldson, 1996).

For Further Consideration

1. In the case of "repressed memories," should clients be told that some techniques are experimental and may produce inaccurate information?
2. Under what conditions, if any, should a therapist express doubt about information "remembered" by a client?
3. Given the high prevalence of child sexual abuse and the indefinite nature of "repressed" memories, how should clinicians proceed if a client discusses early memories of abuse?

---

individuals who report dissociations score high on fantasy proneness and fantasy susceptibility (Giesbrecht, Lynn, Lilienfeld, & Merckelbach, 2008; McNally et al., 2000).

The authenticity of one well-known case of DID, Sybil (mentioned earlier), has actually been questioned (Borch-Jacobsen, 1997). Herbert Spiegel, a hypnotist, worked with Sybil and used her to demonstrate hypnotic phenomena in his classes. He described her as a "Grade 5" or "hypnotic virtuoso," something found in only 5 percent of the population. Sybil told Spiegel that her psychiatrist, Cornelia Wilbur, had wanted her to be "Helen," a name given to a feeling she expressed during therapy. Spiegel later came to believe that Wilbur was using a technique in which different memories or emotions were converted into "personalities." Sybil also wrote a letter denying that she had multiple personalities and stating that the "extreme things" she told about her mother were not true. Tapes of sessions between Wilbur and Sybil indicate that Wilbur may have described personalities for Sybil (Rieber, 2006).

Although iatrogenic influences can be found in any disorder, such effects may be more common with dissociative disorders, in part because of the high levels of hypnotizability and suggestibility found in individuals with these conditions (Simeon et al., 2001). As Goff (1993) states, it is "no coincidence that the field of [multiple-personality disorder] studies in the United States largely originated among practitioners of hypnosis" (p. 604). Hypnosis and other memory-retrieval methods may create rather than uncover personalities in suggestible clients. Although some cases of DID probably are therapist produced, we do not know to what extent iatrogenic influences can account for this disorder. The SCM model (which stresses the importance of exposure to mass media portrayals of DID and therapist suggestions) also has shortcomings. The model fails to explain why only a very small number of individuals who undergo therapy and are aware of the characteristics of DID develop this disorder.

Treatment of Dissociative Disorders

A variety of treatments for the dissociative disorders have been developed, including supportive counseling and the use of hypnosis and personality reconstruction. Currently, there are no specific medications for the dissociative identity disorders. Instead, medications are prescribed to treat concurrent anxiety or depression.

Dissociative Amnesia and Dissociative Fugue

The symptoms of dissociative amnesia and fugue tend to remit, or abate, spontaneously. Moreover, clients typically complain of psychological symptoms other than the amnesia, perhaps because the amnesia interferes only minimally with their day-to-day functioning. It has been noted that depression is often associated with the fugue state and that severe stress is often associated with both fugue and dissociative amnesia (Kopelman, 2002). A reasonable therapeutic approach is to treat these dissociative disorders indirectly by alleviating the depression (with antidepressants or cognitive-behavioral therapy) and the stress (through stress-management techniques).

Depersonalization Disorder

Depersonalization disorder is also subject to spontaneous remission, but at a much slower rate than seen with dissociative amnesia and fugue. Treatment generally concentrates on alleviating the feelings of anxiety or depression or the fear of going insane. Various antidepressants and antianxiety medications have been used to treat the symptoms associated with depersonalization disorder(Janjua, Rapport, & Ferrara, 2010). Occasionally a behavioral approach has been tried. For example, behavior therapy was successfully used to treat depersonalization disorder in a fifteen-year-old girl who had blackouts that she described as "floating in and out." These episodes were associated with headaches and feelings of detachment, but neurological and physical examinations revealed no biological cause. Treatment involved getting increased attention from her family and reinforcement from them when the frequency of blackouts was reduced, training in appropriate responses to stressful situations, and self-reinforcement (Dollinger, 1983).

Dissociative Identity Disorder

The mental health literature contains more information on the treatment of dissociative identity disorder than on all of the other dissociative disorders combined. Treatment for this disorder is not always successful. Chris Sizemore (who was the inspiration for the book and movie *The Three Faces of Eve*) developed additional personalities after therapy but has now recovered. She is a writer, lecturer, and artist. Sybil also recovered (although questions remain regarding her diagnosis)—she became a college art professor and died in Lexington, Kentucky, in 1998 at the age of seventy-five (Miller & Kantrowitz, 1999). Success, however, may be difficult to achieve. Coons (1986) conducted a follow-up study of twenty patients with DID. Each patient was studied for about thirty-nine months after his or her initial assessment. Nine patients achieved partial or full recovery, but only five patients maintained it—the others dissociated again. More than one-third were unable to work because of their disorder. However, a more recent review of sixteen treatment outcome studies found that patients tended to have lower rates of dissociation, suicidality, and depression following treatment. Those who were able to integrate the personalities showed the greatest reduction in symptoms (Brand et al., 2009).

The major goal in the treatment of DID is the fusion and complete integration of all of the individual personalities. In many cases, this cannot be achieved. A hierarchical treatment approach involves (Brand & Loewenstein, 2010; International Society for the Study of Dissociation, 2005):

1. Working on safety issues, stabilization, and the reduction of symptoms
2. Identifying and working through the traumatic memories underlying the disorder
3. Attempting to integrate the personalities

Hypnosis is often used to attempt the fusion or integration. With the client in a hypnotic state, the different personalities are asked to emerge and introduce themselves to the client, to make the client aware of their existence. Then the personalities are asked to help the client recall the traumatic experiences or memories that originally

Debra Lay/Getty Images

A Famous Case of Dissociative Identity Disorder

Chris Sizemore, whose experiences with dissociative identity disorder (DID) inspired the book and movie *The Three Faces of Eve*, is an artist today and no longer shows any signs of her former disorder. How do individuals with DID reconcile having different identities?

triggered the development of new personalities. An important part of this recalling step is to enable the client to experience the emotions associated with the traumatic memories. The therapist then explains to the client that these additional personalities developed to serve a purpose but that alternative coping strategies are available now. The final steps involve piecing together the events and memories of the personalities, integrating them, and continuing therapy to help the client adjust to the new self.

Summary

1. When do physical complaints become a psychological disorder? What are the causes and treatments of these conditions?
    - Complex somatic symptom disorders (CSSD), illness anxiety disorder, and functional neurological symptom disorders involve somatic complaints but no medical condition. The symptoms are distressing and result in significant disruptions in one's life

    - CSSD with somatization is characterized by chronic multiple physical complaints. CSSD with pain is a condition involving reports of severe pain that cannot be fully explained through medical evaluations.
    - Illness anxiety disorder (hypochondriasis) is characterized by health anxiety involving the belief that one has a serious and undetected illness or physical problem.

- Functional neurological symptoms disorder (conversion disorder) involves neurological symptoms that are incompatible with a medical condition.
- Factitious disorders are self-induced or feigned physical complaints.
- Biological explanations have suggested that there is increased vulnerability to somatic symptom disorder when individuals have high sensitivity to bodily sensations, a lower pain threshold, and/or a history of illness or injury. The psychoanalytic view holds that somatic symptom disorders are caused by the repression of sexual conflicts and their conversion into physical symptoms. Other psychological factors include social isolation, high anxiety or stress, and catastrophic thoughts regarding bodily sensations. Social explanations suggest that the role of "being sick" is reinforcing. Parental models for injury or illness can also be influential. From a sociocultural perspective, somatic symptom disorders result from societal restrictions placed on women, who are affected to a much greater degree than men by these disorders. Additionally, social class, limited knowledge about medical concepts, and cultural acceptance of physical symptoms can play a role.
- Treatment includes the use of antidepressants to improve mood and the use of cognitive-behavioral strategies. The process involves psychoeducation about physical complaints, the role of cognitions and their correction, and exercises to tolerate changes in bodily sensations.

2. What are dissociations? What forms can they take? How are they caused, and how are they treated?

- Dissociation involves a disruption in consciousness, memory, identity, or perception and may be transient or chronic.

- Dissociative amnesia and dissociative fugue involve a selective form of forgetting in which the person cannot remember information that is of personal significance. Depersonalization/derealization disorder is characterized by feelings of unreality—distorted perceptions of oneself and one's environment. Dissociative identity disorder (DID) involves the alternation of two or more relatively independent personalities in one individual or an experience of possession.
- Biological explanations for DID have focused on studies finding variations in brain activity when comparing different personalities. Some researchers believe that childhood trauma and chronic stress can result in permanent structural changes in the brain. Psychoanalytic perspectives attribute these disorders to the repression of impulses that are seeking expression and ways of coping with childhood abuse. Sociocultural explanations for dissociation include exposure to media portrayals of dissociation and role enactment. Social explanations include childhood abuse, subtle reinforcement, responding to the expectations of a therapist, or mislabeling dissociative experiences.
- Dissociative amnesia and dissociative fugue tend to be short-lived and remit spontaneously; behavioral therapy has also been used successfully. Dissociative identity disorder has most often been treated with psychotherapy and hypnosis, as well as with behavioral and family therapies.

Media Resources

Psychology CourseMate   Access an interactive eBook, chapter-specific interactive learning tools, including flash cards, quizzes, videos and more in your Psychology CourseMate, accessed through CengageBrain.com.

CENGAGENOW

CengageNOW   CengageNOW is an easy-to-use online resource that helps you study in less time to get the grade you want—NOW. If your textbook does not include an access code card, go to CengageBrain.com to gain access.

CENGAGEbrain.com

CengageBrain   More than just an interactive study guide, WebTutor is an anytime, anywhere customized learning solution with an eBook, keeping you connected to your textbook, instructor, and classmates. Purchase the access chosen by your instructor at CengageBrain.com.

8

Depressive and Bipolar Disorders

Amanda is a forty-year-old homemaker with three young children. Her husband, Jim, is the sales manager for an auto agency. The family does well financially and lives comfortably. For years, family life was stable, cohesive, and loving. However, Jim began to notice that his wife was becoming increasingly unhappy, frequently saying that her life lacked purpose. Jim tried to reassure her and suggested that she find some hobbies or socialize with their neighbors. However, Amanda became progressively more absorbed in her belief that her life was meaningless.

After a while, Amanda no longer bothered to cook, clean, or take care of the children. At first Jim thought that her "bad mood" would pass, but as her lethargy deepened, he became increasingly worried. Amanda told him that she was incredibly tired, that household chores took too much energy, and that she no longer had strong feelings for anything. She often asked to be left alone. Amanda felt guilty about her inability to take care of the children, but everything was simply too overwhelming. Sometimes she cried uncontrollably for hours. Nothing Jim said could improve her spirits or stop her crying. Amanda finally agreed to seek help and is currently receiving medication and psychotherapy to treat her depression.

As we shall see in this chapter, persistent changes in mood are sometimes difficult to explain. In Amanda's case, there was no single event, traumatizing experience, or stressor that caused her depression. A variety of factors, including genetic predisposition, early life events, and other stressors, often interact to produce mood disorders. In this chapter, we first discuss the assessment of mood symptoms followed by a focus on the diagnosis, epidemiology, etiology, and treatment of depressive disorders and bipolar disorders. Suicide, a serious problem associated with mood disorders, is covered in Chapter 9.

Assessing Mood Symptoms

Mood disorders, sometimes referred to as *affective disorders*, are a group of conditions (i.e., depressive and bipolar disorders) that influence emotions, thoughts, and behaviors; cause subjective discomfort; and hinder a person's ability to function. Mood disorders involve symptoms of depression, mania, or a combination of both.

1 What are symptoms of depression and mania, and what are some important considerations in diagnosing mood disorders?

2 Which disorders are considered depressive disorders, what causes these disorders, and how are they treated?

3 What are bipolar disorders, what causes these disorders, and how are they treated?

Depression, characterized by intense sadness, feelings of futility and worthlessness, and withdrawal from others, is a core feature of many mood disorders. Some mood disorders involve mania, a mood-state characterized by increased energy, elevated mood, and other significant changes in behavior. Depression and mania, opposite ends of a continuum that extends from deep sadness to wild elation, represent the extremes of mood.

We have all felt depressed or elated at some time during our lives. The loss of a friendship can result in feelings of sadness or we may feel energized, elated, or even ecstatic when we hear great news. Mood disorders differ from these temporary emotional reactions because they pervade every aspect of a person's life, persist over an extended period of time, often occur for no apparent reason, and are markedly out of proportion to life circumstances. We first describe the *affective* (mood-related), cognitive, behavioral, and physiological changes associated with depression followed by a parallel discussion of the symptoms of mania (Table 8.1). We then discuss diagnostic considerations with depressive and bipolar disorders, an important focus because differential diagnosis of these disorders requires careful consideration of mood symptoms.

Symptoms of Depression

Depression is often evident from a variety of affective, cognitive, behavioral, and physiological changes.

Affective Symptoms

The most striking affective symptom of depression, depressed mood, often involves feelings of sadness, dejection, hopelessness, worthlessness, or low self-esteem. The following case illustrates the hopelessness and emotional detachment characteristic of depression.

Case Study

It's hard to describe the state I was in several months ago. The depression was total—it was as if everything that happened to me passed through this dark filter, and I kept seeing the world through this dark cloud. Nothing was exciting. I felt I was no good, completely worthless, and deserving of nothing. The people who tried to cheer me up just couldn't understand how down I felt.

Individuals who are depressed have limited enthusiasm for things that previously brought pleasure and joy, including social interaction with family and friends. Irritability during depressive episodes is also common (Fava et al., 2009). Feelings of anxiety frequently accompany depressive symptoms (Kessler et al., 2005).

depression a mood state characterized by sadness or despair, feelings of futility and worthlessness, and withdrawal from others

mania mental state characterized by elevated mood and excessive excitement or irritability with resultant impairment in social or occupational functioning

TABLE 8.1 Symptoms of Depression and Mania

Domain	Depression	Mania
Affective	Feelings of sadness, dejection, and worthlessness; apathy; anxiety; brooding	Elation, grandiosity, irritability
Cognitive	Pessimism, guilt, inability to concentrate, negative thinking, loss of interest and motivation, suicidal thoughts	Flighty and pressured thoughts, lack of focus and attention, poor judgment
Behavioral	Social withdrawal, lowered productivity, low energy, anhedonia, neglect of personal appearance, agitation	Overactivity, extreme talkativeness; speech difficult to understand
Physiological	Appetite and weight changes, sleep disturbance, loss of sex drive	High levels of arousal, decreased need for sleep, increased sex drive

Copyright © Cengage Learning 2013

Cognitive Symptoms

Besides feelings of futility, emptiness, and hopelessness, certain thoughts and ideas (cognitive symptoms) are associated with depression. Individuals who are depressed often have profoundly pessimistic beliefs about the present and prospects for the future. Self-denigration (disparaging or belittling oneself) and feelings of incompetence are common, as are thoughts of suicide. Difficulties with memory, concentration, and decision making are often evident. Rumination, continually thinking about certain topics or repeatedly reviewing events that have transpired, is often reported by those who are depressed. Such rumination often involves irrational or unjustified beliefs.

Behavioral Symptoms

Behavioral symptoms such as fatigue, lethargy, social withdrawal, and reduced work productivity are common with depression. In the chapter opening case, Amanda felt constantly tired and complained that she had no energy. Depressed persons often show diminished motivation and exhibit anhedonia, a loss of the capacity to derive pleasure from normally pleasant experiences. Tearfulness may occur in reaction to sadness, frustration, or anger. Unexplained, uncontrollable crying often transpires without a specific precipitant, as was the case for Amanda. Lack of concern for personal cleanliness may also be evident. Speech is often slow and responses may be limited to short phrases. In contrast to such slowing of responses, some who are depressed seem agitated and restless.

Physiological Symptoms

The following physiological or somatic symptoms frequently accompany depression:

1. *Appetite and weight changes.* During depression, some people experience changes in weight due to either increased or decreased eating. Some eat even if they are not hungry, whereas others experience a significant loss of appetite.
2. *Sleep disturbance.* Depression-related insomnia can involve difficulty falling asleep or erratic awakening during the night. Sleep may no longer feel refreshing resulting in *hypersomnia* (extreme day-time sleepiness) despite excessive sleep.
3. *Unexplained aches and pain* Depression is often accompanied by somatic symptoms such as headache or other body aches (Jain, 2009). Such physical symptoms are associated with increased severity and chronicity of depression (Lee et al., 2009; Huijbregts et al., 2010). In some cultural groups, depression is primarily expressed somatically (Kung & Lu, 2008).
4. *Aversion to sexual activity.* Depression often produces dramatically reduced sexual arousal.

Did You Know?

Prevailing cultural norms affect the expression of depressive symptoms. While European Americans show decreased emotional reactivity when depressed (e.g., less smiling), depressed Asian Americans show increased internal physiological reactivity, but no significant changes in outward emotional expression.

Source: Chentsova-Dutton, Tsai, & Gotlib, (2010)

Symptoms of Mania

Case Study

Upon returning to work after a short vacation, Alan, a twenty-six-year-old computer programmer, seemed unusually happy, talkative, and energetic; he bragged that he was getting by on only a few hours of sleep each night by eating sugar. He brought several huge cakes to work and insisted that coworkers eat some of each cake. Initially, everyone was surprised and amused by his antics. However, amusement was soon replaced with irritation when Alan's continual talking and interruptions to share new ideas interfered with their work.

One morning, Alan jumped onto a desk, making obscene remarks and yelling, "Listen! We aren't working on the most important aspects of our data! Erase, re-program, you know what I mean. We've got to examine the total picture based on

self-denigration disparaging or belittling oneself

rumination continually thinking about certain topics or reviewing events that have transpired

anhedonia loss of the capacity to derive pleasure from normally pleasant experiences

the input!" Alan's speech was so rapid and disjointed that it was difficult to understand him. Alan then grabbed a chair and began to smash computers. After several coworkers grabbed him, Alan continued to shout and struggle. Police officers were summoned; they handcuffed Alan to restrain his movements. Within hours, he was taken to a psychiatric hospital for observation.

There are two levels of manic intensity—hypomania and mania (American Psychiatric Association, 2011). The milder form, hypomania, is characterized by significantly increased levels of activity or energy (including decreased need for sleep) combined with an elevated, expansive, or irritable mood. The individual may appear quite distractible, change topics frequently, and generate many disconnected ideas. There may be increased goal-directed behavior—although projects may be started but not finished—and increased creativity. There also may be intense focus on pleasurable activities without concern for consequences. When interacting with others, those experiencing hypomania often talk excessively, dominate the conversation, and act in a self-important manner.

Aside from hypomania being a milder version of mania, another notable difference is that hypomanic episodes do not involve a loss of contact with reality (psychosis), nor do they cause marked impairment in social or occupational functioning or a need for hospitalization. Additionally, the energetic, goal-directed activity in hypomania is sometimes associated with an increase in productivity (Benazzi, 2007). As we saw with Alan, hypomania sometimes progresses into a full manic episode. As with depression, mania involves a variety of affective, cognitive, behavioral, and physiological changes.

Affective Symptoms

Mania is characterized by affective volatility, involving emotions ranging from extreme elation to intense rage. Individuals experiencing an elevated mood may be in extremely high spirits, exhilarated, and full of boundless energy, enthusiasm, and self-assertion. Inappropriate use of humor, lack of restraint in expressing feelings or opinions, and grandiosity (overvaluation of one's importance with related themes of being special, chosen, or superior to others) can result in interpersonal conflicts. Mania can also produce extreme irritability, hostility, and intolerance, a combination that can result in intense agitation, belligerence, aggression, or episodes of rage.

Cognitive Symptoms

Cognitive symptoms of mania include disorientation, intrusive thoughts, lack of focus and attention, poor judgment, and lack of insight regarding the inappropriateness of behaviors or verbalizations. Verbal processes frequently reflect the individual's cognitive state. Speech is often rapid, loud, disjointed, and difficult to interpret. Communication is characterized by frequent changes of topic, irrelevant utterances, or use of idiosyncratic phrases. People experiencing mania have difficulty controlling their attention and focus and are constantly self-distracted by exciting thoughts and ideas.

Poor judgment and failure to evaluate the consequences of decisions can lead to overspending, unsafe sexual practices, or dangerous use of substances. There is often a profound lack of insight regarding the inappropriateness of statements or actions that occur during mania. If concern is expressed about their conduct, those experiencing a manic episode often contend that they are just fine and counter that the person expressing the concern is the one with the problem.

Behavioral Symptoms

In terms of behavioral symptoms, individuals with mania are often uninhibited, engaging in indiscriminate sexual activity or abusive discourse. They may be intolerant of criticism; act impulsively (e.g., gambling, driving recklessly, making poor investments, or spending excessively); and engage in socially disruptive behaviors. Speech is often rapid and incoherent. Impulsivity and difficulty delaying gratification are often present (Strakowski et al., 2010). Wild excitement, ranting, raving (thus, the stereotype of a raving "maniac"),

hypomania a milder form of mania involving increased levels of activity and goal-directed behaviors combined with an elevated, expansive, or irritable mood

grandiosity an overvaluation of one's significance or importance

constant movement, and agitation characterize severe manic episodes. Psychotic symptoms including paranoia, hallucinations, and delusions (false beliefs) may appear. Individuals experiencing extreme mania are often hospitalized after becoming dangerous to themselves or to others.

Physiological Symptoms

Decreased need for sleep and high levels of arousal are the most prominent physiological symptoms of mania. During manic episodes, individuals often experience minimal fatigue and sleep very little. Physiological arousal can result in ongoing restlessness, intense activity, and impulsive behaviors. Increased libido (sex drive) often results in hypersexuality and uncharacteristic sexual indiscretion. Weight loss often occurs due to the high energy expenditure and long periods without adequate sleep.

Diagnostic Considerations with Mood Disorders

Effective treatment of depressive and bipolar disorders is intricately tied to accurate diagnosis and a clear understanding of symptom patterns. Diagnosticians use various specifiers to describe notable features of mood episodes. For example, clinicians determine if mood symptoms are mild, moderate, or severe and ask about the history of previous episodes (including frequency and duration) to determine if mood symptoms have had a recent onset or if they are recurrent or chronic. Because seasonal fluctuations in symptom onset or severity are sometimes seen with mood disorders (Westrin & Lam, 2007a), the clinician inquires about any seasonal changes in mood. They also inquire about the presence of anxiety or melancholia (a pervasive depressive mood involving lack of reaction to pleasurable stimuli, extreme lethargy, intense guilt, and severe weight loss). Melancholia and anxiety symptoms are both associated with increased impairment and increased risk of suicidality. Because individuals with mood disorder often "self-medicate" with substances and because substance-use disorders are frequently comorbid with mood disorders, clinicians also inquire about patterns of alcohol use or other substance use (i.e., illicit drugs or overuse of prescription medications). Other specifiers involving mood symptoms include:

1. *Mixed features.* During depressive or hypomanic/manic episodes, are there symptoms from the other end of the mood continuum? A "mixed features" specifier is given when individuals who experience manic or depressive episodes also exhibit milder symptoms from the opposite pole (e.g., excessive crying, feelings of worthlessness, or talk of suicide during a manic episode). Mixed mood states can alternate or can occur almost simultaneously. (Sleep disturbances, changes in appetite, restlessness, irritability, and difficulty concentrating or making decisions are symptoms seen on both poles and, therefore, are not considered when assessing for mixed features.)

2. *Suicide risk severity.* Are there indicators of past or current suicidality? If so, how severe is the current risk? Mood disorders increase risk of suicide; ongoing substance abuse, prior suicidal acts, impulsivity, or feelings of hopelessness are especially predictive of suicidal behavior among those with mood disorders (Swann et al., 2005; Fiedorowicz et al., 2009). Additionally, sociocultural variables (e.g., Hispanic ethnicity, young age, low income); comorbid anxiety, personality or substance-use disorders; and feelings of worthlessness are associated with increased suicide risk (Bolton, Belik, Enns, Cox, & Sareen, 2008; Bolton, Pagura, Enns, Grant, & Sareen, 2010).

3. *Postpartum onset.* Was the onset of this mood episode within six months of childbirth? Postpartum symptoms can include depressive or hypomanic/manic behaviors as well as mental confusion, anxiety, and insecurity (Beck & Indman, 2005; Sharma, Khan, Corpse, & Sharma, 2008). Postpartum depression, an underdiagnosed condition, is estimated to affect as many as 13 percent of women (Breese-McCoy, 2011); risk is increased with biological vulnerability (e.g., genetics, hypothyroidism); prior history of mood disorder; circumstances

surrounding the pregnancy (e.g., maternal age, unplanned pregnancy); and sociocultural factors (e.g., family size and income, maternal educational and employment status, cultural gender preferences) (Mayberry, Horowitz, & Declercq, 2007; Klainin & Arthur, 2009; Breese-McCoy, 2011). Poor sleep quality increases symptom severity and duration of postpartum depression (Posmontier, 2008). Risk of postpartum psychosis is increased for women with family histories of such episodes; similarly, women with depressive disorders are more likely to have a postpartum relapse (especially in the first two months postpartum) when there is a family history of this pattern (Forty et al., 2006). Postpartum symptoms alone do not constitute a disorder, but are used as an informational specifier when diagnostic criteria are met for a depressive or bipolar disorder.

Clinicians also determine if psychotic symptoms (e.g., hallucinations, delusions) have occurred in conjunction with manic or depressive symptoms and if so, whether the themes are mood congruent (consistent with the individual's mood state). For example, if delusions or hallucinations occur during a depressive episode, the content may be consistent with a depressive mood (e.g., themes of inadequacy, death, guilt, or punishment) or unrelated to mood (e.g., beliefs of being controlled by aliens). Mood incongruent psychotic features indicate more severe illness (Goes et al., 2007). Psychotic symptoms are generally associated with greater cognitive impairment (Levy & Weiss, 2010). Clinicians also note if the client has had characteristics of *catatonia*, a state of apparent unresponsiveness to external stimuli that can include mutism; taking a specific posture and not moving; or extreme agitation with purposeless, excessive motor activity (Seethalakshmi, Dhavale, Suggu, & Dewan, 2008). Catatonia and psychotic features occur most frequently with schizophrenia and are discussed more comprehensively in Chapter 12. In some cases, depressive or manic symptoms occur in addition to indicators of schizophrenia. *Schizoaffective disorder* is diagnosed when someone with a psychotic disorder, such as schizophrenia, also experiences one or more prolonged episodes of mania or major depression.

Clinicians evaluating mood symptoms carefully gather information about the previously described factors in order to increase diagnostic accuracy and plan appropriate treatment. In addition, all individuals with depressive or bipolar disorders are periodically asked about anxiety, suicidality, and substance use because these conditions so frequently accompany mood disorders. Clinicians also inquire about other potential causes of mood symptoms such medication reactions or medical conditions (e.g., thyroid dysfunction). In some cases, intense depression or hypomania/mania represent heightened reactions to substance intoxication or withdrawal.

Depressive and bipolar disorders occur across the lifespan (Figure 8.1). All mood disorders involve symptoms severe enough to cause significant distress or impairment in

Figure 8.1

DEPRESSIVE AND BIPOLAR DISORDERS ACROSS THE LIFESPAN

Biological, psychological, social, and sociocultural factors increase vulnerability to mood disorders during different life stages.

Source: C. B. Nemeroff. Recent Findings in the Pathophysiology of Depression. Focus, January 1, 2008; 6(1): 3–14. http://focus.psychiatryonline.org/content/vol6/issue1/images/large/foc0010821270001.jpeg. Reprinted with permission from Focus, copyright © 2008. American Psychiatric Association.

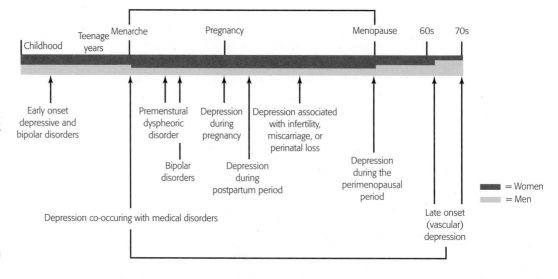

DISORDERS CHART   DEPRESSIVE DISORDERS

TABLE 8.2

Depressive Mood Disorders	Symptoms	Lifetime Prevalence (%)	Gender Difference	Age of Onset
Major Depressive Disorder	• Occurrence of at least one major depressive episode (two week duration) • No history of mania or hypomania	8.0–19.0	Much higher in females	Any age; average onset in 20s
Chronic Depressive Disorder (Dysthymia)	• Depressed mood that has lasted for at least two years (with no more than two months symptom-free)*	6.0	Much higher in females	Often starts in childhood or adolescence
Mixed Anxiety/ Depression	• Multiple symptoms of major depression including depressed mood and/or anhedonia • Anxious distress	No data	More common in females	Often starts in childhood or adolescence
Premenstrual Dysphoric Disorder	• Severe depression, mood swings, anxiety, or irritability occurring before the onset of menses (for at least one year) • Symptoms improve within a few days of menstruation and are minimal or absent following menstruation	2.0–8.0 of women of reproductive age	Most common in women with personal or family history of mood disorder	Late 20's although onset can be earlier
Seasonal Affective Disorder†	• At least two major depressive episodes occurring during fall/winter and remitting in spring/summer • Seasonal episodes of depression outnumber nonseasonal episodes	0.4–2.9	More common in females	Early adulthood, although earlier onset is possible

Source: Data from Kessler, Chiu, Demler, & Walters, (2005); Merikangas et al., 2007; Westrin & Lam, (2007b); Rosenthal, (2009); NIH, (2010); American Psychiatric Association (2011)
*In children and adolescents mood can be irritable and symptoms must have been present for at least one year.
†The American Psychiatric Association (2011) does not recognize Seasonal Affective Disorder as a diagnostic category.

academic, occupational, or social functioning. When making a diagnosis, clinicians pay particular attention to the severity and chronicity of symptoms as well as the presence of symptoms from both poles (i.e., depressive and manic/hypomanic symptoms); such data is critical for accurate differential diagnosis and treatment planning. As you will see, depressive disorders are quite distinct from bipolar disorders. In the next section, we focus on the diagnosis, etiology, and treatment of depressive disorders and conclude the chapter with a discussion of bipolar disorders.

Depressive Disorders

Depressive disorders, a group of related disorders characterized by depressive symptoms, include major depressive disorder, chronic depressive disorder, mixed anxiety/depression, premenstrual dysphoric disorder, and seasonal affective disorder (Table 8.2).

Diagnosis and Classification of Depressive Disorders

Diagnosis is made based on the severity of and chronicity of depressive symptoms as well as the pattern of symptom development. Hypomanic/manic episodes do not occur with depressive disorders. A bipolar disorder diagnosis would be considered if such episodes eventually developed.

Major Depressive Disorder

A diagnosis of major depressive disorder (MDD) requires that a major depressive episode impair functioning most of the day, nearly every day for at least two full weeks. Major depressive episodes involve (1) feelings of sadness or emptiness and/or (2) loss of interest or pleasure in previously enjoyed activities. In addition, weight or appetite changes, changes

major depressive episode two-week period involving pervasive feelings of sadness or emptiness and/or loss of pleasure and other cognitive, behavioral, and physiological changes that impair functioning

in sleep patterns, fatigue or very low energy, observable restlessness or slowing of activity, excessive feelings of guilt or worthlessness, difficulty with concentration and decision making, or recurrent thoughts of death or suicide are often evident (American Psychiatric Association, 2011). As many as 20 percent of individuals with MDD experience psychotic symptoms (Maj, Pirozzi, Magliano, Fiorillo, & Bartoli, 2007); psychotic features increase risk of severe depression, insomnia, agitation, and suicidality (Gaudiano, Young, Chelminski, & Zimmerman, 2008). Nearly one-third of those with MDD also have substance-use disorders; this combination increases suicide risk (Davis, Uezato, Newell, & Frazier, 2008). Additionally, personality disorder, panic disorder, and generalized anxiety disorder are frequently comorbid with MDD (Hasin, Goodwin, Stinson, & Grant, 2005). Approximately 65 percent of those with MDD achieve only partial symptom remission, a characteristic associated with increased risk of suicide and relapse (Trivedi, Hollander, Nutt, & Blier, 2008; Witte, Timmons, Fink, Smith, & Joiner, 2009).

Chronic Depressive Disorder

Chronic depressive disorder (CDD), also referred to as dysthymia, is diagnosed when depressive symptoms are present most of the day for more days than not during a two-year period (with no more than two months symptom-free). CDD involves the ongoing presence of at least two of the following symptoms: feelings of hopelessness, low self-esteem, poor appetite or overeating, low energy or fatigue, difficulty concentrating or making decisions, or sleep difficulties (American Psychiatric Association, 2011). Individuals with chronic MDD also fall in this category. CDD is often associated with a negative worldview and pessimistic outlook on the future. For many, CDD is a lifelong, pervasive disorder with long periods of depression, few periods of remission, and less response to treatment (McCullough et al., 2008; Torpey & Klein, 2008). Those with CDD are more likely to have a family history of mood disorder than those with single or periodic episodes of MDD (Klein et al., 2004).

Did You Know?

Screening of students who visited university health clinics revealed that about one-fourth of the students had significant symptoms of depression.

Source: Mackenzie et al., (2011)

Mixed Anxiety/Depression

Some individuals with depression may simultaneously experience significant anxiety symptoms. The diagnosis of mixed anxiety/depression (MAD) is given when distressing symptoms of major depression (including depressed mood and/or anhedonia) are accompanied by anxious distress (motor tension, difficulty relaxing, pervasive worries or feelings that something catastrophic will occur); the MAD diagnosis is used only when neither anxiety nor depression is clearly predominant. Individuals with MAD exhibit less severe depressive symptoms compared to MDD and fewer somatic symptoms compared to generalized anxiety disorder (Małyszczak & Pawłowski, 2006). However, MAD is associated with longer depressive episodes (Schmidt et al., 2007) and a higher risk of suicide (Boden, Fergusson, & Horwood, 2007).

Seasonal Affective Disorder

Seasonal affective disorder (SAD) refers to major depression that occurs with a seasonal pattern associated with decreasing light. Symptoms typically begin in the fall/winter and remit during the spring/summer. SAD is not yet a diagnostic category recognized by the American Psychiatric Association's Diagnostic and Statistical Manual. However, researchers define SAD as involving at least two seasonal major depressive episodes and a pattern of depressive episodes occurring seasonally more than nonseasonally. Those with SAD typically have a normal mood the rest of the year, although some have mild hypomanic-like symptoms during summer months. Many individuals experience seasonal patterns of mood change, but with only mild to moderate symptoms.

SAD is associated with "vegetative symptoms," including declining energy, lethargy, increased need for sleep, carbohydrate craving and associated weight gain, and social withdrawal. SAD is much more common in regions with less light in the winter months. Individuals with SAD are quite sensitive to environmental light and related circadian rhythm effects

anxious distress symptoms of motor tension, difficulty relaxing, pervasive worries, or feelings that something catastrophic will occur

(Shirani & St Louis, 2009). In fact, some individuals with SAD find that symptoms can increase or reappear with overcast skies at any time of the year. A summer-onset form of SAD (involving loss of appetite and associated weight loss, insomnia, and irritability or agitation) has been described but not adequately studied (Rosenthal, 2009).

Premenstrual Dysphoric Disorder

Premenstrual dysphoric disorder (PMDD) is a controversial diagnostic category; PMDD involves serious symptoms of depression, irritability, and tension that appear the week before menstruation and remit soon after the onset of menses. PMDD requires that at least five symptoms occur during the premenstrual period, including significant mood swings, anger, irritability or increases in interpersonal conflict; depressed mood, sense of hopelessness or self-deprecation; or anxiety or tension. Other premenstrual symptoms include difficulty concentrating; social withdrawal; lack of energy; food cravings or overeating; insomnia or excessive sleepiness; feelings of being overwhelmed; or physical symptoms such as bloating, weight gain, or breast tenderness. These are similar to the physical and emotional symptoms of premenstrual syndrome (PMS); however, PMDD produces significant distress or interference with social and interpersonal relationships or academic/occupational functioning (American Psychiatric Association, 2011).

Seasonal Patterns of Depression

In seasonal affective disorder (SAD), depressive symptoms vary with the seasons. One theory is that inadequate bright light and related circadian rhythm disruptions during the winter months affect neurotransmitters in the brain and subsequently induce depression. The people in this photo are receiving light therapy through exposure to specially designed light boxes. This treatment is effective for many individuals who experience symptoms of SAD. Do you believe that most people feel happier during the summer than winter?

Science Museum/SSPL / The Image Works

Those critical of the designation of PMDD as a disorder contend that PMDD is a socially constructed condition affected by cultural beliefs and conditioned social and gender role expectations. They strongly disagree with designating symptoms of a normal biological function as a psychiatric disorder (Offman & Kleinplatz, 2004; Chekoudjian, 2009).

Epidemiology of Depressive Disorders

Depression is one of the most prevalent psychiatric disorders and a leading cause of worldwide disability (Andrade, 2010). It produces both absenteeism and diminished productivity in the workplace. Moreover, depression is very costly. In the United States, about $50 billion is spent annually on health care services and lost workdays due to depression (Greenberg, Burnham, Lowe, & Corey-Lisle, 2003).

Nearly 15 million Americans will experience a depressive disorder this year. The prevalence of SAD ranges from 0.4 to 2.9 percent of the general population (Westrin & Lam, 2007b; Rosenthal, 2009). Approximately 2 to 8 percent of women in their reproductive years experience PMDD (Vigod & Stewart, 2009; National Institutes of Health [NIH], 2010; American Psychiatric Association, 2011). In a large-scale survey of more than 43,000 adults in the United States, twelve-month and lifetime prevalence of MDD was 5.28 percent and 13.23 percent, respectively (Hasin, Goodwin, Stinson, & Grant, 2005). Another comprehensive study found even higher prevalence rates: 6.6 percent for twelve-month and 16.2 percent for lifetime prevalence (Figure 8.2) (Kessler et al., 2003). In one survey of U.S. college students, more than half reported having experienced depression, 9 percent reported thoughts of suicide, and 1 percent reported attempting suicide since the beginning of college (Furr, Westefeld, McConnell, & Jenkins, 2001). In fact, the suicide risk among individuals with depression is at least eight times higher than that of the general population (Nitzkin & Smith, 2004).

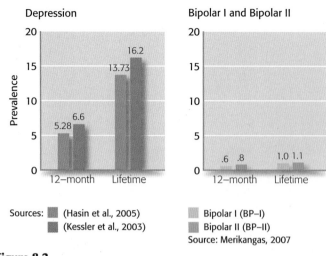

Figure 8.2

TWELVE-MONTH AND LIFETIME PREVALENCE OF DEPRESSIVE AND BIPOLAR DISORDER

Source: Based on Hasin et al., (2005); Kessler et al., (2003); Merikangas et al., (2007)

Being female, Native American, middle-aged, widowed, separated, or divorced, or having a low income increases risk for depression; being Asian, Hispanic, or African American decreases risk (Kessler et al., 2003). In fact, African Americans are 40 percent less likely than whites to experience a major depressive episode during their lifetime, whereas women have a 70 percent increased lifetime risk of experiencing a major depressive episode compared to men (Kessler, Chiu et al., 2005). African Americans, however, tend to have more severe and more chronic depression (Williams et al., 2007; Bailey, Blackmon, & Stevens, 2009; Menke & Flynn, 2009).

After one episode of depression, the likelihood of another is 50 percent; after two episodes, 70 percent; and after three episodes, 90 percent (Munoz et al., 1995). Incomplete remission of depressive symptoms is common, and presents a serious risk of relapse or unremitting course (Conradi, Ormel, & de Jonge, 2010). In one longitudinal survey of individuals with major depression, the most common residual symptoms involved poor concentration, lack of decisiveness, low energy, and sleep difficulties; these symptoms were present 85 to 94 percent of the time during the depressive episode and remained present 39 to 44 percent of the time during remission (Conradi, Ormel, & de Jonge, 2010).

Approximately 15 percent of those treated for depression fail to show any significant remission of symptoms (Berlim & Turecki, 2007); it is believed that many of these cases represent undiagnosed bipolar disorder (Brunoni, Fraguas, & Fregni, 2009; Bowden, 2010). In fact, one group of researchers screened a group of individuals diagnosed with a depressive disorder and found that 7 percent of the group had been misdiagnosed (i.e., they had clear symptoms of bipolar disorder); those misdiagnosed experienced significantly greater impairment and disability, presumably because they were being treated for unipolar depression rather than bipolar disorder (Kamat et al., 2008).

Etiology of Depressive Disorders

Over the years, a variety of explanations have been proposed to account for depression. Consistent with our multipath approach (Figure 8.3), research shows that various biological, psychological, social, and sociocultural factors interact in complex ways to cause depressive disorders. For example, the presence of depression within certain families appears to result from interactions between genetic susceptibility, timing of stressful life events, and the context of the stress (Pemberton et al., 2010). Environmental factors appear to exert greater influence in childhood, whereas hereditary factors exert greater influence in adolescence and adulthood (Harold et al., 2010). The transition between middle and late adolescence is a time during which strength of genetic influence begins to surpass environmental influences on the development of depressive symptoms (Tully, Iacono, & McGue, 2010).

Biological Dimension

Biological explanations regarding depressive disorders generally focus on genetic predisposition, physiological dysfunction, brain structures, or interactions among these factors.

The Role of Heredity   There is now overwhelming evidence that depressive disorders are influenced by genetic factors; however the ultimate phenotypic expression of genes is highly dependent on environmental factors (Leonardo & Hen, 2006). Depression tends to run in families and the same type of depressive disorder is often found among members of the same family (Hettema, 2010). Studies comparing the incidence of depressive disorders

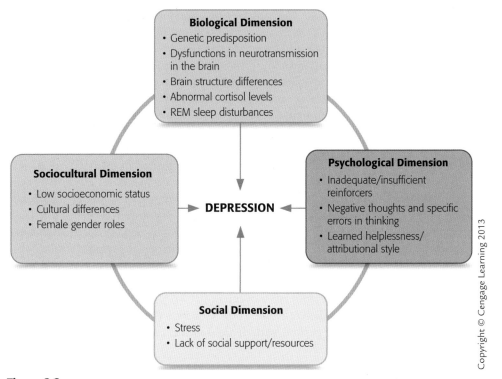

Figure 8.3

MULTIPATH MODEL FOR DEPRESSION

The dimensions interact with one another and combine in different ways to result in depression

among the biological and adoptive families of individuals with depression indicate that the incidence is significantly higher among biological families compared to adoptive families (Levinson, 2006). Studies of monozygotic and dizygotic twins reveal a significantly higher concordance rate for depressive symptoms among monozygotic compared to dizygotic twins. Interestingly, concordance is higher for female than male twins, perhaps indicating gender differences in heritability (Goldberg, 2006).

Genetics also appear to increase anxiety symptoms in some individuals with depression. An extensive study investigating the contribution of genetic and environmental factors to depressive and anxiety disorders (based on data from more than 4,500 pairs of identical and fraternal twins) concluded that there are modest contributions from genetic factors for both depression and anxiety disorders; additionally, there is significant genetic overlap between the disorders that may account for the high comorbidity between anxiety and depression (Kendler & Prescott, 2006).

Overall, it appears that multiple genes, each with relatively small influence, interact with environmental factors to produce depression (Lewis et al., 2010; Lohoff, 2010). For example, as mentioned in Chapter 2, a serotonin transporter gene (5-HTT) has been implicated in depression. Carriers of the shorter allele of this gene release more stress hormone (cortisol) and, when individuals with this gene are mistreated as children, they have increased risk of depression in adulthood (Caspi et al., 2003; Karg et al., 2011). Those with this genetic makeup also have more difficulty absorbing the serotonin circulating in the brain as well as releasing serotonin (Miller et al., 2009). This same gene is also associated with neuroanatomical differences (e.g., enlargement of the thalamus) in those with depression (Young, Bonkale, Holcomb, Hicks, & German, 2008). Genes related to circadian-cycle adaptations also influence brain regions and neurochemical systems associated with mood regulation (McClung, 2007); a circadian-related gene (CRY2) has been implicated in winter-onset depression (Lavebratt et al., 2010; Sjöholm et al., 2010). We now focus on ways various biological factors such as circadian cycles, neuroendocrine regulation, stress circuitry, neurotransmission, and brain structure abnormalities contribute to depression.

Did You Know?

Shorter sleep duration is associated with chronic psychological distress in young adults; as hours of sleep decrease, levels of distress increase.

Source: Glozier et al., (2010)

Circadian Disturbances in Depression   Optimal biological functioning is intricately tied to circadian rhythm, a system allowing adaptation to factors occurring in the external environment. Mood disorders, including depression, are associated with disruptions in this system (Monteleone & Maj, 2008). For example, seasonal circadian disturbances resulting from light-related changes (affecting secretion of the hormone melatonin and serotonin regulation) are implicated in SAD (Rosenthal, 2009).

Impaired sleep and short sleep duration both appear to play a role in the etiology of depression (Lam, 2008). This relationship was investigated in one study that compared depressive symptoms in adolescents who went to sleep at midnight or later with those with parent-designated bedtimes of 10 P.M. or earlier; adolescents with decreased sleep were 24 percent more likely to suffer from depression and 20 percent more likely to report suicidal ideation (Gangwisch et al., 2010). Insomnia and associated sleep deprivation are associated with precipitating and exacerbating depressive symptoms as well as precipitating depressive-relapse (Howland, 2011). Fragmented sleep is strongly linked to the onset of postpartum depression (Goyal, Gay, & Lee, 2009). Adults with depression exhibit increased rapid eye movement (REM) sleep, the stage of sleep during which dreaming occurs (Modell & Lauer, 2007; Goodwin & Guze, 1984). Interestingly, reducing the REM sleep of persons with depression can improve depressive symptoms (Howland, 2011).

Abnormal Cortisol Levels   Considerable research has also focused on possible abnormalities in neuroendocrine regulation in depression. Throughout the world, people with depression register higher blood levels of *cortisol*, a hormone secreted by the adrenal cortex in response to stress (Schnittker, 2010). How cortisol might influence depression is still unclear. In one study, rats developed depression-like behaviors after

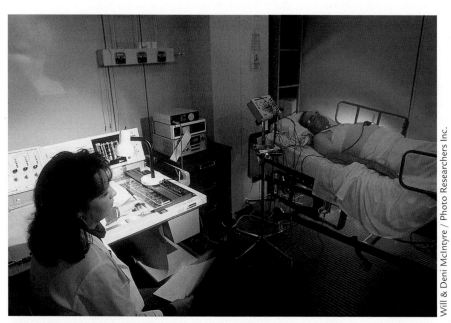

Will & Deni McIntyre / Photo Researchers Inc.

Sleep Disturbances and Depression

Sleep patterns have been linked to depression. For example, rapid eye movement during sleep occurs more often among those who have depression than among those who do not. The reasons for this are unclear. Here, a researcher is monitoring a man's sleep.

receiving repeated injections of a hormone (corticosterone) that simulates chronic stress (Kalynchuk, Gregus, Boudreau, & Perrot-Sinal, 2004). Cortisol may cause depressive symptoms by depleting chemicals necessary for effective neurotransmission, particularly serotonin (Leonard, 2010). Cortisol is also connected to the *inflammation hypothesis* of depression—that depression results from immune system dysfunction. Chronic cortisol-induced immunosuppression can result in brain inflammation and the formation of neurotoxins (Leonard, 2010). Interestingly, increased depressive symptoms have been found in men with biochemical indicators of neuroinflammation (Su et al., 2009).

Gillespie and Nemeroff (2007) observed that many individuals with depression have experienced early life traumas or stressors such as child abuse, neglect, or loss of a parent. Their belief is that exposure to stress during early development affects cortisol levels and the hypothalamic-pituitary-adrenal (HPA) system. This can increase susceptibility to depression in later life, especially among those who have genetic vulnerability. In fact, researchers have linked depression with interactions between childhood adversities and genes that, when triggered by environmental stressors, increase cortisol release (Bradley et al., 2008; Grabe et al., 2010). Thus, stress, the timing of stress, and genetic predisposition may interact to produce depression.

Stress Circuitry and Depression   In explaining stress disorders in Chapter 6, we focused on the stress circuitry of the brain and the HPA axis, a process by which stressors can increase levels of cortisol. As we discussed, the amygdalae recognize environmental stressors and prepare for a rapid response by initiating a cascade of hormones (Figure 8.4). Once a threat is recognized, the amygdalae send signals to the paraventricular nuclei (PVN) of the hypothalamus and corticotropin-releasing factor (CRF) is secreted, stimulating the pituitary gland, a region with many CRF-type 1 receptors (CRFR-1). Once CRF hormonal signals are received, the pituitary gland releases a hormone, adrenocorticotropic hormone (ACTH), into the bloodstream. The ACTH hormones travel to the adrenal glands where glucocorticoids (including cortisol) are released.

Cortisol affects various brain regions associated with depression, most notably the hippocampus; in addition to preparing the body for "fight-or-flight," cortisol also restores homeostasis (metabolic equilibrium) by signaling the brain to dampen HPA activity. Chronic stress and associated high levels of cortisol, however, can damage the hippocampus (i.e., neurons die and fail to regenerate) and result in dysregulation of the stress circuitry (Stahl & Wise, 2008). This dysregulation helps explain the increased vulnerability to depression seen in individuals with multiple lifetime stressors, especially stressors occurring early in life. As discussed in Chapter 6, serotonin levels are affected by both chronic and acute stress. In situations involving acute stress, serotonin is released to facilitate response to the threatening circumstance. However, chronic stress can deplete serotonin. When levels of serotonin are depleted, depression can occur. Additionally, stress can affect the production of enzymes that are necessary for serotonin to be metabolized (Miller et al., 2009).

Neurotransmitters and Depressive Disorders   Abnormalities in neurotransmission are also associated with depression. The availability of neurotransmitters (including serotonin, norepinephrine, and dopamine) is affected both by *reuptake* (reabsorption) of the substances and by *chemical depletion* (resulting from chemical reactions that break down the neurotransmitter). Evidence regarding the importance of neurotransmitters in depression comes from a variety of sources. Years ago, it was accidentally discovered that when the drug reserpine was used to treat hypertension,

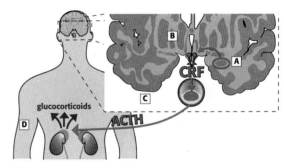

Figure 8.4

STRESS CIRCUITRY: THE HYPOTHALAMIC-PITUITARY-ADRENAL (HPA) AXIS RESPONDING TO STRESS

The amygdala (*A*), recognizing an environmental stressor, initiates a cascade of hormones by signaling the paraventricular nuclei (PVN; *B*) of the hypothalamus. The PVN then secretes corticotropin-releasing factor (CRF) to the pituitary gland (*C*), an area with many CRF-type 1 receptors (CRFR-1). The pituitary gland is thus signaled to release adrenocorticotropic hormone (ACTH) into the bloodstream. ACTH then stimulates the adrenal glands (*D*) to release cortisol. Cortisol prepares the body for "fight-or-flight." Chronic high levels of cortisol are associated with depression.

Source: Nestler et al., 2002; Stahl & Wise, 2008

many patients became depressed (reserpine depletes neurotransmitters). Similarly, the drug iproniazid, given to patients with tuberculosis, elevated the mood of those who were depressed. (Iproniazid inhibits the chemical depletion of neurotransmitters.) Also, as previously noted, a serotonin transporter gene (5-HTT) has been implicated in depression (Caspi et al., 2003). More recently, studies of the effects of antidepressant medications (which increase availability of norepinephrine and serotonin) also implicate neurotransmission. Additionally, antidepressants appear to help normalize HPA function and facilitate regeneration of neurons (Stahl & Wise, 2008).

Neuroanatomy and Depression   Neuroimaging of individuals with depression has documented HPA axis alterations as well as the smaller hippocampal volume that might be predicted by stress dysregulation (Stahl & Wise, 2008). Abnormalities in brain structures (e.g., the nucleus accumbens, amygdala, and regions of the hypothalamus) that are intricately tied to the regulation of motivation, appetite, sleep, energy level, circadian rhythm, and response to rewarding and aversive stimuli have been detected in some individuals with depression (Nestler et al., 2002). Additionally, decreased activation of the prefrontal lobes has been documented in individuals with MDD. Magnetic resonance imaging studies suggest that this decreased brain activity is due, at least in part, to a reduction in gray matter in the brain (Leonardo & Hen, 2006). Abnormalities in brain circuitry have also been implicated in depression. The depression subtype, symptom profile, and affective abnormalities may systematically vary with the brain location and nature of neurological abnormalities (Davidson et al., 2002).

Whether unipolar depressive disorders are caused by circadian system disturbances, deficient neurotransmitter production, or by other brain abnormalities cannot be resolved at this time. It is also possible that because depression is a heterogeneous collection of disorders no single cause will be isolated. Furthermore, the interaction between genetic makeup, stressful experiences, and psychological, social, and sociocultural factors increase etiological complexity.

Did You Know?

Strong adherence to male norms such as having emotional control (i.e., keeping emotions "hidden") and being self-reliant is associated with increased depression among recently unemployed men. Interestingly, men in this group, although depressed, were more likely to find employment.

Source: Syzdek & Addis, (2010)

AP Photo/Karim Kadim

Loss as a Source of Depression

Mourning the death of a loved one occurs in all cultures and societies, as illustrated by these women mourning at the funerals of 13 members of an Iraqi tae kwon do team who were kidnapped and killed in Iraq. In most cultures, severe and incapacitating depression rarely continues longer than three months. What characteristics or symptoms would help one to distinguish between "normal" grief and a depressive disorder?

Psychological Dimension

A number of psychological theories have been proposed to account for the development of depression. In this section we look at behavioral and cognitive theories of depression.

Behavioral Explanations   Behavioral explanations suggest that depression occurs when people receive insufficient social reinforcement (Lejuez, Hopko, Acierno, Daughters, & Pagoto, 2011). This lack of reinforcement may be due to losses such as unemployment, divorce, or death of a friend or family member. Depression thus results from the void created by changes in accustomed levels of reinforcement (e.g., love, affection, companionship). Behaviorists believe depressive symptoms can be reduced by increasing activity that generates environmental reinforcement (Gawrysiak, Nicholas, & Hopko, 2009).

Lewinsohn's model of depression is perhaps the most comprehensive behavioral explanation of depression (Lewinsohn, 1974; Lewinsohn, Munoz, Youngren, & Zeiss, 1994). In addition to the role of reinforcement, Lewinsohn suggests three sets of variables that enhance or hinder a person's access to positive reinforcement. A low rate of positive reinforcement due to any of these factors can increase risk of depression.

1. *The number of events and activities that are potentially reinforcing to the person.* This number depends on personal experiences and characteristics (including biological traits). For example, age, gender, or physical attributes may determine the availability of reinforcers.
2. *The availability of reinforcements in the environment.* Harsh or isolating environments reduce reinforcement.
3. *The instrumental behavior of the individual.* Social interaction can bring about or reduce reinforcement. Individuals experiencing depression often show decreases in social behaviors known to elicit positive reinforcement. They interact with fewer people, respond less, and initiate less conversation. Their discomfort in social situations may result in subdued responses from others. Interestingly, those who tend to have few positive personality traits have more chronic depression, whereas negative personality traits are associated with earlier onset of depression (Robison, Shankman, & McFarland, 2009).

The occurrence of stress also plays a strong role in the theory. Lewinsohn and his colleagues (1985) believe that stressful antecedent events can disrupt predictable and well-established behavioral patterns. Such disruptions can reduce positive reinforcement or increase aversive experiences. If individuals are unable to reverse this pattern, they may experience heightened self-awareness, engage in self-criticism, develop negative expectancies, and lose self-confidence, which then leads to depressed affect. Depressed mood leads to difficulty functioning normally, which further increases vulnerability to depression. Thus, Lewinsohn's model attempts to cover not only behavioral elements but also focuses on the cognitive and emotional consequences of diminished social reinforcement.

Cognitive Explanations   Cognitively oriented psychologists contend that the way people think causes depression. The cognitive view suggests that individuals experiencing depression have negative thoughts and errors in thinking that result in pessimism, negative self-perceptions, feelings of hopelessness, and depression (Emmelkamp, 2004). Those who are depressed often perceive themselves as inept, unworthy, and incompetent and are likely to dismiss personal success as pure luck or forecast eventual failure. Hence a cognitive interpretation of oneself as unworthy may lead to exaggerated, irrational, and catastrophic thinking patterns involving self-blame, self-criticism, and exaggerated ideas of duty and responsibility (Ellis, 1989). For example, it is hypothesized that self-reproach exacerbates irritability, a common symptom of depression (Fava et al., 2010). These depressogenic ways of thinking are believed to result from adverse life experiences such as negative interactions with parents or caregivers (Van Vlierberghe, Braet, Bosmans, Rosseel, & Bogels, 2010; Woolgar & Tranah, 2010).

Beck (1976) developed a major cognitive theory that views depression as a disturbance in *thinking* rather than a disturbance in *mood*; he contends that the manner in which individuals structure and interpret their experiences determines their affective responses. For example, an unpleasant mood is more likely to develop when a situation is viewed as unpleasant. According to Beck, cognitive schemas (cognitive frameworks that help organize and

Dennis MacDonald / PhotoEdit

Magnification of Events

According to cognitive explanations for depression, people may become depressed because of the way they interpret situations. They may overly magnify, selectively abstract, or make into catastrophes events that happen to them. In this photo, an adolescent football player sits alone in a locker room after losing a football game.

schema   a cognitive framework that helps organize and interpret information

Did You Know?

interpret information) can create depression by perpetuating a negative outlook and attention to negative messages. A tendency to focus on (and have difficulty disengaging from) negative information is particularly powerful in generating depression (Gotlib & Joormann, 2010).

According to Beck's theory, individuals experiencing depression tend to have negative self-views, as well as a pessimistic outlook regarding present experiences and future expectations. Four errors in logic typify negative schemas:

1. *Arbitrary inference.* Individuals experiencing depression tend to draw conclusions that are not supported by evidence. For example, if no one initiates conversation on the bus, someone with depression may conclude, "People dislike me".

2. *Selected abstraction.* Individuals may focus on minor incidents or trivial details taken out of context. A minor corrective comment from a supervisor may be construed as implying incompetence—even when the supervisor's overall feedback is highly positive.

3. *Overgeneralization.* Individuals may draw sweeping conclusions about their ability, performance, or worth from a single experience or incident. A job loss due to budgetary cuts may lead to self-perceptions of inadequacy or worthlessness.

4. *Magnification and minimization.* Some individuals magnify (exaggerate) limitations and difficulties and minimize accomplishments, achievements, and capabilities. If asked to evaluate personal strengths and weaknesses, the person may list many shortcomings, but fail to identify any achievements.

Evidence of a link between cognition and depression is strengthened by studies of memory bias. When people with depression are given lists of words that vary in emotional content, they tend to recall more negative words. This may indicate a tendency to attend to, and remember, negative and depressing events (Mineka & Sutton, 1992). Even individuals who have recovered from depression show a more negative cognitive style (Hedlund & Rude, 1995). They presumably have developed negative schemas. Cognitive or perceptual bias was also found when individuals were asked to identify happy faces among a group of morphed faces that varied in degrees of happiness (Joormann, 2006). Those with major depression, compared with nondepressed controls, required greater intensity of facial expression to identify happy faces.

Emotional abuse and neglect in childhood appears to increase the formation of maladaptive schemas involving vulnerability and shame, beliefs that one's relational needs will never be met, feelings of inadequacy in terms of performance, or expectations that loving someone will lead to rejection (Wright, Crawford, & Del Castillo, 2009; Eberhart, 2011). Beliefs such as these can increase depressive symptoms as can be seen in the following case.

Case Study

Gabriel, a twenty-four-year-old college upperclassman, [began] therapy complaining of depressed mood and high anxiety, as well as guilt and disappointment regarding his failure to complete his undergraduate degree on time while his parents continued to pay for his education. . . . Gabriel also felt frustrated because his personal goals were to earn a prestigious scholarship, to study internationally, and to achieve great things in his career. . . . Gabriel had experienced anxieties about school when he was an adolescent, in addition to a depressive episode that he attributed to anticipated difficulties in revealing his homosexuality to his family. Gabriel insisted that this latter problem had been resolved, in spite of the fact that he had never disclosed his sexual orientation to his father. (Newman, 2010, pp. 25–26)

Individuals with depression often tend to cope with stressful circumstances via rumination (repeatedly thinking about concerns or events) rather than active problem solving. Having a ruminative response style predicts depressive symptoms among youth and adults, particularly females and those with anxious tendencies (Hankin, 2008). Co-rumination, the process of constantly talking over problems with peers, has also been linked to increased risk for depression, especially in girls (Stone, Uhrlass, & Gibb, 2010). The tendency to ruminate has been associated with early temperament. In a group of youth followed from birth through adolescence, negative emotionality at age one was associated with self-reported rumination at age 13 and depressive symptoms at ages thirteen and fifteen; the link between rumination and depressive symptoms was particularly strong for girls (Mezulis, Priess, & Hyde, 2011).

Some individuals with depression have a more negative outlook on life and have difficulty using positive events to regulate negative mood (Gotlib & Joormann, 2010). Individuals who experienced a serious life event before the onset of major depression demonstrated more significant declines in negative thinking as their depression remitted compared to individuals experiencing depression without a precipitating event; these finding suggest that the negative cognitive biases seen in the specific-event group were related to a particular incident rather than a pervasive cognitive style (Monroe, Slavich, Torres, & Gotlib, 2007).

Learned Helplessness and Attributional Style   Martin Seligman and colleagues (1975; Nolen-Hoeksema, Girgus, & Seligman, 1992) proposed a unique explanation for depression incorporating behavioral and cognitive-learning theory. The basic assumption of this approach is that both cognitions and feelings of helplessness are learned and that depression results from learned helplessness— an acquired belief that one is helpless and unable to affect outcomes in one's life. People who feel helpless make *causal attributions*, or speculations about why events occur. These attributions can be internal or external, stable or unstable, and global or specific. For instance, suppose that a student in a math course receives low grades despite studying extensively. The student may attribute the low grades to internal or personal factors ("I don't do well in math because I'm scared of math") or to external factors ("The *teacher* doesn't like me, so I can't get a good grade"). The attribution can also be stable ("I'm the type of person who can never do well in math") or unstable ("My low math grade was probably due to my heavy workload this quarter"). Additionally, the attribution can be global or specific. A global attribution ("I'm a lousy student") has broader implications for performance than a specific one ("I'm poor at math but good in other subjects"). Individuals whose attributions are internal, stable, and global are likely to have more pervasive feelings of depression compared to those whose attributions are external, unstable, and specific (Abramson, Seligman, & Teasdale, 1978; Morris, Ciesla, & Garber, 2008).

Both the learned helplessness model and the attributional style approach have generated a great deal of research. There is evidence that people with depression make "depressive" attributions and feel that their lives are less controllable compared to those without depression (Raps, Peterson, Reinhard, Abramson, & Seligman, 1982). One study has also shown that negative self-appraisals by children can predict subsequent level of depression (Hoffman, Cole, Martin, Tram, & Seroczynski, 2000). Cognitive-behavioral and attribution theories make an important contribution to understandings of depression, but appear to only partially explain depression.

Interestingly, Lewinsohn, Joiner, and Rohde (2001) examined the *diathesis-stress process* involved in the Beck and Seligman theories. The diathesis-stress (tendency towards stress) proposed by these theories is believed to be due to negative cognitions (Beck) or pessimistic attributional styles (Seligman). Vulnerability from these cognitive styles combines with stress (negative life events) to produce depression. In a longitudinal study of adolescents, investigators assessed dysfunctional attitudes and negative attributional styles, as well as depressive symptoms. Another

Michael Grecco / Stock Boston

Learned Helplessness and Depression

According to Martin Seligman, feelings of helplessness can lead to depression. Former Major League baseball pitcher Jim Abbott, born without a right hand, fought feelings of helplessness and went on to win multiple awards for his ability to overcome obstacles and adversity through determination and courage. According to Seligman's theory, what can be done to alter feelings of helplessness?

learned helplessness   an acquired belief that one is helpless and unable to affect outcomes

assessment was conducted a year later. The researchers wanted to find out which cognitive theory could better predict the onset of depression from the first to the second assessment. They controlled for initial level of depression, family history of depression, and gender, because these factors are known to be associated with the subsequent development of depression. Results tended to support Beck's theory over that of Seligman. High levels of negative cognitions coupled with stress predicted subsequent depression. Negative attributional style did not result in greater depression even with high levels of stress. Only at low levels of stress did negative attributional styles predict depression (which is somewhat counterintuitive).

Social Dimension

Environmental factors such as childhood maltreatment, death of or abandonment by a parent, and stressful life events have modest and nonspecific effects on the development of depression (Kendler & Prescott, 2006). Parental depression appears to have both a genetic and an environmental influence on intergenerational transmission of depression (Silberg, Maes, & Eaves, 2010). Among a group of children conceived through in vitro fertilization, maternal depression increased the risk of childhood depression for both genetically related and genetically unrelated children (Harold et al., 2010). Adopted infants with genetic vulnerability to depression exhibited heightened reaction to frustrating events only when their adoptive mother demonstrated high levels of anxiety and depression (Leve et al., 2010).

The presence of stress, especially interpersonal stress, is frequently linked with depression (Hammen, 2006). Stressors involving interpersonal problems and dependency (i.e., the need to depend on others) often occur just before the onset of depressive symptoms (Stader & Hokanson, 1998). Other studies have shown that severe psychosocial stress, such as the death of a loved one, a life-threatening medical condition, or frustration regarding major life goals often precedes the onset of major depression (Mazure, 1998).

These findings have led investigators to ask what kinds of stress lead to depression. Brown and Harris (1989) concluded that *severity* is important. One severe stressor is more likely to cause depression than several minor stressors. Additionally, acute stress is even more highly related to depression than chronic stress (Muscatell, Slavich, Monroe, & Gotlib, 2009). However, chronic stress can certainly interact with personal vulnerability to produce depression (Morris, Ciesla, & Garber, 2010). Individuals who are highly conscientious and who have chronic, high work stress and few decision making opportunities tend to be particularly affected by depression (Bonde, 2008; Verboom et al., 2011). *Timing of onset* is also important. Experiences occurring during childhood, including harsh discipline, are associated with increased severity of depression (Lara, Klein, & Kasch, 2000). Finally, the particular *type* of stress is important to consider. For example, stressors such as loss and humiliation are associated with depression, whereas others, such as exposure to dangerous events, are more likely to be associated with anxiety (Kendler, Hettema, Butera, Gardner, & Prescott, 2003). Targeted rejection (active, intentional social exclusion or rejection) has a particularly strong link with onset of depressive symptoms (Slavich, Way, Eisenberger, & Taylor, 2010). Why do some people who encounter stress develop depression, whereas others do not? People appear to differ in their vulnerability to depression. Biological factors, psychosocial factors, or both may increase the vulnerability.

The relationship between stress and depression is complex and interactive. For example, maternal depression has been associated with not only fewer positive but also more negative parent-child interactions; this pattern is hypothesized to initiate a cascade of risk factors that culminate in depression (Foster, Garber, & Durlak, 2008; Garber & Cole, 2010). In a longitudinal study of people with depression, having dysfunctional parents who created stressful home conditions influenced vulnerability to stress. Individuals from such families may fail to acquire adaptive skills and positive self-images, which in turn brings on more stress, which can trigger depression (Hammen, Davilla, Brown,

Ellicott, & Gitlin, 1992). Not only does stress cause depression, but depression can also cause stress. Hammen (2006) has found that individuals who are depressed are more likely to experience stressors that are within their control (e.g., initiating arguments). She believes that depressed persons may create and generate stress for themselves. Liu and Alloy (2010) also contend that *stress generation* (i.e., depressive behaviors that increase susceptibility to stressful events) increases depression. Thus the research suggests that stress and depression are bidirectional.

Finally, stress itself may activate a genetic predisposition for depression; as previously discussed, individuals predisposed to depression (carriers of the short allele of the serotonin transporter gene) were likely to develop depression when exposed to childhood maltreatment (Caspi et al., 2003). This may also explain why some people with genetic predispositions do not develop depression (i.e., significant stressors are absent) and why others who have encountered the same stressors as a depressed person do not suffer from depression (i.e., they do not have the hereditary predisposition).

Social support and social resources appear to serve as a buffer between stress and depression. Personal or family resources (such as helpfulness of family members) can help individuals cope with and adjust to stress (Holahan & Moos, 1991). A ten-year follow-up of individuals with depression (Moos, Cronkite, & Moos, 1998) showed that social resources (e.g., helpful friends, caring family members) were important in remission. Further evidence of the effects of social support was found in a study of gay men with HIV; men who were more satisfied with their social support were less likely to suffer from depression (Hays, Turner, & Coates, 1992). Participation in sports has been found to be protective against depression and suicidal ideation in adolescents (with a risk reduction of up to 25 percent); increased self-esteem and social support mediated this effect (Babiss & Gangwisch, 2009). Social support that meets specific needs (e.g., financial support) is particularly protective against depression (Knowlton & Latkin, 2007).

Sociocultural Dimension

Sociocultural factors found to be significantly associated with depression include socioeconomic status, culture, race/ethnicity, and gender. For example, individuals living in communities that have high rates of poverty and social disorder (e.g., delinquency, drug use) have increased risk for depression (Cutrona et al., 2005).

AP Photo/Mark Lennihan

Major Stressors and Depression

Stress can lead to depression. Circumstances such as failure to reach major life goals, financial insecurity, or loss of social supports often precede depression. Here, individuals struggling with unemployment line up to attend a job fair in New York.

Culture, Ethnicity, and Depression   As noted by Kleinman (2004), culture influences descriptions of depressive symptoms, decisions about treatment, doctor-patient interactions, and the likelihood of outcomes such as suicide. Culture may even turn out to create distinctive environments for gene expression and physiological reaction in depression (Kleinman, 2004). In some cultures, depression may be experienced largely in the form of somatic or bodily complaints, rather than as sadness or guilt. For example, depression may be expressed as "nerves" and headaches in Latino and Mediterranean cultures; weakness, tiredness, or "imbalance" in Chinese and other Asian cultures; problems of the "heart" in Middle Eastern cultures; or being "heartbroken" among the Hopi (American Psychiatric Association, 2000a).

Why do reactions and symptoms differ from culture to culture? Greenberger, Chen, Tally, and Dong (2000) gained some insight into this question. The investigators compared the correlates of depressed mood among adolescents in China and the United States. In both cultures, "culture general" stressors such as parents' illness and family economic losses had similar effects on depressed mood. However, cultural differences emerged for other variables. For instance, correlations between depressed mood and poor relationships with parents or poor academic achievement were higher for Chinese than for Americans, perhaps reflecting the Chinese cultural emphasis on family and achievement. Family disconnection and intergenerational stress appears to be a particularly salient factor for increasing risk of depression in adolescents with immigrant parents (Fornos et al., 2005; Juang, Syed, & Takagi, 2007; Kim, Chen, Li, Huang, & Moon, 2009). Perceived discrimination based on gender, race/ethnicity, or sexual orientation, especially among those who did not talk to others about their experiences, is also associated with depression (Juang & Cookston, 2009; McLaughlin, Hatzenbuehler, & Keyes, 2010). Longitudinal analysis of everyday encounters with discrimination among African American women revealed that increases in such encounters were linked with

Barbara Alper/Stock Boston

Cultural Differences in Symptoms and Treatment

People from different cultures vary in the extent to which they display symptoms commonly associated with depression. Individuals of Chinese descent experiencing depression often report somatic or bodily complaints instead of depressive symptoms, such as sadness or loss of pleasure. They also are more likely to rely on Chinese medicine and acupuncture rather than psychotherapy to treat their symptoms.

increases in depressive symptoms (Schulz et al., 2006). Another study involving African Americans found perceived discrimination to be related to severity of depressive symptoms; discrimination was more stressful for the women than men in the study (Wagner & Abbott, 2007). Concern has been raised in terms of ethnic/racial disparities in treatment for depression (Satre, Campbell, Gordon, & Weisner, 2010). Community-based focus-group discussions involving African American women with major depressive disorder and histories of violent victimization underscored the role of interpersonal violence in the development of depression. Additionally, decisions to seek help for depression were affected by perceptions of racism and mistrust of the health care system as well as a desire to uphold the image of "strong black women" (Nicolaidis et al., 2010).

Gender and Depressive Disorders Depression is far more common among women than among men, regardless of region of the world, race and ethnicity, or social class (Strickland, 1992; Kessler, 2003). Some have wondered if women are simply more likely than men to seek treatment when depressed or to report their depression to physicians or those conducting surveys regarding emotional well-being. That is, the gender differences may reflect differences in self-report of depressive symptoms or willingness to seek treatment rather than differences in actual depression rates. It is also possible that diagnosticians or diagnostic systems are biased toward finding depression among women (Caplan, 1995). Additionally, depression in men may be hidden by other factors such as substance abuse or other addictive behaviors. However, evidence suggests that women do, in fact, have higher rates of depression than men and that the differences are real rather than an artifact of self-reports or biases (Rieker & Bird, 2005). Gender differences in depression begin appearing during adolescence and are greatest during the reproductive years. Attempts to explain these differences have focused on physiological and social psychological factors (Table 8.3).

Multiple research findings suggest that environmental and sociocultural factors interact with biological factors, such as genetic or hormonal differences between the sexes, to influence gender differences in depression. Heritability of depression appears to be higher among women than men, as noted earlier (Goldberg, 2006). It has been suggested that genetic risk factors associated with depression may, in fact, increase some women's likelihood of encountering other stressors such as trauma or divorce (Kendler & Prescott, 2006). Additionally, changes in ovarian hormones and neurotransmitter dysregulation (specifically serotonin) combined with life stress, history of sexual abuse, and gender role and socialization effects have been implicated in the etiology of depression (Vigod & Stewart, 2009). Sexual abuse has a strong association with lifetime diagnosis of depression (Chen et al., 2010).

Did You Know?

You could be living in a "depressed" or a "happy" city. The following rankings were based on antidepressant sales, suicide rates, and the number of days residents reported being depressed ("Depressed? Could Be Where You Live," 2005).

Depressed Cities	Happy Cities
1. Philadelphia, PA	1. Laredo, CA
2. Detroit, MI	2. El Paso, TX
3. St. Petersburg, FL	3. Jersey City, NJ
4. St. Louis, MO	4. Honolulu, HI
5. Tampa, FL	5. San Jose, CA

TABLE 8.3   Possible Explanations for the Increased Rates of Depression Among Women

- **Women may be more willing to acknowledge and seek help for depression.**

- **Genetic or hormonal differences may result in higher rates of depression among women.**

- **Women are subjected to societal factors such as unfulfilling gender roles or limited occupational opportunities that lead to feelings of helplessness and hopelessness.**

- **Cognitive styles (such as ruminating or co-ruminating) that increase depression are more common in women.**

- **Women are more likely to have experienced childhood trauma (sexual abuse, childhood maltreatment) and other stressors associated with depression.**

Gender differences in depression are believed to be influenced by varying hormone levels and hormone secretion patterns beginning in puberty and continuing throughout the transition to menopause (Graziottin & Serafini, 2009); hormonal changes affect systems associated with depression such as the neurotransporter system and hypothalamic-pituitary-adrenal system. Menopause is a time women are particularly vulnerable to severe depression (Graziottin & Serafini, 2009); factors such as working full time, having compromised health, or having negative views on aging can increase risk of depression for women undergoing this transition (Woods, Mitchell, Percival, & Smith-DiJulio, 2009).

Social or psychological factors related to traditional gender roles may also influence the development of depressive disorders. Dedovic, Wadiwalla, Engert, and Pruessner (2009) have suggested that gender socialization and early social learning contribute to gender differences in stress hormone regulation and metabolic effects of stress. Specifically, social modeling and socialization practices can influence gender differences in factors that influence feelings of self-worth. While men are socialized to value autonomy, self-interest, and achievement-oriented goals, females learn to value social goals and interdependent functioning (e.g., caring about others, not wanting to hurt others). Women's self-perceptions are, therefore, more influenced by the opinions of others, a factor that increases vulnerability to interpersonal stress, particularly stressors involving close friends or family. Additionally, gender-role expectations can decrease women's sense of control over life situations and diminish their sense of personal worth.

Nolen-Hoeksema (1987) hypothesized that the way a person responds to depressed moods contributes to the severity, chronicity, and recurrence of depressive episodes. In her view, women tend to ruminate and amplify their depressive moods, whereas men tend to dampen or find means to minimize dysphoria. When individuals tracked their depressed moods and responses to these moods for one month, women were more likely than men to ruminate in response to depressed moods; when tendency to ruminate was statistically controlled, gender differences in duration of depressed moods disappeared (Nolen-Hoeksema, 1991). During adolescence, increases in anxious arousal and rumination have been associated with increases in depressive symptoms among girls (Hankin, 2009). Adolescent girls who are depressed are more likely to generate interpersonal stress, which, in turn, predicts more chronic depression (Rudolph, Flynn, Abaied, Groot, & Thompson, 2009).

Treatment for Depression

Finding the correct treatment or combination of treatments is exceptionally important with depression (Papakostas & Fava, 2008). Treatment planning for individuals with treatment-resistant depression is particularly critical because longer depressive episodes are associated with negative long-term outcome, more frequent depressive episodes and reduced likelihood of symptom remission (Shelton, Osuntokun, Heinloth, & Corya, 2010). When someone is not responding to initial treatment, adjunctive therapy (adding on a therapy) is generally preferred over switching from one therapy to another, particularly if the initial treatment had some effect (Shelton, Osuntokun, Heinloth, & Corya, 2010). Careful diagnostic reassessment of treatment-resistant depression is vital in order to rule out possible misdiagnosis (i.e., to ensure that the person does not, in fact, have a bipolar disorder) (Fornaro & Giosue, 2010). We now turn to various treatment strategies used with depressive disorders.

MYTH: St. John's wort has been proven to be effective in alleviating depression.

REALITY: St. John's wort (*Hypericum perforatum* plant), an herbal supplement, is sometimes used to treat depression. Despite its popularity, little rigorous research has been conducted to establish its effectiveness or possible side effects. The National Center for Complementary and Alternative Medicine (2007) considers St. John's wort to be an unproven treatment for depression.

MYTH VS. REALITY

Biomedical Treatments for Depressive Disorders

Biomedical treatments include the use of medication and other interventions that affect various brain systems such as circadian-related treatments (light therapy and sleep deprivation) and brain stimulation techniques.

Antidepressants and Suicidality: Risk versus Benefit

In 2004, the FDA required manufacturers of certain antidepressants to provide black box warnings regarding the possibility of increased risk for suicidal thinking and behavior in children and adolescents taking these medications. In 2007, the warning was expanded to include those aged 18 to 24. The following is from the FDA (2007):

> Antidepressants increased the risk compared to placebo of suicidal thinking and behavior (suicidality) in children, adolescents, and young adults in short-term studies of major depressive disorder (MDD) and other psychiatric disorders. Anyone considering the use of . . . antidepressants in a child, adolescent, or young adult must balance this risk with the clinical need. . . . All patients being treated with antidepressants for any indication should be monitored appropriately and observed closely for clinical worsening, suicidality, and unusual changes in behavior, especially during the initial few months of a course of drug therapy, or at times of dose changes, either increases or decreases.

What is the relationship between suicidal thoughts, suicide, and antidepressant medication? The findings are consistent for children and adolescents and somewhat mixed for older age groups. The data reviewed by the FDA showed that suicidal thoughts and behaviors occurred among 4 percent of those taking antidepressants compared to 2 percent of those taking placebo. Other reviews have found a modest increase in suicidal thoughts and behaviors in children taking antidepressants (Hammad, Laughren, & Racoosin, 2006). Many studies have shown reduced suicidality for adults taking antidepressants, whereas the emergence or worsening of suicidal behaviors has been found only infrequently (Seemüller et al., 2009). Slight but nonsignificant increases in suicidal thoughts and attempts have been found in adults taking the atypical antidepressant, bupropion (Wightman, Foster, Krishen, Richard, & Modell, 2010). The World Health Organization reports that antidepressants appear to decrease suicide risk for all adults, particularly those older than 65 (Kramer, 2009). The risk of suicide appears to be "strongly age dependent." When compared to placebo, the risk of suicidal thinking or behaviors associated with antidepressant use in young adults (younger than 25) approached that of children and adolescents (i.e., risk almost doubled), was equivalent among adults aged 25 to 64, and was decreased in those older than 65 years of age (Stone et al., 2009).

Some believe the FDA warning has resulted in more harm than good due to the subsequent reduction in the diagnosis and treatment of depression in children, adolescents, and adults (Cuffe, 2007; Brent, 2009). In the year following the FDA warning, the suicide rate in children and adolescents *increased* 18 percent, the first increase in 10 years (Hamilton et al., 2007). Should the FDA warnings regarding antidepressants be reviewed? What factors should be considered when treating children, adolescents, and young adults experiencing depression?

Medication   Antidepressant medications are believed to work by correcting chemical imbalances in the brain. They block the reabsorption of certain neurotransmitters, thus increasing their availability for neural communication. Three classes of antidepressants, the *tricyclics*, the *monoamine oxidase inhibitors (MAOIs)*, and *serotonin norepinephrine reuptake inhibitors (SNRIs)*, block the reabsorption of norepinephrine and serotonin, whereas the *selective serotonin reuptake inhibitors (SSRIs)* block the reuptake of serotonin. *Atypical antidepressants*, a group of unique medications used to treat depressions, affect other neurotransmitters including dopamine. MAOIs are the least frequently used due to concern about serious effects when they are combined with certain foods, beverages, or medications.

The selection of an antidepressant is often rather arbitrary, but can be influenced by prior response to antidepressants (or family patterns of response); desire to avoid certain side effects (e.g., weight gain, sexual side effects, or gastrointestinal problems); or presence of other symptoms such as anxiety or nicotine addiction that might also be helped by certain antidepressants (Brunoni, Fraguas, & Fregni, 2009). All antidepressant medications are considered symptom-suppressive rather than curative; that is, once medication is terminated there is no further protection against the return of symptoms (DeRubeis, Siegle, & Hollon, 2008). For this reason, antidepressants are often continued even if symptoms subside. Antidepressants are not addictive, but they do have a variety of potential side effects. The greatest concern involves possible increases in suicidality in those younger than twenty-five taking certain antidepressants (Berenson, 2006). Additionally, abrupt cessation of certain antidepressants (especially SSRIs and SNRIs) can result in a *discontinuation syndrome*. Individuals with this syndrome experience severe flu-like symptoms; intense fatigue or insomnia; or increased emotionality, including irritability or suicidal thinking due to biochemical changes occurring as the body adjusts to functioning without the medication (Hosenbocus & Chahal, 2011).

Although antidepressants are commonly used in the treatment of depression, questions over their effectiveness remain. Concerns have been raised regarding publication bias in studies on antidepressant medication. One review of studies regarding antidepressant effectiveness found that 94 percent of the studies supportive of antidepressants were submitted for publication and published, whereas many of the studies that did not find antidepressants to be effective were never published or, if they were, were written to give the impression of a positive antidepressant outcome (Turner, Matthews, Linardatos, Tell, & Rosenthal, 2008).

Even with this publication bias, the evidence for antidepressant efficacy is rather weak. Placebos are often as effective as antidepressants in treating minor depression (Barbui, Cipriani, Patel, Ayuso-Mateos, & van Ommeren, 2011). A meta-analytic study evaluating the effectiveness of antidepressant medication concluded the benefit of these medications over placebo for treating mild or moderate depression was "minimal or nonexistent; antidepressants do, however, appear effective for individuals with severe depression" (Fournier et al., 2010). In studies involving antidepressant treatment for major depression, about half show some response to the first antidepressant prescribed, but less than one-third experience full remission of symptoms (Leuchter, Cook, Hunter, & Korb, 2009). Many individuals affected by depression do not respond to antidepressant medications (Ward & Irazoqui, 2010); chronic depression and older age are associated with decreased response (Fournier et al., 2010).

Did You Know?

Many individuals taking SSRIs report feelings of emotional detachment, indifference, diminished positive and negative emotional responsiveness, and personality changes.

Source: Price, Cole, & Goodwin, (2009)

Circadian-Related Treatments   Some treatments for mood disorders involve efforts to reset the circadian clock (McClung, 2007). For example, a night of total sleep deprivation followed by a night of sleep recovery can improve depressive symptoms (Howland, 2011). Additionally, use of bright, visible spectrum or blue wavelength light is an effective and well-tolerated treatment for those with SAD and other depressive disorders (Westrin & Lam, 2007a; Strong et al., 2009). Light therapy appears to influence circadian rhythms by stimulating several photoreceptor systems (Gooley et al., 2010). This therapy involves dawn-light simulation (timer-activated lights that gradually increase in brightness) or daily use of a box, visor, or lighting system that delivers light of a particular intensity for a designated period of time (usually 20 to 60 minutes).

A well-designed study evaluating treatment for SAD compared light therapy alone versus light therapy combined with antidepressants; both groups made similar improvement (67 percent showed improvement and 50 to 54 percent showed remission of symptoms); advantages of light therapy included an absence of side effects and more rapid treatment response (Lam et al., 2006). An analysis of randomized controlled trials suggested that light therapy is as beneficial as antidepressant treatment not only for SAD, but also for nonseasonal depression (Golden et al., 2005). Light therapy is typically continued throughout the low-light season for SAD or depressive patterns involving winter-exacerbation of symptoms (Westrin & Lam, 2007b).

Brain Stimulation Therapies   Electroconvulsive therapy, vagus nerve stimulation, and transcranial magnetic stimulation are sometimes used to treat severe or chronic depression, especially when life-threatening symptoms are present (Andrade et al., 2010).

Electroconvulsive therapy (ECT) is FDA-approved for treatment-resistant depression and is considered a first-line treatment for profound, life-threatening depressive symptoms such as refusal to eat, intense suicidal intent, or unremitting catatonia (Ungvari, Caroff, & Gerevich, 2009; Brunoni et al., 2010; Fink, Shorter, & Taylor, 2010). ECT, which is typically conducted several times weekly, involves application of moderate electrical voltage to the brain in order to produce a convulsion (seizure) lasting at least 15 seconds; appropriate use of anesthetics during ECT treatment minimizes side effects such as headaches, confusion, and memory loss (Mayo, Kaye, Conrad, Baluch, & Frost, 2010). Regularly implemented vagus nerve stimulation (approved for use if four prior treatments for chronic, recurrent depression have failed) has shown therapeutic promise when combined sequentially or concurrently with ECT (Marangell, Martinez, Jurdi, & Zboyan, 2007; Sharma, Chaturvedi, Sharma, & Sorrell, 2009) or when used alone (Nemeroff et al., 2006).

Another controversial technique used with treatment-resistant depression is repetitive transcranial magnetic stimulation, an ECT alternative in which an electromagnetic field stimulates the brain. Although a recent meta-analysis concluded that this technique has sufficient research to support its use for major depressive disorder and for auditory hallucinations (Slotema, Blom, Hoek, & Sommer, 2010), other literature reviews have expressed more skepticism, in part because of the weak design of many studies evaluating the procedure. A factor confounding the research may be intensity of stimulation; high-intensity stimulation appears to produce the most significant results (Levkovitz et al., 2009).

Psychotherapy and Behavioral Treatments for Depressive Disorders

Research has supported the effectiveness of a variety of psychological techniques in treating depression. These therapies can be used alone or in conjunction with biomedical interventions. We cover three approaches that have received extensive research support (behavioral activation, cognitive-behavioral, and interpersonal therapy) and one technique (mindfulness-based cognitive therapy) that has shown promise in treating depression.

Behavioral Activation Therapy Behavioral activation therapy (BAT) is based on the idea that depression results from diminished reinforcement. Consistent with this perspective, the focus of treatment is on increasing exposure to pleasurable events and activities, improving social skills, and facilitating social interactions. The steps involved in treatment include: (1) identifying and rating different activities in terms of pleasure and mastery; (2) performing some of the selected activities, thereby increasing feelings of pleasure or mastery; (3) identifying problems and using behavior techniques to deal with them, and (4) improving social and assertiveness skills (Lejuez, Hopko, Acierno, Daughters, & Pagoto, 2011). Behavioral activation has been shown in one study to be as efficacious as medication and more efficacious than cognitive therapy (Dimidjian et al., 2006).

Interpersonal Psychotherapy Interpersonal therapy (IPT) is an evidence-based approach focused on current problems and the interpersonal context in which they occur. IPT focuses on altering current relationship patterns using strategies found in psychodynamic, cognitive-behavioral, and other forms of therapy. Because IPT presumes that depression occurs within an interpersonal context, relationship issues are the targets of therapy. The focus is on conflicts and problems that occur in four areas (grief, role transitions, role disputes, and interpersonal difficulties). Clients gain insight into their role in interpersonal conflict and strive to change these relationships. For example, by improving communications with others, identifying role conflicts, and increasing social skills, clients come to find relationships more satisfying and pleasant. Although IPT resembles psychodynamic approaches in acknowledging the role of early life experiences and trauma, it is oriented primarily toward present, not past, relationships. It has proven to be an efficacious treatment for acute depression (Levenson et al., 2010) and is as effective as continuing use of antidepressant medication in preventing relapse (Dobson et al., 2008).

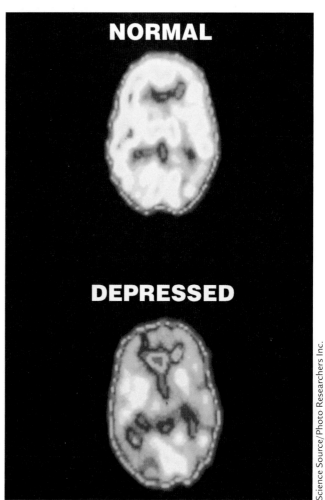

Science Source/Photo Researchers Inc.

Reduced Brain Activity in Depression

These PET scans comparing normal brain activity with the cerebral metabolism of a person suffering from depression reveal the decreased brain activity characteristic of depressive disorders. Research is increasingly directed towards finding ways to use neuroimaging to guide treatment for mental disorders such as depression.

Cognitive-Behavioral Therapy   Cognitive-behavioral therapy (CBT) focuses on altering the habitually negative or extreme thought patterns associated with depression. Cognitive therapists believe that because distorted thinking causes depression, altering thoughts can eliminate depression. CBT helps individuals learn to identify thoughts that precede upsetting emotions, distance themselves from these thoughts, and examine the accuracy of problematic beliefs (DeRubeis, Siegle, & Hollon, 2008). Therefore, clients are taught to:

- Identify negative, self-critical thoughts
- Note the connection between negative thoughts and subsequent feelings
- Examine each negative thought and decide if it is true
- Replace distorted negative thoughts with realistic interpretations

Ruminative positive thoughts (e.g., "Worry helps me overcome my problems") and negative metacognition (e.g., "Other people will reject me if I worry too much") are also linked to depression and are, therefore, targeted in therapy (Liu & Alloy, 2010).

CBT has also been effective for treating adolescents from diverse backgrounds (Marchand, Ng, Rohde, & Stice, 2010) and adapted versions of the therapy have shown promising results in non-Western cultures (Naeem, Waheed, Gobbi, Ayub, & Kingdon, 2011). Although one meta-analysis supported the efficacy of CBT with premenstrual symptoms (Busse, Montori, Krasnik, Patelis-Siotis, & Guyatt, 2009), another systematic review concluded there is a "dearth of evidence" that CBT is effective with PMDD or PMS (Lustyk, Gerrish, Shaver, & Keys, 2009). Overall, individuals treated with CBT are less likely to relapse following treatment termination compared to individuals taking antidepressants (Dobson et al., 2008). Cognitive changes in explanatory styles and alterations in negative self-biases may help prevent recurrence of depressive symptoms (DeRubeis, Siegle, & Hollon, 2008). Cognitive-behavioral treatment has produced changes in the same brain regions affected by the use of SSRI antidepressants. PET scans have revealed changes in the functioning of limbic and cortical regions of the brain following CBT (Goldapple et al., 2004).

Mindfulness-Based Cognitive Therapy   Mindfulness-based cognitive therapy (MBCT) involves calm awareness of one's present experience, thoughts, and feelings and having an attitude of acceptance rather than being judgmental, evaluative, or ruminative. Mindfulness allows one to disrupt the cycle of negative thinking by focusing on the present (Gilbert & Christopher, 2010). Focusing on experiences with curiosity and without judgment prevents the development of maladaptive beliefs and thus prevents depressive thinking (Frewen, Evans, Maraj, Dozios, & Partridge, 2008). In one study, 82 undergraduates participated in three sessions of mindfulness training; the training was effective in reducing depressed mood and heart rate. Clinical studies have found that MBCT reduces residual symptoms in chronic depression, is effective in treatment-resistant depression, and is associated with a decreased risk of relapse or recurrence of depression among recovered depressed patients (Barnhofer et al., 2010; Eisendrath et al., 2008; Godfrin & Heeringen, 2010; Kenny & Williams, 2007).

Combining Biomedical and Psychological Treatments

Unfortunately, current treatments produce symptom remission in less than two-thirds of those treated for depression. Only one-third of those treated for depression achieve sustained recovery from depressive symptoms (DeRubeis, Siegle, & Hollon, 2008). Although there is some evidence that antidepressant medications may be particularly advantageous with severe cases of depression (Lambert & Ogles, 2004), psychotherapies, especially CBT, appear to have longer-lasting effects. That is, effective psychological treatment appears to produce more enduring results, whereas medication relieves depression only during active treatment (Hollon, Stewart, & Strunk, 2006). The changes resulting from cognitive treatment (modifying schemas, correcting negative thoughts, cognitive restructuring) may enable clients to think differently, even after treatment has been terminated. There appear to be some advantages in combined treatments that involve medication and psychotherapy. Medication

Computer-Based Interventions for Depression

Computer-based therapies are being used successfully to treat anxiety disorders. However, are these limited-contact interventions a safe alternative for treating depression, a disorder consistently associated with risk of suicidality? Can symptom severity and suicide risk be adequately monitored? Face-to-face contact is currently not a part of many computer-based interventions; thus, there is no clinician to identify signs of severe depression or suicidality.

Those who support use of computer-based interventions cite the large number of people with depression who receive no treatment (Williams et al., 2007), the accessibility of computer-based interventions, and the research supporting intervention effectiveness for those who participate. In a review of studies, Proudfoot (2004) found a high degree of satisfaction with users of computer therapy programs. Respondents reported greater comfort self-disclosing to a computer and indicated they would be more likely to disclose suicidal plans online rather than to a human. A meta-analysis of various studies using computer-based CBT found therapy effects that were equal to face-to-face CBT and consistently superior to attention-only control conditions; symptom-improvement continued beyond the treatment period and satisfaction with treatment was good (Andrews, Cuijpers, Craske, McEvoy, & Titov, 2010). Similarly, a review of studies using computer-based CBT interventions

for the prevention and treatment of depression in children and adolescents found a reduction in depressive symptoms as well improved behavioral and cognitive functioning (Richardson, Stallard, & Velleman, 2010); however, the lack of randomized controls, high drop out rates, and noncompletion of the full intervention are an ongoing concern (Kaltenthaler et al., 2008). Greater severity and chronicity of depressive symptoms are associated with higher drop out rates; adherence is particularly low with open-access treatment Web sites (Christensen, Griffiths, & Farrer, 2009).

It appears that more research is needed to determine the most appropriate role of computer-based interventions within the context of treating depression (Kaltenthaler et al., 2008) and to understand what accounts for the high drop out rates (Waller & Gilbody, 2009). Data from behavior change research may help researchers develop techniques and modes of delivery that maximize adherence and long-term change (Danaher & Seeley, 2009; Ritterband et al., 2009; Webb, Joseph, Yardley, & Michie, 2010). For example, in studies focused on other health-related behaviors, computerized interventions are most effective when combined with some personal contact and periodic e-mail messages prompting continued involvement (Fry & Neff, 2010). What do you see as advantages and disadvantages of computer-based treatment for depression?

---

tends to produce rapid and reliable reductions in some individuals with severe depression, whereas psychotherapy can enhance social functioning and reduce risk of relapse (Friedman et al., 2004; Hollon & Fawcett, 2001). Additionally, it is likely that effective psychotherapies and antidepressant medications influence similar neural mechanisms, as well as mechanisms unique to each mode of intervention (DeRubeis, Siegle, & Hollon, 2008).

Bipolar Disorders

Earlier, we defined mood disorders as disturbances in emotions that cause subjective discomfort, hinder a person's ability to function, or both. Up to this point, we have discussed depressive disorders, in which only depression occurs. In this section, we discuss bipolar disorders, which involve symptoms of mania/hypomania that may alternate with episodes of depression (see Table 8.4). Depressive disorders and bipolar disorders are considered to be distinct phenomenon. As we will discuss, bipolar disorders have a robust genetic component; in fact, there is strong evidence of physiological overlap between bipolar disorders and schizophrenia (a severe mental health disorder we discuss extensively in Chapter 12). Also, as we will discuss, bipolar disorders respond to medications that have little effect on those with depressive disorders. Additionally, the average age of onset is somewhat earlier for bipolar disorders (late teens and early twenties) compared to depressive disorders (late twenties). Finally, the prevalence of bipolar disorder is much lower than that seen with major depression (see Figure 8.2) (Merikangas, 2007).

Photo by Gregg DeGuire/Wire Image

Advocating Treatment for Mental Illness

Consider this photo of Rebbie Jackson (sister of Michael Jackson) and her daughter, Yashi Brown, who has bipolar disorder. Jackson recently returned to the stage to participate in the "Pick Up the Phone Suicide Prevention Tour," encouraging those with mental illness to seek help. Yashi is the author of a newly released book *Black Daisy in a White Limousine: 77 Poems.*

Diagnosis and Classification of Bipolar Disorders

Bipolar disorders are diagnosed based on the severity and chronicity of hypomanic/manic symptoms as well as the severity and pattern of any depressive symptoms. The essential feature of bipolar disorders is the occurrence of one or more manic or hypomanic

DISORDERS CHART   BIPOLAR DISORDERS

TABLE 8.4

Bipolar Disorders	Symptoms	Lifetime Prevalence (%)	Gender Difference	Age of Onset
Bipolar I Disorder	• At least one week-long manic episode • Most recent episode may be manic, hypomanic, or depressed • Mixed or depressive episodes are common, but not required, for diagnosis • Psychotic features may be present	0.4–1.0	No major difference although rapid-cycling is more common in females	Any age; usually in late adolescence or early adulthood
Bipolar II Disorder	• At least one major depressive episode • At least one hypomanic episode • No history of mania • Most recent episode may be hypomanic or depressed	0.6–1.1	Higher in females	Any age; usually late adolescence or early adulthood
Cyclothymic Disorder	• Numerous hypomanic episodes have alternated with milder depression for at least two years (with no more than two months symptom-free)* • No history of major depression or mania	0.4–1.0	No difference	Often starts in adolescence

Source: Data from Kessler, Chiu, Demler, & Walters, (2005); Merikangas et al., 2007; American Psychiatric Association (2011); Merikangas et al., (2011)
* Symptoms are required to continue for only one year in children and adolescents.

episodes; the term *bipolar* is used because hypomanic/manic symptoms often alternate with depressive episodes. However, depressive episodes are predominant in many cases of bipolar disorder (Kamat et al., 2008) and account for the fact that individuals with bipolar disorder spend much of the time ill (Altshuler et al., 2010). Bipolar disorders include bipolar I, bipolar II, and cyclothymia.

Bipolar I is diagnosed when individuals (with or without a history of major depression) experience at least one manic episode. (Manic symptoms need to be present most of the day, nearly every day for at least one week.) Hypomanic episodes mixed with depression are common in bipolar I, particular in women (Swann, Steinberg, Lijffijt, & Moeller, 2009) and approximately 25 percent of episodes involve rapid-cycling, a pattern involving four or more significant mood swings per year (Solomon et al., 2009). *Bipolar II* is diagnosed when there has been at least one major depressive episode lasting at least two weeks and at least one hypomanic episode lasting at least four consecutive days. Depression is the prominent feature of bipolar II; it is often a mixed depression involving concurrent hypomanic symptoms. In bipolar II, symptoms are usually most severe during depressive episodes, with almost three-fourths of those with bipolar II reporting severe role impairment while depressed (Merikangas et al., 2011). Bipolar II is considered an underdiagnosed disorder; many physicians treat depression without adequately assessing for periods of highly energetic, goal-directed activity and other hypomanic symptoms (Benazzi, 2007). It is estimated that more than 10 percent of those diagnosed with a depressive disorder are eventually diagnosed with a bipolar disorder (Goodwin et al., 2008). Assessment instruments that contain self-ratings of hypomanic/manic symptoms and daily mood monitoring can help avoid misdiagnosis (Picardi, 2009).

The primary distinction between bipolar I and bipolar II is the severity of the symptoms during energized episodes; that is, whether or not (1) symptoms are hypomanic or manic; (2) ongoing for at least one week; and (3) severe enough to significantly impair social or occupational functioning. A history of at least one ongoing manic episode resulting in significantly impaired functioning is required for a bipolar I diagnosis (Benazzi, 2007;

American Psychiatric Association, 2011). Assessment is conducted regarding the severity of hypomanic/manic symptoms and how rapidly moods shift. Some individuals with bipolar disorder exhibit mixed features (concurrent hypomanic/manic and depressive symptoms) or rapid-cycling (four or more mood episodes per year).

Approximately one-third of those with bipolar disorder exhibit both rapid-cycling and mixed features (Koszewska & Rybakowski, 2009). Mixed features are often present in both bipolar I and bipolar II; that is, three or more symptoms of hypomania/mania or depression are seen during an episode from the opposite pole. Hypomanic/manic symptoms that accompany a depressive episode are important prognostic indicators (predicting a more severe course and need for more intensive treatment), but may often go unrecognized due to the prominence of depressive features (Goldberg et al., 2009). A particular danger of hypomanic/manic symptoms occurring with depressive symptoms is increased risk of dangerous, impulsive behaviors such as suicidal actions or substance abuse (Swann et al., 2007).

Rapid-cycling is associated with earlier onset and a more chronic course of the disorder; more days affected by hypomanic/manic symptoms; increased severity of both manic and depressive symptoms; and increased anxiety symptoms (Kupka et al., 2005; Lee et al., 2010; Nierenberg et al., 2010). Both rapid-cycling and anxiety symptoms occur more frequently in women and predict more pervasive depressive episodes (Altshuler et al., 2010). Mood switching can be triggered by a variety of factors including sleep deprivation, antidepressants (especially tricyclics), and corticosteroidal medications (Salvadore et al., 2010).

Cyclothymic disorder is diagnosed when hypomanic episodes are consistently interspersed with depressed moods for at least two years. (The depressive moods do not reach the level of a major depression and the person is never symptom free for more than two months.) Cyclothymic disorder is similar to chronic depressive disorder due to the chronicity of mood symptoms, but differs due to the presence of periodic hypomanic symptoms. The risk that a person with cyclothymia will subsequently develop bipolar I or II is 15 to 50 percent (American Psychiatric Association, 2000a).

Epidemiology of Bipolar Disorders

A large-scale national survey found that the twelve-month and lifetime prevalence rates were 0.6 percent and 1.0 percent, respectively, for bipolar I, and 0.8 percent and 1.1 percent, respectively, for bipolar II (see Figure 8.2). Thus, bipolar disorders are far less prevalent than depressive disorders. Similarly, with lifetime prevalence between 0.4 and 1 percent, cyclothymia is less common than chronic depressive disorder. Although bipolar disorder can begin in childhood, onset more frequently occurs in late adolescence or early adulthood.

Research on gender differences in bipolar disorder is mixed. Most agree there are no marked gender differences in the prevalence of bipolar I (Merikangas et al., 2007), but depressive and mixed episodes, bipolar II, and rapid-cycling occur more frequently in women (Diflorio & Jones, 2010; Ketter, 2010). Women also have a higher risk of symptom recurrence (Suominen et al., 2009). Men are more likely to begin bipolar I with an onset of mania rather than depression (Kawa et al., 2005). As with depressive disorders, reproductive cycle changes, especially childbirth, appear to precipitate or exacerbate depressive bipolar episodes in some women (Arnold, 2003; Diflorio & Jones, 2010). The transition to menopause precipitates increased prevalence of depressive episodes for women with bipolar disorder (Marsh, Ketter, & Rasgon, 2009).

Although bipolar disorders are much less prevalent than depressive disorders, their costs are high. Bipolar disorder is associated with high unemployment and decreased work productivity (Ketter, 2010). Bipolar disorder was associated with 65.5 annual lost workdays per ill worker compared to 27.2 days for those with major depressive disorder; those with bipolar disorder tend to have more severe and persistent depressive episodes (Kessler et al., 2006). Furthermore, the course of bipolar disorder is characterized by frequent relapse and recurrence; as the number of bipolar episodes increases, so does the likelihood of future episodes (Hollon, Stewart, & Strunk, 2006). Bipolar disorder is often comorbid with other conditions, including anxiety disorders (especially panic attacks), attention-deficit/hyperactivity disorder, and substance-use disorders (Merikangas et al., 2011). Anxiety (and episodes with mixed features) appears to increase the severity of both manic and depressive symptoms (Swann, Steinberg, Lijffijt, & Moeller, 2009). Those with coexisting conditions tend to have earlier onset of the disorder and longer episodes, as well as increased suicidal or violent behavior (Baldassano, 2006). Men are more likely to have comorbid substance-use and conduct disorders, whereas women are more likely to have eating disorders (Kawa et al., 2005; Suominen et al., 2009). Substance use is common among those with bipolar disorder and is associated with greater functional impairment (Lagerberg et al., 2010). More than half of one sample of individuals diagnosed with bipolar disorder had a concurrent alcohol-use disorder and suicidal ideation (Oquendo et al., 2010). Bipolar disorder is also associated with increased rates of physical illness such as hypertension, cardiovascular disease, and diabetes as well as increased rates of death from suicide (Leahy, 2007; Fagiolini, 2008; Ketter, 2010). In fact, bipolar disorder is considered the disorder with the greatest risk of suicidal ideation and suicide attempts; an estimated 15 to 19 percent of individuals with bipolar disorder die from suicide (Abreu, Lafer, Baca-Garcia, & Oquendo, 2009).

Etiology of Bipolar Disorders

A number of biological, psychological, social, and sociocultural theories have been proposed to explain how bipolar disorders develop. Many of the etiological factors we have discussed that contribute to the development of depression have also been explored as contributors to depressive episodes in bipolar disorder. In this section, we primarily focus on the unique hereditary and physiological contributions to the hypomanic/manic episodes and mood switching seen in bipolar disorder. We conclude with a brief discussion of the overlap between bipolar disorder and another serious mental illness, schizophrenia.

Biological Dimension

The contribution of genetic factors to bipolar disorder is well established from twin, adoption, and family studies. For example, the concordance rates for bipolar disorders has been found to be 72 percent for identical (monozygotic [MZ]) twins and 14 percent for fraternal (dizygotic [DZ]) twins (Kato, 2007); similar concordance rates are found for bipolar I, bipolar II, and cyclothymia (Edvardsen et al., 2008). Bipolar disorders are believed to have a complex genetic basis involving interactions among multiple genes. Genome-wide studies have implicated several genes influenced by the chemical compound lithium (Baum et al., 2008). Because individuals with bipolar disorder (like those with depressive disorders) have abnormalities in their circadian cycles, genes related to the circadian cycle have been investigated as possible causes of vulnerability to bipolar disorder. In fact, interactions between three genes affecting circadian rhythm (Shi et al., 2008), a dysregulation involving a circadian-related gene (CRY2) (Lavebratt et al., 2010; Sjöholm et al., 2010), and effects from circadian-related genes that contribute to major depression (Soria et al., 2010) have been found to contribute to bipolar disorder.

A variety of biochemical influences appear to affect bipolar symptoms. Tolmunen and his colleagues (2004) found that mania is associated with elevated serotonin transporter availability, a condition that declined with psychotherapy. However, among depressed controls, serotonin availability actually increased with psychotherapy. Some believe that dysregulation in the brain activation system results in the inappropriate affect characteristic of manic episodes (Davidson et al., 2002). Consistent with a dysregulation model, Johnson and her colleagues (2008) found that individuals with bipolar disorders show elevated manic symptoms after experiencing goal-attainment life events (but not just any positive life events). It has been suggested that because those with bipolar disorder have high sensitivity to reward, mania can develop in the course of excessively pursuing additional goals after an objective has been achieved (Miklowitz & Johnson, 2009). Additionally, a ruminative cognitive style has been found to predict depressive episodes, whereas a self-focused, self-conscious style is predictive of hypomanic/manic episodes (Alloy et al., 2009). In a review of the literature, attaining goals, antidepressant medication use, disrupted circadian rhythm, and spring/summer seasonal conditions were all linked to the onset of hypomanic/manic episodes in certain individuals (Proudfoot, Doran, Manicavasagar, & Parker, 2010). Increased levels of glutamate (a neurotransmitter with stimulatory functions) have been found in postmortem studies of individuals with bipolar disorder and major depressive disorder (Hashimoto, Sawa, & Iyo, 2007). Additionally, brain imaging has documented elevated glutamate neurotransmission in the cortex in individuals with bipolar disorder (Eastwood & Harrison, 2010). As with depressive disorder, hormonal influences or disruptions of the neural stress circuitry (HPA axis) appear to contribute to bipolar symptoms. Traumatic brain injury has been found to precipitate manic episodes, especially in individuals with a family history of bipolar disorder (Mustafa, Evrim, & Sari, 2005); these manic episodes are reported to affect up to 9 percent of those with traumatic brain injury (Oster, Anderson, Filley, Wortzel, & Arciniegas, 2007).

Imaging studies have confirmed that disordered brain networks and overactivation of certain brain regions (particularly the amygdala, striatum, and thalamus) are implicated in bipolar disorder (Cerullo, Adler, Delbello, & Strakowski, 2009; Palaniyappan & Cousins, 2010). Abnormalities in white matter connectivity (involving prefrontal and frontal regions and connections both within and between hemispheres) have been found with bipolar disorder (Brambilla, Bellani, Yeh, Soares, & Tansella, 2009; Heng, Song, & Sim, 2010); these abnormalities affect areas involved in the generation and regulation of emotions (Mahon, Burdick, & Szeszko, 2010). Gray matter abnormalities in areas related to emotional processing have also been documented (Ellison-Wright & Bullmore, 2010). These neurological abnormalities apparently develop before the onset of symptoms because they have been documented following the first mood episode in those recently diagnosed with bipolar disorder (Vita, De Peri, & Sacchetti, 2009). Brain imaging of individuals with bipolar disorder has detected brain lesions that appear to result from vascular damage to brain tissue (Beyer, Young, Kuchibhatla, & Krishnan, 2009). Additionally, vascular impairment associated with aging has been hypothesized to contribute to later-onset bipolar disorder (Zanetti, Cordeiro, & Busatto, 2007).

Psychological-sociocultural perspectives have focused primarily on the development of depression rather than on mania. As indicated earlier, biological factors appear to play a more prominent role in the etiology of bipolar disorders compared to depressive disorders. Additionally, evidence is mounting regarding common genetic vulnerabilities between bipolar disorders and schizophrenia.

Commonalities between Bipolar Disorders and Schizophrenia

It is now commonly accepted that bipolar disorder and schizophrenia, both chronic disorders with strong neurological underpinnings, share genetic, neuroanatomical, and cognitive abnormalities. In fact, some contend that bipolar disorders (particularly bipolar I) are much more similar to schizophrenia than they are to depressive disorders (Goldberg, Krueger, Andrews, & Hobbs, 2009). Genome-wide studies have shown that schizophrenia and bipolar disorder have common genetic influences (Goes et al., 2007; Huang et al., 2010). There is substantial overlap in the brain regions affected by schizophrenia and bipolar disorder, including the prefrontal cortex, thalamus, left temporal lobe, and right insula (Yu et al., 2010). Meta-analytic comparisons of the neuroanatomy of schizophrenia and bipolar disorder revealed similar gray matter abnormalities in two brain regions (the anterior cingulate and bilateral insula), with schizophrenia and bipolar disorder also associated with unique deficits in gray matter. In the case of bipolar disorder, the brain regions affected tend to be less extensive and primarily involved areas related to emotional processing (Ellison-Wright & Bullmore, 2010).

Bipolar disorder and schizophrenia also share similarities in cognitive deficits, including poor insight into the inappropriateness of behavior or confused thought processes. In bipolar disorder, lack of insight into the illness is particularly pronounced during manic episodes, whereas insight is adequate during depressive episodes (Cassidy, 2010). Noncompliance with medication regimes is common to both disorders. Poor insight and lack of illness awareness is believed to account for the finding that, on the average, those with schizophrenia or bipolar disorder take only 51 to 70 percent of the medication prescribed for their illness (Velligan et al., 2009). Neurocognitive deficits that affect social competence and daily functioning are also present in both disorders (Bowie et al., 2010), although the deficits tend to be more pervasive in schizophrenia (Jabben, Arts, van Os, & Krabbendam, 2010). Significant psychosocial and vocational impairment is linked to cognitive deficits involving attention, processing speed, and memory common to the two disorders (Bearden, Woogen, & Glahn, 2010). These deficits are most notable on tasks affected by hippocampus function and neurotransmission involving glutamate (Brambilla et al., 2011).

Treatment for Bipolar Disorders

A major goal of therapy with bipolar disorder is complete remission of all symptoms; residual symptoms significantly increase the risk of rapid recurrence of another major mood episode (Judd et al., 2008) and increase the likelihood of ongoing functional impairment (Marangell et al., 2009). Hypomania is also treated to help prevent a hypomania-depression mood cycle (Benazzi, 2007). Thus, intervention with bipolar disorder targets prevention of future manic or depressive episodes. This is often accomplished through a combination of mood stabilizing medications and psychoeducation to help the individual (and family members) understand the importance of regular use of prescribed medications and recognizing early symptoms of mood episodes.

Overcoming Bipolar Disorder

Few people know that actor Ben Stiller has bipolar disorder, as do other members of his family. Following a stressful year and a brief hospital stay for treatment of bipolar II disorder, award-winning actress Catherine Zeta-Jones expressed hope that public revelation of her diagnosis would encourage others struggling with similar symptoms to seek help rather than to suffer silently.

Although antipsychotic medications (like those used with schizophrenia) are prescribed when psychotic symptoms are present, mood stabilizing medications are the foundation of treatment for bipolar disorder (Bowden, 2010; Brooks et al., 2011). Since it was introduced to the United States in 1969, lithium, the only consistently proven preventive treatment targeting depression and hypomania/mania, is often the treatment of choice (Benazzi, 2007). Response rates with lithium range from 60 to 80 percent in "classic" bipolar disorder (Delgado & Gelenberg, 2001); ongoing use of lithium is associated with decreased suicide risk (Goldberg, 2007). Anticonvulsant medications are also used to stabilize mood with bipolar disorder. Lithium or other mood stabilizers are usually used indefinitely to prevent recurrence of hypomania/mania; antidepressants are sometimes added to deal with depressive symptoms (Hollon, Stewart, & Strunk, 2006). However, antidepressants are used cautiously with bipolar disorder; although they target depressive symptoms, they can precipitate or exacerbate hypomanic/manic symptoms (Benazzi, 2007). There is evidence, however, that lithium may reduce antidepressant-induced suicidality (McElroy, Kotwal, Kaneria, & Keck, 2006).

© Lisa O'Connor/ZUMA/Corbis

© Allstar Picture Library / Alamy

The generally positive results achieved with lithium are sometimes overshadowed by serious side effects that can occur if blood levels of lithium are not regularly monitored (Wingo, Wingo, Harvey, & Baldessarini, 2009). Fortunately, accurate measurements of lithium blood levels are easily obtained, and dosages can be adjusted accordingly. Medication adherence contributes significantly to outcome in bipolar disorder (Berk et al., 2010). Unfortunately, noncompliance in taking medication as prescribed is a major problem associated with lithium and other mood stabilizers. Individuals with bipolar disorder often report adjusting their own medication due to weight gain, feelings of sedation, a desire to re-create hypomanic symptoms, a belief medication is no longer needed (especially when judgment is impaired by mania), and doubts about need for continued treatment (Clatworthy et al., 2009; Velligan et al., 2009). Unfortunately, mood stabilizers cannot be manipulated in this manner. When the dosage is decreased, a hypomanic state can quickly progress into a severe manic state or depression. Comorbid substance abuse, negative attitudes toward mood stabilizing medication, and difficulty remembering to take medication also negatively influence compliance (Sajatovic et al., 2009). Psychoeducation that emphasizes the link between medication adherence and long-term prognosis is an important aspect of treatment (Berk et al., 2010).

Although pharmacological treatments are critical in the treatment of bipolar disorder, there is strong evidence that psychoeducation, family-focused therapy, interpersonal therapy, and cognitive-behavioral therapy serve an important role in reducing symptom severity, preventing relapses, and enhancing psychosocial functioning (Rizvi & Zaretsky, 2007). For example, adjunctive family-focused treatment involving psychosocial education about bipolar disorder combined with communication and problem-solving skills training was found to reduce the risk of relapse and hospitalization (Morris, Miklowitz, & Waxmonsky, 2007). *Social rhythm therapy*, a treatment involving the creation of routines in day-to-day life, has been effective in reducing relapse. Examples include setting daily times for sleep, eating, and exercise in order to avoid disruption of bodily rhythm patterns. Treatment adherence and selecting the most appropriate intervention at the different stages of a bipolar episode are critical factors in the effectiveness of treatment. Finally, as noted by Hollon, Stewart, and Strunk (2006), teaching clients to detect early signs of a hypomanic/manic episode and to seek prompt medical assistance have reduced the frequency of onset of full manic episodes; interpersonal therapy has also been found to reduce the frequency of depressive relapse. Light therapy is used cautiously, if at all, in individuals with bipolar disorder, due to concerns about light exposure precipitating hypomanic/manic episodes (McClung, 2007). Finally, ECT is sometimes used to treat severe depression or acute mania.

Summary

1. What are the symptoms of depression and mania, and what are important considerations in diagnosing mood disorders?

    *   Depression involves feelings of sadness or emptiness, social withdrawal, loss of interest in activities, pessimism, low energy, and sleep and appetite disturbances.
    *   Mania produces significant impairment and involves high levels of arousal, elevated or irritable mood, increased activity, poor judgment, grandiosity, and decreased need for sleep. Hypomania refers to milder manic symptoms, which are sometimes accompanied by productive, goal-directed behaviors.

2. Which disorders are considered depressive disorders, what causes these disorders, and how are they treated?

    *   Depressive disorders are diagnosed only when depressive symptoms occur without a history of hypomania/mania. Depressive disorders include major depressive disorder, chronic depressive disorder, mixed anxiety/depression disorder, seasonal affective disorder, and premenstrual dysphoric disorder. Evidence shows that biological factors, including heredity, are important in predisposing one to depression. The functioning of neurotransmitters, brain structure activities, and cortisol levels in the body are associated with depression.

    *   Behavioral explanations for depression focus on reduced reinforcement following losses. Cognitive explanations focus on irrational beliefs and rumination. The learned helplessness theory of depression suggests that susceptibility to depression depends on the person's experience with controlling the environment. Attributional style is also important.
    *   Social explanations focus on relationships and interpersonal stressors that make one vulnerable to depression. Early childhood stressors are particularly important.
    *   Sociocultural explanations have focused on cultural, demographic, and socioeconomic factors, including gender and cultural differences.
    *   Behavioral activation, cognitive-behavioral, and interpersonal therapies have received extensive research support as treatments for depression; mindfulness-based cognitive therapy has shown promising results. Biomedical treatments include sleep deprivation, light therapy, and electrical stimulation of the brain. Antidepressant medications are frequently used to treat depression; they are most effective with severe depression, but they only produce temporary effects. Psychotherapy is more likely to prevent future depression.

3. What are bipolar disorders, what causes these disorders and how are they treated?

- Bipolar disorders are characterized by the occurrence of mania or hypomania. Depressive mood episodes are also common in bipolar disorder.

- Bipolar I involves at least one week-long manic episode. Bipolar II is diagnosed when there is both a history of milder depression and hypomania. Cyclothymic disorder is a chronic bipolar disorder involving hypomanic episodes alternating with depressed mood for at least two years.

- Research has shown that bipolar disorders have a strong genetic basis involving multiple, interacting genes. Biological factors, including neurochemical and neuroanatomical abnormalities and circadian rhythm disturbances, contribute to bipolar disorder. There are many overlaps between bipolar disorder and schizophrenia.

- The most effective treatment for bipolar disorders is ongoing use of mood stabilizing medication combined with psychotherapy and psychosocial interventions.

Media Resources

Psychology CourseMate Access an interactive eBook; chapter-specific interactive learning tools, including flash cards, quizzes, videos; and more in your Psychology CourseMate, accessed through CengageBrain.com.

CENGAGENOW

CengageNow CengageNOW is an easy-to-use online resource that helps you study in less time to get the grade you want—NOW. If your textbook does not include an access code card, go to CengageBrain.com to gain access.

CENGAGEbrain.com

CengageBrain More than just an interactive study guide, WebTutor is an anytime, anywhere customized learning solution with an eBook, keeping you connected to your textbook, instructor, and classmates. Purchase the access chosen by your instructor at CengageBrain.com.

9

Suicide

ate one evening, Carl Johnson, M.D., left his downtown office, got into his
Mercedes S600, and drove toward his expensive suburban home. He was
in no particular hurry because the house would be empty anyway; his
wife had divorced him and moved back east with their two children.
Carl was deeply affected. Although he had been drinking heavily for two years
before the divorce, he had always been able to function at work. For the past
several months, however, his private practice had declined dramatically. He once
found his work rewarding, but now his patients bored and irritated him. Although
he had suffered from depressive episodes in the past, this time he knew things
were different. The future looked bleak and hopeless. Carl knew he had all the
classic symptoms of depression—he was, after all, a psychiatrist.

The garage door opened automatically as he rolled up the
driveway. Carl parked carelessly, not even bothering to press the
switch that closed the garage door. Once in the house, he headed
directly for the bar in his den. There he pulled out a bottle of bour-
bon and three glasses, filled each to the rim, and lined them up
along the bar. He drank them down, one after the other, in rapid
succession. For a good half hour, he stood at the window staring
out into the night. Then Carl sat down at his mahogany desk and
unlocked one of the drawers. Taking a loaded .38-caliber revolver
from the desk drawer, Dr. Carl Johnson held it to his temple and
put a bullet through his brain, which killed him instantly.

hy would someone like Dr. Carl Johnson take his own life?
Granted, he was depressed and obviously feeling the loss of his
family, but most people under similar circumstances are able
to cope and choose life over death. Unfortunately, we will never know
the answer, but our multipath model, as shown in Figure 9.1, does offer clues: There is a strong possibility that the combined influence of
biological, psychological, social, and sociocultural factors contributed
to his suicide. Confining our explanations to only one factor would be
a serious oversimplification and mistake (Leenaars, 2008). First, there
is evidence that Carl had a history of depression; and strong biological factors (biochemical or genetic) are implicated in suicide (Mann,
Arango, Avenevoli et al., 2009). For example, cerebrospinal fluid
levels of people who kill themselves reveal that they have lower levels of
5-HIAA serotonin, found to predict a ten to twenty times higher rate
of suicide (Leonardo & Hen, 2006). Second, psychological factors such

1 What do we know about suicide?

2 What are the major explanations of suicide?

3 Who are the victims of suicide?

4 How can we intervene or prevent suicides?

5 Are there times and situations in which suicide should be an option?

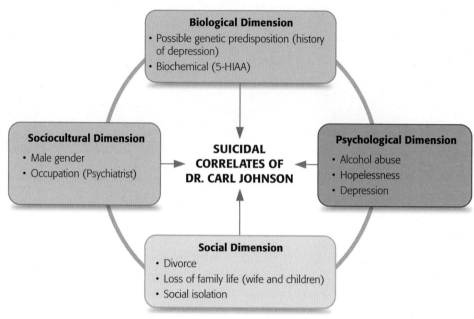

Figure 9.1

MULTIPATH MODEL FOR THE SUICIDE OF DR. CARL JOHNSON

Here you see the interacting multipath dimensions that may have contributed to Dr. Carl Johnson's suicide. Their precise relationship to and interaction with one another is difficult to ascertain, but clearly he was at high risk for suicide.

Copyright © Cengage Learning 2013

as alcohol abuse (Bryan & Rudd, 2006), hopelessness, and depression are often associated with suicide (Jobes, 2006). Third, social factors were evident in Dr. Johnson's pain; a divorce and loss of his family made life no longer meaningful. As we shall see, people who are divorced and lack social relationships are more likely to commit suicide (Rudd, Joiner, & Rajab, 2004). Finally, there are major sociocultural correlates of Dr. Johnson's decision to take his own life. His gender and occupation are significant factors. We know, for example, that men are more likely to kill themselves than women and that, occupationally, psychiatrists have among the highest rates of suicide (Comtois & Linehan, 2006; Klott & Jongsma, 2004). It is clear that Dr. Johnson was at high risk for suicide on a number of risk dimensions. How these four dimensions interact, however, is difficult to ascertain.

There is a saying that goes like this: "We know much about suicide, but we know very little about it." Although this may sound contradictory, this chapter is filled with an impressive array of facts, statistics, and information about many aspects of suicide. We are able to construct fairly accurate portraits of individuals most as risk, delineate protective factors, and even develop intervention strategies in working with suicidal individuals. But, in actuality, we continue to ask: "Why do people kill themselves?"

Suicide—the intentional, direct, and conscious taking of one's own life—is not only a tragic act, it is a baffling and confusing one as well. Most of us have been raised to believe in the sanctity of life, and we operate under strong moral, religious, and cultural sanctions against taking our own lives. Yet suicide is as old as human history itself, and its occurrence no longer seems a rarity. Although explanations abound for suicide, we can never be entirely certain why people knowingly and deliberately end their own lives (Leenaars, 2008; Rudd et al., 2004). The easy and most frequent explanation is that people who kill themselves are suffering from a mental disorder. Yet our increasing understanding of suicide suggests that a single explanation is simplistic. Suicide has many causes, and people kill themselves for many different reasons (Granello, 2010; Rosenfeld, 2004).

suicide the intentional, direct, and conscious taking of one's own life

We have chosen to provide a separate chapter on suicide for several reasons. First, although suicide is not classified as a mental disorder in Diagnostic and Statistical Manual of Mental Disorders, Fifth Edition (DSM-V), the suicidal person usually has clear psychiatric symptoms. Many persons who suffer from depression, alcohol dependence, and schizophrenia exhibit suicidal thoughts or behavior (Bryan & Rudd, 2006; CDC, 2010). Yet suicide does not fall neatly into one of the recognized psychiatric disorders. There is evidence that suicide and suicidal ideation—thoughts about suicide—may represent a separate clinical entity.

The second reason for treating suicide as a separate topic is that increasing interest in suicide and the fact that it is the eleventh leading cause of death for all Americans (Table 9.1) appears to warrant study of this phenomenon in its own right. Every year, there are more deaths due to suicide in the United States than to homicide. However, throughout history, people have traditionally avoided discussing suicide and have participated in a "conspiracy of silence" because of the shame and stigma involved in taking one's life (Maris, Berman, & Silverman, 2000; Rudd et al., 2004). Even mental health professionals find the topic uncomfortable and deeply disturbing (Friedman, 2004). Nearly all therapists encounter a suicidal client in their careers; one fourth will experience an actual client suicide (Granello, 2010). Now, however, we are witnessing increased openness in discussing issues of death and dying, the meaning of suicide, and the right to take one's own life. Some individuals have even gone so far as to advocate a "right to suicide" and the legalization of "assisted suicide." In January 2006, the U.S. Supreme Court upheld the only law in the nation (in Oregon) authorizing doctors to help their terminally ill patients commit suicide.

And, finally, we need to recognize that suicide is an irreversible act. Once the action has been taken, there is no going back, no reconsideration, and no reprieve. Regardless of the moral stand one takes on this position, the decision to commit suicide is often an ambivalent one, clouded by many personal and social stressors. Many mental health professionals believe that the suicidal person, if taught how to deal with personal and social crises, would not consciously take his or her own life. Most do not want to die, but simply want the "pain" to end (Granello & Granello, 2007). As a result, understanding the causes of suicide and what can be done to prevent such an act becomes extremely important to psychologists (Berman, 2006).

TABLE 9.1   Leading Causes of Death in the United States

1. **Diseases of the heart (heart disease)**
2. **Malignant neoplasms (cancer)**
3. **Cerebrovascular diseases (stroke)**
4. **Chronic lower respiratory diseases**
5. **Accidents (unintentional injuries)**
6. **Diabetes mellitus (diabetes)**
7. **Alzheimer's disease**
8. **Pneumonia and influenza**
9. **Nephritis, nephrosis (kidney disease)**
10. **Septicemia (bacterial blood poisoning)**
11. **SUICIDE**
12. **Chronic liver disease and cirrhosis**
13. **Essential hypertension and renal disease**
14. **Parkinson's disease**
15. **Homicide (assault)**

Source: Centers for Disease Control and Prevention Web-based Injury Statistics Query and Reporting System (2005)

Correlates of Suicide

People who commit suicide—who complete their suicide attempts—can no longer inform us about their motives, frames of mind, and emotional states. We have only indirect information, such as case records and reports by others, to help us understand what led them to their tragic act. The systematic examination of existing information for the purpose of understanding and explaining a person's behavior before his or her death is called a psychological autopsy (King & Merchant, 2008). It is patterned on the *medical autopsy*, which is an examination of a dead body to determine the cause or nature of the biological death. The psychological autopsy attempts to make psychological sense of a suicide or homicide by compiling and analyzing case histories of victims, recollections of therapists, interviews with relatives and friends, information obtained from crisis phone calls, and messages left in suicide notes. Unfortunately, these sources are not always available or reliable. Only 12 to 34 percent of victims leave suicide notes, many have never undergone psychotherapy, and the intense feelings of loved ones often cloud their judgments (Black, 1993; Maris, 2001).

suicidal ideation   thoughts about suicide

psychological autopsy   the systematic examination of existing information for the purpose of understanding and explaining a person's behavior before his or her death

CRITICAL THINKING

Is There a Suicidal Crisis on College Campuses?

Have you ever thought about suicide? Do you know of friends or classmates who have talked about taking their lives, made an attempt, or actually committed suicide? Due to high profile suicide-related events on several college campuses, national interest in college-student suicides has increased (Drum, Brownson, Denmark et al., 2009). A wave of suicides at Cornell University, in particular, brought this issue into national consciousness (Spodak, 2010). In 2009, six students committed suicide, a proportion far above the national average. These and a previous cluster of suicides in 1990, have mobilized the Cornell community to institute major suicide prevention and remedial programs on campus.

When you consider how well endowed college students are as a group—with youth, intelligence, and boundless opportunity—you might wonder why students would choose to end their lives. Was the major transition of leaving home, family, and friends too stressful? Did college work prove too difficult and act as a "pressure cooker?" Were they suffering from a pre-existing mental condition like depression and hopelessness? Or, did loneliness, isolation, and alienation play a role in their suicides? As in all suicides, we can never be certain.

Is there a suicidal crisis on our college campuses? According to a major study on college students, suicide rates among their peers are no higher than among a matched noncollege group (Furr et al., 2001). Indeed, in a study conducted over a sixty-year period of twelve colleges and universities, it was found that the rate was nearly half that of a nonstudent group (Schwartz & Whittaker, 1990). But these findings do not tell the entire story. First, the lower rates may be a statistical artifact due to limited access to lethal means such as firearms for students on campus, and the decreasing proportion of males attending colleges (completed suicides for men are twice that of women students) (Drum, et al, 2009; Schwartz, 2006). Second, although suicide is the third leading cause of death for ages 15-24 years, it is the second leading cause of death for college students; nearly 1000 students end their lives in any given year (Centers for Disease Control and Prevention, 2007). Last, counseling centers report a 44 percent increase of severe psychiatric disorders in students seeking services over the past ten years; apparently the effectiveness of psychotropic medication in controlling psychiatric symptoms allows more severely disturbed students to function academically at a marginal level (Gabriel, 2010). Many of these students are considered suicidal.

In one of the most comprehensive studies of college student suicides, 70 participating colleges and universities were surveyed on suicidal ideation, attempts, preparation, and other demographic factors (Drum, et al, 2009). The study revealed the following:

- More than 50 percent of undergraduate and graduate college students reported suicidal thoughts.
- Eighteen percent of undergraduates and 15 percent of graduate students have *seriously considered* attempting suicide. Of those who contemplated suicide seriously in the past 12 months:
- Ninety-two percent of undergraduates and 90 percent of graduate students had a specific plan for killing themselves; most commonly considered were drug or alcohol overdose.
- Fourteen percent of undergraduates and 8 percent of graduate students made an attempt.

- Twenty-three percent of undergraduates and 27 percent of graduate students who made an unsuccessful first attempt were considering a second try.

Factors that contributed to suicidal thoughts/attempts for undergraduates were (listed in order of frequency):
- relief from emotional or physical pain
- problems with romantic relations
- desire to end one's life
- school problems
- friend problems
- family problems
- financial problems

Factors related to whether suicidal students told someone about their thoughts are interesting and potentially helpful in prevention and remedial programs:
- Forty-six percent of undergraduates and 47 percent of graduate students who seriously considered suicide in the past 12 months chose not to tell anyone. Those who did tell someone stated that they found talking to someone and sharing their feelings were either helpful or very helpful to their mental state. The challenge, therefore, is to identify those students who chose not to disclose so that help may be provided.
- The main reasons for not disclosing were fear of being stigmatized or judged, being a burden to others, fear of expulsion from school, fear of forced hospitalization, and not having anyone to tell.
- Sixty-six percent of those who chose to disclose, did so with a peer (romantic partner, roommate, or friend). Not a single student, however, chose to disclose to a professor.

Campus prevention and remediation efforts are of critical importance in identifying students at risk for suicide. Many colleges and universities would be well served to develop programs and resources to (1) identify warning signs related to suicide; (2) have well-established procedures for counselors, faculty, staff, and students in suicide intervention; and (3) clearly identify campus and community resources with expertise in a suicidal crisis.

As a student, however, you can also play a critical role in the prevention effort. Note that approximately 80 percent of students who die by suicide do not go for help on their own to a counseling or psychological services center (Kisch, Leino, & Silverman, 2005), and 45 percent never tell anyone about their serious intentions (Drum et al, 2009). Those who do share their anguish and thoughts of suicide with someone are most likely to do so with a fellow student like you. Further, it is important to note that "verbalizing thoughts of suicide" are not the only signs of suicidal potential (withdrawal, depression, giving prized possessions away, etc.). Two thirds of those who commit suicide communicate their intent in one way or another.

Given this fact, discuss with classmates what you would or should do if a fellow student came to you and shared his/her thoughts about committing suicide. Educate yourself about suicide and become familiar with campus resources. How much do you know about the warning signs of suicide? Are you aware of your campus policy regarding suicides? What resources does the campus provide to help students who are considering taking their own lives (resident hall advisors, counseling centers, suicide hotlines, etc.)? Wouldn't it be a good idea to educate the entire student population about this irreversible and tragic act?

Another strategy involves studying those who survive a suicide attempt. This method, however, assumes that people who attempt suicide are no different from those who succeed. Studies suggest that these two populations differ on many important dimensions. Attempters are more likely to be white female housewives in their twenties and thirties who are experiencing marital difficulties and use primarily barbiturates to attempt suicide. Those who succeed are more likely to be males in their forties or older who suffer from health and depression and shoot or hang themselves (Diekstra, Kienhorst, & de Wilde, 1995; Furr et al., 2001; Shea, 2002).

MYTH Suicides occur more frequently during the holiday seasons because of depression, loneliness, and a feeling of disconnection from significant others.

REALITY Although depressive feelings and loneliness may increase during holidays, suicides do not. The Centers for Health Statistics reports that suicide rates are actually the lowest in December (Annenberg Public Policy Center, [Online], 2009). Suicides are most frequent during the spring and summer months. The holiday suicide myth hampers prevention efforts because it perpetuates misinformation.

MYTH VS. REALITY

Facts about Suicide

In seeking to understand suicide, researchers have focused on events, characteristics, and demographic variables that recur in psychological autopsies and that are highly correlated with the act (Comtois & Linehan, 2006; Lester, 2008). Our first example, Dr. Carl Johnson, fits a particular profile. Higher suicide rates are associated with divorce (Berman, 2006; Bryan & Rudd, 2006) and with certain professions (psychiatry in particular). Alcohol is frequently implicated (Canapary, Bongar, & Cleary, 2002), and men are more likely to kill themselves using firearms than by other means (Centers for Disease Control and Prevention [CDC], 2007e).

Did You Know?

Cleopatra, Kurt Cobain, Ernest Hemingway, Margaux Hemingway, Adolf Hitler, Jim Jones (the People's Temple leader), Marilyn Monroe, Dylan Klebold and Eric Harris (Columbine gunmen), Freddie Prinze, Sr. (comedian), King Saul, and Virginia Woolf all have one thing in common. As you may have guessed, they all committed suicide—the intentional, direct, and conscious taking of one's own life. They differ very much, however, in the reasons for their actions.

Profiles such as these, as well as others described later in this chapter, emerge from our increasing knowledge of facts that are correlated with suicide (Bryan & Rudd, 2006; CDC Web-based Injury Statistics, 2005; Karch, Cosby, & Simon, 2006; King & Merchant, 2008; Leach, 2006). Let's examine some of them in greater detail. But first, look at Table 9.2, which examines some of the characteristics shared by suicidal individuals.

Frequency

Every fifteen minutes or so, someone in the United States takes his or her own life. Approximately 34,000 persons kill themselves each year. Suicide is among the top eleven causes of death in the industrialized parts of the world; it is the eighth leading cause of death among American males, the third leading cause of death among young people ages fifteen to twenty-four, and the second leading cause of death among college students (CDC, 2010; Drum, et al, 2009; Substance Abuse and Mental Health Services Administration, 2010). Some evidence shows that the number of actual suicides is probably 25 to 30 percent higher than that recorded. Many deaths that are officially recorded as accidental—such as single-auto crashes, drownings, or falling from great heights—are actually suicides. According to some estimates, eleven persons attempt suicide for every one person who completes the act (CDC, 2010).

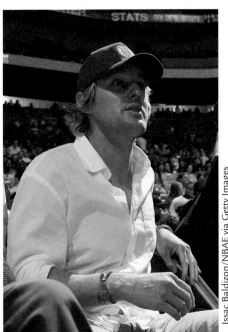

Issac Baldizon/NBAE via Getty Images

Celebrity Attempts at Suicide

Actor Owen Wilson watches a basketball game between the Miami Heat and the Golden State Warriors on March 7, 2008. Less than a year earlier, on August 28, 2007, he attempted suicide with a drug overdose and slitting his wrists.

Children and Young People as Victims

In 2007, suicide was the third leading cause of death for the following age groups: children ages ten to fourteen years (0.9 per 100,000); adolescents ages fifteen to nineteen (6.9 per 100,000), and young adults ages twenty to twenty-four (9.7 per 100,000) (CDC, 2010). Recent reports suggest that about twelve thousand children between the ages of five and twenty-four are admitted to psychiatric hospitals for suicidal behavior every year, and it is believed that twenty times that number actually attempt suicide. Suicides among young people ages fifteen to twenty-four have increased by more than 40 percent in

TABLE 9.2   Ten Common Characteristics of Suicide

1. The common purpose is to seek a solution. People may believe that suicide represents a solution to an insoluble problem. To the suicidal person, taking one's life is not a pointless or accidental occurrence.

2. The cessation of consciousness is a common goal. Consciousness represents constant psychological pain, but suicide represents a termination of distressing thoughts and feelings.

3. The stimulus for suicide is generally intolerable psychological pain. Depression, hopelessness, guilt, shame, and other negative emotions are frequently the basis of a suicide.

4. The common stressor in suicide is frustrated psychological need. The inability to attain high standards or expectations may lead to feelings of frustration, failure, and worthlessness. When progress toward goals is blocked, some individuals become vulnerable to suicide.

5. A common emotion in suicide is hopelessness/helplessness. Pessimism about the future and a conviction that nothing can be done to improve one's life situation may predispose a person to suicide.

6. The cognitive state is one of ambivalence. Although the suicidal person may be strongly motivated to end his or her life, there is usually a desire (in varying degrees) to live as well.

7. The cognitive state is also characterized by "tunnel vision." The person has great difficulty seeing "the larger picture" and can be characterized as suffering from tunnel vision. People intent on suicide seem unable to consider other options or alternatives. Death is the only way out.

8. The common action in suicide is escape. The goal is egression—escape from an intolerable situation.

9. The common interpersonal act in suicide is communication of intention. At least 80 percent of suicides are preceded by either verbal or nonverbal behavioral cues indicating their intentions.

10. The common consistency is in the area of lifelong coping patterns. Patterns or habits developed in coping with crisis generally are the same response patterns that are used throughout life. Some patterns may predispose one to suicide.

Source: Shneidman (1992)

the past decade (50 percent for males and 12 percent for females); suicide is now the second leading cause of death for whites in this age group. College students appear less at risk for suicide than their age-matched noncollege peers, although the highly visible suicides on the campuses of Massachusetts Institute of Technology, New York University, and Cornell seem to indicate it is a major problem (see Critical Thinking section) (Sontag, 2002; Spodak, 2010; Swindler, 2004).

Suicide Publicity and Identification with Victims

Media reports of suicides, especially of celebrities, seem to spark an increase in suicide (Bailey, 2003; Gould, 2007). The twelve-month period following Marilyn Monroe's suicide saw a 12 percent increase. Suicides by young people in small communities or schools seem to evoke copycat suicides in some students. Publicized murder-suicides also seem to be correlated with an increase in car accidents. It is hypothesized that group suicides involving two or more individuals represent an extreme form of personal identification with others. Studies suggest that group suicides are characterized by highly emotional involvements or settings that overcome the desire for self-preservation. Interestingly, publicized natural deaths (as opposed to suicides) of celebrities do not produce similar increases.

Gender

The completed suicide rate for men is about four times that for women, although recent findings suggest that the gap is closing, as many more women are now incurring a higher risk (CDC, 2010). Further, women are more likely to make attempts, but it appears that men are more successful because they use more lethal means. Among people older than sixty-five, the completed suicide rate for men is ten times that for women. However, women in the same age range attempt suicide three times as often as men. The age group beginning at age sixty-five has the highest suicide rate of all. Among younger people, males commit the majority of suicides. For example, among the fifteen to twenty-four age category, more than 70 percent of suicides are men.

Marital Status

Does a stable marriage or relationship immunize people against killing themselves? There are important statistics to suggest an affirmative response, but the precise nature of the relationship is less clear. Being widowed as compared to divorced appears to be associated with higher risk of suicide for white men and women and African American men. At older ages, however, divorce rather than widowhood increases the risk. Interestingly, the pattern reversal occurs much earlier among white women than among men (forty to forty-nine years vs. fifty-five to sixty-five years). Across the life span, the lowest incidence of suicide is found among people who are married (Luoma, Pearson, & Pearson, 2002). The suicide rates for single and widowed or divorced men are about twice those for women of similar marital status. Attempted and completed suicide rates are higher among those who are separated, divorced, or widowed, and they are especially high among single adolescent girls and single men in their thirties.

Occupation

Physicians, lawyers, law enforcement personnel, and dentists have higher than average rates of suicide. Among medical professionals, psychiatrists have the highest rate and pediatricians the lowest. Because medical personnel have easy access to drugs and know what constitutes a fatal dose, they may be more likely to complete a suicide. One in sixteen surgeons in the United States consider suicide, and researchers speculate that "burnout," "stress," and guilt over "medical errors" increases the risk of suicides (Joelving, 2011). Interestingly, the suicide rate of women physicians is four times higher than that of a matched general population. Such marked differences raise the question of whether the specialty influences susceptibility or whether a suicide-prone person is attracted to certain specialties.

Socioeconomic Level

Suicide is represented proportionately among all socioeconomic levels. Level of wealth does not seem to affect the suicide rate as much as do changes in that level. In the Great Depression of the 1930s, suicide was higher among the suddenly impoverished than among those who had always been poor.

Choice of Method

More than 50 percent of suicides are committed by firearms, and 70 percent of attempts are accounted for by drug overdose. Men most frequently choose firearms as the means of suicide; poisoning and asphyxiation via barbiturates are the most common means for women. The violent means (which men are more likely to choose) are more certain to complete the act; this partially explains the

Did You Know?

The primary risk factors for suicide include: previous suicide attempt, history of depression or mental illness, alcohol or drug abuse, family history of suicide or violence, physical illness, feeling alone, and being an elderly male (CDC, 2010).

Did You Know?

Suicide Methods

Firearms: 51.6 percent
Suffocation/Hanging: 22.6 percent
Poisoning: 17.9 percent
Cut/pierce: 1.8 percent
Drowning: 1.1 percent
Other: 5 percent

Source: CDC Web-based Injury Statistics (2007a)

disproportionately greater number of incomplete attempts by women. Recent findings indicate, however, that women are increasingly choosing firearms and explosives as methods (55.9 percent increase; CDC, 2007e). Some have speculated that this change may be related to a change in role definitions of women in society. Among children younger than fifteen, the most common suicide method tends to be jumping from buildings and running into traffic. Older children try hanging or drug overdoses. Younger children attempt suicide impulsively and thus use more readily available means.

Religious Affiliation

Religious affiliation is correlated with suicide rates. Although the U.S. rate is 11.4 per 100,000, in countries in which the influence of the Catholic Church is strong—Latin America, Ireland, Spain, and Italy—the suicide rate is relatively low (less than 10 per 100,000) (CDC, 2010). Islam, too, condemns suicide, but the increase in suicide attacks in the Middle East may affect rates in Arab countries, which are generally low. Where religious sanctions against suicide are absent or weaker—for example, where church authority is weaker, as it is in Scandinavian countries, in the former Czechoslovakia, and in Hungary— higher rates are observed (De Leo, 2009). Indeed, Hungary has the highest recorded rate of suicide, at 40.7 per 100,000, and the former Czechoslovakia's rate was 22.4 per 100,000.

Ethnic and Cultural Variables

Suicide rates vary among ethnic minority groups in the United States. As shown in Figure 9.2, American Indian groups have the highest rate, followed by white Americans, Mexican Americans, African Americans, Japanese Americans, and Chinese Americans.

Bob Daemmrich / The Image Works

© Shepard Sherbell / Corbis

Religion and Suicide

Many religions have strong taboos and sanctions against suicide. In countries in which Catholicism and Islam are strong, for example, the rates of suicide tend to be lower than in countries in which religious sanctions against suicide are not as deeply held.

American Indian and Proud of It

Suicide rates among American Indian youth are extremely high, due perhaps to a lack of validation of their cultural lifestyle. One effort to replenish native pride, shown here, is Camp Walakota, a "spiritual boot camp" for troubled teens from the Cheyenne River Sioux Tribe in South Dakota. Here teens are reacquainted with their cultural heritage as they bond with their elders, who offer many valuable life lessons.

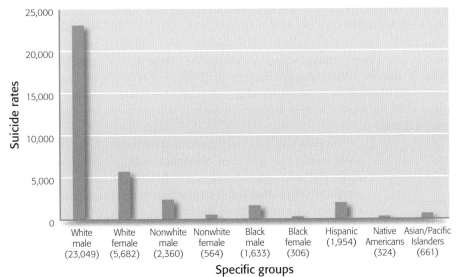

Figure 9.2

RATES OF SUICIDE BY RACE/ETHNICITY

Of all the groups, white men have the highest rates of suicide when men are separated from women. However, as a group (men and women combined), Native Americans have the highest overall group rates, with Asian Americans lowest.

Source: Adapted from American Society of Suicidology (2008)

American Indian youngsters have frighteningly high rates (26 per 100,000) as compared with white youths (14 per 100,000). For American Indians, suicide is the second leading cause of death (CDC, 2010). High rates of alcoholism, a low standard of living, and an invalidation of their cultural lifestyles may all contribute to this tragedy.

Historical Period

Suicide rates tend to decline among the general population during times of war and natural disasters, but they increase during periods of shifting norms and values or social unrest, when traditional expectations no longer apply. Sociologists speculate that during wars, people "pull together" and are less concerned with their own difficulties and conflicts.

Communication of Intent

More than two-thirds of the people who commit suicide communicate their intent to do so within three months of the fatal act. The belief that people who threaten suicide are not serious about it or will not actually make such an attempt is ill founded. It is estimated that 20 percent of persons who attempt suicide try again within one year and that 10 percent finally succeed. Most people who attempt suicide appear to have been ambivalent about death until the suicide. It has been estimated that fewer than 5 percent unequivocally wish to end their lives.

A Multipath Perspective of Suicide

As we have indicated throughout the text, the only viable explanation of mental disorders must come from an integrated and multidimensional analysis. This is truly exemplified in the study of suicide, in which so many different factors seem involved (Leong & Leach, 2008; Lester, 2008). Our biological, psychological, social, and sociocultural multipath model seems especially well suited for this purpose, as it acknowledges the multiple pathways to suicide.

Biological Dimension

Most discussions of the correlates of suicide seem to stress psychological, social, and sociocultural factors. As we will see, all three contribute, but biological factors and the interplay of all four seem to be operating in determining suicides (CDC Web-based Injury Statistics, 2005). Two sets of findings—from biochemistry and from genetics—suggest that suicide may have a strong biological component (Brent & Melhem, 2008; Brezo, Klempan, & Turecki, 2008); Mann, Arango et al., 2009). For example, in Chapter 8 you may recall that there is strong evidence that chemical neurotransmitters are associated with depression and mania. Similar evidence shows that low serotonin levels in the brain influence suicide.

Did You Know?

Air pollution (ambient particulate matter) may actually contribute to higher suicide rates. It has been reported to adversely affect psychological well-being and neuropsychological functioning. In a study of seven cities in the Republic of Korea that included 4,341 suicides in a one year period, mean concentrations of particulate matter was positively related to suicides. Although one cannot conclude that pollution causes suicides, researchers found that a transient increase in air pollution was associated with increased suicide risk (Kim, Jun, Kan et al., 2010).

Evidence of this link began to accumulate in the mid-1970s, when researchers identified a chemical called *5-hydroxyindoleacetic acid* (5HIAA) (Boldrini et al., 2005; Mann, 2003). This chemical is produced when serotonin, a neurotransmitter that affects mood and emotions, is broken down in the body. Moreover, some evidence indicates that the serotonin receptors in the brainstem and frontal cortex may be impaired. And, as noted earlier, the spinal fluid of some depressed and suicidal patients has been found to contain abnormally low amounts of 5HIAA (Laje, Paddock, Manji et al., 2007).

Statistics on patients with low levels of 5HIAA indicate that they are more likely than others to commit suicide; more likely to select violent methods of killing themselves; and more likely to have a history of violence, aggression, and impulsiveness (Brent, 2009a; Mann, Arango et al., 2009). Researchers believe that the tendency toward suicide is not a simple link to depression. We already know that patients suffering from depression also exhibit low levels of 5HIAA. What is startling is that low levels of 5HIAA have been discovered in suicidal people without a history of depression and in suicidal individuals suffering from other mental disorders.

This discovery may lead to a chemical means of detecting people who are at high risk for attempting suicide. However, researchers in this area caution that social and psychological factors also play a role. If, in the future, cerebral serotonin can be detected easily in blood tests, it can be used as a biological marker (a warning sign) of suicide risk. Researchers believe that low 5HIAA content does not cause suicide but that it may make people more vulnerable to environmental stressors. And still another caution is in order: This evidence is correlational in nature; it does not indicate whether low levels of 5HIAA are a cause or a result of particular moods and emotions—or even whether the two are directly related.

There is also evidence to implicate genetics in suicidal behavior, but the relationship is far from clear. There appears to be a higher rate of suicide and suicide attempts among parents and close relatives of people who attempt or commit suicide than among nonsuicidal people (Brent & Melhem, 2008; Brezo, Klempan, & Turecki, 2008). As always, great care must be used in drawing conclusions because it can be argued that modeling by a close member of the family might make a family relative more prone to find suicide an acceptable alternative. Some researchers are hopeful that the Human Genome Project might provide a means of clarifying the genetic markers that may help identify those individuals at risk for suicide.

Psychological Dimension

There are many psychological factors that have been found to be significantly related to suicide. Findings have consistently revealed that a number of individuals who commit suicide suffer from a mental disorder (Bryan & Rudd, 2006). Conversely, more than 90 percent of individuals who kill themselves have risk factors associated with mood disorders, schizophrenia, and substance abuse (CDC, 2010). Those suffering from schizophrenia are most likely to be experiencing an episode of depression, and their suicide methods are usually violent and bizarre; those with personality disorders are usually the emotionally immature with low frustration tolerance, such as those with borderline and antisocial personalities (Mann, Arango et al., 2009). A review of the literature on suicide also reveals a number of other contributing factors, including such experiences as separation and divorce, academic pressures, shame, serious illness, loss of a job, and other life stressors (Granello & Granello, 2007; Rosenfeld, 2004; Substance Abuse & Mental Health Services Administration, 2010).

Depression and Hopelessness

Perhaps the psychological state of mind most correlated with suicide is depression and hopelessness (Berman, 2006; Bryan & Rudd, 2006). For example, interest in suicide usually develops gradually, as a result of pleasure loss and fatigue accompanying a serious depressed mood (Lester, 2008). Shneidman (1993) has described it as a "psychache," an intolerable pain created from an absence of joy. Among both children and adolescents, depression seems to be highly correlated with suicidal behavior (CDC Web-based Injury Statistics, 2005; Eaton et al., 2006).

Such data can lead to the conclusion that depression plays an important role in suicide. But the role depression plays in suicide is far from simple. For example, patients seldom commit suicide while severely depressed. Such patients generally show motor retardation and low energy, which keep them from reaching the level of activity required for suicide. The danger period often comes after some treatment, when the depression begins to lift. Energy and motivation increase, and patients are more likely to carry out the act. Although depression is undeniably correlated with suicidal thoughts and behavior, the relationship seems very complex. Why do some people with depression commit suicide, whereas others do not? The answer may be found in the characteristics of depression and in the factors that contribute to it (Jobes, 2006).

For example, it has been found that an increase in sadness is a frequent mood indicator of suicide, but heightened feelings of anxiety, anger, and shame are also associated. Some researchers believe that hopelessness, or negative expectations about the future, may be the major catalyst in suicide and, possibly, an even more important factor than depression and other moods (Lester, 2008; Weishaar & Beck, 1992). In a classic ten-year study, Beck, Emery, and Greenberg (1985) investigated 207 psychiatric patients who had suicidal thoughts but no recent history of suicide attempts. During the ten-year period, fourteen patients committed suicide, and the test scores of these people were compared with those of the others. The investigators found that the two groups did not differ in terms of depression and suicidal ideation, but they did differ in terms of hopelessness. Those who died were more pessimistic about the future than were those who survived. Although the overall results obtained by the scale did not predict suicide risk, the hopelessness item within the measure did. Some sample statements indicative of hopelessness are "My future seems dark for me"; "I might as well give up because there's nothing I can do about making things better for myself"; "I never get anything I want, so it's foolish to want anything." These findings suggest that therapists should assess all depressed patients' attitudes toward their futures to determine how hopeless they feel.

Alcohol Consumption

One of the most consistently reported correlates of suicidal behavior is alcohol consumption (Canapary et al., 2002; Shea, 2002). As many as 70 percent of suicide attempters drink alcohol before the act, and autopsies of suicide victims suggest that 25 percent are legally intoxicated (Lejoyeux et al., 2008; McCloud et al., 2004). Indeed, a successful suicide unconnected to alcohol abuse is a rare event. Heavy alcohol consumption, such as binge drinking, also seems to deepen feelings of remorse during dry periods, and the person may be at risk even when sober. Many theorists have traditionally argued that alcohol may lower inhibitions related to the fear of death and make it easier to carry out the fatal act.

Several classic studies, however, suggest another explanation of the effects of alcohol: The strength of the relationship between alcohol and suicide is the result of "alcohol-induced myopia," a constriction of cognitive and perceptual processes (Rogers, 1992; Steele & Josephs, 1990). Alcohol use by individuals in psychological conflict may increase rather than decrease personal distress by focusing their thoughts on negative aspects of their personal situations. Alcohol does seem to constrict cognitive and perceptual processes. Although alcohol-induced myopia may relieve depression and anxiety by distracting the person from the problem, it is equally likely to intensify the conflict and distress by narrowing the person's focus on the problem (Cha, Najmi, Park, Finn, & Nock, 2010). Thus, the link between alcohol and suicide may be the result of the myopic qualities of alcohol exaggerating a previously existing constrictive state. If this is true, alcohol is most likely to increase the probability of a suicide in an already suicidal person.

Social Dimension

Case Study

In 1990 the psychology community was shocked by the suicide of one of their very own, Bruno Bettelheim. Bettelheim was a renowned psychologist whose work on autism had influenced the field of mental health and treatment immensely. At eighty-six years, he recently suffered a stroke, was fearful he would suffer another, and he did not want to be kept alive without a purpose. Bettelheim stated he did not want to be a burden to his family or friends, and he could no longer take part in many of the activities that had brought joy and meaning to his life. He believed that he was living on borrowed time and met with a doctor in the Netherlands who was willing to give him a lethal injection.

Ten-year-old Tammy Jimenez was the youngest of three children—a loner who had attempted suicide at least twice in the previous two years. Tammy's parents always seemed to be arguing and threatening divorce. Their alcoholic father constantly abused her and her sisters. In late February 2002, Tammy was struck and killed by a truck when she darted out into the highway that passed by her home. The incident was listed as an accident, but her older sister said Tammy had deliberately killed herself. On the morning of her death, an argument with her father had upset and angered her. Her sister said that seconds before Tammy ran out onto the highway, she had said that she was unwanted and would end her own life.

The influence of social factors in suicides is clearly evident in the two previous cases. Many suicides are interpersonal in nature and are influenced primarily by relationships involving significant others (Jobes, 2006; Leenaars, 2008). There were many reasons why Bruno Bettelheim chose to end his life, but one of the strongest was his desire not to burden his family and friends with his increasing dependency. And suicides and attempted suicides are often related to the quality and nature of our social relationships with people. It has been found that unhappiness over a broken or unhappy love affair, marital discord, disputes with parents, and recent bereavements are correlated with suicides (Rudd et al., 2004).

Family instability, stress, and a chaotic family atmosphere are a factor in suicide attempts by younger children as well. Tammy Jimenez, for example, took her own life because of feeling unloved and abused by her father. Suicidal children seem to have experienced unpredictable traumatic events and to have suffered the loss of a significant parenting figure before age twelve (King & Merchant, 2008).

The interpersonal-psychological theory of suicide by Joiner (2005) has received considerable attention in the psychological literature. In an attempt to integrate the multifactorial factors associated with suicide, he postulates that two social dimensions must be experienced by people before suicide attempts are made: (a) perceived burdensomeness—beliefs or feelings that they are a burden to their family, friends, loved ones, community, and society; and (b) thwarted belongingness—beliefs or feelings that they are not meaningfully connected to others and/or alienated from them (Joiner, 2005; Joiner, Van Orden, Witt et al., 2009). Social factors that separate people or to make them somehow less connected to other people or to their families, to religious institutions, or to their communities can increase susceptibility to suicide (Alcantara & Gone, 2008).

Joiner's theory is quite unique in that he posits a third condition that must exist before a suicide attempt is made: the acquired capacity for suicide (Smith, Cukrowicz, Poindexter, Hobson, & Cohen, 2010). A person must experience a reduction in fear of taking one's own life sufficient to overcome self-preservation reflexes. Repeated exposure to painful life events (abusive childhood, physical abuse, emotional abuse, rape, bullying, exposure to wartime atrocities, etc.) result in habituation to painful life circumstances, and lowering of fear of inflicting self-injury (acquired capacity for suicide). Studies have found that suicide attempters do indeed report the highest levels of fearlessness and pain insensitivity and experiencing greater frequency of painful life events (Smith, Cukrowicz et al., 2010).

Joiner's theory would predict that suicide prevention would be vastly more effective when social support and connectedness are increased and when social isolation is decreased. Conversely, he would expect rates to be higher among the elderly, as their loved ones and friends die off, as they begin to disengage from their work through retirement, and as they sense they are a burden to others. We would also expect that in the divorced, separated, or widowed population, suicide rates would be higher than among those who are married. As we have seen, the research literature supports all of these expectations.

Sociocultural Dimension

In a pioneering work, the French sociologist Emile Durkheim related differences in suicide rates to the impact of sociocultural forces on the person (Durkheim, 1897/1951). From his detailed study of suicides in different countries and across different periods, he proposed one of the first sociocultural explanations of suicide. In Durkheim's view, suicide can result from an inability to integrate oneself with society. Failing to maintain close ties with the community deprives the person of the support systems that are necessary for adaptive functioning. Without such support, and unable to function adaptively, the person becomes isolated and alienated from other people. Some suicidologists believe that modern, mobile, and highly technological society has de-emphasized the importance of extended families and the sense of community. The result, even among young people, has been an increase in suicide rates.

Suicides can also be motivated by the person's desire to further group goals or to achieve some greater good. Someone may give up his or her life for a higher cause (in a religious sacrifice or the ultimate political protest, for example). Group pressures may make such an act highly acceptable and honored. During World War II, Japanese kamikaze pilots voluntarily flew their airplanes into enemy warships "for the Emperor and the glory of Japan." The self-immolation of Buddhist monks during the Vietnam War is likewise in this category. Although likely to arouse considerable disagreement and controversy, a strong case can be made that the suicide bombings now so prevalent in the Middle East, Iraq, Afghanistan and even the 9/11 terrorist attack on the World Trade Center in New York City qualify for this category. From the perspective of those who condone such acts, the perpetrators do not perceive themselves as terrorists but as freedom fighters who willingly give their lives for a greater good.

Sociocultural factors have been shown to account for the differential rates and manifestations of suicides among Asian/Pacific Americans (Leong & Leach, 2008), African Americans (Utsey, Stenard, & Hook, 2008), Latino/Hispanic Americans (Duarte-Velez & Bernal, 2008), American Indians (Alcantara & Gone, 2008), and gays and lesbians (Leach, 2006). As mentioned previously, American Indians have a 70 percent higher rate of suicide than is found among all other groups in American society, including European Americans (Dorgan, 2010). Asian American and Hispanic American rates are significantly lower than that of the white group (Duarte-Velez & Bernal, 2008; Leong & Leach, 2008). Although rates for African

© Bettmann/CORBIS

An Altruistic Suicide

During the Vietnam War, people were horrified by scenes of self-immolation by Buddhist monks as a form of protest against the government. This altruistic suicide in 1963 was witnessed by passersby in the central market of Saigon.

© Stringer/Iraq/Reuters/Corbis

Suicide Bombings

These events have become an all too common sight in Iraq. In the aftermath of a suicide bombing in Baghdad on April 2007, two men try desperately to move a car away to clear the way for help. A suicide truck bomb triggered the incident in an attempt to destroy a satellite television station to take as many lives as possible.

American youngsters have also been traditionally lower than for their white counterparts, reports reveal a dramatic increase over the past two decades (Utsey et al., 2008).

Social change and disorganization, which leads to a breakup in integration with one's community, often predisposes a group to suicide. Suicidologists point to the disorganization imposed on American Indians by Western society: Deprived of their lands, forced to live on reservations, and trapped between the margins of two different cultural traditions, many American Indians become alienated and isolated from both their own communities and the larger society (Goldston, Molock, Whitbeck, Murakami, Zayas, & Hall, 2008).

■■■■■ Victims of Suicide

In this section we briefly discuss two groups of people who are especially victimized by suicide: the very young and the elderly. It is important, however, to realize that those who are left behind may be considered victims as well. Indeed, it is estimated that for every suicide, six others are intimately affected as survivors, such as family members and friends (CDC Web-based Injury Statistics, 2005).

Children and Adolescents

Suicide among the young is an unmentioned tragedy in our society. We have traditionally avoided the idea that some of our young people find life so painful that they consciously and deliberately take their own lives. As in the case of Tammy Jimenez, it may feel easier to call a suicide "an accident." The suicide rate for children younger than fourteen is increasing at an alarming rate, and the rate for adolescents is rising even faster (CDC, 2007e; CDC Web-based Injury Statistics, 2005). Suicide is now the third leading cause of death among teenagers, just behind automobile "accidents" some of which may also really be suicides (Ianelli, 2009; Rudd et al., 2004). After a trend of decreasing rates from 1996 to 2003, teen suicides increased 18 percent in 2004 and 17 percent in 2005; even pre-teens from 6–9 years of age showed an increase (Ianelli, 2009). In a study of high school students in grades 9–12 in 2009, the following was found: 13.8 percent considered suicide in the previous 12 months (17.4 percent females and 10.5 percent males), 6.3 percent reported making at least one attempt (8.1 percent females and 4.5 percent males), and 1.9 percent made an attempt that resulted in an injury, poisoning, or overdose requiring medical attention (2.3 percent females and 1.6 percent males) (CDC, 2010).

There are many reasons postulated for the increase of suicide among young children and teenagers: attempt to regain control of their lives, retaliation or revenge against wrongs, reunion fantasies with a loved one, relief from unbearable pain, being a family scapegoat, distract family from issues such as divorce, and acting out covert or overt desire of parent to be rid of the child. Three, however, seemed to have gained considerable attention in recent years.

The Role of Bullying

"Bullycide" is an increasingly used term to describe bullying that leads to suicides among young people (Ollove, 2010). Such was the case of Phoebe Prince, a 15-year-old freshman, who hanged herself in the stairwell of her home on January 14, 2010. The investigation of her death indicated she was subjected to nearly three torturous months of verbally assaultive behavior, threats of physical harm, cyberbullying, and statutory rape before her suicide. Six of her classmates have been charged with Prince's death for their part in violating her civil rights with bodily injury, harassment, and stalking.

In 2009, bullying statistics reveal that one third of teens reported being bullied at school: 20 percent were teased, 18 percent had rumors or gossip spread about them, 11 percent were physically bullied (spit upon, shoved, or tripped), 6 percent were threatened, 5 percent were excluded, 4 percent were coerced, and 4 percent had belongings destroyed (Bullying Statistics, 2009). It has been found that bully victims are 2 to 9 times

Teens and Suicide

As more and more teens like those shown here find themselves attending the funerals of their peers, it is becoming clear that suicide among high school students is reaching epidemic proportions. To prevent more suicides, schools sometimes initiate programs to help students and faculty cope with their feelings of loss and anger.

more likely to consider suicide than non-victims; nearly 50 percent of young people who commit suicide have experienced bullying (Bullying Statistics, 2009).

Copycat Suicides

Considerable attention has been directed at multiple or so-called "copycat" suicides (suicide contagion), in which youngsters in a particular school or community seem to mimic a previous suicide (Alcantara & Gone, 2008; Phillips, Van Voorhees, & Ruth, 1992). Suggestion and imitation seem to play an especially powerful role. Young people may be especially vulnerable, but studies indicate that highly publicized suicides—such as those of a celebrity, close friend, relative, co-worker, or other well-known person—can increase the number of subsequent suicide attempts (Gould, 2007; Stack, 1987). As we noted earlier, in the months following Marilyn Monroe's death, suicides increased by some 12 percent. When Nirvana's Kurt Cobain committed suicide in 1994, many youth counselors warned about potential imitations by fans. Fans worshiped Cobain, he represented an icon of the "lost generation," and his known psychological problems seemed to endear him to the hearts of many youngsters. According to one study, Cobain's death resulted in an excess of 119 suicides beyond the average number in the one month period following his death (Correspondence, 2010).

Although imitative suicides may not be as common as the media suggest, research has indicated that publicizing the event may have the effect of glorifying and drawing attention to it. Thus, depressed people may identify with a colorful portrayal, increasing the risk of even more suicides. This pattern appears to be especially true for youngsters who may already be thinking about killing themselves. The stable, well-adjusted teenager does not seem to be at risk in these situations.

Adolescence and young adulthood are often periods of confusing emotions, identity formation, and questioning. It is a difficult and turbulent time for most teenagers, and suicide may seem to be a logical response to the pain and stress of growing up. A suicide that occurs in school brings increased risk of other suicides because of its proximity to students' daily lives. In such instances, a suicide prevention program should be implemented to let students vent their feelings in an environment equipped to respond appropriately—and perhaps even to save their lives. Encouragingly, approximately 41 percent of schools have programs aimed at suicide prevention (professional counseling services, peer counseling, and special seminars). It is no longer unusual to hear about school programs that are immediately implemented when a tragedy strikes (such as student suicide, violent death of a student or teacher, or natural disaster) (Freiberg, 1991).

Decrease in Antidepressant Medication

Another explanation for the increase in youth suicides relates to the 2004 Food and Drug Administration (FDA) warning of an increased suicide risk for children taking (SSRI) antidepressants. Although antidepressants are found to help people with depression, the FDA noted an increase in suicidal thoughts/actions in adolescents, and required a "black box" warning on all such medication. There is considerable controversy over the actions of the FDA. Research seems to suggest that SSRIs may increase suicidal thoughts or behaviors for a very select few, that the majority of depressed youths benefit, and that completed suicides (in contrast to suicidal thoughts) are not increased (Brent, 2009b; Ludwig, Marcotte, & Norbert, 2009). In fact, these investigators observe that suicide rates among the young have increased since the black box warnings. They reason that since the notification, parents and doctors have been less inclined to prescribe antidepressant medication, resulting in the increase in suicides. The issue is far from being resolved.

Elderly People

Aging inevitably results in generally unwelcome physical changes, such as wrinkling and thickening skin, graying hair, and diminishing physical strength. In addition, we all encounter a succession of stressful life changes as we grow older. Friends and relatives die, social isolation may increase, and the prospect of death becomes more real. Mandatory retirement rules may lead to the need for financial assistance and the difficulties of living on a fixed and inadequate income. Such conditions make depression one of the most common psychiatric complaints of elderly people. And their depression seems to be involved more with "feeling old" than with their actual age or poor physical health (Rosenfeld, 2004).

Suicide seems to accompany depression for older people. Their suicide rates (especially rates for elderly white American men) are higher than those for the general population; indeed, suicide rates for elderly white men are the highest for any age group (CDC Web-based Injury Statistics, 2005). From 1980 through 1997, the largest relative increases in suicide rates occurred among those eighty to eighty-four years of age. Firearms were the most common method of suicide for both men and women sixty-five years or older. The elderly make fewer attempts per completed suicide, being among the most likely to succeed in taking their lives. In one study comparing rates of suicide among different ethnic groups, it was found that elderly white Americans committed almost 18 percent of all suicides, although they composed only about 11 percent of the population (Leong & Leach, 2008). Suicide rates for elderly Chinese Americans, Japanese Americans, and Filipino Americans are even higher than the rate for elderly white Americans. American Indians and African Americans show the lowest rates of suicide among older adults (although both groups are at high risk for suicide during young adulthood).

Of the Asian American groups, first-generation immigrants were at greatest risk of suicide. One possible explanation for this finding is that newly arrived Asian immigrants intended to earn money and then return to their native countries. When they found they were unable to earn enough either to return home or to bring their families to the United States, they developed feelings of isolation that increased their risk of suicide. This risk has decreased among subsequent generations of Asian Americans (and, probably, among other immigrant groups as well) because of acculturation and the creation of strong family ties.

Christiana Dittmann/Rainbow

A Matter of Respect

Suicide is less likely to occur among the elderly in cultures that revere, respect, and esteem people of increasing age. In Asian and African countries, increasing age is equated with greater privilege and status, such as that shown for an elderly Ghanaian chief; in contrast, in the United States, growing old is often associated with declining worth and social isolation.

▮▮ Preventing Suicide

In almost every case of suicide, there are hints that the act is about to occur. Suicide is irreversible, of course, so preventing it depends very much on early detection and successful intervention (Comtois & Linehan, 2006; Granello, 2010). Mental health professionals involved in suicide prevention efforts operate under the assumption that potential victims are ambivalent about the act. That is, the wish to die is strong, but there is also a wish to live. Potential rescuers are trained to exert their efforts to preserve life. Part of their success in the prevention process is the ability to assess a client's suicide lethality—the probability that a person chooses to end his or her life (Bryan & Rudd, 2006; Rudd et al., 2004).

Working with a potentially suicidal individual is a three-step process that involves (1) knowing which factors are highly correlated with suicide; (2) determining whether there is high, moderate, or low probability that the person will act on the suicide wish; and (3) implementing appropriate actions (Table 9.3) (Isaac, Elias, Katz, Belik et al., 2008). People trained in working with suicidal patients often attempt to quantify the "seriousness" of each factor. For example, a person with a clear suicidal plan who has the means (e.g., a gun) to carry out a suicide threat is considered to be in a more lethal state than a recently divorced and depressed person.

Clues to Suicidal Intent

The prevention of suicide depends very much on the therapist's ability to recognize its signs. Clues to suicidal intent may be demographic or specific. We have already discussed a number of demographic factors, such as the fact that men are three times more likely to

TABLE 9.3   Risk and Protective Factors in Suicide Assessment and Intervention

Risk Factors
• Previous suicide attempt
• Mental disorders such as depression and bipolar disorder
• Co-occurring mental and alcohol and substance abuse disorders
• Family history of suicide
• Hopelessness
• Impulsive and/or aggressive tendencies
• Barriers to accessing mental health treatment
• Relational, social, work, or financial loss
• Physical illness
• Easy access to lethal methods, especially guns
• Unwillingness to seek help because of social stigma
• Family members, peers, or celebrities who have died from suicide
• Cultural or religious beliefs that suicide is a noble resolution
• Local epidemics of suicide that have a contagious influence
• Isolation

Protective Factors
• Effective resources for clinical care for mental, physical, and substance abuse disorders
• Easy access to a variety of clinical interventions and support for seeking help
• Restricted access to lethal means of suicide
• Family and community support
• Good skills in problem solving, conflict resolution, and nonviolent means of handling disputes
• Cultural and religious beliefs that discourage suicide and support self-preservation instincts

Source: Bryan & Rudd (2006); USPHS (1999)

lethality   the probability that a person chooses to end his or her life

kill themselves than are women and that older age is associated with an increased probability of suicide (Bryan & Rudd, 2006). And, although the popular notion is that frequent suicidal gestures are associated with less serious intent, most suicides do have a history of making suicide threats; to ignore them is extremely dangerous. Any suicidal threat or intent must be taken seriously (Berman, 2006).

General characteristics often help detect potential suicides, but individual cases vary from statistical norms. What does one look for in specific instances? The amount of detail involved in a suicide threat can indicate its seriousness. A person who provides specific details, such as method, time, and place, is more at risk than one who describes these factors vaguely. Suicide potential increases if the person has direct access to the means of suicide, such as a loaded pistol. Also, sometimes a suicide may be preceded by a precipitating event. The loss of a loved one, family discord, or chronic or terminal illness may contribute to a person's decision to end his or her life.

A person contemplating suicide may verbally communicate the intent. Some people make very direct statements: "I'm going to kill myself," "I want to die," or "If such and such happens, I'll kill myself." Others make indirect threats: "Goodbye," "I've had it," "You'd be better off without me," and "It's too much to put up with." On the other hand, some cues are frequently very subtle.

Behavioral clues can be communicated directly or indirectly. The most direct clue is a "practice run," an actual suicide attempt. Even if the act is not completed, *it should be taken seriously*; it often communicates deep suicidal intent that may be carried out in the future. Indirect behavioral clues can include actions such as putting one's affairs in order, taking a lengthy trip, giving away prized possessions, buying a casket, or making out a will, depending on the circumstances. In other words, the more unusual or peculiar the situation, the more likely it is that the action is a cue to suicide. Clinicians often divide up warning signs into two categories: (1) early signs, such as depression, statements or expressions of guilt feelings, tension or anxiety, nervousness, insomnia, loss of appetite, loss of weight, and impulsiveness; and (2) critical signs, such as sudden changes in behavior (calmness after a period of anxiety), giving away belongings or putting affairs in order, direct or indirect threats, and actual attempts.

Crisis Intervention

Suicide prevention can occur at several levels, and the mental health profession has now begun to move in several coordinated directions to establish prevention efforts. At the clinical level, attempts are being made to educate staff at mental health institutions and even at schools to recognize conditions and symptoms that indicate potential suicides (Brown & Grumet, 2008; Isaac, Elias, Katz et al., 2009). For example, mental health professionals should recognize a single man who is older than fifty years of age and suffering from a sudden acute onset of depression and expressing hopelessness as being at high risk.

When a psychiatric facility encounters someone who fits a particular risk profile for suicide, crisis intervention strategies are likely to be used to abort or ameliorate the processes that could lead to a suicide attempt. Crisis intervention is aimed at providing intensive short-term help to a patient in resolving an immediate life crisis. Unlike traditional psychotherapy, in which sessions are spaced out and treatment is provided on a more leisurely long-term basis, crisis intervention recognizes the immediacy of the patient's state of mind. The patient may be immediately hospitalized, given medical treatment, and seen by a psychiatric team for two to four hours every day until the person is stabilized and the immediate crisis has passed. In these sessions, the team is very active not only in working with the patient but also in taking charge of the person's personal, social, and professional life outside of the psychiatric facility. Many suicide intervention strategies have been developed through clinical work rather than research because the nature of suicide demands immediate action (Bryan & Rudd, 2006). Waiting for empirical studies is not a luxury the clinician can afford. Figure 9.3 summarizes the process of assessing risk and determining lethality.

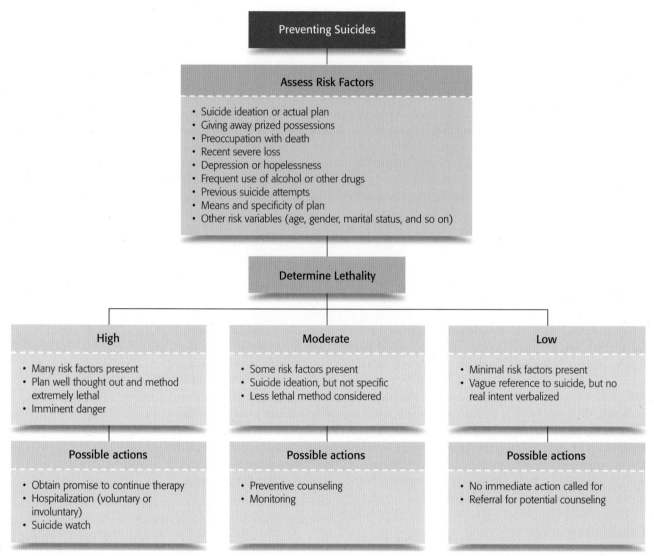

Figure 9.3

THE PROCESS OF PREVENTING SUICIDE

Suicide prevention involves the careful assessment of risk factors to determine lethality—the probability that a person will choose to end his or her life. Working with a potentially suicidal individual is a three-step process that involves (1) knowing what factors are highly correlated with suicide; (2) determining whether there is high, moderate, or low probability that the person will act on the wish; and (3) implementing appropriate actions.

After patients return to a more stable emotional state and the immediate risk of suicide has passed, they are then given more traditional forms of treatment, either on an inpatient or outpatient basis. In addition to the intense therapy they receive from the psychiatric team, relatives and friends may be enlisted to help monitor patients when they leave the hospital. In these cases, the responsible relatives or friends are provided with specific guidelines about how to deal with the patient between treatment team contacts, whom to notify should problems arise outside of the hospital, and so forth.

Suicide Prevention Centers

Crisis intervention can be highly successful if a potentially suicidal patient is either already being treated by a therapist or has come to the attention of one through the efforts of concerned family or friends. Many people in acute distress, however, are not formally being treated. Although contact with a mental health agency may be highly desirable, many people are unaware of the services available to them. Recognizing that suicidal crises may occur at any time and that preventive assistance on a much larger scale may be needed, a number of communities have established suicide prevention centers.

Telephone Crisis Intervention

Suicide prevention centers typically operate twenty-four hours a day, seven days a week. Because most suicide contacts are by phone, a well-publicized telephone number is made available throughout the community for calls at any time of the day or night. Furthermore, many centers provide inpatient or outpatient crisis treatment. Those that lack such resources develop cooperative programs with other community mental health facilities. Most telephone hot lines are staffed by paraprofessionals. All workers have been exposed to crisis situations under supervision and have been trained in crisis intervention techniques such as the following:

1. *Maintain contact and establish a relationship.* The skilled worker who establishes a good relationship with the suicidal caller not only increases the caller's chances of working out an alternative solution but also can exert more influence. Thus, it is important for the worker to show interest, concern, and self-assurance.

2. *Obtain necessary information.* The worker elicits demographic data and the caller's name and address. This information is very valuable in case an urgent need arises to locate the caller.

3. *Evaluate suicidal potential.* The staff person taking the call must quickly determine the seriousness of the caller's self-destructive intent. Most centers use lethality rating scales to help the worker determine suicide potential. These usually contain questions on age, gender, onset of symptoms, situational plight, prior suicidal behavior, and the communication qualities of the caller. Staffers also elicit other demographic and specific information that might provide clues to lethality, such as the information discussed in the section on clues to suicidal intent.

4. *Clarify the nature of the stress and focal problem.* The worker must help callers to clarify the exact nature of their stress, to recognize that they may be under so much duress that their thinking may be confused and impaired, and to realize that there are other solutions besides suicide. Callers are often disoriented, so the worker must be specific to help bring them back to reality.

5. *Assess strengths and resources.* In working out a therapeutic plan, the worker can often mobilize a caller's strengths or available resources. In their agitation, suicidal people tend to forget their own strengths. Their feelings of helplessness are so overwhelming that helping them recognize what they can do about a situation is important. The worker explores the caller's personal resources (family, friends, coworkers), professional resources (doctors, clergy, therapists, lawyers), and community resources (clinics, hospitals, social agencies).

6. *Recommend and initiate an action plan.* Besides being supportive, the worker is highly directive in recommending a course of action. Whether the recommendation entails immediately seeing the person, calling the person's family, or referring the person to a social agency the next day, the worker presents a plan of action and outlines it step by step.

This list implies a rigid sequence, but in fact both the approach and the order of the steps are adjusted to fit the needs of the individual caller.

Today, approximately two hundred suicide prevention centers function in the United States, along with numerous "suicide hot lines" in mental health clinics. Little research has been done on their effectiveness, however, and many of their clients want to remain anonymous. Despite this lack, there is always the

Geri Engberg Photography/The Image Works

Intervening Before It's Too Late

Suicide prevention centers (SPCs) operate twenty-four hours a day, seven days a week, and have well-publicized telephone numbers because most contacts are made by phone. Even though there is controversy about SPC effectiveness, the mental health profession continues to support these centers.

possibility that suicide prevention centers do help. Because life is precious, the mental health profession continues to support them.

■ The Right to Suicide: Moral, Ethical, and Legal Issues

The following letter captured worldwide attention on September 23, 2003, when a twenty-one-year-old paraplegic, Vincent Humbert, wrote a special appeal to French President Jacques Chirac asking to end his own life:

Case Study

Mr. Chirac,

My respects to you, Mr. President.

My name is Vincent Humbert, I am 21. I was in a traffic accident on 24 September 2000. I spent nine months in a coma. I am currently in Helio-Marins hospital in Berck, in the Pas-de-Calais region.

All my vital organs were affected, except for my hearing and my brain, which allows me a little comfort.

I can move my right hand very slightly, putting pressure with my thumb on each letter of the alphabet. These letters make up words and the words form sentences. This is my only method of communication. I currently have a nurse beside me, who spells me the alphabet separating vowels and consonants.

This is how I have decided to write you. The doctors have decided to send me to a specialised clinic. You have the right of pardon and I am asking you for the right to die.

I would like to do this clearly for myself but especially for my mother; she has left her old life to be by my side, here in Berck, working morning and evening after visiting me, seven days out of seven, without a day of rest. And all this to be able to pay the rent for her miserable studio flat.

For the moment she is still young. But in a few years, she will not be able to keep up such a pace of work, that is to say she will not be able to pay her rent and so will be obliged to go back to her apartment in Normandy.

But it is impossible to imagine my remaining here without her by my side, and I think that all patients who are sound of mind are responsible for their actions and have the right to want to continue to live or to die.

I would like you to know that you are my last chance. You should also know that I was a fellow citizen without a history, without any judicial record, a sportsman and a volunteer fireman.

I do not deserve a scenario as terrible as this and I hope that you will read this letter, which is specially addressed to you.

Please accept, Mr. President, my warmest compliments.

In September 2003, after the release of his book *I Ask the Right to Die,* Vincent Humbert's mother administered an overdose of sedatives into his intravenous line, causing his death (Smith, 2003). The case of Vincent Humbert set off a national debate about the morality and legality of euthanasia.

Do people have the right to end their lives if their continued existence would result in psychological and physical deterioration? Surveys of the American public indicate that a majority believe terminally ill individuals should be allowed to take their own lives; in a 1995 survey of physicians working with AIDS patients, over half indicated that they have prescribed lethal doses of narcotics to suicidal patients (Clay, 1997; Drane, 1995). Advocates contend that people should be allowed the choice of dying in a dignified manner, particularly if they suffer from a terminal or severely incapacitating illness that would cause misery for their families and friends (Rosenfeld, 2004).

The act of suicide seems to violate much of what we have been taught regarding the sanctity of life. Many segments of the population consider it immoral and provide strong religious sanctions against it. Suicide is both a sin in the canonical law of the Catholic Church and an illegal act according to the secular laws of most countries. Within the United States, many states have laws against suicide. Of course, such laws are difficult to enforce because the victims are not around to prosecute.

Many are beginning to question the legitimacy of such sanctions, however, and are openly advocating a person's right to suicide. In November 1998, Oregon voters passed a physician-assisted suicide act granting physicians the legal right to help end the lives of terminally ill patients. In 2001, however, U.S. Attorney General John Ashcroft issued a directive intended to overturn the law. In October 2005, the United States Supreme Court ruled 6-3 in favor of upholding the law. Since its passage until 2008, 401 patients have used the act. The average age of patients was 70, with 81.8 percent suffering from malignant neoplasms (cancer), and all involved ingestion of lethal medication. No complications were reported.

Did You Know?

Thomas Szasz (1986) is an outspoken critic of suicide prevention programs. He argues that suicide is an act of a moral agent who is ultimately responsible. Szasz opposes coercive methods (such as involuntary hospitalization) that mental health professionals use to prevent suicide. By taking such actions, Szasz claims practitioners have identified themselves as foes of individual liberty and responsibility.

Recent legislation has intensified the debate over whether it is morally, ethically, and legally permissible to allow relatives, friends, or physicians to provide support, means, and actions to carry out a suicide (Rosenfeld, 2004). Two high-profile individuals have fueled the debate by virtue of their actions. Derek Humphrey, former director of the Hemlock Society (an organization that advocates people's right to end their lives), published a best-selling book, *Final Exit* (1991). It is a manual that provides practical information, such as drug dosages needed to end one's life; when published, it created a national stir. Another individual who has become a household name is Dr. Jack Kevorkian, a physician who has helped nearly 130 people to end their own lives using a device he calls a "suicide machine." Those who see Kevorkian as a courageous physician willing to help others in their search for a dignified death call him a savior; those who oppose his actions refer to him as "Dr. Death."

Ironically, the success of medical science has added fuel to the right-to-die movement. As a part of our remarkably successful efforts to prolong life, this society has also begun to prolong the process of dying. And this prolongation has caused many elderly or terminally ill people to fear the medical decision maker who is intent only on keeping them alive, giving no thought to their desires or dignity. They and many others find it abhorrent to impose on a dying patient a horrifying array of respirators, breathing tubes, feeding tubes, and repeated violent cardiopulmonary resuscitations—procedures that are often futile and against the wishes of the patient and his or her family. Humane and sensitive physicians, who believe that the resulting quality of life will not merit such heroic measures, but whose training impels them to sustain life, are caught in the middle of this conflict. A civil or criminal lawsuit may be brought against the physician who agrees to allow a patient to die.

Proponents of the right to suicide believe that it can be a rational act and that mental health and medical professionals should be allowed to help such patients without fear of legal or professional repercussions. Others argue, however, that suicide is not rational, that many suffer from a mental disorder, or that determining rationality is fraught with hazards. Some are voicing the fear that one result of legalizing suicide may be that patients will fall victim to coercion from relatives intent either on collecting inheritances or on convincing patients that they will overburden their loved ones and friends or become a financial drain on them. Other critics of assisted suicide fear that in this time of medical cost control, medical professionals might encourage the terminally ill to choose to die and that those who are poor and disadvantaged would receive the most encouragement.

Do People Have a Right to Die?

On November 22, 1998, over 15 million viewers of *60 Minutes* watched in either horror or sadness the death by lethal injection of fifty-two-year-old Thomas Youk. This was not, however, a death sentence carried out for a murder conviction but the enactment of a conscious desire and decision of a man suffering from the latter stages of Lou Gehrig's disease.

Youk's wife stated she was "so grateful to know that someone would relieve him of his suffering. . . . I consider it the way things should be done." The man who videotaped the event was Dr. Jack Kevorkian, a retired physician, who has carried on a ten-year battle with the U.S. legal system and society over the right to die.

It is estimated that since 1989 Kevorkian had assisted in the suicides of nearly 130 people (most of them women) with chronic debilitating diseases. The means of death was Kevorkian's "suicide machine," composed of bottles containing chemicals that could be fed intravenously into the arm of the person. The solution could bring instantaneous unconsciousness and quick painless death. His first client, Mrs. J. Adkins, suffered from Alzheimer's disease. She did not want to put her family through the agony of the disease, believed that she had a right to choose death, stated that her act was that of a rational mind, and had the consent of her husband. Many others whom Kevorkian helped commit suicide did not have diseases that threatened to kill them in the immediate future.

Before the CBS taping, charges of homicide had been brought against Kevorkian four previous times, and in each case either the charges were ultimately dropped or he was found innocent. Because of his actions, a Michigan law outlawing "physician-assisted suicides" was passed and used to charge him with manslaughter. Prosecutors contended that Kevorkian's actions in the death of Youk went far beyond what many consider "assistance." Because Thomas Youk was too weak to administer the dose himself, Kevorkian administered it for him. For that act, in 1999, the retired physician was charged with and convicted of second-degree murder, criminal assistance to a suicide, and delivery of a controlled substance. After serving eight years in prison, he was released in 2007 because of failing health, after promising not to engage in assisted suicides.

Carlos Osorio/epa/Corbis

Fighting for the Right to Choose

Dr. Jack Kevorkian, a Michigan physician, was a lifelong advocate who fought for the repeal of laws against assisted suicide. Convicted of second-degree murder of Thomas Youk, who suffered from Lou Gehrig's disease, Kevorkian was released in June 2007 after serving eight years of his sentence. He died in 2011.

For Further Consideration

1. Did Thomas Youk have a right to end his own life? What reasons led you to your answer? Does a doctor—or, for that matter, anyone—have a right to help others terminate their lives?
2. What might motivate someone like Dr. Kevorkian to risk censure and imprisonment to help others to die? Would you be in favor of legislation that would legalize physician-assisted suicides? Why or why not?

Major problems also exist in defining the subjective terms *quality of life* and *quality of humanness* as the criteria for deciding between life and death. At what point do we consider the quality of life sufficiently poor to justify terminating it? Should people who have been severely injured or scarred (through loss of limbs, paralysis, blindness, or brain injury) be allowed to end their own lives? What about mentally retarded or emotionally disturbed people? Could it be argued that their quality of life is equally poor? Moreover, who decides whether a person is terminally ill? There are many recorded cases of "incurable" patients who recovered when new medical techniques or treatments arrested, remitted, or cured their illnesses.

Such questions deal with ethics and human values, and they cannot be answered easily. Yet the mental health practitioner cannot avoid these questions. Like their medical counterparts, clinicians are trained to save people's lives. They have accepted the philosophical assumption that life is better than death and that no one has a right to take his or her own life. Strong social, religious, and legal sanctions support this belief. Therapists work not only with terminally ill clients who wish to take their own lives but also with disturbed clients who may have suicidal tendencies. These latter clients are not terminally ill but may be suffering severe emotional or physical pain; their deaths would bring immense pain and suffering to their loved ones. Moreover, as noted previously, most people who attempt suicide do not want to die, are ambivalent about the act, or find that their suicidal urges pass when their life situations improve.

Clearly, suicide and suicide prevention involve a number of important social and legal issues, as well as the personal value systems of clients and their families, mental health professionals, and those who devise and enforce our laws (Rosenfeld, 2004). And just as clearly, we need to know much more about the causes of suicide and the detection of people who are at high risk for suicide, as well as the most effective means of intervention (Rudd et al., 2004). Life is precious, and we need to do everything possible, within reason, to protect it.

Summary

1. What do we know about suicide?

   - Suicide is the intentional, direct, and conscious taking of one's own life. In the past, it has often been kept hidden, and relatives and friends of the victim did not speak of it. Mental health professionals now realize that understanding the causes of suicide is extremely important.
   - Much is known about the *facts* of suicide, but little about the reasons is understood. Men are more likely to kill themselves than women, although the latter make more attempts; the elderly are at high risk for suicides; religious affiliation, marital status, and ethnicity all influence suicides; and firearms are the most frequent method used.

2. What are the major explanations of suicide?

   - In keeping with the multipath model, suicides appear to be an interaction of biological, psychological, social, and sociocultural factors.
   - More recent evidence has indicated that biological factors may be important: Genetics and biochemical factors are implicated in suicides.
   - Psychological factors include mental disturbance, depression, hopelessness, and excessive alcohol consumption; all are highly correlated with suicide.
   - Lack of positive social relationships can lead to feelings of loneliness and disconnection. The elderly are prone to the loss of loved ones and friends, and divorce or lack of a life partner increases the chances of suicide.
   - Sociocultural factors such as race, culture, ethnicity, social class, gender, and other such demographic variables can either increase or decrease the risk of suicide.
   - The complex relationship between these four dimensions and suicide is not simply one of cause and effect but of an interaction among them.

3. Who are the victims of suicide?

   - In recent years, childhood and adolescent suicides have increased at an alarming rate. A lack of research has limited our understanding of why children take their own lives.
   - Many people tend to become depressed about "feeling old" as they age, and depressed elderly people often think about suicide.

4. How can we intervene or prevent suicides?

- Perhaps the best way to prevent suicide is to recognize its signs and intervene before it occurs. People are more likely to commit suicide if they are older, male, have a history of attempts, describe in detail how the act will be accomplished, and give verbal hints that they are planning self-destruction.

- Crisis intervention concepts and techniques have been used successfully to treat clients who contemplate suicide. Intensive short-term therapy is used to stabilize the immediate crisis.

- Suicide prevention centers operate twenty-four hours a day to provide intervention services to all potential suicides, especially people who are not undergoing treatment. Telephone hot lines are staffed by well-trained paraprofessionals who work with anyone who is contemplating suicide. In addition, these centers provide preventive education to the public.

5. Are there times and situations in which suicide should be an option?

- This question is difficult to answer, particularly when the person is terminally ill and wishes to end his or her suffering. Nevertheless, therapists, like physicians, have been trained to preserve life, and they have a legal obligation to do so.

Media Resources

Psychology CourseMate   Access an interactive eBook, chapter-specific interactive learning tools, including flash cards, quizzes, videos and more in your Psychology CourseMate, accessed through CengageBrain.com.

CENGAGENOW

CengageNow   CengageNOW is an easy-to-use online resource that helps you study in less time to get the grade you want—NOW. If your textbook does not include an access code card, go to CengageBrain.com to gain access.

CENGAGE brain.com

CengageBrain   More than just an interactive study guide, WebTutor is an anytime, anywhere customized learning solution with an eBook, keeping you connected to your textbook, instructor, and classmates. Purchase the access chosen by your instructor at CengageBrain.com.

Eating Disorders

I'm not anorexic, I do eat. Three meals a day, almost every day. Breakfast, lunch, dinner. So I tell myself, my friends, my parents, my boyfriend, I'm OK. "How can you accuse me? You see me eat, I'm not starving myself." It's amazing how much lettuce you can eat and keep below 100 calories, the soups you can make at 50–100 calories per serving. The meals you can make and show people you eat to calm them down. I'm a master at these meals. "I'm not anorexic, I do eat." I'm 5'6" and 99 pounds. I know I'm skinny. I look at myself in the mirror, find the fat, find the places where more pounds can be shed, tell myself that I'm not unhealthy, I'm still safe, there is no reason to stop yet. (Anonymous 5, 2008)

I purge about 4 times a day. . . . I have to be skinny, I want to be skinny. . . . I feel guilty and stupid if I don't purge everything out of my stomach. . . . I've learned that after 3 hours it's very difficult to have anything you ate come up. . . . I'm really scared I don't want to die, but I don't know who to go to. . . . I am not skinny, by the way, I am 5'2 and weigh 123 lbs. I get pains in the inside of my stomach like the inside of my rib cage I think I have a problem with my liver. . . . (Anonymous, 2009)

My friends and I put on weight our first semester of college. . . . We ate dinner as a group, trying to stick to salad and grilled chicken, until one of us said "screw it," and we shared a heaping bowl of our favorite makeshift dessert: marshmallow fluff and butter melted in the dining hall microwave and mixed with sugary cereal and chocolate chips. (Kapalko, 2010, p. 1)

Disturbed eating patterns such as bingeing, purging, and excessive dieting, are increasing in frequency. In this chapter we attempt to determine the reasons for the increase in disordered eating patterns and consider the characteristics, associated features, etiology, and treatment of anorexia nervosa, bulimia nervosa, binge-eating disorder, and eating conditions not elsewhere classified (ECNEC). We also cover obesity because it has important serious physical and psychological consequences (Volkow & O'Brien, 2007).

Eating Disorders

Eating disorders and disordered eating patterns are becoming more prevalent in the United States, even among children and adolescents. These behaviors appear to stem from a variety of factors, including dissatisfaction with body weight or shape. In a sample of 4,745 middle

focus questions

1 What kinds of eating disorders exist?

2 What are some causes of eating disorders?

3 What are some treatment options for eating disorders?

4 What causes obesity?

5 What are some treatment options for obesity?

and high school students, many were unhappy with their bodies (41.5 percent of females; 24.9 percent of males) and had self-esteem issues due to body shape or weight (36.4 percent of females; 23.9 percent of males) (Ackard, Fulkerson, & Neumark-Sztainer, 2007). Data from national surveys indicate that nearly 50 percent of adolescent females and 20 percent of adolescent males diet to control their weight. Weight concerns are so great that a reported 13.4 percent of girls and 7.1 percent of boys have engaged in disordered eating patterns (Table 10.1). Factors associated with disordered eating patterns include excess weight, body dissatisfaction, low self-esteem, depression, substance use, and suicidal ideation (Neumark-Sztainer, Hannan, & Stat, 2000; T. D. Wade, 2007). It is unclear whether these factors are the result or the cause of disordered eating.

Paradoxically, the increasing emphasis on thinness, especially for women, is occurring as the population of the United States is becoming heavier. Currently 68 percent of adults and 16 percent of children are overweight or obese (Flegal, Carroll, Ogden, & Curtin, 2010; Wang & Beydoun, 2007). Weight and body shape concerns are common not only among young white females but also among older women and minorities (Gilbert, 2003; McLean, Paxton, & Wertheim, 2010). Rates of eating disorders are also high among Hispanic American and Native American females and are increasing among immigrant and Asian American females (Gilbert, 2003; Lee & Lock, 2007; Sherwood, Harnack, & Story, 2000; Story et al., 1998; Wax, 2000). Although African American women are less likely than white women to have eating disorders, there is some indication that incidence rates are increasing (Talleyrand, 2006).

Although overeating and being overweight are more socially acceptable for men than for women, there is evidence of increasing body dissatisfaction in males. Some men demonstrate behaviors associated with anorexia, such as exercising excessively and obsessively monitoring their weight (Boodman, 2007). Dennis Quaid, the actor, lost 40 pounds to play a movie role and then kept his weight low. He termed his condition "manorexia." Similarly, actor Billy Bob Thornton battled anorexia, losing 59 pounds. Weight dissatisfaction in adolescent boys and college males often revolves around a desire to be heavier and more muscular (Farquhar & Wasylkiw, 2007; Ricciardelli & McCabe, 2004). In a cross-cultural study involving college men in Germany, France, and the United States (Pope et al., 2000), images of men differing in size and muscularity were shown to a group of research participants. The males were asked to choose images that represented their own bodies, the bodies they would like to have, the body of an average man their age, and the male body they thought women preferred. In all three countries, the men picked an ideal body that was about twenty-eight pounds more muscular than their own. The participants also believed that women preferred a male body thirty pounds more muscular than their current bodies. In actuality, women indicated a preference for an ordinary male body without added muscle. Extreme dissatisfaction with one's muscularity in men is called muscle dysphoria (Murray, Rieger, Touyz, & De la Garza Garcia, 2010).

The body dissatisfaction displayed by both men and women may be due to social comparison processes involving media images of body types that few can achieve. A

TABLE 10.1   Prevalence of Weight Concerns of Youth in Grades 5–12

	Females	Males
Very important not to be overweight	68.5%	54.3%
Ever been on a diet	45.4%	20.2%
Diet recommended by parent	14.5%	13.6%
Diet to "look better"	88.5%	62.2%
Engage in binge/purge behaviors	13.4%	7.1%
Binge/purge at least once a day	8.9%	4.1%

Source: Data from national survey of 6,728 adolescents (Neumark-Sztainer et al., 2000)

muscle dysphoria   extreme dissatisfaction with one's muscularity

study of advertisements in *Sports Illustrated* magazine from 1975 to 2005 revealed that male bodies were increasingly muscular and lean. Male adolescents or college age men exposed to these types of images demonstrate more negative self-evaluations (Farquhar & Wasylkiw, 2007; Hobza & Rochlen, 2009). Perhaps the emphasis on the male body is responsible for the finding that more than 1 percent of 8th and 10th graders, and 2.5 percent of 12th grader males had illicitly used anabolic steroids during the past year (Johnston, Bachman, O'Malley, & Schulenberg, 2011) and that between 6 and 7 percent of males between the ages of fifteen and eighteen reported taking steroids to gain more muscle mass (Kanayama, Pope, & Hudson, 2001).

Disordered eating patterns because of preoccupation with weight and body dimensions sometimes become extreme and lead to an eating disorder—anorexia nervosa, bulimia nervosa, or binge-eating disorder (Table 10.2). The lifetime prevalence rates for anorexia nervosa, bulimia nervosa, and binge-eating disorder are 0.9 percent, 1.5 percent, and 3.5 percent, respectively, for women and 0.3 percent, 0.5 percent, and 2 percent, respectively, for men (Hudson, Hiripi, Pope, & Kessler, 2007). In addition, up to 60 percent of individuals treated in eating disorder programs suffer from disordered eating that does not quite meet the criteria for the other eating disorders (Fairburn et al., 2007; Dalle Grave & Calugi, 2007).

MYTH Females and males can accurately judge the body shape preferred by members of the opposite sex.

REALITY Female heterosexuals desire a body shape that is thinner than the female body type preferred by heterosexual males, while male heterosexuals desire a more muscular body than that preferred by heterosexual females.

MYTH VS. REALITY

Anorexia Nervosa

Case Study

Portia DeGeneres, known for her starring roles in the television shows *Ally McBeal*, *Arrested Development*, and *Better Off Ted* weighed 82 pounds in her mid-twenties. She reports eating only 300 calories per day, taking up to 20 laxatives a day, and exercising for hours. In her autobiography, *Unbearable Lightness: A Story of Loss and Gain*, Portia recounts wanting to be a model. The thin standard became even more important as her acting career took off. She became consumed with bingeing, purging, exercising, dieting, and laxatives. She received a "wake-up call" when her brother broke down and said he was afraid she was going to die. When she collapsed on a movie set, her doctors said her organs were close to failing. These events helped her make changes in her life. With the development of self-confidence, self-acceptance, and coming out as a lesbian, Portia now maintains a normal weight (de Rossi, 2010).

Anorexia nervosa is characterized by a refusal to maintain a body weight above the minimum normal weight for one's age and height; an intense fear of becoming obese that does not diminish with weight loss; body image distortion; and undue self-evaluation based on weight or body shape. Individuals with this puzzling disorder literally engage in self-starvation; they weigh themselves repeatedly and eat only small quantities of certain low-calorie foods (National Institute of Mental Health [NIMH], 2007d).

Although anorexia nervosa has been recognized for more than one hundred years, it is receiving increased attention due to greater public knowledge of the disorder and the apparent increase in its incidence. The disorder occurs primarily in adolescent girls and young women, although 25 percent of those with this condition are male (Hudson, Hiripi, Pope, & Kessler, 2007). Anorexia nervosa is associated with serious medical complications. The mortality rate is six times higher than that of the general population due to suicide, substance abuse, and the physiological effects of starvation (Andersen, 2007; Papadopoulous, Ekbom, Brandt, & Ekselius, 2009). A very frightening characteristic of anorexia nervosa is that most people with this disorder, even when clearly emaciated, continue to insist they are overweight. Some may acknowledge that

anorexia nervosa an eating disorder characterized by low body weight, an intense fear of becoming obese, and body image distortion

DISORDERS CHART   EATING DISORDERS

TABLE 10.2

Eating Disorders	Symptoms	Prevalence and Gender Differences	Age of Onset
Anorexia Nervosa Types: • Restricting • Binge Eating/ Purging	• Restricted caloric intake resulting in body weight significantly below the minimum normal weight for one's age and height • Intense fear of becoming obese, which does not diminish even with weight loss • Body image distortion (not recognizing one's thinness) or self-evaluation unduly influenced by weight	More than 90% are white females; 0.5% to 0.9% prevalence rate	Usually after puberty or late adolescence
Bulimia Nervosa Types: • Purging • Nonpurging	• Recurrent episodes of binge eating • Loss of control of eating behavior when bingeing • Use of vomiting, exercise, laxatives, or dieting to control weight • One or more binges a week, occurring for three or more months • Excess concern with body weight and shape	More than 90% are white females; 1–2% prevalence rate	Late adolescence or early adulthood
Binge-Eating Disorder	• Recurrent episodes of binge eating • Loss of control of eating when bingeing • No regular use of inappropriate compensatory activities to control weight • Binge eating occurs one or more times a week for three months • Concern about the effect of bingeing on body shape and weight • Marked distress over binge eating	1.5 times more prevalent in females than males; about 30% in weight control clinics have this disorder; 0.7–4% prevalence rate	Late adolescence or early 20s

Source: Data from American Psychiatric Association, (2011); Hudson, Hiripi, Pope, & Kessler, (2007); Walsh & Devlin (1998)

they are thin but maintain that some parts of their bodies are "too fat." They may believe that weight loss is a sign of achievement and that gaining weight is a failure of self-control. One eighteen-year-old woman with anorexia nervosa vomited up to ten times daily, took laxatives, and exercised four hours each day. Yet when her friends said, "You look sick," or "You need to eat," she viewed their comments as a sign of jealousy (Tarkan, 1998). Peers sometimes inadvertently provide reinforcement by expressing admiration for thinness. One woman, Rachel, hid her starving body under layers of bulky clothing. Some of her friends commented positively on her figure, which increased her determination to starve (Holahan, 2001). In most cases, the body image disturbance is profound. As one researcher noted more than thirty years ago, people with this disorder "vigorously defend their often gruesome emaciation as not being too thin. . . . They identify with the skeleton-like appearance, actively maintain it, and deny its abnormality" (Bruch, 1978, p. 209).

Subtypes of Anorexia Nervosa
There are two subtypes of anorexia nervosa: the restricting type and the binge-eating/purging type. The restricting type accomplishes weight loss through dieting or exercising. The binge-eating/purging type loses weight through the use of self-induced vomiting, laxatives, or diuretics, often after binge eating. In one study of 105 individuals hospitalized with anorexia, 53 percent had lost weight through constant fasting (restricting type); the remainder had periodically resorted to binge eating followed by vomiting (binge-eating/purging type). Although both groups vigorously pursued thinness, they differed in some aspects. Those with restricting anorexia were more introverted and tended to deny feelings of hunger or psychological distress. Those with the binge-eating/purging type were more extroverted. They reported more anxiety, depression, and guilt; admitted more frequently to having a strong appetite; and tended to be older (Halmi et al., 2000).

Physical Complications

Self-starvation produces a variety of physical complications. Individuals with anorexia often exhibit cardiac arrhythmias because of electrolyte imbalance; most have low blood pressure and slow heart rates. They may be lethargic, have dry skin and brittle hair, exhibit hypothermia, and show enlargement of the salivary glands (from purging) with a resultant chipmunk-like face (NIMH, 2007d). One woman had to wear heavy clothing even when the temperature was over ninety degrees (Bryant, 2001). Portia DeGeneres has osteoporosis and cirrhosis of the liver and was near death with borderline organ failure as a result of her self-starvation. Bone loss also occurs as a result of low caloric intake (Olmos et al., 2010). In addition, the heart muscle is often damaged and weakened because the body may use muscles as a source of protein during starvation. Unfortunately, even with the severe health and emotional damage associated with the disorder, support groups advocating anorexia as a lifestyle choice have appeared on the Internet (Wilson et al., 2006). In fact, eating disorders are sometimes referred to as a "gift" and not a problematic illness (Borzekowski, Schenk, Wilson, & Peebles, 2010, p. 1528).

Course and Outcome

The course of anorexia nervosa is highly variable, with some recovering after one episode, others showing a fluctuating pattern of weight gain and relapse, and others having a chronic and deteriorating course (American Psychiatric Association, 2006). In a five-year follow-up study of ninety-five female adolescents and adults with anorexia, 59 percent of the participants initially had the restricting type and 41 percent the binge-eating/purging type. At follow-up, more than 50 percent no longer had a diagnosable eating disorder, although most still showed disturbed eating patterns, poor body image, and psychosocial difficulties (Ben-Tovim et al., 2001). A study of Finnish women with anorexia nervosa was even more promising. The five-year recovery rate (recovery as evidenced by absence of bingeing and purging, restoration of weight, and menstruation for at least one year) showed that two-thirds had reached either complete or nearly complete recovery, resembling healthy women in weight and on psychological measures (Keski-Rahkonen et al., 2007).

Associated Characteristics

A number of mental disorders and conditions (depression, anxiety, impulse control problems, loss of sexual interest, and substance use) occur concurrently with anorexia nervosa (Hudson, Hiripi, Pope, & Kessler, 2007; Pinheiro et al., 2010). Women with anorexia nervosa often strive for perfection and control over some aspect of their lives: "I'm not eating now and it's kind of a control thing. . . . At least I have control over what I'm eating" (Budd, 2007, p. 100). Another individual noted, "Nothing could prevent my will from controlling my body" (Segall, 2001, p. 22).

Obsessive-compulsive behaviors and thoughts that may or may not involve food or exercise are often reported (Rogers & Petrie, 2001). For example, one woman worried that touching or even breathing around food would cause her to gain weight (Bulik & Kendler, 2000). The manner in which these symptoms are related to anorexia nervosa is unclear because of the possibility that malnutrition or starvation may cause or exacerbate obsessive symptoms. The actor Billy Bob Thornton, however, reports engaging in repetitive, compulsive rituals long before developing anorexia.

Personality disorders and other characteristics have been linked to anorexia nervosa, although the restricting and binge-eating/purging types differ in the characteristics with which they are linked. As noted earlier, the restricting type tends to display traits of introversion, conformity, perfectionism, and rigidity, whereas the bingeing/purging type is more likely to be associated with extroverted, histrionic, emotionally volatile personalities; impulse control problems; and substance abuse. Interpreting these relationships has been difficult, as they could (1) represent the misfortune of having two or more disorders by

© Capital Pictures

Portia DeGeneres

Portia DeGeneres' eating disorder had its roots in attempting to meet an idealized standard of beauty and turmoil over her sexual identity. During this difficult period, she was able to control one area of her life—her eating. Before overcoming anorexia, her weight dropped to 82 pounds. At the time, she believed her weight loss was a demonstration of her "will power"—an accomplishment that nearly killed her.

Anorexia's Web

Drink ice-cold water ("Your body has to burn calories to keep your temperature up") and hot water with bouillon cubes ("only 5 calories a cube, and they taste wonderful") (Springen, 2006, p. 1).

"Starvation is fulfilling. Colors become brighter, sounds sharper, odors so much more savory and penetrating. . . . The greatest enjoyment of food is actually found when never a morsel passes the lips" (Irizarry, 2004).

"I will be thin, at all costs, it is the most important thing, nothing else matters" (Ana Creed; Bardone-Cone & Cass, 2007).

Tips to reduce caloric intake, testimonials on the satisfaction of not eating, and rules to remain thin are part of pro-ana (anorexia) and pro-mia (bulimia) Web sites. These Web sites are easy to access, present information in a manner targeting younger populations, and primarily contain pro-anorexia and pro-bulimia content (Borzekowski, Schenk, Wilson, & Peebles, 2010). Some of the nicknames used in online discussion groups include "thinspiration," "puking pals," "disappearing acts," "anorexiangel," and "chunkee monkee." Web anorexia support group members contend that ultra-thin models and celebrities are fine at their weight and do not need to be treated for eating disorders.

The Web sites include pictures of ultra-thin girls and women, tips for dieting, and ways to conceal thinness from family members and friends. They provide a circle of friends and encouragement. In one study, 43 percent of those who visited the Web sites indicated that they received emotional support. "I kind of lost all of my friends at school and in my neighborhood but I still have my pro-ana and pro-mia friends" (Csipke & Horne, 2007, p. 202). In response to before and after (thinner) pictures, one person wrote: "You're my thinspiration! How did you do it?" Another responded, "Your collarbones are beautiful—nice job" (Hayley, 2004, p. 1). Participants on the Anorexic Nation Web site talk about how it is important to have friends who are like them and argue that anorexia is a lifestyle choice and not an illness. A woman on one site writes, "I am very much for anorexia and this webpage is a reflection of that. If you are recovered or recovering from an eating disorder, please, please, PLEASE do not visit my site. I can almost guarantee it will trigger you! But if you are like me and your eating disorder is your best friend and you aren't ready to give it up, please continue" (Hellmich, 2001, p. 3).

Such Web sites are visited by thousands of people each day and used frequently by adolescents with eating disorders, who reported learning new weight loss and purging methods (Wilson et al., 2006). Medical experts are deeply concerned that the sites are increasing the incidence of eating-disorder cases, especially among susceptible individuals. Judy Sargent, who is recovering from anorexia, says, "These sites don't tell you that you're going to die if you don't get treatment" ("Anorexia's Web," 2001, p. 2). Organizations dedicated to the prevention and treatment of eating disorders are alarmed by these sites and have petitioned Yahoo! and other hosts to remove the forums; however, many sites simply switched to other servers. In fact, in a one-year period (from 2006 to 2007), there was a 470 percent increase in pro-ana and pro-mia

Anorexic Nation

websites (International Internet Trends Study, 2008). Although individuals with eating disorders generally gain a feeling of support when visiting these Web sites, how much danger do they pose to those with and without eating disorders? Should pro-ana and pro-mia Web sites be banned?

chance, (2) indicate that anorexia is an expression of a personality disorder, or (3) be the result of common environmental or genetic factors that underlie both anorexia and the personality disorder (Westen & Harnden-Fischer, 2001).

Bulimia Nervosa

Case Study

"At first, after eating too much, I would just go to the toilet and make myself sick. I hadn't heard of bulimia. . . . I started eating based on how I was feeling about myself. If my hair looked bad, I'd stuff down loads of candy. After a while,

I started exercising excessively because I felt so guilty about eating. I'd run for miles and miles and go to the gym for three hours." (Dirmann, 2003, p. 60)

Bulimia nervosa is an eating disorder characterized by recurrent episodes of binge eating (the rapid consumption of large quantities of food) at least once a week for three months, during which the person loses control over eating. Two subtypes exist: the purging type, in which the individual regularly vomits or uses laxatives, diuretics, or enemas; and the nonpurging type, in which excessive exercise or fasting are used in an attempt to compensate for binges. A persistent focus on body image and weight also characterizes this disorder. Eating episodes sometimes continue until abdominal pain develops or vomiting is induced (American Psychiatric Association, 2011). Individuals with bulimia nervosa judge themselves almost exclusively on their eating and in terms of body shape and weight. They have maladaptive beliefs such as "I am a failure because I am fat" (Jones, Leung, & Harris, 2007). Compared with women of similar weight but without the disorder, women with bulimia exhibited more psychopathology, a greater external locus of control, lower self-esteem, and a lower sense of personal effectiveness (Shisslak, Pazda, & Crago, 1990; Williams, Taylor, & Ricciardelli, 2000).

Those with bulimia realize that their eating patterns are not normal and are frustrated by that knowledge. They become disgusted and ashamed of their eating and hide it from others. The binges, characterized by rapid consumption of food, typically occur in private. Some eat nothing during the day but lose control and binge in the late afternoon or evening. A loss of self-control when eating is characteristic of this disorder, resulting in difficulty curtailing eating once a binge has begun. When the consequences of binge eating are controlled through vomiting or the use of laxatives, this temporary relief from physical discomfort and fear of gaining weight is often followed by feelings of shame and despair. Those with the nonpurging type of bulimia often follow overeating episodes with a commitment to a severely restrictive diet, fasting, or engaging in excessive exercising or physical activity (NIMH, 2007d).

Bulimia is much more prevalent than anorexia. The lifetime prevalence rate for bulimia nervosa, which often begins in adolescence, involves almost 2 percent of women (Hudson, Hiripi, Pope, & Kessler, 2007; Van Hoeken, Seidell, & Hoek, 2003). An additional 10 percent of women report some symptoms but do not meet all the criteria for the diagnosis. The incidence of bulimia appears to be increasing and is especially prevalent in urban areas. Fewer males exhibit the disorder, presumably because there is less cultural pressure for them to remain thin, although up to 25 percent of those affected by this disorder are males (Hudson, Hiripi, Pope, & Kessler, 2007).

Most of those diagnosed with bulimia are of normal weight (Mehler, 2003). Of a sample of forty women with the disorder, twenty-five were of normal weight, two were overweight, one was obese, and twelve were underweight. These women averaged about twelve binges per week, and the estimated calories consumed in a binge could be as high as 11,500. Typical binge foods were ice cream, candy, bread or toast, and donuts (Gordon, 2001).

Physical Complications

As noted earlier, people with bulimia use a variety of measures—fasting, self-induced vomiting, diet pills, laxatives, and exercise—to control the weight gain that accompanies binge eating. Side effects and complications may result from self-induced vomiting or from the excessive use of laxatives. The effects of vomiting include erosion of tooth

Did You Know?

In 2009, millions of Americans underwent cosmetic procedures to enhance their appearance. How many of these procedures may be an attempt to achieve standards of beauty portrayed by the media?

- Liposuction: 198,251
- Breast augmentation and lift: 376,714
- Blepharoplasty (cosmetic eye surgery): 203,309
- Abdominoplasty (tummy tuck): 115,191
- Nose reshaping: 256,000
- Botox injections: 4,795,357

Source: American Society of Plastic Surgeons, (2010)

bulimia nervosa an eating disorder characterized by recurrent episodes of the rapid consumption of large quantities of food and a sense of loss of control over eating that is combined with purging (vomiting, use of laxatives, diuretics, or enemas), and/or excessive exercise or fasting in an attempt to compensate for binges

enamel from vomited stomach acid; dehydration; swollen salivary glands, which produces a puffy facial appearance; and lowered potassium, which can weaken the heart and cause arrhythmia and cardiac arrest (American Dietetic Association, 2001; Nashoni, Yaroslavsky, Varticovschi, Weizman, & Stein, 2010). In rare cases, binge eating can cause the stomach to rupture. Other possible gastrointestinal disturbances include inflammation of the esophagus and gastric and rectal irritation.

Associated Features

Individuals with bulimia often use eating as a way of coping with distressing thoughts or external stressors. Women with this disorder tend to be more likely to perceive events as stressful (Peterson et al., 2010). As one woman stated, "Purging was the biggest part of my day. . . . It was my release from the stress and monotony of my life" (Erdely, 2004, p. 117). There appears to be a close relationship between emotional states and disturbed eating. For example, among individuals with bulimia nervosa, the highest rates of binge eating occur during negative emotional states such as anger or depression (Crosby et al., 2009). Weight preoccupation is also related to the type of coping response an individual shows to life stressors. In a nonclinical sample of university women, those who responded emotionally when facing stressful situations (e.g., "Get angry," "Wish I could change what happened") were more preoccupied with weight than women who responded in a task-oriented style (e.g., "Outline my priorities," "Think about how to solve the problem") (Denisoff & Endler, 2000). A task-oriented approach may diminish stress and, therefore, reduce the need to use food to control one's emotional state.

A number of emotional disorders and features are comorbid with bulimia nervosa. Mood disorders are common, and rates of seasonal affective disorder, a syndrome characterized by depression during the dark winter months followed by remission during the spring and summer months, are higher among those with bulimia nervosa than in the general population (Lam et al., 2001). Characteristics of borderline personality, such as impulsivity, substance abuse, and affective instability, are also found in individuals with bulimia nervosa, although many with this disorder show little evidence of personality disturbances. There may be several subtypes of bulimia nervosa with different etiologies (Wonderlich et al., 2007). Interpreting the meaning of coexisting conditions is difficult because characteristics such as depression and borderline personality traits may precede the eating disorder or may be the consequence of the eating disorder.

Course and Outcome

Bulimia nervosa has a somewhat later onset than anorexia nervosa, beginning in late adolescence or early adult life. The mortality and suicide rate for this disorder is relatively high and is similar to that found in anorexia nervosa (Crow et al., 2009a & b). Outcome studies have shown a mixed course, although the prognosis is more positive than for anorexia nervosa. Based on the results of 27 studies of 5,653 individuals with bulimia nervosa, approximately 45 percent showed full recovery, 27 percent considerable improvement, and 23 percent showed little or no improvement. Positive prognostic signs were positive social support and adjustment, whereas high amounts of psychosocial stress and low social status had a negative influence on outcome (Steinhausen & Weber, 2009).

Binge-Eating Disorder

Case Study

Ms. A was a thirty-eight-year-old African American woman who was single, lived alone, and was employed as a personnel manager. She weighed 292 pounds. Her chief reason for coming to the clinic was that she felt her eating was out of control and, as a result, she had gained approximately 80 pounds over the previous year. A typical binge episode consisted of the ingestion of two pieces of chicken, one small bowl of salad, two servings of mashed potatoes, one hamburger, one large serving of french fries, one large chocolate shake, one large bag of potato chips, and 15 to 20 small cookies—all within a 2-hour period. She was embarrassed by how much she was eating, and felt disgusted with herself and very guilty after eating. (Goldfein, Devlin, & Spitzer, 2000, p. 1052)

Binge-eating disorder (BED) is similar to bulimia nervosa in that it involves the consumption of large amounts of food within a two-hour period, an accompanying feeling of loss of control, and "marked distress" over eating during the episodes. The episodes are not generally followed by "the regular use of compensatory behaviors" such as vomiting, excessive exercise, or fasting, although many women with BED have engaged in these behaviors in the past or do so sporadically (Mond, Peterson, & Hay, 2010). As in the case of bulimia nervosa, the individual with this disordered eating pattern eats large amounts of food, is secretive about this activity, and may eat excessively even when not hungry.

To be diagnosed with BED, an individual must have a history of binge-eating episodes at least once a week for a period of three months. Females are one and a half times more likely to have this disorder than males; the lifetime prevalence rate is 3.5 percent in women and 2 percent in men (Hudson, Hiripi, Pope, & Kessler, 2007). White women make up the vast majority of clinical cases, whereas in community samples, the percentages of African American and white women with BED are roughly equal (Wilfley et al., 2001). Differences have been found between African American and white women with BED. The former are less likely to have been treated for eating problems, are more likely to be obese, and show lower levels of eating, weight concerns, and psychiatric distress (Pike et al., 2001) (Figure 10.1). American Indian women also appear to be at higher risk for BED, with a 10 percent prevalence rate reported in one study (Sherwood et al., 2000).

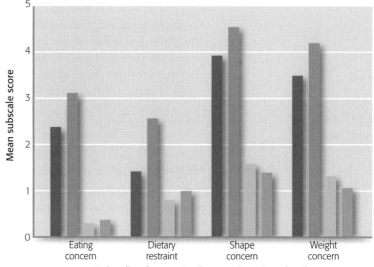

Figure 10.1

BINGE-EATING DISORDER

The comparison of scores on subscales of the Eating Disorder Questionnaire reveal differences between African American and white women with and without binge-eating disorder.

Source: Pike et al., (2001)

Associated Characteristics

In contrast to those with bulimia nervosa, individuals suffering from binge-eating disorder are likely to be overweight (Bull, 2004). It is believed that BED is a contributor to the development of obesity in vulnerable individuals (Yanovski, 2003). It is estimated that from 20 to 40 percent of individuals in weight-control programs have BED. The risk factors associated with this disorder include adverse childhood experiences; parental depression; vulnerability to obesity; and repeated exposure to negative comments from family members about body shape, weight, or eating (Dunkley, Masheb, & Grilo, 2010; Fairburn et al., 1998; Wilfley, Wilson, & Agras, 2003). The binges are often preceded by poor mood, decreased alertness, feelings of poor eating control, and cravings for sweets (Greeno, Wing, & Shiffman, 2000; Hilbert & Tuschen-Caffier, 2007). When weight or shape concerns are triggered, women with BED are more likely than healthy controls to

binge-eating disorder (BED)
an eating disorder that involves the consumption of large amounts of food over a short period of time, an accompanying feeling of loss of control, and distress over the excess eating; inappropriate compensatory behavior following eating are not typically seen with this disorder

report feelings of sadness and anxiety and an increased craving for food (Svaldi, Caffier, Blechert, & Tuschen-Carter, 2009). Complications from this disorder are due to medical conditions associated with obesity, such as high blood pressure, high cholesterol level, and Type 2 diabetes. People with BED are also likely to suffer from depression (Hoffman, 1998; T. D. Wade, 2007).

As with the other eating disorders, various mental disorders are associated with BED. In one study comparing 162 individuals with BED with other psychiatric samples, the lifetime rate for major depressive disorder, obsessive-compulsive personality disorder, and avoidant personality disorder was higher among those with BED. The presence of personality disorders was related to more severe binge eating, and those with avoidant or obsessive-compulsive personality disorders reported higher rates of binge eating one year after treatment (Wilfley et al., 2000). (See Table 10.3 for questions used to assess for an eating disorder.)

Course and Outcome

The onset of binge-eating disorder is similar to that of bulimia nervosa in that it typically begins in late adolescence or early adulthood. The findings are mixed regarding the natural course of BED in women. In one sample, the average duration of the disorder was 14.4 years (Pope et al., 2006). However, in another study, most individuals with BED made a full recovery over a five-year period, even without treatment, with only

---

TABLE 10.3   Do You Have An Eating Disorder?

Questions for Possible Anorexia Nervosa

1. Are you considered to be underweight by others? (What is your weight?)
   (Screening question. If yes, continue to next questions.)

2. Are you intensely fearful of gaining weight or becoming fat even though you are underweight?

3. Do you feel that your body or a part of your body is too fat?

4. If you had periods previously, have they stopped?

Questions for Possible Bulimia Nervosa

1. Do you have binges in which you eat a lot of food?
   (Screening question. If yes, continue to next questions.)

2. When you binge, do you feel a lack of control over eating?

3. Do you make yourself vomit, take laxatives, or exercise excessively because of overeating?

4. Are you very dissatisfied with your body shape or weight?

Questions for Possible Binge-Eating Disorder

1. Do you have binges in which you eat a lot of food?

2. When you binge, do you feel a lack of control over eating?

3. When you binge, do three or more of the following apply?
   a. You eat more rapidly than usual.
   b. You eat until uncomfortably full.
   c. You eat large amounts even when not hungry.
   d. You eat alone because of embarrassment from overeating.
   e. You feel disgusted, depressed, or guilty about binge eating.

4. Do you feel great distress regarding your binge eating?

Note: These questions are derived from the diagnostic criteria for eating disorders (American Psychiatric Association, 2011). For anorexia nervosa, the individual's weight is less than the expected weight for age and height; for bulimia nervosa and binge eating the binges must occur, on average, about once a week for three months. If the full criteria for these disorders are not met and disturbed eating patterns exist, they may represent subclinical forms of the eating disorders or may be diagnosed as eating condition not elsewhere classified.

18 percent demonstrating an eating disorder of clinical severity versus 51 percent of the bulimia nervosa cohort. They also showed improved self-esteem and higher social functioning. However, their weight remained high, and 39 percent eventually met the criteria for obesity (Fairburn et al., 2000).

Eating Conditions Not Elsewhere Classified

According to DSM-5 (American Psychiatric Association, 2011), the category eating conditions not elsewhere classified includes seriously disturbed eating patterns that do not meet all the criteria for anorexia nervosa, bulimia nervosa, binge eating disorder, or other eating problems of clinical significance. Examples of disordered eating that would fit in this category include (American Psychiatric Association, 2011):

Atypical Anorexia Nervosa

In this category, the individual meets the criteria for anorexia nervosa but is of normal weight.

Subthreshold Bulimia Nervosa

Individuals in this category meet the criteria for bulimia nervosa with the exception of either frequency (binge eating and compensatory activities occur less than once a week) and/or duration (less than three months of the disordered eating behaviors).

Subthreshold Binge-Eating Disorder

The criteria for binge-eating disorder are met except binge eating occurs less than once a week and/or has been present for less than three months.

Purging Disorder

The individual does not engage in binge eating, but does use recurrent purging (self-induced vomiting, misuse of laxatives, diuretics, or enemas) as a means to control weight or shape. These individuals are typically of normal weight but suffer from body image distortions and are fearful of becoming fat.

Night-Eating Syndrome

Individuals with this disorder engage in a recurrent pattern of binge eating after awakening from sleep or late at night. The individual is clinically distressed by this eating behavior.

Eating conditions not elsewhere classified, the diagnosis received by 40 to 60 percent of individuals in eating disorders treatment programs (Andersen, Bowers, & Watson, 2001; Dalle Grave & Calugi, 2007), is a problematic diagnostic category because it includes a heterogeneous grouping of symptoms and subthreshold disorders. Many individuals who receive this diagnosis continue on to develop bulimia nervosa or binge-eating disorder (Stice, Marti, Shaw, & Jaconis, 2009) and display a number of emotional and physiological problems (Thomas, Vartanian, & Brownell, 2009). Women with this diagnosis have more weight and shape concerns, dietary restraints, and depressive feelings than controls but less so than women with bulimia nervosa (T. D. Wade, 2007).

▬▬ Etiology of Eating Disorders

The etiology of eating disorders is affected by biological, psychological, social, and sociocultural factors (Becker, 2004; Kaye, 2009; Tylka & Subich, 2004). We examine each of these factors to determine how they might explain the disturbances in body image and the development of either overcontrolled (severe dieting and exercise) or undercontrolled (bingeing) behaviors found in eating disorders. The search for "core" risk factors associated with eating disorders is complicated because biological, psychological, social, and sociocultural factors interact to produce individual vulnerabilities. Understanding etiology involves looking for conditions that precede the development of and maintain

eating conditions not elsewhere classified a category for individuals with problematic eating patterns who do not fully meet the criteria for one of the eating disorders

Figure 10.2

MULTIPATH MODEL FOR EATING DISORDERS

The dimensions interact with one another and combine in different ways to result in an eating disorder.

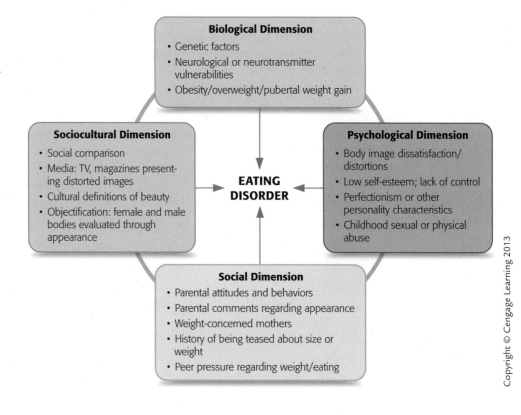

the disorder (Hartmann, Zeeck, & Barrett, 2010). Keeping this in mind, we use the multipath model (Figure 10.2) to consider and evaluate the risk factors associated with eating disorders.

Psychological Dimension

A number of psychological risk factors have been found to increase an individual's chances of developing an eating disorder. These include body dissatisfaction, perfectionism, depression, dysfunctional beliefs, using control to deal with stressors, and low levels of interpersonal competence (Myers & Crowther, 2009).

Body dissatisfaction arises from the discrepancy between one's perceived versus desired body weight or shape. Dissatisfaction with one's body can result in fragile or low self-esteem, depression, and feelings of helplessness. Body dissatisfaction has been found to be a strong predictor of the development of disturbed eating patterns (Johnson & Wardle, 2005). Up to one-third of young people (Crow, Eisenberg, Story, & Neumark-Sztainer, 2008; Mission Australia, 2010) and a large percentage of women between the ages of 35 to 65 (McLean, Paxton, & Wertheim, 2010) indicate significant levels of body dissatisfaction. Women with high body dissatisfaction as compared to body-satisfied women are more likely to compare their bodies to other women and report lower self-evaluation after this process (Trampe, Stapel, & Siero, 2010). Similarly, men who score high on appearance-orientation report lower muscle satisfaction when exposed to commercials with muscular men (Hargreaves & Tiggemann, 2009). Body dissatisfaction is a "robust risk factor" in the development of eating disorders in longitudinal studies and its reduction is associated with increased satisfaction regarding weight and overall appearance (Wade, George, & Atkinson, 2009).

Maladaptive perfectionism has also been identified as a risk factor and may interact with body dissatisfaction to predict not only anorexia but other eating disorders. Maladaptive perfectionism is composed of two dimensions: (1) inflexible high standards, and (2) negative self-evaluations involving mistakes. The presence of both is strongly related to eating disorder symptoms when perfectionist standards are imposed on weight, shape, and/or dieting (Bardone-Cone & Cass, 2007; Bardone-Cone, Sturm, Lawson, Robinson, & Smith, 2010; Boone, Soenens, Braet, & Goossens, 2010). Perceived incompetence or the belief that one is inadequate in social relationships has also been found to be associated with disordered eating (Ferrier & Martens, 2008) and may interact with maladaptive perfection and body dissatisfaction to create even greater risk for an eating disorder (Ferrier-Auerbach & Martens, 2009).

Individuals with eating disorders often appear to use food or weight control as a means of handling stress or anxieties (Schwitzer et al., 2001; Walsh & Devlin, 1998). One anorexic woman stated, "90 percent of you is miserable, and 90 percent of you is depressed, but then there is 10 percent that has this satisfaction in knowing that you weigh such a low weight and that you are getting thinner" (Budd, 2007, p. 102). Dieting may be used to demonstrate self-control and improve self-esteem and body image (Jones, Leung, & Harris, 2007). The element of control appears to provide some satisfaction in dealing with stress. Alternately, binge eating as a source of comfort can be used in an attempt to counteract depression and other negative emotions (Bergstrom & Neighbors, 2006).

Perceived or actual inadequacies in interpersonal skills are also associated with eating disorders. For both men and women, higher scores on characteristics such as passivity, low self-esteem, dependence, and nonassertiveness are associated with higher scores on inventories of disordered eating (Budd, 2007; Lakkis, Ricciardelli, & Williams, 1999). Individuals with eating disorders often display a passive and nonassertive interpersonal style. Severity of this pattern has been related to treatment outcome (Hartmann, Zeeck, & Barrett, 2010). Perceived social incompetence, particularly when combined with maladaptive perfectionism, has been linked with disordered eating patterns (Ferrier-Auerbach & Martens, 2009).

Mood disorders such as depression often accompany eating disorders. Rates of affective disorders such as depression are higher in the relatives of individuals with eating disorders compared with controls, and some investigators believe that eating disorders represent an expression of a mood disorder (Rutter, MacDonald et al., 1990). At this point, we still do not know the precise relationship between affective disorders and eating disorders. Depression may be the result, not the cause, of having an eating disorder.

Myrleen Ferguson Cate/PhotoEdit

Body Consciousness

Females are socialized to be conscious of their bodies. Although most of the attention has been directed to concerns over appearance among young white females, rates of disordered eating and body dissatisfaction are also high among Hispanic American and American Indian girls.

Social Dimension

Interpersonal interaction patterns with parents and peers have also been put forth as explanations for eating disorders. Some with eating disorders report suffering emotional or sexual abuse during childhood (Steiger et al., 2010). It is possible that childhood maltreatment produces a self-critical style as well as depression and body dissatisfaction (Dunkley, Masheb, & Grilo, 2010). In one study, individuals with eating disorders reported that their parents or family members frequently criticized them, had a negative reaction to their eating issues, and blamed them for their condition (Di Paola, Faravelli, & Ricca, 2010).

Unfortunately, the reported findings are difficult to interpret. Most depend on the individual's perceptions regarding their relationships—family interaction patterns may be the result of dealing with an eating disorder rather than the cause. For example, parents may become more "controlling" in an attempt to force the person with the eating disorder to gain weight or to establish a healthier eating pattern (Le Grange, Lock, Loeb, & Nicholls, 2010). At this point we do not know whether the described negative interaction pattern reported in the families of individuals with eating disorders is a causal factor or a consequence of dealing with an individual with an illness. Peers or family members can inadvertently produce pressure to be thin through discussions of weight, encouragement to diet, and the glorification of ultra-slim models (Annus et al., 2007; Jackson & Chen, 2010; McKnight Investigators, 2003; Stice & Bearman, 2001). Peer relationships can either serve as a buffer against eating disorders or produce pressure to lose weight. In a longitudinal study, girls who reported that their friends were "very much" involved in dieting at the beginning of the study were very likely to engage in extreme dieting and unhealthy weight control behaviors five years later (Eisenberg & Neumark-Sztainer, 2010). Perceived pressure from family, friends, dating partners, or the media has been associated with the internalization of a thin ideal and feelings of depression. One woman remembered her mother telling her to "suck in your gut" (Budd, 2007). These messages result in body dissatisfaction and the view that "one should be able to diet or exercise to lose weight"—in other words, that obtaining a slim figure is under voluntary control. Later, eating "too much," unsuccessful dieting, and guilt from purging or loss of control contributes to depressive feelings. Teasing and criticism about body weight or shape by family members has been found to predict ideal-body internalization, body dissatisfaction, dieting, and eating problems (Vincent & McCabe, 2000). Mothers who diet also indirectly transmit the message of the importance of slimness and the thin ideal to their daughters.

Ideal Male Bodies?

Most males would prefer to be heavier and more muscular. Will the increased media focus on physically powerful men produce body image distortion and dissatisfaction among men?

© Yuri Arcurs/shutterstock.com

Sociocultural Dimension

By far, the greatest amount of research has focused on the influence of sociocultural norms and values in the etiology of eating disorders, especially on the development of unrealistic standards of beauty. In the United States and most Western cultures, physical appearance is considered a very important attribute, especially for females. Teenage girls describe their ideal body as five feet seven inches, weighing 110 pounds, and fitting into a size five dress. Although this body type is far from the norm, it is consistent with the image portrayed in the media. It is estimated that only about 5 percent of American women are the size required for fashion models (Irving, 2001). Table 10.4 illustrates data on the average weight of adults in the United States.

Women are socialized to be conscious of their body shape and weight. The APA Task Force on the Sexualization of Girls (2007) points out that women are sexualized through television, music videos, song lyrics, magazines, and advertising. Females are dressed in revealing clothing and objectified. (Figure 10.3 shows how males and females are portrayed in family films.) A narrow standard of physical beauty is emphasized, which affects girls in particular. Following exposure to these messages, girls begin to: (1) believe that their primary value comes from being attractive; (2) define themselves according to the bodily standards shown in media; and (3) see themselves as an object rather than having the capacity for independent action and decision making. As girls and women adopt these unrealistic standards, many develop a *thin-ideal internalization*, which is indicated by strong agreement with statements such as "slender women are more attractive" and "I would like to look like the women that appear in TV shows and movies" (Thompson & Stice, 2004, p. 99). In a random sample of one hundred teenage girls, more than 60 percent reported trying to change their appearance to resemble that of celebrities or actors (Seitz, 2007).

What kind of predisposition or characteristic leads some people to interpret images of thinness in the media as evidence of their own inadequacy? Are people who develop eating disorders chronically self-conscious to begin with, or do they develop eating disorders because their social environment makes them chronically self-conscious? How does exposure to mass media portrayals of thinness influence the values and norms of young people? The development of disordered eating and preoccupation with body image may involve multiple processes (Myers & Crowther, 2009; Harrison, 2001; Tylka & Subich, 2004) (Figure 10.4). A process of *social comparison* occurs in which women and girls begin to evaluate themselves according to external standards. Because these standards are unattainable for the vast majority of women, body dissatisfaction occurs. Self-consciousness and habitual monitoring of one's external appearance can lead to anxiety or shame about the body. Dissatisfaction with one's body leads to disturbed eating patterns and depression (Tiggemann & Kuring, 2004).

Social comparison has been found to trigger negative reactions in women. In one study, female restrained eaters and nonrestrained eaters (classified based on degree of dietary restriction) read descriptions of a peer described either as "thin," "average," or "overweight" and then completed measures of self-evaluation. The restrained eaters showed more negative self-perceptions in response to the description of a thin peer, suggesting they may be more vulnerable to social comparison processes that lead to body dissatisfaction and lower self-esteem (Trottier, Polivy, & Herman, 2007). Although societal emphasis on thinness may increase disordered eating, it is not a sufficient explanation. Only a small percentage of individuals in our media-conscious society develop eating disorders. Protective variables against the impact of media on body image include strong social bonds and social support, personality variables such as self-determination and autonomy, and viewing attractiveness as only one of many qualities that are deemed important (Pelletier & Dion, 2006).

TABLE 10.4 Average Weight for Women and Men (20 to 74 Years) for 1994–2006

	1994	2006
Women		
Weight (pounds)	153.0	164.7
Men		
Weight (pounds)	181.3	194.7
Average weight by ethnicity and gender		
White women	151.4	163.7
African American women	169.7	184.8
Mexican American women	152.6	162.2
White men	183.7	197.4
African American men	181.2	199.8
Mexican American men	172.3	180.5

Source: Ogden et al., (2004); McDowell, Fryar, Ogden, & Flegal, (2008)

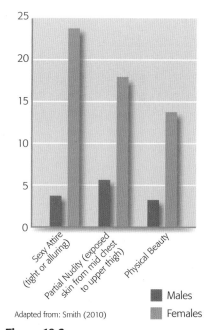

Adapted from: Smith (2010)

Figure 10.3

OBJECTIFICATION OF FEMALES

In family films (those with G, PG, or PG-13 ratings), females often are "scantily clad," very attractive, and have an unrealistic body shape. Does this contribute to the objectification of girls and women?

Source: Smith & Choueiti (2010)

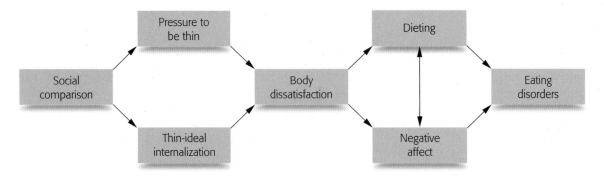

Figure 10.4

ROUTE TO EATING DISORDERS

Social comparison can lead to the development of eating disorders.

Source: Adapted from Stice (2001)

Did You Know?

Do most women want to be ultra-thin?

■ Among overweight and obese women, the amount of weight they would "ideally" like to lose would still place them in the overweight category.

■ Women in the normal weight range want to lose only a few pounds, not the amount needed to be extremely thin.

■ Underweight women believe they are at the ideal weight. This group may be most responsive to messages regarding thinness.

Source: Neighbors & Sobal, (2007)

Adolescent girls gave the following reasons for dieting and concern over their bodies: mass media (magazines, television, advertising, fashions), peer influences (wanting to fit in), and criticisms by family members about their weight (Wertheim et al., 1997). The beginning of dating and mixed-gender social activities is also related to dieting and disordered eating, especially for young women who have recently experienced menarche (Cauffman & Steinberg, 1996). Unfortunately, high school and college females may not be aware of the psychologically harmful effect of the super-slim standard for women. When asked to examine forty magazine ads and indicate which ads featured potentially harmful female stereotypes, they picked out ones that portray women as helpless or dumb, as sex objects, or as using alcohol or cigarettes. They appeared to overlook the ultra-thin models, possibly because they have accepted them as a social-cultural norm (Gustafson, Popovich, & Thomsen, 2001).

Although society's emphasis on body types may lead to general body dissatisfaction, it is important to identify individuals who are most influenced by the standard. The researchers found that among both males and females, those of either gender with low self-esteem displayed the greatest degree of body dissatisfaction. Heterosexual women especially are likely to be inaccurate about the female body preferences of males. In a study that asked "Do men find 'bony' women attractive?" males indicated a preference for a heavier female body type than women thought men preferred (Bergstrom, Neighbors, & Lewis, 2004).

As noted in the beginning of the chapter, mass media portrayals of lean, muscular male bodies are also increasing. For example, male centerfolds displayed in *Playgirl* have become more muscular in recent times (Bergstrom & Neighbors, 2006). There appears to be a gradual shift away from traditional measures of masculinity, such as wealth and power, to physical appearance. If this is true, there may be dramatic increases in eating disorders among men in the near future. In fact, as noted earlier, more cases of muscle dysphoria (dissatisfaction with one's degree of muscularity) have been reported in men (Cafri et al., 2005; Pope et al., 2001).

The gay male subculture places a great deal of value on physical attractiveness, resulting in more concern over body size and appearance and a greater prevalence of disturbed eating patterns than found among heterosexual males (Blashill & Vander Wal, 2009; Strong et al., 2000). Some studies estimate that gay males constitute 30 percent of males with eating disorders (Carlat, Camargo, & Herzog, 1997; Heffernan, 1994). Subcultural influences on attractiveness are also apparent in the fact that lesbians appear to be less concerned about physical appearance and to have a better body image than other females (Boehmer, Bowen, & Bauer, 2007), although the prevalence of eating disorders between lesbian and heterosexual women is similar (Feldman & Meyer, 2007).

Ethnic Minorities and Eating Disorders

Research has also been directed to the influence of cultural standards and values on body dissatisfaction and eating disorders among ethnic minorities. In a meta-analysis of the impact of ethnicity and body dissatisfaction among women in the United States, Grabe and Hyde (2006) came to the following conclusions. First, body dissatisfaction is not just a problem among white women; it also exists among ethnic minority women. Second, Hispanic and Asian American women had levels of body dissatisfaction equivalent to that of white women. Third, black women show body dissatisfaction but at a lower level than all other comparison groups.

African American girls and women tend to be more satisfied with their body size, weight, and appearance than are white females, even though they tend to be heavier than their white counterparts. They also have a lower level of negative attitudes toward body size and weight and less motivation for thinness (Chandler-Laney et al., 2009; Gilbert, 2003; Lovejoy, 2001). Although some show dissatisfaction with their bodies and weight, more African American college students report satisfaction with their appearance, body size, and shape compared with their white peers (Harris, 2006; Powell & Kahn, 1995). Similarly, findings from a national survey of adolescents on dieting and disordered eating supports the view that African American adolescent females appear to be less concerned about their body size and shape than white adolescents (Neumark-Sztainer et al., 2000). Ethnic comparisons suggest that dieting is lowest among African American girls (37.6 percent) and highest among white girls (51.3 percent). Disordered eating patterns (bingeing and purging) were highest among Hispanic American girls (19.1 percent) and lowest among African American girls (11.4 percent). Although the results may indicate that African American girls appear to experience lower levels of body dissatisfaction than girls from other ethnic groups, a substantial percentage of them also diet and binge or purge (Story et al., 1998). Table 10.5 compares some differences in body image and weight concerns between African American and white women.

TABLE 10.5   Differences in Body Image and Weight Concerns among African American and White Females

Concern	African American Females	White American Females
Satisfied with current weight or body shape	70%	11%
Body image	Perceive selves to be thinner than they actually are.	Perceive selves to be heavier than they actually are.
Attitude toward dieting	Belief that it is better to be a little over-weight than underweight (endorsed by 65% of survey respondents).	Belief in importance of dieting to produce a slender body. Fear of being overweight.
Definition of beauty	Well groomed, "style," and overall attractiveness. Beauty is the right "attitude and personality."	Slim; 5'7"; 100 to 110 pounds. Perfect body can lead to success and the good life.
Being overweight	Of those who were overweight, 40% considered their figures attractive or very attractive.	Those who considered selves as not having a weight problem were 6 to 14 pounds under the lower limit of the "ideal" weight range.
Age and beauty	Believed they would get more beautiful with age (65% chose this response).	Beauty is fleeting and decreases with age.

Bryan Bedder/Getty Images

Healthy or Overweight?

In high school, Jamie-Lynn Sigler, who played Meadow on *The Sopranos*, would get up at 4 A.M. to exercise for two hours. Her dinner consisted merely of fat-free yogurt. She was so thin that size 0 clothing was too large for her. Now recovered, she has received criticisms from some fans that she is now overweight!

Did You Know?

In lesbian magazines (e.g., *Curve, Girlfriends, Out*), models are more varied in age and weight compared to models in mainstream magazines (e.g., *Glamour, Elle, Mademoiselle*). Lesbian models are more likely to be advertising activities such as reading or travel, whereas mainstream models are more likely to wear revealing clothing and be associated with products such as clothing or cosmetics (Milillo, 2008).

Why is it that African American women appear to be somewhat insulated from unrealistic standards of thinness? It is possible that African American girls and women are protected by several cultural factors. First, because many do not identify with white women, media messages of thinness may have less impact. Second, their definition of attractiveness is broad, encompassing dress, personality, and confidence, and does not focus solely on external characteristics such as body shape and weight. Third, African American women have characteristics such as being assertive and egalitarian in relationships that allow them to have important roles in the community. In this way, they are less influenced by gender-restrictive messages.

However, not all African American women are immune to majority-culture messages. Those who are acculturated to mainstream values are more at risk for developing an eating disorder (Talleyrand, 2010). The prevalence of eating disorders not elsewhere classified among African American women appears to be equivalent to that found in white American women (Mulholland & Mintz, 2001). And although fewer African American women appear to have either anorexia nervosa or bulimia nervosa, they are as likely as other groups of women to have binge-eating disorder (Lovejoy, 2001; Striegel-Moore et al., 2003). As with white American women, self-esteem and body dissatisfaction among African American women is related to bulimic symptoms. This relationship is greatest among those who have internalized U.S. societal values concerning attractiveness (Grabe & Hyde, 2006; Lester & Petrie, 1998).

Among Hispanic American female college students, weight and adherence to mainstream values were positively related to bulimic symptoms (Lester & Petrie, 1998). Some studies show that American Indian, Asian American, and Hispanic American girls show greater body image dissatisfaction than white females, possibly due to attempts to fit into the societal definition of beauty (Gilbert, 2003). Thus it appears that ethnic minorities are becoming increasingly vulnerable to societal messages regarding attractiveness and may be at especially high risk for developing eating disorders, as a greater percentage of ethnic minority children and adults, especially females, are overweight (Madsen, Weedn, & Crawford, 2010; Ogden et al., 2004).

Cross-Cultural Studies on Eating Disorders

Far fewer reports of eating disorders are found in Latin America, South America, and Asia, whereas they appear to be increasing in European countries, Israel, and Australia (Miller & Pumariega, 2001). Countries or groups that have been exposed to Western values show an increasing concern over eating and body size (Becker, 2004; Steiger & Bruce, 2007). Although the standard of beauty among women in South Africa is based on fuller figures, black teenage girls in this region are drawn to Western standards of thinness, resulting in a dramatic increase in eating disorders among this group (Simmons, 2002). Asian countries that are exposed to Western media also report increases in body shape concerns and distorted eating attitudes (Liao et al., 2010).

Cultural values and norms affect views on body shape and size. Weight normalcy is influenced by cultural beliefs and practices. For example, Micronesians view thinness as a sign of illness. As one parent responded, "The culture on Saipan, the fat one is the healthy one . . . but when they are skinny, 'Oh, my goodness, nobody is feeding that child'" (Bruss, Morris, & Dannison,

Should Underweight Models and Digitally "Enhanced" Photos Be Banned from Advertisements?

Former Ralph Lauren model Filippa Hamilton was fired for being too fat. She is 5'10" tall, weighs 120 pounds, and wears size 4 clothing. "They fired me because they said I was overweight and I couldn't fit in their clothes anymore" (Melago, 2009, p. 1). Later Filippa was shocked to see a digitally retouched picture of herself on an advertisement in which her head appears larger than her hips. (Ralph Lauren has since apologized for this action.) Kate Winslet was digitally slimmed for the cover of *GQ* magazine, as was singer Kelly Clarkson for the cover of *Self* magazine and country singer Faith Hill for *Redbook.* Changing photos to make women appear slimmer on magazine covers and advertisements is a common practice. The digital alteration process generally involves slimming the waist and other parts of the body, boosting cleavage, lengthening the legs, and airbrushing out imperfections on already attractive models or women, thus promoting an unrealistic and unattainable image (Carmichael, 2010).

The Royal College of Psychiatrists in Britain has called on the media to end the use of underweight models and airbrushed photos because the practice leads to unhealthy body images and eating disorders (Berman, 2010).

In Israel, a Knesset bill would ban the use of underweight models (BMI less than 18.5) from appearing in advertisements and require a notice placed on an advertisement when pictures of models are digitally enhanced. Justification for the bill includes the rising incidence of eating disorders in Israel, especially among teenage girls, and research indicating that advertisements play a role in creating body dissatisfaction. It was argued that by using models who are in a "state of unnourishment," the fashion industry has created a distorted image of the "ideal" woman. It was proposed that every violation of the bill result substantial fines (Lis, 2011). Similarly, Australia has encouraged modeling agencies, clothes designers, and magazines to use diverse models rather than ultra thin models. The use of "unrealistic" digital enhancement of pictures of people and rapid weight-loss advertisements are also discouraged. It is also hoped that stores display a wider variety of clothing sizes. Compliance with this voluntary code of conduct earns advertisers, agencies, and stores a "body friendly" recognition award (Ashley, 2010).

The incidence of body dissatisfaction and eating disorders has increased in the United States in recent years. It is clear that the use of underweight models and digitally "enhanced" photos conveys unrealistic messages to girls and women about ideal body size. In a meta-analysis of 77 social comparison research studies, it was found that exposure to pictures of thin models or thin-ideal images, increased depression and body dissatisfaction in young women—a result that subsequently increases the risk of developing an eating disorder (Grabe, Ward, & Hyde, 2008).

Do you think we should ban the use of ultra-thin models and digitally enhanced images in the United States? Would this reduce the incidence of body dissatisfaction and eating disorders? How can we promote a more realistic and healthy body image?

Kate Winslet Photoshopped?

Actress Kate Winslet, pictured on the right, has frequently been the victim of photoshopping. *Harper's Bazaar* has been accused of grafting Kate's head onto another woman's body for the cover shot on the left. Why do magazines go to such lengths in their portrayal of thinness and beauty?

2003). Historically, eating disorders in Chinese populations have been rare because plumpness in females has been considered desirable and attractive. Feeding is an extension of love and care of parents toward their children. Interestingly, in a Hong Kong study, adolescent girls picked an ideal female body size that was somewhat larger than that preferred by boys (Marsh et al., 2007). This finding is in contrast to studies cited earlier in which American girls and women choose ideal body sizes that were thinner than those preferred by males.

However, Lee, Lam, Kwok, and Fung (2010) found that individuals with eating disorders in Hong Kong are increasingly demonstrating a fat phobic pattern similar to that seen in Western countries.

What happens when other cultures are exposed to Western standards of beauty? Becker (2004) reported on the impact of television on adolescent girls living in a rural community in western Fiji. Traditional cultural norms support robust appetites and body sizes. Food and feasts are important aspects of social exchange, and plump bodies are considered to be aesthetically pleasing. After three years of exposure to Western television programs, girls comments revealed admiration for Western standards: "The actresses and all those girls, especially those European girls, I just like, I just admire them and want to be like them. I want their body, I want their size" (p. 546). The girls also paid attention to TV commercials advertising exercise equipment, which portrayed the ease with which weight could be lost. "When they show exercising on TV . . . I feel I should . . . lose my weight" (p. 542).

Although eating disorder increases in developing countries have been associated with rapid transitions in global market economies and heavy media exposure, Anderson-Fye (2004) found that in San Andres, Belize, body size and shape preferences have not changed because of exposure to Western media. In Belize, there is high level of contact with U.S. citizens via tourism. There is also a long history of beauty pageants in Belize. However, girls and women appear to eat freely and show minimum concern with their bodies. They have a broad definition of beauty that involves dress, hairstyle, makeup, and personality. It is believed that adorning oneself "properly" can make nearly any female "beautiful." Girls from different socioeconomic classes, ethnicities, and body shapes have participated in and won pageants. Boys indicate that they prefer girls shaped like "Coca Cola" (hourglass) and "Fanta" (smaller on top and bigger on the bottom). The least preferred shape is the "straight shape." Eating disorders are rare in Belize. It remains to be seen whether the cultural norms and values of Belize will continue to protect against eating disorders.

Biological Dimension

At this point, we have considered psychological, social, and sociocultural risk factors associated with eating disorders. However an "unanswered" question remains, "[I]f all young girls are exposed to these sociocultural pressures, why do only a small fraction go on to develop anorexia nervosa and bulimia nervosa?" (Striegel-Moore & Bulik, 2007, p. 188). A proposed answer to this question is that we need to look at gene × environment interaction. For example, if someone has a genetic predisposition toward severe dieting, the risk of developing an eating disorder is increased by exposure to environmental risk factors. Conversely, those without the predisposition would find severe dieting to be aversive and uncomfortable. In this section we consider possible genetic influences on eating disorders.

Disordered eating appears to run in families, especially among female relatives (Hoffman, 1998; Steiger & Bruce, 2007). Strober and colleagues (2000) examined the lifetime rates of full or partial anorexia nervosa and bulimia nervosa among first-degree relatives of individuals with these eating disorders. The rate was compared with that of relatives of matched, never-ill comparison participants. Support was found for a genetic contribution to disordered eating patterns. Whereas anorexia nervosa and bulimia nervosa were relatively rare among the relatives of the never-ill group, these disorders occurred at significantly high levels among the first-degree relatives of those with eating disorders. Twin studies have attempted to determine additive genetic effects (the effects of many genes), shared environmental factors, and unique environmental factors for eating disorders. Heritability (additive genetic effects) was found to be 41 percent for binge-eating disorder, whereas heritability ranged from 46 percent to 76 percent for anorexia nervosa and from 50 percent to 83 percent for bulimia nervosa (Bulik et al., 2010; Striegel-Moore & Bulik, 2007). Similarly, heritability of restrained eating patterns was found to be 55 percent for both male and female monozygotic (MZ) twins compared with 31 percent and 19 percent among same-sex male and female dizygotic (DZ) twin pairs, respectively (Schur, Noonan, Polivy, Goldberg, & Buchwald, 2009). Genetic influences may be triggered by physical changes such as puberty. In a sample of twins, heritability appeared to be low among preadolescent teens but was substantial after puberty. This suggests that puberty or processes during puberty (such as changes in the body or increasing awareness of sexuality and body shape) may influence the expression of genes for disordered eating through gene × environment interaction. In other words, the eating disorder only shows up when certain environmental factors interact with the presence of genetic risk factors (Culbert, Burt, McGue, Iacono, & Klump, 2009; Klump et al., 2007).

Genetics may influence the neurotransmitters and brain structures, such as the hypothalamus, which are involved in eating behaviors. Research has focused on dopamine, which is thought to be the primary neurotransmitter involved in the reinforcing effects of food (Bello & Hajnal, 2010). Low levels of dopamine are responsible for the desire to consume more food, whereas increased dopamine concentrations can result in a decrease in appetite (Lee & Lin, 2010). Bingeing may be a result of impairments in dopamine detection (Bello & Hajnal, 2010). Differences in dopamine levels may explain why those with bulimia nervosa are more attentive to food stimuli and why individuals with anorexia nervosa show less appetitive response to food images (Brooks, Prince, Stahl, Campbell, & Treasure, 2011).

Some studies have reported differences in the dopamine transporter gene between individuals with eating disorders and healthy controls, with the short allele of the gene being more prevalent among individuals with eating disorders. The researchers (Shinohara et al., 2004) concluded that there is an association between individuals with short or long alleles in this gene and dopamine levels. People with lower levels of dopamine may need greater quantities of food or other rewarding substances, such as drugs, to obtain pleasure. The possible influence of dopamine in eating disorders is being further investigated by examining drugs that affect dopamine levels. For example, some stimulant medications such as methylphenidate appear to decrease appetite by inhibiting dopamine reuptake (Epstein et al., 2007).

Although dopamine seems like a promising lead in explaining eating disorders, other brain regions and neurotransmitters such as serotonin also appear to be involved. Individuals with anorexia nervosa presented with various foods showed different activation patterns within the prefrontal region of the brain compared with controls (Treasure, 2007). The participants with anorexia nervosa also showed less salivation to food cues and reported less preference for fat and sweet substances than did control participants. In the Epstein and colleagues (2007) study, some individuals with the short allele of the dopamine gene

© Mango Productions / Corbis

Beauty Standards

African American females have a greater acceptance of heavier body sizes than white women. In addition, they adopt a broader definition of beauty that includes attitude, personality, and "style."

were ambivalent about eating, whereas others without this genetic variation responded very strongly to food. Of course, it is also possible that changes in eating patterns can alter the amount of specific neurotransmitters in the brain. Although these studies indicate the involvement of genetic and biological factors, more research is needed to determine the precise relationship between genetic factors, brain structures, neurotransmitters, and environmental influences. Epigenetic factors may also play a role. Certain behaviors or environmental factors may change aspects of gene functioning in a manner that increases the risk of developing an eating disorder (Hildebrandt, Alfano, Tricamo, & Pfaff, 2010).

Treatment of Eating Disorders

Prevention programs have been developed to reduce the incidence of eating disorders and disordered eating patterns. Group-based intervention programs generally involve the following components (Chapman, Gilger, & Chestnut, 2010; Daigneault, 2000; Richardson & Paxton, 2010): (1) becoming aware of societal messages of "what it means to be female," and understanding the role of the media's emphasis on appearance; (2) developing a more positive body image by reducing "fat talk" and teasing about body size; (3) developing healthier eating and exercise habits; (4) increasing comfort in expressing feelings to peers, family members, and significant others; (5) developing healthy strategies to deal with stress and pressures; and (6) increasing assertiveness skills. These points are addressed through group discussions and the use of videos, magazines, and examples from mass media.

Similarly, Sands (1998) believes that the social context of eating disorders needs to be acknowledged in any type of treatment. She recommends including a gender analysis by identifying sex role messages such as "Girls must be thin, pretty, and sexy," identifying the consequences of these gender-related messages ("I'm going to starve myself to be thin"), choosing a statement of change and implementing it ("Being healthy is important to me, so I will eat and exercise sensibly"), and developing assertiveness skills to combat patterns of helplessness and submissiveness. These approaches focus on teaching girls and women to re-examine the consequences of gender messages and on the necessity of institutional awareness of the problem. These elements are included in many treatment programs for anorexia nervosa, bulimia nervosa, and binge-eating disorder. The most effective programs include multiple, interactive sessions that address gender-specific issues (Stice & Shaw, 2004).

Treating Anorexia Nervosa

Case Study

A female who began treatment for anorexia nervosa weighing 81 pounds reported, "I did gain 25 pounds, the target weight of my therapist and nutritionist. But every day was really difficult. I would go and cry. A big part of anorexia is fear. Fear of fat, fear of eating. But (my therapist) taught me about societal pressures to be ultra-thin that come from the media, TV, advertising. . . . She talked me through what I was thinking and how I had completely dissociated my mind from my body. . . . I'm slowly reintroducing foods one thing at a time. I'd like to think I am completely better, but I'm not. I'm still extremely self-conscious about my appearance. But I now know I have a problem and my family and I are finding ways to cope with it." (Bryant, 2001, p. B4)

As you have seen, eating disorders, especially anorexia nervosa, can be life threatening. Treatment for anorexia nervosa can be delivered on either an outpatient or an inpatient basis, depending on the weight and health of the individual. Developing a therapeutic alliance through the use of empathy, positive regard, and support is vital because readiness for change is an important predictor of successful treatment (McHugh, 2007). Because anorexia is a complex disorder, there is a need for teamwork between physicians, psychiatrists, and psychotherapists. Treatment typically involves (American Psychiatric Association, 2006):

1. Restoration of a healthy weight. For females, this involves the return of menses and ovulation; for males, the return of normal sexual drive and hormone levels.
2. Treatment of physical complications. These include symptoms related to starvation and physiological reactions during re-feeding.
3. Enhancement of motivation to participate in the treatment program.
4. Psychoeducation about healthy eating patterns and nutrition.
5. Identification of attitudes, dysfunctional thoughts and beliefs, conflicts, and feelings that underlie the eating disorder.
6. Provision of psychotherapy to deal with emotional disturbances related to eating.
7. Mobilization of family support and use of family therapy, when appropriate.
8. Relapse prevention.

Because the individual is starving, the initial goal is to restore weight, a process carefully coordinated with psychological support. During the re-feeding process, the individual's feelings of apathy may begin to fade. Typically, those with anorexia nervosa become terrified of gaining weight and need the opportunity to discuss these reactions. During the weight restoration period, new foods are introduced, supplementing food choices that are not sufficiently high in calories. The physical condition of the person is carefully monitored because sudden and severe physiological reactions can occur during re-feeding. A dental exam is often conducted to assess for damage from purging.

Psychological interventions are used to help the client (1) understand and cooperate with nutritional and physical rehabilitation, (2) identify and understand the dysfunctional attitudes related to the eating disorder, (3) improve interpersonal and social functioning, and (4) address comorbid psychopathology and psychological conflicts that reinforce disordered eating behavior (American Dietetic Association, 2001; American Psychiatric Association, 2006; Walsh & Devlin, 1998). The behavioral approach is designed to correct irrational preoccupation with weight and to encourage weight gain through the use of positive reinforcement such as telephone privileges, visits from family and friends, mail, and access to street clothes. Weight-gain goals generally aim for increases of about two pounds per week (Wilson & Shafran, 2005). Once the individual being treated has gained sufficient weight to become an outpatient, family therapy sessions may be implemented. Experience has shown that this approach helps maintain the treatment gains achieved in the hospital.

Family therapy is often an important component of the treatment plan as seen in this case of an eighteen-year-old girl who failed to respond to inpatient treatment, dietary training, and cognitive-behavioral therapy. Her family was enlisted to participate in a new form of family therapy. The therapy involved (1) having the parents help re-feed their daughter through the planning of meals, (2) reducing parental criticism by understanding anorexia nervosa as a serious disease, (3) negotiating a new pattern of family relationships, and (4) assisting the family with the developmental process of separation and individuation. Parents were encouraged to understand and help their daughter develop the skills, attitudes, and activities appropriate to her developmental stage. This form of family therapy resulted in the girl gaining more than twenty-two pounds (Sim et al., 2004). In another family-focused program, parents are coached to be the deciders about when and how eating will occur. Rather than negotiating or pleading for the child to eat, they are told to put food in front of the child and say, "I know this is difficult for you, but you have to eat this and I'm going to sit here with you until you can" (Neighmond, 2010, p. 1). Overall, family therapy has been found to be successful in treating anorexia nervosa and more effective than individual therapy alone (Halvorsen & Heyerdahl, 2007; Lock et al., 2010; Paulson-Karlsson, Engstrom, & Nevonen, 2009).

Treating Bulimia Nervosa

In bulimia nervosa, treatment goals include (1) reducing or eliminating binge eating and purging; (2) treating any physical complications; (3) motivating the client to participate in the restoration of healthy eating patterns; (4) providing psychoeducation regarding nutrition and eating; (5) identifying dysfunctional thoughts, moods, and conflicts that are associated with eating; (6) providing psychotherapy to deal with these issues; (7) obtaining family support and conducting family therapy, if needed; and (8) preventing relapse (American Psychiatric Association, 2006).

During the initial assessment of individuals with bulimia nervosa, conditions that might contribute to purging, such as esophageal reflux disease, are identified. Physical conditions resulting from purging are treated; these may include dental erosion, muscle weakness, cardiac arrhythmias, dehydration, electrolyte imbalance, or gastrointestinal problems involving the stomach or esophagus. As with anorexia nervosa, treatment involves an interdisciplinary team that includes a physician and psychotherapist. One important goal in treatment is to normalize the eating pattern and to eliminate the binge/purge cycle. A routine of eating three meals a day with one to three snacks a day is used to break up the disordered eating pattern.

The use of antidepressant medication such as selective serotonin reuptake inhibitors (SSRIs) has been helpful in treating this condition (American Psychiatric Association, 2000b, 2006; Wilson & Shafran, 2005). Cognitive-behavioral approaches have also been effective in helping individuals with bulimia and binge-eating disorder develop a sense of self-control (Crow et al., 2009). Common components of cognitive-behavioral treatment plans involve encouraging the consumption of three or more balanced meals a day, reducing rigid food rules and body image concerns, identifying triggers for bingeing, and developing coping strategies. Even with these approaches, only about 50 percent of those with the disorder fully recover. Characteristics associated with treatment failure include poor social adjustment and limited success in reducing purging by the sixth treatment session (Agras et al., 2000). Adding exposure and response prevention (i.e., exposure to bingeing or cues associated with bingeing followed by prevention of purging) to cognitive behavioral strategies appears to improve the long-term outcome of individuals with bulimia nervosa (McIntosh, Carter, Bulik, Frampton, & Joyce, 2010).

Treating Binge-Eating Disorder

Treatments for binge-eating disorder are similar to those for bulimia nervosa, although binge-eating disorder presents fewer physical complications because of the lack of purging. Individuals with binge-eating disorder do differ in some ways from those with bulimia nervosa. Most are overweight and have to deal with prejudices toward overweight individuals. Due to the health consequences of excess weight, some therapy programs also focus on healthy approaches to weight loss.

In general, treatment follows two phases (Ricca et al., 2000; Shelley-Ummenhofer & MacMillan, 2007). First, cognitive factors underlying the eating disorder are determined and then clients are taught to use strategies that reduce eating binges, as seen in the following case.

Case Study

Mrs. A. had very rigid rules concerning eating that, when violated, would result in her "going the whole nine yards." Two types of triggers were identified for her binges—emotional distress (anger, anxiety, sadness, or frustration) and work stress (long hours, deadlines). Interventions were applied to help her develop more flexible rules regarding eating and to deal with her stressors. Information about obesity, proper nutrition, and physical exercise was provided. Her body weight was recorded weekly, and a healthy pattern of three meals and two snacks a day was implemented. She used a food diary to record the type and amount of food consumed and her psychological state preceding eating. Second, cognitive strategies were employed to change distorted beliefs about eating. Mrs. A. was asked to prepare a list of "forbidden" foods and to rank

AP Images/Matt Slocum

Childhood obesity has reached epidemic proportions in developed countries due to a lack of physical activity and the presence of attractive high-calorie foods. At the Children's Medical Center in Texas, children play kickball and other games to help them achieve a healthier weight.

them in order of "dangerousness." Gradually, the foods were introduced into normal eating routines, beginning with those perceived as being less dangerous. Mrs. A. was asked to observe her body in a mirror to help reduce or eliminate cognitive distortions. The prejudices of society about body size were discussed, and realistic expectations about change were addressed. She was asked to observe attractive individuals with a larger body size so that she could consider positive qualities rather than focusing solely on the body. After performing this "homework," Mrs. A. discovered that overweight women can look attractive, and she began to buy more fashionable clothes for herself. She was astonished at the positive reactions and comments from friends and coworkers. Although she had lost twelve pounds, she attributed the attention to her confidence and improved body image (Goldfein, Devlin, & Spitzer, 2000).

Cognitive-behavioral therapy can produce significant reductions in binge eating but is less successful in reducing weight (Shelley-Ummenhofer & MacMillan, 2007; Vocks et al., 2010; Wonderlich et al., 2003).

Obesity

Case Study

When I'm uptight, I often overeat. I know that I often use food to calm me when I'm upset and even find myself feeling that when things don't go my way, I'll just have my way by eating anything and all I want. Like an alcoholic who can't stop drinking once he or she starts, I don't seem to be able to stop myself from eating once I start. (LeCrone, 2007, p. 1)

Obesity is defined as having a body mass index (BMI) greater than 30—BMI is an estimate of body fat calculated on the basis of a person's height and weight. DSM-5 acknowledges eating disorders such as anorexia and bulimia as mental disorders with serious

obesity   a condition involving a body mass index greater than 30

body mass index (BMI)   an estimate of body fat calculated on the basis of a person's height and weight

2000

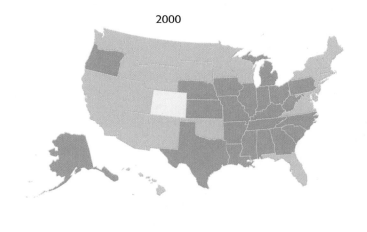

2005

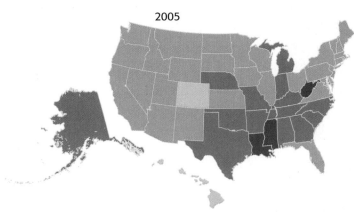

2009

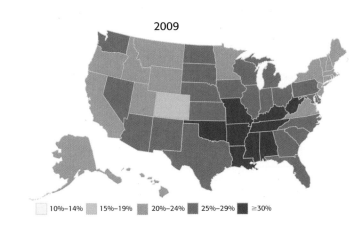

10%–14%   15%–19%   20%–24%   25%–29%   ≥30%

Figure 10.5

STATE-SPECIFIC OBESITY PREVALENCE AMONG ADULTS, INCREASE FROM 1999 TO 2009

The percentage of adults age 18 years and older considered obese, by state.

Source: Vital signs: State-specific obesity prevalence among adults–United States, 2009 (Centers for Disease Control and Prevention, 2010).

adverse outcomes but does not yet recognize obesity as a specific disorder despite its devastating medical and psychological consequences. Some researchers believe that forms of obesity that are characterized by an excessive drive for food should be recognized as a "food addiction" (Volkow & O'Brien, 2007) because characteristics overlap those of substance dependence:

- Development of tolerance—the need to increase the amount consumed to maintain satiety
- Withdrawal symptoms such as distress or dysphoria when dieting
- Larger amount of food ingested than intended
- Considerable time spent thinking about or consuming food
- Overeating despite attempts to curtail the amount consumed
- Overeating despite adverse physical and psychological consequences

We are including obesity in this chapter because it is a condition that is often accompanied by depression and anxiety disorders, low self-esteem, poor body image, and unhealthy eating patterns (Eddy et al., 2007; Rofey et al., 2009). In one study, the majority of obese women surveyed had engaged in binge eating (Bulik & Reichborn-Kjennerud, 2003). Also, obese individuals are five times more likely to display behavior characteristic of night-eating syndrome than those of normal weight (Stunkard et al., 2009). Obesity stems from many causes, including genetic and biological factors, our sedentary modern-day lifestyle, easy access to attractive, high calorie foods, and some of the same disturbed eating patterns seen in eating disorders. Obesity is a worldwide phenomenon that affects more than 300 million individuals (WHO, 2010).

Obesity is second only to tobacco use in terms of being a preventable cause of disease and death. Being overweight or obese increases the risk of high cholesterol or triglyceride levels, Type 2 diabetes, cancer, coronary heart disease, stroke, gallbladder disease, osteoarthritis, sleep apnea, and respiratory problems (Centers for Disease Control and Prevention [CDC], 2010a). By 2019, it is estimated that health care costs related to obesity will reach 343 billion dollars a year (Thorpe, 2009). A reduction of life expectancy of between five and twenty years is also associated with obesity (Fontaine et al., 2003). Being overweight or obese in childhood is related to an increased risk of coronary heart disease in adulthood (Baker, Olsen, & Sorenson, 2007). As compared to normal-weight children, overweight children are more likely to report that they worry a lot, are concerned about how they look, have trouble falling asleep, have headaches, feel angry, and get into fights (American Psychological Association, 2010).

According to BMI standards, 68 percent of American adults are either overweight or obese and 33.8 percent are obese (Flegal, Carroll, Ogden, & Curtin, 2010); 31.7 percent of children and adolescents are either overweight or obese (Ogden, Carroll, Curtin, Lamb & Flegal, 2010). (Figure 10.5 shows the increase in obesity from 2000 to 2009.) In the United States, the prevalence of being overweight and obese has doubled since the

1970s, and it is estimated that by 2015, 75 percent of adults and 24 percent of children and adolescents will fall into one of these categories. Statistics for African Americans, Mexican Americans, American Indians, and women show even higher rates of obesity (CDC, 2009; Wang & Beydoun, 2007). Childhood and adolescent obesity has reached epidemic proportions in developed nations and is a strong risk factor for adult obesity (Singhal, Schwenk, & Kumar, 2007).

Etiology of Obesity

Obesity is a product of biological, psychological, social, and socio-cultural influences, as shown in Figure 10.6. How these dimensions interact is still being investigated. For example, one theory, termed the "thrifty genotype" hypothesis, includes the roles of both genetics and the environment in accounting for the rapid rise in obesity. According to this perspective, certain genes helped our ancestors survive famines by storing fat. These same genes, however, may be dysfunctional in an environment in which high-fat foods are now plentiful (CDC, 2007c). Although "thrifty" genes and access to foods can account for some cases of obesity, other factors must be involved, because rates of obesity also vary according to variables such as class, gender, and race/ethnicity.

Did You Know?

Obesity may be a positive attribute for male political candidates. Undergraduates rated pictures of obese and normal weight men and women. As expected, obese women candidates were rated less favorably than women of normal weight. Surprisingly, obese male candidates were evaluated more positively than normal weight males. Larger body size may be an asset for male candidates (Miller & Lundgren, 2010).

Biological Dimension

Estimates regarding genetic contributions to obesity generally are derived by determining the frequency of obesity among family members and twins. Others have investigated specific genetic variations among the obese. Genes can influence eating behaviors through brain structures and neurochemistry. Hormonal activity within the hypothalamus, specifically the effect of the hormone leptin on the regulation of food consumption and appetite, has been implicated in obesity. A group of children who weighed more than 200 pounds by age 10 were found to have a chromosomal abnormality that affected nine of the genes that influence leptin production (Bochukova et al., 2010). Certain brain regions, such as the cortex, amygdala, and dopamine-sensitive nuclei, are involved in both the inhibitory and motivational processes involved in food consumption (Volkow & O'Brien, 2007). Scientists have begun to focus specifically on the influence of dopamine as it affects food palatability.

Epstein and colleagues (2007) found that about 50 percent of people carry a gene variation affecting dopaminergic activity that appears to increase pleasure in eating. This gene is also associated with addictions such as gambling and the abuse of alcohol and other substances. In their study, obese individuals with this genotype worked harder to be able to get food as a reward. It is hypothesized that individuals with this genetic variation may have to take in more of a substance to achieve the same level of satisfaction or reward as those without this variation. The importance of dopamine has been found in several other studies. Obese individuals were found to have fewer dopamine receptors than those of normal weight, and this decrease was proportional to their BMI (Wang et al., 2001). Similar findings regarding dopamine receptors were found among genetically lean and obese rats (Thanos et al., 2008). It is not clear, however, whether reduced dopamine receptor levels are the cause or effect of obesity. It is possible that overeating may produce lower receptor levels rather than genetically low receptor levels predisposing individuals to overeat. In the study by Thanos and colleagues (2008), restricting food intake in rats caused an increase in dopamine receptors. Also, in the study by Epstein and colleagues (2007), many individuals with the genetic variation associated with obesity did not become overweight, whereas some without the genetic variation became obese. Clearly, additional factors are involved in the etiology of obesity.

Figure 10.6

MULTIPATH MODEL FOR OBESITY

The dimensions interact with one another and combine in different ways to result in obesity.

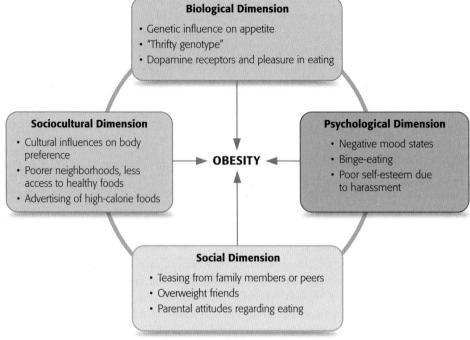

Are the Body Mass Index (BMI) Standards Appropriate?

Brent Hagen, 26, is overweight—according to the body mass index, or BMI, calculation. That is not what he thought. "I don't think of myself as overweight, and I don't think anyone I know has ever thought of me as overweight either." (Mask, 2007, p. 1)

An obesity researcher, Steve Blair, believes that people can be fit and "fat" and that Americans "have been whipped into 'near hysteria' by hype over the 'obesity epidemic.'" He suggests that people concentrate on healthy eating and exercise rather than obsessing about gaining a few extra pounds. (Dunham, 2007)

In 1998, changes were made in the BMI's diagnostic thresholds. The BMI scores were lowered for all weight classes. A consequence of the lowering of the diagnostic thresholds was to immediately increase the prevalence of individuals considered "overweight" or "obese." For example, the BMI cutoff score for the category of "overweight" was lowered from 27 to 25. This resulted in 29 million Americans being added to the overweight category, a 42 percent increase. Although it was hoped that this move would allow for early treatment and disease prevention, the research is mixed in regards to individuals who are mildly overweight. For example, being up to 25 pounds overweight does not seem to be associated with increased mortality. In fact, mortality rates for those slightly overweight are lower than those for individuals of normal weight (Flegal et al., 2007; Flicker et al., 2010). Degree of fitness may be the more important variable.

The current BMI standards are the same for men and women, whereas the past standards separate tables for men and women. The following chart shows the past and present BMI standards. Do the changes seem to make sense?

	1997 BMI Standards		Current BMI Standards
	Women	Men	(Both men and women)
Underweight	<19.1	<20.7	<18.5
Normal weight range	19.1–25.8	20.7–26.4	18.5–24.9
Marginally overweight	25.8–27.3	26.4–27.8	
Overweight	27.3–32.3	27.8–31.1	25–29.9
Obese	>32.3	>31.1	>30

Source: Centers for Disease Control and Treatment (2011)

Are the current standards an improvement over those of the past? Do they provide better information regarding health risks? Should BMI standards consider gender, race, ethnicity, and body type? Calculate your BMI using an online calculator. Which BMI standard (past or current) do you believe most accurately describes your weight category?

Psychological Dimension

Individuals who are obese report negative mood states and poor self-esteem. These responses are likely affected by the weight stigma that exists in society and the resultant harassment, teasing, and discrimination in school, work, and hiring practices (Obesity Action Coalition, 2007). The stigmatization faced by obese children from peers, parents, and teachers is pervasive and often unrelenting (Puhl & Heuer, 2009). Among a sample of 122 overweight youths, many reported being teased about their weight, suffering from mood and anxiety disorders, and internalizing a thin ideal; more than one-third had engaged in recent binge eating (Eddy et al., 2007). It is not clear whether negative mood states are the cause of being overweight, but it is easy to imagine how they can be the result of societal responses to excess weight.

Social Dimension

Family environmental factors have also been associated with excess weight in children and adolescents, including reports of teasing by family members about weight issues (Eddy et al., 2007). Parental eating patterns and attitudes also influence food intake in children (Bruss, Morris, & Dannison, 2003). In families in which a positive mealtime atmosphere was reported, adolescents were less likely to engage in disordered eating (Neumark-Sztainer et al., 2004).

In an interesting study, Christakis and Fowler (2007) followed the social networks of 12,067 adults over a period of thirty-two years to determine social factors associated with obesity. They wanted to see whether friends, siblings, spouses, or neighbors had an impact on weight gain. Some of the findings were quite surprising. If someone a person considers a friend becomes obese, a person's chances of also becoming obese increase by 57 percent. (If both individuals consider each other friends, the chances increase by 171 percent.) The chances for obesity in an individual also increase when one of the following individuals became obese: adult sibling: 40 percent; spouse: 37 percent; neighbors: 0 percent (unless they were also friends). Their social contagion theory hypothesizes that people "infect" others in their social network regarding the acceptability of weight gain and thereby contribute to the increase in obesity (Hill, Rand, Nowak, M. A., & Christakis, N. A., 2010).

> ### Did You Know?
>
> In a twelve-year study of American adults sixty years and older:
>
> - Obese individuals who were fit had lower mortality rates compared to unfit normal-weight or lean individuals.
>
> - Among fit individuals, survival rates were similar for normal weight, overweight, and obese individuals.
>
> - Being overweight and obese was not an independent predictor of death.
>
> - Staying fit may be more important than losing weight.
>
> Source: Sui et al., (2007)

Sociocultural Dimension

Attitudes regarding food and weight normalcy are developed in the home and community. Rates of obesity tend to be highest among ethnic minorities (CDC, 2009). In many ethnic groups, there is less pressure to remain thin, and being overweight is not a big concern unless it is extreme. As noted earlier, among African Americans, there is greater acceptance of fuller figures, and a larger derriere in women is seen as desirable (Foster-Scott, 2007). Rates of obesity also tend to be higher among lower social class individuals and may be a product of limited availability of fruits, vegetables, low-fat food, and opportunities for exercise in poorer neighborhoods (Peralta, 2003). In Mexico, low-income mothers underestimate the weight status of overweight or obese children and do not feel that sweetened drinks and high fat snacks are unhealthy (Jimenez-Cruz et al., 2010). Advertising of high-calorie foods is also seen by some to be a contributor to obesity. Food advertising to children in both Sweden and Quebec was banned more than ten years ago. However, neither region showed any benefit from this action; the childhood obesity rate increased in a manner similar to that of other areas (Adamson & Zywicki, 2007).

Treatments for Obesity

Treatments for obesity have included dieting, lifestyle changes, medications, and surgery. In general, dieting in and of itself may produce short-term weight loss but tends to be ineffective long term; some individuals gain back more weight than was lost. The outcome for children may be somewhat more successful (Moens, Braet, & Van Winckel, 2010). Mann and colleagues (2007) concluded that most adults would be better off not dieting because of the stress on the body as a result of weight cycling. Indeed, the "yo-yo" effect in dieting (cycles of weight gain and loss) is associated with increased risk of cardiovascular disease, stroke, and altered immune functioning. Comprehensive intervention programs appear to be somewhat more promising. In a meta-analysis of studies incorporating "rigorous randomized trials" of obesity treatments that have included a minimum of two years of follow-up, Powell, Calvin, and Calvin (2007) reported the following conclusions:

1. Lifestyle interventions (low-calorie diets and exercise) were successful in producing moderate and sustained reductions in weight. This modest weight loss was associated with a reduction in Type 2 diabetes, blood pressure, and overall mortality rate.

2. Drug treatments such as the use of Orlistat, which blocks the gastrointestinal uptake of about 30 percent of ingested fat, resulted in a sustainable weigh loss of about seven pounds.

3. Gastric bypass surgery for individuals identified as morbidly obese (BMI greater or equal to 35) or obese with serious comorbid disease yielded a weight loss of about fifty to eighty pounds for about 70 percent of the participants. However, in one trial, over a period of five years, 45 percent had sustained only a twenty-two pound loss. It appears that following surgical intervention, it is not unusual for weight gain to occur after the initial period of rapid weight loss.

Thus comprehensive interventions that combine lifestyle changes with drugs and/or surgery appear to be the most effective in sustaining weight loss.

Summary

1. What kinds of eating disorders exist?

   • Individuals with anorexia nervosa suffer from body image distortion. They suffer from the effects of starvation but are still deathly afraid of getting fat.

   • An individual with bulimia nervosa is generally of normal weight; engages in binge eating; feels a loss of control over eating during these periods' and uses vomiting, exercise, or laxatives to attempt to control weight. Some people with anorexia nervosa also engage in binge/purge eating. Although many people have engaged in binge eating, a binge-eating diagnosis is given only when the individual has recurrent episodes in which she or he feels a loss of control over eating and shows marked distress about the activity.

   • Individuals who show atypical patterns of severely disordered eating that do not fully meet the criteria for anorexia nervosa, bulimia nervosa, or binge-eating disorder are given the diagnosis of eating conditions not elsewhere classified.

2. What are some causes of eating disorders?

   • Genetics and neurotransmitter abnormalities are implicated in eating disorders. Research currently is focusing on the role of dopamine in eating disorders.

   • It is believed that the societal emphasis on thinness as being attractive may contribute to the increasing incidence of eating disorder. This is believed to lead to an internalized thin ideal that girls and women aspire to achieve.

- Parental attitudes regarding the importance of thinness are implicated in eating disorders, as is teasing regarding weight, especially among children with low self-esteem or with childhood trauma.
- Countries that are influenced by Western standards also report an increasing incidence of eating disorders in women.

3. What are some treatment options for eating disorders?

- Many of the therapies for eating disorders attempt to teach clients to identify the impact of societal messages regarding thinness and encourage them to develop healthier goals and values.
- For individuals with anorexia nervosa, medical, as well as psychological, treatment is necessary because the body is in starvation mode. The goal is to help clients gain weight, normalize their eating patterns, understand and alter their thoughts related to body image, and develop more healthy methods of dealing with stress.
- With bulimia nervosa, medical assistance may also be required because of the physiological changes associated with purging.

- Because many people with binge-eating disorder are overweight or obese, weight reduction strategies are also included in treatment.
- With both bulimia nervosa and binge-eating disorder, therapy involves normalizing eating patterns, developing a more positive body image, and dealing with stress in a healthier fashion.

4. What causes obesity?

- Obesity is defined as having a body mass index greater than 30. Some researchers believe that obesity should be included in the DSM because it has characteristics of addictive behavior similar to those seen in substance abuse.
- The causes of obesity vary from individual to individual and often involve combinations of biological predispositions and psychological, social, and sociocultural influences.

5. What are some treatment options for obesity?

- In general, dieting alone has been ineffective over the long term. Lifestyle changes that include reduced intake of high-calorie foods combined with exercise have proven more effective. In the case of severely obese individuals, surgery has produced some promising long-term results.

Media Resources

Psychology CourseMate   Access an interactive eBook, chapter-specific interactive learning tools, including flash cards, quizzes, videos, and more in your Psychology CourseMate, accessed through CengageBrain.com.

CENGAGENOW

CengageNow   CengageNOW is an easy-to-use online resource that helps you study in less time to get the grade you want—NOW. If your textbook does not include an access code card, go to CengageBrain.com to gain access.

CENGAGE brain.com

CengageBrain   More than just an interactive study guide, WebTutor is an anytime, anywhere customized learning solution with an eBook, keeping you connected to your textbook, instructor, and classmates. Purchase the access chosen by your instructor at CengageBrain.com.

11

Chip Simons/Taxi/Getty Images

Substance-Use Disorders

Jim, married and father of two teenage sons, is a fifty-four-year-old
alcoholic. He recently lost his job due to his drinking. Jim clearly recalls
the first time he drank. At age fifteen, he attended a party where alcohol
was freely served. Jim took a drink, hoping it would help him feel more
relaxed; he disliked the taste of alcohol, but forced himself to continue drinking to
the point of getting drunk. The next day he was so sick that he swore he would
never drink again, but two weeks later he had a few beers, trying to ease his nerves
before a big test. Over the next several years, Jim acquired the ability to consume
large amounts of alcohol and was proud of his drinking capacity. He remained
anxious about social gatherings, but after a few drinks he was uninhibited and the
"life of the party." His drinking during college was confined to weekend fraternity
parties. He was considered a heavy drinker in the fraternity, but the
drinking did not seem to affect his academic performance.

After graduate school, Jim married and began his career in the
aerospace industry. After accepting a management position, Jim
started drinking throughout the week claiming drinking was the only
way he could relax. He attributed his increased drinking to pressures at work and a desire to feel comfortable in social situations.
It became more difficult for Jim to get up and go to work and to
complete work assignments on time. The drinking continued despite
frequent arguments with his wife and sons regarding alcohol use and
a physician's warning that alcohol was causing liver damage. Jim could
not control his alcohol consumption. Jim and his wife were unaware
that their youngest son, a middle school student, had been using
marijuana and drinking heavily for over a year.

CHAPTER OUTLINE

Substance-Use Disorders

Substance-use disorders can develop in many ways. However, Jim's
story of problem drinking is typical in several respects. He initially
found the taste of alcohol unpleasant, and, after his first bout of
drunkenness, he swore he would never drink again. Nevertheless,
Jim returned to drinking. Heavy drinking served a purpose: It
reduced his anxiety, particularly with respect to work and social situations. His alcohol consumption continued despite obvious negative consequences. His preoccupation with alcohol and deterioration
in social and occupational functioning are also characteristic of

focus questions

1 What are substance-use disorders?

2 What substances are involved in substance-use disorders?

3 Why do people develop substance-use disorders?

4 What kinds of interventions and treatments are available for substance-use disorders, and does treatment work?

problem drinkers. Additionally, Jim's son, like many children of alcoholics, developed a substance-use problem.

Why did Jim force himself to drink when alcohol initially tasted so bad? Even though alcohol may have reduced work and social anxieties, it also increased arguments with his wife and resulted in health problems. Why did he have a hard time limiting how much he drank? What lead him on the path to alcoholism? Would things have turned out differently if Jim had sought professional help for his anxiety rather than trying to self-medicate with alcohol? What might account for his son's early substance use?

Throughout history, people have swallowed, sniffed, smoked, or otherwise taken into their bodies a variety of chemical substances for the purpose of altering mood, levels of consciousness, or behavior. The pervasiveness of substance use in contemporary culture is apparent from our vast consumption of alcohol, tobacco, caffeine, prescription medications, and illegal drugs. Headlines regarding drug busts, "the War on Drugs," and celebrities overdosing or "entering rehab" further highlight the pervasiveness of the issue. The Substance Abuse and Mental Health Services Administration (SAMHSA) obtains annual data regarding the use of alcohol, tobacco, and illicit drugs based on interviews with approximately 67,500 adolescents and adults. Based on 2009 interview data (SAMHSA, 2010a), researchers estimate that 21.8 million adolescents and adults (8.7 percent of the population) used illicit drugs including cannabis, cocaine, heroin, hallucinogens, inhalants, or illicitly obtained prescription drugs. The problem of illicit drug use occurs with greater frequency in some age and some ethnic groups (Figure 11.1 and Figure 11.2). Increases in the nonmedical use of prescription drugs as well as the high rates of heavy drinking and marijuana use reported by young adults (ages 18 to 25) is a particular concern.

Substance-use disorders arise when psychoactive substances, substances that alter moods, thought processes, or other psychological states, are used excessively. Heavy substance use induces changes in the brain that result in the behaviors that characterize

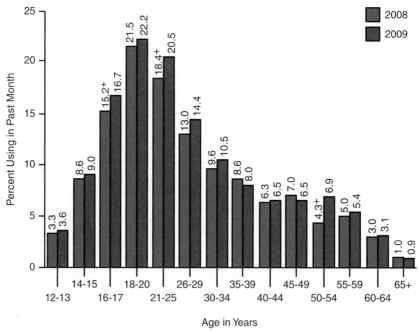

Figure 11.1

TWO YEAR COMPARISON OF PAST MONTH ILLICIT DRUG USE ACROSS AGE GROUPS

In comparing 2008 and 2009, increases in the use of illicit drugs (cannabis, cocaine, heroin, hallucinogens, inhalants, or nonmedical use of prescription drugs) occurred in almost all age groups.

Source: SAMHSA (2010a)

psychoactive substance substance that alters mood, thought processes, or other psychological states

addiction (Kalivas & O'Brien, 2008). Addiction involves compulsive drug-seeking behavior and a loss of control over drug use. It is difficult to stop not only because of the pleasurable feelings that result from substance use, but also the negative feelings that occur when use is discontinued. DSM-5 differentiates substance-use disorders according to the specific substance used. All substance-use disorders involve a maladaptive pattern of recurrent use, extending over a period of at least twelve months. Substance abuse results in notable impairment or distress and continues despite social, occupational, psychological, or physical problems. Substance abuse can cause legal difficulties; jeopardize the safety of the user or others; and affect social relationships and obligations at work, school, or home. The following characteristics are often present:

1. An inability to control use of the substance, despite harmful physical, psychological, or interpersonal effects.
2. Craving for and preoccupation with obtaining and using the substance.
3. The development of tolerance—a need for increasing quantities of the substance to achieve the desired effect.
4. Reduction or cessation of substance intake results in withdrawal (physical or emotional symptoms such as shaking, irritability, and inability to concentrate); withdrawal symptoms may result in resumption of substance use.

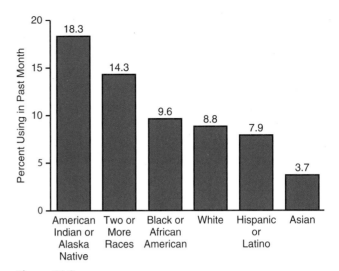

Figure 11.2

ETHNIC GROUPS COMPARISONS IN PAST MONTH ILLICIT DRUG USE

There are significant differences between ethnic groups in the use of illicit drugs (cannabis, cocaine, hallucinogens, inhalants, or nonmedical use of prescription drugs).
Source: SAMHSA (2010a)

Chronic exposure to a substance often results in physiological dependence—the body adapts and begins to accept the presence of the substance as normal. Evidence of either tolerance or withdrawal symptoms indicates that physiological dependence has developed. It is important to remember that substance-use disorders involve much more than physiological dependence alone; in fact, tolerance and withdrawal can occur with moderate doses of many prescription medications.

It is likely that you know someone with a substance-use disorder. Not only is substance use pervasive in our society, so is serious substance abuse. In 2009, an estimated 22.5 million adolescents and adults (8.9 percent of the population) met the criteria for a substance-use disorder at some time during the year; of this group 3.2 million abused alcohol and illicit drugs, 3.9 million abused illicit drugs but not alcohol, and 15.4 million abused only alcohol. Marijuana was the most commonly abused illicit drug followed by pain relievers and cocaine. Substance abuse is twice as prevalent in males, although female abuse rates are almost equal to males among those aged 12 to 17 (Figure 11.3). Additionally, the rate of illicit drug use is much higher among adolescents (with 61 percent reporting illicit drug use) compared to those aged 18 to 25 (38 percent) and those aged 26 or older (25 percent) (SAMHSA, 2010a).

You may wonder which substances are considered the most dangerous. A recent analysis concluded that heroin, crack cocaine, and methamphetamine present the greatest danger for the user, but that alcohol is the most dangerous drug when both personal and societal ramifications are considered (Nutt, King, & Phillip, 2010). As you proceed through this chapter, we hope you consider the personal and societal effects of the substances discussed, as well as the vast numbers affected by substance abuse, both directly and indirectly. We first examine the various substances involved in substance-use disorders. We then use the multipath perspective to understand possible causes of addiction. We conclude by discussing the importance of relapse prevention and treatment efficacy for the most commonly abused substances. As we proceed, keep in mind that these substances activate (and eventually change) psychological reward systems in the pleasure center of the brain and are highly reinforcing to users, especially during initial experimentation when the body has not adapted to the substance.

addiction compulsive drug-seeking behavior and a loss of control over drug use

tolerance decreases in the effects of a substance that occur after chronic use

withdrawal adverse physical and psychological symptoms that occur after reducing or ceasing intake of a substance

physiological dependence state of adaptation that occurs after chronic exposure to a substance; can result in craving and withdrawal symptoms

Figure 11.3

AGE AND GENDER DIFFERENCES IN SUBSTANCE-USE DISORDER DIAGNOSIS

With the exception of those aged 12 to 17, the incidence of past-year substance-use disorder diagnosis is about twice as high for males compared to females.

Source: SAMHSA (2010a)

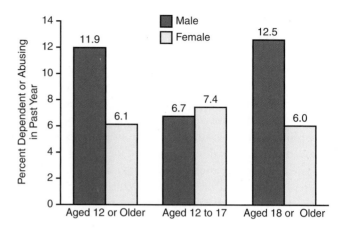

Substances Associated with Abuse

Our national prescription drug abuse problem cannot be ignored. I have worked in the treatment field for the last 35 years, and recent trends regarding the extent of prescription drug abuse are startling. We must work with prescribers, the pharmaceutical industry, and families to help us fight this scourge.

Thomas McLellan, Deputy Director of Office of National Drug Control Policy, 2010.

Misuse of a number of substances can lead to a substance-use disorder. Substances that are abused include prescription medications used to treat anxiety, insomnia, or pain; legal substances such as alcohol, caffeine, tobacco, and household chemicals; and illegal substances such as methamphetamine, cocaine, and heroin. Each of the substances discussed in this chapter can create significant physical; social; psychological; and, sometimes, legal problems. We discuss a variety of substances—including those that tend to overly relax the central nervous system such as alcohol, opioids, tranquilizers, sleeping pills, and antianxiety medications. We also discuss central nervous system stimulants (including caffeine, cocaine, amphetamines, and methamphetamine), hallucinogens (including LSD), dissociative anesthetics (including PCP, ketamine, and dextromethorphan), as well as substances with multiple effects including nicotine, cannabis, Ecstasy, and inhalants. Table 11.1 lists these substances and their effects as well as their addictive potential.

Depressants

Depressants cause generalized depression of the central nervous system and a slowing down of responses. Individuals taking depressants may feel relaxed and sociable due to lowered interpersonal inhibitions. Let's examine in more detail one of the most widely used depressants—alcohol—and then discuss other depressants, including tranquilizers, sleeping pills, and antianxiety medications.

depressant substance that causes a slowing of responses and generalized depression of the central nervous system

moderate drinking a lower-risk pattern of alcohol intake (no more than one or two drinks per day)

binge drinking episodic intake of five or more alcoholic beverages for men or four or more drinks for women

heavy drinking chronic alcohol intake of more than two drinks per day for men and more than one drink per day for women

Alcohol

Slightly more than half of all adolescent and adult Americans report being current drinkers of alcohol. We begin our discussion of alcohol by clarifying terminology. One drink is defined as 12 ounces of beer, 5 ounces of wine, or 1.5 ounces of hard liquor. The term moderate drinking is typically used to describe lower-risk patterns of drinking, generally no more than one or two drinks per day. Binge drinking refers to episodic drinking involving five or more drinks on a single occasion for men and four or more drinks for women. Heavy drinking refers to chronic drinking, usually an average of more than two drinks per day for men and more than one drink per day for women (although the SAMSHA survey defines it as binge drinking five or more days per month).

TABLE 11.1   Commonly Abused Substances

Substance	Short-Term Effects*	Addictive Potential
Central Nervous System Depressants		
Alcohol	Relaxant, loss of inhibitions	High
Opioids	Pain relief, sedation, drowsiness	High
Sedatives/ Hypnotics/Anxiolytics	Sedation, drowsiness, anxiety reduction, impaired judgment	Moderate-High
Central Nervous System Stimulants		
Caffeine	Energizer, attention enhancer	Moderate
Amphetamines	Energizer, euphoriant, attention enhancer	High
Cocaine	Energizer, euphoriant	High
Hallucinogens		
LSD, psilocybin, mescaline	Altered perceptions, sensory distortions	Low
Dissociative Anesthetics		
Phencyclidine (PCP)	Confusion, sensory distortions, feelings ofw detachment	Moderate
Ketamine	Confusion, sensory distortions, feelings of detachment	Moderate
Dextromethorphan (DXM)	Confusion, sensory distortions, feelings of detachment	Moderate
Substances with Multiple Effects		
Nicotine	Energizer, relaxant	High
Cannabis	Relaxant, euphoriant	Moderate
Inhalants	Disorientation	Variable
Ecstasy (MDMA)	Energizer, heightened senses	Moderate
Gamma hydroxybutyrate (GHB)	Depressant, euphoriant, strength enhancer	High

*Specific effects depend on the quantity used, extent of previous use, and other substances concurrently ingested, as well as on the experiences, expectancies, and personality of the person using the substance.

About 70 percent of adults do not drink excessively, either because they abstain or drink in moderation (Hasin et al., 2007). However, nearly one fourth of Americans aged 12 or older binge drink, including 7 percent who binge at least five days per month. Males in all age groups are more likely to consume alcohol and engage in binge and heavy drinking compared to females. Ethnic group data reveals that Asians (followed by African Americans) have the lowest levels of heavy and binge drinking (SAMHSA, 2010a). Native Americans of both genders demonstrate the earliest onset of drinking and highest weekly alcohol consumption, whereas Hispanic men have the highest rates of daily alcohol consumption. Variability exists within ethnic groups: For example, Southwest Indians, especially females, have low rates of alcohol consumption; Pacific Islanders (a subset of Asian Americans) consume twice as much as other Asian groups; and Puerto Rican males and females and Mexican American males have much higher weekly consumption and binge drinking than other Hispanic groups (Chartier & Caetano, 2010).

Let's focus on statistics for the college age population. As illustrated in Figure 11.4, binge drinking and heavy drinking are especially problematic among those aged 21–25. When looking at young adults (ages 18 to 25), the rate of binge drinking is 42 percent, with heavy

Did You Know?

Among college students (ages 18–24) each year:

- 1,700 die from unintentional alcohol-related injuries, including car accidents.

- 599,000 are injured under the influence of alcohol.

- More than 696,000 are assaulted by another student who has been drinking.

- More than 97,000 experience alcohol-related sexual assault or date rape.

- More than 2.1 million drive under the influence of alcohol.

Source: Hingson et al., (2002); Hingson et al., (2005)

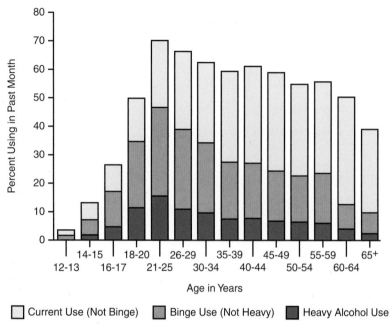

Current Use (Not Binge)   Binge Use (Not Heavy)   Heavy Alcohol Use

Figure 11.4

COMPARISONS IN ALCOHOL USE ACROSS AGE GROUPS

Almost half of those ages 18 to 20 reported underage alcohol use in the past month, including 23 percent who reported binge drinking and 11 percent who were heavy alcohol users. The highest level of binge drinking and heavy alcohol use is seen in the 21 to 25 age group.

Source: SAMHSA (2010a)

drinking reported by 14 percent (SAMSHA, 2010a). Heavy drinking occurs more frequently in 18–22 year olds who attend college full time compared to those who do not (Figure 11.5). A recent online survey revealed that 83 percent of freshman at one university reported recently consuming alcohol, half reported binge-drinking, and many reported drinking at least 6–9 days during the month (Sloane, Burke, Cremeens, Vail-Smith, & Woolsey, 2010).

Approximately 5 percent of those who use alcohol are physiologically dependent (Koob, Kandel, & Volkow, 2008). Alcohol withdrawal symptoms are variable and can include headache, fatigue, sweating, body tremors, and mood changes. Severe withdrawal can produce a life-threatening condition, delirium tremens, that begins with profound anxiety, agitation, and confusion followed by seizures, disorientation, hallucinations, or extreme lethargy. The lifetime prevalence of alcohol abuse is 18 percent. Whites; Native Americans; males; and those who are younger, unmarried, and have lower incomes are most likely to become alcoholic (Hasin, Stinson, Ogburn, & Grant, 2007). Although men are twice as likely to develop an alcohol-use disorder, alcoholism in women progresses more rapidly (Anthenelli, 2010).

Reactions to alcohol often depend on expectancies regarding alcohol use (Witkiewitz & Marlatt, 2004). Short-term psychological effects can include feelings of happiness and loss of inhibitions, as well as anger and negative mood. Once swallowed, alcohol is quickly absorbed into the bloodstream and begins to depress central nervous

---

CRITICAL THINKING

Can Prevention Efforts Combat Societal Messages about Alcohol Use?

There are mixed messages in U.S. society regarding alcohol use. On the one hand, the myth persists that drinking alcohol is the norm, even a rite of passage for adolescents. This erroneous belief persists despite the fact that the majority of American adults consume alcohol only occasionally or not at all. The message of those who market alcohol appears to be much stronger than prevention efforts that attempt to stress the personal and societal risk of excess alcohol consumption and the particular risk of underage alcohol use.

Specialists in the field of addiction are fervently attempting to nullify societal messages that normalize and even glamorize alcohol use and to heighten awareness of risk factors, especially among those who are particularly vulnerable to addiction—adolescents and young adults. Scientists have demonstrated that alcohol (and other substances) has a strong effect on the developing brain and that the effects of alcohol use on neurological development are most profound through the mid-twenties. The college years are a high-risk period for beginning the addiction process. College students who participate in underage alcohol use often drink heavily. Although college-bound high school students are less likely to binge drink, this trend reverses after college entrance;

additionally, students with the greatest genetic risk of developing alcoholism tend to drink the most (Timberlake, Hopfer, Friedman et al., 2007). There is little doubt, given the data on heavy drinking in this age group, that young adults are an important target of prevention efforts. Alcohol-abuse prevention campaigns are attempting to correct social misperceptions about the frequency of behaviors such as drinking and driving (Perkins, Linkenbach, Lewis, & Neighbors, 2010). Unfortunately, as long as societal messages make alcohol consumption look normative, it may be difficult to reverse the trend of increasing alcohol abuse.

For Further Consideration:

1. What mixed messages have you encountered related to alcohol use?
2. Do you feel the college environment plays a role in decisions to participate in heavy or underage drinking?
3. What aspects of alcohol abuse do you think are most relevant to college students, and how can these be incorporated into prevention messages?
4. What kinds of prevention efforts do you think would be the most effective on your college campus?

system functioning. When alcohol content in the blood-stream (blood alcohol level) is about 0.1 percent (for many, the equivalent of drinking three ounces of whiskey or three glasses of beer), muscular coordination and judgment are impaired. Higher levels of blood alcohol (0.3 percent in some individuals) can result in a loss of consciousness or even death.

Our bodies produce "clean-up" enzymes, including aldehyde dehydrogenase (ALDH), to counteract toxins that build up as alcohol is metabolized. Production of ALDH is affected by gender (males, especially younger males, produce more than females), genetic make up (the physiology of some individuals, especially Asians, minimizes ALDH production), and food or medications concurrently in the body. Carbonated beverages and aspirin hasten alcohol absorption and reduce the efficiency of the "clean up," whereas food slows absorption giving the enzymes more time to work. Body weight and the period of time during which alcohol was consumed also affect intoxication. Large amounts of alcohol consumed rapidly can result in impaired breathing, coma, and death; this condition, known as alcohol poisoning, can be exacerbated by the vomiting and dehydration that occur as the body attempts to rid itself of excess alcohol.

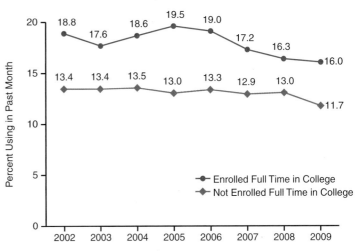

Figure 11.5

TRENDS IN HEAVY ALCOHOL USE IN 18- TO 22-YEAR-OLDS
There are significant differences in heavy alcohol use between 18 to 22-year-olds who attend college full time versus those who attend part time or not at all, with college attendees consistently reporting more heavy drinking.
Source: SAMHSA (2010a)

There are multiple physiological consequences associated with excessive alcohol use. Tolerance to alcohol develops rapidly, so drinkers wanting to feel the effects of alcohol often increase their intake. Unfortunately, tolerance does not decrease the toxicity of alcohol, so heavy drinkers expose their brains and body to greater physiological risk. Neurological effects include impaired motor skills, reduced reasoning and judgment, memory deficits, distractibility, and reduced motivation (Sullivan, Harris, & Pfefferbaum, 2010). Additionally, alcohol affects the entire cardiovascular system and can cause cirrhosis of the liver and alcoholic hepatitis, as well as cancers of the mouth and throat (especially when combined with smoking). Alcoholics who continue to drink demonstrate declines in neurological functioning; sustained abstinence can lead to cognitive improvement although older, heavy drinkers and those with alcohol-related seizures or liver disease demonstrate less recovery (Yeh et al., 2007).

In stark contrast to the stereotype of the skid row alcoholic, many alcoholics are able to function without severe disruption to their life—these so-called "high functioning alcoholics" work, raise families, and maintain social relationships. Although aware of the negative physical and social consequences of their drinking and distressed over their inability to control alcohol intake, they may deny they have a problem with alcohol or hide their drinking (Willenbring, 2010). It is not uncommon for individuals with alcoholism to alternate between periods of excessive drinking and sobriety, often in an attempt to prove they can abstain (Sullivan, Harris, & Pfefferbaum, 2010).

Although many alcoholics recover from dependence, some have a severe, progressive form of alcoholism resulting in significant functional impairment (Willenbring, 2010). In research demonstrating the variable course of alcoholism, Dawson and colleagues (2005) interviewed individuals with past-year alcohol dependence and found that about 75 percent demonstrated considerable recovery; in fact, 36 percent reported complete recovery. Recovery was least likely for those who drank the most. Interviews three years later revealed that alcohol dependence had recurred for about half of those who periodically drank heavily, in 27 percent of those drinking moderately, and in only 7 percent of those who abstained (Dawson, Goldstein, & Grant, 2007). Another three year follow-up of alcoholics found that individuals with psychiatric disorders; a family history of alcoholism; or more chronic, severe drinking were most likely to remain dependent on alcohol (Moss, Chen, & Yi, 2010).

delirium tremens life-threatening withdrawal symptom that can result from chronic alcohol use

alcohol poisoning toxic effects resulting from rapidly consuming alcohol or ingesting a large quantity of alcohol; can result in impaired breathing, coma, and death

Opioids

Case Study

Throughout the evening of June 24, 2009, Michael Jackson was energetically rehearsing for a much-anticipated concert series. The next day he was found in his bedroom, not breathing. Paramedics were unable to revive him. His death appeared to be the result of a drug overdose. Battling a combination of pain, anxiety, and chronic insomnia, Jackson was known to use a variety of prescription medications. His addiction reportedly began with pain medication prescribed after he was burned during a rehearsal. The exact details of his later drug use are debated. Prescription painkillers, stimulants, antianxiety and sleeping medications are often mentioned. Lyrics written by Jackson—"Demerol, oh God he's taking Demerol"—from a song called "Morphine" added to speculation about continued drug use and opioid dependence.

Medications became less effective as Jackson developed tolerance to the drugs. Jackson continued to battle chronic insomnia and was desperate to rest, resorting to more dangerous substances. His ongoing quest for sleep ended the morning of June 25, 2009, when he suffered cardiac arrest. The coroner found multiple medications in Jackson's system including a powerful anesthetic, propofol; it was concluded that Jackson's death resulted from acute propofol intoxication.

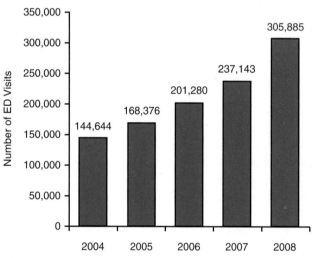

Figure 11.6

EMERGENCY DEPARTMENT CONTACTS RELATED TO ILLICIT USE OF PRESCRIPTION OPIOIDS

The number of emergency department visits due to illicit use of prescription pain medications increased 111 percent between 2004 and 2008, and visits more than doubled in all age groups and for both males and females.

Source: SAMHSA (2010a)

Opioids are painkilling agents that depress the central nervous system. Heroin and opium, both derived from the opium plant, are the most well known of the illicit opioids. All opioids (including morphine, codeine, and oxycodone) are highly addictive and require careful medical management when prescribed for pain and anxiety. Use of prescription opioids obtained through illegal purchase or solicitation of multiple prescriptions is on the increase (Gilson & Kreis, 2010). Almost 20 percent of adults in the United States have used prescription drugs for nonmedical reasons (National Institutes of Health, 2010). Nonmedical use of pain relievers is a leading form of drug abuse, second only to marijuana (SAMHSA, 2010a). The number of emergency department visits due to nonmedical use of pain medications increased 111 percent between 2004 and 2008 (Figure 11.6), led by a 152 percent increase in oxycodone-related visits (SAMHSA, 2010b). Similarly, between 1998 and 2008 there was a 400 percent increase in adolescent and adult treatment admissions for prescription opioid abuse (SAMHSA, 2010c).

Long-term misuse of prescription opioids is linked with significant social problems (Butler et al., 2010). A recent study involving individuals receiving treatment for opioid dependence is particularly disconcerting. Many opioid abusers began their habit with prescribed medication, eventually buying prescription drugs illegally or trying a less expensive and even more lethal opioid—heroin (Canfield et al., 2010). Prescription opioids are considered by some to be the new "gateway" drug (substance leading to the use of more dangerous drugs). An additional concern is that both heroin and *cheese*, a drug combining heroin and over-the-counter cold medications, are being used with increased frequency by adolescents in some areas of the United States.

Opioids produce both feelings of euphoria and drowsiness. Tolerance builds quickly resulting in dependency and a need for increased doses to achieve desired effects. Most opioid overdose deaths are accidental and involve concurrent use of alcohol or other drugs (Okie, 2010). Withdrawal symptoms (including restlessness, muscle pain, insomnia, and cold flashes) are often severe. Symptoms of lethargy, fatigue, anxiety, and disturbed sleep

opioid   painkilling agent that depresses the central nervous system, such as heroin and prescription pain relievers

"gateway" drug   substance that leads to use of even more lethal substances

may persist for months, and drug craving can persist for years. Intravenous heroin use can result in diseases associated with needle sharing such as AIDS and hepatitis. More than 25 percent of AIDS cases involve persons who abuse intravenous drugs (Centers for Disease Control and Prevention, 2007b). The use of adulterants, miscellaneous substances used to increase the bulk of illegal drugs such as heroin, can lead to additional medical complications.

Sedatives, Hypnotics, and Anxiolytics

Sedatives, including hypnotics (sleeping pills) and anxiolytics (antianxiety medications), have calming effects and are used in the treatment of agitation, muscle tension, insomnia, and anxiety. Hypnotics induce sleep and are used during surgical procedures and to combat insomnia. Anxiolytics are used to treat anxiety; they are sometimes referred to as minor tranquilizers, so named to distinguish them from the major tranquilizing medications used with psychotic disorders. The drug classes of barbiturates (such as Seconal and phenobarbital) and benzodiazepines (such as Valium, Ativan, and Xanax) have rapid anxiolytic (anxiety-reducing) effects in moderate doses and hypnotic (sleep-inducing) effects in higher doses. A substance-use disorder can develop with high prescription doses or when medication is misused or obtained illegally. Individuals who have difficulty dealing with stress or who experience anxiety or insomnia are prone to overusing and becoming dependent on sedatives. Although his addiction began with opioids, the case of Michael Jackson illustrates this pattern. Additionally, some use sedatives recreationally or to counteract cocaine withdrawal symptoms (Sola, Chopra, & Rastogi, 2010).

Sedatives are quite dangerous when misused. Even in low doses, they cause drowsiness, impaired judgment, and diminished motor skills. As with opioids, their legal use is carefully monitored due to known risks regarding drug dependence; however, their availability via illegal drug markets makes misuse difficult to control. Nonmedical use of sedatives, anxiolytics, and hypnotics is highest in the 26–35 age group (Sola, Chopra, & Rastogi, 2010). Excessive use of sedatives can lead to accidental overdose and death. Combining alcohol with sedatives can be especially dangerous because alcohol compounds depressant effects, slowing breathing and increasing risk of coma or lethal outcome.

There is high potential for tolerance and physiological dependence with all sedatives; when discontinued, withdrawal symptoms can include insomnia, nervousness, headache, drowsiness, lack of energy, and loss of appetite. Due to concerns regarding addictive potential and lethality with overdose, many medical practitioners avoid prescribing sedatives to treat anxiety, choosing to instead to prescribe nonaddictive medications, such as antidepressants that have anxiolytic properties. Data from a 35,000 participant national survey supports this stance. Individuals prescribed sedatives for anxiety are twice as likely to abuse these drugs (Fenton, Keyes, Martins, & Hasin, 2010). Individuals prescribed sedatives for anxiety disorders, particularly those with a personal or family history of substance abuse, have increased risk of sedative dependence with larger doses or sedative use for more than one month (Sola, Chopra, & Rastogi, 2010).

A well-known sedative, Rohypnol, significantly interferes with cognitive functioning, balance, and short-term memory. Rohypnol is known as a "date rape" drug because unsuspecting individuals given the drug may feel sedated, uninhibited, and not remember recent activities. Rohypnol is illegal in the United States but is available for the treatment of severe insomnia in many countries. It is also used as a recreational drug in combination with alcohol, heroin, or cocaine. Rohypnol can produce dependence; high doses or use with other drugs can be lethal.

Stimulants

Stimulants, substances that speed up central nervous system activity, are used for a variety of reasons: to produce feelings of euphoria and well-being, improve mental and physical performance, reduce appetite, and prevent sleep. Unwanted physiological effects include heart arrhythmias, dizziness, tremors, and sweating. Psychological side effects can include anxiety, restlessness, agitation, hostility, and paranoia. Those who abuse illicit stimulants

adulterants substances used to increase the bulk of illegal drugs before sale

hypnotics medications that induce sleep

anxiolytics medications that reduce anxiety

stimulant substance that is a central nervous system energizer

often demonstrate binge use, with sequential high doses leading to exhaustion and acute psychotic symptoms. Tolerance rapidly leads to increased drug use; withdrawal can result in depression, anxiety, and extreme fatigue. Our discussion begins with a commonly used mild stimulant, caffeine, and then concentrates on amphetamines (including methamphetamine) and cocaine.

Caffeine

Case Study

I use energy drinks to stay awake while I study at night. I am noticing that I need more and more energy drinks to stay awake and keep alert. It's getting to the point where I need over four or five cans to get through a night, when normally it would take me only one can.

Caffeine is a stimulant found in coffee, chocolate, tea, and soft drinks. It is the most widely consumed psychoactive substance in the world, prized by almost every culture for its ability to increase attentiveness. In North America, about 90 percent of adults use caffeine every day. Caffeine can produce restlessness, nervousness, insomnia, gastrointestinal disturbance, and cardiac arrhythmia. Although caffeine is generally consumed in moderate doses (a cup of tea has 40–60 milligrams, coffee 70–175 milligrams, and cola 30–50 milligrams), widespread marketing and consumption of energy drinks has resulted in increased caffeine consumption, especially in younger age groups. Energy drinks, now a billion dollar industry, typically have 80–150 milligrams of caffeine in addition to sweeteners and energy-boosting additives such as the amino acid, taurine. The safety of high levels of taurine has not been documented (Bigard, 2010). Frequent consumption of energy drinks can produce tolerance and side effects such as headache and heart palpitations (Malinauskas et al., 2007). Energy drinks, particularly those that are highly sweetened, are often consumed in succession. They produce a boost in energy followed by feelings of fatigue once blood sugar levels plummet. Heavy consumption of energy drinks has been associated with new-onset seizures in some individuals (Iyadurai & Chung, 2007; Duchan, Patel, & Feucht, 2010).

Amphetamines

Amphetamines, also known as "uppers," significantly speed up central nervous system activity. Prescription amphetamines used to treat attention and sleep disorders (such as Ritalin, Benzedrine, and Dexedrine) are sometimes used illicitly. Nonmedical use of prescription stimulants is increasing in prevalence (Wu et al., 2007), particularly among white adolescents and young adults (Kroutil et al., 2006). About 2 percent of U.S. adults have experienced dependence on amphetamines. Amphetamine abuse is more common among persons from lower socioeconomic groups and among men (American Psychiatric Association, 2000a; SAMHSA, 2007). Addiction is most common in those who take amphetamines intravenously or nasally ("snorting") and in high doses. Although amphetamines can induce feelings of euphoria and confidence, agitation and assaultive or suicidal behaviors also occur. Heavy doses can trigger delusions of persecution that resemble paranoid schizophrenia. Brain damage can result from chronic stimulant abuse (Berman, Kuczenski, McCracken, & London, 2009).

Methamphetamine, a particularly dangerous drug that is taken orally, snorted, injected, or heated and smoked in rock "crystal" form, is used by 0.2 percent of the population (SAMHSA, 2010a). Popular due to its low cost and rapid euphoric effects, methamphetamine has serious health consequences including permanent damage to the heart, lungs, and immune system (Hauer, 2010). Although many are aware of the

CONTROVERSY

Using Stimulants to Improve Performance—A New Source of Addiction?

The nonmedical use of prescription medications is on the rise, including illicit use of stimulant medications (which are usually prescribed for attentional or severe sleep disorders). Stimulants are being illicitly used by high school and college students and young professionals who want to enhance their performance and outperform the competition (Wilens et al., 2008). Eighteen percent of one group of undergraduates reported such use, and another 26 percent of students with an attention deficit/hyperactivity disorder reported overuse of their own medication (Arria et al., 2008); many of these same students also reported extensive marijuana and alcohol use. Medical students, a group who should clearly understand the consequences of nonmedical prescription stimulant use, are also a high-risk population for illicit stimulant use (Tuttle, Scheurich, & Ranseen, 2010). The topic of using stimulants to avoid sleep or enhance performance has generated much debate, due to ethical as well as addiction concerns. What ethical issues arise from the illicit use of prescription medication to improve performance? How would you react if you found out one of your classmates was using stimulants to enhance scholastic achievement?

profound dental and aging effects of methamphetamine (Mooney et al., 2009), psychological changes including psychosis, depression, suicide, and violent behavior are also profound (Darke, Kaye, McKetin, & Duflou, 2008). As with other stimulants, methamphetamine has high potential for abuse and addiction.

Cocaine

Case Study

A 49-year-old woman, previously diagnosed with congestive heart failure, was admitted to the hospital with a severe cough and labored breathing. She reported that she had never smoked cigarettes, consumed alcohol, or used drugs other than cocaine, which she had been smoking for 30 years. Due to her severe emphysema and continued cocaine use, she was not a candidate for heart transplantation. She died from respiratory failure and cardiac arrest (Vahid & Marik, 2007).

Cocaine, a stimulant extracted from the coca plant, induces feelings of energy and euphoria. In 2009, there were an estimated 1.6 million cocaine users (0.7 percent of the population) with a large number of users (1.1 million) demonstrating cocaine dependence (SAMHSA, 2010a). Cocaine users typically prepare the drug by pouring the powder onto a mirror, separating it into "lines," and then "snorting" it from a small spoon, straw, or rolled paper. Crack is a potent form of cocaine produced by heating cocaine with other substances ("freebasing"); it is sold in small, solid pieces ("rocks") and is typically smoked. Crack produces very immediate but short-lived effects. Cocaine has a high potential for addiction, sometimes after only a short period of use. Approximately 20 percent of those who use cocaine are rapidly dependent on the drug (Koob, Kandel, & Volkow, 2008). Due to cocaine's intense effects, withdrawal causes lethargy and depression; users often take multiple doses in rapid succession trying to recreate the "high."

The constant desire for cocaine can impair social and occupational functioning. The high monetary cost of the substance coupled with the need for increased doses to achieve a "high" can cause users to resort to crime to feed their habit. Because cocaine stimulates the sympathetic nervous system, irregular heartbeat, stroke, and death may occur. Cocaine users sometimes experience acute psychiatric symptoms such as psychosis accompanied by delusions, paranoia, and hallucinations; more chronic difficulties such as anxiety, depression, sexual dysfunction, or sleep difficulties also occur. A practice referred to as "speedballing," injecting cocaine mixed with heroin, is particularly dangerous.

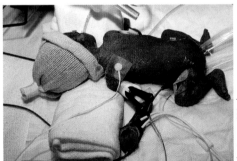

The Image Works

Cocaine Addiction from Mother to Child

Women who use drugs during pregnancy sometimes give birth to drug-addicted, underweight babies who are at risk for serious developmental problems. Pictured here is a newborn baby being monitored as it goes through cocaine withdrawal symptoms.

Hallucinogens

Hallucinogens are substances that produce vivid sensory awareness, heightened alertness, perceptions of increased insight and, sometimes, hallucinations. Extracts from hallucinogenic substances found in plants and fungus have been used for centuries, often during religious ceremonies. The altered state produced by hallucinogens can be a pleasant experience or an extremely traumatic one. "Good trips" are associated with sharpened visual and auditory perception, heightened sensation, and perceptions of profound insight. "Bad trips" can involve severe depression, disorientation, delusions, and sensory distortions that result in fear and panic. Some users also experience "flashbacks," the recurrence of hallucinations or other sensations days or weeks after drug intake. Fatigue, stress, or other drug use can trigger a "flashback." Hallucinogen Persisting Perception Disorder, a rare condition involving persistent flashbacks, can continue for years and significantly affect functioning (Halpern & Harrison, 2003; Espiard, Lecardeur, Abadie, Halbecq, & Dollfus, 2005). Substances that have primarily hallucinogenic effects, including lysergic acid diethylamide (LSD), psilocybin, and mescaline are discussed in this section. Drugs that have hallucinogenic effects combined with other properties (such as PCP, ketamine, and Ecstasy) are discussed later in the chapter. Hallucinogen use, including Ecstasy, was estimated to involve 1.3 million persons (0.5 percent of the adolescent and adult population) in 2009 (SAMHSA, 2010a).

Traditional hallucinogens are derived from natural sources: LSD from a grain-fungus, psilocybin from mushrooms, and mescaline from the peyote cactus. Naturally occurring hallucinogens such as mescaline and psilocybin have been used in cultural ceremonies and religious rites for thousands of years. LSD, however, gained notoriety in the mid-1960s, praised by users as a potent consciousness-expanding psychedelic drug. National surveys reveal that LSD use is not common; mescaline and psilocybin are also used infrequently. The effects and emotional reactions that result from hallucinogens can vary significantly, even for the same person using the same drug. Hallucinogens are not addictive and, therefore, do not cause compulsive drug-seeking behavior. However, tolerance does develop, so users frequently need larger quantities to re-create the initial effects of the drug. In one sample, nearly one in four hallucinogen users showed signs of hallucinogen dependence (Wu, Ringwalt, Weiss, & Blazer, 2009). Large doses are not typically fatal, although there are reports of people who have unwittingly committed suicide while under the influence of hallucinogens.

Dissociative Anesthetics

Case Study

A twenty-year-old man, tied in ropes, was brought to the hospital by his four brothers who explained, "He came home crazy, threw a chair through the window, tore a gas heater off the wall, and ran into the street." Police tried to apprehend him as he stood naked, directing traffic at a busy intersection; however, he escaped from the arresting officers and ran home, screaming threats at his family. His brothers were finally able to subdue him and bring him to the hospital where he remained agitated, his mood fluctuating between fear and anger. He was unable to walk without staggering and his speech was slurred. He continued to behave in a violent and disorganized manner with unpredictable bouts of intense anger, suspiciousness, and slurred speech, punctuated by intervals of lucid thought. Once calm, he denied behaving violently or acting in an unusual manner; he could not remember how he got to the hospital. He stated that he used both alcohol and marijuana socially but denied any recent phencyclidine (PCP) use. His blood and urine tested positive for PCP, a finding that did not surprise his brothers. (Adapted from Sadock & Sadock, 2008, p. 452)

hallucinogen substance that induces perceptual distortions and heightens sensory awareness

Phencyclidine (known as PCP) and ketamine (sometimes referred to as Special K), both highly dangerous and potentially addictive substances, are classified as dissociative anesthetics; used as anesthetics in veterinary medicine, they produce a dream-like detachment in humans. Dextromethorphan (DXM), an active ingredient in many over-the-counter cough suppressants, is another frequently misused dissociative anesthetic. PCP and ketamine are very similar chemically. They have dissociative, stimulant, depressant, amnesic, and hallucinogenic properties. PCP and ketamine are among the most dangerous of the so-called "club drugs," a term that comes from the popular use of certain drugs at dance clubs or "raves." These drugs cause disconnection, perceptual distortion, euphoria, and confusion, as well as delusions, hostility, and violent psychotic behavior, as seen in the earlier case study. Reactions to the drug are influenced by dosage, the individual user, and the circumstances of use. One thing is clear: PCP and ketamine can cause aggressive behavior, violence, or death due to agitation or delusions of invincibility. The cognitive and memory deficits seen in frequent ketamine users increase with ongoing use. Additionally, frequent users demonstrate depressive, dissociative, and delusional symptoms; delusions can persist even after cessation of ketamine use (Morgan, Muetzelfeldt, & Curran, 2010).

Health officials are concerned about the increased abuse of dextromethorphan (DXM), readily available in over-the-counter cold medications and cough suppressants. Despite industry efforts to control misuse of these products, approximately 5 percent of high school teens report using cough and cold medicines to get high (Johnston, Bachman, & O'Malley, 2009). Effects of DXM abuse can include disorientation, confusion, and sensory distortion. The large quantities consumed by those who misuse DXM can result in hyperthermia (a sudden rise in body temperature), high blood pressure, and heart arrhythmia; as with PCP and ketamine, health consequences are intensified when DXM is combined with alcohol or other drugs.

Substances with Mixed Chemical Properties

A number of abused substances have varied effects on the brain and central nervous system. We begin by briefly discussing nicotine, an addictive drug with both depressant and stimulant features. We then discuss cannabis, inhalants, and Ecstasy, as well as the unique dangers involved when substances are combined.

Nicotine

Nicotine, the widely used addictive substance found in tobacco, is most commonly associated with cigarette smoking. Nicotine is a stimulant in low doses and a relaxant in higher doses. In 2009, almost 70 million adults and adolescents (28 percent of the population) used tobacco products; the vast majority (59 million) smoked cigarettes, followed by cigars, smokeless tobacco, and pipes. As seen in Figure 11.7, nicotine use increases significantly during late adolescence, peaking in the twenties. More males (34 percent) than females (22 percent) use tobacco, particularly noncigarette products. Full-time college students (27 percent) are less likely to smoke than their age peers (41 percent); smokeless tobacco, used by 13 percent of males attending college, is increasing in popularity (SAMHSA, 2010a). It has long been known that cigarettes are strongly addictive. Almost 60 percent of current smokers are nicotine dependent (SAMHSA, 2007). A smoker's first cigarette of the day produces the greatest stimulant effect; euphoric effects decrease and tolerance and withdrawal symptoms increase as the day progresses (Benowitz, 2010).

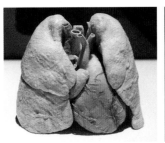

© Nancy Kaszerman/ZUMA/ Corbis

Smoking Effects on the Lungs

An actual view of healthy lungs and heart of a nonsmoker versus the blackened lungs and heart of a smoker at a New York City exhibit of real whole human body specimens. The human body specimens are preserved through a revolutionary technique called polymer preservation. All bodies are from people who died of natural causes.

Nicotine causes both the release of adrenaline, which gives a burst of energy, and the release of dopamine, resulting in feelings of pleasure. Additionally, adrenaline combined

dissociative anesthetic substance that produces a dream-like detachment

Figure 11.7

PAST MONTH CIGARETTE USE AMONG ADOLESCENTS AND ADULTS ACROSS AGE GROUPS

Cigarette smoking increases significantly during late adolescence and peaks between ages 21 and 29.

Source: SAMHSA (2010a)

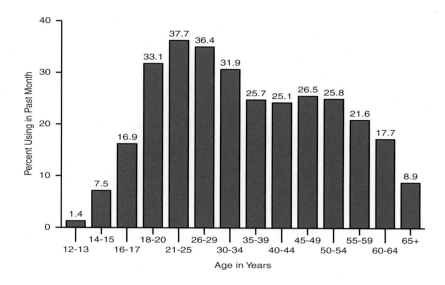

Did You Know?

Researchers have found that feeling "relaxed" immediately after the first puff of a cigarette was the leading predictor of becoming dependent on cigarettes and then being unable to quit. About 29 percent of adolescents interviewed said they had experienced such a feeling after their first cigarette.

Source: DiFranza et al., (2007)

with nicotine-driven releases of insulin result in high blood sugar and a loss of appetite. As tolerance develops, cravings occur and more nicotine is needed to experience the same energy, pleasure, and relaxation. Nicotine withdrawal symptoms include difficulty concentrating, restlessness, anxiety, depressed mood, and irritability. Tobacco smoke, including secondhand smoke, contains 4,000 chemicals, 250 of which are known to be harmful (U.S. Department of Health and Human Services, 2006). Smoking results in multiple health conditions that cause almost 1.5 million deaths annually in the United States (Benowitz, 2010) and 5 million deaths per year worldwide (Hatsukami, Stead, & Gupta, 2008). Smoking is considered the single most preventable cause of premature death (American Cancer Society, 2007).

Cannabis

Cannabis is the botanical name for a plant that contains a chemical (delta-9-tetrahydrocannabinol, referred to as THC) that can produce stimulant, depressant, and hallucinogenic effects. Marijuana is derived from the leaves and flowering top of the cannabis plant, whereas hashish, which contains particularly high levels of THC, comes from the pressed resin. Growing conditions influence the THC content as well as other chemicals in the plant. Concern about dangers with an increasingly popular substance, synthetic marijuana (made from a combination of herbs and chemicals and sold as incense), has resulted in bans on these products in several states and federal efforts to ban chemicals used in their manufacture.

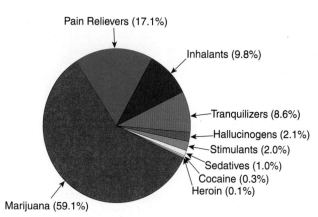

Figure 11.8

DRUGS INVOLVED IN FIRST TIME ILLICIT DRUG USE IN 2009

Among the 3.1 million adolescents and adults who first used an illicit drug during 2009, more than half reported their first drug was marijuana, followed by prescription medications, which accounted for over 25 percent of first drug experiences.

Source: SAMHSA (2010a)

Marijuana is the most commonly used illicit drug both worldwide (United Nations World Drug Report, 2010) and in the United States, where almost 17 million adults and adolescents report current use. Males are more likely than females to use marijuana (8.6 percent vs. 4.8 percent). As seen in Figure 11.8, more than 2 million adolescents and adults tried marijuana for the first time in the past year, representing 60 percent of illegal drug initiates (SAMHSA, 2010a). Marijuana use is particularly widespread among adolescents and young adults, with 21 percent of those aged 18 to 25 reporting current use (SAMHSA, 2010a). The Monitoring the Future Report, based on an annual survey regarding drug use among middle and high school students, revealed that 27 percent of 10th graders and 33 percent of 12th graders used marijuana in the past year (Johnston, Bachman, & O'Malley, 2009); additionally, there was a significant increase in daily marijuana use among 8th, 10th, and 12th graders (Johnston, O'Malley, Bachman, & Schulenberg, 2010c).

Marijuana is the drug most frequently associated with a diagnosis of substance abuse; more than 4 million adolescents and adults demonstrated a cannabis-use disorder in 2009 (SAMHSA, 2010a). It is estimated that approximately 10 percent of those who use marijuana become dependent on the drug (Koob, Kandel, & Volkow, 2008). A unique characteristic of marijuana dependence is a pervasive lack of concern regarding the consequences of drug use (Munsey, 2010). Some suggest that cannabis is a "gateway drug" associated with later use of other illegal substances. Research shows that age of first marijuana use affects later use of other illicit substances. Almost 13 percent of those who first tried marijuana at age 14 or younger later used other illicit substances compared to 2 percent of those who first used marijuana after age 18 (SAMHSA, 2010a). Similarly, Van Gundy and colleagues (2010) found that the gateway effect was lessened when use was initiated after age 21.

Marijuana produces feelings of euphoria, tranquility, and passivity combined with mild perceptual and sensory distortions. Cannabis tends to increase anxiety and depression in females (Fattore & Fratta, 2010). Marijuana use can cause impaired memory, motor coordination, and concentration, as well as hallucinations and short-term psychotic reactions. Some individuals develop chronic, psychotic symptoms following cannabis use, especially when cannabis use occurs at a young age (Degenhardt et al., 2009). Adolescents who use cannabis have an increased risk of developing schizophrenia as well as an earlier age of onset of symptoms (Large, Sharma, Compton, Slade, & Nielssen, 2011). Researchers have found that individuals with a particular genetic variation are most likely to experience gene × environment interactions resulting in this outcome (Caspi et al., 2005).

The American Psychiatric Association (2011) recently recognized cannabis withdrawal syndrome as a diagnostic category citing:

1. Clear patterns of withdrawal, especially for those using cannabis three or more times per week (Copersino et al., 2006; Milin, Manion, Dare, & Walker, 2008);
2. Strong similarities between cannabis withdrawal and the widely recognized tobacco withdrawal syndrome (Budney, Vandrey, Hughes, Thostenson, & Bursac, 2008; Vandrey, Budney, Kamon, & Stanger, 2005); and
3. A clear link between severity of withdrawal symptoms and severity of cannabis dependence (Chung, Martin, Cornelius, & Clark, 2008; Hasin et al., 2008) and relapse (Cornelius, Chung, Martin, Wood, & Clark, 2008).

Approximately 10 percent of those who use marijuana develop dependence (Munsey, 2010). Many users return to cannabis use (Agrawal, Pergadia, & Lynskey, 2008) or resort to using other drugs after experiencing withdrawal symptoms (Copersino et al., 2006).

Long-term use of cannabis is associated with impaired judgment, memory, and concentration. Withdrawal symptoms include irritability, anxiety, insomnia, restlessness, and depression as well as distressing physical symptoms such as stomach pain, tremors, sweating, fever, and headache (American Psychiatric Association, 2010). Diminished cognitive functioning involving attention, memory, and learning often lasts for days after marijuana use (Schweinsburg, Brown, & Tapert, 2008). Adolescents who engage in frequent marijuana use have lower academic achievement (Martins & Alexandre, 2009) and impaired attention, learning, and cognitive processing as well as subtle abnormalities in brain structure (Jacobus, Bava, Cohen-Zion, Mahmood, & Tapert, 2009). These cognitive effects may be more pronounced and persistent in adolescents because their brains are undergoing a critical period of development, thus increasing vulnerability to the effects of drug use (Schweinsburg, Brown, & Tapert, 2008). Negative outcomes increase when marijuana is combined with other drugs such as Ecstasy (Wu, Parrott, Ringwalt, Yang, & Blazer, 2009).

There is speculation that cannabis use is increasing because legalization efforts in many areas of the country are "normalizing" use of marijuana. Cannabis use (even when prescribed for medical purposes) remains illegal at the federal level. However, multiple states and municipalities, in an effort to allow law enforcement efforts to focus on other priorities, have decriminalized the possession of small quantities of marijuana. Various states also allow production and distribution of marijuana for legitimate medical use such as treating side effects from chemotherapy. There has been much debate about the consequences of cannabis use. Some proclaim that cannabis use poses limited physical or psychological risk. However, researchers in the field of substance abuse believe that if marijuana is legalized, more prevalent use will lead to more widespread marijuana dependence (Munsey, 2010).

Inhalants

Case Study

I started when I was eleven. My cousin and his buddies would go down by the creek, and huff, so I would go with them. I saw how they did it, so I just did what they did. That's how I learned how to do it . . . The spray makes me talk slow. Besides the headache I get when I'm not doing it, it makes me slower. The high is good but it makes me slow. When it's wearing off, it makes me like I am stupid. I have to talk slow because the words don't come out.

Sometimes I get suicidal. I don't know why. I just do. I just don't give a damn. I just get out in the street in front of cars. Sometimes I remember that I'm doing it and sometimes I don't know it. When I do know what I'm doing, I don't give a damn. I just want to stop my life because the headaches I get when I stop the spray paint just make me crazy. (Ramos, 1998, pp. 19–39)

Inhalant abusers become intoxicated from chemical vapors found in a variety of common household products, including solvents (paint removers, gasoline, lighter fluid); office supplies (glue, marker pens, correction fluids); aerosol sprays (spray paints, hairspray); and compressed air products (computer and electronics duster sprays). Inhalation of these substances (known as "huffing") is accomplished through sniffing fumes from containers, bags, or balloons; directly inhaling aerosols sprays; or using inhalant-soaked rags. Some adolescents paint intoxicants on their skin, fingernails, or clothing to allow discreet inhalation when adults are present. One group of adolescents reported inhaling gasoline (22 percent), permanent markers (15 percent), computer cleaning spray (15 percent), and spray paint (12 percent) (Howard, Balster, Cottler, Wu, & Vaughn, 2008).

Inhalant use is most common amongst those aged 12 to 17; in 2009, an estimated 1.1 percent of this age group used inhalants in the past month. Of the 813,000 individuals who tried inhalants for the first time in 2009, approximately 68 percent were under age 18 when they first used (SAMHSA, 2010a). In the 2009 Monitoring the Future Survey, lifetime use of inhalants was reported by 15 percent of 8th graders, 12 percent of 10th graders, and 10 percent of 12th graders. Adolescents' perception of risk regarding inhalant use is on the decline; this may explain the higher use by 8th graders (Johnston, O'Malley, Bachman, & Schulenberg, 2010). Experimental use of inhalants in younger adolescents typically occurs before experimentation with tobacco or alcohol. Fortunately, experimentation with inhalants does not appear to be a "gateway" to more serious drug use (Ding, Chang, & Southerland, 2009), although those who chronically abuse inhalants often initiate marijuana and cocaine use. Although boys and girls experiment about equally with inhalants, chronic users are more likely to be male. Most inhalant users are white, although Native Americans and low income Hispanics are increasing rates of use. The pervasive use of inhalants by children and adolescents is considered a silent epidemic;

prevention efforts target parents and teachers, many of whom are unaware of the danger-ousness and extent of inhalant use.

The intoxicating effects of inhalants are brief, resulting in repeated "huffing" to extend intoxication. The immediate effects of inhalants vary depending on the chemicals involved; typical effects include impaired coordination and judgment, euphoria, dizziness, and slurred speech. Hypoxia (oxygen deprivation) results in both acute and persistent cognitive deficits such as severe memory impairment and slow information processing; users are often unable to recall life-threatening events such as physical conflict and suicidal behavior. Any episode of inhalant use, even in first-time users, can result in stroke, acute respiratory distress, or sudden heart failure (referred to as "sudden sniffing death"). Fatal outcome is most common with compressed air products, aerosol sprays, air fresheners, butane, propane, and nitrous oxide (Hall, Edwards, & Howard, 2010; Marsolek, White, & Litovitz, 2010).

Inhalant use produces a number of emotional and interpersonal difficulties. Paranoid thinking and spontaneous violent behavior is problematic because inhalants are typically used in small groups. Suicidal ideation is prevalent among inhalant users, particularly women. In one sample of inhalant abusers, 67 percent had contemplated suicide and 20 percent had attempted suicide (Howard et al., 2010). Additionally, chronic inhalant abuse is associated with high levels of anxiety and depression as well as antisocial behavior and interpersonal violence (Howard et al., 2008; Howard, Perron, Vaughn, Bender, & Garland, 2010; Perron & Howard, 2009).

Ecstasy

Ecstasy (methylenedioxymethamphetamine, or MDMA) has both stimulant and halluci-nogenic properties. Between 2008 and 2009, there was a significant increase in first-time Ecstasy use, with an estimated 1.1 million new users (SAMHSA, 2010a), including signifi-cant increases among high school students (Johnston, O'Malley, Bachman, & Schulenberg, 2010c). Short-term effects of Ecstasy include euphoria, mild sensory and cognitive distor-tion, and feelings of intimacy and well-being, often followed by intense depression. Users frequently experience hyperthermia or the need to suck on lollipops or pacifiers to coun-teract involuntary jaw spasms and teeth clenching.

Although Ecstasy is not typically used on a daily basis, some infrequent users demonst-rate symptoms of drug dependence, suggesting that Ecstasy has unique chemical properties that accelerate the development of dependence (Bruno et al., 2009). In fact, characteristics of hallucinogen dependence were seen in almost 12 percent of one sample of occasional Ecstasy users (Wu, Ringwalt, Mannelli, & Patkar, 2008). In another study, 59 percent of Ecstasy users met the criteria for dependence, with a large number of respondents report-ing withdrawal symptoms and continued use despite physical or psychological problems (Cottle, Leung, & Abdallah, 2009). Adolescent Ecstasy users have a particularly high risk for hallucinogen dependence; in one sample, 39 percent of young users reported symptoms of considerable dependence (Wu, Ringwalt, Weiss, & Blazer, 2009). Those withdrawing from Ecstasy report feeling depressed, irritable, and unsociable. Ecstasy has been linked to long-lasting damage in brain areas critical for thought and memory. Ecstasy use reduces ability to complete challenging cognitive tasks, even with multiple practice opportunities (Brown, McKone, & Ward, 2010). Thus, it is not surprising that Ecstasy use has been strongly associ-ated with low academic achievement in adolescents (Martins & Alexandre, 2009).

A review of 82 cases in which Ecstasy was a cause of death revealed: 83 percent of the decedents were male; the median age was 26; Ecstasy was the sole cause of death in 23 percent of the cases; combined drug toxicity caused 59 percent of deaths; and significant cardiovascular changes contributed to the remaining deaths. Surprisingly, despite the youth of the decedents, atherosclerosis (hardening of the arteries, a condition typically associated with aging) was found in 58 percent of decedents, with 23 percent demonstrating moderate to severe atherosclerosis. This effect, typically seen in cocaine and methamphetamine users, may relate to the stimulant properties of Ecstasy (Kaye, Darke, & Duflou, 2009).

Ecstasy, often produced in multicolored tablets with a variety of logos, is considered a club drug because it is often used in a club or party context. Some of the substances we have already discussed (PCP, ketamine, Rohypnol) are also considered club drugs. Additionally, cocaine is used within the club drug culture. In one large sample of individuals using drugs in a club context, 90 percent reported cocaine use; in fact, 59 percent demonstrated cocaine dependence (Parsons, Grov, & Kelly, 2009). Another common club drug with high addictive potential is GHB (gamma hydroxybutyrate), a substance used primarily by males because of it purported strength enhancing properties. GHB, a central nervous system depressant with strong sedative effects, is particularly dangerous when combined with alcohol.

Club drugs are often used to induce energy and excitement, reduce inhibitions, and create feelings of well-being and connection with others, as well as magnify the effects of the high-energy events known as "raves." Unfortunately, energy exertion in a warm environment intensifies harmful side effects, particularly hyperthermia and dehydration. Although positive effects may last for hours, they are typically followed by a "crash"—lethargy, low motivation, and fatigue. Extreme depression and anxiety (as well as acute physical symptoms due to dehydration or changes in blood pressure and heart rhythm) can occur, particularly when drugs are combined or taken with alcohol. We will discuss the dangerous practice of combining substances in the next section on polysubstance use.

Polysubstance Use

Case Study

Kelly M., age seventeen, lived with her divorced mother. Kelly was hospitalized after her mother found her unconscious from an overdose of tranquilizers; her blood alcohol level was 0.15. The overdose was apparently accidental and not suicidal. Kelly openly discussed her drug use with a therapist, explaining that she had regularly used tranquilizers for over a year. Kelly was unhappy about her parents' divorce, and she began buying the drugs from a classmate. The tranquilizers helped her relax and relieved her stress. Arguments with her mother would precipitate heavy use of the drugs. Eventually she found she needed more of the pills to relax, sometimes stealing money to buy them. She sometimes used alcohol as a substitute for or in combination with the tranquilizers. Her mother reported that she had no knowledge of her daughter's drug or alcohol use. She had noticed that Kelly was increasingly isolated and sleepy. The therapist informed Kelly of the dangers of sedatives, especially when combined with alcohol, and recommended she begin drug treatment.

Kelly's practice of polysubstance use (combining substances) can be extremely dangerous. Chemicals taken simultaneously may exhibit a synergistic effect, interacting to multiply one another's effects. For example, when tranquilizers are combined with alcohol, both depress the central nervous system and the synergistic effect can result in respiratory distress or even death. Similarly, combining alcohol with cocaine results in a very toxic compound called cocaethylene that can significantly impair heart function (Van Amsterdam & van den Brink, 2010). Furthermore, one substance (such as alcohol) may reduce the person's judgment, resulting in excessive (or lethal) use of another substance. Equally dangerous is the use of one drug to counteract the effects of another substance, such as taking stimulants to feel alert and later taking a sleeping pill to counteract insomnia from the stimulant.

Of particular concern is multiple drug use involving Ecstasy. One group of "rave" attendees taking Ecstasy tested positive for an average of four other drugs; those who

synergistic effect   the result of chemicals (or substances) interacting to multiply one another's effects

illicitly manufacture drugs such as Ecstasy often adulterate them with other substances, a factor which may have affected the findings (Black, Cawthon, Moser, Caplan, & Cone, 2009). Three subtypes of Ecstasy users have been described: those who frequently use multiple drugs; those who use marijuana, cocaine, and sometimes amphetamine; and those who report heavy marijuana use combined with prescription drug misuse (Wu, Parrott, Ringwalt, Yang, & Blazer, 2009). Consistent with the forensic toxicology findings we previously discussed regarding deaths associated with Ecstasy, polysubstance use was implicated in the majority of 49 deaths associated with GHB; the mean age was 26 years for male decedents and 21 years for females (Kugelberg, Holmgren, Eklund, & Jones, 2010). Youth advocates feel there is a need to further educate the public about the harmful effects of polysubstance use.

Concern about pre-mixed, flavored alcoholic energy drinks that combine alcohol and high levels of caffeine led to a Food and Drug Administration (2010a) ban on the products and a warning that "the combination of caffeine and alcohol . . . poses a public health concern" because high levels of caffeine combined with alcohol mask cues regarding intoxication. Additionally, dehydration, which increases intoxication, results from the diuretic effects of alcohol and caffeine used together. Findings that college students who combined alcohol and caffeine have increased heavy-drinking episodes, drunkenness, and alcohol-related consequences (sexual assault, physical injury, driving while intoxicated) lend validity to this concern (O'Brien, McCoy, Rhodes, Wagoner, & Wolfson, 2008).

Accidental Overdose

Academy Award-nominated actor Heath Ledger died at age 28 from an apparently accidental overdose of prescription medications including painkillers, anti-anxiety drugs, and sleeping pills.

Etiology of Substance-Use Disorders

Why do people abuse substances, despite having the knowledge (and often the experience) that the misuse of alcohol and drugs can have devastating consequences? In general, progression from initial substance use to substance abuse follows a typical sequence (Walter, 2001). First, an individual decides to experiment with alcohol or drugs—perhaps to experience the effects, enhance self-confidence, rebel against authorities, imitate others, or conform to social pressure. Second, the substance begins to serve an important purpose (such as reducing anxiety, producing feelings of pleasure, or enhancing social relationships) and so consumption continues. Third, brain chemistry becomes altered from chronic use. In many cases, physiological dependency develops resulting in withdrawal symptoms and craving for the substance; it also becomes difficult to experience pleasure without the substance. Fourth, lifestyle changes occur due to chronic substance use. These changes may include loss of interest in previous activities and social relationships and preoccupation with opportunities to use the substance (Figure 11.9). Consistent with the multipath model, in all four phases, biological, psychological, social, and sociocultural influences are involved (Figure 11.10). Let's now turn to research involving the multiple factors that contribute to the development of substance-use disorders.

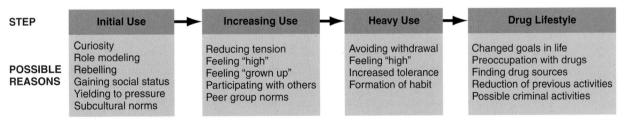

STEP	Initial Use	Increasing Use	Heavy Use	Drug Lifestyle
POSSIBLE REASONS	Curiosity Role modeling Rebelling Gaining social status Yielding to pressure Subcultural norms	Reducing tension Feeling "high" Feeling "grown up" Participating with others Peer group norms	Avoiding withdrawal Feeling "high" Increased tolerance Formation of habit	Changed goals in life Preoccupation with drugs Finding drug sources Reduction of previous activities Possible criminal activities

Figure 11.9

TYPICAL PROGRESSION TOWARD DRUG ABUSE OR DEPENDENCE

The progression from initial substance use to a drug lifestyle typically begins with curiosity about drug effects and casual experimentation.

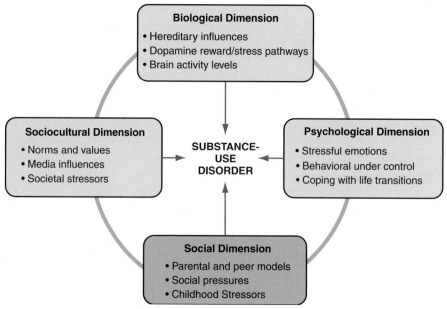

Figure 11.10

MULTIPATH MODEL FOR SUBSTANCE-USE DISORDERS

The dimensions interact with one another and combine in different ways to result in a substance-use disorder.

Copyright © Cengage Learning 2013

Psychological Dimension

Coping with psychological stress and emotional symptoms appears to be a major motive for substance use. Of the 21 million adults with a substance-use disorder in 2009, 43 percent had a concurrent psychiatric disorder. The use of illicit drugs is much higher among mentally ill individuals (27 percent) compared to those without such difficulties (12 percent) (SAMHSA, 2010d). Individuals with psychiatric symptoms often use drugs and alcohol to self-medicate and compensate for stressful emotions such as the depression and anxiety that coexist with substance use. There are high rates of alcoholism in those with stress-related mood and anxiety disorders: Stress is thought to play an important role in both the development of alcoholism and in relapse (Anthenelli, 2010). Individuals with post-traumatic stress disorder (PTSD) report using drugs and alcohol to cope with distressing symptoms (Leeies, Pagura, Sareen, & Bolton, 2010). Severity of marijuana use has been associated with the PTSD symptoms of hyperarousal and re-experiencing the trauma, supporting the self-medication hypothesis (Villagonzalo et al., 2010). Screening of individuals calling a smoking "quitline" revealed that 24 percent had major depression and 17 percent had symptoms of mild depression (Hebert, Cummins, Hernández, Tedeschi, & Zhu, 2011). Anxiety diagnoses are also common among smokers seeking treatment; the thought of quitting often enhances anxiety and increases smoking (Piper et al., 2010). Almost half of a large sample of methamphetamine-dependent individuals had a concurrent mental illness, most commonly mood, anxiety, or antisocial personality disorders; those with psychiatric difficulties had more severe drug use and greater functional impairment (Glasner-Edwards et al., 2010). Coping with family problems was a major reason given for heroin use (Brajevic-Gizdic, Mulic, Pletikosa, & Kljajic, 2009). Those who use heroin have been noted to lack coping strategies, whereas marijuana users want to detach and distance themselves from others (Schindler, Thomasius, Petersen, & Sack, 2009).

Adolescent girls with eating disorders are known to be at high risk for substance abuse; nicotine and stimulants are used to suppress appetite, and depressants are used to cope with bulimic urges (Baker, Mitchell, Neale, & Kendler, 2010). Adolescent girls have increased risk of nonmedical use of prescription medications (Johnston et al., 2010) including stimulants to lose weight and pain medications to deal with stress and depression. Adolescent girls report using substances to help "forget troubles" or "deal with problems at home" (PFDFA/MET, 2010).

The personality characteristic of behavioral undercontrol, associated with rebelliousness, novelty-seeking, risk-taking, and impulsivity, increases risk of substance use. Individuals with these traits are more likely to experiment with substances and continue use because they find the effects rewarding and exciting. An investigation of possible genetic links between substance abuse and impulsivity revealed that siblings of chronic stimulant users tended to be highly impulsive, suggesting that impulsivity may be a behavioral endophenotype that increases risk for stimulant dependence (Ersche et al., 2010).

What psychological factors might account for drug and alcohol use in college students? Undergraduates use drugs and alcohol to cope with anxiety and depression (Grant, Stewart, O'Connor, Blackwell, & Conrod, 2007); in response to academic, social, and financial pressures; and to cope with being away from home for the first time, living in a new environment, and having increased responsibility (Burke, Cremeens, Vail-Smith, & Woolsey, 2010). College students high in behavioral undercontrol, particularly those in fraternities or sororities, are most vulnerable to alcohol dependence (Grekin & Sher, 2006). Impulsivity has a particularly strong association with alcohol abuse among college students who are also poor planners and risk-takers (Mackillop et al., 2007; Siebert & Wilke, 2007).

Social Dimension

The influence of social factors on substance abuse varies across the lifespan, exerting different effects at different ages (Sher et al., 2010). Victimization and stressful events in childhood, especially child neglect, are strongly associated with substance use later in life, especially for those with multiple victimization experiences (McCabe, Wilsnack, West, & Boyd, 2010). In a longitudinal study involving infants documented to have intrauterine substance exposure (a biological risk factor), it was found that exposure to violence between the ages of 8 and 16 was strongly associated with substance use in mid-adolescence (Frank et al., 2010). Similarly, a longitudinal study of children prenatally exposed to cocaine use revealed that caregiver negativity and exposure to violence were related to cocaine use during adolescence (Delaney-Black et al., 2010a). The majority of individuals receiving residential treatment for substance abuse and mental health issues reported childhood trauma (Wu, Schairer, Dellor, & Grella, 2010). Adolescents with alcoholic parents reported drinking heavily and drinking alone with the goal of becoming intoxicated and forgetting problems (Chalder, Elgar, & Bennett, 2006). Inner-city adolescents exposed to environmental stressors are most likely to use substances (Epstein, Banga, & Botvina, 2007).

As you might expect, adolescence and early adulthood are particularly vulnerable periods with respect to social influences on substance use even for those without other life stressors. A variety of social factors appear to affect decisions to drink alcohol or experiment with drugs, including pressure from peers, use of substances to fit in socially and enhance social interactions, attempts to rebel and challenge authority, friendships with peers who have limited parental supervision, desire to assert independence or escape from societal or parental pressures for achievement, and a desire to "have fun" or take risks. Adolescent boys often report that drugs help them "relax socially" and "have more fun at parties" (PFDFA/MET, 2010). Association with friends who get drunk increases high-risk drinking (Siebert & Wilke, 2007).

Family attitudes and behaviors with respect to drinking and drugs (including the use of prescription medication) affect adolescents' likelihood of experimenting with substances. Adolescents exposed to peer and adult drinkers often develop positive expectancies regarding the use of alcohol such as believing that drinking alcohol makes it easier to be part of a group (Cumsille, Sayer, & Graham, 2000). Additionally, adolescents who receive less parental monitoring have increased substance use as well as those whose parents feel unable to enforce rules or influence decisions related to substance use or who believe cultural myths such as "all adolescents experiment" or "it's okay to have teens drink at home" (Wagner et al., 2010).

College presents its own unique set of sociocultural influences. The first year of college is a particularly vulnerable transitional period (Grekin & Sher, 2006; Weitzman, Nelson, & Wechsler, 2003) due to abrupt changes in levels of parental supervision, increased competition and pressure for academic achievement, and exposure to "wet environments" (social or residential settings with easy access to low-cost alcohol), and heavy drinking (Weitzman, Nelson, & Wechsler, 2003). Unofficial social events promoting partying (Paschall & Saltz, 2007) and peers who minimize the consequences of drinking contribute to college drinking (Lee, Geisner, Patrick, & Neighbors, 2010). Additionally, college freshman overestimate the quantity and social acceptability of drinking (LaBrie, Hummer, Grant, & Lac, 2010). In one study, 91 percent of respondents estimated that their peers drank more than themselves (Broadwater, Curtin, Martz, & Zrull, 2006). College athletes' views of social norms and inflated perceptions of alcohol consumption by others, particularly other athletes, predicted their personal alcohol consumption (Dams-O'Connor, Martin, & Martens, 2007). Negative consequences associated with drinking such as forced sexual contact, embarrassment over behavior while intoxicated, or poor academic performance can exacerbate the cycle of college drinking or drug use (Anderson, Martens, & Cimini, 2005; Dams-O'Conner, Martens, & Anderson, 2006).

Eating disorders and associated risks such as stimulant use for appetite control are also encountered in college. Some students skip meals and cut calories so they can drink more or get drunk faster. "Drunkorexia" is a term coined by the media referencing a trend among college women—self-imposed starvation in order to compensate for high-caloric binge drinking. This practice not only hastens intoxication but stresses the body and increases risk of dehydration, blackouts, seizures, or cardiac arrest. In one sample of college freshman, 15 percent reported fasting before drinking; of this subgroup 70 percent were female. The restriction of food for weight control was endorsed by only 39 percent of those who limited food intake, whereas 69 percent reported a desire to hasten intoxication (Burke, Cremeens, Vail-Smith, & Woolsey, 2010).

Sociocultural Dimension

Substance use varies according to sociocultural factors, such as gender, age, socioeconomic status, ethnicity, religion, and nationality. Looking at alcohol use, we know that males and young adults consume more alcohol than females and older adults, respectively. Interestingly, alcohol consumption tends to increase with socioeconomic status, although alcoholism is more frequent in the middle socioeconomic classes (SAMHSA, 2007). In terms of religious affiliation, heavier drinking is found among Catholics compared to Protestants or Jews. Furthermore, drinking behavior varies from country to country. In "wet" cultures, alcohol is widely available and integrated into daily life and activities. In these cultures, abstinence rates are low, and alcohol is consumed with most meals. European countries bordering the Mediterranean have traditionally exemplified wet cultures. In "dry" cultures, access to alcohol is more restricted. Abstinence is more common, but when drinking occurs it is more likely to result in intoxication. The United States, Canada, and Scandinavian countries are considered dry cultures (Bloomfield et al., 2003).

As we have seen from prevalence data, certain substances—alcohol, nicotine, and, to some extent, marijuana and prescription drugs—are an accepted part of U.S. culture. It is common to see marketing and "normalizing" messages regarding tobacco, alcohol, and prescription drug products, as well as depictions of these products in songs, movies, television, and social media. Exposure to positive drug and alcohol information on the Internet is increasing, whereas warnings from parents, schools, or antidrug advertising are on the decrease (PFDFA/MET, 2010). Public debate regarding legalization of marijuana appears to be "normalizing" its social acceptability with resultant increases in use (Johnston, O'Malley, Bachman, & Schulenberg, 2010c). Factors such as perceived prevalence of smoking, exposure to smokers, and exposure to tobacco advertising are all associated with smoking in young adults (Ling, Neilands, & Glantz, 2009; Hanewinkel, Isensee, Sargent, & Morgenstern, 2011). Similarly, exposure to episodes of smoking in movies increases risk of current smoking (Song, Ling, Neilands, & Glantz, 2007). For those who smoke, a direct link has been demonstrated between viewing scenes with smoking and activation of smoking-related addictive responses within the brain and smoking behavior following the viewing (Shmueli, Prochaska, & Glantz, 2010; Wagner, DalCin, Sargent, Kelley, & Heatherton, 2011).

The data suggest that both drug and alcohol use is gaining acceptance among adolescents and is becoming a normative part of adolescent culture. Teen reports of declining concern about personal risk from substance use (Johnston, O'Malley, Bachman, & Schulenberg, 2010b) and increasing peer approval for getting high have been linked to increased use of substances associated with social situations and party environments (PFDFA/MET, 2010). Adolescents whose peer group lacks school commitment and connectedness are particularly prone to substance use (Latimer & Zur, 2010). Not having a high school diploma and being unemployed are strong predictors of later substance use (Van Gundy, Cesar, & Rebellon, 2010).

As we have discussed, alcohol and illicit drug use and abuse varies both within and between ethnic groups. Cultural values affect not only the substances used and amount consumed but also cultural tolerance of substance abuse. African Americans adolescents show lower rates of substance use than whites and Hispanics; in the 8th grade, Hispanics have the highest prevalence of use in all drug categories except stimulants and have the highest levels of crack and methamphetamine use in the 12th grade (Johnston et al., 2010b). A recent study evaluating racial differences in adolescent substance use concluded that among middle school students Hispanics are more likely to smoke cigarettes, consume alcohol, and use marijuana compared to other racial groups, whereas Asian middle-school students were least likely to engage in these activities. Hispanic American students reported less concern about potential negative consequences of substance use and less confidence using refusal skills. Asian American students reported that few of their friends and siblings used substances and that they wanted to respect parental expectations regarding substance use (Shih et al., 2010).

Additional factors affecting variability among ethnic groups include racial discrimination; increased availability of alcohol in urban areas with high ethnic populations; decreased community safety; social and economic disadvantage, including limited job opportunities and inadequate health care; and stress related to acculturation, particularly for Hispanics (Chartier & Caetano, 2010). Interviews conducted within the Filipino American community revealed a connection between perceptions of unfair treatment and illicit drug use and alcohol dependence (Gee, Delva, & Takeuchi, 2007). Similarly, the experience of unfair treatment and racial discrimination among Asian Americans with low ethnic identification increased the chances of alcohol dependence (Chae et al., 2008). African Americans adolescents who perceived racial discrimination reported subsequent willingness to use drugs to cope with their feelings of anger (Gibbons et al., 2010). Although whites are most likely to develop alcohol dependence, the fact that alcoholism involving African Americans and Hispanics is much more likely to be chronic may also result from discrimination (Chartier & Caetano, 2010). Also the target of discrimination, sexual minority youth and adults have increased risk for substance use and abuse (McCabe, Hughes, Bostwick, West, & Boyd, 2009), especially when there is a history of childhood abuse or victimization (McCabe, Wilsnack, West, & Boyd, 2010).

A sociocultural factor recently linked to adolescent substance use is parental incarceration. Researchers found that when a father is incarcerated not only is there increased poverty, school failure, emotional distress, and criminal activity but also more frequent marijuana use among both sons (50 percent using) and daughters (39 percent using) and that sons' cocaine and crystal meth use is double that of their peers, with 25 percent reporting use of these substances. This effect, particularly pronounced in the African American community where there is high prevalence of male incarceration, can further exacerbate the cycle of racial inequality, substance abuse, and imprisonment (Roettger, Swisher, Kuhl, & Chavez, 2011).

Events impacting a society, such as a recession, can increase substance use as individuals cope with unemployment or other financial stressors, at a time when public health resources devoted to prevention and treatment are reduced. Although psychological, social, and sociocultural influences have a pronounced effect on both the initiation of substance use and the continuation of use, the question remains: Why are some individuals able to use drugs or alcohol in moderation, whereas others succumb to heavy use and addiction? Biological explanations provide considerable insight into this issue, as we see in the following section.

Biological Dimension

Biological factors affect the development of substance-use disorders in various ways, most notably through gender differences in physiology, substance-induced changes in brain functioning, and genetic mechanisms. Gender differences in the biological and behavioral effects of substances are frequently observed. Investigation into the neurobiological basis of gender differences in drug dependence, craving, and relapse has implicated the effects of hormonal influence on women's susceptibility to the reinforcing effects of addictive substances (Roth, Cosgrov, & Carroll, 2004; Fattore, Fadda, & Fratta, 2009). Additionally, physiological differences may influence the more rapid progression to alcoholism seen in females (Fattore & Fratta, 2010). Women tend to weigh less, have more fat tissue and less muscle mass; produce fewer enzymes to metabolize alcohol; possess less total body fluid to dilute alcohol in the blood; and are more likely to limit food intake which can further increase toxicity from alcohol (Burke, Cremeens, Vail-Smith, & Woolsey, 2010). Additionally, male-female differences in physiological reactions to stress (combined with differential exposure to traumatic life events) may help explain the more severe course of alcoholism in females (Anthenelli, 2010).

As we have discussed, substance abuse results in changes in brain chemistry and structure. Specifically, addiction results from "pathological changes in brain function

Effects of Cocaine Use

These positron emission tomography (PET) scan images compare the cerebral metabolic activity of a control subject (top row) with those of a cocaine abuser 10 days after discontinuing cocaine (middle row) and after 100 days of abstinence (bottom row). Red and yellow areas reveal efficient brain activity, whereas blue regions indicate minimal brain activity. As you can see, after 100 days of abstinence brain activity is improved but remains far from normal.

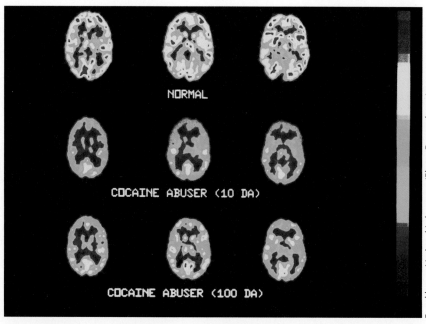

NORMAL

COCAINE ABUSER (10 DA)

COCAINE ABUSER (100 DA)

Brookhaven National Laboratory/Photo Researchers, Inc.

produced by repeated pharmacological insult to the brain circuits that regulate how a person interprets and behaviorally responds to motivationally relevant stimuli. Thus, addictive drugs strongly interact with and change the brain circuits that permit us to learn about and behaviorally adapt to important environmental stimuli, whether it be how to best approach rewards such as food or sex, or to avoid dangerous situations" (Kalivas & O'Brien, 2008, p. 166). Chronic abuse of some substances alters the normal dopamine reward and stress pathways, thus flooding the brain with far more dopamine than is secreted normally. Feelings of euphoria or pleasure ensue. Eventually, substance use crowds out other pleasures and turns into an all-consuming, compulsive desire. As addiction develops, the chronic flooding of dopamine eventually results in the depletion of dopamine and other neurotransmitters involved in stress and reward (Brower, 2006). Consequently, drugs and alcohol (as well as other normally pleasurable activities) bring limited pleasure. Simultaneously, drug tolerance develops and more and more of the substance is needed (Nestler & Malenka, 2004).

Furthermore, substance-induced changes in the area of the brain known as the frontal cortex result in impaired judgment and decision making. When cravings occur, compulsive drug-seeking ensues without consideration of negative consequences (Crews & Boettiger, 2009). In fact, brain imaging documenting reduced activity in the frontal cortex has accurately predicted which methamphetamine addicts will relapse (Paulus, Tapert, & Schuckit, 2005). Adolescence through early adulthood is a critical period for nuanced development of the frontal cortex; drug or alcohol use affecting this process can result in lifelong disruptions in reasoning, goal-setting, and impulse control, which can then lead to further substance abuse (Crews, He, & Hodge, 2007).

Genetic factors also play an important role in the development of substance abuse. For example, there is strong evidence that alcoholism "runs in families" (Piasecki et al., 2005) based on twin studies demonstrating higher rates of alcoholism among identical compared to fraternal twins (Agrawal & Lynskey, 2008), as well as analyses of family patterns of alcoholism (Gelernter & Kranzler, 2009). It is estimated that genetics account for approximately 50–60 percent of the risk of developing alcoholism (Foroud, Edenberg, & Crabbe, 2010). Individuals with a family history of alcohol abuse have a 4.5 times greater lifetime risk of developing alcoholism (Lovallo et al., 2006). However, because family members usually share both genetic and environmental influences, researchers face the challenge of somehow separating the contributions of these two sets of factors (Sher et al., 2010). Kendler and Prescott (2006), using data from more than 4,500 pairs of identical and fraternal twins to isolate genetic and environmental factors involved in substance abuse, concluded that:

- Genetic factors accounted for 56 percent of the risk of alcohol dependence, whereas early environment made no significant contribution to risk.
- Genetic factors accounted for 55 percent of the risk of nicotine dependence, whereas shared early environment made an 11 percent contribution to risk.
- Genetic factors accounted for 75 percent of the risk of illicit drug abuse, with cannabis dependence having the strongest genetic risk; for cocaine and opioid abuse, the genetic contribution was much greater for females than males.

Although collective findings support the importance of heredity in the etiology of substance use, the task of identifying the specific genes involved is complex (Wall et al., 2005). Genetic influences on alcohol dependence include the protective effects of variations in genes that produce the "clean-up" enzyme ALDH (Foroud, Edenberg, & Crabbe, 2010). In individuals with impaired production of ALDH, unpleasant physical reactions result as toxins from metabolized alcohol accumulate; this naturally occurring effect makes alcohol consumption aversive and thus reduces risk of alcoholism (Eng, Luczak, & Wall, 2007). The protective effects of ALDH variations are quite strong—up to a sevenfold lowered risk in some Asian populations (Foroud, Edenberg, & Crabbe, 2010). Similar protective genetic variations are seen in certain regions of the Middle East and Africa. Interestingly, researchers documenting the protective effects of ALDH variations

© Kurt Krieger/Corbis

Family Ties

Drew Barrymore entered rehab at the age of thirteen to deal with her addiction to drugs and alcohol. Although it is difficult to separate environmental and genetic influences in cases of alcohol abuse, both were likely operating in Drew's case. Not only did she experience the stress of young stardom, but she also had a family history of alcohol abuse—her grandfather drank himself to death and her father abused alcohol and drugs.

in Chinese American and Korean American college students, found a subgroup, high in the behavioral trait of undercontrol, who engaged in heavy drinking despite their genetic makeup. Although protective, the ALDH variation does not preclude heavy drinking (Doran, Myers, Luczak, Carr, & Wall, 2007).

Studies have shown that a gene (*DRD2*) affecting the neurotransmitter dopamine appears to increase the risk for alcoholism, as well as for nicotine, cocaine, and opioid dependence. One study assessing substance use in adolescent sons of alcoholics found that those with this genetic variation were more likely to use marijuana and tobacco, as well as drink alcohol to the point of intoxication (Conner et al., 2005). Alcohol abuse in teens was found to be influenced by interactions between the *DRD2* genotype and environmental factors such as permissive parental attitudes toward alcohol consumption (van der Zwaluw et al., 2010) and psychological factors such as drinking to cope with negative feeling (van der Zwaluw, Kuntsche, & Engels, 2011). Similarly, researchers have located genes associated with nicotine dependence, with different genes affecting African Americans compared to European Americans; after smoking is initiated, genetic factors account for about 50 percent of the risk of addiction (Whitten, 2009).

Overall, substance-use disorders are genetically influenced in the following manner:

1. Genes and epigenetic changes affect individual responses to specific drugs (one person may have susceptibility to alcoholism, whereas another has genetic risk of marijuana dependence);

2. Genetic and epigenetic variations influence the degree of pleasure (or aversion) experienced during initial drug use as well as the negative and positive effects of ongoing drug use;

3. Genetics influence personality traits that increase risk, including impulsivity, risk-taking, and novelty-seeking as well as protective characteristics such as self-control (Kendler & Prescott, 2006).

Epigenetic influence on substance abuse is an up-and-coming area of research (Foroud, Edenberg, & Crabbe, 2010). Epigenetic changes affecting the pleasure center of the brain have been documented in chronic cocaine users; these changes are presumed to contribute to both the development and maintenance of addiction (Renthal & Nestler, 2009). It is likely that future research finds that epigenetic changes and networks of genes, rather than individual genes, hold the key to further understanding the mechanisms involved in susceptibility to substance abuse (Foroud, Edenberg, & Crabbe, 2010).

In summary, it is clear that genetic predispositions, as well as epigenetic and physiological changes that result from heavy or chronic substance exposure, affect individual susceptibility to addiction as well as the physiological processes involved in the addiction process. However, there are many factors beyond physiological effects that contribute to the development and maintenance of substance abuse (Baker et al., 2006). The psychological, social, and sociocultural factors previously discussed provide substantial insight into forces involved in decisions to initiate substance use as well as factors affecting continued use.

Methods and Effectiveness of Treatment for Substance-Use Disorders

Half of the all adults and older adolescents in the United States know someone in recovery from addiction to alcohol, illicit drugs, or prescription drugs (SAMHSA, 2008). However, there is a huge disparity between the estimated 23.5 million who need substance-use treatment and the 2.6 million who receive treatment; more than 1 million youth aged 12 to 17 need drug treatment with an additional 1.2 million in need of alcohol treatment (SAMHSA, 2010a). Many who recognize they have a serious substance abuse problem are unable to initiate treatment; cost is often a significant barrier (Figure 11.11). As seen in Figure 11.12 (SAMHSA, 2010a), treatment is most frequently sought for alcohol abuse (2.9 million), followed by cannabis use (1.2 million).

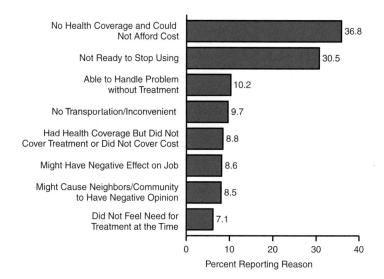

Figure 11.11

REASONS GIVEN FOR NOT RECEIVING SUBSTANCE-USE TREATMENT

Among individuals with a substance abuse problem who indicated that they would like to receive needed treatment, the most prevalent reason given for not initiating treatment was lack of health care coverage and inability to afford treatment.

Source: SAMHSA (2010a)

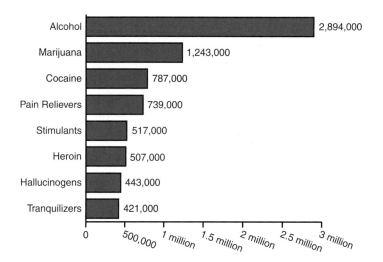

Figure 11.12

SUBSTANCES FOR WHICH TREATMENT WAS RECEIVED

In 2009, Americans sought treatment most frequently for alcohol abuse (2.9 million), followed by cannabis use (1.2 million).

Source: SAMHSA (2010a)

Treatment and supportive intervention take place in a variety of settings, including self-help groups, mental health clinics, and inpatient or outpatient drug and alcohol treatment centers. Many individuals recovering from addiction participate in Alcoholics Anonymous (AA) or Narcotics Anonymous (NA), self-help organizations that use fellowship and spiritual awareness to support abstinence. Self-help group meetings are the most common means of substance abuse intervention in the United States, with almost 2.5 million individuals participating in groups like AA and NA (SAMHSA, 2010a). Self-help groups provide a supportive approach to addiction rather than specialized treatment.

A quality review of traditional drug and alcohol treatment programs produced findings that the authors called "unambiguous and disturbing." Not only were there barriers to access, the majority of programs were not implementing evidence-based care. In fact, many programs relied on a model of treatment that has received minimal research support—AA or NA program attendance combined with lectures and group counseling provided by individuals in recovery from addiction (McLellan & Meyers, 2004). This reliance on poorly trained staff using outdated methods rather than interventions derived from medical and psychological addiction research greatly jeopardizes treatment outcome (Willenbring, 2010). Additionally, these models do not provide the integrated care necessary for those with underlying emotional difficulties (Kuehn, 2010).

Effective treatment requires strategies and pharmaceutical interventions that are research-based (Haaga, McCrady, & Lebow, 2006). In general, broad-spectrum interventions that include different treatment modalities are considered more effective than confining treatment to a single modality. Adolescent treatment programs, for example, address the substance used but also address the developmental, emotional, and social needs of the adolescent, involving family members and developing peer support for abstinence (Williams & Chang, 2000; Sexton, Alexander, & Mease, 2004; Carroll & Onken, 2005). Proponents of multimodal approaches recognize that no single kind of treatment is likely to be totally effective and that successful treatment outcome requires major life changes.

Goals of treatment include achieving sustained abstinence; maintaining a drug-free lifestyle; and functioning productively in family, work, and other environments. This requires changing habits, minimizing thoughts of drugs and drug-related social activities, and learning to cope with daily activities and stressors without the use of drugs. Therefore, effective treatment assists the person in recovery to create a lifestyle that supports abstinence as well as developing a sense of self-efficacy and well-being with respect to educational, career, and leisure activities. Additionally, because drugs so often disrupt multiple aspects of an individual's life, there is a need to rebuild family, friend, and work relationships.

Most alcohol and drug treatment programs have two phases: first, removal of the abusive substance, and second, long-term maintenance without it. In the first phase, called detoxification, the user is immediately or gradually prevented from using the substance. Coping with withdrawal symptoms is a significant focus early in the treatment process. In the second phase, intervention programs focus on preventing relapse, a return to use of the substance. Individuals who have undergone detoxification frequently relapse when ongoing support for recovery is not in place. In the next section we discuss a critical component of all treatment—relapse prevention.

Understanding and Preventing Relapse

Relapse prevention takes into account both physiological effects such as withdrawal symptoms and neurological changes that affect pleasure, motivation, impulsivity, learning, and memory. Neuroplasticity, the ability of the brain to change its structure and function in response to experience, is an important concept in addiction treatment. Just as the brain became conditioned to need a substance, therapy can help recondition the brain, create new neural pathways, and undo changes caused by addiction. Sustained abstinence is essential for maximizing treatment results. Although initial abstinence results in transient alterations in neural functioning, sustained abstinence is necessary for permanent neurological changes to occur (Kalivas & O'Brien, 2008). In other words, the initial changes allow learning of new behavior; subsequent neurological changes make the modifications permanent.

Unfortunately, many individuals with substance-use disorders discontinue treatment, especially when drug craving and a belief that the substance is necessary to "make it through the day" lead to relapse. Therefore, relapse prevention is a critical component of effective treatment. Addiction researchers recognize two types of relapse (Kalivas & O'Brien, 2008). The first, regulated relapse, seen before physiological dependency develops, involves the process of weighing choices and making a conscious decision to use a substance. Compulsive relapse occurs later in the addiction process and involves automatic resumption of drug-seeking behavior in response to stressors or environmental cues associated with substance use. Compulsive relapse, driven by habit or procedural memories, involves the unconscious performance of well-learned, addiction-related behavior. Substances that diminish attention, increase impulsivity, slow cognition, and diminish rational decision making are associated with compulsive relapse. Most pharmaceutical treatments target compulsive relapse: By reducing drug craving they increase the chance of conscious decision making regarding substance

detoxification alcohol or drug treatment phase during which the body is purged of intoxicating substances

relapse return to drug or alcohol use after a period of abstention

neuroplasticity ability of the brain to change its structure and function in response to experience

regulated relapse process of weighing choices and making a conscious decision to use a substance

compulsive relapse automatic resumption of drug-seeking behavior in response to stressors or substance-related cues

use and, in effect, permit the individual to make a choice to abstain. Therapy can then support the choice of abstinence as well as other healthy decisions (Kalivas & O'Brien, 2008).

Although a longer period of initial abstinence reduces the likelihood of relapse, a single lapse in abstinence often leads to complete relapse (Moore & Budney, 2003). Many therapists view relapse not as a treatment failure, but as an indicator that treatment needs to be intensified. Factors associated with relapse include the presence of another psychiatric disorder, younger age at onset of drug use, more extensive involvement with substances, antisocial behavior, minimal connection with school or work, and less support from drug-free family and peers (Walter, 2001). Some researchers have also found that negative emotional states (such as depression, interpersonal conflict, and anxiety) are highly associated with relapse (Cooney et al., 1997). In one group of alcoholics, negative emotional states were a primary factor in major relapse (substantial use of the substance), whereas minor relapse (taking just a beer) was associated with social pressure (Hodgins, El-Guebaly, & Armstrong, 1995). For women, stress, interpersonal conflict, and certain hormonal changes increase the risk of relapse (Wetherington, 2007).

To help minimize withdrawal symptoms and prevent relapse, medications are sometimes prescribed; the goal is to disrupt the physiological mechanisms underlying substance abuse (Jupp & Lawrence, 2010). Medications prescribed vary depending on the substance abused. Currently, most medications produce only modest effects. Therefore, substantial research activity is directed toward the development of new medications to treat addiction (Montoya & Vocci, 2008). Not only are researchers using available information on the physiological mechanisms of addiction, some of the newest research documenting epigenetic changes in chronic substance users has resulted in a search for medicines that can interrupt or reverse these changes. Understanding the genetic and epigenetic aspects of addiction results in a more individualized approach to the use of pharmaceuticals in addiction treatment (Montoya & Vocci, 2008). Additionally, pharmacological investigations are beginning to address sex-differences in the physiological effects of substances (Fattore & Fratta, 2010). It is important to remember that although medication can assist with cravings and withdrawal, given the complexities of addiction, medication alone is not sufficient to prevent relapse.

Contingency management procedures in which participants receive either voucher or cash incentives for verified abstinence, adhering to treatment goals, or taking prescribed medication can significantly reduce relapse (Stitzer & Petry, 2006; Vandrey, Bigelow, & Stitzer, 2007). Incentives can also increase treatment participation and goal-related behaviors that are incompatible with substance use such as exercising, attending school, or learning new job skills (Stitzer, Petry, & Peirce, 2010). Verifying abstinence via toxicology screening is an important component of these interventions (Petry et al., 2006).

An approach that is often used to set the stage for successful treatment and prevent relapse is motivational enhancement therapy (Rollnick, Miller, & Butler, 2008). This method addresses ambivalence about giving up substance use. Unless this ambivalence is resolved, change is slow and short-lived. Motivational interviewing helps clients overcome ambivalence by considering both the advantages and disadvantages of making a change and of the status quo; once there is a commitment to change, therapy moves forward with an emphasis on life-modifications required for abstinence. For example, a therapist helping a client with cannabis dependence might increase motivation for change by asking the client to discuss the advantages and disadvantages of continued marijuana use and the impact marijuana has had on the client's productivity, social relationships, and overall well-being. The client might be asked to articulate how continued drug use is affecting motivation and the accomplishment of goals. Once motivation to change is established, relapse risk is reduced and treatment can focus on lifestyle modifications necessary for sustained abstinence (Carroll & Onken, 2005).

Did You Know?

Life changes needed for long-term recovery include:

- Elimination of cues associated with substance use

- Learning to manage drug craving

- Developing skills to cope with stress, depression, or anxiety

- Learning effective interpersonal skills

- Rebuilding family relationships

- Cultivating friendships with those not using substances

- Developing new hobbies and activities

- Addressing financial issues

- Enhancing job skills

As we have seen from our exploration of the multiple contributors to substance abuse, the development of addiction is a complicated process made even more complex by the addictive characteristics of different substances. What all substances have in common are the long-lasting, difficult-to-reverse physiological and psychological changes that occur with chronic use. Thus, effective treatment targets the involuntary activation of reward circuits in response to drug-associated cues and the resultant drug craving (Kalivas & O'Brien, 2008) as well as the psychological, social, and sociocultural factors that led to initial substance use. In the next section we discuss research validated treatment for the most commonly abused substances: alcohol, nicotine, marijuana, opioids, and stimulants.

Treatment for Alcohol Dependence

Participation in Alcoholics Anonymous (AA) is a common intervention for alcoholism. Alcoholics Anonymous regards alcoholism as a disease and advocates total abstinence. In one of the most rigorous studies investigating the success of AA treatment, strong affiliation with AA predicted better treatment outcome; involvement with AA was associated with feelings of self-efficacy, active coping, and motivation to stop drinking, which, in turn, are associated with positive outcome (Morganstern et al., 1997). Comparing the effects of AA with mental health treatment, Moos and Moos (2006) found both therapy and participation in AA resulted in better outcome during a sixteen-year follow-up period compared to no intervention. Recent research highlighted a strong association between regular AA meeting attendance, increased spirituality, and decreased alcohol use: Additionally, AA members reported new friendships and enhanced mood as well as increased coping skills and motivation for abstinence (Kelly et al., 2011).

Consistent with the position of AA, alcoholism specialists who believe alcoholism is a disease argue that chronic alcoholism changes cerebral functioning in fundamental and long-lasting ways (Nestler & Malenka, 2004) and that recovering alcoholics must completely abstain from drinking because any consumption will set off the disease process

The Cost of Drinking

At a press conference, a mother talks about the death of her son, Dustin Church, 18, who was killed in an alcohol-related car accident. Do you know of anyone who has been injured or killed because of alcohol?

Vizion / The Image Works

(Wollschlaeger, 2007). On the other hand, proponents of controlled drinking assume that, under the right conditions, alcoholics can learn to limit their drinking to appropriate levels. There is evidence that controlled drinking may work for some alcohol abusers (Emmelkamp, 2004). A major task is to discover which individuals can handle controlled drinking without major relapse. Comparing individuals recovered from alcohol dependence who chose to engage in periodic heavy drinking, drink moderately, or abstain from drinking, abstinence significantly increased chances of continued recovery; 51 percent of those who drank heavily and 27 percent of the moderate drinkers were once again dependent on alcohol in a three-year follow-up compared to 7 percent of the abstainers (Dawson, Goldstein, & Grant, 2007).

Medications are frequently used in the treatment of alcohol abuse. Antabuse (disulfiram), a medication that produces an aversion to alcohol, has been used for decades. Antabuse has the effect of blocking the breakdown of alcohol (mimicking the protective genetic effects seen in individuals of Asian descent); if alcohol is consumed while taking Antabuse, acetaldehyde accumulates in the body resulting in highly unpleasant symptoms. Alcoholics often use Antabuse inconsistently due to its adverse effects; few studies support its use (Williams, 2005). Similarly, the medication acamprosate, developed to reduce relapse rates and increase abstinence, does not decrease craving for alcohol (Williams, 2005; Richardson et al., 2008) and has not received strong research support for sustaining abstinence (Anton et al., 2006; Morley et al., 2006). Naltrexone, a medication used to reduce craving for and pleasure in using alcohol, is effective in reducing heavy drinking, especially among individuals with strong cravings for alcohol (Richardson et al., 2008), but it is less effective in sustaining abstinence (Pettinati et al., 2006; Ciraulo, Dong, Silverman, Gastfriend, & Pettinati, 2008).

Given the modest effects seen with pharmaceutical intervention, Mann and Hermann (2010) propose an individualized approach to assessing the effectiveness of medications—assessing medication effects with subgroups of alcoholics based on biologically defined endophenotypes. They give the example of naltrexone being more effective with carriers of a specific gene variant and in those individuals with the strongest MRI evidence of brain reactivity in response to pictures of alcohol. Similarly, Ooteman and colleagues (2009) found that genetic characteristics of individuals undergoing alcohol treatment were associated with differential response to both acamprosate and naltrexone.

Overall, psychological and pharmacological approaches to alcohol treatment demonstrate only modest effects (Mann and Hermann, 2010). Interventions supported by research show the greatest promise. For example, a comprehensive analysis of interventions to decrease college drinking revealed that individual, face-to-face interventions using motivational interviewing and providing information correcting misperceptions of social norms regarding drinking yielded the greatest reduction in alcohol-related problems (Carey, Scott-Sheldon, Carey, & DeMartini, 2007). These methods combined with challenging positive expectancies regarding alcohol use successfully reduced heavy drinking in another group of students (Wood, Capone, Laforge, Erickson, & Brand, 2007).

Not only is there a need for continued research regarding treatments for alcoholism, there is a pressing need to increase access to alcohol treatment. This is particularly important because a decision to enter treatment appears to be a crucial change point for those with alcohol dependence (Willenbring, 2010). In 2009, almost 8 percent of adolescents and adults, more than 19 million individuals, needed treatment for an alcohol-use disorder; however, only about 3 million received treatment (SAMHSA, 2010a).

Treatment for Opioid Dependence

In 2009, almost 3 million Americans received some form of treatment for opioid dependence, including 739,000 individuals addicted to prescription opioids and 507,000 with heroin addiction (SAMHSA, 2010a). Researchers have emphasized the importance of intervening as early as possible with opioid dependence because length of use strongly influences treatment outcome (Butler, Black, Serrano, Wood, & Budman, 2010). Individuals who enter treatment for opioid dependence (compared with those who resist treatment) tend to have more experience with drug treatment, want help with their drug problem, and have a more positive view of methadone (Schwartz, Kelly, O'Grady, Mitchell, & Brown, 2010).

Pharmaceutical treatment is often used to prevent relapse in those undergoing treatment for heroin or prescription opioid abuse. Methadone, a synthetic opioid that minimizes withdrawal symptoms and reduces cravings without producing euphoria, was initially considered a simple solution to a major problem. However, it has an important drawback—tolerance develops, resulting in an addictive need for methadone. The following case illustrates this problem, as well as other facets of treatment for opioid addiction.

Case Study

After several months of denying the seriousness of his heroin habit, Gary B. finally enrolled in a residential treatment program that featured methadone maintenance, peer support, cognitive-behavioral therapy, and job retraining. Although Gary initially responded well to the program, he soon began to feel depressed. The staff reassured him that those recovering from opioid abuse frequently experience depression. A fairly low dose of antidepressant medication was prescribed; Gary also began individual therapy with a psychologist. Psychotherapy helped Gary identify unhealthy relationships in his life. His dependence on these relationships and his dependence on drugs were examined for parallels. His tendency to deny problems and to turn to drugs as an escape was explored. The therapy then focused on practicing refusal skills and exploration of healthy alternatives to drug use. Gary worked hard during his therapy and made considerable progress.

Gary was entirely satisfied with the changes he was making in his life until the day he realized that he was eagerly looking forward to his daily methadone dose. Although Gary had friends who became addicted to methadone, it was a shock when it happened to him. He decided almost immediately to terminate his methadone maintenance program. The withdrawal process was physically and mentally painful, and Gary often doubted his ability to function without methadone. However, by joining a support group composed of others who were discontinuing methadone, he was eventually able to complete methadone withdrawal. Gary had never imagined that the most difficult part of his heroin treatment would be giving up methadone.

Buprenorphine (a synthetic opioid similar to methadone) is a less addictive medication that has been effective in assisting with opioid withdrawal and preventing relapse (Vigezzi et al., 2006). A review of the literature comparing methadone and buprenorphine concluded that they are both effective for treating opioid-use disorder, especially with individualization of dosage (Connock et al., 2007). Naltrexone (the medication designed to block pleasurable sensations in those who use alcohol) is sometimes used with opioid abuse, but a literature review revealed limited effectiveness (Adi et al., 2007). Findings that 36 percent of those using Vivitrol, an injectable form of naltrexone, were able to remain abstinent and stay in treatment for six months compared to 23 percent in a placebo-control group resulted in recent approval of Vivitrol to treat opioid dependence in those who have undergone detoxification (U.S. Food and Drug Administration, 2010).

Opioid addiction is often associated with psychological drug dependence and feelings of being overwhelmed and unable to cope with daily activities. It is not surprising that being married and having a close relationship with one's spouse predicted better treatment outcome for heroin users (Heinz, Wu, Witkiewitz, Epstein, & Preston, 2009). Contingency management with incentives for abstinence (Bickel et al., 1997; Carroll & Onken, 2005) and behaviorally oriented individual and family counseling (Fals-Stewart & O'Farrell, 2003) have improved treatment outcome.

Treatment for Stimulant Dependence

Almost 1.5 million Americans received treatment for stimulant abuse in 2009, including almost 800,000 receiving treatment for cocaine dependence (SAMHSA, 2010a). There are currently no effective pharmacological interventions for stimulant abuse (Montoya & Vocci, 2008); however, the search for effective medications continues (Kampman, 2008). Researchers are testing a vaccine (called TA-CD) to help cocaine-dependent individuals. Antibodies produced from the vaccine prevent cocaine from reaching the brain, thus reducing any pleasurable effects. Unfortunately, many given the vaccine have not produced sufficient antibodies. Additionally, some have responded by using massive doses of cocaine, desperately trying to reach a high, leading to concerns about possible overdose (Kinsey, Kosten, & Orson, 2010).

Prizes for stimulant-free toxicology reports doubled rates of abstinence in a group also receiving pharmacological treatment with methadone (Peirce et al., 2006); similarly, incentives increased rates of continuous abstinence in individuals receiving no pharmaceutical intervention (Stitzer, Petry, & Peirce, 2010). One group of researchers (Rohsenow, Monti, Martin et al., 2000) found that training cocaine users to cope with temptations and high-risk situations was beneficial not only in lowering cocaine use but also in lowering the amount of cocaine used during a relapse. Cocaine users who are married and have a close spousal relationship have better treatment outcome (Heinz et al., 2009).

Treatment for Marijuana Dependence

In 2009, more than 1 million Americans received some form of treatment for cannabis abuse (SAMHSA, 2010a). Increases in treatment admissions and recent recognition of a cannabis-withdrawal syndrome have led to a search for medications to assist in the withdrawal process and to help prevent relapse (Vandrey & Haney, 2009). Research efforts are focusing on the brain systems uniquely affected by marijuana use, particularly the cannabinoid system (Elkashef et al., 2008). The pervasiveness of marijuana use and dependency and the modest results seen with current treatment protocols make research in this area particularly important (Montoya & Vocci, 2008).

Psychological approaches such as brief therapy, cognitive and behavioral therapy, and motivational enhancement have shown promise with cannabis-use disorders (Benyamina, Lecacheux, Blecha, Reynaud, & Lukasiewcz, 2008). However, individuals dependent on marijuana experience difficulty both initiating and maintaining abstinence, highlighting the importance of extended treatment (Moore & Budney, 2003). Because of the ongoing cognitive and motivational deficits associated with marijuana use, some researchers advocate using short, frequent therapy sessions and focusing on increased self-efficacy (Munsey, 2010).

The use of vouchers to reinforce negative urine toxicology has shown some promise (Nordstrom & Levin, 2007). In one study, rewards for verified abstinence initially produced the highest rates of abstinence; however, those who participated in contingency management combined with motivational enhancement and cognitive behavioral therapy had higher abstinence in later follow-up (Kaddena, Littb, Kabela-Cormiera, & Petrya, 2007). A review of outpatient therapies for cannabis dependence revealed low rates of abstinence even with cognitive and contingency management approaches; the researchers concluded that cannabis dependence may not be easily treated in outpatient settings (Denis, Lavie, Fatséas, & Auriacombe, 2006).

Treatment for Nicotine Dependence

It has been estimated that one-third to one-half of those who smoke will die from smoking-related disease (Mitrouska, Bouloukaki, & Siafakas, 2007). Statistics like this highlight the importance of smoking cessation programs. Unfortunately, even once cessation occurs, relapse to smoking remains high, emphasizing the highly addictive nature of nicotine and the need for long-term treatment strategies (Hatsukami, Stead, & Gupta, 2008). Relapse rates and withdrawal-related discomfort are higher in smokers with depression, anxiety, or other substance-use disorders (Weinberger, Desai, & McKee, 2010). Smoking cessation was much more difficult for individuals with major depression seeking help from a quitline compared to those who were mildly depressed or not depressed, emphasizing the importance of addressing underlying emotional issues (Hebert et al., 2011). Smoking cessation programs that provide emotional support and that enhance readiness to change are most likely to result in ongoing abstinence (Grimshaw & Stanton, 2006).

Three pharmaceutical products are used for smoking cessation—nicotine replacement, bupropion, and varenicline. Nicotine replacement therapy (NRT) involves delivering increasingly smaller doses of nicotine using a patch, inhaler, nasal spray, gum, or sublingual tablet. This reduces withdrawal symptoms associated with smoking cessation, thus reducing the urge to smoke. NRT has been found to be fairly effective in smoking cessation (Silagy et al., 2003); those using NRT are three to five times less likely to progress from a one-time smoking lapse to a full-blown relapse (Shiffman et al., 2006).

Bupropion (marketed under the names Zyban as an antismoking agent and Wellbutrin as an antidepressant) is frequently mentioned in the smoking cessation literature. Bupropion affects the release of neurotransmitters and reduces activation of brain regions associated with craving, even in the presence of smoking-related cues (Culbertson et al., 2011). As with other antidepressant medications, caution is urged in the use of bupropion due to concerns about side effects including agitation, depression, and suicidal ideation. Unfortunately, both NRT and bupropion have limited long-term effectiveness (Mitrouska, Bouloukaki, & Siafakas, 2007) even when combined with psychological approaches.

A newer medication, varenicline (marketed as Chantix), has shown success in reducing cue-activated cravings and withdrawal symptoms, as well as decreasing smoking satisfaction in healthy, adult smokers (Garrison & Dugan, 2009; Franklin et al., 2011). A review of research concluded that a smoker taking varenicline is two to three times more likely to achieve cessation four months after initiating treatment compared to a smoker taking bupropion or using NRT (Cahill, Stead, & Lancaster, 2008). Another literature review found significantly higher continuous abstinence rates with 12–24 weeks of varenicline use compared to placebo, bupropion, or NRT; however, due to concerns about agitation, depression, and suicidal thoughts, close monitoring of emotional reactions is recommended for those taking varenicline, especially individuals with coexisting psychiatric disorders (Keating & Lyseng-Williamson, 2010).

A wide range of coping strategies have been helpful in reducing the urge to smoke including learning to cope with negative emotions (O'Connell et al., 2007). Relapse in smoking is strongly affected by a desire to terminate abstinence-induced negative mood; some smokers have particular difficulty tolerating negative moods (Lerman & Audrain-McGovern, 2010). Additionally, intervention to address anxiety issues is very important in smokers with anxiety disorders; they tend to have greater nicotine dependence and are less likely to respond to standard pharmacological interventions (Piper et al., 2010). Virtual reality therapy helps smokers learn to effectively respond to smoking-related cues (Bordnick et al., 2005). With this approach, visual headsets, 3-D earphones, and wired gloves are used to simulate a smoking environment with cues associated with smoking such as alcoholic drinks, other smokers or smells of smoke, and coffee. Participants identify circumstances under which cravings occur and practice methods of coping with cravings during the virtual experience.

Smoking quitlines are usually free and thus easily accessible for those considering smoking cessation; the typically used, research-guided telephone counseling format has proven to be an effective intervention (Lichtenstein, Zhu, & Tedeschi, 2010).

Interventions using the Internet also seem quite promising. Munoz and his colleagues (2006) evaluated the use of a Web-based brochure emphasizing reasons to stop smoking; how to prepare to quit; what to do in case of relapse; how to refuse cigarettes from friends and family; and information on pharmacological aids. Abstinence rates from the online program were similar to those found in traditional interventions such as psychotherapy.

Women have a more difficult time than men with smoking cessation; one variable that affects success is the phase of menstrual cycle at the time of smoking cessation (Allen, Bade, Center, Finstad, & Hatsukami, 2008; Allen, Allen, & Pomerleau, 2009). Other factors that appear to make it more difficult for women to stop smoking include stress and negative mood (Shiffman & Waters, 2004), enjoying the routine of smoking, sensitivity to smoking cues (Perkins, 2009), and fear of weight gain. A study investigating methods to help women concerned about weight gain achieve cessation found success when bupropion was used in combination with cognitive-behavioral therapy focused on the issue of weight control (Levine et al., 2010).

Summary

1. What are substance-use disorders?

   - People often use chemical substances that alter moods, levels of consciousness, or behaviors. The use of such substances is considered a disorder when there is a maladaptive pattern of recurrent use over a twelve-month period; the person is unable to reduce or cease intake of the substance, despite social, occupational, psychological, medical, or safety problems.

2. What substances are involved in substance-use disorders?

   - Substances are largely classified on the basis of their effects. Substances that are abused include depressants, stimulants, hallucinogens, dissociative anesthetics, and substances with multiple properties.
   - Widely used depressants include alcohol, opioids (such as heroin and prescription pain relievers), and prescription medications that produce sedation and relief from anxiety.

   - Stimulants energize the central nervous system, often inducing elation, grandiosity, hyperactivity, agitation, and appetite suppression. Amphetamines, cocaine, and caffeine are all considered stimulants.
   - Hallucinogens, another category of psychoactive substances, produce altered states of consciousness, perceptual distortions, and sometimes hallucinations. Included in this category are LSD, psilocybin, and mescaline.
   - Dissociative anesthetics are substances that produce a dream-like detachment. Phencyclidine (PCP), ketamine, and dextromethorphan (DXM) are included in this category.
   - Substances with multiple chemical properties include nicotine, cannabis, inhalants, and Ecstasy.

3. Why do people develop substance-use disorders?

   - No single factor accounts for the development of a substance-use disorder. Biological, psychological, social, and sociocultural factors are all important.

   - In terms of biological factors, heredity can significantly affect the risk of developing a substance-use disorder. Additionally, chronic drug or alcohol use alters brain chemistry, crowds out other pleasures, impairs decision making, and produces a compulsive desire for the substance.

   - Psychological approaches to understanding substance-use disorders have emphasized personality characteristics such as behavioral undercontrol and self-medicating with substances to cope with stressful emotions and life transitions.

   - Social factors are important in the initiation of substance use. Teenagers and adults use drugs because of parental models, social pressures from peers, and increased feelings of comfort and confidence in social relationships.

   - Sociocultural factors affecting alcohol and drug use include media influences, cultural, and subcultural norms, as well as societal stressors such as discrimination.

4. What kinds of interventions and treatments are available for substance-use disorders, and does treatment work?

   - The complex nature of addiction underscores the importance of a research-based, multifaceted treatment approach that is tailored to the individual's specific substance-use disorder and any concurrent social, emotional, or medical problems.

   - Treatment for substance-use disorders has had mixed success. Intervening earlier in the addiction process increases success. Even after physiological withdrawal from a substance, substance abusers often relapse. Relapse prevention is enhanced through the use of motivational enhancement techniques to increase readiness for change combined with pharmacological products to minimize withdrawal symptoms and incentives for abstinence. Relapse indicates that longer-lasting or more intensive treatment is needed.

Media Resources

Psychology CourseMate   Access an interactive eBook, chapter-specific interactive learning tools, including flash cards, quizzes, videos, and more in your Psychology CourseMate, accessed through CengageBrain.com.

CENGAGENOW

CengageNow   CengageNOW is an easy-to-use online resource that helps you study in less time to get the grade you want—NOW. If your textbook does not include an access code card, go to CengageBrain.com to gain access.

CENGAGEbrain

CengageBrain   More than just an interactive study guide, WebTutor is an anytime, anywhere customized learning solution with an eBook, keeping you connected to your textbook, instructor, and classmates. Purchase the access chosen by your instructor at CengageBrain.com.

12

Schizophrenia and Other Psychotic Disorders

A t the age of eight, Elyn Saks began to experience the hallucinations and fears of being attacked that have accompanied her throughout her life. Elyn understood the importance of not talking openly about what ran through her mind, and she was able to hide her delusional thoughts and hallucinations and maintain top grades throughout college. In graduate school, she experienced full-blown psychotic episodes (e.g., believing that someone had infiltrated her research; dancing on the roof of the law library) that resulted in her hospitalization and subsequent diagnosis of schizophrenia. She once believed her therapist was replaced by an evil person with an identical appearance. In her book *The Center Cannot Hold: My Journey Through Madness*, Elyn recounts her lifelong struggle with mental illness, describing schizophrenia as a "slow fog" that becomes thicker over time (Saks, 2007). Elyn's struggle with the disorder, as well as her experience with forced treatment, resulted in an intense interest in mental health and the law. Her doctors had painted a bleak picture of her future. They believed that she would not complete her degree nor be able to hold a job or get married. However, Elyn Saks did marry and complete graduate school. She is a professor of law, psychology, and psychiatry at the University of Southern California, where she also has served as an associate dean. She is currently training to be a psychoanalyst.

S chizophrenia refers to a group of disorders characterized by psychosis (impaired sense of reality), severely impaired cognitive processes, personality disintegration, affective disturbances, and social withdrawal. It is a heterogeneous clinical syndrome with different etiologies and outcomes (Braff, 2007; Frankenburg, 2010; Heinrichs, 1993; Roth et al., 2004). Like Elyn Saks, individuals with schizophrenia lose contact with reality, see or hear things that are not actually present, or develop false beliefs about themselves or others. A diagnosis of schizophrenia involves deterioration from a previous level of functioning in areas such as work, interpersonal relationships, or self-care together with symptoms such as delusions, hallucinations, disorganized speech, and grossly abnormal psychomotor behavior. Diagnosis requires symptoms to be present most of the time for at least one month, and some of the time for at least six months (American Psychiatric Association, 2011). Neurocognitive disorders, substance use, and mood disorders must be ruled out as causes of the symptoms.

focus questions

1 What are the symptoms of schizophrenia?

2 How do other psychotic disorders differ from schizophrenia?

3 Is there much chance of recovery from schizophrenia?

4 What causes schizophrenia?

5 What treatments are currently available for schizophrenia, and are they effective?

Schizophrenia receives a great deal of attention for several reasons. First, it can be a severely disabling disorder that has a profound impact on the individual and on family members and friends. The prognosis is often much different from the productive life experienced by Elyn Saks. In the following first-person account, Eric Sundstrom presents a personal perspective on the changes he witnessed in his older sister after she developed schizophrenia.

Case Study

My family spent 3 years in Holland when my sister was in middle school. I think she was truly happy then, forming friendships and teaching me about the things she loved. It seems incredible she was once an ordinary girl, full of vibrant personality. I still remember how she taught me to read, using a now-ancient copy of *The Cat in the Hat*. When our family returned to America, all of her friends signed the clogs for her to remember them by. The clogs and a few memories are my only window into who she was then and who she should be now. (Sundstrom, 2004, p. 191)

Eric recalls how his sister developed delusions and violent behavior during her sophomore year in high school. Auditory hallucinations insulted her and commanded her to break things. One day, a change of medication resulted in an intensification of symptoms; his sister destroyed items around the house and had to be hospitalized. After Eric and his brother cleaned up the broken glass and silently began eating their dinner, they realized that their sister had thoughtfully baked quiche for them; one side was filled with vegetables for his brother and the other side was plain, the way Eric liked it. For the relatives of individuals with schizophrenia, the psychotic symptoms shown by their loved ones can be confusing, frightening, and heartwrenching.

Schizophrenia also receives considerable attention because the financial costs of hospitalization, treatment, and loss of productivity caused by schizophrenia are huge—estimated to be $62.7 billion annually (Wu et al., 2005). Because the lifetime prevalence rate of schizophrenia in the United States is about 1 percent, it affects millions of people (McGrath, 2005; National Institute of Mental Health [NIMH], 2007e). In addition, because the causes of schizophrenia are not well understood, it has been difficult to find effective treatments for all individuals diagnosed with the disorder.

Although many individuals with schizophrenia do not fully recover from the illness, some do, as in the case of Elyn Saks. Indeed, there is a move away from the view that schizophrenia is a chronic disorder with an inevitably poor prognosis toward advocacy for a recovery model that envisions substantial return of function for those with schizophrenia. The recovery model, emphasizing optimism and collaborative support targeting each individual's potential for recovery, views schizophrenia as a chronic medical condition, such as diabetes or heart disease, which may interfere with optimal functioning but that does not define the individual (Warner, 2009). The recovery model is based on the following assumptions regarding schizophrenia (Bellack, 2006; Dilks, Tasker, & Wren, 2010):

1. Recovery or improvement in functioning is possible.
2. Healing involves separating one's identity from the illness and developing the ability to cope with psychiatric symptoms.
3. Empowerment of the individual helps correct the sense of powerlessness and dependence that results from traditional mental health care.
4. Establishing or strengthening social connections can facilitate healing.

The recovery model has resulted in social justice actions such as fighting policies that neglect the rights of individuals with schizophrenia; identifying the impact of stigma and discrimination on mental health; and promoting healing, growth, and respect for those

schizophrenia a group of disorders characterized by severely impaired cognitive processes, personality disintegration, affective disturbances, and social withdrawal

psychosis condition involving loss of contact with or distorted view of reality

affected by schizophrenia (Glynn et al., 2006). In this chapter, we present findings regarding the diagnosis, etiology, and treatment of schizophrenia. Other psychotic disorders involving hallucinations, delusions, or cognitive abnormalities are also presented and contrasted with schizophrenia.

The Symptoms of Schizophrenia

The symptoms of schizophrenia fall into four categories: *positive symptoms*, *negative symptoms*, *cognitive symptoms*, and *psychomotor abnormalities*.

Positive Symptoms

> I was convinced that a foreign agency was sending people out to get rid of me. I was so convinced because I kept receiving messages from them via a device planted inside my brain. . . . I decided to strike first: to kill myself so they wouldn't have a chance to carry out their plans and kill me. (Kean, 2011, p. 4)

Positive symptoms of schizophrenia, such as in the previous example, involve unusual thoughts or perceptions such as delusions (false beliefs), hallucinations, disordered thinking (i.e., shifting and unrelated ideas producing incoherent communication), and bizarre behavior. Symptoms can be influenced by the individual's mood and intensified with stress (Smith et al., 2006).

Delusions

Delusions are false personal beliefs that are firmly and consistently held despite disconfirming evidence or logic. Individuals experiencing delusions are not able to distinguish between their private thoughts and external reality. In the following case, therapists attempt to confront the illogical delusion held by a graduate student in neuroscience who believed that rats were inside his head, consuming a section of his brain.

Case Study

"Erin, you are a scientist," they'd begin. "You are intelligent, rational. Tell me then, how can you believe that there are rats inside your brain? They're just too big. Besides, how could they get in?" (Stefanidis, 2006, p. 422)

Erin had no explanation of how rats could enter his brain, but he was certain that he would soon lose functions controlled by the area of the brain that the rats were consuming. To prevent this from happening, he banged his head so that the "activated" neurons would "electrocute" the rats. Realizing he was not losing his sight even though the rats were eating his visual cortex, he entertained two possible explanations. First, his brain had a capacity for rapid regeneration, or second, the remaining brain cells compensated for the loss. Whenever information became too discrepant, Erin depended on his enhanced thought processes or "Deep Meaning," a system he believed transcended scientific logic.

Although some individuals with schizophrenia, like Erin, attempt to maintain some sense of logic, most individuals are either unaware or only moderately aware of the illogical nature of their hallucinations or delusions (Figure 12.1). They may also attribute their symptoms to something other than mental illness (Amador, 2003; Mintz, Dobson, & Romney, 2003). Elyn Saks (2009) did not believe she was mentally ill. She rationalized her psychotic experiences by reasoning that everyone's mind has some chaos and confusion. In addition, she told herself that her symptoms were behaviors of her own choosing. *Poor insight* (i.e., failure to recognize symptoms of one's own

Image courtesy of Elyn Saks. Photo copyright Will Vinet

First-Hand Experience

Elyn Saks, a legal scholar and mental health policy advocate, has written about the forced treatment of the mentally ill based, in part, on her own experiences. She teaches mental health law, has academic appointments at the University of Southern California (USC) and the University of California, San Diego, and has served as an associate dean at USC. She is training to be a psychoanalyst.

positive symptoms symptoms of schizophrenia that involve unusual thoughts or perceptions such as delusions, hallucinations, thought disorder, or bizarre behavior

delusions false beliefs that are firmly and consistently held despite disconfirming evidence or logic

Figure 12.1

Awareness of Psychotic Symptoms by Individuals with Schizophrenia

Source: Amador, X. (2003). Poor insight in schizophrenia: Overview and impact on medication compliance. Downloaded from: http://www .xavieramador.com/file/cns-special-report-on-insight.pdf. Used by permission of Dr. Xavier Amador.

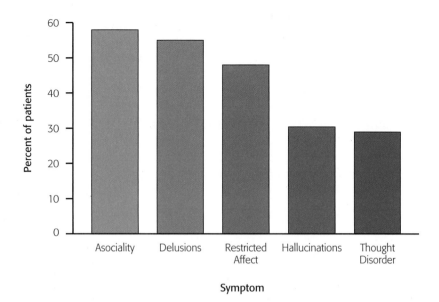

mental illness) is related to greater severity of illness and poorer premorbid adjustment (Campos et al., 2011). Additionally, individuals with schizophrenia may have poor insight regarding psychiatric symptoms but may acknowledge deficits in memory and other cognitive abilities (Gilleen, Greenwood, & David, 2011).

A variety of delusional themes are seen in those with schizophrenia:

- *Delusions of grandeur.* Individuals may believe they are someone famous or powerful (from the present or the past).
- *Delusions of control.* Individuals may believe that other people, animals, or objects are trying to influence or take control of them.
- *Delusions of thought broadcasting.* Individuals may believe that others can hear their thoughts.
- *Delusions of persecution.* Individuals may believe that others are plotting against, mistreating, or even trying to kill them.
- *Delusions of reference.* Individuals may believe they are the center of attention or that all happenings revolve around them.
- *Thought withdrawal.* Individuals may believe that someone or something is removing thoughts from their mind.

Did You Know?

Individuals with severe mental disorders such as schizophrenia have higher rates of violence than healthy people. However, this is true only if they have other risk factors for violent behavior such as substance abuse or a history of violence, physical abuse, or victimization. Severe mental illness alone does not predict violence (Elbogen & Johnson, 2009).

The most common delusion in schizophrenia involves *paranoid ideation*, or suspiciousness about the actions or motives of others (Collip et al., 2010). Those with paranoid ideation often have high levels of anxiety and worry and experience *persecutory delusions* (i.e., beliefs of being targeted) as well as angry reactions to perceived persecution (Startup, Freeman, & Garety, 2006). Those with paranoid delusions often believe that others are plotting against them, are talking about them, or are out to harm them in some way. They are constantly suspicious, and their interpretations of the behavior and motives of others are distorted. A friendly, smiling bus driver is seen as someone who is laughing at them derisively. A busy clerk who fails to offer help is part of a plot to mistreat them. A telephone call that was a wrong number is an act of harassment or an attempt to monitor their comings and goings. Several studies have found that individuals with paranoid delusions externalize their problems (Kinderman & Bentall, 1996, 1997). Paranoid ideation may function to protect self-concept by turning personal problems into accusations that "others are responsible for the bad things that are happening."

A rare delusion is *Capgras syndrome* (named after the person who first reported it). It is the belief in the existence of identical "doubles" who replace significant others, such as Elyn Saks's belief that her therapist had been replaced by an evil double (Dulai & Kelly, 2009). Similarly, the mother of one woman with delusions explained how her daughter would phone her, asking questions such as what she had worn as a Halloween costume at the age of twelve or who had attended a specific birthday party. "She was testing me because she didn't think I was her mother. . . . No matter what question I answered, she was just sobbing" (Stark, 2004, p. A1). The daughter believed that her mother had been replaced by an imposter in a body suit and that her real mother had been kidnapped.

Delusions can produce strong emotional reactions such as fear, depression, or anger. Those with persecutory delusions may respond to perceived threats by leaving "dangerous" situations, avoiding areas where they might be attacked, or becoming more vigilant. Paradoxically, these "safety" behaviors may prevent them from encountering disconfirmatory evidence, thus reinforcing the idea that the lack of catastrophe was due to their cautionary behaviors (Freeman et al., 2007). Delusions may be unconnected or may involve a single theme. One woman had multiple delusions, including a belief that celebrities were talking to her through the television, that her deceased husband was still alive and cheating on her, and that her internal organs were getting infected (Mahgoub & Hossain, 2006b). Delusions may vary from those that are plausible, such as being followed or spied on, to those that are bizarre (e.g., plots to remove internal organs or thoughts being placed in their minds).

In one study (Harrow et al., 2004), nearly half of a group of individuals with delusions had some questions regarding their beliefs, and 21 percent were fully aware that others might view their beliefs as atypical. The strength of delusional beliefs and their effects on the person's life can vary significantly. Delusions have less impact when the individual can acknowledge that the belief may be incorrect; that others may question the accuracy of the belief; and suggest an alternate hypothesis regarding the delusion (Islam, Scarone, & Gambini, 2011; Warman et al., 2007).

Unusual beliefs sometimes develop in individuals with schizophrenia because conclusions are reached based on limited information. Those with delusions appear to make errors during the stages of hypothesis formation and evaluation. They develop unlikely hypotheses due to reduced data gathering and "jump to conclusions" from limited information (Ross, Freeman, Dunn, & Garety, 2011), overestimating the probability that the hypotheses are true (Warman et al., 2007). In one study, individuals with delusions demonstrated a reasoning bias by rating narratives of twenty-five actual delusions involving themes of grandiosity, persecution, thought broadcasting, or thought insertion as "more likely to be true" than matched controls. Interestingly, this reasoning bias did not occur with neutral narratives (e.g., estimating the probability that red or black balls would be picked from a bag with differing proportions of colored balls). To account for these differences, the researchers hypothesized that delusional individuals may have an attentional bias for emotionally salient or threat-related information (McGuire et al., 2001).

People with schizophrenia can be trained to challenge their delusions. One fifty-one-year-old woman believed with almost 100 percent certainty that she was younger than twenty and that she was the daughter of Princess Anne. Her therapist asked her to view her delusion as only one possible interpretation. Then they discussed evidence for her belief, and the therapist presented the inconsistencies and irrationality of the belief, as well as alternative explanations. After this procedure, the woman reported a significantly reduced conviction in her beliefs, stating, "I look 50 and I tire more quickly than I used to; I must be 50" (Lowe & Chadwick, 1990, p. 471). She agreed that she was probably older than Princess Anne and, therefore, could not be her daughter. Belief modification appears to be a helpful procedure for some individuals with schizophrenia.

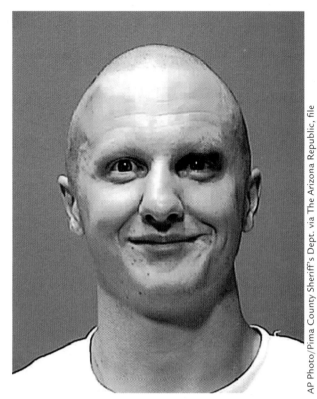

AP Photo/Pima County Sheriff's Dept. via The Arizona Republic, file

Does This Person Appear Mentally Ill?

This photo of Jared Loughner was taken after he was arrested on January 8, 2011, for shooting and killing people attending a political gathering. Four months later, a judge ruled he was incompetent to stand trial. Were there early signs of severe mental illness?

MYTH   Individuals experiencing delusions or hallucinations steadfastly accept them as reality.

REALITY: The strength of hallucinations and delusions can vary significantly among individuals with schizophrenia. Some believe in them 100 percent, whereas others are less certain. Even without treatment, many cope by developing means of re-establishing contact with reality or testing out the reality of their thinking. Some individuals with schizophrenia, such as Elyn Saks, are able to combat delusions and hallucinations through a combination of conscious effort and medication. However, many individuals with schizophrenia require specific cognitive training to develop the skills necessary to question or cope with hallucinations and delusions.

MYTH VS. REALITY

Should We Challenge Delusions and Hallucinations?

The doctor asked a patient who insisted that he was dead: "Look. Dead men don't bleed, right?" When the man agreed, the doctor pricked the man's finger, and showed him the blood. The patient said, "What do you know, dead men do bleed after all." (Walkup, 1995, p. 323)

Clinicians are often unsure about whether to challenge psychotic symptoms. Some contend that delusions and hallucinations serve an adaptive function and that any attempt to change them would be useless or even dangerous. The example of the man who believed he was dead illustrates the apparent futility of using logic with delusions. However, Coltheart, Langdon, and McKay (2007) found that a "gentle and tactful offering of evidence" was successful in treating a man who believed his wife was not his wife but was, instead, his business partner. The man was asked to entertain the possibility that the woman was actually his wife. The therapist pointed out that the woman was wearing a wedding ring identical to the one he had bought for his wife. The man said that the woman probably bought the ring from the same shop. He was then shown the initials engraved in the ring as being those of his wife. Within one week, he accepted the fact that the woman was his wife. Other clinicians (Bak et al., 2003; Beck & Rector, 2000; Chadwick et al., 2000; Freeman et al., 2007; Ross, Freeman, Dunn, & Garety, 2011) have also found that some clients respond well to challenges to their hallucinations and delusions.

The approach has two phases. First, hypothetical contradictions are introduced to assess how open individuals experiencing hallucinations or delusions are to conflicting information. During this phase, clients are presented with information that might contradict their beliefs, a process that often weakens their delusions. For example, one woman, H.J., with auditory hallucinations was asked if her belief in the "voices" would change if it could be determined that they were coming from her. After she agreed, she was given a set of industrial earmuffs to wear; she still reported hearing voices. Another woman who believed that God was commanding her to kill was asked if her belief would be lessened if a priest informed her that God would not ask anyone to kill another person.

In the second phase, the therapist asks clients to give evidence for their beliefs and to develop alternative interpretations. For example, one woman who claimed that voices could accurately tell her when her spouse would return was asked how voices could foretell the future. A man who claimed he would be killed if he did not comply with auditory commands was told that he could resist the voices and would not die.

Alternative explanations are proposed for the hallucinations, including the possibility that the voices are thoughts or "self-talk." After cognitive-behavioral treatment, most participants report a decreased belief in their psychotic symptoms. In H.J.'s case, her degree of certainty about her auditory hallucinations dropped from 100 percent to 20 percent. Although she still heard voices telling her she would die, she learned to disregard them because they were "coming from her head."

For Further Consideration

1. Should we challenge psychotic symptoms? If so, what is the best way of doing so?
2. Might some hallucination or delusions have an adaptive function?

Hallucinations

A hallucination is a sensory perception that is not directly attributable to environmental stimuli; it may involve a single sensory modality or a combination of modalities: hearing (*auditory hallucination*), seeing (*visual hallucination*), smelling (*olfactory hallucination*), feeling (*tactile hallucination*), and tasting (*gustatory hallucination*). Auditory hallucinations are most common and can range from malevolent to benevolent or can involve both qualities (Copolov, Mackinnon, & Trauer, 2004; Stip, 2009). Hallucinations are particularly distressing when they involve dominant, insulting voices or when the individual cannot communicate with the voices (Vaughan & Fowler, 2004).

Case Study

An individual describes his experience with auditory hallucinations while hospitalized for schizophrenia:

"You're alone," an insidious voice told me. "You're going to get what's coming to you." . . . No one moved or looked startled. It was just me hearing the voice. . . . I had seen others screaming back at their voices. . . . I did not want to look mad, like them. . . . Never admit you hear voices. . . . Never question your diagnosis or disagree with your psychiatrist . . . or you will never be discharged. (Gray, 2008, p. 1006)

hallucination a sensory perception that is not directly attributable to environmental stimuli

Auditory hallucinations appear to be "real" to the individual experiencing them and sometimes have relationship-like qualities (Chin, Hayward, & Drinnan, 2009). In one study involving individuals hospitalized with acute psychosis, 61 percent of respondents reported that the voices they heard had a distinct gender; 46 percent believed that the voice was that of a friend, family member, or acquaintance; and 80 percent reported having back-and-forth conversations with the voices. Most believed the voices were independent entities, and some had conducted "research" to test the reality of the voices. One said she initially thought that the voice might be her own but rejected it when the voice called her "mommy," something she would not call herself. Another woman explained, "They are not imaginary. They see what I do. They tell me that I'm baking a cake. They must be there. How else would they know what I'm doing?" (Garrett & Silva, 2003, p. 447). Interestingly, one man with a 25 year history of hallucinations complained about the absence of voices after treatment with medication. He reported feeling lonely, bored, and sad, saying the voices offered companionship (Stip, 2009).

Disorganized Thought and Speech

Disordered thinking is a primary characteristic of schizophrenia. During communication, individuals with schizophrenia may have difficulty focusing on one topic, speak in an unintelligible manner, or reply tangentially to questions. Loosening of associations, also referred to as *cognitive slippage*, is the continual shifting from topic to topic (without any apparent logical or meaningful connection between thoughts) that is characteristic of schizophrenia. Disorganized communication often involves the incoherent speech or bizarre, idiosyncratic responses seen in the following example.

Case Study

INTERVIEWER: "You just must be an emotional person, that's all."
PATIENT (1): "Well, not very much I mean, what if I were dead? It's a funeral age. Well I um. Now I had my toenails operated on. They got infected and I wasn't able to do it. But they wouldn't let me at my tools." (Thomas, 1995, p. 289)

The beginning phrase in the patient's first sentence appears appropriate to the interviewer's comment. However, the reference to death is not. Slippage appears in the comments referring to a funeral age, having toenails operated on, and getting tools. None of these thoughts are related to the interviewer's comment, and they have no hierarchical structure or organization. People with schizophrenia may also respond to words or phrases in a very concrete manner and demonstrate difficulty with abstractions. A saying such as "a rolling stone gathers no moss" might be interpreted as "moss can't grow on a rock that is rolling." These communication difficulties may result from an inability to inhibit contextually irrelevant information (Titone, Levy, & Holzman, 2000).

Individuals with schizophrenia also show over-inclusiveness or abnormal categorization. When asked to sort cards with pictures of animals, fruit, clothing, and body parts into piles of things that go together, one man placed an ear, apple, pineapple, pear, strawberry, lips, orange, and banana together in a self-named category "something to eat." When asked the reason for including ear and lips in the "something to eat" category, he explained that an ear allows you to hear a person asking for fruit, and lips allow you to ask for and eat fruit (Doughty, Lawrence, Al-Mousawi, Ashaye, & Done, 2009).

Grossly Abnormal Psychomotor Behavior

The symptoms of schizophrenia that involve motor functions can be quite bizarre, as is evident in the following case.

Did You Know?

Psychotic-like experiences are not uncommon among the general population. In a sample of 591 young adults, Rossler and colleagues (2007) found:

- 38 percent endorsed the statement "Someone else can control my thoughts."

- 20 percent endorsed the statement "Others are aware of my thoughts."

- 18 percent endorsed the statement "I have thoughts that are not my own."

- 3 percent reported "hearing voices other people don't hear."

In most cases, these beliefs are transient and not clinically relevant unless they become persistent, excessive, or associated with significant distress.

loosening of associations continual shifting from topic to topic without any apparent logical or meaningful connection between thoughts

Prinzhom Sammlung/Psychiatric Hospital in Heidelberg

Prinzhorn Sammlung/Psychiatric Hospital in Heidelberg

Painting by People with Schizophrenia

The inner turmoil and private fantasies of schizophrenics are often revealed in their artwork. The paintings you see here were created by psychiatric patients in European hospitals. They are part of the Prinzhorn Collection at the Psychiatric University Hospital in Heidelberg, Germany. What do you think the paintings symbolize?

catatonia a condition characterized by marked disturbance in motor activity—either extreme excitement or motoric immobility

negative symptoms symptoms of schizophrenia associated with an inability or decreased ability to initiate actions or speech, express emotions, or feel pleasure

Case Study

At age twenty, patient A . . . was found sitting at the edge of the bed for hours, displaying simple repetitive movements of the right hand while simultaneously holding his left hand in a bizarre posture and repeating "I do, I do, I do." (Stober, 2006, pp. 38–39)

Some individuals with schizophrenia exhibit catatonia, a condition involving extremes in activity level (either unusually high or unusually low), peculiar body movements or postures, strange gestures and grimaces, or a combination of these (see Figure 12.2 for symptoms associated with catatonia) (Caroff et al., 2007; Enterman & van Dijk, 2011). People with *excited catatonia* are agitated and hyperactive. They may talk and shout constantly, moving or running until they drop from exhaustion. They sleep little and are continually "on the go." Their behavior can become dangerous and involve violent acts. In sharp contrast, people experiencing *withdrawn catatonia* are extremely unresponsive. They show prolonged periods of stupor and mutism, despite their awareness of all that is going on around them. Some may adopt and maintain strange postures and refuse to move or change position; stand for hours at a time, perhaps with one arm stretched out to the side; or lie on the floor or sit awkwardly on a chair, staring, aware of what is occurring but not responding or moving. Attempts to change the person's position may be persistently resisted. Others exhibit a waxy flexibility, allowing their bodies to be "arranged" in almost any position and then remaining in that position for long periods of time. The extreme withdrawal associated with catatonic episode can be life-threatening when it results in inadequate food intake (Aboraya, Chumber, & Altaha, 2009). Catatonic symptoms can also occur with bipolar and depressive disorders or other medical conditions (Fink, 2009).

Negative Symptoms

Negative symptoms of schizophrenia are associated with an inability or decreased ability to initiate actions or speech, express emotions, or feel pleasure (Messinger et al., 2011). Such symptoms include *avolition* (an inability to take action or focus on goals), *alogia* (a lack of meaningful speech), *asociality* (minimal interest in social relationships), and *restricted affect* (little or no emotion in situations in which emotional reactions are expected). A delusional patient, for instance, might explain in detail how parts of his or her body are rotting away but show absolutely no concern or worry through voice tone or facial expression. Clinicians are careful to distinguish between *primary symptoms* (symptoms that arise from the disease itself) and *secondary symptoms* (symptoms that may develop as a response to medication, institutionalization, or as a result of other conditions such as depression).

In clinical samples, approximately 15 to 25 percent of individuals diagnosed with schizophrenia display primarily negative symptoms (Johnson et al., 2009). Negative symptoms are associated with inferior premorbid (before the onset of illness) social functioning. Restricted affect is more common in men and is associated with poor prognosis and outcome (Addington & Addington, 2009; Gur et al., 2006). One group of individuals with schizophrenia with negative symptoms endorsed beliefs such as "Having friends is not as important as many say," "I attach very little importance to having close friends," "If I show my feelings, others will see my inadequacy," and "Why bother, I'm just going to fail" (Rector, Beck, & Stolar, 2005). These beliefs may contribute to a lack of motivation to interact with others. Poorer insight is associated with more severe negative symptoms (Mutsatsa et al., 2006).

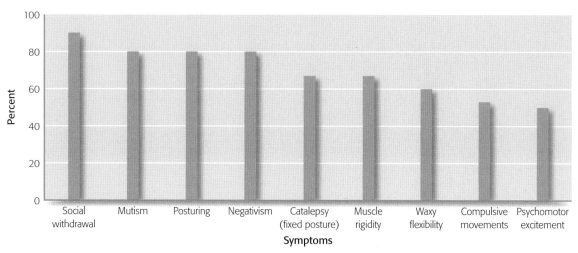

Figure 12.2

PREVALENCE OF SYMPTOMS IN THIRTY YOUNG PATIENTS WITH CATATONIA
Catatonic symptoms can vary significantly.
Source: Cornic, Consoli, & Cohen, (2007)

Cognitive Symptoms

Cognitive symptoms of schizophrenia include problems with attention and memory and difficulty developing a plan of action. As compared with healthy controls, those with schizophrenia have severe to moderately severe cognitive impairment, as evidenced by poor "executive functioning"—deficits in the ability to absorb and interpret information and make decisions based on that information, to sustain attention, and to retain and use recently learned information (Braw et al., 2008; Costafreda et al., 2011; NIMH, 2007e). Difficulties with social-cognitive skills; social perspective-taking; and understanding their own and other's thoughts, motivations, and emotions are also common. Cognitive symptoms are generally present even before the onset of the first psychotic episode (Bailey & Henry, 2010; Pflueger et al., 2007), tend to persist even with treatment, and are found (to a lesser degree) among nonpsychotic relatives of individuals with schizophrenia (Reichenberg & Harvey, 2007). Many researchers consider these cognitive impairments to be a core component of schizophrenia (Keefe & Fenton, 2007). Although most individuals with schizophrenia display cognitive dysfunctions, up to 25 percent show normal or near normal functioning on neuropsychological assessment (Wexler et al., 2009).

Cultural Issues

Culture may affect how symptoms of schizophrenia are viewed. In Japan, for example, schizophrenia is highly stigmatized. Part of the problem is that the condition is called *seishin-bunretsu-byou*, which roughly translates to "a split in mind or spirit." The term conjures up an irreversible condition. Because of this connotation, only about 20 percent of those with schizophrenia were told of their diagnosis in the years preceding 2000 (Kim & Berrios, 2001). In 2002, the name was changed to *togo-shitcho-sho* (integration disorder), which is a less stigmatizing term. With this change, 69.7 percent of psychiatrists surveyed said they would now inform the patient of the diagnosis, although 15.2 percent would continue to withhold the diagnostic information (Takahashi et al., 2011). Similarly, a negative reaction to the term *schizophrenia* is also part of the reason that many psychiatrists in Turkey will not mention the diagnosis to patients or family members (Ucok, 2007).

Did You Know?

In one study, individuals with schizophrenia and healthy controls wore a head-mounted virtual reality display that gave them the sense of going through a neighborhood, a shopping center, and a market. Fifty incoherencies such as a mooing dog, an upside-down house, and a red cloud were presented during the journey. Eighty-eight percent of those with schizophrenia failed to detect these inconsistencies. Even when the inconsistencies were identified, about two-thirds of the participants had difficulty explaining them.

Source: Sorkin, Weinshall, & Peled, (2008)

cognitive symptoms symptoms associated with problems with attention, memory, and difficulty in developing a plan of action

"Studies conducted in the United Kingdom and the United States suggest that schizophrenia may be diagnosed more often in individuals who are African American and Asian American than in other racial groups" (American Psychiatric Association, 2000a, p. 307). Immigrant groups, particularly those of African descent, have the highest rates of schizophrenia in Western Europe; similarly, follow-up of a large birth cohort in the United States revealed that African Americans were three times more likely to be diagnosed with schizophrenia compared to whites. Adjustment of data to account for socioeconomic risk factors still revealed that African Americans were twice as likely to receive a schizophrenia diagnosis (Bresnahan et al., 2007). It is not clear whether these differences reflect actual differences in rates of the disorder or whether they represent clinician bias. Cultural differences between patient and clinician may produce diagnostic errors—the greater the difference, the greater the likelihood of error.

■ Other Psychotic Disorders

Disorders in this group are characterized by psychotic symptoms such as hallucinations, delusions, and disorganized speech but do not meet the diagnosis of schizophrenia. They include brief psychotic disorder, schizophreniform disorder, delusional disorder, attenuated psychosis syndrome, and other specified psychotic disorder.

Brief Psychotic Disorder and Schizophreniform Disorder

"Schizophrenic-like" episodes that last fewer than six months are considered either a brief psychotic disorder (duration of at least one day but less than one month) or schizophreniform disorder (duration of at least one month but less than six months). Diagnosis of these disorders does not require impairment in social or occupational functioning (American Psychiatric Association, 2011). Exposure to psychological trauma can produce brief psychotic episodes. For example, among men who fought in Croatia, 20 percent reported hallucinations and delusions (Kastelan et al., 2007). Brief psychotic disorder has also been reported in cases of Guillain-Barré syndrome, a condition producing temporary paralysis of muscles, including those used for breathing. Among one group of individuals affected by this extremely distressing syndrome, 25 percent developed a psychotic reaction (Weiss et al., 2002). Brief psychotic disorder is relatively uncommon, is more frequent in developing countries, and more frequently occurs in women (Memon & Larson, 2009). Schizophreniform disorder is found equally in men and women and shares some of the anatomical and neural deficits found in schizophrenia (Bhalla, 2009). The lifetime prevalence of schizophreniform disorder is 0.07 percent (Perala et al., 2007) while that of brief psychotic disorder is unknown; many brief psychotic episodes may not persist long enough for a diagnosis.

Differences between these disorders and schizophrenia are shown in Table 12.1. Although they appear to be distinct, these disorders have highly similar characteristics. The diagnoses of brief psychotic disorder and schizophreniform disorder are often considered "provisional." For example, an initial diagnosis of brief psychotic disorder may change to schizophreniform disorder if symptoms last longer than one month and to schizophrenia if they last longer than six months and impair social or occupational functioning. In a follow-up study involving individuals with schizophreniform disorder, 46 percent later received a diagnosis of schizophrenia; 35 percent, a depressive or bipolar disorder; 18 percent, a nonschizophrenic psychotic disorder; and 2 percent, no disorder (Marchesi et al., 2007). Because duration of symptoms is the only accurate means of distinguishing among the disorders, questions about the validity of these categories have been raised.

brief psychotic disorder   psychotic episodes with a duration of at least one day but less than one month

schizophreniform disorder   psychotic episodes with a duration of at least one month but less than six months

TABLE 12.1 Comparison of Brief Psychotic Disorder, Schizophreniform Disorder, and Schizophrenia

	Brief Psychotic Disorder	Schizophreniform Disorder	Schizophrenia
Duration	Less than one month	Less than six months	Six months or more
Psychosocial Stressor	Likely present	Usually present	May or may not be present
Symptoms	Emotional turmoil; psychotic symptoms	Emotional turmoil; psychotic symptoms	Emotional reactions variable; psychotic symptoms
Outcome	Return to premorbid functioning	Possible return to premorbid functioning	Return to premorbid functioning is uncommon
Familial Pattern	No information	Some increased risk of schizophrenia among family members	Higher prevalence of schizophrenia among family members

Delusional Disorder

Delusional disorder is characterized by persistent, nonbizarre delusions (i.e., beliefs that are false, but that could be plausible) that are not accompanied by other unusual or odd behaviors; tactile and olfactory hallucinations related to the delusional theme are sometimes reported (American Psychiatric Association, 2011). Delusional disorder is not considered a form of schizophrenia due to the absence of additional disturbances in thoughts and perceptions or psychosocial impairment. Some contend that delusional disorder represents the midpoint on a continuum between firmly held, extreme beliefs and psychosis. Delusional disorder is rarely diagnosed (.03 to 0.18 percent prevalence); however, it is believed that many with the disorder do not perceive they have a problem and, therefore, do not seek assistance (Chopra & Khan, 2009; Perala et al., 2007). People with delusional disorder behave normally when their delusional ideas are not being discussed. Common themes involved in delusional disorders include:

- *Erotomania*—the belief that someone is in love with the individual; this delusion typically has a romantic rather than sexual focus.
- *Grandiosity*—the conviction that one has great, unrecognized talent; special abilities; or a relationship with an important person or deity.
- *Jealousy*—the conviction that one's spouse or partner is being unfaithful.
- *Persecution*—the belief that one is being conspired or plotted against.
- *Somatic complaints*—convictions of having body odor, being malformed, or being infested by insects or parasites.

Women are more likely to develop erotomanic delusions, whereas men tend to have paranoid delusions involving persecution (Chopra & Khan, 2009). The following cases illustrate some features of delusional disorders:

- A woman was convinced that people were watching her and following her because she saw the same people day after day in her neighborhood and in the stores where she shopped (Muller, 2006).
- A woman complained of insects that wandered in her body; when she scratched her legs, she insisted she saw insects (Mercan et al., 2007).
- A 37-year-old man was arrested for stalking and harassing Tyra Banks, a model and television personality. He had followed her for two months; appeared at her TV studio; made repeated phone calls; and sent multiple letters and flowers, claiming that they had a "thing together" (Serpe, 2009).

Hearing loss or impairment in early adolescence is associated with an increased risk of developing circumscribed delusions (van der Werf et al., 2011). A decreased ability to

delusional disorder involves persistent, nonbizarre delusions without other unusual or odd behaviors; tactile and olfactory hallucinations related to the delusional theme may be present

obtain corrective feedback, combined with pre-existing personality traits of suspiciousness, may increase susceptibility to developing delusional beliefs. Delusional disorder can be treated with antipsychotic medications and/or cognitive-behavior therapy (Chopra & Khan, 2009; Mecan et al., 2007).

In a rare form of delusional disorder (shared psychotic delusion) a person who has a close relationship with an individual with delusional or psychotic beliefs comes to accept those beliefs (Wehmeier, Barth, & Remschmidt, 2003) as seen in the following case.

Case Study

A twenty-eight-year-old woman and her mother both shared the delusion that the daughter had been given poisoned food and was hypnotized by a man so that he could rape her. They appeared at an emergency department together with the mother requesting that the daughter be "dehypnotized" (Mahgoub & Hossain, 2006a).

Shared delusions (sometimes referred to as *folie à deux*) are more prevalent among those who are socially isolated. In the preceding case, the daughter never married, lived with and was submissive to her mother, and had no close relationships with others. The pattern generally involves a family member or partner acquiring the delusional belief from the dominant individual. In many cases, an individual who shares another person's delusional or psychotic beliefs loses faith in those beliefs when the two individuals are separated.

Attenuated Psychosis Syndrome

Attenuated psychosis syndrome involves distressing or disabling delusions, hallucinations, or disorganized speech in combination with intact reality testing; the symptoms must have emerged or gotten progressively worse over the previous year (American Psychiatric Association, 2011). Whether these "milder" signs of psychosis should warrant a psychiatric diagnosis has been a matter of debate. Those in favor make several arguments: (1) Symptoms of attenuated psychosis syndrome occurring in childhood and adolescence increase risk for psychiatric impairment in adulthood (Polanczyk et al., 2010); (2) rapid deterioration often occurs during the early years of psychosis, so early intervention and treatment might diminish the effects of the illness (Amminger et al., 2010; Carpenter, 2010; Crumlish et al., 2009); and (3) this diagnosis allows treatment for people who are highly distressed by their subthreshold psychotic symptoms. In a study to determine the impact of early treatment, McGlashan and colleagues (2006) identified a group of individuals with prodromal symptoms (early symptoms of schizophrenia) and randomly assigned them to a medication or a placebo treatment for a one-year period. Was the treatment with medication useful? Among those who developed full-blown psychosis during the one-year study, 37.9 percent were in the placebo group and 16.1 percent were in the antipsychotic medication group. However, during additional follow-up, many more in the medication group developed psychosis; medication appeared to delay rather than prevent the occurrence of psychosis. Additionally, the majority of participants did not develop schizophrenia during the study or within two follow-up periods.

Opponents of the attenuated psychosis syndrome diagnosis argue that this diagnosis identifies many individuals who will not develop a psychotic disorder ("false positives"), resulting in stigma and unwarranted use of antipsychotic medications. Psychotic-like experiences appear to be present not only in those with schizophrenia and related disorders but also in the general population (Campbell & Morrison, 2007; Kelleher & Cannon, 2010). Among young adults, paranoid ideation is relatively common with 18.6 percent reporting a belief that people were against them, 8.2 percent believing someone was trying to harm them, and 1.8 percent reporting plots against them. In the vast majority, these symptoms were transitory (Freeman et al., 2010). In another study, 845 adolescents were followed for almost nine years. Reports of psychotic symptoms such as beliefs of persecution, thought interference, and auditory hallucinations were quite common but, in

attenuated psychosis syndrome involves early signs of delusions, hallucination, or disorganized speech; for this diagnosis, reality testing must be intact and the symptoms must be distressing or disabling and have emerged or gotten progressively worse over the previous year

most cases, were only transitory (Dominguez, Wichers, Lieb, Wittchen, & van Os, 2011). Depending on the study, 10 to 50 percent with psychotic-like experiences develop schizophrenia or other psychotic disorders (Cornblatt & Correll, 2010; Nelson & Yung, 2011). Recurrence of psychotic symptoms is associated with greater likelihood of a psychotic disorder (Dominguez et al., 2011).

Other Specified Psychotic Disorder

This category of "other specified psychotic disorder" includes individuals who have psychotic symptoms (e.g., hallucinations, delusions, disorganized speech, grossly disorganized behavior, or catatonia) that are not significant enough to meet the criteria for a specific psychotic disorder (American Psychiatric Association, 2011). Examples are postpartum psychosis not associated with a depressive or bipolar disorder, persistent auditory hallucination in the absence of other symptoms, nonbizarre hallucinations that overlap with fluctuating mood symptoms, and psychotic symptoms of unknown etiology.

CONTROVERSY

Morgellons Disease: Delusional Parasitosis or Physical Disease?

More than ten years ago, "Mary Leitao plucked a fiber that looked like a dandelion fluff from a sore under her two-year-old son's lips. . . . Sometimes the fibers were white, and sometimes they were black, red, or blue" (DeVita-Raeburn, 2007, p. 1). Leitao was frustrated by the inability of physicians to diagnose her son's skin condition. In fact, many of the professionals Leitao consulted indicated that they could find no evidence of disease or infection. Frustrated by the medical establishment, Leitao put a description of the condition on a Web site in 2001, calling it Morgellons disease after a seventeenth-century French medical study involving children with similar symptoms (Mason, 2006). The Web site has since compiled 12,000 worldwide reports of the condition among adults and children. Sufferers report granules and fiber-like threads emerging from the skin at the site of itching; sensations of crawling, stinging, or biting; and rashes and skin lesions that do not heal (Paquette, 2007). Some describe the fibers as "inorganic but alive" and report that the fibers pull back from a lit match (Browne, 2011, p. 2). Symptoms of vision changes, joint pain, fatigue, mental confusion, and short-term memory difficulties have also been reported in connection with Morgellons disease (Centers for Disease Control [CDC], 2011a & b). Although Morgellons disease has been reported throughout the United States and in at least 15 other countries, the greatest numbers of reported cases come from California, Florida, and Texas (Ho & Cummins, 2008).

What could cause this disorder? Many dermatologists, physicians, and psychiatrists believe that Morgellons disease results from self-inflicted injury or is a somatic type of delusional disorder such as *delusional parasitosis*, a condition in which individuals (often those with psychosis or a substance-use disorder) maintain a delusional belief that they are afflicted with living organisms or other pathogens (Freudenmann & Lepping, 2009). In examining individuals with Morgellons disease, physicians report being unable to find fibers at the sites of "infection" but often describe inflamed skin that appears to result from scratching or picking (DeVita-Raeburn, 2007). Stephen Stone, past president of the American Academy of Dermatology, does not believe Morgellons disease is real.

He argues that the Internet community is allowing individuals with somatic delusions to band together (Marris, 2006). Some physicians, however, believe there is an underlying physical disorder, citing those with Morgellons symptoms who test positive for Lyme disease or whose symptoms are alleviated with antibacterial or antiparasitic medications (Savely, Leitao, & Stricker, 2006). Focusing on differential diagnosis to rule out delusional parasitosis, one group of physicians gathered comprehensive medical histories, laboratory tests, and physical examinations on 25 self-defined sufferers of Morgellons disease; they found that in all cases the "delusions" began following physical symptoms and that the patients had immune system deficiency and markers of chronic inflammation, which are evidence of infectious disease (Harvey et al., 2009).

Vitaly Citovsky, a member of the Morgellons Research Foundation Medical Advisory Board, professor of molecular and cell biology and authority on *Agrobacterium* (a soil bacterium used in the genetic engineering of plants; this bacterium is known to be capable of transforming human cells) has entered the debate citing not-yet-published findings from his research team indicating that *Agrobacterium* was detected in skin biopsies from individuals with symptoms of Morgellons, but not in biopsies from healthy controls (Ho & Cummins, 2008). Some say that it was this report combined with the increasing number of complaints to the Centers for Disease Control (CDC) from sufferers of the condition that prompted a CDC-initiated investigation focused on characteristics and epidemiologic data related to Morgellons disease. The study included environmental analysis, examination of skin biopsies, and laboratory study of fibers or threads obtained from people with the condition (CDC, 2011b). Results of the investigations, begun early in 2008, have been submitted for publication in a peer-reviewed scientific journal but have not yet been publically released.

For Further Consideration:

1. Are Internet discussions of Morgellons disease allowing a population of vulnerable, delusional individuals to receive reinforcement for their illness, or do they provide comfort for those with an actual disease?

The Course of Schizophrenia

It is popularly believed that overwhelming stress can cause a well-adjusted and relatively normal person to experience a psychotic breakdown or develop schizophrenia. There are, in fact, recorded instances of the sudden onset of psychotic behaviors in previously well-functioning people (Kastelan et al., 2007). In most cases, however, the person's *premorbid personality* (personality before the onset of major symptoms) shows some impairment. Similarly, most people with schizophrenia recover gradually rather than suddenly. The typical course of schizophrenia consists of three phases: prodromal, active, and residual.

The *prodromal phase* includes the onset and buildup of schizophrenic symptoms. Social withdrawal and isolation, peculiar behaviors, inappropriate affect, poor communication patterns, and neglect of personal grooming may become evident during this phase. Of eleven individuals with schizophrenia who were interviewed in one study (Campo et al., 1998), nine indicated that they had drastically changed their appearances (cutting or changing hairstyles; wearing multiple pants, dresses, coats, or other items of clothing at the same time) just before the onset of the schizophrenic episode. They said the changes were an attempt to maintain their identities. Friends and relatives often considered such behavior odd or peculiar.

Often, psychosocial stressors or excessive demands on an individual with schizophrenia in the prodromal phase result in the onset of prominent psychotic symptoms, or the *active phase* of schizophrenia. In this phase, the person shows full-blown symptoms of schizophrenia, including severe disturbances in thinking, deterioration in social relationships, and flat or markedly inappropriate affect.

At some later time, the person may enter the *residual phase*, in which the symptoms are no longer prominent. In the residual phase, the symptom severity declines, and the individual may show milder impairment similar to that seen in the prodromal phase. Although long-term studies have shown that many people with schizophrenia can lead productive lives, complete recovery is rare. (Figure 12.3 illustrates different courses schizophrenia may take.)

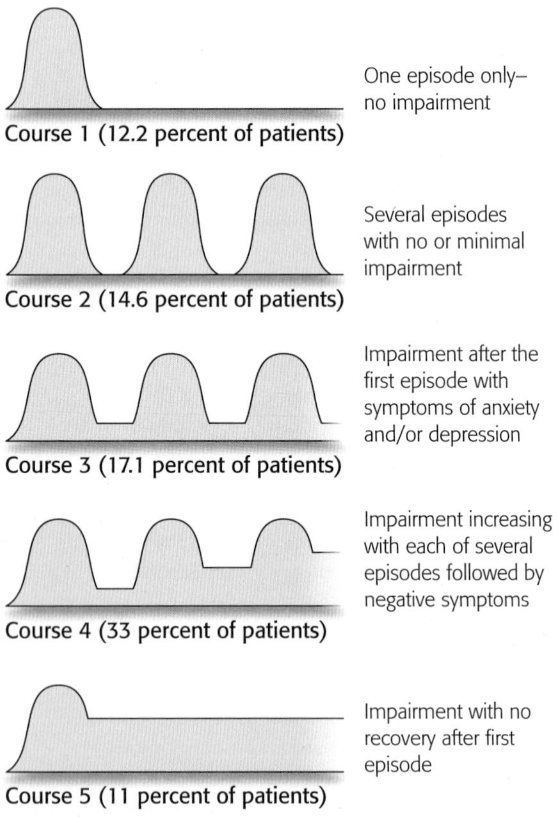

Long-Term Outcome Studies

What are the chances for recovery from or improvement in schizophrenia? The chances for improvement or recovery are difficult to definitively evaluate because of recent improvements in both psychotherapy and medication. In a ten-year follow-up study of individuals hospitalized for schizophrenia, the majority of participants improved over time, whereas a minority appeared to deteriorate (Rabinowitz et al., 2007). Similarly, during a fifteen-year follow-up involving individuals with schizophrenia, the following were found (Harrow et al., 2005):

- More than 40 percent showed one or more periods of recovery (defined as the absence of psychotic activity and negative symptoms, working half time or more, and no psychiatric hospitalization during the period of evaluation).
- A sizable minority were not on any medication.

An earlier follow-up study (Wiersma et al., 1998) also reported that about one-quarter of a group of individuals diagnosed with schizophrenia showed complete remission of symptoms, even though about half of the group had had more than one psychotic episode. About 50 percent showed partial remission of symptoms accompanied by either anxiety and depression or negative symptoms, and 11 percent showed no recovery after the initial psychotic episode. Relapses occurred in two-thirds of this sample, after which about one in six showed no remission of symptoms. Factors associated with a positive outcome include gender (women have a better outcome),

Course 1 (12.2 percent of patients) — One episode only—no impairment

Course 2 (14.6 percent of patients) — Several episodes with no or minimal impairment

Course 3 (17.1 percent of patients) — Impairment after the first episode with symptoms of anxiety and/or depression

Course 4 (33 percent of patients) — Impairment increasing with each of several episodes followed by negative symptoms

Course 5 (11 percent of patients) — Impairment with no recovery after first episode

Figure 12.3

VARYING OUTCOMES WITH SCHIZOPHRENIA
This figure shows five of the many outcomes possible with schizophrenia. These outcomes were observed in individuals during a fifteen-year follow-up study.
Source: Wiersma et al., (1998)

higher levels of education, being married, and having a higher premorbid level of functioning (Irani & Siegel, 2006). In a ten-year follow-up study examining baseline predictors associated with recovery from schizophrenia, researchers found that fewer negative symptoms, a prior history of good work performance and ability to live independently, and lower levels of depression and aggression were all associated with improved outcome (Shrivastava, Shah, Johnston, Stitt, & Thakar, 2010). Peer support, work opportunities, and reducing the stigma of schizophrenia all play an important role in the recovery process (Warner, 2009). An eight-year follow-up of adults with first-episode psychosis documented the effectiveness of comprehensive intervention early in the course of the illness; such intervention increased chance of remission, reduced positive symptoms, and resulted in an overall more favorable course of the illness (Mihalopoulos, Harris, Henry, Harrigan, & McGorry, 2009). Intervention to decrease stress from issues such as self-stigmatization, negative beliefs, and social skills deficits can significantly enhance recovery (Tsang et al., 2010). Having a social network with friends and being single or married as opposed to separated or divorced are also associated with a more positive outcome (Sibitz, Unger, Woppmann, Zidek, & Amering, 2011).

■ Etiology of Schizophrenia

Case Study

A thirteen-year-old boy who was having behavioral and academic problems in school was taking part in a series of family therapy sessions. Family communication was negative in tone, with a great deal of blaming. Near the end of one session, the boy suddenly broke down and cried out, "I don't want to be like her." He was referring to his mother, who had been receiving treatment for schizophrenia and was taking antipsychotic medication. He had often been frightened by her bizarre behavior, and he was concerned that his friends would "find out" about her condition. But his greatest fear was that he would inherit the disorder. Sobbing, he turned to the therapist and asked, "Am I going to be crazy, too?"

If you were the therapist, how would you respond? At the end of this section on the etiology of schizophrenia, you should be able to reach your own conclusion about what to tell the boy.

Schizophrenia and other psychotic conditions are best understood using a multipath model that integrates heredity (genetic influences on brain structure and neurotransmitters), personal vulnerability such as depression or other characteristics, cognitive processes (e.g., faulty psychological processing of information can maintain delusional ideas), and social adversities (such as low social or economic status) (van der Gaag, 2006). To develop an accurate etiological framework, all of these dimensions must be taken into consideration, as shown in Figure 12.4.

In the following section, we discuss the biological, psychological, social, and sociocultural dimensions separately, remembering that each dimension interacts with the others. For example, emotional or sexual abuse; cannabis use; and exposure to trauma (physical threat, serious accident) have all been hypothesized to affect dopamine levels and neurocognitive functioning. In one sample, the probability of persistent psychotic symptoms was influenced by each of these factors, especially among individuals who were exposed to all three influences (Cougnard et al., 2007). The interactive model illustrated in Figure 12.5 demonstrates how an underlying biological vulnerability combined with other risk characteristics (e.g., male gender, younger age) can result in the development of prodromal symptoms of schizophrenia. As time progresses, psychotic features may appear or intensify if additional environmental risk factors (e.g., cannabis use, trauma) occur. If the environmental exposures are chronic or severe, the risk of developing schizophrenia increases. We now begin the discussion of specific risk factors associated with schizophrenia.

Figure 12.4

MULTIPATH MODEL FOR SCHIZOPHRENIA

The dimensions interact with one another and combine in different ways to result in schizophrenia.

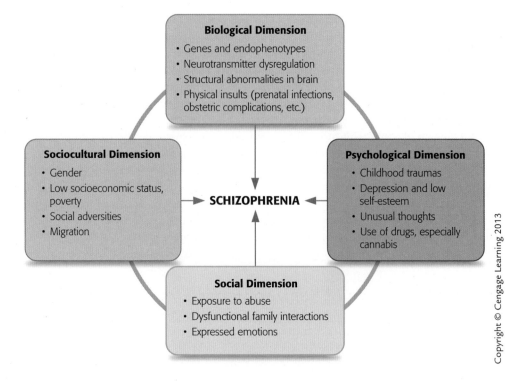

Copyright © Cengage Learning 2013

Did You Know?

Individuals who recently experienced a psychotic breakdown attributed their emotional collapse to drug use (especially cannabis); adult trauma (e.g., sexual assault, violence, or abuse); personal sensitivity (e.g., not fitting in, bottling up feelings, discomfort around others); or developmental problems (e.g., being teased or bullied as a child, childhood abuse, personal loss).

Source: Dudley, Siitarinen, James, & Dodson, (2009)

Biological Dimension

Case Study

The coupling of sufficient genetic bias with stressful input from the environment is the modern formulation of how nature and nurture conspire to produce schizophrenia.

Stahl, 2007 (p. 583)

Past research was focused on the attempt to identify the specific gene or genes that cause schizophrenia (Williamson, 2007). The disorder is now understood to be the result of as many as twenty different genes and their interactions; specific genes appear to make only minor contributions toward the illness (Lyon et al., 2011). That schizophrenia is a result of genetic influences is not disputed. Researchers have found the disorder more often among close relatives of people diagnosed with schizophrenia than among more distant relatives (Figure 12.6). The data show that closer

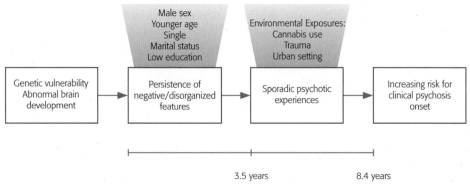

Figure 12.5

INTERACTIVE VARIABLES AND THE ONSET OF CLINICAL PSYCHOSIS

Source: Dominguez, M. D. G., Saka, M. C., Lieb, R., Wittchan, H.-U., & Van Os, J. (2010). Early expression of negative/disorganized symptoms predicting psychotic experiences and subsequent clinical psychosis: A 10-year study. *American Journal of Psychiatry, 167,* 1075–1082. Reprinted with permission from the American Journal of Psychiatry, copyright © 2010. American Psychiatric Association.

blood relatives of individuals diagnosed with schizophrenia run a greater risk of developing the disorder. Thus the boy described earlier who was concerned about becoming schizophrenic like his mother has a 16 percent chance of being diagnosed with schizophrenia, whereas his mother's nieces or nephews have only a 4 percent chance. (It should be noted that the risk for the general population is 1 percent.) However, even among monozygotic (identical) twins, if one twin receives the diagnosis of schizophrenia, the risk of the second twin developing the disorder is less than 50 percent. Thus environmental influences also play a significant role in genetic expression of the disorder (Gottesman, 1978, 1991).

Endophenotypes

Currently, the strategy in genetic research has moved from demonstrating that heredity is involved in schizophrenia to attempts to identify the genes that are responsible for specific characteristics or traits that are evident in this disorder. This approach involves the identification and study of endophenotypes—characteristics that are quantifiable, heritable, and trait-related (Braff, Freedman, Schork, & Gottesman, 2007). Endophenotypes (also being researched with respect to an array of mental and physical disorders) are hypothesized to underlie the illness and exist in the individual before, during, and following remission of the disorder. It would be expected that these characteristics be found with higher frequency, although in milder forms, among "non-ill" relatives of individuals with schizophrenia (Gur et al., 2007). Researchers have identified several possible endophenotypes related to impairment in function in both those with schizophrenia and unaffected biological relatives. The traits involved include working memory, executive functions, sustained attention, and verbal memory (Chan, Di, McAlonan, & Gong, 2011; Reichenberg & Harvey, 2007; Turetsky et al., 2007).

Neurostructures

How do genes produce a vulnerability to schizophrenia? Clues to the ways that genes might increase susceptibility to developing schizophrenia have involved the identification of structural and neurochemical differences between those with schizophrenia and healthy controls. A number of studies (Borgwardt et al., 2010; Kim et al., 2007; Sim et al., 2006; Tregellas et al., 2007) have reported that individuals with schizophrenia have smaller cortical structures (hippocampal and medial temporal lobes, orbitofrontal cortices, and prefrontal lobes) and ventricle enlargement (enlarged spaces in the brain) (Lawrie et al., 2008; Staal et al., 2001). Ventricular enlargement may primarily indicate an increased susceptibility to schizophrenia, because healthy siblings of individuals with schizophrenia also show ventricle enlargement (Staal et al., 2001). In an interesting longitudinal study of brain changes among youths with and without schizophrenia, those with the disorder showed a striking loss of gray brain matter over a period of six years. The loss was so rapid that it was likened to a "forest fire" (Thompson et al., 2001). Interestingly, healthy siblings of adolescents with child-onset schizophrenia also showed cortical loss (Gogtag, 2008).

How might decreased volumes in cortical structures and enlarged ventricles predispose someone to the development of schizophrenia? These structural characteristics may result in aberrant or weak connectivity between the various brain regions, leading to reductions in the integrative function of the brain and impaired cognitive processing (Salgado-Pineda et al., 2007). Thus the ineffectiveness of communication within the different brain systems may lead to the cognitive symptoms (e.g., impairment in memory, decision making, and problem solving), negative symptoms (e.g., lack of drive or initiative), and positive symptoms (e.g., delusions and hallucinations) that are found in schizophrenia. However, the differences in brain structure between individuals with and without schizophrenia are relatively small, and decreased cortical volumes have also been found in healthy individuals and individuals with other disorders. In addition, some of the abnormalities found in

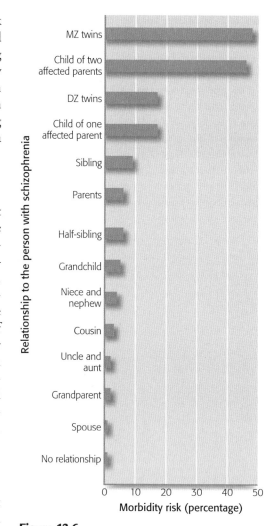

Figure 12.6

RISK OF SCHIZOPHRENIA AMONG BLOOD RELATIVES OF INDIVIDUALS DIAGNOSED WITH SCHIZOPHRENIA

This figure reflects the estimate of the lifetime risk of developing schizophrenia—a risk that is strongly correlated with the degree of genetic influence.

Source: Data from Gottesman, (1978, 1991)

Rate of Gray Matter Loss in Teenagers with Schizophrenia

Male and female adolescents with schizophrenia show progressive loss of gray matter in the parietal, frontal, and temporal areas of the brain that is much greater than that found in "normal" adolescents. A similar pattern of gray matter loss in the different brain regions is found among males and females with schizophrenia. How would you interpret this finding?

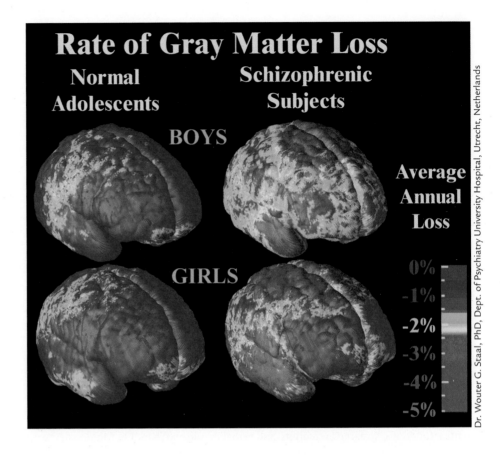

the brain of individuals with schizophrenia may not be due to the disorder, but may result from the use of antipsychotic medication (Ho et al., 2011; Montcrieff & Leo, 2010).

Neurotransmitters

Abnormalities in neurotransmitters (chemicals that allow brain cells to communicate with one another) such as dopamine, serotonin, GABA, and glutamate have also been linked to schizophrenia (Benes, 2009; Tan et al., 2007). Considerable attention has been focused on the neurotransmitter dopamine (Borda & Sterin-Borda, 2006; Howes et al., 2009; Lyon et al., 2011). According to the dopamine hypothesis, schizophrenia may result from excess dopamine activity at certain synaptic sites. Support for the dopamine hypothesis has come from research with three types of drugs: phenothiazines, L-dopa, and amphetamines.

- *Phenothiazines* are conventional antipsychotic drugs that decrease the severity of disordered thinking, decrease social withdrawal, alleviate hallucinations, and improve the mood of individuals with schizophrenia. Evidence shows that the phenothiazines reduce dopamine activity in the brain by blocking dopamine receptor sites in postsynaptic neurons.
- *L-dopa* is generally used to treat symptoms of Parkinson's disease, such as muscle and limb rigidity and tremors. The body converts L-dopa to dopamine, and the drug sometimes produces schizophrenic-like side effects. In contrast, the phenothiazines, which reduce dopamine activity, can produce side effects that resemble Parkinson's disease.
- *Amphetamines* are stimulants that increase the availability of dopamine and norepinephrine (another neurotransmitter) in the brain. When individuals not diagnosed with schizophrenia are given continual doses of amphetamines, they show symptoms very much like those of acute paranoid schizophrenia. Also, very small doses of amphetamine can increase the severity of symptoms in individuals diagnosed with schizophrenia.

dopamine hypothesis   the suggestion that schizophrenia may result from excess dopamine activity at certain synaptic sites

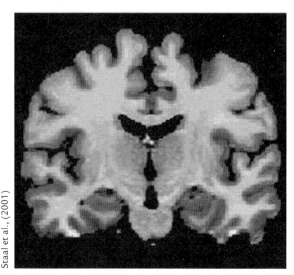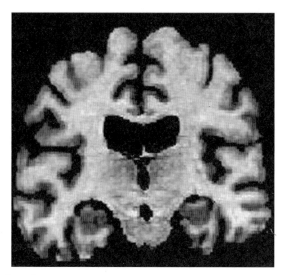

Staal et al., (2001)

Coronal Sections of the Brain in a Patient with Schizophrenia

Structural brain abnormalities have been found in most individuals with schizophrenia. The degree and extent of the abnormalities appear to be related to outcome. Patients with poor outcome (represented by the right photo) show significantly greater loss of cerebral gray matter and greater enlargement of the ventricles than those with less severe symptoms (represented by the photo on the left).

Thus one group of drugs that blocks dopamine reception has the effect of reducing the severity of schizophrenic symptoms, whereas two drugs that increase dopamine availability either produce or worsen these symptoms. Such evidence suggests that excess dopamine may be responsible for schizophrenic symptoms.

The evidence is not clear-cut, however. For example, the dopamine hypothesis might lead us to expect that treating schizophrenia with phenothiazines would be effective in almost all cases of schizophrenia, which is not the case. Additionally, whereas conventional antipsychotics influence dopamine levels by binding tightly to dopamine receptors, second-generation (newer) antipsychotics—most of which work by blocking serotonin receptors, as well as slowing dopamine availability by loosely binding with dopamine receptors—are also effective in treating schizophrenia (Canas, 2005). This suggests that researchers may be looking for an oversimplified explanation by focusing on dopamine alone without considering the interactive functioning of the brain and the biochemical system as a whole. As was indicated earlier, other neurotransmitters also play a major role in schizophrenia (Tan et al., 2007).

Because the concordance rate—the likelihood that both members of a twin pair show the same characteristic—is less than 50 percent when one identical twin has schizophrenia, nonshared environmental influences (physical, psychological, social) between the twins must also play a role. Conditions influencing brain structure or prenatal or postnatal neurodevelopment that have been associated with schizophrenia include prenatal infections, obstetric complications, and head trauma (Compton, 2005; Jablensky et al., 2005; Stahl, 2007; Mittal, Ellman, & Cannon, 2008). Numerous studies have documented an association between early developmental delay and later development of schizophrenia; one large prospective population study recently reported that infants who later developed schizophrenia were slower to smile, lift their heads, sit, crawl, and walk compared to healthy controls (Sørensen et al., 2010). Early behavioral disturbances and cognitive and language deficits have similarly been associated with development of the disorder (Welham, Isohanni, Jones, & McGrath, 2009).

Research has consistently found up to a tenfold increase in prevalence of schizophrenia in areas with colder climates and increased latitude, particularly in individuals with darker skin and regions with lower fish consumption; this research has led to questions about the role of vitamin D deficiency in the development of the disorder (Kinney et al., 2009). Retroviruses have also been implicated in sudden-onset schizophrenia in adults (Karlsson et al., 2001). Although a variety of biological influences appear to increase susceptibility to

concordance rate the likelihood that both members of a twin pair show the same characteristic

schizophrenia by changing or altering brain structures or neurotransmitters, specific psychological, social, and sociocultural variables can also influence development of schizophrenia. We now examine these influences as possible contributors to the disorder.

Psychological Dimension

The psychological dimension includes behaviors, attitudes, and attributes that contribute to the symptoms of schizophrenia by increasing the vulnerability of predisposed individuals. The use of cocaine, amphetamines, alcohol, and especially cannabis appear to increase the chances of developing a psychotic disorder. The onset of psychosis is nearly three years earlier in cannabis users than nonusers (Large, Sharma, Compton, Slade, & Nielssen, 2011). Adolescents who tried cannabis were more likely to report prodromal symptoms (e.g., "Something strange is taking place in me," "I feel that I am being followed," or "I am being influenced in a special way") (Miettunen et al., 2008). Several interpretations are possible to explain the relationship between cannabis use and psychosis, including (1) the increased risk of developing psychosis may be due to the substance use itself, (2) individuals with a predisposition for psychosis may also have a predisposition to substance use, or (3) individuals with prodromal symptoms or psychotic-like experiences may use cannabis to self-medicate these symptoms (Thirthalli & Benegal, 2006; Foti, Kotov, Guey, & Bromet, 2010). Additionally, cannabis may influence dopamine levels and thereby increase vulnerability through interactions with environmental stressors.

Individuals who develop schizophrenia report certain cognitive patterns and unusual beliefs that precede the onset of psychotic symptoms (Solano & De Chavez, 2000). Subclinical disordered thinking (e.g., misattributions and catastrophic interpretations) may evolve into a clinical disorder (Coltheart, Langdon, & McKay, 2007; Nothard, Morrison, & Wells, 2008). For example, negative symptoms such as avolition, anhedonia, and restricted affect may be due to individuals' beliefs that they are "worthless" or "failures" and that their condition is "hopeless" (Rector, Beck, & Stolar, 2005). The combination of low expectancy for pleasure and success, combined with reduced expectancies due to their illness, may maintain the negative symptoms. In fact, some researchers believe that it is the interpretation of events that causes the distress and disability associated with schizophrenia rather than the experience itself (Garety et al., 2007). These pessimistic interpretations can produce and maintain negative symptoms. See Table 12.2 for patterns of thinking associated with negative symptoms.

Social Dimension

Social relationships have long been considered to play a role in the development of schizophrenia. Until the 1900s, biological factors were not considered to have etiological importance (Walker & Tessner, 2008). Instead, it was believed that schizophrenia

TABLE 12.2　Negative Expectancy Appraisals Associated with Negative Symptoms

Negative Symptoms	Low Self-Efficacy (Success)	Low Satisfaction (Pleasure)	Low Acceptance	Low Available Resources
Restricted Affect	If I show my feelings, others will see my inadequacy.	I don't feel the way I used to.	My face appears stiff and contorted to others.	I don't have the ability to express my feelings.
Alogia	I'm not going to find the right words to express myself.	I take so long to get my point across that it's boring.	I'm going to sound weird, stupid, or strange.	It takes too much effort to talk.
Avolition	Why bother, I'm just going to fail.	It's more trouble than it's worth.	It's best not to get involved.	It takes too much effort to try.

Source: From Rector, Beck, & Stolar, (2005), p. 254

was the result of exposure to specific dysfunctional family patterns. However, as Lehman and Steinwachs (1998) note, "Research has failed to substantiate hypothesized causal links between family dysfunction and the etiology of schizophrenia" (p. 8). It is quite probable that among individuals with a biological predisposition, the social environment may contribute to risk of schizophrenia. In this section, we consider social factors as either the cause of or a contributor to schizophrenia.

Certain social conditions appear to influence the appearance of psychotic disorders. For example, being in a traumatic accident has been associated with slightly increased risk of psychotic symptoms (Figure 12.7) (Arseneault et al., 2011). Individuals with psychosis were three times more likely to report severe physical abuse from mothers before 12 years of age compared to matched controls (Fisher et al., 2010). In contrast, among adolescents with symptoms that appeared to put them "at imminent risk" for the onset of psychosis, positive remarks and warmth expressed by caregivers were associated with improvement in negative and disorganized symptoms and social functioning (O'Brien et al., 2006). Children at higher biological risk for schizophrenia may be more sensitive to the effects of both adverse and healthy childrearing patterns (Tienari et al., 2004). However, parenting style may also be influenced by how "sick" the child is, a possibility we consider later in the chapter.

In a longitudinal study focused on 2,232 twins, those who experienced maltreatment by an adult or bullying by peers had a higher risk of psychotic symptoms at the age of 12; children who reported being bullied were 2.5 times more likely to develop psychotic symptoms, and risk was 5.68 times greater for those exposed to both bullying and maltreatment. In another sample of 12-year-old children who had been tracked since the age of 7, the risk of psychotic symptoms doubled for those who had been victims of bullying between the ages of 8 and 10; the association was stronger with more severe or chronic forms of bullying (Schreier et al., 2009). Maltreatment during childhood may alter neurodevelopment in a manner that increases the susceptibility to schizophrenia or other disorders.

Expressed emotion (EE), a negative communication pattern found among some relatives of individuals with schizophrenia, has been associated with higher relapse rates in individuals diagnosed with schizophrenia. Levels of EE index are determined by the number of critical comments made by a relative (criticism); the number of statements of dislike or resentment directed toward the individual with schizophrenia by family members (hostility); and the number of statements reflecting emotional overinvolvement, overconcern, or overprotectiveness with respect to the family member with schizophrenia. For example, relatives high in EE are likely to make statements such as "You are a lazy person" or "You've caused our family a lot of trouble" (Rosenfarb et al., 1995). Relatives high in EE may be more critical because they are more likely than relatives low in EE to believe that the psychotic symptoms are under the personal control of the individual with schizophrenia (Weisman et al., 2000). The EE construct strongly predicts relapse and the overall course of the disorder (Breitborde, Lopez, & Nuechterlein, 2009; Miklowitz, 1994).

However, the EE construct may have less meaning for different cultural groups. Family criticism scores were not associated with relapse for Mexican Americans with schizophrenia (Lopez et al., 2004; Rosenfarb, Bellack, & Aziz, 2006). Interestingly, in a sample of African Americans with schizophrenia, high levels of critical and intrusive behavior by family members were associated with better outcome over a two-year period than were low levels of such behavior. Among African Americans, seemingly

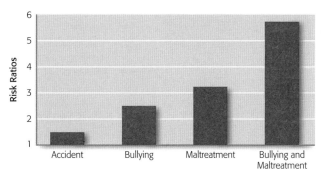

Figure 12.7

RISK OF PSYCHOTIC SYMPTOMS AT AGE 12 ASSOCIATED WITH CUMULATIVE CHILDHOOD TRAUMA

Youth exposed to both bullying and childhood maltreatment demonstrate a significantly increased risk of developing psychotic symptoms.

Source: Arseneault, L., Cannon, M., Fisher, H. L., Polanczyk, G., Moffitt, T. E., & Caspi, A. (2011). Childhood trauma and children's emerging psychotic symptoms: A genetically sensitive longitudinal cohort study. American Journal of Psychiatry, 168, 65–72. Reprinted with permission From the American Journal of Psychiatry, copyright © 2011. American Psychiatric Association.

Did You Know?

A meta-analysis of thirty-five studies reached the following conclusions:

- Risk of psychosis is increased by 40 percent in marijuana users.

- "Heavy pot user" increases risk of psychosis by 50 to 200 percent.

- Psychotic symptoms are not due to the transitory effects of intoxication.

- It is estimated that 14 percent of the cases of psychosis might not have occurred if marijuana had not been used.

Source: Moore et al., (2007); Nordentoft & Hjorthoj, (2007)

expressed emotion (EE) a negative communication pattern found among some relatives of individuals with schizophrenia

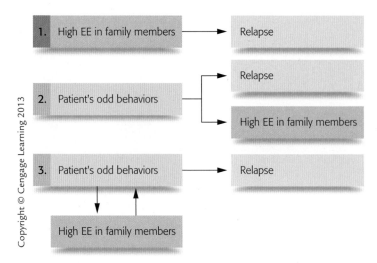

Figure 12.8

POSSIBLE RELATIONSHIPS BETWEEN HIGH RATES OF EXPRESSED EMOTION AND RELAPSE RATES IN PATIENTS WITH SCHIZOPHRENIA

Although some researchers believe that high expressed emotions among family members are related to relapse rates in schizophrenic patients, the precise relationship has not been determined. This figure shows several ways in which expressed emotions and relapse rates can be related.

negative communication may, in fact, reflect caring and concern. Cultural factors determine the specific symptoms that are appraised as burdensome by relatives, as well as the relationship among psychiatric symptoms, burden of care, and relatives' negative attitudes and behavior. White relatives felt more burdened by and had more negative attitudes toward their mentally ill family members than did African American relatives (Rosenfarb, Bellack, & Aziz, 2006). Lopez and his associates (2004) concluded that family communication processes such as emotional overprotection or overinvolvement may be interpreted differently by different cultural groups. In fact, therapists who focus on reducing critical and intrusive communication patterns in African American families may inadvertently increase family stress.

Although high EE has been associated with an increased risk of relapse, the studies are correlational in nature and are therefore subject to different interpretations. Figure 12.8 indicates three possible interpretations:

1. A high EE environment is stressful and may lead directly to relapse in the family member who has schizophrenia. Those with schizophrenia whose parents are rated high in EE are more likely to recount negative and stressful memories involving their parents than those whose parents are low on EE (Cutting & Docherty, 2000).

2. A more severely ill individual may cause more negative or high EE communication patterns in relatives. The severity of the illness means that the chances of relapse are high. Schreiber, Breier, and Pickar (1995) found some support for this pattern. They examined parental emotional response in families who had children both with and without schizophrenia. The parents often showed differential reactions to their children, with more EE communication being directed toward the child with schizophrenia. The researchers hypothesize that expressed emotions may be a parental response to the "chronic disabling aspect of this illness, and a belief by the parents that increased involvement would facilitate increased functioning of the child" (p. 649).

3. In the bidirectional model, odd behaviors or symptoms on the part of the individual with schizophrenia may cause family members to attempt to exert control and to react to the symptoms with frustration, which in turn produces increases in psychotic symptoms. An examination of communication patterns in families of individuals with schizophrenia also shows some support for this view (Rosenfarb et al., 1995).

High EE communication patterns have also been found in the families of individuals with depression, bipolar disorder, and eating disorders (Butzlaff & Hooley, 1998; Kavanagh, 1992). In addition, although EE has been found to be related to relapse, little evidence supports the idea that deviant family communication patterns are, by themselves, sufficient to produce schizophrenia.

Sociocultural Dimension

Although the prevalence of schizophrenia is roughly equal between men and women, gender differences in the age of onset of the disorder have been found. The age of onset of schizophrenia is earlier in males than in females. The gender ratio shifts by the mid-forties and fifties, when the percentage of women receiving the diagnosis exceeds that of men. This trend is especially pronounced in the mid-sixties and later (Howard et al., 2000; Thorup et al., 2007). Researchers have hypothesized that the later age of onset found in women is due to the protective effects of estrogen, which diminish after menopause (Grigoriadis & Seeman, 2002; Hafner et al., 1998). In a study of premenopausal women with schizophrenia, significant improvements in psychotic symptoms were observed during the luteal phase of their menstrual cycle (the period after ovulation) when estradiol (a type of estrogen) levels were higher (Bergemann et al., 2008). Estrogen may affect either dopamine levels or dopamine sensitivity, which have been associated with schizophrenia. Estrogen replacement therapy has also resulted in improved cognitive functioning among women with schizophrenia (Bergmann et al., 2008).

A number of social factors have been identified as risk factors for schizophrenia, such as lower educational level of parents, lower occupational status of fathers, and living in poorer residential areas at birth (Werner, Malaspina, & Rabinowitz, 2007; Wicks, Hjern, & Dalman, 2010). These forms of social adversity, especially in children who are exposed to other risk factors, appear to produce a threefold increase in the risk of developing schizophrenia as opposed to children who are exposed to none of these adversities (Wicks, Hjern, Gunnell, Lewis, & Dalman, 2005). Migration was also a risk factor for schizophrenia among first- and second-generation immigrants to the United Kingdom, especially for those with African ancestry (Bourque, van der Ven, & Malla, 2010; Selten, Cantor-Graae, & Kahn, 2007; Schofield, Ashworth, & Jones, 2010).

Similarly, the incidence of schizophrenia has been found to be very high among several ethnic groups in the Netherlands, particularly Moroccan immigrants (Veling et al., 2007). Experiences with social adversity may contribute to the increased incidence of the disorder. Among immigrants, there is no evidence of selective migration of individuals with a predisposition to schizophrenia (Selten, Cantor-Graae, & Kahn, 2007), but migration and experiences of discrimination as a visible minority may act as an additional stressor to predisposed individuals. How social stress might increase the risk for the disorder is not known, although there is a belief that stressors may cause dopamine deregulation or sensitization (Selten, Cantor-Graae, & Kahn, 2007).

Culture also affects the way disorders are viewed, as evidenced in the case of a thirteen-year-old child of a Tongan mother and Caucasian father living in the United States. The girl appeared to have visual hallucinations, had become isolative, exhibited echolalia,

© SHANNON STAPLETON/Reuters/Corbis

Abandoned Building in Camden, New Jersey

Schizophrenia is much more prevalent in poorer neighborhoods. Some believe that the increased stress from living in poverty may be the cause; others believe that individuals with schizophrenia move into poor neighborhoods because of their decreased ability to function in society. How would you determine which view has the most validity?

TABLE 12.3   Explanatory Models of Illness in Schizophrenia among Four Ethnic Groups

Cause of Illness	Biological	Social	Supernatural	Nonspecific
African Caribbean	6.7%	60%	20%	23.3%
Bangladeshi	0.0%	42.3%	26.9%	30.8%
West African	10.7%	31%	28.6%	21.4%
White (in the United Kingdom)	34.5%	31%	0.0%	34.5%

From McCabe & Priebe, (2004)

could be observed conversing with herself, and reported hearing voices of a woman who sounded like her mother and a man who sounded like her dead grandfather. Although some improvement was observed with antipsychotic medication, the girl still reported being disturbed by ghosts and reported ideas of reference—that people were talking about her. The mother decided that her daughter suffered from "fakama-haki," a culture-bound syndrome in which deceased relatives can inflict illness or possess the living when customs have been neglected. She took her daughter to Tonga to be treated. For five days, a traditional healer ("witch doctor") treated the girl with herbal potions. Vomiting was induced to remove toxins from the body. She also visited her grandfather's grave site to allow proper mourning. The girl returned to the United States and was re-evaluated. No symptoms of psychosis could be found. Follow-up contact revealed that the girl was continuing to do well. This case is interesting because medication was only minimally successful, whereas traditional healing seemed to be effective. It is also conceivable that the disorder was time-limited, but it is important to consider how folk medicine might account for successful treatment of severe mental disorders (Takeuchi, 2000).

As noted throughout this book, the study of cross-cultural perspectives on psychopathology is important because indigenous belief systems influence views of etiology and treatment. In India, for example, the belief in supernatural causation of schizophrenia is very widespread, leading to consultation and treatment by indigenous healers (Banerjee & Roy, 1998). In a study of individuals with schizophrenia from four ethnic groups (whites in the United Kingdom, African Caribbeans, Bangladeshi, and West Africans), distinct differences in explanatory models were found for the disorder (Table 12.3) (McCabe & Priebe, 2004). The different models included biological (e.g., physical illness/substance abuse); social (e.g., interpersonal problems, stress, negative childhood events, personality); supernatural (e.g., evil forces, evil magic); and nonspecific (do not know/other). The white group as compared to the other ethnic groups was the most likely to attribute biological causes for their condition. None identified supernatural causes as a potential causal factor—an explanation selected by a substantial minority of individuals from the other ethnic groups. The particular etiological model also influenced the response to treatment type. Those who cited biological causes believed they were receiving the right treatment (medications). Bangladeshis who supported a supernatural explanatory model wanted more alternative forms of treatment, such as religious activities. Thus views of etiology affect an individual's ideas regarding the nature of his or her problem, its severity, prognosis, and appropriate treatment.

The Treatment of Schizophrenia

Through the years, schizophrenia has been "treated" by a variety of means, including prefrontal lobotomy, a surgical procedure in which the frontal lobes are disconnected from the remainder of the patient's brain, and "warehousing" severely disturbed patients in overcrowded asylums. Such inhumane treatment was generally abandoned in the 1950s, when the beneficial effects of antipsychotic drugs were discovered. Today schizophrenia is typically treated with antipsychotic medication, along with some type of psychosocial therapy. In recent years, the research and clinical perspective on people with schizophrenia has shifted from a focus on disease and deficit to one of recovery and promotion of health, competencies, independence, and self-determination (Bellack, 2006). This change of focus is affecting therapists' roles, their views of clients and their families, and appropriate treatments (Glynn et al., 2006). We first discuss medication in the treatment of schizophrenia and then the psychological and social therapies.

Antipsychotic Medication

Case Study

Peter, a twenty-nine-year-old man, was diagnosed with chronic paranoid schizophrenia. . . . When on medication, he heard voices talking about him and felt that his phone was bugged. When off medication, he had constant hallucinations and his behavior became unpredictable. . . . He was on 10 milligrams of haloperidol (Haldol) three times a day. . . . Peter complained that he had been quite restless, and did not want to take the medication. Over the next six months, Peter's psychiatrist gradually reduced Peter's medication to 4 milligrams per day. . . . At this dose, Peter continued to have bothersome symptoms, but they remained moderate. . . . He was no longer restless. (Liberman, Kopelowicz, & Young, 1994, p. 94)

The use of medication in Peter's case illustrates several points. First, antipsychotic medications can reduce intensity of symptoms; second, dosage levels should be carefully monitored; and third, side effects can occur as a result of medication.

Many consider the 1955 introduction of *Thorazine*, the first antipsychotic drug, to be the beginning of a new era in treating schizophrenia. For the first time, a medication was available that sufficiently relaxed even those most severely affected by schizophrenia and helped organize their thoughts to the point that straitjackets were no longer needed for physical restraint. Although medications have improved the lives of many with schizophrenia, they do not cure the disorder. Nearly five decades later, conventional antipsychotics are still viewed as effective treatments for schizophrenia, although their use has been largely supplanted by newer, atypical antipsychotics. Conventional antipsychotic medications (chlorpromazine/Thorazine, haloperidol/Haldol, perphenazine/Trilafon, and fluphenazine/Prolixin) have dopaminergic receptor-blocking capabilities (i.e., they reduce dopamine levels), which led to the dopamine hypothesis of schizophrenia.

The newer atypical antipsychotics (such as clozapine/Clozaril, risperidone/Risperdal, olanzapine/Zyprexa, quetiapine/Seroquel, and ziprasidone/Geodon) act on multiple dopamine and serotonin receptors and are purportedly less likely to produce side effects such as the rigidity, persistent muscle spasms, tremors, and restlessness that are found with the older antipsychotic medications (Canas, 2005; Caroff, Hurford, Lybrand, & Campbell, 2011). However, questions are being raised about the side effects of these second-generation antipsychotic medications (Foley & Morley, 2011; Miller et al., 2008; Jeste et al., 2009; Lewin, Storch, & Storch, 2010).

Did You Know?

In a randomized, double-blind study, 81 adolescents at high risk for developing psychosis were given either omega 3 fatty acids (fish oil) or a placebo and followed up for 12 months. In the placebo group, 11 developed psychosis as opposed to only 2 in the fish oil group. Could treatment be this easy? Why would it be effective?

Source: Amminger et al., (2010)

Both types of antipsychotic medications can effectively reduce the severity of the positive symptoms of schizophrenia, such as hallucinations, delusions, bizarre speech, and thought disorders. Most, however, offer little relief from the negative symptoms such as social withdrawal, apathy, and impaired personal hygiene (Carpenter, Conley, Buchanan, Breier, & Tamminga, 1995; Strous et al., 2004). As Green (2007) noted, "Optimism that second-generation antipsychotics would yield cognitive improvements has progressively been tempered. . . . [T]he high hopes for beneficial cognitive effects from antipsychotic medications are now hanging by threads" (p. 992). Moreover, a "relatively large group" of people with schizophrenia do not benefit at all from antipsychotic medication and cessation rates are high (Almerie, Matar, Essali, Alkhateeb, & Rezk, 2008; Wiesel, 1994). Because of the side effects of the medications, treatment adherence is poor, especially among those who are younger or African American (Valenstein et al., 2004).

Newer antipsychotic medications cost ten times more than older antipsychotics. Are these newer antipsychotic medications more effective than first-generation antipsychotics? Are they less likely to produce side effects? Answers to these questions were sought in a large, comprehensive nationwide comparative drug study, known as CATIE (Clinical Antipsychotic Trials of Intervention Effectiveness). The effectiveness of an older antipsychotic (perphenazine) was compared with several newer antipsychotic medications (olanzapine, quetiapine, risperidone, or ziprasidone) in the treatment of chronic schizophrenia (average length of illness in the participants was 14.4 years). The following conclusions were reached (Lieberman et al., 2005):

- Surprisingly, the older, less expensive medication (perphenazine) used in the study generally performed as well as the four newer medications. With all antipsychotics, there were high rates of discontinuation due to intolerable side effects or failure to control symptoms. (Nearly three-quarters of the participants discontinued their assigned drugs and switched to another.)
- Olanzapine was slightly more effective but was associated with significant weight gain.
- Contrary to expectations, the newer drugs did not produce significantly fewer extrapyramidal symptoms (movement side effects, rigidity, stiff movements, tremor, and muscle restlessness).

These findings question the assumption that the newer antipsychotic medications are more effective and produce fewer side effects than older antipsychotic medications. (It should be noted that the older antipsychotic, perphenazine, was chosen for its more limited side effects.) Some early findings that suggested that second-generation antipsychotics are superior in alleviating cognitive problems may, in fact, be due to assessment practice effects. For example, healthy individuals showed the same "improvement" on cognitive tasks as individuals with schizophrenia when undergoing repeated testing (Goldberg et al., 2007), presumably because of practice effects. The findings from the CATIE study prompted one researcher, Green (2007), to suggest the need to identify new drugs that work through different neuropharmacological mechanisms.

As was mentioned earlier, most individuals treated with antipsychotic medications develop extrapyramidal symptoms, which include *Parkinsonism* (muscle tremors, shakiness, and immobility), *dystonia* (slow and continued involuntary movements of the limbs and tongue), *akathesis* (motor restlessness), and *neuroleptic malignant syndrome* (muscle rigidity and autonomic instability, which can be fatal if untreated). Other symptoms may involve the loss of facial expression, immobility, shuffling gait, tremors of the hand, rigidity of the body, and poor postural stability; these symptoms are usually reversible (Casey, 2006). Although these symptoms are reduced with atypical antipsychotics, they still occur. Antipsychotic medications are also associated with increased risk of metabolic syndrome (a condition associated with obesity, diabetes, high cholesterol, and hypertension) (Shirzadi & Ghaemi, 2006). (See Controversy Box, "The Marketing of Atypical Antipsychotic Medication.")

The Marketing of Atypical Antipsychotic Medications

The woman in the Abilify ad says, "I'm taking an antidepressant but I think I need more help." According to the ad, two out of three individuals taking an antidepressant alone still have symptoms of depression. The ad goes on to suggest that Abilify can be helpful when combined with current antidepressant medications. Abilify is an atypical antipsychotic medication, but that fact is not mentioned (Westburg, 2011).

What is the top selling class of medications in the United States? Surprisingly, it is atypical antipsychotic medications, a drug class accounting for $13 billion of U.S. prescriptions in 2007; quetiapine (Seroquel), aripiprazole (Abilify), olanzapine (Zyprexa), and risperidone (Risperdal) each had more than $1 billion in annual sales in the United States (Alexander, Gallagher, Mascola, Moloney, & Stafford, 2011). These profitable drugs are heavily promoted by the pharmaceutical companies, with resultant increases in the number of people taking both antidepressants and antipsychotics. However, many of these combinations are of "unproven efficacy" (Mojtabai & Olfson, 2010).

Even more problematic is that off-label use (i.e., prescribing medication for unapproved indications such as for treatment of a different disorder or age group) of atypical antipsychotics has increased dramatically. Antipsychotics are increasingly prescribed for a range of mental disorders including attention-deficit hyperactivity disorder and conduct and anxiety disorders, although they have never been evaluated for use with these disorders (Crystal, Olfson, Huang, Pincus, & Gerhard, 2009). Among one sample of nursing home residents, 29 percent were prescribed at least one antipsychotic medication; many of this group had no clinical indication for the medication (Chen et al., 2010). Findings such as this are of particular concern because the use of antipsychotic medication can compromise the health of individuals with dementia (Treloar, 2010). More than half of the prescriptions in 2008 for atypical antipsychotic medications were off-label and of "uncertain efficacy" (Alexander, Gallagher, Mascola, Moloney, & Stafford, 2011).

Physicians are often unaware that the medication they prescribed off-label do not have FDA approval for the disorder they are treating (Chen, Wynia, Molney, & Alexander, 2009).

The atypical antipsychotics replaced older antipsychotic medications because they were presumed to be more effective and have fewer side effects. Surprisingly, the largest comparative drug study yet conducted found that the older antipsychotic medications were as effective and did not have any more side effects than the atypical antipsychotic medications that cost ten times more. The increased use of atypical antipsychotic medications is of particular concern due to their association with troublesome side effects. After only twelve weeks on Abilify, Risperdal, Seroquel, or Zyprexa, children were found to gain up to nineteen pounds (Correll et al., 2010). In a five-year study of atypical antipsychotics in middle-aged and older individuals with schizophrenia, 29.7 percent had serious adverse physical effects that were probably or possibly due to the medication. Increases in cholesterol levels and weight gain have been found in individuals taking atypical antipsychotic medications for as little as three months (Foley & Morley, 2011). Quetiapine was recently excluded from an NIMH-funded drug comparison study involving middle-aged and older participants due to concern about significantly increased rates of pneumonia in those taking the drug (Jeste et al., 2009). The FDA has warned that infants born to mothers taking antipsychotic medications during the third trimester of pregnancy are at high risk of having abnormal muscle tone, tremors, sleepiness, severe difficulty breathing, and difficulty sucking (FDA, 2011).

Should regulations be in place to protect consumers from the increasing off-label use of antipsychotic medications? Should advertisements promoting atypical antipsychotic medications identify them as such? Should physicians and psychiatrists inform patients when they are writing off-label prescriptions?

A more chronic or permanent condition, tardive dyskinesia, may develop. This condition is characterized by involuntary and rhythmic movements of the tongue; chewing, lip smacking, and other facial movements; and jerking movements of the limbs. The risk of developing this disorder is greatest for those who have been treated with antipsychotic medications over an extended period of time. The elderly appear to be especially vulnerable to antipsychotic medications' side effects (Meltzer, 2000; Zayas & Grossberg, 1998). Women tend to have both more frequent and more severe tardive dyskinesia than do men (American Psychiatric Association, 1997; Yassa & Jeste, 1992).

Regulation and monitoring of antipsychotic drugs is especially important, as is using the minimum effective dose possible (Lehman et al., 2004). However, a study of 719 individuals diagnosed with schizophrenia revealed that the dosage levels of their antipsychotic medications were often outside the recommended treatment ranges and that minority group members were more likely than whites to be prescribed a higher dosage (Lehman & Steinwachs, 1998). Equally disturbing, clinicians are often unaware of possible reactions to the drugs, which include tremors, motor restlessness, anxiety, agitation, extreme terror, and even impulsive suicide attempts (Hirose, 2003; Lehman & Steinwachs, 1998). In one study (Weiden et al., 1987), many clinicians did not identify motor side effects such as restlessness, rigidity, and tremors in individuals taking prescribed antipsychotic medication. In fact, the clinicians accurately identified only one of ten patients showing tardive dyskinesia. Although antipsychotic medications are still considered to be an effective treatment for schizophrenia, they must be carefully monitored in terms of dosage, effectiveness, and side effects.

Psychosocial Therapy

Case Study

Philip's psychotic symptoms had been reduced with medication. However, he was unable to obtain employment because of cognitive and behavioral peculiarities. Philip did not seem to understand what was considered to be appropriate conversational topics and attire. His counselor suggested that his clothing (sweatshirt, exercise pants, head band, and worn sneakers) might be inappropriate for a job interview. Field trips were planned to allow Philip to observe attire worn by individuals in different businesses. He was trained in conversational topics and practiced job interviews with his counselor. After deciding to apply for landscape work, Philip wore a work shirt, blue jeans, and construction boots, and was hired by the landscaping contractor (Heinssen & Cuthbert, 2001).

Many individuals with schizophrenia behave "strangely," do not have positive conversational skills, and display faulty thinking. Social communication is problematic because many exhibit consistent deficits in emotional perception and in understanding the beliefs and attitudes of others (Combs et al., 2007). Heinssen and Cuthbert (2001) found that eccentricities in appearance, attire, and communication patterns or lack of discretion in discussing their illness can impede employment or the establishment of social networks. Psychotherapeutic approaches have been tailored to address these issues, allowing many individuals with schizophrenia to acquire competitive employment.

Most clinicians today agree that the most beneficial treatment for schizophrenia is a combination of antipsychotic medication and psychotherapy. But even as medications are introduced that effectively reduce many symptoms of schizophrenia, one vital fact is clear. Individuals with schizophrenia discharged from protective hospital environments often return to stressful home or work situations. Dealing with chronic stress can result in the return of psychotic symptoms and rehospitalization; medication alone is often not enough to help those with schizophrenia function in their natural environments. Clinicians realize that antipsychotic medication must be supplemented with psychotherapy. Such therapy includes traditional institutional approaches, cognitive-behavioral therapies, and interventions based on family communication.

Inpatient Approaches

Both milieu therapy and behavioral therapy can be beneficial for those receiving inpatient treatment. In milieu therapy, the hospital environment operates as a community within which those with schizophrenia exercise a wide range of responsibilities and help make decisions. Psychosocial skills training focuses on increasing appropriate self-care behaviors, conversational skills, and job skills. Undesirable behaviors such as "crazy talk" or social isolation are decreased through reinforcement and modeling techniques. Both approaches have been shown to be effective in helping many people with schizophrenia achieve independent living. Living in community homes (halfway houses) can also assist with the transition from inpatient programs to community living. In a study of nearly 100 individuals with chronic schizophrenia placed in community facilities, almost all improved (Leff, 1994).

Cognitive-Behavioral Therapy

Major advances have been made in the use of cognitive and behavioral strategies in treating the symptoms of schizophrenia, especially among those who have not been fully helped through medication. Therapeutic interventions often target positive and negative symptoms with the goal of reducing their frequency, severity and associated distress. Therapists teach coping skills that allow clients to manage their positive and negative symptoms as well as the cognitive deficits found in schizophrenia (Hansen, Kingdon, & Turkington, 2006; Zimmermann et al., 2005). An 18 month follow-up of 216 individuals with persisting psychotic symptoms found that those receiving cognitive-behavior therapy demonstrated 183 days of normal functioning compared to 106 days of normal functioning for those who received treatment as usual (van der Gaag et al., 2011).

The following case provides an example of symptoms of schizophrenia which might be effectively addressed with cognitive-behavioral treatment strategies.

Case Study

A young African American woman with auditory hallucinations, paranoid delusions, delusions of reference, and a history of childhood verbal and physical abuse and adult sexual assault felt extremely hopeless about her prospects for developing social ties. She believed that her persecutors had informed others of her socially undesirable activities.... She often loudly screamed at the voices she was hearing.... When she did leave her home, she often covered her head with a black kerchief and wore dark sunglasses, partly in an effort to disguise herself from her persecutors. (Cather, 2005, p. 260)

Cognitive-behavioral treatment of schizophrenia often includes the following steps (Addington & Haarmans, 2006; Hansen, Kingdon, & Turkington, 2006):

- *Engagement.* The therapist explains the therapy and works to foster a safe and collaborative method of looking at causes of distress, drawing out the client's understanding of stressors and ways of coping. The relationship between stress, anxiety, and severity of symptoms is discussed.
- *Assessment.* Clients are encouraged to discuss their fears and anxieties; the therapist shares information about how symptoms are formed and maintained. In the preceding case, the therapist helped the woman make sense of her persecutory experiences. It was explained that victims of abuse often internalize beliefs that they are responsible for the abuse and how her view that she was "bad" led to expectations of negative reactions from others and the need to disguise herself.
- *Identification of negative beliefs.* The therapist explains the link between personal beliefs and emotional distress to the patient and how beliefs such as "Nobody will like me if I tell them about my voices" (p. 50), can be disputed and changed to "I can't demand that everyone like me. Some people will and some won't" (p. 50). This reinterpretation often leads to less sadness and isolation (Hansen, Kingdon, & Turkington et al., 2006).
- *Normalization.* The therapist works with the client to normalize and decatastrophize the psychotic experiences. Information that many people can have unusual experiences can reduce a client's sense of isolation.
- *Collaborative analysis of symptoms.* Once a strong therapeutic alliance has been established, the therapist begins critical discussions of the client's symptoms, such as "If voices come from your head, why can't others hear them?" Evidence for and against the maladaptive beliefs is discussed, combined with information about how beliefs are maintained through cognitive distortions or inferences.
- *Developing alternative explanations.* The therapist helps the client develop alternatives to previous maladaptive assumptions, using the client's ideas whenever possible.

More recently, instead of trying to eliminate or combat hallucinations, clients are taught to accept them in a nonjudgmental manner. In mindfulness training, clients are taught to let go of angry or fearful responses to psychotic symptoms; instead, the client is taught to let the psychotic symptoms come into consciousness without reacting. This process enhances feelings of self-control and significantly reduces negative emotions (Dannahy et al., 2011; Chadwick, Hugh, Russell, Russell, & Dagnan, 2009). The approach was used with men who had heard malevolent and powerful voices for more than thirty years. Their attempts to stop the voices or to distract themselves were ineffective. After undergoing mindfulness training, the men were less distressed with the voices and more confident in their ability to live with the voices (Taylor, Harper, & Chadwick, 2009). Similarly, malevolent and persecuting voices became less disturbing when individuals with schizophrenia learned to access positive emotions such as warmth and contentment during psychotic episodes (Mayhew & Gilbert, 2008).

A form of cognitive therapy, *integrated psychological therapy (IPT)*, has also produced promising results. IPT specifically targets deficits found in individuals with schizophrenia, such as basic impairments in neurocognition (e.g., attention, verbal memory, cognitive flexibility, concept formation), deficits in social cognition (e.g. social-emotional perception, emotional expression), interpersonal communication (e.g., verbal fluency and executive functioning), and problem-solving skills. In a meta-analysis of IPT, Roder and colleagues (2006) concluded: "IPT is an effective rehabilitation approach for schizophrenia that is robust across a wide range of patients and treatment conditions" (p. 81).

Interventions Focusing on Family Communication and Education

A serious mental illness such as schizophrenia can have a powerful effect on family members, who may feel stigmatized or responsible for the disorder. As one woman stated:

> All family members are affected by a loved one's mental illness. The entire family system needs to be addressed. To assure us that we are not to blame and the situation is not hopeless. To point us to the people and places that can help our loved one. The impact still lingers on. (Marsh & Johnson, 1997)

Siblings without the disorder also display a variety of emotional reactions to the mental illness experienced by their sibling—love ("She's really kind and loves me so very much

Family Communication and Education

Therapy that includes the family members of individuals with schizophrenia reduces relapse rates and is more effective than drug treatment alone.

Bruce Ayers/Getty Images

it's never been a problem."); loss ("Somehow I've lost my sister the way she was before and I think I won't get her back."); anger ("Yes, it's hell. . . . She's incredibly mean to our mother and she sure as hell doesn't deserve that."); guilt and shame ("Yes, you can think about how he got ill and I didn't."); and fear ("You worry a lot about getting it yourself.") (Stalberg, Ekerwald, & Hultman, 2004, p. 450).

More than half of those recovering from a psychotic episode return to live with their families, and new psychological interventions address this fact. Family intervention programs have not only reduced relapse rates but have also lowered the cost of care. They have been beneficial for families with and without communication patterns such as EE. Most programs include the following components (Glynn et al., 2006; Mueser et al., 2001):

1. Normalizing the family experience
2. Demonstrating concern, empathy, and sympathy to all family members
3. Educating family members about schizophrenia
4. Avoiding blaming the family or pathologizing their coping efforts
5. Identifying the strengths and competencies of the client and family members
6. Developing skills in problem solving and managing stress
7. Teaching family members to cope with the symptoms of mental illness and its repercussions on the family
8. Strengthening the communication and problem-solving skills of family members

Family approaches and social skills training are much more effective in preventing relapse than drug treatment alone (Xia, Merinker, & Belgamwar, 2011). Combining cognitive-behavioral strategies, family counseling, and social skills training seems to produce the most positive result (Penn et al., 2004). The use of medication combined with psychosocial interventions has provided hope for many of those with schizophrenia. In fact, recent research suggests that "optimism about outcome from schizophrenia is justified" and that "a substantial proportion of people with the illness will recover completely and many more will regain good social functioning" (Warner, 2009, p. 374).

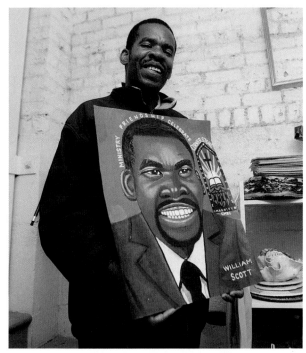

AP Images

Artwork to Demonstrate Creative Talents

A self-portrait by artist William Scott is displayed at the Creative Growth Art Center in Oakland, California. The artist, diagnosed with schizophrenia and an autism spectrum disorder, has had his paintings and sculptures sold around the world in the trendiest galleries. The program hopes to decrease the stigma associated with mental illness by highlighting creative talents.

Summary

1. What are the symptoms of schizophrenia?

   • Positive symptoms of schizophrenia involve unusual thoughts or perceptions, such as delusions, hallucinations, thought disorder, and bizarre behavior.

   • Negative symptoms of schizophrenia are associated with an inability or decreased ability to initiate actions or speech, express emotions, or feel pleasure. Such symptoms include *avolition* (an inability to take action or become goal oriented), *alogia* (a lack of meaningful speech), and *restricted affect* (little or no emotion in situations in which strong reactions are expected).

   • Cognitive symptoms of schizophrenia include problems with attention, memory, and difficulty developing a plan of action.

2. How do other psychotic disorders differ from schizophrenia?

   • Brief psychotic disorder is characterized by psychotic symptoms that last less than one month.

   • Schizophreniform disorder is characterized by psychotic symptoms that are usually associated with a stressor and that last from one to six months.

   • Delusional disorder is characterized by persistent nonbizarre delusions and the absence of other unusual or odd behaviors.

   • Attenuated psychosis syndrome is characterized by early subthreshold psychotic symptoms that have developed or increased over the past year. Many in this category do not go on to develop a psychotic disorder.

   • Other specified psychotic disorder is characterized by psychotic symptoms that are not significant enough to meet the criteria for a specific psychotic disorder.

3. Is there much chance of recovery from schizophrenia?

   • Prognosis for schizophrenia is variable and is associated with premorbid levels of functioning. Many individuals with schizophrenia experience minimal or no lasting impairment. Most individuals with schizophrenia recover enough to lead relatively productive lives.

4. What causes schizophrenia?

   • The best conclusion is that genetics and environmental factors (physical, psychological, or social) combine to cause the disorder. Genetic factors may contribute to biological risk factors such as neurotransmitter or structural brain abnormalities. Certain negative family patterns involving parental characteristics or intrafamilial communication processes have been hypothesized to result in schizophrenia. They function as risk factors in vulnerable individuals, but there is little evidence that psychological factors in and of themselves can cause the condition.

5. What treatments are currently available for schizophrenia, and are they effective?

   • Schizophrenia seems to involve both biological and psychological factors, and treatment programs that combine drugs with psychotherapy appear to hold the most promise.

   • Drug therapy usually involves conventional antipsychotics or the newer atypical antipsychotics.

   • The accompanying psychosocial therapy consists of either supportive counseling or behavior therapy, with an emphasis on cognitive and social skills training and changing communication patterns among those with schizophrenia and family members.

Media Resources

Psychology CourseMate Access an interactive eBook; chapter-specific interactive learning tools, including flashcards, quizzes, videos; and more in your Psychology CourseMate, accessed through CengageBrain.com.

CENGAGENOW

CengageNow CengageNOW is an easy-to-use online resource that helps you study in less time to get the grade you want—NOW. If your textbook does not include an access code card, go to CengageBrain.com to gain access.

CENGAGE brain.com

CengageBrain More than just an interactive study guide, WebTutor is an anytime, anywhere customized learning solution with an eBook, keeping you connected to your textbook, instructor, and classmates. Purchase the access chosen by your instructor at CengageBrain.com.

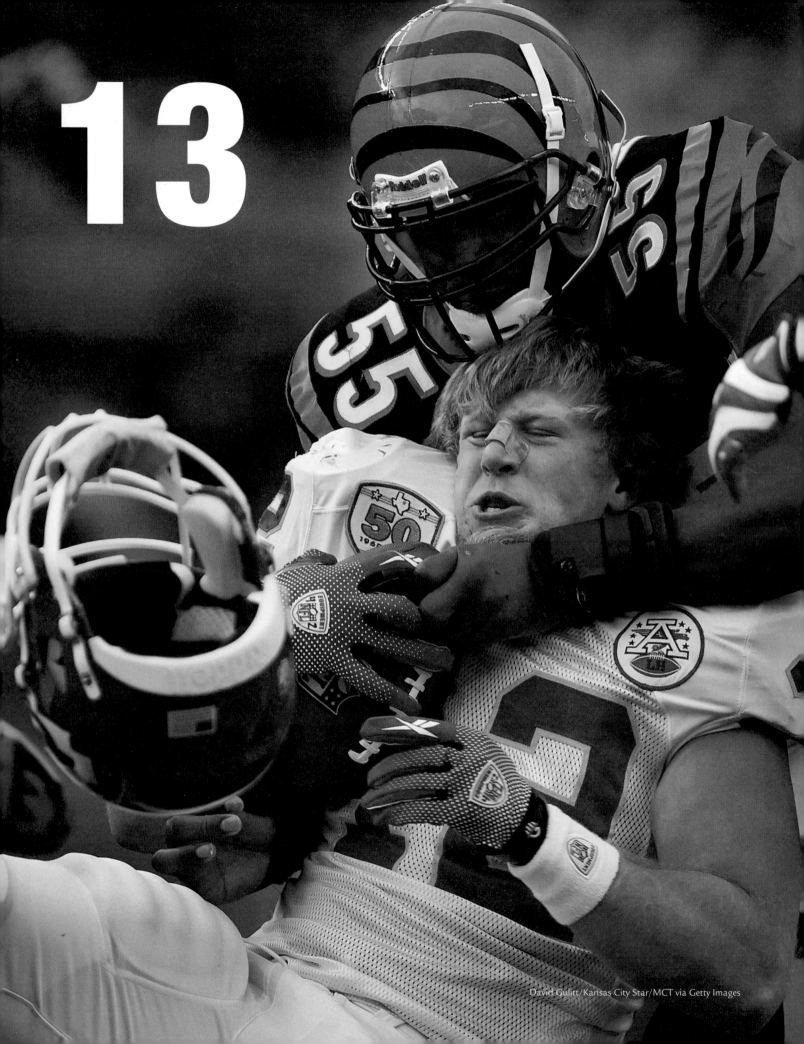

13

David Gulitt/Kansas City Star/MCT via Getty Images

Neurocognitive Disorders

Mr. C., age 42, was in a coma for two weeks after falling from a ladder. Before his fall, he was both conscientious and easygoing. After the fall, socially inappropriate and impulsive behaviors, such as getting into arguments and groping female coworkers, interfered with all aspects of his life. A psychiatric evaluation involving brain scans and psychological testing documented residual brain injury, including damage to the frontal lobe of his brain, an area associated with impulse control. Although additional rehabilitation resulted in significant improvement, residual effects from the injury prevented complete recovery (Rao et al., 2007).

Like many other individuals, Mr. C. suffers from a neurocognitive disorder—a condition resulting from transient or permanent damage to the brain. DSM-5 (American Psychiatric Association, 2011) characterizes neurocognitive disorders as conditions that affect thinking processes, memory, consciousness, and perception that are attributable to changes in brain structure, function, or chemistry. Changes in behavior and emotional functioning, as seen in the case of Mr. C., are commonly seen in neurocognitive disorders.

DSM-5 classifies cognitive disorders into three major categories: (1) mild neurocognitive disorder, (2) major neurocognitive disorder, and (3) delirium (Table 13.1).

Possible causes of neurocognitive disorders include degenerative conditions such as Parkinson's and Alzheimer's disease (Table 13.2) or relatively sudden events such as stroke, head trauma, or infection (Table 13.3). Although the symptoms of neurocognitive disorders result from specific brain pathology, they are also influenced by social and psychological factors. People with similar types of brain damage may recover quite differently, depending on their premorbid personalities, their coping skills, and the availability of resources such as rehabilitation and family support systems. Emotional reactions are intricately tied to brain functioning. The disruptions in brain function seen in neurocognitive disorders can lead to a variety of behavioral and emotional changes including apathy, depression, anxiety, or difficulty with impulse control (Rosen & Levenson, 2009). Furthermore, others may treat people with cognitive impairments with insensitivity, which may add to their stress. This stress can exacerbate symptoms that stem from the brain pathology itself. Thus, biological, psychological, social, and sociocultural factors interact in complicated ways to produce the symptoms seen in individuals with neurocognitive disorders. We discussed the structure of the human brain in Chapter 2; in this chapter, we focus on the assessment of brain damage, subtypes of neurocognitive disorders and their etiology, and treatment and prevention considerations.

CHAPTER OUTLINE

focus questions

1 How can we determine whether someone has a neurocognitive disorder?

2 What are the different types of neurocognitive disorders?

3 What are the causes of neurocognitive disorders?

4 What kinds of interventions can be used to treat people with neurocognitive disorders?

TABLE 13.1 Neurocognitive Disorders

Disorder	Symptoms
Mild Neurocognitive Disorder	Minor decline in performance in one or more cognitive area; compensatory strategies may be required to maintain independence
Major Neurocognitive Disorder*	Significant decline in performance in one or more cognitive area; severity of deficit interferes with independence
Delirium**	Sudden changes in cognition, including diminished awareness and impaired attention and focus

*Mild and major neurocognitive disorder are sometimes earlier and later stages of the same disorder.

**Delirium is often seen in major and mild neurocognitive disorder but also occurs independent of these disorders.

Source: American Psychiatric Association, (2011)

TABLE 13.2 Neurodegenerative Disorders

Etiology	Characteristics
Alzheimer's Disease	Declining cognitive functioning, including early, prominent memory impairment
Dementia with Lewy Bodies	Visual hallucinations, fluctuating cognitive impairment, decline in motor skills
Parkinson's Disease	Tremor, muscle rigidity, and slow movement; possible cognitive decline
Huntington's Disease	Involuntary movement, cognitive decline, and emotional instability
Frontotemporal Lobar Degeneration	Brain degeneration in frontal or temporal lobes affecting language and behavior
Vascular Cognitive Impairment	Brain degeneration due to cardiovascular factors
AIDS-Dementia Complex	Cognitive decline due to HIV or AIDS

Copyright © Cengage Learning 2013

TABLE 13.3 Other Causes of Neurocognitive Disorders

Etiology	Characteristics
Ischemic stroke	Blockage of blood flow in brain
Hemorrhagic stroke	Bleeding within the brain
Traumatic brain injury	Head wounds or trauma
Substance abuse	Effects of intoxication, withdrawal, oxygen deprivation, or chronic substance use
Meningitis	Infection-produced inflammation of tissues surrounding the brain and spinal cord
Encephalitis	Infection-produced brain inflammation
Epilepsy	Seizures

Copyright © Cengage Learning 2013

neurocognitive disorder a disorder caused by brain dysfunction that affects thinking processes, memory, consciousness, and perception

The Assessment of Brain Damage

To screen for neurocognitive disorders, clinicians gather background information, paying particular attention to declines in cognitive functioning. They may conduct a mental status examination (see Chapter 3) to assess memory, attentional skills and orientation to time and place; they also carefully appraise general functioning; personality characteristics; coping skills; behaviors and emotional reactions, alert for departures from prior functioning. Comprehensive assessment provides the information about brain dysfunction needed for planning treatment or further evaluation. Psychologists often use both psychological and neuropsychological tests and inventories to evaluate specific cognitive functions such as memory and thought processes. Testing detects signs of cognitive difficulty such as *aphasia* (difficulty understanding or using language), *apraxia* (cognitive inability to carry out motor activities), *agnosia* (cognitive inability to recognize objects, sounds or smells), or disturbances in higher level thought processes.

Neurological testing is frequently used to assess neurocognitive functioning. The Glasgow Coma Scale, a screening tool used to objectively measure consciousness following head injury or stroke, helps localize and evaluate the extent of brain damage. Areas assessed include motor responsiveness, verbalization, and control over eye movements. The electroencephalograph (EEG) measures the firing of neurons via electrodes placed on the scalp; EEGs can detect irregular electrical activity and brain waves patterns. Newer *neuroimaging techniques* allow medical professionals to noninvasively visualize brain structures and monitor activity within the brain. Computerized axial tomography (CT or CAT) involves computer analysis of multiple, cross-sectional x-rays of the brain taken from various angles. A newer version of this technique, spiral CT, increases image detail through a very rapid scanning and image construction procedure. Magnetic resonance imaging (MRI) also uses computer processing and a layer-by-layer scanning technique to produce detailed images of the brain without the radiation exposure and cancer risk seen with CT scans (Brenner & Hall, 2007; Berrington de González et al., 2009). Instead of radiation, MRI uses a powerful magnetic field and radio frequency pulses to create brain images.

Although CT and MRI scans provide images of brain structure, nuclear imaging provides information on metabolic processes within the brain. In a positron emission tomography (PET) scan, the metabolism of glucose in the brain is monitored. Through snippets of data regarding brain activity and subtle metabolic changes, PET imaging can determine if disease is active or dormant or if tumors are benign or malignant. Single photon emission computed tomography (SPECT) imaging provides longer but less detailed images of metabolic activity and blood flow patterns within the brain. Each of these neuroimaging techniques has strengths and weaknesses in terms of costs, benefits, and possible side effects. An appraisal of procedural risks and benefits guides decisions regarding which tools to use for diagnosis, treatment, and assessment of progress.

Types of Neurocognitive Disorders

Three categories of neurocognitive disorder are listed in DSM-5: mild neurocognitive disorder, major neurocognitive disorder, and delirium. With each, clinicians indicate the underlying medical circumstances causing the disorder, if the cause is known.

© Betteman / CORBIS

Still a Champion, but at What Cost?

Muhammad Ali, one of the greatest heavyweight champion boxers ever, developed Parkinson's-like symptoms, such as slurred speech, shuffling when walking, expressionless facial appearance, and occasional memory lapses. The repeated blows to the head suffered by Ali during his boxing career are believed to have caused chronic traumatic encephalopathy (also called boxer's dementia or punch-drunk syndrome), a condition resulting in these symptoms.

electroencephalograph (EEG) measures the firing of neurons via electrodes placed on the scalp

computerized axial tomography (CT or CAT) brain images are produced from multiple, cross-sectional x-rays of the brain

magnetic resonance imaging (MRI) produces images of the brain using a magnetic field

positron emission tomography (PET) nuclear imaging scan that assesses glucose metabolism in the brain

Single photon emission computed tomography (SPECT) nuclear imaging scan that provides longer but less detailed images of metabolic activity within the brain

MRI Scans

A technician observing the MRI scan of a patient. In MRI, radio waves produce pictures of the brain that are not obscured by bone. With striking resolution, they can reveal detailed anatomical areas of the brain. However, the procedure is expensive and requires patients to remain perfectly still while the imaging is taking place. What advantages do you see in using the MRI over other procedures, such as PET or CT scans?

Neurocognitive disorders may be due to a specific medical condition, a substance-induced condition, or may result from multiple etiologies. Following explanation of the neurocognitive disorder categories, we discuss some subtypes of neurocognitive disorders.

Major Neurocognitive Disorder

Case Study

Ms. B., an 80-year-old woman became increasingly agitated, screaming, spitting, striking staff.... Her speech was loud, disarticulate.... She repeatedly yelled "get out." Ms. B. had recently moved to an assisted-living facility due to her declining language, social, and self-care skills (Bang, Price, Prentice, & Campbell, 2008, p. 379).

Individuals diagnosed with major neurocognitive disorder show significant decline in:

1. One or more cognitive areas (Table 13.4), including complex attention, decision making and judgment, learning and memory, visual perception, or social skills and behavior, *and*

2. Ability to independently meet the demands of daily living

Direct observation, interviews, and psychological or neuropsychological testing are used to objectively document that skills are significantly lower than would be expected based on the individual's age, gender, educational and cultural background, and levels of prior functioning. A deficit in one cognitive area is needed for diagnosis; however, deficits in multiple areas are common. The cognitive slowing sometimes seen in normal aging is distinct from declines seen in major neurocognitive disorder (see comparisons in Table 13.5); for example, periodic memory difficulties (e.g., forgetting names or phone numbers, misplacing objects) are common occurrences and not signs of a neurocognitive disorder.

Dementia is a term used to describe the memory impairment and declining cognitive functioning (i.e., the symptoms of neurocognitive disorder) resulting from degenerative brain conditions. People with dementia may forget the names of significant others or past events. They may also display difficulties with impulse control, and demonstrate behaviors such as disrobing in public or making sexual advances to strangers. Dementia is characterized by gradual onset and continuing cognitive decline. Age is the best studied and the strongest risk factor for dementia. The longer one lives,

TABLE 13.4 Areas of Possible Neurocognitive Dysfunction

Cognitive Domain	Skills Affected
Complex attention	Planning, working memory
Executive ability	Decision making, mental flexibility
Learning and memory	Long-term, immediate, and recent memory
Language	Understanding and use of language
Visual-perceptual ability	Construction and visual perception
Social cognition	Recognition of emotions, behavioral regulation

Source: American Psychiatric Association, (2011)

dementia pervasive deterioration in cognition and independent functioning

TABLE 13.5   Normal Aging or Neurocognitive Disorder?

Normal Aging	Major Neurocognitive Disorder
Independent in most activities	Requires assistance with daily activities
Occasionally misplaces things and locates them after searching	Places items in unusual locations; may not recall objects are missing
Occasionally forgets a name, word, or appointment	Frequently forgets words or recently learned information; uses incorrect words
Usually follows written or verbal directions without difficulty	Difficulty following written or verbal directions
Slower to complete mental or physical activities	Difficulty performing familiar tasks
Concern about occasional forgetfulness	Unaware or unconcerned about memory difficulties
Occasional distractibility	Poor judgment; fails to remember important details
Continues interacting socially; occasionally tired	Decreasing social skills, declining social engagement, passivity
Occasionally gets lost	Increasing disorientation and confusion
Normal changes in mood	Personality changes, drastic mood shifts

the greater the chance of developing dementia. Women usually live longer than men, so they are more likely to develop dementia. Among sixty-five-year-olds, the lifetime risk of developing dementia is estimated to be 11 percent for men and 19 percent for women (Gatz, 2007).

Mild Neurocognitive Disorder

A mild neurocognitive disorder also involves deficits in at least one major cognitive area (see Table 13.4), although to a lesser degree of severity than that seen in major neurocognitive disorder. Individuals with this diagnosis may struggle with familiar tasks or use *compensatory strategies* to complete tasks (e.g., keeping lists or paying someone to do complex mental tasks). Extra effort to maintain independence may be required; however, overall independent functioning is not compromised. Early diagnosis of mild neurocognitive disorder sometimes allows for medical intervention before more significant brain damage occurs.

The primary distinction between major and mild neurocognitive disorder is the severity of cognitive decline and related decline in independent functioning. In fact, mild and major neurocognitive disorders are sometimes earlier and later stages of the same disorder. For example, someone in the early stages of a neurodegenerative disorder such as Alzheimer's disease may initially present with minor declines in functioning that do not interfere with independence; as the disease progresses, symptoms may increase in severity or affect additional cognitive areas. On the other hand, recovery from infection-induced brain damage, stroke, traumatic brain injury, or substance abuse might result in improved cognitive skills and a change in diagnosis from major to mild cognitive disorder. The functioning of individuals with

Did You Know?

Veterans diagnosed with post-traumatic stress disorder (PTSD) have a greater risk for dementia than veterans without PTSD (including veterans who received traumatic wartime injuries). It is unclear if PTSD is a risk factor for dementia or if another factor increases risk of both disorders.

Source: Qureshi et al., (2010)

either major or mild neurocognitive disorder can be temporarily compromised if they experience an episode of delirium, the third category of neurocognitive disorder.

Delirium

Case Study

Police brought an eighteen-year-old high school senior to the emergency department after being picked up wandering in traffic. He was angry, agitated, and aggressive. In a rambling, disjointed manner he explained that he had been using "speed." In the emergency room he had difficulty focusing his attention, frequently needed questions repeated, and was disoriented as to time and place. (Spitzer et al., 1994, p. 162)

Delirium is an acute state of confusion characterized by diminished awareness (including disorientation) and impaired attentional skills. Although delirium can emerge in the context of a major or mild neurocognitive disorder, it also appears independently. Delirium is distinguished from mild and major neurocognitive disorder based on its core characteristics (disturbance in awareness and inability to direct, focus, sustain, and shift attention) as well as its acute onset and fluctuating course. Delirium typically develops rather rapidly over a course of hours or days. Symptoms can be mild or quite severe. There may be impaired orientation to time and place; disorganized patterns of thinking; and rambling, irrelevant, or incoherent speech. Psychotic symptoms such as delusions or hallucinations may be present. Symptoms of delirium fluctuate and can range from agitation and combativeness to drowsy, unresponsive behavior.

Treatment of delirium involves identifying the underlying cause which may include high fever; severe dehydration or malnutrition; acute infection; medication side effects or synergistic (interactive) effects of multiple medications; alcohol, drug, or inhalant intoxication; physiological withdrawal from alcohol, sedatives, or sleeping medications; or brain changes associated with neurocognitive disorder. Additionally, when people are ill or elderly, they have less cerebral reserve and are more likely to develop delirium with medical illness, stress conditions, or surgical procedures (Wise, Hilty, & Cerda, 2001; American Geriatric Society, 2010). Given the multiple vulnerabilities of those in the hospital (illness, recovery from surgery, use of new medications, sleep deprivation), episodes of delirium are not uncommon (Miller & Ely, 2007). Delirium associated with hospitalization is illustrated in the following case studies.

Case Study

Following a lung cancer diagnosis, Annie, a smoker since age 18, had surgery to remove the diseased portion of her lung. After her surgery, she was quite agitated, begging to leave immediately, convinced that the doctors and nurses were trying to kill her. Annie's confusion and paranoia continued for the next few days, but resolved when she returned home.

delirium an acute state of confusion involving diminished awareness, disorientation, and impaired attentional skills

Case Study

Justin Kaplan, an alert 84-year-old Pulitzer Prize-winning historian hospitalized after contracting pneumonia, describes an episode of delirium in which he fought with aliens: "Thousands of tiny little creatures, some on horseback, waving arms, carrying weapons like some grand Renaissance battle." In an attempt to "attack the aliens' television production studio," Mr. Kaplan fell out of bed, injuring himself. He later threatened to kill his wife and kicked a nurse who was trying to restrain him. Once his medical condition improved, the delirium subsided. (Belluck, 2010)

The severe symptoms of hospital delirium can distress loved ones, especially because there is usually no prior history of such behavior. Hospital delirium can result in longer hospital stays and lower rates of survival as well as increased risk of persistent cognitive impairment in vulnerable individuals (Girard, Pandharipande, & Ely, 2008). Fortunately, many hospitals attempt to detect and intervene with delirium in its earliest stages (American Geriatric Society, 2010).

Etiology of Neurocognitive Disorders

Neurocognitive disorders result from a variety of medical conditions. Rather than an etiological discussion using our multipath model, we focus on some of the *sources* of neurocognitive disorders. We do this because neurocognitive disorders involve conditions in which the cause and expected symptoms and course of the disorder are already known. We also discuss factors that increase the risk of developing a neurocognitive disorder. From the perspective of our multipath model, the specific brain pathology is the primary biological factor for each condition; however, other factors interact with the neurological condition to affect outcome as shown in Figure 13.1.

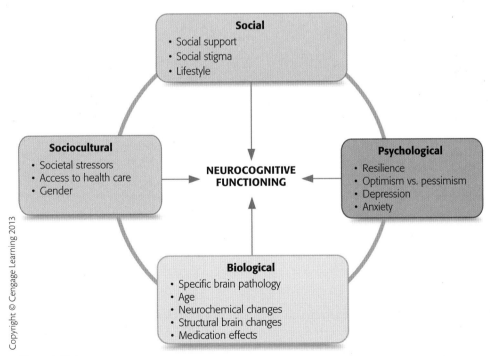

Copyright © Cengage Learning 2013

Figure 13.1

MULTIPATH MODEL FOR NEUROCOGNITIVE DISORDERS
The dimensions interact with specific brain pathology to produce the symptoms and pattern of recovery seen in various neurocognitive disorders.

Head Injury: What Do Soldiers Need to Know?

Case Studies

- A 28-year-old soldier with six separate blast-related concussions reports that he has daily headaches and difficulty performing simple mental tasks.

- After a bomb explosion hurled an Army enlistee against a wall, he continued working despite being dazed and suffering shrapnel wounds. Confusion, headaches, and problems with balance persisted for months; he later developed seizures.

- The driver of a vehicle hit by a roadside bomb did not appear to be seriously injured. However, in the months following the explosion, his speech was slurred and he had difficulty reading and completing simple tasks. (Miller & Zwerdling, 2010)

A confidential survey conducted by the Rand Corporation (2010) revealed that almost 20 percent of veterans returning from Iraq and Afghanistan reported experiencing probable traumatic brain injury (TBI) during combat; injuries often involve blasts from hidden land mines and improvised explosive devices (IEDs). These explosions cause complex brain damage including: 1) diffuse brain injury resulting from shock waves that bruise the brain and damage nerve pathways; 2) penetrating, focal injury from fragments of shrapnel or flying debris; and 3) injury from being thrown by the blast (Taber, Warden, & Hurley, 2006; Champion, Holcomb, & Young, 2009). Just what are the long-term risks from head injuries sustained in combat? The answer depends on many factors, including the source, location, and intensity of the injury, as well as interventions following the injury. Civilians treated for TBI are encouraged to allow the brain to rest to facilitate full recovery. However, in combat situations, mild head injuries are often not recognized, documented, and treated; subsequently, soldiers return immediately to combat (Murray et al., 2005).

The importance of early and comprehensive intervention to minimize the neurocognitive sequelae of TBI is widely accepted. However, some are concerned that soldiers are not receiving quality, evidence-based care for TBI in a timely manner (Miller & Zwerdling, 2010). Additionally, because the short and long-term implications of brain injury following blast exposure are unclear (Cernak, 2005), some wonder if soldiers exposed to multiple blast injuries are at risk for degenerative neurocognitive conditions such as *chronic traumatic encephalopathy* (Gavett, Stern, Cantu, Nowinski, & McKee, 2010). Should standard recommendations for TBI for civilians also apply to soldiers? What protocols might be beneficial to ensure that soldiers in combat receive appropriate care for TBI sustained in battle?

Traumatic Brain Injury

Case Study

United States Congresswoman Gabrielle Giffords, age 40, was shot in the head at point-blank range on January 8, 2011. The bullet entered and exited from the left side of her brain. Following surgery, Congresswoman Giffords remained in a medically induced coma, a state of deep sedation that allows time for the brain to heal. Part of her skull was removed to accommodate the anticipated swelling of her brain and to prevent further damage. Giffords' purposeful movements and responsiveness to simple commands were early, encouraging signs. Specialized cognitive and physical rehabilitation are helping to maximize her recovery.

Case Study

At age 53, H.N. sustained multiple injuries, including mild bleeding in the brain, when he was hit by a car. Although his initial delirium subsided, other behavioral changes, including pervasive apathy punctuated by angry outbursts, persisted for months. Subsequent MRI scans revealed damage in the orbitofrontal cortex, an area of the brain involved in emotion and decision making. (Adapted from Namiki et al., 2008, p. 475)

Case Study

PJM, a 38-year-old female, remained in a coma for several weeks after a bicycle accident. After regaining consciousness, she had severe short and long-term memory deficits (including no recall of the year before her accident) and difficulty using the right side of her body. Despite some improvement, PJM remains unable to drive or return to her work as a university professor. (Adapted from Rathbone, Moulin, & Conway, 2009, pp. 407–408)

Traumatic brain injury (TBI) can result from a physical wound or bump, jolt, or blow to the head. Approximately 1.7 million people sustain a TBI each year in the United States; infants and young children, older adolescents, and older adults have the highest incidence of TBI (Centers for Disease Control [CDC], 2011). Head injury contributes to almost one-third of injury-related deaths (Faul, Xu, Wald, & Coronado, 2010). Falls, vehicle accidents, and striking or being struck by objects are the leading causes of TBI (Figure 13.2).

Effects of TBI can be temporary or permanent and can result in mild to severe cognitive impairment. We are often amazed by stories of remarkable recovery of brain function following TBI. United States Congresswoman Gabrielle Giffords' much-publicized progress after her injury reinforces the capacity for brain recovery, particularly given immediate intervention, an excellent rehabilitation program, personal resilience, and social support during the recovery process. Similar conditions facilitated the recovery of well-known news anchor Bob Woodruff, who sustained a life-threatening brain injury in 2006 from a roadside bomb explosion encountered while he was on assignment in Iraq. After surgery, he spent 36 days in a medically induced coma. He underwent extensive rehabilitation and has since returned to work. In both cases, almost immediate medical attention and surgery played an important role in survival and recovery. A far different outcome resulted from what initially appeared to be a minor head injury sustained actress Natasha Richardson. Her first symptom, a headache, did not appear until almost an hour after hitting the back of her head during a ski lesson; however, unrecognized neurological injury (i.e., bleeding between the skull and brain) resulted in rapid death. Sometimes referred to as the "talk and die" syndrome, such injury can have severe, even fatal, consequences. All of these stories highlight the importance of immediate medical intervention when there is head injury.

As seen in the case examples, the severity, duration, and symptoms of TBI can vary significantly, depending on the extent and location of the neural damage. Symptoms can include headaches, disorientation, confusion, memory loss, deficits in attention, poor concentration, fatigue, and irritability as well as changes in behavior and emotionality. Generally, the greater the tissue damage, the more impaired the functioning. Chronic traumatic encephalopathy (CTE) is a progressive, degenerative condition diagnosed when autopsy reveals diffuse brain damage resulting from ongoing head trauma. CTE is seen in individuals who have had multiple episodes of head trauma such as athletes who participate in sports such as boxing or football. CTE is associated with psychological symptoms such as depression and poor impulse control as well as a significantly increased risk of dementia in later adulthood (Gavett, Stern, Cantu, Nowinski, & McKee, 2010).

Acute head injuries include concussions, contusions, and cerebral lacerations. *Concussion,* the most common form of traumatic brain injury, is a trauma-induced alteration in brain

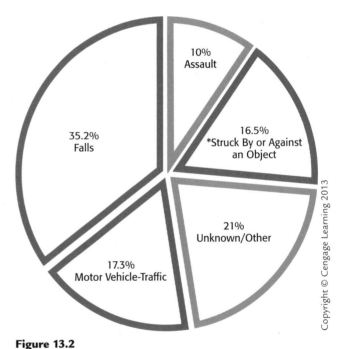

10%
Assault

16.5%
*Struck By or Against
an Object

35.2%
Falls

21%
Unknown/Other

17.3%
Motor Vehicle-Traffic

Copyright © Cengage Learning 2013

Figure 13.2

LEADING CAUSES OF TRAUMATIC BRAIN INJURY*

*This data does not include injuries occurring during military deployment.

traumatic brain injury (TBI) a physical wound or internal injury to the brain

chronic traumatic encephalopathy (CTE) progressive, degenerative condition involving brain damage from multiple episodes of head trauma

CRITICAL THINKING

Insidious Head Injury: Just How Safe Are Contact Sports?

How important is it for those involved in sports to know about concussion? Although the potential of brain damage with sports such as boxing is fairly well known, injuries resulting from team sports are beginning to spark public concern. The suicide of a Pennsylvania college football player Owen Thomas, age 21, garnered attention when his autopsy revealed evidence of the degenerative brain condition, chronic traumatic encephalopathy (CTE), likely resulting from chronic head injury incurred while playing football. In fact, CTE has been found on autopsy in at least 20 former professional football players, including two who committed suicide (Schwartz, 2010). After dying from fall-related head trauma, former Cincinnati Bengals player Chris Henry, age 26, was also found to have CTE. Amazingly, neither Thomas nor Henry had ever been diagnosed with a concussion during their years in football. How could such significant brain damage occur at such a young age, particularly with no history of concussion?

A groundbreaking study involving a high school football team (Talavage et al., 2010) sheds some light on the issue. Researchers compared computer-based cognitive testing and brain imaging studies of the players (obtained before, during, and after the football season) with data regarding the frequency and intensity of head impact (obtained by equipping helmets with special impact-monitoring sensors) during the football season. Players who had experienced a concussion during the season showed MRI changes and related cognitive

declines, but so did half of the other players; based on sensor data it was found that those players with brain changes but no recorded concussions had sustained multiple impacts (up to 1,600 subconcussive collisions) during the season. These results lead to the question: Should we be more concerned about the intensity of head injuries, about the effect of cumulative impacts to the head, or equally concerned about both?

Professional organizations such as the American Academy of Pediatrics and American Academy of Neurology have created guidelines for school-age athletes who are suspected of having a concussion. Recommendations include immediate removal from play, restricting physical activity for at least 7 to 10 days, and evaluation by a physician knowledgeable about head injury before return to play (American Academy of Neurology, 2010; Halstead & Walter, 2010). These guidelines have the potential to significantly change coaching practices and increase safety for athletes. Additionally, some have proposed nationwide guidelines regarding concussions. Careful monitoring of athletes with possible neurological damage (e.g., headache, confusion, poor balance, speech, vision or hearing difficulties) is certainly a step in the right direction. However, are adequate protections in place for those who receive multiple blows to the head while playing contact sports? Are the potential dangers of concussion and head injuries in contact sports and other activities such as basketball, soccer, baseball, hockey, cycling, and motorbiking receiving sufficient attention?

functioning, typically caused by a blow to the head. The injury effects the functioning of neurons and causes disorientation or loss of consciousness. Symptoms of concussion can include headache, dizziness, nausea, impaired coordination, or sensitivity to light. Once more severe brain injury is ruled out, individuals with a concussion are advised to rest and minimize stimulation and mentally challenging activities, refrain from any activity that can produce subsequent head injury, and immediately report any significant cognitive changes. Although symptoms are usually temporary, lasting no longer than a few weeks, in some cases, symptoms persist for much longer.

When someone receives a blow to the head or if the head hits another object, brain injury often occurs both at the site of impact and on the opposite side of the brain; bruising of the brain (called a *contusion*) results when the brain strikes the skull with sufficient force to cause bruising. Unlike the disruption in cellular functioning seen in a concussion, contusions involve actual tissue damage in the areas bruised. Swelling of the brain often results from a contusion so treatment includes preventing edema. Symptoms are similar to those seen with a concussion. Contusions and concussions commonly occur together. Brain imaging is frequently used to document areas of brain damage and monitor swelling. For example, CT and MRI scans are used to document *shaken baby syndrome*—a form of child abuse in which brain damage results from the violent shaking of an infant or young child. However, CT or MRI imaging cannot always detect the more subtle damage caused by closed head injury such as damage to neurons, mild bruising of brain tissue, or mild bleeding within the brain.

A *cerebral laceration* is an open head injury in which brain tissue is torn, pierced, or ruptured, usually from a skull fracture or an object that has penetrated the skull. Similar to a contusion, damage is localized and immediate medical care focuses on reducing bleeding and preventing swelling. As in the cases of Congresswoman Gifford and Bob Woodruff, a *craniectomy* (removal of part of the skull) may be performed to prevent pressure on other parts of the brain. As with other brain injuries, symptoms of open head injury can be quite serious,

Danger Just a Tumble Away

More than 8 million Americans suffer head injuries each year, such as concussions, contusions, and lacerations. In order to reduce the risk of head injuries, individuals are advised to wear helmets while skateboarding, rollerblading, and bicycling. If you engage in these activities, do you wear a helmet?

depending on the extent of damage to the brain tissue, the amount of hemorrhaging or swelling within the brain, and the medical care received. Severe brain trauma can have long-term negative consequences and recovery does not always ensure a return to prior levels of functioning. Along with the physical or cognitive difficulties produced by the injury, motivational and emotional effects and reactions can affect recovery.

Cognitive Vascular Disorders

Case Study

Kate McCarron's stroke symptoms started on a Friday, with a little tingle in her leg. On Saturday, McCarron, age 46, felt uncharacteristically tired. Sunday she seemed a bit under the weather. Monday, her left side felt numb. Tuesday morning, she couldn't move her left side. She was rushed to the hospital. A small blood vessel leading to a deep part of her brain was closing, choking off a region of her brain that controlled motion. (Dworkin, 2009, p. 1)

Neurocognitive vascular disorders can result from a one-time cardiovascular event such as a stroke or from insidious, ongoing disruptions to the cardiovascular system. The majority begins with *atherosclerosis*, clogging of the arteries resulting from a build-up of plaque. This plaque (comprised of fat, cholesterol, and other substances) accumulates over time and causes thickening and narrowing of the arterial walls and eventual reductions in blood flow and oxygen to the brain and other organs. If blood clots form or plaque breaks free of the artery wall, blood flow to or within the brain is obstructed and a stroke occurs. (Some refer to stroke as a "brain attack" due to similarities in how stroke and heart attack occur.)

The sudden halt of blood flow that occurs during a stroke results in a loss of brain function. An ischemic stroke results from reduced blood flow caused by a clot or severe narrowing of the arteries; approximately 85 percent of strokes are ischemic strokes (Lloyd-Jones et al.,

stroke a sudden halting of blood flow to a portion of the brain, leading to brain damage

ischemic stroke stroke due to reduced blood supply caused by a clot or severe narrowing of the arteries supplying blood to the brain

2009). A transient ischemic attack (TIA) is a "mini-stroke" resulting from temporary blockage of arteries; TIAs produce temporary symptoms, but no long-term damage. Seeking medical attention for a TIA reduces risk of a major stroke. Additionally, if emergency medical care is sought immediately following a clot-produced ischemic stroke, medications (i.e., thrombolytics) can dissolve the clot and prevent serious brain damage. A condition not related to plaque build-up, a hemorrhagic stroke, involves leakage of blood into the brain; the intracranial bleeding seen when a cerebral aneurysm bursts is an example of a hemorrhagic stroke. In either case, brain damage occurs when brain cells are deprived of blood and oxygen (Figure 13.3). Stroke is the fourth leading cause of death in the United States; about 137,000 deaths result from stroke every year (Heron et al., 2009; CDC, 2011). Careful monitoring and management of neurological complications from stroke (e.g., bleeding or swelling within the brain) reduces mortality and improves prognosis (Balami, Chen, & Grunwald, 2011).

Only a fraction of strokes occur in individuals younger than 50 years of age; younger individuals who experience stroke typically have risk factors such as hypertension, diabetes, high cholesterol, smoking, or exposure to secondhand smoke (Balci, Utku, Asil, & Celik, 2011). Cigarette smoking is considered the primary contributor to up to one-fourth of all strokes; however, when young adults experience a *cryptogenic ischemic stroke* (stroke without a clear physiological etiology), the contribution of smoking approaches 50 percent. Use of oral contraceptives can increase stroke risk, particularly when combined with smoking (Girot, 2009). A study assessing the relationship between smoking and ischemic stroke risk in young women revealed that as number of cigarettes smoked per day increases there is a corresponding increase in stroke risk (Bhat et al., 2008). Worldwide data pertaining to stroke risk implicates hypertension; smoking; abdominal obesity; a high intake of salt and saturated fats; limited physical activity, stress, or depression; and heavy or binge drinking (O'Donnell et al., 2010). Prevention efforts focus on these modifiable risk factors because they account for almost 90 percent of the risk of stroke (Hankey, 2011).

Stroke is not only a leading cause of death but also a significant cause of disability (Young & Tolentino, 2011). Prompt medical intervention vastly improves prognosis

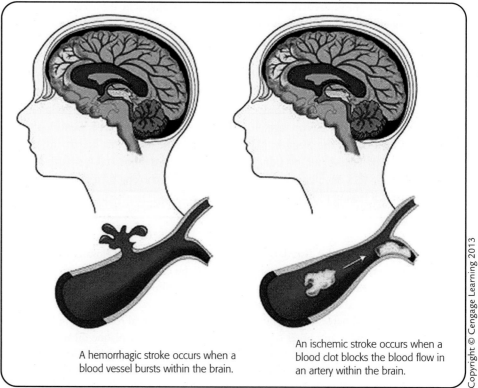

A hemorrhagic stroke occurs when a blood vessel bursts within the brain.

An ischemic stroke occurs when a blood clot blocks the blood flow in an artery within the brain.

Copyright © Cengage Learning 2013

Figure 13.3

TYPES OF STROKE

Ischemic strokes resulting from a blocked artery account for approximately 85 percent of all strokes.

(Ahmed et al., 2010); this underscores the importance of recognizing a stroke (Table 13.6). Because many people do not recognize stroke symptoms (e.g., slurred speech, blurry vision, or numbness on one side of the body) or hesitate to treat these symptoms as an emergency, public health campaigns continue to stress the importance of immediate intervention (Fussman et al., 2010).

Stroke survivors who do not receive immediate intervention often require long-term care due to a variety of physical and psychological symptoms that impair independent functioning. Strokes damaging the left side of the brain typically affect speech and language proficiency as well as physical movement on the right half of the body. Strokes occurring within the right hemisphere can impair judgment and short-term memory, increase impulsivity, and affect visual-spatial skills (e.g., fastening buttons or judging distance and speed while driving) and motor movement on the left side of the body. Visual problems (blurry or double vision) are sometimes seen in those with a right-hemisphere stroke, including *spatial-visual neglect*, a failure to attend to or process large portions of what is seen, most frequently in the left field of vision. Cognitive, behavioral, and emotional changes that occur following stroke depend not only on the area affected by the stroke and the extent of brain damage, but also on the individual's personality, emotional resilience, and coping skills. Some stroke survivors are frustrated and depressed by the difficulties they experience attempting to perform activities of daily living, whereas others actively and optimistically participate in therapeutic rehabilitation activities.

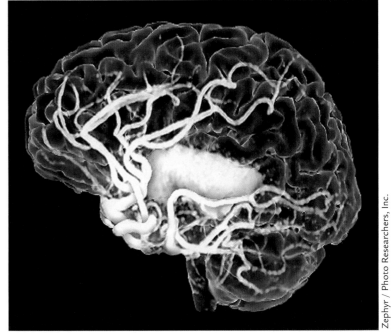

Results of Stroke on the Brain

Stroke is brain damage caused by the interruption of the brain's blood supply or by the leakage of blood through blood vessel walls. The two main causes of stroke are high blood pressure and narrowing of the arteries. Here, a three-dimensional magnetic resonance angiogram scan shows a human brain after a stroke. Major arteries are shown in white. The central region in yellow is an area in which bleeding occurred.

Zephyr / Photo Researchers, Inc.

A series of small strokes or a chronic decrease in blood flow can lead to a degenerative condition known as vascular cognitive impairment (sometimes referred to as vascular dementia), which is characterized by uneven deterioration of intellectual abilities. The specific symptoms of this condition depend on the area and extent of the brain damage (Bowler, 2007). Both physical and cognitive functioning may be impaired. Vascular cognitive impairment, estimated to affect 8 to 15 percent of those with dementia, often coexists with Alzheimer's disease because both have similar lifestyle risk factors (Jellinger, 2008). Recent analyses concluded that hypertension (Sharp, Aarsland, Day, Sonnesyn, & Ballard, 2010), diabetes (Launer, 2009), and smoking (Rusanen et al., 2010) all significantly increase the risk of both vascular dementia and Alzheimer's disease; regular physical activity has been found to prevent both conditions (Aarsland, Sardahaee, Anderssen, & Ballard, 2010).

TABLE 13.6 Knowing When to Act: Stroke Symptoms

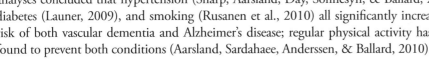

- **Numbness or weakness, especially on one side of the body**

- **Confusion, trouble speaking or understanding speech**

- **Vision difficulty in one or both eyes**

- **Dizziness, loss of balance or coordination**

- **Severe headache with no known cause**

Emergency medical attention immediately following onset of stroke symptoms can significantly improve outcome for both ischemic and hemorrhagic strokes.

vascular cognitive impairment cognitive skills decline due to chronic or sporadic cardiovascular events affecting blood flow to the brain

Experiencing a Stroke

Neuroanatomist Jill Bolte Taylor is shown holding a human brain and spinal cord. At age 38, Dr. Taylor experienced a massive stroke caused by a congenital abnormality in the blood vessels of her brain. After regaining consciousness, she could not talk, understand language, or remember her life. She felt completely disabled. After recovering from the stroke, Taylor described the outcome of her experience as positive. It shifted her out of left hemisphere-dominated thinking (which emphasizes language and focuses on the past and future) to the consciousness of her right hemisphere, which thinks in pictures and exists in the present moment. When her left hemisphere was damaged from the stroke, her right hemisphere became dominant. Taylor became a different person. Shifting away from her intense focus on academics, career, and achievement, she has become more compassionate and humane. Her values have shifted toward helping those in need such as people with mental disorders, the homeless, and those who are incarcerated.

neurodegeneration declining brain function due to brain atrophy and death of neurons

Alzheimer's disease (AD) dementia involving memory loss and other declines in cognitive and adaptive functioning

Neurodegenerative Disorders

In contrast with the recovery often seen in cases of stroke or traumatic brain injury, individuals with neurodegenerative disorders show decline in function rather than progress. Neurodegeneration refers to declining functioning due to progressive loss of brain structure, neurochemical abnormalities, and/or death of neurons. We focus on a variety of disorders with very distinct symptoms, including some that appear in later life and some that can occur during early adulthood. Neurodegenerative disorders vary greatly in terms of age of onset, skills affected, and course of the disorder. We begin our discussion with the most well-known neurodegenerative disorder, Alzheimer's disease.

Alzheimer's Disease

Alzheimer's disease (AD), the most prevalent neurodegenerative disorder, affects about five million Americans. AD is the sixth leading cause of death in the United States (CDC, 2011). The cost of care for those currently diagnosed is $172 billion per year. It has been estimated that by 2030 almost eight million will have AD, with the prevalence reaching 16 million by 2050 (Alzheimer's Association, 2010; Hebert, Scherr, Bienias, Bennett, & Evans, 2003). Although AD can strike adults in their thirties, forties, or fifties, risk of the disease significantly increases with age; those who are 65 have a 1 percent risk, whereas there is a 40 to 50 percent risk at the age of 95 (Wang & Ding, 2008).

The course of AD disease is characterized by gradual onset and ongoing cognitive decline. The core feature of AD is memory impairment. However, caution is used in making an Alzheimer's diagnosis based only on early signs of memory impairment; unless the individual has clear genetic indicators (e.g., evidence of genetic mutations or biomarkers associated with AD) it is still not possible to reliably predict who among those with mild cognitive decline might eventually develop AD (Ballard, Corbett, & Jones, 2011). Individuals who seek treatment for impaired memory develop AD at a rate of 12 to 15 percent per year; however, among individuals with memory impairment in the general population (i.e., not just those who seek treatment) there is a lower rate of progression and, in some cases, a reversal of symptoms (American Psychiatric Association, 2011).

Characteristics of Alzheimer's Disease AD is characterized by insidious onset and progressive decline in cognitive, physical, and social functioning (Gatz, 2007). The physiological processes that produce AD begin years before the onset of symptoms (Brooks & Loewenstein, 2010). As early symptoms—memory dysfunction, irritability, and cognitive impairment—gradually worsen, other symptoms, such as social withdrawal, depression, apathy, delusions, impulsive behaviors, and neglect of personal hygiene often appear. Some individuals with AD become loving and child-like, whereas others become increasingly agitated and combative. At present, no curative or disease-reversing interventions exist for AD. From the time of diagnosis, those with AD survive about half as long as those of similar age without dementia (Larson et al., 2004). However, slower rates of cognitive decline predict longer survival (Doody et al., 2010).

> **Case Study**
>
> Elizabeth R., a forty-six-year-old woman diagnosed with AD, is trying to cope with her increasing memory difficulties. She writes notes to herself and rehearses conversations, anticipating what might be said. After reading only a few sentences, she forgets what she has read. She sometimes forgets where the bathroom is located in her own house and is depressed by the realization that she is becoming a burden to her family. (Clark et al., 1984, p. 60)

The deterioration of memory is one of the most poignant and disturbing symptoms for those who have AD. At first they may forget appointments, phone numbers, and addresses, but as AD progresses, they lose track of the time of day, have trouble remembering

AP Photo/Ron Schumacher

Did Alzheimer's Disease Affect His Presidency?

Former President Ronald Reagan was diagnosed with Alzheimer's disease at age 83. There has been debate regarding whether or not he began to show symptoms of the disease, such as memory difficulties, while still in office. Five years prior to the diagnosis, Reagan was treated for a traumatic head injury that occurred when he was thrown from a horse. Some have speculated that this head injury accelerated the progression of his Alzheimer's disease.

recent and past events, and forget who they are. But even when memory is gone, emotions remain. In fact, researchers have found that although those with AD may forget details of an emotional event (such as the plot of a sad movie), the emotions of the experience continue (Feinstein, Duff, & Tranela, 2010).

Other Factors Affecting Memory Loss   A common concern of older adults is whether occasional memory lapses are signs of AD. Memory loss occurs for a variety of reasons. It can, in fact, be a symptom of AD or other neurodegenerative disorders. However, occasional lapses of memory are common in healthy adults. As we age, neurons are gradually lost, the brain becomes smaller and information is processed more slowly. For some, this brain atrophy leads to declining memory and difficulty learning new material (Mormino et al., 2008). This normal process is why some older adults experience declines in perception, attention, and memory as they age; more rapid atrophy is associated with more rapid cognitive decline (Smith et al., 2010). The reason that many older adults experience minimal decline in cognitive function despite brain atrophy is because, as we age, the brain reorganizes itself in a way that maximizes cognitive functioning (Population Reference Bureau, 2007).

Memory loss and confusion can also result from acute conditions such as an infection or reactions to prescription drugs. Prescription medications can interact with one another or with certain foods to produce negative side effects, including memory impairment. In addition, cardiac, metabolic, and endocrine disorders and nutritional deficiencies can produce memory loss and symptoms resembling dementia. Acute conditions are often easily treated and reversed once diagnosed. Declining cognitive skills and ongoing memory difficulties may, however, be signs of AD.

Alzheimer's Disease and the Brain   Comparisons of the brains of persons with AD and those who are free of AD reveal a number of differences. First, persons with AD have increased atrophy of brain tissue. In a prospective study, accelerated atrophy of the hippocampus and amygdala among cognitively intact elderly people was predictive of the subsequent development of AD and dementia (den Heijer et al., 2006). Second, the brain of those with AD becomes clogged with two abnormal structures, *neurofibrillary tangles* and *senile plaques*. Neurofibrillary tangles are twisted masses of protein fibers found inside nerve cells. Senile plaques are composed of parts of neurons (e.g., patches of degenerated nerve endings) surrounding a group of proteins called beta-amyloid deposits. Both conditions, which are detected on autopsy, are believed to produce AD symptoms by disrupting the transmission of impulses between neurons. It is hypothesized that these plaques cause *oxidative injury* (damage due to release of free radicals during cellular metabolism), inflammation, and alterations in neurotransmitters, eventually resulting in the death of neurons and brain atrophy.

Recent research has led to speculation that interference in connections between the entorhinal cortex (an "information hub" located in the temporal lobe), where senile plaques and beta-amyloid deposits first accumulate, and the hippocampus (a region involved in memory) results in the memory loss seen in the earliest stages of AD (Harris et al., 2010). Additionally, it appears that rather than overproduction of beta-amyloid protein fragments, AD results from inefficient clearance of these proteins once they are produced (Kwasi et al., 2010). Higher blood levels of the amino acid, homocysteine, are associated with increased risk of AD. Certain vitamins, such as B vitamins, can decrease homocysteine levels. In a sample of individuals with mild cognitive impairment, the progression of brain atrophy (documented by MRI scans) was slowed by about 30 percent in those taking high doses of B vitamins over a two year period; not surprisingly, atrophy was reduced most (up to 53 percent) in those with the highest initial levels of homocysteine (Smith et al., 2010).

Did You Know?

Difficulty identifying smells such as lemon, banana, and cinnamon may be the first sign of Alzheimer's disease (Wilson, Schneider et al., 2007). Does this occur because of changes occurring in brain regions related to smell or because individuals with Alzheimer's disease cannot remember the words associated with the odors? (Razani, Nordin, Chan, & Murphy, 2010)

Although multiple indicators (e.g., cognitive symptoms and imaging documenting brain atrophy) are suggestive of AD, it has not been possible to definitively diagnose AD before autopsy. However, the Food and Drug Administration is close to approving use of a special dye that allows senile plaques to be detected via PET imaging. Such definitive information will facilitate the search for medications to slow or halt the progression of AD. Additionally, because AD diagnoses sometime prove to be inaccurate on autopsy, the ability to definitively confirm or rule out AD will guide interventions for those who do not, in fact, have AD and will increase the validity of AD research by insuring that study participants, in fact, have the disease.

Etiology of Alzheimer's Disease   The etiology of AD is believed to be a product of hereditary and environmental factors (Rocchi, Orsucci, Tognoni, Ceravolo, & Siciliano, 2009). It appears that a number of factors (or interaction between factors) increase risk of AD.

We do know that several genes have been associated with increased incidence of AD, although the exact role of these genes is not known (Boustani et al., 2003). The risk of developing AD is 1.8 to 4.0 times higher for those with a family history of the disorder than for those without (Gatz, 2007). In a comparison of dizygotic (DZ) and monozygotic (MZ) twins with AD, several important findings emerged: (1) heritability for the disease is high, (2) gender differences do not appear to be significant, and (3) environmental influences are also important and should be the focus of interventions to reduce risk or delay onset of the disease (Gatz et al., 2006). A small number of families have a generational pattern of what is called *autosomal-dominant Alzheimer's disease (ADAD)*; family members who inherit one of three very rare genetic mutations develop early-onset AD (Zetzsche, Rujescu, Hardy, & Hampel, 2010). Those with ADAD typically develop the disorder between the ages of 30 and 50.

Did You Know?

A comprehensive, 17-year longitudinal study concluded that depression is associated with an increased risk of both Alzheimer's and other dementias; multiple episodes of depression appear to further heighten this risk.

Source: Dotson, Beydoun, & Zonderman, (2010); Saczynski et al., (2010)

A much more common gene that increases risk for later-onset AD is the APOE-e4 gene. Those with this *risk gene* (thought to contribute to approximately 25 percent of all AD) have an increased likelihood of developing AD but will not necessarily develop the disorder; risk is further increased when the gene is inherited from both parents. A study using MRI imaging found that non-symptomatic carriers of this gene had atypical connections within the brain (Sheline et al., 2010) and biomarkers typical of AD such as changes in how the brain metabolizes glucose and abnormalities in the cerebrospinal fluid (Zetzsche et al., 2010). Efforts to detect the genes and biomarkers of the early physiological processes involved in AD continue, with the ultimate goal of developing methods to prevent the development and progression of this devastating disease (Brooks & Loewenstein, 2010; Bateman et al., 2011).

Prevention and Intervention with Alzheimer's Disease Maintaining a healthy cardiovascular system by exercising and eating a healthy diet can help reduce risk of AD and other disorders involving dementia (Baker et al., 2010). Changes in lifestyle may, in fact, help slow the progression of AD (Rolland, van Kan, & Vellas, 2010). Among one group of adults with early-stage AD, those with good cardiovascular fitness had less brain atrophy compared to those who did not exercise regularly (Honea et al., 2009). Some investigators assessing the role of cerebral immune system responses in the development of AD have suggested that anti-inflammatory drugs may slow the accumulation of proteins implicated in AD (Zotova, Nicoll, Kalaria, Holmes, & Boche, 2010). Cholinesterase inhibitors have reduced the rate of cognitive decline (Boustani et al., 2003) and have helped facilitate new learning (Rokem & Silver, 2010) in some individuals with AD. However, caution is urged with these medications due to increased risk of slowed heart rate and sudden loss of consciousness (Gill et al., 2009).

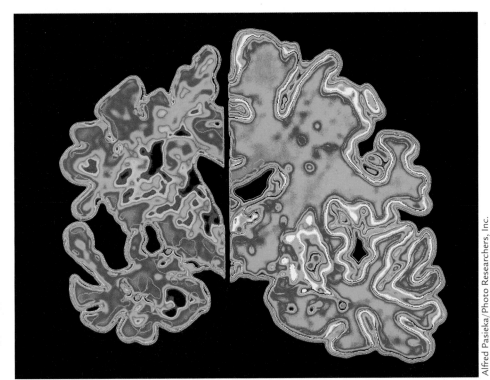

Alfred Pasieka/Photo Researchers, Inc.

Normal Brain and Alzheimer's Brain

This image shows a computer graphic of a vertical slice through the brain of an Alzheimer patient (at left) compared with a normal brain (at right). The Alzheimer's disease brain is considerably shrunken, due to the degeneration and death of nerve cells. Tangled protein filaments (neurofibrillary tangles) are found within nerve cells and patients also develop brain lesions of beta-amyloid protein. Symptoms of Alzheimer's disease include memory loss, disorientation, and personality change.

Lewy Body Dementia (LBD)

Lewy body dementia (LBD), the second most common form of dementia, results in the progressive cognitive decline seen in AD as well a milder presentation of the atypical movements seen in Parkinson's disease. Although the onset of LBD tends to be more rapid than that of AD, the two diseases have a similar survival rate of approximately eight years after diagnosis. Characteristics of LBD include: 1) significant fluctuations in attention and alertness (e.g., staring spells and periods of extreme drowsiness); 2) recurrent, detailed visual hallucinations; 3) impaired movement, including frequent falls, a shuffling gait, muscular rigidity, and slowed movement; and 4) sleep disturbance, including acting out dreams (Lewy Body Dementia Association, 2008). Depression is frequently seen in those with LBD. Compared to cognitive deficits associated with AD, memory and language skills are unusually more intact in those with LBD, whereas visual-spatial tasks (such a reproducing a drawing) are more impaired.

Lewy body dementia (LBD) dementia involving visual hallucinations, cognitive fluctuations, and atypical movements

Individuals with LBD have the same irregularities in neurons (affecting cognition and motor movement) that are seen in Parkinson's disease (Goldmann, Siderowf, & Hurtig, 2008). These unique cell structures are called Lewy bodies after the researcher, Frederick Lewy, who first discovered them. These abnormal neurons are found in the midbrain of those with Parkinson's and in the cortex and midbrain of individuals with LBD. LBD is diagnosed when cognitive decline begins at the same time (or within a year of) the Parkinson's-like motor symptoms. If dementia begins more than a year after a Parkinson's diagnosis, it is considered to be Parkinson's disease with dementia. Individuals with LBD often have the plaques and tangles characteristic of AD, and some with AD sometimes have Lewy bodies. LBD can only be confirmed by autopsy because brain imaging techniques cannot yet detect Lewy bodies (National Institute of Neurological Disorders and Stroke, 2011).

LBD is estimated to account for up to 30 percent of all dementias; however, prevalence data is compromised by the overlap in symptoms with other dementias and with Parkinson's disease; additionally, professionals who are not dementia specialists are often less familiar with LBD. Differential diagnosis is quite important, however, because those with LBD sometimes experience serious reactions to medications used to treat psychotic symptoms. Although specific genes associated with LBD have not been detected, LBD and its core symptoms have been found to occur more frequently in some families (Nervi et al., 2011).

Frontotemporal Lobar Degeneration

Frontotemporal lobar degeneration (FTLD), the fourth leadng cause of dementia, is characterized by progressive declines in language and behavior; the deficits result from degeneration in the frontal and temporal lobes of the brain (Rabinovici & Miller, 2010). FTLD presents in three distinct ways, depending on the area of the brain undergoing neuronal loss: 1) significant changes in behavior and personality (e.g., extreme disinhibition or intense apathy); 2) progressive difficulty using words and naming objects; or 3) difficulty forming words and using language. Mean age of onset is in midlife, making it the second leading cause of dementia in those younger than age 65 (Johnson et al., 2005). Both diagnosis and treatment of FTLD are complicated by the variety of cognitive areas and physiological processes involved in the disorder. FTLD has a significant genetic component (Bigio, 2008). Recently, scientists have been able to identify biomarkers of FTLD in cerebrospinal fluid, a finding that will further FTLD research (Borroni et al., 2010; Rabinovici & Miller, 2010).

Parkinson's Disease

Parkinson's disease (PD) is a progressive disorder characterized by four primary symptoms: 1) tremor of the hands, arms, legs, jaw, or face; 2) rigidity of the limbs and trunk; 3) slowness in initiating movement; and 4) postural instability, or impaired balance and coordination (National Institute of Neurological Disorders and Stroke, 2007b). Cognitive impairment and dementia are common in the later stages of PD, eventually affecting up to 75 percent of those with the disorder; risk for dementia is highest in those who develop PD later in life (Aarsland et al., 2003). Neurological changes in those with PD often affects ability to recognize emotional cues, such as recognizing an upset face or voice, a factor that can strain interpersonal interactions (Gray & Tickle-Degnen, 2010). Many individuals with PD, especially those with more severe motor symptoms and those diagnosed at younger ages, are affected by depression and anxiety (Dissanayaka et al., 2010). Psychotic symptoms may also be present, particularly among those with dementia (Weintraub, Comella, & Horn, 2008).

PD is associated with Lewy bodies in the motor area of the brainstem, accelerated aging of neurons, and loss of dopamine-producing brain cells (Goldmann, Siderowf,

Kevin Mazur/WireImage/Getty Images

Parkinson's Disease

Actor Michael J. Fox, who has Parkinson's disease, performs at a benefit for The Michael J. Fox Foundation for Parkinson's Research in New York City.

frontotemporal lobar degeneration (FTLD) brain degeneration in the frontal and temporal lobes resulting in progressive declines in language and behavior

Parkinson's disease (PD) progressive disorder characterized by poorly controlled motor movements

& Hurtig, 2008). The disease is the second most common neurodegenerative disorder in the United States (Dobkin, Allen, & Menza, 2006), affecting about 500,000 individuals. PD strikes about 50 percent more men than women, but the reasons for this discrepancy are unclear. In some persons, the disorder may be influenced by infections of the brain, toxins, cerebrovascular disorders, and brain trauma. PD occurs more frequently in the northern Midwest and Northeast and in urban settings; this geographic distribution has raised questions about the impact of environmental toxins common to these areas (Willis et al., 2010). Researchers are searching for physiological explanations for the pattern of brain cell death seen in PD; genetic mutations account for only 5 percent of PD cases (Stoessl, 2011; Syed et al., 2011). Researchers have discovered that an interaction between one genetic mutation and diets low in vitamin B_6 accounts for the low dopamine levels seen in some individuals with PD (Tan, Ho, Tan, Prakash, & Zhao, 2010).

Although medication can help control some PD symptoms, pharmacological treatment is often delayed until it is certain that the benefits clearly outweigh the risks. Side effects of medications for physical symptoms can produce or exacerbate hallucinations and other psychotic symptoms, and psychiatric medications can increase difficulties with movement (Weintraub & Hurtig, 2007). For some patients, high-technology surgical procedures on the brain or the implantation of electrodes to continuously stimulate areas of the brain have been helpful (Hartman-Stein, 2004).

Huntington's Disease

Huntington's disease (HD) is a rare, genetically transmitted degenerative disorder characterized by involuntary movement, progressive dementia, and emotional instability. Age of onset is variable, ranging from childhood to late in life; onset most typically occurs during midlife (Roos, 2010). Initial physical symptoms of HD can include twitches in the fingers or facial grimaces. As the disorder progresses, abrupt, repetitive movements often develop. Changes in personality and emotional stability are frequently seen early in the disease process; many individuals with HD become uncharacteristically moody and quarrelsome. Other psychiatric symptoms include agitation, hypersexuality, and psychosis. Cognitive deficits and dementia are often the last symptoms to appear. As the disease progresses, the severity of motor and cognitive impairment results in total dependency and the need for full-time care (Roos, 2010). Severity of depression and impairment in day-to-day functioning have the strongest influence on quality of life for those with HD (Ho, Gilbert, Mason, Goodman, & Barker, 2009). Medication can reduce symptom severity, including depression associated with the disorder. HD cannot be cured; death typically occurs 15 to 20 years after the onset of symptoms. Suicide is a common cause of death among those with HD (Roos, 2010).

Because HD is transmitted from parent to child through a dominant genetic mutation, approximately 50 percent of the offspring of an affected individual develop the condition; symptoms are more severe in those who inherit the disease from their father. Predictive genetic testing is available for offspring who want to know if they have inherited the disorder. Genetic counseling is extremely important in preventing transmission of the disease.

AIDS Dementia Complex

The general public knows about the serious consequences of AIDS, or acquired immunodeficiency syndrome—susceptibility to diseases, physical deterioration, and death. Relatively few people, however, know that dementia may be the first sign of HIV infection or AIDS. Symptoms can include an inability to concentrate, difficulty with complex mental tasks, tremors, poor balance, and increasing apathy and lethargy. In more serious cases, a diagnosis of *AIDS dementia complex (ADC)* is made. Prevalence of ADC among persons with HIV infection is between 10 and 20 percent in Western countries (Grant, Sacktor, & McArthur, 2005).

Did You Know?

Evidence of a genetic mutation that causes Huntington's disease has been found in some individuals whose primary symptom is major depression (Perlis et al., 2010).

© Mark Peterson / Corbis

Major Discovery

Dr. Nancy Wexler helped to develop the first test to determine who was carrying the gene for Huntington's disease. Her mother died of the disease.

Huntington's disease genetically transmitted degenerative disease characterized by involuntary twitching movements and eventual dementia

CONTROVERSY

Genetic Testing: Helpful or Harmful?

DNA testing is now available to provide information regarding risk for a variety of neurocognitive disorders. Genotyping (gathering information about specific genes by examining an individual's DNA sequence) brings up a number of interconnected issues and divergent opinions. When genotyping is performed on individuals who have a family member with a *genetically determined* condition such as Huntington's disease or early-onset, autosomal-dominant Alzheimer's disease, the outcome of the test reveals life-changing information—certainty as to whether or not they will develop the neurodegenerative disorder afflicting other members of their family. In other cases (e.g., the APOE-e4 genotype associated with later-onset Alzheimer's disease) genetic tests only indicate *possible* risk. Clinicians often lean toward discouraging testing in such circumstances (Howe, 2010), contending that knowledge of *possible risk* can be more harmful than helpful (Howard & Filley, 2009).

Those who approach genetic testing cautiously cite concerns about social and economic stigma associated with genetically transmitted conditions such as Huntington's disease (The Lancet Neurology, 2010) combined with the lack of specific treatments or interventions if Huntington's or Alzheimer's mutations are detected. Advocates of testing for those who may carry *deterministic genes* (e.g., Huntington's) emphasize benefits such as reproductive planning as well as decreasing uncertainty about the future. Regarding testing for genes that only increase risk (e.g., the APOE-e4 genotype), it is argued that confirmatory information does not, in fact, increase distress (Cassidy et al., 2008); uncertainty about

disease risk can be a chronic stressor, and confirmatory information may motivate lifestyle changes that ultimately reduce the risk of developing Alzheimer's.

To test the issue of psychological impact of genotyping for the APOE-e4 allele, researchers (Green et al., 2009) worked with a group of healthy adults who had a parent with Alzheimer's disease; after DNA testing, genotyping results were disclosed to half of the participants. Professionally guided psychoeducation and genetic counseling (Howard & Filley, 2009) included explanations to all participants that not all of those with APOE-e4 develop Alzheimer's and that everyone has some risk of developing Alzheimer's. Testing did not appear to cause any significant short-term psychological distress for the participants; the group who received DNA results confirming an APOE-e4 genotype did not report any greater anxiety, depression, or distress compared to other participants. Genotyping continues to guide research aimed at developing interventions to prevent or slow the progression of neurodegenerative diseases (Sleegers et al., 2010). Once such interventions exist, some of the debate may subside.

For Further Consideration:

1. If your parent had Huntington's disease or autosomal-dominant Alzheimer's disease, would you want to know if you would eventually develop the disorder?
2. If your family members had later-onset Alzheimer's disease, would you want to know if you carried the APOE-e4 allele that would increase your risk of developing the disorder?

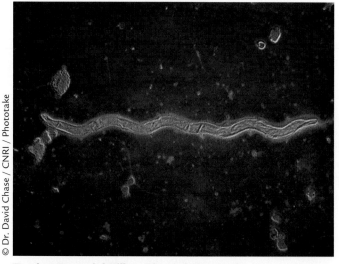

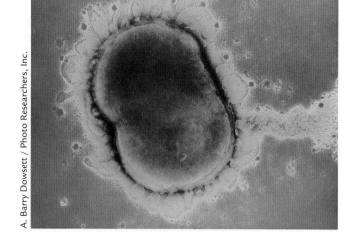

Taming Potential Killers Through Research

Shown at left is the syphilis spirochete *Treponema pallidum*, the bacterium responsible for the development of syphilis and, if untreated, significant neurocognitive impairment; shown at right is the spherical bacterium *Neisseria meningitidis*, which causes bacterial meningitis in humans. Both can cause destruction of brain tissue, seizures, and ultimately death.

ADC develops when the HIV virus reaches the brain at some phase of the infection. When it becomes active, the virus can affect mental, as well as physical, processes. Also, because AIDS affects the immune system, AIDS-related infections may cause infected cells to release toxic substances that cause changes in brain-controlled physiological processes. Some degree of cerebral atrophy is present in almost all HIV patients with dementia. The antiretroviral therapy used to aggressively treat HIV and AIDS can prevent or delay the onset of ADC. Strengthened immune system functioning is a key to decreasing the impact of HIV on neurocognitive functioning; however, antiretroviral therapy carries its own risk of contributing to HIV-associated dementia (Wright, 2009). There are currently no medications proven to improve symptoms once ADC has developed (Uthman & Abdulmalik, 2008).

Other Diseases and Infections of the Brain

A variety of diseases and infections can lead to the development of neurocognitive disorders. In the following section, we discuss a few of these conditions.

Meningitis and Encephalitis

Meningitis and encephalitis can both develop as a result of a virus or bacteria. Some types of bacterial meningitis and encephalitis are contagious. Meningitis is an inflammation of the *meninges*, the membrane that surrounds the brain and spinal cord, whereas encephalitis involves inflammation of the brain itself. The symptoms of meningitis vary with age. In neonates and young infants, the symptoms are nonspecific (bulging fontanel, jaundice, lethargy, poor eating, and irritability) making diagnosis difficult. In patients older than one year, symptoms often include stiffness of the neck, headache, sudden high fever, and sensitivity to light and noise (Curtis, Stobart, Vandermeer, Simel, & Klassen, 2010). Diagnosis of suspected meningitis is confirmed through microscopic analysis of cerebrospinal fluid. Meningitis can result in the localized destruction of brain tissue; severity is greatest with bacterial meningitis and when meningitis is contracted during the neonatal period. Residual effects of bacterial meningitis can include partial or complete hearing loss and ongoing cognitive difficulties. Seizures are associated with more serious outcome (Zoons et al., 2007). The availability of vaccines has helped reduce the incidence of bacterial meningitis (Hunt, 2010); however, death and disability remain a significant concern for those who contract it (Gammelgaard, Colding, Hartze, & Penkowa, 2011).

Encephalitis can produce mild symptoms that resemble the stomach flu. Severe encephalitis can create lethargy, drowsiness, fever, vomiting, and delirium. The infection that results in encephalitis can come from a variety of sources, including viruses (including the herpes virus) and insect bites. Most severe cases follow a rapidly developing course that begins with headache and diminished consciousness. Although seizures, headache, fatigue, memory difficulties, and impaired decision making can be long-term effects of encephalitis, many individuals make a complete recovery.

Epilepsy

Epilepsy is a chronic neurological condition characterized by *seizures*—intermittent periods of altered consciousness resulting from uncontrolled electrical discharge within the brain. It is the most common neurological disorder: 1 to 2 percent of the population has

Erich Lessing / Art Resource, NY

The Most Common Neurological Disorder

Epilepsy refers to any disorder that is characterized by intermittent periods of altered consciousness, often accompanied by seizures. It also seems to be one of the earliest recognized organic brain syndromes. Among those who suffered from the disease was Vincent van Gogh, shown here in a self-portrait painted sometime after he had cut off his ear.

meningitis inflammation of the membrane surrounding the brain and spinal cord

encephalitis brain inflammation

epilepsy disorder characterized by seizures and uncontrolled electrical discharge from brain cells

A Cerebral Tumor

The neuroimaging technique computerized axial tomography (known as a CT or CAT scan) involves analysis of cross-sectional x-rays of the brain taken from various angles. CT scan can detect a variety of brain abnormalities, including cerebral tumors such as the one shown in this image. Cerebral tumors result from abnormal tissue growing within the brain. Symptoms depend on the size and location of the tumor.

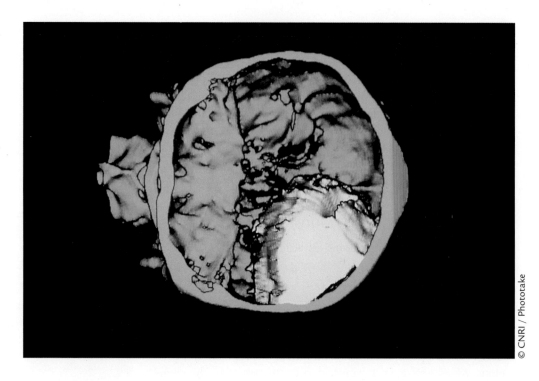

© CNRI / Phototake

had at least one epileptic seizure. Epilepsy affects an estimated 2.7 million people in the United States and costs about $15.5 billion in medical expenses and lost or reduced earnings and productivity each year (CDC, 2011).

Epilepsy is most frequently diagnosed during childhood. It can have no apparent etiology, or it can arise from such causes as brain tumors, injury, degenerative diseases, or substance abuse. Head trauma is the most common cause of new-onset epilepsy in young adults; penetrating head injury can increase risk of epilepsy in the short term or years later (Raymont et al., 2010). Epileptic seizures and unconsciousness may last from a few seconds to several hours; they may occur only a few times during the patient's entire life or many times in one day. Seizures can produce momentary changes in consciousness or violent convulsions lasting for hours. Researchers continue to look for ways to help the approximately 30 percent of individuals with epilepsy whose seizures do not improve with medication (Radwa et al., 2010; French & Friedman, 2011).

Substance Abuse

Use or abuse of psychoactive substances can result in delirium or the chronic brain dysfunction seen in major or mild neurocognitive disorders. Although substance-induced neurocognitive disorders are most common among those with a history of heavy substance use, significant neurocognitive dysfunction can occur when larger quantities of drugs or alcohol are ingested; when multiple substances are taken simultaneously; or with inhalant use (due to oxygen deprivation or the toxicity of substances inhaled). Delirium can occur during acute intoxication or during drug or alcohol withdrawal. Some of the neurological damage caused by substance abuse can be reversed. Although sustained abstinence allows new neural pathways to be created, older individuals and chronic users demonstrate less recovery (Yeh et al., 2007).

Treatment and Prevention Considerations

Because neurocognitive disorders have many different causes and are associated with different symptoms and dysfunctions, treatment approaches vary widely. In general, the major interventions for neurocognitive disorders include rehabilitative, medical, and psychological techniques.

Rehabilitation

The key to recovery often involves participation in comprehensive, sustained rehabilitation services. Physical, occupational, speech, and language therapy help individuals relearn skills or compensate for lost abilities. Rehabilitative interventions are often guided by the individual's strengths as well as their deficits. The individual's commitment to and participation in therapy also plays an important role in recovery. Depression, pessimism, and anxiety can stall progress. Fortunately, in many cases, survivors are encouraged when the brain begins to reorganize and skills return as the brain compensates for the damage sustained. Brain changes achieved through rehabilitation can now be documented with imaging techniques (Young & Tolentino, 2010); imaging studies are sometimes used to determine which physical and occupational therapies most effectively enhance brain adaptation (Lin et al., 2010). For example, very encouraging signs of brain reorganization and related recovery of motor function have been documented in individuals treated with constraint-induced therapy, a technique that encourages repeated and intensive use of the side of the body affected by brain damage; use of the unaffected side is physically prohibited by means such as putting the individual's "good arm" in a sling (Lin et al., 2010). This technique helps prevent the "learned nonuse" frequently seen in those with brain damage. Additionally, therapy provided by robotic devices has shown promising results (Young & Tolentino, 2010).

Medication

Medications can help prevent, control, or reduce the symptoms of some neurocognitive disorders. Some medications target physical symptoms of conditions such as epilepsy, PD, or LBD, whereas others help delay the inevitable cognitive decline associated with dementia. Medication can also help prevent recurrence of stroke by treating hypertension or diabetes. Antidepressants are sometimes used to alleviate the depression associated with neurocognitive disorders. In one study, individuals with moderate to severe motor impairment resulting from an ischemic stroke took an antidepressant (fluoxetine) for three months. This group not only regained more muscle function compared to a placebo-control group, but also reported fewer depressive symptoms; the antidepressant may have enhanced progress by reducing cerebral inflammation, improving neurotransmitter functioning, or enhancing participation in physical therapy due to improved mood (Chollet et al., 2011). Although low doses of antipsychotic medication are sometimes used to reduce neurocognitive symptoms such as paranoia, hallucinations, and agitation, the use of antipsychotic medications for the treatment of dementia is discouraged (Treloar, 2010). As mentioned previously, it is often necessary to balance the positive effects and side effects of medications, taking particular care to monitor medication response and potential interactions of multiple medications.

Cognitive and Behavioral Approaches

Cognitive deficits resulting from neurocognitive disorders (e.g., emotional reactivity and diminished ability to concentrate) can hinder recovery or interfere with well-being; psychotherapy can enhance coping and participation in rehabilitation efforts. For example, a cognitive-behavioral treatment targeting depression in individuals with PD included identifying life stressors, training in self-care stress management, relaxation techniques, and cognitive restructuring. The treatment was found to be both feasible and effective (Dobkin et al., 2006).

Cognitive and behavioral techniques are also used to reduce the frequency or severity of problem behaviors, such as aggression or socially inappropriate conduct, or to improve functional skills. Strategies may include social skills training, reducing complex tasks (e.g., dressing or eating) into simpler steps, or simplifying the environment to avoid confusion.

David Young-Wolff / PhotoEdit

Help for People Who Experience Memory Problems

Memory loss can be extremely frustrating. Affected individuals may require constant attention and aid from others in locating items. With labels like the ones shown on the cupboards here, those with memory problems are able to function more independently.

Lifestyle Changes

Lifestyle changes can help prevent or reduce progression of some neurocognitive disorders. For example, treatment for vascular neurocognitive disorders often involves lifestyle changes and interventions (e.g., smoking cessation; weight reduction; and blood sugar, cholesterol, or blood pressure control) to minimize the risk of further damage (Gatz, 2007).

Mental stimulation has been found to both prevent and reduce cognitive decline in some individuals. In a population-based study of elderly individuals in Taiwan, researchers found that participating in social activities (e.g., playing games or volunteering) helped preserve cognitive function over a seven-year follow-up period (Glei et al., 2005). Another large-scale study concluded that mental exercises can improve memory, reasoning ability, and information-processing speed in older adults (Willis et al., 2006). Beneficial activities include playing computer games (Tárraga et al., 2006), reading a newspaper, visiting a library, playing games such as chess or checkers (Wilson, Scherr et al., 2007), or exposure to novel and cognitively challenging tasks (Greenwood & Parasuraman, 2010).

Environmental and Caregiver Support

Although rehabilitation can be very effective with acute conditions such as TBI or stroke, neurodegenerative disorders involving dementia are irreversible and best managed by providing a supportive environment. In many cases, care within a nursing or assisted-living facility is required during the final stages of neurodegenerative conditions, especially those involving dementia, as profound cognitive losses often precede death by a number of years. There are many ways to help those with declining abilities to feel happier and live comfortably and with dignity. Bright lighting has been shown to improve mood and slow cognitive decline in those with dementia (Riemersma-van der Lek et al., 2008). Techniques such as writing answers to questions that are repeatedly asked or labeling family photos can decrease frustration resulting from memory difficulties. Family visits enhance the lives of those with dementia because emotional memories (e.g., happiness seeing a loved one) persist even when the visit itself is no longer recalled (Feinstein, Duff, & Tranela, 2010). Modifying the environment can increase safety and comfort while decreasing confusion and agitation.

Family and friends who provide care may themselves need support. They may feel overwhelmed, helpless, frustrated, anxious, or even angry at having to take care of someone with neurocognitive impairment. Sometimes, agonizing decisions must be made about whether the affected individual can live at home or with relatives versus living in a nursing home or assisted-living facility. Caregivers can benefit from support such as groups composed of other caregivers (Dobkin et al., 2006).

Summary

1. How can we determine whether someone has a neurocognitive disorder?

   - Neurocognitive disorders result from transient or permanent damage to the brain. The effects of brain damage vary greatly.
   - The most common symptoms include impaired consciousness and memory, impaired judgment, orientation difficulties, and attentional deficits.
   - The assessment of brain damage is performed using interviews, psychological tests, brain scans and imaging, and other observational or biological measures.

2. What are the different types of neurocognitive disorders?

   - DSM-5 lists three major types of neurocognitive disorders: major cognitive disorder, mild cognitive disorder, and delirium. In major neurocognitive disorder, significant decline in independent-care skills and cognitive functioning are noted. In mild neurocognitive disorder, cognitive declines are more mild and independent functioning is not compromised.
   - Delirium is characterized by diminished awareness (including disorientation) and impaired attentional skills.

3. What causes neurocognitive disorders?

   - Many different agents can cause neurocognitive disorders; among these are physical wounds or injuries to the brain, substance abuse, processes of aging, and diseases that destroy brain tissue (e.g., meningitis, encephalitis, AIDS).
   - As we age, the proportions of persons with memory problems and cognitive disorders increase. However, many older adults do not suffer from any major cognitive decline.
   - Neurocognitive disorders caused by neurodegenerative processes include conditions characterized by dementia (e.g., Alzheimer's disease, vascular dementia, dementia with Lewy bodies, frontotemporal lobar degeneration) and disorders such as Parkinson's and Huntington's disease that begin with specific symptoms of motor dysfunction.

4. What kinds of interventions can be used to treat people with neurocognitive disorders?

   - Treatment strategies include rehabilitative efforts and cognitive and behavioral therapy. Medication is sometimes used to control the symptoms of the various neurocognitive disorders. Family and caregivers often provide assistance to loved ones with neurocognitive disorders.

Media Resources

Psychology CourseMate   Access an interactive eBook, chapter-specific interactive learning tools, including flash cards, quizzes, videos, and more in your Psychology CourseMate, accessed through CengageBrain.com.

CENGAGENOW

CengageNow   **CengageNOW** is an easy-to-use online resource that helps you study in less time to get the grade you want—NOW. If your textbook does not include an access code card, go to CengageBrain.com to gain access.

CENGAGEbrain.com

CengageBrain   More than just an interactive study guide, WebTutor is an anytime, anywhere customized learning solution with an eBook, keeping you connected to your textbook, instructor, and classmates. Purchase the access chosen by your instructor at CengageBrain.com.

14

© Ariel Skelley/Blend Images/Corbis

moodboard / Alamy

Sexual Dysfunction and Gender Dysphoria

hristina and Jeremiah had been referred for sex therapy by their primary care physician after only eight months of marriage. Both were extremely dissatisfied with their lovemaking: (1) Jeremiah complained that Christina never initiated sex, found excuses to avoid it, and appeared to fake her orgasms during intercourse; and (2) Christina complained that Jeremiah's lovemaking was often brief, perfunctory, and without affection. During the sessions, it became clear that Christina had never had a strong interest in sex and would seldom become aroused during intercourse. Although Jeremiah had never had difficulty with maintaining an erection, sex with Christina had become progressively worrisome, as he often had difficulty getting hard enough for penetration. Before initiating sex, Jeremiah drank heavily to give him "courage" to approach Christina and to alleviate his guilt in "forcing her to have sex." These encounters were often humiliating, as he felt that Christina only agreed to sex due to pity and sufferance.

"I am a woman." This declaration has been frequently voiced by Lana Lawless since her sex reassignment surgery in 2005. Before that date, she had worked for 18 years as a "male" police officer for Rialto, California, in their "gang unit" where Lawless achieved a reputation for being a burly, mean, 245-pound tough cop. "People didn't want to mess with me," she stated. Lawless indicates that beneath her callous exterior, she was always compassionate and sensitive on the inside: "I was always hiding in a straight world. . . . I wanted to be a normal girl." Lawless is notable for another reason as well: She filed and won a lawsuit forcing the Ladies Professional Golf Association (L. P. G. A.) to allow her and transgender persons to compete in their tours (Thomas, 2010) (see Controversy box).

From early childhood, Peter F., a forty-one-year-old man, had fantasies of being mistreated, humiliated, and beaten. He recalls how he would become sexually excited when envisioning such activities. As he grew older, he experienced difficulty achieving an orgasm unless he was able to experience pain inflicted by his sexual partners. He was obsessed with masochistic sexual acts, which made it difficult for him to concentrate on other matters. He had been married and divorced three times because of his proclivity for demanding that his wives engage in "sex games" that involved having them hurt him. These games involved being bound spread-eagled on his bed

focus questions

1 What are normal and abnormal sexual behaviors?

2 What does the normal sexual response cycle tell us about sexual dysfunctions?

3 What causes sexual dysfunctions?

4 What types of treatments are available for sexual dysfunctions?

5 How does aging affect the sexual activity of the elderly?

6 What causes gender dysphoria, and how is it treated?

7 What are the paraphilic disorders, what causes them, and how are they treated?

8 Is rape an act of sex or aggression?

and tortured by whippings, biting of his upper thighs, the sticking of pins into his legs, and other forms of torture. During these sessions, he could ejaculate.

These cases illustrate some of the sexual dysfunctions and disorders we present in this chapter. We discuss the following categories listed in DSM-IV-TR (American Psychiatric Association, 2000a) and also changes in the proposed DSM-5 (DSM-5 Workgroups, 2011):

- *Sexual dysfunctions*, which involve problems in the normal sexual response cycle that affect sexual interest, arousal, and response. The case of Christina and Jeremiah seems to fall into this category.
- *Gender dysphoria/identity disorder*, which involves an incongruity or conflict between one's anatomical sex and one's psychological feeling of being male or female. Lana Lawless had such a conflict.
- *Paraphilic disorders*, which involve sexual urges and fantasies about situations, objects, or people that cause significant distress to self or others, and are not part of the usual arousal pattern leading to reciprocal and affectionate sexual activity. Peter F.'s activities place him in this category.

Before we begin these discussions, however, let's consider another question: How do we decide what constitutes "normal" sexual functioning?

What Is "Normal" Sexual Behavior?

Of all the psychological or psychiatric disorders discussed in this text, sexual dysfunctions and disorders present the greatest difficulty for those attempting to distinguish between "abnormal" (maladaptive) behavior and nonharmful variations that reflect personal values and tastes that are markedly different from social norms (Balon, Segraves, & Clayton, 2007). The definitions of normal sexual behavior vary widely and are influenced by both moral and legal judgments. For example, the laws of some states define oral-genital sex as a "crime against nature." This view is reflected in a California statute that was only repealed in 1976:

Oral Sex Perversion—Any person participating in an act of copulating the mouth of one person with the sexual organ of another is punishable by incarceration in the state prison for a period not exceeding fifteen years, or by imprisonment in the county jail not to exceed one year.

It would be difficult today to justify the classification of oral sex as a "perversion." The pioneering work of Alfred Kinsey and colleagues revealed that oral sex is widespread, especially among the more highly educated part of the population (Kinsey, Pomeroy, Martin, & Gebhard, 1953). In one of the most comprehensive studies conducted on the sexual behavior of 5,865 Americans, 53 percent of men ages 20 to 24 reported giving and 63 percent receiving oral sex from female partners, and 74 percent of women ages 20 to 24 reported giving and 70 percent receiving oral sex from men over a one year period (Herbenick et al., 2010). The percentage is much higher when lifetime rates are reported: 97 percent of men and 88 percent of women ages 25 to 44 have engaged in oral sex with an opposite-sex partner (Herbenick et al., 2010; Mosher, Chandra, & Jones, 2005).

The codification of sexual behavior into law is often based on lack of information regarding normal sexual practices (Table 14.1). For example, in the 1943 *Dittrick v. Brown County* Minnesota Supreme Court ruling, the court upheld the conviction of a father of six as a sexual psychopath because he had an "uncontrollable craving for sexual intercourse with his wife." This "craving" amounted to three or four times a week. If he were tried today, Mr. Dittrick could base his defense on the views of some current researchers who believe that not having sex often *enough* indicates a sexual interest/arousal disorder.

Did You Know?

Sexual activities vary widely among people of different ages, marital status, and nationalities.

- People across the world have sex an average of 97 times a year.

- Fifty-nine percent claim to have sex at least once a week; 4 percent claim to have sex every day.

- Twenty-one- to 34-year-olds have sex the most (113 times/year) compared with 70 for those older than 45.

- Unmarried people living together have more sex (113 times/year) than those married (100) or single (86).

- One in 10 people has never had sex.

Source: Durex (2001, 2005)

Cultural Influences and Sexuality

Sexuality is influenced by how it is viewed in different cultures. Some societies have very rigid social, cultural, and religious taboos associated with exposure of the human body, whereas other societies are more open. Note the contrast between the Muslim and American teens shown here.

Classification of normal and abnormal behavior becomes especially difficult when one compares Western and non-Western cultures or different time periods within a particular culture (Rathus, Nevid, & Fichner-Rathus, 2005). For example, the Japanese have significantly less sexual intercourse than Americans (70 percent less), as is the case in many Asian countries (Durex, 2005). Should we conclude that Asians are more prone to sexual interest/arousal disorders, or do cultural factors account for the lower rate? In ancient Greece, homosexuality was not only accepted but encouraged. In many countries, sex with animals is fairly common among rural youths but is rare among urban boys. Thus it is clear that definitions of sexual disorders are also strongly influenced by cultural norms and values.

If legal, moral, and, statistical models fall short of the viable definition of normal sexual behavior that is needed, can we resolve the controversy by simply stating that sexual behavior is deviant if it is a threat to society, causes distress to participants, or impairs social or occupational functioning? Using this definition, there would be no objection to our considering rape as deviant behavior; it includes the elements of nonconsent, force, and victimization. But what about sexual arousal to an inanimate object (fetishism), low sexual drive, or gender dysphoria? These conditions are not threats to society, they may not cause distress to people who experience them, and they may not result in impaired social or occupational functioning. They are deviant simply because they do not fall within "normal arousal and activity patterns." And they are considered deviant even though what constitutes a normal sexual pattern is the subject of controversy (Balon, Segraves, & Clayton, 2007; Gierhart, 2006). This concern has been voiced by many that paraphilias (sexual attraction and fantasies to nonhuman objects, nonconsenting persons, or suffering and humiliation), for example, are not *ipso facto* psychiatric disorders (Blanchard, Lykins, Wherret, Kuban, Cantor, & Blak, 2009). They may be non-normative behaviors, but not pathological. In short, ambiguities surround all the classification systems, and the controversies become more obvious as we discuss the three groups of sexual disorders and rape in the remainder of this chapter.

Did You Know?

In a national survey of eighteen- to forty-four-year-olds, 90 percent of men identified themselves as heterosexual, 2.3 percent homosexual, 1.8 percent bisexual, and 3.9 percent something else; 1.8 percent did not respond. For women the responses were nearly identical: 90 percent heterosexual, 1.3 percent homosexual, 2.8 percent bisexual, and 3.8 percent something else; 1.8 percent did not answer.

Source: Mosher, Chandra, & Jones, (2005)

The Study of Human Sexuality

Because sexual behavior is such an important part of our lives and because so many taboos and myths surround it, people have great difficulty dealing with the topic in an open and direct manner (Ohl, 2007). To some extent, Freud made the discussion of sexual topics more acceptable when he made sex (libido) an important part of psychoanalytic theory.

TABLE 14.1   Percentage of Americans Performing Certain Sexual Behaviors in the Past Year (N = 5865)

Sexual Behaviors	Age Groups									
	14–15		16–17		18–19		20–24		25–29	
	Men	Women	Men	Women	Men	Women	Men	Women	Men	Women
Masturbated Alone	62%	40%	75%	45%	81%	60%	83%	64%	84%	72%
Masturbated with Partner	5%	8%	15%	19%	43%	36%	44%	36%	49%	48%
Received Oral from Women	12%	1%	31%	5%	54%	4%	63%	9%	77%	3%
Received Oral from Men	1%	10%	3%	24%	6%	58%	6%	70%	5%	72%
Gave Oral to Women	8%	2%	18%	7%	51%	2%	55%	9%	74%	3%
Gave Oral to Men	1%	12%	2%	22%	4%	59%	7%	74%	5%	76%
Vaginal Intercourse	9%	11%	30%	30%	53%	62%	63%	80%	86%	87%
Received Penis in Anus	1%	4%	1%	5%	4%	18%	5%	23%	4%	21%
Inserted Penis into Anus	3%		6%		6%		11%		27%	

Source: Herbenick et al., (2010).

His knowledge of sexual practices and behavior, however, was largely confined to his clinical cases and his speculations from the understanding of social mores.

Our contemporary understanding of human sexual physiology and sexual practices and customs is based on the works of Alfred Kinsey and his colleagues (Kinsey, Pomeroy, & Martin, 1948; Kinsey, Pomeroy, Martin, & Gebhard, 1953), William Masters and Virginia Johnson in their seminal works *Human Sexual Response* (1966) and *Human Sexual Inadequacy* (1970), on the *Janus Report* (Janus & Janus, 1993), the findings of the National Survey of Sexual Health and Behavior (Reese, Herbinick, Schick, Sanders, Dodge, & Fortenberry, 2010), and on the work of other contemporary sex researchers. Although the nature of the subject matter and the means used to obtain the information proved controversial and provocative, these studies dispelled myths and provided explicit evidence of human sexual responsiveness, attitudes, and practices.

The Sexual Response Cycle

Treating human sexual dysfunction requires an understanding of the normal sexual response cycle, which traditionally consists of four stages: appetitive (interest), arousal, orgasm, and resolution (Figure 14.1). Originally, Masters and Johnson (1966) proposed only three stages; they included the appetitive stage with the arousal phase. Because of the clinical work of sex therapist Helen Singer Kaplan (1974), most models of sexual response have identified the appetitive or desire stage as distinct. But empirical findings suggest that it is difficult to distinguish between desire and subjective arousal, that they overlap, and that desire may precede or follow arousal (Brotto, 2009; Graham, Sanders, Milhausen, & McBride, 2004; Hartmann et al., 2002). Thus, although we maintain the four stage description, it is best to perceive the appetitive and arousal stages as intertwined and interactive.

1. The *appetitive phase* is characterized by the person's interest in sexual activity. The person begins to have thoughts or fantasies surrounding sex. He or she may begin to feel attracted to another person and to daydream increasingly about sex.
2. The *arousal phase*, which may follow or precede the *appetitive phase*, is heightened and intensified when specific and direct—but not necessarily physical—sexual stimulation occurs. Heart rate, blood pressure, and respiration rate increase. In the male, blood flow increases in the penis, resulting in an erection (Figure 14.2). The ridge around the head of the penis turns deep purple,

Age Groups									
30–39		40–49		50–59		60–69		70+	
Men	Women	Men	Women	Men	Women	Men	Women	Men	Women
80%	63%	76%	65%	72%	54%	61%	47%	46%	33%
45%	43%	38%	35%	28%	18%	17%	13%	13%	5%
78%	5%	62%	2%	49%	1%	38%	1%	19%	2%
6%	59%	6%	52%	8%	34%	3%	25%	2%	8%
69%	4%	57%	3%	44%	1%	34%	1%	24%	2%
5%	59%	7%	53%	8%	34%	3%	25%	2%	8%
85%	74%	74%	70%	58%	51%	54%	42%	43%	22%
3%	22%	4%	12%	5%	6%	1%	4%	2%	1%
24%		21%		11%		6%		2%	

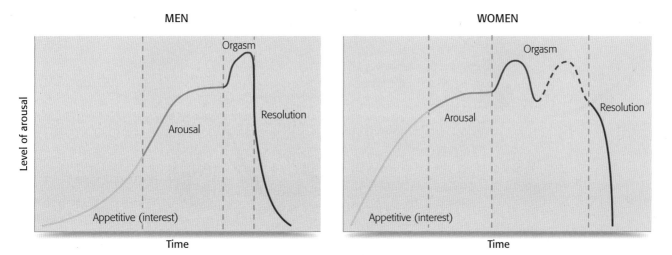

Figure 14.1

HUMAN SEXUAL RESPONSE CYCLE

The studies of Masters and Johnson reveal similar normal sexual response cycles for men and women. Note that women may experience more than one orgasm. Sexual disorders may occur at any of the phases, but seldom at the resolution phase.

Copyright © Cengage Learning, 2013

and the testes enlarge and elevate in preparation for ejaculation. In the female, the breasts swell, nipples become erect, blood engorges the genital region, and the clitoris expands (Figure 14.3). Vaginal lubrication reflexively occurs, and a sex flush may appear on the skin (usually later in this phase).

3. The *orgasm phase* is characterized by involuntary muscular contractions throughout the body and the eventual release of sexual tension. In the man, muscles at the base of the penis contract, propelling semen through the penis. In the woman, the outer third of the vagina contracts rhythmically. Following orgasm, men enter a refractory period during which they are unresponsive to sexual stimulation. However, women are capable of multiple orgasms with continued stimulation.

4. The *resolution phase* is characterized by relaxation of the body after orgasm. Heart rate, blood pressure, and respiration return to normal.

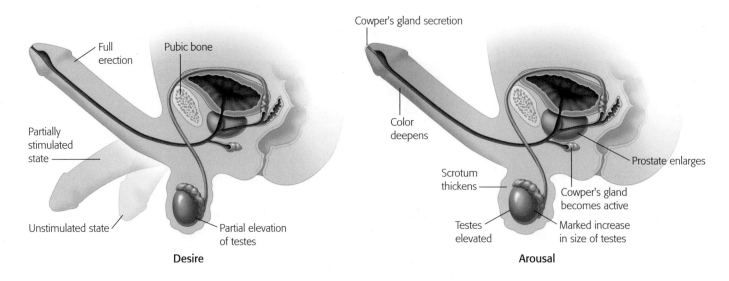

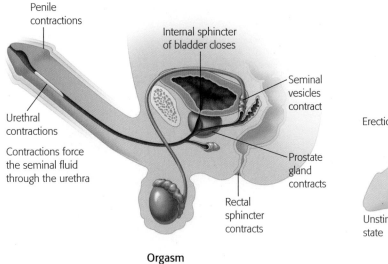

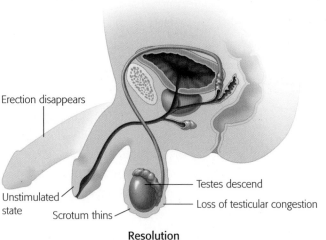

Figure 14.2

GENITAL CHANGES ASSOCIATED WITH STAGES OF THE HUMAN MALE SEXUAL RESPONSE CYCLE
Although we often focus on the differences between men and women, Masters and Johnson found that the physiological responses of both to sexual stimulation are quite similar. (Compare this figure with Figure 14.3.)

Copyright © Cengage Learning, 2013

Problems may occur in any of the phases of the sexual response cycle, although they are rare in the resolution phase. If problems related to interest, arousal, or orgasm are recurrent and persistent, they may be diagnosed as dysfunctions.

Sexual Dysfunctions

A sexual dysfunction is a disruption of any part of the normal sexual response cycle that affects sexual interest, arousal, and response. Problems in sexual functioning, such as early (premature) ejaculation, low sexual interest/arousal, and difficulties in achieving orgasm, are quite common in our society. Epidemiological data suggest that 40 to 45 percent of adult women and 20 to 30 percent of adult men suffer from at least one sexual dysfunction (Lewis et al., 2004). Lifetime prevalence of sexual problems in adults at some time in their lives is summarized in Table 14.2.

sexual dysfunction a disruption of any part of the normal sexual response cycle that affects sexual desire, arousal, and response

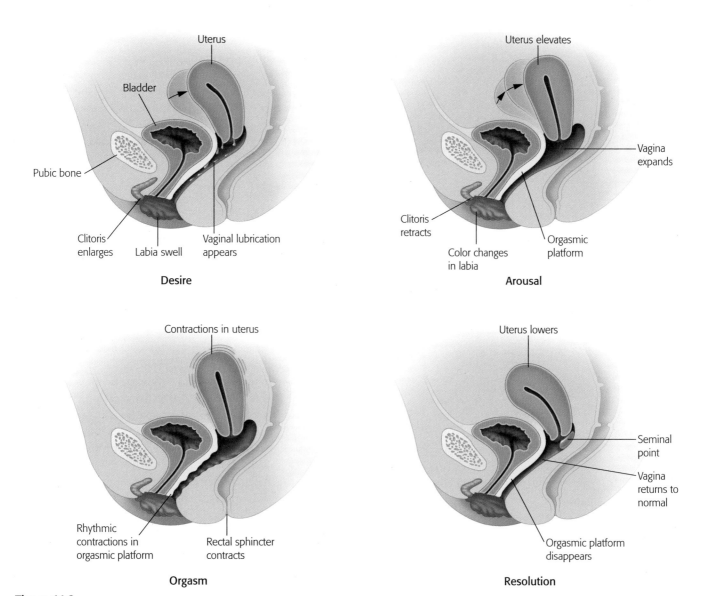

Figure 14.3

GENITAL CHANGES ASSOCIATED WITH STAGES OF THE HUMAN FEMALE SEXUAL RESPONSE CYCLE
Although we often focus on the differences between men and women, Masters and Johnson found that the physiological responses of both to sexual stimulation are quite similar. (Compare this figure with Figure 14.2.)
Copyright © Cengage Learning, 2013

TABLE 14.2 Lifetime Prevalence of Sexual Disorders in Men and Women in the 40–80 Age Range for Non-European Countries

Condition	Women	Men
Lack of interest in sex	32.9%	17.6%
Inability to reach orgasm	25.2%	14.5%
Orgasm too quickly	10.5%	27.4%
Pain during sex	14.0%	3.5%
Sex not pleasurable	21.5%	12.1%
Trouble lubricating	27.1%	N/A

Source: Laumann, Glasser, Neves, & Moreira, (2009)

Understanding Sexuality

Through their clinical research and well-known publications, *Human Sexual Response* (1966) and *Human Sexual Inadequacy* (1970), William Masters and Virginia Johnson have done much to further understanding and dispel myths of human sexuality.

To be diagnosed as a dysfunction, the disruption must be recurrent and persistent. DSM-IV-TR also requires that such factors as frequency, chronicity, subjective distress, and effect on other areas of functioning be considered in the diagnosis. As indicated in Table 14.3, the DSM-IV-TR categories for sexual dysfunctions are *sexual desire disorders, sexual arousal disorders, orgasmic disorders*, and *sexual pain disorders*. Prevalence of the sexual dysfunctions is summarized here as well. Please note that DSM-5 is proposing minor classification changes in May 2013 that are not necessarily reflected on the table.

Sexual Interest/Arousal Disorders

Sexual interest/arousal disorders in women and men are related to the appetitive and arousal phases and are characterized by a lack of sexual interest/arousal over a prolonged period of time. These disorders are problems that occur during the excitement phase and that relate to difficulties with feelings of sexual pleasure or with the physiological changes associated with sexual excitement. In DSM-IV they include *hypoactive sexual desire disorder*, characterized by little or no interest in sexual activities, either actual or fantasized; *sexual aversion disorder*, characterized by an avoidance of and aversion to sexual intercourse; and for women, *female sexual arousal disorder*, an inability to attain or maintain physiological response and/or psychological arousal during sexual activity. The DSM-5 Work Group (2011) is proposing to (a) remove *sexual aversion disorder* from this category, and (b) make distinct, separate, and parallel diagnoses for *sexual interest/arousal disorders in women* and *sexual interest/arousal disorders in men*.

Despite the direction they elect to take, sexual interest/arousal disorders in men and women can be lifelong or acquired or generalized or situational and caused by relationship factors and/or a combination of psychological and biological factors (Hackett, 2008; Perlman, Martin, Hirdes, & Curtin-Telegdi, 2007; van Lankveld, 2008). For women, this disorder is often the result of negative attitudes about sex or early sexual experiences. Receiving negative information about sex, having been sexually assaulted or molested, and having conflicts with a sexual partner can contribute to the disorder (Perlman, Martin, Hirdes, & Curtin-Telegdi, 2007). Some people may report low sexual interest because of inexperience. Many of these people may not have learned to label or identify their own arousal levels, may not know how to increase their arousal, and may have a limited expectation for their ability to be aroused (van Lankveld, 2008).

Some clinicians estimate that 40 to 50 percent of all sexual dysfunctions involve deficits in interest, and it is now the most common complaint of couples seeking sex therapy (Laumann, Glasser, Neves, & Moreira, 2009; McAnulty & Burnette, 2004). Although people with sexual interest/arousal disorders are often capable of experiencing orgasm, they claim to have little interest in, or to derive no pleasure from, sexual activity. In the following case, relationship problems contributed to the sexual dysfunction.

Case Study

Rhonda and Michael had been married for five years and sought sex therapy because of their unsatisfactory sexual encounters. Although they had enjoyed sex for the first five to six months of their marriage, sexual intercourse had progressively declined: For the past three years they have had little or no sexual

TABLE 14.3   Sexual Dysfunctions

Sexual Dysfunction	Symptoms	Prevalence	Age of Onset	Course
Sexual Interest Disorders	—**Problems during the appetitive phase** —**Hypoactive sexual desire disorder** Absent or low sexual interest/desire —**Sexual aversion disorder** Avoidance of/aversion to sexual intercourse	20% of adult population; women have higher rates (20–35%) than men (15%)	Usually noticed in adulthood by a partner who complains	May be lifelong or acquired; treatment may help
Sexual Arousal Disorders	—**Problems of sexual pleasure or physiological changes involving sexual excitement** —**Erectile disorder (ED)** Inability to attain/maintain an erection sufficient for sexual intercourse and/or psychological arousal during sexual activity —**Female sexual arousal disorder** Inability to attain/maintain physiological response and/or psychological arousal during sexual activity	10% of men report ED; some 50% have experienced "transient" conditions; 10–50% of women suffer from arousal lubrication problems	Can occur at age of sexual maturity but increases with age, especially in men	Most can be helped by psychological or medical treatment
Orgasmic Disorders	—**Problems with the orgasm phase** —**Female/male orgasmic disorder** Persistent delay or inability to achieve orgasm after reaching excitement phase —**Early (premature) ejaculation** Ejaculation with minimal sexual stimulation before, during, or shortly after penetration	Early (premature) ejaculation estimates from 30–50%; 3–10% of nonclinical population suffer from inhibited male orgasm; 10% of women have never experienced an orgasm	At age of sexual maturity	In men, often related to performance anxiety; in women, lack of foreplay is most frequent reason
Genital-Pelvic Pain/ Penetration Disorders	—**Dyspareunia** Genital pain in a man or woman not primarily due to lack of lubrication in the vagina or vaginismus —**Vaginismus** Involuntary spasm of the outer third of the vaginal wall that prevents or interferes with sexual intercourse	Dyspareunia is relatively rare in men but more common in women (17–19%); vaginismus occurs in less than 1% of females	Can occur because of medical problems (such as injury to the pelvis) or traumatic event	Most have physical causes and can be treated

Source: Data from American Psychiatric Association, (2000a); Spector & Carey, (1990); LoPiccolo, (1995, 1997); Hooper, (1998); Paik & Laumann, (2006)

contact. Rhonda found that gentle fondling was enjoyable to both of them, but as their relationship progressed to genital caressing, she became more anxious, despite being easily orgasmic. Michael described her as "punitive, angry, and a vengeful person" and believed she was punishing him for a brief affair he had with a coworker. Rhonda described Michael as "unloving, cold, angry, controlling, and demanding." Naturally, she did not feel loving or sexually interested or receptive. Correspondingly, he felt angry, resentful, and cheated of a "normal sex life."

In this case, Rhonda was diagnosed as suffering from a sexual dysfunction because of her low sexual desire and interest toward Michael. Many people, however question the legitimacy of such a diagnosis. They challenge the idea that sexual problems stemming from a troubled relationship or from job or academic stress are sufficient to indicate a disorder (Balon, Segraves, & Clayton, 2007).

hypoactive sexual desire disorder sexual dysfunction that is related to the appetitive phase of the sexual response cycle and is characterized by a lack of sexual desire

sexual arousal disorder disorder characterized by problems occurring during the excitement phase of the sexual response cycle and relating to difficulties with feelings of sexual pleasure or with the physiological changes associated with sexual excitement

female sexual arousal disorder the inability to attain or maintain physiological response and/or psychological arousal during sexual activity

There is an even larger issue in diagnosing these problems. As noted earlier in this chapter, we do not really know what constitutes "normal" sexual interest, and we know little about what frequency of sexual fantasies or what activities are "normal." Kinsey and colleagues (1948) found tremendous variation in reported total sexual outlet, or release. One man reported that he had ejaculated only once in thirty years; another claimed to have averaged thirty orgasms per week for thirty years. However, using some average frequency of sexual activity does not seem appropriate for categorizing people as having low sexual interest. One person may have a high sex drive but not engage in sexual activities; another may not have sexual interest or fantasies but may engage in frequent sexual behaviors for the sake of his or her partner.

Furthermore, using number of orgasms (intercourse or masturbation) or desire for orgasms may introduce gender bias into the definition of "normal" sexual desire. The *Janus Report* indicated that, for all age groups, men masturbate and experience orgasms more than women do (Janus & Janus, 1993). Does this mean that women's sexual interest is less than that of men? Until we can decide on a normal range of sexual interest and desire, we can hardly discover the causes of sexual interest disorders or develop treatment programs for them.

Did You Know?

Men think about sex significantly more often than women.

Thoughts of Sex	Once or Several Times a Day	Weekly or Monthly	Less Than Once a Month/Never
Men	54%	43%	4%
Women	19%	67%	14%

Adapted from Michael, Gagnon, Laumann, & Kolata, (1994)

Erectile Disorder

In men, inhibited sexual excitement takes the form of an erectile disorder (ED), an inability to attain or maintain an erection sufficient for sexual intercourse and/or psychological arousal during sexual activity (Segraves, 2010). The man may feel fully aroused, but he cannot finish the sex act. In the past, such a dysfunction has been attributed primarily to psychological causes ("It's all in the head"). Masters and Johnson (1970), for example, estimated that only about 5 percent of erectile dysfunctions were due to physical conditions. However, studies indicate that from 30 percent to as many as 70 percent of erectile dysfunctions are caused by some form of vascular insufficiency, such as diabetes, atherosclerosis, or traumatic groin injury, or by other physiological factors (Lewis, Yuan, & Wang, 2008; Lewis et al., 2004). A primary reason that DSM includes general medical conditions as a factor in sexual dysfunctions is that a man may also have a minor organic impairment that makes him more vulnerable to experiencing ED because of other psychological, social, or sexual stressors.

Distinguishing between erectile dysfunctions that are primarily biological and those that are primarily psychological has been difficult (Lewis, Yuan, & Wang, 2008) (Table 14.4). For example, one procedure involves recording nocturnal penile tumescence (NPT). During sleep, men have frequent erections. If, however, they suffer from an organic problem, they are not able to have erections during the waking state. Psychological distress is minimized during sleep and should not impair erections. Thus men who do not display adequate spontaneous erections during sleep suffer from an organic impairment, and psychological causes are thought to predominate in men who have such erections. Unfortunately, considerable overlap in NPT scores has been found between samples of diabetic men with erectile difficulties and normally functioning men in control groups (Lewis, Yuan, & Wang, 2008; Lue, 2002). Therefore, some people diagnosed with organic impotence may actually have a psychologically based impotence. The reverse could also be true.

Primary erectile dysfunction is the diagnosis for a man who has never been able to engage successfully in sexual intercourse. This difficulty often has a clear psychological origin, because many men with this dysfunction can get an erection and reach orgasm during masturbation and can show erection during the REM (rapid eye movement) phase of sleep. In *secondary erectile dysfunction*, the man has had at least one successful instance of sexual intercourse but is currently unable to achieve an erection and penetration in 25 percent or more of his sexual attempts (Masters & Johnson, 1970).

TABLE 14.4   Some Possible Physical/Neurogenic Causes of Erectile Disorder

- **Alcoholism (neuropathy)**
- **Diabetes mellitus**
- **Arterial disease**
- **Renal failure**
- **Carcinomatosis**
- **Neurosyphilis**
- **Hypothalamo-pituitary dysfunction**
- **Liver failure**
- **Multiple sclerosis**
- **Parkinson's disease**
- **Stroke**
- **Alzheimer's disease**
- **Penile injury**
- **Aging**

Source: Lewis, Yuan, & Wang, (2008)

erectile disorder (ED)   an inability to attain or maintain an erection sufficient for sexual intercourse and/or psychological arousal during sexual activity

Case Study

A twenty-year-old college student was suffering from secondary erectile dysfunction. His first episode of erectile difficulty occurred when he attempted sexual intercourse after drinking heavily. Although to a certain extent he attributed the failure to alcohol, he also began to have doubts about his sexual ability. During a subsequent sexual encounter, his anxiety and worry increased. When he failed in this next coital encounter, even though he had not been drinking, his anxiety level rose even more. The client sought therapy after the discovery that he was unable to have an erection even during petting.

The prevalence rate of ED is difficult to determine because it is often unreported. Clinicians estimate that approximately 50 percent of men have experienced transient impotence (Feldman, Goldstein, Hatzichristou, Krane, & McKinlay, 1994). Of 448 men with sexual dysfunctions treated at the Masters and Johnson sex clinic, 32 were suffering from primary ED and 213 from secondary ED. Before the introduction of drugs such as Cialis, Levitra, and Viagra, the generally accepted figure of ED among men was between 10 million and 15 million (Leary, 1992). Current estimates of erectile problems place the figure at approximately 30 million (Hooper, 1998). Several factors may be contributing to this increase in the number of reported cases: (1) an increasing acceptance that the dysfunction may be caused by some physical condition and not by feelings of "psychological inadequacy"; (2) the availability of drugs such as Viagra as a nonintrusive successful treatment; (3) an increasing willingness among men to talk about this problem; and (4) a greater acceptance of women's right to expect satisfaction in sexual relationships.

Hypersexual Disorder?

Is there such a thing as sexual addiction or a compulsion to have sex? Can a person be "oversexed" and have a sexual appetite that requires frequent sex in order to be satisfied? Golfer Tiger Woods, actor David Duchovny (*X-Files*), and TV reality star Jesse James (ex-husband of actress Sandra Bullock) have admitted to suffering from sex addiction, and entered rehabilitation centers for treatment. In all three cases, their "compulsions" to have sex with multiple partners resulted in marital/pair-bond dysfunctions and/or negative personal/professional consequences. Is sexual addiction a real disease or simply an excuse?

Most sex therapists are in agreement that some individuals seem obsessed with sex, feel compelled to engage in frequent sexual activity, and find their behavior causes them personal distress. Even the Masters and Johnson Therapy Clinic has a residential treatment center for sexual addiction and has used such terms as *hypersexuality, erotomania, nymphomania*, and *satyriasis* to refer to this phenomenon. More than 4 percent of people claim to have sex every day; 2 percent of married men and 1 percent of married women have intercourse more than once a day (Durex, 2001, 2005). By statistical standards, would these people be considered abnormal?

Compulsive sexual behavior is a term used by many sex therapists to describe individuals who seem to crave constant sex at the expense of relationships, work productivity, and daily activities. These individuals may spend excessive time thinking about sexual fantasies and urges and planning for and engaging in one or more of the following sexual behaviors: masturbation, watching or reading pornography, having sex with multiple consenting adults, engaging in cybersex, engaging in telephone sex, and attending strip clubs (Kafka, 2009; McBride, Reece, & Sanders, 2008). Although the current DSM does not recognize the existence of sexual addiction per se, the DSM-5 Work Group is considering a new diagnostic category called hypersexual disorder.

Sufficient clinical and research findings support the existence of individuals who seem to suffer from a hypersexual disorder. These people seem to exhibit recurrent sexual fantasies, urges, and behaviors manifested in the following ways: (1) excessive time consumed by sexual urges and thoughts; (2) repetitively engaging in sexual fantasies and behaviors in response to dysphoric mood states like depression, anxiety, boredom,

hypersexual disorder individuals who seem to crave constant sex at the expense of relationships, work productivity, and daily activities

and irritability; (3) repetitively engaging in sexual urges and behaviors due to stressful life events; (4) repetitive unsuccessful attempts to reduce or control sexual urges, activities, and fantasies; and (5) repetitively engaging in sexual urges and behaviors while disregarding the risk for physical/emotional harm to self or others (DSM-5 Work Group, 2011). In addition to personal psychological distress (guilt, shame, anxiety, depression, and loss of control), the consequences of the disorder may include relationship problems, divorce/separation, increased rate of sexually transmitted disease, unintended pregnancies, excessive spending on sexual services, and school/employment dysfunction (Kafka, 2009; Reid, Harper, & Anderson, 2009; McBride, Reece, & Sanders, 2008).

There is a significant gap in knowledge as to the causes of a hypersexual disorder. Some might argue that the disorder is simply an excuse to escape responsibility for immoral conduct like infidelity. Further, developmental risk factors, family history, cognitive markers, and the direct neurobiological substrates are relatively unknown for the disorder. Kafka (2009), however, argues that enough evidence exists to warrant the existence of hypersexual disorder as a separate and distinct diagnostic criterion in DSM-5. It appears that by whatever name we call it, hypersexual disorders can cause real harm to not only the individual, but to others as well.

Did You Know?

Some people take pride in claiming they are hypersexual. A strong sexual libido is often valued by our society because it connotes potency, power, attractiveness, sensual pleasure, and health. Indeed, the search for aphrodisiacs in the form of powdered animal genitals, herbs, secret concoctions, and even drugs such as Viagra is a multibillion-dollar industry. So there are many in our society who would value a strong sex drive, especially if they do not experience personal distress over their behaviors and if it does not interfere with their ability to function in their many roles in life.

Orgasmic Disorders

An orgasmic disorder may be manifested in several different ways. In women there may be a marked delay, infrequency, or an inability to achieve an orgasm after entering the excitement phase and receiving adequate sexual stimulation, and/or a marked reduced intensity of orgasmic sensation. Men may suffer from two forms of an orgasmic disorder: (1) delayed ejaculation even in the face of adequate stimulation, or (2) early (premature) ejaculation with minimal stimulation, leading to dissatisfaction and lack of fulfillment of one or both partners.

Female Orgasmic Disorder

A woman with female orgasmic disorder (FOD) experiences persistent delay or inability to achieve an orgasm with stimulation that is "adequate in focus, intensity, and duration" after entering the excitement phase. If an orgasm occurs, she may report it as "greatly diminished in intensity and pleasure." Whether the lack of orgasm or reduced pleasure is categorized as a dysfunction or as a "normal variant" is left to the judgment of the clinician. Again, the criteria that define adequate functioning during sexual intercourse are quite controversial (Balon, 2008).

Female orgasmic disorders may be termed *primary*, to indicate that orgasm has never been experienced, or *secondary*, to show that orgasm has been experienced. FOD is the second most frequently reported sexual problem for women (Meston, Seal, & Hamilton, 2008). Primary orgasmic dysfunction is considered relatively common in women: Approximately 10 percent of all women have never achieved an orgasm (Rosen & Lieblum, 1995). This disorder is not equivalent to primary orgasmic disorder in males, who often can achieve orgasm through masturbation or by some other means.

female orgasmic disorder a sexual dysfunction in which the woman experiences persistent delay or inability to achieve an orgasm with stimulation that is adequate in focus, intensity, and duration after entering the excitement phase; also known as *inhibited female orgasm*

delayed ejaculation (male orgasmic disorder) persistent delay or inability to achieve an orgasm after the excitement phase has been reached and sexual activity has been adequate in focus, intensity, and duration; usually restricted to an inability to ejaculate within the vagina; also known as *inhibited male orgasm*

Delayed Ejaculation (Male Orgasmic Disorder)

Delayed ejaculation (male orgasmic disorder) is the persistent delay or inability to achieve an orgasm after the excitement phase has been reached and sexual activity has been adequate in focus, intensity, and duration. The DSM-5 Work Group (2011) is considering renaming male orgasmic disorder to "delayed ejaculation" because it is a more accurate descriptor. The term is usually restricted to the delay or inability to ejaculate within the vagina, even with full arousal and penile erection. As noted, men who have this dysfunction can usually ejaculate when masturbating. Inhibited orgasm in males is relatively rare, and little is known about it (McAnulty & Burnette, 2004). Treatment is often urged by the wife, who may want to conceive or who may feel (because of the husband's lack of orgasm) that she is unattractive. Delayed ejaculation is probably the least understood, least common, and least researched of all the sexual dysfunctions (Perelman & Rowland, 2008).

Early Ejaculation

The inability to satisfy a sexual partner is a source of anguish for many men. Early ejaculation (premature) is ejaculation with minimal sexual stimulation before, during, or shortly after penetration. It is believed to be the most common type of male sexual dysfunction, affecting 21 to 33 percent of men (Walling, 2007). Table 14.5 provides comparison responses between a group of men with and without early ejaculation problems. The DSM-5 Work Group (2011) is considering the use of a dimensional assessment scale to measure rapid ejaculation: 0 = 60 seconds or more; 1 = between 45 and 60 seconds; 2 = between 30 and 45 seconds; 3 = between 15 and 30 seconds; 4 = start of sexual activity; and 5 = prior to start of sexual activity. Sex researchers and therapists, however, differ in their criteria for prematurity. Kaplan (1974) defined *prematurity* as the inability of a man to tolerate high (plateau) levels of sexual excitement without ejaculating reflexively. Kilmann and Auerbach (1979) suggested that ejaculation less than five minutes after coital entry is a suitable criterion of prematurity. Masters and Johnson (1970) contended that a man who is unable to delay ejaculation long enough during sexual intercourse to produce an orgasm in the woman 50 percent of the time is a premature ejaculator. The difficulty with the latter definition is the possibility that a man may be "premature" with one partner but entirely adequate for another.

Genital-Pelvic Pain/Penetration Disorder

Genital-pelvic pain/penetration disorders can be manifested in both males and females in a condition termed dyspareunia, which is a recurrent or persistent pain in the genitals before, during, or after sexual intercourse. It is estimated that the lifetime prevalence rate is 17 to 19 percent (Paik & Laumann, 2006). Dyspareunia is not caused exclusively by lack of lubrication or by vaginismus, which is an involuntary spasm of the outer third of the vaginal wall that prevents or interferes with sexual intercourse. The incidence of vaginismus is not known, but it is considered very rare. The DSM-5 Work Group (2011) has observed that the reliability of differentiating between dyspareunia and vaginismus is difficult and unreliable. Thus, they are proposing that these conditions be described under a broader overarching umbrella: genital-pelvic pain/penetration disorder.

early ejaculation ejaculation with minimal sexual stimulation before, during, or shortly after penetration

genital-pelvic pain/penetration disorder includes previous diagnoses of vaginismus and dyspareunia and involves physical pain or discomfort associated with intercourse/penetration; fear, anxiety and distress is also usually present

dyspareunia recurrent or persistent pain in the genitals before, during, or after sexual intercourse

vaginismus involuntary spasm of the outer third of the vaginal wall that prevents or interferes with sexual intercourse

TABLE 14.5 Mean Responses of Men with and without Early Ejaculation

Item	Early	Controls
1. **Over the past month, was your control over ejaculation during sexual intercourse? (0 = very poor; 4 = good)**	0.9	3.0
2. **Over the past month, was your satisfaction with sexual intercourse? (0 = very poor; 4 = very good)**	1.9	3.3
3. **How distressed are you by how fast you ejaculate during intercourse? (4 = extremely distressed; 0 = not at all)**	2.9	0.7
4. **To what extent does how fast you ejaculate cause difficulty in your relationship with your partner? (4 = extremely; 0 = not at all)**	1.9	0.3

Source: Items taken from the Premature Ejaculation Profile, Rowland et al., (2007)

■ Etiology of Sexual Dysfunctions

There is perhaps no other group of mental disorders in which the interaction of biological, psychological, social, and sociocultural dimensions are as clearly demonstrated as in the etiology of sexual dysfunctions. Nor are there disorders that so directly illustrate how these dimensions can interact with one another to create sexual problems (Lussier, McCann, & Beauregard, 2008; Ohl, 2007). Let's return to the case of Jeremiah and Christina in our chapter opener to illustrate how various etiological factors can contribute to sexual dysfunctions. (You may wish to reread the case in order to follow our multipath analysis.)

Recall that both came for sex therapy because Christina did not seem to desire nor enjoy sex and Jeremiah was experiencing erection difficulties during their lovemaking. Christina was diagnosed as suffering from a sexual interest arousal disorder and Jeremiah from an erectile disorder. The possibility that Christina could also be suffering from an orgasmic disorder was entertained but eliminated as therapy progressed. It appeared that she was quite capable of being aroused and orgasmic under the right conditions.

Studies suggest that sexual interest/desire is due to a combination of biological, psychological, social, and sociocultural factors (Heard-Davison, Heiman, & Briggs, 2004; Nanda, 2008). On the biological level, hormones such as prolactin, testosterone, and estrogen affect high or low levels of sexual desire (Hyde, 2005; van Lankveld, 2008). On a psychological level, negative childhood experiences such as sexual abuse, strict moralistic upbringing, and positive or negative attitudes toward sex affect fantasy and desire ("Study Confirms Importance of Sexual Fantasies," 2007). Likewise, social and sociocultural factors such as a dysfunctional partner or marital relationships that are full of anger or resentment and gender scripts ("Good girls do not initiate sex" or "They enjoy it as much as men") can affect desire.

A similar analysis can be applied to Jeremiah and his problems with maintaining an erection during intercourse. His past sexual history revealed no significant erectile problems until his marriage to Christina. Although his increasing ED seems more related to psychological causes, his heavy drinking affects his biological sexual response cycle. Although consumption of alcohol might decrease inhibition (and thereby increase his courage), it is a central nervous system suppressant that makes it more difficult for any man to achieve an erection. For Jeremiah, it is clear that he is also suffering from guilt, humiliation, and anger toward Christina, whom he may blame for his problem. As a man, he may also operate from a *cultural script*—a social and cultural belief and expectation that guides our behaviors regarding sex—that equates masculinity with sexual potency. Given these facts, the following multipath explanation of the couple's sexual difficulties might be operative (Figure 14.4).

Case Study

Jeremiah and Christina's sexual disorders are intertwined in their relationship (social) and cannot be viewed in isolation (interactive). Christina's low sexual interest (biological) makes Jeremiah doubt his own sexual attractiveness (psychological) and increases his anxiety levels so that it affects his ability to achieve an erection. He drinks heavily to reduce his anxiety and to decrease his inhibitions about initiating sex. Alcohol and his anxiety affect his ability to achieve and maintain an erection (biological). When he does achieve an erection, he quickly enters Christina for fear of losing it (psychological), and in turn becomes "brief and perfunctory in lovemaking." The brevity of the sexual encounter does not allow Christina to become sexually aroused, to become sufficiently lubricated (biological; intercourse becomes painful), or to achieve an orgasm, so she "fakes it" in order to please him. Jeremiah, however, knows it is faked and not only blames himself for the failure (psychological) but feels humiliated by her "pity." He may begin to equate his inability to satisfy Christina with "not being a real man" (sociocultural). Both find the encounter unpleasant (social). The cycle then repeats itself.

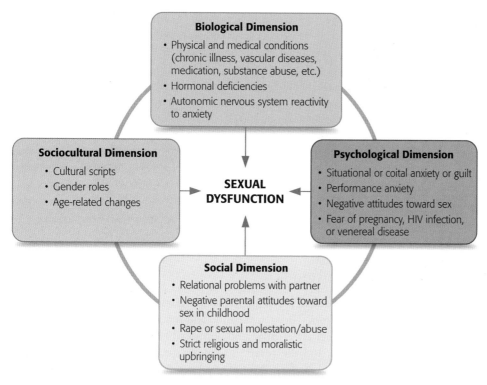

Figure 14.4

MULTIPATH MODEL FOR SEXUAL DYSFUNCTIONS

The dimensions interact with one another and combine in different ways to result in a specific sexual dysfunction. The importance and influence of each dimension varies from individual to individual.

Copyright © Cengage Learning, 2013

Biological Dimension

As has been indicated, lower levels of testosterone or higher levels of estrogens such as prolactin (or both) have been associated with lower sexual interest in both men and women and with erectile difficulties in men (Hyde, 2005; van Lankveld, 2008). Drugs that suppress testosterone levels appear to decrease sexual desire in men (Lewis, Yuan, & Wang, 2008). Conversely, the administration of androgens is associated with reports of increased sexual desire in both men and women. However, the relationship between hormones and sexual behavior is complex and difficult to understand. Many people with sexual dysfunctions have normal testosterone levels (Hyde, 2005).

Medications given to treat ulcers, glaucoma, allergies, and convulsions have also been found to affect the sex drive. Drugs such as antihypertensive medication and alcohol are also associated with sexual dysfunctions, as are illnesses and other physical conditions (Lewis, Yuan, & Wang, 2008; McAnulty & Burnette, 2004). Indeed, some believe that alcohol abuse is the leading cause of erectile disorders, as well as of early ejaculation (Arackal & Benegal, 2007). But again, not everyone who takes antihypertensive drugs, consumes alcohol, or is ill has a sexual dysfunction. In some people these factors may combine with a predisposing personal history or current stress to produce problems in sexual function. A complete physical workup—including a medical history, physical exam, and laboratory evaluation—is a necessary first step in assessment before treatment decisions are made.

For some, a lack of sexual desire may be physiological (Paik & Laumann, 2006). In one early study (Wincze, Hoon, & Hoon, 1978), a group of women who reported no feelings of anxiety about or aversion to sexual intercourse showed significantly lower sexual arousal during exposure to erotic stimuli than did sexually active women and no increase in responsiveness after participation in therapy. The researchers concluded that the absence of sexual arousal in these women was biological and that the appropriate treatment for this condition was unknown. Penile hypersensitivity to physical stimulation has been found to affect sexual functioning in men. Men who ejaculate early seem to have difficulty determining when ejaculation is inevitable once the sympathetic nervous system is triggered and seem to be "hardwired" to have a sensitive and more easily triggered sensory/response system (Rowland & McMahon, 2008).

The amount of blood flowing into the genital area is also associated with orgasmic potential in women and erectile functioning in men. In women, masturbation training and Kegel exercises (tightening muscles in the vagina) may increase vascularization of the labia, clitoris, and vagina. In men, vascular surgery to increase blood flow to the penis is successful when used appropriately. Unfortunately, if the problem is due to arteriosclerosis, which affects a number of the small blood vessels, vascular surgery meets with little success.

Psychological Dimension

Sexual dysfunctions may be due to psychological factors alone or to a combination of psychological and biological factors. They may be mild and transient or lifelong and chronic. Studies indicate that neurological, vascular, and hormonal factors are important in many cases of sexual dysfunctions, and they may also render sexual functioning more susceptible to psychological or social stresses. Psychological causes for sexual dysfunctions may include predisposing or historical factors, as well as more current problems and concerns. Guilt, anger, or resentment toward a partner, fear of pregnancy, fear of catching a sexually transmitted disease, and anxiety can all interfere with sexual performance (Westheimer & Lopater, 2005).

Traditional psychoanalysts have stressed the role of unconscious conflicts in sexual dysfunctions. For example, erectile difficulties and early ejaculation represent a man's hostility to women due to unresolved early developmental conflicts involving his parents. Likewise, a woman's lack of desire or arousal may also represent repressed hostility toward her partner or an attempt to punish him.

Cognitive theorists stress the interaction of performance anxiety and the spectator role in the etiology of sexual dysfunctions. For example, a man may experience a rare erection problem and begin to worry that it will happen again. Instead of enjoying the next sexual encounter and becoming aroused, he monitors or observes his own reactions ("Am I getting an erection?") and becomes a spectator who is anxious and detached from the situation. The result is potential failure and greater anxiety for future sexual encounters. Men with psychological erectile dysfunction often report anxiety over sexual overtures, including a fear of failing sexually, a fear of being seen as sexually inferior, and anxiety over the size of their genitals.

Early psychosexual experiences may shape a man's expectations and sexual responses as well. Men who suffer from early ejaculation, for example, have been found to have less sexual intercourse than their functional counterparts (Rowland and McMahon, 2008). Even in normal functioning men, longer intervals between sex result in greater excitement when intercourse occurs. For men with early ejaculation, it is possible that fewer sexual experiences predispose them to higher excitement and arousal, and they have fewer opportunities to learn how to delay an ejaculatory response. It is important to note that one successful form of sexual therapy for early ejaculation directs patients to attend more to somatic feedback and to adjust their cognitions and behaviors to influence an impending ejaculation.

Situational or coital anxiety can also interrupt sexual functioning in women. Factors associated with orgasmic dysfunction in women include having a sexually inexperienced or dysfunctional partner; a crippling fear of performance failure, of never being able to attain orgasm, pregnancy, or venereal disease; an inability to accept the partner, either emotionally or physically; and misinformation or ignorance about sexuality or sexual techniques.

Social Dimension

Social upbringing and current relationships have been identified as important in sexual functioning. It seems plausible that the attitudes parents display toward sex and affection and toward each other can influence their children's attitudes. Being raised in a strict religious environment is also associated with sexual dysfunctions in both men and women (Masters & Johnson, 1970). Traumatic sexual experiences involving incestuous molestations during childhood or adolescence or rape are also factors to consider (Lussier, McCann, & Beauregard, 2008). Adults who have been molested as a child or women who have been raped may suffer from a post-traumatic stress disorder, distrust men, find it difficult to establish intimacy, and exhibit sexual dysfunctions (Lussier, McCann, & Beauregard, 2008).

Relationship issues are often at the forefront of sexual disorders among and between men and women. As we saw in the case study of Jeremiah and Christina, current marital or relationship problems may interfere with sexual function. Marital satisfaction, for example, is associated with greater levels of sexual arousal and frequency between partners (Graham et al., 2004), whereas relationship dissatisfaction is linked to sexual difficulties (interest, arousal, and orgasm) among couples (Laumann et al., 1994). Specifically, relationships that are caring, warm, and affectionate, and in which there is more communication about sex and sexual activities seem to predict much more sexual satisfaction (Meston, Seal, & Hamilton, 2008). It is important to note that sexual satisfaction may be defined differently between the sexes. For women it is determined more by "closeness" to a partner than in the number or orgasms or the intensity of sexual arousal.

> ## Did You Know?
>
> Frequency of yearly sex varies among countries, nationalities, and regions:
>
> - Americans have the most sex (124 times/year), followed by Greeks (117 times/year), South Africans and Croatians (116 times/year), and New Zealanders (115 times/year).
>
> - People in Japan (36 times/year), Hong Kong (63 times/year), Taiwan (65 times/year), and China (72 times/year) have sex the least.
>
> **Source:** Durex, (2001, 2005)

Sociocultural Dimensions

From our earlier discussion, it is clear that sexual behavior and functioning are influenced by gender, age, cultural scripts, educational level, and country of origin. Although the human sexual response cycle is similar for women and men, gender differences are clearly present: Women (1) are capable of multiple orgasms, (2) entertain different sexual fantasies than men, (3) have a broader arousal pattern to sexual stimuli, (4) are more attuned to relationships in the sexual encounter, and (5) take longer than men to become aroused (Safarinejad, 2006; "Study Suggests Difference Between Female and Male Sexuality," 2003; "Study Confirms Importance of Sexual Fantasies," 2007). Likewise, sexual dysfunctions differ because of biological differences and gender role expectations: Women are more likely than men to be diagnosed as suffering from sexual interest disorders, and they differ as to the manifestation of an arousal disorder (erectile disorder for men vs. lubrication problems for women). In our society, men are taught to be the sexual aggressors, whereas women are taught not to initiate sex directly but in a more subtle and indirect manner. It is important to note that sex researchers and clinicians who do not consider biological differences and cultural scripts may unfairly portray women as suffering from sexual interest disorders.

Sexual orientation is also an important sociocultural influence on understanding sexual responsiveness among gays and lesbians. Although there are no physiological differences in sexual arousal and response between homosexuals and heterosexuals, it is also important to note that sexual issues may differ quite dramatically. For example, problems among heterosexuals most often focus on sexual intercourse, whereas gay and lesbian sexual concerns focus on other behaviors (e.g., aversion toward anal eroticism and cunnilingus). Lesbians and gay men must also deal with societal or internalized homophobia, which often inhibits open expression of their affection toward one another (Schneider, Brown, & Glassgold, 2002). Finally, gay men are forced to deal with the association between sexual activity and HIV infection. These broader contextual issues may create diminished sexual interest/desire, sexual aversion, and negative feelings toward sexual activity (Croteau et al., 2005).

Sexual Flirtation Common among Teens

Direct expressions of sexual interest are often discouraged in various cultures. Flirting, however, allows for indirect, playful, and romantic sexual overtures toward others. It may occur through verbal communication (tone of voice, pace, and intonation) and/or body language (eye contact, open stances, flicking the hair, or brief touching).

Earlier, we mentioned how cultural scripts, the social and cultural beliefs and expectations that guide our behaviors regarding sex, can have a major impact on sexual functioning. This perspective states that most of us are socialized into both domestic and international cultural scripts that vary from being quite explicit to being implicit. Some domestic scripts for men in the United States may be "Sexual potency in men is a sign of masculinity," implying that "impotence" is a sign of not being a "real man"; "The bigger the sex organ, the better"; and "Strong and virile men do not show feelings." For women, scripts include "Nice women don't initiate sex"; "Nice women are restrained and proper in lovemaking"; and "It is the woman's responsibility to take care of contraception." Likewise, other nations also vary in the cultural scripts they communicate to their citizens. For example, people in Asian countries consistently report the lowest frequency of sexual intercourse. It would be a serious mistake to believe that an entire nation can suffer from a sexual interest/arousal disorder. Rather, some suggest that these countries are more conservative, restrained, and restrictive in their attitudes toward sex (Sue & Sue, 2008a). In conclusion, it is clear that sexual functioning (and dysfunction) may be strongly influenced by sociocultural forces.

▪▪▪ Treatment of Sexual Dysfunctions

Many approaches have been used to treat sexual dysfunctions, including biological interventions and psychological treatment approaches.

Biological Interventions

Biological interventions may include hormone replacement and special medications or mechanical means to improve sexual functioning. For example, men with organic erectile dysfunction may be treated with vacuum pumps, suppositories, or penile implants. The penile prosthesis is an inflatable or semirigid device that, once inflated, produces an erection sufficient for intercourse and ejaculation (Table 14.6). It has been found that approximately 89 percent of men and 70 percent of their partners expressed satisfaction with penile implants (Center for Male Reproductive Medicine and Microsurgery, 2005) and that most would choose the treatment again.

Another form of medical treatment for ED is the injection of substances into the penis (Lewis, Yuan, & Wang, 2008). Within a very short time the man gets a very stiff

TABLE 14.6   Treating Erectile Disorders: Medical Interventions

Treatment	Primary Agent	Effects	Drawbacks
Oral medication	Viagra (sildenafil)	Taken as a pill. Some 70% to 80% of users achieve erections normal for their ages. Viagra enhances blood flow and retention by blocking an enzyme found primarily in the penis. The drug must be taken an hour before sex, and stimulation is needed for an erection.	Headaches and diarrhea; a drop in blood pressure; temporary blue-green-tinted vision.
Surgery	Vascular surgery	Corrects venous leak from a groin injury by repairing arteries to boost blood supply in the penis. Restores the ability to have a normal erection.	Minimal problems when used appropriately with diagnosed condition.
Suppository	Muse (alprotadil)	A tiny pellet is inserted into the penis by means of an applicator 5 to 10 minutes before sex. Erections can last an hour. Some 65% of users show some tumescence.	Penile aching, minor urethral bleeding or spotting, dizziness, and leg-vein swelling.
Injection therapy	Vasodilating drugs, including Caverject (alprotadil), Edex (alprostadil), and Invicorp (VIP and phentolamine)	Drug is injected directly into the base of the penis 10 minutes to 2 hours before sex, depending on the drug. The drug helps relax smooth-muscle tissues and creates an erection in up to 90% of patients. Erection lasts about an hour.	Pain, bleeding, and scar tissue formation. Erections may not readily subside.
Devices	Vacuum pump	Creates negative air pressure around the penis to induce the flow of blood, which is then trapped by an elastic band encircling the shaft. Pump is used just before sex. Erection lasts until band is removed.	Some difficulty in ejaculation. Penis can become cool and appear constricted in color. Apparatus can be clumsy to use.
	Penile implants	Considered a court of last resort. A penile prosthesis is implanted in the penis, enabling men to literally "pump themselves up" by pulling blood into it.	Destruction of spongy tissue inside the penis.

erection, which may last from one to four hours. Although men and their mates have reported general satisfaction with the method, it does have some side effects. There is often bruising of the penis and the development of nodules. Some men find the prolonged erection disturbing in the absence of sexual stimulation.

Oral medications such as Viagra, Levitra, and Cialis have been found to be an attractive alternative in minimizing the negative effects of injection therapy. Viagra made headlines in 1998 as a "miracle cure" for the 30 million men suffering from erectile dysfunctions (Tuller, 2004). The early clinical trials on 4,500 men indicated between 50 and 80 percent effectiveness; users' testimony of its "instantaneous success" has added to the hype (Hooper, 1998; Leland, 1997). There have even been reports that, by increasing blood flow to the genital areas, the pill can increase sexual desire in women. Recently, Pfizer reported that Viagra has not proven effective for women, but this has not hindered drug companies for continuing their search for a female alternative to Viagra.

Unlike injectables, Viagra and its competitors do not produce an automatic erection in the absence of sexual stimuli. If a man becomes aroused, the drugs enable the body to follow through the sexual response cycle to completion. Urologists claim that for individuals with no sexual dysfunction, taking Viagra, for example, does not improve their erections; in other words, Viagra does not provide physiological help that will enable normally functioning men to improve their sexual functioning, nor does it lead to a stiffer erection. These drugs may aid sexual arousal and performance by stimulating men's expectations and fantasies; this psychological boost may then lead to subjective feelings of enhanced pleasure.

Psychological Treatment Approaches

In addition to biological forms of treatment, most general psychological treatment approaches include the following components:

- **Education** The therapist replaces sexual myths and misconceptions with accurate information about sexual anatomy and functioning.
- **Anxiety reduction** The therapist uses procedures such as desensitization or graded approaches to keep anxiety at a minimum. The therapist explains that constantly "observing and evaluating" one's performance can interfere with sexual functioning.
- **Structured behavioral exercises** The therapist gives a series of graded tasks that gradually increase the amount of sexual interaction between the partners. Each partner takes turns touching and being touched over different parts of the body except for the genital regions. Later the partners fondle the body and genital regions without making demands for sexual arousal or orgasm. Successful sexual intercourse and orgasm is the final stage of the structured exercises.
- **Communication training** The therapist teaches the partners appropriate ways of communicating their sexual wishes to each other and also teaches them conflict resolution.

Some specific nonmedical treatments for other dysfunctions are as follows:

1. *Female orgasmic dysfunction* Both structured behavioral exercises and communication training have been successful in treating sexual arousal disorders in women and erectile disorders in men. Masturbation appears to be the most effective way for orgasmically dysfunctional women to have an orgasm. The procedure involves education about sexual anatomy, visual and tactile self-exploration, using sexual fantasies and images, and masturbation, both individually and with a partner. High success rates have been reported with this procedure for women with primary orgasmic dysfunction. This approach does not necessarily lead to the woman's ability to achieve orgasm during sexual intercourse.

2. *Early ejaculation* In one technique, the partner stimulates the penis while it is outside the vagina until the man feels the sensation of impending ejaculation. At this point, the partner stops the stimulation for a short period of time and then continues it again. This pattern is repeated until the man can tolerate increasingly greater periods of stimulation before ejaculation. Masters and Johnson (1970) and Kaplan (1974) used a similar procedure, called the "squeeze technique." They reported a success rate of nearly 100 percent. The treatment is easily learned. Although the short-term success rate for treating premature ejaculation is very high, relapses were common.

3. *Vaginismus* The results of treatment for vaginismus have been uniformly positive. The involuntary spasms or closure of the vaginal muscle can be deconditioned by first training the woman to relax and by then inserting successively larger dilators while she is relaxed, until insertion of the penis can occur.

▮▮▮▮ Aging, Sexual Activity, and Sexual Dysfunctions

Aging has been found to be one of the most powerful predictors of changing sexual functioning (decreases in sexual interest, arousal, and activity) even when the effects of illness, medication, and psychopathology are controlled (Gooren, 2008). Physiological aspects of male and female aging are evident in the neural, endocrinological, and cardiovascular functioning of the body; this is often compounded by psychological adjustments related to the aging process and relationship changes (close friends or even a partner may die) (Brotto & Luria, 2008).

In the most comprehensive study of sexuality and health among older adults in the United States ages fifty-seven to eighty-five, 3,005 participants (1,550 women and 1,455 men) were surveyed, with the following findings (Lindau et al., 2007):

- Sexual activity declined with age (73 percent among fifty-seven- to sixty-four-year-olds; 53 percent among sixty-five- to seventy-four-year-olds; 25 percent among seventy-five- to eighty-five-year-olds).
- Women were far more likely to report less sexual activity at all ages.
- Among men and women who were sexually active, approximately 50 percent reported at least one bothersome sexual problem.
- The most frequently reported sexual problems for women included low sexual interest/desire (43 percent), problems with vaginal lubrication (39 percent), and inability to climax (34 percent).
- Among men the most frequent problems were erectile difficulties (37 percent).

It is important for us to understand how the aging process affects sexuality. When women reach menopause, estrogen levels drop, and women may experience vaginal dryness and thinning of the vaginal wall (Brotto & Luria, 2008). This may result in discomfort during sexual activity. Likewise, older men are at higher risk for prostate problems that may increase the risk of ED (Gooren, 2008). Both sexes are also at higher risk for illnesses that affect sexual performance and interest (diabetes, high blood pressure, rheumatism, and heart disease). Hormone replacement therapy, drugs for ED (Cialis, Levitra, and Viagra), and other medical procedures may help minimize the effects of these organic problems on sexual activity. For example, older men and women who rate their health as poor are less likely to be sexually active, and 14 percent of men report using medication to improve their sexual performance (Lindau et al., 2007).

MYTH: Sex is unimportant to the elderly. They are averse to being sexually active and are conservative in sexual behavior.

REALITY: Although sexual activity does decline with age, a 2007 major survey of adults ages fifty-seven to eighty-five found that many older people are sexually active well into their sixties, seventies, and eighties. Fifty-four percent reported having sex at least twice a month, and 23 percent reported once a week or more. Approximately 50 percent of men and women younger than age seventy-five had engaged in oral sex in the previous two months.

MYTH VS. REALITY

David Young-Wolff / PhotoEdit

Sexual Behavior among Seniors

Contrary to the belief that the elderly lose their sexual desire, studies reveal that sexual desire, activity, and enjoyment remain high in the older population.

Some additional findings reported by the American Association of Retired Persons (AARP, 1999) were the following:

• Although most men and women report that satisfying sex is important in their lives, they found relationships to be more important than sex.

• Sexual activity is affected by the "partner gap." Whereas 80 percent of those surveyed between the ages of forty-five and fifty-nine have partners, only 58 percent of men and 21 percent of women older than seventy-five had partners.

• Both men and women report that sexual activity declines with advancing age due to health problems; yet, 64 percent of men and 68 percent of women with sexual partners report being satisfied with their sex lives.

Sexuality during old age is an area of intolerance in our youth-oriented society, in which sexual activity is simply not associated with the elderly. Nevertheless, a large percentage of older Americans clearly have active sex lives. In one study (Diokno, Brown, & Herzog, 1990), investigators found a clear relationship between the reported frequency of intercourse at younger ages and at the present time among sixty- to seventy-nine-year-old married men. The most active respondents reported a present frequency that was 61 percent of their frequency between ages forty and fifty-nine, whereas the least active reported a present frequency of only 6 percent of that between ages forty and fifty-nine. The most active also indicated that they became aroused on seeing women in public situations and in response to visual stimuli. The vast majority (69 percent) felt that sex was important for good health, and most (63 percent) looked on masturbation as an acceptable outlet. Sexual dysfunctions were also more prevalent in the older groups than in younger ones, and the prevalence was affected by the individuals' prior and present sexual activity levels. Of the least active, 21 percent suffered from premature ejaculation, and 75 percent were either impotent or had erectile difficulties. For the most active group, the corresponding percentages were 8 and 19 percent. The results of this study are summarized in Figure 14.5.

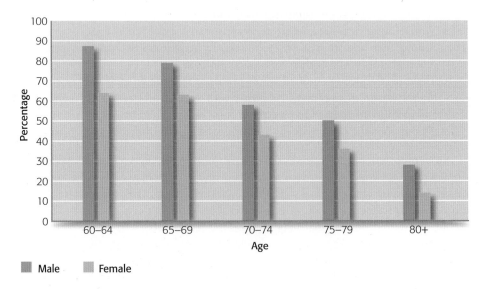

Figure 14.5

PERCENTAGES OF MEN AND WOMEN REMAINING SEXUALLY ACTIVE, AGES 60 AND OLDER

Contrary to many myths about aging and reduced sexual activity, studies reveal that elderly people are surprisingly sexually active. At all age levels, however, men continue to be more sexually active than women.

Source: Data from Diokno, Brown, & Herzog (1990, pp. 197–200)

A comprehensive survey (Janus & Janus, 1993) suggested that sexual activity and enjoyment among the older population remains surprisingly high. The Janus' survey found that (1) the sexual activity of people ages sixty-five and older declined little from that of their thirty- to forty-year-old counterparts, (2) their ability to reach orgasm and have sex diminished very little from their early years, and (3) their desire to continue a relatively active sex life was unchanged. These findings are supported by a poll of 1,292 Americans (534 men and 758 women) ages sixty or older who reported that their interest in sex remains high, that over half engage in sexual activity at least once a month, and that half rated their sexual activity to be physically better now than in their youth (National Council on Aging, 1998).

Aside from sexual outlook and behavior, physiologically based changes in patterns of sexual arousal and orgasm have been found in people older than age sixty-five (Masters & Johnson, 1966). For both men and women, sexual arousal takes longer (Brotto & Luria, 2008; McAnulty & Burnette, 2003). Erection and vaginal lubrication are slower to occur, and the urgency for orgasm is reduced. Both men and women are fully capable of sexual satisfaction if no physiological conditions interfere. Many elderly individuals felt that such changes allowed them to experience sex more fully. They reported that they had more time to spend on a seductive buildup, felt positively about their ability to experience unhurried sex-for-joy, and experienced more warmth and intimacy after the sex act (Janus & Janus, 1993).

■ Gender Dysphoria

In contrast to the sexual dysfunctions, which involve any disruption of the normal sexual response cycle, gender dyphoria—previously called **gender identity disorder (GID)** or **transsexualism**—is characterized by a marked incongruence between one's experienced/expressed gender and assigned gender as a male or female (Meyer-Behburg, 2009). It is important to note that gender dysphoria and sexual orientation are not the same thing—the sexual orientation of a transsexual can thus be heterosexual, homosexual, or bisexual (Zucker & Cohen-Ketteris, 2008).

Gender dysphoria involves the person experiencing strong and persistent gender dysphoria and a dislike and/or desire to be rid of one's sexual anatomy. Gender dysphoria may or may not be manifested in significant impairment in social, occupational, or other important areas of functioning. People with this disorder hold a lifelong conviction that nature has placed them in the body of the wrong gender. This feeling produces a preoccupation with eliminating the "natural" physical and behavioral sexual characteristics and acquiring those of the opposite sex (Lawrence, 2008).

People with gender dysphoria tend to exhibit gender-role incongruence at an early age and to report transsexual feelings in childhood, some as early as two years old (McAnulty & Burnette, 2004; Zucker, 2009). A boy may claim that he will grow up to be a woman, demonstrate disgust with his penis, and be exclusively preoccupied with interests and activities considered "feminine." Boys with this disorder are frequently labeled "sissies" by their male peers. They prefer playing with girls and generally avoid the rough-and-tumble activities in which boys are traditionally encouraged to participate. They are more likely than other boys to play with "feminine" toys.

Girls with a dysphoria may insist that they have a penis or will grow one and may exhibit an avid interest in rough-and-tumble play. Female transsexuals report being labeled "tomboys" during their childhoods. Although it is not uncommon for girls to be considered tomboys, the strength, pervasiveness, and persistence of the gender incongruence are the distinguishing features. Children who may engage in traditional opposite sex role activities (feminine or masculine) should not be prematurely diagnosed as having gender dysphoria. Nonconformity to stereotypical sex role behavior should not, for example, be confused with the pervasiveness of the opposite gender wishes, interests, and activities of gender dysphoria.

gender dysphoria/gender identity disorder (GID)/transsexualism disorder characterized by conflict between a person's anatomical sex and his or her gender identity, or self-identification as male or female

Etiology of Gender Dysphoria

The etiology of gender dysphoria is unclear. Because the disorder is quite rare, investigators have focused more attention on other sexual disorders. Gender dysphoria appears to be more common in males than in females and may appear in both adults and children (Lawrence, 2008). In all likelihood, a number of variables interact to produce gender dysphoria. Again, a multipath analysis reveals multiple influences, but biological factors seem to be strongly implicated.

A Case of Sex Reassignment

Chaz Bono, born Chastity Bono is the only child of famous entertainers Sonny and Cher. In 2008, Bono began undergoing a physical gender transition from female to male. Bono made a documentary film, *Becoming Chaz*, about his sex change which premiered at the 2011 Sundance Film Festival. Chastity Bono is shown on the left prior to her sex change. On the right, Chaz Bono is seen in a practice session with his female partner competing on the September 2011 *Dancing with the Stars*.

Biological Influences

The research in this area suggests that neurohormonal factors, genetics, and possible brain differences may be involved in the etiology of gender dysphoria. In animal studies, for example, the presence or absence of testosterone early in life appears to influence the organization of brain centers that govern sexual behavior. In human females, early exposure to male hormones has resulted in a more masculine behavior pattern. Thus it does appear that gender orientation can be influenced by a lack or excess of sex hormones. Genetics and differences in areas of the hypothalamus have also been found to correlate with the development of gender dysphoria (Henningsson et al., 2005; Zhou, Hofman, Gooren, & Swaab, 1995). These studies suggest that gender dysphoria may run in families and that there are differences in the size of brain clusters in regions of the hypothalamus between men with and men without gender dysphoria (Swaab, 2005).

It is important to note, however, that limited research in this area makes conclusions about hormonal, genetic, and brain structure explanations very hazardous. Some researchers believe that gender identity is malleable. For example, most transsexual children have normal hormone levels, and their opposite-gender orientation raises doubt that biology alone determines male-female behaviors. Although neurohormonal levels are important, their degree of influence on gender identity in human beings may be minor.

Psychological and Social Influences

Psychological and social explanations of gender dysphoria must also be viewed with caution. In psychodynamic theory, all sexual deviations symbolically represent unconscious conflicts that began in early childhood. They occur because the Oedipus complex is not fully resolved. The male or female child has a basic conflict between the wish for and the dread of maternal re-engulfment. The conflict results from a failure to deal successfully with separation-individuation phases of life, which creates a gender incongruence problem. Although psychodynamic theorists adhere to such an explanation, research support is lacking.

Some researchers have hypothesized that childhood experiences influence the development of gender dysphoria (Zucker & Cohen-Ketteris, 2008). Factors thought to contribute to the disorder in boys include parental encouragement of feminine behavior, discouragement of the development of autonomy, excessive attention and overprotection by the mother, the absence of an older male as a model, a relatively powerless or absent father figure, a lack of exposure to male playmates, and encouragement to cross-dress.

Treatment of Gender Identity Disorder

Psychotherapy and hormone therapy have been used for many persons with GID. For some, however, sex reassignment surgery is chosen. According to DSM-IV, 1 in 30,000 adult males and 1 in 100,000 adult females seek sex-reassignment surgery. For men, the surgery involves altering the male genitalia to be more similar to the opposite sex through what can be described as "penis inversion." Then plastic surgery constructs female genitalia, including a vagina and clitoris. The skin of the penis is used in this construction because the sensory nerve endings that are preserved enable most transsexuals to experience orgasm. The male-to-female operation is nearly perfected, and affirms the gender identity of the individual. Research suggests that genital surgery can produce happier lives. Women who want to become men generally request operations to remove their breasts and some ask for an artificial penis to be constructed. This procedure is much more complicated and expensive than the male-to-female conversion.

CONTROVERSY

Are Transgendered People Suffering from a Mental Disorder?

Do you believe that people born a male or female, but who experience themselves as members of the opposite gender and desire to live their lives as such, are normal? Or do you believe they qualify as suffering from a mental disorder? DSM-IV-TR classifies transgendered persons as suffering from a gender identity disorder (now labeled gender dysphoria). But this diagnosis has come under heavy criticism from transgendered mental health consumer advocacy groups who believe they are allowed minimal opportunity for meaningful input into a diagnosis that affects their ability to live a stigma-free and nonprejudiced life (Frese & Myrick, 2010). Labeling gender dysphoria or GID as a disorder stirs up major conflicts and issues regarding the accuracy of psychological diagnosis, the scientific foundations of the disorder, the challenge it brings to our bimodal concepts of gender identity, inherent social stigma, and even civil rights issues. The battle over removing GID as a disorder intensified during the 2009 meeting of the American Psychiatric Association in San Francisco where the DSM-5 Task Force on Sexual and Gender Identity Disorders met to consider changes. Protesters both inside and outside of the meeting focused on the "biased" attitudes of the psychiatric establishment and denounced the oppressive harm and stigma placed on transgendered persons.

Critics of the DSM inclusion of gender identity disorder point out the oppressive harm it places on this class of people: (a) The maligning terminology is hurtful and damaging because it disregards their experienced gender identities, denies affirmed gender roles, and relegates them to their assigned birth sex; (b) It pathologizes ordinary behaviors and confuses cultural nonconformity with mental illness; and (c) It potentially denies equal access and opportunity to transgendered people (Winters, 2007; Granderson, 2010). This latter concern is most evident in sports where for years the International Olympic Committee denied the right of transgender people to compete until 2004 (unless they had undergone sex reassignment surgery and had at least two years of postoperative hormone-replacement therapy). Many others sports organizations have passed their own policies permitting transgender folks to complete, but it was only recently in 2010, that the LPGA allowed transgendered people to compete because of a lawsuit filed against the organization. Discrimination in health care, employment, and education are often experienced due to prejudice and discrimination. Transgendered individuals are often portrayed as less than human, an anomaly, and referred to as "shims" or "shemales."

Like the struggle to remove homosexuality as a mental disorder, the battle being waged by many transgendered persons contains numerous parallels too difficult to ignore. First, many who allegedly have gender identity disorder do not regard their transgender feelings and desires as abnormal (Granderson, 2010; Winters, 2007). In some Asian and Pacific Islander cultures, gender roles that include homosexuality and transexuality are accepted and considered normal (Park & Manzon-Santos, 2000). Second, in May 2009, after years of study and debate, the government of France declared that a transsexual gender identity is not a psychiatric condition: "It is not a mental illness" (Le Monde, 2009). Third, with the next revision of the DSM, some experts have advocated the removal of gender identity disorder (gender dysphoria) as a psychiatric diagnosis (Winters, 2007). They cite the following in support of their contention: (a) lack of reliability and validity supporting the GID diagnostic criteria in DSM-IV-TR, (b) the psychological distress experienced by sons and daughters is often created by parental and societal negative reactions and not the result of pathology, (c) some therapeutic approaches are often similar to "reparative therapies," and (d) there is little evidence of pathology in GID children (Hausman, 2003). Finally, there are some who believe that gender identity can best be conceptualized along a spectrum rather than a bimodal curve. Like sexual orientation, gender identity is a basic and important aspect of our total being. Gender dysphoria challenges our basic notions of the dichotomy between male and female identities.

For Further Consideration:

1. What makes a person a "man" or a "woman?" Is it based on one's anatomy?
2. With the removal of homosexuality as a mental disorder, what are your thoughts about removing transsexualism as a disorder?
3. What criteria should be used to determine whether being a transsexual is normal or abnormal?

Some studies of transsexuals indicate positive outcomes for sex reassignment surgery. Most females who "changed" to males express satisfaction over the outcome of surgery, although males who "changed" to females are less likely to feel satisfied (Lawrence, 2008). It has been suggested that adjusting to life as a man is easier than adjusting to life as a woman, or perhaps others may react less negatively to woman-to-man changes than man-to-woman changes (APA, 2000).

▉ Paraphilic Disorders

Paraphilic disorders are sexual disorders of at least six months' duration in which the person has either acted on and is severely distressed by recurrent urges or fantasies involving any of the following three categories (Table 14.7): (1) nonhuman objects, as in fetishistic and transvestic disorders; (2) nonconsenting others, as in exhibitionistic, voyeuristic, frotteuristic disorders (rubbing against others for sexual arousal), and pedo-hebephilic; and (3) real or simulated suffering or humiliation, as in sexual sadism and sexual masochism disorders. The DSM-5 Work Group (2011) is proposing to make a distinct separation between paraphilias and paraphilic disorders. First, they note that a paraphilia in and of itself may not cause personal distress or harm to others, thus psychiatric intervention is not justified. Such a distinction would prevent labeling a nonnormative behavior as pathological. Thus, they propose adding the word "disorder" to all the paraphilias. In other words, paraphilias in and of themselves are not necessarily abnormal. Just as a person may gamble for recreation purposes, the activity must be distinguished from a gambling addiction. Second, in order to diagnose a paraphilic order, they are considering a minimal number of separate victims in order to prevent too many false positives (i.e., inaccurately diagnosing someone with an exhibitionistic disorder because of a low threshold).

It is not unusual for people in this category to possess multiple paraphilic disorders (Langstrom & Zucker, 2005). In one study of sex offenders, researchers found that nearly 50 percent had engaged in a variety of sexually deviant behaviors, averaging between three and four paraphilic, disorders and had committed more than five hundred deviant acts (Rosenfield, 1985). Men who had committed incest, for example, had also molested non-relatives, exposed themselves, raped adult women, and engaged in voyeurism and frotteurism. In most cultures, paraphilias seem to be much more prevalent in males than in females (Gijs, 2008). This finding has led some to speculate that biological factors may account for the unequal distribution.

Paraphilic Disorders Involving Nonhuman Objects

Under this category, two forms of paraphilic disorders are evident: an attraction or arousal related to a nonliving object (the "fetish") or transvestic disorder that involves cross-dressing.

Fetishistic Disorder

Fetishistic disorder comprises an extremely strong sexual attraction to and fantasies involving inanimate objects such as female undergarments. The fetish is often used as a sexual stimulus during masturbation or sexual intercourse. The disorder causes significant distress to self or others and is most common in men, and the disorder is rare among women.

paraphilic disorders   sexual disorders of at least six months' duration in which the person has either acted on or is severely distressed by recurrent urges or fantasies involving nonhuman objects, nonconsenting persons, or suffering or humiliation

fetishistic disorder   sexual attraction and fantasies involving inanimate objects such as female undergarments

Case Study

Mr. D. met his wife at a local church and was strongly attracted to her because of her strong religious convictions. When they dated, occasional kissing and petting took place but never any other sexual contact. He had not masturbated before marriage because he was taught by moralistic parents who believed it a sin. Although Mr. D.

TABLE 14.7   Paraphilic Disorders

Paraphilia Category	Symptoms	Prevalence	Age of Onset	Course
Nonhuman Objects	**Fetishistic disorder** Sexual attraction and fantasies involving nonliving objects such as female undergarments	Primarily a male disorder; rare in women; exact figures unavailable	Usually adolescence	Causes are difficult to pinpoint; conditioning and learning seem likely
	Transvestic disorder Intense sexual arousal by cross-dressing	Exact figures difficult to obtain because cross-dressing often goes unreported and is acceptable in many societies	Begins as early as puberty	Cross-dressing is not usually associated with major psychiatric problems
Nonconsenting Persons	**Exhibitionistic disorder** Urges, acts, or fantasies involving exposure of genitals to a stranger	Almost exclusively a male activity; best estimates are 4.1% of men and 2.1% of women	Begins in teens; exhibitionist is most likely in 20s	Most likely to have doubts about his masculinity; likes to shock; many have an erection during act; most masturbate after exposure
	Voyeuristic disorder Urges, acts, or fantasies of observing an unsuspecting person disrobing or engaging in sexual activity	Difficult to determine; 11.4% are men and 3.9% for women	Begins around age 15; tends to be chronic	Voyeurs tend to be young males; they may masturbate during or after the episode
	Frotteuristic disorder Urges, acts, or fantasies of touching or rubbing against a nonconsenting person	Difficult to determine; most are men	Begins in adolescence or earlier	Usually decreases after age 25
	Pedophebephilic disorder Urges, acts, or fantasies involving sexual contact with a prepubescent child	Primarily men; exact figures not available	Must be at least 16; pedophiles tend to be in late 20s/30s	Prefer children who are at least 5 years younger than they are and usually less than 13 years old; pedophiles often have poor social skills
Pain or Humiliation	**Sexual sadism disorder** Sexually arousing urges, fantasies, or acts associated with inflicting physical or psychological suffering	Usually male; rates unknown, however, 22% of men and 12% of women in one study report some sexual arousal from sadistic stories	Begins in early childhood with sexual fantasies	Fantasies begin in childhood; sadistic acts usually develop in adulthood and can stay at the same level of cruelty or, more rarely, increase to problematic proportions
	Sexual masochism disorder Sexual urges, fantasies, or acts associated with being humiliated, bound, or made to suffer	Precise figures difficult to obtain	Males report first interests around 15 and women at 22	Not all suffering arouses; usually it must be produced in a specific way; classical conditioning strongly implicated as causal

and his wife loved each other very much, he was unable to have sexual intercourse with her because he could not obtain an erection. However, he had fantasies involving an apron and was able to get an erection while wearing one. His wife was upset over this discovery but was persuaded to accept it because she wanted children. Using the apron allowed them to consummate their marriage, but Mrs. D. was distressed about what she considered to be a perversion. Mr. D. remembers during his childhood years being forced by his mother to wear an apron and help her in the kitchen. As time went by, Mrs. D. could no longer tolerate the situation and both sought sex therapy.

Most males find the sight of female undergarments sexually arousing and stimulating; this does not constitute a fetish. An interest in such inanimate objects as panties,

AP Images

Not Necessarily What You Might Think

The etiology and behavioral symptoms of gender identity disorder go far beyond enjoying dressing as the opposite sex; more important is persistent cross-gender identification and discomfort with one's own anatomical sex.

stockings, bras, and shoes becomes a sexual disorder when the person is often sexually aroused to the point of erection in the presence of the fetish item, needs this item for sexual arousal during intercourse, chooses sexual partners on the basis of their having the item, or collects these items. To qualify as a paraphilic disorder, it must also cause the individual or others significant distress. In many cases, the fetish item is enough by itself for complete sexual satisfaction through masturbation, and the person does not seek contact with a partner. Common fetishes include aprons, shoes, undergarments, and leather or latex items. As a group, people diagnosed with a fetishistic disorder are not dangerous, nor do they tend to commit serious crimes.

Transvestic Disorder

A diagnosis of fetishistic disorder is not made if the inanimate object is an article of clothing used only in cross-dressing. In such cases, the appropriate diagnosis would be transvestic disorder—intense sexual arousal obtained through cross-dressing (wearing clothes appropriate to the opposite gender). This disorder should not be confused with gender identity disorder (transsexualism), in which one *identifies* with the opposite gender. Although some transsexuals and homosexuals cross-dress, most transvestites are exclusively heterosexual and married. Again, to be classified as a transvestic disorder, the person must have clinically significant distress or impairment in important areas of functioning. Several aspects of transvestism are illustrated in the following case study:

Case Study

A twenty-six-year-old graduate student referred himself for treatment after he failed an exam in one of his courses. He had been cross-dressing since the age of ten and attributed his exam failure to the excessive amount of time that he spent doing so (four times a week). When he was younger, his cross-dressing had taken the form of masturbating while wearing his mother's high-heeled shoes, but it had gradually expanded to the present stage, in which he dressed completely as a woman, masturbating in front of a mirror. At no time had he experienced a desire to obtain a sex-change operation. He had neither homosexual experiences nor homosexual fantasies. Heterosexual contact had been restricted to heavy petting with occasional girlfriends. (Lambley, 1974, p. 101)

Sexual arousal while cross-dressing is an important criterion in the diagnosis of a transvestic disorder. If arousal is not present or has disappeared over time, a more appropriate diagnosis may be gender dysphoria. This distinction, however, may be difficult to make. Some transsexuals show penile erections to descriptions of cross-dressing. The occurrence of sexual arousal in cross-dressing, therefore, may not serve as a valid distinction between transsexualism and a transvestic disorder. If the cross-dressing occurs only during the course of a gender identity disorder, the person is not considered in the category of transvestic disorder.

Many transvestites believe that they have alternating masculine and feminine personalities. In a feminine role, they can play out such behavior patterns as buying nightgowns and trying on fashionable clothes. They may introduce their wives to their female personalities and urge them to go on shopping trips together as women. Other transvestites cross-dress only for the purposes of sexual arousal and masturbation and

transvestic disorder   intense sexual arousal obtained through cross-dressing (wearing clothes appropriate to the opposite gender); not to be confused with transsexualism

do not fantasize themselves as members of the opposite sex. Male transvestites often wear feminine garments or undergarments during sexual intercourse with their wives.

Paraphilic Disorders Involving Nonconsenting Persons

This category of disorders involves persistent and powerful sexual fantasies about unsuspecting strangers or acquaintances. The victims are nonconsenting in that they do not choose to be the objects of the attention or sexual behavior.

Exhibitionistic Disorder

Exhibitionistic disorder is characterized by urges, acts, or fantasies of exposing one's genitals to a stranger, often with the intent of shocking the unsuspecting victim. The person is clinically distressed with his/her behavior and may experience impairment in important areas of life functioning.

Case Study

A nineteen-year-old single white college man reported that he had daily fantasies of exposing himself and had done so on three occasions. The first occurred when he masturbated in front of the window of his dormitory room when women would be passing by. The other two acts occurred in his car; in each case he asked young women for directions and then exposed his penis and masturbated when they approached. He felt a great deal of anxiety in the presence of women and dated infrequently. (Hayes, Brownell, & Barlow, 1983)

Exhibitionistic disorder is relatively common. The exhibitionist is most often male and the victim female. A high number of young women have been victims of exhibitionists, although most women did not report any long-lasting psychological traumas associated with the episodes. It is more likely to cause moderate distress, although a smaller number believed the incidents had negatively affected their attitudes toward men (Lussier, McCann, & Beauregard, 2008).

The main goal of the exhibitionist seems to be the sexual arousal he gets by exposing himself; most exhibitionists want no further contact. Exhibitionists may expect to produce surprise, sexual arousal, or disgust in the victim. The act may involve exposing a limp penis or masturbating an erect penis. Most exhibitionists are in their twenties—far from being the "dirty old men" of popular myth. Most are married. Their exhibiting has a compulsive quality to it, and they report that they feel a great deal of anxiety about the act. A typical exposure sequence involves the person first entertaining sexually arousing memories of previous exposures and then returning to the area where previous exposures took place. Next, the person locates a suitable victim, rehearses the exposure mentally, and finally exposes himself. As the person moves through this sequence, self-control weakens and disappears. Many exhibitionists use alcohol before exposing themselves, perhaps to reduce inhibitions.

Voyeuristic Disorder

Voyeuristic disorder comprises urges, acts, or fantasies of observing an unsuspecting person disrobing or engaging in sexual activity. "Peeping," as voyeurism is sometimes termed, is considered deviant when it includes serious risk, is done in socially unacceptable circumstances, or is preferred to coitus. The typical voyeur is not interested in looking at his wife or girlfriend; an overwhelming number of voyeurism acts involve

Did You Know?

Some social scientists believe that the United States is an exhibitionistic and voyeuristic society that contributes to such disorders. Reality television and access to the Internet (MySpace, Facebook, YouTube, etc.) encourage people to reveal intimate aspects of their lives to strangers. Some even claim that modern architecture reflects the "peek-a-boo effect" such that glass-walled condominiums and office buildings allow residents to see out and be seen in a "Webcam" manner.

exhibitionistic disorder characterized by urges, acts, or fantasies about the exposure of one's genitals to strangers

voyeuristic disorder urges, acts, or fantasies involving observation of an unsuspecting person disrobing or engaging in sexual activity

Jerry Lee Lewis: Pedophiliac or Something Else?

When musician Jerry Lee Lewis married a thirteen-year-old girl in the 1950s, it created a furor in Great Britain, where many considered him a pedophiliac. The public's outrage resulted in the cancellation of many of his concerts, forcing him to return to New York. Lewis was twenty-two at the time of this marriage and not yet divorced from his second wife.

strangers. Observation alone produces sexual arousal and excitement, and the voyeur often masturbates during this surreptitious activity.

The voyeur is like the exhibitionist in that sexual contact is not the goal; viewing an undressed body is the primary motive. However, a voyeur may also exhibit or use other indirect forms of sexual expression. Because the act is repetitive, arrest is predictable. Usually an accidental witness or a victim notifies the police.

The proliferation of sexually oriented television programs, "romance" paperbacks, explicit sexual magazines, and NC-17–rated movies all point to the voyeuristic nature of our society. The growing number of "night clubs" featuring male exotic dancers that are attended by women and female interest in the male body have become quite common and acceptable.

Frotteuristic Disorder

Whereas physical contact is not the goal of voyeurism, contact is the primary motive in frotteuristic disorder. Frotteuristic disorder involves recurrent and intense sexual urges, acts, or fantasies of touching or rubbing against a nonconsenting person. The touching, not the coercive nature of the act, is the sexually exciting feature. As in the case of the other paraphilic disorders, the diagnosis is made when the person has acted on the urges or is markedly distressed by them.

Pedophebephilic Disorder

Pedophebephilic disorder involves an adult obtaining erotic gratification through urges, acts, or fantasies of sexual contact with a prepubescent child. According to DSM-IV-TR, to be diagnosed with this disorder, the person must be at least sixteen years of age (although DSM-5 Work Group recommends 18 years) and at least five years older than the victim. Pedophiles may victimize their own children (incest), stepchildren, or those outside the family. Despite the large number of high profile cases of abuse of boys by Catholic priests and in scouting, most pedophiles prefer girls, although a few choose prepubertal boys.

Sexual abuse of children is common (Phillips & Daniluk, 2004). Between 20 and 30 percent of women report having had a childhood sexual encounter with an adult man. And, contrary to the popular view of the child molester as a stranger, most pedophiles are relatives, friends, or casual acquaintances of their victims (Lussier, McCann, & Beauregard, 2008). In most cases of abuse, only one adult and one child are involved, but cases involving several adults or groups of children have been reported.

Child victims of sexual abuse show a variety of physical symptoms, such as urinary tract infections, poor appetite, and headaches. Reported psychological symptoms include nightmares, difficulty sleeping, decline in school performance, acting-out behaviors, and sexually focused behavior. Some child victims show the symptoms of post-traumatic stress disorder. The effects of sexual abuse can be lifelong. One study of women who were victims of childhood sexual abuse revealed a "contaminated identity" characterized by self-loathing, shame, and powerlessness (Phillips & Daniluk, 2004).

frotteuristic disorder characterized by recurrent and intense sexual urges, acts, or fantasies or touching or rubbing against a nonconsenting person

pedophebephilic disorder a disorder in which an adult obtains erotic gratification through urges, acts, or fantasies involving sexual contact with a prepubescent child

incest a form of pedophilic disorder; can also be sexual relations between people too closely related to marry legally

Incest

DSM-IV-TR considers childhood incest to be a form of pedophilia disorder. Incest, however, can also occur between adults too closely related to marry legally; it is nearly universally taboo in society. The cases of incest most frequently reported to law enforcement agencies are those between a father and his daughter or stepdaughter. However, the most common incestuous relationship is brother-sister incest, not parent-child incest. Mother-son incest seems to be rare. Sexual activities between siblings are relatively frequent. Although brother-sister incest is more common, most research has focused on father-daughter incest. This type of incestuous relationship generally begins when the daughter is between six and eleven years old. Unlike sex between siblings (which may or may not be exploitative), father-daughter incest is always exploitative. The girl is especially vulnerable because she depends on her father for emotional support. As a result, the victims often feel guilty and powerless. Their problems continue into adulthood and are reflected in their high rates of drug abuse, sexual dysfunction, and psychiatric problems (McAnulty & Burnette, 2003).

Paraphilic Disorders Involving Pain or Humiliation

Pain and humiliation do not appear to be related to normal sexual arousal. In sadism and masochism, however, they play a prominent role. Sexual sadism disorder is a form of paraphilic disorder in which sexually arousing urges, fantasies, or acts are associated with inflicting physical or psychological suffering on others. The word *sadism* was coined from the name of the Marquis de Sade (1740–1814), a French nobleman who wrote extensively about the sexual pleasure he received by inflicting pain on women. The Marquis himself was so cruel to his sexual victims that he was declared insane and jailed for twenty-seven years. Sadistic behavior may range from the pretended or fantasized infliction of pain through mild to severe cruelty toward partners to an extremely dangerous pathological form of sadism that may involve mutilation or murder.

Sexual masochism disorder is another paraphilic disorder in which sexual urges, fantasies, or acts are associated with being humiliated, bound, or made to suffer. The word *masochism* is derived from the name of a nineteenth-century Austrian novelist, Leopold von Sacher-Masoch, whose fictional characters obtained sexual satisfaction only when pain was inflicted on them. Because of their passive roles, masochists are not considered dangerous.

For some sadists and masochists, coitus becomes unnecessary; pain or humiliation alone is sufficient to produce sexual pleasure. As with other paraphilic disorders, DSM-IV-TR specifies that to receive the diagnosis the person must have acted on the urges and must be markedly distressed by them.

Most sadomasochists (men and women) engage in and enjoy both submissive and dominant roles (Lussier, McCann, & Beauregard, 2008). Only 16 percent are exclusively dominant or submissive. Many engaged in spanking, whipping, and bondage (Table 14.8). Approximately 40 percent engaged in behaviors that caused minor pain using ice, hot wax, biting, or face slapping. Fewer than 18 percent engaged in more harmful procedures, such as burning or piercing. Nearly all respondents reported sadomasochistic (S&M) activities to be more satisfying than "straight" sex. Most sadomasochists who have been studied report that they do not seek harm or injury but that they find the sensation of utter helplessness appealing (Baumeister, 1988). S&M activities are often carefully scripted and involve role playing and mutual consent by the participants. In addition, fantasies involving sexual abuse, rejection, and forced sex are not uncommon among both male and female college students. Most sadomasochistic behavior among college students involves very mild forms of pain (such as in biting or pinching) that are accepted in our society.

Sadomasochistic behavior is considered deviant when pain, either inflicted or received, is necessary for sexual arousal and orgasm. According to Kinsey and his associates (1953), 22 percent of men and 12 percent of women reported at least some sexual response to sadomasochistic stories. Janus and Janus (1993) reported that 14 percent of men and 11 percent of women have had at least some sadomasochistic experiences.

Some cases of sadomasochism appear to be the result of an early experience associating sexual arousal with pain. One masochistic man reported that as a child he was often

sexual sadism disorder a disorder in which sexually arousing urges, fantasies, or acts are associated with inflicting physical or psychological suffering on others

sexual masochism disorder a disorder in which sexual urges, fantasies, or acts are associated with being humiliated, bound, or made to suffer

TABLE 14.8   Sadomasochistic Activities Ranked by Samples of Male and Female Participants

Activity	Male (percentage)	Female (percentage)
Spanking	79	80
Master-slave relationships	79	76
Oral sex	77	90
Bondage	67	88
Humiliation	65	61
Restraint	60	83
Anal sex	58	51
Pain	51	34
Whipping	47	39
Use of rubber or leather	42	42
Enemas	33	22
Torture	32	32
Golden showers (urination)	30	37

Note: These sadomasochistic sexual preferences were reported by both male and female respondents. Many more men express a preference for S&M activities, but women who do so are likely to engage in this form of sexual behavior more frequently and with many more partners.

Source: Data from Brewslow, Evans, & Langley, (1986)

"caned" on the buttocks by a school headmaster as his "attractive" wife looked on (Money, 1987). He reported, "I got sexual feelings from around the age of twelve, especially if she was watching" (p. 273). He and some of his schoolmates later hired prostitutes to spank them. Later yet, he engaged in self-whipping.

In addition to the paraphilic disorders covered here, DSM-IV-TR lists many others under the category of paraphilia "not otherwise specified." They include *telephone scatalogia* (making obscene telephone calls) and sexual urges involving corpses (*necrophilia*), animals (*zoophilia*), or feces (*coprophilia*).

Etiology and Treatment of Paraphilias

All etiological theories for the paraphilias attempt to answer three questions: (1) What produced the deviant arousal pattern?; (2) Why does the person not develop a more appropriate outlet for his or her sexual drive?; (3) Why is the behavior not deterred by normative and legal prohibitions? As the multipath model suggests, there are multiple contributing causes, but the state of our knowledge provides only partial answers.

Earlier, we noted that investigators have attempted to find genetic, neurohormonal, and brain anomalies that might be associated with sexual disorders. Some of the research findings conflict; others need replication and confirmation. There is evidence, however, that some men may be biologically predisposed to pedophilia ("Are Some Men Predisposed to Pedophilia?," 2007), as they have been found to have deficits in brain activation and less white matter. In any event, researchers need to continue applying advanced technology in the study of the biological influences on sexual disorders.

Even if biological factors are found to be important in the causes of sexual disorders, psychological factors are also likely to contribute in important ways. Among early attempts to explain paraphilic disorders, psychodynamic theorists proposed that all sexual deviations symbolically represent unconscious conflicts that began in early childhood (Schrut, 2005). Castration anxiety is hypothesized to be an important etiological factor underlying transvestic fetishism, exhibitionism, sadism, and masochism. This anxiety occurs because the Oedipal complex is not fully resolved. Because the boy's incestuous desires are only partially repressed, he fears retribution from his father in the form of castration. If this is the case, many sexual deviations can be seen as attempts to protect the person from castration anxiety. For example, in transvestic disorder, acknowledging that women lack a penis raises the fear of castration. To refute this possibility, the male transvestite "restores" the penis to women through cross-dressing. In this manner, he unconsciously represents a "woman who has a penis" and therefore reduces the fear of castration. An item of clothing or a particular fetish is selected because it represents a phallic symbol.

Similarly, according to psychodynamic theorists, an exhibitionist exposes to reassure himself that castration has not occurred. The shock that registers on the faces of others assures him that he still has a penis. A sadist may protect himself from castration anxiety by inflicting pain (power equals penis). A masochist may engage in self-castration through the acceptance of pain, thereby limiting the power of others to castrate him. Because castration anxiety stems from an unconscious source, the fear is never completely allayed, so the person feels compelled to repeat deviant sexual acts. The psychodynamic treatment of sexual deviations involves helping the patient understand the relationship between the deviation and the unconscious conflict that produced it.

Learning theorists stress the importance of early conditioning experiences in the etiology of sexually deviant behaviors. For example, if a person with poor social skills masturbates while engaged in sexually deviant fantasies, the conditioning may hamper the development of normal sexual patterns. A young boy may develop a fetish for women's panties after he becomes sexually excited watching girls come down a slide with their underpants exposed. He begins to masturbate to fantasies of girls with their panties showing and may develop a fetish into adulthood. Accidental association between sexual arousal and exposure to situations, events, acts, or objects may result in the development of paraphilias and/or a paraphilic disorder. In other words, classical conditioning, operant conditioning, and/or observational learning can account for the development of paraphilias.

Learning approaches to treating sexual deviations have generally involved one or more of the following elements: (1) weakening or eliminating the sexually inappropriate behaviors through processes such as extinction or aversive conditioning; (2) acquiring or strengthening sexually appropriate behaviors; and (3) developing appropriate social skills. The following case illustrates this multiple approach:

Case Study

A twenty-seven-year-old man with a three-year history of pedophilic activities (fondling and cunnilingus) with four- to seven-year-old girls was treated through the following procedure. The man first masturbated to orgasm while exposed to stimuli involving adult females. He then masturbated to orgasm while listening to a relaxation tape, and then he masturbated (but not to orgasm) to deviant stimuli. The procedure allowed the strengthening of normal arousal patterns and lessened the ability to achieve an orgasm while exposed to deviant stimuli (extinction). Measurement of penile tumescence when exposed to the stimuli indicated a sharp decrease to pedophilic stimuli and high arousal to heterosexual stimuli. These changes were maintained over a twelve-month follow-up period. (Alford, Morin, Atkins, & Schuen, 1987)

One of the more unique treatments for exhibitionism is the *aversive behavior rehearsal (ABR) program* (Wickramasekera, 1976), in which shame or humiliation is the aversive stimulus. The technique requires that the patient exhibit himself in his usual manner to a preselected audience of women. During the exhibiting act, the patient must verbalize a conversation between himself and his penis. He must talk about what he is feeling emotionally and physically and must explain his fantasies regarding what he supposes the female observers are thinking about him. One premise of the ABR program is that exhibitionism often occurs during a state similar to hypnosis, when the exhibitionist's fantasies are extremely active and his judgment is impaired. The ABR method forces him to experience and examine his act while being fully aware of what he is doing.

The results of behavioral treatment have been generally positive, but the majority of the studies involved single participants. Few control groups were included. Another problem in interpreting the results of these studies becomes apparent when we examine the approaches that were employed. For the most part, several different behavioral techniques were used within each study, so evaluation of a particular technique is impossible.

■ Rape

Although it is not considered a DSM disorder, we believe that the magnitude and seriousness of problems related to rape in our society warrant such discussion. Public awareness of these problems has heightened in the wake of highly publicized allegations of sexual assault or harassment made against public figures such as basketball player Kobe Bryant, boxer Mike Tyson, NFL quarterback Ben Roethlisberger, conservative talk show host Bill O'Reilly, Supreme Court Justice Clarence Thomas, and actor Mel Gibson.

Rape is a form of sexual aggression that refers to *sexual activity* (oral-genital sex, anal intercourse, and vaginal intercourse) performed against a person's will through the use of force, argument, pressure, alcohol or drugs, or authority (McAnulty & Burnette, 2004). With a child younger than the age of consent, however, the law recognizes what is called *statutory rape*. Rape is an act surrounded by many myths and misconceptions (Table 14.9). Considerable controversy exists over whether rape is primarily a crime of violence or of sex. Feminists have challenged the belief that rape is an act of sexual deviance; they make a good case that it is truly an act of violence and aggression against women. The principal motive, they believe, is that of power, not sex (Marsh, 1988).

The number of rapes in the United States has risen dramatically, with an average of 1.3 rapes every minute, 78 rapes in one hour, 1,872 rapes in one day, 56,160 rapes each month, and 683,280 rapes each year (CEASE, 2011). It is estimated that 1 in 3 women will be sexually assaulted in their lifetime. However, in past decades, only about 16 percent of reported cases resulted in a conviction for rape, with another 4 percent of those cases producing convictions for lesser offenses. This low conviction rate and the humiliation and shame of a rape trial keep many women from reporting rapes, so the actual incidence of the crime is probably much higher than reported.

Most rape victims are young women in their teens or twenties; in approximately one-half of all rape cases, the victim is at least acquainted with the rapist and is attacked in the home or in an automobile. One in seven women will be raped by their husband. About 90 percent of rapists attack persons of the same race; most rapes are planned and not impulsive. The most frequent form of rape reported is "acquaintance" or "date" rape.

Date rape may account for the majority of all rapes. Many victims may be reluctant to report such an attack; they feel responsible—at least in part—because they made a date with their attacker. Statistics vary as to the incidence of date rapes. Between 8 and 25 percent of female college students have reported that they had "unwanted sexual intercourse," and studies have generally found that most college women experienced some unwanted sexual activity (Aardvark, 2011). Men who try to coerce women into intercourse share certain characteristics (Hall, Windover, & Maramba, 1998; Lussier, McCann, & Beauregard, 2008). They tend to (1) actively create the situation in which sexual encounters may occur; (2) interpret women's friendliness as provocation or their protests as insincerity; (3) try to

Did You Know?

Early explanations attributed rape to an unusually quick sexual arousal response and impulsivity that was considered a natural reaction. Thus excuses were made for men: "Boys will be boys." Conversely, women were often blamed for enticing rape through flirtatious behaviors and/or revealing dress. In reality, rape is an act of aggression and control, not sex. Most rapists are deliberate and often plan their attacks.

rape a form of sexual aggression that refers to sexual activity (oral-genital sex, anal intercourse, and vaginal intercourse) performed against a person's will through the use of force, argument, pressure, alcohol or drugs, or authority

TABLE 14.9   The Facts about Rape

- **Anyone can be raped.** Rape happens among all age groups, from infants to elderly women; among all economic classes, from rich to poor; among all ethnic groups/races of people; and in heterosexual and same-sex relationships.

- **Rape happens to both males and females.** Statistics show that 1 in 4 girls and 1 in 6 boys are sexually assaulted before they reach the age of eighteen. About 1 in 6 women and 1 in 11 men are raped after turning eighteen.

- **Rape is not sex.** Rape is an act of violence. Rape is used as a way of dominating, humiliating, and terrifying another person.

- **Rape is never the fault of the victim.** It has nothing to do with what the victim wore, where the victim went, what the victim did, or whether they are "attractive." Only the person committing the assault is to blame. Rape is painful, humiliating, and hurtful. No one ever asks to be raped.

- **A rapist can be someone you know.** Most rapes happen between people of the same race or ethnicity. You are also much more likely to be raped by someone you know than a stranger. Approximately 75 percent of rapes are committed by someone the survivor knows.

- **You have the right to say "No" anytime.** You can be raped by someone you've had sex with before, even your spouse or partner. Each time you are asked to have sex, you have the right to say "no," even if you've said "yes" before. You also have the right to stop having sex at any time.

- **Rape is against the law.** Not only is rape always wrong, it's also a crime.

Source: San Francisco Women Against Rape, 3543 18th Street, San Francisco, CA 94110, 415-861-2024 (http://www.sfwar.org/facts.html, retrieved January 9, 2011)

manipulate women into sexual favors by using alcohol (some 70 percent of rapes are associated with alcohol intoxication) or "date rape drugs" such as rohypnol and GHB; (4) attribute failed attempts at sexual encounters to perceived negative features of the woman, thereby protecting their egos; (5) come from environments of parental neglect or physical or sexual abuse; (6) initiate coitus earlier than men who are not sexually aggressive; and (7) have more sexual partners than males who are not sexually aggressive. Many men who do not rape may also have these characteristics. Indeed, when asked to indicate the likelihood that they would rape if assured that they would not be caught and punished, approximately one-third of college males reported some likelihood.

Sexual aggression by men is quite common. Fifteen percent of a sample of college men reported that they forced intercourse at least once or twice. In a survey of students enrolled in thirty-two universities in the United States, more than 50 percent of women reported being the victims of sexual aggression, and 8 percent of men admitted to committing sexual acts that met the legal definition of rape (Hall, 1996; Koss, Gidycz, & Wisniewski, 1987). Women seldom reported episodes of date rape. Many universities are conducting workshops for students to help them understand that intercourse without consent during a date or other social activity is rape.

Did You Know?

Approximately two of every three rapes occur in the victim's home or that of a friend, relative, or neighbor.

Source: CEASE (2011)

Effects of Rape

Rape victims may experience a cluster of emotional reactions known as the rape trauma syndrome; they include psychological distress, phobic reactions, and sexual dysfunction (Lussier, McCann, & Beauregard, 2008; Gijs, 2008). These reactions appear consistent with post-traumatic stress disorder. Two phases have been identified in rape trauma syndrome (Koss, 1993):

1. *Acute Phase: Disorganization* During this period of several or more weeks, the rape victim may have feelings of self-blame, fear, and depression. The victim may believe

rape trauma syndrome   a two-phase syndrome that rape victims may experience, including such emotional reactions as psychological distress, phobic reactions, and sexual dysfunction

Protesting Rape

In South Africa it is reported that half a million women are victims of sexual violence, but only one in nine women who are raped will report it. Antirape and crime activists stage a mock crucifixion in Johannesburg to protest the reported recent assault of a woman raped by nine men and to highlight the unacceptable high numbers of women who are raped in the country.

he or she was responsible for the rape (for example, by not locking the door, not wearing provocative clothing, or by being overly friendly toward the attacker). The victim may have a fear that the attacker will return and anxiety that she may again be raped or even killed. The victim may express these emotional reactions and beliefs directly as anger, fear, rage, anxiety, and/or depression, or conceal them, appearing amazingly calm. Beneath this exterior, however, are signs of tension, including headaches, irritability, restlessness, sleeplessness, and jumpiness.

2. *Long-Term Phase: Reorganization* This second phase may last for several years. The victim begins to deal directly with her feelings and attempts to reorganize her life. Lingering fears and phobic reactions continue, especially to situations or events that remind the victim of the traumatic incident. A host of reactions may be present. Many women report one or more sexual dysfunctions as the result of the rape; fear of sex and lack of desire or arousal appear most common. Some women recover quickly, but others report problems years after the rape. Victims may experience selective fears involving things such as darkness and enclosed places—conditions likely to be associated with rape. Duration and intensity of fear also appear to be related to perceptions of danger. Many women drastically alter their feelings of safety and personal vulnerability; they feel unsafe in many situations and over an extended period of time. It is clear that the impact of rape has long-lasting consequences and that family, friends, and acquaintances need to exercise patience and understanding of the victim as she goes through the healing process.

Etiology of Rape

Rape is not specifically listed in the DSM as a mental disorder because of the controversy regarding whether rape is an act of aggression or sex. In an influential study of 133 rapists that supported the former viewpoint, Groth, Burgess, and Holstrom (1977) distinguished three motivational types:

1. The *power rapist*, comprising 55 percent of those studied, is primarily attempting to compensate for feelings of personal or sexual inadequacy by intimidating his victims.

2. The *anger rapist*, comprising 40 percent of those studied, is angry at women in general; the victim is merely a convenient target.
3. The *sadistic rapist*, comprising only 5 percent of those studied, derives satisfaction from inflicting pain and may torture or mutilate the victim.

These findings are used to support the contention that rape has more to do with power, aggression, and violence than with sex. More recent formulations and findings suggest that there is, however, support that rape is partially sexually motivated (Abel & Rouleau, 1990; LeVay & Valente, 2006; Lussier, McCann, & Beauregard, 2008): (a) Although women with all degrees of physical attractiveness are raped, most victims are in their teens or twenties (considered most sexually attractive), (b) most rapists name sexual motivation as the primary reason for their actions, and (c) many rapists seem to have multiple paraphilias. Thus, it appears that sexual motivation may play some role in some rapes.

Researchers are raising questions about the effect that media portrayals of violent sex, especially in pornography, have on rape rates. Exposure to such material may affect attitudes and thoughts and influence patterns of sexual arousal. These media portrayals may reflect and affect societal values concerning violence and women. A "cultural spillover" theory—namely, that rape tends to be high in cultures or environments that encourage violence—has been proposed (Baron, Straus, & Jaffee, 1988). The investigators studied the relationship between cultural support for violence, as well as demographic characteristics and rates of rapes in all fifty states. Results indicated that cultural support for violence was significantly related to the rate of rape: When violence is generally encouraged or condoned, there is a "spillover" effect on rape. Interestingly, the United States has been described as a violent and sexually oriented society; it has the highest rape rates of countries reporting such statistics (CEASE, 2011). It is four times higher than Germany, thirteen times higher than England, and twenty times higher than Japan.

Treatment for Rapists

Many believe that sex offenders are not good candidates for treatment. High recidivism rates are often associated with sexual aggression, and the most frequent action is punishment (incarceration). Both conventional and more controversial treatments have been used or proposed.

Conventional Treatment

Imprisonment has been the main form of treatment for rapists. However, it is more accurate to describe it as punishment, as the majority of convicts receive little or no treatment in prison. Behavioral treatment for sexual aggressors (rapists and pedophiles) generally involves the following steps (Federoff, 2008; Lussier, McCann, & Beauregard, 2008):

1. Assessing sexual preferences through self-report and measuring erectile responses to different sexual stimuli
2. Reducing deviant interests through aversion therapy (e.g., the man receives electric shock when deviant stimuli are presented)
3. Orgasmic reconditioning or masturbation training to increase sexual arousal to appropriate stimuli
4. Social skills training to increase interpersonal competence
5. Assessment after treatment

Treatments for sex offenders are becoming increasingly sophisticated. They involve identifying risk factors and attempting to develop intervention strategies directly attuned to them. These risk factors are (1) *dispositional*, such as psychopathic or antisocial personality characteristics; (2) *historical*, such as prior history of crime and violence and developmental trauma; (3) *criminogenic*, such as deviant social networks and lack of positive social supports; and (4) *clinical*, such as indicators of substance abuse, psychiatric problems, and poor social functioning (Ward & Stewart, 2003). Treatment as previously outlined attempts to use the most empirically sound strategies to alter or minimize the risk factors (Polaschek, 2003). For example, if a person has a deviant social network, attempts are made to remove the person from such an environment.

Although treatment is becoming more sophisticated, questions remain about the effectiveness of these programs. Some treatment programs have been effective with child molesters and exhibitionists, but treatment outcomes have tended to be poor for rapists. Public revulsion and outrage against incest offenders, pedophiles, and rapists have resulted in calls for severe punishment, although there is no agreement as to what this should entail.

CRITICAL THINKING

Why Do Men Rape Women?

In 1995, former world heavyweight boxing champ Mike Tyson was released from prison after serving a sentence for raping a beauty contestant in his hotel room. During his trial, "talk radio" and the print media were filled with speculations about his motives and responsibility for the event. Some claimed that Tyson was only minimally responsible because the woman had willingly gone to his hotel room. (This reasoning was also offered to excuse Los Angeles Lakers basketball star Kobe Bryant of the alleged rape of a young hotel worker.) Others placed the blame on certain sports such as boxing, saying the activity condones aggression, even sexual aggression. Still others speculated that Tyson was oversexed, that his testosterone levels were high, or that he acted out because of steroid use.

Sociocultural Perspective

A variety of views of the causes of rape have been proposed. Some researchers theorized that rape was committed by mentally disturbed men, and studies were initiated to find personality characteristics that might be associated with committing rape. The sociocultural view of rape gained favor with the finding that a significant proportion of men would consider rape if they could get away with it. The view that rapists were simply mentally disturbed individuals began to change. Many argued that rape was a means of control and dominance whereby men keep women in a perpetual state of intimidation. This view emphasized a "culture" of male dominance rather than a sexual motive as a primary reason for sexual assault (McAnulty & Burnette, 2004).

Other theorists believe that social myths embedded in our culture reinforce themes that underlie rape: (1) that women have an unconscious desire to be overpowered and raped; (2) that women "ask for it" by dressing in provocative clothing, visiting a man's room, or going where they should not go; (3) that women could avoid rape if they wanted to; (4) that only "bad girls" get raped; and (5) that women only "cry rape" for revenge.

Sociobiological Perspective

Another explanation of rape and sexual aggression is posited by sociobiological models. Sexual aggression, according to this view, has an evolutionary basis. Sex differences have evolved as a means of maximizing the reproduction of the human species: Men have much more to gain in reproductive terms by being able to pass on their genes rapidly to a large number of women,

which increases their chances of having offspring (L. Ellis, 1991). Men's advantage is women's disadvantage, however. Because women must bear much more of the investment in each offspring before and after birth, natural selection would favor women whose mates are likely to supply a greater share of the investment in offspring. Therefore, it would be advantageous for women to avoid multiple partners and to seek male commitment. Ellis also argued that men's sex drive is stronger than women's and cited as evidence these three points:

1. Men in all societies have higher self-reported desires for copulation and other forms of sexual experiences.
2. Males (including males in other species of primates) masturbate more, especially in the absence of sex partners.
3. Women are more likely than men to report having sexual intercourse for reasons other than sexual gratification.

Ellis took issue with the view that rape is not a sexual crime. He agreed that rapists often try to obtain sex by actions such as getting women drunk and falsely pledging love; that they use physical force only after these other tactics fail; and that fewer men than women believe rape is motivated by power and anger. Nevertheless, sociobiological theories have difficulty explaining rates of rape in different societies or changes in rates of rape over time without references to cultural conditions or experiential factors. Ellis believes that the motivation for sexual assault is unlearned but that the behavior surrounding sexual assault is learned. Thus sexual motivation (including the drive to rape) is innate. If sexual aggression is reinforced (or not punished), forced copulatory attempts persist.

Isolating and testing different propositions concerning sexual assault have been difficult. Even so, no one—not even those who believe that men have a stronger biological sexual drive—can excuse or condone such behavior. Research findings suggest that changes in the way men and women relate to one another, attitudes toward violence, and cultural practices can reduce the incidence of rape.

For Further Consideration:

1. Can you give examples that support or disprove the sociocultural perspective?
2. Does the sociocultural perspective seem accurate to you?
3. Do you think punishment is an effective deterrent to rape?
4. Does the sociobiological perspective seem accurate to you?

Controversial Treatments

Surgical castration has been used to treat sexual offenders in many European countries, and results indicate that rates of relapse have been low (Federoff, 2008). Rapists, heterosexual pedophiles, homosexual pedophiles, bisexual pedophiles, and a sexual murderer who are surgically castrated do report a decrease in sexual intercourse, masturbation, and frequency of sexual fantasies. However, some of these men do remain sexually active.

Chemical therapy, usually involving the hormone Depo-Provera, reduces self-reports of sexual urges in pedophiles but not the ability to show genital arousal. Drugs appear to reduce psychological desire more than actual erection capabilities. The effectiveness of biological treatment such as surgery and chemotherapy is not known, and controversy obviously continues over the appropriate treatment for incest offenders, pedophiles, and rapists.

Summary

1. **What are normal and abnormal sexual behaviors?**
   - One of the difficulties in diagnosing abnormal sexual behavior is measuring it against a standard of normal sexual behavior. No attempt to establish such criteria has been completely successful, but these attempts have produced a better understanding of the normal human sexual response cycle.

2. **What does the normal sexual response cycle tell us about sexual dysfunctions?**
   - The human sexual response cycle has four stages: the appetitive, arousal, orgasm, and resolution phases. Each may be characterized by problems, which may be diagnosed as disorders if they are recurrent and persistent.
   - Sexual dysfunctions are disruptions of the normal sexual response cycle. They are fairly common in the general population and may affect a person's ability to become sexually aroused or to engage in intercourse. Many result from fear or anxiety regarding sexual activities; the various treatment programs are generally successful.

3. **What causes sexual dysfunctions?**
   - The multipath model illustrates how biological (hormonal variations and medical conditions), psychological (performance anxieties), social (parental upbringing and attitudes), and sociocultural (cultural scripts) dimensions contribute to sexual dysfunctions.

4. **What types of treatments are available for sexual dysfunctions?**
   - Depending on the specific dysfunction, treatments vary: Biological interventions such as hormone replacement are used in the treatment of low sexual desire; Penile implants or drugs like Viagra are used for erectile dysfunction; education and communications training are used to combat negative attitudes or misinformation about sex; and structured sexual exercises are prescribed for learning new behaviors and warding off performance anxieties.

5. How does aging affect the sexual activity of the elderly?

- Despite myths to the contrary, sexuality extends into old age. However, sexual dysfunction becomes increasingly prevalent with aging, and the frequency of sexual activity typically declines.

6. What causes gender dysphoria, and how is it treated?

- Gender dysphoria involves strong and persistent cross-gender identification. Transsexuals feel a severe psychological conflict between their sexual self-concepts and their genders. Children with this problem identify with members of the opposite gender, deny their own physical attributes, and often cross-dress.
- Some transsexuals seek sex-conversion surgery, although behavioral therapies are increasingly being used. For children, treatment generally includes the parents and is behavioral in nature.

7. What are paraphilic disorders, what causes them, and how are they treated?

- The paraphilic disorders are of three types, characterized by (1) a preference for nonhuman objects for sexual arousal, (2) repetitive sexual activity with nonconsenting partners, or (3) the association of real or simulated suffering with sexual activity.
- Biological factors such as hormonal or brain processes have been studied as the cause of paraphilic disorders, but the results have not been consistent enough to permit strong conclusions about the role of biological factors in the paraphilias. Psychological factors also play a role.
- Treatments are usually behavioral and are aimed at eliminating the deviant behavior while teaching more appropriate behaviors.

8. Is rape an act of sex or aggression?

- Rape is not listed in DSM, but it is a serious problem. There appears to be no single cause of rape, and rapists seem to have different motivations and personalities.
- Some researchers feel that sociocultural factors can encourage rape and violence against women; others believe that biological factors coupled with sociocultural factors are important in explaining rape.

Media Resources

Psychology CourseMate   Access an interactive eBook; chapter-specific interactive learning tools, including flash cards, quizzes, videos; and more in your Psychology CourseMate, accessed through CengageBrain.com.

CENGAGENOW

CengageNow   CengageNOW is an easy-to-use online resource that helps you study in less time to get the grade you want—NOW. If your textbook does not include an access code card, go to CengageBrain.com to gain access.

CENGAGEbrain.com

CengageBrain   More than just an interactive study guide, WebTutor is an anytime, anywhere customized learning solution with an eBook, keeping you connected to your textbook, instructor, and classmates. Purchase the access chosen by your instructor at CengageBrain.com.

15

Personality Psychopathology

A college senior in his final year at Oregon State University, Aaron Kopinsky was known as a "loner" by classmates. He seldom participated in social activities, had few friends in his dormitory, and even avoided any type of social relationship with his roommate. His favorite pastime seemed to be sitting in front of the TV and watching programs in the lounge. It mattered little what program was playing, as he never made an effort to change the channel. Few things seem to interest Aaron; he did not read the newspaper, didn't go to movies, and had few hobbies or activities that seemed to give him joy. Yet, he did not appear lonely. As his college major was in "forestry," he frequently went on "outings" that required long periods of time in the forests. While some of his classmates would huddle around a campfire during the evenings for companionship, Aaron preferred to be by himself.

Jennifer Wang, a thirty-four-year-old project manager for a small technology start-up company, was always described by family, friends, and coworkers as being excessively compulsive. At team meetings she was demanding, insistent that things be done correctly in a prescribed manner, and would drive employees "crazy" with her detailed lists, tasks, and posted schedules. Team members were expected to check off tasks (which were always written in red) posted on the bulletin board when completed; they had to do so with a blue colored marker. Any other color would not do. Jennifer would become upset when even the most trivial tasks or schedules were not completed or followed. Everything had to be done flawlessly without errors or faults.

Jordan Mitchell was "clubbing" with friends in San Francisco when he met an attractive prostitute who invited him to a nearby hotel for sex. Despite being warned by friends to use a condom because of the high incidence of HIV infection in the neighborhood, he failed to do so. He did not believe he was in any danger of catching HIV and was willing to take the risk. Throughout his life, Jordon exhibited a high degree of recklessness and impulsivity. He enjoyed risky and dangerous activities such a racing his car against other willing drivers at intersections, and discharging his firearm into the sky at night within city limits. Jordan seemed to bore easily and constantly needed excitement. It was difficult for him to keep his mind on any one task or activity and to follow a plan to completion. Follow through was a major problem because his impulsivity, distractibility, and constant need for change would sidetrack him.

focus questions

1 Can one's personality be pathological?

2 What criteria are used to assess personality disorders?

3 Are there certain personality disorder types?

4 How does the multipath model explain antisocial personality disorder?

5 What types of therapy are used in treating antisocial personality disorder?

6 What personality traits are important in determining pathology?

A aron Kopinsky, Jennifer Wang, and Jordan Mitchell all possess an organized set of characteristic patterns of behaviors, thoughts, and feelings that typify how they generally respond to life situations. These behavioral and mental characteristics make each of them unique and are said to form the basis of their personalities. The concept of "personality" in psychology encompasses three assumptions. First, it refers to an individual's recognizable behaviors in which a pattern, order, and regularity can be identified. Aaron, for example, prefers spending time by himself; he is a loner, probably introverted, and avoids almost all social interactions or situations. Jennifer might be described as detail oriented, perfectionistic, and quite inflexible. Jordan, however, is impulsive, a thrill seeker, and a risk taker. Essentially, all three exhibit a consistency in how they respond to similar, or even different, situations. Second, personality is a psychological construct, but as we shall shortly see, research suggests that it is also influenced by biological processes and needs (Kuo & Linehan, 2009; Sterzer, 2010). People, for example, have been found at birth to exhibit different levels of physiological reactivity to outside stimulation (Glenn et al., 2009). This may account for why some people seek or avoid new and novel situations. Third, personality not only influences how we respond in the world, but it *causes* us to act in certain ways.

If we assume that Aaron, Jennifer, and Jordan are not suffering from any form of mental disorder, can their personalities be pathological?; that is, "Can people's characteristic style of responding prove problematic to themselves or others?" Certainly, social isolation and being friendless may be bothersome to most of us, but Aaron does not appear bothered by it. He prefers solitary tasks and situations, and perhaps his major in forestry and desire to become a forest ranger may be the perfect occupational match. Jennifer's compulsivity may be maddening to coworkers, but there are upsides and downsides to this prominent trait. Being orderly and attentive to details are assets in many situations (accurate record keeping, accounting, etc.). Being rule- and habit-governed, however, may mean a sacrifice of creativity and adaptability to unexpected problems or situations. On the other hand, Jordan's need for excitement, impulsivity, and risk-taking actions may place both him and others in danger. His personality traits are more likely to become problematic than perhaps that of Aaron and Jennifer.

As we shall see in this chapter, when personality characteristics result in an adaptive failure in life, when they cause personal problems to self or others, and when they are quite pronounced, the person may be suffering from personality psychopathology or a personality disorder. People with personality psychopathology often function well enough to get along without aid from others. They often fall under the radar and are simply described as odd, peculiar, dramatic, or unusual. They may not see themselves as having a problem. For example, a person with a pronounced tendency to avoid social interactions like Aaron is described as "shy" (avoidant personality disorder type); a person with a strong self-orientation is described as "selfish" (prominent personality traits of narcissism, manipulativeness, and callousness); and a person with a preference to be alone is described as a "hermit" (prominent personality traits of social withdrawal, detachment, and intimacy avoidance).

Indeed, as we have mentioned, some pronounced personality traits may actually serve as an asset in certain situations. For these reasons, many people with personality psychopathology rarely come to the attention of mental health professionals, seldom seek help, and often terminate prematurely when in therapy (Millon et al., 2004). As a result, the incidence of personality disorders has been difficult to ascertain, but available statistics indicate that these disorders account for 5 to 15 percent of admissions to hospitals and outpatient clinics. The overall lifetime prevalence of personality disorders is 9 to 13 percent, which suggests that these disorders are relatively common in the general population (Lenzenweger et al., 2007; Phillips, Yen, & Gunderson, 2004).

personality disorder a disorder characterized by inflexible, long-standing, and maladaptive personality traits that cause significant functional impairment, subjective distress, or a combination of both for the individual

Diagnosing Personality Psychopathology

Personality disorders can be diagnosed through two different routes: (1) through being categorized as showing characteristics from one of six specific personality disorder types, or (2) through possessing certain specific personality traits that impair functioning. Both

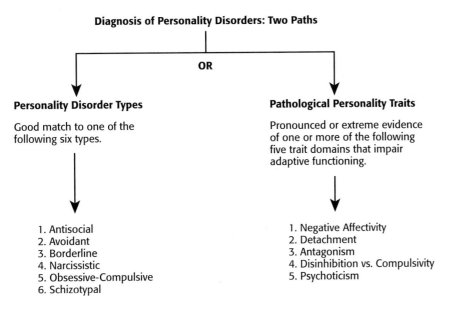

Figure 15.1

DIAGNOSING PERSONALITY DISORDERS: TWO PATHS

personality types and descriptive personality traits must be pronounced, and a good match with the individual. Further, the person's impairment or problem in adaptation must be relatively stable across time and situations (i.e., its manifestation can be traced to at least adolescence). Adaptive failures or problems related to personality must not due to the presence of another mental disorder or to the physiological effects of substance use or to a general medical condition. Figure 15.1 outlines the two major paths by which a diagnosis of a personality disorder may be made.

All of us have characteristic ways of responding, thinking, and feeling when encountering situations or other people. Some of us are outgoing, sociable, and adventurous in new or unfamiliar situations. Others of us are more cautious, laid back, and hesitant to form new relationships until we have adequately familiarized ourselves with our surrounding environment. In other words, most of us have a degree of consistency and predictability in our outlook on life and in how we approach people and situations (Millon et al., 2004). Yet all of us possess a degree of flexibility in how we respond to similar or different situations. A shy coworker, for example, is not necessarily shy in all situations or when he or she gets to know other employees. People with personality psychopathology, however, possess rigid patterns of responding that are inflexible, long-standing, and enduring and that can extend into the elderly years (Abrams & Bromberg, 2007); they are shy and withdrawn in nearly all situations and continue to be uncomfortable even with people they know well. Personality disorders begin early in life and generally become evident in adolescence (Weston & Riolo, 2007), and there are frequently telltale signs in childhood (Gao et al., 2010; Lahey et al., 2005; Sterzer, 2010).

Levels of Personality Functioning

According to DSM-5, personality disorders represent a significant impairment or adaptive failure in the individual's *self functioning (identity and self-direction issues)* and in his or her ability to engage in *effective interpersonal functioning (empathy and intimacy issues)*. In other words, the key element in this definition is "impairment" and adaptive failure because both concepts implicitly acknowledge that everyone has a personality and that how it is used determines whether it is adaptive or maladaptive. The possible *interpersonal failures* of Aaron, Jennifer, and Jordan are quite clear. Problems of intimacy (Aaron), cooperativeness (Jennifer), and social responsibility (Jordan) may ultimately result in dysfunctional relationships with others. All three also seem to possess potential *self-identity problems* (e.g., identity integration, integrity of self-concept, and self-directness). A case can be made, for example, that Jordan's adaptive failure in self-identity can be seen as a lack of direction, meaning, and purpose in life. He possesses low self-directness and is unable to set or achieve satisfying and rewarding goals. The general diagnostic criteria in DSM-5 for a personality disorder are outlined in Table 15.1.

TABLE 15.1 General Diagnostic Criteria for Personality Disorder

A personality disorder represents impairments in personality (self and interpersonal) functioning and the presence of pathological personality traits. To diagnose a personality disorder, the impairments must meet all of the following criteria.

A. Significant impairments in **self (identity or self direction)** and **interpersonal (empathy or intimacy)** functioning.

B. One or more pathological personality trait domains or trait facets.

C. Impairments and trait expression are relatively stable across time and consistent across situations.

D. Impairments and trait expressions are not better understood as normative for the person's developmental stage or socio-cultural environment.

E. Impairments and trait expressions not due solely to direct physiological effects of a substance (e.g., medication, drug abuse) or medical condition (e.g., severe head trauma).

Adapted from DSM-5.org, (accessed August 9, 2011)

In diagnosing a personality disorder, clinicians would approach the task by asking the following questions: (a) Does the person have impairment in personality functioning and if so, how severe is it? (b) If present, is it manifested in one of the six personality disorder types or in one of the five pathological personality traits (see Figure 15.1)?

The absence or degree of impairment in personality functioning is measured on a 5-point scale on the Level of Personality Functioning continuum: 0 = no impairment; 1 = mild impairment; 2 = moderate impairment; 3 = serious impairment; and 4 = extreme impairment. Impairment is assessed in self (identity and self-direction) and interpersonal (empathy and intimacy) functioning. For Aaron, Jennifer, and Jordan, a clinician would use these criteria to determine the degree of impairment the three would experience on the self and interpersonal functioning continuum.

Sociocultural Considerations

In diagnosing a personality disorder, DSM-5 recognizes the importance of culture and ethnicity by stressing that what is considered "impairment or adaptive" is based on the individual's contextual norms and expectations. It acknowledges that culture shapes habits, customs, values, and personality characteristics, so that expressions of personality in one culture may differ from those in another culture. Asians, for example, are more likely to exhibit shyness and collectivism, whereas Americans are more likely to show assertiveness and individualism (Sue & Sue, 2008a). Japanese people and Asian Indians (South Asians) often display more overt dependent, submissive, and social conformance behaviors than Americans or Europeans. In essence, these three traits in U.S. society often possess negative connotations. Does this mean that people in Japan and India are more likely to have this type of personality disorder? More likely, the high incidence of these behaviors reflects the influence of other factors, one of which may be cultural bias in the classification system.

In one study conducted in the United Kingdom, it was found that whites were 2.8 times more likely to be given a diagnosis of antisocial personality disorder than African Caribbeans (Mikton & Grounds, 2007). The diagnosis varied not only with the race of the client but also with that of the clinician. The three possible explanations of bias were (1) belief that antisocial and criminal behavior is more "normal" among African Caribbean men, (2) tendency to attribute antisocial behavior to environmental factors for blacks, and (3) reluctance to attribute pathology to blacks because of sensitivity to risks of prejudice and stigmatization. Anyone making judgments about personality functioning and disturbance must consider the individual's cultural, ethnic, and social background (DSM-5.org).

Gender implications are also important in the diagnosis of personality disorders, although there are some inconsistencies due primarily to the year of the studies and the locations from which the populations are drawn (Millon et al., 2004). One major study found that men are more likely than women to be diagnosed as having antisocial personality disorder (Grant et al., 2004), whereas women more often receive diagnoses of borderline personality disorder (Kuo & Linehan, 2009), possession of psychopathological traits associated with excessive dependency, and emotional lability (Millon et al., 2004; Torgersen, Kringlen, & Cramer, 2001). The existence of gender differences in the diagnosis of certain personality disorders is widely known in the profession. The question, however, is whether these differences are attributable to biases (Widiger & Coker, 2002).

Gender bias occurs when diagnostic categories are not valid and when they have a different impact on men and women. The mere fact that men and women have different prevalence rates for a particular disorder is not sufficient to prove gender bias. Rates may differ because of actual biological conditions (e.g., a genetic predisposition) or social conditions (e.g., stressors) that affect one gender more than another. For the diagnostic system to be biased, the differences must be attributable to errors or problems in the categories or diagnostic criteria. Debate over what these differences mean continues.

Personality Type and Personality Trait Disorders: A Hybrid Approach

In the past, the multiaxial classification of mental disorders listed all the clinical disorders on Axis I, whereas personality disorders, mental retardation, and long-standing defenses are noted on Axis II. Under the new DSM-5, this separation appears less important and may eventually be eliminated, although the distinction between personality psychopathology and the clinical disorders remains: (1) Personality disorders are chronic, developmental, and relatively inflexible patterns of responding that are less likely to be successfully changed in treatment; and (2) it is entirely possible for a personality disorder to coexist with one or more clinical disorders. For example, a person with a personality disorder may also be diagnosed with schizophrenia or alcohol dependency. Usually, people with personality disorders are hospitalized only when a second clinical disorder (e.g., schizophrenia, depression, etc.) so impairs social functioning that they require inpatient care. In fact, the treatment outcome for people with clinical disorders who also have personality disorders is worse than for those who have only clinical disorders (Benjamin & Karpiak, 2002; Clarkin & Levy, 2004).

DSM-5 uses a hybrid approach in conceptualizing personality disorders. There is recognition that some disorders are more categorical in nature, whereas others are more accurately described on a continuum of traits. We discuss the personality trait means of determining personality impairment shortly, but we first concentrate on personality disorder types. Of the ten personality disorders identified by DSM-IV-TR, only six seem to possess sufficient research support to be considered semi-categorical in nature: antisocial, avoidant, borderline, narcissistic, obsessive-compulsive, and schizotypal types (DeFife, 2010; Skodol & Bender, 2009; Westen et al., 2010). The other four types (paranoid, schizoid, histrionic, and dependent) appear to better fit a dimensional trait description rather than as freestanding entities (Haslam, 2003; Science Daily, 2010). There is considerable controversy, however, about whether to retire these four or maintain them in the original personality types.

■ Personality Disorder Types

As Figure 15.1 reveals, one path by which a person may be diagnosed as having a personality disorder is through matching a categorical type. Research supports the existence of six specific personality disorder types (Table 15.2): schizotypal, borderline, avoidant, narcissistic, obsessive-compulsive, and antisocial. To diagnose a personality disorder type, clinicians use a brief DSM-5 description of the disorder and determine the degree of "match" with the individual.

DISORDERS CHART   PERSONALITY DISORDER TYPES

TABLE 15.2

Personality Disorder	Symptoms	Gender Differences	Prevalence
Schizotypal type	• Peculiar thoughts and behaviors, poor interpersonal relationships	Higher in males	2.0–4.0%
Borderline type	• Intense fluctuations in mood, self-image, and interpersonal relationships	Higher in females	1.0–5.9%
Avoidant type	• Fear of rejection and humiliation, reluctance to enter into social relationships	None	0.3–2.0%
Narcissistic type	• Exaggerated sense of self importance, exploitativeness, relationships largely superficial	Higher in males	1.0–2.0%
Obsessive-compulsive type	• Perfectionism, interpersonally controlling, devotion to details, and rigidity	Higher in males	1% (DSM-IV-TR); 7.9% (Grant et al., 2004)
Antisocial type	• Failure to conform to social or legal codes, lack of anxiety and guilt, irresponsible behaviors	Higher in males	2.0–3.6%

Note: In all of the personality disorders, early symptoms appear in childhood or adolescence. Personality disorders tend to be stable and to endure over time, although symptoms of antisocial and borderline personality disorders tend to remit with age.

Source: Based on American Psychiatric Association, (2000a); Bollini & Walker, (2007); Grant et al., (2004); Kuo & Linehan, (2009); O'Connor, (2008). Prevalence figures and gender differences have varied from study to study, and investigators may disagree on these rates. Because the definition of personality psychopathology has moved to a continuous description of types, it is possible that these rates will change in future prevalence studies.

Schizotypal Type

People with the schizotypal type of personality disorder manifest odd, eccentric, peculiar thoughts and behaviors and have poor interpersonal relationships. Many believe they possess magical thinking abilities or special powers (e.g., "I can predict what people will say before they say it"), and some are subject to recurrent illusions (e.g., "I feel that my dead father is watching me"). Speech oddities, such as frequent digression or vagueness in conversation, are often present. The disorder occurs in approximately 2 to 4 percent of the population, more frequently among men than women. Again, the evaluation of individuals must take into account their cultural milieu. Superstitious beliefs, delusions, and hallucinations may be condoned or encouraged in certain religious ceremonies or other cultures.

The peculiarities seen in schizotypal types stem from distortions or difficulties in cognition (Bollini & Walker, 2007; Goodman et al., 2007). That is, these people seem to have problems in thinking and perceiving. People with this disorder often show social isolation, hypersensitivity, and inappropriate affect (emotions). They seem to lack pleasure from social interactions (Blanchard et al., 2000). The prevailing belief is that the disorder is defined primarily by cognitive distortions and that affective and interpersonal problems are secondary. Research has demonstrated some cognitive processing abnormalities in individuals with this disorder that help to explain many of the symptoms (Goodman et al., 2007; Stone, 2001).

The man described in the following case was diagnosed as having schizotypal personality disorder type.

schizotypal type a personality disorder characterized by peculiar thoughts and behaviors and by poor interpersonal relationships

Case Study

A forty-one-year-old man was referred to a community mental health center's activities program for help in improving his social skills. He had a lifelong pattern of social isolation, with no real friends, and spent long hours worrying that his angry thoughts about his older brother would cause his brother harm. During one interview, the patient was distant and somewhat distrustful. He described in elaborate and often irrelevant detail his rather uneventful and routine daily life.... For two days he had studied the washing instructions on a new pair of jeans—Did "wash before wearing" mean that the jeans were to be washed before wearing the first time, or did they need, for some reason, to be washed each time before they were worn? ... He asked the interviewer whether, if he joined the program, he would be required to participate in groups. He said that groups made him very nervous because he felt that if he revealed too much personal information, such as the amount of money that he had in the bank, people would take advantage of him or manipulate him for their own benefit. (Spitzer et al., 1994, pp. 289–290)

The man's symptoms included absence of close friends, magical thinking (worrying that his thoughts might harm his brother), being distant in the interview, and social anxiety. These symptoms are associated with schizotypal types.

Many characteristics of schizotypal types resemble those of schizophrenia, although in less serious form. For example, people with schizophrenia exhibit problems in personality characteristics, psychophysiological responses, and information processing— deficits that have also been observed among persons with schizotypal personality disorder (Goodman et al., 2007; Lenzenweger, 2001). Some evidence is consistent with a genetic interpretation of the link between the two disorders (Bollini & Walker, 2007). There appears to be a higher risk of schizotypal personality disorder among relatives of people diagnosed with schizophrenia than among members of a control group. In general, family, twin, and adoption studies support the genetic relationship between schizophrenia and schizotypal personality disorder type. Despite the possibility of genetic influence in the disorder, early environmental enrichment for children (i.e., two years of enhanced nutrition, education, and physical exercise) has been found to reduce schizotypal personality disorder and symptoms compared with a nonenriched group of children (Raine et al., 2003).

Various psychotherapies have been used to treat schizotypal types of personality disorders, such as dynamic therapy, supportive therapy, and cognitive-behavioral approaches, as well as group psychotherapy. For clients who are experiencing a great deal of anxiety, small doses of anxiolytics (a class of antianxiety drugs) may be used (Stone, 2001).

Borderline Type

A borderline type of personality disorder has a very fragile self-concept that may become easily disrupted and fragmented under stress. Self-identity is amorphous or lacking. Borderline types are also characterized by intense fluctuations in mood, self-image, and interpersonal relationships (Selby & Joiner, 2009). Persons with this disorder are impulsive, have chronic feelings of emptiness, and form unstable and intense interpersonal relationships (Goodman et al., 2007). They may be quite friendly one day and quite hostile the next. Many perceive their early childhoods as having malevolent others—others who were hostile or physically violent (Nigg et al., 1992). Many exhibit recurrent suicidal behaviors or gestures (Yen et al., 2003), and the probability of suicide attempts and completions are higher than average among those who have this disorder (Sherry & Whilde, 2008). Self-destructive behaviors, such as suicide attempts and self-harm (cutting and self-mutilation), are often triggered by interpersonal conflicts and events (Welch, Shaw, & Linehan, 2002). Sexual difficulties, such as sexual preoccupation, dissatisfaction, and depression, have also been

Did You Know?

Many well-known individuals have been described as having borderline personality disorder—Adolf Hitler, Marilyn Monroe, and even Princess Diana. Biographer and journalist Sally Bedell-Smith (1999) consulted a psychologist, who agreed that Princess Diana's rapid mood swings, preoccupation with real or imagined abandonment, dissatisfaction, depression, self-harm such as cutting, and suicide attempts fit the category well. It is important to note, however, that people with personality disorders may also suffer from other mental disorders.

borderline type a personality disorder characterized by intense fluctuations in mood, self-image, and interpersonal relationships

Chris Smith/PhotoEdit

Did Princess Diana Suffer from a Borderline Personality Disorder?

Princess Diana, smiling happily in this picture, was known to suffer from rapid mood swings, depression, and suicide attempts. Her emotional and behavioral traits, such as impulsiveness, marked fluctuations in mood, chronic feelings of emptiness, and unstable and intense interpersonal relationships, are consistent with a diagnosis of borderline personality disorder. Why do women receive this diagnosis far more frequently than do men?

observed (Zanarini et al., 2003). Although no single feature defines borderline type personality disorder, its essence can be captured in the capriciousness of behaviors and the lability of moods (Millon et al., 2004).

The prevalence of borderline type is about 1.4–5.9 percent of the population, with females three times as likely as males to receive the diagnosis (Kuo & Linehan, 2009; Lenzenweger et al., 2007). This is the most commonly diagnosed personality disorder in both inpatient and outpatient settings (Oldham, 2006). Some researchers believe that the prevalence of the disorder is increasing because our society makes it difficult for people to maintain stable relationships and a sense of identity.

The following example illustrates some of the many facets of borderline personality type.

Case Study

Bryan was a twenty-three-year-old graduate student majoring in sociology at a prestigious university. He was active in student government and was viewed as charismatic, articulate, and sociable. When he met other students for the first time, he could often persuade them to participate in the campus activities that interested him. Women were quite attracted to him because of his charm and self-disclosing nature. They described him as exciting, intense, and different from other men. Bryan could form close relationships with others very quickly.

Bryan could not, however, maintain his social relationships. Sometimes he would have a brief but intense affair with a woman and then abruptly and angrily ask himself what he ever saw in her. At other times, the woman would reject him after a few dates because she thought Bryan was moody, self-centered, and demanding. He often called his friends after midnight because he felt lonesome, empty, and bored and wanted to talk. Several times he threatened to commit suicide. He gave little thought to the inconvenience he was causing. Once he organized a group of students to protest the inadequate student parking the university provided. The morning of the planned protest demonstration, he announced that he no longer supported the effort. He said he was not in the right mood for the protest, much to the consternation of his followers, who had spent weeks preparing for the event. Bryan's intense but brief relationships, the marked and continual shifts in moods, and boredom with others in spite of his need for social contacts all point to borderline type of personality disorder.

People who have borderline type personality disorder may exhibit psychotic symptoms, such as auditory hallucinations (e.g., hearing imaginary voices that tell them to commit suicide), but the symptoms are usually transient (Sieswerda & Arntz, 2007). They also usually have an ego-dystonic reaction to their hallucinations (Oldham, 2006). That is, they recognize their imaginary voices or other hallucinations as being unacceptable, alien, and distressful. By contrast, a person with a psychotic disorder may not realize that his or her hallucinations are pathological. Some researchers (Trull et al., 2008) have found that individuals with borderline personality features are more likely to show dysfunctional moods, interpersonal problems, poor coping skills, and cognitive distortions than are people without borderline personality characteristics (Franklin et al., 2009). Again, it is important to note that borderline types may be better viewed as a continuous rather than a categorical disorder (Rothschild et al., 2003; Widiger & Mullins-Sweatt, 2005). Rather than either having or not having the disorder, people differ in the degree of borderline type characteristics they exhibit (Gunderson, 2010).

Although diverse models have been used to conceptualize borderline type personality disorder, most of the literature comes from researchers with psychodynamic perspectives. For example, Kernberg (1976) proposed the concept of object splitting—that people with borderline personality disorder perceive others as all good or all bad at different times. This split results in emotional fluctuations toward others.

Another perspective looks at the disorder from a social learning viewpoint. One view (Millon et al., 2004) is that borderline personality is caused by a faulty self-identity, which affects the development of consistent goals and accomplishments. As a result, persons with this disorder have difficulty coping with their own emotions and with life in general. They then develop a conflict between the need to depend on others and the need to assert themselves. A similar model (Sable, 1997) views the conflict as a desire for proximity and attachment versus a dread and avoidance of engagement, but it attributes the conflict to traumatic attachment experiences that occurred early in life, not to a faulty self-identity.

A third possibility is that the fluctuations in emotions or dysfunctions in emotional regulation are at the core of the disorder (Kuo & Linehan, 2009). Such emotional dysregulations have been observed in different populations of people with this disorder, including adolescents (Gratz et al., 2009; Santisteban et al., 2003). An interesting aspect of this approach is the idea that biological factors may be responsible for the emotional dysregulation among individuals with borderline personality disorder. In fact, MRI and PET scans reveal structural abnormalities in the prefrontal cortex and a different pattern of activation in the amygdala in the working brain of people with borderline personality disorder (Goodman et al., 2007; Prossin et al., 2010). Both are implicated in mood and motor disinhibition.

Cognitive-oriented approaches have also been used. There appear to be two core aspects of borderline personality: difficulties in regulating emotions and unstable and intense interpersonal relationships (Franklin et al., 2009; Oldham, 2006). According to this approach, these two aspects are affected by distorted or inaccurate attributions (explanations for others' behaviors or attitudes). Cognitive-behavioral therapy for borderline personality disorders, therefore, attempts to change the way clients think about and approach interpersonal situations (Sieswerda & Arntz, 2007). Another cognitive theorist, Aaron Beck, argued that an individual's basic assumptions (that is, thoughts) play a central role in influencing perceptions, interpretations, and behavioral and emotional responses (Beck et al., 1990). Individuals with borderline personality disorder seem to have three basic assumptions: (1) "The world is dangerous and malevolent," (2) "I am powerless and vulnerable," and (3) "I am inherently unacceptable." Believing in these assumptions, individuals with this disorder become fearful, vigilant, guarded, and defensive. For these reasons, they are difficult to treat. Regardless of therapeutic approach, most individual psychotherapies end with the borderline patient's dropping out of treatment (Gunderson & Links, 2001).

Finally, Linehan (1993) has developed *dialectical behavior therapy* (*DBT*) specifically for clients with borderline personality disorder. Patients are taught skills that include emotional regulation, distress tolerance, and interpersonal effectiveness (Benjamin & Karpiak, 2002; Harned et al., 2009). Linehan's goals, in descending order of priority, are to change (1) suicidal behaviors, (2) behaviors that interfere with therapy, (3) behaviors that interfere with quality of life, (4) behavioral skills acquisition, (5) post-traumatic stress behavior, and (6) self-respect behaviors. Thus she targets as priorities possible suicidal behaviors in clients and the therapist-client relationship. Her treatment has been found to decrease dropping out and suicidal behaviors and to be generally effective (Emmelkamp, 2004). Because of positive treatment outcomes, DBT has been increasingly used as a treatment procedure (Harned et al., 2009).

These diverse theoretical perspectives on this disorder reflect the strong interest in borderline personality. In contrast to the theoretical contributions, empirical research is sparse. Some investigators have found that individuals with the disorder have a history of chaotic family environments, including physical and sexual abuse (Goodman et al., 2009; Golier et al., 2003; Phillips & Gunderson, 1999) and family history of mood and substance-use disorders (Morey & Zanarini, 2000). Such family experiences may affect perceptions of self and others.

Again, mood changes, intense and unstable interpersonal relationships, identity problems, and other characteristics associated with borderline personality disorder can be observed in all persons to a greater or lesser extent. In fact, although borderline personality disorder is associated with relationship dysfunctions and problems, so are other personality disorders (Daley, Burge, & Hammen, 2000). As is the case with other personality disorders, diagnosis is difficult, and formulations about the causes of the disorder must rely on what we know about personality development in general. We return to that topic later in this chapter.

Avoidant Personality Type

The essential features of avoidant personality type are fears of rejection and humiliation and a reluctance to enter into social relationships. Persons with this disorder tend to have a negative sense of self, low self-esteem, and a strong sense of inadequacy. They tend to avoid social situations and relationships and are perceived as socially inept, shy, and withdrawn. Avoidant types are overly sensitive to criticisms, fear humiliation, blame themselves for things that go wrong, and seem to find little pleasure in life. A study of childhood antecedents of persons with avoidant personality disorder revealed that they engaged in fewer extracurricular activities, hobbies, and leadership roles; had less athletic ability; and were less popular in school (Rettew, Zanarini, & Yen, 2003; Weston & Riolo, 2007). Unlike some individuals who avoid others because they lack interest, and unlike persons who are shy because of their cultural background, people with avoidant personality disorder do not desire to be alone. On the contrary, they crave affection and an active social life. They want—but fear—social contacts, and this ambivalence may be reflected in different ways. For example, many people with this disorder engage in intellectual pursuits, wear fine clothes, or are active in the artistic community. Their need for contact and relationships is often woven into their activities. Thus an avoidant person may write poems expressing the plight of the lonely or the need for human intimacy. A primary defense mechanism is fantasy, whereby wishes are fulfilled to an excessive degree in the person's imagination (Millon et al., 2004).

Avoidant personality disorder occurs in less than 1 percent of the population, and no gender differences are apparent (American Psychiatric Association, 2000a). People with this disorder are caught in a vicious cycle: Because they are preoccupied with rejection, they are constantly alert to signs of derogation or ridicule. This concern leads to many perceived instances of rejection, which cause them to avoid others. Their social skills may then become deficient and invite criticism from others. In other words, their very fear of criticism may lead to criticism. People with avoidant personality disorder often feel depressed, anxious, angry at themselves, inferior, and inadequate into their elderly years (Mahgoub & Hossain, 2007).

Case Study

Jenny L., an unmarried twenty-seven-year-old bank teller, showed several features of avoidant personality disorder. Although she functioned adequately at work, Jenny was extremely shy, sensitive, and quiet with fellow employees. She perceived others as being insensitive and gross. If the bank manager joked with other tellers, she felt that the manager preferred them to her. Although Jenny tried to be friendly, she did not interact much with anyone because of the possibility of them criticizing or rejecting her.

Jenny had very few hobbies. A great deal of her time was spent watching television and eating chocolates. As a result, she was about forty pounds overweight. Television romances were her favorite programs; after watching one, she tended to daydream about having an intense romantic relationship. Jenny eventually sought treatment for her depression and loneliness.

avoidant personality type   a personality disorder characterized by fear of rejection and humiliation and reluctance to enter into social relationships

Some researchers believe that the disorder is on a continuum with social phobia disorder, whereas others see it as a distinct disorder that simply has features in common with social phobia. Little research has been conducted on the etiology of avoidant type of personality disorders. It may be that the avoidant type results from a complex interaction of early childhood environmental experiences and innate temperament. For example, parental rejection and censure, reinforced by rejecting peers, may be contributing factors in the disorder

Because of the fear of rejection and scrutiny, clients may be reluctant to disclose personal thoughts and feelings. It is important for the therapist to establish rapport and a therapeutic alliance, or the client may fail to return for treatment. A number of different therapies have been used, such as cognitive-behavioral, psychodynamic, interpersonal, and psychopharmacological treatments.

Narcissistic Type

The clinical characteristics of **narcissistic personality disorder** are an exaggerated sense of self-importance, an exploitative attitude, and a lack of empathy. People with this disorder require constant attention and admiration, and have difficulty accepting personal criticism. In conversations, they talk mainly about themselves and show a lack of interest in others. Many have fantasies about power or influence, and they constantly overestimate their talents and importance.

Case Study

Roberto J. was a well known sociologist at the local community college. He was flamboyant, attention seeking, and was known for frequently bragging about himself to anyone who would listen. His wardrobe, which cost him a fortune, was extremely eye-catching and colorful although the dress was inappropriate for most college events. Most people found him superficial and so self-centered that any type of meaningful conversation was nearly impossible. His expertise was in critical race theory and he had published a few minor articles on topics of racism in professional journals. He saw himself as a great scholar and would often talk about his "accomplishments" to colleagues; Roberto frequently nominated himself for numerous awards, and asked colleagues to write letters on his behalf. Because

Topham/The Images Works

Narcissistic Behavior

Miranda Priestly (Meryl Streep) in the movie *The Devil Wears Prada* illustrates some of the symptoms of narcissistic personality disorder, including an exaggerated sense of self-importance, an excessive need for admiration, and an inability to accept criticism or rejection. Do you think that narcissistic personality disorder is increasing among young people?

his accomplishments were considered mediocre by academic standards, Roberto seldom received any of the awards. Nevertheless, he continued to present himself as a "giant" and "pioneer" in the field of race relations.

Roberto came for couple counseling on the request of his young wife, a former undergraduate student. In his classes, she was attracted to his apparent confidence, outgoing nature, sense of humor, and "supposed achievements." After several months of marriage, however, she found his self-centered behavior and constant self-orientation alienating. He seemed not to notice her presence, and when she complained about his inability to relate and empathize with her situation, Roberto became angry. He stated that his work was demanding and that he was on the verge of a major theoretical breakthrough in his field. Their spats and disagreements were not important in light of his work. "You just had to understand." After nearly a year of therapy without significant change in Roberto, his wife filed for divorce.

Individuals diagnosed with this disorder show reflective responses and idealization involving unlimited success, a sense of entitlement, and a sense of self-importance. Owing to their sense of self-importance, people with narcissistic personality disorder expect to be the superior participants in all relationships. For example, they may be impatient and irate if others arrive late for a meeting but may frequently be late themselves and think nothing of it. They are seldom concerned with the plight or feelings of others.

Narcissistic traits are common among adolescents and do not necessarily imply that a teenager has the disorder (American Psychiatric Association, 2000a). However, it was found that people later diagnosed with this disorder were more likely to experience feelings of invulnerability, to display risk taking behavior, and to have strong feelings of uniqueness as adolescents (Weston & Riolo, 2007). The prevalence of narcissistic personality disorder is about 1 to 2 percent, although some studies have found lower rates (Grant et al., 2004). More males than females are given the diagnosis.

As in the case of most of the personality disorders, no controlled treatment studies for narcissistic personality disorder have been conducted, and treatment recommendations are therefore based on clinical experience (Groopman & Cooper, 2001). Individual psychotherapy and group therapy have been used and are generally recommended. Unfortunately, narcissistic personality disorders are considered very difficult to treat; most forms of therapy have tried to help increase empathic abilities, to focus on the opinion of others, and to break self-involvement (Leahy et al., 2005; Beck et al., 2004). Unfortunately, none of these treatments have met with much success.

Obsessive-Compulsive Type

The characteristics of obsessive-compulsive personality type are perfectionism, a marked tendency to be interpersonally controlling, strong devotion to details, and rigidity. Again, these traits are found in many normal people. Unlike normal people, however, individuals with obsessive-compulsive personality disorder show marked impairment in occupational or social functioning. Their relationships with others may be quite stiff, formal, and distant (McCullough & Maltsberger, 2001). Further, the extent of the character rigidity is greater among people who have this disorder.

Obsessive-compulsive type (OCT), as presented in this chapter, is distinct from obsessive-compulsive disorder (OCD), as discussed in the chapter on anxiety disorders. The two disorders have similar names, but the clinical manifestations of these disorders are quite different. OCT is not characterized by the presence of obsessions (intrusive and repetitive anxiety-arousing thoughts) or compulsions (a need to perform acts or to dwell on mental acts repetitively). Rather, OCT involves a preoccupation with orderliness, perfectionism, and control. Persons with OCD experience tremendous

obsessive-compulsive personality type a personality disorder characterized by perfectionism, a tendency to be interpersonally controlling, devotion to details, and rigidity

anxiety related to specific preoccupations, which are perceived as threatening. They usually recognize that their obsessions or compulsions are irrational or senseless. In OCT, it is one's dysfunctional philosophy that produces anxiety, discomfort, and frustration. OCT is a pervasive characterological disturbance. People with the disorder genuinely see their way of functioning as the "correct" way. Their overall style of relating to the world around them is processed through their own strict standards. Research also shows that OCT symptoms are related to anger and depression, and those with these symptoms are more prone to suppress their anger (Whiteside & Abramowitz, 2004).

The preoccupation with details, rules, and possible errors leads to indecision and an inability to see "the big picture." There is heightened concern with being in control, not only over the details of their lives but also over their emotions and other people. Coworkers may find individuals with this disorder too demanding, inflexible, miserly, and perfectionistic. They may actually be ineffective on the job, despite long hours of devotion, as in the following case.

Sony Pictures/Everett Collection

As Good As It Gets

Jack Nicholson in *As Good As It Gets* tries to woo Helen Hunt, a woman he finds very attractive. Suffering from obsessive-compulsive type personality disorder, however, his preoccupation with details and rules and overconcern with being in control interferes with his emotions toward Ms. Hunt. Many find people with obsessive-compulsive personality disorders to be too demanding, inflexible, miserly, and perfectionistic.

Case Study

His graduate adviser referred Cecil, a third-year medical student, for therapy. The adviser told the therapist that Cecil was in danger of being expelled from medical school because of his inability to get along with patients and other students. Cecil often berated patients for failing to follow his advice. In one instance, he told a patient with a lung condition to stop smoking. When the patient indicated he was unable to stop, Cecil angrily told the patient to go for medical treatment elsewhere—that the medical center had no place for such a "weak-willed fool." Cecil's relationships with others were similarly strained. He considered many members of the faculty to be "incompetent old deadwood," and he characterized fellow graduate students as "partygoers."

The graduate adviser told the therapist that Cecil had not been expelled only because several faculty members thought that he was brilliant. Cecil studied and worked sixteen hours a day. He was extremely well read and had an extensive knowledge of medical disorders. Although he was always able to provide a careful and detailed analysis of a patient's condition, it took him a great deal of time to do so. His diagnoses tended to cover every disorder that each patient could conceivably have, on the basis of all possible combinations of symptoms.

Obsessive-compulsive type occurs in about 1 percent of the population according to DSM-IV-TR, but a more recent study places it at

Did You Know?

These are the primary differences and similarities between OCT and OCD:

Characteristics	OCT	OCD
Rigidity in personality	Yes	Not usual
Preoccupation in thinking	Yes	Yes
Orderliness in general	Yes	Not usual
Control	Yes	Not usual
Perfectionism	Yes	Not usual
Indecisiveness	Yes	Not usual
Intrusive thoughts/ behaviors	Not usual	Yes
Need to perform acts	Not usual	Yes
Recognition of irrationality	Not usual	Yes

Crime Bosses and Antisocial Personality Disorders

Vito Corleone (played by Marlon Brando) in *The Godfather* and Boss Tony Soprano (played by James Gandolfini) in the TV series *The Sopranos* are both men who exhibit many of the traits of an antisocial personality disorder. Both men evidenced a callous disregard for the rights of others and showed little regret or remorse for cheating, lying, breaking the law, or even murder. However, they also revealed characteristics that are at odds with the diagnosis. Both had deep family relationships, revealed intense loyalty and emotional commitment to their families, evidenced flashes of guilt; Tony Soprano even sought psychiatric help for his anxiety attacks.

7.9 percent (Grant et al., 2004). It is about twice as prevalent among males as females, according to DSM-IV-TR. Cognitive-behavioral therapy, as well as supportive forms of psychotherapy, have helped some clients (Barber et al., 1997; Beck et al., 1990). No medications specific to obsessive-compulsive type are currently available (McCullough & Maltsberger, 2001).

Antisocial Type

The characteristics of the antisocial type are arrogance, self-centeredness, feelings of entitlement, and an exaggerated sense of self-importance (Decuyper et al., 2009). Those with this disorder seek power over others and like to manipulate, deceive, exploit and con others for their own needs and purposes. Chronic antisocial behavioral patterns, such as a failure to conform to social or legal codes, a lack of anxiety and guilt, and irresponsible behaviors, typify this type. People with this disorder show little guilt for their wrongdoing, which may include lying, using other people, and aggressive sexual acts. Their relationships with others are superficial and fleeting and involve little loyalty.

Cleckley's (1976) classic description of the disorder included the following characteristics:

1. Superficial charm and good intelligence
2. Shallow emotions and lack of empathy, guilt, or remorse
3. Behaviors indicative of little life plan or order
4. Failure to learn from experiences and absence of anxiety
5. Unreliability, insincerity, and untruthfulness

antisocial type a personality disorder characterized by a failure to conform to social and legal codes, a lack of anxiety and guilt, and irresponsible behaviors

Some research now suggests that psychopathy is composed of three factors: arrogant and deceitful interpersonal style, deficient affective experience, and impulsive and irresponsible behavioral style (Cooke & Michie, 2001). Psychopaths are prone to engage in

People with an
not voluntarily see
with a doctor, and
ment (Meloy, 2001
populations, which
questionable, how
psychopathic popu
general community
they are infrequent

■ **For**

Originally, ten per
clinical evidence d
personality disorde
Justification for the
absence of research
(Skodol & Bender,
tients are often diag
(Zimmerman, Rotl
(Grillo, 2004) mak
these as distinct cat
tinuum of personali
personality disorde
person possesses tra

Does eliminati
dependent persons
Table 15.3 outline
their DSM-IV-TR
would be used to d
the domain-trait ap

TABLE 15.3

DSM-IV-TR
Categorical
Diagnosis:

DSM-5 Continuum
Trait Description:

DSM-IV-TR
Categorical
Diagnosis:

DSM-5 Continuum
Trait Description:

unlawful and criminal behavior and have no compunction about violating moral, ethical, or legal codes of conduct (Hare & Neumann, 2009). The following case of Robert T. exemplifies many of these characteristics.

Case Study

The epitome of a hard-driven, successful businessman, Robert T. seemed to have it all: enormous financial wealth; influence with politicians; a private jet; a young, beautiful wife; and, despite his reputation as a ruthless corporate raider, he enjoyed high regard from associates for his business acumen. Then, in less than a year, he lost everything, including his wife, who filed for divorce. Stockholders raised questions about nonstandard accounting practices, inappropriate personal use of funds for family vacations, and unauthorized purchase of properties in the name of his wife. When banks refused to loan him funds on a prospective takeover bid and creditors demanded repayment of loans, his financial world collapsed. Lawsuits from investors against Robert and his company followed, with the trustees finally demanding his resignation. Robert refused to resign and launched a campaign against his own board of directors, accusing them of a personal vendetta and of conspiring against him. He hired a private detective to "dig up dirt" on certain trustees and their families, and tried to use that information to intimidate and discredit them. In cases where embarrassing information was lacking, he had no qualms about spreading false rumors. These attempts, however, failed and Robert was eventually removed from his post.

Only with his downfall did the facts about Robert's tendency to exaggerate and distort the truth become known. He was not a graduate of the Wharton School of Business, as his resume had indicated; he had told people that he was divorced once, but in fact he had been married four times (two of the marriages ended in divorce before age twenty); and his fortune did not come from "old money" but from a series of questionable business schemes in real estate that often left investors holding bad debts, which he referred to as "collateral damage." People who knew him in the past often described him as arrogant, deceitful, cunning, and calculating. He showed a disregard for the rights of others, manipulated them, and then discarded them when they served no further use to him. These attributes were evident even in his early years. For example, he had married a sixteen-year-old girl from a wealthy family, but when her father refused to support them, Robert blamed his wife and constantly belittled her until their divorce three months later. He never expressed regret or remorse for any of his actions but operated from a belief that "this is a dog-eat-dog world" and "do unto others before they do unto you." He had never been in therapy, but school records revealed a pattern of juvenile alcohol use, poor grades, frequent lying, and petty theft. At age fourteen, he was tentatively diagnosed with a conduct disorder when school officials became concerned with his fascination for setting fires in the restroom toilets. Nevertheless, it is interesting that the school psychologist described Robert as "charming, very bright, persuasive, and with high potential for future success."

Robert T. typifies our definition of an individual with an antisocial type of personality disorder. He exhibits little empathy for others, views them as objects to be manipulated, and has difficulty establishing meaningful and intimate relationships. He also seems to suffer from self-identity integration problems in that he believes that the self he presents to the world is a façade or a fake. Robert pushes the boundaries of social convention and often violates moral, legal, and ethical rules for his own personal gain, with little regard for the feelings of others. His characteristic way of handling things is long-standing and developmental in nature evident in his early teens (Dolan & Fullam, 2010; Weston & Riolo, 2007). Although these traits can be

Behavior Pattern
Diagnosis

Individuals who en
or civil disobedien
as having antisoci
Although some m
other features of a
disorder—chronic
deceitfulness, for
absent. In this pho
als demonstrate to
the war in Iraq. Ar
well as antisocial
more common am
older adults?

TABLE 15.3   Former DSM-IV-TR Personality Disorders Versus DSM-5 Domain-Trait Descriptions—*cont'd*

	3. Histrionic Personality Disorder
DSM-IV-TR Categorical Diagnosis:	People with **histrionic personality disorder** engage in self-dramatization, exaggerated expression of emotions, and attention-seeking behaviors. The desire for attention may lead to flamboyant acts or flirtatious behaviors. Despite superficial warmth and charm, the histrionic person is typically shallow and egocentric. Individuals from different cultures vary in the extent to which they display their emotions, but the histrionic person goes well beyond cultural norms. The categorical nature of this diagnosis is that a person has or doesn't have this personality disorder depending on whether he/she meets an arbitrary threshold.
DSM-5 Continuum Trait Description:	There is no recognition of a histrionic personality type, but a person may exhibit features similar to those just described. They, however, are described in terms of prominent personality traits such *emotional lability* and *histrionism*.
	5. Dependent Personality Disorder
DSM-IV-TR Categorical Diagnosis:	People with **dependent personality disorder** lack self-confidence and subordinate their needs to those of the people on whom they depend. They are fearful of taking the initiative on most matters and are afraid of disrupting their relationships with others. Dependent personalities have two deeply ingrained assumptions that affect their thoughts, perceptions, and behaviors. First, they see themselves as inherently inadequate and unable to cope. Second, they conclude that their course of action should be to find someone who can take care of them. Depression, helplessness, and suppressed anger are often present in dependent personality disorder.
DSM-5 Continuum Trait Description:	There is no recognition of a dependent personality type, but a person may exhibit features similar to those just described. They, however, are described in terms of prominent personality traits such *submissiveness*, *anxiousness*, and *separation insecurity*.

 ## Multipath Analysis of One Personality Disorder: Antisocial Type

Research on personality disorders has been quite limited, although anecdotal, clinical, and theoretical speculation abound (Millon et al., 2004). As mentioned previously, research on antisocial/psychopathic personality disorder type is perhaps more developed because of its higher visibility and association with criminality. Thus, to give you a broader view and an appreciation of the wide range of explanatory views that can be proposed for personality disorders in general, we have chosen to concentrate our etiological analysis on the antisocial type. Using our multipath model, we survey how the four dimensions (biological, psychological, social, and sociocultural) explain antisocial type development and their possible interacting contributions, as shown in Figure 15.2. In this way, we hope to provide a prototype for understanding the multidimensional development of other personality disorders as well.

Biological Dimension

An extraordinary amount of research has been devoted to trying to uncover the biological basis of antisocial type. Indeed, early researchers concentrated primarily on using genetics, central nervous system abnormalities, and autonomic nervous system abnormalities to explain the disorder.

Genetic Influences

Throughout history, many people have speculated that some individuals are born to "raise hell." It is not uncommon for casual observers to remark that antisocials, criminals, and sociopaths appear to have an inborn temperament toward aggressiveness, sensation seeking, impulsivity, and disregard for others. These speculations are difficult to test because of the problems involved in distinguishing between the influences of environment and heredity on behavior (Sterzer, 2010). Nevertheless, considerable support indicates genetic influences on antisocial behavior, even across childhood and adolescence (Van Hulle et al., 2009). For

Did You K

Beck and colleagu
es of the behaviora
that characterize th

Disorder
Antisocial type
Avoidant type
Obsessive-compulsive type

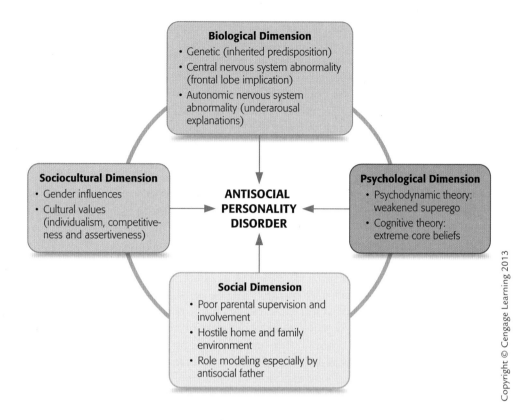

Figure 15.2

MULTIPATH MODEL FOR ANTISOCIAL PERSONALITY DISORDER

The dimensions interact with one another and combine in different ways to result in antisocial personality disorder.

example, antisocial type is five times more common among first-degree biological relatives (immediate blood-relative family members) of males and ten times more common among first-degree biological relatives of females than among the general population (American Psychiatric Association, 2000a). But is this due to heredity or environment?

Support for the former is found in studies comparing concordance rates for identical or monozygotic (MZ) twins with those for fraternal or dizygotic (DZ) twins. MZ twins share exactly the same genes, whereas DZ twins are genetically no more alike than any two siblings. Most studies show that MZ twins do tend to have a higher concordance rate than DZ twins for antisocial tendencies, delinquency, and criminality (Eley, Lichtenstein, & Moffitt, 2003; Gottesman & Goldsmith, 1994). Further, adoptees separated from their biological parents who have antisocial/psychopathic personalities and were raised by parents without such a diagnosis still exhibited higher rates of antisocial characteristics.

Although this body of evidence seems to show a strong causal pattern, it should be examined carefully for several reasons. First, although the newer definition of antisocial type seems to entertain a broader inclusion of antisocial criteria for the disorder, many of the studies fail to clearly distinguish between antisocial/psychopathic personalities and criminals; they may draw research participants only from distinctly criminal populations. Truly representative samples of people with antisocial/psychopathic type should be investigated.

Second, the evidence supporting a genetic basis for antisocial tendencies does not preclude the environment as a factor. Antisocial personality is undoubtedly caused by environmental, as well as genetic, influences (Moffitt, 2005). The fact that crime has increased fivefold or more in most industrialized Western countries over the past fifty years has to be attributed to environmental influences, because gene pools cannot change that quickly. As noted in our multipath model, heredity and environment may interact in complex ways. Ineffective parenting, for example, does not appear to be related to conduct problems in children with antisocial temperamental characteristics, but for children without such characteristics, ineffective parenting increased conduct disorders (Wootton et al., 1997).

Third, studies indicating that genetic factors are important do not provide much insight into how antisocial type is inherited. What exactly is transmitted genetically?

MYTH: Antisocial personality type problems are primarily caused by genetic factors. Some people seem born to "raise hell."

REALITY: Although genetic factors are related to antisocial type, a wide range of family patterns can influence the development of the disorder. For example, dysfunctional aspects of family life, such as severe parental discord, a parent's maladjustment or criminality, overcrowding, and even large family size, can predispose a child to antisocial personality disorder, especially if the child does not have a loving relationship with at least one parent (Millon et al., 2004).

Genetic factors do not influence crime and antisocial behavior directly, but they seem to affect the probability that such behavior occurs (Moffitt, 2005). Hence there is no specific "gene for crime."

Some investigators suggest that adults with antisocial personalities tend to have abnormal brain wave activity similar to that of young children (Elliott & Gillett, 1992; Hare, 1993). Perhaps these abnormalities indicate brain pathology, specially in the frontal lobes (Goodman et al., 2007; Sterzer, 2010). Neuroimaging MRI and PET scans) of brains of individuals with antisocial personalities reveal structural and activity abnormalities in the prefrontal portion of the brain and the limbic amygdala circuitry (Gao et al., 2010). These regions are known to underlie emotional processing (Brambilla et al., 2004; Frankle, Lombardo, & New, 2005). Such pathology could inhibit the capacity of people with antisocial personalities to learn how to avoid punishment and could render them unable to learn from experience (Glenn et al., 2009).

In a major longitudinal study based on data collected some 20 years ago, Gao and colleagues (2010) reasoned that fear conditioning was the primary mechanism that linked antisocial behavior to negative consequences (punishment). Poor fear conditioning would predispose individuals to antisocial behavior and should be detectable in early life. They tested fear conditioning in children at age 3 and probed the association with adult criminal behavior at age 23. They found that those who had criminal records at a later age failed to show fear conditioning in early childhood. They also reasoned that the amygdala is the part of the brain in which the circuitry determines fear conditioning and the perception of threatening stimuli. Deficient amygdala functioning may render the individual unable to recognize cues that signal threats, making them fearless.

This explanation is plausible, but there simply is not enough evidence to support its unbridled acceptance. Many persons diagnosed with antisocial/psychopathic personalities do not show activity abnormalities in these regions of the brain. In addition, physiological measures of conditioning (e.g., skin conductance, heart rate, and the electroencephalogram [EEG]) are imprecise diagnostic correlates. Abnormal brain wave activity in people with antisocial personalities, for example, may simply be correlated with, rather than a cause of, disturbed behavior.

Autonomic Nervous System Abnormalities

Other interesting research points to the involvement of the autonomic nervous system (ANS) in the prominent features of antisocial personalities: the inability to learn from experience, the absence of anxiety, and the tendency to engage in thrill-seeking behaviors (Glenn et al., 2009). Two lines of investigation can be identified, both based on the assumption that people with antisocial personalities have ANS deficiencies or abnormalities (Crozier et al., 2008). The first states that ANS abnormalities make antisocial personalities less susceptible to anxiety and therefore less likely to learn from their experiences in situations in which aversive stimuli (or punishment) are involved. The second explanation suggests that ANS abnormalities could keep antisocial people emotionally underaroused. To achieve an optimal level of arousal or to avoid boredom, underaroused individuals might seek excitement and thrills and fail to conform to conventional behavioral standards. The two premises—lack of anxiety and underarousal—may, of course, be related because underarousal could include underaroused anxiety (Newman et al., 2010).

Genetic Predisposition to Fearlessness or Lack of Anxiety

Lykken (1982) was among the first to maintain that genetic predisposition affects people's levels of fearlessness. Antisocial behavior may develop because of fearlessness or low anxiety levels (Newman et al., 2010). People who have high levels of fear avoid risks, stress, and strong stimulation; relatively fearless people seek thrills and adventures. Fearlessness is associated with heroes (such as those who volunteer for dangerous military action or who risk their lives to save others), as well as with individuals with antisocial personalities who may engage in risky criminal activities or impulsively violate norms and rules (Sterzer, 2010; Gao et al., 2010).

Lykken's (1957) classic research suggested that, because psychopaths do not become conditioned to aversive stimuli as readily as nonpsychopaths do, they fail to acquire avoidance behaviors, experience little anticipatory anxiety, and consequently have fewer inhibitions about engaging in antisocial behavior. There is evidence that low anxiety among psychopaths is associated with more errors in learning tasks (Newman & Schmitt, 1998), inhibited social learning, and poor fear conditioning (Gao et al., 2010).

Arousal, Sensation-Seeking, and Behavioral Perspectives

Lykken and others suggest that individuals with antisocial personality may have deficiencies in learning because of lower anxiety. Another line of research proposes that they simply have lower levels of ANS reactivity and are underaroused (Glenn et al., 2009). According to this view, the sensitivity of individuals' reticular cortical systems varies, although there is an optimal level for each person. The system regulates the tonic level of arousal in the cortex so that some people have high and some have low levels of arousal. Those with low sensitivity need more stimulation to reach an optimal level of arousal. If psychopaths are underaroused, it may take a more intense stimulus to elicit a reaction in them than in nonpsychopaths (Newman et al., 2010). The lowered levels of reactivity may cause psychopaths to show impulsive, stimulus-seeking behaviors to avoid boredom.

Zuckerman (1996) believes that a trait he calls *impulsive unsocialized sensation seeking* can help explain not only antisocial/psychopathic personalities but also other disorders. Those with this trait want to seek adventures and thrills and are disinhibited and susceptible to boredom. Psychopaths score high for this trait. Early on, Farley (1986) proposed that people vary in their degree of thrill-seeking behaviors. At one end of the thrill-seeking continuum are the "Big T's"—the risk takers and adventurers who seek excitement and stimulation. Because of their low levels of CNS or ANS arousal, Big T's need stimulation to maintain an optimal level of arousal. On the other end of the continuum are "Little t's"—people with high arousal who seek low levels of stimulation to calm their hyped-up nervous systems. In contrast to Big T's, Little t's prefer certainty, predictability, low risk, familiarity, clarity, simplicity, low conflict, and low intensity.

Psychological Dimension

Psychological explanations of personality disorders and specifically antisocial personalities tend to fall into three camps: psychodynamic, cognitive, and social learning.

Psychodynamic Perspectives

According to psychodynamic approaches, the psychopath's absence of guilt and frequent violation of moral and ethical standards are the result of faulty superego development (Fenichel, 1945). Although the ego develops adequately, the personalities of people with antisocial personalities are dominated by id impulses that operate primarily from the pleasure principle in seeking immediate (impulsive) gratification with minimal regard for others (egocentricity). Because the infantile id is dominated

Ross Woodhall/Getty Images

Sensation Seeking and Antisocial Personality Disorder

Lykken theorized that people with low anxiety levels are often thrill seekers. The difference between the psychopath who takes risks and the adventurer may largely be a matter of whether the thrill-seeking behaviors are channeled into destructive or constructive acts. In this picture, we see a female skier launching herself from an almost vertical cliff. It is believed, however, that men are more likely to be risk takers than women. Do you believe there are gender differences in thrill-seeking behaviors? If so, what can account for the gender differences?

Did You Know?

It's possible that heroes and psychopaths are two sides of the same coin because they both share one characteristic: fearlessness. They tend to choose frightening or challenging situations, push the boundaries of acceptable behavior, and may use deception to attain goals. The difference seems to be that heroes channel their fearlessness into socially approved activities and are socialized in families that emphasize loving relationships rather than punishment.

primarily by sex and aggression, so are people with this disorder who act out these impulses on others (Millon et al., 2004). People exhibiting antisocial behavior patterns presumably did not adequately identify with their parents and thus did not internalize the morals and values of society. It is believed that frustration, rejection, or inconsistent discipline resulted in fixation at an early stage of development.

Cognitive Perspectives

Cognitive explanations of antisocial disorder stress the relationship of core beliefs that influence behavior (Beck et al., 1990). These core beliefs operate on an unconscious level, occur automatically, and influence emotions and behaviors. Beck and colleagues has summarized the typical cognitions most likely found in antisocial people:

- I have to look out for myself.
- Force or cunning is the best way to get things done.
- We live in a jungle and the strong person is the one who survives.
- People will get at me if I don't get them first.
- It is not important to keep promises or honor debts.
- Lying and cheating are OK as long as you don't get caught.
- I have been unfairly treated and am entitled to get my fair share by whatever means I can.
- Other people are weak and deserve to be taken.
- If I don't push other people, I will get pushed around.
- I should do whatever I can get away with.
- What others think of me doesn't really matter.
- If I want something, I should do whatever is necessary to get it.
- I can get away with things so I don't need to worry about bad consequences.
- If people can't take care of themselves, that's their problem. (p. 361)

These thoughts arise from what Beck and colleagues (1990) refer to as a "predatory strategy." It is built around a need to perceive oneself as strong and independent, necessary attributes for survival in a competitive, hostile, and unforgiving world.

Learning Perspectives

Learning theories stress a number of different forces in explaining antisocial personalities: (1) inherent neurobiological characteristics that delay or impede learning, (2) lack of positive role models in developing prosocial behaviors, or (3) presence of poor role models. In all cases, whether we are speaking about classical conditioning, operant conditioning, or social modeling, it is proposed that biology or social/developmental factors combine in unique ways to influence the development of antisocial personalities.

As we have seen earlier, some believe that learning deficiencies among individuals with antisocial disorders are caused by the absence of anxiety and by lowered autonomic reactivity. If so, is it possible to improve their learning by increasing their anxiety or arousal ability? In a now classic study, researchers designed two conditions in which psychopaths, a mixed group, and nonpsychopaths would perform an avoidance learning task, with electric shock as the unconditioned stimulus (Schachter & Latané, 1964). Under one condition, participants were injected with adrenaline, which presumably increases arousal; under the other, they were injected with a placebo. Psychopaths receiving the placebo made more errors in avoiding the shocks than did nonpsychopaths; psychopaths receiving adrenaline, however, tended to perform better than nonpsychopaths. These findings imply that psychopaths do not react to the same amount of anxiety as do nonpsychopaths and that their learning improves when their anxiety is increased.

The *kind* of punishment used in avoidance learning is also an important consideration in evaluating psychopaths' learning deficiencies. Whereas psychopaths may show learning deficits when faced with physical (electric shock) or social (verbal feedback) punishments, they learn as well as nonpsychopaths when the punishment is monetary loss. Figure 15.3

shows the effects of the three types of punishment for incorrect responses in Schmauk's (1970) classic study of convicted psychopaths.

Social modeling or observational learning is a complex form of learning that involves the social dimension in our multipath model. As with our understanding of the reciprocal interaction between autonomous nervous system reactivity and learning processes, so too a strong relationship exists between how learning occurs through the social dimension of antisocial/psychopathic type. It is impossible to discuss one without the other.

Social Dimension

Among the many factors that have been implicated in the development of personality disorders, relationships within the family—the primary agent of socialization—are paramount in the development of antisocial patterns. A number of social factors and conditions have been implicated in increased antisocial behaviors and lowered prosocial behaviors among children (Coyne et al., 2009; Franklin, Heilbron, et al., 2009; Jaffe et al., 2002). Children from impoverished backgrounds were twice as likely to develop antisocial personalities as those from higher socioeconomic status (Lahey et al., 2005). Poor parental supervision and involvement were good predictors of antisocial behaviors (Loeber, 1990). The risk of psychosocial dysfunction is increased with a corresponding increase in antisocial behavior in adulthood for children in families characterized by neglect, maltreatment, and abuse (Jaffe, Caspi, Moffitt, & Taylor, 2004). Antisocial personality, according to this view, results from children who are exposed to family environments of neglect, hostility, indifference, and physical abuse (Millon et al., 2004). Children from such environments learn that the world is cold, unforgiving, and punitive. Struggle and survival become part of their outlook on life, and they respond in an aggressive fashion to control and manipulate the world.

Rejection or deprivation by one or both parents may mean that the child has little opportunity to learn socially appropriate behaviors or that the value of people as socially reinforcing agents is diminished. There is also evidence that family structure, predictability of expectations, and dependability of family roles are related to lower antisocial tendencies (Tolan et al., 1997). Parental separation or absence and assaultive or inconsistent parenting are related to antisocial personality (Phillips & Gunderson, 1999). Children may have been traumatized or subjected to a hostile environment during the parental separation, or the hostility in such families may result in interpersonal hostility among the children. Such situations may lead to little satisfaction in close or meaningful relationships with others. Individuals with antisocial types tend to misperceive the motives and behaviors of others and have difficulty being empathetic (Benjamin, 1996).

It has been long established that people with antisocial personality disorder can learn and use social skills very effectively, as shown in their adeptness at manipulation, lying, and cheating and their ease at being charming and sociable. The difficulty is that, in many areas of learning, these individuals do not pay attention to social stimuli (Newman et al., 2010), and their schedules of reinforcement differ from those of most other people. Perhaps this relatively diminished attention stems from inconsistent reinforcement from parents or inadequate feedback on behaviors.

Sociocultural Dimension

The study of culture and personality has always been of fascination to early anthropologists, who believed that culture shapes the development of personality or that culture represents an expanded extension of personality (Benedict, 1934; Kardiner, 1939; Mead,

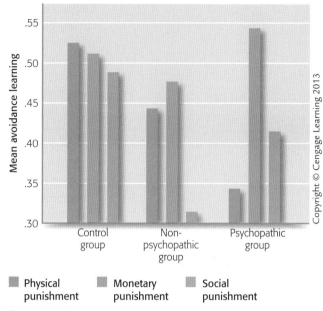

Copyright © Cengage Learning 2013

Figure 15.3

EFFECT OF TYPE OF PUNISHMENT ON PSYCHOPATHS AND OTHERS

The effects of three different types of punishment on an avoidance learning task are shown for three groups of participants. Although physical or social punishment had little impact on psychopaths' learning, monetary punishment was quite effective.

Source: Schmauk, (1970)

1928). Little doubt exists that our lives are influenced by the values, traditions, and institutions of our society and that such factors as social class, race, gender, and other sociodemographic variables are important in both normal and abnormal development (Sue & Sue, 2008a). Determining the relative impact of specific sociocultural factors, however, is a complicated procedure. We have already seen that gender and larger cultural values (individualism and collectivism) may have a profound impact on personality development and in the manifestation of behavior disorders (Ivey et al., 2007; Millon et al., 2004).

Gender

Because males are more likely to exhibit both conduct disorders and antisocial personalities than females, there is a strong possibility that different pathways to development exist along gender lines. For example, although parental conflict and disharmony are often implicated in antisocial development, studies suggest that they do not predict antisocial behavior for men but do predict it for women (Mulder et al., 1994). Further, the specific manner of expression of antisocial/personality seems influenced by gender as well: Men were found to exhibit job problems, violence, and traffic offenses, whereas women were more likely to report relationship problems, job problems, and violence.

Because the sex role for women emphasizes a less assertive and more people-focused orientation, the term *relational aggression* has been coined to describe the behavior of females with antisocial personality disorder (Millon et al., 2004). Whereas men are believed to engage in direct acting-out behaviors (e.g., physical aggression), women express themselves by more indirect or passive means (e.g., spreading rumors or false gossip and rejecting others from their social group). As gender role differences have narrowed, however, female antisocial behaviors have become progressively similar to those of their male counterparts. Social learning models indicate that children often copy the behaviors of a parent who socializes them into the values of the larger society. The parental influence on antisocial behaviors in children may be a result of traditional gender role training. Males have traditionally received more encouragement to engage in aggressive behaviors than females, and antisocial patterns are more prevalent among men than among women. As traditional gender roles change, one might reasonably expect that antisocial tendencies will increase among females and that mothers will play a greater role in the development of antisocial behaviors in children.

Cultural Values

To be born and raised in the United States is to be exposed to the standards, beliefs, and values of United States society. One dominant value is that of "rugged individualism," which is composed of two assumptions: (1) Healthy functioning is equated with individualism and independence, and (2) people can and should master and control their own lives and the universe (Sue & Sue, 2008a). Striving, competition, and ability to manipulate the environment are considered pathways to success; achievements are measured by surpassing the attainment of others. In the extreme, this psychological orientation may cause and/or fuel the aggressive and violent behavior of antisocials.

Other societies, such as those in some Asian countries, possess values and beliefs that are often at odds with individualistic values: Collectivism and interdependence are valued, concern is with group rather than self-development, and being in harmony with the universe is preferred over mastering it. Some have observed that antisocial behavior (e.g., crime and violence) is less likely to occur in Japan and China than in the United States because of these countries' collectivistic orientation, in which harmony and relationship with others are valued (Ivey et al., 2007). Such findings also seem to be present among Asian Americans and Hispanic Americans in the United States. Because traditional Asian values, for example, value harmony, subtlety, and restraint of strong feelings, Asian American clients who seek therapy are less likely than their white European American counterparts to evidence acting-out disorders (e.g., overt expressions of anger, physical aggression, verbal hostility, substance abuse, and criminal behavior) (Sue & Sue, 2008a). Thus it is clear that the sociocultural dimension is a powerful determinant in the etiology and manifestation of personality disorders.

Treatment of Antisocial Personality Disorder

As you have seen, evidence is growing that low anxiety and low autonomic reactivity characterize individuals with antisocial personalities. But we still do not know whether these characteristics are products of inherited temperament, of an acquired congenital defect, or of social and environmental experiences during childhood. The theory that psychopaths have developed a defense against anxiety is intriguing, but the factors behind the development of such a defense have not been pinpointed. Because people with antisocial personality disorder feel little anxiety, they are poorly motivated to change themselves; they are also unlikely to see their behaviors as "bad" and may try to manipulate or "con" therapists. Thus traditional treatment approaches, which require the genuine cooperation of the client, may be ineffective for antisocial personality disorder. Few treatment outcome studies have been conducted for this disorder. In some studies, drugs with tranquilizing effects (e.g., phenothiazines and Dilantin) have been helpful in reducing antisocial behavior. People with antisocial personality disorder, however, are not likely to follow through with self-medication. Moreover, drug treatment is effective in only a few cases, and it can result in side effects such as blurred vision, lethargy, and neurological disorders.

It may be that successful treatment can occur only in a setting in which behavior can be controlled. That is, treatment programs may need to provide enough control so that those with antisocial personalities cannot avoid confronting their inability to form close and intimate relationships and the effect of their behaviors on others. Such control is sometimes possible for psychopaths who are imprisoned for crimes or who, for one reason or another, are hospitalized. Intensive group therapy may then be initiated to help clients with antisocial personalities in the required confrontation.

Mary Kate Denny / PhotoEdit

Treating Antisocial Behaviors

Peers and family are critically important in the treatment of antisocial youths and in maintaining progress made in treatment. Here, a group led by a peer counselor is exploring some of the issues troubling these young people. What would you do as a peer counselor to help these youths open up and talk about their own problems?

Some behavior modification programs have been tried, especially with delinquents who behave in antisocial ways. The most useful treatments are skill based and behavioral (Meloy, 2001). Money and tokens that can be used to purchase items have been given as rewards to young people who show appropriate behaviors (e.g., discussion of personal problems, good study habits, punctuality, and prosocial and nondisruptive behaviors). This use of material rewards has been fairly effective in changing antisocial behaviors (Van Evra, 1983). Once the young people leave the treatment programs, however, they are likely to revert to antisocial behavior unless their families and peers help them maintain the appropriate behaviors.

Cognitive approaches have also been used. Because individuals with antisocial personalities may be influenced by dysfunctional beliefs about themselves, the world, and the future, they vary in skills for anticipating and acting on possible negative outcomes of their behaviors. Beck and colleagues (1990) have advocated that the therapist build rapport with the client, attempting to guide the patient away from thinking only in

What Are Impulse Control Disorders?

Definitions of personality disorders include the major characteristic of impulsivity. Yet certain impulse control disorders occupy a distinct category. Although they may be long-standing and unvarying behavioral patterns, they are not considered personality disorders. Three such disorders are recognized under impulse control disorders: *intermittent explosive disorder, kleptomania,* and *pyromania.* Controversy, however, surrounds the issue of whether this category is clinically useful and whether they should not be classified elsewhere.

People with impulse control disorders tend to share three characteristics: (1) They fail to resist an impulse or temptation, despite knowing the act is wrong or harmful to them or others; (2) they experience tension or arousal before the act; and (3) they feel a sense of excitement, gratification, or release after committing the act. Guilt or regret may or may not follow. The core feature of the disorder is the repeated expression of impulsive acts that lead to physical or financial damage to the individual or another person, often resulting in a sense of relief or release of tension. We briefly describe them here.

1. Intermittent explosive disorder describes people who experience separate and discrete episodes of loss of control over their aggressive impulses, resulting in serious assaults on others or the destruction of property. The aggressiveness is grossly out of proportion to any precipitating stress that may have occurred. People with this disorder show no signs of general aggressiveness between episodes and may genuinely feel remorse for their actions. The disorder is apparently rare and believed to be much more common among males than females.

2. Kleptomania is characterized by a recurrent failure to resist impulses to steal objects. People with this disorder do not need the objects for personal use and do not steal them for their monetary value; indeed, they usually have enough money to buy the objects and typically discard, give away, or surreptitiously return them. The individual feels irresistible urges and tension before stealing or shoplifting and then an intense feeling of relief or gratification after the theft. The stealing is not committed to express anger or vengeance and is not in response to a delusion or hallucination. The disorder appears to be more common among females than among males.

3. Pyromania is characterized by deliberate and purposeful fire setting on more than one occasion. Fire and burning objects fascinate people with this disorder, who get intense pleasure or relief from setting the fires, watching things burn, or observing firefighters and their efforts to put out fires. Their fire-setting impulses are driven by this fascination rather than by motives involving revenge, sabotage, or financial gains. Fire setters have been reported to have high rates of mood and substance-use disorders (McElroy & Arnold, 2001).

There is some debate about whether impulse control disorders are more appropriately considered symptoms and manifestation of some other disturbance, such as related to nonsubstance addiction or obsessive-compulsive disorders. This controversy has been recently reinvigorated by a move to declare Internet addiction a new impulse control disorder or a nonsubstance addiction in the DSM-5. In one major survey, it was found that 15 percent of client youths described being addicted to the Internet and that they used the Internet so frequently that they isolated themselves from family and friends (Cynkar, 2007). Many children and adults not only feel a compulsion to constantly surf the Internet but also describe the cyberworld as their new social environment, in which they enter chat rooms, instant message one another, post their profiles on Facebook, visit YouTube or pornography sites, and play virtual games (Bishop, 2005; DeAngelis, 2007), to the detriment of relationships with significant others and of their education or jobs.

Opponents believe that an overly broad approach to the definition of addiction opens the floodgates to declaring every compensatory behavior an impulse control disorder, such as fingernail biting, frequent sexual activities, or even excessive use of cell phones.

For Further Consideration:

1. Can you make a case for and against the existence of impulse control disorders as distinct from other forms of compulsive activities?

2. What are your thoughts about Internet addiction? Have you ever found yourself so preoccupied with Internet use that other aspects of your life have suffered?

terms of self-interest and immediate gratification and toward higher levels of thinking. These higher levels would include, for example, recognizing the effects of one's behaviors on others and developing a sense of responsibility. Because cognitive and behavioral approaches assume that antisocial behaviors are learned, treatment programs may target these behaviors by setting rules and enforcing consequences for rule violations, substituting new behaviors for undesirable ones, and learning to anticipate consequences of behaviors (Meloy, 2001).

Because current treatment programs do not seem very effective, new strategies must be used. These strategies should focus on antisocial youths who seem amenable to treatment, and treatment programs should broaden the base of intervention to involve not only the young clients but also their families and peers. Because people with antisocial personality disorder may seek thrills (Big T's), they may respond to intervention programs that provide the physical and mental stimulation they need (Farley, 1986). Longitudinal studies show that the prevalence of this disorder diminishes with age as these individuals become more aware of the social and interpersonal maladaptiveness of their social behaviors (Phillips & Gunderson, 1999).

■■■■■ Personality Disorder Trait Specified (PDTS)

As we have emphasized, DSM-5 uses a hybrid approach (personality types and pathological personality traits) that combine both categorical and dimensional characteristics to the diagnosis of personality disorders. An exclusive categorical approach has limitations because it uses an "all-or-none" approach to classification (Reed, 2010). Further, it is based on an arbitrary diagnostic threshold and does not recognize the continuous nature of personality traits (Westen et al., 2010). In reality, people may "have" a personality trait or disorder to varying degrees or at various times (see advantages of moving to a continuous description of personality disorders in Table 15.4). We all exhibit some of the traits that characterize personality disorders—for example, suspiciousness, dependency, sensitivity to rejection, or compulsiveness.

For this reason, many investigators (Bienenfeld, 2007b; Skodol & Bender, 2009; Widiger, 2007) prefer to view personality disorders as the extremes of underlying dimensions of normal personality traits. They argue that dimensions such as extraversion (sociability), agreeableness (nurturance), neuroticism, conscientiousness, and openness to experience may be used to describe personality disorders (Costa & McCrae, 2005). Because people differ in the extent to which they possess a trait, a clinician may have trouble deciding when a client exhibits a trait to a degree that could be considered a symptom of a disorder (Millon et al., 2004). For example, rather than considering the existence of a schizoid personality disorder in a client, it is more accurate to describe that person as possessing varying degrees of personality traits associated with social withdrawal, social detachment, intimacy avoidance, and so forth. These can be assessed on a scaled continuum. Even with disorders that seem to better fit a type category (high validity and reliability), DSM-5 uses a 5-point "degree of match" between the description of a personality disorder type and the client (see Critical Thinking Box "What Domain Traits Best Apply to This Man?").

Another argument against a solely categorical approach to assessing personality psychopathology lies in the issue of diagnostic accuracy. Although diagnosticians show excellent reliability in diagnosing *whether* a particular client has a personality disorder, they show much lower reliability when they must classify clients as to the precise *type* of personality disorder (Costa & McCrae, 2005; Reed, 2010; Zimmerman, Rothschild, & Chelminski, 2005). Co-occurrence is common in that a person diagnosed with one personality disorder often meets criteria for others as well (Rothman, Ahn, Sanislow, & Kim, 2009; Widiger, 2007). Because people can have more than one type of personality disorder, the problems in accurately distinguishing these disorders are formidable. Moreover, although the distinction between personality disorders and other disorders is valid, many individuals have symptoms that do not neatly characterize a particular disorder and that overlap with different disorders (Westen et al., 2010).

impulse control disorders disorders in which the person fails to resist an impulse or temptation to perform some act that is harmful to the person or to others; the person feels tension before the act and release after it

intermittent explosive disorder impulse control disorder characterized by separate and discrete episodes of loss of control over aggressive impulses, resulting in serious assaults on others or destruction of property

kleptomania an impulse control disorder characterized by a recurrent failure to resist impulses to steal objects

pyromania an impulse control disorder having as its main feature deliberate and purposeful fire setting on more than one occasion

Internet addiction a new impulse control disorder in the 2012 edition of DSM-5 characterized by persons using the Internet so frequently that they isolate themselves from family and friends

TABLE 15.4   Reasons to Use a Dimensional and Continuous Diagnosis of Personality Psychopathology

DSM-5 utilizes a dimensional rather than a sole categorical approach to diagnosing personality disorders. Research, conceptual, and therapeutic reasons suggest that most personality disorders are better seen as continuous in nature (Skodol & Bender, 2009; Westen et al., 2010; Widiger, 2007)

Advantages	Reasons
Minimizing pejorative connotations	Once diagnosed with a personality disorder, there is an assumption that the disorder is relatively unchangeable even in therapy. Insurance carriers are reluctant to provide coverage. To be diagnosed with such a condition gives the impression that there is little prospect of improvement, even though research provides compelling evidence that meaningful change can occur in many with lower manifestations of the disorder. By moving to a trait description, and by recognizing the **degree** to which disorders exist in the client, the all-or-none stigma is minimized.
Reducing excessive diagnostic co-occurrence and improving accurate diagnosis	A major problem with DSM-IV-TR is that it proposes the existence of ten personality disorders; they are considered distinct entities (categories). First, some of the personality disorders lack a research base. Thus, it is not unusual for a person to meet criteria for an excessive number of personality disorders. In other words, a person with a borderline personality disorder under the old system might also be diagnosed with histrionic and narcissistic disorders. Which one does he or she have? Second, it is just not true that there are only ten personality disorders. DSM-5 recognizes five major types but the domain-trait model allows mawny diagnostic combinations.
Acknowledging differences among those sharing the same diagnosis	People possessing the same diagnosis of a personality disorder often appear very different from one another; they rarely share the same personality features. Allowing clinicians to consider the degree of match between a diagnostic type and rating prominent personality traits on a scale facilitates seeing clients in a more unique manner.
Reducing inconsistent and arbitrary diagnosis	Under a categorical system, the boundaries used to determine normal personality features and personality disorders are inconsistent, subjective, and arbitrary. No clear rationale is given for establishing these boundaries. Although a dimensional approach also establishes criteria to determine abnormality, it is rooted in impairment or adaptive failure in life circumstances.
Scientific support for the existence of six types of personality disorders, and the dimensional trait analysis	Many of the personality disorders identified in DSM-IV-TR lack a research base for their formulation and description. They are based primarily on subjective clinical formulations. Only some of the ten personality disorders such as antisocial and borderline seem to possess such a research base

Copyright © Cengage Learning 2013

AP Images

Eluding Capture Aided by Schizoid Personality Features of a Unabomber

It took many years for authorities to track down and arrest Ted Kaczynski, the Unabomber, who killed many people over an 18-year period. Formerly a University of California, Berkeley, math professor, Kaczynski is believed to have a schizoid personality disorder and to have eluded capture because of his "hermit-like" existence. He was a loner and did not seem interested in socializing with people. He was finally arrested in his isolated cabin, where he had lived alone for many years.

The DSM-5 Work Group uses an overarching dimensional diagnostic system of five domain traits for assessing personality disorders. The use of the word *trait* refers to a specific personality characteristic possessed by an individual (distractibility, anxiousness, perfectionism, etc.). Traits may be organized around a *domain*, which represents a higher order or superordinate grouping of related traits like introversion (includes traits of social withdrawal, social detachment, intimacy avoidance, etc.) The term *dimension* simply refers to a scaled continuum that can be used to measure (match) the degree to whether a person possesses certain traits. The five domain traits are outlined in Table 15.5 and briefly described. The existence of one or more of these domain traits that impair self or interpersonal functioning is sufficient to indicate a personality disorder.

TABLE 15.5   DSM-5 Five-Domain Traits and Their Specific Trait Facets

1. **Negative affectivity** refers to people who experience a wide range of negative emotions such as anxiety, depression, guilt, shame, worry, and so forth and the behavioral or interpersonal manifestations of those experiences. The specific traits associated with this domain are:
   - Emotional lability, anxiousness, separation insecurity, perseveration, submissiveness, hostility, depressivity, suspiciousness, and restricted affectivity.

2. **Detachment** is descriptive of people who withdraw from others whether the relationships are with intimate acquaintances or strangers. They have restricted or limited affective experiences and expressions and are limited in their hedonic capacity (i.e., inability to experience pleasure or joys in life). The specific traits associated with this domain are:
   - Restricted affectivity, depressivity, suspiciousness, withdrawal, anhedonia, and intimacy avoidance.

3. **Antagonism** relates to people who feel and behave negatively toward others and have a corresponding exaggerated sense of self-importance. The specific traits associated with this domain are:
   - Manipulativeness, deceitfulness, grandiosity, attention seeking, callousness, and hostility.

4. **Disinhibition** describes a person who seeks immediate gratification, is present oriented and responds primarily to immediate or current internal and external stimuli. The past (past learning) and the future (future consequences) appear to be minimally important in motivation or behaviors. Compulsivity is the opposite end of this domain. The specific traits associated with this domain are:
   - Irresponsibility, impulsivity, distractibility, risk taking, rigid perfectionism or lack of it.

5. **Psychoticism** is the domain that includes behaviors and cognitions (includes perception, content, and belief) considered odd, unusual or bizarre. The specific traits associated with this domain are:
   - Unusual beliefs and experiences, egocentricity, and cognitive and perceptual dysregulation.

What Domain Traits Best Apply to This Man?

CRITICAL THINKING

The following case describes the behavior of a teenager, Roy W. He exhibits some very prominent personality traits that appear bothersome. After reading the case, look closely at the six domains in Table 15.5 to determine which domain(s) you believe apply to Roy. Use the following scale to ascertain the degree of match between the descriptions given and the behaviors of Roy W.: 0 = very little or not at all, 1 = mildly descriptive, 2 = moderately descriptive, and 3 = extremely descriptive. A rating of moderately or extremely descriptive with one or more of the trait-domains would suggest a personality disorder. What are your conclusions?

Case Study

Roy W. was an eighteen-year-old high school senior who was referred by juvenile court for diagnosis and evaluation. He was arrested for stealing a car, something he had done on several other occasions. The court agreed with Roy's mother that he needed evaluation and perhaps psychotherapy. During his interview with the psychologist, Roy was articulate, relaxed, and even witty. He said that stealing was wrong but that none of the cars he stole was ever damaged. The last theft occurred because he needed transportation to a beer party (which was located only a mile from his home) and his leg was sore from playing basketball. When the psychologist asked Roy how he got along with young women, he grinned and said that he was very outgoing and could easily "hustle" them. He then related the following incident:

"About three months ago, I was pulling out of the school parking lot real fast and accidentally sideswiped this other car. The girl who was driving it started to scream at me. God, there was only a small dent on her fender! Anyway, we exchanged names and addresses and I apologized for the accident. When I filled out the accident report later, I said that it was her car that pulled out from the other side and hit my car. How do you like that? Anyway, when she heard about my claim that it was her fault, she had her old man call me. He said that his daughter had witnesses to the accident and that I could be arrested. Bull, he was just trying to bluff me. But I gave him a sob story—about how my parents were ready to get a divorce, how poor we were, and the trouble I would get into if they found out about the accident. I apologized for lying and told him I could fix the dent. Luckily he never checked with my folks for the real story. Anyway, I went over to look at the girl's car. I really didn't have any idea of how to fix that old heap so I said I had to wait a couple of weeks to get some tools for the repair job.

"Meanwhile, I started to talk to the girl. Gave her my sob story, told her how nice I thought her folks and home were. We started to date and I took her out three times. Then one night I laid her. The crummy thing was that she told her folks about it. Can you imagine that? Anyway, her old man called and told me never to get near his precious little thing again. She's actually a slut.

"At least I didn't have to fix her old heap. I know I shouldn't lie but can you blame me? People make such a big thing out of nothing."

Summary

1. Can one's personality be pathological?

    *   Yes. Personality disorders are enduring, inflexible, long-standing personality traits or types that cause impairment or adaptive failure in the person's everyday life. They are usually extreme and manifest in adolescence and continue into adulthood.

2. What criteria are used to assess personality disorders?

    *   Impairments in **self** and in **interpersonal functioning** are used to diagnose a personality disorder. They must meet criteria for a personality disorder type or be sufficiently extreme in one of the five personality domain traits   as to cause impairment.

    *   Personality types or traits must also be relatively stable across time and consistent across situations, are not better explained as norm of the person's culture, and not due to a physiological or medical condition.

3. Are there certain personality disorder types?

    *   Yes. Research and therapeutic findings support the existence of six types of personality disorders: schizotypal, borderline, avoidant, narcissistic, obsessive-compulsive, and antisocial.

4. How does the multipath model explain antisocial personality disorder?

    *   Because personality is at the core of the disorder, etiological explanations focus on factors that influence personality. Genetics and neurobiological factors (e.g., underarousal of ANS and low anxiety), psychodynamic, cognitive and learning formulations, social or parental and family environments, and sociocultural factors (e.g., gender, race, and culture) all seem to contribute in a highly complex fashion.

5. What types of therapy are used in treating antisocial personality disorder?

    *   Traditional treatment approaches are not particularly effective with antisocial personalities. It may be that successful treatment can occur only in a setting in which behavior can be controlled. That is, treatment programs may need to provide enough control so that those with antisocial personalities cannot avoid confronting their inability to form close and intimate relationships and the effect of their behaviors on others.

6. What personality traits are important in determining pathology?

    *   Increasingly personality disorders are being viewed less categorically but in a dimensional manner (e.g., extremes on a continuum of normal personality traits).

    *   The five domain traits used to determine personality psychopathology are negative affectivity, detachment, antagonism, disinhibition vs. compulsivity, and psychoticism. Numerous specific traits are associated with each domain.

Media Resources

Psychology CourseMate   Access an interactive eBook, chapter-specific interactive learning tools, including flash cards, quizzes, videos, and more in your Psychology CourseMate, accessed through CengageBrain.com.

CENGAGENOW

CengageNow   CengageNOW is an easy-to-use online resource that helps you study in less time to get the grade you want—NOW. If your textbook does not include an access code card, go to CengageBrain.com to gain access.

CENGAGEbrain.com

CengageBrain   More than just an interactive study guide, WebTutor is an anytime, anywhere customized learning solution with an eBook, keeping you connected to your textbook, instructor, and classmates. Purchase the access chosen by your instructor at CengageBrain.com.

16

Disorders of Childhood and Adolescence

"Please Don't Leave Me Alone"

Eight-year-old Nina cannot tolerate having her mother out of sight. Upon arriving at school, Nina clings to her mother, refusing to leave the car. Even when her mother walks her to the classroom, Nina cries, screams, and begs her mother not to leave.

Diagnosis: separation anxiety disorder

"No, I Won't"

Ten-year-old Casey's parents are frustrated by Casey's continuing defiance and constant arguments. Today Casey is refusing to come out of his bedroom to meet friends and relatives attending his mother's surprise birthday party. He shouts at his parents, "You can't make me do anything!"

Diagnosis: oppositional defiant disorder

"Sit Still and Pay Attention"

Sitting in the psychologist's office, the mother explained that ever since he was in preschool, her ten-year-old son Tyrone has disrupted classroom instruction. He has difficulty concentrating, is often reprimanded for talking and is failing most subjects. Throughout the session, Tyrone fidgets in his seat and interrupts his mother. He is quite remorseful when he accidentally breaks an item on the psychologist's desk.

Diagnosis: attention-deficit/hyperactivity disorder

"Leave Me Alone"

Five-year-old Ahmed sits apart from the other children, spinning the wheels of a toy truck and humming aloud as if to mimic the sound. Ahmed seems to live in a world of his own, interacting with those around him as if they are inanimate objects.

Diagnosis: autism spectrum disorder

In this chapter, we discuss problems that arise during childhood and adolescence. Accurate assessment of childhood disorders requires understanding of normal child development and child temperament, as well as knowledge about psychiatric disorders. Familiarity with

1 What internalizing disorders occur in childhood and adolescence?

2 What are the characteristics of externalizing disorders?

3 What are elimination disorders, and what is their prognosis?

4 What are neurodevelopmental disorders, and what are their characteristics?

child psychopathology (how psychological disorders manifest in children and adolescents) is essential because characteristics that signify mental illness in adults often occur in normally developing children. Additionally, symptoms of some disorders are quite different in children compared to adults.

Anxiety about a parent leaving, oppositional behavior, or high levels of activity combined with a short attention span are viewed quite differently depending on the age of the child. These behaviors would be considered rather typical in a two or three-year-old, but would be of concern in a ten-year-old. Additionally, children differ in their natural temperament; some are cautious and slow to warm to new situations, whereas others are energetic, strong-willed, and intense in their reactions. To determine if a child has an actual disorder, clinicians consider the child's age and developmental level as well as environmental factors, asking questions such as: Is the child's behavior significantly different from other children the same age? Are the symptoms likely to subside as the child matures? Are the behaviors present in most contexts or only in particular settings? Are the symptoms occurring because adults are expecting too much or too little of the child? Diagnoses are approached cautiously, weighing the potential effects of "labeling" on a child's future development with the knowledge that untreated disorders can develop into lifelong patterns that create ongoing distress.

Childhood disorders are not rare; about one in five children have a serious emotional or behavioral problem (Koppelman, 2004). Face-to-face diagnostic assessment of a representative sample of more than 10,000 U.S. adolescents (ages 13 to 18) found that almost half had experienced significant mental health concerns. Nearly one-third (31.9 percent) reported symptoms of an anxiety disorder, 19.1 percent demonstrated a behavior disorder, and 14 percent reported symptoms of a mood disorder. Twenty-two percent of the sample reported severe impairment due to their symptoms. Depressive and bipolar disorder symptoms caused the greatest distress. (See Table 16.1 for prevalence, severity, and gender comparisons of specific disorders.) Females reported more depression and post-traumatic stress disorder (PTSD), whereas males demonstrated more inattention/hyperactivity symptoms; more than 40 percent of those surveyed met diagnostic criteria for more than one disorder (Merikangas et al., 2010). Like adults, children and adolescents often have coexisting disorders (Yoo, Brown, & Luthar, 2009). Unfortunately, in a national sample of 6,483

TABLE 16.1 Lifetime Prevalence of Psychiatric Disorders in Adolescents

Disorder	Females	Males	Percent with Severe Impairment
Generalized Anxiety Disorder	3.0	1.5	30
Social Phobia	11.2	7.0	14
Specific Phobia	22.1	16.7	3
Panic Disorder	2.6	2.0	9
Post-Traumatic Stress Disorder	8.0	2.3	30
Depression	16.9	7.7	74
Bipolar Disorder	3.3	2.6	89
Attention-Deficit/Hyperactivity	4.2	13.0	48
Oppositional-Defiant Disorder	11.3	13.9	52
Conduct Disorder	5.8	7.9	32

Lifetime prevalence (in percentages) of various mental disorders in a sample of youth ages 13 to 18 and percentage of those with each disorder experiencing severe impairment.

Source: Merikangas et al., (2010)

child psychopathology the emotional and behavioral manifestation of psychological disorders in children and adolescents

Are We Overmedicating Children?

Many medications are prescribed to treat childhood disorders, including tranquilizers, stimulants, and antipsychotics (Parens & Johnston, 2010). As with adults, medication prescriptions for children and adolescents have increased dramatically (Thomas, Conrad, Casler, & Goodman, 2006; Mojtabai & Olfson, 2010). Controversy continues regarding overdiagnosis of some disorders in youth, the "quick fix" nature of medication, and the tendency to use medication without first attempting psychotherapy or interventions in the academic or home environment (Berman, Kuczenski, McCracken, & London, 2009). Additionally, many medications prescribed for youth have only been tested on adults; thus, there is insufficient information regarding how these medications might affect the extensive brain development that occurs throughout childhood and adolescence (Kern, 2009).

Many believe that medication should be considered only after comprehensive diagnostic evaluation and implementation of nonpharmaceutical interventions. Certainly, if medication is prescribed, it is important to educate parents about the specific symptoms being treated and the plan for monitoring progress and possible side effects (American Academy of Child and Adolescent Psychiatry, 2009). How can we determine if medications are prescribed too freely and if their use with children is safe? How can we ensure that adequate assessment and consideration of nonpharmaceutical interventions occur before medication is prescribed?

adolescents (ages 13 to 18), almost two-thirds of those with mental illness received no treatment (Merikangas et al., 2011). Of particular concern are the low treatment rates for youth experiencing major depression; this lack of intervention is particularly pronounced for black, Hispanic, and Asian American adolescents (Cummings & Druss, 2011).

Psychiatric disorders among youth often affect multiple aspects of daily life; diagnosis requires that symptoms cause significant impairment in daily functioning over an extended period of time. We begin our discussion with disorders with internalizing (i.e., emotions directed inward) and externalizing (i.e., disruptive) symptoms followed by a brief review of elimination disorders. We conclude with a look at neurodevelopmental disorders (childhood disorders involving impaired neurological development). The field of child psychopathology is extensive. Our goal in this chapter is to expose readers to the characteristics, etiology, and treatment of some of the most significant disorders.

Did You Know?

Childhood behaviors and emotional problems differ from culture to culture. For example, in Thailand, where parenting techniques prolong dependence and slow psychological maturation, children display problems involving dependence and immaturity that are not seen in the United States. Sociocultural factors can significantly affect definitions and characteristics of childhood disorders.

Source: Weisz et al., (2006)

Internalizing Disorders of Childhood

In this section, we focus on internalizing disorders in childhood or adolescence (i.e., disorders involving emotional symptoms directed inward). As with adults, children and adolescents with internalizing disorders display heightened reactions to trauma, stressors, or negative events as well as difficulty regulating their emotions. Anxiety and depressive disorders are prevalent in early life (see Table 16.1) and are of particular concern because symptoms of these disorders often precede adolescent substance use and abuse (O'Neil, Conner, & Kendall, 2011). We will focus on the anxiety, trauma and stressor-related disorders, and mood presentations unique to childhood and adolescence followed by a discussion of nonsuicidal self-injury.

Anxiety, Trauma, and Stressor-Related Disorders in Early Life

Anxiety, trauma, and stressor-related disorders in childhood or adolescence typically result from a combination of innate reactivity and exposure to environmental influences. Anxiety disorders are the most common mental health disorder in childhood and adolescence (Rockhill et al., 2010). Among the 32 percent of adolescents who have experienced an anxiety disorder, specific phobias (19 percent) and social phobia (9 percent) are most common (Merikangas et al., 2010). Specific phobias often begin in early to middle childhood, whereas social phobias typically begin in early to middle adolescence

neurodevelopmental

disorders conditions involving impaired development of the brain and central nervous system that are evident early in a child's life

(Rapee, Schniering, & Hudson, 2009). Childhood anxiety can significantly affect academic, social, and interpersonal functioning (Sakolsky & Birmaher, 2008) and can lead to adult anxiety disorders (Essex et al., 2010). An inhibited, fearful temperament increases risk for anxiety disorders in childhood, particularly when exacerbated by overprotective parenting practices, controlling parental behavior, low parental warmth, or perceived parental rejection (DiBartolo & Helt, 2007; Lindhout et al., 2009; Bayer et al., 2011). Anxiety disorders specific to childhood include school phobia (e.g., fear of attending school), separation anxiety disorder (e.g., severe distress about leaving home, being alone, or being separated from a parent), and selective mutism (e.g., consistent failure to speak in certain situations). Children with these disturbances display exaggerated autonomic responses and are apprehensive in new situations, preferring to stay at home or in other familiar environments. Childhood phobias and anxiety disorders are most effectively treated with individual, group, and family-focused cognitive-behavior therapy (Silverman, Pina, & Viswesvaran, 2008).

Post-traumatic Stress Disorder in Childhood

The effects of trauma and resultant post-traumatic stress disorder (PTSD) can be particularly distressing in childhood as illustrated in the following case:

Case Study

Several months after witnessing her father seriously injure her mother during a domestic dispute, Jenna remained withdrawn; she spoke little and rarely played with her toys. Although a protection order prevented her father from returning home, Jenna startled whenever she heard the door open and frequently woke up screaming "Stop!" She refused to enter the kitchen, the site of the violent assault.

Youth with PTSD experience recurrent, distressing memories of a shocking experience. The trauma that precipitates PTSD can include threats of or direct experience with death, serious injury, or sexual violation. Witnessing or hearing about the victimization of others can also result in PTSD, especially when a primary caregiver is involved. Memories of the event may entail: (1) distressing dreams; (2) intense physiological or psychological reactions to thoughts or cues associated with the event and avoidance of such cues; (3) episodes of playacting the event (sometimes without apparent distress); or (4) dissociative reactions, in which the child appears to re-experience the trauma or appears unaware of present surroundings. Traumatized children often display negative affect (e.g., shame, guilt, fear); social withdrawal; diminished positive affect; and disinterest in previously enjoyed activities. Behavioral evidence of PTSD includes angry, aggressive behavior or temper tantrums; difficulty sleeping or concentrating; and exaggerated startle response or vigilance for possible threats (American Psychiatric Association, 2011). Lifetime prevalence of PTSD among adolescents is 8 percent for females and 2.3 percent for males; approximately one-third report severe PTSD symptoms (Merikangas et al., 2010). Trauma-focused and school-based cognitive-behavior therapies have proven to be effective in treating childhood PTSD (Silverman et al, 2008).

Attachment Disorders

Infants and children with early-life exposure to stressful environments devoid of predictable caretaking and nurturing sometimes demonstrate significant difficulties with emotional attachment and social relationships. We begin by discussing a pattern of inhibited responding, referred to as *reactive attachment disorder*, and then discuss *disinhibited social engagement disorder*. These disorders are evident before age five and are diagnosed only when early circumstances prevented the child from forming stable attachments. Situations that can disrupt attachment include persistent neglect of physical or psychological safety (e.g., physical abuse or lack of comfort, stimulation, and affection) or frequent changes in primary caregiver (e.g., living in multiple foster care settings). As you will see, symptoms of the disorders are quite distinct; however, they both result from early experiences characterized by disrupted or unreliable care, social deprivation, and emotional neglect.

Infants or children with reactive attachment disorder (RAD) appear to have little trust that their needs will be attended to and do not readily seek or respond to comfort, attention, or nurturing. They appear to use avoidance or ambivalence as a psychological defense; have great difficulty with age-appropriate responding to or initiation of social or emotional interactions; and often behave in a very inhibited, watchful, or avoidant manner, even with family and caregivers. Children with RAD often show limited positive emotion and may demonstrate irritability, sadness, or fearfulness when interacting with adults (American Psychiatric Association, 2011).

In stark contrast, children with disinhibited social engagement disorder (DSED) socialize effortlessly, but indiscriminately, and readily become superficially "attached" to strangers or casual acquaintances. They easily approach and interact with unfamiliar adults in an overly familiar manner (both verbally and physically) and demonstrate such eagerness for interpersonal contact that they frequently venture away from caregivers. Children with DSED often have a history of harsh punishment or inconsistent parenting in addition to emotional neglect and limited attachment opportunities (American Psychiatric Association, 2011). Children exposed to maltreatment or maternal psychiatric hospitalizations are particularly vulnerable to DSED (Lyons-Ruth, Bureau, Riley, & Atlas-Corbett, 2009).

The course of these disorders depends on the severity of the abuse, neglect, or disruption of attachments and subsequent events in the child's life. Symptoms of RAD often disappear if children are provided an opportunity for predictable caretaking and nurturance, whereas symptoms of DSED are more persistent (Zeanah & Gleason, 2010). Issues of mistrust and difficulties with intimate relationships may, in some cases, continue into adulthood. Once RAD or DSED is identified, therapeutic support can focus on building emotional security (Hornor, 2008). Some children subjected to abuse or trauma show neurobiological changes that can, in fact, be reversed with intervention (Rick & Douglas, 2007). Unfortunately, research on treatment for attachment disorders is limited (Cornell & Hamrin, 2008), and unsubstantiated treatment methods such as rebirthing therapy (as discussed in Chapter 4) may put vulnerable children at risk (Newman & Mares, 2007). Effective intervention includes providing a secure and nurturing environment, exposure to positive parenting practices, and opportunities to develop interpersonal trust and social relationship skills. It should be noted that many children raised under difficult circumstances do not show signs of these disorders.

Depressive Disorders in Early Life

Depressive disorders affect a large number of youth, particularly females and older adolescents. Thirteen percent of one sample of adolescents reported symptoms of major depression, with 74 percent reporting severe symptoms (Merikangas et al., 2010). Children are especially vulnerable to environmental factors because they lack the maturity and skills to deal with stressors. Conditions such as childhood maltreatment, parental illness, or loss of an attachment figure can increase vulnerability to depression. Like adults, youth with mood disorders have more negative self-concepts and are more likely to engage in self-blame and self-criticism. Early-onset of depressive symptoms tends to predict a more chronic and severe course (Merikangas et al., 2010).

Evidence-based treatment for depression in youth includes individual, group, or school-based cognitive-behavior therapy; parent involvement and programs focused on building resilience based on positive psychology principles are also beneficial

(David-Ferndon & Kaslow, 2008). Intervention is critical because of the strong association between depressive disorders and adolescent suicidal ideation and suicide attempts (Chronis-Tuscano et al., 2010). However, concerns about selective serotonin reuptake inhibitors (SSRIs) increasing suicidality led to FDA warnings regarding the use of certain antidepressants for treatment of depression in youth (Hammad, Laughren, & Racoosin, 2006). Subsequent data analysis has indicated that although SSRIs may have only a moderate effect on depressive symptoms, they appear superior to some cognitive-behavioral therapies, especially in the first months of treatment, and that the benefits of using SSRIs (particularly fluoxetine) may outweigh the risk of increased suicidality (Bridge et al., 2007; Vitiello, 2009). Best practices support careful monitoring of suicidality in all children and adolescents who are depressed, with particular attention to those taking antidepressants (Reid et al., 2010).

Pediatric Bipolar Disorder

Careful monitoring of suicidality is also important in *pediatric bipolar disorder* (*PBD*), a debilitating disorder that parallels the mood variability and significant departure from the individual's typical functioning characteristic of adult bipolar disorder (Rich et al., 2008; Algorta et al., 2011). PBD is illustrated in the following case:

Case Study

Anna was a fairly cooperative, engaging child throughout her early years. However, around her tenth birthday, her behavior changed significantly. At times, she experienced periods of extreme moodiness, depression, and high irritability; on other occasions, she seemed to have almost boundless energy and talked incessantly, often moving rapidly from one topic to another as she described different ideas and plans. During her energetic periods, she could go for several weeks with minimal sleep and, despite protests from her parents, insisted on calling various friends in the middle of the night.

Youth with PBD typically display (1) recurring depression; (2) rapid mood changes; and (3) distinct periods of abnormally elevated mood involving diminished need for sleep, increased activity, distractibility, talkativeness, and inflated self-esteem (Stringaris et al., 2010) (Table 16.2). Pervasive lack of pleasure during periods of irritability and depression alternate with exaggerated pleasure-seeking and goal-directed activity during periods of hypomania (Dickstein et al., 2007). Males and females have equal incidence of PBD; lifetime prevalence in adolescents is estimated to be 3 percent, with 89 percent of those with PBD reporting severe impairment (Merikangas et al., 2010).

As with the diagnosis of adult bipolar disorder, manic episodes involve symptoms that are present most of the day, nearly every day for at least one week; hypomanic episodes involve symptoms that are consistently present for at least four consecutive days (American Psychiatric Association, 2011). Youth with PBD often demonstrate rapid cycling of moods combined with neurocognitively based difficulties processing emotional stimuli and regulating behavior and social-emotional functioning (Rosen & Rich, 2010). They also show elevated neurological responsiveness to emotional stimuli, reduced volume in the amygdala (Kalmar et al., 2009) and other brain abnormalities (James et al., 2011). Symptoms of PBD can develop gradually or emerge suddenly. PBD often occurs in families with a history of the illness and is likely to evolve into adult bipolar disorder or another chronic psychiatric disorder (Brotman et al., 2007). Medications used with adult bipolar disorder are often combined with psychosocial intervention to treat PBD (Parens & Johnston, 2010); however, many contend that further research is needed to ensure the safety of lithium or antipsychotic medications in pediatric populations (Thomas, Stansifer, & Findling, 2011).

DISORDERS CHART   DISRUPTIVE MOOD DYSREGULATION DISORDER AND PEDIATRIC BIPOLAR DISORDER

TABLE 16.2

Disorder	Symptoms	Prevalence	Age of Onset	Course
Disruptive Mood Dysregulation Disorder (DMDD)	• Recurrent episodes of temper, including verbal rage or physical aggression • Anger response is exaggerated in intensity and duration • Typical mood is irritable, angry, or sad	3%; more frequently diagnosed in boys	Symptoms are present before age 10 and may be present in early childhood	May improve with maturity; may evolve into a depressive disorder
Pediatric Bipolar Disorder	• Distinct periods of abnormally elevated mood (i.e., manic or hypomanic symptoms) • Periodic mood and behavioral changes (e.g., irritability, depression, increased activity, distractibility, or talkativeness; inflated self-esteem)	3%; equally affects boys and girls	Onset is around age 10, about 5 years later than TDD	Poor prognosis; often evolves into a chronic psychiatric disorder

Source: Brotman et al., (2006); Meyer et al., (2009); Merikangas et al., (2010); American Psychiatric Association, (2011).

Non-suicidal Self Injury

Case Study

For the past year, Maria has been secretly cutting her forearms and thighs with a razor blade. She has tried to stop, but when she feels anxious or depressed she thinks of the razor blade and the relief she experiences once she feels the cutting. She doesn't underst and why she cuts; she just knows it's how she copes when she feels overwhelmed. The more life hurts, the more she cuts.

Non-suicidal self injury (NSSI) is a relatively new phenomenon that involves the induction of bleeding, bruising, or pain by means of intentional, self-inflicted injury. Youth who engage in NSSI cut, burn, stab, hit, or excessively rub themselves to the point of pain and injury, but without suicidal intent. Intense negative affect or cognitions (e.g., depressive, anxious, angry, or self-critical thoughts) and a preoccupation with engaging in self-harm (often accompanied by a desire to resist the impulse to self-injure) typically precede episodes of NSSI. Those engaging in NSSI often expect that it will improve their mood and many report a respite from uncomfortable feelings or a temporary sense of calm and well-being following self-harm (American Psychiatric Association, 2011). Two-thirds of those who engage in NSSI begin the behavior in adolescence. NSSI occurs with similar frequency in both genders, although males are more likely to hit or burn themselves while females more frequently cut themselves. It is estimated that approximately 14 to 17 percent of adolescents and young adults have engaged in self-injury at least once; only a minority engage in repeated self-injury. Those who engage in repeated NSSI tend to be highly self-critical and have difficulty expressing their emotions (Klonsky & Glenn, 2011). NSSI is associated with increased risk of attempted suicide (Kerr, Muehlenkamp, & Turner, 2010), particularly among those who have more depressive symptoms, lower self-esteem, and limited parental support (Nock et al., 2006; Brausch & Gutierrez, 2010). Treatment for those who engage in repeated NSSI often includes teaching problem solving, coping, and emotional regulation skills as well as a focus on emotional expression and improving interpersonal relationship skills (Klonsky & Muehlenkamp, 2007).

Externalizing Disorders of Childhood

Externalizing disorders (sometimes called disruptive behavior disorders) include disruptive mood dysregulation disorder (DMDD), oppositional defiant disorder (ODD), and conduct disorder (CD), conditions associated with symptoms that are socially disturbing and distressing to others. Parenting a child with externalizing behaviors can be challenging and can result in negative parent-child interactions, high family stress, and negative feelings about parenting; this can further exacerbate behavioral difficulties. Early intervention is necessary to interrupt the negative course of these disorders. However, diagnosis involving disruptive behaviors can be controversial. It is sometimes difficult to distinguish externalizing disorders from one another and from the defiance and noncompliance that can typically occur during childhood and adolescence. Gender, sociocultural, and age-related developmental factors all need to be considered when defining normative behavior. Diagnosis of externalizing disorders requires a pattern of behavior that is (1) atypical for the child's age and developmental level; (2) persistent (occurring consistently for at least one year); and (3) severe enough to cause significant impairment in social, academic, or vocational functioning.

Disruptive Mood Dysregulation Disorder

Case Study

As an infant and toddler, Juan was irritable and difficult to please. Temper tantrums, often involving attempts to hit his parents, occurred multiple times daily. Juan's parents had hoped he would outgrow this behavior; now eight, Juan is still "grumpy" and has continued temper outbursts. These rages are particularly pronounced when he is hungry or tired.

Temper Disruptive Mood Dysregulation Disorder (DMDD) is characterized by chronic irritability and severe mood dysregulation, including recurrent episodes of temper triggered by common childhood stressors (e.g., interpersonal conflict, being denied a request). Anger reactions (e.g., verbal rage and physical aggression towards people and property) are significantly exaggerated in both intensity and duration. DMDD is considered a depressive disorder; although behavioral symptoms are directed outwards, they are reflective of an irritable, angry, or sad mood state. Although behavior patterns associated with DMDD often begin in early childhood, diagnosis requires that symptoms persist beyond age six; the onset of symptoms must occur before age ten (American Psychiatric Association, 2011). These age distinctions ensure that diagnosis is not based on the erratic moods associated with puberty or early childhood (e.g., "the terrible twos"). A lifetime prevalence of 3.3 percent for DMDD was reported in one sample of children ages 10 to 19. The pervasive negative affect associated with DMDD is predictive of later depression (Brotman et al., 2006). Clinicians making a DMDD diagnosis need to rule out PBD due to the overlapping symptoms involving depression and mood changes (see Table 16.2); this differential diagnosis is important because interventions with PBD are quite different from those for DMDD (Dickstein et al., 2009).

Oppositional Defiant Disorder

Case Study

Mark's parents and teachers know that when requests are made, Mark often refuses to comply. He has been irritable and oppositional since he was a toddler. His parents have given up trying to enlist cooperation; they vacillate between ignoring Mark's hostile, defiant behavior and threatening punishment. If punished, Mark finds ways to retaliate.

Oppositional defiant disorder (*ODD*) is characterized by a negativistic, argumentative, and hostile behavior pattern. Children with this disorder often lose their temper, argue, and defy adult requests, but do not demonstrate the serious violations of societal norms seen with conduct disorder (Table 16.3). Defiant behavior is primarily directed toward parents, teachers, and others in authority. Angry, resentful, blaming, spiteful, and vindictive behaviors are common. Although ODD sometimes evolves into conduct disorder, the symptoms of ODD often resolve, especially with early intervention. ODD appears to have two components, one involving negative affect (e.g., angry, irritable mood) and the other involving oppositional behavior; negative affect is predictive of future depressive symptoms, whereas oppositional behaviors are more predictive of conduct disorder (First, 2007). Additionally, approximately half of those with ODD also have attention-deficit/hyperactivity disorder (McBurnett & Pfiffner, 2009).

Conduct Disorders

Case Study

Ben, well-known for his ongoing bullying and aggressive behavior, was expelled from school after stabbing another student. Two months later, he was arrested for armed robbery and placed in juvenile detention. Peer relationships at the facility were strained because of Ben's ongoing attempts to intimidate others.

A Troubled Teen

Conduct disorders involve a persistent pattern of antisocial behaviors. Here a teenager wearing a red plaid shirt watches for security as he shoplifts in a music store.

Bill Aron/PhotoEdit

Conduct disorders are characterized by a persistent pattern of antisocial behavior that violates the rights of others. These behaviors reflect dysfunction within the individual and include serious violations of rules and social norms; cruelty and deliberate aggression towards people or animals; and theft, deceit, or vandalism. A callous and unemotional subtype refers to those with CD who display minimal guilt or remorse and who are consistently unconcerned about the feelings of others, their own wrongdoing, or poor performance at school or work. With this subtype, emotional expression is very superficial and is used primarily to manipulate others (American Psychiatric Association, 2011). MRI imaging documented this callousness in one sample of adolescents with CD—they demonstrated strong pleasure responses to video clips of people experiencing pain and distress (Decety, Michalska, Akitsuki, & Lahey, 2009).

DISORDERS CHART OPPOSITIONAL DEFIANT DISORDER AND CONDUCT DISORDER

TABLE 16.3

Disorder	Symptoms	Prevalence	Age of Onset	Course
Oppositional Defiant Disorder	• Angry, irritable mood • Hostile, defiant, and vindictive behavior • Often loses temper, argues, and defies adult requests • Does not take responsibility for actions; blames others	6–13%; more common in males	Childhood	May resolve, or evolve into a conduct disorder or depressive disorder
Conduct Disorder	• Aggression and cruelty to people or animals • Often bullies, threatens, or initiates physical fights • Serious violations of rules and societal norms (e.g., lying, stealing, cheating, property destruction)	2–9% of children; more common in males; more common in urban settings	Childhood or adolescence	Prognosis poor, especially with childhood onset; often leads to criminal behaviors, antisocial acts, and problems in adult adjustment

Source: American Psychiatric Association (2011); Froehlich et al., (2007); Tynan, (2008); Tynan, (2010); Merikangas et al., (2010)

Did You Know?

Among a group of three-year-olds followed longitudinally, those who demonstrated a limited sense of fear as young children had frequent arrests for criminal activity in early adulthood; individuals who aren't inhibited by fear may have difficulty learning from negative consequences associated with inappropriate behavior.

Source: Gao et al., (2010)

Approximately 2 to 9 percent of youth meet diagnostic criteria for CD; incidence of CD increases from childhood to adolescence (Tynan, 2010). Approximately 50 percent of those with CD also have ADHD (Tynan, 2010). Males with CD are often involved in confrontational aggression (e.g., fighting, vandalism), whereas females are more likely to display truancy, substance abuse, or chronic lying. CD tends to be more persistent than other childhood disorders. In particular, childhood-onset CD is associated with chronic, serious offenses and poor prognosis, including criminal behavior and substance abuse during adulthood (Tynan, 2010). Those with callous disregard of societal rules and other individuals often exhibit antisocial personality disorder in adulthood (Tynan, 2010). The behaviors and criminal acts associated with CD present a significant concern to the public. Some youth advocates endorse widespread screening for CD among young children and maintain that early intervention and treatment can successfully modify the course of the disorder (Wilson, Minnis, Puckering, & Gillberg, 2009).

Etiology of Externalizing Disorders

Externalizing disorders often begin in early childhood. The etiology of these disorders involves an interaction between biological, psychological, social, and sociocultural factors. Biological factors appear to exert the greatest influence on the development of CD (Figure 16.1). Aggressive behavior has been linked to abnormal neural circuitry and resultant deficits in social-information processing as well as reduced activity in the amygdala in situations associated with fear (Sterzer, Stadler, & Front, 2009; Sterzer, 2010); these deficits may result in a decreased ability to learn from socializing punishment (Gao et al., 2010). CD risk is particularly increased when carriers of the genotype "low MAOA" (an allele associated with fear-regulating circuitry in the amygdala) are subjected to childhood maltreatment (First, 2007). Reduced autonomic nervous system activity (associated with increased need for stimulation to

Figure 16.1

MULTIPATH MODEL FOR CONDUCT DISORDER

The dimensions interact with one another and combine in different ways to result in a conduct disorder.

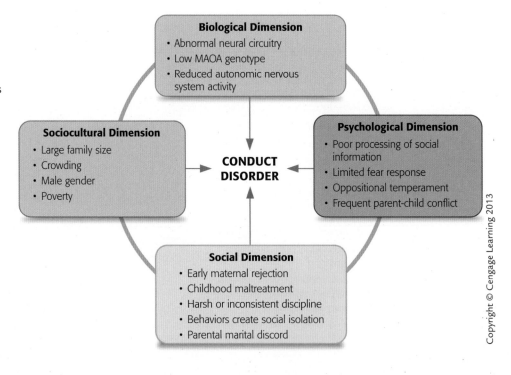

Biological Dimension
- Abnormal neural circuitry
- Low MAOA genotype
- Reduced autonomic nervous system activity

Sociocultural Dimension
- Large family size
- Crowding
- Male gender
- Poverty

CONDUCT DISORDER

Psychological Dimension
- Poor processing of social information
- Limited fear response
- Oppositional temperament
- Frequent parent-child conflict

Social Dimension
- Early maternal rejection
- Childhood maltreatment
- Harsh or inconsistent discipline
- Behaviors create social isolation
- Parental marital discord

achieve optimal arousal) is also associated with CD in males; this may account for the increased risk-taking associated with the disorder (van Goozen et al., 2007; El-Sheikh, Keiley, & Hinnant, 2009). Elevated stress hormones (cortisol) are associated with symptoms of impulsive aggression, whereas low cortisol levels have been linked with callous-unemotional traits and predatory aggression (Barzman, Patel, Sonnier, & Strawn, 2010).

Both family and social context play a large role in the development of externalizing disorders (Parens & Johnston, 2010). Disruptive behavior is associated with large families, marital breakdown, economic stress, crowded living conditions, harsh or inconsistent discipline, and maternal or peer rejection (Costello et al., 2003; van Goozen et al., 2007). Parents experiencing depression, anxiety or other psychiatric conditions may behave in a punitive, inconsistent, or impatient manner in response to typical demands of parenting (Tynan, 2010). Parent-child conflict and power struggles can exacerbate disruptive behaviors. Patterson (1986) formulated a classic psychological-behavioral model of disruptive behavior associated with the following patterns of parental failure to effectively intervene with misbehavior:

1. The parent addresses misbehavior or makes an unpopular request.
2. The child responds by arguing or counterattacking.
3. The parent withdraws from the conflict or gives in to the child's demands.

The child subsequently does not learn to respect authority. An alternate pattern that can occur involves a vicious cycle of harsh, punitive parental responses to misbehavior, resulting in defiance and disrespect on the part of the child and further coercive parental behaviors (Tynan, 2008). Disruptive behaviors are also exacerbated by limited parental supervision, increased parental attention for negative behavior, inconsistent disciplinary practices, and failure to teach prosocial skills and use positive management techniques.

Difficult child temperament (e.g., irritable, resistant, impulsive tendencies) contributes to behavioral conflict and increases the need for parents to learn and consistently apply appropriate management skills. Similarly, these temperamental tendencies can lead to rejection by peers and a blaming, negative worldview, sometimes accompanied by aggressive behavior. Underlying emotional issues are common in disruptive behavior disorders. For example, many youth with ODD have underlying anxiety disorders (Mireault, Rooney, Kouwenhoven, & Hannan, 2008). Additionally, depression frequently coexists with ODD and DMDD and can be exacerbated by the social alienation created by disruptive behaviors (First, 2007).

Treatment of Externalizing Disorders

Significant improvement can occur when interventions consider the family and social context of behaviors as well as psychosocial skills deficits (Parens & Johnston, 2010). CD is particularly difficult to treat (Tynan, 2010); treatment is most effective when implemented before patterns of disruptive behavior are firmly established (Conner at al., 2006). A well-established intervention for externalizing disorders is parent education (Eyberg, Nelson, & Boggs, 2008). Behavior management programs teach parents to establish appropriate rules, consistently implement consequences, increase positive interactions, and encourage positive behaviors. Parents practice their newly learned skills with simple problems, addressing more difficult behaviors as they become more proficient with behavior management techniques; relationship-building skills are also directly taught (Hanisch et al., 2010).

Youth involvement in psychosocial interventions that focus on assertiveness-training; anger management techniques; and building empathy, communication,

Did You Know?

Boys are more likely to show direct forms of bullying—intimidating, controlling, or assaulting other children—whereas girls demonstrate more relational aggression, such as using threats of social exclusion (Leff & Crick, 2010).

AP Images

Resisting Bullying

In this photo, sixth-grade students participate in a skit is designed to demonstrate ways in which victims and bystanders can stand up to bullying. The skit is part of an anti-bullying program sponsored by the Delaware State Attorney General's office.

social and problem-solving skills can also produce marked and durable changes in disruptive behaviors (Eyberg, Nelson, & Boggs, 2008). For those needing extensive intervention, short-term, full day treatment programs using evidence-based strategies can significantly improve behavior (Jerrott, Clark, & Fearon, 2010). These interventions are particularly powerful when combined with parent education regarding child management techniques and when implemented early (Eyberg, Nelson, & Boggs, 2008). Intervention with adolescents can be challenging. Group interventions need to carefully consider possible "deviancy training effects;" that is, group members may extend their repertoire of misbehaviors and demonstrate increases in antisocial or aggressive behavior (Dishion, McCord, & Poulin, 1999). Family intervention or mobilizing adult mentors are powerful alternatives, especially when mentors or parents are coached to demonstrate empathy, warmth, and acceptance (Kazdin, Whitley, & Marciano, 2006).

Elimination Disorders

Although most children handle the developmental milestone of achieving full control over elimination without difficulty, some children experience enuresis or encopresis, which are disorders involving bladder or bowel control. Many children with elimination disorders experience significant distress and apprehension, sensitivity to real or imagined parental disappointment and disapproval, and fear of peer ridicule. They may withdraw from peer relationships or may be ostracized by other children. Unsympathetic or impatient parents who pressure the child can increase anxiety and feelings of failure, further exacerbating the problem (Nevéus, 2011).

Enuresis

Enuresis involves periodic voiding of urine during the day or night into one's clothes or bed, or onto the floor. Enuresis is usually involuntary, although in rare situations it may be intentional (von Gontard, 2011). Enuresis is most likely to occur during sleep. To be diagnosed with enuresis, the child must be at least five years old and must void inappropriately at least twice per week for at least three months. In epidemiological studies, 4.9 to 10.5 percent of seven to seventeen-year-olds were enuretic (Klages et al., 2005; Loening-Baucke, 2007). Most children outgrow the disorder by adolescence, although 1 percent of individuals with enuresis continue to have symptoms in adulthood (American Psychiatric Association, 2000a).

Both psychological and biological factors are associated with enuresis. Psychological stressors (e.g., life situations such as death of a parent or birth of a new sibling), disturbed family patterns, or the presence of other emotional problems can increase risk (Joinson et al., 2006). Although severe nocturnal enuresis is usually due to hereditary factors, more sporadic bedwetting is associated with social and emotional stressors (Sureshkumar, Jones, Caldwell, & Craig, 2009). Biological influences affected by genetics include delays in maturation of the urinary tract and development of normal rhythms of urine production and a hypersensitive or small bladder. Providing support to the parents and child,

enuresis elimination disorder involving voiding of urine

Child Maltreatment

Case Study

Because the three-year-old boy had soiled his pants, the mother forced him to sit on the toilet. She told her son that he would not be allowed to get up or eat unless he had a bowel movement. When the son could not comply, the mother pulled him from the toilet seat and lashed his buttocks, until they were raw and bleeding.

Parents, social scientists, and politicians repeat sentiments such as, "Children are our most precious resource." Yet child neglect and the physical, emotional, and sexual abuse of children remain a significant national problem. Despite legislation requiring mental health professionals, teachers, and doctors to report suspected child abuse or neglect, maltreatment of the young persists. In the United States, 702,000 cases of child abuse and neglect were confirmed in 2009, including 1,770 deaths from child abuse (U.S. Department of Health and Human Services, 2009). As seen in Figure 16.2, many fatalities from abuse involve children aged three or younger. Children with mental health or neurodevelopmental disorders have increased risk of experiencing abuse (Cuevas, Finkelhor, Ormrod, & Turner, 2008).

Why would parents abuse or neglect their own children? We know that multiple factors, including poverty, parental immaturity, and lack of parenting skills, contribute to child maltreatment and that many adults who abuse were themselves abused as children. Many parents involved in maltreatment are young, high school dropouts, and under severe stress. Many have personality disorders, low tolerance for frustration, and abuse alcohol and other substances (Child Welfare Information Gateway, 2006).

The physical consequences of abuse range from mild bruises and lacerations to severe brain damage resulting in death or lifelong disability. Child abuse can lead to physical symptoms such as hypertension and chronic headaches in adulthood (Stein et al., 2010; Tietjen et al., 2010); it can also cause the alterations in neural circuits regulating emotion (specifically the amygdala and the hypothalamic-pituitary-adrenal axis) that have been linked to depression, anxiety, and PTSD (Bradley et al., 2008; Gillespie, Phifer, Bradley, & Ressler, 2009). Additionally, childhood sexual abuse is associated with increased risk of somatic disorders, anxiety, depression, eating disorders, and PTSD (Chen et al., 2010; Paras et al., 2009). The effects of emotional maltreatment often persist into adulthood (Shaffer, Huston, & Egeland, 2008). The more maltreatment a child encounters, the greater the risk of subsequent psychiatric illness (Benjet, Borges, & Medina-Mora, 2010; Green et al., 2010; McLaughlin et al., 2010). Researchers suspect that children exposed to childhood maltreatment undergo epigenetic changes that can, in fact, result in genetic vulnerability in their own children (Neigh, Gillespie, & Nemeroff, 2009).

A continual debate in the field of child protection is the balance between child safety and maintaining the family (U.S. Department of Health and Human Services, 2009). Many communities offer parent education and support groups, especially for "at risk" families. There is a particular need for programs to prevent the maltreatment of infants and young children (Turner et al., 2010). Therapeutic intervention (e.g., efforts to modify internalized schema of the self as worthless, others as abusive, or the world as dangerous) can help to reduce the emotional damage caused by maltreatment and dysfunctional parenting (Sher, 2008; Weich, Patterson, Shaw, & Stewart-Brown, 2009; Wright, Crawford, & Del Castillo, 2009). What are additional short-term and long-term consequences of child maltreatment? Why might those who are mistreated as children become abusers?

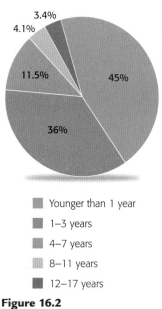

■ Younger than 1 year
■ 1–3 years
■ 4–7 years
■ 8–11 years
■ 12–17 years

Figure 16.2

FATALITIES FROM CHILD ABUSE OR NEGLECT BY AGE, 2004

The youngest are the most vulnerable.

Source: Child Welfare Information Gateway, (2006)

---

setting up reward systems, or using a bedtime urine alarm can all produce successful results (Wootton & Norfolk, 2010; Nevéus, 2011). Medication (e.g., desmopressin) is sometime used to reduce urine output (Saldano et al., 2007). Relapse following treatment is less likely with the alarm (12 percent relapse) versus medication (50 percent relapse) (Kwak, Lee, Park, & Baek, 2010).

Encopresis

Encopresis involves defecating onto one's clothes, the floor, or other inappropriate places. To be diagnosed with encopresis, the child must be at least four years old and must have defecated inappropriately at least once a month for at least three months. Epidemiological studies report a 0.7 to 4.4 percent prevalence of encopresis in children (Klages et al., 2005;

encopresis elimination disorder involving defecation

Loening-Baucke, 2007). Intermittent episodes of encopresis can persist for years. The typical pattern for children with encopresis is a history of constipation, resulting in painful defecation and subsequent withholding of bowel movements; this leads to additional constipation, fecal leakage, and involuntary soiling (Dobson & Rogers, 2009). Higher rates of ODD, CD, inattention, hyperactivity, and obsessive-compulsive symptoms have been found among children with encopresis, particularly those who soil frequently (Joinson et al., 2006). Intense social problems can arise due to shame, embarrassment, or attempts to conceal the disorder. Ostracism by peers, anger on the part of caregivers, and overall rejection can compound the problem (Dobson & Rogers, 2009). The most common means of treatment include proper medical evaluation, increasing fluid intake, and parent and child education about toileting regimens (Kuhl et al., 2010).

Neurodevelopmental Disorders

Neurodevelopmental disorders involve impaired development of the brain and central nervous system; symptoms (e.g., learning, communication and behavioral difficulties) become increasing evident as the child grows and develops (Table 16.4). We begin our discussion with an overview of tic disorders (including Tourette's disorder), attention-deficit/hyperactivity disorder and autism spectrum disorders followed by a discussion of intellectual and learning disorders. We conclude by focusing on the high comorbidity among neurodevelopmental disorders and support options for individuals significantly affected by these disorders.

Tics and Tourette's Disorder

Case Study

James Durbin, a contestant on American Idol, had facial and vocal tics as a child and was diagnosed with Tourette's disorder. During his school years he was bullied and teased because of his tics. However, when he would sing, he felt free because his tics completely disappeared. (Healy, 2011)

Tics are involuntary, repetitive movements or vocalizations. Motor tics involve various physical behaviors including eye blinking, facial grimacing, head jerking, foot tapping, flaring of the nostrils, and contractions of the shoulders or abdominal muscles. Vocal tics include coughing; grunting; throat clearing; sniffling; or sudden, repetitive, and stereotyped outbursts of words. Short-term suppression of a tic is sometimes

DISORDERS CHART NEURODEVELOPMENTAL DISORDERS

TABLE 16.4	Disorder	Prevalence	Characteristics/Course
	Tic Disorders	2–5% 4:1 (male to female)	Involuntary, repetitive movements or vocalizations; occasionally persists into adulthood
	Attention-Deficit/ Hyperactivity Disorder	8–9% 2:1 (male to female)	Inattention, hyperactivity, and impulsivity; some symptoms may persist into adulthood
	Autism Spectrum Disorder	0.6–1% 4:1 (male to female)	Qualitative impairment in social communication; restricted, stereotyped interest and activities; course depends on severity, presence of intellectual disability, and intervention
	Intellectual Disability	1–2% 1.5:1 (male to female)	Mild, moderate, severe, or profound deficits in intellectual functioning and adaptive behavior are lifelong
	Learning Disorder	5% 1.75:1 (male to female)	Normal intelligence with significant deficits in basic reading, writing, or basic math skills; may improve with intervention or persist into adulthood

Source: Wolanczyk et al., (2008); Robertson, (2010); Centers for Disease Control [CDC], (2009); CDC, (2010); U.S. Department of Education, (2010)

Eliminating Asperger's Disorder: Why the Uproar?

I have aspergers (diagnosed) and my brother has classic autism. I can read and write, I've got a degree, I can dress myself in the morning. My brother however has no communication, bowel problems, he is a man in his 20s who is trapped with the mind of a two year old. He needs help with every aspect of his life. It doesn't do me any good or him any good by you trying to merge what we've got into one condition. (David, 2010)

Asperger's disorder, a syndrome with characteristics similar to mild autism, is characterized by average to above average cognitive skills; intense focus on narrow interests; and eccentric, one-sided social interactions (e.g., poor understanding of rules of social engagement; asking inappropriate or intrusive questions) (Newschaffer et al., 2007; Ghaziuddin, 2010). Although affected by debilitating social difficulties, individuals with Asperger's disorder often make significant intellectual contributions as adults. It is believed that many individuals have the social deficits, idiosyncratic behaviors, depression, and loneliness commonly associated with Asperger's disorder (Whitehouse, Durkin, Jaquet, & Ziatas, 2009) but are never diagnosed.

Those revising DSM-5 concluded that the social communication abnormalities (Hofvander et al., 2009), interpersonal relationship difficulties, desire for sameness, and narrow interests seen in Asperger's syndrome are, in fact, an extension of the autism spectrum continuum; contending that a separate diagnostic category is redundant, they eliminated the Asperger's diagnosis (American Psychiatric Association, 2011). This decision generated strong reactions from individuals diagnosed with Asperger's, who embrace their uniqueness and have found social connection within the Asperger's community. They argue that Asperger's is clearly distinct from autism and that stigma associated with autism might discourage individuals with milder symptoms from seeking assessment and treatment. Some experts also supported maintaining the Asperger's category with modifications in diagnostic criteria to include unique features not previously identified such as socially insensitive communication; verbose, one-sided conversations pertaining to areas of restricted interests; and difficulty with practical use of language (Ghaziuddin, 2010). Do individuals with Asperger's have a point—that they are different from those with autism and that including them in the autism category will result in increased stigma?

possible, but often results in subsequent increases in the tic. Some report feeling tension build before a tic, followed by a sense of relief after the tic occurs. A physician with tics described it this way: "This urge comes in the form of a sensation. . . a sensation that is somehow incomplete. To complete and resolve the sensation, the tic must be executed, which provides almost instant relief. . . the relief is very transient. . . the sensation comes back again, but often more intensely than before (Turtle & Robertson, 2008, p. 451).

Most tics in children are transient and disappear without treatment. Stress can increase the frequency and intensity of tics. When a tic has been present for less than a year, a diagnosis of *provisional tic disorder* is given; *chronic motor or vocal tic disorder* refers to tics lasting more than a year (American Psychiatric Association, 2011). Chronic tics sometimes continue throughout adolescence and into adulthood. Tic disorders are four to five times more prevalent in boys (Lanzi et al., 2004; Robertson, 2010). In one sample of children, 2.6 percent met the criteria for provisional tic disorder, 3.7 percent had a chronic tic disorder, and 0.6 percent had Tourette's disorder (Wolanczyk et al., 2008).

Tourette's disorder (*TD*) is characterized by multiple motor tics (e.g., eye blinking, facial grimacing, shoulder shrugging, head or shoulder jerking) and one or more vocal tics (e.g., repetitive throat clearing, sniffing, or grunting). Onset is before the age of eighteen, and both motor and vocal tics must be present for at least one year, although not necessarily concurrently (American Psychological Association, 2011). Usually, the first symptoms are noticed between the ages of seven and ten, with symptoms increasing in the middle teen years and improving in early adulthood; about 8 percent of those with TD eventually show a complete remission of symptoms (National Institute of Neurological Disorders and Stroke [NINDS], 2010). Symptoms of TD can be severe or mild (Rivera-Navarro, Cubo, & Almazan, 2009). Involuntary *coprolalia* (uttering swear words) or motor movements involving self-harm (e.g., punching oneself) occur in less than 10 percent of those with TD (NIH, 2005). Comorbid conditions include poor anger control, attention-deficit/hyperactivity disorder, obsessive-compulsive disorder, impulsive behavior, and poor social skills (Dugdale, Jasmin, & Zieve, 2010).

Both chronic tic disorder and TD appear to be genetically transmitted. Because TD is highly comorbid with obsessive-compulsive disorder, similar physiological mechanisms involving the basal ganglia and orbital frontal cortex are likely involved (Mathews & Grados, 2011). Because some antipsychotic medications reduce the severity of TD symptoms, abnormalities involving neurotransmitters are hypothesized to be involved in the disorder (Robertson, 2010). Although antipsychotic medication is sometimes used to treat severe vocal tics (Kuwabara, Kono, Shimada, & Kano, 2011), medication is not typically used to treat tic disorders. Psychotherapy can help with the distress caused by tic symptoms.

Attention-Deficit/Hyperactivity Disorder

Case Study

Ron, always on the go as a toddler and preschooler, has had many injuries resulting from his continual climbing and risk-taking. In kindergarten, Ron talked incessantly and could not stay seated for group work. In the first grade, his distractibility and off-task behavior persisted despite ongoing efforts to help him focus. As part of a comprehensive assessment, his parents took him for a psychological evaluation and a complete physical examination.

Did You Know?

Children who are the youngest in their class are more likely to receive an ADHD diagnosis; in fact, one study found that the youngest children in fifth and eighth grade classrooms were almost twice as likely as older classmates to take medication for ADHD. What might account for these differences?

Source: Elder, (2010)

Attention-deficit/hyperactivity disorder (ADHD) is characterized by attentional problems and/or impulsive, hyperactive behaviors that are atypical for the child's age and developmental level and that significantly interfere with social, academic, or occupational activities. An ADHD diagnosis requires that symptoms begin before age twelve and persist for at least six months. Those with ADHD can have problems involving (1) inattention; (2) hyperactivity and impulsivity; or (3) a combination of these characteristics. The distractibility and intense focus on irrelevant environmental stimuli seen in ADHD are due to poor regulation of attentional processes (Montauk & Mayhall, 2010). Symptoms of hyperactivity and impulsivity involve a combination of excessive movement and tendencies to act without considering the consequences. See Table 16.5 for characteristics associated with ADHD.

ADHD can be difficult to diagnose, especially in early childhood when limited attentional skills and high levels of energy are common. Although standardized tests of motor speed and response processing are sometimes used to differentiate children with ADHD from those with other disorders (Udal et al., 2009), diagnosis relies primarily on observations and input from parents, school personnel, and others knowledgeable about the child's behaviors. To receive a diagnosis of ADHD, the child must display symptoms in two or more settings (American Psychiatric Association, 2011). When presented with parental concern about ongoing inattentive, hyperactive, and impulsive behaviors, it is necessary to determine if the behaviors are (1) typical for the child's age, gender, and overall level of development; (2) a normal temperamental variant involving higher than average energy and impulsivity; or (3) an actual disorder involving significantly atypical behaviors that interfere with day-to-day functioning in multiple settings.

Hyperactive is a confusing term because it is frequently used to describe all highly energetic children. In fact, even family physicians often make ADHD diagnoses and prescribe medication when symptoms of inattention, hyperactivity, and impulsivity do not meet DSM diagnostic criteria (Parens & Johnston, 2009). Another confusing aspect of ADHD is the apparent inconsistency of symptoms; some children

attention-deficit/hyperactivity disorder (ADHD) disorder characterized by inattention and/or hyperactivity and impulsivity

with ADHD, for example, seem unusually active in the classroom, but may not differ from peers during play activities. Other characteristics, however, might be apparent in these settings.

ADHD is the most frequently diagnosed disorder in school-aged children (Banerjee, Middleton, & Faraone, 2007). Prevalence in one national sample of youth (ages 8 to 15) was 8.7 percent (Froehlich et al., 2007), whereas in a broader sample, parent-reported prevalence (ages 6 to 17) was 8.2 percent (Larson et al., 2011). Another national survey of parent-reported ADHD among youth (ages 4 to 17) revealed a 21.8 percent increase in ADHD prevalence between 2003 (7.8 percent prevalence) and 2007 (9.5 percent prevalence); in this sample, 46.7 percent of those identified as having ADHD were reported to have mild symptoms, 39.5 percent had moderate symptoms, and 13.8 percent had severe symptoms (CDC, 2010). Boys are more than twice as likely as girls to be diagnosed with ADHD (Bloom & Cohen, 2007; CDC, 2010). Although symptoms of ADHD often improve in late adolescence, follow-up studies suggest that between 30 and 50 percent of those diagnosed with ADHD experience continued symptoms of inattention or fidgeting, difficulty sitting still, and impulsive actions throughout adulthood (Spencer, Biederman, & Mick, 2007; Montauk & Mayhall, 2010).

ADHD is associated with behavioral and academic problems, including disciplinary referrals and increased rates of detention and expulsion; low grades, poor test scores, and grade retention; and lower rates of high school graduation and post-secondary education (Loe & Feldman, 2007; Larson et al., 2011). Children with ADHD have the most difficulty in unstructured situations, with activities demanding sustained attention, and when there is insufficient stimulation (Kooistra et al., 2010). Peer relationships and maintaining friendships are also challenging (CDC, 2010). Data regarding more than 62,000 U.S. youth (ages 6 to 17) revealed that two-thirds of those with ADHD have other mental health conditions (including CD, ODD, anxiety, and depression) or learning disabilities and other neurodevelopmental disorders; the risk of coexisting conditions is almost four times greater among children living in poverty (Larson et al., 2011).

TABLE 16.5 Characteristics of Attention-Deficit/ Hyperactivity Disorder

Inattention	Hyperactivity and Impulsivity
Poor attention to detail	Fidgets
Difficulty sustaining attention	Restless
Does not seem to listen	Moves excessively
Poor follow-through	Excessively loud
Difficulty organizing tasks	Talks excessively
Avoids sustained mental effort	Blurts out answers
Loses objects	Difficulty waiting for a turn
Easily distracted	Interrupts or intrudes on others
Forgetful	Impatient

Note: With ADHD, these characteristics occur more frequently than would be expected based on age, gender, and developmental level

Source: American Psychiatric Association, (2011)

Etiology

Like many other disorders, ADHD symptoms result from multiple etiological factors (Parens & Johnston, 2009). ADHD is an early-onset disorder with clear biological as well as psychological, social, and sociocultural etiology.

Biological Dimension   ADHD is a highly heritable disorder with up to 80 percent of ADHD symptoms explainable by genetic factors (Coghill & Banaschewski, 2009; Durston, 2010). The exact nature of genetic transmission is unclear because no specific genes strongly link to ADHD symptoms (Faraone & Mick, 2010; Stergiakouli & Thapar, 2010); however, rare, inherited gene mutations (Elia et al., 2010), chromosomal DNA deletions and duplications (Williams et al., 2010), and genes affecting the regulation of the neurotransmitter dopamine (Montauk & Mayhall, 2010) have been implicated. It is likely that many of the symptoms seen in ADHD involve multiple genes, each with small effects, and subsequent gene × gene or gene × environment interactions (Ficks & Waldman, 2009; Franke, Neale, & Faraone, 2009; Plomp, Van Engeland, & Durston, 2009).

AP Images

Interventions for Attention-Deficit/Hyperactivity Disorder

A mother is shown interacting with her six-year-old son. He is enrolled in a study called Project Achieve in which parents and teachers are taught strategies to help minimize problem behaviors. New research shows that providing more structure throughout a child's day can offer a nondrug alternative to help children with attention-deficit/hyperactivity disorder.

Different hypotheses regarding neurological mechanisms that produce ADHD symptoms include:

1. Reduced activity in the prefrontal cortex when tasks require inhibition of responses; this low arousal of inhibitory mechanisms can affect impulsivity, organizational planning, working memory, and attentional processes (Montauk & Mayhall, 2010).

2. Differences in brain structure and circuitry in the frontal cortex, cerebellum, and parietal lobes; neuroimaging has confirmed these differences (Cherkasova & Hechtman, 2009), including smaller frontal lobe size in children with ADHD, especially in children with more severe symptoms (Montauk & Mayhall, 2010). Additionally, some children with ADHD show slower development of the cerebrum, particularly prefrontal regions associated with attention and motor planning (Shaw et al., 2007); this delay (and subsequent catch-up) in neurological developmental may explain why many children with ADHD eventually outgrow their disorder.

3. Inadequate dopamine and associated neurotransmitters that affect signal flow to and from the frontal lobes (Stergiakouli & Thapar, 2010); medications used to treat ADHD target these neurotransmitters (Spencer, Biederman, & Mick, 2007).

Other biological factors implicated in the development of ADHD include prematurity, oxygen deprivation during birth, and very low birth weight (Aarnoudse-Moens et al., 2009); lead and PCB exposure (Abelsohn & Sanborn, 2010; Eubig, Aguiar, & Schantz, 2010); viral infections, meningitis, and encephalitis (Millichap, 2008); and maternal smoking or drug or alcohol use during pregnancy (Froehlich et al., 2009; National Institute of Mental Health [NIMH], 2007b). Some believe that certain food additives produce hyperactive behaviors. Although previous research concluded that eliminating food additives does not reduce hyperactive behaviors (NIMH, 2007b), a study involving three hundred British children concluded that certain food dyes could cause hyperactive behavior (McCann et al., 2007). Although this study was criticized because a chemical preservative was added to the food dye (thus confounding the results), it served to rekindle the debate regarding food additives (Wallis, 2007). In fact, despite assurances that synthetic food dyes are highly regulated in the United States, the FDA agreed to respond to public concerns and hold a hearing on the topic (Deardorff, 2011).

Psychological, Social, and Sociocultural Dimensions   Many psychological, social, and sociocultural factors have been associated with ADHD. Sociocultural and social adversity (e.g., family stress, severe marital discord, low social class, large family size, family conflicts, maternal psychopathology, paternal criminality, maternal mental disorder, and foster care placement) seem to contribute to ADHD (Spencer, Biederman, & Mick, 2007; Ray, Croen, & Habel, 2009). Additionally, parents of children with ADHD report stressors such as reduced work productivity; strained family relationships; and difficulty coping with consistently demanding, disruptive, and impulsive behaviors and their effect on family routines and school adjustment (Coghill et al., 2008). We know that children who are inattentive, hyperactive, or impulsive often encounter negative reactions from others. These negative reactions and associated interpersonal conflict may result in psychological reactions (e.g., stress, low self-esteem, rebelliousness) that further exacerbate symptoms

(Deault, 2010). Some argue that differing cultural and regional expectations regarding high activity, inattentiveness, and academic achievement can affect the prevalence of ADHD diagnosis (Figure 16.3). Similarly, parenting practices that encourage exercise and outdoor activity or help prevent children from getting over-tired or over-aroused may decrease the likelihood of ADHD symptoms (Parens & Johnston, 2009).

Treatment

For decades, stimulants such as methylphenidate (Ritalin) have been used to treat ADHD symptoms (Findling, 2008); these medications continue to receive the most evidenced-based support for ADHD treatment (Greydanus, Nazeer, & Patel, 2009). Stimulants work by normalizing neurotransmitter functioning and increasing neurological activation in the frontal cortex, thereby increasing attention and reducing impulsivity. Treatment trends emphasizing initiation of treatment at an early age; using medication throughout the day (rather than just during school hours) (Buitelaar & Medori, 2010); and continuing medication, if needed, throughout the lifespan have resulted in increased lifetime medication exposure (Parens & Johnston, 2009). These trends, combined with increased rates of ADHD diagnoses, likely account for the continued increases in stimulant medication use in the United States (Figure 16.4). In a recent national survey regarding youth ages four to seventeen diagnosed with ADHD, 66.3 percent were taking medication for the disorder, with the proportion taking medication ranging from 56.4 percent for those with mild symptoms to 85.9 percent for those with severe symptoms (CDC, 2010). Due to the frequency of misuse and diversion (i.e., giving, selling, or trading) of prescribed short-acting stimulant medications (Arria et al., 2008; Wilens et al., 2008), the use of longer-acting stimulants or other medications with less abuse potential is increasing (Faraone & Wilens et al., 2007; Kollins, 2008). Additionally, the search continues for other medications to assist in treating symptoms of the disorder, particularly for those who do not respond to current medications (May & Kratochvil, 2010).

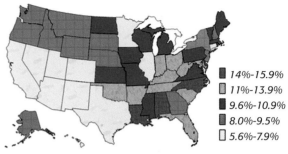

14%–15.9%
11%–13.9%
9.6%–10.9%
8.0%–9.5%
5.6%–7.9%

Figure 16.3

PREVALENCE OF YOUTH (AGES 4–17) DIAGNOSED WITH ATTENTION-DEFICIT/ HYPERACTIVITY DISORDER BY STATE, 2007–2008

The prevalence of parent-reported attention-deficit/hyperactivity disorder (ADHD) varies significantly from state-to-state, ranging from a low of 5.6 percent in Nevada to a high of 15.6 percent in North Carolina. What might account for the variability in ADHD diagnoses that we see from state to state?

Source: Centers for Disease Control and Prevention, 2010

Did You Know?

The prevalence of ADHD diagnosis (based on parent report) ranges from 5.6 percent in Nevada to 15.6 percent in North Carolina, whereas the prevalence of children receiving medication for ADHD ranges from 2.1 percent in California to 6.5 percent in Arkansas.

Source: CDC, (2010)

Brendan Smialowski/Getty Images

Interventions for Older Kids with Attention-Deficit/Hyperactivity Disorder

Students eat while camping out at the Center for Attention and Related Disorders camp in Connecticut. The four-week camp matches one instructor for every two campers and provides the structure, discipline, and social order that are helpful for children who have attention-deficit/hyperactivity disorder (ADHD) and similar disorders.

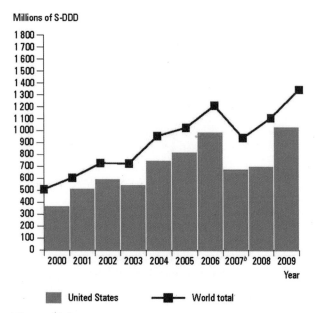

Figure 16.4

MEDICAL CONSUMPTION OF METHYLPHENI-DATE IN THE UNITED STATES AND WORLDWIDE, 2000–2009

Methylphenidate is a medication frequently prescribed for attention-deficit/hyperactivity disorder (ADHD). This graph demonstrates that the United States accounts for a large percentage of the use of this medication worldwide and that from 2000–2009 the amount of methylphenidate consumed more than doubled both in the United States and worldwide.

Source: International Narcotics Control Board (2010) Report 2010: Statistics for 2009. Retrieved from http://www.incb.org/pdf/technical-reports/psychotropics/2010/psy 2010 EFS Part2 E comments.pdf

There is strong and consistent evidence that behavioral and psychosocial treatments (e.g., behavioral parent training, classroom management strategies and reward systems, behavioral interventions involving peers, self-control training) are highly effective in producing both short and long-term reductions in ADHD symptoms (Pelham & Fabiano, 2008; Fabiano et al., 2009). In fact, some argue that these approaches should be used before considering medication, particularly for those with milder symptoms (Parens & Johnston, 2009). Additionally, modifying the environment or social context (e.g., allowing movement or opportunities to optimize cognitive stimulation) can enhance feelings of competence, motivation, and self-efficacy for those with ADHD (Gallichan & Curle, 2008). In fact, simply providing recess breaks can reduce inappropriate behaviors among children with ADHD (Ridgway et al., 2003).

Interventions are most successful when educational, medical, mental health, and social support systems coordinate services and when the child's unique characteristics and social and family circumstances are considered (Larson et al., 2011). Some propose that symptom severity should guide treatment decisions with interventions ranging from environmental modifications for mild symptoms to intensive, combined treatment (e.g., behavior management, parenting strategies, and stimulant medication) for severe ADHD symptoms (Daly et al., 2007; Pelham & Fabiano, 2008). It is hoped that greater understanding of the genetic underpinnings of ADHD and how they interact with environmental risk factors will allow for more targeted treatment (Wallis, Russell, & Muenke, 2008).

Autism Spectrum Disorders

Autism spectrum disorder (ASD) is characterized by significant impairment in social communication skills and the display of stereotyped interests and behaviors (Ozonoff et al., 2010). ASD symptoms range from mild to severe. ASD, estimated to affect approximately 1 out of 100–110 children, has been increasing; ASD occurs four to five times more frequently in boys than in girls (Landa, 2008; Kogan et al., 2009; CDC, 2009). Students with ASD make up 0.6 percent of the public school population (U.S. Department of Education, 2010). Approximately 1 in every 500 children displays severe autistic symptoms (Newschaffer et al., 2007). Autism can significantly affect cognitive development; approximately two-thirds of those with autism have concurrent intellectual impairment (Kaufman, Ayub, & Vincent, 2010). We begin our discussion with an overview of characteristics of ASD.

Symptoms of Autism

Case Study

During the first and part of the second year of her life, Amy showed normal development, smiling, laughing, babbling, waving to parents, and playing peek-a-boo. By age two, she was withdrawn and spoke no words except meaningless phrases from songs. She spent her time rocking back and forth or spinning her toys.

Case Study

Danny B. wants chicken and potatoes. He asks for it once, twice . . . ten times. . . . His mother patiently explains that she is fixing spaghetti. "Mom," he asks in a monotone,

autism spectrum disorder (ASD) disorder characterized by impairment in social communication and restricted, stereotyped interests and activities

"why can't we have chicken and potatoes?" If Danny were a toddler, his behavior would be nothing unusual. But Danny is twenty years old. "That's really what life with autism is like," says his mom. "I have to keep laughing. Otherwise, I would cry." (Kantrowitz & Scelfo, 2006, p. 47)

At the beginning of this chapter, we introduced Ahmed, a young child with autism. In the cases of Amy and Danny, we again get a glimpse of how ASD presents early in life and in early adulthood. What is autism, and what causes this baffling disorder? In 1943, Leo Kanner, a child psychiatrist, identified a triad of behaviors that have come to define the essential features of autism: extreme isolation and inability to relate to people, a need for sameness, and significant difficulties with communication. Kanner called the syndrome *infantile autism*, from the Greek *autos* ("self"), to reflect the profound aloneness and detachment of these children.

ASD is diagnosed when, based on multiple sources of information, including observation by a trained professional, there is persistent evidence of the following characteristics (American Psychiatric Association, 2011):

1. Deficits in social communication and social interaction
   a. *Atypical social-emotional reciprocity*: Interest in social interaction may be limited or totally lacking. For example, infants with autism are often content to be left alone and show no anticipatory responding when picked up. In adulthood, milder symptoms may include one-sided domination of conversation focused on narrow self-interests and failure to understand the "back and forth" of typical conversations.
   b. *Atypical nonverbal communication*: There may be little to no eye contact and an absence of meaningful gestures or facial expressions. Milder symptoms may include unusual nonverbal communication (e.g., pushing a person aside as if they were an object), intrusive behavior and poor social boundaries or failure to understand others intentions.
   c. *Difficulties developing and maintaining relationships*: There may be a lack of interest in others or failure to recognize people's identity or emotions, including treating people as objects, and failure to seek physical or emotional responses from caretakers. Those with milder symptoms may have no interest in imaginative play, may be socially inept, and have difficulty adjusting their behavior to the social context.
2. Repetitive behavior or restricted interests or activities involving at least two of the following:
   a. *Repetitive speech, movement, or use of objects*: Rhythmical, repetitive, apparently purposeless movements (e.g., head banging, arm flapping, rocking the body, spinning objects, whirling in circles, rhythmically moving fingers) are common symptoms. Those with ASD sometimes repetitively stack or spin objects or move them from side-to-side. There may be repetitive use of language, including *echolalia* (echoing what has previously been said); incessant repetition of sounds, words, or phrases or nonsensical word combinations; or repetitive, one-sided conversations involving topics of fixated interest.
   b. *Intense focus on rituals or routines and strong resistance to change*: Common rituals may involve objects (e.g., lining up or dropping toys) or insistence on the same foods, order of events, or desired routine. Even small changes in routine can produce extreme distress or intense reactions.
   c. *Intense fixations or restricted interests*: This may involve fascination with certain objects or a repetitive focus on a narrow range of interests.
   d. *Atypical sensory reactivity*: There may be a lack of reactivity (e.g., apparent indifference to pain, heat, or cold); over-reactivity to sensory input

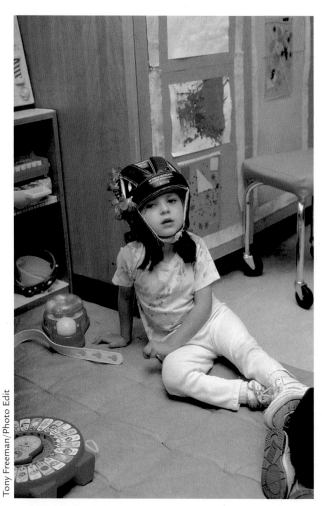

Tony Freeman/Photo Edit

Autistic Girl Wearing a Helmet

Besides having problems with social interactions and communication, children with an autism spectrum disorder can show a variety of symptoms, such as impulsivity, temper tantrums, and self-injurious behavior. Here a child is wearing a helmet to prevent damage from head banging.

(e.g., aversion to touch or certain sounds); or an unusual focus on sensory aspects of objects (e.g., licking or smelling objects or intense interest in a moving fan).

The symptoms seen in ASD are not simply developmental delays but reflect differences in development that cause impairment in everyday functioning (Kabot, Masi, & Segal, 2003). Table 16.6 summarizes the range of symptoms found in ASD. Approximately two-thirds of those with ASD have IQ scores lower than 70 (Kaufman, Ayub, & Vincent, 2010). However, some display *splinter skills*—that is, they do well on isolated tasks such as drawing, puzzle construction, or rote memory but perform poorly on verbal tasks and tasks requiring language skills and symbolic thinking. These children are referred to as autistic savants.

Although ASD might seem easy to diagnose given its unique characteristics, diagnosis can be complicated because there are currently no medical tests to confirm autism and because of the confounding effects of intellectual impairment. Typical evaluation procedures include clinical observations, parent interviews, developmental histories, autism screening inventories, speech and language assessment, and psychological testing. Some researchers are hopeful that neuroimaging, which has shown some preliminary differences in metabolic brain activity in individuals with autism, will soon be available for diagnostic purposes (Lange et al., 2010).

Although behavioral differences are sometimes evident in infancy (Martínez-Pedraza & Carter, 2009), autism is often not diagnosed until age three or later (Barbaro & Dissanayake, 2009). In some cases, infants later diagnosed with ASD seemed "different" from birth (Volkmar, Charwarska, & Klin, 2005)—unresponsive to people, but focusing intently on objects for long periods of time. Unlike typically developing infants, infants with autistic symptoms fail to attend to human motion, such as a parent's movement (Klin, Lin, Gorrindo, Ramsay, & Jones, 2009), or demonstrate interest in human faces (Chawarska, Volkmar, & Klin, 2010). ASD symptoms sometimes appear following a period of apparently normal social and intellectual development, with deterioration of skills beginning around 6–12 months of age (Ozonoff et al., 2008; Rogers, 2009; Ozonoff et al., 2010). Children with this pattern of regression often develop more severe symptoms, especially repetitive

TABLE 16.6 Continuum of Symptoms Associated with Autism Spectrum Disorder

Level of Impairment	Social Communication	Fixated Interests and Repetitive Behaviors
Severe (Requires very substantial support)	Minimal or absent communication or response to attempts at social interaction	Ongoing repetitive behaviors; intense preoccupation with rituals; interference with rituals can produce extreme distress
Moderate (Requires substantial support)	Limited social communication; interactions noticeably atypical	Fixated interests and frequent repetitive behaviors and rituals that interfere with functioning
Mild* (Requires support)	Atypical social interaction; difficulty initiating or responding to social communication	Repetitive behaviors and fixated interests cause some interference with everyday functioning
Symptoms not severe enough for ASD diagnosis	Some atypical behaviors and mild social communication deficit; social deficits do not limit and impair everyday functioning	Ritualized behavior, odd mannerisms, or excessive preoccupations do not interfere with daily functioning
Variation of normal	Socially isolated and awkward	Odd preoccupations or mannerisms

*Mild autism is sometimes referred to as high-functioning autism or Asperger's syndrome.
Adapted from American Psychiatric Association, (2011)

behaviors, compared to autistic children without this pattern (Meilleur & Fombonne, 2009).

Although we are learning more about autism, many questions remain. What causes the puzzling abnormalities seen in ASD? What causes the regression seen in some children with ASD? Can the symptoms of autism be reversed? We now discuss the causes and treatment of ASD.

Etiology

A great deal of research has focused on the causes of ASD with the hope of developing early diagnostic procedures and interventions that can prevent, halt, or reverse autistic symptoms (Zwaigenbaum, 2010). ASD is unique because symptoms sometimes appear following a period of relatively normal development and because, among some children, intervention has reversed progression of the disorder. Although psychological effects are important in understanding the course of the disorder, biological factors play the most critical role.

Biological Dimension   Researchers are approaching the biological etiology of autism from a variety of perspectives: documenting biological mechanisms (biomarkers) involved in the development of the disorder; confirming genetic and environmental risk factors; and, most importantly, gene × environment interactions. There have been unprecedented advances in the identification of genes and risk alleles associated with ASD (Carayol et al., 2010; Oliver et al., 2010). Although the exact mechanisms by which genetic defects translate into impaired brain functioning are not known, research has linked ASD with numerous neurological findings including:

- Unique patterns of metabolic brain activity (Lange et al., 2010)
- Poor connectivity involving the amygdala (Gaigg & Bowler, 2007; Ashwin et al., 2007) and other brain regions associated with autistic symptoms (Anderson et al., 2010)

Will and Deni McIntyre/Photo Researchers Inc.

Therapist Signs to a Boy with Autism

Sign language is often used to enhance their receptive and expressive communication skills of individuals with an autism spectrum disorder. Can you think of additional means of communication that might be useful in working with individuals with autism?

MYTH: Childhood vaccinations cause autism.

REALITY: This widespread rumor has been proven completely false. Concerns about vaccinations originated from a 1998 study that claimed the measles-mumps-rubella (MMR) vaccine caused autism. However, the study has been deemed fraudulent based on evidence that the lead author manipulated data for monetary gain. No subsequent study has found any connection whatsoever between vaccinations and the onset of autism (Godlee, Smith, & Marcovitch, 2011)

MYTH VS. REALITY

Cary Wolinsky/Aurora Photos

Communicating Through Art

Twenty-year-old Tito Mukhopadhyay is severely autistic but can communicate his thoughts and feelings through prose and poetry. He is pictured here with his mother Soma, who gave up a career in chemistry to devote her life to teaching her son.

- Correlations between levels of certain biochemicals in the amygdala and severity of symptoms (Kleinhans et al., 2009)
- Abnormally high levels of serotonin, particularly in males with ASD and those with high-functioning autism (Brasic & Wong, 2010)
- Longitudinal evidence of decreasing size of the occipital cortex, a region responsible for visual processing (Hardan et al., 2009)

Accelerated head growth may, in fact, be an endophenotype (biological marker) for autism (Constantino et al., 2010). Male infants later diagnosed with ASD exhibited a pattern of rapid head growth 6–9 months after birth (Fukumoto et al., 2010); increased head circumference (as well as rapidly increasing height) has been found not only in children with ASD but also in children who develop other psychiatric disorders (Rommelse et al., 2011). Children who later "recover" from autism following intensive early treatment have also been found to possess this trait (Mraz et al., 2009). MRI imaging with toddlers diagnosed with ASD has confirmed extra growth in multiple regions of the brain; girls with autism have the most pronounced abnormal brain growth (Schumann et al., 2010). The period of accelerated head growth in infancy has been found to precede and overlap the onset of behavioral symptoms. Additionally, a subsequent period of decelerated growth corresponds with the increasing severity of symptoms often seen in the second year of life (Dawson et al., 2007).

Recent research has focused on the much higher rate of *mitochondrial dysfunction* found in children with ASD (Giulivi et al., 2010). Mitochondrial dysfunction affects the energy-producing function of cells, a process critically important to neural development; some biomarkers of mitochondrial dysfunction correlate with severity of autistic symptoms, especially in children with a history of developmental regression (Rossignol & Frye, 2011). In fact, some children with ASD appear to have genetically based mitochondrial disease (Haas, 2010).

Genetic mutations have been implicated in familial autism (Korvatska et al., 2011). Different genetic factors involving multiple brain regions, including the cerebellum and frontal and temporal lobes, appear to influence different autistic symptoms (Abrahams & Geschwind, 2010; Nijmeijer et al., 2010). Also, a fairly common genetic variant that affects synaptic connections occurs with 20 percent greater frequency in those with ASD (Pinto et al., 2010).

Concordance rates for autism are much higher for MZ (monozygotic) twins than DZ (dizygotic) twins, with heritability estimated to be around 0.73 percent for males and 0.87 percent for females (Taniai et al., 2008). Furthermore, ASD affects 2 to 14 percent of the siblings of those with ASD, a much higher prevalence than seen in the general population. Additionally, some siblings show atypical social and communication skills in infancy as well as an increased prevalence of social and behavioral difficulties (Orsmond & Seltzer, 2007). Taken together, twin and family studies clearly establish that genetic susceptibility to autism exists. However, because MZ concordance is less than 100 percent and the degree of impairment varies markedly among MZ twins with ASD, other factors are etiologically significant as well (Newschaffer et al., 2007).

Children who develop ASD appear to have an innate vulnerability that is triggered by environmental factors (Herbert, 2010). Environmental toxins associated with the development of ASD include mercury (Dufault et al., 2009; Geier, Kern, & Geier, 2009; Kern et al., 2011), certain pesticides (Roberts et al., 2007), heavy metals toxins (Desoto & Hitlan, 2010), maternal smoking, poor indoor ventilation, and PVC flooring (Larsson et al., 2009). Why do environmental toxins cause ASD in some children and not others? A partial answer to this question may come from research showing that typically developing children appear to have similar blood levels of both lead (Tian et al., 2011) and mercury (Stamova et al., 2011) as children with ASD; however, autistic children appear to metabolize these toxins differently. It is unclear if toxins or other effects account for the demographic variance in ASD across the United States (Figure 16.5) (Newschaffer et al., 2007).

Other factors associated with ASD include nutritional deficiencies (Dufault et al., 2009); changes in the immune system (Careaga, Van de Water, & Ashwood, 2010), and abnormal immune responses (Chez & Guido-Estrada, 2010); obstetric complications (Brasic & Holland, 2007); and closely spaced pregnancies (Cheslack-Postava, Liu, & Bearman, 2011). Biological mechanisms may also account for the fact that autistic symptoms sometimes improve and then abruptly return when children with ASD have a fever (Curran et al., 2007). Most researchers agree that autism is a heterogeneous disorder with multiple causes. Fortunately, biological researchers and experts in the field of autism are working together to search for interventions that produce documentable biological changes (Llaneza et al., 2010); they are encouraged by the neuroplasticity seen in some children who have received intensive, early intervention (Landa, Holman, O'Neill, & Stuart, 2011).

Psychological Dimension From a psychological perspective, autism affects the way a child interacts with the world, which, in turn, affects how others interact with the child. Autism affects a child's attentional and perceptual systems, including recognition of and response to qualities of others such as age or gender. Normally developing infants can distinguish between male and female and between child and adult, an ability that suggests responsiveness and attention to social cues. In contrast, children with ASD differentiate between pictures of buildings but have poor face recognition (Boucher & Lewis, 1992). Autistic children seldom make eye contact, seek social connectedness, or bid for attention with gestures or vocalizations; they are usually content being alone, do not engage in play, and ignore parental efforts at connection (Johnson et al., 2007). Individuals with ASD are described as lacking a "theory of the mind;" that is, they seem unable to understand that others think and have beliefs. All of these psychological characteristics affect interactions with peers and family members; without reciprocal social interaction, attempts to maintain social connection often diminish, further adding to the child's isolation. Additionally, behavioral characteristics associated with ASD can create additional stress and further affect interactions within a family, particularly when parents have limited respite from the day-to-day demands of caretaking (Taylor & Seltzer, 2010b).

Early psychological theories pointed to deviant parent-child interactions as the cause of autism. In fact, Kanner (1943), who named the syndrome, originally concluded that cold and unresponsive parenting was responsible for the development of autism, describing parents of autistic children as cold, humorless perfectionists who preferred reading, writing, playing music, or thinking. Kanner later came to believe that autism is "innate." It is now widely concluded that although psychological and social factors such as child-rearing practices, parent-child interactions, and reactions from peers play a role in the manifestation of symptoms, autism is primarily influenced by the wide variety of biological factors discussed in the previous section.

Intervention and Treatment

The prognosis for children with ASD is mixed. Most children diagnosed with autism retain their diagnosis and require support throughout their lifetime. Those with milder symptoms may be self-sufficient, successfully employed, and function reasonably well in adulthood, although social awkwardness, restrictive interests, or atypical behaviors may

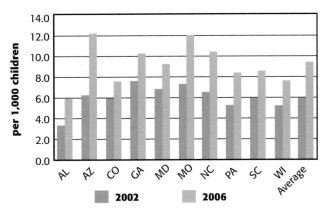

Changes in Prevalence of ASDs among Children 8 Years Old, 2002 to 2006

Figure 16.5

CHANGES IN THE PREVALENCE OF AUTISM SPECTRUM DISORDER AMONG EIGHT-YEAR-OLD CHILDREN IN TEN STATES, 2002 TO 2006

The prevalence of autism spectrum disorder among eight-year-old children increased between 2002 and 2006 in all ten state sites monitored. What might account for these increases as well as the state-to-state variations in prevalence of the disorder?

Source: Centers for Disease Control and Prevention, 2009

Did You Know?

In a study involving 600,000 sibling pairs, children born less than one year after the birth of a sibling were almost 300 percent more likely to develop autism compared to children born at least four years after a sibling.

Source: Cheslack-Postava, Liu, & Bearman, (2011)

persist (Johnson et al., 2007). In general, those with higher levels of cognitive-adaptive functioning fare better than those with intellectual disability and severe autistic symptoms. A significant degree of recovery has been seen in some children (including some with severe symptoms) who received intense early intervention, with the most impressive results occurring among children with higher cognitive and language skills (Dawson et al., 2010). After intensive intervention, some children no longer meet ASD diagnostic criteria; however, even among children who have "recovered," comormid conditions such as depression, anxiety, inattention, and hyperactivity often remain (Helt et al., 2008) and interfere with optimal performance in learning environments (Ashburner, Ziviani, & Rodger, 2010).

A variety of medications are used in an effort to decrease anxiety, repetitive behaviors, and hyperactivity in those with ASD (Myers et al., 2007); however, such intervention is only minimally effective (Oswald & Sonenklar, 2007) and some medications (such as SSRIs) can, in fact, be harmful (Williams, Wheeler, Silove, & Hazell, 2010). Only one medication, the antipsychotic risperidone, has received FDA approval for the treatment of ASD; however, other treatments (such as melatonin and antioxidants) have received substantial research support (Rossignol, 2009). Additionally, some preliminary research has found that that administration of oxytocin, a naturally occurring hormone that affects social bonding, can increase social interactions in adults and adolescents with mild ASD (Andari et al., 2010; Guastella et al., 2010).

ASD causes major disruption in families and unfulfilled lives for many affected children. However, comprehensive treatment programs have enabled many children with ASD to develop more functional skills (Eldevik et al., 2010). Because of the communication and social impairments associated with autism, skill building in these areas is often a target of intervention. Specialized programs for children with autism often include:

- A high degree of structure through elements such as predictable routine, visual activity schedules, and clear physical boundaries to minimize distractions
- Intensive, systematically planned, developmentally appropriate educational activities
- Behavior modification procedures to eliminate echolalia and repetitive behaviors and to increase attending behaviors, verbalizations, and social play (Lovaas, 2003; Myers et al., 2007)
- Parent education regarding behavior management and enhancing communication
- Opportunities to apply learned skills to new environments, including interactions with typically developing peers

Interventions that result in the most significant gains involve emphasis on social communication and social imitation, environmental enrichment, reinforcement of appropriate attention and response to social stimuli, prevention of repetitive behaviors, sustained practice of weaker skills, reduction of environmental stress, and strategies to improve sleep and nutrition (Helt et al., 2008). Explicit training focused on skills such as emotional recognition, social interaction, verbal and nonverbal communication, and social perspective-taking has improved the social communication skills of adolescents with high-functioning autism (De Rosier et al., 2010; Hopkins et al., 2011).

Diagnosing Intellectual Disabilities

Intellectual disability (ID) involves lifelong cognitive deficits characterized by significant limitations in intellectual functioning and adaptive behaviors. Approximately 1 percent of students in public schools in the United States are identified as having an ID (U.S. Department of Education, 2010). Low and middle-income countries have double the prevalence of ID compared to higher income countries (Maulik et al., 2011). Many individuals with ID have coexisting conditions such as ASD or depression (Morin et al., 2010); approximately

intellectual disability (ID) disorder characterized by limitations in intellectual functioning and adaptive behaviors

one-fourth have a seizure disorder (World Health Organization [WHO], 2011). Intellectual disability is defined as involving:

1. Significantly subaverage general intellectual functioning (ordinarily interpreted as an IQ score of 70 or less on an individually administered IQ test)
2. Deficiencies in adaptive behavior (e.g., skills required for communication, self-care, social interactions, health and safety, work, and leisure activities) that are lower than would be based expected based on age or cultural background

ID is diagnosed only when low intelligence is accompanied by impaired adaptive functioning (e.g., functional use of academic skills; self-care; understanding health and safety issues; ability to live, work, plan leisure activities, and use community resources). Psychologists have traditionally identified four distinct categories of ID based on IQ score ranges and adaptive behaviors. These categories are: (1) *mild* (IQ score 50–55 to 70); (2) *moderate* (IQ score 35–40 to 50–55); (3) *severe* (IQ score 20–25 to 35–40); and (4) *profound* (IQ score below 20–25). Table 16.7 summarizes functional characteristics associated with each of these categories; social, vocational, and adaptive behaviors can vary significantly not only between categories, but also within each category.

TABLE 16.7 Adaptive Characteristics Associated with Intellectual Disability

Level	Approximate IQ Range	Characteristics
Mild	50–70	Daily living and social interactions skills mildly affected; adaptive difficulties involve conceptual and academic understanding; may need assistance with job skills or independent living; may marry and raise children
Moderate	35–49	May have functional self-care skills and ability to communicate basic needs; may read a few basic words; lifelong support and supervision required (e.g., supervised meal preparation, sheltered work)
Severe	20–34	May recognize familiar people; limited communication skills; lifelong support required
Profound	Below 20	Similar to severe intellectual disability

The American Association of Intellectual and Developmental Disabilities (AAIDD, 2007) asserts that, although IQ scores may be used to approximate intellectual functioning for diagnostic purposes, it is much more important to focus on adaptive functioning and the nature of psychosocial supports needed to maximize adaptive functioning. The AAIDD makes the following assumptions about diagnosis and intervention for those with intellectual disabilities:

1. Identified deficits should be considered within the context of the individual's age, peer group, culture, and community environment.
2. Assessment should always take into account cultural and linguistic diversity, as well as ability to communicate and sensory, motor, behavioral factors.
3. Every individual possesses strengths as well as limitations.
4. The purpose of identifying limitations is to plan for providing needed support.
5. Given ongoing, individualized support, the overall functioning of individuals with ID will improve.

These assumptions focus on the individuality and humanity of all people with ID, regardless of level of impairment. More severe ID, often associated with significant

CRITICAL THINKING

Risks of Substance Use in Pregnancy

It is common knowledge that alcohol and other drugs can affect a developing fetus. The effects depend on timing (i.e., the stage of fetal development) as well as the type and amount of substance used. Pregnant women are advised to avoid alcohol throughout pregnancy to prevent the physical and cognitive abnormalities associated with fetal alcohol syndrome, the leading cause of preventable intellectual disability (Thomas, Warren, & Hewitt, 2010). Use of marijuana, cocaine, heroin, or methamphetamine can also lead to neurodevelopmental disorders (Campolongo et al., 2009; Lu et al., 2009; Delaney-Black et al., 2010; Sowell et al., 2010). Of course, in utero substance exposure is often associated with other prenatal and childhood risk factors such as poor nutrition; limited prenatal care; chaotic home environment; and abuse, neglect, or other stressors that can affect brain development (Schempf & Strobino, 2008; Lester et al., 2010).

Researchers are attempting to find diagnostic tools to detect drug or alcohol use during pregnancy and to identify newborns affected by maternal substance use; their hope is that early detection will allow for early intervention (Ismail et al., 2010). What are the health, legal, and moral implications of these efforts to detect substance use? Are there other ways to reach out to women who are using substances during pregnancy?

developmental delay, communication difficulties, and neurological disorders, was once considered a hopeless condition requiring institutionalization. We now know that the effects of ID are variable and that individuals with mild or moderate ID often function independently or semi-independently in adulthood. Additionally, with support and intervention, those with more severe ID can make cognitive and social gains and have improved life satisfaction.

Etiology of Intellectual Disabilities

The etiology of ID differs, to some extent, depending on the level of intellectual impairment. Mild ID is often *idiopathic* (having no known cause), whereas more pronounced ID is typically related to genetic factors, brain abnormalities, or brain injury. Although a variety of biological factors are implicated in intellectual disability, psychological, social, and sociocultural factors also play an important role in intellectual development and adaptive functioning.

Genetic Factors   Genetic factors that exert an influence on ID include both genetic variations and genetic abnormalities. ID caused by normal genetic variation reflects the fact that in a normal distribution of any trait, some individuals fall in the upper range and some in the lower. The normal range of intelligence is considered to lie between the IQ scores of 70 and 130 (the "average" IQ is 100); some individuals with ID have an IQ that falls at or slightly below the lower end of this normal range. Most people with mild ID are otherwise physically and emotionally healthy and have no specific physiological anomaly associated with their cognitive and adaptive difficulties.

The genetic anomalies associated with ID include chromosomal abnormalities as well as conditions resulting from inheritance of a single gene. Although genetic abnormalities result in varying degrees of ID, many genetically affected persons have significant impairment (Raymond et al., 2007). The most common inherited form of ID is *fragile X syndrome*, a condition resulting in limited production of proteins required for brain development. Fragile X syndrome results in mild to severe ID. Females generally have less impairment; males are prone to having communication and social difficulties including anxious, inattentive, fearful, or aggressive behavior. Symptoms of autism occur in some individuals with fragile X syndrome (National Institute of Child Health and Human Development [NICHHD], 2011a).

Down syndrome (*DS*) is the most common and most easily recognized chromosomal disorder resulting in ID (Shin et al., 2009). In the vast majority of cases, an extra copy of chromosome 21 originates during gamete development (involving either the egg or the sperm); this extra chromosome produces unregulated expression of certain genes and the resulting physical and neurological characteristics associated with DS (Gardiner et al., 2010). DS occurs once in approximately every 800–1,000 live births ("Down Syndrome," 2007). The chance of an egg containing an extra copy of chromosome 21 increases significantly with increasing maternal age. The incidence of DS births for women younger than 30 is less than 1 in 1,000; the incidence increases to 1 in 400 at age 35; 1 in 60 at age 42, and 1 in 12 at age 49. However, because more than 90 percent of all pregnancies occur in women younger than age 35, over 75 percent of the babies born with DS have young mothers (NICHHD, 2011b).

The distinctive physical characteristics associated with DS include a single crease across the palm of the hand, extra skin at the inner corners of the eyelids, slanted eyes, a protruding tongue, harsh voice, and incomplete or delayed sexual development. The majority of individuals with DS have mild to moderate ID; however, negligible intellectual impairment or severe impairment is also possible. With support, many adults with DS have jobs and live semi-independently. Individuals with DS have significantly increased incidence of childhood leukemia and infectious diseases, hearing loss, congenital heart disease, and premature aging (NICHHD, 2011b). Dementia can begin as early as age 35; those with DS have a significantly increased risk of early-onset Alzheimer's disease (National Down Syndrome Society, 2011). Because researchers are identifying specific genes associated with symptoms of DS, medical treatment targeted at minimizing negative effects associated with Trisomy 21, including premature aging, may be forthcoming (Mégarbané et al., 2009). Already, medical intervention has improved health outcome and increased life expectancy for those with DS (Weijerman & de Winter, 2010). Prenatal detection of DS is possible through different techniques, including *amniocentesis*, a screening procedure involving withdrawal of amniotic fluid from the fetal sac. This procedure, performed between the fourteenth and eighteenth week of pregnancy, involves some risk for both mother and fetus, so it is employed primarily when the chance of finding DS is high (e.g., with women 35 or older). Regional and cultural differences in use of genetic screening and decisions regarding termination of pregnancy have resulted in ethnic/racial differences in DS incidence, with Hispanic mothers being the most likely to give birth to a child with DS (Shin et al., 2009).

In up to 80 percent of the cases of ID, the underlying cause is unknown (Xiang et al., 2008; Kaufman, Ayub, & Vincent, 2010). It is believed that not-yet-identified genetic factors are responsible for many of these cases; in particular, researchers are working to identify genes that are related to learning and memory. Also, due to the increased incidence of ID in males, a great deal of research has focused on genes residing on the X chromosome; of the 40 genes that have been identified as contributing to ID, approximately 80 percent are, in fact, on the X chromosome (Kaufman, Ayub, & Vincent, 2010).

Nongenetic Biological Factors ID can result from a variety of environmental influences during the prenatal (from conception to birth), perinatal (during the birth process), or postnatal (after birth) period. Many of the circumstances that can cause ID (as well as other neurodevelopmental disorders) are preventable or controllable (Table 16.8). During the prenatal period, the developing fetus is susceptible to viruses and infections (e.g., tuberculosis or German measles), drugs and alcohol, radiation, and poor nutrition. Some risk factors can cause ID both prenatally and after birth. For example, iodine deficiency either during pregnancy or during early infancy can impair intellectual development (Angermayr & Clar, 2004). In fact, worldwide, iodine deficiency is the single most preventable cause of ID, primarily affecting countries where food and soil are deficient in iodine, where supplemental iodization of salt is not available, and where diets are low in selenium and vitamin A (WHO, 2011).

Similarly, phenylketonuria (PKU), an inherited condition affecting metabolism, can have prenatal or postnatal effects; if pregnant women with PKU ingest protein or artificial

TABLE 16.8   Preventable or Controllable Causes of
Neurodevelopmental Disorders

Timing and Cause of Effects
Prenatal (Before Birth)
Severe malnutrition
Alcohol or illicit drugs; prescription medications
Iodine or folic acid deficiency*
Maternal infections such as rubella* or syphilis
Toxoplasmosis parasites (from cat feces, undercooked meats, unwashed produce)
Exposure to radiation
Blood incompatibility (Rh factor)
Chronic disease in the mother (heart or kidney disease, diabetes)
Untreated phenylketonuria (PKU)
Perinatal (Just Before or During Birth)
Severe prematurity
Birth trauma
Asphyxia (lack of oxygen)
Infancy and Childhood
Untreated phenylketonuria (PKU)
Nutritional deficiencies*
Iodine deficiency
Severe lack of stimulation
Chronic lead exposure*
Other environmental toxins*
Brain infections (e.g., meningitis and encephalitis)
Head injury

*This factor has been implicated in the etiology of autism.
Adapted from the World Health Organization, (2011)

sweeteners, the resultant build-up of a substance called phenylalanine can cause significant intellectual impairment in a developing fetus. This can be prevented if a special diet is followed. Similarly, phenylalanine build-up from undetected and untreated PKU in an infant can cause postnatal brain damage. ID resulting from PKU can be prevented when routine PKU screening is implemented (as is done in the United States, Canada, and many developed countries) and dietary recommendations are followed.

Alcohol intake can significantly affect embryonic and fetal development. Although there is a continuum of detrimental neurological and behavioral effects resulting from alcohol consumption during pregnancy (referred to as *fetal alcohol spectrum disorders*), the greatest concern is for those children who have *fetal alcohol syndrome* (*FAS*). FAS is estimated to occur in less than 1 percent of live births, and 2 to 5 percent of the United States population is estimated to have fetal alcohol effects (May et al., 2009). Fetal alcohol spectrum disorders are associated with reduced cognitive functioning, attentional difficulties, slower information processing, and poor working memory (Kodituwakku, 2009), whereas FAS results in retarded growth, facial abnormalities, central nervous system dysfunction, and altered brain development (Thomas, Warren, & Hewitt, 2010). Children with FAS experience difficulty with attention, learning, memory, regulation of emotions, and executive functioning, all of which are associated with the frontal lobe of the brain (Green et al., 2009); overstimulation appears to have a particularly negative effect on children with FAS (Kooistra et al., 2010). Markedly delayed development in adaptive behavior, particularly skills of daily living, is also common (Crocker, Vaurio, Riley, & Mattson, 2009).

During the perinatal period, ID can result from birth trauma, prematurity, or asphyxiation. The most common birth condition associated with ID is prematurity and low birth weight. Although most premature infants develop normally, some have neurological problems resulting in learning disabilities and ID. Extremely low birth weight is also a risk factor for conditions such as blindness, hearing loss, and cerebral palsy (Whitaker et al., 2006). After birth or during the postnatal period, factors such as head injuries, brain infections, tumors, and prolonged malnutrition can cause brain damage and consequent ID. Exposure to environmental toxins is an increasing concern. Lead, a well-known neurotoxin, is associated with both ID and hyperactivity (Abelsohn & Sanborn, 2010); researchers have warned that there is no safe level of lead exposure (Bellinger, 2008). In the United States, lead exposure involves lead paint in toys and in older homes, whereas worldwide many children are exposed to a variety of industrial and commercial sources of lead (Nevin, 2009).

Psychological, Social, and Sociocultural Dimensions   Psychological, social, and sociocultural factors can affect both intellectual and adaptive functioning. A child's genetic background interacts with environmental factors; children from socioeconomically advantaged homes are often provided enriching experiences that enhance cognitive development. In contrast, crowded living conditions, lack of adequate health care, poor nutrition, and inadequate educational opportunities place children living in poverty at an intellectual disadvantage and can influence whether they reach their genetic potential. A longitudinal study evaluating the development of 750 sets of twins from varying socioeconomic backgrounds found skill development at age 10 months was fairly equal across socioeconomic levels; however, by age 2, children from socioeconomically advantaged backgrounds were outperforming children from less advantaged backgrounds. In effect, those from impoverished homes had less opportunity to reach their genetic potential (Tucker-Drob et al., 2011). Similarly, children raised by parents with mild ID may begin their lives with less learning opportunity, further contributing to a generational pattern of lower intellectual functioning. Additionally, the long-term effects of prematurity appear to be moderated by sociocultural factors such as socioeconomic status and parenting style; supportive parenting or increased socioeconomic resources can enhance ultimate cognitive functioning (Anderson & Doyle, 2008).

An enriching and encouraging home environment as well as ongoing educational intervention focused on targeted cognitive, academic, self-care, social, and problem-solving skills can have a strong and positive influence on the development of children with ID (Thomas, Warren, & Hewitt, 2010). Coping strategies and seeking help when raising a child with ID can be highly influenced by sociocultural context. Additionally, religious or cultural beliefs may affect parents' perceptions of their child's condition; for example, some parents may attribute ID to factors such as personal wrongdoing or a curse placed on their family, whereas others believe a child with special needs is a gift from God (Durà-Vilà, Dein, & Hodes, 2010).

Learning Disorders

A learning disorder (LD) is diagnosed when someone with at least average intellectual abilities demonstrates basic math, reading, or writing skill development that is substantially below levels that would be expected based on the person's chronological age, educational background, and intellectual disability. LD primarily interferes with academic achievement and activities of daily living in which reading, writing, or math skills are required. As with any testing, when an assessment for LD is conducted, care is taken to ensure that testing procedures take the child's linguistic and cultural background into consideration. Specific learning disorders include *dyslexia* (significant difficulties with accuracy or fluency of reading), *dyscalculia* (significant difficulties in understanding quantities, number symbols, or basic arithmetic calculations) and disorders of written expression.

learning disorder   academic disability characterized by reading, writing, and math skill deficits that are substantially below levels that would be expected based on the person's age, intellectual ability and educational background

Approximately 5 percent of students in public schools in the United States are identified as having LD (U.S. Department of Education, 2010); boys are almost twice as likely as girls to have LD (CDC, 2011). Many children with LD have concurrent ADHD. Some individuals appear to mature out of their academic difficulties, whereas, for others, it is a lifelong condition. Severity of the disorder varies, and some individuals continue to cope with severe academic deficits in adulthood. Because adults with severe LD may experience problems with employment, it is beneficial when their career choice capitalizes on their abilities and strengths.

Etiology

Little is currently known about the precise causes of LD. Children with LD that eventually resolves appear to have slower brain maturation (with eventual catch-up). However, others have lifelong differences in neurological processing of information related to basic academic skills. Etiological possibilities for chronic LD include many of the same biological explanations for ID and ADHD (see Table 16.8) such as prematurity (Aarnoudse-Moens et al., 2009) and alcohol use during pregnancy (Kodituwakku, 2009). Additionally, LD tends to run in families, suggesting a genetic component. Some also link the higher prevalence of LD in English-speaking countries to the irregular spelling, pronunciation, and structure of the English language.

Comorbidity of Neurodevelopmental Disorders

It is clear from our etiological discussions that there are many overlapping environmental influences during pregnancy, birth, or early childhood that can significantly affect brain development and cause a neurodevelopmental disorder. Outcome is likely related not only to the strength and the timing of the environmental impact, but also on the genetic makeup of the child. Researchers are focusing on the comorbidity of neurodevelopmental disorders and genetic similarities between disorders; it is hoped that ongoing genome analysis will identify alleles linked to attention and cognitive development (Anney et al., 2010).

Some argue that the strong similarities between autism and more severe ID (i.e., social and communication difficulties, repetition of meaningless movements) and the high frequency of ID in those with ASD result from overlapping genetic influences (Kaufman, Ayub, & Vincent, 2010). Additionally, one-half of those with ASD also have symptoms of ADHD (Yerys et al., 2009). Family and twins studies suggest that ASD and ADHD may originate from similar transmittable genetic factors (Rommelse et al., 2010) and that a repeated allele of one gene (DRD4) appears to increase the risk of ASD in those with ADHD (Reiersen & Todorov, 2011). Some of the chromosomal deletions or replications found in genome studies targeting ADHD are identical to defects associated with both ASD and schizophrenia (Williams et al., 2010). Additionally, ADHD is frequently seen in individuals with chronic tics and Tourette's disorder (Erenberg, 2005). Cross-ethnic research is particularly important because preliminary neurodevelopmental research suggests differential gene effects between ethnic groups (Gabriela et al., 2009). As research progresses, it is likely that we will learn more about genetic overlap among neurodevelopmental disorders and the influence of gene × environment interactions on early brain development.

Support for Individuals with Neurodevelopmental Disorders

Because many neurodevelopmental disorders produce lifelong disability, the goal of intervention is to build skills and develop each individual's potential to the fullest extent possible. For those with moderate to severe ID or ASD, such support often begins in infancy and extends across the lifespan. In the case of ASD, early targeted intervention can result in moderately to significantly improved linguistic, intellectual, adaptive, and social functioning (Dawson et al., 2010; Virués-Ortega, 2010). For children with ADHD, LD, milder ID, or milder ASD, support may occur primarily in the school setting. Interventions for LD and mild ID typically involve remedial interventions targeting the area of academic difficulty, whereas supports for ASD and more severe intellectual impairment are generally more comprehensive.

Support in Childhood

When ASD or ID is identified early, children often participate in individualized home-based or school-based programs focused on decreasing inappropriate behaviors and maximizing skill development in areas such as movement; communication; and, when appropriate, pre-academic skills. Parent involvement is an integral part of early intervention programs; parent follow-through with home activities that capitalize on the child's strengths can enhance cognitive, social, and communication development. Educational programs, offered from early childhood through the high school years, typically involve comprehensive services involving school psychologists, specially trained teachers, and therapists that specialize in communication and motor skill development. Adaptive behavior and self-care skills, social skills and pre-vocational skills are frequently included in educational plans for older students.

In the United States, if academic progress is significantly compromised by the disability, children with ASD, ID, LD, or ADHD are entitled to free educational services from age 3 to age 21 (or until high school graduation for those with milder impairment). In accordance with federal law, each child is entitled to a comprehensive evaluation of skills every three years and an annual individualized education plan (IEP) that is developed by a team that includes parents and school professionals. The IEP summarizes the child's current level of functioning in academics, communication, motor skills, social skills, adaptive behaviors; identifies annual goals; and specifies the supports needed for the child to meet the stated goals. Some of the supports offered might include specialized preschool programming or special education services targeting academic skills, behavior, social skills and life skills. For those with mild ID or LD, the plan may include academic tutoring, modified classroom assignments, or explicitly teaching the skills necessary to complete assignments. Pre-vocational skills are often incorporated into the IEP beginning in early adolescence. In general, school services are individualized to meet the needs of the child and to maximize learning opportunities, including skills needed for independent or semi-independent living (National Dissemination Center for Children with Disabilities, 2007). Unfortunately, rates of improvement often decrease once school programs are completed; programs terminate following high school graduation or at age 21 for those with more significant impairment (Taylor & Seltzer, 2010a).

Support in Adulthood

A number of programs are available for young adults with moderate neurodevelopmental disabilities to learn vocational skills or to participate in work opportunities in a specialized setting. These programs focus on specific job skills, social skills for interacting with coworkers and supervisors, and completing work-related tasks with speed and quality (American Association on Intellectual and Developmental Disabilities [AAIDD], 2007). There is a clear need for more support for those with milder ID or ASD as they make the transition from high school to out-of-school activities, especially for those who are unable to obtain employment without support (Taylor & Seltzer, 2010b).

Institutionalization of adults with neurodevelopmental disorders is rare. Many adults with special needs live with family members; others live independently or semi-independently within the community. The idea is to provide the "least restrictive environment" possible; that is, as much independence and personal choice as is safe and practical. Although group arrangements vary considerably from setting to setting (Perry & Felce, 2005), most normalized living arrangements produce benefits such as increased adaptive functioning, improved language development, and socialization. Many assisted-living

© Mika/Corbis

Work Opportunities for Those with Neurodevelopmental Disorders

Many people with Down syndrome and other neurodevelopmental disorders can function well in a supportive work environment. Here a baker's assistant is proudly displaying fresh bread.

environments promote social interaction with the larger community and continue to support the development of personal competence and independence.

Persons with ID are at higher risk of developing a depressive disorder than are members of the general population (Morin et al., 2010), and individuals with ASD frequently experience comorbid depression and anxiety as well as behaviors that interfere with optimal functioning (Hofvander et al., 2009; Skokauskas & Gallagher, 2010). Intervention to help those who have social, behavioral, depressive, or anxiety symptoms in adulthood includes environmental modification and cognitive or behavioral therapy (often targeting social and coping skill development) adapted to the individual's level of functioning.

Summary

1. What internalizing disorders occur in childhood and adolescence?

   - Anxiety disorders are the most common internalizing disorders in youth.
   - Depression and bipolar disorder can occur in childhood, but they are more prevalent during adolescence.
   - Nonsuicidal self injury is most likely to emerge during adolescence.
   - Attachment disorders develop early in life due to persistent neglect, abuse, or frequent changes in primary caregiver.

2. What are the characteristics of externalizing disorders?

   - Disruptive mood dysregulation disorder involves negative affect and exaggerated responses to anger.
   - Oppositional defiant disorder involves a pattern of hostile, defiant behavior toward authority figures.
   - Conduct disorders involve serious antisocial behaviors and violations of the rights of others.

3. What are elimination disorders, and what is their prognosis?

   - Enuresis involves the voiding of urine and encopresis involves the expulsion of feces. Both elimination disorders usually abate with increasing age.

4. What are neurodevelopmental disorders, and what are their characteristics?

   - Motor and vocal tics and Tourette's disorders involve involuntary repetitive movements or vocalizations.
   - Attention-deficit/hyperactivity disorder (ADHD) is characterized by inattention, hyperactivity, and impulsivity.
   - Autism spectrum disorders involve impairment in social communication and restricted, stereotyped interests and activities.
   - Intellectual disability involves limitations in intellectual functioning and adaptive behaviors.
   - Learning disorders involve basic reading, writing, or math skills that are substantially below expectations based on age, intelligence, and educational experiences.

Media Resources

Psychology CourseMate   Access an interactive eBook; chapter-specific interactive learning tools, including flash cards, quizzes, videos; and more in your Psychology CourseMate, accessed through CengageBrain.com.

CENGAGENOW

CengageNow   CengageNOW is an easy-to-use online resource that helps you study in less time to get the grade you want—NOW. If your textbook does not include an access code card, go to CengageBrain.com to gain access.

CENGAGEbrain.com

CengageBrain   More than just an interactive study guide, WebTutor is an anytime, anywhere customized learning solution with an eBook, keeping you connected to your textbook, instructor, and classmates. Purchase the access chosen by your instructor at CengageBrain.com.

17

Brett Coomer-Pool/Getty Images

Legal and Ethical Issues in Abnormal Psychology

O n June 30, 2001, Andrea Yates waited until her husband left for work, filled the bathtub to the very top, and proceeded to kill her five children (ages seven months to seven years). She drowned each child in the bathtub, carried them to a bedroom, laid them out next to one another, and covered them with a sheet. Yates then called 911 and asked for the police. She called her husband and stated, "You need to come home.... It's time. I did it." When asked what she meant, Yates responded "It's the children ... all of them." When the police arrived, Yates calmly explained how she had killed her five young children. Police report that the children struggled vigorously as the mother held each under the water until they drowned.

The case of Andrea Yates shocked the nation. How could a mother possibly commit such an unthinkable act? Although filicides (killing one's child or children) are often reported in the news media, this one was especially heinous because it involved five children and was carried out in such a methodical manner. During Yates's trial, the prosecution asked for the death penalty, but the defense contended that she was psychotic, suffering from postpartum depression, insane, and should not be held accountable for her actions. The jury, however, found her guilty. An appeals court subsequently overturned the verdict, and on July 26, 2006, another Texas jury found her not guilty by reason of insanity.

Questions: What criteria are used to determine sanity and insanity? Is being mentally ill the same as being insane?

On June 5, 2002, 14-year-old Elizabeth Smart was kidnapped at knife-point from her Salt Lake City, Utah, home by Brian David Mitchell. The incident set off a massive search effort, evoked intense media coverage, was showcased in *America's Most Wanted* TV program, became the subject of a book, and resulted in a made-for-TV movie, *The Elizabeth Smart Story.* Smart was found nine months later after enduring a horrendous experience, which included a forced polygamous marriage, frequent rapes, and constant threats to her life. Mitchell, a former street preacher, was arrested for the crime, but claimed that God had commanded him to abduct Smart, to enter into a celestial marriage, and to form a religious society of younger females.

Despite being captured, arrested, and charged with kidnapping nearly 9 years ago, the trial of Mitchell only began in November 2010. The delays in his trial have been due to one primary reason: In three separate court hearings, Mitchell was judged "mentally incapable of assisting in his own defense." In the courtroom he would sing hymns and scream at the judge "forsake those robes and kneel in the dust." His behavior was so bizarre that he was banished from the courtroom several times. As a result, Mitchell was ordered to be hospitalized indefinitely until he was capable of understanding the proceedings. To improve his condition and render him competent, psychiatrists attempted to administer antipsychotic drugs. However, in December 2008, a ruling forbid the State of Utah from legally forcing Mitchell to take medication; it was "unnecessary and needlessly harsh," infringed on his civil liberties, and Mitchell had a constitutional right to refuse treatment.

On March 1, 2010, U.S. District Judge Dale Kimball effectively circumvented this argument when he ruled that Mitchell was exaggerating his symptoms and thus, mentally competent to stand trial. As a result, Mitchell was convicted of kidnapping and transporting a minor across state lines on December 10, 2010.

Questions: Is being insane at the commission of a crime different from being mentally incompetent to stand trial? If medication will improve people's mental state, shouldn't they be forced to take it? Do people have a right to refuse treatment?

She was only known as BL ("bag lady") in the downtown Oakland, California, area. By night, she slept on any number of park benches and in storefronts. By day she could be seen pushing her Safeway shopping cart full of boxes, extra clothing, and garbage, which she collected from numerous trash containers. According to her only surviving sister, the woman had lived this way for nearly ten years and had been tolerated by local merchants.

Over the past six months, however, BL's behavior had become progressively intolerable. She had always talked to herself, but recently she had begun shouting and screaming at anyone who approached her. Her use of profanity was graphic, and she often urinated and defecated in front of local stores. Although she never physically assaulted anyone, her menacing behavior frightened many pedestrians, customers, and shopkeepers. She was occasionally arrested and detained for short periods of time by local law-enforcement officials, but she always returned to her familiar haunts. Finally, her sister and several merchants requested that the city take action to commit her to a mental institution.

Questions: How do we determine whether people are dangerous to others? Can we commit them even if they have not committed a crime? Under what conditions can they be confined (committed) against their will?

In 1968, Prosenjit Poddar, a graduate student from India studying at the University of California, Berkeley, sought therapy from the student health services for depression. Poddar was apparently upset over what he perceived to be a rebuff from a female student, Tatiana Tarasoff, whom he claimed to love. During the course of treatment, Poddar informed his therapist that he intended to purchase a gun and kill Tarasoff. Judging Poddar to be dangerous, the psychologist breached the confidentiality of the professional relationship by informing the campus police. The police detained Poddar briefly but freed him because he agreed to stay away from Tarasoff. On October 27, Poddar went to Tarasoff's home and killed her, first wounding her with a gun and then stabbing her repeatedly with a knife. Because of this case, the California Supreme Court made a landmark 1976 ruling popularly known as the "duty-to-warn"; the therapist should have warned not only the police but the intended victim as well.

Questions: What are the limits of therapeutic confidentiality? What legal obligations do therapists have in reporting whether clients pose a threat to themselves or to others? If confidentiality cannot be absolutely guaranteed, how will it affect patient self-disclosures?

The Insanity Defense

Naveed Haq, a Pakistani American, invaded the downtown office of the Jewish Federation of Greater Seattle railing against Israel and the Iraq war. He fired at workers, killing one woman and wounding five. He appears here on April 14, 2008, the first day of his trial. Haq is pleading innocent by reason of insanity. His family and a psychiatrist testified that he has a long history of mental illness and that Haq was in a manic state on the morning of the rampage. In June 2008, the jury became hopelessly deadlocked and a mistrial was declared. He was eventually retried and convicted in 2009.

Psychologists and mental health professionals are increasingly becoming involved in the legal system and must deal with the multiple questions posed here. They are playing important roles in determining the state of mind of individuals and are participating in decisions and actions of the legal system that affect human relationships (Simon & Gold, 2004; Werth, Weilfel, & Benjamin, 2009). In the past, psychologists dealt primarily with evaluation of competency and issues related to criminal cases such as those of Andrea Yates and Brian David Mitchell. Now, however, their expanded roles include giving expert opinions on child custody, organic brain functioning, traumatic injury, suicide, and even deprogramming activities (Table 17.1). The American Psychological Association has even taken on the role of *amicus curiae* (friend of the court) by filing briefs to act in an advisory capacity on issues of importance to social science questions (Clay, 2010). And just as psychologists influence decisions in the legal system, they have also been influenced by mental health laws passed at local, state, and federal levels (Pope & Vasquez, 2007).

All four of the preceding examples fit the definition of abnormal behavior, and we can clearly see many of their clinical implications. What is less clear to many is that clinical or mental health issues can often become legal and ethical ones as well. This is evident in the Elizabeth Smart abduction, for which court psychiatrists ruled that Brian Mitchell was not competent to stand trial. It was only after a judge ruled that Mitchell was feigning that his trial finally proceeded. Yet how do we determine whether a person is competent to stand trial or whether someone like Yates is insane or sane? What criteria do we use? If we call on experts, we find that professionals often disagree with one another (Koocher & Keith-Spiegel, 2008). Further, might defendants in criminal trials attempt to fake mental disturbances to escape guilty verdicts? The task of determining sanity is even more difficult because many lawyers are using clients' claims of child abuse, domestic violence, and other psychological traumas to explain the criminal actions of their clients.

The example of BL leads us into the area of civil and criminal commitments, and legal rulings that force mental health practitioners to go beyond clinical concepts defined in the DSM. Some of her behaviors are extreme, but should a person who has committed no crime be institutionalized because she appears severely disturbed? Certainly, defecating and urinating in public are disgusting to most people and are truly unusual behaviors, but are these enough to deprive her of her civil liberties? Does being a nuisance or a "potential danger" to oneself or others constitute grounds for commitment? What are the procedures for civil commitment? What happens to people once they are committed?

In the first three case examples, the focus of legal and ethical issues tends to be on the individual, or defendant. Mental health issues become legal ones when (1) competence to stand trial is in doubt, (2) an accused person bases his or her criminal defense on insanity or diminished mental capacity, (3) decisions must be made about involuntary commitment to mental hospitals, and (4) the rights of mental patients are legally tested.

In the *Tarasoff* case, the focus of legal and ethical concern shifts to the therapist. When is a therapist legally and ethically obligated to breach patient-therapist confidentiality? In this case, had the therapist done enough to prevent a potentially dangerous situation from occurring? According to all codes of conduct before 1976 issued by professional organizations such as the American Psychological Association, and according to accepted practice in the field at the time, many psychologists would have answered yes. Yet in 1976 the California Supreme Court ruled that the therapist should have warned not only the police but also the likely victim.

TABLE 17.1   The Intersection of Psychology and the Law

Psychologists are finding that their expertise is either being sought in the legal system or being influenced by the law. Only a few of these roles and activities are described.

Assessing Dangerousness	Determination of Sanity or Insanity
• Assess suicide and homicide potential, child endangerment, civil commitment, and so on. • Be knowledgeable about the clinical and research findings affecting such determinations.	• Asked by the court, prosecution, or defense to determine the sanity or insanity of someone accused of a crime. • Present findings via a private hearing to the judge or expert testimony in front of a jury.
Child Custody Evaluations in Divorce Proceedings	**Determination of Competency to Stand Trial**
• Provide expertise to help courts and social service agencies determine the "best interests of the child." • May advise on parental arrangements, termination of parental rights, and issues of neglect and abuse in custody cases.	• Determine whether an individual is mentally competent or sufficiently rational to stand trial and to aid in his or her defense.
Psychological Evaluations in Child Protection Matters	**Jury Selection**
• Attempt to determine whether abuse or neglect has occurred; whether the child is at risk for harm; and what, if any, corrective action should be recommended.	• Aid attorneys to determine whether prospective jurors might favor one side or the other. • Use clinical knowledge in an attempt to screen out individuals who might be biased against their clients.
Repressed/Recovered or False Memory Determinations	**Profiling of Serial Killers, Mass Murderers, or Specific Criminals**
• Asked to determine the accuracy and validity of repressed memories—claims by adults that they have recovered memories of childhood abuse.	• Work hand in hand with law enforcement officials in developing profiles of criminals.
Civil Commitment Determination	**Testifying in Malpractice Suits**
• Become involved in the civil commitment of an individual or the discharge of a person who has been so confined. • Determine whether the person is at risk of harm to him- or herself or others, is too mentally disturbed to take care of him- or herself, or lacks the appropriate resources for care if left alone.	• Testify in a civil suit on whether another practicing clinician failed to follow the "standards of the profession" and is thus guilty of negligence or malpractice. • Determine whether the client bringing the suit suffered psychological harm or damage as a result of the clinician's actions.
Filing Amicus Briefs	**Protection of Patient Rights**
• Using psychological science to help inform the court as to relevant social science research to a particular pending litigation. • Act as a friend of the court by filing amicus briefs (pleadings) that have psychological implications in possible court rulings.	• Become involved in seeing that patients are not grievously wronged by the loss of their civil liberties on the grounds of mental health treatment. • Advise on the right to receive treatment, to refuse treatment, and to live in the least restrictive environment.

That ruling has major implications for therapists in the conduct of therapy today: How does a therapist predict that another person is dangerous (to him- or herself, to others, or to society)? To protect themselves from being sued, do therapists report all threats of homicide or suicide? Should psychologists warn clients that not everything they say is privileged or confidential? How does this affect the clinical relationship?

We cover these and other topics in this chapter, and we begin by examining some of the issues of criminal and civil commitment. Then we look at patients' rights and deinstitutionalization. We end by exploring the legal and ethical parameters of the therapist-client relationship, taking a final look at ethical issues related to cultural competence in mental health.

Criminal Commitment

criminal commitment incarceration of an individual for having committed a crime

A basic premise of criminal law is that all of us are responsible beings who exercise free will and are capable of choices. If we do something wrong, we are responsible for our actions and should suffer the consequences. Criminal commitment is the incarceration of an individual

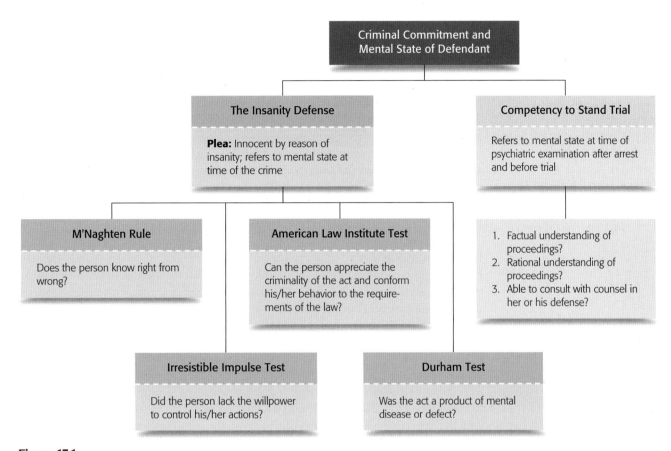

Figure 17.1

LEGAL STANDARDS THAT ADDRESS THE MENTAL STATE OF DEFENDANTS

Copyright © Cengage Learning 2013

for having committed a crime. Abnormal psychology accepts different perspectives on free will; criminal law does not. Yet criminal law does recognize that some people lack the ability to discern the ramifications of their actions because they are mentally disturbed. Although they may be technically guilty of a crime, their mental state at the time of the offense exempts them from legal responsibility. Let us explore the landmark cases that have influenced this concept's evolution and application. Standards arising from these cases and some other important guidelines are summarized in Figure 17.1.

The Insanity Defense

The concept of "not guilty by reason of insanity" (NGRI) has provoked much controversy among legal scholars, mental health practitioners, and the general public. The insanity defense is a legal argument used by defendants who admit they have committed a crime but plead not guilty because they were mentally disturbed at the time the crime was committed. The insanity plea recognizes that under specific circumstances people may not be held accountable for their behavior.

The fear that a guilty individual might use such a plea to escape criminal responsibility has been frequently exploited in popular media for dramatic effect. For example, the Hollywood film *Primal Fear* features actor Richard Gere, playing a high-powered attorney, who was duped into believing that his client suffered from a dissociative identity disorder. The client was found NGRI at the trial, only to have Gere's character discover

MYTH: Defendants who are found "not guilty by reason of insanity" spend less time in custody than those who are convicted. That is the reason why the plea is overused.

REALITY: As a rule, defendants found not guilty by reason of insanity spend significantly more time in custody than those who are convicted. They often face a lifetime of postrelease judicial oversight. Further, the plea is infrequently used (less than 1 percent of cases) and seldom successful.

MYTH VS. REALITY

insanity defense the legal argument used by defendants who admit they have committed a crime but who plead not guilty because they were mentally disturbed at the time the crime was committed

the ghastly truth. His client had convincingly faked his insanity. In reality, however, only 0.25 of a percent of NGRI defenses are successful (law.jrank.org, 2010). Many of the cases discussed in this chapter are the exception to the rule because they are pivotal to the discussion of abnormal behavior and the law. These are the same cases that received media attention that help construct this popular misconception.

In real life, most defendants who plead NGRI have a long history of mental illness. Those who fake it are seldom successful. Confessed Hillside Strangler Kenneth Bianchi, for example, attempted to fake mental illness for his part in raping, torturing, and murdering a number of young women in the late 1970s. Wanting to use the insanity plea to get a reduced sentence, Bianchi tried to convince psychiatrists that he suffered from multiple personality disorder (now called dissociative identity disorder). Psychologist and hypnosis expert Dr. Martin Orne exposed his scheme as a fake, and Bianchi was found guilty of murder and sentenced to life in prison without parole.

Legal Precedents

In this country, a number of different standards are used as legal tests of insanity. One of the earliest is the M'Naghten Rule. In 1843, Daniel M'Naghten, a grossly disturbed woodcutter from Glasgow, Scotland, claimed that he was commanded by God to kill the English Prime Minister, Sir Robert Peel. He killed a lesser minister by mistake and was placed on trial, at which it became obvious that M'Naghten was quite delusional. Out of this incident emerged the M'Naghten Rule, popularly known as the "right-wrong" test, which holds that people can be acquitted of a crime if it can be shown that, at the time of the act, they (1) had such defective reasoning that they did not know what they were doing or (2) were unable to comprehend that the act was wrong. The M'Naghten Rule has come under tremendous criticism from some who regard it as being exclusively a cognitive test (knowledge of right or wrong), which does not consider volition, emotion, and other mental activity. Further, it is often difficult to evaluate a defendant's awareness or comprehension.

The second major precedent that strengthened the insanity defense was the irresistible impulse test. In essence, the doctrine says that a defendant is not criminally responsible if he or she lacked the will power to control his or her behavior. Combined with the M'Naghten Rule, this test broadened the criteria for using the insanity defense. In other words, a verdict of NGRI could be obtained if it was shown that the defendant was unaware of or did not comprehend the act (M'Naghten Rule) or was irresistibly impelled to commit the act. Criticisms of the irresistible impulse defense revolve around what constitutes an irresistible impulse. We can ask the question: "When is a person unable to exert control (irresistible impulse) and choosing not to exert control (unresisted impulse)? For example, is a person with a history of antisocial behavior unable to resist his or her impulses, or is he or she choosing not to exert control? Neither the mental health profession nor the legal profession has answered this question satisfactorily.

In the case of *Durham v. United States* (1954), the U.S. Court of Appeals broadened the M'Naghten Rule with the so-called products test or Durham standard. An accused person is not considered criminally responsible if his or her unlawful act was the *product* of mental disease or defect. The intent of the ruling was to (1) give the greatest possible weight to expert evaluation and testimony and (2) allow mental health professionals to define mental illness. The Durham standard also has its drawbacks. The term *product* is vague and difficult to define because almost anything can cause anything (as you have learned by studying the many theoretical viewpoints in this text). Leaving the task of defining mental illness to mental health professionals often results in having to define mental illness in every case. In many situations, relying on psychiatric testimony serves only to confuse the issues, because both the prosecution and defense bring in psychiatric experts, who often present conflicting testimony (Koocher & Keith-Spiegel, 2008).

In 1962, the American Law Institute (ALI), in its Model Penal Code, produced guidelines to help jurors determine the validity of the insanity defense on a case-by-case basis. The guidelines combined features from the previous standards.

M'Naghten Rule a cognitive test of legal insanity that inquires whether the accused knew right from wrong when he or she committed the crime

irresistible impulse test a doctrine that states that a defendant is not criminally responsible if he or she lacked the will power to control his or her behavior

Durham standard a test of legal insanity known as the products test—an accused person is not responsible if the unlawful act was the product of mental disease or defect

American Law Institute (ALI) Model Penal Code a test of legal insanity that combines both cognitive criteria (diminished capacity) and motivational criteria (specific intent); its purpose is to give jurors increased latitude in determining the sanity of the accused

1. A person is not responsible for criminal conduct if at the time of such conduct as a result of mental disease or defect he lacks substantial capacity either to appreciate the criminality of his conduct or to conform his conduct to the requirements of the law.
2. As used in the Article, the terms "mental disease or defect" do not include an abnormality manifested by repeated criminal or otherwise antisocial conduct (Sec. 401, p. 66).

It is interesting to note that the second point was intended to eliminate the insanity defense for people diagnosed as antisocial personalities.

With the attempt to be more specific and precise, the ALI guidelines moved the burden of determining criminal responsibility back to the jurors. As we have seen, previous standards, particularly the Durham standard, gave great weight to expert testimony, and many feared that it would usurp the jury's responsibilities. By using phrases such as "substantial capacity," "appreciate the criminality of his conduct," and "conform his conduct to the requirements of the law," the ALI standard was intended to allow the jurors the greatest possible flexibility in ascribing criminal responsibility.

In some jurisdictions, the concept of *diminished capacity* has also been incorporated into the ALI standard. As a result of a mental disease or defect, a person may lack the *specific intent* to commit the offense. For example, a person under the influence of drugs or alcohol may commit a crime without premeditation or intent; a person who is grief-stricken over the death of a loved one may harm the one responsible for the death. Although diminished capacity has been used primarily to guide the sentencing and disposition of the defendant, it is now introduced in the trial phase as well.

Such was the trial of Dan White, a San Francisco supervisor who killed Mayor George Moscone and Supervisor Harvey Milk on November 27, 1978. White blamed both individuals for his political demise. During the trial, his attorney used the now-famous "Twinkie defense" (White gorged himself on junk food such as Twinkies, chips, and soda) as a partial explanation for his client's actions. White's attorney attempted to convince the jury that the high sugar content of the junk food affected his cognitive and emotional state and was partially to blame for his actions. Because of the unusual defense (the junk food diminished his judgment), White was convicted only of voluntary manslaughter and sentenced to less than eight years in jail. Of course, the citizens of San Francisco were outraged by the verdict and never forgave Dan White. Facing constant public condemnation, he eventually committed suicide after his release.

Guilty, but Mentally Ill

Perhaps no other trial has more greatly challenged the use of the insanity plea than the case of John W. Hinckley, Jr. Hinckley's attempt to assassinate President Ronald Reagan and his subsequent acquittal by reason of insanity outraged the public, as well as legal and mental health professionals. Even before the shooting, the increasingly successful use of the insanity defense had been a growing concern in both legal circles and the public arena. Many had begun to believe that the criteria for the defense were too broadly interpreted. These concerns were strong, even though findings indicate that the insanity defense is used in less than 1 percent of cases and successful only 25 percent of the time, and, as stated earlier, few defendants fake or exaggerate their psychological disorders (law.jrank.org, 2010; Steadman et al., 1993).

For quite some time, the Hinckley case aroused such strong emotional reaction that calls for reform were rampant. The American Psychiatric Association (1983), the American Medical Association (Kerlitz & Fulton, 1984), and the American Bar Association (1984) all advocated a more stringent interpretation of insanity. As a result, Congress passed the Insanity Reform Act of 1984, which based the definition of insanity totally on the individual's ability to understand what he or she did. The American Psychological Association's position on the insanity defense ran counter to these changes. Its position is that even though a given verdict might be wrong, the standard is not necessarily wrong.

© Bettman/CORBIS

Not Guilty by Reason of Insanity

John Hinckley, Jr., was charged with the attempted murder of President Ronald Reagan. His acquittal by reason of insanity created a furor among the American public over use of the insanity defense. The outrage forced Congress to pass the Insanity Reform Act.

Nevertheless, in the wake of the *Hinckley* verdict, some states have adopted alternative pleas, such as "culpable and mentally disabled;" "mentally disabled, but neither culpable nor innocent;" and "guilty, but mentally ill." These pleas are attempts to separate mental illness from insanity and to hold people responsible for their acts. Such pleas allow jurors to reach a decision that not only convicts individuals for their crimes and holds them responsible but also ensures that they are given treatment for their mental illnesses. Despite attempts at reform, however, states and municipalities continue to use different tests of insanity with varying outcomes, and the use of the insanity plea remains controversial.

Competency to Stand Trial

The term competency to stand trial refers to a defendant's mental state at the time of psychiatric examination after arrest and before trial. It has nothing to do with the issue of criminal responsibility, which refers to an individual's mental state or behavior at the time of the offense. If you recall from the case of Brian David Mitchell, court-appointed psychiatrists in the past declared Mitchell not competent to stand trial. In such cases, our system of law states that an accused person cannot be tried unless three criteria are satisfied (Fitch, 2007):

competency to stand trial a judgment that a defendant has a factual and rational understanding of the proceedings and can rationally consult with counsel in presenting his or her own defense; refers to the defendant's mental state at the time of the psychiatric examination

1. Does the defendant have a factual understanding of the proceedings?
2. Does the defendant have a rational understanding of the proceedings?
3. Can the defendant rationally consult with counsel in presenting his or her own defense?

Given this third criterion, a defendant who is suffering from paranoid delusions could not stand trial because a serious impairment exists.

It is clear that many more people are committed to prison hospitals because of incompetency determinations than are acquitted on insanity pleas (Stafford & Wygant, 2005; Zapf & Roesch, 2006). It is estimated, for example, that some forty thousand people in the United States are evaluated for their competency to stand trial and as many as 75 percent are determined to be incompetent. Determination of competency to stand trial is meant to ensure that a person understands the nature of the proceedings and is able to help in his or her own defense. This effort is an attempt to protect mentally disturbed people and to guarantee preservation of criminal and civil rights. But being judged incompetent to stand trial may have unfair negative consequences as well. A person may be committed for a long period of time, denied the chance to post bail, and isolated from friends and family, all without having been found guilty of a crime.

Such a miscarriage of justice was the focus of a U.S. Supreme Court ruling in 1972 in the case of *Jackson v. Indiana*. In that case, a severely retarded, brain-damaged person who could neither hear nor speak was charged with robbery but was determined incompetent to stand trial. He was committed indefinitely, which in his case probably meant for life, because it was apparent by the severity of his disorders that he would never be competent. His lawyers filed a petition to have him released on the basis of deprivation of due process—the legal checks and balances that are guaranteed to everyone, such as the right to a fair trial, the right to face accusers, the right to present evidence, the right to counsel, and so on. The U.S. Supreme Court ruled that a defendant cannot be confined indefinitely solely on the grounds of incompetency. After a reasonable time, a determination must be made as to whether the person is likely or unlikely to regain competency in the foreseeable future. If, in the hospital's opinion, the person is unlikely to do so, the hospital must either release the individual or initiate civil commitment procedures.

■ Civil Commitment

Sometimes action seems necessary when people are severely disturbed and exhibit bizarre behaviors that can pose a threat to themselves or others. Government has a long-standing precedent of *parens patriae* ("father of the country" or "power of the state"), in which it has authority to commit disturbed individuals for their own best interest. Civil commitment is the involuntary confinement of individuals judged to be a danger to themselves or others, even though they have not committed a crime. Factors relevant to civil commitment are displayed in Figure 17.2. The commitment of a person in acute distress may be viewed as a form of protective confinement and concern for the psychological and physical well-being of that person or others. Hospitalization is considered in the case of potential suicide or assault, bizarre behavior, destruction of property, and severe anxiety leading to loss of impulse control.

Involuntary hospitalization should, however, be avoided if at all possible because it has many potentially negative consequences. It may result in the lifelong social stigma associated with psychiatric hospitalization, major interruption in the person's life, losing control of his or her life and dependency on others, and loss of self-esteem and self-concept. To this we would add a possible loss or restriction of civil liberties—a point that becomes even more glaring when we consider that the person has actually committed no crime other than being a nuisance or assailing people's sensibilities. The "bag lady" (BL), described earlier, had committed no crime, although she violated many social norms. But at what point do we confine people simply because they fail to conform to our standards of "decency" or "socially appropriate" behavior?

due process legal checks and balances that are guaranteed to everyone (e.g., the right to a fair trial, the right to face accusers, the right to present evidence, the right to counsel, and so on)

civil commitment the involuntary confinement of a person judged to be a danger to himself or herself or to others, even though the person has not committed a crime

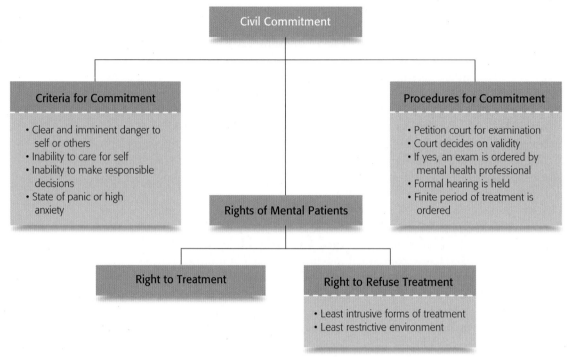

Figure 17.2

FACTORS IN THE CIVIL COMMITMENT OF A NONCONSENTING PERSON

Copyright © Cengage Learning 2013

Criteria for Commitment

States vary in the criteria used to commit a person, but there does appear to be certain general standards. It is not enough that a person is mentally ill; additional conditions need to exist before hospitalization is considered (Corey, Callanan, & Corey, 2010).

1. *The person presents a clear and imminent danger to him- or herself or others.* An example is someone who is displaying suicidal or bizarre behavior (such as walking out on a busy freeway) that places the individual in immediate danger. Threats to harm someone or behavior viewed to be assaultive or destructive are also grounds for commitment.

2. *The person is unable to care for himself or herself or does not have the social network to provide for such care.* Most civil commitments are based primarily on this criterion. The details vary, but states generally specify an inability to provide sufficient forms of the following:
   - Food (person is malnourished, food is unavailable, and person has no feasible plan to obtain it)
   - Clothing (attire is not appropriate for climate or is dirty or torn, and person has no plans for obtaining others)
   - Shelter (person has no permanent residence, insufficient protection from climatic conditions, and no logical plans for obtaining adequate housing)

3. *The person is unable to make responsible decisions about appropriate treatment and hospitalization.* As a result, there is a strong chance of deterioration.

4. *The person is in an unmanageable state of fright or panic.* Such people may believe and feel that they are on the brink of losing control.

In the past, commitments could be obtained solely on the basis of mental illness and a person's need for treatment, which was often determined arbitrarily. Increasingly, the courts have tightened up civil commitment procedures and have begun to rely more on a determination of whether the person presents a danger to him- or herself or others.

How do we determine this possibility? Many people would not consider BL a danger to herself or others. Some, however, might believe that she could be assaultive to others and injurious to herself. Disagreements among the public may be understandable, but are trained mental health professionals more accurate in their predictions? Let's turn to that question.

Assessing Dangerousness

As noted earlier, mental health professionals have difficulty predicting whether their clients will commit dangerous acts, and they often overpredict violence (Levin, 2008; Werth, Weifel, & Benjamin, 2009). The fact that civil commitments are often based on a determination of dangerousness—the person's potential for doing harm to himself or herself or to others—makes this conclusion even more disturbing. The difficulty in predicting this potential seems linked to four factors.

1. *The rarer something is, the more difficult it is to predict.* As a group, psychiatric patients are not dangerous! Although some evidence suggests that individuals suffering from severe psychotic disorders may have slightly higher rates of violent behavior (Elbogen & Johnson, 2009; Junginger, 1996), the risk is not considered a major concern. A frequent misconception shared by both the public and the courts is that mental illnesses are in and of themselves dangerous. Studies have indicated that approximately 90 percent of people suffering from mental disorders are neither violent nor dangerous (Swanson et al., 1990), and few psychotic patients are assaultive. Homicide is even more rare.

2. *Violence seems as much a function of the context in which it occurs as a function of the person's characteristics.* Although it is theoretically possible for a psychologist to accurately assess an individual's personality, we can have little idea about the situations in which people find themselves. Behavior is almost always influenced by characteristics of the situation. A person may be relatively "meek and mild" but when driving in heavy traffic experience uncontrollable road rage.

3. *The best predictor of dangerousness is probably past criminal conduct or a history of violence or aggression.* Such a record, however, is frequently ruled irrelevant or inadmissible by mental health commissions and the courts.

4. *The definition of dangerousness is itself unclear.* Most of us would agree that murder, rape, torture, and physical assaults are dangerous. But are we confining our definition to physical harm only? What about psychological abuse or even destruction of property?

Procedures in Civil Commitment

Despite the difficulties in defining dangerousness, once someone believes that a person is a threat to himself or herself or to others, civil commitment procedures may be instituted. The rationale for this action is that it (1) prevents harm to the person or to others, (2) provides appropriate treatment and care, and (3) ensures due process of law (that is, a legal hearing). In most cases, people deemed in need of protective confinement can be persuaded to *voluntarily* commit themselves to a period of hospitalization. This process is fairly straightforward, and many believe that it is the preferred one. *Involuntary* commitment occurs when the client does not consent to hospitalization.

Involuntary commitment can be a temporary emergency action or a longer period of detention that is determined at a formal hearing. Although states vary in the process and standards, all recognize that cases arise in which a person is so grossly disturbed that immediate detention is required (Bindman & Thornicroft, 2008). Because formal hearings may take a long time, delaying commitment might prove adverse to the person or to other individuals.

Formal civil commitment usually follows a similar process, regardless of the state in which it occurs. First, a concerned person, such as a family member, therapist, or family

dangerousness a person's potential for doing harm to himself or herself or to others

A Tragic Case of Failing to Predict Dangerousness

Convicted serial killer Jeffrey Dahmer killed at least seventeen men and young boys over a period of many years. Besides torturing many of his victims, Dahmer admitted to dismembering and devouring their bodies. Although Dahmer had been imprisoned in 1988 for sexual molestation, it would have been difficult to predict his degree of dangerousness. Despite an attempt to use the insanity plea, Dahmer was found guilty in 1994 and imprisoned. Another inmate subsequently killed him.

physician, petitions the court for an examination of the person. If the judge believes there is responsible cause for this action, he or she orders an examination. Second, the judge appoints two professionals with no connection to each other to examine the person. In most cases, the examiners are physicians or mental health professionals. Third, a formal hearing is held in which the examiners testify to the person's mental state and potential danger. Others, such as family members, friends, or therapists, may also testify. The person is allowed to speak on his or her own behalf and is represented by counsel. Fourth, if it is determined that the person must enter treatment, a finite period may be specified; periods of six months to one year are common. Some states, however, have indefinite periods subject to periodic review and assessment.

Protection against Involuntary Commitment

We have said that involuntary commitment can lead to a violation of civil rights. Some have even argued that criminals have more rights than the mentally ill. For example, a person accused of a crime is considered innocent until proven guilty in a court of law. Usually, he or she is incarcerated only after a jury trial, and only if a crime is committed (not if there is only the possibility or even high probability of crime). Yet a mentally ill person may be confined without a jury trial and without having committed a crime if it is thought possible that he or she might do harm to him- or herself or others. In other words, the criminal justice system will not incarcerate people because they *might* harm someone (they must already have done it), but civil commitment is based on possible future harm. It can be argued that in the former case, confinement is punishment, whereas in the latter case it is treatment (for the individual's benefit). For example, it is often argued that mentally ill people may be incapable of determining their own treatment, and that, once treated, they will be grateful for the treatment they received. If people resist hospitalization, they are thus being irrational, which is a symptom of their mental disorder.

Critics do not accept this reasoning. They point out that civil commitment is for the benefit of those initiating commitment procedures (society) and not for the individual. Even after treatment, people rarely appreciate it. These concerns have raised and heightened sensitivity toward patient welfare and rights, resulting in a trend toward restricting the powers of the state over the individual.

Rights of Mental Patients

Many people in the United States are concerned about the balance of power among the state, our mental institutions, and our citizens. The U.S. Constitution guarantees certain "inalienable rights" such as trial by jury, legal representation, and protection against self-incrimination. The mental health profession has great power, which may be used wittingly or unwittingly to abridge individual freedom. In recent decades, some courts have ruled that commitment for any purpose constitutes a major deprivation of liberty that requires due process protection.

Until 1979, the level of proof required for civil commitments varied from state to state. In a case that set a legal precedent, a Texas man claimed that he was denied due process because the jury that committed him was instructed to use a lower standard than "beyond a reasonable doubt" (more than 90 percent certainty). The appellate court agreed with the man, but when the case finally reached the Supreme Court in April 1979 (*Addington v. Texas*), the Court ruled that the state must provide only "clear and convincing evidence" (approximately 75 percent certainty) that a person is mentally ill and potentially dangerous before that person can be committed. Although these standards for confinement are higher than those advocated by most mental health organizations, this ruling nevertheless represented the first time that the Supreme Court considered any aspect of the civil commitment process.

Predicting Dangerousness: The Case of Serial Killers and Mass Murderers

CRITICAL THINKING

Seung Hui Cho (Virginia Tech shooter), Jeffrey Dahmer (killer of 17 young men), Kenneth Bianchi (Hillside Strangler), and Eric Harris and Dylan Klebold (Columbine High School killers) were all either serial killers or mass murderers. Were there signs these individuals were potentially dangerous? Jeffrey Dahmer tortured animals as a small boy and was arrested in 1988 for molesting a child. Even though his father suspected his son was dangerous, Jeffrey Dahmer was released. And there appears to be sufficient evidence to suggest that mass murderer Cho was a deeply disturbed young man who harbored great resentment and anger waiting to explode. Harris and Klebold created a Web site that seemed to foretell their proclivity toward violence. In all three situations, aberrant thoughts and behaviors appeared to go unrecognized or ignored.

Lest we be too harsh on psychologists and law enforcement officials, it is important to realize that few serial killers or mass murderers willingly share their deviant sexual or asocial fantasies. Furthermore, many of the problems in predicting whether a person will commit dangerous acts lie in (1) limited knowledge concerning the characteristics associated with violence, (2) lack of a one-to-one correspondence between danger signs and possible violence, (3) increasing knowledge that violent behavior is most often the result of many variables, and (4) recognition that incarceration—both criminal and civil—cannot occur on the basis of "potential danger" alone. Nevertheless, our limited experiences with mass murderers and serial killers have produced patterns and profiles of interest to mental health practitioners and law enforcement officials. Although similar, the profiles of mass murderers and serial killers also differ in some major ways.

Profile of Serial Killers

Serial killers are usually white males, and they often suffer from some recognized psychiatric disorder, such as sexual sadism, antisocial personality, extreme narcissism, and borderline personality disorder. Few are psychotic, and psychoses do not appear to be the cause of their compulsion to kill. Almost all, however, entertain violent sexual fantasies and have experienced traumatic sex at a young age. Their earlier years are troubled with family histories of abuse, alcoholism, and criminal activity. Dahmer, for example, was sexually molested as a youngster. Most serial killers seem to exhibit little remorse for their victims, have little incentive to change, and seem to lack a value system.

The compulsion to kill is often associated with what has been described as "morbid prognostic signs" (Schlesinger, 1989): breaking and entering for nonmonetary purposes; unprovoked assaults and mistreatment of women; a fetish for female undergarments and destruction of them; showing hatred, contempt, or fear of women; violence against animals, especially cats; sexual identity confusion; a "violent and primitive fantasy life"; and sexual inhibitions and preoccupation with rigid standards of morality (Youngstrom, 1991, p. 32).

Although we have come a long way in being able to compile a composite description of serial killers, some have challenged the accuracy of such profiles. In the 2002 Washington, D.C., sniper case, in which ten innocent people were shot (eight fatally), John Allen Muhammad and teenager Lee Boyd Malvo did not fit the descriptions profiled by experts, either. They were originally thought to be angry white men, with no military background and probably local residents. As it turned out, the snipers were African Americans, one had combat experience, and they were drifters.

Profile of Mass Murderers

Mass murderers are usually men who are socially isolated and seem to exhibit inadequate social and interpersonal skills. They have been found to be quite angry and to be filled with rage. The anger appears to be cumulative and is triggered by some type of event, usually a loss. For example, they may view the end of a job or a relationship as a catastrophic loss. Most have strong mistrust of people and entertain paranoid fantasies, such as a wide-ranging conspiracy against them.

They tend to be rootless and have few support systems such as family, friends, or religious or fraternal groups. Many researchers believe that the number of mass murders will increase as firearms proliferate in our society. Other social correlates affecting mass murders are an increasing sense of rootlessness in the country, general disenchantment, and loneliness. The more random the killings, the more disturbed, delusional, and paranoid the person is likely to be.

What criteria would you use to determine whether someone is dangerous or not? Can you identify the weaknesses or possible dangers to using this set of criteria? Can you give specific examples of cases in which they would prove problematic to apply? How does one balance applying and implementing criteria of dangerousness with the loss of civil liberties of citizens?

Due to decisions in several other cases (*Lessard v. Schmidt*, 1972, Wisconsin Federal Court; and *Dixon v. Weinberger*, 1975), states must provide the least restrictive environment for people. This means that people have a right to the least restrictive alternative to freedom that is appropriate to their condition. Only patients who cannot adequately care for themselves are confined to hospitals. Those who can function acceptably should be given alternative choices, such as boarding homes and other shelters.

Right to Treatment

One of the primary justifications for commitment is that treatment improves a person's mental condition and increases the likelihood that he or she is able to return to the community. If we confine a person involuntarily and do not provide the means for release

least restrictive environment a person's right to the least restrictive alternative to freedom that is appropriate to his or her condition (therapy), isn't this deprivation of due process? Several cases have raised this problem as a constitutional issue. Together, they have determined that mental patients who have been involuntarily committed have a right to treatment—a right to receive therapy that would improve their emotional state.

In 1966, in a lawsuit brought against St. Elizabeth's Hospital in Washington, D.C. (*Rouse v. Cameron*), the court held that (1) right to treatment is a constitutional right and (2) failure to provide treatment cannot be justified by lack of resources. In other words, a mental institution or the state could not use lack of funding facilities or labor power as reasons for not providing treatment. Although this decision represented a major advance in patient rights, the ruling provided no guidelines for what constitutes treatment.

U.S. District Court Judge Frank Johnson in the Alabama federal court finally addressed this issue in 1972. The case (*Wyatt v. Stickney*) involved a boy with mental retardation who not only was not given treatment but also was made to live in an institution that was unable to meet even minimum standards of care. Indeed, the living conditions in two of the hospital buildings resembled those found in early asylums of the eighteenth century. Less than 50 cents a day was spent on food for each patient; the toilet facilities were totally inadequate and filthy; patients were crowded in group rooms with minimal or no privacy; and personnel (one physician per two thousand patients) and patient care were practically nonexistent.

Judge Johnson not only ruled in favor of the right to treatment but also specified standards of adequate treatment, such as staff-patient ratios, therapeutic environmental conditions, and professional consensus about appropriate treatment. The court also made it clear that mental patients could not be forced to work (scrub floors, cook, serve food, wash laundry, and so on) or to engage in work-related activities aimed at maintaining the institution in which they lived. This practice, widely used in institutions, was declared unconstitutional. Moreover, patients who volunteered to perform tasks had to be paid at least the minimum wage to do them instead of merely being given token allowances or special privileges.

This landmark decision ensures treatment beyond custodial care and protection against neglect and abuse.

Another important case (tried in the U.S. District Court in Florida), *O'Connor v. Donaldson* (1975), has also had a major impact on the right-to-treatment issue. It involved Kenneth Donaldson, who at age forty-nine was committed for twenty years to the Chattahoochee State Hospital on petition by his father. He was found to be mentally ill, unable to care for himself, easily manipulated, and dangerous. Throughout his confinement, Donaldson petitioned for release, but Dr. O'Connor, the hospital superintendent, determined that the patient was too dangerous. Finally, Donaldson threatened a lawsuit and was reluctantly discharged by the hospital after fourteen years of confinement. He then sued both O'Connor and the hospital, winning an award of $20,000. The monetary award is insignificant compared with the significance of the ruling. Again, the court reaffirmed the client's right to treatment. It ruled that Donaldson did not receive appropriate treatment and said that the state cannot constitutionally confine a nondangerous person who is capable of caring for himself or herself outside of an institution or who has willing friends or family to help. Further, it said that physicians, as well as institutions, are liable for improper confinements.

One major dilemma facing the courts in all cases of court-ordered treatment is determining what constitutes treatment. Treatment can range from rest and relaxation to psychosurgery, medication, and aversion therapy. Mental health professionals believe that they are in the best position to evaluate the type and efficacy of treatment, a position supported by the case of *Youngberg v. Romeo* (1982). The court ruled that Nicholas Romeo, a boy with mental retardation, had a constitutional right to "reasonable care and safety," and it deferred judgment to the mental health professional as to what constitutes therapy.

right to treatment the concept that mental patients who have been involuntarily committed have a right to receive therapy that would improve their emotional state

Right to Refuse Treatment

Brian David Mitchell, the man who kidnapped Elizabeth Smart, refused antipsychotic drugs over a period of nine years. As you recall, he was declared mentally incompetent to stand trial, and he refused to take medication to make him competent. His attorneys, however, supported his right to refuse treatment and fought government officials on this point. It was only after a judge believed Mitchell was manipulating the system that he was judged competent in 2009.

The right to refuse treatment occasionally poses ironies. For example, a Supreme Court ruling (*Ford vs. Wainwright*) concluded that the government cannot execute an incompetent convict. Thus it would seem ironic for any prisoner to agree to medication only to be executed. Some courts have ordered prisoners to take medication on the likelihood that they will improve. In June 2003, however, the Supreme Court placed strict limits on the ability to medicate mentally ill defendants forcibly to make them competent to stand trial. Such actions must be, according to the court, in the "best interest of the defendant." What this means will have to be played out in the future.

Although it may be easy for us to surmise the reason for Mitchell's attorneys refusing treatment to make him better, does it make sense for others? Patients frequently refuse medical treatment on religious grounds or because the treatment would only prolong a terminal illness. In many cases, physicians are inclined to honor such refusals, especially if they seem to be based on reasonable grounds. But should mental patients have a right to refuse treatment? At first glance, it may appear illogical. After all, why commit patients for treatment and then allow them to refuse it? Furthermore, isn't it possible that mental patients may be incapable of deciding what is best for themselves? For example, a man with a paranoid delusion may refuse treatment because he believes the hospital staff is plotting against him. If he is allowed to refuse medication or other forms of therapy, his condition may deteriorate more. The result is that the client may become even more dangerous or incapable of caring for himself outside of hospital confinement.

Did You Know?

In a 2010 decision, the U.S. Supreme Court ruled that certain sex offenders can be civilly committed and confined **even after finishing their prison sentence**. The law allows the government to detain prisoners who have engaged in sexually violent conduct, suffered from a mental illness, and have difficulty controlling themselves. The ruling is believed by some to have dangerous civil liberties implications and that it is unconstitutional (Liptak, 2010).

AP Images

Job Training for the Mentally Challenged

Increasingly, it is recognized that the mentally challenged or those suffering from mental disorders can be helped if they are taught functional skills in self-care and those related to employment. Here we see such a program in action, in which basic skills such as cooking, grooming, and conversation starters are taught.

Proponents of the right to refuse treatment argue, however, that many forms of treatment, such as medication or electroconvulsive therapy (ECT), may have long term side effects, as discussed in earlier chapters. They also point out that involuntary treatment is generally much less effective than treatment accepted voluntarily. People forced into treatment seem to resist it, thereby nullifying the potentially beneficial effects.

The case of *Rennie v. Klein* (1978) involved several state hospitals in New Jersey that were forcibly medicating patients in nonemergency situations. The court ruled that people have a constitutional right to refuse treatment (psychotropic medication) and to be given due process. In another related case, *Rogers v. Okin* (1979), a Massachusetts court supported these guidelines. Both cases made the point that psychotropic medication was often used only to control behavior or as a substitute for treatment. Further, the decisions noted that drugs might actually inhibit recovery.

In these cases, the courts supported the right to refuse treatment under certain conditions and extended the least restrictive alternative principle to include *least intrusive forms of treatment*. Generally, psychotherapy is considered less intrusive than somatic or physical therapies (e.g., ECT and medication). Although this compromise may appear reasonable, other problems present themselves. First, how do we define *intrusive treatment*? Are insight therapies as intrusive as behavioral techniques (punishment and aversion procedures)? Second, if patients are allowed to refuse certain forms of treatment and if the hospital does not have alternatives for them, can clients sue the institution? These questions remain unanswered.

▉ Deinstitutionalization

Deinstitutionalization is the shifting of responsibility for the care of mental patients from large central institutions to agencies within local communities. When originally formulated in the 1960s and 1970s, the concept excited many mental health professionals. Since its inception, the mental hospital population of patients has dropped 75 percent, the number of state-run mental hospitals has declined dramatically, and there has been a 75 percent decrease in the average daily number of committed patients (Geller, 2006; Lamb & Weinberger, 2005). The impetus behind deinstitutionalization came from several quarters.

First, there was (and still is) a feeling that large hospitals provide mainly custodial care, that they produce little benefit for the patient, and that they may even impede improvement. Court cases discussed earlier (*Wyatt v. Stickney* and *O'Connor v. Donaldson*) exposed the fact that many mental hospitals are no better than "warehouses for the insane." Institutionalization was accused of fostering dependency, promoting helplessness, and lowering self-sufficiency in patients. The longer patients were hospitalized, the more likely they were to remain hospitalized, even if they had improved. Further, symptoms such as flat affect and nonresponsiveness, which were thought to be clinical signs of schizophrenia, may actually result from hospitalization.

Second, the issue of patient rights was receiving increased attention. Mental health professionals became very concerned about keeping patients confined against their will and began to discharge patients whenever they approached minimal competencies. It was believed that mainstreaming—integrating mental patients as soon as possible back into the community—could be accomplished by providing local outpatient or transitory services (such as board-and-care facilities, halfway houses, and churches). In addition, advances in tranquilizers and other drug treatment techniques made it possible to medicate patients, which made them manageable once discharged.

Third, insufficient funds for state hospitals almost forced these institutions to release patients back into communities. Overcrowded conditions made mental health administrators view the movement favorably; state legislative branches encouraged the trend, especially because it reduced state costs and funding.

What has been the impact of deinstitutionalization on patients? Its critics believe that deinstitutionalization is a policy that allows states to relinquish their responsibility to care for patients unable to care for themselves. There are alarming indications that

deinstitutionalization   the shifting of responsibility for the care of mental patients from large central institutions to agencies within local communities

mainstreaming   integrating mental patients as soon as possible back into the community

© Gideon Mendel/Corbis

The Downside of Deinstitutionalization

Homelessness has become one of the great social problems of urban communities. Many believe that deinstitutionalization has contributed to the problem, although it is not clear what proportion of homeless people are mentally ill who were previously institutionalized. Scenes such as this one, however, are becoming all too common in large urban areas.

deinstitutionalization has been responsible for placing or "dumping" on the streets many former patients who should have remained institutionalized (Rosenberg & Rosenberg, 2006). Critics believe that the "bag lady" (BL) of Oakland, California, is an example of the human cost and tragedy of such a policy. Most of these people appear severely disabled, have difficulty coping with daily living, suffer from schizophrenia, and are alcoholic. It appears that millions of mentally ill individuals have joined the ranks of the homeless and that existing programs are woefully fragmented and inadequate in delivering needed services.

Thus it is becoming apparent that many mentally ill people are not receiving treatment. Many live on the streets where conditions can be cruel and harsh, and where they are prone to violent victimization. Others live in nursing homes, board-and-care homes, or group residences. The quality of care in many of these places is marginal, forcing continuing and periodic rehospitalization of their residents. It is estimated that 30 to 70 percent of the homeless population suffers from a mental disorder (Cougnard et al., 2006; Mojtabai, 2005).

Much of the problem with deinstitutionalization appears to be the community's lack of preparation and resources to care for people with chronic mental illness. Many patients lack family or friends who can help them make the transition back into the community; many state hospitals do not provide patients with adequate skills training; many discharged patients have difficulty finding jobs; many find substandard housing that is worse than the institutions from which they came; many are not adequately monitored and receive no psychiatric treatment; and many become homeless.

It is difficult to estimate how many discharged mental patients have been added to the burgeoning ranks of the homeless. We do know that homelessness in the United States, especially in large, urban areas, is increasing at an alarming pace. Certainly, it is not difficult to see the number of people who live in transport terminals, parks, flophouses, homeless shelters, cars, and storefronts. It is hard to determine how many of these homeless people were deinstitutionalized before adequate support services were present in a community. We do know, however, that the homeless have significantly poorer psychological adjustment and higher arrests and conviction records (U.S. Department of Health and Human Services, 2003). The solution, although complex, probably does not call for a return to the old institutions of the 1950s but rather for the provision of more and better community-based treatment facilities and alternatives.

For patients involved in alternative community programs, the picture appears somewhat more positive. A recent study concluded that programs providing permanent housing, special care and concerned community treatment can reduce homelessness and improve well-being (Nelson et al., 2007; Padgett et al., 2006). These special programs are few, however, and much remains to be done if deinstitutionalized patients are to be provided with the best supportive treatment.

■ The Therapist-Client Relationship

The therapist-client relationship involves a number of legal, moral, and ethical issues. Three primary concerns are issues of confidentiality and privileged communication; the therapist's duty to warn others of a risk posed by a dangerous client; and the therapist's obligation to avoid sexual intimacies with clients.

Confidentiality and Privileged Communication

Basic to the therapist-patient relationship is the premise that therapy involves a deeply personal association in which clients have a right to expect that whatever they say is kept private. Therapists believe that genuine therapy cannot occur unless clients trust their therapists and believe that they will not divulge confidential communications. Without this guarantee, clients may not be completely open with their thoughts and may thereby lose the benefits of therapy.

Confidentiality is an ethical standard that protects clients from disclosure of information without their consent. The importance of confidentiality is also shared by the public; in one study it was found that 74 percent of respondents thought everything told to a therapist should be confidential; indeed, 69 percent believed that whatever they discussed was never disclosed (Miller & Thelen, 1986). Confidentiality, however, is an ethical, not a legal, obligation. Privileged communication, a narrower legal concept, protects privacy and prevents the disclosure of confidential communications without a client's permission (Corey, Callahan, & Corey, 2010). An important part of this concept is that the "holder of the privilege" is the client, not the therapist. In other words, if a client waives this privilege, the therapist has no grounds for withholding information. Our society recognizes how important certain confidential relationships are and protects them by law. These relationships are the husband-wife, attorney-client, pastor-congregant, and therapist-client relationships. Psychiatric practices are regulated in all fifty states and the District of Columbia, and most have privileged-communication statutes.

Exemptions from Privileged Communication

Although states vary considerably, all states recognize certain situations in which communications can be divulged (Brown & Srebalus, 2003). Corey and associates (Corey & Corey, 2010; Corey, Callahan, & Corey, 2010) summarized these conditions:

1. In situations that deal with civil or criminal commitment or competency to stand trial, the client's right to privilege can be waived.
2. Disclosure can also be made when a client sees a therapist and introduces his or her mental condition as a claim or defense in a civil action.
3. When the client is younger than sixteen years of age or is a dependent elderly person and information leads the therapist to believe that the individual

confidentiality   an ethical standard that protects clients from disclosure of information without their consent; an ethical obligation of the therapist

privileged communication   a therapist's legal obligation to protect a client's privacy and to prevent the disclosure of confidential communications without a client's permission

"Doc, I Murdered Someone": Client Disclosures of Violence to Therapists

CONTROVERSY

Basic to a therapeutic relationship is the belief that whatever a client discloses is kept private. However, confidentiality and privilege is not absolute. Most of these exemptions are mandated by law and include child abuse, neglect of minors, and abuse of the elderly and certain classes of "vulnerable" adults (Fisher, 2009). The *Tarasoff* ruling also makes it clear that when clients disclose a potential to harm to identifiable third parties, therapists have a legal obligation to take actions to ward off the danger. The duty-to-warn principle applies to *future threats of harm*. But, what are the legal obligations of therapists who hear from clients that they have committed a *past crime*? What if clients disclose they have assaulted, raped, or even killed someone?

These questions deal with not only legal issues, but moral and ethical ones as well. It may be shocking to many students to know that the law is not clear on this matter. The prevailing consensus is that mental health professionals are not legally mandated to breach confidentiality when clients inform them that they have committed past crimes (Handelsman et al., 2001) and that doing so would create liability for them.

But how often do therapists experience confessions from their clients about past criminal conduct? The answer is that *although not common, it is not infrequent* as well. In a recently conducted survey (Walfish, Barnett, Marlyere, & Zielke, 2010), the incidents of clients informing their therapists of committing violent crimes were reported. It is important to note that these crimes were never reported elsewhere. Out of a sample of 162 doctoral-level psychologists, mostly full-time psychotherapists, the following statistics were uncovered:

- Confessions of murder: 13 percent
- Sexual assaults/rape: 33 percent
- Physical assaults: 69 percent

In therapy, clients are likely to reveal very intimate secrets about their past feelings, thoughts, and actions. The likelihood that something shocking, distasteful, or even frightening may be disclosed is not rare. These researchers believe it important that therapists be prepared to respond in an appropriate legal, moral, and therapeutic manner.

For Further Consideration:

1. Shouldn't therapists be required to report a past crime like murder?
2. Can the *Tarasoff* ruling be interpreted to allow therapists latitude in reporting past crimes? How?
3. If you were the therapist and heard a murder confession, how do you think it would affect you and the therapeutic relationship? Would you want to continue working with the client? What would you do and why?

---

has been a victim of crime (e.g., incest, rape, or child and elder abuse), the therapist must provide that information to the appropriate protective services agency.

4. When the therapist has reason to believe that a client presents a danger to himself or herself (possible injury or suicide) or may potentially harm someone else, the therapist must act to ward off the danger.

Privilege in communication is not absolute. Rather, it strikes a delicate balance between the individual's right to privacy and the public's need to know certain information. Problems arise when we try to determine what the balance should be and how important various events and facts are in individual cases.

The Duty-to-Warn Principle

At the beginning of the chapter, we briefly described the case of Prosenjit Poddar (*Tarasoff v. Board of Regents of the University of California*, 1976), a graduate student who killed Tatiana Tarasoff after notifying his therapist that he intended to take her life. Before the homicide, the therapist had decided that Poddar was dangerous and likely to carry out the threat, so he had notified the director of the psychiatric clinic that Poddar was dangerous. He also informed the campus police, hoping that they would detain the student. Surely the therapist had done all that could be reasonably expected. Not so, ruled the California Supreme Court. In the *Tarasoff* ruling, the court stated that when a therapist determines, according to the standards of the mental health profession, that a patient presents a serious danger to another, the therapist is obligated to warn the *intended victim*. The court went on to say that protective privilege ends where public peril begins. In general, courts have ruled that therapists have a responsibility to protect the public from dangerous acts of violent clients and have held therapists accountable for (1) failing to diagnose or predict dangerousness, (2) failing to warn potential victims, (3) failing to commit dangerous individuals, and (4) prematurely discharging dangerous clients from a hospital.

***Tarasoff* ruling** often referred to as the "duty-to-warn" principle; obligates mental health professionals to break confidentiality when their clients pose clear and imminent danger to another person

A Duty to Warn

Tatiana Tarasoff, a college student, was stabbed to death in 1969 by Prosenjit Poddar, a graduate student at the University of California, Berkeley. Although Poddar's therapist notified the university that he thought Poddar was dangerous, the California Supreme Court ruled that the therapist should have warned the victim as well.

Criticism of the Duty-to-Warn Principle

The *Tarasoff* ruling seems to place the therapist in the unenviable role of being a double agent (Bednar et al., 1991). Therapists have an ethical and legal obligation to their clients, but they also have legal obligations to society. Not only can these dual obligations conflict with one another, but they can also be quite ambiguous. Many situations exist in which state courts must rule to clarify the implications and uncertainties of the "duty-to-warn" rule.

When the ruling came out, Siegel (1979) loudly criticized the *Tarasoff* decision, stating that the outcome was a hollow victory for individual parties, but it was devastating for the mental health professions. He reasoned that if confidentiality had been an absolute policy, if had been applied to all situations, Poddar might have been kept in treatment, thus ultimately saving Tarasoff's life. Other mental health professionals have echoed this theme in one form or another (Levin, 2008; Werth, Weifel, & Benjamin, 2009). Hostile clients with pent-up feelings and emotions may be less likely to act out or become violent when allowed to vent their thoughts. The irony, according to critics, is that the duty-to-warn principle may actually be counterproductive to its intent to protect the potential victim.

The Family Educational Rights and Privacy Act and Confidentiality of College Student Life

Elizabeth Shin, a nineteen-year-old sophomore at the Massachusetts Institute of Technology (MIT), was believed to have set fire to herself and died on April 14, 2000. Two years after the death, her parents filed a $27 million wrongful death suit against MIT, accusing them of breach of contract, medical malpractice, and negligence on the part of university psychiatrists, student life staff, and campus police. The Shins contend that MIT knew their daughter had made suicide attempts, cut herself frequently, and suffered from depression but failed to inform them of her deteriorating mental state. Had they done so, they assert, Elizabeth Shin might still be alive today. They further claim that MIT broke the "business contract" with the family, which they say is implied in their daughter's college enrollment at MIT.

Not unlike the *Tarasoff* case, the outcome of the Shins' lawsuit had the power to set legal precedent and potentially radically change the Family Educational Rights and Privacy Act that prevents colleges and universities from disclosing any personal information about students, even to their parents. Colleges and universities generally assume that students are adults, and if they were required to report every problem to parents, they would infantilize students by sending the wrong message. Students may also be less inclined to share personal information with school officials if they knew that such information may be reported back to their parents. Yet institutions of higher education are very aware that they are grappling to minister to an undergraduate population that seems to require more mental health care than ever before. One national study of counseling center client problems over thirteen years reveals that students are entering college with more severe problems than in the past (Benton et al., 2003). The lawsuit never tested the issue of student confidentiality and privacy because the case was settled out of court in 2005 for an undisclosed sum and an agreement by MIT that the Shins' daughter died by accident rather than suicide to protect both parties involved.

Sexual Relationships with Clients

Therapeutic practice can also be legally regulated by civil lawsuits brought by clients against their therapists for professional malpractice. To be successful, however, these lawsuits must satisfy four conditions: (1) the plaintiff must have been involved in a professional therapeutic relationship with the therapist, (2) there must have been negligence in the care of the client, (3) demonstrable harm must have occurred, and (4) there must be a cause-effect relationship between the negligence and harm. If these four conditions are demonstrated, a jury may find the therapist guilty and award the plaintiff monetary damages. Although malpractice claims can be brought in any number of situations, by far the most common type involves sexual intimacies with a current or former client (Corey, Callanan, & Corey, 2010; Pope & Vasquez, 2007).

Traditionally, mental health practitioners have emphasized the importance of separating their personal and professional lives. They reasoned that therapists need to be objective and removed from their clients because becoming emotionally involved with them was nontherapeutic. A therapist in a personal relationship with a client may be less confrontative, may fulfill his or her own needs at the expense of the client's, and may unintentionally exploit the client because of his or her position (Corey & Corey, 2010). Although some people question the belief that a social or personal relationship is necessarily antitherapeutic, matters of personal relations with clients, especially those dealing with erotic and sexual intimacies, are receiving increasing attention.

Sexual misconduct of therapists is considered to be one of the most serious of all ethical violations. Indeed, virtually all professional organizations condemn sexual intimacies in the therapist-client relationship. The American Psychological Association (2010) states explicitly, "Psychologists do not engage in sexual intimacies with current therapy clients/patients."

But how do practitioners view sexual intimacies with clients? How often do such intimacies really occur? Who does what to whom? Being sexually attracted to a client or engaging in sexual fantasy about one is not uncommon among therapists (Pope & Vasquez, 2007). Furthermore, complaints to state licensing boards about sexual misconduct by therapists have increased significantly. Although these are indisputable facts, the vast majority of psychologists are able to control their sexual feelings and to behave in a professional manner.

■ Cultural Competence and the Mental Health Profession

Many mental health professionals assert that the prevailing concepts of mental health and mental disorders are culture bound and that contemporary theories of therapy are based on values specific to a middle class, white, highly individualistic, and ethnocentric population

(American Psychological Association, 2003; Sue & Sue, 2008a). There are strong concerns that the services offered to culturally different clients are frequently antagonistic or inappropriate to their life experiences and that these services not only lack sensitivity and understanding but may also be oppressive and discriminating toward minority populations. These assertions about counseling and psychotherapy are echoed by other marginalized groups (women, gays/lesbians, disabled, etc.) in our society as well.

The American Psychological Association (2010), in its most recent Ethical Principles of Psychologists and Code of Conduct, has made it clear that working with culturally different clients is unethical unless the mental health professional has adequate training and expertise in multicultural psychology. Such a position has resulted in the development of "Guidelines for Providers of Psychological Services to Ethnic, Linguistic, and Culturally Diverse Populations" (American Psychological Association, 1993) and "Guidelines for Psychotherapy with Lesbian, Gay, and Bisexual Clients" (American Psychological Association, 2000).

In a historic move by the American Psychological Association (2003), the Council of Representatives passed "Guidelines on Multicultural Education, Training, Research,

Matthew H. Starling Photography

Changing Demographics and Therapy

The Teaching Tolerance program, founded in 1991 by the Southern Poverty Law Center, supports the efforts of K–12 teachers and other educators to promote respect for differences and appreciation of diversity. This photo was taken at the Mix It Up at Lunch Day program, which encourages students to step outside their social boundaries through various activities.

Practice, and Organizational Change for Psychologists." This document has now become official policy of the American Psychological Association and extends to nearly every realm of psychological practice. One of the most comprehensive guidelines on racial/ethnic minorities to be proposed, the document makes it clear that service providers need to become aware of how their own culture, life experiences, attitudes, values, and biases have influenced them. It also emphasizes the importance of cultural and environmental factors in diagnosis and treatment, and it insists that therapists respect and consider using traditional healing approaches intrinsic to a client's culture. Finally, it suggests that therapists learn more about cultural issues and seek consultation when confronted with culture-specific problems.

Inherent in all these documents is their call for "cultural competence" and the conclusion that psychotherapy may represent biased, discriminatory, and unethical treatment if the racial/cultural backgrounds of clients are ignored and if the therapist does not possess adequate training in working with a culturally diverse population. From this perspective, mental health professionals have a moral and professional responsibility to become culturally competent if they work with people who differ from them in terms of race, culture, ethnicity, gender, sexual orientation, and so forth. To become culturally competent requires mental health professionals to strive toward attaining three goals (Sue & Sue, 2008a): (1) to become aware of and deal with the biases, stereotypes, and assumptions that affect their practice; (2) to become aware of the culturally different client's values and worldview; and (3) to develop appropriate intervention strategies that take into account the social, cultural, historical, and environmental influences on culturally different clients. As we have seen, the increased awareness of multicultural influences in our understanding of abnormal psychology is reflected in the *Diagnostic and Statistical Manual of Mental Disorders* of the American Psychiatric Association (DSM-IV-TR; American Psychiatric Association, 2000a) and in the proposed DSM-5.

Summary

1. **What are the criteria used to judge insanity, and what is the difference between being insane and being incompetent to stand trial?**

   - Insanity is a legal concept. Historically, several standards have been used.
   - The M'Naghten Rule holds that people can be acquitted of a crime if it can be shown that their reasoning was so defective that they were unaware of their actions or, if aware of their actions, were unable to comprehend the wrongness of them. The irresistible impulse test holds that people are innocent if they are unable to control their behavior. The *Durham* decision acquits people if their criminal actions were products of mental disease or defects. The American Law Institute guidelines state that people are not responsible for a crime

   if they lack substantial capacity to appreciate the criminality of their conduct or to conform their conduct to the requirements of the law.
   - The phrase "competency to stand trial" refers to defendants' mental state at the time they are being examined. It is a separate issue from criminal responsibility, which refers to past behavior at the time of the offense. Accused people are considered incompetent if they have difficulty understanding the trial proceedings or cannot rationally consult with attorneys in their defense. Although competency to stand trial is important in ensuring fair trials, being judged incompetent can have negative consequences, such as unfair and prolonged denial of civil liberties.

2. Under what conditions can a person be involuntarily committed to a mental institution?

- People who have committed no crime can be confined against their will if it can be shown that (1) they present a clear and imminent danger to themselves or others, (2) they are unable to care for themselves, (3) they are unable to make responsible decisions about appropriate treatment and hospitalization, and (4) they are in an unmanageable state of fright or panic.
- Courts have tightened criteria and rely more than ever on the concept of dangerousness. Mental health professionals have great difficulty in predicting dangerousness because dangerous acts depend as much on social situations as on personal attributes and because the definition is unclear.

3. What rights do mental patients have with respect to treatment and care issues?

- Concern with patients' rights has become an issue because many practices and procedures seem to violate constitutional guarantees. As a result, court rulings have established several important precedents. Among these are the right to treatment and the right to refuse treatment.

4. What is deinstitutionalization?

- During the 1960s and 1970s, the policy of deinstitutionalization became popular: the shifting of responsibility for the care of mental patients from large central institutions to agencies within the local community. Deinstitutionalization was considered a promising answer to the "least restrictive environment" ruling and to monetary problems experienced by state governments. Critics, however, have accused the states of "dumping" former patients and avoiding their responsibilities under the guise of mental health innovations.

5. What legal and ethical issues govern the therapist-client relationship?

- Most mental health professionals believe that confidentiality is crucial to the therapist-client relationship. Exceptions to this privilege include situations that involve (1) civil or criminal commitment and competency to stand trial, (2) a client's initiation of a lawsuit for malpractice or a civil action in which the client's mental condition is introduced, (3) the belief that child or elder abuse has occurred, (4) a criminal action, or (5) the danger a client poses to himself or herself or to others.
- Although psychologists have always known that privileged communication is not an absolute right, the *Tarasoff* decision makes therapists responsible for warning a potential victim to avoid liability.
- Sexual misconduct by therapists is considered to be one of the most serious of all ethical violations by virtually all professional organizations.

6. What is cultural competence in the mental health profession?

- Major demographic changes are forcing mental health professionals to consider culture, ethnicity, gender, and socioeconomic status as powerful variables in (1) the manifestation of mental disorders and (2) the need to provide culturally appropriate intervention strategies for minority groups. Increasingly, mental health organizations are taking the position that it is unethical to treat members of marginalized groups without adequate training and expertise in multicultural psychology.

Media Resources

Psychology CourseMate   Access an interactive eBook; chapter-specific interactive learning tools, including flash cards, quizzes, videos; and more in your Psychology CourseMate, accessed through CengageBrain.com.

CENGAGENOW

CengageNow   CengageNOW is an easy-to-use online resource that helps you study in less time to get the grade you want—NOW. If your textbook does not include an access code card, go to CengageBrain.com to gain access.

CENGAGEbrain.com

CengageBrain   More than just an interactive study guide, WebTutor is an anytime, anywhere customized learning solution with an eBook, keeping you connected to your textbook, instructor, and classmates. Purchase the access chosen by your instructor at CengageBrain.com.

Glossary

abnormal behavior a behavioral or psychological syndrome or pattern that reflects an underlying psychobiological dysfunction, that is associated with distress or disability, and that is not merely an expectable response to common stressors or losses

abnormal psychology the scientific study whose objectives are to describe, explain, predict, and modify behaviors that are considered strange or unusual

acute stress disorder (ASD) disorder characterized by anxiety and dissociative symptoms that occur within one month after exposure to a traumatic stressor

addiction compulsive drug-seeking behavior and a loss of control over drug use

adulterants substances used to increase the bulk of illegal drugs before sale

agoraphobia an intense fear of being in public places where escape or help may not be readily available

alcohol poisoning toxic effects resulting from rapidly consuming alcohol or ingesting a large quantity of alcohol; can result in impaired breathing, coma, and death

Alzheimer's disease (AD) neurodegenerative disorder involving memory loss and other declines in cognitive and adaptive functioning

American Law Institute (ALI) Model Penal Code a test of legal insanity that combines both cognitive criteria (diminished capacity) and motivational criteria (specific intent); its purpose is to give jurors increased latitude in determining the sanity of the accused

analogue study an investigation that attempts to replicate or simulate, under controlled conditions, a situation that occurs in real life

anhedonia loss of the capacity to derive pleasure from normally pleasant experiences

anorexia nervosa an eating disorder characterized by low body weight, an intense fear of becoming obese, and body image distortion

antisocial/psychopathic type a personality disorder characterized by a failure to conform to social and legal codes, a lack of anxiety and guilt, and irresponsible behaviors

anxiety a fundamental human emotion that produces bodily reactions that prepare us for "fight or flight;" anxiety is anticipatory; the dreaded event or situation has not yet occurred

anxiety disorder condition involving fear or anxiety symptoms that interfere with an individual's day-to-day functioning

anxiolytics medications that reduce anxiety

anxious distress symptoms of motor tension, difficulty relaxing, pervasive worries, or feelings that something catastrophic will occur

assessment the process of gathering information and drawing conclusions about the traits, skills, abilities, emotional functioning, and psychological problems of an individual

asthma chronic inflammatory disease of the airways in the lungs

attention-deficit/hyperactivity disorder (ADHD) disorder characterized by inattention and/or hyperactivity and impulsivity

attenuated psychosis syndrome condition involving early signs of delusions, hallucination, or disorganized speech; for this diagnosis, reality testing must be intact and the symptoms must be distressing or disabling and have emerged or gotten progressively worse over the previous year

autism spectrum disorder (ASD) disorder characterized by impairment in social communication and restricted, stereotyped interests and activities

avoidant personality type a personality disorder characterized by fear of rejection and humiliation and reluctance to enter into social relationships

axon extension on the cell body that sends signals to neurons

base rate the rate of natural occurrence of a phenomenon in the population studied

behavioral models models of psychopathology concerned with the role of learning in abnormal behavior

behaviorism psychological perspective that stresses the importance of learning and behavior in explanations of normal and abnormal development

binge drinking episodic intake of five or more alcoholic beverages for men or four or more drinks for women

binge-eating disorder (BED) an eating disorder that involves the consumption of large amounts of food over a short period of time, an accompanying feeling of loss of control, and distress over the excess eating; inappropriate compensatory behavior following eating are not typically seen with this disorder

biofeedback training a physiological and behavioral approach in which an individual receives information regarding particular autonomic functions and is rewarded for influencing those functions in a desired direction

biological (organic) view the belief that mental disorders have a physical or physiological basis

biopsychosocial model a model in which mental disorders are viewed as the result of an interaction of biological, psychological, and social factors

body mass index (BMI) an estimate of body fat calculated on the basis of a person's height and weight

borderline type a personality disorder characterized by intense fluctuations in mood, self-image, and interpersonal relationships

brain pathology a dysfunction or disease of the brain

brief psychotic disorder psychotic episodes with a duration of at least one day but less than one month

bulimia nervosa an eating disorder characterized by recurrent episodes of the rapid consumption of large quantities of food and a sense of loss of control over eating that is combined with purging (vomiting, use of laxatives, diuretics, or enemas), and/or excessive exercise or fasting in an attempt to compensate for binges

case study an intensive study of one individual that relies on clinical data, such as observations, psychological tests, and historical and biographical information

catatonia a condition characterized by marked disturbance in motor activity—either extreme excitement or motoric immobility

cathartic method a therapeutic use of verbal expression to release pent-up emotional conflicts

child psychopathology the emotional and behavioral manifestation of psychological disorders in children and adolescents

chronic traumatic encephalopathy (CTE) progressive, degenerative condition involving brain damage from multiple episodes of head trauma

civil commitment the involuntary confinement of a person judged to be a danger to himself or herself or to others, even though the person has not committed a crime

classical conditioning a process in which responses to new stimuli are learned through association

cluster headache excruciating stabbing or burning sensations located in the eye or cheek

cognitive models models based on the assumption that conscious thought mediates an individual's emotional state and/or behavior in response to a stimulus

cognitive restructuring cognitive strategy that attempts to alter unrealistic thoughts that are believed to be responsible for phobias

cognitive symptoms symptoms associated with problems with attention, memory, and difficulty in developing a plan of action

comorbidity co-occurrence of different disorders

competency to stand trial a judgment that a defendant has a factual and rational understanding of the proceedings and can rationally consult with counsel in presenting his or her own defense; refers to the defendant's mental state at the time of the psychiatric examination

complex somatic symptom disorder (CSSD) with pain features reports of severe or lingering pain that appears to have no physical basis

complex somatic symptom disorder (CSSD) with somatization features chronic complaints of specific bodily symptoms that have no physical basis

complex somatic symptom disorders a group of disorders involving physical symptoms or complaints that have no physiological basis; believed to occur due to an underlying psychological conflict or need

compulsion the need to perform acts or to dwell on thoughts to reduce anxiety

compulsive relapse automatic resumption of drug-seeking behavior in response to stressors or substance-related cues

computerized axial tomography (CT or CAT) brain images are produced from multiple, cross-sectional x-rays of the brain

concordance rate the likelihood that both members of a twin pair show the same characteristic

conditioned response (CR) in classical conditioning, a learned response to a previously neutral stimulus that has acquired some of the properties of another stimulus with which it has been paired

conditioned stimulus (CS) in classical conditioning, a previously neutral stimulus that has acquired some of the properties of another stimulus with which it has been paired

confidentiality an ethical standard that protects clients from disclosure of information without their consent; an ethical obligation of the therapist

coronary heart disease (CHD) the narrowing of cardiac arteries, resulting in the restriction or partial blockage of the flow of blood and oxygen to the heart

correlation the extent to which variations in one variable are accompanied by increases or decreases in a second variable

couples therapy a treatment aimed at helping couples understand and clarify their communications, role relationships, unfulfilled needs, and unrealistic or unmet expectations

criminal commitment incarceration of an individual for having committed a crime

cultural relativism the belief that lifestyles, cultural values, and worldviews affect the expression and determination of behavior

cultural universality the assumption that a fixed set of mental disorders exists whose obvious manifestations cut across cultures

dangerousness a person's potential for doing harm to himself or herself or to others

defense mechanism in psychoanalytic theory, an ego-protection strategy that shelters the individual from anxiety, operates unconsciously, and distorts reality

deficit model early attempt to explain differences in minority groups that contends that differences are the result of "cultural deprivation"

deinstitutionalization the shifting of responsibility for the care of mental patients from large central institutions to agencies within local communities

delayed ejaculation (male orgasmic disorder) persistent delay or inability to achieve an orgasm after the excitement phase has been reached and sexual activity has been adequate in focus, intensity, and duration; usually restricted to an inability to ejaculate within the vagina; also known as *inhibited male orgasm*

delirium an acute state of confusion involving diminished awareness, disorientation, and impaired attentional skills

delirium tremens life-threatening withdrawal symptom that can result from chronic alcohol use

delusional disorder involves persistent, nonbizarre delusions without other unusual or odd behaviors; tactile and olfactory hallucinations related to the delusional theme may be present

delusions false beliefs that are firmly and consistently held despite disconfirming evidence or logic

dementia pervasive deterioration in cognition and independent functioning

dendrite short rootlike structure on the cell body whose function is to receive signals from other neurons

dependent variable a variable that is expected to change when an independent variable is manipulated in a psychological experiment

depersonalization disorder disorder characterized by feelings of unreality concerning the self and the environment

depressant substance that causes a slowing of responses and generalized depression of the central nervous system

depression a mood state characterized by sadness or despair, feelings of futility and worthlessness, and withdrawal from others

detoxification alcohol or drug treatment phase during which the body is purged of intoxicating substances

diathesis-stress theory theory that holds that people do not inherit a particular abnormality but rather a *predisposition to develop illness* (diathesis) and that certain environmental forces, called *stressors*, may activate the predisposition, resulting in a disorder

dissociative amnesia partial or total loss of important personal information due to psychological factors; may involve failure to recall all events that occurred during the period of time involving a highly painful or disturbing event

dissociative anesthetic substance that produces a dream-like detachment

dissociative disorders a group of disorders, including dissociative amnesia, dissociative fugue, dissociative identity disorder, and depersonalization disorder, all of which involve some sort of dissociation, or separation, of a part of the person's consciousness, memory, or identity

dissociative fugue confusion over personal identity, often involving complete loss of memory of one's entire life, unexpected travel to a new location, and the partial or complete assumption of a new identity

dissociative identity disorder (DID) a condition in which two or more relatively independent personality states appear to exist in one person or an experience of possession; also known as multiple-personality disorder

dopamine hypothesis the suggestion that schizophrenia may result from excess dopamine activity at certain synaptic sites

due process legal checks and balances that are guaranteed to everyone (e.g., the right to a fair trial, the right to face accusers, the right to present evidence, the right to counsel, and so on)

Durham standard a test of legal insanity known as the products test—an accused person is not responsible if the unlawful act was the product of mental disease or defect

dyspareunia recurrent or persistent pain in the genitals before, during, or after sexual intercourse

early ejaculation ejaculation with minimal sexual stimulation before, during, or shortly after penetration

eating conditions not elsewhere classified a category for individuals with problematic eating patterns who do not fully meet the criteria for one of the eating disorders

electroencephalograph (EEG) measures the firing of neurons via electrodes placed on the scalp

encephalitis medical condition involving brain inflammation

encopresis elimination disorder involving defecation

endophenotypes measurable characteristics (neurochemical, endocrinological, neuroanatomical, cognitive, or neuropsychological) that can give clues regarding the specific genes involved in disorders

enuresis elimination disorder involving voiding of urine

epidemiological research the study of the rate and distribution of mental disorders in a population

epigenetics reciprocal gene-environment interactions that modify the expression of the genome

epilepsy disorder characterized by seizures and uncontrolled electrical discharge from brain cells

erectile disorder (ED) an inability to attain or maintain an erection sufficient for sexual intercourse and/or psychological arousal during sexual activity

etiology cause of a disorder

exhibitionistic disorder characterized by urges, acts, or fantasies about the exposure of one's genitals to strangers

existential approach a set of attitudes that has many commonalities with humanism but is less optimistic, focusing (1) on human alienation in an increasingly technological and impersonal world, (2) on the individual in the context of the human condition, and (3) on responsibility to others, as well as to oneself

exorcism treatment method used by groups including the early Greeks, Chinese, Hebrews, and Egyptians in which prayers, noises, emetics, flogging, and starvation were used to cast evil spirits out of an afflicted person's body

experiment a technique of scientific inquiry in which a prediction—an experimental hypothesis—is made about two variables; the independent variable is then manipulated in a controlled situation, and changes in the dependent variable are measured

experimental hypothesis a prediction concerning how an independent variable will affect a dependent variable in an experiment

expressed emotion (EE) a negative communication pattern found among some relatives of individuals with schizophrenia

exposure therapy treatment that involves gradually introducing the client to increasingly difficult encounters with a feared situation

external validity the degree to which findings of a particular study can be generalized to other groups or conditions

factitious disorder symptoms of physical or mental illnesses are deliberately induced

or simulated with no apparent external incentive

factitious disorder imposed on another person a pattern of falsification of physical or psychological symptoms in another individual

family systems model model that assumes that the behavior of one family member directly affects the entire family system

female orgasmic disorder a sexual dysfunction in which the woman experiences persistent delay or inability to achieve an orgasm with stimulation that is adequate in focus, intensity, and duration after entering the excitement phase; also known as *inhibited female orgasm*

female sexual arousal disorder the inability to attain or maintain physiological response and/or psychological arousal during sexual activity

fetishistic disorder sexual attraction and fantasies involving inanimate objects such as female undergarments

field study an investigative technique in which behaviors and events are observed and recorded in their natural environment

flooding a technique that involves inducing a high anxiety level through continued actual or imagined exposure to a fear-arousing situation

free association psychoanalytic therapeutic technique in which the client says whatever comes to mind for the purpose of revealing his or her unconscious

frontotemporal lobar degeneration (FTLD) brain degeneration in the frontal and temporal lobes resulting in progressive declines in language and behavior

frotteuristic disorder characterized by recurrent and intense sexual urges, acts, or fantasies or touching or rubbing against a nonconsenting person

functional neurological symptom disorder (conversion disorder) impairments in sensory or motor functioning controlled by the voluntary nervous system that suggest a neurological disorder but with no underlying medical cause

"gateway" drug substance that leads to use of even more lethal substances

gender dysphoria/gender identity disorder (GID)/transsexualism disorder characterized by conflict between a person's anatomical sex and his or her gender identity, or self-identification as male or female

genetic linkage studies studies that attempt to determine whether a disorder follows a genetic pattern

genital-pelvic pain/penetration disorder includes previous diagnoses of vaginismus and dyspareunia and involves physical pain or discomfort associated with intercourse/penetration; fear, anxiety and distress is also usually present

genome all the genetic material in the chromosomes of a particular organism

genotype person's genetic makeup

grandiosity an overvaluation of one's significance or importance

group therapy a form of therapy that involves the simultaneous treatment of two or more clients and may involve more than one therapist

hallucination a sensory perception that is not directly attributable to environmental stimuli

hallucinogen substance that induces perceptual distortions and heightens sensory awareness

heavy drinking chronic alcohol intake of more than two drinks per day for men and more than one drink per day for women

hemorrhagic stroke stroke involving leakage of blood into the brain

humanism a philosophical movement that emphasizes human welfare and the worth and uniqueness of the individual

humanistic perspective the optimistic viewpoint that people are born with the ability to fulfill their potential and that abnormal behavior results from disharmony between the person's potential and his or her self-concept

Huntington's disease genetically transmitted degenerative disease characterized by involuntary twitching movements and eventual dementia

hypersexual disorder individuals with this condition seem to crave constant sex at the expense of relationships, work productivity, and daily activities

hypertension a chronic condition characterized by blood pressure of 140 (systolic) over 90 (diastolic) or higher

hypnotics medications that induce sleep

hypoactive sexual desire disorder sexual dysfunction that is related to the appetitive phase of the sexual response cycle and is characterized by a lack of sexual desire

hypomania a milder form of mania involving increased levels of activity and goal-directed behaviors combined with an elevated, expansive, or irritable mood

hypothesis a conjectural statement that usually describes a relationship between two variables

iatrogenic effects unintended effects of an intervention—such as an unintended change in behavior resulting from a medication or a psychological technique used in treatment

illness anxiety disorder (hypochondriasis) persistent health anxiety and concern that one has an undetected physical illness, even in the face of physical evaluations that reveal no organic problems

impulse control disorders disorders in which the person fails to resist an impulse or temptation to perform some act that is harmful to the person or to others; the person feels tension before the act and release after it

incest a form of pedophilic disorder; can also be sexual relations between people too closely related to marry legally

incidence the onset or occurrence of a given disorder over some period of time

independent variable a variable or condition that an experimenter manipulates to determine its effect on a dependent variable

inferiority model early attempt to explain differences in minority groups that contends that racial and ethnic minorities are inferior in some respect to the majority population

insanity defense the legal argument used by defendants who admit they have committed a crime but who plead not guilty because they were mentally disturbed at the time the crime was committed

intellectual disability (ID) disability characterized by limitations in intellectual functioning and adaptive behaviors

intermittent explosive disorder impulse control disorder characterized by separate and discrete episodes of loss of control over aggressive impulses, resulting in serious assaults on others or destruction of property

Internet addiction an impulse control disorder characterized by persons using the Internet so frequently that they isolate themselves from family and friends

internal validity the degree to which changes in the dependent variable are due solely to the effect of changes in the independent variable

irresistible impulse test a doctrine that states that a defendant is not criminally responsible if he or she lacked the will power to control his or her behavior

ischemic stroke stroke due to reduced blood supply caused by a clot or severe narrowing of the arteries supplying blood to the brain

kleptomania an impulse control disorder characterized by a recurrent failure to resist impulses to steal objects

learned helplessness an acquired belief that one is helpless and unable to affect life outcomes

learning disorder academic disability characterized by reading, writing, and math skills that are substantially below levels that would be expected based on the person's age, intellectual ability and educational background

least restrictive environment a person's right to the least restrictive alternative to freedom that is appropriate to his or her condition

lethality the degree of probability that a person chooses to end his or her life

Lewy body dementia (LBD) dementia involving visual hallucinations, cognitive fluctuations, and atypical movements

lifetime prevalence the percentage of people in the population who have had a disorder at some point in their life

localized amnesia lack of memory for a specific event or events

loosening of associations symptom of schizophrenia involving continual shifting from topic to topic without any apparent logical or meaningful connection between thoughts

magnetic resonance imaging (MRI) brain imaging procedure that produces images of the brain using a magnetic field

mainstreaming integrating individuals with intellectual disabilities or mental illness into age-appropriate school or community settings

major depressive episode two-week period involving pervasive, disabling feelings of sadness or emptiness and/or loss of pleasure and other cognitive, behavioral, and physiological changes

managed health care the industrialization of health care, whereby large organizations in the private sector control the delivery of services

mania mental state characterized by elevated mood and excessive excitement or irritability with resultant impairment in social or occupational functioning

mass madness group hysteria in which a great many people exhibit similar symptoms that have no apparent physical cause

meningitis medical condition involving inflammation of the membranes surrounding the brain and spinal cord

migraine headache moderate to severe pain resulting from constriction of the cranial arteries followed by dilation of the cerebral blood vessels

M'Naghten Rule a cognitive test of legal insanity that inquires whether the accused knew right from wrong at the time the crime was committed

model an analogy used by scientists, usually to describe or explain a phenomenon or process they cannot directly observe

modeling process of learning by observing others engaged in a behavior (and later imitating them)

modeling therapy procedures (including filmed modeling, live modeling, and participant modeling) that are used to treat certain phobias

moderate drinking a lower-risk pattern of alcohol intake (no more than one or two drinks per day)

moral treatment movement movement instituted by Philippe Pinel that resulted in a shift to more humane treatment of the mentally disturbed

multicultural model a systematic approach that views racial and cultural differences as important in explaining normal and abnormal behaviors

multicultural psychology an approach that stresses the importance of culture, race, ethnicity, gender, age, socioeconomic class, and other sociodemographic variables in understanding human development

multipath model a model that provides an organizational framework for understanding the numerous causes of mental disorders, the complexity of their interacting components, and the need to view disorders from a holistic framework

multiple-baseline study a single-participant experimental design in which baselines on two or more behaviors or the same behavior in two or more settings are obtained prior to intervention

muscle dysphoria extreme dissatisfaction with one's muscularity

narcissistic type a personality disorder characterized by an exaggerated sense of self-importance, exploitative attitude and a lack of empathy.

negative symptoms symptoms of schizophrenia associated with an inability or decreased ability to initiate actions or speech, express emotions, or feel pleasure

neurocognitive disorder a disorder caused by brain dysfunction that affects thinking processes, memory, consciousness, and perception

neurodegeneration declining brain function due to brain atrophy and death of neurons

neurodevelopmental disorders conditions involving impaired development of the brain and central nervous system that are evident early in a child's life

neuron nerve cell that transmits messages throughout the body

neuroplasticity ability of the brain to change its structure and function in response to experience

neurotransmitter chemical substance released by the axon of the sending neuron and involved in the transmission of neural impulses to the dendrite of the receiving neuron

obesity a condition involving a body mass index greater than 30

observational learning theory theory that suggests that an individual can acquire new behaviors by watching other people perform them

obsession intrusive, repetitive thought or image that produces anxiety

obsessive-compulsive personality type a personality disorder characterized by perfectionism, a tendency to be interpersonally controlling, devotion to details, and rigidity

operant behavior a voluntary and controllable behavior, such as walking or thinking, that "operates" on an individual's environment

operant conditioning a theory of learning that holds that behaviors are controlled by the consequences that follow them

operational definitions concrete definitions of the variables that are being studied

opioid painkilling agent that depresses the central nervous system, such as heroin and prescription pain relievers

optimal human functioning qualities such as subjective well-being, happiness, optimism, resilience, hope, courage, ability to cope with stress, self-actualization, and self-determinism

panic attack intense fear accompanied by symptoms such as a pounding heart, trembling, shortness of breath, fear of losing control or dying

paraphilic disorders sexual disorders of at least six months' duration in which the person has either acted on or is severely distressed by recurrent urges or fantasies involving nonhuman objects, nonconsenting persons, or suffering or humiliation

Parkinson's disease (PD) neurodegenerative disorder characterized by poorly controlled motor movements

pedophebephilic disorder a disorder in which an adult obtains erotic gratification through urges, acts, or fantasies involving sexual contact with a prepubescent child

personality disorder a disorder characterized by inflexible, long-standing, and maladaptive personality traits that cause significant impairment in self and interpersonal functioning

phenotype observable physical and behavioral characteristics caused by the interaction between the genotype and the environment

phobia a strong, persistent, and unwarranted fear of a specific object or situation

physiological dependence state of adaptation that occurs after chronic exposure to a substance; can result in craving and withdrawal symptoms

pleasure principle according to psychodynamic theory, the impulsive, pleasure-seeking aspect of our being from which the id operates

positive psychology the philosophical and scientific study of positive human functioning and the strengths and assets of individuals, families, and communities

positive symptoms symptoms of schizophrenia that involve unusual thoughts or perceptions such as delusions, hallucinations, thought disorder, or bizarre behavior

positron emission tomography (PET) nuclear imaging scan that assesses glucose metabolism in the brain

posttraumatic stress disorder (PTSD) disorder characterized by anxiety, dissociative, and other symptoms that last for more than one month and that occur as a result of exposure to extreme trauma

prevalence the percentage of people in a population who suffer from a disorder at a given point in time

privileged communication discussions between a therapist and client are confidential due to the therapist's legal obligation to protect a client's privacy and to prevent the disclosure of confidential communications without the client's permission

projective personality test testing involving responses to ambiguous stimuli, such as inkblots, pictures, or incomplete sentences

psychiatric epidemiology the study of the prevalence of mental illness in a society

psychoactive substance substances that alter mood, thought processes, or other psychological states

psychoanalysis a therapeutic approach involving efforts to uncover repressed material, to help clients achieve insight into inner motivations and desires, and to resolve childhood conflicts that affect current relationships

psychodiagnosis an attempt to describe, assess, and systematically draw inferences about an individual's psychological disorder

psychodynamic model model that views disorders as the result of childhood trauma or anxieties and that holds that many of these childhood-based anxieties operate unconsciously

psychological autopsy the systematic examination of existing information for the purpose of understanding and explaining a person's behavior before his or her death

psychological view the belief that mental disorders are caused by psychological and emotional factors rather than organic or biological ones

psychopathology a term clinical psychologists use as a synonym for *abnormal behavior*

psychophysiological disorder any physical disorder that has a strong psychological basis or component

psychosexual stages in psychodynamic theory, the sequence of stages—oral, anal, phallic, latency, and genital—through which human personality develops

psychosis condition involving loss of contact with or distorted view of reality

pyromania an impulse control disorder having as its main feature deliberate and purposeful fire setting on more than one occasion

rape a form of sexual aggression that refers to sexual activity (oral-genital sex, anal intercourse, and vaginal intercourse) performed against a person's will through the use of force, argument, pressure, alcohol or drugs, or authority

rape trauma syndrome a two-phase syndrome that rape victims may experience, including emotional reactions such as psychological distress, phobic responses, and sexual dysfunction

reality principle according to psychodynamic theory, the ego operates based on an awareness of the demands of the environment and the need to adjust behavior to meet these demands

regulated relapse process of weighing choices and making a conscious decision to use a substance

relapse return to drug or alcohol use after a period of abstention

relaxation training therapeutic technique in which a person acquires the ability to relax the muscles of the body in almost any circumstance

reliability the degree to which a procedure or test yields the same results repeatedly under the same circumstances

resistance during psychoanalysis, a client may unconsciously attempt to impede the analysis by preventing the exposure of repressed material

right to treatment the concept that mental patients who have been involuntarily committed have a right to receive therapy that would improve their emotional state

rumination continually thinking about certain topics or reviewing events that have transpired

schema a cognitive framework that helps organize and interpret information; schema are heavily influenced by a person's experiences, values, and perceived capabilities

schizophrenia a group of disorders characterized by severely impaired cognitive processes, personality disintegration, affective disturbances, and social withdrawal

schizophreniform disorder psychotic episodes with a duration of at least one month but less than six months

schizotypal type a personality disorder characterized by peculiar thoughts and behaviors and by poor interpersonal relationships

scientific method a method of inquiry that provides for the systematic collection of data, controlled observation, and the testing of hypotheses

self-actualization an inherent tendency to strive toward the realization of one's full potential

self-concept an individual's assessment of his or her own value and worth

self-denigration disparaging or belittling oneself

sensitized autonomic system condition in which the nervous system has become highly reactive to fear and stress

sexual arousal disorder disorder characterized by problems occurring during the excitement phase of the sexual response cycle and relating to difficulties with feelings of sexual pleasure or with the physiological changes associated with sexual excitement

sexual dysfunction a disruption of any part of the normal sexual response cycle

that affects sexual desire, arousal, and response

sexual masochism disorder a disorder in which sexual urges, fantasies, or acts are associated with being humiliated, bound, or made to suffer

sexual sadism disorder a disorder in which sexually arousing urges, fantasies, or acts are associated with inflicting physical or psychological suffering on others

single-participant experiment an experiment performed on a single individual in which some aspect of the person's behavior is used as a control or baseline for comparison with future behaviors

Single photon emission computed tomography (SPECT) nuclear imaging scan that provides longer but less detailed images of metabolic activity within the brain

social phobia an intense fear of being scrutinized in one or more social or performance situations

specific phobia an extreme fear of a specific object (such as snakes) or situation (such as being in an enclosed place)

spirituality the animating life force or energy of the human condition that is broader than but inclusive of religion

standardization the use of identical procedures in the administration of tests or the establishment of a norm or comparison group to which an individual's test performance can be compared

stimulant substance that is a central nervous system energizer

stress an internal psychological or physiological response to a difficult life circumstances

stressor an external event or situation that places a physical or psychological demand on a person

stroke a sudden halting of blood flow to a portion of the brain, leading to brain damage

suicidal ideation thoughts about suicide

suicide the intentional, direct, and conscious taking of one's own life

syndrome a constellation of symptoms that collectively characterize a disease or condition

synapse minute gap that exists between the axon of the sending neuron and the dendrites of the receiving neuron

synergistic effect the result of chemicals (or substances) interacting to multiply one another's effects

systematic desensitization exposure strategy that uses muscle relaxation to reduce the anxiety associated with specific and social phobias

Tarasoff ruling often referred to as the "duty-to-warn" principle; obligates mental health professionals to break confidentiality when their clients pose clear and imminent danger to another person

tension headache headache produced by prolonged contraction of the scalp and neck muscles, resulting in vascular constriction and steady pain

theory a group of principles and hypotheses that together explain some aspect of a particular area of inquiry

therapy a program of systematic intervention with the purpose of improving a client's behavioral, affective (emotional), and/or cognitive state

tolerance decreases in the effect of a substance that occur after chronic use

transference in psychoanalysis, the process by which a client reenacts early conflicts by applying to the analyst feelings and attitudes that the client had toward significant others in the past

transient ischemic attack (TIA) "mini-stroke" resulting from temporary blockage of arteries

transvestic disorder disorder involving intense sexual arousal obtained through cross-dressing (wearing clothes appropriate to the opposite gender)

traumatic brain injury (TBI) a physical wound or internal injury to the brain

trephining a surgical method from the Stone Age in which part of the skull was chipped away to provide an opening through which an evil spirit could escape

unconditioned response (UCR) in classical conditioning, the unlearned response made to an unconditioned stimulus

unconditioned stimulus (UCS) in classical conditioning, the stimulus that elicits an unconditioned response

Universal Shamanic Tradition a set of belief and practices from nonwestern indigenous psychologies that assume special healers are blessed with the power to act as intermediaries or messengers between the human and spirit worlds

vaginismus involuntary spasm of the outer third of the vaginal wall that prevents or interferes with sexual intercourse

validity the extent to which a test or procedure actually performs the function it was designed to perform

vascular cognitive impairment decline in cognitive skills due to chronic or sporadic cardiovascular events affecting blood flow to the brain

voyeuristic disorder urges, acts, or fantasies involving observation of an unsuspecting person disrobing or engaging in sexual activity

withdrawal adverse physical and psychological symptoms that occur after reducing or ceasing intake of a substance

References

AARDVARC. (2011). Quick stats from the Dept. of Justice Bureau of Justice Statistics. An Abuse, Rape and Domestic Violence Aid and Resource Collection. Retrieved from http://www.aardvarc.org/rape/about/statistics.shtml

Aarnoudse-Moens, C. S., Weisglas-Kuperus, N., van Goudoever, J. B., & Oosterlaan, J. (2009). Meta-analysis of neurobehavioral outcomes in very preterm and/or very low birth weight children. *Journal of Pediatrics, 124,* 717–728.

Aarsland, D., Andersen, K., Larsen, J. P., Lolk, A. L., & Kragh-Sorensen, P. (2003). Prevalence and characteristics of dementia in Parkinson disease: An 8-year prospective study. *Archives of Neurology, 60,* 387–392.

Aarsland, D., Sardahaee, F. S., Anderssen, S., & Ballard, C. (2010). Is physical activity a potential preventive factor for vascular dementia? A systematic review. *Aging and Mental Health, 14,* 386–395.

Abel, G. G., & Rouleau, J. L. (1990). The nature and extent of sexual assault. In W. L. Marshall, D. R. Laws, & H. E. Barbaree (Eds.), *Handbook of sexual assaults: Issues, theories and treatment of the offender* (pp. 9–22). New York: Plenum.

Abeles, N., & Victor, T. (2003). Unique opportunities for psychology in mental health care for older adults. *Clinical Psychology: Science and Practice, 10,* 120–124.

Abelsohn, A. R., & Sanborn, M. (2010). Lead and children: Clinical management for family physicians. *Canadian Family Physician, 56,* 531–535.

Aboa-Eboule, C., Brisson, C., Maunsell, E., Masse, B., Bourbonnais, R., . . . Dagenais, G. R. (2007). Job strain and risk of recurrent coronary heart disease events. *Journal of the American Medical Association, 298,* 1652–1660.

Aboraya, A. (2010a). Recommendations for DSM-V: A proposal for adding causal specifiers to Axis 1 diagnoses. *Psychiatry, 7,* 24–27.

Aboraya, A. (2010b). Scientific forum on the Diagnostic and Statistical Manual of Mental Disorders, Fifth Edition (DSM-V)—An invitation. *Psychiatry, 7,* 32–35.

Aboraya, A., Chumber, P., & Altaha, B. (2009). The treatment-resistant catatonia patient. *Current Psychiatry, 8,* 66–69.

Abrahams, B. S., & Geschwind, D. H. (2010). Connecting genes to brain in the autism spectrum disorders. *Archives of Neurology, 67,* 395–399.

Abramowitz, J. S., & Braddock, A. E. (2011). *Hypochondriasis and health anxiety: Advances in psychotherapy—Evidence-based practice.* Cambridge, MA: Hogrefe Publishing.

Abramowitz, J. S., Foa, E. B., & Franklin, M. E. (2003). Exposure and ritual prevention for obsessive-compulsive disorder: Effects of intensive versus twice-weekly sessions. *Journal of Consulting and Clinical Psychology, 71,* 394–398.

Abramowitz, J. S., & Larsen, J. E. (2007). Exposure therapy for obsessive-compulsive disorder. In D. C. Richard & D. Lauterach (Eds.), *Handbook of exposure therapies* (pp. 185–208). New York: Academic Press.

Abramowitz, J. S., Metzer-Brody, S., Leserman, J., Killenberg, S., Rinaldi, K. . . . Pedersen, C. (2010). Obsessional thoughts and compulsive behaviors in a sample of women with postpartum mood symptoms. *Archives of Women's Mental Health, 13,* 523–530.

Abramowitz, J. S., & Moore, E. L. (2007). An experimental analysis of hypochondriasis. *Behaviour Research and Therapy, 45,* 413–424.

Abrams, R. C., & Bromberg, C. E. (2007). Personality disorders in the elderly. *Psychiatric Annals, 37*(2), 123–127.

Abramson, L. Y., Metalsky, G. I., & Alloy, L. B. (1989). Hopelessness in depression: A theory-based subtype of depression. *Psychological Review, 96*(2), 358–372.

Abramson, L. Y., Seligman, M. E. P., & Teasdale, J. D. (1978). Learned helplessness in humans: Critique and reformulation. *Journal of Abnormal Psychology, 87,* 49–74.

Abreu, L. N., Lafer, B., Baca-Garcia, E., & Oquendo, M. A. (2009) Suicidal ideation and suicide attempts in bipolar disorder type I: An update for the clinician. *Journal of the Brazilian Psychiatric Association, 31,* 271–280.

Ackard, D. M., Fulkerson, J. A., & Neumark-Sztainer, D. (2007). Prevalence and utility of DSM-IV eating disorder diagnostic criteria among youth. *International Journal of Eating Disorders, 40,* 409–417.

Adamson, J., & Zywicki, T. J. (2007). Food advertising to children. *Regulation, 30,* 5.

Addington v. Texas, 99 S. Ct. 1804 (1979).

Addington, J., & Addington, D. (2009). Three-year outcome of treatment in an early psychosis program. *Canadian Journal of Psychiatry, 54,* 626–630.

Addington, J., & Haarmans, M. (2006). Cognitive-behavioral therapy for individuals recovering from a first-episode psychosis. *Journal of Contemporary Psychotherapy, 36,* 43–49.

Adelman, H. S., & Taylor, L. (2004). Mental health in schools: A shared agenda. *Report on Emotional and Behavioral Disorder in Youth, 4,* 59–62, 76–78.

Adi, Y., Juarez-Garcia, A., Wang, D., Jowett, S., Frew, E., . . . Burls, A. (2007). Oral naltrexone as a treatment for relapse prevention in formerly opioid-dependent drug users: A systematic review and economic evaluation. *Health Technology Assessment, 11,* iii–iv, 1–85.

Adler, J., & Rogers, A. (1999, January 11). The new war against migraines. *Newsweek,* pp. 46–52.

Administration on Aging. (2007). *Statistics: A profile of older Americans 2006—The older population.* Retrieved from www.aoa.gov/prof/Statistics/profile/2006/2.asp

Agras, W. S., Crow, S. J., Halmi, K. A., Mitchell, J. E., Wilson, G. T., & Kraemer, H. C. (2000). Outcome predictors for the cognitive behavior treatment of bulimia nervosa: Data from a multisite study. *American Journal of Psychiatry, 157,* 1302–1308.

Agras, W. S., Rossiter, E. M., Arnow, B., Schneider, J. A., Telch, C. F., . . . Koran, L. M. (1992). Pharmacologic and cognitive-behavioral treatment for bulimia nervosa: A controlled comparison. *American Journal of Psychiatry, 149,* 82–87.

Agrawal, A., & Lynskey, M. T. (2008). Are there genetic influences on addiction: Evidence from family, adoption and twin studies. *Addiction, 103,* 1069–1081.

Agrawal, A., Pergadia, M. L., & Lynskey, M. T. (2008). Is there evidence for symptoms of cannabis withdrawal in the national epidemiologic survey of alcohol and related conditions? *American Journal on Addictions, 17,* 199–208.

R-1

Ahmed, N., Wahlgren, N., Grond, M., Hennerici, M., Lees, K. R., . . . Ringleb, P. (2010). Implementation and outcome of thrombolysis with alteplase 3-4.5 h after an acute stroke: An updated analysis from SITS-ISTR. *Lancet Neurology, 9,* 866–874.

Akimova, E., Lanzenberger, R., & Kasper, S. (2009). The serotonin-1A receptor in anxiety disorders. *Biological Psychiatry, 66,* 627–635.

Akinbami, L. J., Moorman, J. E., & Liu, X. (2011). Asthma prevalence, health care use, and mortality: United States, 2005–2009. *National Health Statistics Report, 12*(32), 1–14.

Alao, A. O., & Chung, C. (2007). West Nile virus and conversion disorder. *Psychosomatics, 48,* 176.

Albee, G. W. (2002). Just say no to psychotropic drugs! *Journal of Clinical Psychology, 58,* 635–648.

Albert, M. A., Glynn, R. G., & Buring, J. (2010). *Women with high job strain have 40 percent increased risk of heart disease.* Presented at the Annual Meetings of the American Heart Association, November 15, 2010, Chicago, Illinois.

Albert, P. R., & Francois, B. L. (2010). Modifying 5-HT1A receptor gene expression as a new target for antidepressant therapy. *Frontiers of Neuroscience, 4,* 35.

Alcantara, C., & Gone, J. P. (2008). Suicide in Native American communities. In F. Leong & M. M. Leach (Eds.), *Ethnic suicides* (pp. 173–199). New York: Routledge.

Aldridge-Morris, R. (1989). *Multiple personality: An exercise in deception.* Hove, UK: Erlbaum.

Alexander, F. G., & Selesnick, S. T. (1966). *The history of psychiatry.* New York: Harper & Row.

Alexander, G. C., Gallagher, S. A., Maswcola, A., Moloney, R. M., & Stafford, R. S. (2011). Increasing off-label use of antipsychotic medications in the United States, 1995–2008. *Pharmacoepidemiology and Drug Safety, 20*(2), 177–184. doi:10.1002/pds.2082

Alexander, J. F., Holtzworth-Munroe, A., & Jameson, P. (1994). The process and outcome of marital and family therapy: Research review and evaluation. In A. E. Bergin & S. L. Garfield (Eds.), *Handbook of psychotherapy and behavior change* (pp. 595–630). New York: Wiley.

Alexander, J. R., Lerer, B., & Baron, M. (1992). Ethical issues in genetic linkage studies of psychiatric disorders. *British Journal of Psychiatry, 160,* 98–102.

Alford, G. S. (1980). Alcoholics Anonymous: An empirical outcome study. *Addictive Behaviors, 5,* 359–370.

Alford, G. S., Morin, C., Atkins, M., & Schuen, L. (1987). Masturbatory extinction of deviant sexual arousal: A case study. *Behavior Therapy, 18,* 265–271.

Algorta, G. P., Youngstrom, E. A., Frazier, T. W., Freeman, A. J., Youngstrom, J. K., & Findling, R. L. (2011). Suicidality in pediatric bipolar disorder: Predictor or outcome of family processes and mixed mood presentation? *Bipolar Disorder, 13,* 76–86.

Ali, S., Jabeen, S., Arain, A., Wassef, T., & Ibrahim, A. (2011). How to use your clinical judgment to screen for and diagnose psychogenic nonepileptic seizures without video electroencephalogram. *Innovations in Clinical Neuroscience, 8,* 36–41.

Allanson, J., Bass, C., & Wade, D. T. (2002). Characteristics of patients with persistent severe disability and medically unexplained neurological symptoms: A pilot study. *Journal of Neurology, Neurosurgery and Psychiatry, 73,* 307–309.

Allen, L. A., Gara, M. A., Escobar, J. I., Waitzkin, H., & Silver, R. C. (2001). Somatization: A debilitating syndrome in primary care. *Psychosomatics, 42,* 63–67.

Allen, L. A., Woolfolk, R. L., Escobar, J. I., Gara, M. A., & Hamer, R. M. (2006). Cognitive-behavioral therapy for somatization disorder. *Archives of Internal Medicine, 166,* 1512–1518.

Allen, S. S., Allen, A. M., & Pomerleau, C. S. (2009). Influence of phase-related variability in premenstrual symptomatology, mood, smoking withdrawal, and smoking behavior during ad libitum smoking, on smoking cessation outcome. *Addictive Behavior, 34,* 107–111.

Allen, S. S., Bade, T., Center, B., Finstad, D., & Hatsukami, H. (2008). Menstrual phase effects on smoking relapse. *Addiction, 103,* 809–821.

Allenou, C., Olliac, B., Bourdet-Loubere, S., Brunet, A., Annie-Claude, D., Claudet, I., . . . Birmes, P. (2010). Symptoms of traumatic stress in mothers of children victims of a motor vehicle accident. *Depression and Anxiety, 27,* 652–657.

Allgeier, E. R., & Allgeier, A. R. (1998). *Sexual interactions.* Boston: Houghton Mifflin.

Allgulander, C., Hartford, J., Russell, J., Ball, S., Erickson, J., Raskin, J., & Rynn, M. (2007). Pharmacotherapy of generalized anxiety disorder: Results of duloxetine treatment from a pooled analysis of three clinical trials. *Current Medical Research and Opinion, 23,* 1245–1252.

Alloy, L. B., Abramson, L. Y., Flynn, M., Liu, R. T., Grant, D. A., Jager-Hyman, S., & Whitehouse, W. G. (2009). Self-focused cognitive styles and bipolar spectrum disorders: concurrent and prospective associations. *International Journal of Cognitive Therapy, 2,* 354–372.

Almerie, M. Q., Matar, H. E.-D., Essali, A., Alkhateeb, H., & Rezk, E. (2008). Cessation of medication for people with schizophrenia already stable on chlorpromazine. *Schizophrenia Bulletin, 34,* 13–14.

Altshuler, L. L., Kupka, R. W., Hellemann, G., Frye, M. A., Sugar, C. A., . . . Suppes, T. (2010). Gender and depressive symptoms in 711 patients with bipolar disorder evaluated prospectively in the Stanley Foundation bipolar treatment outcome network. *American Journal of Psychiatry, 167,* 708–715.

Alzheimer's Association. (2010). 2010 Alzheimer's disease facts and figures. Retrieved from http://www.alz.org/documents_custom/report_alzfactsfigures2010.pdf

Amador, X. (2003). Poor insight in schizophrenia: Overview and impact on medication compliance.

Retrieved from http://www.xavieramador.com/files/cns-special-report-on-insight.pdf

Amador, X. F., Falum, M., Andreasen, N. C., Strauss, D. H., Yale, S. A., Clark, S. C., & Gorman, J. M. (1994). Awareness of illness in schizophrenia and schizoaffective and mood disorders. *Archives of General Psychiatry, 51,* 826–836.

American Academy of Child and Adolescent Psychiatry. (2009). Practice parameter on the use of psychotropic medication in children and adolescents. *Journal of the American Academy of Child and Adolescent Psychiatry, 48,* 961–973.

American Academy of Neurology. (2010). Practice parameter: The management of concussion in sports. Retrieved from http://www.aan.com/professionals/practice/guidelines/pda/Concussion_sports.pdf

American Association of Retired Persons. (1999, September–October). Sex and sexuality [Special issue]. *Modern Maturity.*

American Association on Intellectual and Developmental Disabilities. (2007). *Mental retardation is no more—New name is* intellectual and developmental disabilities. Retrieved from www.aamr.org/About_AAIDD/MR_name_change.htm

American Bar Association Standing Committee on Association Standards for Criminal Justice. (1984). *Criminal justice and mental health standards.* Chicago: Author.

American Cancer Society. (2007). *Cigarette smoking.* Retrieved from www.cancer.org/docroot/PED/content/PED_10_2X_Cigarette_Smoking.asp?sitearea=PED

American Dietetic Association. (2001). Position of the American Dietetic Association: Nutrition intervention in the treatment of anorexia nervosa, bulimia nervosa, and eating disorders not otherwise specified (EDNOS). Journal of the *American Dietetic Association, 101,* 810–819.

American Heart Association. (2007). *Cardiovascular disease statistics.* Retrieved from www.americanheart.org/presenter.jhtml?identifier=4478

American Heart Association. (2010). *Heart disease and stroke statistics: 2010 update.* Dallas, TX: American Heart Association.

American Heritage Dictionary. (2007). Retrieved from http://education.yahoo.com/reference/dictionary/entry/disease;_ylt=ApxvYfTk1i88x 9OTzaJG1Oarg MMF

American Geriatric Society. (2010). Preventing and effectively treating delirium in elderly can save seniors' lives and may also lower their risks of permanent cognitive loss. *AGS Newsletter* (3rd quarter). Retrieved from http://www.americangeriatrics.org/press/ags_newsletter_2010_third_quarter

American Law Institute. (1962). *Model penal code: Proposed official draft.* Philadelphia: Author.

American Psychiatric Association. (1983). American Psychiatric Association statement on the insanity defense. *American Journal of Psychiatry, 140,* 681–688.

American Psychiatric Association. (1987). *Diagnostic and statistical manual of mental disorders* (3rd ed., rev.). Washington, DC: Author.

American Psychiatric Association. (1994). *Diagnostic and statistical manual of mental disorders* (4th ed.). Washington, DC: Author.

American Psychiatric Association. (1997). Practice guidelines for the treatment of patients with schizophrenia. *American Journal of Psychiatry, 154,* 1–40.

American Psychiatric Association. (2000a). *Diagnostic and statistical manual of mental disorders* (4th ed., text rev.). Washington, DC: Author.

American Psychiatric Association. (2000b). Practice guideline for the treatment of patients with eating disorders (revision). *American Journal of Psychiatry, 157,* 1–39.

American Psychiatric Association. (2006). Treatment recommendations for patients with eating disorders. *American Journal of Psychiatry, 163,* 5–54.

American Psychiatric Association. (2007). Practice guideline for the treatment of patients with obsessive-compulsive disorder. *American Journal of Psychiatry, 164,* 1–56.

American Psychiatric Association. (2010). Eating disorders. Retrieved from http://www.dsm5.org/ProposedRevisions/Pages/EatingDisorders.aspx

American Psychiatric Association. (2011). DSM-5: The future of psychiatric diagnosis. Downloaded from: http://www.dsm5.org/Pages/Default.aspx

American Psychological Association. (1990). In the Supreme Court of the United States: Price Waterhouse v. Ann B. Hopkins. Amicus Curiae Brief for the American Psychological Association. *American Psychologist, 46,* 1061–1070.

American Psychological Association. (1993). Guidelines for providers of psychological services to ethnic, linguistic, and culturally diverse populations. *American Psychologist, 48,* 45–48.

American Psychological Association. (1995). *Ethical principles of psychologists and code of conduct.* Washington, DC: Author.

American Psychological Association. (2000). Guidelines for psychotherapy with lesbian, gay, and bisexual clients. *American Psychologist, 55*(12), 1440–1451.

American Psychological Association. (2002). Ethical principles of psychologists and code of conduct. *American Psychologist, 57,* 1060–1073.

American Psychological Association. (2003). Guidelines on multicultural education, training, research, practice, and organizational change for psychologists. *American Psychologist, 58,* 377–402.

American Psychological Association. (2007). *Report of the task force on the sexualization of girls.* Retrieved from www.apa.org/pi/wpo/sexualization.html

American Psychological Association. (2010a). *Stress in America.* Washington, D.C.: American Psychological Association.

American Psychological Association. (2010b). *Ethical principles of psychologists and code of conduct.* Washington, D.C.: American Psychological Association.

American Psychological Association Task Force on Socioeconomic Status. (2006, April). *Draft report of the APA Task Force on socioeconomic status.* Washington, D.C: American Psychological Association.

American Society for Asthetic Plastic Surgery. (2008). *11.7 cosmetic procedures in 2007.* Retrieved from http://www.surgery.org/press/news-release.php?iid=491

American Society of Plastic Surgeons. (2010). 2000/2008/2009 National Plastic Surgery Statistics. Retrieved from http://www.plasticsurgery.org/Documents/Media/statistics/2009-US-cosmeticreconstructiveplasticsurgeryminimally-invasive-statistics.pdf

American Society of Suicidology. (2008, January 17). *USA suicide: 2005 final data.* Retrieved from http://www.suicidology.org/associations/1045/files/2005datapgs.pdf

Amodio, D. M., Jost, J. T., Master, S. L., & Yee, C. M. (2007). Neurocognitive correlates of liberalism and conservatism. *Nature Neuroscience, 10,* 1246–1247.

Amminger, G. P., Schafer, M. R., Papageorgiou, K., Klier, C. M., Cotton, S. M., . . . Berger, G. E. (2010). Long-chain omega-3 fatty acids for indicated prevention of psychotic disorders: A randomized, placebo-controlled trial. *Archives of General Psychiatry, 67,* 146–154.

Anastasi, A. (1982). *Psychological testing.* New York: Macmillan.

Anda, R. F., Felitti, V. J., Bremner, J. D., Walker, J. D., Whitfield, C. H., . . . Giles, W. H. (2006). The enduring effects of abuse and related experiences in childhood: A convergence of evidence from neurobiology and epidemiology. *European Archives of Psychiatry and Clinical Neuroscience, 256,* 174–186.

Andari, E., Duhamel, J. R., Zalla, T., Herbrecht, E., Leboyer, M., & Sirigu, A. (2010). Promoting social behavior with oxytocin in high-functioning autism spectrum disorders. *Proceedings of the National Academy of Science, 107,* 4389–4394.

Andersen, A. E. (2001). Progress in eating disorders research. *American Journal of Psychiatry, 158,* 515–517.

Andersen, A. E. (2007). Eating disorders and coercion. *American Journal of Psychiatry, 164,* 9–11.

Andersen, A. E., Bowers, W. A., & Watson, T. (2001). A slimming program for eating disorders not otherwise specified: Reconceptualizing a confusing, residual diagnostic category. *Psychiatric Clinics of North America, 24,* 272–280.

Andersen, B. L., & Cyranowski, J. M. (1995). Women's sexuality: Behaviors, responses, and individual differences. *Journal of Consulting and Clinical Psychology, 63,* 891–906.

Anderson, P. J., & Doyle, L. W. (2008). Cognitive and educational deficits in children born extremely preterm. *Seminars in Perinatology, 32,* 51–58.

Anderson, D. A., Martens, M. P., & Cimini, M. P. (2005). Do female college students who purge report greater alcohol use and negative alcohol-related consequences? *International Journal of Eating Disorders, 37,* 65–68.

Anderson, J. S., Druzgal, T. J., Froehlich, A., Dubray, M. B., Lange, N., . . . Lainhart, J. E. (2011). Decreased interhemispheric functional connectivity in autism. *Cerebral Cortex, 21*(5), 1134–1146. doi: PMID: 20943668

Anderson, K. W., Taylor, S., & McLean, P. H. (1996). Panic disorder associated with blood-injury reactivity: The necessity of establishing functional relationships among maladaptive behaviors. *Behavior Therapy, 27,* 463–472.

Anderson, T., & Strupp, H. H. (1996). The ecology of psychotherapy research. *Journal of Consulting and Clinical Psychology, 64,* 776–782.

Anderson-Fye, E. P. (2004). A "coca-cola" shape: Cultural change, body image, and eating disorders in San Andres, Belize. *Culture, Medicine and Psychiatry, 28,* 561–595.

Andreasen, N. C. (1989). Nuclear magnetic resonance imaging. In N. C. Andreasen (Ed.), *Brain imaging: Applications in psychiatry* (pp. 67–121). Washington, DC: American Psychiatric Press.

Andreasen, N. C. (Ed.). (2005). *Research advances in genetics and genomics: Implications for psychiatry.* Washington, DC: American Psychiatric Association.

Andrade, P., Noblesse, L. H., Temel, Y., Ackermans, L., Lim, L. W., Steinbusch, H. W., & Visser-Vandewalle, V. (2010). Neurostimulatory and ablative treatment options in major depressive disorder: A systematic review. *Acta Neurochirugia, 152,* 565–577.

Andrews, G., Cuijpers, P., Craske, M. G., McEvoy, P., & Titov, N. (2010). Computer therapy for the anxiety and depressive disorders is effective, acceptable and practical health care: A meta-analysis. *PLoS One, 5,* e13196.

Andrews, G., Hobbs, J. J., Borkovec, T. D., Beesdo, K., Craske, M. G., . . . Stanley, M. A. (2010). Generalized worry disorder: A review of DSM-IV generalized anxiety disorder and options for DSM-V. *Depression and Anxiety, 27,* 137–147.

Angermayr, L., & Clar, C. (2004). Iodine supplementation for preventing iodine deficiency disorders in children. *Cochrane Database of Systematic Reviews,* Issue 2, No. CD003819. doi: 10.1002/14651858.CD003819.pub2

Annenberg Public Policy Center. (2009). The holiday-suicide link: The myth persists. Retrieved from http://www.annenbergpublicpolicycenter.org/NewsDetails.aspx?myId=331

Anney, R., Klei, L., Pinto, D., Regan, R., Conroy, J., . . . Hallmayer, J. (2010). A genome-wide scan for common alleles affecting risk for autism. *Human Molecular Genetics, 19,* 4072–4082.

Annus, A. M., Smith, G. T., Fischer, S., Hendricks, M., & Williams, S. F. (2007). Associations among family-of-origin food-related experiences, expectancies, and disordered eating. *International Journal of Eating Disorders, 40,* 179–184.

Anonymous (2009). Bingeing and purging forum. Retrieved from http://www.caloriesperhour.com/forums/forum25/656.html

Anonymous 5. (2008). *Anorexia nervosa: Feeding the lie.* Retrieved from http://www.eating.ucdavis.edu/speaking/told/anorexia/a37feeding.html

Anorexia's web. (2001, September 7). *Current Events, 101,* 1–3.

Anthenelli, R. M. (2010). Focus on: Comorbid mental health disorders. *Alcohol Research & Health*. Retrieved from http://findarticles.com/p/articles/mi_m0CXH/is_1-2_33/ai_n55302109/

Anton, R. F., O'Malley, S. S., Ciraulo, D. A., Cisler, R. A., Couper, D., . . . COMBINE Study Research Group (2006a). Combined pharmacotherapies and behavioral interventions for alcohol dependence: The COMBINE study: A randomized controlled trial. *Journal of the American Medical Association, 295,* 2003–2017.

Anton, R. F., O'Malley, S., Ciraulo, D. A., Cisler, R. A., Couper, D., . . . Zweben, A. (2006b). Effect of combined pharmacotherapies and behavioral interventions for alcohol dependence. *Journal of the American Medical Association, 295,* 2003–2017.

Antonuccio, D. O., Burns, D. D., & Danton, W. G. (2002). *Antidepressants: A triumph of marketing over science?* Retrieved from http://psycnet.apa.org/index.cfm?fa=browsePA.volumes&jcode=pre&

Antony, M. M., Brown, T. A., & Barlow, D. H. (1997). Heterogeneity among specific phobia types in DSM-IV. *Behaviour Research and Therapy, 35,* 1089–1100.

Anxiety Disorders Association of America. (2007). *Statistics and facts about anxiety disorders.* Retrieved from www.adaa.org/aboutADAA/PressRoom/Stats&Facts.asp

Aoki, H., Kato, R., Hirano, K., Suzuki, T., Kato, K., & Inuma, M. (2003). A case of sudden unexplained nocturnal death from overlooked Brugada syndrome at a pre-employment check-up. *Journal of Occupational Health, 45,* 70–73.

Aplin, D. Y., & Kane, J. M. (1985). Variables affecting pure tone and speech audiometry in experimentally simulated hearing loss. *British Journal of Audiology, 19,* 219–228.

Applebaum, P. S. (1987). The right to refuse treatment with antipsychotic medications: Retrospect and prospect. *American Journal of Psychiatry, 145,* 413–419.

Arackal, B. S., & Benegal, V. (2007). Prevalence of sexual dysfunction in male subjects with alcohol dependence. *Indian Journal of Psychiatry, 49,* 109–120.

Are some men predisposed to pedophilia? (2007, October 23). *Science Daily.* Retrieved from www.sciencedaily.com/releases/2007/10/071022120203.htm

Armstrong, J. G., Putnam, F. W., Carlson, E. B., Libero, D. Z., & Smith, S. R. (1997). Development and validation of a measure of adolescent dissociation: The Adolescent Dissociation Scale. *Journal of Nervous and Mental Disease, 185,* 491–497.

Arndt, W. B., Jr. (1991). *Gender disorders and the paraphilias.* Madison, CT: International Universities Press.

Arnett, J. J. (2008). The neglected 95%. Why American psychology needs to become less American. *American Psychologist, 63,* 602–614.

Arnold, I. A., de Waal, M. W. M., Eekhoff, J. A. H., & van Hemert, A. M. (2006). Somatoform disorder in primary care: Course and the need for cognitive-behavioral treatment. *Psychosomatics, 47,* 498–503.

Arnold, L. M. (2003). Gender differences in bipolar disorder. *Psychiatric Clinics of North America, 26,* 595–620.

Arria, A. M., Caldeira, K. M., O'Grady, K. E., Vincent, K. B., Johnson, E. P., & Wish, E. D. (2008). Nonmedical use of prescription stimulants among college students: Associations with attention-deficit-hyperactivity disorder and polydrug use. *Pharmacotherapy, 28,* 156–169.

Arseneault, L., Cannon, M., Fisher, H. L., Polanczyk, G., Moffitt, T. E., & Caspi, A. (2011). Childhood trauma and children's emerging psychotic symptoms: A genetically sensitive longitudinal cohort study. *American Journal of Psychiatry, 168,* 65–72.

Artman, L. K., & Daniels, J. A. (2010). Disability and psychotherapy practice: Cultural competence and practical tips. *Professional Psychology: Research and Practice, 41,* 442–448.

Ashburner, J., Ziviani, J., & Rodger, S. (2010). Surviving in the mainstream: Capacity of children with autism spectrum disorders to perform academically and regulate their emotions and behavior at school. *Research in Autism Spectrum Disorders, 4,* 18–27.

Ashwin, C., Baron-Cohen, S., Wheelwright, S., O'Riordan, M., & Bullmore, E. T. (2007). Differential activation of the amygdala and the 'social brain' during fearful face-processing in Asperger Syndrome. *Neuropsychologia, 45,* 2–14.

Asian American Federation of New York. (2003). *Asian American mental health: A post-September 11th needs assessment.* New York: Author.

Askew, C., Kessock-Philip, H., & Field, A. P. (2008). What happens when verbal threat information and vicarious learning combine? *Behavioural and Cognitive Psychotherapy, 36,* 491–505.

Asmundson, G. J. G., & Norton, G. R. (1993). Anxiety sensitivity and its relationship to spontaneous and cued panic attacks in college students. *Behaviour Research and Therapy, 31,* 199–201.

Associated Press. (1998, August 14). Psychiatrist is sued over multiple bad personalities. *Seattle Post Intelligencer,* p. A12.

Associated Press. (2001, April 22). Two therapists found guilty in rebirthing therapy death. *Bellingham Herald,* p. A3.

Associated Press. (2007a, November 6). *Being a little heavy may have some benefits.* Retrieved November from www.msnbc.msn.com/id/21655928/print/1/displaymode

Associated Press. (2007b, January 26). *Man loses memory, wanders for 25 days.* Retrieved from www.msnbc.msn.com/id/16829260/print/1/displaymode/1098

Associated Press. (2007c, August 10). *Too many studies use college students as guinea pigs.* Retrieved from www.printthis.clickability.com/pt/cpt?action=cpt&title=Psych

Asthma and Allergy Foundation of America. (2007). *Asthma facts and figures.* Retrieved from www.aafa.org/display.cfm?id=8&sub=42

Astin, M. C., Ogland-Hand, S. M., Foy, D. W., & Coleman, E. M. (1995). Posttraumatic stress disorder and childhood abuse in battered women: Comparisons with maritally distressed women. *Journal of Consulting and Clinical Psychology, 63,* 308–312.

Auerbach, J., Geller, V., Lezer, S., Shinwell, E., Belmaker, R. H., Levine, J., & Ebstein, R. (1999). Dopamine D4 receptor (D4DR) and serotonin transporter promoter (5-HTTLPR) polymorphisms in the determination of temperament in 2-month-old infants. *Molecular Psychiatry, 4,* 369–373.

Auerbach, J. G., Faroy, M., Ebstein, R., Kahana, M., & Levine, J. (2001). The association of the dopamine D4 receptor gene (DRD4) and the serotonin transport promoter gene (5-HTTLPR) with temperament in 12-month-old infants. *Journal of Child Psychology and Psychiatry, 42,* 777–783.

Ausubel, D. P. (1961). Causes and types of narcotic addiction: A psychosocial view. *Psychiatric Quarterly, 35,* 523–531.

Avedisova, A., Borodin, V., Zakharova, K., & Aldushin, A. (2009). Effect of milnacipran on suicidality in patients with mild to moderate depressive disorder. *Neurophychiatric Disorder and Treatment, 5,* 415–420.

Avia, M. D., & Ruiz, M. A. (2005). Recommendations for the treatment of hypochondriac patients. *Journal of Contemporary Psychotherapy, 35,* 301–313.

Ayala, E. S., Meuret, A. E., & Ritz, T. (2009). Treatments for blood-injury-injection phobia: A critical review of current evidence. *Journal of Psychiatric Research, 43,* 1235–1242.

Ayers, C. R., Sorrell, J. T., Thorp, S. R., & Wetherell, J. L. (2007). Evidence-based psychological treatments for late-life anxiety. *Psychology and Aging, 22,* 8–17.

Azar, B. (2010). Your brain on culture. *Monitor on Psychology, 41*(10) 44–47.

Babiss, L. A., & Gangwisch, J. E. (2009). Sports participation as a protective factor against depression and suicidal ideation in adolescents as mediated by self-esteem and social support. *Journal of Developmental and Behavioral Pediatrics, 30,* 376–384.

Bagby, R. M., Rogers, R., Nicholson, R. A., Buis, T., Seeman, M. V., & Rector, N. A. (1997). The effectiveness of the MMPI-2 validity indicators in the detection of defensive responding in clinical and nonclinical samples. *Psychology Assessment, 9,* 406–413.

Bailey, D. S. (2003). Help the media prevent copycat suicides. *Monitor, 34,* 14.

Bailey, P. E., & Henry, J. D. (2010). Separating component processes of theory of mind in schizophrenia. *British Journal of Clinical Psychology, 49,* 43–52.

Bailey, R. K., Blackmon, H. L., & Stevens, F. L. (2009). Major depressive disorder in the African American population: Meeting the challenges of stigma, misdiagnosis, and treatment disparities. *Journal of National Medical Association, 101,* 1084–1089.

Bak, M., Myin-Germeys, I., Hanssen, M., Bijl, R., Volleberg, W., Delespaul, P., & van Os, J. (2003). When does experience of psychosis result in a need for care? A prospective general population study. *Schizophrenia Bulletin, 29,* 349–356.

Baker, J. H., Mitchell, K. S., Neale, M. C., & Kendler, K. S. (2010). Eating disorder symptomatology and substance use disorders: Prevalence and shared risk in a population based twin sample. *International Journal of Eating Disorders, 43,* 648–658.

Baker, J. L., Olsen, L. W., & Sorensen, T. I. A. (2007). Childhood body-mass index and the risk of coronary heart disease in adulthood. *New England Journal of Medicine, 357,* 2329–2337.

Baker, K. (2010). "It's not me" to "it was me, after all." *Psychoanalytic Social Work, 17,* 79–98.

Baker, L. A., & Clark, R. (1990). Introduction to special feature on genetic origins of behavior: Implications for counselors. *Journal of Counseling and Development, 68,* 597–605.

Baker, L. D., Frank, K., Foster-Schubert, K., Green, P. S., Wilkinson, C. W., . . . Craft, S. (2010). Effects of aerobic exercise on mild cognitive impairment: A controlled trial. *Archives of Neurology, 67,* 71–79.

Baker, T. B., Japuntich, S. J., Hogle, J. M., McCarthy, D. E., & Curtin, J. J. (2006). Pharmacologic and behavioral withdrawal from addictive drugs. *Current Directions in Psychological Science, 15,* 232–236.

Baker, T. B., McFall, R. M., & Shoham, V. (2008). Current status and future prospects of clinical psychology: Toward a scientifically principled approach to mental and behavioral health care. *Psychological Science in the Public Interest, 9,* 67–103.

Bakker, A., Spinhoven, P., Van Balkom, A. J. L. M., & Van Dyck, R. (2002). Relevance of assessment of cognitions during panic attacks in the treatment of panic disorder. *Psychotherapy and Psychosomatics, 71,* 158–162.

Balami, J. S., Chen, R., & Grunwald, I. Q. (2011). Neurological complications of acute ischaemic stroke. *The Lancet Neurology, 10*(4), 357–371. doi: 10.1016/S1474-4422(10)70313-6C

Balci, K., Utku, U., Asil, T., & Celik, Y. (2011). Ischemic stroke in young adults: risk factors, subtypes, and prognosis. *Neurologist, 17,* 16–20.

Baldassano, C. F. (2006). Illness course, comorbidity, gender, and suicidality in patients with bipolar disorder. *Journal of Clinical Psychiatry, 67*(Suppl 11), 8–11.

Bale, T. L., Baram, T. Z., Brown, A. S., Goldstein, J. M., Insel, T. R., McCarthy, M. M., . . . Nestler, E. J. (2010). Early life programming and neurodevelopmental disorders. *Biological Psychiatry, 68,* 314–319.

Ball, J. D., Archer, R. P., Gordon, R. A., & French, J. (1991). Rorschach depression indices with children and adolescents: Concurrent validity findings. *Journal of Personality Assessment, 57,* 465–476.

Ballard, C., Corbett, A., & Jones, E. L. (2011). Dementia: challenges and promising developments. *The Lancet Neurology, 10,* 7–9.

Ballenger, J. C., Davidson, J. R. T., Lecrubier, Y., Nutt, D. J., Borkovec, T. D., . . . Wittchen, H. U. (2000). Consensus statement on generalized anxiety disorder from the International Consensus Group on depression and anxiety. *Journal of Clinical Psychiatry, 62,* 53–58.

Ballew, L., Morgan, Y., & Lippmann, S. (2003). Intravenous diazepam for dissociative disorder: Memory lost and found. *Psychosomatics, 44,* 346–349.

Balon, R. (2008). The DSM criteria of sexual dysfunction: Need for a change. *Journal of Sex and Marital Therapy, 34,* 186–197.

Balon, R., Segraves, R. T., & Clayton, A. (2007). Issues of DSM-V: Sexual dysfunctions, disorder, or variation along normal distribution: Toward rethinking DSM criteria of sexual dysfunctions. *American Journal of Psychiatry, 164,* 198–200.

Bande, C. S., & Garcia-Alba, C. (2008). Munchausen syndrome by proxy: A dilemma for diagnosis. *Roschachiana, 29,* 183–200.

Bandura, A. (1997). *Self-efficacy: The exercise of self-control.* New York: Freeman.

Banerjee, G., & Roy, S. (1998). Determinants of help-seeking behaviour of families of schizophrenic patients attending a teaching hospital in India: An indigenous explanatory model. *International Journal of Social Psychiatry, 44,* 199–214.

Banerjee, T. D., Middleton, F., & Faraone, S. V. (2007). Environmental risk factors for attention-deficit hyperactivity disorder. *Acta Paediatrica, 96,* 1269–1274.

Bang, J., Price, D., Prentice, G., & Campbell, J. (2009). ECT treatment for two cases of dementia-related pathological yelling. *Journal of Neuropsychiatry and Clinical Neuroscience, 20,* 379–380.

Barbaro, J., & Dissanayake, C. (2009). Autism spectrum disorders in infancy and toddlerhood: A review of the evidence on early signs, early identification tools, and early diagnosis. *Journal of Developmental and Behavioral Pediatrics, 30,* 447–459.

Barber, J. P., & Luborsky, L. (1991). A psychodynamic view of simple phobias and prescriptive matching: A commentary. *Psychotherapy, 28,* 469–472.

Barber, J. P., Morse, J. Q., Krakauer, I. D., Chittams, J., & Crits-Cristoph, K. (1997). Change in obsessive-compulsive and avoidant personality disorders following time-limited supportive-expressive therapy. *Journal of Psychotherapy, 34,* 133–143.

Barbui, C., Cipriani, A., Patel, V., Ayuso-Mateos, J. L., & van Ommeren, M. (2011). Efficacy of antidepressants and benzodiazepines in minor depression: Systematic review and meta-analysis. *British Journal of Psychiatry, 198,* 11–16.

Barclay, L. (2004, September 14). Call for mandatory clinical trial registration, open access to results. *Medscape Medical News.* Retrieved from www.medscape.com/viewarticle/489219

Bardone-Cone, A. M., & Cass, K. M. (2007). What does viewing a pro-anorexia website do? An experimental examination of website exposure and moderating effects. *International Journal of Eating Disorders, 40,* 537–548.

Bardone-Cone, A. M., Sturm, K., Lawson, M. A., Robinson, D. P., & Smith, R. (2010). Perfectionism across stages of recovery from eating disorders. *International Journal of Eating Disorders, 43,* 139–148.

Barkley, R. A., Anastopoulous, A. D., Guevremont, D. C., & Fletcher, K. E. (1992). Adolescents with attention deficit hyperactivity disorder: Mother-child-adolescent interactions, family beliefs and conflicts, and psychopathology. *Journal of Abnormal Child Psychology, 20,* 263–288.

Barlow, D. H., Gorman, J. M., Shear, M. K., & Woods, S. W. (2000). Cognitive-behavioral therapy, imipramine, or their combination for panic disorder: A randomized controlled trial. *Journal of the American Medical Association, 283,* 2529–2536.

Barnhofer, T., Crane, C., Hargus, E., Amarasinghe, M., Winder, R., & Williams, J. M. G. (2010). Mindfulness-based cognitive therapy as a treatment for chronic depression: A preliminary study. *Behavior Research and Therapy, 47,* 366–373.

Baron, L., Straus, M. A., & Jaffee, D. (1988). Legitimate violence, violent attitudes, and rape: A test of the cultural spillover theory. In R. A. Prentky & V. L. Quisey (Eds.), *Annals of the New York Academy of Sciences: Vol. 528. Human sexual aggression: Current perspectives* (pp. 79–110). Salem, MA: New York Academy of Sciences.

Baron, R. M., & Kenny, D. A. (1986). The moderator-mediator variable distinction in social psychological research: Conceptual, strategic, and statistical considerations. *Journal of Personality and Social Psychology, 51,* 1173–1182.

Barraclough, B. M., Jennings, C., & Moss, J. R. (1977). Suicide prevention by the Samaritans: A controlled study of effectiveness. *Lancet, 2,* 237–238.

Barrera, T. L., & Norton, P. J. (2010). Quality of life impairment in generalized anxiety disorder, social phobia, and panic disorder. *Journal of Anxiety Disorders, 23,* 1086–1090.

Barrett, G. V., & Depinet, R. L. (1991). A reconsideration of testing for competence rather than for intelligence. *American Psychologist, 46,* 1012–1024.

Barsky, A. J. (1991). Amplification, somatization and somatoform disorders. *Psychosomatics, 33,* 28–34.

Barsky, A. J., & Ahern, D. K. (2004). Cognitive behavior therapy for hypochondriasis: A randomized controlled trial. *Journal of the American Medical Association, 291,* 1464–1470.

Barsky, A. J., Wool, C., Barnett, M. C., & Cleary, P. D. (1995). Histories of childhood trauma in adult hypochondriacal patients. *American Journal of Psychiatry, 151,* 397–401.

Barsky, A. J., & Wyshak, G. (1990). Hypochondriasis and somatosensory amplification. *British Journal of Psychiatry, 157,* 404–409.

Barton, J. (2004, September 29). Mental health centers feel storm surge: Calls for help climb after hurricanes. *Columbian,* p. A3.

Barzman, D. H., Patel, A., Sonnier, L., & Strawn, J. R. (2010). Neuroendocrine aspects of pediatric aggression: Can hormone measures be clinically useful? *Journal of Neuropsychiatric Disease and Treatment, 6,* 691–697.

Baschnagel, J. S., Gudmundsdottir, B., Hawk Jr., L. W., & Beck, J. G. (2009). Post-trauma symptoms following indirect exposure to the September 11th terrorist attacks: The predictive role of dispositional coping. *Journal of Anxiety Disorders, 23,* 915–922.

Basoglu, M., Livanou, M. L., & Salcioglu, E. (2003). A single session with an earthquake simulator for traumatic stress in earthquake survivors. *American Journal of Psychiatry, 160,* 788–790.

Bassil, N., & Grossberg, G. T. (2010). Alzheimer's disease. *Current Psychiatry, 9,* 23–36.

Bateman, P., Aisen, B., De Strooper, N. C., Fox, C. A., . . . Chengjie Xiong, C. (2011). Autosomal-dominant Alzheimer's disease: A review and proposal for the prevention of Alzheimer's disease. *Alzheimers Research and Therapy.* Retrieved from http://alzres.com/content/2/6/35

Baum, A. E., Akula, N., Cabanero, M., Cardona, I., Corona, W., . . . McMahon, F. J. (2008). A genome-wide association study implicates diacylglycerol kinase eta (DGKH) and several other genes in the etiology of bipolar disorder. *Molecular Psychiatry, 13,* 197–207.

Baumeister, R. F. (1988). Masochism as escape from self. *Journal of Sex Research, 25,* 28–59.

Baxter, L. R., Jr., Schwartz, J. M., Bergman, K. S., Szuba, M. P., Guze, B. H., . . . Phelps, M. E. (1992). Caudate glucose metabolic rate changes with both drug and behavior therapy for obsessive-compulsive disorder. *Archives of General Psychiatry, 49,* 681–689.

Bayer, J. K., Rapee, R. M., Hiscock, H., Ukoumunne, O. C., Mihalopoulos, C., & Wake, M. (2011). Translational research to prevent internalizing problems early in childhood. *Depression and Anxiety, 28,* 50–57.

BBC News. (2001). *Artificial brain to spot schizophrenia.* Retrieved from http://news.bbc.co.uk/2/hi/health/1182065.stm

Beard, C., Moitra, E., Weisberg, R. B., & Keller, M. B. (2010). Characteristics and predictors of social phobia course in a longitudinal study of primary-care patients. *Depression and Anxiety, 27,* 839–845.

Bearden, C. E., Woogen, M., & Glahn, D. C. (2010). Neurocognitive and neuroimaging predictors of clinical outcome in bipolar disorder. *Current Psychiatry Reports, 12,* 499–504.

Beck, A., Beidel, D. C., Rao, P. A., Scharfstein, L., Wong, N., & Alfano, C. A. (2010). Social skills and social phobia: An investigation of DSM-IV subtypes. *Behaviour Research and Therapy, 48,* 992–1001.

Beck, A. T. (1976). *Cognitive therapy and emotional disorders.* New York: International Universities Press.

Beck, A. T. (1985). Cognitive therapy, behavior therapy, psychoanalysis, and pharmacotherapy: A cognitive continuum. In M. Mahoney & A. Freeman (Eds.), *Cognition and psychotherapy* (pp. 197–220). New York: Plenum Press.

Beck, A. T. (1997). Cognitive therapy: Reflections. In J. K. Zeig (Ed.), *The evolution of psychotherapy: The third conference.* New York: Brunner/Mazel.

Beck, A. T., Emery, G., & Greenberg, R. L. (1985). *Anxiety disorders and phobias: A cognitive perspective.* New York: Basic Books.

Beck, A. T., Freeman, A. F., & Associates. (1990). *Cognitive therapy of personality disorders.* New York: Guilford Press.

Beck, A. T., Freeman, A., & Davis, D. D. (2004). *Cognitive therapy of personality disorders.* New York: Guilford Press.

Beck, A. T., & Rector, N. A. (2000). Cognitive therapy of schizophrenia: A new therapy for the new millennium. *American Journal of Psychotherapy, 54,* 291–300.

Beck, A. T., Rush, A., Shaw, B., & Emery, G. (1979). *Cognitive therapy of depression.* New York: Guilford Press.

Beck, A. T., Ward, C. H., Mendelson, M., Mock, J. E., & Erbaugh, J. (1961). An inventory for measuring depression. *Archives of General Psychiatry, 4,* 561–571.

Beck, A. T., & Weishaar, M. E. (1989). Cognitive therapy. In R. J. Corsini & D. Wedding (Eds.), *Current psychotherapies* (pp. 285–320). Itasca, IL: Peacock.

Beck, A. T., & Weishaar, M. E. (2010). Cognitive therapy. In R. J. Corsini & D. Wedding (Eds.), *Current Psychotherapies* (pp. 301–322) (9th ed.). Belmont, CA: Brooks/Cole.

Beck, C. T., & Indman P. J. (2005). The many faces of postpartum depression. *Journal of Obstetric, Gynecological and Neonatal Nursing, 34,* 569–576.

Becker, A. E. (2004). Television, disordered eating, and young women in Fiji: Negotiating body image and identity during rapid social change. *Cultural Medical Psychiatry, 28,* 533–559.

Bedell-Smith, S. (1999). *Diana in search of herself.* New York: Random House.

Bednar, R. L., Bednar, S. C., Lambert, M. J., & Waite, D. R. (1991). *Psychotherapy with high-risk clients: Legal and professional standards.* Pacific Grove, CA: Brooks/Cole.

Beers, M. H., & Berkow, R. (Eds.). (1999). *The Merck manual of diagnosis and therapy* (17th ed.). Whitehouse Station, NJ: Merck.

Beinenfeld, D. (2007). Personality disorders. *Psychiatric Annals, 37,* 84–86.

Bellack, A. S. (2006). Scientific and consumer models of recovery in schizophrenia: Concordance, contrasts, and implications. *Schizophrenia Bulletin, 32,* 432–442.

Bellinger, D. C. (2008). Very low lead exposures and children's neurodevelopment. *Current Opinions in Pediatrics, 20,* 172–177.

Bello, N. T., & Hajnal, A. (2010). Dopamine and binge eating behaviors. *Pharmacology, Biochemistry and Behavior, 97,* 25–33.

Belloch, A., Cabedo, E., & Carrio, C. (2008). Cognitive versus behaviour therapy in the individual treatment of obsessive-compulsive disorder: Changes in cognitions and clinically significant outcomes at post-treatment and one-year follow-up. *Behavioural and Cognitive Psychotherapy, 36,* 521–540.

Bellodi, L., Cavallini, M. C., Bertelli, S., Chiapparino, D., Riboldi, C., & Smeraldi, E. (2001). Morbidity risk for obsessive-compulsive spectrum disorders in first-degree relatives of patients with eating disorders. *American Journal of Psychiatry, 158,* 563–569.

Belluck, P. (2010, June 20). Hallucinations in hospital pose risk to elderly. *The New York Times.* Retrieved from http://www.nytimes.com/2010/06/21/science/21delirium.html?_r=1&pagewanted=printune

Benazzi, F. (2007). Bipolar II disorder: epidemiology, diagnosis and management. *CNS Drugs.21,* 727–40.

Bender, L. (1938). A visual motor gestalt test and its clinical use. *Research Monograph of the American Orthopsychiatric Association, 3*(11), 176.

Benedict, J. G., & Donaldson, D. W. (1996). Recovered memories threaten all. *Professional Psychology: Research and Practice, 27,* 427–428.

Benedict, R. (1934). *Patterns of culture.* New York: Houghton Mifflin.

Benjamin, L. S. (1996). *Interpersonal diagnosis and treatment of personality disorders.* New York: Guilford Press.

Benjamin, L. S., & Karpiak, C. P. (2002). Personality disorders. In J. C. Norcross (Ed.), *Psychotherapy relationships that work* (pp. 423–440). New York: Oxford University Press.

Benjamin, L. S., & Wonderlich, S. A. (1994). Social perceptions and borderline personality disorder: The relation to mood disorders. *Journal of Abnormal Psychology, 103,* 610–624.

Benes, F. M. (2009). Neural circuitry models of schizophrenia: Is it dopamine, GABA, glutamate, or something else? *Biological Psychiatry, 65,* 1003–1005.

Benjet, C., Borges, G., & Medina-Mora, M. E. (2010). Chronic childhood adversity and onset of psychopathology during three life stages: Childhood, adolescence and adulthood. *Journal of Psychiatric Research, 44,* 732–740.

Bennett, M. P., & Lengacher, C. A. (2006). Humor and laughter may influence health. *Evidence Based Complementary Alternative Medicine, 3,* 61–63.

Bennett, M. P., Zeller, J. M., Rosenberg, L., & McCann, J. (2003). The effect of mirthful laughter on stress and natural killer cell activity. *Alternative Therapies in Health and Medicine, 9,* 38–45.

Bennett, S. A., Beck, J. G., & Clapp, J. D. (2009). Understanding the relationship between post-traumatic stress disorder and trauma cognitions: The impact of thought control strategies. *Behaviour Research and Therapy, 47,* 1018–1023.

Benowitz, N. L. (2010). Nicotine addiction. *New England Journal of Medicine, 362,* 2295–2303.

Bentler, P. M. (2007). Can scientifically useful hypotheses be tested with correlations? *American Psychologist, 62,* 772–782.

Benton, S. A., Robertson, J. M., Tseng, W.-C., Newton, F. B., & Benton, S. L. (2003). Changes in counseling center client problems across 13 years. *Professional Psychology: Research and Practice, 34,* 66–72.

Ben-Tovim, D. I., Walker, K., Gilchrist, P., Freeman, R., Kalucy, R., & Esterman, A. (2001). Outcome in patients with eating disorders: A five-year study. *Lancet, 357,* 1254–1257.

Benyamina, A., Lecacheux, M., Blecha, L., Reynaud, M., & Lukasiewcz, M. (2008). Pharmacotherapy and psychotherapy in cannabis withdrawal and dependence. *Expert Reviews in Neurotherapy, 8,* 479–491.

Beratis, S., Gabriel, J., & Hoidas, S. (1994). Age at onset in subtypes of schizophrenic disorders. *Schizophrenic Bulletin, 20,* 287–296.

Berenbaum, H., Raghavan, C., Le, H., Vernon, L. L., & Gomez, J. J. (2003). A taxonomy of emotional disturbances. *Clinical Psychology: Science and Practice, 10,* 206–226.

Berenson, A. (2006, January 1). Study bolsters antidepression drugs. *Sacramento Bee,* A21.

Bergemann, N., Parzer, P., Jaggy, S., Auler, B., Mundt, C., & Maier-Braunleder, S. (2008). Estrogen and comprehension of metaphoric speech in women suffering from schizophrenia: Results of a double-blind, placebo-controlled trial. *Schizophrenia Bulletin, 34,* 1172–1181.

Bergemann, N., Parzer, P., Runnebaum, B., Resch, F., & Mundt, C. (2007). Estrogen, menstrual cycle phases, and psychopathology in women suffering from schizophrenia. *Psychological Medicine, 37,* 1427–1436.

Berger, M. (2010). 'It's the sight not the bite': A model and reinterpretation of visually-based developmental fears. *Clinical Psychology Review, 30,* 779–793.

Bergstrom, R. L., & Neighbors, C. (2006). Body image disturbance and the social norms approach: An integrative review of the literature. *Journal of Social and Clinical Psychology, 25,* 975–1000.

Bergstrom, R. L., Neighbors, C., & Lewis, M. A. (2004). Do men find "bony" women attractive? Consequences of misperceiving opposite sex perceptions of attractive body image. *Body Image, 1,* 183–191.

Berk, L., Hallam, K. T., Colom, F., Vieta, E., Hasty, M., Macneil, C., & Berk, M. (2010). Enhancing medication adherence in patients with bipolar disorder. *Human Psychopharmacology, 25,* 1–16.

Berkman, L. F., & Syme, S. L. (1979). Social networks, host resistance, and mortality: A nine-year follow-up of Alameda County residents. *American Journal of Epidemiology, 109,* 186–204.

Berlim, M. T., & Turecki, G. (2007). Definition, assessment, and staging of treatment-resistant refractory major depression: a review of current concepts and methods.. *Canadian Journal of Psychiatry, 52,* 46–54.

Berman, A. L. (2006). Risk management with suicidal patients. *Journal of Clinical Psychology: In Session, 62,* 171–184.

Berman, J. (2010). The media's contribution to eating disorders. Retrieved from http://doctorjenn.com/wordpress/tag/royal-college-of-psychiatrists/

Berman, S. M., Kuczenski, R., McCracken, J. T., & London, E. D. (2009). Potential adverse effects of amphetamine treatment on brain and behavior: A review. *Molecular Psychiatry, 14,* 123–142.

Bernard, J. (1976). Homosociality and female depression. *Journal of Social Issues, 32,* 213–238.

Bernsburg, J. G., & Krohn, M. D. (2003). Labeling, life chances, and adult crime: The direct and indirect effects of official intervention in adolescence on crime in early adulthood. *Criminology, 4,* 1287–1318.

Berrington de González, A., Mahesh, M. Kim, K., Bhargavan, M., Lewis, R., Mettler, F., & Land, C. (2009). Projected cancer risks from computed tomographic scans performed in the United States in 2007. *Archives of Internal Medicine, 169,* 2071–2077.

Berrios, G. E. (1989). Obsessive-compulsive disorder: Its conceptual history in France during the 19th century. *Comprehensive Psychiatry, 30,* 283–295.

Bersoff, D. N. (1981). Testing and the law. *American Psychologist, 36,* 1047–1057.

Beyer, J. L., Young, R., Kuchibhatla, M., & Krishnan, K. R. (2009). Hyperintense MRI lesions in bipolar disorder: A meta-analysis and review. *International Review of Psychiatry, 21,* 394–409.

Bhadrinath, B. R. (1990). Anorexia nervosa in adolescents of Asian extraction. *British Journal of Psychiatry, 156,* 565–568.

Bhalla, R. N. (2009). *Schizophreniform disorder.* Retrieved from http://emedicine.medscape.com/article/292885-print

Bhat, V. M., Cole, J. W., Sorkin, J. D., Wozniak, M. A., Malarcher, A. M., . . . Kittner, S. J. (2008). Dose-response relationship between cigarette smoking and risk of ischemic stroke in young women. *Stroke, 39,* 2439–2443.

Bhugra, D. (2005). The global prevalence of schizophrenia. *PLoS Medicine, 2,* 372–373.

Bickel, W. K., Amass, L., Higgins, S. T., Badger, G. J., & Esch, R. A. (1997). Effects of adding behavioral treatment to opioid detoxification with buprenorphine. *Journal of Consulting and Clinical Psychology, 65,* 803–810.

Bienenfeld, D. (2007a). Cognitive therapy of patients with personality disorders. *Psychiatric Annals, 37*(2), 133–139.

Bienenfeld, D. (2007b). Personality disorders. *Psychiatric Annals, 37*(2), 84–85.

Bienvenu, O. J., Davydow, D. S., & Kendler, K. S. (2011). Psychiatric 'diseases' vs behavioral disorders and degree of genetic influence. *Psychological Medicine, 41,* 33–40.

Bigard, A. (2010). Risks of energy drinks in youth. *Archives of Pediatrics, 17,* 1625–1631.

Bigio, E. H. (2008). Update on recent molecular and genetic advances in frontotemporal lobar degeneration. *Journal of Neuropathology and Experimental Neurology, 67,* 635–648.

Bindman, J., & Thornicroft, G. (2008). Strategies for engagement and treatment. In K. T. Mueser & D. V. Jeste (Eds.), *Clinical handbook of schizophrenia* (pp. 516–523). New York: Guilford Press.

Binzer, M., Eisenmann, M., & Kullgren, G. (1998). Illness behavior in the acute phase of motor disability in neurological disease and in conversion disorder: A comparative study. *Journal of Psychosomatic Research, 44,* 657–666.

Biondi, M., & Picardi, A. (2003). Attribution of improvement to medication and increased risk of relapse of panic disorder with agoraphobia: Reply. *Psychotherapy and Psychosomatics, 72,* 110–111.

Bishop, G. E., Enkelmann, H. C., Tong, E. M. W., Why, Y. P., Diong, S. M., Ang, J., & Khader, M. (2003). Job demands, decisional control, and cardiovascular responses. *Journal of Occupational Health Psychology, 8,* 146–156.

Bishop, J. (2005). *Does Internet addiction exist?* Retrieved from www.jonathanbishop.com/Weblog/Display. aspx?Item=75

Biskupic, J. (2007, November 12). A new page in O'Connors' love story. *USA Today.* Retrieved from www.usatoday.com/news/nation/2007-11-12-court_N.htm

Bjornsson, A. S., Dyck, I., Moitra, E., Stout, R. L., Weisberg, R., . . . Phillips, K. A. (2011). The clinical course of body dysmorphic disorder in the Harvard/Brown anxiety research project (HARP). *Journal of Nervous and Mental Disease, 199,* 55–57.

Black, D. L., Cawthon, B., Robert, T., Moser, F., Caplan, Y. H., & Cone, E. J. (2009). Multiple drug ingestion by ecstasy abusers in the United States. *Journal of Analytical Toxicology, 33,* 143–147.

Black, S. T. (1993). Comparing genuine and simulated suicide notes: A new perspective. *Journal of Consulting and Clinical Psychology, 67,* 699–702.

Blanchard, J. J., Gangestad, S. W., Brown, S. A., & Horan, W. P. (2000). Hedonic capacity and schizotypy revisited: A taxometric analysis of social anhedonia. *Journal of Abnormal Psychology, 109,* 87–95.

Blanchard, R., Lykins, A. D., Wherrett, D., Kuban, M. E., Cantor, J. M., . . . Klassen, P. E. (2009). Pedophilia, hebephilia, and the DSM-V. *Archives of Sexual Behavior, 38,* 335–350.

Blanchard, R., Racansky, I. G., & Steiner, B. W. (1986). Phallometric detection of fetishistic arousal. *Journal of Sex Research, 22,* 452–462.

Blashill, A. J., & Vander Wal, J. S. (2009). Mediation of gender role conflict and eating pathology in gay men. *Psychology of Men and Masculinity, 10,* 204–207.

Bleichhardt, G., Timmer, B., & Reif, W. (2005). Hypochondriasis among patients with multiple somatoform symptoms: Psychopathology and outcome of a cognitive-behavioral therapy. *Journal of Contemporary Psychotherapy, 35,* 239–340.

Blier, P., Szabo, S. T., Haddjeri, N., & Dong, J. (2000). Orbitofrontal cortex-basal ganglia system in OCD. *International Journal of Neuropsychopharmacology, 3,* 1–14.

Block, J. J. (2006). Ethical concerns regarding olanzapine versus placebo in patients prodromally symptomatic for psychosis. *American Journal of Psychiatry, 163,* 1838.

Bloom, B., & Cohen, R. A. (2007). Summary health statistics for U.S. children: National Health Interview Survey, 2006. *National Center for Health Statistics. Vital Health Statistics,* 10, 2007.

Bloomberg, D. (2000, January/February). Bennett Braun case settled: Two-year loss of license, five years probation. *Skeptical Inquirer,* 7–8.

Bloomfield, K., Stockwell, T., Gerhard, F., & Rhen, N. (2003). International comparisons of alcohol consumption. *Alcohol Research and Health, 27,* 95–109.

Blouin, A., Blouin, J., Aubin, P., Carter, J., Goldstein, C., Boyer, H., & Perez, E. (1992). Seasonal patterns of bulimia nervosa. *American Journal of Psychiatry, 149,* 73–81.

Bochukova, E. G., Huang, N., Keogh, J., Henning, E., Purmann, C., . . . Farooqui, I. S. (2010). Large, rare chromosomal deletions associated with severe early-onset obesity. *Nature, 463,* 666–669.

Bock, M. A. (2007). The impact of social-behavioral learning strategy training on the social interaction skills of four students with Asperger syndrome. *Focus on Autism and Other Developmental Disabilities, 22,* 88–95.

Boden, J. M., Fergusson, D. M., & Horwood, J. (2007). Anxiety disorders and suicidal behaviours in adolescence and young adulthood: Findings from a longitudinal study. *Psychological Medicine, 37,* 431–440.

Boehmer, U., Bowen, D. J., & Bauer, G. R. (2007). Overweight and obesity in sexual-minority women: Evidence from population-based data. *American Journal of Public Health, 29,* 1134–1140.

Bohne, A., Keuthen, N. J., Wilhelm, S., Deckersbach, T., & Jenike, M. A. (2002). Prevalence of symptoms of body dysmorphic disorder and its correlates: A cross-cultural comparison. *Psychosomatics, 43,* 486–490.

Bokszczanin, A. (2008). Parental support, family conflict, and overprotectiveness: Predicting PTSD symptom levels of adolescents 28 months after a natural disaster. *Anxiety, Stress, & Coping, 21,* 325–335.

Boldrini, M., Underwood, M. D., Mann, J. J., & Arango, V. (2005). More tryptophan hydroxylase in the brainstem dorsal raphe nucleus in depressed suicides. *Brain Research, 104,* 19–28.

Boll, T. J. (1983). Neuropsychological assessment. In I. B. Weiner (Ed.), *Clinical methods in psychology.* New York: Wiley.

Bollini, A. M., & Walker, E. F. (2007). Schizotypal personality disorder. In W. O. Donohus, K. A. Fowler, & S. O. Lilienfeld (Eds.), *Personality disorders: Toward the DSM-V.* Los Angeles: Sage Publications.

Bolton, J. M., Belik, S. L., Enns, M. W., Cox, B. J., & Sareen, J. (2008). Exploring the correlates of suicide attempts among individuals with major depressive disorder: findings from the national epidemiologic survey on alcohol and related conditions. *Journal of Clinical Psychiatry, 69,* 1139–1149.

Bolton, J. M., Pagura, J., Enns, M. W., Grant, B., & Sareen, J. (2010). A population-based longitudinal study of risk factors for suicide attempts in major depressive disorder. *Journal of Psychiatric Research, 44,* 817–826.

Bonde, J. P. (2008). Psychosocial factors at work and risk of depression: A systematic review of the epidemiological evidence. *Occupational and Environmental Medicine, 65,* 438–445.

Bongar, B. (1991). *The suicidal patient: Clinical and legal standards of care.* Washington, DC: American Psychological Association.

Bongar, B. (1992). Effective risk management and the suicidal patient. *Register Report, 18,* 1–3, 21–27.

Boodman, S. G. (2007). Eating disorders: Not just for women. Retrieved from http://www.washingtonpost.com/wp-dyn/content/article/2007/03/09/AR2007030901870.html

Boon, S., & Draijer, N. (1993). Multiple personality disorder in the Netherlands: A clinical investigation of 71 patients. *American Journal of Psychiatry, 150,* 489–494.

Boone, L., Soenens, B., Braet, C., & Goossens, L. (2010). An empirical typology of perfectionism in early-to-mid adolescents and its relation with eating disorder symptoms. *Behaviour Research and Therapy, 48,* 686–691.

Booth, R., & Rachman, S. (1992). The reduction of claustrophobia: I. *Behaviour Research and Therapy, 30,* 207–221.

Bootzin, R. R., & Bailey, E. T. (2005). Understanding placebo, nocebo, and iatrogenic treatment effects. *Journal of Clinical Psychology, 61,* 87.

Borch-Jacobsen, M. (1997). Sybil—The making of a disease: An interview with Dr. Herbert Spiegel. *New York Review of Books, 44,* 60–64.

Borda, T., & Sterin-Borda, L. (2006). Novel insight into neuroimmunogenic factors in the etiology of schizophrenia. *Psychiatric Annals, 36,* 102–108.

Bordnick, P. S., Graap, K. M., Copp, H. L., Brooks, J., & Ferrer, M. (2005). Virtual reality cue reactivity assessment in cigarette smokers. *Cyberpsychology and Behavior, 8,* 487–492.

Borgwardt, S. J., Picchioni, M. M., Ettinger, U., Toulopoulou, T., Murray, R., & McGuire, P. K. (2010). Regional gray matter volume in monozygotic twins concordant and disconcordant for schizophrenia. *Biological Psychiatry, 67,* 956–964.

Borkovec, T. D., & Ruscio, A. M. (2001). Psychotherapy for generalized anxiety disorder. *Journal of Clinical Psychiatry, 62,* 37–42.

Bornstein, R. F. (1997). Dependent personality disorder in the DSM-IV and beyond. *Clinical Psychology, 4,* 175–187.

Bornstein, R. F. (1998). Reconceptualizing personality disorder diagnosis in the DSM-V: The discriminant validity challenge. *Clinical Psychology, 5,* 333–343.

Borroni, B., Alberici, A., Archetti, S., Magnani, E., Di Luca, M., & Padovani, A. (2010). New insights into biological markers of frontotemporal lobar degeneration spectrum. *Current Medical Chemistry, 17,* 1002–1009.

Borzekowski, D. L. G., Schenk, S., Wilson, J. L., & Peebles, R. (2010). e-Ana and e-Mia: A content analysis of pro-eating disorder web sites. *American Journal of Public Health, 100,* 1526–1534.

Boucher, J., & Lewis, Y. (1992). Unfamiliar face recognition in relatively able autistic children. *Journal of Child Psychology and Psychiatry, 33,* 843–859.

Boudreault, S. (2011). Top six Charlie Sheen rantings, with analysis. Retrieved from http://celebs.gather.com/viewArticle.action?articleId=281474979115776

Bourne, D., Watts, S., Gordon, T., & Figueroa-Garcia, A. (2006). Analysis: One year after hurricane Katrina—Issues of social disadvantage and political process. *Communique, 3,* 9.

Bourque, F., van der Ven, E., & Malla, A. (2010). A meta-analysis of the risk for psychotic disorders among first- and second-generation immigrants. *Psychological Medicine, 41*(5), 897–910. doi:10.1017/S0033291710001406

Boustani, M., Peterson, B., Hanson, L., Harris, R., & Lohr, K. (2003). Screening for dementia in primary care: A summary of the evidence for the U.S. Preventive Services Task Force. *Annals of Internal Medicine, 138,* 927–937.

Bouvard, M. A., Milliery, M., & Cottraux, J. (2004). Management of obsessive compulsive disorder. *Psychotherapy and Psychosomatics, 73,* 149–157.

Bowden, C. L. (2010a). Diagnosis, treatment, and recovery maintenance in bipolar depression. *Journal of Clinical Psychiatry, 71,* e01.

Bowden, C. L. (2010b). Treatment strategies for bipolar depression. *Journal of Clinical Psychiatry, 71,* e10.

Bowie, C. R., Depp, C., McGrath, J. A., Wolyniec, P., Mausbach, B. T., . . . Pulver, A. E. (2010). Prediction of real-world functional disability in chronic mental disorders: a comparison of schizophrenia and bipolar disorder. *American Journal of Psychiatry, 167,* 1116–1124.

Bowler, J. V. (2007). Modern concept of vascular cognitive impairment. *British Medical Bulletin, 83,* 291–305.

Braaten, E. B., & Rosen, L. A. (2000). Self-regulation of affect in attention deficit-hyperactivity disorder (ADHD) and non-ADHD boys: Differences in empathic responding. *Journal of Consulting and Clinical Psychology, 68,* 313–321.

Bradley, R. G., Binder, E. B., Epstein, M. P., Tang, Y., Nair, H. P., . . . Ressler, K. J. (2008). Influence of child abuse on adult depression: Moderation by the corticotrophin-releasing hormone receptor gene. *Archives of General Psychiatry, 65,* 190–200.

Bradley, S. J. (1995). Psychosexual disorders in adolescence. In J. M. Oldham & M. B. Riba (Eds.), *American Psychiatric Press Review of Psychiatry* (Vol. 14). Washington, DC: American Psychiatric Press.

Braff, D. L. (2007). Introduction: The use of endophenotypes to deconstruct and understand the genetic architecture, neurobiology, and guide future treatments of the group of schizophrenias. *Schizophrenia Bulletin, 33,* 19.

Braff, D. L., Freedman, R., Schork, N. J., & Gottesman, I. I. (2007). Deconstructing schizophrenia: An overview of the use of endophenotypes in order to understand a complex disorder. *Schizophrenia Bulletin, 33,* 21–25.

Brajevic-Gizdic, I., Mulic, R., Pletikosa, M., & Kljajic, Z. (2009). Self-perception of drug abusers and addicts and investigators' perception of etiological factors of psychoactive drug addiction. *Collegium Antropologicum, 33,* 225–231.

Brambilla, P., Bellani, M., Yeh, P. H., Soares, J. C., & Tansella, M. (2009). White matter connectivity in bipolar disorder. *International Review of Psychiatry, 21,* 380–386.

Brambilla, P., Cerruti, S., Bellani, M., Perlini, C., Ferro, A., . . . Diwadkar, V. A. (2011). Shared impairment in associative learning in schizophrenia and bipolar disorder. *Progress in Neuropsychopharmacolgy and Biological Psychiatry, 35*(4), 1093–1099.

Brambilla, P., Soloff, P. H., Sala, M., Nocoletti, M. A., Keshavan, M. S., & Soares, J. C. (2004). Anatomical MRI study of borderline personality disorder patients. *Psychiatric Research: Neuroimaging, 131,* 125–132.

Brand, B., Classen, C., Lanins, R., Loewenstein, R., McNary, S., . . . Putnam, F. (2009). A naturalistic study of dissociative identity disorder and dissociative disorder not otherwise specified patients treated by community clinicians. *Psychological Trauma: Theory, Research, Practice, and Policy, 1,* 153–171.

Brand, B. L., Classen, C. C., McNary, S. W., & Zaveri, P. (2009). A review of dissociative disorders treatment studies. *Journal of Nervous and Mental Disease, 197,* 646–654.

Brand, B., & Lowenstein, R. J. (2010). Dissociative disorders: An overview of assessment, phenomenology, and treatment. *Psychiatric Times.* Retrieved from https://www.cmellc.com/landing/pdf/A10001101.pdf

Brandsma, J. (1979). *Outpatient treatment of alcoholism.* Baltimore: University Park Press.

Brannigan, G. G., Decker, S. L., & Madsen, D. H. (2004). *Innovative features of the Bender-Gestalt II and expanded guidelines for the use of the Global Scoring System* (Bender Visual-Motor Gestalt Test, 2nd ed., Assessment Service Bulletin No. 1). Itasca, IL: Riverside.

Brannon, G. E. (2011). History and mental status exam. Retrieved from http://emedicine.medscape.com/article/293402-print

Brasic, J. R., & Holland, J. A. (2007). A qualitative and quantitative review of obstetric complications and autistic disorder. *Journal of Developmental and Physical Disabilities, 19,* 337–364.

Brasic, J. R., & Wong, D. F. (2010). PET Scanning in autism spectrum disorders. Retrieved from http://emedicine.medscape.com/article/1155568-overview

Bratiotis, C., Otte, S., Steketee, G., Muroff, J., & Frost, R. O. (2009). Hoarding fact sheet. Retrieved from http://www.ocfoundation.org/uploadedFiles/Hoarding%20Fact%20Sheet.pdf?n=3557

Braucht, G. (1982). Problem drinking among adolescents: A review and analysis of psychosocial research. In National Institute on Alcohol Abuse and Alcoholism, *Alcohol Monograph 4: Special Population Issues.* Washington, DC: U.S. Government Printing Office.

Braun, P., Kochonsky, G., Shapiro, R., Greenberg, S., Gudeman, J. E., Johnson, S., & Shore, M. F. (1981). Overview: Deinstitutionalization of psychiatric patients: A critical review of outcome studies. *American Journal of Psychiatry, 138,* 736–749.

Brausch, A. M., & Gutierrez, P. M. (2010). Differences in non-suicidal self-injury and suicide attempts in adolescents. *Journal of Youth and Adolescents, 39,* 233–242.

Braw, Y., Bloch, Y., Mendelovich, S., Ratzoni, G., Gal, G., . . . Levkovitz, Y. (2008). Cognition in young schizophrenia outpatients: Comparison of first-episode with multiepisode patients. *Schizophrenia Bulletin, 34,* 544–554.

Brawman-Mintzer, O., Lydiard, R. B., Rickels, K., & Small, G. W. (1997). Biological basis of generalized anxiety disorder: Discussion. *Journal of Clinical Psychology, 58,* 16–23.

Bray, J. H., Adams, G. J., Getz, J. G., & McQueen, A. (2003). Individuation, peers, and adolescent alcohol use: A latent growth analysis. *Journal of Consulting and Clinical Psychology, 71,* 553–564.

Breese-McCoy, S. J. (2011). Postpartum depression: An essential overview for the practitioner. *Southern Medical Journal, 104,* 128–132.

Breitborde, N. J. K., Lopez, S. R., & Nuechterlein, K. H. (2009). Expressed emotion, human agency, and schizophrenia: Toward a new model for the EE-relapse association. *Cultural and Medical Psychiatry, 33,* 41–60.

Bremner, J. D., Southwick, S. M., Johnson, D. R., Yehuda, R., & Charney, D. S. (1993). Childhood physical abuse and combat-related posttraumatic stress disorder in Vietnam veterans. *American Journal of Psychiatry, 150,* 235–239.

Brenner, D. J., & Hall, E. J. (2007). Computed tomography—An increasing source of radiation exposure. *New England Journal of Medicine, 357,* 2277–2284.

Brent, D. A. (2009a). Youth depression and suicide: Selective serotonin reuptake inhibitors treat the former and prevent the latter. *Canadian Journal of Psychiatry, 54,* 76–77.

Brent, D. A. (2009b). In search of endophenotypes for suicidal behavior. *American Journal of Psychiatry, 166,* 1087–1089.

Brent, D. A., Bridge, J., Johnson, B. A., & Connolly, J. (1996). Suicidal behavior runs in families: A controlled family study of adolescent suicide victims. *Archives of General Psychiatry, 53,* 1145–1152.

Brent, D. A., & Melhem, N. (2008). Familial transmission of suicidal behavior. *Psychiatric Clinics of North America, 31,* 157–177.

Brent, D. A., Perper, J. A., & Allman, C. J. (1987). Alcohol, firearms, and suicide among youth. *Journal of the American Medical Association, 257,* 3369–3372.

Breslau, N., Davis, G. C., & Andreski, P. (1995). Risk factors for PTSD-related traumatic events: A prospective analysis. *American Journal of Psychiatry, 152,* 529–535.

Bresnahan, M., Begg, M. D., Brown, A., Schaefer, C., Sohler, N., . . . Susser, E. (2007). Race and risk of schizophrenia in a US birth cohort: Another example of health disparity? *International Journal of Epidemiology, 36,* 751–758.

Breuer, J., & Freud, S. (1957). *Studies in hysteria.* New York: Basic Books. (Original work published 1895)

Brewin, C. R., Andrews, B., & Valentine, J. D. (2000). Meta-analysis of risk factors for posttraumatic stress disorder in trauma-exposed adults. *Journal of Consulting and Clinical Psychology, 68,* 748–766.

Brewslow, N., Evans, L., & Langley, J. (1986). Comparisons among heterosexual, bisexual, and homosexual male sadomasochists. *Journal of Homosexuality, 13,* 83–107.

Brezo, J., Klempan, T., & Turecki, G. (2008). The genetics of suicide: A critical review of molecular studies. *Psychiatric Clinics of North America, 31,* 179–203.

Bride, B. E. (2007). Prevalence of secondary traumatic stress among social workers. *Social Work, 52,* 63–70.

Bridge, J. A., Iyengar, S., Salary, C. B., Barbe, R. P., Birmaher, B., . . . Brent, D. A. (2007). Clinical response and risk for reported suicidal ideation and suicide attempts in pediatric antidepressant treatment: A meta-analysis of randomized controlled trials. *Journal of the American Medical Association, 297,* 1683–1696.

Briere, J. (1992). Methodological issues in the study of sexual abuse effects. *Journal of Consulting and Clinical Psychology, 60,* 196–203.

Briggs, E. S., & Price, I. R. (2009). The relationship between adverse childhood experience and obsessive-compulsive symptoms and beliefs: The role of anxiety, depression, and experiential avoidance. *Journal of Anxiety Disorders, 23,* 1037–1046.

Brim, S. N., Rudd, R. A., Funk, R. H., & Callahan, D. B. (2008). Asthma prevalence among US children in underrepresented minority populations: American Indian/Alaska Native, Chinese, Filipino, and Asian Indian. *Pediatrics, 122,* 217–222.

Brislin, R. (1993). *Understanding culture's influence on behavior.* New York: Harcourt Brace Jovanovich.

Bristol, M. M., Cohen, D. J., Costello, E. J., Deckla, M. B., Eckberg, T. J., . . . Spence, M. A. (1996). State of the science in autism: Report to the National Institute of Health. *Journal of Autism and Developmental Disorders, 26,* 121–154.

Britton, J. C., Lissek, S., Grillon, C., Norcross, M. A., & Pine, D. S. (2011). Development of anxiety: The role of threat appraisal and fear learning. *Depression and Anxiety, 28,* 5–17.

Broadwater, K., Curtin, L., Martz, D. M., & Zrull, M. C. (2006). College student drinking: Perception of the norm and behavioral intentions. *Addictive Behaviors, 31,* 632–640.

Broeren, S., Lester, K. J., Muris, P., & Field, A. P. (2011). They are afraid of the animal, so therefore I am too: Influence of peer modeling on fear beliefs and approach–avoidance behaviors towards animals in typically developing children. *Behaviour Research and Therapy, 49,* 50–57.

Brooks, J. O. Goldberg, J. F., Ketter, T. A., Miklowitz, D. J., Calabrese, J. R., Bowden, C. L., & Thase, M. E. (2011). Safety and tolerability associated with second-generation antipsychotic polytherapy in bipolar disorder: findings from the systematic treatment enhancement program for bipolar disorder. *Journal of Clinical Psychiatry, 72,* 240–247.

Brooks, L. G., & Loewenstein, D. A. (2010). Assessing the progression of mild cognitive impairment to Alzheimer's disease: Current trends and future directions. *Alzheimer's Research & Therapy, 2,* 28. Retrieved from http://alzres.com/content/2/5/28

Brooks, S., Prince, A., Stahl, D., Campbell, I. C., & Treasure, J. (2011). A systematic review and meta-analysis of cognitive bias to food stimuli in people with disordered eating behavior. *Clinical Psychology Review, 31,* 37–51.

Brooks-Harris, J. E. (2008). *Integrative multitheoretical psychotherapy.* Boston: Lahaska Press.

Brotman, M. A., Schmajuk, M., Rich, B. A., Dickstein, D. P., Guyer, A. E., . . . Leibenluft, E. (2006). Prevalence, clinical correlates, and longitudinal course of severe mood dysregulation in children.

Brotman, M. A., Kassem, L., Reising, M. M., Guyer, A. E., Dickstein, D. P., . . . Leibenluft, E. (2007). Parental diagnoses in youth with narrow phenotype bipolar disorder or severe mood dysregulation. *American Journal of Psychiatry, 164,* 1238–1241. *Biological Psychiatry, 60,* 991–997.

Brotto, L. A. (2009). The DSM diagnostic criteria for hypoactive sexual desire disorder. *Archives of Sexual Behavior.* doi: 10.1007/s10508-009-9543-1

Brotto, L. A., & Luria, M. (2008). Menopause, aging, and sexual response in women. In D. Rowland & L. Incrocci (Eds.), *Handbook of sexual and gender identity disorders* (pp. 251–283). Hoboken, NJ: Wiley.

Brower, V. (2006). Loosening addiction's deadly grip. *EMBO Reports, 7,* 140–142.

Brown, D., & Srebalus, D. J. (2003). *Introduction to the counseling profession.* Boston: Allyn & Bacon.

Brown, E. C., Catalano, R. F., Fleming, C. B., Haggerty, K. P., & Abbott, R. D. (2005). Adolescent substance use outcomes in the Raising Healthy Children Project: A two-part latent growth curve analysis. *Journal of Consulting and Clinical Psychology, 73,* 699–710.

Brown, G. L., Ebert, M., Goyer, P., Jimerson, D. C., Klein, W. J., Bunney, W. E., & Goodwin, F. K. (1982). Aggression, suicide, and serotonin: Relationships to CSF amine metabolites. *American Journal of Psychiatry, 139,* 741–746.

Brown, G. R., & Anderson, B. (1991). Psychiatric morbidity in adult inpatients with childhood histories of sexual and physical abuse. *American Journal of Psychiatry, 148,* 55–61.

Brown, G. W., & Harris, T. O. (1989). Depression. In G. W. Brown & T. O. Harris (Eds.), *Life events and illness* (pp. 49–93). New York: Guilford Press.

Brown, J. (2004, December 14). "Magic" opening for Burger King. *Miami Times,* p. 1a.

Brown, J., McKone, E., & Ward, J. (2010). Deficits of long-term memory in ecstasy users are related to cognitive complexity of the task. *Psychopharmacology, 209,* 51–67.

Brown, J., O'Brien, P. M., Marjoribanks, J., & Wyatt, K. (2009). Selective serotonin reuptake inhibitors for premenstrual syndrome. *Cochrane Database Systematic Review.* Retrieved from http://onlinelibrary.wiley.com/o/cochrane/clsysrev/articles/CD001396/frame.html

Brown, T. A. (2007). Temporal course and structural relationships among dimensions of temperament and DSM-IV anxiety and mood disorder constructs. *Journal of Abnormal Psychology, 116,* 313–328.

Brown, T. A., & Cash, T. F. (1990). The phenomenon of nonclinical panic: Parameters of panic, fear, and avoidance. *Journal of Anxiety Disorders, 4,* 15–29.

Brown, T. A., Chorpita, B. R., & Barlow, D. H. (1998). Structural relationships among dimensions of the DSM-IV anxiety and mood disorder and dimensions of negative affect, positive affect, and autonomic arousal. *Journal of Abnormal Psychology, 107,* 179–192.

Brown, T. A., Di Nardo, P. A., Lehman, C. L., & Campbell, L. A. (2001). Reliability of DSMIV anxiety and mood disorders: Implications for the classification of emotional disorders. *Journal of Abnormal Psychology, 110,* 49–58.

Browne, B. (2011). Sinister secrets in the sky. Retrieved from http://www.cyprus-mail.com/conspiracy-theories/sinister-secrets-sky/20110202

Bruch, H. (1978). Obesity and anorexia nervosa. *Psychosomatics, 19,* 208–221.

Bruch, M. A., Fallon, M., & Heimberg, R. G. (2003). Social phobia and difficulties in occupational adjustment. *Journal of Counseling Psychology, 50,* 109–117.

Bruch, M. A., & Heimberg, R. G. (1994). Differences in perceptions of parental and personal characteristics between generalized and nongeneralized social phobics. *Journal of Anxiety Disorders, 8,* 155–168.

Bruno, R., Matthews, A. J., Topp, L., Degenhardt, L., Gomez, R., & Dunn, M. (2009). Can the severity of dependence scale be usefully applied to 'ecstasy'? *Neuropsychobiology, 60,* 137–147.

Brunoni, A. R., Fraguas, R., & Fregni, F. (2009). Pharmacological and combined interventions for the acute depressive episode: Focus on efficacy and tolerability. *Journal of Therapeutics and Clinical Risk Management, 5,* 897–910.

Brunoni, A. R., Teng, C. T., Correa, C., Imamura, M., Brasil-Neto, J. P., . . . Diwadkar, V. A. (2010). Neuromodulation approaches for the treatment of major depression: challenges and recommendations from a working group meeting. *Arquivos de Neuro-Psiquiatria, 68*(3), 433–451.

Bruss, M. B., Morris, J., & Dannison, L. (2003). Prevention of childhood obesity: Sociocultural and familial factors. *Journal of the American Dietetic Association, 103,* 1042–1045.

Bryan, C. J., & Rudd, D. (2006). Advances in the assessment of suicide risk. *Journal of Clinical Psychology: In Session, 62,* 185–200.

Bryant, K. (2001, February 20). Eating disorders: In their own words. *Atlanta Journal-Constitution,* p. B4.

Bryant, R. A., Felmingham, K. L., Falconer, E. M., Pe Benito, L., Dobson-Stone, C., Pierce, K. D., & Schofield, P. R. (2010). Preliminary evidence of the short allele of the serotonin transporter gene predicting poor response to cognitive behavior therapy in posttraumatic stress disorder. *Biological Psychiatry, 67,* 1217–1219.

Buchanan, A. (1997). The investigation of acting on delusions as a tool for risk assessment in the mentally disordered. *British Journal of Psychiatry, 170,* 12–14.

Budd, G. (2007). Disordered eating: Young women's search for control and connection. *Journal of Child and Adolescent Nursing, 20,* 96–106.

Budney, A. J., Vandrey, R. G., Hughes, J. R., Thostenson, J. D., & Bursac, Z. (2008). Comparison of cannabis and tobacco withdrawal: Severity and contribution to relapse. *Journal of Substance Abuse Treatment, 35,* 362–368.

Buitelaar, J., & Medori, R. (2010). Treating attention-deficit/hyperactivity disorder beyond symptom control alone in children and adolescents: A review of the potential benefits of long-acting stimulants. *European Child and Adolescent Psychiatry, 19,* 325–340.

Bulik, C. M., & Kendler, K. S. (2000). "I am what I (don't) eat": Establishing an identity independent of an eating disorder. *American Journal of Psychiatry, 157,* 1755–1760.

Bulik, C. M., & Reichborn-Kjennerud, T. (2003). Medical morbidity in binge eating disorder. *International Journal of Eating Disorders, 34,* S39–S46.

Bulik, C. M., Thornton, L. M., Root, T. L., Pisetsky, E. M., Lichtenstein, P., & Pedersen, N. L. (2010). Understanding the relation between anorexia nervosa and bulimia nervosa in a Swedish national twin sample. *Biological Psychiatry, 67,* 71–77.

Bull, C. B. (2004). Binge eating disorder. *Current Opinion in Psychiatry, 17,* 43–48.

Bullying Statistics (2009). Retrieved from http://www.bullyingstatistics.org/content/bullying-statistics-2009.html

Bunce, D., Kivipelto, M., & Wahlin, A. (2004). Utilization of cognitive support in episodic free recall as a function of apolipoprotein E and vitamin B12 or folate among adults aged 75 years and older. *Neuropsychology, 18,* 362–370.

Bunney, W. E., Pert, A., Rosenblatt, J., Pert, C. B., & Gallaper, D. (1979). Mode of action of lithium: Some biological considerations. *Archives of General Psychiatry, 36,* 898–901.

Buodo, G., Ghisi, M., Novara, C., Scozzari, S., Di Natale, A., & Sanavio, E. (2011). Assessment of cognitive functions in individuals with post-traumatic symptoms after work-related accidents. *Journal of Anxiety Disorders, 25,* 64–70.

Burgess, A. W., & Holmstrom, L. L. (1979). Rape: Sex disruption and recovery. *American Journal of Orthopsychiatry, 49,* 648–657.

Burghart, G., & Finn, C. A. (2010). *Handbook of MRI scanning.* New York: Mosby.

Burgy, M. (2001). The narcissistic function in obsessive-compulsive neurosis. *American Journal of Psychotherapy, 55,* 65–73.

Burham, J. J. (2009). Contemporary fears of children and adolescents: Coping and resiliency in the 21st century. *Journal of Counseling and Development, 87,* 28–33.

Burke, S. C., Cremeens, J., Vail-Smith, K., & Woolsey, C. (2010). Drunkorexia: Calorie restriction prior to alcohol consumption among college freshman. *Journal of Alcohol & Drug Education.* Retrieved from http://findarticles.com/p/articles/mi_go2545/is_2_54/ai_n55140635/

Burke, W. J., & Bohac, D. L. (2001). Amnestic disorder due to a general medical condition and amnestic disorder not otherwise specified. In G. O. Gabbard (Ed.), *Treatment of psychiatric disorders* (pp. 609–624). Washington, DC: American Psychiatric Press.

Burman, B., Mednick, S. A., Machon, R. A., Parnas, J., & Schulsinger, F. (1987). Children at high risk for schizophrenia: Parents and offspring perceptions of family relationships. *Journal of Abnormal Psychology, 96,* 364–366.

Burruss, J. W., Travella, J. I., & Robinson, R. G. (2001). Vascular dementia. In G. O. Gabbard (Ed.), *Treatment of psychiatric disorders* (pp. 515–534). Washington, DC: American Psychiatric Press.

Burstein, M., & Ginsburg, G. S. (2010). The effect of parental modeling of anxious behaviors and cognitions in school-aged children: An experimental pilot study. *Behaviour Research and Therapy, 48,* 506–515.

Burt, V. L., Whelton, P., Roccella, E. J., Higgins, M., Horan, M. J., & Labarthe, D. (1995). Prevalence of hypertension in the U.S. adult population: Results from the Third National Health and Nutrition Examination Survey, 1988–1991. *Hypertension, 25,* 305–313.

Burton, C., McGorm, K., Weller, D., & Sharpe, M. (2010). Depression and anxiety in patients repeatedly referred to secondary care with medically unexplained symptoms: A case-control study. *Psychological Medicine, 41*(3), 555–563. doi:10.1017/S0033291710001017

Bush, A., & Beail, N. (2004). Risk factors for dementia in people with Down syndrome: Issues in assessment and diagnosis. *American Journal on Mental Retardation, 109,* 83–97.

Busse, J. W., Montori, V. M., Krasnik, C., Patelis-Siotis, I., & Guyatt, G. H. (2009). Psychological intervention for premenstrual syndrome: A meta-analysis of randomized controlled trials. *Psychotherapy and Psychosomatics, 78,* 6–15.

Butcher, J. N. (1990). *The MMPI-2 in psychological treatment.* New York: Oxford University Press.

Butcher, J. N. (1995). Item content in the interpretation of the MMPI-2. In J. N. Butcher (Ed.), *Clinical personality assessment: Practical approaches* (pp. 302–316). New York: Oxford University Press.

Butler, L. D., Duran, R. E. F., Jasiukaitis, P., Koopman, C., & Spiegel, D. (1996). Hypnotizability and traumatic experience. *American Journal of Psychiatry, 153,* 42–59.

Butler, S. F., Black, R., Serrano, J., Wood, M., & Budman, S. (2010). Characteristics of prescription opioid abusers in treatment: Prescription opioid use history, age, use patterns, and functional severity. *Journal of Opioid Management, 6,* 239–41, 246–52.

Butzlaff, R. L., & Hooley, J. M. (1998). Expressed emotion and psychiatric relapse: A metaanalysis. *Archives of General Psychiatry, 55,* 547–553.

Buwalda, F. M., & Bouman, T. K. (2008). Predicting the effect of psychoeducational group treatment for hypochondriasis. *Clinical Psychology and Psychotherapy, 15,* 396–403.

Bystritsky, A., Kerwin, L., Noosha, N., Natoli, J. L., Abrahami, N., . . . Young, A. S. (2010). Clinical and subthreshold panic disorder. *Depression and Anxiety, 27,* 381–389.

Caccavale, J. (2002). Opposition to prescriptive authority: Is this a case of the tail wagging the dog? *Journal of Clinical Psychology, 58,* 623–633.

Cadoret, R. J., & Cain, C. (1981). Environmental and genetic factors in predicting adolescent antisocial behavior in adoptees. *Psychiatric Journal of the University of Ottawa, 6,* 220–225.

Cadoret, R. J., & Wesner, R. B. (1990). Use of the adoption paradigm to elucidate the role of genes and environment and their interaction in the genesis of alcoholism. In C. R. Cloninger & H. Begleiter (Eds.), *Genetics and biology of alcoholism* (pp. 31–42). Cold Spring Harbor, NY: Cold Spring Harbor Laboratory Press.

Cafri, G., Thompson, J. K., Ricciardelli, L., McCabe, M., Smolak, L., & Yesalis, C. (2005). Pursuit of the muscular ideal: Physical and psychological consequences and putative risk factors. *Clinical Psychology Review, 25,* 215–239.

Cahill, K., Stead, L. F., & Lancaster, T. (2008). Nicotine receptor partial agonists for smoking cessation. *Cochrane Database Systematic Review, 16,* CD006103.

California Birth Defects Monitoring Program. (2007). *Down syndrome.* Retrieved from http://www.cbdmp.org/bd_down_syn.htm

Callahan, L. A., Steadman, H. J., McGreevy, M. A., & Robbins, P. C. (1991). The volume and characteristics of insanity defense pleas: An eight-state study. *Bulletin of the American Academy of Psychiatry and the Law, 19,* 331–338.

Camara, W. J., Nathan, J. S., & Puente, A. E. (2000). Psychological test usage: Implications in professional psychology. *Professional Psychology: Research and Practice, 31,* 141–154.

Cameron, A., Palm, K., & Follette, V. (2010). Reaction to stressful life events: What predicts symptom severity? *Journal of Anxiety Disorders, 24,* 645–649.

Cameron, R. P., Grabill, C. M., Hobfoll, S. E., Crowther, J. H., Ritter, C., & Lavin, J. (1996). Weight, self-esteem, ethnicity, and depressive symptomatology during pregnancy. *Health Psychology, 15,* 293–297.

Campbell, M. L. C., & Morrison, A. P. (2007). The role of unhelpful appraisals and behaviours in vulnerability to psychotic–like phenomenon. *Behavioural and Cognitive Psychotherapy, 35,* 555–567.

Campbell, R. J. (1981). *Psychiatric dictionary* (5th ed.). New York: Oxford University Press.

Campo, J. A., Frederikx, M., Nijman, H., & Merckelback, H. (1998). Schizophrenia and changes in physical appearance. *Journal of Clinical Psychiatry, 59,* 197–198.

Campolongo, P., Trezza, V., Palmery, M., Trabace, L., & Cuomo, V. (2009). Developmental exposure to cannabinoids causes subtle and enduring neurofunctional alterations. *International Review of Neurobiology, 85,* 117–133.

Campos, M. S., Garcia-Jalon, E., Gilleen, J. K., David, A. S., Peralta, V., & Cuesta, M. J. (2011). Premorbid personality and insight in first-episode psychosis. *Schizophrenia Bulletin, 37,* 2011.

Canapary, D., Bongar, B., & Cleary, K. M. (2002). Assessing risk for completed suicide in patients with alcohol dependence: Clinicans' views of critical factors. *Professional Psychology: Research and Practice, 33,* 464–469.

Canas, F. (2005). Mechanisms of action of atypical antipsychotics. *CNS Spectrums, 8,* 5–11.

Canavera, K. E., Ollendick, May, J. T. E., & Pincus, D. B. (2010). Clinical correlates of comorbid obsessive-compulsive disorder and depression in youth. *Child Psychiatry and Human Development, 41,* 583–594.

Canfield, M., Keller, C., Frydrych, L., Ashrafioun, L., Purdy, Christopher, H., & Blondell, R., (2010). Prescription opioid use among patients seeking treatment for opioid dependence. *Journal of Addiction Medicine, 4,* 108–113.

Cannon, T. D., Cadenhead, K., Comblatt, B., Woods, S. W., Addington, J., . . . Heinssen, R. (2008). Prediction of psychosis in youth at high clinical risk: A multisite longitudinal study in North America. *Archives of General Psychiatry, 65,* 28–32.

Cantor, D. W., & Fuentes, M. A. (2008). Psychology's response to managed care. *Professional Psychology: Research and Practice, 39,* 638–645.

Caplan, P. J. (1995). *They say you're crazy.* Reading, MA: Addison-Wesley.

Capodilupo, C. M., Nadal, K. L., Corman, L., Hamit, S., Lyons, O. B., & Weinberg, A. (2010). The manifestation of gender microaggressions. In D. W. Sue (Ed.), *Microaggressions and marginality: Manifestation, dynamics and impact* (pp. 193–213). Hoboken, NJ: Wiley.

Cardemil, E., & Barber, J. P. (2001). Building a model for prevention practice: Depression as an example. *Professional Psychology: Research and Practice, 32,* 392–401.

Cardena, E., & Weiner, L. A. (2004). Evaluation of dissociation throughout the lifespan.

Psychotherapy: Theory, Research, Practice, Training, 41, 496–508.

Careaga, M., Van de Water, J., & Ashwood, P. (2010). Immune dysfunction in autism: A pathway to treatment. *Neurotherapeutics, 7,* 283–292.

Carels, R. A., Cacciapaglia, H., Perez-Benitez, C. I., Douglass, O., Christie, S., & O'Brien, W. H. (2003). The association between emotional upset and cardiac arrhythmias during daily life. *Journal of Consulting and Clinical Psychology, 71,* 613–618.

Carey, B. (2007, August 1). Man regains speech after brain stimulation. *The New York Times.* Retrieved from http://www.nytimes.com/2007/08/02/health/02brain.html

Carey, K. B., Scott-Sheldon, L., Carey, M. P., & DeMartini, K. S. (2007). Individual-level interventions to reduce college student drinking: A meta-analytic review. *Addictive Behaviors, 32,* 2469–2494.

Carey, G., & DiLalla, D. L. (1994). Personality and psychopathology: Genetic perspectives. *Journal of Abnormal Psychology, 103,* 32–43.

Carey, K. B., & Carey, M. P. (1995). Reasons for drinking among psychiatric outpatients: Relationship to drinking patterns. *Psychology of Addictive Behavior, 9,* 251–257.

Carlat, D. J., Camargo, C. A., & Herzog, D. B. (1997). Eating disorders in males: A report on 135 patients. *American Journal of Psychiatry, 154,* 1127–1132.

Carlin, A. S., Hoffman, H. G., & Weghorst, S. (1997). Virtual reality and tactile argumentation in the treatment of spider phobia: A case report. *Behaviour Research and Therapy, 35,* 153–158.

Carlson, E. B., & Rosser-Hogan, R. (1991). Trauma experiences, posttraumatic stress, dissociation, and depression in Cambodian refugees. *American Journal of Psychiatry, 148,* 1548–1551.

Carlson, L. E., Speca, M., Faris, P., & Patel, K. D. (2007). One year pre-post intervention follow-up of psychological, immune, endocrine and blood pressure outcomes of mindfulness-based stress reduction (MBSR) in breast and prostate cancer outpatients. *Brain and Behavioral Immunology, 21,* 1038–1049.

Carmichael, S. (2010). Debenhams reveals tricks of the trade and axes digitally enhanced models. Downloaded from: http://www.thisislondon.co.uk/standard/article-23846949-debenhams-reveals-tricks-of-the-trade-and-axes-digitally-enhanced-models.do

Carnes, P. (1983). *Out of the shadows: Understanding sexual addiction.* Minneapolis, MN: CompCare.

Carney, R. M., Freedland, K. E., & Veith, R. C. (2005). Depression, the autonomic nervous system, and coronary heart disease. *Psychosomatic Medicine, 67,* 29–33.

Caroff, S. N., Hurford, I., Lybrand, J., & Cabrina, C. E. (2011). Movement disorders induced by antipsychotic drugs: Implications of the CATIE schizophrenia trial. *Neurologic Clinics, 29,* 127–148.

Caroff, S. N., Ungvari, G. S., Bhati, M. T., Datto, C. J., & O'Reardon, J. P. (2007). Catatonia and prediction of response to electroconvulsive therapy. *Psychiatric Annals, 37,* 57–64.

Carpenter, W. T., Conley, R. R., Buchanan, R. W., Breier, A., & Tamminga, C. A. (1995). Patient response and resource management: Another view of clozapine treatment of schizophrenia. *American Journal of Psychiatry, 152,* 827–832.

Carpenter, W. T., Jr. (2010). Conceptualizing schizophrenia through attenuated symptoms in the population. *American Journal of Psychiatry, 167,* 1013–1016.

Carroll, K. M., & Onken, L. S. (2005). Behavioral therapies for drug abuse. *American Journal of Psychiatry, 162,* 1452–1460.

Carter, C. S., & Krug, M. K. (2009). The functional neuroanatomy of dread: Functional magnetic resonance imaging insights into generalized anxiety disorder and treatment. *American Journal of Psychiatry, 166,* 263–265.

Casey, B. J., Ruberry, E. J., Libby, V., Glatt, C. E., Hare, T., . . . Tottenham, N. (2011). Transitional and translational studies of risk for anxiety. *Depression and Anxiety, 28,* 18–28.

Casey, D. E. (2006). Implications of the CATIE trial on treatment: Extrapyramidal symptoms. *CNS Spectrums, 11,* 25–31.

Cash, R. (1998). Losing it? *Essence, 28,* 34–37.

Caspi, A., Sugden, K., Moffitt, T. E., Taylor, A., Craig, I. W., . . . Poulton, R. (2003). Influence of life stress on depression: Moderation by a polymorphism in the 5-HTT gene. *Science, 301,* 386–389.

Caspi, A., Moffitt, T. E., Cannon, M., McClay, J., Murray, R., . . . Craig, I. W. (2005). Moderation of the effect of adolescent-onset cannabis use on adult psychosis by a functional polymorphism in the catechol-O-methyltransferase gene: Longitudinal evidence of a gene X environment interaction. *Biological Psychiatry, 57*(10), 1117–1127.

Cassidy, F. (2010). Insight in bipolar disorder: Relationship to episode subtypes and symptom dimensions. *Journal of Neuropsychiatric Disease and Treatment, 6,* 627–631.

Cassidy, M. R., Roberts, J. S., Thomas D., Steinbart, E. J., Cupples, L. A., . . . Green, R. C. (2008). Comparing test-specific distress of susceptibility versus deterministic genetic testing for Alzheimer's disease. *Alzheimer's & Dementia: The Journal of the Alzheimer's Association, 4,* 406–413.

Castro-Blanco, D. R. (2005). Cultural sensitivity in conventional psychotherapy: A comment on Martinez-Taboas. *Psychotherapy: Theory, Research, Practice, Training, 42,* 14–16.

Catapano, F., Sperandeo, R., Perris, F., Lanzaro, M., & Maj, M. (2001). Insight and resistance in patients with obsessive-compulsive disorder. *Psychopathology, 34,* 62–69.

Cather, C. (2005). Functional cognitive-behavioural therapy: A brief, individual treatment for functional impairments resulting from psychotic symptoms in schizophrenia. *Canadian Journal of Psychiatry, 50,* 258–263.

Cauffman, E., & Steinberg, L. (1996). Interactive effects of menarcheal status and dating on dieting and disordered eating among adolescent girls. *Developmental Psychology, 32,* 631–635.

Cautela, J. R. (1966). Treatment of compulsive behavior by covert sensitization. *Psychological Record, 16,* 33–41.

Cavedini, P., Zorzi, C., Piccinni, M., Cavallini, M. C., & Bellodi, L. (2010). Executive dysfunctions in obsessive-compulsive patients and unaffected relatives: Searching for a new intermediate phenotype. *Biological Psychiatry, 67,* 1178–1184.

Center for Male Reproductive Medicine and Microsurgery. (2005). *Penile implants (prosthesis) surgery.* Retrieved from www.maleinfertility.org/penileimplants.html

Centers for Disease Control. (2005). State-specific prevalence of obesity among adults—United States, 2005. *Morbidity and Mortality Weekly Report, 55,* 985–988.

Centers for Disease Control and Prevention. (2006, June 5). Alcohol and public health. Retrieved from www.cdc.gov/alcohol/

Centers for Disease Control and Prevention. (2007a). Epilepsy. Retrieved from www.cdc.gov/epilepsy/index.htm

Centers for Disease Control and Prevention. (2007b, June). HIV/AIDS statistics and surveillance report: Cases of HIV infection and AIDS in the United States and dependent areas, 2005. Retrieved from www.cdc.gov/hiv/topics/surveillance/resources/reports/2005report/default.htm

Centers for Disease Control and Prevention. (2007c). Obesity and overweight. Retrieved from www.cdc.gov/needphp/dnpa/obesity/index.htm

Centers for Disease Control and Prevention. (2007d). Prevalence of autism spectrum disorders: Autism and developmental disabilities monitoring network, six sites, United States, 2000. *Morbidity and Mortality Weekly Report, 55*(SS-1).

Centers for Disease Control and Prevention (2007e). Suicide: Facts at a glance. Retrieved September 30, 2007, from www.cdc.gov/ncipc/dvp/suicide/

Centers for Disease Control and Prevention. (2007f). Traumatic brain injury. Retrieved January 11,2008, from www.cdc.gov/ncipc/factsheets/tbi.htm

Centers for Disease Control and Prevention. (2007g). Suicide prevention: Youth suicide. Retrieved from http://www.cdc.gov/ncipc/dvp/Suicide/youthsuicide.htm

Centers for Disease Control (CDC). (2009a). Difference in prevalence of obesity among black, white, and Hispanic adults—United States, 2006–2008. *MMWR, 58,* 740–744.

Centers for Disease Control and Prevention (CDC). (2009c). Prevalence of autism spectrum disorders—Autism and Developmental Disabilities Monitoring Network, United States, 2006. Retrieved from http://www.cdc.gov/mmwr/preview/mmwrhtml/ss5810a1.htm

Centers for Disease Control. (2010a). Health, United States, 2010. Downloaded April 16, 2011, from http://www.cded.gov/nchs/data/hus/hus10.pdf#066

Centers for Disease Control and Prevention (CDC). (2010b). Web-based Injury Statistics Query and

Reporting System (WISQARS). Retrieved from http://www.cdc.gov/injury/wisqars/index.html

Centers for Disease Control. (2010c). Youth risk behavior Surveillance—United States, 2009. *Morbidity and Mortality Weekly Report Surveillance Summary, 59*(SS-5), 1–142.

Centers for Disease Control. (2010d). Overweight and obesity: Health consequences. Retrieved from http://www.cdc.gov/obesity/causes/health.html

Centers for Disease Control. (2010e). Vital signs: State-specific obesity prevalence among adults—United States, 2009. *MMRW, 59,* 1–5.

Centers for Disease Control. (2010f). Increasing prevalence of parent-reported attention-deficit/hyperactivity disorder among children—United States, 2003 and 2007. *Morbidity and Mortality Weekly Report, 59,* 1439–1443.

Centers for Disease Control (CDC). (2011a). Unexplained dermopathy (also called "Morgellons"). Retrieved from http://www.cdc.gov/unexplaineddermopathy/

Centers for Disease Control (CDC). (2011b). CDC investigation of unexplained dermopathy. Retrieved from http://www.cdc.gov/unexplaineddermopathy/

Centers for Disease Control and Prevention (CDC). (2011c). Leading causes of death. Retrieved from http://www.cdc.gov/nchs/fastats/lcod.htm

Centers for Disease Control and Prevention (CDC). (2011d). Attention-deficit/hyperactivity disorders: Facts and statistics. Retrieved from http://www.cdc.gov/ncbddd/adhd/data.html

Centers for Disease Control and Prevention Web-based Injury Statistics Query and Reporting System. (2005). Injury statistics. Retrieved from www.cdc.gov/ncipc/wisqars/default.htm.

Centers for Disease Control and Prevention Web-based Injury Statistics Query and Reporting System. (2007a). Fatal injury reports. Retrieved from www.cdc.gov/ncipc/wisquars

Centers for Disease Control and Prevention Web-based Injury Statistics Query and Reporting System. (2007b). Leading causes of death reports. Retrieved from www.cdc.gov/ncipc/wisquars

Centers for Disease Control and Treatment. (2011). Downloaded June 10, 2011 from: http://www.cdc.gov/healthyweight/assessing/bmi/adult_bmi/index.html

Cernak, I. (2005). Blast (explosion)-induced neurotrauma: A myth becomes reality. *Restorative Neurology and Neuroscience, 23,* 139–140.

Cerullo, M. A., Adler, C. M., Delbello, M. P., & Strakowski, S. M. (2009). The functional neuroanatomy of bipolar disorder. *International Review of Psychiatry, 21,* 314–322.

Cha, C. B., Najmi, S., Park, J. M., Finn, C. T., & Nock, M. K. (2010). Attentional bias toward suicide-related stimuli predicts suicidal behavior. *Journal of Abnormal Psychology, 119,* 616–622.

Chadwick, P., Hughes, Russell, D., Russell, I., & Dagnan, D. (2009). Mindfulness groups for distressing voices and paranoia: A replication and randomized feasibility trial. *Behavioral and Cognitive Psychotherapy, 37,* 403–412.

Chadwick, P., Sambrooke, S., Rasch, S., & Davies, E. (2000). Challenging the omnipotence of voices: Group cognitive behavior therapy for voices. *Behaviour Research and Therapy, 38,* 993–1003.

Chae, D. H., Takeuchi, D. T., Barbeau, E. M., Bennett, G. G., Lindsey, J. C., Stoddard, A. M., & Krieger, N. (2008). Alcohol disorders among Asian Americans: Associations with unfair treatment, racial/ethnic discrimination, and ethnic identification (the national Latino and Asian Americans study, 2002–2003). *Journal of Epidemiology and Community Health, 62,* 973–979.

Chalder, M., Elgar, F. J., & Bennett, P. (2006). Drinking and motivations to drink among adolescent children of parents with alcohol problems. *Alcohol and Alcoholism, 41,* 107–113.

Challacombe, F., & Salkovskis, P. (2009). A preliminary investigation of the impact of maternal obsessive-compulsive disorder and panic disorder on parenting and children. *Journal of Anxiety Disorders, 23,* 848–847.

Chamberlain, S. R., Fineberg, N. A., Menzies, L. A., Blackwell, A. D., Bullmore, E. T., Robbins, T. W., & Sahakian, B. J. (2007). Impaired cognitive flexibility and motor inhibition in unaffected first-degree relatives of patients with obsessive-compulsive disorder. *American Journal of Psychiatry, 164,* 335–338.

Chambless, D. M. (1993). Division 12 Board of Clinical Psychology, Task Force on Promotion and Dissemination of Psychological Procedures. *Report adopted by the Division 12 Board—October 1993.* Unpublished document.

Champion, H. R., Holcomb, J. B., & Young L. A. (2009). Injuries from explosions. *Journal of Trauma, 66,* 1468–1476.

Chan, R. C. K., Di, X., McAlonan, G. M., & Gong, Q.-y. (2011). Brain anatomical abnormalities in high-risk individuals, first-episode, and chronic schizophrenia: An activiation likelihood estimation meta-analysis of illness progression. *Schizophrenia Bulletin, 37,* 177–188.

Chandler-Laney, P. C., Hunter, G. R., Ard, J. D., Roy, J. L., Brock, D. W., & Gower, B. A. (2009). Perception of others' body size influences weight loss and regain for European American but not African American women. *Health Psychology, 28,* 414–418.

Chapman, C., Gilger, K., & Chestnutt, A. (2010). The challenge of eating disorders on a college campus. *Counseling Today, 53,* 44–45.

Chapman, L. J., & Chapman, J. P. (1967). Genesis of popular but erroneous psychodiagnostic observations. *Journal of Abnormal Psychology, 72,* 193–204.

Chapman, L. K., & Steiger, M. F. (2010). Race and religion: Differential prediction of anxiety symptoms by religious coping in African American and European American young adults. *Depression and Anxiety, 27,* 316–322.

Charman, I., Swettenham, J., Baron-Cohen, S., Cox, A., Baird, G., & Drew, A. (1997). Infants with autism: An investigation of empathy, pretend play, joint attention and imitation. *Developmental Psychology, 33,* 781–789.

Chartier, K., & Caetano, R. (2010). Ethnicity and health disparities in alcohol research. *Alcohol Research & Health.* Retrieved from http://findarticles.com/p/articles/mi_m0CXH/is_1–2_33/ai_n55302113/

Chassin, L. C., Pillow, D. R., Curran, P. J., Molina, B. S., & Berrera, M. (1993). Relation of parental alcoholism to early adolescent substance use: A test of three mediating mechanisms. *Journal of Abnormal Psychology, 102,* 3–19.

Chaturvedi, S. K., Desai, G., & Shaligram, D. (2010). Dissociative disorders in a psychiatric institute in India—A selected review and patterns over a decade. *International Journal of Social Psychiatry, 56,* 533–539.

Chawarska, K., Volkmar, F., & Klin, A. (2010). Limited attentional bias for faces in toddlers with autism spectrum disorders. *Archives of General Psychiatry, 67,* 178–185.

Chekoudjian, C. B. (2009). The subjective experience of PMS: A sociological analysis of women's narratives (Unpublished masters thesis). University of South Florida: Tampa, FL. Retrieved from http://scholarcommons.usf.edu/etd/1895

Chen, E., Bloomberg, G. R., Fisher, E. B., & Strunk, R. C. (2003). Predictors of repeat hospitalizations in children with asthma: The role of psychosocial and socioenvironmental factors. *Health Psychology, 22,* 12–18.

Chen, E., Matthews, K. A., & Boyce, W. T. (2002). Socioeconomic differences in children's health: How and why do these relationships change with age? *Psychological Bulletin, 128,* 295–329.

Chen, D. T., Wynia, M. K., Moloney, R. M., & Alexander, G. C. (2009). U.S. physician knowledge of the FDA-approved indications and evidence base for commonly prescribed drugs: Results of a national survey. *Pharmacoepidemiology and Drug Safety, 18*(11), 1094–1100.

Chen, L. P., Murad, M. H., Paras, M. L., Colbenson, K. M., Sattler, A. L., . . . Zirakzadeh, A. (2010). Sexual abuse and lifetime diagnosis of psychiatric disorders: Systematic review and meta-analysis. *Mayo Clinic Proceedings, 85,* 618–629.

Chen, Y., Briesacher, B. A., Field, T. S., Tjia, J., Lau, D. T., & Gurwitz, J. H. (2010). Unexplained variation across US nursing homes in antipsychotic prescribing rates. *Archives of Internal Medicine, 170,* 89–95.

Chentsova-Dutton, Y. E., Tsai J. L., & Gotlib, I. H. (2010). Further evidence for the cultural norm hypothesis: Positive emotion in depressed and control European American and Asian American women. *Cultural Diversity and Ethnic Minority Psychology, 16,* 284–295.

Cherkasova, M. V., & Hechtman, L. (2009). Neuroimaging in attention-deficit hyperactivity disorder: Beyond the frontostriatal circuitry. *Canadian Journal of Psychiatry, 54,* 651–664.

Cheslack-Postava, K., Liu, K., & Bearman, P. S. (2011). Closely spaced pregnancies are associated with increased odds of autism in California sibling births. *Pediatrics, 127,* 246–253.

Cheyne, R. (2010). Literary, cultural, & disability studies: A tripartite approach to postcolonialism.

Journal of Literary & Cultural Disability Studies, 4, 201–204.

Chez, M. G., & Guido-Estrada, N. (2010). Immune therapy in autism: Historical experience and future directions with immunomodulatory therapy. *Neurotherapeutics, 7,* 293–301.

Child Welfare Information Gateway. (2006). *Child abuse and neglect fatalities: Statistics and interventions.* Retrieved from www.childwelfare.gov/pubs/factsheets/fatality.cfm

Chin, J. T., Hayward, M., & Drinnan, A. (2009). 'Relating' to voices: Exploring the relevance of this concept to people who hear voices. Psychology and Psychotherapy: *Theory, Research and Practice, 81,* 1–17.

Chobanian, A. V., Bakris, G. L., Black, H. R., Cushman, W. C., Green, L. A., . . . National High Blood Pressure Education Program Coordinating Committee. (2003). Seventh report of the Joint National Committee on Prevention, Detection, Evaluation, and Treatment of High Blood Pressure. *Hypertension, 42,* 1206–1274.

Chodoff, P. (1987). [Letter to the editor]. *American Journal of Psychiatry, 144,* 124.

Choi, P. Y. L., Pope, H. G., Jr., Olivardia, R., & Cash, T. F. (2002). Muscle dysphoria: A new syndrome in weightlifters. *British Journal of Sports Medicine, 36,* 375–377.

Chollar, S. (1988). Food for thought. *Psychology Today, 22,* 30–34.

Chollet, F., Tardy, J., Albucher, J., Thalamas, C., Berard, E., . . . Loubinoux, I. (2011). Fluoxetine for motor recovery after acute ischaemic stroke (FLAME): A randomised placebo-controlled trial. *The Lancet Neurology, 10*(2), 123–130. doi: 10.1016/S1474-4422(10)70314-8

Chopra, S., & Khan, R. A. (2009). Delusional disorder. Retrieved from http://emedicine.medscape.com/article/292991

Chorpita, B. F., & Barlow, D. H. (1998). The development of anxiety: The role of control in the early environment. *Psychological Bulletin, 124,* 3–21.

Christakis, N. A., & Fowler, J. H. (2007). The spread of obesity in a large social network over 32 years. *New England Journal of Medicine, 357,* 370–379.

Christensen, H., Griffiths, K.M., & Farrer, L. (2009). Adherence in internet interventions for anxiety and depression. *Journal of Medical Internet Research, 11,* e13.

Christensen, L., & Duncan, K. (1995). Distinguishing depressed from nondepressed individuals using energy and psychosocial variables. *Journal of Consulting and Clinical Psychology, 63,* 495–498.

Christiansen, S. C., Martin, S. B., Schleicher, N. C., Koziol, J. A., & Zuraw, B. L. (1996). Current prevalence of asthma-related symptoms in San Diego's predominantly Hispanic inner-city children. *Journal of Asthma, 33,* 17–26.

Christie, A. M., & Barling, J. (2009). Disentangling the indirect links between socioeconomic status and health: The dynamic roles of work stressors and personal control. *Journal of Applied Psychology, 94,* 1466–1478.

Chronis-Tuscano, A., Brooke, S. G., Molina, W. E., Pelham, B., Applegate, A., . . . Lahey, B. B. (2010). Very early predictors of adolescent depression and suicide attempts in children with attention-deficit/hyperactivity disorder. *Archives of General Psychiatry, 67,* 1044–1051.

Chung, R., & Okazaki, S. (1991). Counseling Americans of Southeast Asian descent: The impact of the refugee experience. In C. C. Lee & B. L. Richardson (Eds.), *Multicultural issues in counseling: New approaches to diversity* (pp. 107–126). Alexandria, VA: American Association for Counseling and Development.

Chung, T., Martin, C. S., Cornelius, J. R., & Clark, D. B. (2008). Cannabis withdrawal predicts severity of cannabis involvement at 1-year follow-up among treated adolescents. *Addiction, 103,* 787–799.

Cicero, D. C., Kerns, J. G., & McCarthy, D. M. (2010). The aberrant salience inventory: A new measure of psychosis proneness. *Psychological Assessment, 22,* 688–701.

Cinciripini, P. M., Lapitsky, L., Seay, S., Wallfisch, A., Kitchens, K., & Van Vunakis, H. (1995). The effects of smoking schedules on cessation outcome: Can we improve on common methods of gradual and abrupt nicotine withdrawal? *Journal of Consulting and Clinical Psychology, 63,* 388–400.

Ciraulo, D. A., Dong, Q., Silverman, B. L., Gastfriend, D. R., & Pettinati, H. M. (2008). Early treatment response in alcohol dependence with extended-release naltrexone. *Journal of Clinical Psychiatry, 69,* 190–195.

Cisler, J. M., Adams, T. G., Brady, R. E., Bridges, A. J., Lohr, J. M., & Olatunji, B. O. (2011). Unique affective and cognitive processes in contamination appraisals: Implications for contamination fear. *Journal of Anxiety Disorders, 25,* 28–35.

Cisler, J. M., Olatunji, B. O., & Lohr, J. M. (2009). Disgust, fear, and the anxiety disorders: A critical review. *Clinical Psychology Review, 29,* 34–46.

Clark, D. A., & Beck, A. T. (2009). *Cognitive therapy for anxiety disorders.* New York: Guilford Press.

Clark, L. A. (2005). Temperament as a unifying basis for personality and psychopathology. *Journal of Abnormal Psychology, 114,* 505–521.

Clark, M., Gosnell, M., Witherspoon, J., Huck, J., Hager, M., . . . Robinson, T. L. (1984, December 3). A slow death of the mind. *Newsweek,* pp. 56–62.

Clark, R. (2006). Perceived racism and vascular reactivity in Black college women: Moderating effects of seeking social support. *Health Psychology, 25,* 20–25.

Clarkin, J. F., Hurt, S. W., & Mattis, S. (1999). Psychological and neurological assessment. In R. E. Hales, S. C. Yudofsky & J. A. Talbott (Eds.), *Textbook of psychiatry* (pp. 253–280). Washington, DC: American Psychiatric Press.

Clarkin, J. F., & Levy, K. N. (2004). The influence of client variables on psychotherapy. In M. J. Lambert (Ed.), *Bergin and Garfield's handbook of psychotherapy and behavior change* (pp. 194–226). New York: Wiley.

Clarkin, J. F., Marziali, E., & Munroe-Blum, H. (1991). Group and family treatments for borderline personality disorder. *Hospital and Community Psychiatry, 42,* 1038–1043.

Classon, G. S., Buhlmann, U., Tolin, D. F., Rao, S. R., Reese, H. E., . . . Wilhelm, S. (2010). Need for speed: Evaluating slopes of OCD recovery in behavior therapy enhanced with D-cycloserine. *Behaviour Research and Therapy, 48,* 675–679.

Clatworthy, J., Bowskill, R., Parham, R., Rank, T., Scott, J., & Horne, R. J. (2009). Understanding medication non-adherence in bipolar disorders using a necessity-concerns framework. *Affective Disorders, 116,* 51–55.

Clay, R. A. (1997, April). Is assisted suicide ever a rational choice? *APA Monitor, 28,* 1, 43.

Clay, R. A. (2001). Marijuana youth treatment study produces promising results. *SAMHSA News, 9*(1), 17–19.

Clay, R. A. (2010). Psychology's voice is heard. *APA Monitor, 41,* 22.

Clay, R. A. (2011). Revising the DSM. *Monitor on Psychology, 41,* 54–55.

Cleckley, J. (1976). *The mask of sanity* (5th ed.). St. Louis, MO: Mosby.

Clemmensen, L. H. (1990). The "real-life test" for surgical candidates. In R. Blanchard & B. W. Steiner (Eds.), *Clinical management of gender identity disorders in children and adults* (pp. 119–136). Washington, DC: American Psychiatric Press.

Cloitre, M., Stovall-McClough, K. C., Nooner, K., Zorbas, P., Cherry, S., Jackson, C. L., . . . Petkova, E. (2010). Treatment for PTSD related to childhood abuse: A randomized control trial. *American Journal of Psychiatry, 167,* 915–924.

Cloninger, C. R., & Dokucu, M. (2008). Somatoform and dissociative disorders. In S. H. Fatemi & P. J. Clayton (Eds.). *The medical basis of psychiatry* (pp. 181–194). Totowa, NJ: Humana Press.

Cloninger, C. R., Reich, T., Sigvardsson, S., Von Knorring, A. L., & Bohman, M. (1986). The effects of changes in alcohol use between generations or the inheritance of alcohol abuse. In American Psychological Association (Ed.), *Alcoholism: A medical disorder: Proceedings of the 76th annual meeting of the American Psychological Association.* Washington, DC: Author.

Cloud, J. (2010, February 13). The DSM: How psychiatrists define 'disordered.' *Time.* Retrieved from http://www.time.com/time/health/article/0,8599,1964196,00.html?xid=rsstopstories#ixzz0fRfQE5B9

Coaley, K. (2010). *An introduction to psychological assessment and psychometrics.* Thousand Oaks, CA: Sage.

Coalition About Educating Against Sexual Endangerment (CEASE). (2011). Rape statistics. Retrieved from http://oak.cats.ohiou.edu/~ad361896/anne/cease/numberspage.html

Coelho, C. M., & Purkis, H. (2009). The origins of specific phobias: Influential theories and current perspectives. *Review of General Psychology, 13,* 335–348.

Coffman, J. A. (1989). Computed tomography in psychiatry. In N. C. Andreasen (Ed.), *Brain imaging: Applications in psychiatry* (pp. 1–65). Washington, DC: American Psychiatric Press.

Coghill, D., & Banaschewski, T. (2009). The genetics of attention-deficit/hyperactivity disorder. *Expert Review of Neurotherapeutics, 9,* 1547–1565.

Coghill, D., Soutullo, C., d'Aubuisson, C., Preuss, U., Lindback, T., Silverberg, M., & Buitelaar, J. (2008). Impact of attention-deficit/hyperactivity disorder on the patient and family: Results from a European survey. *Child and Adolescent Psychiatry and Mental Health, 2,* 31.

Cohen, N. (2009, July 28). A Rorschach cheat sheet on Wikipedia? *The New York Times.* Retrieved from http://www.nytimes.com/2009/07/29/technology/internet/29inkblot.html

Cohen, S., Frank, E., Doyle, W. J., Skoner, D. P., Rabin, B. S., & Gwaltney, J. M. (1998). Types of stressors that increase susceptibility in the common cold in healthy adults. *Health Psychology, 17,* 214–223.

Cohen, S., & Herbert, T. B. (1996). Health psychology: Psychological factors and physical disease from the perspective of human psychoneuroimmunology. *Annual Review of Psychology, 47,* 113–123.

Cohen, S., & Lemay, E. P. (2007). Why would social networks be linked to affect and health practices? *Health Psychology, 26,* 410–417.

Cole, D. A. (2004). Taxometrics in psychopathology research: An introduction to some of the procedures and related methodological issues. *Journal of Abnormal Psychology, 113,* 3–9.

Cole, M. (2006). Internationalism in psychology. Why we need it now more than ever. *American Psychologist, 61,* 904–917.

Coles, M. E., & Coleman, S. L. (2010). Barriers to treatment seeking for anxiety disorders: Initial data on the role of mental health literacy. *Depression and Anxiety, 27,* 63–71.

Collip, D., Oorschot, M., Thewissen, V., Van Os, J., Bentall, R., & Myin-Germeys, I. (2010). Social world interactions: how company connects to paranoia. *Psychological Medicine, 41*(5), 911–921. Advance online publication. doi:10.1017/S003329170001558

Collishaw, S., Pickles, A., Messer, J., Rutter, M., Shearer, C., & Maughan, R. (2007). Resilience to adult psychopathology following childhood mistreatment: Evidence from a community sample. *Child Abuse and Neglect, 31,* 211–229.

Colt, G. H., & Hollister, A. (1998, April). Were you born that way? *Life,* pp. 39–48.

Coltheart, M., Langdon, R., & McKay, R. (2007). Schizophrenia and monothematic delusions. *Schizophrenia Bulletin, 33,* 642–647.

Combs, D. R., Adams, S. D., Penn, D. L., Roberts, D., Thiegreen, J., & Stem, P. (2007). Social cognition and interaction training (SCIT) for inpatients with schizophrenia spectrum disorders: Preliminary findings. *Schizophrenia Research, 91,* 112–116.

Comings, D. E., Comings, B. G., Muhleman, G., Dietz, B., Shahbahrami, D., . . . Flanagan, S. D. (1991). The dopamine D2 receptor locus as a modifying gene in neuropsychiatric

disorders. *Journal of the American Medical Association, 266,* 1793–1800.

Compton, M. T. (2005). Risk factors and risk markers for schizophrenia. *Medscape Psychiatry and Mental Health, 8,* 1–5.

Comtois, K. A., & Linehan, M. M. (2006). Psychosocial treatments of suicidal behaviors: A practice-friendly review. *Journal of Clinical Psychology: In Session, 62,* 161–170.

Conklin, C. A., & Perkins, K. A. (2005). Subjective and reinforcing effects of smoking during negative mood induction. *Journal of Abnormal Psychology, 114,* 153–164.

Conner, B. T., Noble, E. P., Berman, S. M., Ozkaragoz, T., Ritchie, T., Antolin, T., & Sheen, C. (2005). DRD2 genotypes and substance use in adolescent children of alcoholics. *Drug and Alcohol Dependence, 79,* 379–387.

Conners, M. E., & Morse, W. (1993). Sexual abuse and eating disorders: A review. *International Journal of Eating Disorders, 13,* 1–11.

Connock, M., Juarez-Garcia, A., Jowett, S., Frew, E., Liu, Z., . . . Taylor, R. S. (2007). Methadone and buprenorphine for the management of opioid dependence: A systematic review and economic evaluation. *Health Technology Assessment, 11,* 1–171.

Conradi, H. J., Ormel, J., & de Jonge, P. (2010). Presence of individual (residual) symptoms during depressive episodes and periods of remission: A 3-year prospective study. *Psychological Medicine, 8,* 1–10.

Constantino, J. N., Majmudar, P., Bottini, A., Arvin, M., Virkud, Y., Simons, P., & Spitznagel, E. J. (2010). Infant head growth in male siblings of children with and without autism spectrum disorders. *Neurodevelopmental Disorders, 2,* 39–46.

Cook, E. W., III, Hodes, R. L., & Lang, P. J. (1986). Preparedness and phobia: Effects of stimulus content on human visceral conditioning. *Journal of Abnormal Psychology, 95,* 195–207.

Cooke, D. J., & Michie, C. (2001). Refining the construct of psychopathy: Towards a hierarchical model. *Psychological Assessment, 13,* 171–188.

Cooney, N. L., Litt, M. D., Morse, P. A., Bauer, L. O., & Gaupp, L. (1997). Alcohol cue reactivity, negative-mood reactivity, and relapse in treated alcoholic men. *Journal of Abnormal Psychology, 106,* 243–250.

Coons, P. M. (1986). Treatment progress in twenty patients with multiple personality disorder. *Journal of Nervous and Mental Disease, 174,* 715–721.

Coons, P. M. (1988). Misuse of forensic hypnosis: A hypnotically elicited false confession with the apparent creation of a multiple personality. *International Journal of Clinical and Experimental Hypnosis, 36,* 1–11.

Coons, P. M. (1994). Confirmation of childhood abuse in child and adolescent cases of multiple personality disorder and dissociative disorder not otherwise specified. *Journal of Nervous and Mental Disease, 182,* 461–464.

Cooper, A. J. (1969). A clinical study of coital anxiety in male potency disorders. *Journal of Psychosomatic Research, 13,* 143–147.

Cooper, M., & Osman, S. (2007). Metacognition in body dysmorphic disorder—A preliminary exploration. *Journal of Cognitive Psychotherapy: An International Quarterly, 21,* 148–155.

Cooper, M. L., Russell, M., & George, W. H. (1988). Coping, expectancies, and alcohol abuse: A test of social learning formulations. *Journal of Abnormal Psychology, 97,* 218–230.

Copeland, W. E., Keeler, G., Angold, A., & Costello, E. J. (2010). Posttraumatic stress without trauma in children. *American Journal of Psychiatry, 167,* 1059–1065.

Copersino, M. L., Boyd, S. J., Tashkin, D. P., Huestis, M. A., Heishman, S. J., . . . Gorelick, D. A. (2006). Cannabis withdrawal among non-treatment-seeking adult cannabis users. *American Journal of Addiction, 15,* 8–14.

Copolov, D. L., Mackinnon, A., & Trauer, T. (2004). Correlates of the affective impact of auditory hallucinations in psychotic disorders. *Schizophrenic Bulletin, 30,* 163–169.

Corbitt, E. M., & Widiger, T. A. (1995). Sex differences among the personality disorders: An exploration of the data. *Clinical Psychology: Science and Practice, 2,* 225–238.

Cordova, M. J., Cunningham, L. L. C., Carlson, C. R., & Andrykowski, M. A. (2001). Social constraints, cognitive processing, and adjustment to breast cancer. *Journal of Consulting and Clinical Psychology, 69,* 706–711.

Corey, G. (2001). *Theory and practice of counseling and psychotherapy* (6th ed.). Belmont, CA: Brooks/Cole.

Corey, G. (2004). *Theory and practice of group counseling* (6th ed.). Belmont, CA: Brooks/Cole.

Corey, G. (2005). *Theory and practice of counseling and psychotherapy* (7th ed.). Belmont, CA: Brooks/Cole.

Corey, G. (2007). *Theory and practice of group counseling* (7th ed.). Belmont, CA: Brooks/Cole.

Corey, G. (2008). *Theory and practice of counseling and psychotherapy* (8th ed.). Belmont, CA: Brooks/Cole.

Corey, G., & Corey, M. S. (2010). *Codes of ethics for the helping professions.* Belmont, CA: Brooks/Cole.

Corey, G., Callanan, P., & Corey, M. S. (2010). *Issues and ethics in the helping professions.* Belmont, CA: Brooks/Cole.

Corey, G., Corey, M. S., & Callanan, P. (1998). *Issues and ethics in the helping professions.* Pacific Grove, CA: Brooks/Cole.

Corey, G., Corey, M. S., & Callanan, P. (2003). *Issues and ethics in the helping professions* (6th ed.). Pacific Grove, CA: Brooks/Cole.

Cormier, J. F., & Thelen, M. H. (1998). Professional skepticism of multiple personality disorder. *Professional Psychology: Research and Practice, 29,* 163–167.

Cormier, W. H., & Cormier, L. S. (1998). *Interviewing strategies for helpers: Fundamental skills and cognitive behavioral interventions* (4th ed.). Pacific Grove, CA: Brooks/Cole.

Cornah, D. (2006). *The impact of spirituality on mental health: A review of the literature.* London: Mental Health Foundation.

Cornblatt, B. A., & Correll, C. U. (2010). Psychosis risk syndrome or attenuated psychotic symptoms syndrome and DSM-5. Downloaded from http://www.medscape.com/viewarticle/727682_print

Cornelius, J. R., Chung, T., Martin, C., Wood, D. S., & Clark, D. B. (2008). Cannabis withdrawal is common among treatment-seeking adolescents with cannabis dependence and major depression, and is associated with rapid relapse to dependence. *Addictive Behavior, 33,* 1500–1505.

Cornell, T., & Hamrin, V. (2008). Clinical interventions for children with attachment problems. *Journal of Child and Adolescent Psychiatric Nursing, 21,* 35–47.

Cornic, F., Consoli, A., & Cohen, D. (2007). Catatonia in children and adolescents. *Psychiatric Annals, 37,* 19–26.

Cornish, M. A., & Wade, N. G. (2010). Spirituality and religion in group counseling: A literature review with practice guidelines. *Professional Psychology: Research and Practice, 41,* 398–404.

Correll, C. U., Manu, P., Olshanskiv, Napolitano, B., Kane, J. M., & Malhotra, A. K. (2010). Cardiometabolic risk of second-generation antipsychotic medications during first-time use in children and adolescents. *Journal of the American Medical Association, 302,* 1765–1773.

Corrigan, P. W., & Watson, A. C. (2005). Mental illness and dangerousness: Fact or misperception, and implications for stigma. In P. W. Corrigan (Ed.), *On the stigma of mental illness: Practical strategies for research and social change* (pp. 165–179). Washington, DC: American Psychological Association.

Cortina, L. M., & Kubiak, S. P. (2006). Gender and posttraumatic stress: Sexual violence as an explanation for women's increased risk. *Journal of Abnormal Psychology, 115,* 753–759.

Cosand, B. J., Bourque, L. B., & Kraus, J. F. (1982). Suicide among adolescents in Sacramento County, California 1950–1979. *Adolescence, 17,* 917–930.

Cosgrove, L., Bursztajn, H. J., Kupfer, D. J., & Regier, D. A. (2009). Toward credible conflict of interest policies in clinical psychology. *Psychiatric Times, 26,* 1–3.

Costa, P. T., Jr., & McCrae, R. R. (2005). A five-factor model perspective on personality disorders. In S. Strack (Ed.), *Handbook of personality and psychopathology* (pp. 442–461). Hoboken, NJ: Wiley.

Costafreda, S. G., Fu, C. H., Picchioni, M., Touloupoulou, T., McDonald, C., Walshe, M., . . . McGuire, P. K. (2011). Pattern of neural responses to verbal fluency shows diagnostic specificity for schizophrenia and bipolar disorder. *BioMed Central Psychiatry, 11,* 18. doi:10.1186/1471-244X-11-18

Costello, E. J., Mustillo, S., Erkanli, A., Keeler, G., & Angold, A. (2003). Prevalence and development of psychiatric disorders in childhood and adolescence. *Archives of General Psychiatry, 60,* 837–844.

Cottler, L. B., Leung, K. S., & Abdallah, A. B. (2009). Test-re-test reliability of DSM-IV adopted criteria for 3,4-methylenedioxymethamphetamine (MDMA) abuse and dependence: A cross-national study. *Addiction, 104,* 1679–1690.

Cottone, R. R. (1992). *Theories and paradigms of counseling and psychotherapy.* Boston: Allyn & Bacon.

Cougnard, A., Marcelis, M., Myin-Germeys, I., De Graaf, F., Vollebergh, W., . . . Van Os, J. (2007). Does normal developmental expression of psychosis combine with environmental risk to cause persistence of psychosis? A psychosis proneness-persistence model. *Psychological Medicine, 37,* 513–527.

Cougnard, A., Grolleau, S., Lamarque, F., Beitz, C., Brugere, S., & Verdoux, H. (2006). Psychotic disorders among homeless subjects attending a psychiatric emergency service. *Social Psychiatry and Psychiatric Epidemiology, 41,* 904–910.

Council on Scientific Affairs. (1985). Scientific status of refreshing recollection by the use of hypnosis. *Journal of the American Medical Association, 253,* 1918–1923.

Courtet, P. (2010). Suicidality: Risk factors and the effects of antidepressants. *Neuropsychiatric Disorders and Treatment, 6,* 3–8.

Cousins, N. (1979). *Anatomy of an illness.* New York: Norton.

Cowen, P. J. (2002). Cortisol, serotonin and depression: All stressed out? *British Journal of Psychiatry, 180,* 99–100.

Cowley, G., & Underwood, A. (1997, May 26). Why Ebonie can't breathe. *Newsweek,* 58–63.

Cox, D. J., & McMahon, B. (1978). Incidence of male exhibitionism in the United States as reported by victimized college students. *International Journal of Law and Psychiatry, 1,* 453–457.

Cox, W. M., & Klinger, E. (1988). A motivational model of alcohol use. *Journal of Abnormal Psychology, 97,* 168–180.

Coyne, J. C., Stefanek, M., & Palmer, S. C. (2007). Psychotherapy and survival in cancer: The conflict between hope and evidence. *Psychological Bulletin, 133,* 367–394.

Coyne, S. M., Nelson, D. A., Graham-Kevan, N., Keister, E., & Grant, D. M. (2009). Mean on the screen: Psychopathy, relationship aggression, and aggression in the media. *Personality and Individual Differences, 48,* 288–293.

Craig, M. E. (1990). Coercive sexuality in dating relationships: A situational model. *Clinical Psychology Review, 10,* 395–424.

Creveling, C. C., Varela, R. E., Weems, C. F., & Corey, D. M. (2010). Maternal control, cognitive style, and childhood anxiety: A test of a theoretical model in a multi-ethnic sample. *Journal of Family Psychology, 24,* 439–448.

Crews, F., He, J., & Hodge, C. (2007). Adolescent cortical development: A critical period of vulnerability for addiction. *Pharmacology Biochemistry and Behavior, 86,* 189–199.

Crews, F. T., & Boettiger, C. A. (2009). Impulsivity, frontal lobes and risk for addiction. *Pharmacology Biochemistry and Behavior, 88,* 237–247.

Crimlisk, H. L., Bhatia, K., Cope, H., & David, A. (1998). Slater revisited: Six-year follow-up study of patients with medically unexplained motor symptoms. *British Medical Journal, 316,* 582–586.

Crocker, N., Vaurio, L., Riley, E. P., & Mattson, S. N. (2009). Comparison of adaptive behavior in children with heavy prenatal alcohol exposure or attention-deficit/hyperactivity disorder. *Alcoholism: Clinical and Experimental Research, 33,* 2015–2023.

Crosby, R. D., Wonderlich, S. A., Engel, S. G., Simonich, H., Smyth, J., & Mitchell, J. E. (2010). Daily mood patterns and bulimic behaviors in the natural environment. *Behaviour Research and Therapy, 47,* 181–188.

Croteau, J. M., Lark, J. S., Lidderdale, M. A., & Chung, Y. B. (2005). *Deconstructing heterosexism in the counseling professions.* Thousand Oaks, CA: Sage.

Crow, S. J., Mitchell, J. E., Crosby, R. D., Swanson, S. A., Wonderlich, S., & Lancaster, K. (2009a). The cost-effectiveness of cognitive behavioral therapy for bulimia nervosa delivered via telemedicine versus face to face. *Behaviour Research and Therapy, 47,* 451–453.

Crow, S. J., Peterson, C. B., Swanson, S. A., Raymond, N. C., Specker, S., Eckert, E. D., & Mitchell, J. E. (2009b). Increased mortality in bulimia nervosa and other eating disorders. *American Journal of Psychiatry, 166,* 1342–1346.

Crowson, J. J., & Cromwell, R. L. (1995). Depressed and normal individuals differ both in selection and in perceived tonal quality of positive-negative messages. *Journal of Abnormal Psychology, 104,* 305–311.

Crozier, J. C., Dodge, K. A., Fontaine, R. G., Lansford, J. E., Bates, J. E, Pettit, G. S., & Levenson, R. W. (2008). Social information processing and cardiac predictors of adolescent antisocial behavior. *Journal of Abnormal Psychology, 117,* 253–267.

Cruess, D. G., Antoni, M. H., Schneiderman, N., Ironson, G., McCabe, P., . . . Kumar, M. (2000). Cognitive-behavioral stress management increases free testosterone and decreases psychological distress in HIV-seropositive men. *Health Psychology, 19,* 12–20.

Crumlish, N., Whitty, P., Clarke, M., Browne, S., Karnali, M., . . . O'Callahan, E. (2009). Beyond the critical period: Longitudinal study of 8-year outcome in first-episode non-affective psychosis. *British Journal of Psychiatry, 194,* 18–24.

Cruz, I. Y., & Dunn, M. E. (2003). Lowering risk for early alcohol use by challenging alcohol expectancies in elementary school children. *Journal of Consulting and Clinical Psychology, 71,* 493–503.

Crystal, S., Olfson, M., Huang, C., Pincus, H., & Gerhard, T. (2009). Broadened use of atypical antipsychotics: Safety, effectiveness, and policy challenges. *Health Affairs, 28,* 770–781.

Csipke, E., & Horne, O. (2007). Pro-eating disorder websites: Users' opinions. *European Eating Disorders Review, 15,* 196–206.

Cuevas, C. A., Finkelhor, D., Ormrod, R., & Turner, H. (2009). Psychiatric diagnosis as a risk marker for victimization in a national sample of children. *Journal of Interpersonal Violence, 24,* 636–652.

Cuffe, S. P. (2007). Suicide and SSRI medications in children and adolescents: An update. *American Academy of Child and Adolescent Psychiatry.* Retrieved from http://www.aacap.org/cs/root/developmentor/suicide_and_ssri_medications_in_children_and_adolescents_an_update

Culbert, K. M., Burt, S. A., McGue, M., Iacono, W. G., & Klump, K. L. (2009). Puberty and the genetic diathesis of disordered eating attitudes and behaviors. *Journal of Abnormal Psychology, 118,* 788–796.

Culbertson, C. S., Bramen, J., Cohen, M. S., London, E. D, Olmstead, R. E., . . . Brody, A. L. (2011). Effect of bupropion treatment on brain activation induced by cigarette-related cues in smokers. *Archives of General Psychiatry, 68*(5), 505–515. doi:10.1001/archgenpsychiatry.2010.193

Cummings, N. A. (1995). Behavioral health after managed care: The next golden opportunity for professional psychology. *Register Report, 20*(1), 30–33.

Cummings, J. R., & Druss, B. G. (2011). Racial/ethnic differences in mental health service use among adolescents with major depression. *Journal of the American Academy of Child and Adolescent Psychiatry, 50,* 106–107.

Cumsille, P. E., Sayer, A. G., & Graham, J. W. (2000). Perceived exposure to peer and adult drinking as predictors of growth in positive alcohol expectancies during adolescence. *Journal of Consulting and Clinical Psychology, 68,* 531–536.

Curran, L. K., Newschaffer, C. J., Lee, L. C., Crawford, S. O., Johnston, M. V., & Zimmerman, A. W. (2007). Behaviors associated with fever in children with autism spectrum disorders. *Pediatrics, 120,* 1386–1392.

Curran, P. J., Stice, E., & Chassin, L. (1997). The relation between adolescent alcohol use and peer alcohol use: A longitudinal random coefficients model. *Journal of Consulting and Clinical Psychology, 65,* 130–140.

Curry, V. (2001, May 20). School shooting affects students after three years. *Columbian,* p. C3.

Curtis, S., Stobart, K., Vandermeer, B., Simel, D. L., & Klassen, T. (2010). Clinical features suggestive of meningitis in children: A systematic review of prospective data. *Pediatrics, 126,* 952–960.

Cutrona, C. E., Russell, D. W., Brown, P. A., Clark, L. A., Hessling, R. M., & Gardner, K. A. (2005). Neighborhood context, personality, and stressful life events as predictors of depression among African American women. *Journal of Abnormal Psychology, 114,* 3–15.

Cutting, L. P., & Docherty, N. M. (2000). Schizophrenia outpatients' perceptions of their parents: Is expressed emotion a factor? *Journal of Abnormal Psychology, 109,* 266–272.

Cynkar, A. (2007, November). Socially wired. *Monitor on Psychology, 38*(10), 47–49.

Dahlstrom, W. G., & Welsh, G. S. (1965). *An MMPI handbook.* Minneapolis: University of Minnesota Press.

Daigneault, S. D. (2000). Body talk: A school-based group intervention for working with disordered eating behaviors. *Journal for Specialists in Group Work, 25,* 191–213.

Daley, S. E., Burge, D., & Hammen, C. (2000). Borderline personality disorder symptoms as predictors of four-year romantic relationship dysfunction in young women: Addressing issues of specificity. *Journal of Abnormal Psychology, 109,* 451–460.

Dalle Grave, R., & Calugi, S. (2007). Eating disorder not otherwise specified in an inpatient unit: The impact of altering the DSM-IV criteria for anorexia and bulimia nervosa. *European Eating Disorders Review, 15,* 340–349.

Dalrymple, K. L., & Zimmerman, M. (2011). Age of onset of social anxiety disorders in depressed outpatients. *Journal of Anxiety Disorders, 25,* 131–137.

Daly, B. P., Creed, T., Xanthopoulos, M., & Brown, R. T. (2007). Psychosocial treatments for children with attention deficit/hyperactivity disorder. *Neuropsychological Review, 17,* 73–89.

Dammeyer, M. D., Nightingale, N. N., & McCoy, M. L. (1997). Repressed memory and other controversial origins of sexual abuse allegations: Beliefs among psychologists and clinical social workers. *Child Maltreatment, 2,* 252–263.

Dams-O'Connor, K., Martin, J. L., & Martens, M. P. (2007). Social norms and alcohol consumption among intercollegiate athletes: The role of athlete and nonathlete reference groups. *Addictive Behaviors, 32,* 2657–2666.

Dams-O'Conner, K., Martens, M. P., & Anderson, D. A. (2006). Alcohol-related consequences among women who want to lose weight. *Eating Behaviors, 7,* 188–195.

Dana, R. H. (1998). *Understanding cultural identity in intervention and assessment.* Thousand Oaks, CA: Sage.

Danaher, B. G., & Seeley, J. R. (2009). Methodological issues in research on web-based behavioral interventions. *Annals of Behavior Medicine, 38,* 28–39.

Dance, A. (2007, June 16). Veterans have higher suicide risk than civilians, study finds. *Los Angeles Times,* p. A12.

Dannahy, L., Hayward, M., Strauss, C., Turton, W., Harding, E., & Chadwick, P. (2011). Group person-based cognitive therapy for distressing voices: Pilot data from nine groups. *Journal of Behavior Therapy and Experimental Psychiatry, 42,* 111–116.

Dar, R., Rish, S., Hermesh, H., Taub, M., & Fux, M. (2000). Realism of confidence in obsessive-compulsive checkers. *Journal of Abnormal Psychology, 109,* 673–678.

Dardick, H. (2004, February 13). Psychiatric patient tells of ordeal in treatment. *Chicago Tribune,* p. 1.

Darrach, D. (1976, March 8). Poetry and poison. *Time.*

Davey, G. C. L., McDonald, A. S., Hirisave, U., Prabhu, G. G., Iwawaki, S., . . . Reimann, B. C. (1998). A cross-cultural study of animal fears. *Behaviour Research and Therapy, 36,* 735–750.

David (2010, March 19). Child Psychology Research Blog: Autism and Asperger's in the DSM-V: Thoughts on clinical utility. [Web log comment]. Retrieved from http://www.childpsych.org/2010/02/autism-and-aspergers-in-the-dsm-v-going-beyond-the-politics.html

David, A. S. (2010). Why we need more debate on whether psychotic symptoms lie on a continuum with normality. *Psychological Medicine, 40,* 1935–1942.

David-Ferndon, C., & Kaslow, N. J. (2008). Evidence-based psychosocial treatments for child and adolescent depression. *Journal of Clinical Child & Adolescent Psychology, 37,* 62–104.

Davidson, D., Gulliver, S. B., Longabaugh, R., Wirtz, P. W., & Swift, R. (2007). Building better cognitive-behavioral therapy: Is broad-spectrum treatment more effective than motivational-enhancement therapy for alcohol-dependent patients treated with naltrexone? *Journal of Studies on Alcohol and Drugs, 68,* 238–247.

Davidson, J. R. T. (2000). Pharmacotherapy of posttraumatic stress disorder: Treatment options, long-term follow-up and predictors of outcome. *Journal of Clinical Psychiatry, 61,* 52–56.

Davidson, J. R. T. (2001). Pharmacotherapy of generalized anxiety disorder. *Journal of Clinical Psychiatry, 62,* 46–50.

Davidson, J. R. T., Foa, E. B., Huppert, J. D., Keefe, F. J., Franklin, M. E., . . . Gadde, K. M. (2004). Fluoxetine, comprehensive cognitive behavioral therapy, and placebo in generalized social phobia. *Archives of General Psychiatry, 61,* 1005–1013.

Davidson, K. W., Mostofsky, E., & Whang, W. (2010). Don't worry, be happy: positive affect and reduced 10-year incident coronary heart disease: The Canadian Nova Scotia Health Survey. *European Heart Journal, 31,* 1065–1070.

Davidson, R. J., Pizzagalli, D., Nitschke, J. B., & Putnam, K. (2002). Depression: Perspectives from affective neuroscience. *Annual Review of Psychology, 53,* 545–574.

Davies, P. G., Spencer, S. J., & Steele, C. M. (2005). Clearing the air: Identity safety moderates the effects of stereotype threat on women's leadership aspirations. *Journal of Personality and Social Psychology, 88,* 276–287.

Davis, K. L., Kahn, R. S., & Ko, G. (1991). Dopamine in schizophrenia: A review and reconceptualization, *American Journal of Psychiatry, 148,* 1474–1486.

Davis, L., Uezato, A., Newell, J. M., & Frazier, E. (2008). Major depression and comorbid substance use disorders. *Current Opinions in Psychiatry, 21,* 14–18.

Davis, M. C., Mathews, K. A., Meilahn, E. N., & Kiss, J. E. (1995). Are job characteristics related to fibrinogen levels in middle-aged women? *Health Psychology, 14,* 310–318.

Davis, P. J., & Gibson, M. G. (2000). Recognition of posed and genuine facial expressions of emotion in paranoid and nonparanoid schizophrenia. *Journal of Abnormal Psychology, 109,* 445–450.

Dawson, D. A., Goldstein, R. B., & Grant, B. F. (2007). Rates and correlates of relapse among individuals in remission from DSM-IV alcohol dependence: A 3-year follow-up. *Alcoholism: Clinical and Experimental Research, 31,* 2036–2045.

Dawson, D. A., Grant, B. F., Stinson, F. S., Chou, P. S., Huang, B., & Ruan, W. J. (2005). Recovery from DSM-IV alcohol dependence: United States, 2001–2002. *Addiction, 100,* 281–292.

Dawson, G., & Castelloe, P. (1992). Autism. In C. E. Walker (Ed.), *Clinical psychology: Historical and research foundations.* New York: Plenum.

Dawson, G., Munson, J., Webb, S. J., Nalty, T., Abbott, R., & Toth, K. (2007). Rate of head growth decelerates and symptoms worsen in the second year of life in autism. *Biological Psychiatry, 61,* 458–464.

Dawson, G., Rogers, S., Munson, J., Smith, M., Winter, J., Greenson, J., Donaldson, A., & Varley, J. (2010). Randomized, controlled trial of an intervention for toddlers with autism: The Early Start Denver Model. *Pediatrics, 125,* 17–23.

Day, S. X., & Rottinghause, P. (2003). The healthy personality. In W. B. Walsh (Ed.), *Counseling psychology and optimal human functioning* (pp. 1–23). Mahwah, NJ: Lawrence Erlbaum Associates.

DeAngelis, T. (2007, November). Creating a place for MySpace. *Monitor on Psychology, 38*(10), 49.

Deardorff, J. (2011). FDA will hold hearings on possible effects of food dyes. *Chicago Tribune.* Retrieved from http://www.dailycamera.com/health-fitness/ci_17195935

Deault, L. C. (2010). A systematic review of parenting in relation to the development of comorbidities and functional impairments in children with attention-deficit/hyperactivity disorder (ADHD). *Child Psychiatry and Human Development, 41,* 168–192.

Decety, J., Michalska, K. J., Akitsuki, Y., & Lahey, B. B. (2009). Atypical empathic responses in adolescents with aggressive conduct disorder: A functional MRI investigation. *Biological Psychology, 80,* 203–211.

Declaration of Helsinki. (2004). Ethical principles for medical research involving human subjects. Retrieved from http://ohsr.od.nih.gov/guidelines/helsinki.html

De Coteau, T., Anderson, J., & Hope, D. (2006). Adapting manualized treatments: Treating anxiety disorders among Native Americans. *Cognitive and Behavioral Practice, 13,* 304–309.

Decuyper, M., De Pauw, S., De Fruyt, F., De Bolle, M., & De Clercq, B. J. (2009). A meta-analysis of psychopathy, antisocial PD- and FFM associations. *European Journal of Personality, 23,* 531–565.

Dedovic, K., D'Aguiar, C., & Pruessner, J. C. (2009). What stress does to your brain: A review of neuroimaging studies. *Canadian Journal of Psychiatry, 54,* 5–15.

Deepika, S., Damsa, C., Ruether, K. A., Moussaly, K., Adam, E., Vaney, C., & Berclaz, O. (2009). Greater evidence of dissociative symptoms noted in general practitioners attending an educational session on dissociation. *American Journal of Psychiatry, 166,* 1190–1191.

DeFife, J. (2010, February 10). DSM-V offers new criteria for personality disorders. *Psychology Today.* Retrieved from http://www.psychologytoday.com

De Geus, E. J. C., Kupper, N., Boomsma, D. I., & Snieder, H. (2007). Bivariate genetic modeling of cardiovascular stress reactivity: Does stress uncover genetic variance? *Psychosomatic Medicine, 69,* 356–364.

de Jong, P. J., Vorage, I., & van den Hout, M. A. (2000). Counterconditioning in the treatment of spider phobia: Effects on disgust, fear and valence. *Behaviour Research and Therapy, 38,* 1055–1069.

de Simone, V., Kaplan, L., Patronas, N., Wassermann, E. M., & Grafman, J. (2006). Driving abilities in frontotemporal dementia patients. *Dementia and Geriatric Cognitive Disorders, 23,* 1–7.

Deckel, A. W., Hesselbrock, V. M., & Bauer, L. (1996). Antisocial personality disorder, childhood delinquency, and frontal brain functioning: EEG and neuropsychological findings. *Journal of Clinical Psychology, 52,* 639–650.

Delaney-Black, V., Chiodo, L. M., Hannigan, J. H., Greenwald, M. K, Janisse, J., . . . Sokol, R. J. (2011). Prenatal and postnatal cocaine exposure predict teen cocaine use. *Neurotoxicology and Teratology, 33*(1), 110–119.

Delaney-Black, V., Chiodo, L. M., Hannigan, J. H., Greenwald, M. K., Janisse, J., . . . Sokol, R. J. (2010). Just say "I don't": Lack of concordance between teen report and biological measures of drug use. *Pediatrics, 126,* 887–893.

Delahanty, D. L. (2007). Are we prepared to handle the mental health consequences of terrorism? *American Journal of Psychiatry, 164,* 189–191.

Delgado, P. L., & Gelenberg, A. J. (2001). Antidepressant and antimanic medications. In G. O. Gabbard (Ed.), *Treatment of psychiatric disorders* (pp. 1137–1179). Washington, DC: American Psychiatric Press.

DeLisi, L. E., Maurizio, A., Yost, M., Papparozzi, C. F., Flulchino, C., . . . Stevens, P. (2003). A survey of New Yorkers after the Sept. 11, 2001, terrorist attacks. *American Journal of Psychiatry, 160,* 780–783.

Dell, P. F., & Eisenhower, J. W. (1990). Adolescent multiple personality disorder: A preliminary study of eleven cases. *Journal of the American Academy of Child and Adolescent Psychiatry, 29,* 359–366.

Demaray, M. K., & Malecki, C. K. (2003). Perceptions of the frequency and importance of social support by students classified as victims, bullies, and bully/victims in an urban middle school. *School Psychology Review, 32,* 471–489.

den Heijer, T., Geerlings, M. I., Hoebeek, F. E., Hofman, A., Koudstaal, P. J., & Breteler, M. M. (2006). Use of hippocampal and amygdalar volumes on magnetic resonance imaging to predict dementia in cognitively intact elderly people. *Archives of General Psychiatry, 63,* 57–62.

DeLisi, I. E., & Fleischbaker, W. (2007). Schizophrenia research in the era of the genome. *Current Opinion in Psychiatry, 20,* 109–110.

Denisoff, E., & Endler, N. S. (2000). Life experiences, coping, and weight preoccupation in young adult women. *Canadian Journal of Behavioural Science, 32,* 97–103.

Dennis, M., Godley, S. H., Diamond, G., Tims, F. M., Babor, T., . . . Funk, R. (2004). The Cannabis Youth Treatment (CYT) Study: Main findings from two randomized trials. *Journal of Substance Abuse Treatment, 27,* 197–213.

Denov, M. S. (2004). The long-term effects of child sexual abuse by female perpetrators: A qualitative study of male and female victims. *Journal of Interpersonal Violence, 19,* 1137–1156.

Dent, C. W., Sussman, S., Stacy, A. W., Craig, S., Burton, D., & Flay, B. R. (1995). Two-year behavior outcomes of Project Towards No Tobacco Use. *Journal of Consulting and Clinical Psychology, 63,* 676–677.

Depressed? Could be where you live. (2005). *National Psychologist, 14,* 24.

De Rosier, M., Swick, D., Davis, N., McMillen, J., & Matthews, R. (2010). The efficacy of a social skills group intervention for improving social behaviors in children with high functioning autism spectrum disorders. *Journal of Autism and Developmental Disorders.* doi: 10.1007/s10803-010-1128-2

de Rossi, P. (2010). *Unbearable lightness: A story of loss and gain.* Chicago, IL: Atria

DeRubeis, R. J., Siegle, G. J., & Hollon, S. D. (2008). Cognitive therapy vs. medications for depression: Treatment outcomes and neural mechanisms. *National Review of Neuroscience, 9,* 788–796.

Desmond, S., Price, J., Hallinan, C., & Smith, D. (1989). Black and White adolescents' perceptions of their weight. *Journal of School Health, 59,* 353–358.

Desoto, M. C., & Hitlan, R. T. (2010). Sorting out the spinning of autism: Heavy metals and the question of incidence. *Acta Neurobiologae Experimentalis, 70,* 165–176.

Deutsch, A. (1949). *The mentally ill in America* (2nd ed.). New York: Columbia University Press.

DeVellis, B. M., & Blalock, S. J. (1992). Illness attributions and hopelessness depression: The role of hopelessness expectancy. *Journal of Abnormal Psychology, 101,* 257–264.

Devinsky, O. (1994). *A guide to understanding and living with epilepsy.* Philadelphia: Davis.

DeVita-Raeburn, E. (2007). *The Morgellon mystery.* Retrieved from http://psychologytoday.com/articles/index.php?term=pto-20070227-000003.html

DeVoe, J. F., Peter, K., Kaufman, P., Miller, A., Noonan, M., Snyder, T. D., & Baum, K. (2004). *Indicators of school crime and safety: 2004* (NCES 2005-002/NCJ 205290). Washington, DC: U.S. Government Printing Office.

DeVries, R., Anderson, M. S., & Martinson, B. C. (2006). Normal misbehavior: Scientists talk about the ethics of research. *Journal of Empirical Research on Human Research Ethics, 1,* 43–50.

DeWaal, M. W. M., Arnold, I. A., Eekhof, J. A. H., & Van Hemert, A. M. (2004). Somatoform disorders in general practice. *British Journal of Psychiatry, 184,* 470–476.

Diamond, A. (2009). The interplay of biology and the environment broadly defined. *Developmental Psychology, 45,* 1–8.

Diaz-Asper, C. M., Schretlen, D. J., & Pearlson, G. D. (2004). Should clinicians use intelligence as a means of estimating expected neuropsychological test performance? *Journal of the International Neuropsychological Society, 10,* 82–90.

DiBartolo, P. M., & Helt, M. (2007). Theoretical models of affectionate versus affectionless control in anxious families: A critical examination based on observations of parent-child interactions. *Clinical Child and Family Psychology Review, 10,* 253–274.

Dick, D. M., & Rose, R. J. (2002). Behavior genetics: What's new? What's next? *Current Directions in Psychological Science, 11,* 70–74.

Dickerson, S. S., & Kemeny, M. E. (2004). Acute stressors and cortisol responses: A theoretical integration and synthesis of laboratory research. *Psychological Bulletin, 130,* 355–391.

Dickey, R., & Steiner, B. (1990). Hormone treatment and surgery. In R. Blanchard & B. W. Steiner (Eds.), *Clinical management of gender identity disorders in children and adults* (pp. 137–158). Washington, DC: American Psychiatric Press.

Dickstein, D. P., Nelson, E. E., McClure, E., Grimley, M. E., Knopf, L., . . . Leibenluft, E. (2007). Cognitive flexibility in phenotypes of pediatric bipolar disorder. *Journal of the American Academy of Child and Adolescent Psychiatry, 46,* 341–355.

Dickstein, D. P., Towbin, K. E., Van Der Veen, J. W., Rich, B. A., Brotman, M. A., . . . Leibenluft, E. (2009). Randomized double-blind placebo-controlled trial of lithium in youth with severe mood dysregulation. *Journal of Child and Adolescent Psychopharmacology, 19,* 61–73.

Diekstra, R. F., Kienhorst, C. W. M., & de Wilde, E. J. (1995). Suicide and suicidal behaviour among adolescents. In M. Rutter & D. J. Smith (Eds.), *Psychological disorders in young people.* Chichester, UK: Wiley.

Diflorio, A., & Jones, I. (2010). Is sex important? Gender differences in bipolar disorder. *International Review of Psychiatry, 22,* 437–452.

DiFranza, J. R., Savageau, J. A., Fletcher, K., Pbert, L., O'Loughlin, J., . . . Wellman, R. J. (2007). Susceptibility to nicotine dependence: The Development and Assessment of Nicotine Dependence in Youth 2 study. *Pediatrics, 120,* 974–983.

DiGrande, L., Neria, Y., Brackbill, M., Pulliam, P., & Galea, S. (2011). Long-term posttraumatic stress symptoms among 3,271 civilian survivors of the September 11, 2001, terrorist attacks on the World Trade Center. *American Journal of Epidemiology, 173,* 271–281.

Dilks, S., Tasker, F., & Wren, B. (2010). Managing the impact of psychosis: A grounded theory exploration of recovery processes in psychosis. *British Journal of Clinical Psychology, 49,* 87–107.

Dimidjian, S., Hollon, S. D., Dobson, K. S., Schmaling, K. B., Kohlenberg, R., . . . Jacobson, N. S. (2006). Randomized trial of behavioral activation, cognitive therapy, and antidepressant medication in the acute treatment of adults with major depression. *Journal of Consulting and Clinical Psychology, 74,* 658–670.

Ding, K., Chang, G. A., & Southerland, R. (2009). Age of inhalant first time use and its association to the use of other drugs. *Journal of Drug Education, 39,* 261–272.

Dingfelder, S. (2010). What's behind the imposter delusion? *Monitor on Psychology, 41,* 10. Retrieved from http://www.apa.org/monitor/2010/10/imposter.aspx

Diokno, A. C., Brown, M. B., & Herzog, A. R. (1990). Sexual function in the elderly. *Archives of Internal Medicine, 150,* 197–200.

Di Paola, F., Faravelli, C., & Ricca, V. (2010). Perceived expressed emotion in anorexia nervosa, bulimia nervosa, and binge-eating disorder. *Comprehensive Psychiatry, 51,* 401–405.

Dirmann, T. (2003, September 8). Ex-Spice Girl Geri Halliwell: How I beat my eating disorder. *US Weekly,* 60.

Dishion, T. J., McCord, J., & Poulin, F. (1999). When interventions harm: Peer groups and problem behavior. *American Psychologist, 54,* 755–764.

Dissanayaka, N., Sellbach, A., Matheson, M., O'Sullivan, J. D., Silburn, P. A., . . . Mellick, G. (2010). Anxiety disorders in Parkinson's disease: Prevalence and risk factors. *Movement Disorders, 25,* 838–845.

Dixon v. Weinberger 498 F. 2d 202 (1975).

Dobbs, D. (2009). The post-traumatic stress trap. *Scientific American, 300*(4), 64–69.

Dobkin, R. D., Allen, L. A., & Menza, M. (2006). A cognitive-behavioral treatment package for depression in Parkinson's disease. *Psychosomatics, 47,* 259–263.

Dobson, K. S., Hollon, S. D., Dimidjian, S., Schmaling, K. B., Kohlenberg, R. J., . . . Jacobson, N. S. (2008). Randomized trial of behavioral activation, cognitive therapy, and antidepressant medication in the prevention of relapse and recurrence in major depression. *Journal of Consulting and Clinical Psychology, 76,* 468–477.

Dobson, P., & Rogers, J. (2009). Assessing and treating faecal incontinence in children. *Nursing Standards, 24,* 49–56.

Dodick, D. W., & Gargus, J. J. (2008). Why migraines strike. *Scientific American, 299*(2), 56–63.

Dogden, D. (2000). Science policy and the protection of children. *American Psychologist, 55,* 1034–1035.

Dolan, M. C., & Fullam, R. (2010). Emotional memory and psychopathic traits in conduct disordered adolescents. *Personality and Individual Differences, 48,* 327–331.

Dollinger, S. J. (1983). A case of dissociative neurosis (depersonalization disorder) in an adolescent treated with family therapy and behavior modification. *Journal of Consulting and Clinical Psychology, 15,* 479–484.

Dominguez, M. D. G., Wichers, M., Lieb, R., Wittchen, H.-U. & van Os, J. (2011). Evidence that the outcome of progressively more persistent subclinical psychotic experiences: A 8-year cohort study. *Schizophrenia Bulletin, 37,* 84–93.

Domschke, K., Stevens, S., Pfleiderer, B., & Gerlach, A. L. (2010). Interoceptive sensitivity in anxiety and anxiety disorders: An overview and integration of neurobiological findings. *Clinical Psychology Review, 30,* 1–11.

Donenberg, G., & Baker, B. L. (1993). The impact of young children with externalizing behaviors on their families. *Journal of Abnormal Child Psychology, 21,* 179–198.

Dong, Q., Yang, B., & Ollendick, T. H. (1994). Fears in Chinese children and adolescents and their relations to anxiety and depression. *Journal of Child Psychology and Psychiatry, 35,* 351–363.

Doody, R. S., Pavlik, V., Massman, P., Rountree, S., Darby, E., & Chan, W. (2010). Predicting progression of Alzheimer's disease. *Alzheimer's Research & Therapy, 2,* 2. Retrieved from http://alzres.com/content/2/1/2

Doran, N., Myers, M. G., Luczak, S. E., Carr, L. G., & Wall, T. L. (2007). Stability of heavy episodic drinking in Chinese- and Korean-American college students: Effects of aldh2 gene status and behavioral undercontrol. *Journal of Studies On Alcohol And Drugs, 68,* 789–797.

Dotson, V. M., Beydoun, M. A., & Zonderman, A. B. (2010). Recurrent depressive symptoms and the incidence of dementia and mild cognitive impairment. *Neurology, 75,* 27–34.

Doughty, O. J., Lawrence, V. A., Al-Mousawi, A., Ashaye, K., & Done, D. J. (2009). Overinclusive thought and loosening of associations are not unique to schizophrenia and are produced in Alzheimer's dementia. *Cognitive Neuropsychiatry, 14,* 149–164.

Dovidio, J. F., Kawakami, K., Smoak, N., & Gaertner, S. L. (2009). Implicit measures of attitudes. In R. Petty, R. Faxio, & P. Brinol (Eds.), *Implicit measures* (pp. 165–192). New York: Psychology Press.

Down syndrome. (2007). Retrieved from http://ghr.nlm.nih.gov/condition=downsyndrome

Dragt, S., Nieman, D. H., Becker, H. E., van de Fliert, R., Dingemans, P. M., . . . Linszen, D. H. (2010). Age of onset of cannabis use is associated with age of onset of high-risk symptoms for psychosis. *Canadian Journal of Psychiatry, 55,* 165–171.

Draguns, J. G. (1996). Multicultural and cross-cultural assessment: Dilemmas and decisions. In G. R. Sodowsky & J. C. Impara (Eds.), *Multicultural assessment in counseling and clinical psychology* (pp. 37–84). Lincoln, NE: Buros Institute of Mental Measurements.

Drake, R. E., & Ehrlich, J. (1985). Suicide attempts associated with akathisia. *American Journal of Psychiatry, 142,* 499–501.

Drane, J. (1995). Physician-assisted suicide and voluntary active euthanasia: Social ethics and the role of hospice. *American Journal of Hospice and Palliative Care, 12,* 3–10.

Drugs and talk therapy. (2004, October). *Consumer Reports*, 22–29.

Drum, D. J., Brownson, C., Denmark, A. B., & Smith, S. E. (2009). New data on the nature of suicidal crisis in college students: Shifting the paradigm. *Professional Psychology: Research and Practice, 40*, 213–222.

Drzezga, A., Grimmer, T., Peller, M., Wermke, M., Siebner, H., . . . Kurz, A. (2005). Impaired cross-modal inhibition in Alzheimer disease. *PLoS Medicine, 2*, e288.

DSM-V Work Groups (2011). Retrieved from www.DSM5.org

Duarte-Velez, Y. M., & Bernal, G. (2008). Suicide risk in Latino and Latina adolescents. In F. Leong & M. M. Leach (Eds.), *Ethnic suicides* (pp. 81–115). New York: Routledge.

Duberstein, P. R., & Conwell, Y. (1997). Personality disorders and completed suicide: A methodological and conceptual review. *Clinical Psychology 4*, 502–504.

Dubovsky, S., Franks, R., Lifschitz, M., & Coen, R. (1982). Effectiveness of verapamil in the treatment of a manic patient. *American Journal of Psychiatry, 139*, 502–504.

Dubovsky, S. L., & Buzan, R. (1999). Mood disorders. In R. E. Hales, S. C. Yudofsky, & J. A. Talbott (Eds.), *Textbook of psychiatry* (pp. 479–565). Washington, DC: American Psychiatric Press.

Duchan, E., Patel, N. D., & Feucht, C. (2010). Energy drinks: A review of use and safety for athletes. *The Physician and Sports Medicine, 38*, 171–179.

Dudley, R., Siitarinen, J., James, I., & Dodson, G. (2009). What do people with psychosis think caused their psychosis? A Q methodology study. *Behavioural and Cognitive Psychotherapy, 37*, 11–24.

Dufault, R., Schnoll, R., Lukiw, W. J., Leblanc, B., Cornett, C., . . . Crider, R. (2009). Mercury exposure, nutritional deficiencies, and metabolic disruptions may affect learning in children. *Behavior and Brain Functioning, 27*, 44.

Dugas, M. J., & Ladouceur, R. (2000). Treatment of GAD: Targeting intolerance of uncertainty in two types of worry. *Behavior Modification, 24*, 635–657.

Dugdale, D. C., Jasmin, L., & Zieve, D. (2010). *Gilles de la Tourette syndrome.* Retrieved from http://www.ncbi.nlm.nih.gov/pubmedhealth/PMH0001744

Dulai, R., & Kelly, S. L. (2009). A case of the body snatchers. *Current Psychiatry, 8*, 56–65.

Dunham, W. (2007). Being fat and fit is better than being thin and sedentary, study says. Downloaded from: http://www.boston.com/news/nation/articles/2007/12/05/being_fat_and_fit_is_better_than_being_thin_and_sedentary_study_says/

Dunkley, D. M., Masheb, R. M., & Grilo, C. M. (2010). Child maltreatment, depressive symptoms, and body dissatisfaction in patients with binge eating disorder: The mediating role of self-criticism. *International Journal of Eating Disorders, 43*, 274–281.

Durà-Vilà, G., Dein, S., & Hodes, M. (2010). Children with intellectual disability: A gain not a loss: Parental beliefs and family life. *Clinical Child Psychology and Psychiatry, 5*, 171–184.

Durex. (2001). *Global sex survey.* Retrieved from http://www.durex.com/uk/globalsexsurvey/2005results.asp

Durex. (2005). *Global sex survey 2005 results.* Retrieved from www.durex.com/uk/globalsexsurvey/2005results.asp

Durham v. United States, 214 F.2d, 862, 874-875 (D.C. Cir. 1954).

Durkheim, E. (1951). *Suicide.* New York: Free Press. (Original work published 1897)

Durston, S. (2010). Imaging genetics in ADHD. *Neuroimage, 53*, 832–838.

Dworkin, A. (2009, Nov 11). After stroke, Portland woman's brain on the rebound. Retrieved from http://blog.oregonlive.com/health-impact/printhtml?entry+/2009/11

Dworkin, S., VonKorff, M., & LeResche, L. (1990). Multiple pains and psychiatric disturbance. *Archives of General Psychiatry, 47*, 239–244.

Dyer, O. (2004). GlaxoSmithKline faces US lawsuit over concealment of trial results. *British Medical Journal, 328*, 1395.

Dykens, E. M., & Hodapp, R. M. (1997). Treatment issues in genetic mental retardation syndromes. *Professional Psychology: Research and Practice, 28*, 263–270.

Dzokoto, A. A., & Adams, G. (2005). Understanding genital-shrinking epidemics in West Africa: Koro, Juju, or mass psychogenic illness? *Culture, Medicine and Psychiatry, 29*, 53–78.

Eaker, E. D., Sullivan, L. M., Kelly-Hayes, M., D'Agostino, R. B., Sr., & Benjamin, E. J. (2007). Marital status, marital strain, and risk of coronary heart disease or total mortality: The Framingham Offspring Study. *Psychosomatic Medicine, 69*, 509–515.

Eastwood, S. L., & Harrison, P. J. (2010). Markers of glutamate synaptic transmission and plasticity are increased in the anterior cingulate cortex in bipolar disorder. *Biological Psychiatry, 7*, 1010–1016.

Eaton, D. K., Kann, L., Kinchen, S. A., Ross, J. G., Hawkins, J., & Harris, W. A. (2006). Youth risk behavior surveillance—United States, 2005. *Morbidity and Mortality Weekly Report, 55*(No. SS-5), 1–108.

Eberhart, N. K. (2011). Maladaptive schemas and depression: Tests of stress generation and diathesis-stress models. *Journal of Social and Clinical Psychology, 30*, 75–104.

Eddy, K. T., Tanofsky-Kraff, M., Thompson-Brenner, H., Hertzog, D. B., Brown, T. A. & Ludwig, D. S. (2007). Eating disorder pathology among overweight treatment-seeking youth: Clinical correlates and cross-sectional risk modeling. *Behaviour Research and Therapy, 45*, 2360–2367.

Edlund, A., Lundstrom, M., Sandberg, O., Bucht, G., Brannstrom, B., & Gustafson, Y. (2007). Symptom profile of delirium in older people with and without dementia. *Journal of Geriatric Psychiatry and Neurology, 20*, 166–171.

Edman, G., Asberg, M., Levander, S., & Schalling, D. (1986). Skin conductance habituation and cerebrospinal fluid 5-hydroxyindoleactic acid in suicidal patients. *Archives of General Psychiatry, 43*, 586–592.

Edvardsen, J., Torgersen, S., Røysamb, E., Lygren, S., Skre, I., Onstad, S., & Oien, P. A. (2008). Heritability of bipolar spectrum disorders. Unity or heterogeneity? *Journal of Affective Disorders, 106*, 229–40.

Edwards, S., & Dickerson, M. (1987). On the similarity of positive and negative intrusions. *Behaviour Research and Therapy, 25*, 207–211.

Egeland, J. A., & Hostetter, A. M. (1983). Amish study: I. Affective disorders among the Amish. *American Journal of Psychiatry, 140*, 56–61.

Ehringer, M. A., Rhee, S. H., Young, S., Corley, R., & Hewitt, J. K. (2006). Genetic and environmental contributions to common psychopathologies of childhood and adolescence: A study of twins and their siblings. *Journal of Abnormal Child Psychology, 34*, 1–17.

Ehrlich, S., Pfeiffer, E., Salbach, H., Lenz, K., & Lehmkuhl, U. (2008). Factitious disorder in children and adolescents: A retrospective study. *Psychosomatics, 49*, 392–398.

Eigenmann, P., & Haenggeli, C. (2004). Food colourings and preservatives: Allergy and hyperactivity. *Lancet, 364*, 823–824.

Eisen, A. R., & Silverman, W. K. (1998). Prescriptive treatment for generalized anxiety disorder in children. *Behaviour Therapy, 29*, 105–121.

Eisenberg, M. E., & Neumark-Sztainer, D. (2010). Friends' dieting and disordered eating behaviors among adolescents five years later: Findings from Project EAT. *Journal of Adolescent Health, 47*, 67–73.

Eisendrath, S. J., Delucchi, K., Bitner, R., Fenimore, P., Smit, M., & McLane, M. (2008). Mindfulness-based cognitive therapy for treatment-resistant depression: A pilot study. *Psychotherapy and Psychosomatics, 77*(5), 319–320.

Elbogen, E. B., & Johnson, S. C. (2009). The intricate link between violence and mental disorder. *Archives of General Psychiatry, 66*, 152–161.

Elder, T. (2010). The importance of relative standards in ADHD diagnosis: Evidence based on exact birth dates. *Journal of Health Economics, 29*, 641–656.

Eldevik, S., Hastings, R. P., Hughes, J. C., Jahr, E., Eikeseth, S., & Cross, S. (2010). Using participant data to extend the evidence base for intensive behavioral intervention for children with autism. *American Journal of Intellectual and Developmental Disabilities, 115*, 381–405.

El-Gabalawy, R., Cox, B., & Mackenzie, C. (2010). Assessing the validity of social anxiety disorder subtypes using a nationally representative sample. *Journal of Anxiety Disorders, 24*, 244–249.

Eley, T. C., Lichtenstein, P., & Moffitt, T. E. (2003). A longitudinal behavioral genetic analysis of the etiology of aggressive and nonaggressive antisocial behavior. *Development and Psychopathology, 15*, 383–402.

Elkashef, A., Vocci, F., Huestis, M., Haney, M., Budney, A., Gruber, A., & el-Guebaly, N. (2008). Marijuana neurobiology and treatment. *Substance Abuse, 29,* 17–29.

Elkin, I. (1994). The NIMH Treatment of Depression Collaborative Research Program: Where we began and where we are. In A. E. Bergin & S. L. Garfield (Eds.), *Handbook of psychotherapy and behavior change* (4th ed., pp. 114–142). New York: Wiley.

Elkin, I., Gibbons, R. D., Shea, M. T., Sotsky, S. M., Watkins, J. T., Pilkonis, P. A., & Hedeker, D. (1995). Initial severity and differential treatment outcome in the National Institute of Mental Health Treatment of Depression Collaborative Research Program. *Journal of Consulting and Clinical Psychology, 63,* 841–847.

Ellason, J. W., & Ross, C. A. (1997). Two-year follow-up of inpatients with dissociative identity disorder. *American Journal of Psychiatry, 154,* 832–839.

Elliott, C., & Gillett, G. (1992). Moral insanity and practical reason. *Philosophical Psychology, 5,* 53–67.

Ellis, A. (1989). Rational-emotive therapy. In R. J. Corsini & D. Wedding (Eds.), *Current psychotherapies* (pp. 197–238). Itasca, IL: Peacock.

Ellis, A. (1991). Rational-emotive treatment of simple phobias. *Psychotherapy, 28,* 452–456.

Ellis, A. (1997). The evolution of Albert Ellis and rational emotive behavior therapy. In J. K. Zeig (Ed.), *The evolution of psychotherapy: The third conference.* New York: Brunner/Mazel.

Ellis, A. (2008). Rational emotive behavior therapy. In R. J. Corsini & D. Wedding (Eds.), *Current Psychotherapies,* (8th ed.). Belmont, CA: Brooks/Cole.

Ellis, D. M., & Hudson, J. L. (2010). The metacognitive model of generalized anxiety disorder in children and adolescents. *Clinical Child and Family Psychology Review, 13,* 151–163.

Ellis, L. (1991). A synthesized (biosocial) theory of rape. *Journal of Consulting and Clinical Psychology, 59,* 631–642.

Ellis, A. (2008). Rational emotive behavior therapy. In R. J. Corsini & D. Wedding (Eds.), *Current Psychotherapies,* (8th ed.). Belmont, CA: Brooks/Cole.

Ellis, L., & Ames, M. A. (1987). Neurohormonal functioning and sexual orientation: A theory of homosexuality-heterosexuality. *Psychological Bulletin, 101,* 233–258.

Ellison-Wright, I., & Bullmore, E. (2010). Anatomy of bipolar disorder and schizophrenia: A meta-analysis. *Schizophrenia Research, 117,* 1–12.

Elsevier (2010, August 18). Early life influences risk for psychiatric disorders. *ScienceDaily.* Retrieved from http://www.sciencedaily.com/releases/2010/08/100818090012.htm

El-Sheikh, M., Keiley, M., & Hinnant J. B. (2009). Developmental trajectories of skin conductance level in middle childhood: Sex, race, and externalizing behavior problems as predictors of growth. *Biological Psychology, 83,* 116–124.

Elvish, J., Simpson, J., & Ball, L. J. (2010). Which clinical and demographic factors predict poor insight in individuals with obsessions and/or compulsions. *Journal of Anxiety Disorders, 24,* 231–237.

Elwood, L. S., Mott, J., Lohr, J. M., & Galovski, T. E. (2011). Secondary trauma symptoms in clinicians: A critical review of the construct, specificity, and implications for trauma-focused treatment. *Clinical Psychology Review, 31,* 25–36.

Ely, D. L., & Mostardi, R. A. (1986). The effects of recent life events stress, life assets, and temperament pattern on cardiovascular risk factors for Akron city police officers. *Journal of Human Stress, 12,* 77–91.

Emmelkamp, P. M. (2004). Behavior therapy with adults. In M. J. Lambert (Ed.), *Bergin and Garfield's handbook of psychotherapy and behavior change* (5th ed., pp. 393–446). New York: Wiley.

Endler, N. (1982). *Holiday of darkness.* New York: Wiley.

Enea, V., & Dafinoiu, I. (2008). Posthypnotic amnesia and autobiographical memory in adolescents. *Journal of Cognitive and Behavioral Psychotherapies, 8,* 201–215.

Eng, M. Y., Luczak, S. E., & Wall, T. L. (2007). ALDH2, ADH1B, and ADH1C genotypes in Asians: A literature review. *Alcohol Research and Health, 30,* 22–27.

Engelhard, I. M., de Jong, P. J., van den Hout, M. A., & van Overveld, M. (2009). Expectancy bias and the persistence of posttraumatic stress. *Behaviour Research and Therapy, 47,* 887–892.

Engh, J. J. (2006). *In the name of heaven: 3,000 years of religious persecution.* Amherst, NY: Prometheus Books.

Enterman, J. H., & van Dijk, D. (2011). The curious case of a catatonic patient. *Schizophrenia Bulletin, 37,* 235–237.

Epstein, J. A., Banga, H., & Botvina, G. J. (2007). Which psychosocial factors moderate or directly affect substance use among inner-city adolescents? *Addictive Behaviors, 32,* 700–713.

Epstein, L. H., Leddy, J. J., Temple, J. L., & Faith, M. S. (2007). Food reinforcement and eating: A multilevel analysis. *Psychological Bulletin, 133,* 884–906.

Erdely, S. R. (2004, March). What women sacrifice to be thin. *Redbook,* 114–120.

Erenberg, G. (2005). The relationship between Tourette's syndrome, attention deficit hyperactivity disorder, and stimulant medication: A critical review. *Seminars in Pediatric Neurology, 12,* 217–221.

Eriksson, A. S., & de Chateau, P. (1992). Brief report: A girl aged two years and seven months with autistic disorder videotaped from birth. *Journal of Autism and Developmental Disorders, 22,* 127–129.

Eronen, M., Angermeyer, M. C., & Schulze, B. (1998). The psychiatric epidemiology of violent behavior. *Social Psychiatry and Psychiatric Epidemiology, 33*(Suppl. 1), S13–S23.

Ersche, K. D., Turton, A. J., Pradhan, S., Bullmore, E. T., & Robbins, T. W. (2010). Drug addiction endophenotypes: Impulsive versus sensation-seeking personality traits. *Biological Psychiatry, 68,* 770–773.

Eschleman, K. J., Bowling, N. A., & Alarcon, G. M. (2010). A meta-analytic examination of hardiness. *International Journal of Stress Management, 17,* 277–307.

Eshun, S., & Gurung, R. A. R. (Eds.). (2009). *Introduction to culture and psychopathology, in culture and mental health: Sociocultural influences, theory, and practice.* Oxford, UK: Wiley-Blackwell. doi: 10.1002/9781444305807.ch1

Essex, M. J., Klein, M. H., Slattery, M. J., Goldsmith, H., & Kalin, N. H. (2010). Early risk factors and developmental pathways to chronic high inhibition and social anxiety disorder in adolescence. *American Journal of Psychiatry, 167,* 40–46.

Evans, C., Mezey, G., & Ehlers, A. (2009). Amnesia for violent crime among young offenders. *Journal of Forensic Psychiatry and Psychology, 20,* 85–106.

Eubig, P. A., Aguiar, A., & Schantz, S. L. (2010). Lead and PCBs as risk factors for attention deficit/hyperactivity disorder. *Environmental Health Perspectives, 118,* 1654–1667.

Ewing, C. P. (1998, February). Indictment fuels repressed-memory debate. *APA Monitor,* p. 52.

Exner, J. E. (1983). Rorschach assessment. In I. B. Weiner (Ed.), *Clinical methods in psychology.* New York: Wiley.

Exner, J. E. (1990). *A Rorschach workbook for the comprehensive system* (2nd ed.). Asheville, NC: Rorschach Workshops.

Exner, J. E. (1995). Assessment of personality disorders. In J. N. Butcher (Ed.), *Clinical personality assessment: Practical approaches* (pp. 10–18). New York: Oxford University Press.

Eyberg, S. M., Nelson, M. M., & Boggs, S. R. (2008). Evidence-based psychosocial treatments for children and adolescents with disruptive behavior. *Journal of Clinical Child and Adolescent Psychology, 37,* 215–237.

Fabiano, G. A., Pelham, W. E., Coles, E. K., Gnagy, E. M., Chronis-Tuscano, A., & O'Connor, B. C. (2009). A meta-analysis of behavioral treatments for attention-deficit/hyperactivity disorder. *Clinical Psychology Review, 29,* 129–140.

Fagiolini, A. (2008). Medical monitoring in patients with bipolar disorder: A review of data. *Journal of Clinical Psychiatry, 69,* e16.

Fairburn, C. G., Cooper, Z., Bohn, K., O'Connor, M. E., Doll, H. A., & Palmer, R. L. (2007). The severity and status of eating disorders NOS: Implications for DSM-V. *Behaviour Research and Therapy, 45,* 1705–1715.

Fairburn, C. G., Cooper, Z., Doll, H. A., Norman, P., & O'Connor, M. (2000). The natural course of bulimia nervosa and binge eating disorder in young women. *Archives of General Psychiatry, 57,* 659–665.

Fairburn, C. G., Doll, H. A., Welch, S. L., Hay, P. J., Davies, B. A., & O'Connor, M. E. (1998). Risk factors for binge eating disorder: A community-based, case-control study. *Archives of General Psychiatry, 55,* 425–429.

Falloon, I. R. J., Boyd, J. L., & McGill, C. W. (1984). *Family care of schizophrenia.* New York: Guilford Press.

Fals-Stewart, W., & O'Farrell, T. J. (2003). Behavioral family counseling and naltrexone for male opioid-dependent patients. *Journal of Consulting and Clinical Psychology, 71*, 432–442.

Fama, J. M. (2010). Skin picking disorder fact sheet. Retrieved from http://www.ocfoundation.org/uploadedFiles/MainContent/Find_Help/Skin%20Picking%2Disorder%20Fact%20Sheet.pdf

Fang, C. Y., & Myers, H. F. (2001). The effects of racial stressors and hostility on cardiovascular reactivity in African American and Caucasian men. *Health Psychology, 20*, 64–70.

Faraone, S. V., Kremen, W. S., & Tsuang, M. T. (1990). Genetic transmission of affective disorders: Quantitative models and linkage analysis. *Psychological Bulletin, 108*, 109–127.

Faraone, S. V., & Mick, E. (2010). Molecular genetics of attention deficit hyperactivity disorder. *Psychiatric Clinics of North America, 33*, 159–180.

Faraone, S. V., & Wilens, T. E. (2007). Effect of stimulant medications for attention-deficit/hyperactivity disorder on later substance use and the potential for stimulant misuse, abuse, and diversion. *Journal of Clinical Psychiatry, 68*(Suppl 11), 15–22.

Farberow, N. L. (1970). Ten years of suicide prevention: Past and future. *Bulletin of Suicidology, 6*, 5–11.

Farley, F. (1986). World of the type T personality. *Psychology Today, 20*, 45–52.

Farmer, E. M. Z. (1995). Extremity of externalizing behavior and young adult outcomes. *Journal of Child Psychology and Psychiatry, 36*, 617–632.

Farquhar, J. C., & Wasylkiw, L. (2007). Media images of men: Trends and consequences of body conceptualization. *Psychology of Men and Masculinity, 8*, 145–160.

Farrell, A. D., Stiles-Camplair, P., & McCullough, L. (1987). Identification of target complaints by computer interview: Evaluation of the computerized assessment system for psychotherapy evaluation research. *Journal of Consulting and Clinical Psychology, 55*, 691–700.

Farrell, A. D., & White, K. S. (1998). Peer influences and drug use among urban adolescents: Family structure and parent-adolescent relationship as protective factors. *Journal of Consulting and Clinical Psychology, 66*, 248–252.

Farrugia, D., & Fetter, H. (2009). Chronic pain: Biological understanding and treatment suggestions for mental health counselors. *Journal of Mental Health Counseling, 31*, 189–200.

Fattore, L., & Fratta, W. (2010). How important are sex differences in cannabinoid action? *British Journal of Pharmacology, 160*, 544–548.

Faul, M., Xu, L., Wald, M. M., & Coronado, V. G. (2010). Traumatic brain injury in the United States: Emergency department visits, hospitalizations, and deaths 2002–2006. Atlanta, GA: Centers for Disease Control and Prevention, National Center for Injury. http://www.cdc.gove/traumaticbraininjury/tbi_ed.html

Fauman, M. A. (2006). Defining a DSM infrastructure. *American Journal of Psychiatry, 163*, 1873–1874.

Fava, G. A., Fabbri, S., Sirri, L., & Wise, T. N. (2007). Psychological factors affecting medical condition: A new proposal for DSM-V. *Psychosomatics, 48*, 103–111.

Fava, G. A., & Wise, T. N. (2007). Issues for DSM-V: Psychological factors affecting either identified or feared medical conditions: A solution for somatoform disorders. *American Journal of Psychiatry, 164*, 1002–1003.

Fava, G. A., Zielezny, M., Savron, G., & Grandi, S. (1995). The long-term behavioral treatment for panic disorder with agoraphobia. *British Journal of Psychiatry, 166*, 87–92.

Fava, L., & Morton, J. (2009). Causal modeling of panic disorder theories. *Clinical Psychology Review, 29*, 623–637.

Fava, M., Hwang, I., Rush, A. J., Sampson, N., Walters, E. E., & Kessler, R. C. (2009). The importance of irritability as a symptom of major depressive disorder: results from the National Comorbidity Survey Replication. *Molecular Psychiatry, 15*, 856–867.

Federal Bureau of Investigation. (1996). *Uniform crime reports for the United States, 1995.* Washington, DC: Government Printing Office.

Federal Interagency Forum on Aging-Related Statistics. (2006). *Older Americans update 2006: Key indicators of well-being.* Washington, DC: Author.

Fedoroff, J. P. (2008). Treatment of paraphilic sexual disorders. In D. Rowland & L. Incrocci (Eds.). *Handbook of sexual and gender identity disorders* (pp. 563–586). Hoboken, NJ: Wiley.

Feingold, B. F. (1977). Behavioral disturbances linked to the ingestion of food additives. *Delaware Medical Journal, 49*, 89–94.

Feinstein, J. S., Adolphs, R., Damasio, A., & Tranel, D. (2011). The human amygdala and the induction and experience of fear. *Current Biology, 21*, 1–5.

Feinstein, J. S., Duff, M. C., & Tranela, D. (2010). Sustained experience of emotion after loss of memory in patients with amnesia. *Proceedings of the National Academy of Sciences, 107*, 7674–7679.

Feldman, H. A., Goldstein, I., Hatzichristou, D. G., Krane, R. J., & McKinlay, J. B. (1994). Impotence and its medical and psychosocial correlates: Results of the Massachusetts Male Aging Study. *Journal of Urology, 151*, 54–61.

Feldman, M. B., & Meyer, I. H. (2007). Eating disorders in diverse lesbian, gay, and bisexual populations. *International Journal of Eating disorders, 40*, 218–226.

Feldman-Summers, S., & Pope, K. S. (1994). The experience of "forgetting" childhood abuse: A national survey of psychologists. *Journal of Consulting and Clinical Psychology, 62*, 636–639.

Fenichel, O. (1945). *The psychoanalytic theory of neuroses.* New York: Norton.

Fenton, M. C., Keyes, K. M., Martins, S. S., & Hasin, D. S. (2010). The role of a prescription in anxiety medication use, abuse, and dependence. *American Journal of Psychiatry, 167*, 1247–1253.

Fergusson, D. M., Horwood, L. J., & Lynskey, M. T. (1995). The stability of disruptive childhood behaviors. *Journal of Abnormal Child Psychology, 23*, 379–396.

Ferrao, Y. A., Miguel, E. C., & Stein, D. J. (2011). Tourette's syndrome, trichotillomania, and obsessive-compulsive disorder: How closely are they related? In E. Hollander, J. Zohar, P. J. Sirovatka, & D. A. Regier (Eds.), *Obsessive-compulsive spectrum disorders: Refining the research agenda for DSM-V* (pp. 57–88). Washington, D.C.: American Psychiatric Association.

Ferrier, A. G., & Martens, M. P. (2008). Perceived incompetence and disordered eating among college students. *Eating Behaviors, 9*, 111–119.

Ferrier-Auerbach, A. G., & Martens, M. P. (2009). Perceived incompetence moderates the relationship between maladaptive perfectionism and disordered eating. *Eating Disorders, 17*, 333–344.

Ferster, C. B. (1965). Classification of behavior pathology. In L. Krasner & L. P. Ullman (Eds.), *Research in behavior modification.* New York: Holt, Rinehart & Winston.

Ficks, C. A., & Waldman, I. D. (2009). Gene-environment interactions in attention-deficit/hyperactivity disorder. *Current Psychiatry Reports, 11*, 387–392.

Fiedorowicz, J. G., Leon, A. C., Keller, M. B., Solomon, D. A., Rice, J. P., Coryell, W. H. (2009). Do risk factors for suicidal behavior differ by affective disorder polarity? *Psychological Medicine, 39*, 763–771.

Field, A. P., Ball, J. E., Kawycz, N. J., & Moore, H. (2007). Parent-child relationships and verbal information pathway to fear in children: Two preliminary experiments. *Behavioural and Cognitive Psychotherapy, 35*, 473–486.

Fields, R. (2004). *Drugs in perspective: A personalized look at substance use and abuse* (5th ed.). New York: McGraw-Hill.

Findling, R. L. (2008). Evolution of the treatment of attention-deficit/hyperactivity disorder in children: A review. *Clinical Therapy, 30*, 942–957.

Findorff, M. J., Wyman, J. F., & Gross, C. R. (2009). Predictors of long-term exercise adherence in a community-based sample of older women. *Journal of Womens Health (Larchmont), 18*(11), 1769–1776.

Fink, M. (2009). Catatonia: A syndrome appears, disappears, and is rediscovered. *Canadian Journal of Psychiatry, 54*, 437–445.

Fink, M., Shorter, E., & Taylor, M. A. (2010). Catatonia is not schizophrenia: Kraepelin's error and the need to recognize catatonia as an independent syndrome in medical nomenclature. *Schizophrenia Bulletin, 36*, 314–320.

Finkelhor, D. (1980). Sex among siblings: A survey on prevalence, variety, and effects. *Archives of Sexual Behavior, 9*, 171–194.

Finkelhor, D., Ormrod, R., Turner, H., & Hamby, S. L. (2005). The victimization of children and youth: A comprehensive national survey. *Child Maltreatment, 10*, 5–25.

Finkelstein, E. A., Fiebelkorn, I. C., & Wang, G. (2004). State-level estimates of annual medical expenditures attributable to obesity. *Obesity Research, 12*, 18–24.

First, M. B. (2007). Externalizing disorders of childhood (attention-deficit/hyperactivity disorder, conduct disorder, oppositional-defiant disorder, juvenile bipolar disorder). Retrieved from http://www.psych.org/MainMenu/Research/DSMIV/DSMV/DSMRevisionActivities/ConferenceSummaries/ExternalizingDisordersofChildhood.aspx

Fischer, M., Barkley, R. A., Smallish, L., & Fletcher, K. (2005). Executive function in hyperactive children as young adults: Attention, inhibition, response perseveration, and the impact of co-morbidity. *Developmental Neuropsychology, 27,* 107–133.

Fischer, S., Stojek, M., & Hartzell, E. (2010). Effects of multiple forms of childhood abuse and adult sexual assault on current eating disorder symptoms. *Eating Behaviors, 11,* 190–192.

Fischer, P. J., & Breakey, W. R. (1991). The epidemiology of alcohol, drug, and mental disorders among homeless persons. *American Psychologist, 46,* 1115–1128.

Fisher, H. L., Jones, P. B., Fearon, P., Craig, T. K., Dazzan, P., . . . Morgan, C. (2010). The varying impact of type, timing and frequency of exposure to childhood adversity on its association with adult psychotic disorder. *Psychological Medicine, 40,* 1967–1978.

Fisher, M. A. (2009). Replacing "who is the client?" with a different ethical question. *Professional Psychology: Research and Practice, 40,* 1–7.

Fitch, W. L. (2007). AAPL practice guidelines for the forensic psychiatric evaluation of competence to stand trial: An American legal perspective. *Journal of American Psychiatric Law, 35,* 509–513.

Flaherty, M. L., Infante, M., Tinsley, J. A., & Black, J. L., III. (2001). Factitious hypertension by pseudoephedrine. *Psychosomatics, 42,* 150–153.

Flavin, D. K., Franklin, J. E., & Frances, R. J. (1990). Substance abuse and suicidal behavior. In S. J. Blumenthal & D. J. Kupfer (Eds.), *Suicide over the life cycle: Risk factors, assessment, and treatment of suicidal patients.* Washington, DC: American Psychiatric Press.

Fleet, R. P., Lavoie, K. L., Martel, J.-P., Dupuis, G., Marchand, A., & Beitman, B. D. (2003). Two-year follow-up status of emergency department patients with chest pain: Was it a panic disorder? *Journal of the Canadian Association of Emergency Physicians, 5,* 247–252.

Flegal, K. M., Carroll, M. D., Ogden, C. L., & Curtin, L. R. (2010). Prevalence and trends in obesity among US adults, 1999–2008. *Journal of the American Medical Association, 303,* 235–240.

Flegal, K. M., Graubard, B. I., Williamson, D. F., & Gail, M. H. (2007). Cause-specific excess deaths associated with underweight, overweight, and obesity. *Journal of the American Medical Association, 298,* 2028–2037.

Fleming, I., Baum, A., Davidson, L. M., Rectanus, E., & McArdle, S. (1987). Chronic stress as a factor in physiologic reactivity to challenge. *Health Psychology, 6,* 221–237.

Flicker, L., McCaul, K. A., Hankey, G. J., Jamrozik, K., Brown, W. J., Byles, J. E., & Almeida, O. P. (2010). Body mass index and survival in men and women aged 70 to 75. *Journal of the American Geriatric Society, 58,* 234–241.

Flink, I. K., Nicholas, M. K., Boersma, K., & Linton, S. J. (2009). Reducing the threat value of chronic pain: A preliminary replicated single-case study of interoceptive exposure versus distraction in six individuals with chronic back pain. *Behaviour Research and Therapy, 47,* 721–728.

Flores, E., Tschann, J. M., Dimas, J. M., Pasch, L. A., & de Groat, C. L. (2010). Perceived racial/ethnic discrimination, posttraumatic stress symptoms, and health risk behaviors among Mexican American adolescents. *Journal of Counseling Psychology, 57,* 264–273.

Foa, E. B. (2000). Psychosocial treatment of posttraumatic stress disorder. *Journal of Clinical Psychiatry, 61,* 43–53.

Foa, E. B., Dancu, C. V., Hembree, E. A., Jaycox, L. H., Meadows, E. A., & Street, G. P. (1999). A comparison of exposure therapy, stress inoculation training, and their combination in reducing posttraumatic stress disorder in female assault victims. *Journal of Consulting and Clinical Psychology, 67,* 194–200.

Foa, E. B., Ehlers, A., Clark, D. M., Tolin, D. F., & Orsillo, S. M. (1999). The Posttraumatic Cognitions Inventory (PTCI): Development and validation. *Psychological Assessment, 11,* 303–314.

Foa, E. B., & Kozak, M. J. (1995). DSM-IV field trial: Obsessive-compulsive disorder. *American Journal of Psychiatry, 152,* 90–96.

Fogel, E. R. (2003). Biofeedback-assisted musculoskeletal therapy. In K. West & F. Andrasik (Eds.), *Biofeedback: A practitioner's guided* (3rd Ed., pp. 515–544). New York: Guilford Press.

Foley, D. L., & Morley, K. I. (2011). Systematic review of early cardiometabolic outcomes of the first treated episode of psychosis. *Archives of General Psychiatry.* doi: 10.1001/archigenpsychiatry.2011.2

Follette, W. C., & Houts, A. C. (1996). Models of scientific progress and the role of theory in taxonomy development: A case study of the DSM. *Journal of Consulting and Clinical Psychology, 64,* 1120–1132.

Fombonne, E. (2003). Epidemiological surveys of autism and other pervasive developmental disorders: An update. *Journal of Autism and Developmental Disorders, 33,* 365–382.

Fontaine, K. R., Redden, D. T., Wang, C., Westfall, A. O., & Allison, D. B. (2003). Years of life lost due to obesity. *Journal of the American Medical Association, 289,* 187–193.

Fontenelle, L. F., Telles, L. L., Nazar, B. P., de Menezes, G. B., do Nascimento, A. L., Mendlowicz, M. V., & Versiani, M. (2006). A sociodemographic, phenomenological, and long-term follow-up study of patients with body dysmorphic disorder in Brazil. *International Journal of Psychiatry in Medicine, 36,* 243–259.

Foote, B., Smolin, Y., Kaplan, M., Legatt, M. E., & Lipschitz, D. (2006). Prevalence of dissociative disorders in psychiatric outpatients. *American Journal of Psychiatry, 163,* 623–629.

Forbes, G. B., Adams-Curtis, L. E., Rade, B., & Jaberg, P. (2001). Body dissatisfaction in women and men: The role of gender-typing and self-esteem. *Sex Roles, 44,* 461–484.

Ford v. Wainwright 477 U.S. 399 (1986).

Fornaro, M., & Giosue, P. (2010). Current nosology of treatment resistant depression: A controversy resistant to revision. *Clinical Practice and Epidemiology in Mental Health, 6,* 20–24.

Forno, E., & Celedón, J. C. (2009). Asthma and minorities: Socioeconomic status and beyond. *Current Opinion in Allergy and Clinical Immunology, 9,* 154–160.

Fornos, L. B., Mika, V. S., Bayles, B., Serrano, A. C., Jimenez, R. L., & Villarreal, R. (2005). A qualitative study of Mexican American adolescents and depression. *Journal of School Health, 75,* 162–170.

Foroud, T., Edenberg, H. J., & Crabbe, J. C. (2010). Genetic research: Who is at risk for alcoholism? *Alcohol Research & Health.* Retrieved from http://findarticles.com/p/articles/mi_m0CXH/is_1-2_33/ai_n55302105/

Forsyth, J. P., Eifert, G. H., & Thompson, R. N. (1996). Systemic alarms in fear conditioning: II. An experimental methodology using 20 percent carbon dioxide inhalation as an unconditioned stimulus. *Behavior Therapy, 27,* 391–415.

Forty, L., Jones, L., Macgregor, S., Caesar, S., Cooper, C., . . . Jones, I. (2006). Familiality of postpartum depression in unipolar disorder: Results of a family study. *American Journal of Psychiatry, 163,* 1549–1553.

Foster, C. J., Garber, J., & Durlak, J. A. (2008). Current and past maternal depression, maternal interaction behaviors, and children's externalizing and internalizing symptoms. *Journal of Abnormal Child Psychology, 36,* 527–537.

Foster, J. A., & MacQueen, G. (2008). Neurobiological factors linking personality traits and major depression. *La Revue Canadienne de Psychiatrie, 53,* 6–13.

Foster-Scott, L. (2007). Sociological factors affecting childhood obesity. *Journal of Physical Education, Recreation and Dance, 78,* 29–47.

Foti, D. J., Kotov, R., Guey, L. T., & Bromet, E. J. (2010). Cannabis use and the course of schizophrenia: 10 year follow-up after first hospitalization. *American Journal of Psychiatry, 167,* 987–993.

Fournier, J. C., DeRubeis, R. J., Hollon, S. D., Dimidjian, S., Amsterdam, J. D., & Fawcett, J. (2010). Antidepressant drug effects and depression severity: A patient-level meta-analysis. *Journal of the American Medical Association, 303,* 47–53.

Fowler, K. B. (2007). Snapshots: The first symptoms of psychosis. *Schizophrenia Bulletin, 33,* 16–18.

Fox, N. A., Nichols, K. E., Henderson, H. A., Rubin, K., Schmidt, L., . . . Pine, D. S. (2005). Evidence for a gene-environment interaction in predicting behavioral inhibition in middle childhood. *Psychological Science, 16,* 921–926.

Fox, R. E., & Sammons, M. T. (1998). A history of prescription privileges. *Monitor on Psychology, 29,* 1–5.

Foxhall, K. (2001, March). How psychopharmacology training is enhancing some psychology practices. *Monitor on Psychology, 27,* 50–52.

Foxx, R., & Brown, R. (1979). Nicotine fading and self-monitoring for cigarette abstinence or controlled smoking. *Journal of Applied Behavior Analysis, 12,* 111–125.

Frances, A. (2011a). DSM-5 promotes a 60% jump in the rate of alcohol use disorders. *Psychiatric Times, 28,* 1–2.

Frances, A. (2011a). A warning sign on the road to DSM-V: Beware of its unintended consequences. *Psychiatric Times, 26,* 1–7.

Frank, D. A., Rose-Jacobs, R., Crooks, D., Cabral, H. J., Gerteis, J., . . . Heeren, T. (2010). Adolescent initiation of licit and illicit substance use: Impact of intrauterine exposures and post-natal exposure to violence. *Neurotoxicology and Teratology, 33*(1), 100–109.

Franke, B., Neale, B. M., & Faraone, S. V. (2009). Genome-wide association studies in ADHD. *Human Genetics, 126,* 13–50.

Frankenburg, F. R. (2010). Schizophrenia. Retrieved from http://emedicine.medscape.com/article/288259-print

Frankle, W. G., Lombardo, I., & New, A. S. (2005). Brain serotonin transporter distribution in subjects with impulsive aggressivity: A positron emission study [11C] McN 5652. *American Journal of Psychiatry, 162,* 915–923.

Franklin, D. (1987). The politics of masochism. *Psychology Today, 21,* 51–57.

Franklin, K. (2011). Forensic psychiatrists vote no on proposed paraphilias. *Psychiatric Times, 27,* 1–2.

Franklin, J. E., & Frances, R. J. (1999). Alcohol and other psychoactive substance use disorders. In R. E. Hales, S. C. Yudofsky, & J. A. Talbott (Eds.), *Textbook of psychiatry* (pp. 363–423). Washington, DC: American Psychiatric Press.

Franklin, J. C., Heilbron, N., Guerry, J. D., Bowker, K. B., & Blumenthal, T. D. (2009). Antisocial and borderline personality disorder symptomalogies are associated with decreased prepulse inhibition: The importance of optimal experimental parameters. *Personality and Individual Differences, 47,* 439–443.

Franklin, M. E., Abramowitz, J. S., Kozak, M. J., Levitt, J. T., & Foa, E. B. (2000). Effectiveness of exposure and ritual prevention for obsessive-compulsive disorder: Randomized compared with nonrandomized samples. *Journal of Consulting and Clinical Psychology, 68,* 594–602.

Franklin, T., Wang, Z., Suh, J. J., Hazan, R., Cruz, J., . . . Childress, A. R. (2011). Effects of varenicline on smoking cue-triggered neural and craving responses. *Archives of General Psychiatry, 68*(5), 516–526. doi: 10.1001/archgenpsychiatry.2010.190

Franklin, T. B., Russig, H., Weiss, I. C., Graff, J., Linder, N. . . . Michalon, A. (2010). Epigenetic transmission of the impact of early stress across generations. *Biological Psychiatry, 68,* 408–415.

Frazier, P., Anders, S., Perera, S., Tomich, P., Tennen, H., Park, C., & Tashiro, T. (2009). Traumatic events among undergraduate students: Prevalence and associated symptoms. *Journal of Counseling Psychology, 56,* 450–460.

Freed, G. L., Clark, S. J., Butchart, A. T., Singer, D. C., & Davis, M. M. (2010). Parental vaccine safety concerns in 2009. *Pediatrics, 125,* 654–659.

Freeland, A., Manchanda, R., Chiu, S., Sharma, V., & Merskey, H. (1993). Four cases of supposed multiple personality disorder: Evidence of unjustified diagnoses. *Canadian Journal of Psychiatry, 23,* 245–247.

Freeman, D., Garety, P. A., Kuipers, E., Fowler, D., Bebbington, P. E., & Dunn, G. (2007). Acting on persecutory delusions: The importance of safety seeking. *Behaviour Research and Therapy, 45,* 89–99.

Freeman, D., McManus, S., Brugha, T., Meltzer, H., Jenkins, R., & Bebbington, P. (2010). Concomitants of paranoia in the general population. *Psychological Medicine, 41*(5):923–936. doi:10.1017/S003329171000546

Freeman, D., Pugh, K., Antley, A., Slater, M., Bebbington, P., . . . Garety, P. (2008). Virtual reality study paranoid thinking in the general population. *British Journal of Psychiatry, 192,* 258–263.

Freeston, M. H., & Ladouceur, R. (1993). Appraisal of cognitive intrusions and response style: Replication and extension. *Behaviour Research and Therapy, 31,* 185–191.

Freeston, M. H., & Ladouceur, R. (1997). What do patients do with their obsessive thoughts? *Behaviour Research and Therapy, 35,* 335–347.

Freiberg, P. (1991). Suicide in family, friends is familiar to too many teens. *APA Monitor, 22,* 36–37.

French, J., & Friedman, D. (2011). Epilepsy: From newly diagnosed to treatment-resistant disease. *The Lancet Neurology, 10,* 9–11.

Frese, F. J., & Myrick, K. J. (2010). On consumer advocacy and the diagnosis of mental disorders. *Professional Psychology: Research and Practice, 41,* 495–501.

Frewen, P. A., Evans, E. M., Maraj, N., Dozois, D. J. A., & Partridge, K. (2008). Letting go: Mindfulness and negative automatic thinking. *Cognitive Therapy Research, 32,* 758–774.

Freinkel, A., Koopman, C., & Spiegel, D. (1994). Dissociative symptoms in media eyewitnesses of an execution. *American Journal of Psychiatry, 151,* 1335–1339.

Freud, S. (1909). Analysis of a phobia of a five-year-old boy. In *The Pelican Freud Library* Vol 8, Case Histories 1 (1977, pp. 169–306).

Freud, S. (1938). The psychopathology of everyday life. In A. B. Brill (Ed.), *The basic writings of Sigmund Freud.* New York: Modern Library.

Freud, S. (1949). *An outline of psychoanalysis.* New York: Norton.

Freud, S. (1955). *Mourning and melancholia.* In J. Strachey (Ed. & Trans.), *The standard edition of the complete psychological works of Sigmund Freud* (Vol. 14, pp. 737–858). London: Hogarth Press. (Original work published 1917)

Freud, S. (1959). *Beyond the pleasure principle.* New York: Bantam. (Original work published 1909)

Freud, S. (1909/1977). Analysis of a phobia of a five year old boy. In *The Pelican Freud Library: Case histories 1.* (Vol. 8) (pp. 169–306). London: Penguin.

Freudenmann, R. W., & Lepping, P. (2009). Delusional infestation. *Clinical Microbiology Reviews, 22,* 690–732.

Freyer, T., Kloppel, S., Tuscher, O., Kordon, A., Zurowski, B., . . . Voderhotzer, U. (2011). Frontostriatal activation in patients with obsessive-compulsive disorder before and after cognitive behavior therapy. *Psychological Medicine, 41,* 211–216.

Frick, P. J., & Lahey, B. B. (1991). Nature and characteristics of attention-deficit hyperactivity disorder. *School Psychology Review, 20,* 163–173.

Friedman, J. H., & LaFrance, W. C., Jr. (2010). Psychogenic disorders: the need to speak plainly. *Archives of Neurology, 67,* 753–755.

Friedman, M. A., Detweiler-Bedell, J. B., Leventhal, H. E., Horne, R., Keitner, G. I., & Miller, I. W. (2004). Combined psychotherapy and pharmacotherapy for the treatment of major depressive disorder. *Clinical Psychology: Science and Practice, 11,* 47–68.

Friedman, R. A. (2004, October 18). A patient's suicide, a psychiatrist's pain. *New York Times,* p. F6.

Friedrich, W. N., Fisher, J., Broughton, D., Houston, M., & Shafran, C. (1998). Normative sexual behavior in children: A contemporary sample. *Pediatrics, 101,* 1–8.

Frieling, H., Romer, K. D., Scholz, S., Mittelbach, F., Wilhelm, J., . . . Bleich, S. (2010). Epigenetic dysregulation of dopaminergic genes in eating disorders. *International Journal of Eating Disorders, 43,* 577–583.

Fritz, G. K., Rubenstein, S., & Lewiston, N. J. (1987). Psychological factors in fatal childhood asthma. *American Journal of Orthopsychiatry, 57,* 253–257.

Froehlich, T. E., Lanphear, B. P., Auinger, P., Hornung, R., Epstein, J. N., Braun, J., & Kahn, R. S. (2009). Association of tobacco and lead exposures with attention-deficit/hyperactivity disorder. *Pediatrics, 124,* e1054–1063.

Froehlich, T. E., Lanphear, B. P., Epstein, J. N., Barbaresi, W. J., Katusic, S. K., & Kahn, R. S. (2007). Prevalence and treatment of ADHD in a national sample of U.S. children. *Archives of Pediatrics and Adolescent Medicine, 161,* 857–864.

Frohm, K. D., & Beehler, G. P. (2010). Psychologists as change agents in chronic pain management practice: Cultural competence in the health care system. *Psychological Services, 7,* 115–125.

Frojd, S., Ranta, K., Kaltiala-Heino, R., & Marttunen, M. (2011). Associations of social phobia and general anxiety with alcohol and drug use in a community sample of adolescents. *Alcohol and Alcoholism, 46*(2), 192–199. doi: 10.1093/alcalc/agq096

Fry, J. P., & Neff, R. A. (2010). Periodic prompts and reminders in health promotion and health behavior interventions: Systematic review. *Journal of Medical Internet Research, 11,* e16.

Fukumoto, A., Hashimoto, T., Mori, K., Tsuda, Y., Arisawa, K., & Kagami, S. (2010). Head circumference and body growth in autism spectrum disorders. *Brain Development.* In press.

Fulero, S. M. (1988). Tarasoff: 10 years later. *Professional Psychology: Research and Practice, 19,* 184–190.

Fulkerson, J. A., Strauss, J., Neumark-Sztainer, D., Story, M., & Boutelle, K. (2007). Correlates of psychosocial well-being among overweight adolescents: The role of the family. *Journal of Consulting and Clinical Psychology, 75,* 181–186.

Fullana, M. A., Mataix-Cols, D., Caspi, A., Harrington, H., Grisham, J. R., . . . Poulton, R. (2009). Obsessions and compulsions in the community: Prevalence, interference, help-seeking, developmental stability, and co-occurring psychiatric conditions. *American Journal of Psychiatry, 166,* 329–336.

Furer, P., & Walker, J. R. (2005). Treatment of hypochondriasis with exposure. *Journal of Contemporary Psychotherapy, 35,* 251–267.

Furness, P., Glazebrook, C., Tay, J., Abbas, K., & Slaveska-Hollis, K. (2009). Medically unexplained physical symptoms in children: Exploring hospital staff perceptions. *Child Clinical Psychology and Psychiatry, 14,* 575–587.

Furr, S. R., Westefeld, J. S., McConnell, G. N., & Jenkins, J. M. (2001). Suicide and depression among college students: A decade later. *Professional Psychology: Research and Practice, 32,* 97–100.

Fussman, C., Rafferty, A. P., Lyon-Callo, S., Morgenstern, L. B., & Reeves, M. J. (2010). Lack of association between stroke symptom knowledge and intent to call 911: A population-based survey. *Stroke, 41,* 1501–1507.

Gabbard, G. O. (2000). A neurobiologically informed perspective on psychotherapy. *British Journal of Psychiatry, 177,* 117–122.

Gabbard, G. O. (2001). Psychodynamic psychotherapies. In G. O. Gabbard (Ed.), *Treatment of psychiatric disorders* (pp. 1227–1245). Washington, DC: American Psychiatric Press.

Gabriel, T. (2010, December 19). Serious mental health needs seen growing at colleges. *The New York Times,* http://www.nytimes.com/2010/12/20/health/20campus.html?_r=1&scp=1&sq=mental%20health&st=cse

Gabriela, M. L., John, D. G., Magdalena, B. V., Ariadna, G. S., Francisco, L. P., . . . Carlos, C. F. (2009). Genetic interaction analysis for DRD4 and DAT1 genes in a group of Mexican ADHD patients. *Neuroscience Letter, 451,* 257–260.

Gagnon, J. H. (1990). The explicit and implicit use of the scripting perspective in sex research. *Annual Review of Sex Research, 1,* 1–43.

Galea, S., Ahern, J., Resnick, H., Kilpatrick, D., Bucuvalas, M., Gold, J., & Vlahov, D. (2002). Psychological sequelae of the September 11 terrorist attacks in New York City. *New England Journal of Medicine, 346,* 982–987.

Gallant, D. (2001). Alcoholism. In G. O. Gabbard (Ed.), *Treatment of psychiatric disorders*

(pp. 665–678). Washington, DC: American Psychiatric Press.

Gallichan, D. J., & Curle, C. (2008). Fitting square pegs into round holes: The challenge of coping with attention-deficit hyperactivity disorder. *Clinical Child Psychology and Psychiatry, 13,* 343–363.

Gallup Organization. (2009). Religion. Retrieved from http://www.gallup.com/poll/1690/Religion.aspx

Gamble, E., & Elder, S. (1983). Multimodal biofeedback in the treatment of migraine. *Biofeedback and Self-Regulation, 8,* 383–392.

Gammelgaard, L. K., Colding, H., Hartzen, S. H., & Penkowa, M. (2011). Meningococcal disease and future drug targets. *CNS & Neurological Disorders—Drug Targets, 10,* 140–145.

Gangadhar, B., Kapur, R., & Kalyanasundaram, S. (1982). Comparison of electroconvulsive therapy with imipramine in endogenous depression: A double blind study. *British Journal of Psychiatry, 141,* 367–371.

Ganguli, M., Du, Y., Dodge, H. H., Ratcliff, G. G., & Chang, C. C. (2006). Depressive symptoms and cognitive decline in late life: A prospective epidemiologic study. *Archives of General Psychiatry, 63,* 153–160.

Gangwisch, J. E., Babiss, L. A., Malaspina, D., Turner, J. B., Zammit, G. K., & Posner, K. (2010). Earlier parental set bedtimes as a protective factor against depression and suicidal ideation. *Sleep, 33,* 97–106.

Gan, W., & Petkova, E. (2010). Treatment for PTSD related to childhood abuse: A randomized control trial. *American Journal of Psychiatry, 167,* 915–924.

Gao, Y., Raine, A., Venables, P. H., Dawson, M. E., & Mednick, S. A. (2010). Association of poor childhood fear conditioning and adult crime. *American Journal of Psychiatry, 167,* 56–60.

Garb, H. N. (2003). Dear Dr. Antony [Letter to the editor]. *Clinical Psychologist, 56,* 5.

Garb, H. N., Wood, J. M., Lilienfeld, S. O., & Nezworski, T. (2005). Roots of the Rorschach controversy. *Clinical Psychology Review, 25,* 97–118.

Garber, J., & Cole, D. A. (2010). Intergenerational transmission of depression: A launch and grow model of change across adolescence. *Developmental Psychopathology, 22,* 819–830.

Gardiner, K., Herault, Y., Lott, I. T., Antonarakis, S. E., Reeves, R. H., & Dierssen, M. (2010). Down syndrome: From understanding the neurobiology to therapy. *Journal of Neuroscience, 30,* 14943–14945.

Gardner, A. (2011). Is Charlie Sheen bipolar? Retrieved from http://news.health.com/2011/03/01/charlie-sheen-bipolar/

Garety, P. A., Bebbington, P., Fowler, D., Freeman, D., & Kuipers, E. (2007). Implications for neurobiological research of cognitive models of psychosis: A theoretical paper. *Psychological Medicine, 37,* 1377–1391.

Garfinkel, B. D., Froese, A., & Hood, J. (1982). Suicide attempts in children and adolescents. *American Journal of Psychiatry, 139,* 1257–1261.

Garfinkel, B. D., & Golumbek, H. (1983). Suicidal behavior in adolescence. In H. Golumbek & B. D. Garfinkel (Eds.), *The adolescent and mood disturbance.* New York: International Universities Press.

Garrett, M., & Silva, R. (2003). Auditory hallucinations, source monitoring, and the belief that "voices" are real. *Schizophrenia Bulletin, 29,* 445–451.

Garrison, M. J. (2009). *A measure of failure: The political origins of standardized testing.* New York: University of New York Press.

Gass, C. S. (2002). Personality assessment of neurologically impaired patients. In J. N. Butcher (Ed.), *Clinical personality assessment: Practical approaches* (pp. 208–224). New York: Oxford University Press.

Gavett, B. E., Stern, R. A., Cantu, R. C., Nowinski, C. J., & McKee, A. C. (2010). Mild traumatic brain injury: A risk factor for neurodegeneration. *Alzheimer's Research & Therapy, 2,* 18. Retrieved from http://alzres.com/content/2/3/18

Gatz, M. (1990). Interpreting behavioral genetic results: Suggestions for counselors and clients. *Journal of Counseling and Development, 68,* 601–605.

Gatz, M. (2007). Genetics, dementia, and the elderly. *Current Directions in Psychological Science, 16,* 123–127.

Gatz, M., Reynolds, C. A., Fratiglioni, L., Johansson, B., Mortimer, J. A., . . . Pederson, N. L. (2006). The role of genes and environments for explaining Alzheimer's disease. *Archives of General Psychiatry, 63,* 168–174.

Gaub, M., & Carlson, C. L. (1997). Behavioral characteristics of DSM-IV ADHD subtypes in a school-based population. *Journal of Abnormal Child Psychology, 25,* 103–111.

Gaudiano, B. A., Young, D., Chelminski, I., & Zimmerman, M. (2008). Depressive symptom profiles and severity patterns in outpatients with psychotic vs nonpsychotic major depression. *Comprehensive Psychiatry, 49,* 421–429.

Gawin, F. H. (1991). Cocaine addiction: Psychology and neurophysiology. *Science, 251,* 1580–1586.

Gawrysiak, M., Nicholas, C., & Hopko, D. R. (2009). Behavioral activation for moderately depressed university students: Randomized controlled trial. *Journal of Counseling Psychology, 56,* 468–475.

Gee, G. C., Delva, J., & Takeuchi, D. T. (2007). Relationships between self-reported unfair treatment and prescription medication use, illicit drug use, and alcohol dependence among Filipino Americans. *American Journal of Public Health, 97,* 933–940.

Geier, D. A., Kern, J. K., & Geier, M. R. (2009). A prospective blinded evaluation of urinary porphyrins verses the clinical severity of autism spectrum disorders. *Journal of Toxicology and Environmental Health, 72,* 1585–1591.

Gelernter, J., & Kranzler, H. (1999). D2 dopamine receptor gene (DRD2) allele and haplotype frequencies in alcohol dependent and control subjects: No association with phenotype or severity of phenotype. *Neuropsychopharmacology, 20,* 640–649.

Gelernter, J., & Kranzler, H. R. (2009). Genetics of alcohol dependence. *Human Genetics, 126,* 91–99.

Geller, D. A. (2006). Obsessive-compulsive and spectrum disorders in children and adolescents. *Psychiatric Clinics of North America, 29,* 353–370.

Gelson, C. J., & Woodhouse, S. (2003). Toward a positive psychotherapy: Focus on human strength. In W. B. Walsh (Ed.), *Counseling psychology and optimal human functioning* (pp. 171–197). Mahwah, NJ: Lawrence Erlbaum Associates.

Genes and stressed-out parents lead to shy kids. (2007, March 5). *Science Daily.* Retrieved from www.sciencedaily.com/releases/2007/03/070302111100.htm

George, M. S., Trimble, M. R., Ring, H. A., Sallee, F. R., & Robertson, M. M. (1993). Obsessions in obsessive-compulsive disorder with and without Gilles de la Tourette's syndrome. *American Journal of Psychiatry, 150,* 93–97.

Geller, J. L. (2006). A history of private psychiatric hospitals in the USA: From start to finish. *Psychiatric Quarterly, 77,* 1–41.

Gever, J. (2010). Big changes for DSM-V, the psychiatrist's bible. Retrieved from http://abcnews.go.com/Health/MindMoodNews/psychiatrist-bible-revisions-diagnostic-statistical-manual-mental-disorders/story?id=9795049

Ghaemi, S. N. (2010a). Levels of evidence. *Psychiatric Times, 27,* 1–4.

Ghaemi, S. N. (2010b). *The rise and fall of the biopsychosocial model: Reconciling art and science in psychiatry.* Baltimore, MD: John Hopkins University Press.

Gharaibeh, N. (2009). Dissociative identity disorder: Time to remove it from DSM-V? *Current Psychiatry, 8,* 30–37.

Ghaziuddin, M. (2010). Should the DSM-V drop Asperger syndrome? *Journal of Autism and Developmental Disorders, 40,* 1146–1148.

Ghaziuddin, M., & Mountain-Kimchi, K. (2004). Defining the intellectual profile of Asperger syndrome: Comparison with high-functioning autism. *Journal of Autism and Developmental Disorders, 34,* 279–284.

Ghisi, M., Chiri, L. R., Marchetti, I., Sanavio, E., & Sica, C. (2010). In search of specificity: "Not just right experiences" and obsessive-compulsive symptoms in non-clinical and clinical Italian individuals. *Journal of Anxiety Disorders, 24,* 879–886.

Giancola, P. R., & Zeichner, A. (1997). The biphasic effects of alcohol on human physical aggression. *Journal of Abnormal Psychology, 106,* 598–607.

Gibbons, F., Etcheverry, P. E., Stock, M. L., Gerrard, M., Weng, C., . . . O'Hara, R. E. (2010). Exploring the link between racial discrimination and substance use: What mediates? What buffers? *Journal of Personality and Social Psychology, 99,* 785–801.

Gibbons, R. D., Brown, C. H., Hur, K., Marcus, S. M., Bhaumik, D. K., . . . Mann, J. J. (2007).

Early evidence on the effects of regulators' suicidality warnings on SSRI prescriptions and suicide in children and adolescents. *American Journal of Psychiatry, 164,* 1356–1363.

Gierhart, B. S. (2006). When does a "less than perfect" sex life become female sexual dysfunction? *Obstetrics and Gynecology, 107,* 750–751.

Giesbrecht, T., Lynn, S. J., Lilienfeld, S. O., & Merckelbach, H. (2008). Cognitive processes in dissociation: An analysis of core theoretical assumptions. *Psychological Bulletin, 134,* 617–647.

Gijs, L. (2008). Paraphilia and parphilia-related disorders: An introduction. In D. Rowland & L. Incrocci (Eds.), *Handbook of sexual and gender identity disorders* (pp. 491–528). Hoboken, NJ: Wiley.

Gilbert, B. D., & Christopher, M. S. (2010). Mindfulness-based attention as a moderator of the relationship between depressive affect and negative cognitions. *Cognitive Therapy and Research, 34,* 514–521.

Gilbert, S. C. (2003). Eating disorders in women of color. *Clinical Psychology: Science and Practice, 10,* 1–16.

Gilbertson, M. W., Paulus, L. A., Williston, S. K., Gurvits, T. V., Lasko, N. B., Pittman, R. K., & Orr, S. P. (2006). Neurocognitive function in monozygotic twins discordant for combat exposure: Relationship to posttraumatic stress disorder. *Journal of Abnormal Psychology, 115,* 484–495.

Gill, S. S., Anderson, G. M., Fischer, H. D., Bell, C. M., Li, P., . . . Normand, S. L. (2009). Syncope and its consequences in patients with dementia receiving cholinesterase inhibitors: A population-based cohort study. *Archives of Internal Medicine, 169,* 867–873.

Gilleen, J., Greenwood, K., & David, A. S. (2011). Domains of awareness in schizophrenia. *Schizophrenia Bulletin, 37,* 61–72.

Gillespie, C. F., & Nemeroff, C. B. (2007). Corticotropin-releasing factor and the psychobiology of early-life stress. *Current Directions in Psychological Science, 16,* 85–89.

Gillespie, C. F., Phifer, J., Bradley, B., & Ressler, K. J. (2009). Risk and resilience: Genetic and environmental influences on development of the stress response. *Depression and Anxiety, 26,* 984–992.

Gillis, J. J., Gilger, J. W., Pennington, B. F., & DeFries, J. C. (1992). Attention deficit in reading-disabled twins: Evidence for a genetic etiology. *Journal of Abnormal Child Psychology, 20,* 303–315.

Gilson, A. M., & Kreis, P. G. (2009). The burden of the nonmedical use of prescription opioid analgesics. *Pain Medication, Suppl 2,* S89–100.

Ginzburg, K., & Solomon, Z. (2010). Trajectories of stress reactions and somatization symptoms among war veterans: A 20-year longitudinal study. *Psychological Medicine, 41,* 353–362.

Girard, T. D., Pandharipande, P. P., & Ely, E. W. (2008). Delirium in the intensive care unit. *Critical Care, 12*(Suppl 3), S3.

Girot, M. (2009). Smoking and stroke. *La Presse Medicale, 38,* 1120–1125.

Giulivi, C., Zhang, Y., Omanska-Klusek, A. Ross-Inta, C. Wong, S., . . . Pessah, I. N. (2010). Mitochondrial dysfunction in autism. *Journal of the American Medical Association, 304,* 2389–2396.

Glasner-Edwards, S., Mooney, L. J., Marinelli-Casey, P., Hillhouse, M., Ang, A., & Rawson, R. A. (2010). Psychopathology in methamphetamine-dependent adults 3 years after treatment. *Drug and Alcohol Review, 29,* 12–20.

Glass, K. C. (2008). Ethical obligations and the use of placebo controls. *Canadian Journal of Psychiatry, 53,* 428–429.

Gleaves, D. H. (1996). The sociocognitive model of dissociative identity disorder: A reexamination of the evidence. *Psychological Bulletin, 120,* 42–59.

Glei, D. A., Landau, D. A., Goldman, N., Chuang, Y., Rodríguez, G., & Weinstein, M. (2005). Participating in social activities helps to preserve cognitive function: An analysis of a longitudinal, population-based study of the elderly. *International Journal of Epidemiology, 34,* 864–871.

Glenn, A. L., & Raine, A., Venables, P. H., & Mednick, S. A. (2007). Early temperamental and psychophysiological precursors of adult psychopathic personality. *Journal of Abnormal Psychology, 116*(3), 508–518.

Glozier, N., Martiniuk, A., Patton, G., Ivers, R., Li, Q., . . . Stevenson, M. (2010). Short sleep duration in prevalent and persistent psychological distress in young adults: The DRIVE study. *Sleep, 33,* 1139–1145.

Glynn, S. M., Cohen, A. N., Dixon, L. B., & Niv, N. (2006). The potential impact of the recovery movement on family interventions for schizophrenia: Opportunities and obstacles. *Schizophrenia Bulletin, 32,* 451–463.

Godfrin, K. A., & van Heeringen, C. (2010). The effects of mindfulness-based cognitive therapy on recurrence of depressive episodes, mental health and quality of life: A randomized controlled study. *Behaviour Research and Therapy, 48,* 738–746.

Godlee, F., Smith, J., & Marcovitch, H. (2011). Wakefield's article linking MMR vaccine and autism was fraudulent. *British Medical Journal.* Retrieved from http://www.bmj.com/content/342/bmj.c7452.full

Godoy, A., & Haynes, S. N. (2011). Clinical case formulation. *European Journal of Psychological Assessment, 27,* 1–3.

Goes, F. S., Zandi, P. P., Miao, K., McMahon, F. J., Steele, J., . . . Potash, J. B. (2007). Mood-incongruent psychotic features in bipolar disorder: familial aggregation and suggestive linkage to 2p11-q14 and 13q21-33. *American Journal of Psychiatry, 164,* 236–247.

Goff, D. C. (1993). Reply to Dr. Armstrong. *Journal of Nervous and Mental Disease, 181,* 604–605.

Goff, D. C., & Simms, C. A. (1993). Has multiple personality disorder remained consistent over time? *Journal of Nervous and Mental Disease, 181,* 595–600.

Gogtag, N. (2008). Cortical brain development in schizophrenia: Insights from neuroimaging studies in childhood-onset schizophrenia. *Schizophrenia Bulletin, 34,* 30–36.

Golafshani, N. (2003). Understanding reliability and validity in qualitative research. *The Qualitative Report, 8,* 597–607.

Goldapple, K., Segal, Z., Garson, C., Lau, M., Bieling, P., Kennedy, S., & Mayberg, H. (2004). Modulation of cortical-limbic pathways in major depression: Treatment-specific effects of cognitive behavior therapy. *Archives of General Psychiatry, 61,* 34–41.

Goldberg, C. (2009). The mental status exam (MSE). Retrieved from http://meded.ucsd.edu/clinicalmed/mental.htm

Goldberg, D. (1996). Psychological disorders in general medical settings. *Social Psychiatry, 31,* 1–2.

Goldberg, D. (2006). The aetiology of depression. *Psychological Medicine, 36,* 1341–1347.

Goldberg, D. P., Krueger, R. F., Andrews, G., & Hobb, M. J. (2009). Emotional disorders: Cluster 4 of the proposed meta-structure for DSM-V and ICD-11. *Psychological Medicine, 39,* 2043–2059.

Goldberg, J. F. (2007). What psychotherapists should know about pharmacotherapies for bipolar disorder. *Journal of Clinical Psychology: In Session, 63,* 475–490.

Goldberg, J. F., Perlis, R. H., Bowden, C. L., Thase, M. E., Miklowitz, D. J., . . . Sachs, G. S. (2009). Manic symptoms during depressive episodes in 1,380 patients with bipolar disorder: Findings from the STEP–BD. *American Journal of Psychiatry, 166,* 173–181.

Goldberg, T. E., Goldman, R. S., Burdick, K. E., Malhotra, A. K., Lencz, T., . . . Robinson, D. G. (2007). Cognitive improvement after treatment with second-generation antipsychotic medications in first-episode schizophrenia: Is it a practice effect? *Archives of General Psychiatry, 64,* 1115–1122.

Golden, C. J. (1989). The Nebraska Neuropsychological Children's Battery. In C. R. Reynolds & E. Fletcher-Janzen (Eds.), *Handbook of clinical child neuropsychology* (pp. 193–204). New York: Plenum Press.

Golden, C. J., Graber, B., Blose, I., Berg, R., Coffman, J., & Bloch, S. (1981). Differences in brain densities between chronic alcoholic and normal control patients. *Science, 211,* 508–510.

Golden, J. (1988). A second look at a case of inhibited sexual desire. *Journal of Sex Research, 25,* 304–306.

Golden, R. N., Gaynes, B. N., Ekstrom, R. D., Hamer, R. M., Jacobsen, F. M., . . . Nemeroff, C. B. (2005). The efficacy of light therapy in the treatment of mood disorders: A review and meta-analysis of the evidence. *American Journal of Psychiatry, 162,* 656–662.

Goldfein, J. A., Devlin, M. J., & Spitzer, R. L. (2000). Cognitive behavioral therapy for the treatment of binge eating disorder: What constitutes success? *American Journal of Psychiatry, 157,* 1051–1056.

Goldfried, M. R., & Davison, G. C. (1976). *Clinical behavior therapy.* San Francisco: Holt, Rinehart & Winston.

Goldin, P. R., Manber-Ball, T., Werner, K., Heimberg, R., & Gross, J. J. (2009). Neural mechanisms of cognitive reappraisal of negative self-beliefs in social anxiety disorder. *Biological Psychiatry, 66,* 1091–1099.

Goldman, H. H. (1988). Psychiatric epidemiology and mental health services research. In H. H. Goldman (Ed.), *Review of general psychiatry* (pp. 143–156). Norwalk, CT: Appleton & Lange.

Goldmann, G. R., Siderowf, A., & Hurtig, H. I. (2008). Cognitive impairment in Parkinson's disease and dementia with lewy bodies: A spectrum of disease. *Neuro-Signals, 16,* 24–34.

Goldstein, G., & Beers, S. (2004). *Comprehensive handbook of psychological assessment, intellectual and neuropsychological assessment* (Vol. 1). New York: John Wiley.

Goldston, D. B., Molock, S. D., Whitbeck, L. B., Murakami, J. L., Zayas, L. H., & Hall, G. C. N. (2008). Cultural considerations in adolescent suicide prevention and psychosocial treatment. *American Psychologist, 63,* 14–31.

Goleman, D. (1992). Therapies offer hope for sex offenders. *New York Times,* pp. C1, C11.

Golier, J. A., Yehuda, R., Bierer, L. M., Mitropoulou, V., New, A. S., & Schmeidler, J. (2003). The relationship of borderline personality disorder to posttraumatic stress disorder and traumatic events. *American Journal of Psychiatry, 160,* 2018–2024.

Goma, M., Perez, J., & Torrubia, R. (1988). Personality variables in antisocial and prosocial disinhibitory behavior. In T. E. Moffitt & S. A. Mednick (Eds.), *Biological contributions to crime causation* (pp. 211–222). Boston: Nijhoff.

Gonsiorek, J. C., Richards, P. S., Pargament, K. I., & McMinn, M. R. (2009). Ethical challenges and opportunities at the edge: Incorporating spirituality and religion into psychotherapy. *Professional Psychology: Research and Practice, 40,* 385–395.

Goodheart, C. D. (2010). More accurate diagnoses ahead. *Monitor on Psychology, 41,* 5.

Goodman, M., Hazlett, E. A., New, A. S., Koenigsberg, H. W., & Siever, L. (2009). Quieting the affective storm of borderline personality disorder. *American Journal of Psychiatry, 166,* 522–528.

Goodman, M., Triebwasser, J., Shah, S., & New, A. S. (2007). Neuroimaging in personality disorders: Current concepts, findings, and implications. *Psychiatric Annals, 37,* 100–104, 107–108.

Goodwin, D. W. (1979). Alcoholism and heredity. *Archives of General Psychiatry, 36,* 57–61.

Goodwin, D. W., & Guze, S. B. (1984). *Psychiatric diagnosis* (3rd ed.). New York: Oxford University Press.

Goodwin, G. M., Anderson, I., Arango, C., Bowden, C. L., Henry, C., . . . Wittchen, H. U. (2008). ECNP consensus meeting. Bipolar depression. *Europena Neuropsychopharmacolgy, 18,* 535–549.

Gooley, J. J., Rajaratnam, S. M., Brainard, G. C., Kronauer, R. E., Czeisler, C. A., & Lockley S. W. (2010). Spectral responses of the human circadian system depend on the irradiance and duration of exposure to light. *Science Translational Medicine, 2,* 31–33.

Gooren, L. (2008). Androgens and endocrine function in aging men: Effects on sexual and general health. In D. Rowland & L. Incrocci (Eds.), *Handbook of sexual and gender identity disorders* (pp. 122–153). Hoboken, NJ: Wiley.

Gordon, A. (2001). Eating disorders: 2. Bulimia nervosa. *Hospital Practice, 36,* 71–73.

Gorman, J. M. (1996). Comorbid depression and anxiety spectrum disorders. *Depression and Anxiety, 4,* 160–168.

Gorman, J. M. (2001). Generalized anxiety disorder. *Clinical Cornerstone, 3,* 37–46.

Gorman, J. M., Kent, J. M., Sullivan, G. M., & Coplan, J. D. (2000). Neuroanatomical hypothesis of panic disorder, revised. *American Journal of Psychiatry, 157,* 493–505.

Gotlib, I. H. (1992). Interpersonal and cognitive aspects of depression. *Current Directions in Psychological Science, 1*(5), 149–154.

Gotlib, I. H., & Joormann, J. (2010). Cognition and depression: Current status and future directions. *Annual Review of Clinical Psychology, 6,* 285–312.

Gottesman, I. I. (1978). Schizophrenia and genetics: Where are we? Are you sure? In L. C. Wynne, R. L. Cromwell, & S. Matthysse (Eds.), *The nature of schizophrenia: New approaches to research and treatment* (pp. 59–69). New York: Wiley.

Gottesman, I. I. (1991). *Schizophrenia genesis.* New York: Freeman.

Gottesman, I. I., & Goldsmith, H. H. (1994). Developmental psychopathology of antisocial behavior: Inserting genes into its ontogenesis and epigenesis. In C. A. Nelson (Ed.), *Threats to optimal development.* Hillside, NJ: Erlbaum.

Gottesman, I. I., & Gould, T. D. (2003). The endophenotype concept in psychiatry: Etymology and strategic intentions. *American Journal of Psychiatry, 160,* 636–645.

Gould, M. S. (2007). *Suicide contagion (clusters).* Retrieved from http://suicideandmentalhealthassociationinternational.org/suiconclus.html

Goyal, D., Gay, C., & Lee, K. (2009). Fragmented maternal sleep is more strongly correlated with depressive symptoms than infant temperament at three months postpartum. *Archives of Womens Mental Health, 12,* 229–237.

Grabe, H. J., Schwahn, C. Appel, K., Mahler, J., Schulz, A., . . . Freyberger, H. J. (2010). Childhood maltreatment, the corticotropin-releasing hormone receptor gene and adult depression in the general population. *American Journal of Medical Genetics Part B: Neuropsychiatric Genetics, 153B,* 1483–1493.

Grabe, S., & Hyde, J. S. (2006). Ethnicity and body dissatisfaction among women in the United States: A meta-analysis. *Psychological Bulletin, 132,* 622–640.

Grabe, S., Ward, L. M., & Hyde, J. S. (2008). The role of the media in body image concerns among women: A meta-analysis of experimental and correlational studies. *Psychological Bulletin, 134,* 460–476.

Graham, C. A., Sanders, S. A., Milhausen, R. R., & McBride, K. R. (2004). Turning on and turning off: A focus group study of the factors that affect women's sexual arousal. *Archives of Sexual Behavior, 33,* 527–538.

Graham, J. R. (1990). *MMPI-2: Assessing personality and psychopathology.* New York: Oxford University Press.

Graham, J. R. (2005). *MMPI-2: Assessing personality and psychopathology* (4th ed.). New York: Oxford University Press.

Gramling, S. E., Clawson, E. P., & McDonald, M. K. (1996). Perceptual and cognitive abnormality of hypochondriasis: Amplification and physiological reactivity in women. *Psychosomatic Medicine, 58,* 423–431.

Granderson, L. Z. (2010, December 3). Sports, gender, questions and hate. Retrieved from http://sports.espn.go.com/espn/commentary/news/story?id=6879536

Granello, D. H. (2010). The process of suicide risk assessment: Twelve core principles. *Journal of Counseling and Development, 88,* 363–370.

Granello, D. H., & Granello, P. F. (2007). *Suicide: An essential guide for helping professionals and educators.* Boston, MA: Allyn & Bacon.

Grange, L. L., Hojnowski, N., & Nesterova, S. (2007). Personality correlates of alcohol consumption and aggression in a Hispanic College population. *Hispanic Journal of Behavioral Sciences, 29*(4), 570–580.

Grann, M., & Langstrom, N. (2007). Actuarial risk assessment: To weigh or not to weigh? *Criminal Justice and Behavior, 34,* 22–36.

Grant, B. F., Stinson, F. S., Dawson, D. A., Chou, S. P., Dufour, M. C., . . . Kaplan, K. (2004). Prevalence and co-occurrence of substance use disorders and independent mood and anxiety disorders. *Archives of General Psychiatry, 61,* 807–816.

Grant, I., & Adams, K. M. (2009). *Neuropsychological assessment of neuropsychiatric and neuromedical disorders* (3rd ed.). New York: Oxford University Press.

Grant, I., Sacktor, H., & McArthur, J. (2005). HIV neurocognitive disorders. In H. E. Gendelman, I. Grant, I. Everall, S. A. Lipton, & S. Swindells (Eds.), *The neurology of AIDS* (pp. 357–373). London: Oxford University Press.

Grant, J. E., Kim, S. W., & Crow, S. J. (2001). Prevalence and clinical features of body dysmorphic disorder in adolescent and adult psychiatric inpatients. *Journal of Clinical Psychiatry, 62,* 517–522.

Grant, V. V., Stewart, S. H., O'Connor, R. M., Blackwell, E., & Conrod, P. J. (2007). Psychometric evaluation of the five-factor modified drinking motives questionnaire—revised in undergraduates. *Addictive Behaviors, 32*(11), 2611–2632.

Gratz, K. L, Rosaenthal, M. Z., Tull, M. T., Lejuez, C. W., & Gunderson, J. G. (2006). An experimental investigation of emotion dysregulation in borderline personality disorder. *Journal of Abnormal Psychology, 115*(4), 850–855.

Gray, B. (2008). Hidden demons: A personal account of hearing voices and the alternative of the hearing voices movement. *Schizophrenia Bulletin, 34,* 1006–1007.

Gray, H. M., & Tickle-Degnen, L. (2010). A meta-analysis of performance on emotion recognition tasks in Parkinson's disease. *Neuropsychology, 24,* 176–191.

Graziottin, A., & Serafini, A. (2009). Depression and the menopause: Why antidepressants are not enough? *Menopause International, 15,* 76–81.

Green, C. R., Mihic, A. M., Nikkel, S. M., Stade, B. C., Rasmussen, C., Munoz, D. P., & Reynolds, J. N. (2009). Executive function deficits in children with fetal alcohol spectrum disorders (FASD) measured using the Cambridge Neuropsychological Tests Automated Battery. *Journal of Child Psychology and Psychiatry, 50,* 688–697.

Green, J. G., McLaughlin, K. A., Berglund, P. A., Gruber, M. J., Sampson, N. A., Zaslavsky, A. M., & Kessler, R. C. (2010). Childhood adversities and adult psychiatric disorders in the national comorbidity survey replication I: Associations with first onset of DSM-IV disorders. *Archives of General Psychiatry, 67,* 113–123.

Green, M. F. (2007). Cognition, drug treatment, and functional outcome in schizophrenia: A tale of two transitions. *American Journal of Psychiatry, 164,* 992–994.

Green, R. (1987). *The "sissy boy syndrome" and the development of homosexuality.* New Haven: Yale University Press.

Green, R. C., Roberts, J. S., Cupples, L. A., Relkin, N. R., Whitehouse, P. J., . . . Brown, T. (2009). Disclosure of APOE genotype for risk of Alzheimer's disease. *New England Journal of Medicine, 361,* 245–254.

Greenan, D. E., & Tunnell, G. (2003). *Couple therapy with gay men.* New York: Guilford Press.

Greenberg, B. D., Altemus, M., & Murphy, D. L. (1997). The role of neurotransmitters and neurohormones in obsessive-compulsive disorder. *International Review of Psychiatry, 9,* 31–44.

Greenberg, P. E., Burnham, H. G., Lowe, S. W., & Corey-Lisle, P. K. (2003). The economic burden of depression in the United States: How did it change from 1990 to 2000? *Journal of Clinical Psychiatry, 64,* 1465–1475.

Greenberg, W. M. (2010). Obsessive-compulsive disorder. Retrieved from http://emedicine.medscape.com/article/287681-print

Greenberger, E., Chen, C., Tally, S. R., & Dong, Q. (2000). Family, peer, and individual correlates of depressive symptomatology among U.S. and Chinese adolescents. *Journal of Consulting and Clinical Psychology, 68,* 209–219.

Greene, R. L. (1991). *The MMPI-2/MMPI: An interpretive manual.* Boston: Allyn & Bacon.

Greeno, C. G., Wing, R. R., & Shiffman, S. (2000). Binge eating antecedents in obese women with and without binge eating disorder. *Journal of Consulting and Clinical Psychology, 68,* 95–102.

Greenwood, P. M., & Parasuraman, R. (2010). Neuronal and cognitive plasticity: A neurocognitive framework for ameliorating cognitive aging. *The Frontiers in Aging Neuroscience, 2,* 150. Retrieved from http://www.frontiersin.org/aging_neuroscience/10.3389/fnagi.2010.00150/full

Gregory, R. J., & Jindal, S. (2006). Factitious disorder on an inpatient psychiatry ward. *American Journal of Orthopsychiatry, 76,* 31–36.

Grekin, E. R., & Sher, K. J. (2006). Alcohol dependence symptoms among college freshmen: Prevalence, stability and person-environment interactions. *Experimental and Clinical Psychopharmacology, 14,* 329–338.

Grenier, S., Preville, M., Boyer, R., & O'Connor, K. (2009). Prevalence and correlates of obsessive-compulsive disorder among older adults living in the community. *Journal of Anxiety Disorders, 23,* 858–865.

Greydanus, D. E., Nazeer, A., & Patel, D. R. (2009). Psychopharmacology of ADHD in pediatrics: Current advances and issues. *Journal of Neuropsychiatric Disease and Treatment, 5,* 171–181.

Griffith, E. E., Gonzalez, C. A., & Blue, H. C. (1999). The basics of cultural psychiatry. In R. E. Hales, S. C. Yudofsky & J. A. Talbott (Eds.), *Textbook of psychiatry* (pp. 1463–1492). Washington, DC: American Psychiatric Press.

Grigoriadis, S., & Seeman, M. V. (2002). The role of estrogen in schizophrenia: Implications for schizophrenia practice guidelines for women. *Canadian Journal of Psychiatry, 47,* 437–442.

Grillo, C. M., Shea, M. T., Sanislow, C. A., Skodol, A. E., Gunderson, J. G., . . . McGlashan, T. H. (2004). Two-year stability and change in schizotypal, borderline, avoidant and obsessive-compulsive personality disorders. *Journal of Consulting and Clinical Psychology, 72,* 767–775.

Grimshaw, G. M., & Stanton, A. (2006). Tobacco cessation interventions for young people. *Cochrane Database Systematic Review, 18*(4), CD003289.

Grisham, J. R., Norberg, M. M., William, A. D., Certoma, S. P., & Kadib, R. (2010). Categorization and cognitive deficits in compulsive hoarding. *Behaviour Research and Therapy, 48,* 866–872.

Groopman, L. C., & Cooper, A. M. (2001). Narcissistic personality disorder. In G. O. Gabbard (Ed.), *Treatment of psychiatric disorders* (pp. 2309–2326). Washington, DC: American Psychiatric Press.

Groth, A. N., Burgess, A. W., & Holstrom, L. (1977). Rape: Power, anger, and sexuality. *American Journal of Psychiatry, 134,* 1239–1243.

Groth-Marnat, G. (2009). *Handbook of psychological assessment* (5th ed.). New York: John Wiley.

Gu, Q., Dillon, C. F., & Burt, V. L. (2010). Prescription drug use continues to increase: U.S. prescription drug data for 2007–2008. *NCHS Data Brief, 42.* Retrieved from http://www.cdc.gov/nchs/data/databriefs/db42.htm

Guastella, A. J., Einfeld, S. L., Gray, K. M., Rinehart, N. J., Tonge, B. J., Lambert, T. J., & Hickie, I. B. (2010). Intranasal oxytocin improves emotion recognition for youth with autism spectrum disorders. *Biological Psychiatry, 67,* 692–694.

Gunderson, J. G. (2010). Revising the borderline diagnosis for DSM-V: An alternative proposal. *Journal of Personality Disorders, 24,* 694–708.

Gunderson, J. G., & Links, P. S. (2001). Borderline personality disorder. In G. O. Gabbard (Ed.), *Treatment of psychiatric disorders* (pp. 2273–2291). Washington, DC: American Psychiatric Press.

Gupta, S., & Bonanno, G. A. (2010). Trait self-enhancement as a buffer against potentially traumatic events: A prospective study. *Psychological Trauma: Theory, Research, Practice, and Policy, 2,* 83–92.

Gur, R. E., Calkins, M. E., Gur, R. C., Horan, W. P., Nuechterlein, K. H., Seidman, L. J., & Stone, W. S. (2007). The Consortium on the Genetics of Schizophrenia: Neurocognitive endophenotypes. *Schizophrenia Bulletin, 33,* 49–55.

Gur, R. E., Kohler, C. G., Ragland, J. D., Siegel, S. J., Lesko, K., Bilker, W. B., & Gur, R. C. (2006). Flat affect in schizophrenia: Relation to emotion processing and neurocognitive measures. *Schizophrenia Bulletin, 32,* 279–287.

Gustafson, R., Popovich, M., & Thomsen, S. (2001). Subtle ad images threaten girls more. *Marketing News, 35,* 12–13.

Gutierrez, P. M., & Silk, K. R. (1998). Prescription privileges for psychologists: A review of the psychological literature. *Professional Psychology: Research and Practice, 29,* 213–222.

Guyll, M., Cutrona, C., Burzette, R., & Russell, D. (2010). Hostility, relationship quality, and health among African American couples. *Journal of Consulting and Clinical Psychology, 78,* 646–654.

Haaga, D. A., McCrady, B., & Lebow, J. (2006). Integrative principles for treating substance use disorders. *Journal of Clinical Psychology, 62,* 675–684.

Haas, K., & Haas, A. (1993). *Understanding human sexuality.* St. Louis, MO: Mosby.

Haas, R. H. (2010). Autism and mitochondrial disease. *Developmental Disabilities Research Review, 16,* 144–153.

Hackett, G. I. (2008). Disorders of male sexual desire. In D. Rowland & L. Incrocci (Eds.), *Handbook of sexual and gender identity disorders* (pp. 154–187). Hoboken, NJ: Wiley.

Haenen, M. A., de Jong, P. J., Schmidt, A. J. M., Stevens, S., & Visser, L. (2000). Hypochondriacs' estimation of negative outcomes: Domain-specificity and responsiveness to reassuring and alarming information. *Behaviour Research and Therapy, 38,* 819–833.

Hafner, H., an der Heiden, W., Behrens, S., Gattaz, W. F., Hambrecht, M., . . . Stein, A. (1998). Causes and consequences of gender difference in age at onset of schizophrenia. *Schizophrenia Bulletin, 24,* 99–113.

Hage, S. M. (2004). A closer look at the role of spirituality in psychology training programs. *Professional Psychology: Research and Practice, 37,* 303–310.

Hagen, M. A. (2003). Faith in the model and resistance to research. *Clinical Psychology: Science and Practice, 10,* 172–178.

Haggard-Grann, U. (2007). Assessing violence risk: A review and clinical recommendations. *Journal of Counseling and Development, 85,* 294–301.

Halderman, D. C. (2002). Gay rights, patient rights: The implications of sexual orientation conversion therapy. *Professional Psychology: Research and Practice, 33,* 260–264.

Haley, J. (1963). *Strategies of psychotherapy.* New York: Grune & Stratton.

Haley, J. (1980). *Leaving home.* New York: McGraw-Hill.

Haley, J. (1987). *Problem-solving therapy* (2nd ed.). New York: Jossey-Bass.

Haley, J. (2003, October 31). Defendant's wife testifies about his multiple personas. *Bellingham Herald,* p. B4.

Hall, G. C. (1996). *Theory-based assessment, treatment, and prevention of sexual aggression.* New York: Oxford University Press.

Hall, G. C., Windover, A. K., & Maramba, G. C. (1998). Sexual aggression among Asian Americans: Risk and protective factors. *Cultural Diversity and Mental Health, 4,* 305–318.

Hall, J. E. (1995). A perspective on the evolving health care environment: Quality, integrity, reliability and value. *Register Report, 20,* 2–3.

Hallak, J. E. C., Crippa, J. A. S., & Zuardi, A. W. (2000). Treatment of koro with citalopram. *Journal of Clinical Psychology, 61,* 951–952.

Hall, M. T., Howard, M. O., & McCabe, S. E. (2010). Subtypes of adolescent sedative/anxiolytic misusers: A latent profile analysis. *Addictive Behavior, 35,* 882–889.

Hall, M. T., Edwards, J. D., & Howard, M. O. (2010). Accidental deaths due to inhalant misuse in North Carolina: 2000–2008. *Substance Use and Misuse, 45,* 1330–1339.

Halmi, K. A., Sunday, S. R., Strober, M., Kaplan, A., Woodside, D. B., . . . Kaye, W. H. (2000). Perfectionism in anorexia nervosa: Variation by clinical subtype, obsessionality, and pathological eating disorder. *American Journal of Psychiatry, 157,* 1799–1805.

Halpern, H. H., & Harrison, G. (2003). Hallucinogen persisting perception disorder: What do we know after 50 years? *Drug and Alcohol Dependence, 69,* 109–119.

Halstead, M. E., & Walter, K. D. (2010). Clinical report—sport-related concussion in children and adolescents. *Pediatrics, 126,* 597–615.

Halvorsen, I., & Heyerdahl, S. (2007). Treatment perception in adolescent onset anorexia nervosa: Retrospective views of patients and parents. *International Journal of Eating Disorders, 40,* 629–639.

Hamelsky, S. W., & Lipton, R. B. (2006). Psychiatric comorbidity of migraine. *Headache, 46,* 1327–1333.

Hamer, M., O'Donnell, K., Lahiri, A., & Steptoe, A. (2010). Salivary cortisol responses to mental stress are associated with coronary artery calcification in healthy men and women. *European Heart Journal, 31,* 424–429.

Hamilton, B. E., Miniño, A. M., Martin, J. A., Kochanek, K. D., Strobino, D. M., & Guyer, B. (2007). Annual summary of vital statistics: 2005. *Pediatrics, 119,* 345–360.

Hammad, T. A., Laughren, T., & Racoosin, J. (2006). Suicidality in pediatric patients treated with antidepressant drugs. *Archives of General Psychiatry, 63,* 332–339.

Hammen, C. (2006). Stress generation in depression: Reflections on origins, research, and future directions. *Journal of Clinical Psychology, 62,* 1065–1082.

Hammen, C., Davilla, J., Brown, G., Ellicott, A., & Gitlin, M. (1992). Psychiatric history and stress: Predictors of severity of unipolar depression. *Journal of Abnormal Psychology, 101,* 45–52.

Hammen, C., & Peters, S. (1978). Interpersonal consequences of depression: Responses to men and women enacting a depressed role. *Journal of Abnormal Psychology, 87,* 322–332.

Hammen, C. L. (1985). Predicting depression: A cognitive-behavioral perspective. In P. Kendall (Ed.), *Advances in cognitive-behavioral research and therapy* (Vol. 4). New York: Academic Press.

Hanback, J. W., & Revelle, W. (1978). Arousal and perceptual sensitivity in hypochondriacs. *Journal of Abnormal Psychology, 87,* 523–530.

Handelsman, M., Walfish, S., & Hess, A. K. (Eds.). (2001). *Learning to become ethical: Succeeding in graduate school: The career guide for psychology students.* Wahwah, NJ: Erlbaum.

Hanewinkel, R., Isensee, B., Sargent, J. D., & Morgenstern, M. (2011). Cigarette advertising and teen smoking initiation. *Pediatrics, 127*(2), e271–278. doi:10.1542/peds.2010–2934

Haney, M., Hart, C. L., Vosburg, S. K., Comer, S. D., Reed, S. C., & Foltin, R. W. (2008). Effects of THC and lofexidine in a human laboratory model of marijuana withdrawal and relapse. *Psychopharmacology, 197,* 157–168.

Hanisch, C., Freund-Braier, I., Hautmann, C., Jänen, N., Plück, J., Brix, G., Eichelberger, I., & Döpfner, M. (2010). Detecting effects of the indicated prevention Programme for Externalizing Problem behaviour (PEP) on child symptoms, parenting, and parental quality of life in a randomized controlled trial. *Behavioral and Cognitive Psychotherapy, 38,* 95–112.

Hankey, G. J. (2011). Stroke: Fresh insights into causes, prevention, and treatment. *The Lancet Neurology, 10,* 2–3.

Hankin, B. L. (2008). Rumination and depression in adolescence: Investigating symptom specificity in a multiwave prospective study. *Journal of Clinical Child and Adolescent Psychology, 37,* 701–713.

Hankin, B. L. (2009). Development of sex differences in depressive and co-occurring anxious symptoms during adolescence: Descriptive trajectories and potential explanations in a multiwave prospective study. *Journal of Clinical Child and Adolescent Psychology, 38,* 460–472.

Hankin, B. L., Fraley, C. R., Lahey, B. B., & Waldman, I. D. (2005). Is depression best viewed as a continuum or discrete category? A taxometric analysis of childhood and adolescent depression in a population-based sample. *Journal of Abnormal Psychology, 114,* 96–110.

Hansen, L., Kingdon, D., & Turkington, D. (2006). The ABCs of cognitive-behavioral therapy for schizophrenia. *Psychiatric Times, 23,* 49–53.

Hardan, A. Y., Libove, R. A., Keshavan, M. S., Melhem, N. M., & Minshew, N. J. (2009). A preliminary longitudinal magnetic resonance imaging study of brain volume and cortical thickness in autism. *Biological Psychiatry, 66,* 320–326.

Hare, R. D. (1993). *Without conscience: The disturbing world of the psychopaths among us.* New York: Pocket Books.

Hare, R. D., & Neumann, C. S. (2009). Psychopathy: Assessment and forensic implications. *The Canadian Journal of Psychiatry, 54,* 791–802.

Harenstam, A., Theorell, T., & Kaijser, L. (2000). Coping with anger-provoking situations, psychosocial working conditions, and the ECG-detected signs of coronary heart disease. *Journal of Occupational Health Psychology, 5,* 191–203.

Hargreaves, D. A., & Tiggemann, M. (2009). Muscular ideal media images and men's body image: Social comparison processing and individual vulnerability. *Psychology of Men and Masculinity, 10,* 109–119.

Hariri, A. R., & Brown, S. M. (2006). Serotonin. *American Journal of Psychiatry, 163,* 1.

Hariri, A. R., Drabant, E. M., Munoz, K. E., Kolachana, B. S., Mattay, V. S., Egan, M. F., & Weinberger, D. R. (2005). A susceptibility gene for affective disorders and the response of the human amygdala. *Archives of General Psychiatry, 62,* 146–152.

Hariri, A. R., Mattay, V. S., Tessitore, A., Kolachana, B., Fera, F., Goldman, D., . . . Weinberger, D. R. (2002). Serotonin transporter genetic variation and the response of the human amygdala. *Science, 297,* 400–403.

Harlow, H. F., & Harlow, M. (1962). Social deprivation in monkeys. *Scientific American, 207*(5), 136–146.

Harlow, J. M. (1868). Recovery from the passage of an iron bar through the head. *Publication of the Massachusetts Medical Society, 2,* 327.

Harned, M. S., Chapman, A. L., Dexter-Mazza, E. T., Murray, A., Comtois, K. A., & Linehan, M. M. (2008). Treating co-occurring axis I disorders in recurrently suicidal women with borderline personality disorder: A 2-year randomized trial of dialectical behavior therapy vs. community treatment by experts. *Journal of Consulting and Clinical Psychology, 76*(6), 1068–1075.

Harold, G. T., Rice, F., Hay, D. F., Boivin, J., van den Bree, M., & Thapar, A. (2010). Familial transmission of depression and antisocial behavior symptoms: Disentangling the contribution of inherited and environmental factors and testing the mediating role of parenting. *Psychological Medicine, 22,* 1–11.

Harris, E. C., & Barraclough, B. (1997). Suicide as an outcome for mental disorders. *British Journal of Psychiatry, 170,* 205–228.

Harris, J. A., Devidze, N., Verret, L., Ho, K., Halabisky, B., . . . Mucke, L. (2010) Transsynaptic progression of amyloid-β-induced neuronal dysfunction within the entorhinal-hippocampal network. *Neuron, 68,* 428–441.

Harris, J. C. (2001). Psychiatric disorders in mentally retarded persons. In G. O. Gabbard (Ed.), *Treatment of psychiatric disorders* (pp. 75–107). Washington, DC: American Psychiatric Press.

Harris, J. C. (2004). Anxiety (angst). *Archives of General Psychiatry, 61,* 15.

Harris, S. M. (2006). Body image attitudes, physical attributes and disturbed eating among African American college women. *Race, Gender and Class, 13,* 46–56.

Harrison, K. (2001). Ourselves, our bodies: Thin-ideal media, self-discrepancies, and eating disorder symptomatology in adolescents. *Journal of Social and Clinical Psychology, 20,* 289–299.

Harrow, M., Grossman, L. S., Jobe, T. H., & Herbener, E. S. (2005). Do patients with schizophrenia ever show periods of recovery? A 15-year multi-follow-up study. *Schizophrenia Bulletin, 31,* 723–734.

Harrow, M., Herbener, E. S., Shanklin, A., Jobe, T. H., Rattenbury, F., & Kaplan, K. J. (2004). Followup of psychotic outpatients: Dimensions of delusions and work functioning in schizophrenia. *Schizophrenia Bulletin, 30,* 147–161.

Hartmann, A., Zeeck, A., & Barrett, M. S. (2010). Interpersonal problems in eating disorders. *International Journal of Eating Disorders, 43,* 619–627.

Hartmann, U., Heiser, K., Ruffer-Hesse, C., & Kloth, G. (2002). Female sexual desire disorders: Subtypes, classification, personality factors and new directions for treatment. *World Journal of Urology, 20,* 79–88.

Hartman-Stein, P. (2004). Psychologists develop new roles with Parkinson's patients. *National Psychologist, 13,* 4–5.

Harvey, A. G., Clark, D. M., Ehlers, A., & Rapee, R. M. (2000). Social anxiety and self-impression. *Behaviour Research and Therapy, 38,* 1183–1192.

Harvey, W. T., Bransfield, R. C., Mercer, D. E., Wright, A. J., Ricchi, R. M., & Leitao M. M. (2009). Morgellons disease, illuminating an undefined illness: A case series. *Journal of Medical Case Reports, 3,* 8243.

Hashimoto, K., Sawa, A., Iyo, M. (2007). Increased levels of glutamate in brains from patients with mood disorders. *Biological Psychiatry, 62,* 1310–1316.

Hasin, D. S., Goodwin, R. D., Stinson, F. S., & Grant, B. F. (2005). Epidemiology of major depressive disorder: Results from the National Epidemiologic Survey on Alcoholism and Related Conditions. *Archives of General Psychiatry, 62,* 1097–1106.

Hasin, D. S., Keyes, K. M., Alderson, D., Wang, S., Aharonovich, E., & Grant, B. F. (2008). Cannabis withdrawal in the United States: Results from NESARC. *Journal of Clinical Psychiatry, 69,* 1354–1363.

Hasin, D. S., Stinson, F. S., Ogburn, E., & Grant, B. F. (2007). Prevalence, correlates, disability, and comorbidity of DSM-IV alcohol abuse and dependence in the United States: Results from the National Epidemiologic Survey on Alcohol and Related Conditions. *Archives of General Psychiatry, 64,* 830–842.

Haslam, N. (2003). The dimensional view of personality disorders: A review of the taxometric evidence. *Clinical Psychology Review, 23,* 75–93.

Hastings, J. D., & Robbennolt, J. K. (2004). Physician-assisted suicide. *Monitor, 35*(9), 86.

Hathaway, S. R., & McKinley, J. C. (1943). *Manual for the Minnesota Multiphasic Personality Inventory.* New York: Psychological Corporation.

Hatsukami, D. K., Stead, L. F., & Gupta, P. C. (2008). Tobacco addiction. *Lancet, 371,* 2027–2038.

Hauer, P. (2010). Systemic affects of methamphetamine use. *South Dakota Medicine: Journal of the South Dakota State Medical Association, 63*(8), 285–287.

Haug Schnabel, G. (1992). Daytime and nighttime enuresis: A functional disorder and its ethological decoding. *Behavior, 120,* 232–262.

Haugaard, J. J. (2000). The challenge of defining child sexual abuse. *American Psychologist, 55,* 1036–1039.

Hausman, K. (2003). Controversy continues to grow over DSM's GID diagnosis. *Psychiatric News, 38*(14), 25.

Havens, J., Young, A., & Havens, C. E. (2011). Nonmedical prescription drug use in a nationally representative sample of adolescents. *Archives of Pediatric and Adolescent Medicine, 165*(3), 250–255. doi:10.1001/archpediatrics.2010.217.

Hayes, S. C., Brownell, K. D., & Barlow, D. H. (1983). Heterosexual skills training and covert sensitization: Effects on social skills and sexual arousal in sexual deviants. *Behaviour Research and Therapy, 21,* 383–392.

Hayes, S. C., & Chang, G. (2002). Invasion of the body snatchers: Prescription privileges, professional schools, and the drive to create a new behavioral health profession. *Clinical Psychology: Science and Practice, 9,* 264–275.

Hayley, M. (2004, July 21). Type "pro-ana" into any internet search engine and you'll get disturbing glimpse of a deadly obsession with thin. *Canadian Press Newswire,* p. 1.

Haynes, S. N. (2001). Clinical applications of analogue behavioral observation: Dimensions of psychometric evaluation. *Psychological Assessment, 13,* 73–85.

Hays, P. A. (2009). Integrating evidence-based practice, cognitive-behavior therapy, and multicultural therapy: Ten steps for culturally competent practice. *Professional Psychology: Research and Practice, 40,* 354–360.

Hays, R. B., Turner, H., & Coates, T. J. (1992). Social support, AIDS-related symptoms, and depression among gay men. *Journal of Consulting and Clinical Psychology, 60*(3), 463–469.

Hayward, P., Wardie, J., & Higgitt, A. (1989). Benzodiazepine research: Current findings and practical consequences. *British Journal of Psychiatry, 28,* 307–327.

Headaches. (2006). *Journal of the American Medical Association, 295,* 2320–2322.

Healy, D., & Whitaker, C. (2010). Does taking antidepressants lead to suicide? In Brent Slife (Ed.) *Taking Sides: Clashing Views on Psychological Issues*

(16th ed.) (pp. 272–291). New York: McGraw-Hill/Dushkin.

Healy, M. (2011). 'Idol' finalist Durbin is singing through Tourette's. Downloaded from http://yourlife.usatoday.com/health/medical/conditions/story/2011/03/Idol-finalist-Durbin-is-singing-through-Tourettes/44650354/1.

Heard-Davison, A., Heiman, J. R., & Briggs, B. (2004). Sexual disorders affecting women. In L. J. Haas (Ed.)., *Handbook of primary care psychology* (pp. 495–509). New York: Oxford University Press.

Hebert, K. K., Cummins, S. E., Hernández, S., Tedeschi, G. J., & Zhu, S. (2011). Current major depression among smokers using a state quitline. *American Journal of Preventive Medicine, 40,* 47–53.

Hebert, L. E., Scherr, P. A., Bienias, J. L., Bennett, D. A., & Evans, D. A. (2003). Alzheimer disease in the U.S. population: Prevalence estimates using the 2000 census. *Archives of Neurology, 60,* 1119–1122.

Hedlund, S., & Rude, S. S. (1995). Evidence of latent depressive schemas in formerly depressed individuals. *Journal of Abnormal Psychology, 104,* 517–525.

Heffernan, K. (1994). Sexual orientation as a factor in risk for binge eating and bulimia nervosa: A review. *International Journal of Eating Disorders, 16,* 335–347.

Heiman, J. R. (2002). Sexual dysfunction: Overview of prevalence, etiological factors, and treatments. *Journal of Sex Research, 39,* 1–19.

Heinrichs, R. W. (1993). Schizophrenia and the brain. *American Psychologist, 48,* 221–233.

Heinssen, R. K., & Cuthbert, B. N. (2001). Barrier to relationship formation in schizophrenia: Implications for treatment, social recovery, and translational research. *Psychiatry, 64,* 126–132.

Heinz, A. J., Wu, J., Witkiewitz, K., Epstein, D. H., & Preston K. L. (2009). Marriage and relationship closeness as predictors of cocaine and heroin use. *Addictive Behavior, 34,* 258–263.

Hellmich, N. (2001, July 25). Super-thin, super-troubling. *USA Today,* p. D7.

Hellstrom, K., Fellenius, J., & Öst, L.-G. (1996). One versus five sessions of applied tension in the treatment of blood phobia. *Behaviour Research and Therapy, 34,* 101–112.

Helmich, I., Latini, A., Sigwalt, A., Carta, M. G., Machado, S., . . . Budde, H. (2010). Draft for clinical practice and epidemiology in mental health neurobiological alterations induced by exercise and their impact on depressive disorders. *Clinical Practice and Epidemiology in Mental Health, 6,* 115–125.

Helms, J. E. (1992). Why is there no study of cultural equivalence in standardized cognitive ability testing? *American Psychologist, 47,* 1083–1101.

Helt, M., Kelley, E., Kinsbourne, M., Pandey, J., Boorstein, H., Herbert, M., & Fein, D. (2008). Can children with autism recover? If so, how? *Neuropsychological Review, 18,* 339–366.

Hendin, H. (1995). Assisted suicide, euthanasia, and suicide prevention: The implications for the Dutch experience. *Suicide and Life-Threatening Behavior, 25,* 193–205.

Hendrie, H. C. (2001). Exploration of environmental and genetic risk factors for Alzheimer's disease: The value of cross-cultural studies. *Current Directions in Psychological Science, 10,* 98–101.

Heng, S., Song, A. W., & Sim, K. J. (2010). White matter abnormalities in bipolar disorder: Insights from diffusion tensor imaging studies. *Journal of Neural Transmission, 117,* 639–654.

Henningsson, S., Westberg, L., Nilsson, S., Lundstrom, B., Ekselius, L., Bodlund, O., . . . Landén, M. (2005). Sex steroid-related genes and male-to-female transsexualism. *Psychoneuroendocrinology, 30,* 657–664.

Herbenick, D., Reece, M., Schick, V., Sanders, S. A., Dodge, B., & Fortenberry, J. D. (2010). Sexual behavior in the United States from a national probability sample of men and women ages 14–94. *Journal of Sexual Medicine, 7,* 255–265.

Herbert, M. R. (2010). Contributions of the environment and environmentally vulnerable physiology to autism spectrum disorders. *Current Opinions in Neurology, 23,* 103–110.

Herlicky, B., & Sheeley, V. L. (1988). Privileged communication in selected helping professions: A comparison among statutes. *Journal of Counseling and Development, 65,* 479–483.

Herman, J., & Hirschman, L. (1981). Families at risk for father-daughter incest. *American Journal of Psychiatry, 38,* 967–970.

Hermes, G. L., Rosenthal, L., Montag, A., & McClintock, M. K. (2006). Social isolation and the inflammatory response: Sex differences in the enduring effects of a prior stressor. *American Journal of Physiology—Regulatory, Integrative and Comparative Physiology, 290,* 273–282.

Hernandez, A., & Sachs-Ericsson, N. (2006). Ethnic differences in pain reports and the moderating role of depression in a community sample of Hispanic and Caucasian participants with serious health problems. *Psychosomatic Medicine, 68,* 121–127.

Heron, M. P., Hoyert, D. L., Murphy, S. L., Xu, J. Q., Kochanek, K. D., & Tejada-Vera, B. (2009). Deaths: Final data for 2006. *National Vital Statistics Reports, 57,* 1–15. Retrieved from http://www.cdc.gov/nchs/data/nvsr/nvsr57/nvsr57_14.pdf

Herrnstein, R. J., & Murray, C. (1994). *The bell curve: Intelligence and class structure in American life.* New York: Free Press.

Herschell, A. D., McNeil, C. B., & McNeil, D. W. (2004). Clinical child psychology's progress in disseminating empirically supported treatments. *Clinical Psychology: Science and Practice, 11,* 267–288.

Herzog, W., Kronmuller, K.-T., Hartmann, M., Bergmann, G., & Kroger, F. (2000). Family perception of interpersonal behavior as a predictor in eating disorders: A prospective, six-year follow-up study. *Family Process, 39,* 359–374.

Hessl, D., Dyer-Friedman, J., Glaser, B., Wisbeck, J., Barajas, R. G., Taylor, A., & Reiss, A. L. (2001). The influence of environmental and genetic factors on behavior problems and autistic symptoms in boys and girls with Fragile X syndrome. *Pediatrics, 108,* 88.

Hester, R. K., & Miller, W. R. (Eds.). (2003). *Handbook of alcoholism treatment approaches: Effective alternatives.* Boston: Allyn & Bacon.

Hettema, J. M. (2010). Genetics of depression. *Focus, 8,* 316–322.

Hettema, J. M., Annas, P., Neale, M. C., Kendler, K. S., & Frederikson, M. (2003). A twin study of the genetics of fear conditioning. *Archives of General Psychiatry, 60,* 702–708.

Hicks, T. V., Leitenberg, H., Barlow, D. H., & Gorman, K. M. (2005). Physical, mental, and social catastrophic cognitions as prognostic factors in cognitive-behavioral and pharmacological treatments for panic disorder. *Journal of Consulting and Clinical Psychology, 73,* 506–514.

Hilbert, A., & Tuschen-Caffier, B. (2007). Maintenance of binge eating through negative mood: A naturalistic comparison of binge eating disorder and bulimia nervosa. *International Journal of Eating Disorders, 40,* 521–527.

Hildebrandt, T., Alfano, L., Tricamo, M., & Pfaff, D. W. (2010). Conceptualizing the role of estrogens and serotonin in the development and maintenance of bulimia nervosa. *Clinical Psychology Review, 30,* 655–668.

Hill, A. J., & Bhatti, R. (1995). Body shape perception and dieting in preadolescent British Asian girls: Links with eating disorders. *International Journal of Eating Disorders, 17,* 175–183.

Hill, A. L., Rand, D. G., Nowak, M. A., & Christakis, N. A. (2010). Infectious disease modeling of social contagion in networks. *PLoS Computational Biology, 6.* Retrieved from http://www.ploscompbiol.org/article/info.doi/10.1371/journal.pcbi.1000968

Hill, C. E., & Lambert, M. J. (2004). Methodological issues in studying psychotherapy processes and outcomes. In M. J. Lambert (Ed.), *Bergin and Garfield's handbook of psychotherapy and behavior change* (pp. 84–135). New York: Wiley.

Hiller, W., Leibbrand, R., Rief, W., & Fichter, M. M. (2002). Predictors of course and outcome in hypochondriasis after cognitive-behavioral treatment. *Psychotherapy and Psychosomatics, 71,* 318–327.

Hilsenroth, M. J., Fowler, J. C., Padawer, J. R., & Handler, L. (1997). Narcissism in the Rorschach revisited: Some reflections on empirical data. *Psychological Assessment, 9,* 113–121.

Hingson, R., Heeren, T., Winter, M., & Wechsler, H. (2005). Magnitude of alcohol-related mortality and morbidity among U.S. college students ages 18–24: Changes from 1998 to 2001. *Annual Review of Public Health, 26,* 259–279.

Hingson, R. W., Heeren, T., Zakocs, R. C., Kopstein, A., & Wechsler, H. (2002). Magnitude of alcohol-related mortality and morbidity among U.S. college students ages 18–24. *Journal of Studies on Alcohol, 63,* 136–144.

Hirose, S. (2003). The causes of underdiagnosing akathisia. *Schizophrenia Bulletin, 29,* 547–552.

Hirshfeld-Becker, D. R., Masek, B., Henin, A., Blakely, L. R., Pollock-Wurman, R. A., . . . Biderman, J. (2010). Cognitive behavioral therapy for 4–7 year-old children with anxiety disorders. *Journal of Consulting and Clinical Psychology, 78,* 498–510.

Ho, A. K., Gilbert, A. S., Mason, S. L., Goodman, A. O., & Barker, R. A. (2009). Health-related quality of life in Huntington's disease: Which factors matter most? *Movement Disorders, 24,* 574–578.

Ho, B.-C., Andreasen, N. C., Ziebell, S., Pierson, R., & Magnotta, V. (2011). Long-term antipsychotic treatment and brain volumes. *Archives of General Psychiatry, 68,* 128–137.

Ho, D. D., Neumann, A. U., Perelson, A. S., Chen, W., Leonard, J. M., & Markowitz, M. (1995). Rapid turnover of plasma virions and CD4 lymphocytes in HIV-1 infection. *Nature, 373,* 123–126.

Ho, E. D. F., Tsang, A. K. T., & Ho, D. Y. F. (1991). An investigation of the calendar calculation ability of a Chinese calendar savant. *Journal of Autism and Developmental Disorders, 21,* 315–327.

Ho, M., & Cummins, J. (2008). Agrobacterium & Morgellons Disease, A GM Connection? Downloaded from http://www.globalresearch.ca/index.php?context=va&aid=9891

Hobza, C. L., & Rochlen, A. B. (2009). Gender role conflict, drive for muscularity, and the impact of ideal media portrayals on men. *Psychology of Men & Masculinity, 10,* 120–130.

Hodgins, D. C., El-Guebaly, N., & Armstrong, S. (1995). Prospective and retrospective reports of mood states before relapse to substance use. *Journal of Consulting and Clinical Psychology, 63,* 400–407.

Hodgins, S., Mednick, S. A., Brennan, P. A., Schulsinger, F., & Engberg, M. (1996). Mental disorder and crime. *Archives of General Psychiatry, 53,* 489–496.

Hoehn-Saric, R., McLeod, D. R., Funderburk, F., & Kowalski, P. (2004). Somatic symptoms and physiologic responses in generalized anxiety disorder and panic disorder: An ambulatory monitor study. *Archives of General Psychiatry, 61,* 913–921.

Hoehn-Saric, R., Pearlson, G. D., Harris, G. J., Machlin, S. R., & Camargo, E. E. (1991). Effects of fluoxetine on regional cerebral blood flow in obsessive-compulsive patients. *American Journal of Psychiatry, 148,* 1243–1245.

Hoff, A. L., Kremen, W. S., Weineke, M. H., Lauriello, J., Blankfeld, H., . . . Nordahl, T. E. (2001). Association of estrogen levels with neuropsychological performance in women with schizophrenia. *American Journal of Psychiatry, 158,* 1134–1139.

Hoffman, B. M., Papas, R. K., Chatkoff, D. K., & Kerns, R. D. (2007). Meta-analysis of psychological interventions for chronic low back pain. *Health Psychology, 26,* 1–9.

Hoffman, K. B., Cole, D. A., Martin, J. M., Tram, J., & Seroczynski, A. D. (2000). Are the discrepancies between self- and others' appraisals of competence predictive or reflective of depressive symptoms in children and adolescents? A longitudinal study: Part 2. *Journal of Abnormal Psychology, 109,* 651–662.

Hoffman, L. (1998). *Eating disorders.* Rockville, MD: National Institutes of Health.

Hofmann, S. G. (2000). Self-focused attention before and after treatment of social phobia. *Behaviour Research and Therapy, 38,* 717–725.

Hofmann, S. G., Lehman, C. L., & Barlow, D. H. (1997). How specific are specific phobias? *Journal of Behavior Therapy and Experimental Psychiatry, 28,* 233–240.

Hofmann, S. G., Meuret, A. E., Rosenfield, D., Suvak, M. K., Barlow, D. H., . . . Woods, S. W. (2007). Preliminary evidence for cognitive mediation during cognitive-behavioral therapy of panic disorder. *Journal of Consulting and Clinical Psychology, 75,* 374–379.

Hofmann, S. G., Moscovitch, D. A., Kim, H.-J., & Taylor, A. N. (2004). Changes in self-perception during treatment of social phobia. *Journal of Consulting and Clinical Psychology, 72,* 588–596.

Hofvander, B., Delorme, R., Chaste, P., Nydén, A., Wentz, E., Ståhlberg, O., . . . Leboyer, M. (2009). Psychiatric and psychosocial problems in adults with normal-intelligence autism spectrum disorders. *BMC Psychiatry, 9,* 35.

Hoge, C. W., Castro, C. A., Messer, S. C., McGurk, D., Cotting, D. I., & Koffman, R. L. (2004). Combat duty in Iraq and Afghanistan, mental health problems and barriers to care. *New England Journal of Medicine, 351,* 13–22.

Holahan, C. (2001, August 28). Hidden eating disorders concealment is growing, specialists say. *Boston Globe,* p. C4.

Holahan, C. J., & Moos, R. H. (1991). Life stressors, personal and social resources, and depression: A four-year structure model. *Journal of Abnormal Psychology, 100,* 31–38.

Holcomb, H. H., Links, J., Smith, C., & Wong, D. (1989). Positron emission tomography: Measuring the metabolic and neurochemical characteristics of the living human nervous system. In N. C. Andreasen (Ed.), *Brain imaging: Applications in psychiatry* (pp. 235–370). Washington, DC: American Psychiatric Press.

Hollender, M. H. (1980). The case of Anna O.: A reformulation. *American Journal of Psychiatry, 137,* 797–800.

Hollon, S. D., DeRubeis, R. J., & Seligman, M. E. P. (1992). Cognitive therapy and the prevention of depression. *Applied and Preventive Psychology, 1,* 89–95.

Hollon, S. D., & Fawcett, J. (2001). Combined medication and psychotherapy. In G. O. Gabbard (Ed.), *Treatment of psychiatric disorders* (pp. 1247–1266). Washington, DC: American Psychiatric Press.

Hollon, S. D., Stewart, M. O., & Strunk, D. (2006). Enduring effects for cognitive behavior therapy in the treatment of depression and anxiety. *Annual Review of Psychology, 57,* 285–315.

Hollon, S. D., Thase, M. E., & Markowitz, J. C. (2002). Treatment and prevention of depression. *Psychological Science in the Public Interest, 3,* 39–77.

Holloway, J. D. (2003). Understanding compulsive sexual behavior. *APA Monitor, 34,* 20.

Holloway, J. D. (2004). Lawsuits could change managed-care landscape. *Monitor on Psychology, 35*(3), 30–31.

Holroyd, K. A., France, J. L., Cordingley, G. E., & Rockicki, L. A. (1995). Enhancing the effectiveness of relaxation-thermal biofeedback training with propranolol hydrochloride. *Journal of Consulting and Clinical Psychology, 63,* 327–330.

Holroyd, S., & Baron-Cohen, S. (1993). Brief report: How far can people with autism go in developing a theory of mind? *Journal of Autism and Developmental Disorders, 23,* 379–385.

Holt-Lunstad, J., Smith, T. B., & Layton, B. (2010). Social relationships and mortality risk: A meta-analytic review. *PLoS Medicine, 7*(7), e1000316. doi:10.1371/journal.pmed.1000316

Honda, K., & Goodwin, R. D. (2004). Cancer and mental disorders in a national community sample. *Psychotherapy and Psychosomatics, 73,* 235–242.

Honea, R. A., Thomas, G. P., Harsha, A., Anderson, H. S., Donnelly, J. E., Brooks, W. M., & Burns, J. M. (2009). Cardiorespiratory fitness and preserved medial temporal lobe volume in Alzheimer disease. *Alzheimer Disease and Associated Disorders, 23,* 188–197.

Hooper, J. (1998, August). Science in the sack: Beyond Viagra. *Health and Fitness,* pp. 108–113.

Hopkins, I. M., Gower, M. W., Perez, T. A., Smith, D. S., Amthor, F. R., Casey-Wimsatt, F., & Biasini, F. J. (2011). Avatar assistant: Improving social skills in students with an ASD through a computer-based intervention. *Journal of Autism Developmental Disorders.* In press.

Hornor, G. (2008). Reactive attachment disorder. *Journal of Pediatric Health Care, 22,* 234–239.

Horowitz, M. J. (2001). Histronic personality disorder. In G. O. Gabbard (Ed.), *Treatment of psychiatric disorders* (pp. 2293–2307). Washington, DC: American Psychiatric Press.

Horwath, E., & Weissman, M. M. (1997). Epidemiology of anxiety disorders across cultural groups. In S. Friedman (Ed.), *Cultural issues in the treatment of anxiety* (pp. 21–39). New York: Guilford Press.

Hosenbocus, S., & Chahal, R. (2011). SSRIs and SNRIs: A review of the discontinuation syndrome in children and adolescents. *Journal of the Canadian Academy of Child and Adolescent Psychiatry, 20,* 60–67.

Hougaard, E., Madsen, S. S., Hansen, L. M., Jensen, M., Katborg, G. S., . . . Piet, J. (2008). Novel group therapeutic format in cognitive behavioural treatment for clients with social phobia in a training session: A case study of one treatment group with nine clients. *Pragmatic Case Studies in Psychotherapy, 4,* 1–52.

House, J. S., Landis, K. R., & Umberson, D. (1988). Social relationships and health. *Science, 241,* 540–545.

Hovanitz, C. A., & Wander, M. R. (1990). Tension headache: Disregulation at some levels of stress. *Journal of Behavioral Medicine, 13,* 539–560.

Howard, K. L., & Filley, C. M. (2009). Advances in genetic testing for Alzheimer's disease. *Review of Neurological Diseases, 6,* 26–32.

Howard, M. O., Balster, R. L., Cottler, L. B., Wu, L. T., & Vaughn, M. G. (2008). Inhalant use among incarcerated adolescents in the United States: Prevalence, characteristics, and correlates of use. *Drug and Alcohol Dependence, 93,* 197–209.

Howard, M. O., Perron, B. E., Sacco, P., Ilgen, M., Vaughn, M. G., Garland, E., & Freedentahl, S. (2010). Suicide ideation and attempts among inhalant users: Results from the national epidemiologic survey on alcohol and related conditions. *Suicide and Life Threatening Behavior, 40,* 276–286.

Howard, M. O., Perron, B. E., Vaughn, M. G., Bender, K. A., & Garland, E. (2010). Inhalant use, inhalant-use disorders, and antisocial behavior: Findings from the National Epidemiologic Survey on Alcohol and Related Conditions (NESARC). *Journal of Studies on Alcohol and Drugs, 71,* 201–209.

Howard, R. (1992). Folie à deux involving a dog. *American Journal of Psychiatry, 149,* 414.

Howard, R., Rabins, P. V., Seeman, M. V., & Jeste, D. V. (2000). International late onset schizophrenia group: Late-onset schizophrenia and very-late-onset schizophrenia-like psychosis—An international consensus. *American Journal of Psychiatry, 157,* 172–178.

Howe, E. (2010). What psychiatrists should know about genes and Alzheimer's disease. *Psychiatry, 7,* 45–51.

Howes, O. D., Montgomery, A. J., Asselin, M. C., Murray, R. M., Valli, I., . . . Graspy, P. M. (2009). Elevated striatal dopamine function linked to prodromal signs of schizophrenia. *Archives of General Psychiatry, 66,* 13–20.

Howland, R. H. (2011). Sleep interventions for the treatment of depression. *Journal of Psychosocial Nursing and Mental Health Services, 49,* 17–20.

Howlett, S., & Reuber, M. (2009). An augmented model of brief psychodynamic interpersonal therapy for patients with nonepileptic seizures. *Psychotherapy: Research, Practice, Training, 46,* 125–138.

Hu, S., Pattatucci, A. M. L., & Patterson, C. L. L. (1995, November). Linkage between sexual orientation and chromosome Xq28 in males but not in females. *Nature Genetics, 11,* 248–256.

Huang, J., Perlis, R. H., Lee, P. H., Rush, A. J., Fava, M., . . . Smoller, J. W. (2010). Cross-disorder genomewide analysis of schizophrenia, bipolar disorder, and depression. *American Journal of Psychiatry, 167,* 1254–1263.

Hudson, J. I., Hiripi, E., Pope, H. G., & Kessler, R. C. (2007). The prevalence and correlates of eating disorders in the National Comorbidity Survey Replication. *Biological Psychiatry, 61,* 348–358.

Hudson, J. I., Manoach, D. S., Sabo, A. N., & Sternbach, S. E. (1991). Recurrent nightmares in posttraumatic stress disorder: Association with sleep paralysis, hypnopompic hallucinations, and REM sleep. *Journal of Nervous and Mental Disease, 179,* 572–573.

Huijbregts, K. M., van der Feltz-Cornelis, C. M., van Marwijk, H. W., de Jonge, F. J., van der Windt, D. A., & Beekman, A. T. (2010). Negative association of concomitant physical symptoms with the course of major depressive disorder: A systematic review. *Journal of Psychosomatic Research, 68,* 511–519.

Humphrey, D. (1991). *Final exit.* Eugene, OR: Hemlock Society.

Hunfeld, J., Perquin, C., Hazebroek-Kampschrueur, A., Passchier, J., Suiklekom-Smit, L., & van der Wouden, J. (2002). Physically unexplained chronic pain and its impact on children and their families: The mother's perception. *Psychology and Psychotherapy: Theory and Practice, 75,* 251–260.

Hunsley, J. (2007). Addressing key challenges in evidence-based practice in psychology. *Professional Psychology: Research and Practice, 38,* 113–121.

Hunt, W. G. (2010). Meningitis and encephalitis in adolescents. *Adolescent Medicine State of the Art Review, 21,* 287–317, ix–x.

Hunter, R., & Macalpine, I. (1963). *Three hundred years of psychiatry, 1535–1860.* London: Oxford University Press.

Huntjens, R. J. C., Peters, M. L., Woertman, L., van der Hart, O., & Postma, A. (2007). Memory transfer for emotionally valenced words between identities in dissociative identity disorder. *Behaviour Research and Therapy, 45,* 775–789.

Huppert, J. D., Schultz, L. T., Foa, E. B., Barlow, D. H., Davidson, J. R. T., . . . Woods, S. W. (2004). Differential response to placebo among patients with social phobia, panic disorder, and obsessive-compulsive disorder. *American Journal of Psychiatry, 161,* 1485–1487.

Hurley, R. A., Saxena, S., Rauch, S. L., Hoehn-Saric, R., & Taber, K. H. (2002). Predicting treatment response in obsessive-compulsive disorder. *Journal of Neuropsychiatry and Clinical Neurosciences, 14,* 249–255.

Hussong, A. M., Hicks, R. E., Levy, S. A., & Curran, P. J. (2001). Specifying the relations between affect and heavy alcohol use among young adults. *Journal of Abnormal Psychology, 110,* 449–461.

Hyde, J. S. (2005). *Biological substrates of human sexuality.* Washington, DC: American Psychological Association.

Ingersoll, R. E., & Previts, S. B. (2001). Prevalence of childhood disorders. In E. Welfel & R. E. Ingersoll (Eds.), *The mental health desk reference: A sourcebook for counselors* (pp. 155–162). New York: Wiley.

International Internet Trends Study. (2008). Retrieved from http://www.optenet.com/mailing/pdfs/TrendReport.pdf

International Narcotics Control Board. (2010). Psychotropic Substances – Technical Reports – Report 2010: Statistics for 2009. Retrieved from http://www.incb.org/pdf/technical-reports/psychotropics/2010/Psy_2010_EFS_Part2_E_comments.pdf

International Society for the Study of Dissociation. (2005). Guidelines for treating dissociative identity disorder in adults. *Journal of Trauma and Dissociation, 6,* 69–149.

Irani, F., & Siegel, S. J. (2006). Predicting outcome in schizophrenia. *Psychiatric Times, 23,* 69–71.

Irizarry, L. (2004, August 8). Widespread starvation: A proliferation of web sites are promoting anorexia, which shows that sometimes, there is no safety in numbers. *Times-Picayune,* p. 1.

Irving, L. M. (2001). Media exposure and disordered eating: Introduction to the special section. *Journal of Social and Clinical Psychology, 20,* 259–263.

Irwin, H. J. (1998). Attitudinal predictors of dissociation: Hostility and powerlessness. *Journal of Psychology, 132,* 389–404.

Isenberg, S. A., Lehrer, P. M., & Hochron, S. (1992). The effects of suggestion and emotional arousal on pulmonary function in asthma: A review and a hypothesis regarding vagal medication. *Psychosomatic Medicine, 54,* 192–216.

Islam, L., Scarone, S., & Gambini, O. (2011). First- and third-person perspectives in psychotic disorder and mood disorders with psychotic features. *Schizophrenia Research and Treatment.* doi:10.1155/2011/769136

Ismail, S., Buckley, S., Budacki, R., Jabbar, A., & Gallicano, I. (2010). Screening, diagnosing and prevention of fetal alcohol syndrome: Is this syndrome treatable? *Developmental Neuroscience, 32,* 91–100.

Issenman, R. M., Filmer, R. B., & Gorski, P. A. (1999). A review of bowel and bladder control development in children: How gastrointestinal and urologic conditions relate to problems in toilet training. *Pediatrics, 103,* 1346–1352.

Ivey, A. E., D'Andrea, M., Ivey, M. B., & Simek-Morgan, L. (2007). *Theories of counseling and psychotherapy: A multicultural perspective.* Boston: Allyn & Bacon.

Iyadurai, S., & Chung, S. (2007). New-onset seizures in adults: Possible association with consumption of popular energy drinks. *Epilepsy & Behavior, 10,* 504–508.

Jabben, N., Arts, B., van Os, J., Krabbendam, L. (2010). Neurocognitive functioning as intermediary phenotype and predictor of psychosocial functioning across the psychosis continuum: Studies in schizophrenia and bipolar disorder. *Journal of Clinical Psychiatry, 71,* 764–774.

Jablensky, A. V., Morgan, V., Zubrick, S. R., Bower, C., & Yellachich, L.-A. (2005). Pregnancy, delivery, and neonatal complications in a population cohort of women with schizophrenia and major affective disorder. *American Journal of Psychiatry, 162,* 79–91.

Jackson, B., & Farrugia, D. (1997). Diagnosis and treatment of adults with attention deficit hyperactive disorder. *Journal of Counseling and Development, 75,* 312–319.

Jackson, G., Kubzansky, L. D., Cohen, S., & Jacobs, D. R., Jr. (2007). Does harboring hostility hurt? Associations between hostility and pulmonary function in the coronary artery risk development in (young) adults (CARDIA) study. *Health Psychology, 26*, 333–340.

Jackson, M., & Claridge, G. (1991). Reliability and validity of a psychotic traits questionnaire (STQ). *British Journal of Psychiatry, 30*, 311–323.

Jackson, T. (2003, December 17). Malvo's case in hands of Va. jury: Insanity argued in sniper case. *The Washington Post*, p. A01.

Jackson, T., & Chen, H. (2010). Sociocultural experiences of bulimic and non-bulimic adolescents in a school-based Chinese sample. *Journal of Abnormal Child Psychology, 38*, 69–76.

Jacobs, D., & Klein, M. E. (1993). The expanding role of psychological autopsies. In A. A. Leenaars (Ed.), *Suicidology*. Northvale: Aronson.

Jacobsen, P. B., Bovbjerg, D. H., Schwartz, M. D., Hudis, C. A., Gilewski, T. A., & Norton, L. (1995). Conditioned emotional distress in women receiving chemotherapy for breast cancer. *Journal of Consulting and Clinical Psychology, 63*, 108–114.

Jacobson, E. (1938). *Progressive relaxation*. Chicago: University of Chicago Press.

Jacobson, E. (1967). *Tension in medicine*. Springfield, IL: Thomas.

Jacobson, S., & Alex, P. (2001, February 19). Waist management: Men aren't immune to eating disorders, but they do their best to disguise them. *Record*, p. 1.

Jacobus, J., Bava, S., Cohen-Zion, M., Mahmood, O., & Tapert, S. F. (2009). Functional consequences of marijuana use in adolescents. *Pharmacology Biochemistry and Behavior, 92*, 559–565.

Jaffe, S. R., Moffitt, T. E., Caspi, A., & Taylor, A. (2004). Physical maltreatment victim to antisocial child: Evidence of an environmentally mediated process. *Journal of Abnormal Psychology, 113*, 44–55.

Jaffe, S. R., Moffitt, T. E., Caspi, A., Taylor, A., & Arsenault, L. (2002). Influence of adult domestic violence on children's externalizing and internalizing problems: An environmentally informative twin study. *Journal of the American Academy of Child and Adolescent Psychiatry, 41*, 1095–1103.

Jagdeo, A., Cox, B. J., Stein, M. B., & Sareen, J. (2009). Negative attitudes toward help seeking for mental illness in 2 population-based surveys from the United States and Canada. *The Canadian Journal of Psychiatry, 54*, 757–766.

Jain, R. (2009). The epidemiology and recognition of pain and physical symptoms in depression. *Journal of Clinical Psychiatry, 70*, e04.

James, A., Hough, M., James, S., Burge, L., Winmill, L., Nijhawan, S., Matthews, P. M., & Zarei, M. (2011). Structural brain and neuropsychometric changes associated with pediatric bipolar disorder with psychosis. *Bipolar Disorders, 13*, 16–27.

James, R. K., & Gilliland, B. E. (2003). *Counseling and psychotherapy*. Boston: Allyn & Bacon.

Janjua, A., Rapport, D., & Ferrara, G. (2010). The woman who wasn't there. *Current Psychiatry, 9*, 62–72.

Janssen, K. (1983). Treatment of sinus tachycardia with heart-rate feedback. *Psychiatry and Human Development, 17*, 166–176.

Janssens, T., Verleden, G., De Peuter, S., Van Diest, I., & Van den Bergh, O. (2009). Inaccurate perception of asthma symptoms: A cognitive-affective framework and implications for asthma treatment. *Clinical Psychology Review, 29*, 317–327.

Janus, S. S., & Janus, C. L. (1993). *The Janus report on sexual behavior*. New York: Wiley.

Jason, L. A. (1998). Tobacco, drug and HIV prevention media interventions. *American Journal of Community Psychology, 26*, 151–187.

Jawed, S. Y. (1991). A survey of psychiatrically ill Asian children. *British Journal of Psychiatry, 158*, 268–270.

Jellinek, E. M. (1971). Phases of alcohol addiction. In G. Shean (Ed.), *Studies in abnormal behavior*. Chicago: Rand McNally.

Jellinger, K. A. (2008). Morphologic diagnosis of "vascular dementia"—A critical update. *Journal of Neurological Science, 270*, 1–12.

Jenike, M. A. (2001). A forty-five-year-old woman with obsessive-compulsive disorder. *Journal of the American Medical Association, 285*, 2121–2128.

Jenner, F. A., Gjessing, L. R., Cox, J. R., Davies Jones, A., Hullin, R. R., & Hanna, S. M. (1967). A manic-depressive psychotic with a persistent forty-eight-hour cycle. *British Journal of Psychiatry, 113*, 895–910.

Jensen, P. S. (2003). Foreword. In S. Ozonoff, S. J. Rogers, & R. L. Hendren (Eds.), *Autism spectrum disorders: A research review for practitioners* (pp. xv–xix). Arlington, VA: American Psychiatric.

Jerrott, S., Clark, S. E., & Fearon, I. (2010). Day treatment for disruptive behaviour disorders: Can a short-term program be effective? *Journal of the Canadian Academy of Child and Adolescent Psychiatry, 19*, 88–93.

Jeste, D. V., Jin, H., Golshan, S., Mudaliar, S., Glorioso, D., Fellows, I., . . . Arndt, S. (2009). Discontinuation of quetiapine from an NIMH funded trial due to serious adverse effects. *American Journal of Psychiatry, 166*, 937–938.

Jilek, W. G. (2001, July). *Cultural factors in psychiatric disorders*. Paper presented at the Twenty-sixth Congress of the World Federation for Mental Health, Vancouver, British Columbia, Canada.

Jobes, D. A. (2006). *Managing suicidal risk: A collaborative approach*. New York: Guilford Press.

Joelving, F. (2011). One in 16 U.S. surgeons consider suicide: Survey. *Archives of Surgery*. Retrieved from bit.ly/f50r53 and bit.ly/gOMRz3

Johns, L. C., Cannon, M., Singleton, N., Murray, R. M., Farrell, M., Brugha, T., . . . Metzer, H. (2004). Prevalence and correlates of self-reported psychotic symptoms in the British population. *British Journal of Psychiatry, 185*, 298–305.

Johnson, C. P., Myers, S. M., & the Council on Children with Disabilities. (2007). Identification and evaluation of children with autism spectrum disorders. *Pediatrics, 120*, 1183–1215.

Johnson, D. P., Penn, D. L., Fredrickson, B. L., Meyer, P. S., Kring, A. M., & Brantley, M. (2009). Loving-kindness meditation to enhance recovery from negative symptoms of schizophrenia.

Journal of Clinical Psychology: In Session, 65, 499–509.

Johnson, D. W., & Johnson, F. P. (2003). *Joining together*. Boston: Allyn & Bacon.

Johnson, F., & Wardle, J. (2005). Dietary restraint, body dissatisfaction, and psychological distress: A prospective analysis. *Journal of Abnormal Psychology, 114*, 119–125.

Johnson, J. G., Cohen, P., Smailes, E. M., Kasen, S., & Brook, J. S. (2002). Television viewing and aggressive behavior during adolescent and adulthood. *Science, 295*, 2468–2471.

Johnson, J. K., Diehl, J., Mendez, M. F., Neuhaus, J., Shapira, J. S., . . . Miller B. L. (2005). Frontotemporal lobar degeneration: Demographic characteristics of 353 patients. *Archives of Neurology, 62*, 925–930.

Johnson, S. L., Cuellar, A. K., Ruggero, C., Winett-Perlman, C., Goodnick, P., White, R., & Miller, I. J. (2008). Life events as predictors of mania and depression in bipolar I disorder. *Journal of Abnormal Psychology, 117*, 268–277.

Johnson, S. L., Sandrow, D., Meyer, B., Winters, R., Miller, I., Solomon, D., & Keitner, G. (2000). Increases in manic symptoms after life events involving goal attainment. *Journal of Abnormal Psychology, 109*, 721–727.

Johnston, L. D., Bachman, J. G., & O'Malley, P. M. (2009). *Monitoring the future: questionnaire responses from the nation's high school seniors, 2008*. Ann Arbor, MI: Institute for Social Research.

Johnston, L. D., O'Malley, P. M., Bachman, J. G., & Schulenberg, J. E. (2006, December 21). *Teen drug use continues down in 2006, particularly among older teens; but use of prescription-type drugs remains high*. Ann Arbor: University of Michigan News and Information Services.

Johnston, L. D., O'Malley, P. M., Bachman, J. G., & Schulenberg, J. E. (2010a). *Monitoring the future national survey results on drug use, 1975–2009. Volume I: Secondary school students* (NIH Publication No. 10–7584). Bethesda, MD: National Institute on Drug Abuse.

Johnston, L. D., O'Malley, P. M., Bachman, J. G., & Schulenberg, J. E. (2010b). *Demographic subgroup trends for various licit and illicit drugs, 1975–2009* (Monitoring the Future Occasional Paper No. 73). Ann Arbor, MI: Institute for Social Research. Retrieved from http://www.monitoringthefuture.org/

Johnston, L. D., O'Malley, P. M., Bachman, J. G., & Schulenberg, J. E. (2010c). Marijuana use is rising; ecstasy use is beginning to rise; and alcohol use is declining among U.S. teens. Ann Arbor, MI: University of Michigan News Service. Retrieved from http://www.monitoringthefuture.org

Johnston, L. D., O'Malley, P. M., Bachman, J. G., & Schulenberg, J. E. (2009, December 14). "Smoking continues gradual decline among U.S. teens, smokeless tobacco threatens a comeback." University of Michigan News Service: Ann Arbor, MI. Retrieved from http://www.monitoringthefuture.org

Johnston, L. D., O'Malley, P. M., Bachman, J. G., & Schulenberg, J. E. (2010). *Monitoring the future national results on adolescent drug use: Overview of key findings, 2009* (NIH Publication No. 10–7583). Bethesda, MD: National Institute on Drug Abuse.

Joiner, T. E. (2005). *Why people die by suicide.* Cambridge, MA: Harvard University Press.

Joiner, T. E., Van Orden, K. A., Witte, T. K., Selby, E. A., Ribeiro, J. D., Lewis, R., & Rudd, M. D. (2009). Main predictions of the interpersonal-psychology theory of suicidal behavior: Empirical tests in two samples of young adults. *Journal of Abnormal Psychology, 118,* 634–646.

Joinson, C., Heron, J., Butler, U., & von Gontard, A. (2006). Psychological differences between children with and without soiling problems. *Pediatrics, 117,* 1575–1584.

Joinson, C., Heron, J., & von Gontard, A. (2006). Psychological problems in children with daytime wetting. *Pediatrics, 118,* 1985–1993.

Jones, C., Leung, N., & Harris, G. (2007). Dysfunctional core beliefs in eating disorders: A review. *Journal of Cognitive Psychotherapy: An International Quarterly, 21,* 156–171.

Jones, D. R., Harrell, J. P., Morris-Prather, C. E., Thomas, J., & Omowale, N. (1996). Affective and physiological responses to racism: The role of Afrocentrism and mode of presentation. *Ethnicity and Disease, 6,* 109–122.

Jones, J. M., Bennett, S., Olmsted, M. P., Lawson, M. L., & Rodin, G. (2001). Disordered eating attitudes and behaviours in teenaged girls: A school-based study. *Canadian Medical Association Journal, 165,* 547–551.

Joormann, J. (2006). Is this happiness I see? Biases in the identification of emotional facial expressions in depression and social phobia. *Journal of Abnormal Psychology, 115,* 705–714.

Jorm, A. F., Mather, K., Butterworth, P., Anstey, K. J., Christensen, H., & Easteal, S. (2007). APOE genotype and cognitive functioning in a large age-stratified population sample. *Neuropsychology, 21,* 1–8.

Joseph, E. (1991). Psychodynamic personality theory. In K. Davis, H. Klar, & J. J. Coyle (Eds.), *Foundations of psychiatry.* Philadelphia: Saunders.

Jovanovic, T., Norrholm, S. D., Blanding, N. Q., Davis, M., Duncan, E., Bradley, B., & Ressler, K. J. (2010). Impaired fear inhibition is a biomarker of PTSD but not depression. *Depression and Anxiety, 27,* 244–251.

Juang, L. P., & Cookston, J. T. (2009). Acculturation, discrimination, and depressive symptoms among Chinese American adolescents: A longitudinal study. *Journal of Primary Prevention, 30,* 475–496.

Juang, L. P., Syed, M., & Takagi, M. (2007). Intergenerational discrepancies of parental control among Chinese American families: Links to family conflict and adolescent depressive symptoms. *Journal of Adolescence, 30,* 965–975.

Judd, L. L., Schettler, P. J., Akiskal, H. S., Coryell, W., Leon, A. C., Maser, J. D., & Solomon, D. A. (2008). Residual symptom recovery from major affective episodes in bipolar disorders and rapid episode relapse/recurrence. *Archives of General Psychiatry, 65,* 386–394.

Junginger, J. (1996). Psychosis and violence: The case for a content analysis of psychotic experience. *Schizophrenia Bulletin, 22,* 91–103.

Jupp, B., & Lawrence, A. J. (2010). New horizons for therapeutics in drug and alcohol abuse. *Pharmacological Therapy, 125,* 138–168.

Kabot, S., Masi, W., & Segal, M. (2003). Advances in the diagnosis and treatment of autism spectrum disorders. *Professional Psychology: Research and Practice, 34,* 26–33.

Kaddena, R. M., Littb, M. D., Kabela-Cormiera, E., & Petrya, N. M. (2007). Abstinence rates following behavioral treatments for marijuana dependence. *Addictive Behaviors, 32,* 1220–1236.

Kafka, M. P. (2009). Hypersexual disorder: A proposed diagnosis for DSM-V. *Archives of Sexual Behavior, 39*(2), 377–400. doi: 10.1007/s10508-009-9574-7

Kahn, A. U., Staerk, M., & Bonk, C. (1974). Role of counterconditioning in the treatment of asthma. *Journal of Psychosomatic Research, 18,* 88–92.

Kalivas, P. W., & O'Brien, C. (2008). Drug addiction as a pathology of staged neuroplasticity. *Neuropsychopharmacology Reviews, 33,* 166–180.

Kalivas, P. W., & Volkow, N. D. (2005). The neural basis of addiction: A pathology of motivation and choice. *American Journal of Psychiatry, 162,* 1403–1413.

Kalmar, J. H., Wang, F., Chepenik, L. G., Womer, F. Y., Jones, M. M., . . . Blumberg, H. P. (2009). Relation between amygdala structure and function in adolescents with bipolar disorder. *Journal of American Academy of Child and Adolescent Psychiatry, 48,* 636–642.

Kaltenthaler, E., Parry, G., Beverley, C., & Ferriter, M. (2008). Computerised cognitive-behavioural therapy for depression: Systematic review. *British Journal of Psychiatry, 193,* 181–184.

Kalynchuk, L. E., Gregus, A., Boudreau, D., & Perrot-Sinal, T. S. (2004). Corticosterone increases depression-like behavior with some effects on predator odor-induced defensive behavior in male and female rats. *Behavioral Neuroscience, 118,* 1365–1377.

Kamarck, T. W., Muldoon, M. F., Shiffman, S. S., & Sutton-Tyrrell, K. (2007). Experiences of demand and control during daily life are predictors of carotid progression among healthy men. *Health Psychology, 26,* 324–332.

Kamarck, T. W., Muldoon, M. F., Shiffman, S., Sutton-Tyrrell, K., Gwaltney, C., & Janicki, D. L. (2004). Experiences of demand and control in daily life as correlates of subclinical carotid atherosclerosis in a healthy older sample. *Health Psychology, 23,* 24–32.

Kamat, S. A., Rajagopalan, K., Pethick, N., Willey, V., Bullano, M., & Hassan, M. J. (2008). Prevalence and humanistic impact of potential misdiagnosis of bipolar disorder among patients with major depressive disorder in a commercially insured population. *Academy of Managed Care Pharmacy, 14,* 631–642.

Kamphuis, J. H., & Telch, M. J. (2000). Effects of distraction and guided threat reappraisal on fear reduction during exposure-based treatments for specific fears. *Behaviour Research and Therapy, 38,* 1163–1181.

Kampman, K. M. (2008). The search for medications to treat stimulant dependence. *Addiction Science & Clinical Practice, 4,* 28–35.

Kanaan, R., Armstrong, D., & Wesseley, S. (2009). Limits to truth-telling: Neurologists' communication in conversion disorder. *Parent Education and Counseling, 77,* 296–301.

Kanas, N. (1988). Psychoactive substance use disorders: Alcohol. In H. H. Goldman (Ed.), *Review of general psychiatry* (pp. 286–298). Norwalk, CT: Appleton & Lange.

Kanaya, T., Scullin, M. H., & Ceci, S. J. (2003). The Flynn effect and U.S. policies: The impact of rising IQ scores on American society via mental retardation diagnoses. *American Psychologist, 58,* 778–790.

Kanayama, G., Pope, H. G., Jr., & Hudson, J. I. (2001). "Body image" drugs: A growing psychosomatic problem. *Psychotherapy and Psychosomatics, 70,* 61–64.

Kanfer, F. H., & Phillips, J. S. (1969). A survey of current behavior therapies and a proposal for classification. In C. M. Franks (Ed.), *Behavior therapy: Appraisal and status.* New York: Wiley.

Kannai, R. (2009). Munchausen by mommy. *Families, Systems, & Health, 27,* 105–112.

Kanner, L. (1943). Autistic disturbances of affective content. *Nervous Child, 2,* 217–240.

Kanner, L., & Lesser, L. I. (1958). Early infantile autism. *Pediatric Clinics of North America, 5,* 711–730.

Kantrowitz, B., & Scelfo, J. (2006, November 27). What happens when they grow up? *Newsweek,* 47–53.

Kapalko, J. (2010). Pro-ana websites abound. Retrieved from http://www.salon.com/print.html?URL=mwt/broadsheet/2010/06/

Kaplan, H. S. (1974). No nonsense therapy for six sexual malfunctions. *Psychology Today, 8,* 76–80, 83, 86.

Kaplan, H. S. (1979). *Disorders of sexual desire.* Levittown, PA: Brunner/Mazel.

Kaplan, M. (1983). A woman's view of DSM-III. *American Psychologist, 38,* 786–792.

Karch, D., Cosby, A., & Simon, T. (2006). Toxicology testing and results for suicide victims: 13 states, 2004. *Morbidity and Mortality Weekly Report, 55,* 1245–1248.

Kardiner, A. (1939). *The psychological frontiers of society.* New York: Columbia University Press.

Karg, K., Burmeister, M., Shedden, K., & Sen, S. (2011). The serotonin transporter promoter variant (5–HTTLPR), stress, and depression meta-analysis revisited: Evidence of genetic moderation. *Archives of General Psychiatry, 68*(5), 444–454. doi:10.1001/archgenpsychiatry.2010.189

Karlsson, H., Bachmann, S., Schroder, J., McArthur, J., Torrey, E. F., & Yolken, R. H. (2001). Retroviral RNA identified in the cerebrospinal fluids and brains of individuals with schizophrenia. *Proceedings of the National Academy of Science, 98,* 4634–4639.

Karno, M., & Golding, J. M. (1991). Obsessive-compulsive disorder. In L. N. Robins & D. A. Regier (Eds.), *Psychiatric disorders in America: The Epidemiologic Catchment Area study* (pp. 204–219). New York: Free Press.

Karno, M., Hough, R. L., Burnam, A., Escobar, J. I., Timbers, D. M., Santana, F., & Boyd, J. H. (1987). Lifetime prevalence of specific psychiatric disorders among Mexican Americans and non-Hispanic whites in Los Angeles. *Archives of General Psychiatry, 44,* 695–701.

Kaslow, N. J., & Aronson, S. G. (2004). Recommendations for family interventions following a suicide. *Professional Psychology: Research and Practice, 35,* 240–246.

Kastelan, A., Franciskovic, T., Moro, L., Roncevic-Grzeta, I., Grkovic, J., . . . Girotto, I. (2007). Psychotic symptoms in combat-related posttraumatic stress disorder. *Military Medicine, 172,* 273–277.

Kato, T. (2007). Molecular genetics of bipolar disorder and depression. *Psychiatry and Clinical Neurosciences, 61,* 3–19.

Katon, W. (2010). Asthma, suicide risk, and psychiatric comorbidity. *American Journal of Psychiatry, 167,* 1020–1022.

Katon, W. J. (2006). Panic attacks. *New England Journal of Medicine, 354,* 2360–2368.

Kaufman, A. S., & Kaufman, N. L. (2004). *Kaufman Assessment Battery for Children—Manual* (2nd ed.). Circle Pines, MN: AGS.

Kaufman, A. S., Kamphaus, R. W., & Kaufman, N. L. (1985). The Kaufman Assessment Battery for Children (K-ABC). In C. S. Newmark (Ed.), *Major psychological assessment instruments* (pp. 249–276). Boston: Allyn & Bacon.

Kaufman, L., Ayub, M., & Vincent, J. B. (2010). The genetic basis of non-syndromic intellectual disability: A review. *Journal of Neurodevelopmental Disorders, 2,* 182–209.

Kavanagh, D. J. (1992). Recent developments in expressed emotions and schizophrenia. *British Journal of Psychiatry, 160,* 601–620.

Kawa, I., Carter, J. D., Joyce P. R., Doughty, C. J., Frampton, C. M., . . . Olds, R. J. (2005). Gender differences in bipolar disorder: Age of onset, course, comorbidity, and symptom presentation. *Bipolar Disorders, 7,* 119–125.

Kaye, S., Darke, S., & Duflou, J. (2009). Methylenedioxymethamphetamine (MDMA)-related fatalities in Australia: Demographics, circumstances, toxicology and major organ pathology. *Drug and Alcohol Dependence, 104,* 254–261.

Kaye, W. (2009). Eating disorders: Hope despite mortal risk. *American Journal of Psychiatry, 166,* 1309–1311.

Kaye, W. H., Fudge, J. L., & Paulus, M. (2009). New insights into symptoms and neurocircuit function of anorexia nervosa. *Nature Reviews, 10,* 573–582.

Kazdin, A. E., Whitley, M., & Marciano, P. L. (2006). Child-therapist and parent-therapist alliance and therapeutic change in the treatment of children referred for oppositional, aggressive, and antisocial behavior. *Journal of Child Psychology and Psychiatry, 47,* 436–445.

Keating, G. M., & Lyseng-Williamson, K. A. (2010). Varenicline: A pharmacoeconomic review of its use as an aid to smoking cessation. *Pharmacoeconomics, 28,* 231–254.

Keefe, R. S. E., & Fenton, W. S. (2007). How should DSM-V criteria for schizophrenia include cognitive impairment? *Schizophrenia Bulletin, 33,* 912–920.

Keel, P. K., Mitchell, J. E., Miller, K. B., Davis, T. L., & Crow, S. J. (1999). Long-term outcome of bulimia nervosa. *Archives of General Psychiatry, 56,* 63–69.

Kelleher, I., & Cannon, M. (2010). Psychotic-like experiences in the general population: Characterizing a high-risk group for psychosis. *Psychological Medicine, 41*(1), 1–6. doi:10.1017/S0033291710001005

Keller, R. M., & Calgay, C. E. (2010). Microaggressive experiences of people with disabilities. In D. W. Sue (Ed.), *Microaggressions and marginality: Manifestation, dynamics and impact* (pp. 241–267). Hoboken, NJ: Wiley.

Kellner, R. (1985). Functional somatic symptoms and hypochondriasis. *Archives of General Psychiatry, 42,* 821–833.

Kellner, R., Hernandez, J., & Pathak, D. (1992). Hypochondriacal fears and beliefs, anxiety, and somatization. *British Journal of Psychiatry, 160,* 525–532.

Kelly, J. F., Stout, R. L., Magill, Tonigan, J. S. . . . Pagano, M. E. (2011). Spirituality in Recovery: A Lagged Mediational Analysis of Alcoholics Anonymous' Principal Theoretical Mechanism of Behavior Change. *Alcoholism: Clinical & Experimental Research, 35,* 454–463.

Kelly, R. E., Jr., Cohen, L. J., Semple, R. J., Bialer, P., Lau, A., . . . Galynker, I. I. (2006). Relationship between drug company funding and outcomes of clinical psychiatric research. *Psychological Medicine, 36,* 1647–1656.

Kelly, V. L., Barker, H., Field, A. P., Wilson, C., & Reynolds, S. (2010). Can Rachman's indirect pathways be used to un-learn fear? A prospective paradigm to test whether children's fears can be reduced using positive information and modeling a non-anxious response. *Behaviour Research and Therapy, 48,* 164–170.

Keltner, N. G., & Dowben, J. S. (2007). Psychobiological substrates of posttraumatic stress disorder: Part 1. *Perspectives in Psychiatric Care, 43,* 97–101.

Kendall, P. C., Holmbeck, G., & Verduin, T. (2004). Methodology, design, and evaluation in psychotherapy research. In M. J. Lambert (Ed.), *Bergin and Garfield's handbook of psychotherapy and behavior change* (pp. 16–43). New York: Wiley.

Kendall, P. C., Khanna, M. S., Edson, A., Cummings, C., & Harris, M. S. (2011). Computers and psychosocial treatment for child anxiety: Recent advances and ongoing efforts. *Depression and Anxiety, 28,* 58–66.

Kendall-Tackett, K. (2009). Psychological trauma and physical health: A psychoneuroimmunology approach to etiology of negative health effects and possible interventions. *Psychological Trauma: Theory, Research, Practice, and Policy, 1,* 35–48.

Kendall-Tackett, K., & Klest, B. (2009). Causal mechanisms and multidirectional pathways between trauma, dissociation, and health. *Journal of Trauma, 10,* 129–134.

Kendall-Tackett, K. A., Williams, L. M., & Finkelhor, D. (1993). Impact of sexual abuse on children: A review and synthesis of recent empirical studies. *Psychological Bulletin, 113,* 164–180.

Kendler, K. S. (1988). Familial aggregation of schizophrenia and schizophrenic spectrum disorders. *Archives of General Psychiatry, 45,* 377–383.

Kendler, K. S., & Prescott, C. A. (2006). *Genes, environment, and psychopathology: Understanding the causes of psychiatric and substance use disorders.* New York: Guilford Press.

Kendler, K. S., Gallagher, T. J., Abelson, J. M., & Kessler, R. C. (1996). Lifetime prevalence, demographic risk factors, and diagnostic validity of nonaffective psychosis as assessed in a US community sample: The National Comorbidity Survey. *Archives of General Psychiatry, 53,* 1022–1031.

Kendler, K. S., Heath, A. C., Neale, M. C., Kessler, R. C., & Eaves, L. J. (1992). A population-based twin study of alcoholism in women. *Journal of the American Medical Association, 268,* 1877–1882.

Kendler, K. S., Hettema, J. M., Butera, F., Gardner, C. O., & Prescott, C. A. (2003). Life event dimensions of loss, humiliation, entrapment and danger in the prediction of onsets of major depression and generalized anxiety. *Archives of General Psychiatry, 60,* 789–796.

Kendler, K. S., MacLean, C., Neale, M., Kessler, R., Heath, A., & Eaves, L. (1991). The genetic epidemiology of bulimia nervosa. *American Journal of Psychiatry, 148,* 1627–1637.

Kendler, K. S., Myers, J., Prescott, C. A., & Neale, M. C. (2001). The genetic epidemiology of irrational fears and phobias in men. *Archives of General Psychiatry, 58,* 257–265.

Kendler, K. S., Neale, M. C., Kessler, R. C., Heath, A. C., & Eaves, L. J. (1992). Generalized anxiety disorder in women. *Archives of General Psychiatry, 49,* 267–271.

Kendler, K. S., Silberg, J. L., Neale, M. C., Kessler, R. C., Heath, A. C., & Eaves, L. J. (1991). The family history method: Whose psychiatric history is being measured? *American Journal of Psychiatry, 148,* 1501–1504.

Kennard, B. D., Silva, S. G., Mayes, T. L., Rohde, P., Hughes, J. L., Vitiello, B., . . . March, J. S. (2009). Assessment of safety and long-term outcomes of initial treatment with placebos in TADS. *American Journal of Psychiatry, 166,* 337–344.

Kennedy, R. (2002). PTSD: The trauma after the trauma. *Medscape Psychiatry and Mental Health, 2.* Retrieved from www.medscape.com/viewarticle/441133

Kenny, M. A., & Williams, J. M. G. (2007). Treatment-resistant depressed patients show a good response to mindfulness-based cognitive therapy. *Behaviour Research & Therapy, 45,* 617–625.

Kent, M. M., & Haub, C. (2005). Global demographic divide. *Population Bulletin, 60,* 1–24.

Kerlitz, I., & Fulton, J. P. (1984). *The insanity defense and its alternatives: A guide to policy makers.* Williamsburg, VA: National Center for State Courts.

Kern, J. K., Geier, D. A., Adams, J. B., Mehta, J. A., Grannemann, B. D., & Geier, M. R. (2011). Toxicity biomarkers in autism spectrum disorder: A blinded study of urinary porphyrins. *Pediatrics International, 53,* 147–153.

Kern, S. E. (2009). Challenges in conducting clinical trials in children: Approaches for improving performance. *Expert Review of Clinical Pharmacology, 2*(6), 609–617.

Kernberg, O. (1976). Technical considerations in the treatment of borderline personality organization. *Journal of the American Psychoanalytic Association, 24,* 795–829.

Kernberg, O. F. (1975). *Borderline conditions and pathological narcissism.* New York: Aronson.

Kerr, P. L, Muehlenkamp, J. J., & Turner, J. M. (2010). Nonsuicidal self-injury: A review of current research for family medicine and primary care physicians. *The Journal of the American Board of Family Medicine, 23,* 240–259.

Keski-Rahkonen, A., Hoek, H. W., Susser, E. S., Linna, M. S., Sihvola, E., . . . Rissanen, A. (2007). Epidemiology and course of anorexia nervosa in the community. *American Journal of Psychiatry, 164,* 1259–1266.

Kessler, R. C. (2003). Epidemiology of women and depression. *Journal of Affective Disorders, 74,* 5–13.

Kessler, R. C., Akiskal, H. S., Ames, M., Birnbaum, H., Greenberg, P., . . . Wang, P. S. (2006). Prevalence and effects of mood disorders on work performance in a nationally representative sample of U.S. workers. *American Journal of Psychiatry, 163,* 1561–1568.

Kessler, R. C., Berglund, P., Demler, O., Jin, R., Koretz, D., . . . National Comorbidity Survey Replication (2003). The epidemiology of major depressive disorder: Results from the National Comorbidity Survey Replication (NCS-R). *Journal of the American Medical Association, 289,* 3095–3105.

Kessler, R. C., Berglund, P., Demler, O., Jin, R., Merikangas, K. R., & Walters, E. E. (2005). Lifetime prevalence and age-of-onset distribution of DSM-IV disorders in the National Comorbidity Survey Replication. *Archives of General Psychiatry, 62,* 593–602.

Kessler, R. C., Chiu, W. T., Demler, O., & Walters, E. E. (2005). Prevalence, severity, and comorbidity of 12-month DSM-IV disorders in the National Comorbidity Survey Replication. *Archives of General Psychiatry, 62,* 617–627.

Kessler, R. C., McGonagle, K. A., Zhao, S., Nelson, C. B., Hughes, M., Eshleman, S., . . . Kendler, K. S. (1994). Lifetime and twelve-month prevalence of DSM-III-R psychiatric disorders in the United States. *Archives of General Psychiatry, 51,* 8–19.

Kessler, R. C., Stein, M. B., & Berglund, P. (1998). Social phobia subtypes in the National Comorbidity Survey. *American Journal of Psychiatry, 155,* 613–619.

Ketter, T. A. (2010). Diagnostic features, prevalence, and impact of bipolar disorder. *Journal of Clinical Psychiatry, 71,* e14.

Kiecolt-Glaser, J. (2009). Is stress a risk factor for cancer? Retrieved from http://health. usnews.com/health-news/blogs/health-advice/2009/02/19/is-stress-a-risk-factor-for-cancer_print.html

Kiecolt-Glaser, J. K., & Glaser, R. (1993). Mind and immunity. In D. Goleman & J. Gurin (Eds.), *Mind/body medicine* (pp. 39–64). New York: Consumer Reports Books.

Kiecolt-Glaser, J. K., Glaser, R., Cacioppo, J. T., MacCallum, R. C., Snydersmith, M., Kim, C., & Malarkey, W. B. (1997). Marital conflict in older adults: Endocrinological and immunological correlates. *Psychosomatic Medicine, 59,* 339–349.

Kiecolt-Glaser, J. K., Glaser, R., Dyer, C., Shuttleworth, E. C., Ogrocki, P., & Speicher, C. E. (1987). Chronic stress and immune function in family caregivers of Alzheimer's disease victims. *Psychosomatic Medicine, 49,* 523–535.

Kienhorst, I. C., de Wilde, E. J., Diekstra, R. F. W., & Wolters, W. H. G. (1995). Adolescents' image of their suicide attempt. *Journal of the American Academy of Childhood and Adolescent Psychiatry, 34,* 623–628.

Kiesler, C. A. (1991). Homelessness and public policy priorities. *American Psychologist, 46,* 1245–1252.

Kiesler, D. J. (1996). *Contemporary interpersonal theory and research: Personality, psychopathology, and psychotherapy.* New York: Wiley.

Killen, J. D., Robinson, T. N., Haydel, K. F., Hayward, C., Wilson, D. M., . . . Taylor, C. B. (1997). Prospective study of risk factors for the initiation of cigarette smoking. *Journal of Consulting and Clinical Psychology, 65,* 1011–1016.

Kilmann, P., Sabalis, R., Gearing, M., Bukstel, L., & Scovern, A. (1982). The treatment of sexual paraphilias: A review of the outcome research. *Journal of Sex Research, 18,* 193–252.

Kilmann, P. R., & Auerbach, R. (1979). Treatments of premature ejaculation and psychogenic impotence: A critical review of the literature. *Archives of Sexual Behavior, 8,* 81–100.

Kilpatrick, D. G., Amstadter, A. B., Resnick, H. S., & Ruggiero, K. J. (2007). Rape-related PTSD: Issues and interventions. *Psychiatric Times, 24,* 1–3.

Kim, C., Jun, S. H., Kang, D. R., Kim, H. C., Moon, K. T., . . . Suh, I. (2010). Ambient particulate matter as a risk factor for suicide. *American Journal of Psychiatry, 167,* 1100–1107.

Kim, J.-J., Kim, D.-J., Kim, T.-G., Seok, J.-H., Chun, J. W., Oh, M.-K., & Park, A. J. (2007). Volumetric abnormalities in connectivity-based subregions of the thalamus in patients with chronic schizophrenia. *Schizophrenia Research, 97,* 226–235.

Kim, S.-J., Kim, B-N., Cho, S. C., Kim, J.-W., Shin, M.-S., . . . Kim, H. W. (2010). The prevalence of specific phobia and associated co-morbid features in children and adolescents. *Journal of Anxiety Disorders, 24,* 629–634.

Kim, S. Y., Chen, Q., Li, J., Huang, X., & Moon, U. J. (2009). Parent-child acculturation, parenting, and adolescent depressive symptoms in Chinese immigrant families. *Journal of Family Psychology, 23,* 426–437.

Kim, U., & Berry, J. W. (1993). *Indigenous psychologies.* Newbury Park, CA: Sage.

Kim, Y., & Berrios, G. E. (2001). Impact of the term schizophrenia on the culture of ideograph: The Japanese experience. *Schizophrenia Bulletin, 27,* 181–185.

Kinderman, P., & Bentall, R. P. (1996). Self-discrepancies and persecutory delusions: Evidence for a model of paranoid ideation. *Journal of Abnormal Psychology, 105,* 106–113.

Kinderman, P., & Bentall, R. P. (1997). Casual attributions in paranoia and depression: Internal, personal, and situational attributions for negative events. *Journal of Abnormal Psychology, 106,* 341–345.

King, C. A., & Merchant, C. R. (2008). Social and interpersonal factors relating to adolescent suicidality: A review of the literature. *Archives of Suicide Research, 12,* 181–196.

King, G., Yerger, V. B., Whembolua, G., Bendel, R. B., Kittles, R., & Moolchan, E. T. (2009). Link between facultative melanin and tobacco use among African Americans. *Pharmacology, Biochemistry and Behavior, 92,* 589–596.

King, K. M., & Chassin, L. (2004). Mediating and moderated effects of adolescent behavioral undercontrol and parenting in the prediction of drug use disorders in emerging adulthood. *Psychology of Addictive Behavior, 18,* 239–249.

King, N. J., Clowes-Hollins, V., & Ollendick, T. H. (1997). The etiology of dog phobia. *Behaviour Research and Therapy, 35,* 77.

King, N. J., Eleonora, G., & Ollendick, T. H. (1998). Etiology of childhood phobias: Current status of Rachman's three pathways theory. *Behavior Research and Therapy, 36,* 297–309.

King, S. M., Burt, S. A., Malone, S. M., McGue, M., & Iacono, W. G. (2005). Etiological contributions to heavy drinking from late adolescence to young adulthood. *Journal of Abnormal Psychology, 114,* 587–598.

Kinney, D. K., Teixeira, P., Hsu, D., Napoleon, S. C., Crowley, D. J., . . . Huang E. (2009). Relation of schizophrenia prevalence to latitude, climate, fish consumption, infant mortality, and skin color: A role for prenatal vitamin D deficiency and infections? *Schizophrenia Bulletin, 35,* 582–595.

Kinsey, A. C., Pomeroy, W. B., & Martin, C. E. (1948). *Sexual behavior in the human male.* Philadelphia: Saunders.

Kinsey, A. C., Pomeroy, W. B., Martin, C. E., & Gebhard, P. H. (1953). *Sexual behavior in the human female.* Philadelphia: Saunders.

Kinsey, B. M., Kosten, T. R., & Orson, F. M. (2010). Anti-cocaine vaccine development. *Expert Review of Vaccines, 9,* 1109–1114.

Kirkpatrick, B., Fenton, W. S., Carpenter, W. T., Jr., & Marder, S. R. (2006). The NIMH-MATRICS consensus statement on negative symptoms. *Schizophrenia Bulletin, 32,* 214–219.

Klages, T., Geller, B., Tillman, R., Bolhofner, K., & Zimerman, B. (2005). Controlled study of encopresis and enuresis in children with a prepubertal and early adolescent bipolar I disorder phenotype. *Journal of the American Academy of Child and Adolescent Psychiatry, 44,* 1050–1057.

Klainin, P., & Arthur, D. G. (2009). Postpartum depression in Asian cultures: A literature review. *International Journal of Nursing Studies, 46,* 1355–1373.

Klauke, B., Deckert, J., Reif, A., Pauli, P., & Domschke, K. (2010). Life events in panic disorder—An update on "candidate stressors." *Depression and Anxiety, 27,* 716–730.

Klein, D. M., Shankman, S. A., Lewinsohn, P. M., Rohde, P., & Seeley, J. R. (2004). Family study of chronic depression in a community sample of young adults. *American Journal of Psychiatry, 161,* 646–653.

Klein, D. N., Norden, K. A., Ferro, T., Leader, J. B., Kasch, K. L., . . . Aronson, T. A. (1998). Thirty-month naturalistic follow-up study of early-onset dysthymic disorder: Course, diagnostic stability, and prediction of outcome. *Journal of Abnormal Psychology, 107,* 338–348.

Kleinhans, N. M., Richards, T., Weaver, K. E., Liang, O., Dawson, G., & Aylward, E. (2009). Brief report: Biochemical correlates of clinical impairment in high functioning autism and Asperger's disorder. *Journal of Autism and Developmental Disorders, 39,* 1079–1086.

Kleinman, A. (1997). Triumph or pyrrhic victory? The inclusion of culture in DSM-IV. *Harvard Review of Psychiatry, 4,* 343–344.

Kleinman, A. (2004). Culture and depression. *New England Journal of Medicine, 351,* 951–953.

Klerman, G. L. (1982). Practical issues in the treatment of depression and mania. In E. S. Paykel (Ed.), *Handbook of affective disorders.* New York: Guilford Press.

Klerman, G. L., Weissman, M. M., Markowitz, J., Glick, I., Wilner, P. J., Mason, B., et al. (1994). Medication and psychotherapy. In A. E. Bergin & S. L. Garfield (Eds.), *Handbook of psychotherapy and behavior change* (pp. 734–782). New York: Wiley.

Klerman, G. L., Weissman, M. M., Rounsavelle, B. J., & Chevron, E. S. (1984). *Interpersonal psychotherapy of depression.* New York: Basic Books.

Klin, A., Lin, D. J., Gorrindo, P., Ramsay, G., & Jones, W. (2009). Two-year-olds with autism orient to nonsocial contingencies rather than biological motion. *Nature, 459,* 257–261.

Kline, T. J. (2005). *Psychological testing: A practical approach to design and evaluation.* Thousand Oaks, CA: Sage.

Klonsky, E. D., & Muehlenkamp, J. J. (2007). Self-injury: A research review for the practitioner. *Journal of Clinical Psychology/In Session, 63,* 1045–1056.

Klonsky, E. D., & Glenn, C. R. (2011). Non-suicidal self-injury: What independent practitioners should know. Retrieved from http://www.42online.org/node/163

Klopfer, B., & Davidson, H. (1962). *The Rorschach technique.* New York: Harcourt, Brace & World.

Klott, J., & Jongsma, A. E. (2004). *The suicide and homicide risk assessment and prevention treatment planner.* Hoboken, NJ: Wiley.

Kluft, R. P. (1987). Dr. Kluft replies. *American Journal of Psychiatry, 144,* 125.

Kluger, J. (2003). Medicating young minds. *Time, 162,* 48–58.

Klump, K. L., Suisman, J. L., Burt, S. A., McGue, M., & Iacono, W. G. (2009). Genetic and environmental influences on disordered eating: An adoption study. *Journal of Abnormal Psychology, 118,* 797–805.

Knapik, G. P., Martsolf, D. S., Draucker, C. B., & Strickland, K. D. (2010). Attributes of spirituality described by survivors of sexual violence. *Qualitative Report, 15,* 644–657.

Knopf, I. J. (1984). *Childhood psychopathology* (2nd ed.). Englewood Cliffs, NJ: Prentice-Hall.

Knowlton, A. R., & Latkin, C. A. (2007). Network financial support and conflict as predictors of depressive symptoms among a disadvantaged population. *Journal of Community Psychology, 35,* 13–28.

Knox, S., Catlin, L., Casper, M., & Schlosser, L. Z. (2005). Addressing religion and spirituality in psychotherapy: Clients' perspectives. *Psychotherapy Research, 15,* 287–303.

Kockott, G., & Fahrner, E.-M. (1987). Transsexuals who have not undergone surgery: A follow-up study. *Archives of Sexual Behavior, 16,* 511–522.

Kodituwakku, P. W. (2009). Neurocognitive profile in children with fetal alcohol spectrum disorders. *Developmental Disabilities Research Reviews, 15,* 218–224.

Koenen, K. C. (2010). Developmental origins of posttraumatic stress disorder. *Depression and Anxiety, 27,* 413–416.

Kogan, M. D. Blumberg, S. J., Schieve, L. A., Boyle, C. A., Perrin, J. M., . . . van Dyck, P. C. (2009). Prevalence of parent-reported diagnosis of autism spectrum disorder among children in the US, 2007. *Pediatrics, 124,* 1395–1403.

Kohler, J. (2001, March 30). Therapists on trial in death of girl, 10. *Washington Post,* p. A19.

Kohn, S. W., & Scorcia, D. (2007). Personality and behavioral assessment: Considerations for culturally and linguistically diverse individuals. In G. Esquivel, E. C. Lopez, & S. G. Nahari (Eds.), *Handbook of multicultural school psychology: An interdisciplinary perspective* (pp. 289–307). Mahwah, NJ: Erlbaum.

Kohon, G. (1987). Fetishism revisited. *International Journal of Psychoanalysis, 68,* 213–228.

Kolassa, I.-T., Ertl, V., Eckart, C., Kolassa, S., Onyut, L. P., & Elbert, T. (2010). Spontaneous remission from PTSD depends on the number of traumatic event types experienced. *Psychological Trauma: Theory, Research, Practice, and Policy, 2,* 169–174.

Kolb, B., Gibb, R., & Robinson, T. E. (2003). Brain plasticity and behavior. *Current Directions in Psychological Science, 12,* 1–4.

Kolko, D. J., Loar, L. L., & Sturnick, D. (1990). Inpatient social-cognitive skills training groups with conduct disordered and attention deficit disordered children. *Journal of Child Psychology and Psychiatry, 31,* 734–748.

Kollins, S. H. (2008). A qualitative review of issues arising in the use of psycho-stimulant medications in patients with ADHD and co-morbid substance use disorders. *Current Medical Research Opinions, 24,* 1345–1357.

Kondratas, A. (1991). Ending homelessness. *American Psychologist, 46,* 1226–1231.

Koob, G. F., Kandel, D., & Volkow, N. D. (2008). Pathophysiology of addiction. In A. Tasman, J. Kay, J. A. Lieberman, M. B. First, & M. Maj (Eds.), *Psychiatry, Volume 1,* (3rd ed.) (pp. 354–378). Hoboken, NJ: Wiley.

Koocher, G. P., & Keith-Spiegel, P. (2008). *Ethics in psychology and the mental health profession: Standards and cases* (3rd ed.). Oxford, UK: Oxford University Press.

Kooistra, L., Crawford, S., Gibbard, B., Ramage, B., & Kaplan, B. J. (2010). Differentiating attention deficits in children with fetal alcohol spectrum disorder or attention-deficit-hyperactivity disorder. *Developmental Medicine & Child Neurology, 52,* 205–211.

Kopelman, M. D. (2002). Disorders of memory. *Brain, 125,* 2152–2190.

Koppelman, J. (2004, June 4). Children with mental disorders: Making sense of their needs and the systems that help them. *National Health Policy Forum Issue Brief,* No. 799, 1–23.

Koran, L., Thienemann, M., & Davenport, R. (1996). Quality of life for patients with obsessive-compulsive disorder. *British Journal of Psychiatry, 156,* 51–54.

Koren, D., Hemel, D., & Klein, E. (2006). Injury increases the risk for PTSD: An examination of potential neurobiological and psychological mediators. *CNS Spectrums, 11,* 616–624.

Kornman, L., Chambers, H., Nisbet, D., & Liebelt, J. (2002). Pre-conception and antenatal screening for the fragile site on the X-chromosome. *Cochrane Database of Systematic Reviews,* Issue 1, No. CD001806. doi: 10.1002/14651858. CD001806.

Korvatska, O., Estes, A., Munson, J., Dawson, G., Bekris, L. M., . . . Raskind, W. H. (2011). Mutations in the TSGA14 gene in families with autism spectrum disorders. *American Journal of Medical Genetics: Part B Neuropsychiatric Genetics.* In press.

Koss, M. P. (1993). Detecting the scope of rape: A review of prevalence research methods. *Journal of Interpersonal Violence, 8,* 198–222.

Koss, M. P., Gidycz, C. A., & Wisniewski, N. (1987). The scope of rape: Incidence and prevalence of sexual aggression and victimization in a national sample of higher education students.

Journal of Consulting and Clinical Psychology, 55, 162–170.

Koszewska, I., & Rybakowski, J. K. (2009). Antidepressant-induced mood conversions in bipolar disorder: A retrospective study of tricyclic versus non-tricyclic antidepressant drugs. *Neuropsychobiology, 59,* 12–16.

Koszycki, D., Taljaard, M., Segal, Z., & Bradwejn, J. (2011). A randomized trial of sertraline, self-administered cognitive behavior therapy, and their combination for panic disorder. *Psychological Medicine, 41,* 371–381.

Kottler, J. A. (2002). *Theories in counseling and therapy.* Boston: Allyn & Bacon.

Kottler, J. A., & Brown, R. W. (1992). *Introduction to therapeutic counseling.* Belmont, CA: Brooks/Cole.

Kraemer, H. C., Kupfer, D. J., Narrow, W. E., Clarke, D. E., & Regier, D. A. (2010). Moving toward DSM-5: The field trials. *American Journal of Psychiatry, 167,* 1158–1160.

Kraepelin, E. (1923). *Textbook of psychiatry* (8th ed.). New York: Macmillan. (Original work published 1883)

Kramer, P. D. (2009). Antidepressants and suicide: WHO scientists weigh in. Retrieved from http://www.psychologytoday.com/blog/in-practice/200902/antidepressants-and-suicide-who-scientists-weigh-in

Kramer, U. (2009). Individualizing exposure therapy for PTSD: The case of Caroline. *Pragmatic Case Studies in Psychotherapy, 5,* 1–24.

Krampe, H., Stawicki, S., Wagner, T., Bartels, C., Aust, C., . . . Ehrenreich, H. (2006). Follow-up of 180 alcoholic patients for up to 7 years after outpatient treatment: Impact of alcohol deterrents on outcome. *Alcoholism, Clinical and Experimental Research, 30,* 86–95.

Krantz, S. E., & Moos, R. H. (1988). Risk factors at intake predict nonremission among depressed patients. *Journal of Consulting and Clinical Psychology, 56,* 863–869.

Kranzler, H. R., & Anton, R. F. (1994). Implications of recent neuropsychopharmacologic research for understanding the etiology and development of alcoholism. *Journal of Consulting and Clinical Psychology, 62,* 1116–1126.

Kraus, R. P., & Nicholson, I. R. (1996). AIDS-related obsessive compulsive disorder: Deconditioning based in fluoxetine-induced inhibition of anxiety. *Journal of Behavior Therapy and Experimental Psychiatry, 27,* 51–56.

Kresin, D. (1993). Medical aspects of inhibited sexual desire disorder. In W. O'Donohue & J. Geer (Eds.), *Handbook of sexual dysfunctions.* Boston: Allyn & Bacon.

Kroenke, K., Sharpe, M., & Sykes, R. (2007). Revising the classification of somatoform disorders: Key questions and preliminary recommendations. *Psychosomatics, 48,* 277–285.

Kroutil, L. A., Van Brunt, D. L., Herman-Stahl, M. A., Heller, D. C., Bray, R. M., & Penne, M. A. (2006). Nonmedical use of prescription stimulants in the United States. *Drug and Alcohol Dependence, 84,* 135–43.

Krueger, R. F., Caspi, A., Moffitt, T. E., & Silva, P. A. (1998). The structure and stability of common mental disorders (DSM-III-R): A longitudinal-epidemiological study. *Journal of Abnormal Psychology, 107,* 216–227.

Kubany, E. S., Hill, E. E., Owens, J. A., Iannce-Spencer, C., McCaig, M. A., Tremayne, K. J., & William, P. L. (2004). Cognitive trauma therapy for battered women with PTSD (CTT-BW). *Journal of Consulting and Clinical Psychology, 72,* 3–18.

Kubiszyn, T. W., Meyer, G. J., Finn, S. E., Eyde, L. D., Kay, G. G., Moreland, K. L., . . . Eisman, E. (2000). Empirical support for psychological assessment in clinical health care settings. *Professional Psychology: Research and Practice, 31,* 119–130.

Kuehn, B. M. (2010). Integrated care key for patients with both addiction and mental illness. *Journal of the American Medical Association, 303,* 1905–1907.

Kuehnle, K., & Connell, M. (2009). *The evaluation of child sexual abuse allegations: A comprehensive guide to assessment and testimony.* Hoboken, NJ: John Wiley.

Kuhl, E. S., Hoodin, F., Rice, J., Felt, B. T, Rausch, J. R., & Patton, S. R. (2010). Increasing daily water intake and fluid adherence in children receiving treatment for retentive encopresis. *Journal of Pediatric Psychology, 35,* 1144–1151.

Kuhn, B., Marcus, B., & Pitner, S. (1999). Treatment guidelines for primary nonretentive encopresis and stool toileting refusal. *American Family Physician, 59,* 2171–2178.

Kumanyika, S., Wilson, J., & Guilford-Davenport, M. (1993). Weight-related attitudes and behaviors of Black women. *Journal of the American Dietetic Association, 93,* 416–422.

Kumari, V. (2006). Do psychotherapies produce neurobiological effects? *Acta Neuropsychiatrica, 18,* 61–70.

Kumperscak, H. G., Paschke, E., Gradisnik, P., Vidmar, J., & Bradac, S. U. (2005). Adult metachromatic leukodystrophy: Disorganized schizophrenia-like symptoms and postpartum depression in 2 sisters. *Neuroscience, 30,* 33–36.

Kung, W. W., & Lu, P. C. (2008). How symptom manifestations affect help seeking for mental health problems among Chinese Americans. *Journal of Nervous and Mental Disease, 196,* 46–54.

Kuo, C.-J., Chen, V. C.-H., Lee, W.-C., Chen, W. J., Ferri, C. P., . . . Ko, Y.-C. (2010). Asthma and suicide mortality in young people: A 12-year follow-up study. *American Journal of Psychiatry, 167,* 1092–1099.

Kuo, J. R., & Linehan, M. M. (2009). Disentangling emotion processes in borderline personality disorder: Physiological and self-reported assessment of biological vulnerability, baseline intensity, and reactivity to emotionally evocative stimuli. *Journal of Abnormal Psychology, 118,* 531–544.

Kupka, R. W., Luckenbaugh, D. A., Post, R. M., Suppes, T., Altshuler, L. L., . . . Nolen, W. A. (2005). Comparison of rapid-cycling and non-rapid-cycling bipolar disorder based on prospective mood ratings in 539 outpatients. *American Journal of Psychiatry, 162,* 1273–1280.

Kurth, J. H., & Kurth, M. C. (1994). Role of monoamine oxidase genetics in the etiology of Parkinson's disease. In A. Lieberman, C. W. Olanow, M. B. Youdin, & K. Tipton (Eds.), *Monoamine oxidase inhibitors in neurological diseases* (pp. 113–126). New York: Dekker.

Kusek, K. (2001). Could a fear wreak havoc on your life? *Cosmopolitan, 230,* 182–184.

Kuwabara, H., Kono, T., Shimada, T., & Kano, Y. (2011). Factors affecting clinicians' decision as to whether to prescribe psychotropic medications or not in treatment of tic disorders. *Brain Development.* Retrieved from: http://www.sciencedirect.com/science/article/pii/S038776411000076

Kwak, K. W., Lee, Y. S., Park, K. H., & Baek, M. (2010). Efficacy of desmopressin and enuresis alarm as first and second line treatment for primary monosymptomatic nocturnal enuresis: Prospective randomized crossover study. *Journal of Urology, 184,* 2521–2526.

Kwasi, G., Mawuenyega, W., Sigurdson, K., Ovod, V., Munsell, L., . . . Bateman, R. J. (2010). Decreased clearance of CNS β-Amyloid in Alzheimer's disease. *Science, 330,* 1774.

Lab, D. D., & Moore, E. (2005). Prevalence and denial of sexual abuse in a male psychiatric inpatient population. *Journal of Traumatic Stress, 18,* 323–330.

Lader, M., & Bond, A. J. (1998). Interaction of pharmacological and psychological treatments of anxiety. *British Journal of Psychiatry, 173,* 41–48.

Ladouceur, R., Freeston, M. H., Fournier, S., Rheaume, J., Dugas, M. J., . . . Fournier, S. (2000). Strategies used with intrusive thoughts: A comparison of OCD patients with anxious and community controls. *Journal of Abnormal Psychology, 109,* 179–187.

Lagerberg, T. V., Andreassen, O. A, Ringen, P. A., Berg, O., Larsson, S., . . . Melle, I. (2010). Excessive substance use in bipolar disorder is associated with impaired functioning rather than clinical characteristics, a descriptive study. *BMC Psychiatry, 10,* 9.

La Greca, A. M., & Silverman, W. K. (2006). Children and disasters and terrorism. In P. C. Kendall (Ed.), *Child and adolescent therapy: Cognitive-behavioral procedures* (3rd ed., pp. 356–382). New York: Guilford Press.

La Greca, A. M., Silverman, W. K., Lai, B., & Jaccard, J. (2010). Hurricane-related exposure experiences and stressors, other life events, and social support: Concurrent and prospective impact on children's persistent posttraumatic stress symptoms. *Journal of Consulting and Clinical Psychology, 78,* 794–805.

La Greca, A. M., & Stringer, S. A. (1985). The Wechsler Intelligence Scale for Children–Revised. In C. S. Newmark (Ed.), *Major psychological assessment instruments* (pp. 277–322). Boston: Allyn & Bacon.

Lahey, B., Hartdagen S. E., Frick, P. J., McBurnett, K., Connor, R., & Hynd, G. W.

(1988). Conduct disorder: Parsing the confounded relation to parental divorce and antisocial personality. *Journal of Abnormal Psychology, 97*, 334–337.

Lahey, B. B., Loeber, R., Burke, J. D., & Applegate, B. (2005). Predicting future antisocial personality disorder in males from a clinical assessment in childhood. *Journal of Consulting and Clinical Psychology, 73*, 389–399.

Lahmann, C., Loew, T. H., Tritt, K., & Nickel, M. (2008). Efficacy of functional relaxation and patient education in the treatment of somatoform heart disorders: A randomized controlled clinical investigation. *Psychosomatics, 49*, 378–385.

Lai, J. Y., & Linden, W. (1992). Gender, anger expression style, and opportunity for anger release determine cardiovascular reaction to and recovery from anger provocation. *Psychosomatic Medicine, 54*, 297–310.

Laird, J., & Green. R. J. (1996). *Lesbians and gays in couples and families.* San Francisco: Jossey-Bass.

Laje, G., Paddock, S., Manji, H., Rush, A. J., Wilson, A. F., Charney, D., & McMahon, F. J. (2007). Genetic markers of suicidal ideation emerging during citolopram treatment of major depression. *American Journal of Psychiatry, 164*, 1530–1538.

Lakkis, J., Ricciardelli, L. A., & Williams, R. J. (1999). Role of sexual orientation and gender-related traits in disordered eating. *Sex Roles, 41*, 1–16.

Lam, R. W. (2008). Addressing circadian rhythm disturbances in depressed patients. *Journal of Psychopharmacology, 22*, 13–28.

Lam, R. W., Lee, S. K., Tam, E. M., Grewal, A., & Yatham, L. N. (2001). An open trial of light therapy for women with seasonal affective disorder and comorbid bulimia nervosa. *Journal of Clinical Psychiatry, 62*, 164–168.

Lam, R. W., Levitt, A. J., Levitan, R. D., Enns, M. W., Morehouse, R., Michalak, E. E., & Tam, E. M. (2006). The Can-SAD study: A randomized controlled trial of the effectiveness of light therapy and fluoxetine in patients with winter seasonal affective disorder. *American Journal of Psychiatry, 163*, 805–812.

Lamb, H. R. (1984). Deinstitutionalization and the homeless mentally ill. *Hospital Community Psychiatry, 35*, 899–907.

Lamb, H. R., & Weinberger, I. E. (2005). One year follow up of persons discharged from a locked intermediate care facility. *Psychiatric Services, 56*, 198–201.

Lambert, E. W., Wahler, R. G., Andrade, A. R., & Bickman, L. (2001). Looking for the disorder in conduct disorder. *Journal of Abnormal Psychology, 110*, 110–123.

Lambert, M. J., & Ogles, B. M. (2004). The efficacy and effectiveness of psychotherapy. In M. J. Lambert (Ed.), *Bergin and Garfield's handbook of psychotherapy and behavior change* (5th ed., pp. 139–193). New York: Wiley.

Lambert, K. G., & Kingsley, G. H. (2005). *Clinical neuroscience: Neurobiological foundations of mental health.* New York: Worth Publishers.

Lambley, P. (1974). Treatment of transvestism and subsequent coital problems. *Journal of Behavior Therapy and Experimental Psychiatry, 5*, 101–102.

The Lancet Neurology (2010). Dispelling the stigma of Huntington's disease. *The Lancet Neurology, 9*, 751. Retrieved from http://www.thelancet.com/journals/laneur/article/PIIS1474-4422%2810%2970170-8/fulltext

Landa, R. J. (2008). Diagnosis of autism spectrum disorders in the first 3 years of life. *Nature Clinical Practice Neurology, 4*, 138–147.

Landa, R. J., Holman, K. C., O'Neill, A. H., Stuart, E. A. (2011). Intervention targeting development of socially synchronous engagement in toddlers with autism spectrum disorder: A randomized controlled trial. *Journal of Child Psychology and Psychiatry, 52*, 22–23.

Landrigan, P. J. (2010). What causes autism? Exploring the environmental contribution. *Current Opinions in Pediatrics, 22*, 219–225.

Landro, L. (2010). Hidden heart disease. Retrieved from http://online.wsj.com/articles/SB10001424052748703514904575602382290981078.html

Laney, C., & Loftus, E. F. (2005). Traumatic memories are not necessarily accurate memories. *Canadian Journal of Psychiatry, 50*, 823–828.

Lange, N., Du Bray, M. B., Lee, J. E., Froimowitz, M. P., Froehlich, A., . . . Lainhart, J. E. (2010). Atypical diffusion tensor hemisphere asymmetry in autism. *Autism Research, 3*(6), 350–358. doi: 10.1002/aur.162

Langer, E. J., & Rodin, J. (1976). The effects of choice and enhanced personal responsibility for the aged: A field experiment in an institutional setting. *Journal of Personality and Social Psychology, 34*, 191–198.

Langstrom, N., & Zucker, K. J. (2005). Transvestic fetishism in the general population: Prevalence and correlates. *Journal of Sex and Marital Therapy, 31*, 87–95.

Lanzi, G., Zambrino, C. A., Termine, C., Palestra, M. Ferrari, O., Orcesi, S., Manfredi, P., & Beghi, E. (2004). Prevalence of tic disorders among primary school students in the city of Pavia, Italy. *Archives of Disorders of Childhood, 89*, 45–47.

Lara, M. E., Klein, D. N., & Kasch, K. L. (2000). Psychosocial predictors of the short-term course and outcome of major depression: A longitudinal study of a nonclinical sample with recent-onset episodes. *Journal of Abnormal Psychology, 109*, 644–650.

Laraia, M. T., Stuart, G. W., Frye, L. H., Lydiard, R. B., & Ballenger, J. C. (1994). Childhood environment of women having panic disorder with agoraphobia. *Journal of Anxiety Disorders, 8*, 1–17.

Large, M., Sharma, S., Compton, M. T., Slade, T., & Nielssen, O. (2011). Cannabis use and earlier onset of psychosis: A systematic meta-analysis. *Archives of General Psychiatry*. doi:10.1001/archgenpsychiatry.2011.5

Larkin, K. T., & Zayfert, C. (1996). Anger management training with mild essential hypertensive patients. *Journal of Behavioral Medicine, 19*, 415–433.

La Roche, M. J., & Christopher, M. S. (2009). Changing pradigms from empirically supported treatments to evidence-based practice: A cultural perspective. *Professional Psychology: Research and Practice, 40*, 396–402.

Larson, C. A., & Carey, K. B. (1998). Caffeine: Brewing trouble in mental health settings? *Professional Psychology, Research and Practice, 29*, 373–376.

Larson, E. B., Shadlen, M. F., Wang, L., McCormick, W. C., Bowen, J. D., Teri, L., & Kukall, W. A. (2004). Survival after initial diagnosis of Alzheimer disease. *Annals of Internal Medicine, 140*, 501–509.

Larson, K., Russ, S. A., Kahn, R. S., & Halfon, N. (2011). Patterns of comorbidity, functioning, and service use for US children with ADHD, 2007. *Pediatrics, 127*(3), 462–470. doi: 10.1542/peds.2010-0165

Larsson, M., Weiss, B., Janson, S., Sundell, J., & Bornehag, C. G. (2009). Associations between indoor environmental factors and parental-reported autistic spectrum disorders in children 6-8 years of age. *Neurotoxicology, 30*, 822–831.

Lassek, W. D., & Gaulin, S. J. C. (2006). Changes in body fat distribution in relation to parity in American women: A correct form of maternal depletion. *American Journal of Physical Anthropology, 131*, 295–302.

Lassek, W. D., & Gaulin, S. J. C. (2008). Waist-hip ratio and cognitive ability: Is gluteofemoral fat a privileged store of neurodevelopmental resources? *Journal of Evolution and Human Behavior, 29*, 26–34.

Laumann, E. O., Gagnon, J. H., Michael, R. T., & Michaels, S. (1994). *The social organization of sexuality.* Chicago: University of Chicago Press.

Laumann, E. O., Glasser, D. B., Neves, R. C. S., & Moreira, E. D. (2009). A population-based survey of sexual activity, sexual problems and associated help-seeking behavior patterns in mature adults in the United States of America. *International Journal of Impotence Research, 21*, 171–178.

Launer, L. J. (2009). Diabetes: Vascular or neurodegenerative an epidemiologic perspective. *Stroke, 40*, S53.

Lavakumar, M., Garlow, S. J., & Schwartz, A. C. (2011). A case of returning psychosis. *Current Psychiatry, 10*, 51–57.

Lavebratt, C., Sjöholm, L. K., Soronen, P., Paunio, T., Vawter, M. P., . . . Schalling, M. (2010). CRY2 is associated with depression. *PLoS One, 5*, e9407.

Law.jrank.org. Excuse: Insanity—Empirical data and myths. Retrieved from http://law.jrank.org/pages/1136/Excuse-Insanity-Empirical-data-myths.html

Lawrie, S. M., McIntosh, A. M., Hall, J., Owens, D. G. C., & Johnstone, E. C. (2008). Brain structure and function changes during the development of schizophrenia: The evidence from studies of subjects at increased genetic risk. *Schizophrenia Bulletin, 34*, 330–340.

Lawrence, A. A. (2008). Gender identity disorders in adults: Diagnosis and treatment. In D. Rowland & L. Incrocci (Eds.), *Handbook of sexual and gender identity disorders* (pp. 423–456). Hoboken, NJ: Wiley.

Lazarus, P. (2001, May). Breaking the code of silence: What schools can do about it. *NASP Communique, 28–29.*

Leach, M. M. (2006). *Cultural diversity and suicide: Ethnic, religious, gender and sexual orientation perspectives.* Binghamton, NY: Haworth.

Leahy, R. L. (2007). Bipolar disorder: Causes, contexts, and treatments. *Journal of Clinical Psychology: In Session, 63,* 417–424.

Leahy, R. I., Beck, J., & Beck, A. T. (2005). Cognitive therapy for the personality disorders. In S. Strack (Ed.). Handbook of personality and psychopathology (pp. 442–461). Hoboken, NJ: Wiley.

Leary, P. M. (2003). Conversion disorder in childhood: Diagnosed too late, investigated too much? *Journal of the Royal Society of Medicine, 96,* 436–444.

Leary, W. E. (1992, December 10). Medical panel says most sexual impotence in men can be treated without surgery. *The New York Times,* p. D20.

Leckman, J. F., & King, R. A. (2007). A developmental perspective on the controversy surrounding the use of SSRIs to treat pediatric depression. *American Journal of Psychiatry, 164,* 1304–1306.

LeCrone, H. (2007). *BED sometimes thought of as overeating takes over one's life.* Retrieved from http://proquest.umi.com. ezproxy.library.wwu.edu/pqdweb?index=2

Lee, C. C., & Armstrong, K. L. (1995). Indigenous models of mental health intervention: Lessons from traditional healers. In J. G. Ponterotto, J. M. Casas, L. A. Suzuki, & C. M. Alexander (Eds.), *Handbook of multicultural counseling.* Thousand Oaks, CA: Sage.

Lee, C. C., Oh, M. Y., & Montcastle, A. R. (1992). Indigenous models of helping in nonwestern countries: Implications for multicultural counseling. *Journal of Multicultural Counseling and Development, 20,* 1–10.

Lee, C. M., Geisner, I. M., Patrick, M. E., & Neighbors, C. (2010). The social norms of alcohol-related negative consequences. *Psychology of Addictive Behaviors, 24*(2), 342–348.

Lee, H.-Y. & Lock, J. (2007). Anorexia nervosa in Asian-American adolescents: Do they differ from their non-Asian peers? *International Journal of Eating Disorders, 40,* 227–231.

Lee, P., Zhang, M., Hong, J. P., Chua, H. C., Chen, K. P., . . . Dossenbach, M. (2009). Frequency of painful physical symptoms with major depressive disorder in Asia: Relationship with disease severity and quality of life. *Journal of Clinical Psychiatry, 70,* 83–91.

Lee, T. M. C., Chen, E. Y. H., Chan, C. C. H., Paterson, J. G., Janzen, H. L., & Blashko, C. A. (1998). Seasonal affective disorder. *Clinical Psychology: Science and Practice, 5,* 275–290.

Lee, S., Lam, K., Kwok, K., & Fung, C. (2010). The changing profile of eating disorders at a tertiary psychiatric clinic in Hong Kong (1987–2007). *International Journal of Eating Disorders, 43,* 307–314.

Lee, S., Tsang, A., Kessler, R. C., Jin, R., Sampson, N., . . . Petukhova, M. (2010). Rapid-cycling bipolar disorder: Cross-national community study. *British Journal of Psychiatry, 196,* 217–225.

Lee, S., Tsang, A., Von Korff, M., de Graaf, R., Bejet, C., Haro, J. M., . . Kessler, R. C. (2009). Association of headache with childhood adversity and mental disorder: Cross-national study. *British Journal of Psychiatry, 194,* 111–116.

Lee, Y., & Lin, P.-Y. (2010). Association between serotonin transporter gene polymorphism and eating disorders: A meta-analytic study. *International Journal of Eating Disorders, 43,* 498–504.

Leeies, T. M., Pagura, J., Sareen, J., & Bolton, J. M. (2010). The use of alcohol and drugs to self-medicate symptoms of posttraumatic stress disorder. *Depression and Anxiety, 27*(8), 731–736.

Leenaars, A. A. (1992). Suicide notes, communication, and ideation. In R. W. Maris, A. L. Berman, J. T. Maltsberger, & R. I. Yufit (Eds.), *Assessment and prediction of suicide.* New York: Guilford Press.

Leenaars, A. A. (2008). Suicide: A cross-cultural theory. In F. Leong & M. M. Leach (Eds.), *Ethnic suicides* (pp. 13–37). New York: Routledge.

Leff, J. (1994). Working with the families of schizophrenic patients. *British Journal of Psychiatry, 164,* 71–76.

Leff, S. S., & Crick, N. R. (2010). Interventions for relational aggression: Innovative programming and next steps in research and practice. *School Psychology Review, 39,* 504–507.

Le Grange, D., Lock, J., Loeb, K., & Nicholls, D. (2010). Academy for eating disorders position paper: The role of the family in eating disorders. *International Journal of Eating Disorders, 43,* 1–5.

Lehman, A. F., Kreyenbuhl, J., Buchanan, R. W., & Dickerson, F. B. (2004). The schizophrenia patient outcome research team (PORT): Updated treatment recommendations 2003. *Schizophrenia Bulletin, 30,* 193–207.

Lehman, A. F., & Steinwachs, D. M. (1998). At issue: Translating research into practice: The schizophrenia patient outcome research team (PORT) treatment recommendations. *Schizophrenia Bulletin, 24,* 1–10.

Lehmann, H. E. (1985). Affective disorders: Clinical features. In H. I. Kaplan & B. J. Sadock (Eds.), *Comprehensive textbook of psychiatry* (Vol. 4, pp. 786–810). Baltimore: Williams & Wilkins.

Lehrer, P. M., Vaschillo, E., Vaschillo, B., Lu, S.-E., Scardella, A., Siddique, M., & Habib, R. H. (2004). Biofeedback treatment for asthma. *Chest, 126,* 352–361.

Leibbrand, R., Hiller, W., & Fichter, M. M. (2000). Hypochondriasis and somatization: Two distinct aspects of somatoform disorders. *Journal of Clinical Psychology, 56,* 63–72.

Leiblum, S. R., & Rosen, R. C. (1991). Couples therapy for erectile disorders: Conceptual and clinical considerations. *Journal of Sex and Marital Therapy, 17,* 147–159.

Leiknes, K. A., Finset, A., Moum, T., & Sandanger, I. (2008). Overlap, comorbidity, and stability of somatoform disorders and the use of current versus lifetime criteria. *Psychosomatics, 49,* 152–162.

Lejoyeux, M., Huet, F., Claudon, M., Fichelle, A., Casalino, E., & Lequen, V. (2008). Characteristics of suicide attempts preceded by alcohol consumption. *Archives of Suicide Research, 12,* 30–38.

Lejuez, C. W., Hopko, D. R., Acierno, R., Daughters, S. B., & Pagoto, S. L. (2011). Ten year revision of the brief behavioral activation treatment for depression: Revised treatment manual. *Behavior Modification, 35,* 111–161.

Leland, J. (1997). A risky Rx for fun. *Newsweek,* 74.

Lemonick, M. D. (2007). The science of addiction. *Time, 170,* 42–48.

Lenzenweger, M. F. (2001). Reaction time slowing during high-load, sustained-attention task performance in relation to psychometrically identified schizotypy. *Journal of Abnormal Psychology, 110,* 290–296.

Lenzenweger, M. F., Lane, M. C., Loranger, A. W., & Kessler, R. C. (2007). Personality disorders in the National Comorbidity Survey Replication. *Biological Psychiatry, 62,* 553–564.

Leonard, B. E. (2010). The concept of depression as a dysfunction of the immune system. *Current Opinion in Immunology, 6,* 205–212.

Leonardo, E. D., & Hen, R. (2006). Genetics of affective and anxiety disorders. *Annual Review of Psychology, 57,* 117–137.

Leong, F. T., & Leach, M. M. (2008). *Ethnic suicides.* New York: Routledge.

Lerman, C., & Audrain-McGovern, J. (2010). Reinforcing effects of smoking: More than feeling. *Biological Psychiatry, 67,* 699–701.

Lervolino, A. C., Perroud, N., Fullana, M. A., Guipponi, M., Cherkas, L., Collier, D. A., & Mataix-Cols, D. (2009). Prevalence and heritability of compulsive hoarding: A twin study. *American Journal of Psychiatry, 166,* 1156–1161.

Leserman, J., Petitto, J. M., Golden, R. N., Gaynes, B. N., Gu, H., . . . Evans, D. L. (2000). Impact of stressful life events, depression, social support, coping, and cortisol on progression to AIDS. *American Journal of Psychiatry, 157,* 1221–1228.

Leshner, A. I. (2001). Addiction is a brain disease. *Monitor on Psychology, 32,* 19.

Leskin, G. A., & Sheikh, J. I. (2004). *Gender differences in panic disorder.* Retrieved from www.psychiatrictimes/p040165.html

Leslie, R. (1991, July/August). Psychotherapist-patient privilege clarified. *California Therapist,* 11–19.

Lessard v. Schmidt 349 F. Supp. 1078 (E.D. Wis. 1972).

Lester, B. M., Lagasse, L. L., Shankaran, S., Bada, H. S., Bauer, C. R., & Lin, R. (2010). Prenatal cocaine exposure related to cortisol stress reactivity in 11-year-old children. *The Journal of Pediatrics, 157,* 288–295.e1.

Lester, D. (1989). *Can we prevent suicide?* New York: AMS Press.

Lester, D. (1991). Do suicide prevention centers prevent suicide? *Homeostasis in Health and Disease, 33*(4), 190–194.

Lester, D. (2008). Theories of suicide. In F. Leong & M. M. Leach (Eds.), *Ethnic suicides* (pp. 39–53). New York: Routledge.

Lester, K. J., Seal, K., Nightingale, Z. C., & Field, A. P. (2010). Are children's own interpretations of ambiguous situations based on how they perceive their mothers have interpreted ambiguous situations for them in the past? *Journal of Anxiety Disorders, 24,* 102–108.

Lester, R., & Petrie, T. A. (1998). Physical, psychological, and societal correlates of bulimic symptomatology among African American college women. *Journal of Counseling Psychology, 45,* 315–321.

Leuchter, A. F., Cook, I. A., Hunter, A., & Korb, A. (2009). Use of clinical neurophysiology for the selection of medication in the treatment of major depressive disorder: The state of the evidence. *Clinical EEG and Neuroscience, 40,* 78–83.

Leuchter, A., Cook, J. A., Witte, E. A., Morgan, M., & Abrams, M. (2002). Changes in brain function of depressed subjects during treatment with placebo. *Journal of Psychiatry, 159,* 122–129.

LeVay, S., & Valente, S. M. (2006). *Human sexuality.* Sunderland, MA: Sinauer Associates.

Leve, L. D., Kerr, D. C., Shaw, D., Ge, X., Neiderhiser, J. M., . . . Reiss, D. (2010). Infant pathways to externalizing behavior: Evidence of Genotype x Environment interaction. *Child Development, 81,* 340–356.

Levenson, J. C., Frank, E., Cheng, Y., Rucci, P., Janney, C. A., . . . Fagiolini, A. (2010). Comparative outcomes among the problem areas of interpersonal psychotherapy. *Depression and Anxiety, 27,* 434–440.

Levin, A. (2008, June 20). Psychiatrists lack crystal balls to predict patient violence. *Psychiatric News, 43,* 4.

Levine, D., & Mishna, F. (2007). A self psychology and relational approach to group therapy for university students with bulimia. *International Journal of Group Psychotherapy, 57,* 167–185.

Levine, I. S., & Rog, D. J. (1990). Mental health services for homeless mentally ill persons: Federal initiatives and current service trends. *American Psychologist, 45,* 963–968.

Levine, M. D., Perkins, K. A., Kalarchian, M. K., Cheng, Y., Houck, P. R., Slane, J. D., & Marcus, M. D. (2010). Bupropion and cognitive behavioral therapy for weight-concerned women smokers. *Archives of Internal Medicine, 170,* 543–550.

Levinson, D. F. (2006). The genetics of depression: A review. *Biological Psychiatry, 60,* 84–92.

Levinthal, C. F. (2005). *Drugs, behavior, and modern society.* New York: Allyn & Bacon.

Levkovitz, Y., Harel, E. V., Roth, Y., Braw, Y., Most, D., & Zangen, A. (2009). Deep transcranial magnetic stimulation over the prefrontal cortex: Evaluation of antidepressant and cognitive effects in depressive patients. *Brain Stimulation, 2,* 188–200.

Levy, B., & Weiss, R. D. (2010). Neurocognitive impairment and psychosis in bipolar I disorder during early remission from an acute episode of mood disturbance. *Journal of Clinical Psychiatry, 71,* 201–206.

Lewin, A. B., Storch, E. A., & Storch, A. D. (2010). Risks from antipsychotic medications in children and adolescents. *Journal of the American Medical Association, 303,* 729–730.

Lewinsohn, P. M. (1974). A behavioral approach to depression. In R. J. Friedman & M. M. Katz (Eds.), *The psychology of depression: Contemporary theory and research.* New York: Wiley.

Lewinsohn, P. M., Hoberman, H. M., & Rosenbaum, M. (1988). A prospective study of risk factors for unipolar depression. *Journal of Abnormal Psychology, 97,* 251–264.

Lewinsohn, P. M., Hoberman, H. M., Teri, L., & Hautzinger, M. (1985). An integrative theory of depression. In S. Reiss & R. R. Bootzin (Eds.), *Theoretical issues in behavioral therapy* (pp. 331–359). Orlando, FL: Academic Press.

Lewinsohn, P. M., Joiner, T. E., & Rohde, P. (2001). Evaluation of cognitive diathesis-stress models in predicting major depressive disorder in adolescents. *Journal of Abnormal Psychology, 110,* 203–215.

Lewinsohn, P. M., Munoz, R. F., Youngren, M. A., & Zeiss, A. M. (1994). *Control your depression* (Revised ed.). New York: Fireside.

Lewinsohn, P. M., Pettit, J. W., Joiner, T. E., & Seeley, J. R. (2003). The symptomatic expression of major depressive disorder in adolescents and young adults. *Journal of Abnormal Psychology, 112,* 244–252.

Lewinsohn, P. M., Zeiss, A. M., & Duncan, E. M. (1989). Probability of relapse after recovery from an episode of depression. *Journal of Abnormal Psychology, 97,* 387–398.

Lewis, C. M., Ng, M. Y., Butler, A. W., Cohen-Woods, S., Uher, R., . . . McGuffin, P. (2010). Genome-wide association study of major recurrent depression in the U.K. population. *American Journal of Psychiatry, 167,* 949–957.

Lewis, R. W., Fugl-Meyer, K. S., Bosch, R., Fugl-Meyer, A. R., Laumann, E. O., Lizza, E., Martin-Morales, A. (2004). Epidemiology/risk factors of sexual dysfunction. *Journal of Sexual Medicine, 1,* 35–39.

Lewis-Fernàndez, R., Hinton, D. E., Laria, A. J., Patterson, E. H., Hofmann, S. G., . . . Liao, B. (2010). Culture and the anxiety disorders: Recommendations for DSM-V. *Depression and Anxiety, 27,* 212–229.

Lewy, A. J., Emens, J. S., Songer, J. B., Sims, N., Laurie, A. L., Fiala, S. C., & Buti, A. L. (2009). Winter depression: Integrating mood, circadian rhythms, and the sleep/wake and light/dark cycles into a bio-psycho-social-environmental model. *Journal of Clinical Sleep Medicine, 4,* 285–299.

Lewy Body Dementia Association. (2008). Current issues in lewy body dementia. Retrieved from http://www.lbda.org/

Liao, Y., Knoesen, N. P., Castle, D. J., Tang, J., Deng, Y., . . . Liu, T. (2010). Symptoms of disordered eating, body shape, and mood concerns in the male and female Chinese medical students. *Comprehensive Psychiatry, 51,* 516–523.

Liberini, P., Faglia, L., Salvi, F., & Grant, R. P. J. (1993). Cognitive impairment related to conversion disorder: A two-year follow-up study. *Journal of Nervous and Mental Disease, 181,* 325–327.

Liberman, R. P., Kopelowicz, A., & Young, A. S. (1994). Biobehavioral treatment and rehabilitation of schizophrenia. *Behavior Therapy, 25,* 89–107.

Lichtenstein, E., Zhu, S., & Tedeschi, G. J. (2010). Smoking cessation quitlines: An underrecognized intervention success story. *American Psychologist, 65,* 252–261.

Lickey, M. E., & Gordon, B. (1991). *Medicine and mental illness.* New York: Freeman.

Lieberman, J. A., Stroup, T. S., McEvoy, J. P., Swartz, M. S., Rosenheck, R. A., . . . Clinical Antipsychotic Trials of Intervention Effectiveness (CATIE) Investigators. (2005). Effectiveness of antipsychotic drugs in patients with chronic schizophrenia. *New England Journal of Medicine, 353,* 1209–1223.

Lilienfeld, S. O., Fowler, K. A., & Lohr, J. M. (2003). And the band played on: Science, pseudoscience, and the Rorschach Inkblot Method. *Clinical Psychologist, 56,* 6–7.

Lilienfeld, S. O., Lynn, S. J., Kirsch, I., Chaves, J. F., Sarbin, T. R., Ganaway, G. K., & Powell, R. A. (1999). Dissociative identity disorder and the sociocognitive model: Recalling the lessons of the past. *Psychological Bulletin, 125,* 507–523.

Lilienfeld, S. O., Lynn, S. J., & Lohr, J. M. (2004). *Science and pseudoscience in clinical psychology.* New York: Guilford.

Lilienfeld, S. O., Wood, J. M., & Garb, H. N. (2000). The scientific status of projective techniques. *Psychological Science in the Public Interest, 1,* 27–61.

Lilliecreutz, C., & Josefsson, A. (2008). Prevalence of blood and injection phobia among pregnant women. *Acta Obstetrics and Gynecology Scandinavia, 87,* 1276–1279.

Lilly, M. M., Pole, N., Best, S. R., Metzler, T., & Marmar, C. R. (2009). Gender and PTSD: What can we learn from female police officers. *Journal of Anxiety Disorders, 23,* 767–774.

Lin, E. C., & Alavi, A. (2009). *PET and PET/CT: A clinical guide* (2nd ed.). New York: Thieme Medical Publishers.

Lin, K. C., Chung, H. Y., Wu, C. Y., Liu, H. L., Hsieh, Y. W., . . . Wai, Y. Y. (2010). Constraint-induced therapy versus control intervention in patients with stroke: A functional magnetic resonance imaging study. *American Journal of Physical and Medical Rehabilitation, 89,* 177–185.

Lind, C., & Boschen, M. J. (2009). Intolerance of uncertainty mediates the relationship between responsibility beliefs and compulsive checking. *Journal of Anxiety Disorders, 23,* 1047–1052.

Lindau, S. T., Schumm, L. P., Laumann, E. O., Levinson, W., O'Muircheartaigh, C. A., & Waite, L. J. (2007). A study of sexuality and health among older adults in the United States. *New England Journal of Medicine, 357,* 762–774.

Lindhout, I. E., Markus, M. T., Borst, S. R., Hoogendijk, T. H., Dingemans, P. M., & Boer, F. (2009). Childrearing style in families of anxiety-disordered children: Between-family and within-family differences. *Child Psychiatry and Human Development, 40,* 197–212.

Linehan, M. M. (1987). Dialectical behavior therapy for borderline personality disorder: Theory and method. *Bulletin of the Menninger Clinic, 51,* 261–276.

Linehan, M. M. (1993). *Cognitive-behavioral treatment of borderline personality disorder.* New York: Guilford Press.

Ling, P. M., Neilands, T. B., & Glantz, S. A. (2009). Young adult smoking behavior: A national survey. *American Journal of Preventive Medicine, 36*(5), 389–394.

Linn, V. (2004, June 26). Headache "beast" holds tight grip on sufferers. *Seattle Post-Intelligencer,* p. A1.

Lipsitt, D., & Starcevic, V. (2006). Psychotherapy and pharmacotherapy in the treatment of somatoform disorders. *Psychiatric Annals, 36,* 341–348.

Lipsitz, J. D. (2006). Psychotherapy for social anxiety disorder. *Psychiatric Times, 23,* 53–58.

Liptak, A. (2010, May 17). Extended civil commitment of sex offenders is upheld. *The New York Times,* A3.

Lipton, R. B., Bigal, M. E., Diamond, M., Freitag, F., Reed, M. L., & Stewart, W. F. (2007). Migraine prevalence, disease burden, and the need for preventive therapy. *Neurology, 68,* 343–349.

Lis, J. (2011). Ban on stick-thin models passes Knesset hurdle. Downloaded from: http://www.haaretz.com/print-edition/news/ban-on-stick-thin-models-passes-knesset-hurdle-1.362195

Listerine drinker arrested for DUI. (2005, January 16). Retrieved from http://alcoholism.about.com/b/a/139765.htm

Listernick, R. (2007). A 9-year-old girl who is unable to walk. *Pediatric Annals, 36,* 379–382.

Liu, R. T., & Alloy, L. B. (2010). Stress generation in depression: A systematic review of the empirical literature and recommendations for future study. *Clinical Psychology Review, 30,* 582–593.

Liu, W. M., Ali, S. R., Soleck, G., Hopps, J., Dunston, K., & Pickett, T. (2004). Using social class in counseling psychology research. *Journal of Counseling Psychology, 51,* 3–18.

Llaneza, D. C., DeLuke, S. V., Batista, M., Crawley, J. N., Christodulu, K. V., & Frye, C. A. (2010). Communication, interventions, and scientific advances in autism: A commentary. *Physiology and Behavior, 100,* 268–276.

Lloyd-Jones, D., Adams, R., Carnethon, M., De Simone, G., Bruce Ferguson, T., ... American Heart Association Statistics Committee and Stroke Statistics Subcommittee. Heart disease and stroke statistics—2009 update. A report from the American Heart Association Statistics Committee and Stroke Statistics Subcommittee. *Circulation, 119,* e21–e181. Retrieved from http://circ.ahajournals.org/cgi/reprint/CIRCULATIONAHA.108.191261v1

Lock, J., LeGrange, D., Agras, S., Moye, A., Bryson, S. W., & Jo, B. (2010). Randomized clinical trial comparing family-based treatment with adolescent-focused individual therapy for adolescents with anorexia nervosa. *Archives of General Psychiatry, 67,* 1025–1032.

Loe, I. M., & Feldman, H. M. (2007). Academic and educational outcomes of children with ADHD. *Journal of Pediatric Psychology, 32,* 643–654.

Loeber, R. (1990). Development and risk factors of juvenile antisocial behavior and delinquency. *Clinical Psychology Review, 10,* 1–42.

Loening-Baucke, V. (2000). Clinical approach to fecal soiling in children. *Clinical Pediatrics, 39,* 603–607.

Loening-Baucke, V. (2007). Prevalence rates for constipation and faecal and urinary incontinence. *Archives of Disease in Childhood, 92,* 486–489.

Loesch, D. Z., Bui, Q. M., Grigsby, J., Butler, E., Epstein, J., . . . Hagerman, R. J. (2003). Effect of the fragile X status categories and the fragile X mental retardation protein levels on executive functioning in males and females with fragile X. *Neuropsychology, 17,* 646–657.

Loewenstein, R. (1994). Diagnosis, epidemiology, clinical course, treatment, and cost effectiveness of treatment for dissociative disorders and MPD: Report submitted to the Clinton administration task force on health care reform. *Dissociation, 7,* 3–11.

Loftus, E. (2003). Memory in Canadian courts of law. *Canadian Psychology, 44,* 207–212.

Loftus, E. F., Garry, M., & Feldman, J. (1994). Forgetting sexual trauma: What does it mean when 38 percent forget? *Journal of Consulting and Clinical Psychology, 62,* 1177–1181.

Loftus, E. F., Garry, M., & Hayne, H. (2008). Repressed and recovered memory. In E. Borgida & S. T. Fiske (Eds.). *Beyond common sense: Psychological science in the courtroom* (pp. 177–194). Malden, MA: Blackwell Publishing.

Lohoff, F. W. (2010). Overview of the genetics of major depressive disorder. *Current Psychiatry Reports, 12,* 539–546.

Lommen, M. J. J., Sanders, A. J. M. L., & Arntz, A. (2009). Psychosocial predictors of chronic post-traumatic stress disorder in Sri Lankan tsunami survivors. *Behaviour Research and Therapy, 47,* 60–65.

Long, L. L., Allen, J. J. B., & Glisky, E. L. (2008). Interidentity memory transfer in dissociative identity disorder. *Journal of Abnormal Psychology, 117,* 686–692.

Longstaffe, S., Moffatt, M. E., & Whalen, J. C. (2000). Behavioral and self-concept changes after six months of enuresis treatment: A randomized, controlled trial. *Pediatrics, 105,* 935–940.

Lopez, S. R., & Hernandez, P. (1987). When culture is considered in the evaluation and treatment of Hispanic patients. *Psychotherapy, 24,* 120–126.

Lopez, S. R., Hipke, K. N., Polo, A. J., Jenkins, J. H., Karno, M., Vaughn, C., & Snyder, K. S. (2004). Ethnicity, expressed emotion, attributions, and course of schizophrenia: Family warmth matters. *Journal of Abnormal Psychology, 113,* 428–439.

LoPiccolo, J. (1995). Sexual disorders and gender identity disorders. In R. J. Comer (Ed.), *Abnormal psychology* (pp. 411–435). New York: Freeman.

LoPiccolo, J. (1997). Sex therapy: A postmodern model. In S. J. Lynn & J. P. Garske (Eds.), *Contemporary psychotherapies: Models and methods* (pp. 485–494). New York: Guilford Press.

LoPiccolo, J., & Stock, W. E. (1986). Treatment of sexual dysfunction. *Journal of Consulting and Clinical Psychology, 54,* 158–167.

Lovaas, O. I. (Ed.). (2003). *Teaching individuals with developmental delays: Basic intervention techniques.* Austin, TX: PRO-ED.

Lovallo, W. R., Yechiam, E., Sorocco, K. H., Vincent, A. S., & Collins, F. L. (2006). Working memory and decision-making biases in young adults with a family history of alcoholism: Studies from the Oklahoma Family Health Patterns Project. *Alcoholism: Clinical and Experimental Research, 30,* 763–773.

Lovejoy, M. (2001). Disturbances in the social body: Differences in body image and eating problems among African American and white women. *Gender and Society, 15,* 239–261.

Low, C. A., Thurston, R. C., & Matthews, K. A. (2010). Psychosocial factors in the development of heart disease in women: Current research and future directions. *Psychosomatic Medicine, 72,* 842–854.

Lowe, C. F., & Chadwick, P. D. J. (1990). Verbal control of delusions. *Behavior Therapy, 21,* 461–479.

Lu, L. H., Johnson, A., O'Hare, E., Bookheimer, S., Smith, L. M., O'Connor, M. J., & Sowell, E. R. (2009). Effects of prenatal methamphetamine exposure on verbal memory revealed with functional magnetic resonance imaging. *Journal of Developmental & Behavioral Pediatrics, 30*(3), 185–192.

Luborsky, L., Diguer, L., Seligman, D. A., Rosenthal, R., Krause, E. D., . . . Schweizer, E. (1999). The researcher's own therapy allegiances: A "wild card" in comparisons of treatment efficacy. *Clinical Psychology: Science and Practice, 6,* 95–106.

Lue, T. F. (2002). Physiology of penile erection and pathophysiology of erectile dysfunction and priapism. In P. C. Walsh, A. B. Retik, & E. D. Vaughan, Jr. (Eds.), *Campbell's urology* (8th ed.) (pp. 1610–1696). Philadelphia: Saunders.

Lucchelli, J. P., Bondolfi, G., & Bertschy, G. (2006). Body dysmorphic disorder, psychosis and insight: A report of four cases. *Psychopathology, 39,* 130–135.

Luchian, S. A., McNally, R. J., & Hooley, J. M. (2007). Cognitive aspects of nonclinical obsessive-compulsive hoarding. *Behaviour Research and Therapy, 45,* 1657–1662.

Ludwig, J., Marcotte, D. E., & Norberg, K. (2009). Anti-depressants and suicide. *Journal of Health Economics, 28,* 659–676.

Luoma, J. B., Pearson, M. A., & Pearson, J. L. (2002). Suicide and marital risk in the United States, 1991–1996: Is widowhood a risk factor? *American Journal of Public Health, 92,* 1518–1522.

Lussier, P., McCann, K., & Beauregard, E. (2008). The etiology of sexual deviance. In D. Rowland & L. Incrocci (Eds.), *Handbook of sexual and gender identity disorders* (pp. 529–562). Hoboken, NJ: Wiley.

Lustyk, M. K., Gerrish, W. G., Shaver, S., & Keys, S. L. (2009). Cognitive-behavioral therapy for premenstrual syndrome and premenstrual dysphoric disorder: A systematic review. *Archives of Women's Mental Health, 12,* 85–96.

Lydiard, R. B., Brady, K. T., & Austin, L. S. (1994). [To the editor]. *American Journal of Psychiatry, 151,* 462.

Lyke, M. L. (2004, August 27). Once a "people person," vet couldn't leave home. *Seattle Post-Intelligencer,* p. A8.

Lykken, D. T. (1957). A study of anxiety in the sociopathic personality. *Journal of Abnormal and Social Psychology, 55,* 6–10.

Lykken, D. T. (1982). Fearlessness: Its carefree charm and deadly risks. *Psychology Today, 16,* 20–28.

Lyon, G. J., Abi-Dargham, A., Moore, H., Lieberman, J. A., Javitch, J. A., & Sulzer, D. (2011). Presynaptic regulation of dopamine transmission in schizophrenia. *Schizophrenic Bulletin, 37,* 108–117.

Lyons-Ruth, K., Bureau, J., Riley, C. D., & Atlas-Corbett, A. F. (2009). Socially indiscriminate attachment behavior in the strange situation: Convergent and discriminant validity in relation to caregiving risk, later behavior problems, and attachment insecurity. *Development and Psychopathology, 21,* 355–367.

Lynch, T. B. (2007). *PET/CT in clinical practice.* London: Springer-Verlag.

Mace, C. J., & Trimble, M. R. (1996). Ten-year prognosis of conversion disorder. *British Journal of Psychiatry, 169,* 282–288.

Machon, R. A., Mednick, S. A., & Huttunen, M. O. (1997). Adult major affective disorder after prenatal exposure to an influenza epidemic. *Archives of General Psychiatry, 54,* 322–328.

Machover, K. (1949). *Personality projection in the drawing of the human figure: A method of personality investigation.* Springfield, IL: Thomas.

Mackenzie, S., Wiegel, J. R., Mundt, M., Brown, D., Saewyc, E., . . . Fleming, M. (2011). Depression and suicide ideation among students accessing campus health care. *American Journal of Orthopsychiatry, 81,* 101–107.

Mackenzie, T. B., & Popkin, M. K. (1987). Suicide in the medical patient. *International Journal of Psychiatry in Medicine, 17,* 3–22.

Mackillop, J., Mattson, R. E., Anderson, E. J., Mackillop, E. J., Castelda, B. A., & Donovick, P. J. (2007). Multidimensional assessment of impulsivity in undergraduate hazardous drinkers and controls. *Journal of Studies on Alcohol and Drugs, 68,* 785–788.

Maddi, S. R. (2002). The story of hardiness: Twenty years of theorizing, research and practice. *Consulting Psychology Journal, 54,* 173–185.

Madsen, K. A., Weedn, A. E., & Crawford, P. B. (2010). Disparities in the peaks, plateaus, and declines in prevalence of high BMI among adolescents. *Pediatrics, 126,* 434–442.

Maher, W. B., & Maher, B. A. (1985). Psychopathology: I. From ancient times to the eighteenth century. In G. A. Kimble & K. Schlesinger (Eds.), *Topics in the history of psychology* (Vol. 2). Hillsdale, NJ: Erlbaum.

Mahgoub, N., & Hossain, A. (2006a). A 28-year-old woman and her 58-year-old mother with a shared psychotic disorder. *Psychiatric Annals, 36,* 306–309.

Mahgoub, N., & Hossain, A. (2006b). A 73-year-old woman with Parkinson's disease, psychotic symptoms. *Psychiatric Annals, 36,* 598–602.

Mahgoub, N., & Hossain, A. (2007). A 60-year-old woman with avoidant personality disorder. *Psychiatric Annals, 37*(1), 10–12.

Mahon, K., Burdick, K. E., & Szeszko, P. R. (2010). A role for white matter abnormalities in the pathophysiology of bipolar disorder. *Neuroscience and Biobehavioral Reviews, 34,* 533–554.

Mahoney, D. M. (2000). Panic disorder and self states: Clinical and research illustrations. *Clinical Social Work Journal, 28,* 197–212.

Maines, R. P. (1999). *The technology of orgasm: "Hysteria," the vibrator, and women's sexual satisfaction.* Baltimore: Johns Hopkins University Press.

Maj, M., Pirozzi, R., Magliano, L., Fiorillo, A., & Bartoli, L. (2007). Phenomenology and prognostic significance of delusions in major depressive disorder: A 10-year prospective follow-up study. *Journal of Clinical Psychiatry, 68,* 1411–1417.

Malamuth, N. M. (1981). Rape proclivity among males. *Journal of Social Issues, 37,* 138–157.

Malhotra, S., Singh, G., & Mohan, A. (2005). Somatoform and dissociative disorders in children and adolescents: A comparative study. *Indian Journal of Psychiatry, 47,* 39–43.

Malinauskas, B. M., Aeby, V. G., Overton, R. F., Carpenter-Aeby, T., & Barber-Heidal, K. (2007). A survey of energy drink consumption patterns among college students. *Nutrition Journal, 6,* 35.

Mallinckrodt, B., McCreary, B. A., & Robertson, A. K. (1995). Co-occurrence of eating disorders and incest: The role of attachment, family environment, and social competencies. *Journal of Counseling Psychology, 42,* 178–186.

Malyszczak, K., & Pawłowski, T. (2006). Distress and functioning in mixed anxiety and depressive disorder. *Psychiatry and Clinical Neuroscience, 60,* 168–173.

Man accused of stalking Kournikova. (2005, February 9). *Bellingham Herald,* p. B2.

Mancuso, C. E., Tanzi, M. G., & Gabay, M. (2004). Paradoxical reactions to benzodiazepines: Literature review and treatment options. *Pharmacotherapy, 24,* 1177–1185.

Mancuso, S. P., Knoesen, N. P., & Castle, D. J. (2010). Delusional versus nondelusional body dysmorphic disorder. *Comprehensive Psychiatry, 51,* 177–182.

Manderscheid, R. W., & Sonnenschein, M. A. (1992). *Mental health, United States, 1992.* Rockville, MD: U.S. Department of Health and Human Services.

Mann, J. J. (1989). Neurobiological models. In J. J. Mann (Ed.), *Models of depressive disorders: Psychological, biological, and genetic perspectives* (pp. 143–177). New York: Plenum Press.

Mann, J. J. (2003). Neurobiology of suicidal behavior. *Nature Reviews Neuroscience, 4,* 819–828.

Mann, J. J., Arango, V. A., Avenevoli, S., Brent, D. A., Champagne, F. A., . . . Wenzel, A. (2009). Candidate endophenotypes for genetic studies of suicidal behavior. *Biological Psychiatry, 65,* 556–563.

Mann, J. J., & Haghihgi, F. (2010). Genes and environment: Multiple pathways to psychopathology. *Biological Psychiatry, 68,* 403–404.

Mann, K., & Hermann, D. (2010). Individualized treatment in alcohol-dependent patients. *European Achieves of Psychiatry and Clinical Neuroscience, 2,* S116–120.

Mann, T., Tomiyama, A. J., Westling, E., Lew, A.-M., Samuels, B., & Chatman, J. (2007). Medicare's search for effective obesity treatments: Diets are not the answer. *American Psychologist, 62,* 220–233.

Marantz, S., & Coates, S. (1991). Mothers of boys with gender identity disorder: A comparison of matched controls. *Journal of the American Academy of Child and Adolescent Psychiatry, 30,* 310–315.

Marangell, L. B., Dennehy, E. B., Miyahara, S., Wisniewski, S. R., Bauer, M. S., Rapaport, M. H., & Allen, M. H. (2009). The functional impact of subsyndromal depressive symptoms in bipolar disorder: ata from STEP-BD. *Journal of Affective Disorders, 114,* 58–67.

Marangell, L. B., Martinez, M., Jurdi, R. A., & Zboyan, H. (2007). Neurostimulation therapies in depression: A review of new modalities. *Acta Psychiatrica Scandinavica, 116,* 174–181.

Marchand, A., Roberge, P., Primiano, S., & Germain, V. (2009). A randomized controlled clinical trial of standard group and brief cognitive-behavioral therapy for panic disorder with agoraphobia: A two–year follow-up. *Journal of Anxiety Disorders, 23,* 1139–1147.

Marchand, E., Ng, J., Rohde, P., & Stice, E. (2010). Effects of an indicated cognitive-behavioral depression prevention program are similar for Asian American, Latino, and European American adolescents. *Behavior Research and Therapy, 48,* 821–825.

Marchesi, C., Paini, M., Ruju, L., Rosi, L., Turrini, G., & Maggini, C. (2007). Predictors of the evolution towards schizophrenia or mood disorder in patients with schizophreniform disorder. *Schizophrenia Research, 97,* 1–5.

Marcus, J., Hans, S. L., Nagler, S., Auerbach, J. G., Mirsky, A. F., & Aubrey, A. (1987). Review of the NIMH Israeli kibbutz-city study and the Jerusalem Infant Developmental study. *Schizophrenia Bulletin, 13,* 425–437.

Marcus, M. D., & Kalarchian, M. A. (2003). Binge eating in children and adolescents. *International Journal of Eating Disorders, 34,* S47–S57.

Marcus, S. M., Gorman, J., Shear, M. K., Lewin, D., Martinez, J., . . . Woods, S. (2007). A comparison of medication side effect reports by panic disorder patients with and without concomitant cognitive behavior therapy. *American Journal of Psychiatry, 164,* 273–275.

Margolin, G., & Gordis, E. B. (2004). Children's exposure to violence in the family and community. *Current Directions in Psychological Science, 13,* 152–155.

Margraf, J., Barlow, D. H., Clark, D. M., & Telch, M. J. (1993). Psychological treatment of panic: Work in progress on outcome, active ingredients, and follow-up. *Behaviour Research and Therapy, 31,* 1–8.

Margraf, J., Ehlers, A., Roth, W. T., Clark, D. B., Sheikh, J., Agras, W. S., & Taylor, C. B. (1991). How "blind" are double-blind studies? *Journal of Consulting and Clinical Psychology, 59,* 184–187.

Maris, R. W. (2001). Suicide. In H. S. Friedman (Ed.), *Specialty articles from the encyclopedia of mental health.* San Diego: Academic Press.

Maris, R. W., Berman, A. L., & Silverman, M. M. (2000). *Comprehensive textbook of suicidology.* New York: Guilford Press.

Markarian, Y., Larson, M. J., Aldea, M. A., Baldwin, S. A., Good, D., . . . McKay, D. (2010). Multiple pathways to functional impairment in obsessive-compulsive disorder. *Clinical Psychology Review, 30,* 78–88.

Marlatt, G. A. (1978). Craving for alcohol, loss of control and relapse: A cognitive-behavioral analysis. In P. E. Nathan & G. A. Marlatt (Eds.), *Experimental and behavioral approaches to alcoholism.* New York: Plenum.

Marlatt, G. A. (1983). The controlled-drinking controversy: A commentary. *American Psychologist, 38,* 1097–1110.

Marlatt, G. A., Baer, J. S., Kivlahan, D. R., Dimeff, L. A., Larimer, M. E., . . . Williams, E. (1998). Screening and brief intervention for high-risk college student drinkers: Results from a two-year follow-up assessment. *Journal of Consulting and Clinical Psychology, 66,* 604–615.

Marlatt, G. A., Demming, B., & Reid, J. (1973). Loss-of-control drinking in alcoholics: An experimental analogue. *Journal of Abnormal Psychology, 81,* 233–241.

Marmar, C. R. (1988). Personality disorders. In H. H. Goldman (Ed.), *Review of general psychiatry* (pp. 401–424). Norwalk, CT: Appleton & Lange.

Marmot, M. G., & Syme, S. L. (1976). Acculturation and coronary heart disease in Japanese-Americans. *American Journal of Epidemiology, 104,* 225–247.

Marquardt, W. H. (2000). Update on migraine management. *Journal of the American Academy of Physician Assistants, 13,* 60–72.

Marr, A. J. (2006). Relaxation and muscular tension: A biobehavioristic explanation. *International Journal of Stress Management, 13,* 131–153.

Marris, E. (2006). Mysterious "Morgellons disease" prompts U.S. investigation. *Nature, 12,* p. 982.

Marsa, L. (2000, April 3). Children's health issue—The drug dilemma: The increased use of powerful psychiatric medicines in children under six has

raised concerns about over-medication and long-term effects. *Los Angeles Times,* p. S1.

Marsella, A. J. (1988). Ethnocultural issues in the assessment of psychopathology. In S. Wetzler (Ed.), *Measuring mental illness* (pp. 7–21). Washington, DC: American Psychiatric Press.

Marsh, D. T., & Johnson, D. L. (1997). The family experience of mental illness: Implications for intervention. *Professional Psychology: Research and Practice, 28,* 229–237.

Marsh, H. W., Hau, K. T., Sung, R. Y. T., & Yu, C. W. (2007). Childhood obesity, gender, actual-ideal body image discrepancies, and the physical self-concept in Hong Kong children: Cultural differences in the value of moderation. *Developmental Psychology, 43,* 647–662.

Marshall, J. (1998, February 23). Memoir of anorexia and bulimia is a harrowing story. *Seattle Post-Intelligencer,* pp. D1–D2.

Marshall, S. A., Landau, M. E., Carroll, C. G., Schwieters, B. (2008). *Conversion disorder.* Downloaded from: http://emedicine.medscape.com/article/287464-overview

Marsh, J. C. (1988). What have we learned about legislative remedies for rape? In R. A. Prentky & V. L. Quisey (Eds.), *Annals of the New York Academy of Sciences: Vol. 528. Human sexual aggression: Current perspectives* (pp. 79–110). Salem, MA: New York Academy of Sciences.

Marsh, W. K., Ketter, T. A., & Rasgon, N. L. (2009). Increased depressive symptoms in menopausal age women with bipolar disorder: Age and gender comparison. *Journal of Psychiatric Research, 43,* 798–802.

Marshall, R. D., Bryant, R. A., Amsel, L., Suh, E. J., Cook, J. M., & Neria, Y. (2007). The psychology of ongoing threat: Relative risk appraisal, the September 11 attacks, and terrorism-related fears. *American Psychologist, 62,* 304–316.

Marshall, W. L. (1988). Behavioral indices of habituation and sensitization during exposure to phobic stimuli. *Behaviour Research and Therapy, 26,* 67–77.

Marshall, W. L., Jones, R., Ward, T., Johnston, P., & Barbaree, H. E. (1991). Treatment outcome with sex offenders. *Clinical Psychology Review, 11,* 465–486.

Marsolek, M. R., White, N. C., & Litovitz, T. L. (2010). Inhalant abuse: Monitoring trends by using poison control data, 1993–2008. *Pediatrics, 125,* 906–913.

Martin, P. R., & MacLeod, C. (2009). Behavioral management of headache triggers: Avoidance of triggers is an inadequate strategy. *Clinical Psychology Review, 29,* 483–495.

Martin, P. R., & Seneviratne, H. M. (1997). Effects of food deprivation and a stressor on head pain. *Health Psychology, 16,* 310–318.

Martínez-Pedraza, F. L., & Carter, A. S. (2009). Autism spectrum disorders in young children. *Child and Adolescent Psychiatric Clinics of North America, 18,* 645–663.

Martins, S. S., & Alexandre, P. K. (2009). The association of ecstasy use and academic achievement among adolescents in two US national surveys. *Addictive Behaviors, 34,* 9–16.

Martinez, A. G., Piff, P. K., Mendoza-Denton, R., & Hinshaw, S. P. (2011). The power of a label: Mental illness diagnoses, ascribed humanity, and social rejection. *Journal of Social & Clinical Psychology, 30,* 1–23.

Martinez-Mallen, E., Castro-Fornieles, J., Lazaro, L., Moreno, E., Morer, A., . . . Toro, J. (2007). Cue exposure in the treatment of resistant adolescent bulimia nervosa. *International Journal of Eating Disorders, 40,* 596–601.

Martinez-Taboas, A. (2005). Psychogenic seizures in an espiritismo context: The role of culturally sensitive psychotherapy. *Psychotherapy: Theory, Research, Practice, Training, 42,* 6-13.

Marx, B. P., Foley, K. M., Feinstein, B. A., Wolf, E. J., Kaloupek, D. G., & Keane, T. M. (2010). Combat-related guilt mediates the relations between exposure to combat-related abuse violence and psychiatric diagnosis. *Depression and Anxiety, 27,* 287–293.

Mask, A. (2007). *A little extra weight is health help in some situations.* Retrieved from www.wral.com/lifestyles/healthteam/story/2009863

Maslow, A. H. (1954). *Motivation and personality.* New York: Harper & Row.

Mason, M. (2006, October 24). Is it disease or delusion? U.S. takes on a dilemma. *The New York Times.* Retrieved from http://www.nytimes.com/2006/10/24/health/24cons.html

Masserman, J., Yum, K., Nicholson, J., & Lee, S. (1944). Neurosis and alcohol: An experimental study. *American Journal of Psychiatry, 101,* 389–395.

Masterman, D. L., & Cummings, J. L. (2001). Alzheimer's disease. In G. O. Gabbard (Ed.), *Treatment of psychiatric disorders* (pp. 481–514). Washington, DC: American Psychiatric Press.

Masters, W. H., & Johnson, V. E. (1966). *Human sexual response.* Boston: Little, Brown.

Masters, W. H., & Johnson, V. E. (1970). *Human sexual inadequacy.* London: Churchill.

Masters, W. H., & Johnson, V. E. (1979). *Homosexuality in perspective.* Boston: Little, Brown.

Masters, W. H., Johnson, V. E., & Kolodny, R. C. (1992). *Human sexuality.* New York: Harper-Collins.

Masterson, J. F. (1981). *The narcissistic and borderline disorders: An integrated developmental approach.* New York: Brunner/Mazel.

Mataix-Cols, D., Frost, R. O., Pertusa, A., Clark, L. A., Saxena, S., . . . Wilhelm, S. (2010). Hoarding disorder: A new diagnosis for DSM-V? *Depression and Anxiety, 27,* 556–572.

Mataix-Cols, D., Marks, I. M., Greist, J. H., Kobak, K. A., & Baer, L. (2002). Obsessive compulsive symptom dimensions as predictors of compliance with and response to behavior therapy: Results from a controlled trial. *Psychotherapy and Psychosomatics, 71,* 255–261.

Mataix-Cols, D., Wooderson, S., Lawrence, N., Brammer, M. J., Speckens, A., & Phillips, M. L. (2004). Distinct neural correlates of washing, checking, and hoarding symptom dimensions in obsessive-compulsive disorder. *Archives of General Psychiatry, 61,* 564–576.

Materka, P. R. (1984). Families caring, coping with Alzheimer's disease. *Michigan Today, 16,* 13–14.

Mather, M., Canli, T., English, T., Whitfield, S., Wais, P., . . . Carstensen, L. L. (2004). Amygdala responses to emotionally valenced stimuli in older and younger adults. *Psychological Science, 15,* 259–263.

Mathews, C. A., & Grados, M. A. (2011). Familiality of Tourette syndrome, obsessive-compulsive disorder and attention-deficit/hyperactivity disorder: Heritability analysis in a large sib-pair sample. *Journal of the American Academy of Child and Adolescent Psychiatry, 50,* 46–54.

Maulik, P. K., Mascarenhas, M. N., Mathers, C. D., Dua, T., & Saxena, S. (2011). Prevalence of intellectual disability: A meta-analysis of population-based studies. *Research on Developmental Disabilities, 32,* 419–436.

May, D. E., & Kratochvil, C. J. (2010). Attention-deficit hyperactivity disorder: Recent advances in paediatric pharmacotherapy. *Drugs, 70,* 15–40.

May, P. A., Gossage, J. P., Kalberg, W. O, Robinson, L. K., Buckley, D., Manning, M., & Hoyme, H. E. (2009). Prevalence and epidemiologic characteristics of FASD from various research methods with an emphasis on recent in-school studies. *Developmental Disabilities Research Reviews, 15,* 176–192.

May, R. (1967). *Psychology and the human dilemma.* New York: Van Nostrand.

Mayberry, L. J., Horowitz, J. A., & Declercq, E. J. (2007). Depression symptom prevalence and demographic risk factors among U.S. women during the first 2 years postpartum. *Journal of Obstetric, Gynecological and Neonatal Nursing, 36,* 542–549.

Mayhew, S. L., & Gilbert, P. (2008). Compassionate mind training with people who hear malevolent voices: A case series report. *Clinical Psychology and Psychotherapy, 15,* 113–138.

Mayo, C., Kaye, A. D., Conrad, E., Baluch, A., & Frost, E. (2010). Update on anesthesia considerations for electroconvulsive therapy. *Middle Eastern Journal of Anesthesiology, 20,* 493–498.

Mazure, C. M. (1998). Life stressors as risk factors in depression. *Clinical Psychology: Science and Practice, 5,* 291–313.

McAnulty, R. D., & Burnette, M. M. (2003). *Fundamentals of human sexuality: Making healthy decisions.* New York: Allyn & Bacon.

McAnulty, R. D., & Burnette, M. M. (2004). *Exploring human sexuality: Making healthy decisions.* New York: Allyn & Bacon.

McBride, K. R., Reece, M., & Sanders, S. (2008). Using the sexual compulsivity scale to predict outcomes of sexual behavior in young adults. *Sexual Addiction & Compulsivity, 15,* 97–115.

McBurnett, K., & Pfiffner, L. J. (2009). Treatment of aggressive ADHD in children and adolescents: Conceptualization and treatment of comorbid behavior disorders. *Postgraduate Medicine, 121,* 158–165.

McCabe, H. T., Wilsnack, S. E., West, B. T., & Boyd, C. J. (2010). Victimization and substance use disorders in a national sample of heterosexual and sexual minority women and men. *Addiction, 105*(12), 2130–2140. doi: 10.1111/j.1360–0443.2010.03088.x

McCabe, R., & Priebe, S. (2004). Explanatory models of illness in schizophrenia: Comparison of four ethnic groups. *British Journal of Psychiatry, 185,* 25–30.

McCabe, R. E., Miller, J. L., Laugesen, N., Antony, M. M., & Young, L. (2010). The relationship between anxiety disorders in adults and recalled childhood teasing. *Journal of Anxiety Disorders, 24,* 238–243.

McCabe, S. E., Hughes, T. L., Bostwick, W. B., West, B. T., & Boyd, C. J. (2009). Sexual orientation, substance use behaviors and substance dependence in the United States. *Addiction, 104,* 1333–1345.

McCabe, S. E., West, B. T., Morales, M., Cranford, J. A., & Boyd, C. J. (2007). Does early onset of non-medical use of prescription drugs predict subsequent prescription drug abuse and dependence? Results from a national study. *Addiction, 102,* 1920–1930.

McCann, D., Barrett, A., Cooper, A., Crumpler, D., Dalen, L., . . . Stevenon, J. (2007). Food additives and hyperactive behaviour in 3-year-old and 8/9-year-old children in the community: A randomised, double-blinded, placebo-controlled trial. *Lancet, 370,* 1560–1567.

McCarron, R. M. (2006). Somatization in the primary care setting. *Psychiatric Times, 23,* 32–36.

McCarthy, K. (2002). Family dynamics affect asthma in at-risk kids. *Psychology Today, 35,* 30–31.

McLellan, A. T., & Meyers, K. (2004). Contemporary addiction treatment: A review of systems problems for adults and adolescents. *Biological Psychiatry, 56,* 764–770.

McCloud, A., Barnaby, B., Omu, N., Drumond, C., & Aboud, A. (2004). Relationship between alcohol use disorders and suicidality in a psychiatric population. *British Journal of Psychiatry, 184,* 439–445.

McClung, C. A. (2007). Circadian genes, rhythms and the biology of mood disorders. *Pharmacology and Therapeutics, 114,* 222–232.

McCracken, L. M., & Larkin, K. T. (1991). Treatment of paruresis with in vivo desensitization: A case report. *Journal of Behavior Therapy and Experimental Psychiatry, 22,* 57–62.

McCrady, B. S. (1994). Alcoholics Anonymous and behavior therapy: Can habits be treated as diseases? Can diseases be treated as habits? *Journal of Consulting and Clinical Psychology, 62,* 1159–1166.

McCullough, J. P., Klein, D. N., Borian, F. E., Howland, R. H., Riso, L. P., Keller, M. B., & Banks, P. (2008). Group comparisons of DSM-IV subtypes of chronic depression: Validity of the distinctions Part II. *Journal of Abnormal Psychology, 112,* 614–622.

McCullough, P. K., & Maltsberger, J. T. (2001). Obsessive-compulsive personality disorder. In G. O. Gabbard (Ed.), *Treatment of psychiatric disorders* (pp. 2341–2351). Washington, DC: American Psychiatric Press.

McDaniel, S. H., & Speice, J. (2001). What family psychology has to offer women's health: The examples of conversion, somatization, infertility treatment, and genetic testing. *Professional Psychology: Research and Practice, 32,* 44–51.

McDowell, M. A., Fryar, C. D., Ogden, C. L., & Flegal, K. M. (2008). Anthropometric reference data for children and adults: United States, 2003–2006. *National Health Statistics Reports, 10.*

McElroy, S. L., & Arnold, L. M. (2001). Impulse-control disorders. In G. O. Gabbard (Ed.), *Treatment of psychiatric disorders* (pp. 2435–2471). Washington, DC: American Psychiatric Press.

McElroy, S. L., Kotwal, R., Kaneria, R., & Keck, P. E. (2006). Antidepressants and suicidal behavior in bipolar disorder. *Bipolar Disorders, 8,* 596–617.

McFarlane, A. C., Ellis, N., Barton, C., Browne, D., & Van Hooff, M. (2008). The conundrum of medically unexplained symptoms: Questions to consider. *Psychosomatics, 49,* 369–377.

McGorm, K., Burton, C., Weller, D., Murray, G., and Sharpe, M. (2010). Patients repeatedly referred to secondary care with symptoms unexplained by organic disease: Prevalence, characteristics, and referral pattern. *Family Practice, 27,* 479–486.

McGilley, B. M., & Pryor, T. L. (1998). Assessment and treatment of bulimia nervosa. *American Family Physician, 57,* 2743–2750.

McGlashan, T. H. (2006). Dr. McGlashan replies. *American Journal of Psychiatry, 163,* 1038.

McGlashan, T. H., Addington, J., Cannon, T., Heinimaa, M., McGorry, P., O'Brien, M., . . . Yung, A. (2007). Recruitment and treatment practices for help-seeking "prodomal" patients. *Schizophrenia Bulletin, 33,* 715–726.

McGlashan, T. H., Zipursky, R. B., Perkins, D., Addington, J., Miller, T., Woods, S. W., . . . Breier, A. (2006). Randomized, double-blind trial of olanzapine versus placebo in patients prodromally symptomatic for psychosis. *American Journal of Psychiatry, 163,* 790–799.

McGoldrick, M., Giordano, J., & Garcia-Preto, N. (2005). *Ethnicity and family therapy.* New York: Guilford Press.

McGonagle, K. A., & Kessler, R. C. (1990). Chronic stress, acute stress, and depressive symptoms. *American Journal of Community Psychology, 18,* 681–706.

McGrath, J., Welham, J., Scott, J., Varghese, D., Degenhardt, L., Hayatbakhsh, M. R., . . . Najman, J. M. (2010). Association between cannabis use and psychosis-related outcomes using sibling pair analysis in a cohort of young adults. *Archives of General Psychiatry, 67,* 440–447.

McGrath, M. (2005). *A systematic review of the prevalence of schizophrenia.* Retrieved from http://medicine. plosjournals.org/perlserv/?request=getdocument&doi=10.1371/journal.pmed. 0020145

McGue, M., & Christensen, K. (1997). Genetic and environmental contributions to depression symptomology: Evidence from Danish twins 75 years of age and older. *Journal of Abnormal Psychology, 106,* 439–448.

McGue, M., Pickens, R. W., & Svikis, D. S. (1992). Sex and age effects on the inheritance of alcohol problems: A twin study. *Journal of Abnormal Psychology, 101,* 3–17.

McGuire, L., Junginger, J., Adams, S. G., Burright, R., & Donovick, P. (2001). Delusions and delusional reasoning. *Journal of Abnormal Psychology, 110,* 259–266.

McGuire, R. J., Carlisle, J. M., & Young, B. G. (1965). Sexual deviations as conditioned behavior: A hypothesis. *Behavior Research and Therapy, 2,* 185–190.

McHugh, M. D. (2007). Readiness for change and short-term outcomes of female adolescents in residential treatment for anorexia nervosa. *International Journal of Eating Disorders, 40,* 602–605.

McHugh, P. R. (2009). Multiple personality disorder (dissociative identity disorder). Retrieved from http://www.psycom.net/mchugh.html

McIntosh, J. L. (1991). Epidemiology of suicide in the U.S. In A. A. Leenaars (Ed.), *Lifespan perspectives of suicide.* New York: Plenum.

McIntosh, J. L. (1992). Epidemiology of suicide in the elderly. *Suicide and Life-Threatening Behavior, 22,* 15–35.

McIntosh, V. V. W., Carter, F. A., Bulik, C. M., Frampton, C. M. A., & Joyce, P. R. (2010). Five-year outcome of cognitive behavioral therapy and exposure with response: Prevention for bulimia nervosa. *Psychological Medicine, 41(5),* 1061–1071. doi: 10.1017/S0033291710001583

McKnight Investigators. (2003). Risk factors for the onset of eating disorders in adolescent girls: Results of the McKnight longitudinal risk factor study. *American Journal of Psychiatry, 160,* 248–254.

McLaughlin, K. A., Green, J. G., Gruber, M. J., Sampson, N. A., Zaslavsky, A. M., & Kessler, R. C. (2010). Childhood adversities and adult psychiatric disorders in the national comorbidity survey replication II: Associations with persistence of DSM-IV disorders. *Archives of General Psychiatry, 67(2),* 124–132.

McLaughlin, K. A., & Hatzenbuehler, M. L. (2009). Stressful life events, anxiety sensitivity, and internalizing symptoms in adolescents. *Journal of Abnormal Psychology, 118,* 659–669.

McLaughlin, K. A., Hatzenbuehler, M. L., & Keyes, K. M. (2010). Responses to discrimination and psychiatric disorders among Black, Hispanic, female, and lesbian, gay, and bisexual individuals. *American Journal of Public Health, 100,* 1477–1484.

McLaughlin, K. A., Mennin, D. S., & Farach, F. J. (2007). The contributory role of worry in emotion generation and dysregulation in generalized anxiety disorder. *Behavior Research and Therapy, 45,* 1735–1752.

McLean, C. P., & Anderson, E. R. (2009). Brave men and timid women? A review of gender differences in fear and anxiety. *Clinical Psychology Review, 29,* 496–505.

McLean, S. A., Paxton, S. J., & Wertheim, E. H. (2010). Factors associated with body dissatisfaction and disordered eating in women in midlife. *International Journal of Eating Disorders, 43,* 527–536.

McMillan, D., & Lee, R. (2010). A systematic review of behavior experiments vs. exposure alone in the treatment of anxiety disorders: A case of exposure while wearing the emperor's new clothes? *Clinical Psychology Review, 30,* 467–478.

McNally, R. J. (2007). Dispelling confusion about traumatic dissociative amnesia. *Mayo Clinic Proceedings, 82,* 1083–1087.

McNally, R. J., Clancy, S. A., Schacter, D. L., & Pitman, R. K. (2000). Personality profiles, dissociation, and absorption in women reporting repressed, recovered, or continuous memories of childhood sexual abuse. *Journal of Consulting and Clinical Psychology, 68,* 1033–1037.

McNamee, H. B., Mello, N. K., & Mendelson, J. H. (1968). Experimental analysis of drinking patterns of alcoholics: Concurrent psychiatric observations. *American Journal of Psychiatry, 124,* 1063–1069.

McNiel, D. E., & Binder, R. L. (1991). Clinical assessment of the risk of violence among psychiatric inpatients. *American Journal of Psychiatry, 148,* 1317–1321.

McWilliams, N. (2006). A movement toward more clinically relevant assessment. *National Psychologist, 15,* 6–7.

Mead, M. (1928). *Coming of age in Samoa.* New York: Blue Ribbon Press.

Meehl, P. (1970). Psychology and criminal law. *University of Richmond Law Review, 5,* 1–30.

Meehl, P. E. (1962). Schizotaxia, schizotypia, schizophrenia. *American Psychologist, 17,* 827–838.

Meeks, J. (2004). *AFPPA 2003: Headache management—Evaluation and treatment.* Retrieved from www.medscape.com/viewarticle/467744

Mégarbané, A., Ravel, A., Mircher, C., Sturtz, F., Grattau, Y., . . . Mobley W. C. (2009). The 50th anniversary of the discovery of trisomy 21: The past, present, and future of research and treatment of Down syndrome. *Genetic Medicine, 11,* 611–616.

Mehler, P. S. (2003). Bulimia nervosa. *New England Journal of Medicine, 349,* 875–881.

Meilleur, A. A., & Fombonne, E. J. (2009). Regression of language and non-language skills in pervasive developmental disorders. *Intellectual Disabilities Research, 53,* 115–124.

Meiser-Stedman, R., Dalgleish, T., Gluckman, E., Yule, W., & Smith, P. (2009). Maladaptive cognitive appraisals mediate the evolution of post-traumatic stress reactions: A 6-month follow-up of child and adolescent assault and motor vehicle accident survivors. *Journal of Abnormal Psychology, 118,* 778–787.

Meissner, W. W. (2001). Paranoid personality disorder. In G. O. Gabbard (Ed.), *Treatment of psychiatric disorders* (pp. 2227–2236). Washington, DC: American Psychiatric Press.

Melchert, T. P. (2007). Strengthening the scientific foundations of professional psychology: Time for the next steps. *Professional Psychology: Research and Practice, 38,* 34–43.

Melgo, C. (2009). Ralph Lauren model Filippa Hamilton: I was fired because I was too fat. *New York Daily News.* Retrieved from http://www.nydailynews.com/lifestyle/fashion/2009/10/14/2009

Melka, S. E., Lancaster, S. L., Adams, L. J., Howarth, E. A., & Rodriguez, B. F. (2010). Social anxiety across ethnicity: A confirmatory factor analysis of the FNE and SAD. *Journal of Anxiety Disorders, 24,* 680–685.

Meloy, J. R. (2001). Antisocial personality disorder. In G. O. Gabbard (Ed.), *Treatment of psychiatric disorders* (pp. 2251–2271). Washington, DC: American Psychiatric Press.

Meltzer, H. Y. (2000). Side effects of antipsychotic medications: Physician's choice of medication and patient compliance. *Journal of Clinical Psychiatry, 61,* 3–4.

Memon, M. A., & Larson, M. (2009). Brief psychotic disorder. Retrieved from http://emedicine.medscape.com/article/294416-print

Mendlowicz, M. V., Rapaport, M. H., Fontenelle, L., Jean-Louis, G., & De Morales, T. M. (2002). Amnesia and neonaticide. *American Journal of Psychiatry, 159,* 498.

Menke, R., & Flynn, H. (2009). Relationships between stigma, depression, and treatment in white and African American primary care patients. *Journal of Nervous and Mental Diseases, 197,* 407–411.

Menkedick, S. (2010). Does BMI really reflect health? Retrieved from http://womensrights.change.org/blog/view/does_bmi_really_reflect_health

Menzies, R. G., & Clarke, J. C. (1995). Danger expectancies and insight in acrophobia. *Behaviour Research and Therapy, 33,* 215–221.

Mercan, S., Altunay, I. K., Taskintuna, N., Ogutcen, O., & Kayaoglu, S. (2007). Atypical antipsychotic drugs in the treatment of delusional parasitosis. *International Journal of Psychiatry in Medicine, 37,* 29–37.

Merikangas, K. R., Akiskal, H. S., Angst, J., Greenberg, P. E., Hirschfeld, R. M., Petukhova, M., & Kessler, R. C. (2007). Lifetime and 12-month prevalence of bipolar spectrum disorder in the National Comorbidity Survey replication. *Archives of General Psychiatry, 64,* 543–552.

Merikangas, K. R., He, Jian-ping, Burstein, M., Swanson, S. A., Avenevoli, S., Cui, L., . . . Swendsen, J. (2010). Lifetime prevalence of mental disorders in U.S. Adolescents: Results from the National Comorbidity Survey Replication-Adolescent Supplement (NCS-A). *Journal of the Academy of Child & Adolescent Psychiatry, 49,* 980–989.

Merikangas, K. R., He, J.-P., Burstein, M., Swanson, S. A., Avenevoli, S., . . . Swendsen, J. (2011a). Lifetime prevalence of mental disorders in U.S. adolescents: Results from the National Comorbidity Survey Replication—Adolescent Supplement (NCS-A). *Journal of American Academy of Child and Adolescent Psychiatry, 49,* 980–989.

Merikangas, K. R., Jin, R., He, J. P., Kessler, R. C., Lee, S., . . . Zarkov, Z. (2011b). Prevalence and correlates of bipolar spectrum disorder in the world mental health survey initiative. *Archives of General Psychiatry, 68,* 241–51.

Merikangas, K. R., He, J., Burstein, M., Swendsen, J., Avenevoli, S., Case, B., . . . Olfson, M. (2011c). Service utilization for lifetime mental disorders in U.S. adolescents: Results of the National Comorbidity Survey-Adolescent Supplement (NCS-A). *American Academy of Child and Adolescent Psychiatry, 50,* 32–45.

Merritt, M. M., Bennett, G. G., Jr., Williams, R. B., Edwards, C. L., & Sollers, J. J., III (2006). Perceived racism and cardiovascular reactivity and recovery to personally relevant stress. *Health Psychology, 25,* 364–369.

Merryman, K. (1997, July 17). Medical experts say Roberts may well have amnesia: Parts of her life match profile of person who might lose memory. *News Tribune,* pp. A8–A9.

Merskey, H. (1992). The manufacture of personalities: The production of multiple personality disorder. *British Journal of Psychiatry, 160,* 327–340.

Merskey, H. (1995). Multiple personality disorder and false memory syndrome. *British Journal of Psychiatry, 166,* 281–283.

Merten, J., & Brunnhuber, S. (2004). Facial expression and experience of emotions in psychodynamic interviews with patients suffering from a pain disorder. *Psychopathology, 37,* 266–271.

Messer, S. B. (2001). Empirically supported treatments: What's a nonbehaviorist to do? In B. D. Slife, R. N. Williams, & S. H. Barlow (Eds.), *Critical issues in psychotherapy* (pp. 45–59). Thousand Oaks, CA: Sage.

Messinger, J. W., Tremeau, F., Antonius, D., Mendelsohn, E., Prudent, V., . . . Malaspina, D. (2011). Avolition and expressive deficits capture negative symptom phenomenology: Implications for DSM-V and schizophrenia research. *Clinical Psychology Review, 31,* 161–168.

Meston, C. M., Seal, B. N., & Hamilton, L. D. (2008). Problems with arousal and orgasm in women. In D. Rowland & L. Incrocci (Eds.), *Handbook of sexual and gender identity disorders* (pp. 188–219). Hoboken, NJ: Wiley.

Meuret, A. E., Rosenfield, D., Hofman, S. G., Seidel, A., & Bhaskara (2010). Respiratory and cognitive mediators of treatment change in panic disorder: Evidence for intervention specificity. *Journal of Consulting and Clinical Psychology, 78,* 691–704.

Mewton, L., Slade, T., McBride, O., Grove, R., & Teesson, M. (2011). An evaluation of the proposed DSM-5 alcohol use disorder criteria using Australian national data. *Addiction, 106*(5), 941–950. doi: 10.111/j.1360–0443.2010.03340.x

Meyer, G. J., Finn, S. E., Eyde, L. D., Kay, G. G., Moreland, K. L., . . . Reed, G. M. (2001). Psychological testing and psychological assessment: A review of evidence and issues. *American Psychologist, 56,* 128–165.

Meyer, G. J., Finn, S. E., Eyde, L. D., Kay, G. G., Moreland, K. L., Dies, R. R., et al. (2003). Psychological testing and psychological assessment: A review of the evidence and issues. In A. E. Kazdin (Ed.), *Methodological issues and strategies in clinical research* (pp. 265–345). Washington, DC: American Psychological Association.

Meyer, J., & Peter, D. (1979). Sex reassignment: Follow-up. *Archives of General Psychiatry, 36,* 1010–1015.

Meyer, R. G., & Osborne, Y. V. H. (1982). *Case studies in abnormal behavior.* Boston: Allyn & Bacon.

Meyer, S. E, Carlson, G. A., Youngstrom, E., Ronsaville, D. S., Martinez, P. E., . . . Radke-Yarrow, M. (2009). Long-term outcomes of youth who manifested the CBCL-pediatric bipolar disorder phenotype during childhood and/or adolescence. *Journal of Affective Disorders, 113,* 227–235.

Meyer, W. S., & Keith, C. R. (1991). Homosexual and preoedipal issues in the psychoanalytic psychotherapy of a female-to-male transsexual. In C. W. Socarides & V. D. Volkan (Eds.), *The homosexualities and the therapeutic process* (pp. 75–96). Madison, CT: International Universities Press.

Meyer-Bahlburg, H. F. L. (2009). From mental disorder to iatrogenic hypogonadism: Dilemmas in conceptualizing gender identity variants as psychiatric conditions. *Archives of Sexual Behavior, 39*(2), 461–476. doi:10.1007/s10508-009-9532-4

Meyers, B. S., Flint, A. J., Rothschild, A. J., Mulsant, B. H., Whyte, E. M., . . . Heo, M. (2009). A double-blind randomized controlled trial of olanzapine plus sertraline vs olanzapine plus placebo for psychotic depression: The study of pharmacotherapy of psychotic depression (STOP-PD). *Archives of General Psychiatry, 66,* 838–847.

Meyers, W. A. (1991). A case history of a man who made obscene telephone calls and practiced frotteurism. In G. I. Fogel & W. A. Myers (Eds.), *Perversions and near-perversions in clinical practice* (pp. 109–126). New Haven, CT: Yale University Press.

Mezulis, A., Funasaki, K., Charbonneau, A., & Hyde, J. (2010). Gender differences in the cognitive vulnerability-stress model of depression in the transition to adolescence. *Cognitive Therapy and Research, 34,* 501–514.

Mezulis, A. H., Priess, H. A., & Hyde, J. S. (2011). Rumination mediates the relationship between infant temperament and adolescent depressive symptoms. *Depression Research and Treatment,* 487873.

Mezzich. (2002). International surveys on the use of ICD-10 and related diagnostic systems. *Psychopathology, 35,* 72–75.

Michael, R. T., Gagnon, J. H., Laumann, E. O., & Kolata, G. (1994). *Sex in America: A definitive survey.* New York: Little, Brown.

Midei, A. J., & Matthews, K. A. (2009). Social relationships and negative emotional traits are associated with central adiposity and arterial stiffness in health adolescents. *Health Psychology, 28,* 347–353.

Miettunen, J., Tormanen, S., Murray, G. K., Jones, P. B., Maki, P., . . . Veijola, J. (2008). Association of cannabis use with prodromal symptoms of psychosis in adolescence. *British Journal of Psychiatry, 192,* 470–471.

Mihalopoulos, C., Harris, M., Henry, L., Harrigan, S., & McGorry, P. (2009). Is early intervention in psychosis cost-effective over the long term? *Schizophrenia Bulletin, 35,* 909–918.

Miklowitz, D. J. (1994). Family risk indicators in schizophrenia. *Schizophrenia Bulletin, 20,* 137–148.

Miklowitz, D. J., & Johnson, S. L. (2009). Social and familial factors in the course of bipolar disorder: Basic processes and relevant interventions. *Clinical Psychology, 16,* 281–296.

Mikton, C., & Grounds, A. (2007). Cross-cultural clinical judgment bias in personality disorder diagnosis by forensic psychiatrists in the UK: A case-vignette study. *Journal of Personality Disorders, 21,* 400–417.

Mikulas, W. L. (2006). Integrating the world's psychologies. In L. T. Hoshman (Ed.), *Culture, psychotherapy and counseling* (pp. 91–111). Thousand Oaks, CA: Sage.

Mileno, M. D., Barnowski, C., Fiore, T., Gormley, J., Rich, J. D., Emgushov, R.-T., & Carpenter, C. C. (2001). Factitious HIV syndrome in young women. *AIDS Reader, 11,* 263–268.

Milillo, D. (2008). Sexuality sells: A content analysis of lesbian and heterosexual women's bodies in magazine advertisements. *Journal of Lesbian Studies, 12,* 381–386.

Milin, R., Manion, I., Dare, G., & Walker, S. (2008). Prospective assessment of cannabis withdrawal in adolescents with cannabis dependence: A pilot study. *Journal of American Academy of Child and Adolescent Psychiatry, 47,* 174–178.

Miller, A. H. (2010). Depression and immunity: A role for T cells? *Brain, Behavior and Immunity, 24,* 1–8.

Miller, B. J., & Lundgren, J. D. (2010). An experimental study of the role of weight bias in candidate evaluation. *Obesity, 18,* 712–718.

Miller, D. D., Caroff, S. N., Davis, S. M., Rosenheck, R. A., McEvoy, J. P., . . . Liberman, J. A. (2008). Extrapyramidal side-effects of antipsychotics in a randomized trial. *British Journal of Psychiatry, 193,* 279–288.

Miller, D. J., & Thelen, M. H. (1986). Knowledge and beliefs about confidentiality in psychotherapy. *Professional Psychology, 17,* 15–19.

Miller, G. A., & Keller, J. (2000). Psychology and neuroscience: Making peace. *Current Directions in Psychological Science, 9,* 212–215.

Miller, G. E., Chen, E., & Zhou, E. S. (2007). If it goes up, must it come down? Chronic stress and the hypothalamic-pituitary-adrenocortical axis in humans. *Psychological Bulletin, 133,* 25–45.

Miller, H. L., Coombs, D. W., & Leeper, J. D. (1984). An analysis of the effects of suicide prevention facilities on suicide rates in the United States. *American Journal of Public Health, 74,* 340–343.

Miller, J. M., Brennan, K. G., Ogden, T. R., Oquendo, M. A., Sullivan, G. M., Mann, J. J., & Parsey, R. V. (2009). Elevated serotonin 1A binding in remitted major depressive disorder: Evidence for a trait biological abnormality. *Neuropsychopharmacology, 34,* 2275–2284.

Miller, J. N., & Ozonoff, S. (2000). The external validity of Asperger disorder: Lack of evidence from the domain of neuropsychology. *Journal of Abnormal Psychology, 109,* 227–238.

Miller, M., & Kantrowitz, B. (1999, January 25). Unmasking Sybil. *Newsweek,* pp. 66–68.

Miller, M. N., & Pumariega, A. J. (2001). Culture and eating disorders: A historical and cross-cultural review. *Psychiatry, 64,* 93–110.

Miller, R. R., & Ely, E. W. (2007). Delirium and cognitive dysfunction in the intensive care unit. *Current Psychiatry Reports, 9,* 26–34.

Miller, S. B., Friese, M., Dolgoy, L., Sita, A., Lavoie, K., & Campbell, T. (1998). Hostility, sodium consumption, and cardiovascular response to interpersonal stress. *Psychosomatic Medicine, 60,* 71–77.

Millichap, J. G. (2008). Etiologic classification of attention-deficit/hyperactivity disorder. *Pediatrics, 121,* e358–65.

Millon, T., Grossman, S., Millon, C., Meagher, S., & Ramnath, R. (2004). *Personality disorders in modern life.* Hoboken, NJ: Wiley.

Miller, T. C., & Zwerdling, D. (2010, June 9) With traumatic brain injuries, soldiers face battle for care. *National Public Radio.* Retrieved from http://www.npr.org/templates/story/story.php?storyId=127542820

Milrod, B., Leon, A. C., Busch, F., Rudden, M., Schwalberg, M., . . . Shear, M. K. (2007). A randomized controlled clinical trial of psychoanalytic psychotherapy for panic disorder. *American Journal of Psychiatry, 164,* 265–272.

Milstein, V. (1988). EEG topography in patients with aggressive violent behavior. In T. E. Moffitt & S. A. Mednick (Eds.), *Biological contributions to crime causation* (pp. 121–134). Boston: Nijhoff.

Milstone, C. (1997). Sybil minds. *Saturday Night, 112,* 35–42.

Mineka, S., & Sutton, S. K. (1992). Cognitive biases and the emotional disorders. *Psychological Science, 3*(1), 65–69.

Mineka, S., & Zinbarg, R. (2006). A contemporary learning theory perspective on the etiology of anxiety disorders. *American Psychologist, 61,* 10–26.

Mintz, A. R., Dobson, K. S., & Romney, D. M. (2003). Insight in schizophrenia: A meta-analysis. *Schizophrenia Research, 61,* 75–88.

Mintz, J., Mintz, L., & Goldstein, M. (1987). Expressed emotion and relapse in first episodes of schizophrenia. *British Journal of Psychiatry, 151,* 314–320.

Minuchin, S. (1974). *Families and family therapy.* Cambridge, MA: Harvard University Press.

Mireault, G., Rooney, S., Kouwenhoven, K., & Hannan, C. (2008). Oppositional behavior and anxiety in boys and girls: A cross-sectional study in two community samples. *Child Psychiatry and Human Development, 39,* 519–527.

Mission Australia. (2010). National survey of young Australians 2010. Retrieved from https://www.missionaustralia.com.au/downloads/national-survey-of-young-australians/271-2010

Mitchell, A. (1998, June 17). Controversy over Lott's view of homosexuality. *The New York Times,* p. 24.

Mitrouska, I., Bouloukaki, I., & Siafakas, N. M. (2007). Pharmacological approaches to smoking cessation. *Pulmonary Pharmacological Therapy, 20,* 220–32.

Mittal, V. A., Ellman, L. M., & Cannon, T. D. (2008). Gene-environment interaction and covariation in schizophrenia: The role of obstetric complications. *Schizophrenia Bulletin, 34,* 1083–1094.

Modell, S., & Lauer, C. J. (2007). Rapid eye movement (REM) sleep: An endophenotype for depression. *Current Psychiatry Reports, 9,* 480–485.

Modestin, J. (1992). Multiple personality disorder in Switzerland. *American Journal of Psychiatry, 149,* 88–92.

Moens, E., Braet, C., & Van Winckel, M. (2010). An 8 year follow-up of treated obese children: Children's process and parental predictors of successful treatment. *Behaviour Research and Therapy, 48,* 626–633.

Moffitt, T. E. (2005). The new look of behavioral genetics in developmental psychopathology: Gene-environment interplay in antisocial behaviors. *Psychological Bulletin, 131,* 533–554.

Mogg, K., Philippot, P., & Bradley, B. P. (2004). Selective attention to angry faces in clinical social phobia. *Journal of Abnormal Behavior, 113,* 160–165.

Mohr, D. C., & Beutler, L. E. (1990). Erectile dysfunction: A review of diagnostic and treatment procedures. *Clinical Psychology Review, 10,* 123–150.

Mohr, D. C., Cox, D., & Merluzzi, N. (2005). Self-injection anxiety training: Successful treatment for patients unable to self-inject injectable medication. *Multiple Sclerosis, 11,* 182–185.

Mojtabai, R. (2005). Perceived reasons for loss of housing and continued homelessness among homeless persons with mental illness. *Psychiatric Services, 56,* 172–178.

Mojtabai, R., & Olfson, M. (2010). National trends in psychotropic medication polypharmacy in office-based psychiatry. *Archives of General Psychiatry, 67,* 26–36.

Mommersteeg, P. M. G., Keijsers, G. P. J., Heijnen, C. J., Verbraak, M. J. P. M., & van Doornen, L. J. P. (2006). Cortisol deviations in people with burnout before and after psychotherapy: A pilot study. *Health Psychology, 25,* 243–248.

Monahan, J. (1981). *The clinical prediction of violent behavior.* Rockville, MD: National Institute of Mental Health.

Monahan, J. (1993). Limiting therapist exposure to Tarasoff liability: Guidelines for risk containment. *American Psychologist, 48,* 242–250.

Monahan, J., & Walker, L. (Eds.). (1990). *Social science in law: Cases and materials* (2nd ed.). Westbury, NJ: Foundation Press.

Mond, J. M., Peterson, C. B., & Hay, P. J. (2010). Prior use of extreme weight-control behaviors in a community sample of women with binge eating disorder or subthreshold binge eating disorder: A descriptive study. *International Journal of Eating Disorders, 43,* 440–446.

Le Monde (2009, May 16). La transsexualité ne sera plus classée comme affectation psychiatrique. *Le Monde.* Retrieved from http://www.lemonde.fr/societe/article/2009/05/16/la-transsexualite-ne-sera-plus-classee-comme-affectation-psychiatrique_1193860_3224.html

Money, J. (1987). Masochism: On the childhood origin of paraphilia, opponent-process theory, and antiandrogen therapy. *Journal of Sex Research, 23,* 273–275.

Money, J. (1996). *Lovemaps: Clinical concepts of sexual/erotic health and pathology, paraphilia, and gender transpositions in childhood, adolescence, and maturity.* New York: Irvington.

Monk, C. S., Nelson, E. E., McClure, E. B., Mogg, K., Bradley, B. P., . . . Pine, D. S. (2006). Ventrolateral prefrontal cortex activation and attentional bias in response to angry faces in adolescents with generalized anxiety disorder. *American Journal of Psychiatry, 163,* 1091–1097.

Monopoli, J. (2005). Managing hypochondriasis in elderly clients. *Journal of Contemporary Psychotherapy, 35,* 285–300.

Monot, M. J., Quirk, S. W., Hoerger, M., & Brewer, L. (2009). Racial bias in personality assessment: Using the MMPI-2 to predict psychiatric diagnosis of African American and Caucasian chemical dependency inpatients. *Psychological Assessment, 21,* 137–151.

Monroe, S. M., Slavich, G. M., Torres, L. D., & Gotlib, I. H. (2007). Severe life events predict specific patterns of change in cognitive biases in major depression. *Psychological Medicine, 37,* 863–871.

Monroe, S. M., Thase, M. E., & Simons, A. D. (1992). Social factors and the psychobiology of depression: Relations between life stress and rapid eye movement sleep latency. *Journal of Abnormal Psychology, 101,* 528–537.

Montauk, S. L., & Mayhall, C. A. (2010). Attention deficit hyperactivity disorder. Retrieved from http://emedicine.medscape.com/article/912633-print

Montcrieff, J., & Leo, J. (2010). A systematic review of the effects of antipsychotic drugs on brain volume. *Psychological Medicine, 40,* 1409–1422.

Monteith, T., & Sprenger, T. (2010). Tension type headache in adolescence and childhood: Where are we now? *Current Pain and Headache Reports, 14,* 424–430.

Monteleone, P., & Maj, M. (2008). The circadian basis of mood disorders: recent developments and treatment implications. *European Neuropsychopharmacology, 18,* 701–711.

Montoya, I. D., & Vocci, F. (2008). Novel medications to treat addictive disorders. *Current Psychiatry Reports, 10,* 392–398.

Moodley, R. (2005). Shamanic performances: Healing through magic and the supernatureal. In R. Moodley & W. West (Eds.). *Integrating traditional healing practices into counseling and psychotherapy* (pp. 2–14). Thousand Oaks, CA: Sage.

Mooney, L. J., Glasner-Edwards, S., Marinelli-Casey, P., Hillhouse, M., Ang, A., . . . Rawson, R. A. (2009). Health conditions in methamphetamine-dependent adults 3 years after treatment. *Journal of Addiction Medicine, 3,* 155–163.

Moore, B. A., & Budney, J. (2003). Relapse in outpatient treatment for marijuana dependence. *Journal of Substance Abuse Treatment, 25,* 85–89.

Moore, K. (2009). 'Amnesia girl' drained bank account before vanishing. Retrieved from http://www.king5.com/home/NYC-amnesia-teen-identified-as-Kitsap-Co-resident—65981942.html

Moore, T. H. M., Zammit, S., Lingford-Hughes, A., Barnes, T. R. E., Jones, P. B., Burke, M., & Lewis, G. (2007). Cannabis use and risk of psychotic or affective mental health outcomes: A systematic review. *Lancet, 370,* 319–328.

Moos, R. H. (2005). Iatrogenic effects of psychosocial interventions for substance use disorders: Prevalence, predictors, prevention. *Addiction, 100,* 595–604.

Moos, R. H., Cronkite, R. C., & Moos, B. S. (1998). Family and extrafamily resources and the ten-year course of treated depression. *Journal of Abnormal Psychology, 107,* 450–460.

Moos, R. H., & Moos, B. S. (2006). Participation in treatment and Alcoholics Anonymous: A 16-year follow-up of initially untreated individuals. *Journal of Clinical Psychology, 62,* 735–750.

Morales, A. T., & Sheafor, B. W. (2004). *Social work* (10th ed.). Boston: Allyn & Bacon.

Morenz, B., & Becker, J. V. (1995). The treatment of youthful sex offenders. *Applied and Preventive Psychology, 4,* 247–256.

Morey, L. C., & Ochoa, E. S. (1989). An investigation of adherence to diagnostic criteria: Clinical diagnosis of the DSM-III personality disorders. *Journal of Personality Disorders, 3,* 180–192.

Morey, L. C., & Zanarini, M. C. (2000). Borderline personality: Traits and disorder. *Journal of Abnormal Psychology, 109,* 733–737.

Morgan, C. J., Muetzelfeldt, L., & Curran, H. V. (2010). Consequences of chronic ketamine self-administration upon neurocognitive function and psychological wellbeing: A 1-year longitudinal study. *Addiction, 105,* 121–133.

Morgan, D. L., & Morgan, R. K. (2001). Single-participant research design: Bringing science to managed care. *American Psychologist, 56,* 119–127.

Morgan, W. J., Crain, E. F., Gruchalla, R. S., O'Connor, G. T., Kattan, M., . . . Inner-City Asthma Study Group. (2004). Results of a home-based environmental intervention among urban children with asthma. *New England Journal of Medicine, 351,* 1068–1080.

Morganstern, J., Labouvie, E., McCrady, B. S., Kahler, C. W., & Frey, R. M. (1997). Affiliation with Alcoholics Anonymous after treatment: A study of its therapeutic effects and mechanisms of action. *Journal of Consulting and Clinical Psychology, 65,* 768–777.

Morin, D., Cobigo, V., Rivard, M., & Lépine, M. (2010). Intellectual disabilities and depression: How to adapt psychological assessment and intervention. *Canadian Psychology, 51,* 185–193.

Morihisa, J. M., Rosse, R. B., Cross, C. D., Balkoski, V., & Ingraham, C. A. (1999). Laboratory and other diagnostic tests in psychiatry. In R. E. Hales, S. C. Yudofsky, & J. A. Talbott (Eds.), *Textbook of psychiatry* (pp. 281–316). Washington, DC: American Psychiatric Press.

Morillo, C., Belloch, A., & Garcia-Soriano, G. (2007). Clinical obsessions in obsessive-compulsive patients and obsession-relevant intrusive thoughts in non-clinical, depressed and anxious subjects: Where are the differences? *Behaviour Research and Therapy, 45,* 1319–1333.

Morley, K. C., Teesson, M., Reid, S. C., Sannibale, C., Thomson, C., Phung, N., Weltman, M., Bell, J. R., Richardson, K., & Haber, P. S. (2006). Naltrexone versus acamprosate in the treatment of alcohol dependence: A multi-centre, randomized, double-blind, placebo-controlled trial. *Addiction, 101,* 1451–1462.

Mormino, E. C., Kluth, J. T., Madison, C. M., Rabinovic, G. D., Baker, S. L., . . . Jagust, W. J. (2008). Episodic memory loss is related to hippocampal-mediated beta-amyloid deposition in elderly subjects. *Brain, 132,* 1310–1323.

Morris, C. D., Miklowitz, D., & Waxmonsky, J. A. (2007). Family-focused treatment for bipolar disorder in adults and youth. *Journal of Clinical Psychology: In Session, 63,* 433–445.

Morris, M. W., Ciesla, J. A., & Garber, J. (2008). A prospective study of the cognitive-stress model of depressive symptoms in adolescents. *Journal of Abnormal Psychology, 117,* 719–734.

Morris, M. C., Ciesla, J. A., & Garber, J. (2010). A prospective study of stress autonomy versus stress sensitization in adolescents at varied risk for depression. *Journal of Abnormal Psychology, 119,* 341–354.

Moser, C., & Levitt, E. E. (1987). An exploratory-descriptive study of a sadomasochistically oriented sample. *Journal of Sex Research, 23,* 322–337.

Moser, G., Wenzal-Abatzi, T.-A., Stelzeneder, M., & Wenzel, T. (1998). Globus sensation: Pharyngoesophageal function, psychometric and psychiatric findings, and follow-up in eighty-eight patients. *Archives of Internal Medicine, 158,* 1365–1372.

Mosher, W. D., Chandra, A., & Jones, J. (2005, September 15). Sexual behavior and selected health measures: Men and women 15–44 years of age, United States, 2002. *Advance Data from Vital and Health Statistics,* No. 362. Hyattsville, MD: National Center for Health Statistics.

Moss, H. B., Chen, C. M., & Yi, H. Y. (2010). Prospective follow-up of empirically derived alcohol dependence subtypes in wave 2 of the National Epidemiologic Survey on Alcohol and Related Conditions (NESARC): Recovery status, alcohol use disorders and diagnostic criteria, alcohol consumption behavior, health status, and treatment seeking. *Alcoholism: Clinical and Experimental Research, 34*(6), 1073–1083.

Moukheiber, A., Rautureau, G., Perez-Diaz, F., Soussignan, R., Dubal, S., . . . Pelissolo, A. (2010). Gaze avoidance in social phobia: Objective measure and correlates. *Behaviour Research and Therapy, 48,* 147–151.

Mraz, K. D., Dixon, J., Dumont-Mathieu, T., & Fein, D. (2009). Accelerated head and body growth in infants later diagnosed with autism spectrum disorders: A comparative study of optimal outcome children. *Journal of Child Neurology, 24,* 833–845.

Mueller, A., Mitchell, J. E., Crosby, R. D., Glaesmer, H., & de Zwaan, M. (2009). The prevalence of compulsive hoarding and its association with compulsive buying in a German population-based sample. *Behaviour Research and Therapy, 47,* 705–709.

Mueser, K. T., Sengupta, A., Schooler, N. R., Bellack, A. S., Xie, H., Glick, I. D., & Keith, S. J. (2001). Family treatment and medication dosage reduction in schizophrenia: Effects on patient social functioning, family attitudes, and burden. *Journal of Consulting and Clinical Psychology, 69,* 3–12.

Muhlberger, A., Wiedemann, G., Herrmann, M. J., & Pauli, P. (2006). Phylo- and ontogenetic fears and expectations of danger: Differences between spider- and flight-phobic subjects in cognitive and physiological responses to disorder-specific stimuli. *Journal of Abnormal Psychology, 115,* 580–589.

Mukai, T. (1996). Mothers, peers, and perceived pressure to diet among Japanese adolescent girls. *Journal of Research on Adolescence, 6,* 309–324.

Mulder, R. T., Wells, J. F., Joyce, P. R., & Bushnell, J. A. (1994). Antisocial women. *Journal of Personality Disorders, 8,* 279–287.

Mulholland, A. M., & Mintz, L. B. (2001). Prevalence of eating disorders among African American women. *Journal of Counseling Psychology, 48,* 111–116.

Mulkens, S. A. N., de Jong, P. J., & Merckelbach, H. (1996). Disgust and spider phobia. *Journal of Abnormal Psychology, 105,* 464–468.

Muller, R. J. (2006). A woman who refused treatment for a paranoid psychosis. *Psychiatric Times, 23,* 422–424.

Mullins-Sweatt, S. N., & Widiger, T. A. (2009). Clinical utility and DSM-V. *Psychological Assessment, 21,* 302–312.

Mumford, D. B., Whitehouse, A. M., & Choudry, I. Y. (1992). Survey of eating disorders in English-medium schools in Lehore, Pakistan. *International Journal of Eating Disorders, 11,* 173–184.

Munoz, R. F., Lenert, L. L., Delucchi, K., Stoddard, J., Pérez, J. E., Penilla, C., & Pérez-Stable, E. J. (2006). Toward evidence-based Internet interventions: A Spanish/English Web site for international smoking cessation trials. *Nicotine and Tobacco Research, 8,* 77–87.

Munoz, R. F., Ying, Y. W., Bernal, G., Perez-Stable, E. J., Sorenson, J. L., . . . Miller, R. S. (1995). Prevention of depression with primary care patients: A randomized controlled trial. *American Journal of Community Psychology, 23,* 199–222.

Munsey, C. (2010). Medicine or menace?: Psychologists' research can inform the growing debate over legalizing marijuana. *APA Monitor, 41*(6), 50.

Muris, P., & Merckelbach, H. (2000). How serious are common childhood fears? II. The parent's point of view. *Behaviour Research and Therapy, 38,* 813–818.

Muris, P., Merckelbach, H., & Clavan, M. (1997). Abnormal and normal compulsions. *Behaviour Research and Therapy, 35*, 249–252.

Muris, P., Merckelbach, H., & Collaris, R. (1997). Common childhood fears and their origins. *Behaviour Research and Therapy, 35*, 929–936.

Muris, P., Merckelbach, H., & de Jong, P. J. (1995). Exposure therapy outcome in spider phobics: Effects of monitoring and blunting coping styles. *Behaviour Research and Therapy, 33*, 461–464.

Muris, P., Merckelbach, H., Ollendick, T. H., King, N. J., & Bogie, N. (2001). Children's nighttime fears: Parent-child ratings of frequency, content, origins, coping behaviors and severity. *Behaviour Research and Therapy, 39*, 13–28.

Muris, P., van Zwol, L., Huijding, J., & Mayer, B. (2010). Mom told me scary things about this animal: parents installing fear beliefs in their children via the verbal information pathway. *Behaviour Research and Therapy, 48*, 341–346.

Murray, C. K., Reynolds, J. C., Schroeder, J. M., Harrison, M. B., Evans, O. M., & Hospenthal, D. R. (2005). Spectrum of care provided at an Echelon II medical unit during Operation Iraqi Freedom. *Military Medicine, 170*, 516–520.

Murray, H. A., & Morgan, H. (1938). *Explorations in personality.* New York: Oxford University Press.

Murray, S. B., Reiger, E., Touyz, S. W., & De la Garza Garcia, Y. (2010). Muscle dysmorphia and the DSM-V conundrum: Where does it belong? A review paper. *International Journal of Eating Disorders, 43*, 483–491.

Muscatell, K. A., Slavich, G. M., Monroe, S. M., & Gotlib, I. H. (2009). Stressful life events, chronic difficulties, and the symptoms of clinical depression. *Journal of Nervous and Mental Diseases, 197*, 154–c160.

Muse, K., McManus, F., Hackmann, A., Williams, M., & Williams, M. (2010). Intrusive imagery in severe health anxiety: Prevalence, nature and links with memory and maintenance cycles. *Behaviour Research and Therapy, 48*, 792–798.

Mustafa, B., Evrim, O., & Sari, A. (2005). Secondary mania following traumatic brain injury. *Journal of Neuropsychiatry and Clinical Neuroscience 17*, 122–124.

Mutsatsa, S. H., Joyce, E. M., Hutton, S. B., & Barnes, T. R. E. (2006). Relationship between insight, cognitive function, social function and symptomatology in schizophrenia. *European Archives of Psychiatry and Clinical Neuroscience, 256*, 356–363.

Myers, S. M., Johnson, C. P., & the Council on Children with Disabilities. (2007). Management of children with autism spectrum disorders. *Pediatrics, 120*, 1162–1182.

Myers, T. A., & Crowther, J. H. (2009). Social comparison as a predictor of body satisfaction. *Journal of Abnormal Psychology, 118*, 683–698.

Myers, W. (2011). 9 top signs of hoarding. Retrieved from http://www.everydayhealth.com/printview.aspx?puid=F4C04DE3-4746-4F93-948C-7406ACFBCBAF

Nacasch, N., Foa, E. B., Fostick, L., Polliack, M., Dinstein, Y., . . . Zohar, J. (2007). Prolonged exposure therapy for chronic combat-related PTSD: A case report of five veterans. *CNS Spectrums, 12*, 690–695.

Nademanee, K., Veerakul, G., Nimmannit, S., Chaowakul, V., Bhuripanyo, K., . . . Tatsanavivat, P. (1997). Arrhythmogenic marker for sudden unexplained death syndrome in Thai men. *Circulation, 96*, 2595–2600.

Naeem, F., Waheed, W., Gobbi, M., Ayub, M., & Kingdon, D. (2011). Preliminary evaluation of culturally sensitive CBT for depression in Pakistan: Findings from Developing Culturally Sensitive CBT Project (DCCP). *Behavioral and Cognitive Psychotherapy, 39*, 165–173.

Nagano, J., Kakuta, C., Motomura, C., Odajima, H., Sudo, N., Nishima, S., & Kubo, C. (2010). The parenting attitudes and the stress of mothers predict the asthmatic severity of their children: A prospective study. *BioPsychosocial Medicine,* http://www.ncbi.nlm.nih.gov/pmc/articles/PMC2959059/?tool=pubmed

Nagin, D. S., & Tremblay, R. E. (2001). Parental and early childhood predictors of persistent physical aggression in boys from kindergarten to high school. *Archives of General Psychiatry, 58*, 389–397.

Naglieri, J. A., Drasgow, F., Schmit, M., Handler, L., Prifitera, A., Margolis, A., & Velasquez, R. (2004). Psychological testing on the Internet: New problems, old issues. *American Psychologist, 59*, 150–162.

Nakao, M., Nomura, S., Shimosawa, T., Yoshiuchi, K., Kumano, H., . . . Fujita, T. (1997). Clinical effects of blood pressure biofeedback treatment on hypertension by autoshaping. *Psychosomatic Medicine, 59*, 331–338.

Namiki, C., Yamada, M., Yoshida, H., Hanakawa, T., Fukuyama, H., & Murai, T. (2008). Small orbitofrontal traumatic lesions detected by high resolution MRI in a patient with major behavioral changes. *Neurocase, 14*, 474–479.

Nanda, S. (2008). Cross-cultural issues. In D. Rowland & L. Incrocci (Eds.), *Handbook of sexual and gender identity disorders* (pp. 457–485). Hoboken, NJ: Wiley.

Naqvi, N. H., Rudrauf, D., Damasio, H., & Bechara, A. (2007). Damage to the insula disrupts addiction to cigarette smoking. *Science, 315*, 531–534.

Nash, J. M. (1997, March 24). Gift of love. *Time,* pp. 81–82.

Nash, J. R., Sargent, P. A., Rabiner, E. A., Hood, S. D., Argyopoulos, S. V., . . . Nutt, D. J. (2008). Serotonin 5-HT receptor binding in people with panic disorder: Positron emission tomography study. *British Journal of Psychiatry, 193*, 229–234.

Nashoni, E., Yaroslavsky, A., Varticovschi, P., Weizman, A., & Stein, D. (2010). Alterations in QT dispersion in the surface electrocardiogram of female adolescent inpatients diagnosed with bulimia nervosa. *Comprehensive Psychiatry, 51*, 406–411.

Nasim, A., Robert, A., Harrell, J. P., & Young, H. (2005). Non-cognitive predictors of academic achievement for African Americans across cultural contexts. *Journal of Negro Education, 74*, 344–358.

Nasrallah, H. A. (2009). Diagnosis 2.0. Are mental illnesses diseases, disorders, or syndromes? *Current Psychiatry, 8*, 14–16.

Nathan, P. E. (1988). The addictive personality is the behavior of the addict. *Journal of Consulting and Clinical Psychology, 56*, 183–188.

Nathan, P. E. (1998). Practice guidelines: Not yet ideal. *American Psychologist, 53*, 290–299.

National Academy of Sciences, National Academy of Engineering, & Institute of Medicine. (2006). *Beyond bias and barriers: Fulfilling the potential of women in academic science and engineering.* Washington, DC: National Academies Press.

National Association of Anorexia Nervosa and Associated Disorders. (2004). *Eating disorder information.* Retrieved from http://www.anad.org/site/anadweb/content.php?type1&id=6982

National Association of Social Workers. (2007). *School violence.* Retrieved from www.naswdc.org/resources/abstracts/abstracts/schoolviolence.asp

National Center for Children Exposed to Violence. (2006, March 20). *School violence.* Retrieved from www.nccev.org/violence/school.html#statistics

National Center for Complementary and Alternative Medicine. (2007). *St. John's wort* (NCCAM Publication No. D269). Bethesda, MD: Author.

National Center for Health Statistics. (2007). Asthma prevalence, health care use and mortality: United States, 2003–2005. Retrieved from www.cdc.gov/nchs/products/pubs/pubd/hestats/asthma03–05/asthma03–05.htm

National Council on Aging. (1998, September 29). Want to understand how Americans view long-term care? *San Francisco Chronicle,* A4.

National Dissemination Center for Children with Disabilities. (2007). Mental retardation. Retrieved from www.nichcy.org/pubs/factshe/fs8txt.htm

National Down Syndrome Society. (2011). Alzheimer's and Down Syndrome. Retrieved from http://www.ndss.org/index.php?option=com_content&view=article&id=180&showall=1

National Heart Lung and Blood Institute. (2009). What is coronary artery disease? Retrieved from http://www.nhlbi.nih.gov/health/dci/Diseases/Cad/CAD_WhatIs.html

National Institute of Child Health and Human Development (NICHHD). (2011a). What is Fragile X syndrome? Retrieved from http://www.nichd.nih.gov/health/topics/fragile_x_syndrome.cfm

National Institute of Child Health and Human Development (NICHHD). (2011b). Facts about Down Syndrome. Retrieved from http://www.nichd.nih.gov/health/topics/fragile_x_syndrome.cfm

National Institute of Mental Health. (1985). *Mental health: United States, 1985.* Washington, DC: U.S. Government Printing Office.

National Institute of Mental Health. (1995). Mental illness in America: The National Institute of Mental Health agenda. Rockville, MD: Author.

National Institute of Mental Health. (1999). *Facts about panic disorder.* Washington, DC: Author.

National Institute of Mental Health. (2007a). *Anxiety disorders*. Retrieved from www.nimh.nih.gov/publicat/NIMHanxiety.pdf

National Institute of Mental Health. (2007b). *Attention deficit hyperactivity disorder*. Retrieved from www.nimh.nih.gov/health/publications/adhd/completepublication.shtml

National Institute of Mental Health. (2007c). *Autism spectrum disorders (pervasive developmental disorders)*. Retrieved from http://www.nimh.nih.gov/health/publications/autism/complete-index.shtml

National Institute of Mental Health. (2007d). *Eating disorders*. Bethesda, MD: Author.

National Institute of Mental Health. (2007e). *Schizophrenia*. Retrieved from http://www.nimh.nih.gov/health/publications/schizophrenia/schizophrenia-booklet—2006.pdf

National Institute of Mental Health. (2007f). *When unwanted thoughts take over: Obsessive-compulsive disorder*. Retrieved from www.nimh.nih.gov/publicat/NIMHocd.cfm

National Institute of Mental Health. (2010). *The numbers count: Mental disorders in America*. Bethesda, MD: National Institute of Mental Health.

National Institute of Neurological Disorders and Stroke. (2007a). *Headache: Hope through research*. Retrieved from http://www.ninds.nih.gov/disorders/headache/detail_headache.htm

National Institute of Neurological Disorders and Stroke. (2007b). *Parkinson's disease: Hope through research*. Retrieved from www.ninds.nih.gov/disorders/parkinsons_disease/detail_parkinsons_disease.htm#90593159

National Institute of Neurological Disorders and Stroke (NINDS). (2010). Tourette syndrome fact sheet. Retrieved from http://www.ninds.nih.gov/disorders/tourette/detail_tourette.htm

National Institute of Neurological Disorders and Stroke (NINDS). (2011). NINDS dementia with Lewy bodies information page. Retrieved from http://www.ninds.nih.gov/disorders/dementiawithlewybodies/dementiawithlewybodies.htm

National Institutes of Health (NIH). (2010). Premenstrual dysphoric disorder. Retrieved from http://www.ncbi.nlm.nih.gov/pubmedhealth/PMH0004461/

National Institute on Alcohol Abuse and Alcoholism. (2003). *Assessing alcohol problems: A guide for clinicians and researchers* (2nd ed.). NIH Pub. No. 03–3745. Washington, DC: U.S. Department of Health and Human Services, Public Health Service. Retrieved from www.niaaa.nih.gov/publications/protraining.htm

National Institute on Alcohol Abuse and Alcoholism. (2005). *Helping patients who drink too much: A clinician's guide*. NIH Pub No. 05–3769. Bethesda, MD.

Neal, D. J., & Fromme, K. (2007). Hook 'em horns and heavy drinking: Alcohol use and collegiate sports. *Addictive Behaviors, 32*, 2681–2693.

Neal-Barnett, A., Flessner, C., Franklin, M. E., Woods, D. W., Keuthen, N. J., & Stein, D. W. (2010). Ethnic differences in trichotillomania: Phenomenology, interference, impairment, and treatment efficacy. *Journal of Anxiety Disorders, 24*, 553–558.

Nedic, A., Zivanovic, O., & Lisulov, R. (2011). Nosological status of social phobia: Contrasting classical and recent literature. *Current Opinion in Psychiatry, 24*, 61–66.

Neerakal, I., & Srinivasan, K. (2003). A study of the phenomenology of panic attacks in patients from India. *Psychopathology, 36*, 92–97.

Neigh, G. N., Gillespie, C. F., & Nemeroff, C. B. (2009). The neurobiological toll of child abuse and neglect. *Trauma Violence Abuse, 10*(4), 389–410.

Neighbors, C., Walters, S. T., Lee, C. M., Vader, A. M., Vehige, T., Szigethy, T., & DeJong, W. (2007). Event-specific prevention: Addressing college student drinking during known windows of risk. *Addictive Behaviors, 32*, 2667–2680.

Neighbors, L., & Sobal, J. (2007). Prevalence and magnitude of body weight and shape dissatisfaction among university students. *Eating Behaviors, 9*, 429–439.

Neighmond, P. (2010). Parents can make a difference with anorexic teens. *National Public Radio.* Retrieved from http://www.npr.org/templates/story/story.php?storyID=130342901

Nelson, B., & Yung, A. R. (2011). Should a risk syndrome for first episode psychosis be included in the DSM-5? *Current Opinion in Psychiatry, 24*, 128–133.

Nelson, C. B., Heath, A. C., & Kessler, R. C. (1998). Temporal progression of alcohol dependence symptoms in the U.S. household population: Results from the National Comorbidity Survey. *Journal of Consulting and Clinical Psychology, 66*, 474–483.

Nelson, G., Aubry, T., & Lawrence, A. (2007). A review of the literature on the effectiveness of housing and support, assertive community treatment, and intensive case management interventions for persons with mental illness who have been homeless. *American Journal of Orthopsychiatry, 77*, 350–361.

Nelson, T. D. (2009). *Handbook of prejudice, stereotyping, and discrimination*. New York: Taylor and Frances.

Nelson-Gray, R. O. (1991). DSM-IV: Empirical guidelines from psychometrics. *Journal of Abnormal Psychology, 100*, 308–315.

Nemeroff, C. B. (1998). Psychopharmacology of affective disorders in the twenty-first century. *Biological Psychiatry, 44*, 517–525.

Nemeroff, C. B. (2008). Recent findings in the pathophysiology of depression. *Focus, 6*, 3–14.

Nemeroff, C. B., Mayberg, H. S., Krahl, S. E., McNamara, J., Frazer, A., . . . Brannan, S. K. (2006). VNS therapy in treatment-resistant depression: Clinical evidence and putative neurobiological mechanisms. *Neuropsychopharmacology, 31*, 1345–1355.

Nervi, A., Reitz, C., Tang, M. X., Santana, V., Piriz, A., . . . Mayeux, R. (2011). Familial aggregation of dementia with lewy bodies. *British Archives of Neurology, 68*, 90–93.

Nestler, E. J., Barrot, M., DiLeone, R. J., Eisch, A. J., Gold, S. J., & Monteggia, L. M. (2002). Neurobiology of depression. *Neuron, 34*, 13–25.

Nestler, E. J., & Malenka, R. C. (2004). The addicted brain. *Scientific American, 290*, 50–57.

Netting, J. (2001, February 17). The newly sequenced genome bares all. *Science News.* Retrieved from www.findarticles.com

Neugebauer, R. (1979). Medieval and early modern theories of mental illness. *Archives of General Psychiatry, 36*, 477–483.

Neumark-Sztainer, D., Hannan, P. J., & Stat, M. (2000). Weight-related behaviors among adolescent girls and boys. *Archives of Pediatric Adolescent Medicine, 154*, 569–577.

Neumark-Sztainer, D., Wall, M., Story, M., & Fulkerson, J. A. (2004). Are family meal patterns associated with disordered eating behaviors among adolescents? *Journal of Adolescent Health, 35*, 350–359.

Neumeister, A., Bain, E., Nugent, A. C., Carson, R. E., Bonne, O., . . . Drevets, W. C. (2004). Reduced serotonin Type 1A receptor binding in panic disorder. *Journal of Neuroscience, 24*, 589–591.

Nevéus, T. (2011). Nocturnal enuresis-theoretic background and practical guidelines. *Pediatric Nephrology.* In press.

Nevid, J. S., Fichner-Rathus, L., & Rathus, S. A. (1995). *Human sexuality.* Boston: Allyn & Bacon.

Nevin, R. (2009). Trends in preschool lead exposure, mental retardation, and scholastic achievement: Association or causation? *Environmental Research, 109*, 301–310.

New report opens old debate about the nature of mental illness. (2005). *National Psychologist, 14*, 23.

Newman, C. F. (2010). The case of Gabriel: Treatment with Beckian cognitive therapy. *Journal of Constructivist Psychology, 23*, 25–41.

Newman, J. P., Curtin, J. J., Bertsch, J. D., & Baskin-Sommers, A. R. (2010). Attention moderates the fearlessness of psychopathic offenders. *Biological Psychiatry, 67*, 66–70.

Newman, J. P., & Schmitt, W. A. (1998). Passive avoidance in psychopathic offenders: A replication and extension. *Journal of Abnormal Psychology, 107*, 527–532.

Newman, L., & Mares, S. (2007). Recent advances in the theories of and interventions with attachment disorders. *Current Opinions in Psychiatry, 20*, 343–348.

Newmark, C. S. (1985). The MMPI. In C. S. Newmark (Ed.), *Major psychological assessment instruments* (pp. 11–64). Boston: Allyn & Bacon.

Newschaffer, C. J., Croen, L. A., Daniels, J., Giarelli, E., Grether, J. K., . . . Windham, G. C. (2007). The epidemiology of autism spectrum disorders. *Annual Review of Public Health, 28*, 235–258.

Neziroglu, F., & Yaryura-Tobias, J. A. (1997). A review of cognitive behavioral and pharmacological treatment of body dysmorphic disorder. *Behavior Modification, 21*, 324–340.

Niaura, R. S., Rohsenow, D. J., Binkoff, J. A., Monti, P. M., Pedraza, M., & Abrams, D. B. (1988).

Relevance of cue reactivity to understanding alcohol and smoking relapse. *Journal of Abnormal Psychology, 97,* 133–152.

Nichols, M. P., & Schwartz, R. C. (2005). *The essentials of family therapy.* New York: Allyn & Bacon.

Nicholson, R. A., & Kugler, K. E. (1991). Competent and incompetent criminal defendants: A quantitative review of comparative research. *Psychological Bulletin, 109,* 355–370.

Nicolaidis, C., Timmons, V., Thomas, M. J. Waters, A. S., Wahab, S., . . . Mitchell, R. (2010). "You don't go tell white people nothing": African American women's perspectives on the influence of violence and race on depression and depression care. *American Journal of Public Health, 100,* 1470–1476.

Niendam, T. A., Bearden, C. E., Zinberg, J., Johnson, J. K., O'Brien, M., & Cannon, T. D. (2007). The course of neurocognition and social functioning in individuals at ultra high risk for psychosis. *Schizophrenia Bulletin, 33,* 772–781.

Nierenberg, A. A., Akiskal, H. S., Angst, J., Hirschfeld, R. M., Merikangas, K. R., Petukhova, M., & Kessler, R. C. (2010). Bipolar disorder with frequent mood episodes in the national comorbidity survey replication (NCS-R). *Molecular Psychiatry, 15,* 1075–1087.

Nigg, J. T., Lohr, N. E., Westen, D., Gold, L. J., & Silk, K. R. (1992). Malevolent object representations in borderline personality disorder and major depression. *Journal of Abnormal Psychology, 101,* 61–67.

Nijmeijer, J. S., Arias-Vasquez, A., Rommelse, N. N., Altink, M. E., Anney, R. J., Asherson, P. . . . Hoekstra, P. J., et al. (2010). Identifying loci for the overlap between attention-deficit/hyper-activity disorder and autism spectrum disorder using a genome-wide QTL linkage approach. *Journal of the American Academy of Child and Adolescent Psychiatry, 49,* 675–685.

Nillni, Y. I., Rohan, K. J., Bernstein, A., & Zvolensky, M. J. (2010). Premenstrual distress predicts panic-relevant responding to a CO2 challenge among young adult females. *Journal of Anxiety Disorder, 24,* 416–422.

Nir, Y., Paz, A., Sabo, E., & Potasman, I. (2003). Fear of injections in young adults: Prevalence and associations. *American Journal of Tropical Medicine and Hygiene, 68,* 341–344.

Nisbett, R. E. (2005). Heredity, environment, and race differences in IQ: A commentary on Rushton and Jensen (2005). *Psychology, Public Policy, and Law, 11,* 302–310.

Nitzkin, J., & Smith, S. A. (2004). *Clinical preventive services in substance abuse and mental health update: From science to services* (DHHS Publication No. SMA 04-3906). Rockville, MD: Substance Abuse and Mental Health Services Administration, Center for Mental Health Services.

Noble, E. P. (1990). Alcoholic fathers and their sons: Neuropsychological, electrophysiological, personality, and family correlates. In C. R. Cloninger & H. Begleiter (Eds.), *Genetics and biology of alcoholism* (pp. 159–170). Cold

Spring Harbor, NY: Cold Spring Harbor Laboratory Press.

Nock, M. K., Joiner, T. E. Jr, Gordon, K. H., Lloyd-Richardson, E., & Prinstein, M. J. (2006). Non-suicidal self-injury among adolescents: Diagnostic correlates and relation to suicide attempts. *Psychiatry Research, 144*(1), 65–72.

Nolen-Hoeksema, S. (1987). Sex differences in unipolar depression: Evidence and theory. *Psychological Bulletin, 101,* 259–282.

Nolen-Hoeksema, S. (1991). Responses to depression and their effects on the duration of depressive episodes. *Journal of Abnormal Psychology, 100,* 569–582.

Nolen-Hoeksema, S. (2004). Gender differences in depression. In T. F. Oltmanns & R. E. Emery (Eds.), *Current directions in abnormal psychology* (pp. 49–55). Upper Saddle River, NJ: Prentice Hall.

Nolen-Hoeksema, S., Girgus, J. S., & Seligman, M. E. (1992). Predictors and consequences of childhood depressive symptoms: A 5-year longitudinal study. *Journal of Abnormal Psychology, 101,* 405–422.

Noll, J. G., Shenk, C. E., & Putnam, K. T. (2009). Childhood sexual abuse and adolescent pregnancy: A meta-analytic update. *Journal of Pediatric Psychology, 34,* 366–378.

Norcross, J. C. (2004). Empirically supported treatments (ESTS): Context, consensus, and controversy. *Register Report, 30,* 12–14.

Norcross, J. C., & Newman, C. F. (1992). Psychotherapy integration: Setting the context. In J. C. Norcross & M. R. Goldfried (Eds.), *Handbook of psychotherapy integration* (pp. 3–45). New York: Basic Books.

Nordentoft, M., & Hjorthoj, C. (2007). Cannabis use and risk of psychosis in later life. *Lancet, 370,* 293–294.

Nordstrom, B. R., & Levin, F. R. (2007). Treatment of cannabis use disorders: A review of the literature. *American Journal of Addiction, 16,* 331–342.

Norfleet, M. A. (2002). Responding to society's needs: Prescription privileges for psychologists. *Journal of Clinical Psychology, 58,* 599–610.

North, C. S., Smith, E. M., & Spitznagel, E. L. (1997). One-year follow-up of survivors of a mass shooting. *American Journal of Psychiatry, 154,* 1696–1702.

Norton, P. J., & Hope, D. A. (2001). Analogue observational methods in the assessment of social functioning in adults. *Psychological Assessment, 13,* 59–72.

Nothard, S., Morrison, A. P., & Wells, A. (2008). Identifying specific interpretations and exploring the nature of safety behaviours for people who hear voices: An exploratory study. *Behavioural and Cognitive Psychotherapy, 36,* 353–357.

Noveck, J., & Tompson, T. (2007). Poll: Family, friends make youths happy. *Sacramento Bee, 295,* A1, A14.

Noyes, R., Jr., Holt, C. S., Happel, R. L., Kathol, R. G., & Yagla, S. J. (1997). A family study of hypochondriasis. *Journal of Nervous and Mental Disease, 185,* 223–232.

Noyes, R., Jr., Langbehn, D. R., Happel, R. L., Stout, L. R., Muller, B. A., & Longley, S. L. (2001). Personality dysfunction among somatizing patients. *Psychosomatics, 42,* 320–329.

Noyes, R., Jr., Stuart, S., Watson, D. B., & Langbehn, D. R. (2006). Distinguishing between hypochondriasis and somatization disorder: A review of the existing literature. *Psychotherapy and Psychosomatics, 75,* 270–281.

Nussbaum, N. L., & Bigler, E. D. (1989). Halstead-Reitan neuropsychological test batteries for children. In C. R. Reynolds & E. Fletcher-Janzen (Eds.), *Handbook of clinical child neuropsychology* (pp. 181–191). New York: Plenum Press.

Nutt, D. J. (2001). Neurobiological mechanisms in generalized anxiety disorder. *Journal of Clinical Psychiatry, 62,* 22–27.

Nutt, D. J., King, L. A., & Phillip, L. D. (2010). Drug harms in the UK: A multicriteria decision analysis. *The Lancet, 376*(9752), 1558–1565.

Nystul, M. S. (2003). *Introduction to counseling.* Boston: Allyn & Bacon.

Oaten, M., Stevenson, R. J., & Case, T. I. (2009). Disgust as a disease-avoidance mechanism. *Psychological Bulletin, 135,* 303–321.

Obesity Action Coalition. (2007). *Understanding obesity stigma.* Retrieved from www.obesityaction. org/resources/Stigma%20Brochure.pdf

O'Brien, M. C., McCoy, T. P., Rhodes, S. D., Wagoner, A., & Wolfson M. (2008). Caffeinated cocktails: Energy drink consumption, high-risk drinking, and alcohol-related consequences among college students. *Academic Emergency Medicine, 5*(5), 453–460.

O'Brien, M. P., Gordon, J. L., Bearden, C. E., Lopez, S. R., Kopelowicz, A., & Cannon, T. D. (2006). Positive family environment predicts improvement in symptoms and social functioning among adolescents at imminent risk for onset of psychosis. *Schizophrenia Research, 81,* 269–275.

O'Brien, W. H., & Carhart, V. (2011). Functional analysis in behavioral medicine. *European Journal of Psychological Assessment, 27,* 4–16.

O'Connell, K. A., Hosein, V. L., Schwartz, J. E., & Leibowitz, R. Q. (2007). How does coping help people resist lapses during smoking cessation? *Health Psychology, 26,* 77–84.

O'Connor v. Donaldson, 95 S. Ct. 2486 (1975).

O'Connor, B. P. (2008). Other personality disorders. In M. Hersen & J. Rosqvist (Eds.). *Handbook of psychological assessment, case conceptualization and treatment. Vol. 1: Adults.* (pp. 438–462). Hoboken, NJ: Wiley.

O'Donnell, M. J., Xavier, D., Liu, L., Zhang, H., Chin, S. L., Rao-Melacini, P., . . . Yusuf, S. (2010). Risk factors for ischaemic and intracerebral haemorrhagic stroke in 22 countries (the INTERSTROKE study): A case-control study. *Lancet, 376,* 112–123.

O'Donohue, W. T., Mosco, E. A., Bowers, A. H., & Avina, C. (2006). Sexual harassment as diagnosable PTSD trauma. *Psychiatric Times, 23,* 50–62.

Odlaug, B. L., Kim, S. W., & Grant, J. E. (2010). Quality of life and clinical severity in pathological skin picking and trichotillomania. *Journal of Anxiety Disorders, 24,* 823–829.

Office of National Drug Control Policy. (2010). New data reveal 400% increase in substance abuse treatment admissions for people abusing prescription drugs. Retrieved from http://www.whitehousedrugpolicy.gov/news/press10/071510.html

Offman, A., & Kleinplatz, P. J. (2004). Does PMDD belong in the DSM? Challenging the medicalization of women's bodies. *Canadian Journal of Human Sexuality, 13.* Retrieved from http://findarticles.com/p/articles/mi_go1966/is_1_13/ai_n7459081/

Ofshe, R. J. (1992). Inadvertent hypnosis during interrogation: False confession due to dissociative state; misidentified multiple personality and the satanic cult hypothesis. *International Journal of Clinical and Experimental Hypnosis, 40,* 125–156.

Ogden, C. L., Carroll, M. D., Curtin, L. R., Lamb, M. M., & Flegal, K. M. (2010). Prevalence of high body mass in US Children and adolescents, 2007–2008. *Journal of the American Medical Association, 303,* 242–249.

Ogden, C. L., Fryar, C. D., Carroll, M. D., & Flegal, K. M. (2004). Mean body weight, height, and body mass index, United States 1960–2002: Advance data from vital and health statistics (no. 347). Hyattsville, MD: National Center for Health Statistics.

Ohaeri, J. U., & Odejide, O. A. (1994). Somatization symptoms among patients using primary health care facilities in a rural community in Nigeria. *American Journal of Psychiatry, 151,* 728–731.

O'Hara, M. W. (2003). Postpartum depression. *Clinician's Research Digest, 29,* 12.

Ohl, L. E. (2007). Essentials of female sexual dysfunction from a sex therapy perspective. *Urologic Nursing, 27,* 57–63.

Ohman, A., & Hultman, C. M. (1998). Electrodermal activity and obstetric complications in schizophrenia. *Journal of Abnormal Psychology, 107,* 228–237.

Ohman, A., & Mineka, S. (2001). Fears, phobias, and preparedness: Toward an evolved module of fear and fear learning. *Psychological Review, 108,* 483–522.

Okazaki, S. (1997). Sources of ethnic differences between Asian American and white American college students on measures of depression and social anxiety. *Journal of Abnormal Psychology, 106,* 52–60.

Okazaki, S., Liu, J. F., Longworth, S. L., & Minn, J. Y. (2002). Asian American-White American differences in expressions of social anxiety: A replication and extension. *Cultural Diversity and Ethnic Minority Psychology, 8,* 234–247.

Okie, S. (2010). A flood of opioids, a rising tide of deaths. *New England Journal of Medicine, 363,* 1981–1985.

Olarte, S. W. (1997). Sexual boundary violations. In *The Hatherleigh guide to ethics in therapy* (pp. 195–209). New York: Hatherleigh Press.

Olatunji, B. O., Elwood, L. S., Williams, N. L., & Lohr, J. M. (2008). Mental pollution and PTSD symptoms in victims of sexual assault: A preliminary examination of the mediating role of trauma-related cognitions. *Journal of Cognitive Psychotherapy: An International Quarterly, 22,* 37–47.

Oldham, J. M. (2006). Integrated treatment for borderline personality disorder. *Psychiatric Annals, 36,* 361–362, 364–369.

Oldham, J. M. (2009). Borderline personality disorder comes of age. *American Journal of Psychiatry, 166,* 509–511.

Oleary, E. M. M., Barrett, P., & Fjermestad, K. W. (2009). Cognitive-behavioral family treatment for childhood obsessive-compulsive disorder: A 7-year follow-up study. *Journal of Anxiety Disorder, 23,* 973–978.

Olfson, M., & Marcus, S. C. (2008). A case-control study of antidepressants and attempted suicide during early phase treatment of major depressive episodes. *Journal of Clinical Psychiatry, 69,* 425–432.

Olivardia, R., Pope, H. G., Jr., & Hudson, J. I. (2000). Muscle dysphoria in male weight-lifters: A case-control study. *American Journal of Psychiatry, 157,* 1291–1296.

Oliver, C., Berg, K., Moss, J., Arron, K., & Burbidge, C. (2010). Delineation of behavioral phenotypes in genetic syndromes: Characteristics of autism spectrum disorder, affect and hyperactivity. *Journal of Autism and Developmental Disorders.* In press.

Olkin, R. (1999). *What psychotherapists should know about disability.* New York: Guilford Press.

Ollendick, T. H., & King, N. J. (1998). Empirically supported treatments for children with phobic and anxiety disorders: Current status. *Journal of Clinical Child Psychology, 27,* 156–167.

Ollendick, T. H., Ost-L.-G., Reuterskiold, L., Cosa, N., Cederlund, R., . . . Jarrett, M. A. (2009). One-session treatment of specific phobias in youth: A randomized clinical trial in the United States and Sweden. *Journal of Consulting and Clinical Psychology, 77,* 504–516.

Olmos, J. M., Valero, C., Gomez del Barrio, A., Amando, J. A., Hernandez, J. L., Menendez-Arango, J., & Gonzalez-Macia, J. (2010). Time course of bone loss in patients with anorexia nervosa. *International Journal of Eating Disorders, 43,* 537–542.

Olsson, A., Nearing, K. I., & Phelps, E. A. (2007). Learning fears by observing others: The neural systems of social fear transmission. *Scan, 2,* 3–11.

Olsson, S. E., & Moller, A. (2006). Regret after sex reassignment surgery in male-to-female transsexual: A long-term follow-up. *Archives of Sexual Behavior, 35,* 501–506.

O'Neil, K. A., Conner, B. T., & Kendall, P. C. (2011). Internalizing disorders and substance use disorders in youth: Comorbidity, risk, temporal order, and implications for intervention. *Clinical Psychology Review, 31,* 104–112.

Ooteman, W., Naassila, M., Koeter, M. W., Verheul, R., Schippers, G. M., Houchi, H., Daoust, M., & van den Brink, W. (2009). Predicting the effect of naltrexone and acamprosate in alcohol-dependent patients using genetic indicators. *Addictive Biology, 14,* 328–337.

Oquendo, M. A., Currier, D., Liu, S. M., Hasin, D. S., Grant, B. F., & Blanco, C. (2010). Increased risk for suicidal behavior in comorbid bipolar disorder and alcohol use disorders: Results from the National Epidemiologic Survey on Alcohol and Related Conditions (NESARC). *Journal of Clinical Psychiatry, 71,* 902–909.

Oren, D. A., & Rosenthal, N. E. (2001). Light therapy. In G. O. Gabbard (Ed.), *Treatment of psychiatric disorders* (pp. 1295–1306). Washington, DC: American Psychiatric Press.

Orr, S. P., Lasko, N. B., Shalev, A. Y., & Pitman, R. K. (1995). Physiologic responses to loud tones in Vietnam veterans with posttraumatic stress disorder. *Journal of Abnormal Psychology, 104,* 75–82.

Orr, S. P., Metzger, L. J., Lasko, N. B., Macklin, M. L., Peri, T., & Pitman, R. K. (2000). De Novo conditioning in trauma-exposed individuals with and without posttraumatic stress disorder. *Journal of Abnormal Psychology, 109,* 290–298.

Orsmond, G. I., & Seltzer, M. M. (2007). Siblings of individuals with autism spectrum disorders across the life course. *Mental Retardation and Developmental Disabilities Research Review, 13,* 313–320.

Ortega, A. N., McQuaid, E. L., Canino, G., Goodwin, R. D., & Fritz, G. K. (2004). Comorbidity of asthma and anxiety and depression in Puerto Rican children. *Psychosomatics, 45,* 93–99.

Osbourne, L. (2001, May 6). Regional disturbances. *New York Times Magazine,* pp. 6–14.

Öst, L.-G. (1987). Age of onset in different phobias. *Journal of Abnormal Psychology, 96,* 223–229.

Öst, L.-G. (1992). Blood and injection phobia: Background and cognitive, physiological, and behavioral variables. *Journal of Abnormal Psychology, 101,* 68–74.

Öst, L.-G., Alm, T., Brandberg, M., & Breitholtz, E. (2001). One vs. five sessions of exposure and five sessions of cognitive therapy in the treatment of claustrophobia. *Behaviour Research and Therapy, 39,* 167–183.

Öst, L.-G., & Hugdahl, K. (1981). Acquisition of phobias and anxiety response patterns in clinical patients. *Behaviour Research and Therapy, 19,* 439–447.

Ostchega, Y., Yoon, S. S., Hughes, J., & Louis, T. (2008). Hypertension awareness, treatment, and control—continued disparities in adults: United States, 2005–2006. *National Center for Health Statistics, 3,* 1–8.

Oster, T. J., Anderson, C. A., Filley, C. M., Wortzel, H. S., & Arciniegas, D. B. (2007). Quetiapine for mania due to traumatic brain injury. *CNS Spectrums, 12,* 764–769.

Oswald, D. P., & Sonenklar, N. A. (2007). Medication use among children with autism spectrum disorders. *Journal of Child and Adolescent Psychopharmacology, 17,* 348–355.

Othmer, E., & Othmer, S. C. (1994). *The clinical interview using DSM-IV: Volume 1. Fundamentals.* Washington, DC: American Psychiatric Press.

Otto, M. W., McHugh, R. K., Simon, N. M., Farach, F. J., Worthington, J. J., & Pollack, M. H. (2010). Efficacy of CBT for benzodiazepine discontinuation in patients with panic disorder: Further evaluation. *Behaviour Research and Therapy, 48,* 720–727.

Otto, M. W., Pollack, M. H., & Sabatino, S. A. (1996). Maintenance of remission following cognitive behavior therapy for panic disorder: Possible deleterious effects of concurrent medication treatment. *Behavior Therapy, 27,* 473–482.

Otto, R. K. (1989). Bias and expert testimony of mental health professionals in adversarial proceedings: A preliminary investigation. *Behavioral Science and Law, 7,* 267–273.

Ozer, E. J., Best, S. R., Lipsey, T. L., & Weiss, D. S. (2003). Predictors of posttraumatic stress disorder and symptoms in adults: A meta-analysis. *Psychological Bulletin, 129,* 52–73.

Ozonoff, S., Heung, K., Byrd, R., Hansen, R., & Hertz-Picciotto, I. (2008). The onset of autism: Patterns of symptom emergence in the first years of life. *Autism Research, 1,* 320–328.

Ozonoff, S., Iosif, A. M., Baguio, F., Cook, I. C., Hill, M. M., . . . Sigman, M. (2010). A prospective study of the emergence of early behavioral signs of autism. *Journal of American Academy of Child and Adolescent Psychiatry, 49,* 256–266.

Ozonoff, S., & Rogers, S. J. (2003). From Kanner to the millennium. In S. Ozonoff, S. J. Rogers, & R. L. Hendren (Eds.), *Autism spectrum disorders: A research review for practitioners* (pp. 3–36). Arlington, VA: American Psychiatric.

Padgett, D. K., Hawkins, R. L., Abrams, C., & Davis, A. (2006). In their own words: Trauma, and substance abuse in the lives of formerly homeless women with serious mental illness. *American Journal of Orthopsychiatry, 76,* 461–467.

Paik, A., & Laumann, E. O. (2006). Prevalence of women's sexual problems in the USA. In I. Goldstein, C. M. Meston, S. R. Davis, & A. M. Traish (Eds.), *Women's sexual function and dysfunction* (pp. 23–33). London: Taylor & Francis.

Pajonk, F-G., Wobrock, T., Gruber, O., Scherk, H., Berner, D., Kaizi, I., . . . Falkai, P. (2010). Hippocampal plasticity in response to exercise in schizophrenia. *Archives of General Psychiatry, 67,* 133–143.

Palaniyappan, L., & Cousins, D. A. (2010). Brain networks: foundations and futures in bipolar disorder. *Journal of Mental Health, 19,* 157–167.

Pallack, M. (1995). Managed care's evolution during the health care revolution. *National Psychologist, 4,* 12.

Palmatier, T. J. (2010, December 1). Narcissistic personality disorder and histrionic personality disorder to be eliminated in the DSM-V: Starbuck's Diagnostics 101. Retrieved from http://www.shrink4men.com/2010/12/01/narcissistic-personality-disorder-and-histrionic-personality

Palmieri, P. A., Weathers, F. W., Difede, J., & King, D. W. (2007). Confirmatory factor analysis of the PTSD Checklist and the Clinician-Administered PTSD Scale in disaster workers exposed to the World Trade Center Ground Zero. *Journal of Abnormal Psychology, 116,* 329–341.

Panagiotopoulos, C., McCrindle, B. W., Hick, K., & Katzman, D. K. (2000). Electrocardiographic findings in adolescents with eating disorders. *Pediatrics, 105,* 1100–1105.

Papadopoulous, F. C., Ekbom, A., Brandt, L., & Ekselius, L. (2009). Excess mortality, causes of death and prognostic factors in anorexia nervosa. *British Journal of Psychiatry, 194,* 10–17.

Papakostas, G. I., & Fava, M. (2008). Predictors, moderators, and mediators (correlates) of treatment outcome in major depressive disorder. *Dialogues in Clinical Neuroscience, 10,* 439–451.

Paquette, M. (2007). Morgellons: Disease or delusions? *Perspectives in Psychiatric Care, 43,* 67–68.

Paquette, V., Levesque, J., Mensour, V., Leroux, J. M., Beaudoin, G., Bourgouin, P., & Beauregard, M. (2003). "Change the mind and you change the brain": Effects of cognitive-behavioral therapy on the neural correlates of spider phobias. *Neuro-Image, 18,* 401–409.

Paras, M. L., Murad, M. H., Chen, L. P., Goranson, E. N., Sattler, A. L., . . . Zirakzadeh, A. (2009). Sexual abuse and lifetime diagnosis of somatic disorders: A systematic review and meta-analysis. *Journal of the American Medical Association, 302*(5), 550–561.

Parens, E., & Johnston, J. (2009). Facts, values, and attention-deficit hyperactivity disorder (ADHD): An update on the controversies. *Child and Adolescent Psychiatry and Mental Health, 3,* 1–17.

Parens, E., & Johnston, J. (2010). Controversies concerning the diagnosis and treatment of bipolar disorder in children. *Childhood and Adolescent Psychiatry and Mental Health, 10,* 4–9.

Parents Television Council. (2007). *The alarming family hour . . . No place for children.* Retrieved from www.parentstv.org/PTC/publications/reports/familyhour/exs

Paris, J. (2009). Psychiatry and neuroscience. *The Canadian Journal of Psychiatry, 54,* 513–517.

Parish, B. S., & Yutzy, S. H. (2011). Somatoform disorders. In R. E. Hales, S. C. Yudofsky, & G. O. Babbard (Eds.). *Essentials of psychiatry* (3rd ed.). (pp. 229–254). Arlington, VA: American Psychiatric Publishing, Inc.

Park, L. E., Calogero, R. M., Young, A. F., & Diraddo, A. M. (2010). Appearance-based rejection sensitivity predicts body dysmorphic disorder symptoms and cosmetic surgery acceptance. *Journal of Social and Clinical Psychology, 29,* 489–509.

Park, P., & Manzon-Santos (2000). Issues of transgendered Asian Americans and Pacific Islanders. Retrieved from http://www.apiwellness.org/article_tg_issues.html

Parker, S., Nichter, M., Vuckovic, N., Sims, C., & Ritenbaugh, C. (1995). Body image and weight concerns among African-American and White adolescent females: Differences that make a difference. *Human Organization, 54,* 103–114.

Parrott, C. (1998). Treating binge eating disorder. *Counseling Psychology Quarterly, 11,* 265–281.

Parsons, J. T., Grov, C., & Kelly, B. C. (2009). Club drug use and dependence among young adults recruited through time-space sampling. *Public Health Reports, 124*(2), 246–254.

Partnership for a Drug-Free America and MetLife Foundation (PFDFA/MET). (2010). *2009 Parents and Teens Attitude Tracking Study.* Retrieved from http://drugfreetexas.org/wp-content/files_flutter/1267570941PATS_Full_Report_2009_PDF.pdf

Paschall, M. J., & Saltz, R. F. (2007). Relationships between college settings and student alcohol use before, during and after events: A multi-level study. *Drug and Alcohol Review, 26*(6), 635–644.

Pascoe, E. A., & Richman, L. S. (2009). Perceived discrimination and health: A meta-analytic review. *Psychological Bulletin, 135,* 531–554.

Patterson, C., & Seligman, M. (2005). *Character strengths and virtue: A handbook and classification.* New York: Oxford University Press.

Patterson, G. R. (1986). Performance models for antisocial boys. *American Psychologist, 41,* 432–444.

Paulson-Karlsson, G., Engstrom, I., & Nevonen, L. (2009). A pilot study of a family-based treatment for adolescent anorexia nervosa: 18- and 36-month follow-ups. *Eating Disorders, 17,* 72–88.

Paulus, M. P., Tapert, S. F., & Schuckit, M. A. (2005). Neural activation patterns of methamphetamine-dependent subjects during decision making predict relapse. *Archives of General Psychiatry, 62,* 761–768.

Paykel, E. S. (Ed.). (1982). *Handbook of affective disorders.* New York: Guilford Press.

Paykel, E. S., Abbott, R., Jenkins, R., Brugha, T., & Meltzer, H. (2003). Urban-rural mental health differences in Great Britian: Findings from the National Morbidity Survey. *International Review of Psychiatry, 15,* 97–107.

Pearson, K. A., Watkins, E. R., & Mullan, E. G. (2010). Submissive interpersonal style mediates the effect of brooding on future depressive symptoms. *Behaviour Research and Therapy, 48,* 966–973.

Peirce, J. M., Petry, N. M., Stitzer, M. L., Blaine, J., Kellogg, S., . . . Li, R. (2006). Effects of lower-cost incentives on stimulant abstinence in methadone maintenance treatment: A National Drug Abuse Treatment Clinical Trials Network study. *Archives of General Psychiatry, 63,* 201–208.

Pelham, W. E., & Fabiano, G. A. (2008). Evidence-based psychosocial treatment for ADHD: An update. *Journal of Clinical Child and Adolescent Psychology, 37,* 184–214.

Pelletier, L. G., & Dion, S. C. (2007). An examination of general and specific motivational mechanisms for the relations between body dissatisfaction and eating behaviors. *Journal of Social and Clinical Psychology, 26,* 303–333.

Pemberton, C. K, Neiderhiser, J. M., Leve, L. D., Natsuaki, M. N., Shaw, D. S., Reiss, D., & Ge, X. (2010). Influence of parental depressive symptoms on adopted toddler behaviors: An emerging developmental cascade of genetic and environmental effects. *Developmental Psychopathology, 22,* 803–818.

Penava, S. J., Otto, M. W., Maki, K. M., & Pollack, M. H. (1998). Rate of improvement during cognitive-behavioral group treatment for panic disorder. *Behaviour Research and Therapy, 36,* 665–673.

Pendery, M. L., Maltzman, I. M., & West, L. J. (1982). Controlled drinking by alcoholics? New findings and a reevaluation of a major affirmative study. *Science, 217,* 169–175.

Penn, D. L., Mueser, K. T., Tarrier, N., Gloege, A., Cather, C., Serrano, D., & Otto, M. W. (2004). Supportive therapy for schizophrenia: Possible mechanisms and implications for adjunctive psychosocial treatments. *Schizophrenia Bulletin, 30,* 101–112.

Penninx, B. W., Beekman, A. T., Honig, A., Deeg, D. J., Schoevers, R. A., Van Eijk, J. T., & van Tilburg, W. (2001). Depression and cardiac mortality: Results from a community-based longitudinal study. *Archives of General Psychiatry, 58,* 221–227.

Perala, J., Suvisaari, J., Saarni, S. I., Kuoppasalmi, K., Isometsa, E., . . . Lonnqvist, J. (2007). Lifetime prevalence of psychotic and bipolar I disorders in a general population. *Archives of General Psychiatry, 64,* 19–28.

Peralta, R. L. (2003). Thinking sociologically about sources of obesity in the United States. *Gender Issues, 21,* 5–16.

Perelman, M. A., & Rowland, D. L. (2008). Retarded and inhibited ejaculation. In D. Rowland & L. Incrocci (Eds.), *Handbook of sexual and gender identity disorders* (pp. 100–121). Hoboken, NJ: Wiley.

Perez, J. E. (1999). Clients deserve empirically supported treatments, not romanticism. *American Psychologist, 54,* 205–206.

Perkins, H. W., Linkenbach, J. W., Lewis, M. A., & Neighbors, C. (2010). Effectiveness of social norms media marketing in reducing drinking and driving: A statewide campaign *Addictive Behaviors, 35*(10), 866–874.

Perkins, K. A. (2009). Sex differences in nicotine reinforcement and reward: Influences on the persistence of tobacco smoking. *The Motivational Impact of Nicotine and its Role in Tobacco Use: Nebraska Symposium on Motivation, 55,* 1–27.

Perlis, R. H., Ostacher, M., Fava, M., Nierenberg, A. A., Sachs, G. S., & Rosenbaum, J. F. (2010). Assuring that double-blind is blind. *American Journal of Psychiatry, 167,* 250–252.

Perlis, R. H., Smoller, J. W., Mysore, J., Sun, M., Gillis, T., . . . Gusella, J. (2010). Prevalence of incompletely penetrant Huntington's disease alleles among individuals with major depressive disorder. *American Journal of Psychiatry, 167,* 574–579.

Perlman, C. M., Martin, L., Hirdes, J. P., & Curtin-Telegdi, N. (2007). Prevalence and predictors of sexual dysfunction in psychiatric inpatients. *Psychosomatics, 48,* 309–318.

Perner, L. E. (2001, August). *Literal detours: Propositions on abstraction in high functioning autistic individuals.* Paper presented at the meeting of the American Psychological Association, San Francisco.

Perron, B. E., & Howard, M. O. (2009). Adolescent inhalant use, abuse and dependence. *Addiction, 104,* 1185–1192.

Perry, J., & Felce, D. (2005). Factors associated with outcome in community group homes. *American Journal on Mental Retardation, 110,* 121–135.

Perry, J. C. (2001). Dependent personality disorder. In G. O. Gabbard (Ed.), *Treatment of psychiatric disorders* (pp. 2353–2368). Washington, DC: American Psychiatric Press.

Perse, T. L., Greist, J. H., Jefferson, J. W., Rosenfeld, R., & Dar, R. (1987). Fluvoxamine treatment of obsessive-compulsive disorder. *American Journal of Psychiatry, 144,* 1543–1548.

Petersen, L., & Brown, D. (1994). Integrating child injury and abuse-neglect research: Common histories, etiologies, and solutions. *Psychological Bulletin, 116,* 293–315.

Peterson, C. B., Thuras, P., Ackard, D. M., Mitchell, J. E., Berg, K., . . . Crow, S. J. (2010). Personality dimensions in bulimia nervosa, binge eating disorder, and obesity. *Comprehensive Psychiatry, 51,* 31–36.

Peterson, R. A. (2001). On the use of college students in social science research: Insights from a second-order meta-analysis. *Journal of Consumer Research, 28,* 450–461.

Petrovic, P., Kalso, E., Peterson, K. M., & Ingvar, M. (2002). Placebo and opioid analgesia: Imaging a shared neural network. *Science, 295,* 1737–1740.

Petry, N. M., Alessi, S. M., Carroll, K. M., Hanson, T., MacKinnon. S., Rounsaville, B., & Sierra, S. (2006). Contingency management treatments: Reinforcing abstinence versus adherence with goal-related activities. *Journal of Consulting and Clinical Psychology, 74,* 592–601.

Petry, N. M., Martin, B., Cooney, J. L., & Kranzler, H. R. (2000). Give them prizes, and they will come: Contingency management for treatment of alcohol dependence. *Journal of Consulting and Clinical Psychology, 68,* 250–257.

Pettinati, H. M., O'Brien, C. P., Rabinowitz, A. R., Wortman, S. P., Oslin, D. W., . . . Dackis, C. A. (2006). The status of naltrexone in the treatment of alcohol dependence: Specific effects on heavy drinking. *Journal of Clinical Psychopharmacology, 26,* 610–625.

Pettus, A. (2008). Repressed memory: A cultural symptom? *Harvard Magazine.* Retrieved from: http://harvardmagazine.com/2008/01/repressed-memory.html

Peveler, R. (1998). Understanding medically unexplained physical symptoms: Faster progress in the next century than in this? *Journal of Psychosomatic Research, 45,* 93–97.

Pezawas, L., Meyer-Lindenberg, A., Drabant, E. M., Verchinski, B. A., Munoz, K. E., . . . Weinberger, D. R. (2005). 5-HTTLPR polymorphism impacts human cingulated amygdala interactions: A genetic susceptibility mechanism for depression. *Nature Neuroscience, 8,* 828–834.

Pezdek, K., Blandon-Gitlin, I., & Gabbay, P. (2006). Imagination and memory: Does imagining implausible events lead to false autobiographical memories? *Psychonomic Bulletin and Review, 13,* 764–769.

Pflueger, M. O., Gschwandtner, U., Stieglitz, R.-D., & Riecher-Rossler, A. (2007). Neuropsychological deficits in individuals with an at risk mental state for psychosis: Working memory as a potential trait marker. *Schizophrenia Research, 97,* 14–24.

Pfuhlmann, B., & Stober, G. (1997). The importance of differentiated psychopathology of catatonia. *Acta Psychiatrica Scandinavia, 95,* 357–359.

Phelps, B. J. (2000). Dissociative identity disorder: The relevance of behavior analysis. *Psychological Record, 50,* 235–249.

Phelps, L., Brown, R. T., & Power, T. J. (2002). *Pediatric psychopharmacology: Combining medical and psychosocial interventions.* Washington, DC: American Psychological Association.

Phillips, A., & Daniluk, J. C. (2004). Beyond "survivor": How childhood sexual abuse informs the identity of adult women at the end of the therapeutic process. *Journal of Counseling and Development, 82,* 177–184.

Phillips, D. P., Van Voorhees, C. A., & Ruth, T. E. (1992). The birthday: Lifeline or deadline? *Psychosomatic Medicine, 54,* 532–542.

Phillips, K. A., & Gunderson, J. G. (1999). Personality disorders. In R. E. Hales, S. C. Yudofsky, & J. A. Talbott (Eds.), *Textbook of psychiatry* (pp. 795–823). Washington, DC: American Psychiatric.

Phillips, K. A., & Rasmussen, S. A. (2004). Change in psychosocial functioning and quality of life of patients with body dysmorphic disorder treated with fluoxetine: A placebo-controlled study. *Psychosomatics, 45,* 438–444.

Phillips, K. A., McElroy, S. L., Dwight, M. M., Eisen, J. L., & Rasmussen, S. A. (2001). Delusionality and response to open-label fluvoxamine in body dysmorphic disorder. *Journal of Clinical Psychiatry, 62,* 87–91.

Phillips, K. A., McElroy, S. L., Keck, P. E., Pope, H. G., Jr., & Hudson, J. I. (1993). Body dysmorphic disorder: Thirty cases of imagined ugliness. *American Journal of Psychiatry, 150,* 302–308.

Phillips, K. A., Pagano, M. E., Menard, W., & Stout, R. L. (2006). A 12-month follow-up study of the course of body dysmorphic disorder. *American Journal of Psychiatry, 163,* 907–912.

Phillips, K. A., Stein, D. J., Rauch, S. L., Hollander, E., Fallon, B. A., . . . Leckman, J. (2010). Should an obsessive-compulsive spectrum grouping of disorders be included in DSM-V? *Depression and Anxiety, 27,* 528–555.

Phillips, K. A., Wilhelm, S., Koran, L. M., Didie, E. R., Fallon, B. A., . . . Stein, D. J. (2010). Body dysmorphic disorder: Some key issues for DSM-V. *Depression and Anxiety, 27,* 573–591.

Phillips, K. A., Yen, S., & Gunderson, J. G. (2004). Personality disorders. In R. E. Hales & S. C. Yudofsky (Eds.), *Essentials of clinical psychiatry* (2nd ed., pp. 567–589). Washington, DC: American Psychiatric.

Piasecki, T. M., Sher, K. J., Slutske, W. S., & Jackson, K. M. (2005). Hangover frequency and risk for alcohol use disorders: Evidence from a longitudinal high-risk study. *Journal of Abnormal Psychology, 114*, 223–234.

Picardi, A. (2009). Rating scales in bipolar disorder. *Current Opinions in Psychiatry, 22*, 42–49.

Piefke, M., Pestinger, M., Arin, T., Kohl, B., Kastrau, F., Schnitker, R., . . . Flatten, G. (2007). The neurofunctional mechanism of traumatic and non-traumatic memory in patients with acute PTSD following accident trauma. *Neurocase, 13*, 342–357.

Pies, R. (2011). How to eliminate narcissism overnight: DSM-V and the death of narcissistic personality disorder. *Innovations in Clinical Neuroscience, 8*, 23–27.

Pigott, T. A., & Murphy, D. L. (1991). In reply. *Archives of General Psychiatry, 48*, 858–859.

Pigott, T. A., & Seay, S. (1997). Pharmacotherapy of obsessive-compulsive disorder. *International Review of Psychiatry, 9*, 133–147.

Pike, J. L., Smith, T. L., Hauger, R. L., Nicassio, P. M., Patterson, T. L., . . . Irwin, M. R. (1997). Chronic life stress alters sympathetic, neuroendocrine, and immune responsivity to an acute psychological stressor in humans. *Psychosomatic Medicine, 59*, 447–457.

Pike, K. M., Dohm, F.-A., Streigel-Moore, R., Wilfley, D. E., & Fairburn, C. G. (2001). A comparison of black and white women with binge eating disorder. *American Journal of Psychiatry, 158*, 1455–1461.

Pincus, A. L. (2011). Some comments on nosology, diagnostic process, and narcissistic personality disorder in DSM-5: Proposal for personality and personality disorders. *Personality Disorders, Theory, Research, and Treatment, 2*, 41–53.

Pincus, D. B., May, J. E., Whitton, S. W., Mattis, S. G., & Barlow, D. H. (2010). Cognitive-behavioral treatment of panic disorder in adolescence. *Journal of Clinical Child and adolescent Psychology, 39*, 638–649.

Pinheiro, A. P., Raney, T. J., Thornton, L. M., Fichter, M. M., Berrentini, W. H., . . . Bulik, C. M. (2010). Sexual functioning in women with eating disorders. *International Journal of Eating Disorder, 43*, 123–129.

Pinto, D., Pagnamenta, A. T., Klei, L., Anney, R., Merico, D., . . . Betancur, C. (2010). Functional impact of global rare copy number variation in autism spectrum disorders. *Nature, 466*, 368–372.

Piper, A., & Mersky, H. (2004). The persistence of folly: A critical examination of dissociative identity disorder. Part 1. The excesses of an improbable concept. *Canadian Journal of Psychiatry, 49*, 592–600.

Piper, M. E., Cook, J. W., Schlam, T. R., Jorenby, D. E., & Baker, T. B. (2010). Anxiety diagnoses in smokers seeking cessation treatment: Relations with tobacco dependence, withdrawal, outcome and response to treatment. *Addiction, 106*(2), 418–427. doi: 10.1111/j.1360-0443.2010.03173.x

Pizarro, J., Silver, R. C., & Prause, J. (2006). Physical and mental health costs of traumatic war experiences among Civil War veterans. *Archives of General Psychiatry, 63*, 193–200.

Plomin, R., & Crabbe, J. (2000). DNA. *Psychological Bulletin, 126*, 806–828.

Plomin, R., & McGuffin, P. (2003). Psychopathology in the postgenomic era. *Annual Review of Psychology, 54*, 205–228.

Plomin, R., Owen, M. J., & McGuffin, P. (1994). The genetic basis of complex human behaviors. *Science, 264*, 1733–1739.

Plomp, E., Van Engeland, H., & Durston, S. (2009). Understanding genes, environment and their interaction in attention-deficit hyperactivity disorder: Is there a role for neuroimaging? *Neuroscience, 164*, 230–240.

Polanczyk, G., Moffitt, T. E., Arseneault, L., Cannon, M., Ambler, A., Keefe, R. S. E., . . . Caspi, A. (2010). Etiological and clinical features of childhood psychotic symptoms: Results from a birth cohort. *Archives of General Psychiatry, 67*, 328–338.

Polaschek, D. L. L. (2003). Relapse prevention, offense process models, and the treatment of sexual offenders. *Professional Psychology: Research and Practice, 34*, 361–367.

Poleshuck, E. L., Gamble, S. A., Cort, N., Hoffman-King, D., Cerrito, B., Rosario-McCabe, L., & Giles, D. E. (2010). Interpersonal psychotherapy for co-occurring depression and chronic pain. *Professional Psychology: Research and Practice, 41*, 312–318.

Pollard, C. A., Pollard, H. J., & Corn, K. J. (1989). Panic onset and major events in the lives of agoraphobics: A test of continuity. *Journal of Abnormal Psychology, 98*, 318–321.

Ponterotto, J. G., & Casas, J. M. (1991). *Handbook of racial/ethnic minority counseling research.* Springfield, IL: Thomas.

Ponterotto, J. G., Utsey, S. O., & Pedersen, P. B. (2006). *Preventing prejudice.* Thousand Oaks, CA: Sage.

Pop, H. G., Jr., & Hudson, J. I. (1992). Is childhood sexual abuse a risk factor for bulimia nervosa? *American Journal of Psychiatry, 149*, 455–463.

Pope, H. G., Jr., & Hudson, J. I. (2007). "Repressed memory" challenge. Retrieved from www.butterfliesandwheels.com/printer_friendly.php?num=177

Pope, H. G., Jr., Barry, S., Bodkin, A., & Hudson, J. I. (2006). Tracking scientific interest in the dissociative disorders: A study of scientific publication output, 1984–2003. *Psychotherapy and Psychosomatics, 75*, 19–24.

Pope, H. G., Jr., Gruber, A. J., Mangweth, B., Bureau, B., deCol, C., Jouvent, R., & Hudson, J. I. (2000). Body image perception among men in three countries. *American Journal of Psychiatry, 157*, 1297–1301.

Pope, H. G., Jr., & Hudson, J. I. (1992). Is childhood sexual abuse a risk factor for bulimia nervosa? *American Journal of Psychiatry, 149*, 455–463.

Pope, H. G., Jr., Lalonde, J. K., Pindyck, L. J., Walsh, T., Bulik, C. M., . . . Hudson, J. I. (2006). Binge eating disorder: A stable syndrome. *American Journal of Psychiatry, 163*, 2181–2183.

Pope, H. G., Jr., Mangweth, B., Negrao, A. B., Hudson, J. I., & Cordas, T. A. (1994). Childhood sexual abuse and bulimia nervosa: A comparison of American, Austrian, and Brazilian women. *American Journal of Psychiatry, 151*, 732–737.

Pope, H. G., Jr., Olivardia, R., Borowiecki, J. J., III, & Cohane, G. H. (2001). The growing commercial value of the male body: A longitudinal survey of advertising in women's magazines. *Psychotherapy and Psychosomatics, 70*, 189–193.

Pope, K. S., & Tabachnick, B. G. (1993). Therapists' anger, hate, fear, and sexual feelings: National survey of therapist responses, client characteristics, critical events, formal complaints, and training. *Professional Psychology: Research and Practice, 24*, 142–152.

Pope, K. S., Tabachnick, B. G., & Keith-Spiegel, P. (1987). Ethics of practice: The beliefs and behaviors of psychologists as therapists. *American Psychologist, 42*, 993–1166.

Pope, K. S., & Vasquez, M. J. T. (2007). *Ethics in psychotherapy and counseling.* Hoboken, NJ: Wiley.

Popper, C., & West, S. A. (1999). Disorders usually first diagnosed in infancy, childhood, or adolescence. In R. E. Hales, S. C. Yudofsky, & J. A. Talbott (Eds.), *Textbook of psychiatry* (pp. 825–954). Washington, DC: American Psychiatric Press.

Population Reference Bureau. (2007). Cognitive aging: Imaging, emotion, and memory. *Today's Research on Aging, 5*, 1–5.

Poulton, R., Trainor, P., Stanton, W., McGee, R., Davies, S., & Silva, P. (1997). The (in)stability of adolescent fears. *Behaviour Research and Therapy, 35*, 159–163.

Poulton, R., Waldie, K. E., Craske, M. G., Menzies, R. G., & McGee, R. (2000). Dishabituation processes in height fear and dental fear: An indirect test of the non-associative model of fear acquisition. *Behaviour Research and Therapy, 38*, 909–919.

Pound, E. J. (1987). Children and prematurity. In A. Thomas & J. Grimes (Eds.), *Children's needs: Psychological perspectives* (pp. 441–450). Washington, DC: National Association of School Psychologists.

Posmontier, B. (2008). Sleep quality in women with and without postpartum depression. *Journal of Obstetric, Gynecological and Neonatal Nursing, 37*, 722–735.

Powell, A. D., & Kahn, A. S. (1995). Racial differences in women's desires to be thin. *International Journal of Eating Disorders, 17*, 191–195.

Powell, L. H., Calvin, J. E., III, & Calvin, J. E., Jr. (2007). Effective obesity treatments. *American Psychologist, 62*, 234–246.

Powers, M. B., Halpern, J. M., Ferenschak, M. P., Gillihan, S. J., & Foa, E. B. (2010). A meta-analytic review of prolonged exposure for posttraumatic stress disorder. *Clinical Psychology Review, 30*, 635–641.

Prati, G., & Pietrantoni, L. (2009). Optimism, social support, and coping strategies as factors contributing to posttraumatic growth: A meta-analysis. *Journal of Loss and Trauma, 14*, 364–388.

Preece, M. H., Horswill, M. S., & Geffen, G. M. (2010). Driving after concussion: The acute effect of mild traumatic brain injury on drivers' hazard perception. *Neuropsychology, 24,* 493–503.

President's New Freedom Commission on Mental Health. (2003). *Achieving the promise: Transforming mental health care in America: Final Report* (DHHS Publication No. SMA03-3832). Rockville, MD: U.S. Department of Health and Human Services.

Pribor, E. F., & Dinwiddie, S. H. (1992). Psychiatric correlates of incest in childhood. *American Journal of Psychiatry, 149,* 52–56.

Price, J., Cole, V., & Goodwin, G. M. (2009). Emotional side effects of selective serotonin reuptake inhibitors: Qualitative study. *British Journal of Psychiatry, 195,* 211–217.

Price, T. R. P., Goetz, K. L., & Lovell, M. R. (2002). Neuropsychiatric aspects of brain tumors. In S. E. Yudowfsky & R. E. Hales (Eds.), *The American Psychiatric Publishing textbook of neuropsychiatry and clinical neurosciences* (pp. 753–781). Washington, DC: American Psychiatric.

Prichard, J. C. (1837). *Treatise on insanity and other disorders affecting the mind.* Philadelphia: Haswell, Barrington, & Haswell.

Priester, M. J., & Clum, G. A. (1992). Attributional style as a diathesis in predicting depression, hopelessness, and suicide ideation in college students. *Journal of Psychopathology and Behavioral Assessment, 14,* 111–122.

Prisciandaro, J. J., & Roberts, J. E. (2005). A taxometric investigation of unipolar depression in the National Comorbidity Survey. *Journal of Abnormal Psychology, 114,* 718–728.

Prochaska, J. O., & Norcross, J. C. (1999). *Systems of psychotherapy: A transtheoretical analysis* (4th ed.). Pacific Grove, CA: Brooks/Cole.

Prossin, A. R., Love, T. M., Koeppe, R. A., Zubieta, J. K. & Silk, K. R. (2010). Dysregulation of regional endogenous opioid function in borderline personality disorder. *American Journal of Psychiatry, 167,* 925–933.

Proudfoot, J., Doran, J., Manicavasagar, V., & Parker, G. (2010). The precipitants of manic/hypomanic episodes in the context of bipolar disorder: A review. *Journal of Affective Disorders.* In press.

Proudfoot, J. G. (2004). Computer-based treatment for anxiety and depression: Is it feasible? Is it effective? *Neuroscience and Biobehavioral Reviews, 28,* 353–363.

Psychosomatic medicine: Doctors see positive effects of humor on health. (2004, June 16). *Immunotherapy Weekly,* 135.

Public Health Service. (1991). *Depression: What you need to know* (NIMH Publication No. 60-FL-1481-0). Rockville, MD: U.S. Government Printing Office.

PubMed (2010). Narcissistic personality disorder. Retrieved from http://www.ncbi.nlm.nih.gov/pubmedhealth/PMH0001930/

PubMed Health. (2010). Trichotillomania. Retrieved from http://www.ncbi.nlm.nih.gov/pubmedhealth/PMH0002485

Puhl, R. M., & Heuer, C. A. (2009). The stigma of obesity: A review and update. *Obesity, 17,* 941–964.

Puhl, R. M., & Latner, J. D. (2007). Stigma, obesity, and the health of the nation's children. *Psychological Bulletin, 133,* 557–580.

Purdon, C. (1999). Thought suppression and psychopathology. *Behavior Research and Therapy, 37,* 1029–1054.

Purdon, C., & Clark, D. A. (2005). *Overcoming obsessional thoughts.* Oakland, CA: New Harbinger.

Queinec, R., Beitz, C., Contrand, B., Jougla, E., Leffondré, K., Lagarde, E., & Encrenaz, G. (2010). Copycat effect after celebrity suicides: Results from the French, national death register. *Psychological Medicine, 40,* 1–4.

Qureshi, S. U., Kimbrell, T., Pyne, J. M., Magruder, K. M., Hudson, T. J., . . . Kunik, M. E. (2010). Greater prevalence and incidence of dementia in older veterans with posttraumatic stress disorder. *Journal of the American Geriatrics Society.* Retrieved from http://onlinelibrary.wiley.com/doi/10.1111/j.1532-5415.2010.02977.x/full

Rabinovici, G. D., & Miller, B. L. (2010). Frontotemporal lobar degeneration: Epidemiology, pathophysiology, diagnosis and management. *CNS Drugs, 24,* 375–398.

Rabinowitz, J., Levine, S. Z., Haim, R., & Hafner, H. (2007). The course of schizophrenia: Progressive deterioration, amelioration or both? *Schizophrenia Research, 91,* 254–258.

Rachman, S. (1966). Sexual fetishism: An experimental analogue. *Psychological Record, 16,* 293–296.

Rachman, S., Elliott, C. M., Shafran, R., & Radomsky, A. S. (2009). Separating hoarding from OCD. *Behaviour Research and Therapy, 47,* 520–522.

Rachman, S., Marks, I. M., & Hodgson, R. (1973). The treatment of obsessive compulsive neurotics by modeling and flooding in vivo. *Behaviour Research and Therapy, 11,* 463–471.

Radwa, A. B., Badawy, R. A., Macdonell, L., Berkovic, S. F., Newton, M. R., & Jackson, G. D. (2010). Predicting seizure control: Cortical excitability and antiepileptic medication. *Annals of Neurology, 67,* 64–73.

Raikkonen, K., Matthews, K. A., & Salomon, K. (2003). Hostility predicts metabolic syndrome risk factors in children and adolescents. *Health Psychology, 22,* 279–286.

Raine, A., Mellingen, K., Liu, J., Venables, P., & Mednick, S. A. (2003). Effect of environmental enrichment at ages 3–5 years on schizotypal personality and antisocial behavior at ages 17 and 23 years. *American Journal of Psychiatry, 160,* 1627–1635.

Ramos, R. (1998). *An ethnographic study of Mexican American inhalant abusers in San Antonio.* Austin, TX: Texas Commission on Alcohol and Drug Abuse. Retrieved from http://www.dshs.state.tx.us/sa/research/populations/Inhale98S.pdf

Rand Corporation. (2010). Understanding invisible wounds: The research challenge. Retrieved from http://www.rand.org/pubs/research_briefs/RB9336/index1.html

Rand, C., & Kuldau, J. (1990). The epidemiology of obesity and self-defined weight problem in the general population: Gender, race, age, and social class. *International Journal of Eating Disorders, 9,* 329–343.

Rao, V., Handel, S., Vaishnavi, S., Keach, S., Robbins, B., Spiro, J., Ward, J., & Berlin, F. (2007). Psychiatric sequelae of traumatic brain injury: A case report. *American Journal of Psychiatry, 164,* 728–735.

Rapaport, K., & Burkhart, B. R. (1984). Personality attitudinal characteristics of sexually coercive college males. *Journal of Abnormal Psychology, 93,* 216–221.

Rapee, R. M., Schniering, C. A., & Hudson, J. L. (2009). Anxiety disorders during childhood and adolescence: Origins and treatment. *Annual Review of Clinical Psychology, 5,* 311–341.

Rapp, M. A., Schneider-Beeri, M., Grossman, H. T., Sano, M., Perl, D. P., . . . Haroutunian, V. (2006). Increased hippocampal plaques and tangles in patients with Alzheimer disease with a lifetime history of major depression. *Archives of General Psychiatry, 63,* 161–167.

Rappaport, J., & Cleary, C. P. (1980). Labeling theory and the social psychology of experts and helpers. In M. S. Gibbs, J. R. Lachenmeyer, & J. Sigal (Eds.), *Community psychology: Theoretical and empirical approaches.* New York: Gardner Press.

Raps, C. S., Peterson, C., Reinhard, K. E., Abramson, L. Y., & Seligman, M. E. P. (1982). Attributional styles among depressed patients. *Journal of Abnormal Psychology, 91,* 102–108.

Rashid, T., & Ostermann, R. F. (2009). Strength-based assessment in clinical practice. *Journal of Clinical Psychology, 65,* 488–498.

Rassin, E., Muris, P., Schmidt, H., & Merckelbach, H. (2000). Relationships between thought-action fusion, thought suppression and obsessive-compulsive symptoms: A structural equation modeling approach. *Behaviour Research and Therapy, 38,* 889–897.

Rathbone, C. J., Moulin, C. J., & Conway, M. A. (2009). Autobiographical memory and amnesia: Using conceptual knowledge to ground the self. *Neurocase: The Neural Basis of Cognition, 15,* 405–418.

Rathus, S. A., Nevid, J. S., & Fichner-Rathus, L. (2005). *Abnormal psychology.* New York: Allyn & Bacon.

Ratican, K. L. (1992). Sexual abuse survivors: Identifying symptoms and special treatment considerations. *Journal of Counseling and Development, 71,* 33–38.

Rauch, S. L., Shin, L. M., & Wright, C. I. (2003). Neuroimaging studies of amygdala function in anxiety disorders. *Annals of the New York Academy of Sciences, 985,* 389–410.

Rausch, S. M., Gramling, S. E., & Auerbach, S. M. (2006). Effects of a single session of large-group meditation and meditation and progressive muscle relaxation training on stress reduction, reactivity, and recovery. *International Journal of Stress Management, 13,* 273–290.

Ray, G. T., Croen, L. A., & Habel, L. A. (2009). Mothers of children diagnosed with attention-deficit/hyperactivity disorder: Health conditions and medical care utilization in periods before and after birth of the child. *Medical Care, 47,* 105–114.

Ray, S., Britschgi, M., Herberr, C., Takeda-Uchimura, Y., Boxer, A., . . . Wyss-Coray, T. (2007). Classification and prediction of clinical Alzheimer's diagnosis based on plasma signaling proteins. *Nature Medicine, 13,* 1359–1362.

Raymond, F. L., Tarpey, P. S., Edkins, S., Tofts, C., O'Meara, S., . . . Futreal, P. A. (2007). Mutations in ZDHHC9, which encodes a palmitoyl-transferase of NRAS and HRAS, cause X-linked mental retardation associated with a marfanoid habitus. *American Journal of Human Genetics, 80,* 982–987.

Raymont, V., Salazar. A. M., Lipsky, R., Goldman, D., Tasick, G., & Grafman, J. (2010). Correlates of posttraumatic epilepsy 35 years following combat brain injury. *Neurology, 75,* 224–229.

Razani, J., Nordin, S., Chan, A., & Murphy, C. (2010). Semantic networks for odors and colors in Alzheimer's disease. *Neuropsychology, 24,* 291–299.

Read, J. P., Kahler, C. W., & Stevenson, J. F. (2001). Bridging the gap between alcoholism treatment research and practice: Identifying what works and why. *Professional Psychology: Research and Practice, 32,* 227–238.

Reading, C., & Mohr, P. (1976). Biofeedback control of migraine: A pilot study. *British Journal of Social and Clinical Psychology, 15,* 429–433.

Rechlin, T., Loew, T. H., & Joraschky, P. (1997). Pseudoseizure "status." *Journal of Psychosomatic Research, 42,* 495–498.

Recovered Memory Project. (2007). *Case information and scholarly resources.* Retrieved from www.brown.edu/Departments/Taubman_Center/Recovmem

Rector, N. A., Beck, A. T., & Stolar, N. (2005). The negative symptoms of schizophrenia: A cognitive perspective. *Canadian Journal of Psychiatry, 50,* 247–257.

Reed, G. M. (2010). Toward ICD-11: Improving the clinical utility of WHO's International Classification of Mental Disorders. *Professional Psychology: Research and Practice, 41,* 457–464.

Reese, M., Herbenick, D., Schick, V., Sanders, S. A., Dodge, B., & Fortenberry, J. D. (2010). Background and considerations on the National Survey of Sexual Health and Behavior (NSSHB) from the investigators. *Journal of Sexual Medicine, 7,* 243–245.

Regier, D. A., Narrow, W. E., Rae, D. S., Mander-scheid, R. W., Locke, B. Z., & Goodwin, F. K. (1993). The de facto U.S. Mental and Addictive Disorders Service System: Epidemiologic Catchment Area prospective one-year prevalence rates of disorders in services. *Archives of General Psychiatry, 50,* 85–94.

Reichenberg, A., & Harvey, P. D. (2007). Neuro-psychological impairments in schizophrenia: Integration of performance-based and brain imaging findings. *Psychological Bulletin, 133,* 833–858.

Reid, J. M., Storch, E. A., Murphy, T. K., Bodzin, D., Mutch, . . . Goodman, W. K. (2010). Development and psychometric evaluation of the treatment-emergent activation and suicidality assessment profile. *Child and Youth Care Forum, 39,* 113–124.

Reid, R. C., Harper, J. M., & Anderson, E. H. (2009). Coping strategies used by hypersexual patients to defend against the painful effects of shame *Clinical Psychology and Psychotherapy, 16,* 125–138.

Reiersen, A. M., & Todorov, A. A. (2011). Association between DRD4 genotype and autistic symptoms in DSM-IV ADHD. *Journal of Canadian Academy of Child and Adolescent Psychiatry, 20,* 15–21.

Reilly, D. (1984). Family therapy with adolescent drug abusers and their families: Defying gravity and achieving escape velocity. *Journal of Drug Issues, 14,* 381–389.

Reinders, A. A. T. S., Nijenhuis, E. R. S., Paans, A. M. J., Korf, J., Willemsen, A. T. M., & den Boers, J. A. (2003). One brain, two selves. *Neuroimage, 20,* 2119–2125.

Reinhold, N., & Markowitsch, H. J. (2009). Retrograde episodic memory and emotion: A perspective from patients with dissociative amnesia. *Neuropsychologia, 47,* 2197–2206.

Reiser, D. E. (1988). The psychiatric interview. In H. H. Goldman (Ed.), *Review of general psychiatry* (pp. 184–192). Norwalk, CT: Appleton & Lange.

Reiss, S., & McNally, R. J. (1985). The expectancy model of fear. In S. Reiss & R. Bootzin (Eds.), *Theoretical issues in behavior therapy* (pp. 107–121). San Diego, CA: Academic Press.

Reiss, S., Peterson, R. A., Gursky, D. M., & McNally, R. J. (1986). Anxiety sensitivity, anxiety frequency, and the prediction of fearfulness. *Behaviour Research and Therapy, 24,* 1–8.

Rennie v. Klein, 462 F. Supp. 1131 (D.N.J. 1978).

Renthal, W., & Nestler, E. J. (2009). Histone acetylation in drug addiction. *Seminars in Cell and Developmental Biology, 20,* 387–394.

Report of the Virginia Tech Review Panel. (2007, August). *Mass shootings at Virginia Tech, April 16, 2007.* Commonwealth of Virginia: Governor's Office.

Resick, P. A., Galovski, T. E., Uhlmansick, M. O., Scher, C. D., Clum, G. A., & Young-Xu, Y. (2008). A randomized clinical trial to dismantle components of cognitive processing therapy for posttraumatic stress disorder in female victims of interpersonal violence. *Journal of Consulting and Clinical Psychology, 76,* 243–248.

Resnick, M., Yehnuda, R., & Pitts, R. K. (1992, March 24). *JAMA* cited in young Indians prone to suicide, study finds. *The New York Times,* D24.

Ressler, K. J. (2010). Amygdala activity, fear, and anxiety: Modulation by stress. *Biological Psychiatry, 67,* 1117–1119.

Rettew, D. C., Zanarini, M. C., & Yen, S. (2003). Childhood antecedents of avoidant personality disorder: A retrospective study. *Journal of the American Academy of Child and Adolescent Psychiatry, 42,* 1122–1130.

Reus, V. I. (1988). Affective disorders. In H. H. Goldman (Ed.), *Review of general psychiatry* (pp. 332–348). Norwalk, CT: Appleton & Lange.

Reynolds, C. R., Kamphaus, R. W., & Rosenthal, B. L. (1989). Applications of the Kaufman Assessment Battery for Children (KABC) in neuropsychological assessment. In C. R. Reynolds & E. Fletcher-Janzen (Eds.), *Handbook of clinical child neuropsychology* (pp. 181–191). New York: Plenum Press.

Rhee, S. H., Waldman, I. D., Hay, D. A., & Levy, F. (1999). Sex differences in genetic and environmental influences in DSM-III-R ADHD. *Journal of Abnormal Psychology, 108,* 24–41.

Rhodes, L., Bailey, C. M., & Moorman, J. E. (2004). Asthma prevalence and control characteristics by race/ethnicity: United States, 2002. *Morbidity and Mortality Weekly Report, 53,* 145–148.

Ricca, V., Mannucci, E., Zucchi, T., Rotella, C. M., & Faravelli, C. (2000). Cognitive-behavioral therapy for bulimia nervosa and binge eating disorder: A review. *Psychotherapy and Psychosomatics, 69,* 287–295.

Ricciardelli, L. A., & McCabe, M. P. (2004). A biopsychosocial model of disordered eating and the pursuit of muscularity in adolescent boys. *Psychological Bulletin, 130,* 179–205.

Rich, B. A., Fromm, S. J., Berghorst, L. H., Dickstein, D. P., Brotman, M. A., Pine, D. S., & Leibenluft, E. (2008). Neural connectivity in children with bipolar disorder: Impairment in the face emotion processing circuit. *Journal of Child Psychology and Psychiatry, 49,* 88–96.

Richards, E. P. (2010). Phenotype v. genotype: Why identical twins have different fingerprints. Retrieved from http//www.forensic-evidence.com/site/ID/ID_Twins.html

Richards, J. C., Alvarenga, M., & Hof, A. (2000). Serum lipids and their relationships with hostility and angry affect and behaviors in men. *Health Psychology, 19,* 393–398.

Richardson, L. F. (1998). Psychogenic dissociation in childhood: The role of the counseling psychologist. *Counseling Psychologist, 26,* 69–100.

Richardson, T., Stallard, P., & Velleman, S. (2010). Computerised cognitive behavioural therapy for the prevention and treatment of depression and anxiety in children and adolescents: A systematic review. *Clinical Child and Family Psychology Review, 13,* 275–290.

Richwine, L. (2004b). *U.S. reviewer claims pressure in antidepressant probe.* Retrieved from www.medscape.com/viewarticle/489987

Rick, S., & Douglas, D. H. (2007). Neurobiological effects of childhood abuse. *Journal of Psychosocial Nursing and Mental Health Services, 45,* 47–54.

Ridenour, T., Maldonado-Molina, M., Compton, W., Spitznagel, E., & Cottlerc, L. (2005). Factors associated with the transition from abuse to dependence among substance abusers: Implications for a measure of addictive liability. *Drug and Alcohol Dependence, 80*(1), 1–14.

Ridgway, A. R., Northup, J., Pellegrin, A., LaRue, R., & Hightshoe, A. (2003). The benefits of recess for children with and without attention-deficit/hyperactivity disorder. *School Psychology Quarterly, 18,* 253–268.

Ridley, C. R. (1995). *Overcoming unintentional racism in counseling and therapy: A practitioner's guide to intentional intervention.* Thousand Oaks, CA: Sage.

Ridley, C. R. (2005). *Overcoming unintentional racism in counseling and therapy* (2nd ed.). Thousand Oaks, CA: Sage.

Rieber, R. W. (2006). *The bifurcation of the self: The history and theory of dissociation and its disorders.* New York: Springer.

Rief, W., & Hiller, W. (2003). A new approach to the assessment of the treatment effects of somatoform. *Psychosomatics, 44,* 492–496.

Rieker, P. P., & Bird, C. E. (2005). Rethinking gender differences in health: Why we need to integrate social and biological perspectives. *Journal of Gerontology, 60,* S40–S47.

Riemann, B. C. (2006). Cognitive behavioral treatment for obsessive-compulsive disorder. *Psychiatric Times, 23,* 65–67.

Rietveld, S., Everaerd, W., & van Beest, I. (2000). Excessive breathlessness through emotional imagery in asthma. *Behaviour Research and Therapy, 38,* 1005–1014.

Rinck, M., & Becker, E. S. (2006). Spider fearful individuals attend to threat, then quickly avoid it: Evidence from eye movements. *Journal of Abnormal Psychology, 115,* 231–238.

Rind, B., Tromovitch, P., & Bauserman, R. (1998). A meta-analysis examination of assumed properties of child sexual abuse using college samples. *Psychological Bulletin, 124,* 22–53.

Riskind, J. H. (2005). Cognitive mechanism in generalized anxiety disorder: A second generation of theoretical perspectives. *Cognitive Therapy and Research, 29,* 1–5.

Riskind, J. H., Moore, R., & Bowley, L. (1995). The looming of spiders: The fearful perceptual distortion of movement and menace. *Behaviour Research and Therapy, 33,* 171–178.

Ritter, M. (2010). Spiders, snakes? Brain-damaged woman knows no fear. Retrieved from http://www.cell.com/current-biology

Ritterband, L. M., Thorndike, F. P., Cox, D. J., Kovatchev, B. P., & Gonder-Frederick, L. A. (2009). A behavior change model for internet interventions. *Annals of Behavioral Medicine, 38,* 18–27.

Rivas-Vazquez, R. A. (2001). Cholinesterase inhibitors: Current pharmacological treatments for Alzheimer's disease. *Professional Psychology: Research and Practice, 32,* 433–436.

Rivas-Vazquez, R. A., & Blais, M. A. (1997). Selective serotonin reuptake inhibitors and atypical antidepressants: A review and update for psychologists. *Professional Psychology: Research and Practice, 28,* 526–536.

Rivera, R. P., & Borda, T. (2001). The etiology of body dysmorphic disorder. *Psychiatric Annals, 31,* 559–564.

Rivera-Navarro, J., Cubo, E., & Almazan, J. (2009). The diagnosis of Tourette's syndrome:

Communication and impact. *Clinical Child Psychology and Psychiatry, 14,* 13–23.

Rivers v. Katz (67 N.Y. 2d 485, 1986).

Rizvi, S., & Zaretsky, A. E. (2007). Psychotherapy through the phases of bipolar disorder: Evidence for general efficacy and differential effects. *Journal of Clinical Psychology: In Session, 63,* 491–506.

Roberts, A. L., Austin, S. B., Corliss, H. L., Vandermorris, A. K., & Koenenn, K. C. (2010). Pervasive traumatic exposure among US sexual orientation minority adults and risk of posttraumatic stress disorder. *American Journal of Public Health, 100,* 2433–2441.

Roberts, A. L., Gilman, S. E., Breslau, J., Breslau, N., & Koenen, K. C. (2010). Race/ethnic differences in exposure to traumatic events, development of post-traumatic stress disorder, and treatment-seeking for post-traumatic stress disorder in the United States. *Psychological Medicine, 41*(1), 71–83. doi: 10.1017/S0033291710000401

Roberts, E. M., English, P. B., Grether, J. K., Windham, G. C., Somberg, L., & Wolff, C. (2007). Maternal residence near agricultural pesticide applications and autism spectrum disorders among children in the California Central Valley. *Environmental Health Perspectives, 115,* 1482–1489.

Roberts, W. (1995). Postvention and psychological autopsy in the suicide of a 14-year-old public school student. *School Counselor, 42,* 322–330.

Robertson, W. C., Jr. (2010). Tourette syndrome and other tic disorders. Retrieved from http://emedicine.medscape.com/article/1182258-overview

Robins, L. N. (1966). *Deviant children growing up: A sociological and psychiatric study of sociopathic personality.* Baltimore: Williams & Wilkins.

Robins, L. N., & Regier, D. A. (Eds.). (1991). *Psychiatric disorders in America: The Epidemiologic Catchment Area study.* New York: Free Press.

Robins, L. N., Tipp, J., & Przybeck, T. (1991). Antisocial personality. In L. N. Robins & D. A. Regier (Eds.), *Psychiatric disorders in America: The Epidemiologic Catchment Area study* (pp. 258–290). New York: Free Press.

Robinson, J. P., Shaver, P. R., & Wrightsman, L. S. (Eds.). (1991). *Measures of personality and social psychological attitudes.* San Diego, CA: Academic Press.

Robinson, J. S., & Larson, C. (2010). Are traumatic events necessary to elicit symptoms of post-traumatic stress? *Psychological Trauma: Theory, Research, and Policy, 2,* 71–76.

Robison, E. J., Shankman, S. A., & McFarland, B. R. (2009). Independent associations between personality traits and clinical characteristics of depression. *Journal of Nervous and Mental Disease, 197,* 476–483.

Rocchi, A., Orsucci, D., Tognoni, G., Ceravolo, R., & Siciliano, G. (2009). The role of vascular factors in late-onset sporadic Alzheimer's disease. *Current Alzheimer Research, 6,* 224–237.

Rockhill, C., Kodish, I., DiBattisto, C., Macias, M., Varley, C., & Ryan, S. (2010). Anxiety disorders in children and adolescents. *Current Problems in Pediatric and Adolescent Care, 40,* 66–99.

Rodebaugh, T. L. (2009). Social phobia and perceived friendship quality. *Journal of Anxiety Disorders, 23,* 872–878.

Roder, V., Mueller, D. R., Mueser, K. T., & Brenner, H. D. (2006). Integrated psychological therapy (IPT) for schizophrenia: Is it effective? *Schizophrenia Bulletin, 32,* 81–93.

Roelofs, J., Huibers, M., Peeters, F., Arntz, A., & van Os, J. (2008). Rumination and worrying as possible mediators in the relation between neuroticism and symptoms of depression and anxiety in clinically depressed individuals. *Behavior Research and Therapy, 46,* 1283–1289.

Roettger, M. E., Swisher, R. R., Kuhl, D. C., & Chavez, J. (2011). Paternal incarceration and trajectories of marijuana and other illegal drug use from adolescence into young adulthood: Evidence from longitudinal panels of males and females in the United States. *Addiction, 106,* 121–132.

Rofey, D. L., Kolko, R. P., Iosif, A.-M., Silk, J. S., Bost, J. E., . . . Dahl, R. E. (2009). A longitudinal study of childhood depression and anxiety in relation to weight gain. *Child Psychiatry and Human Development, 40,* 517–526.

Rogers v. Okin (1979). 478 F.Supp.1342(D. Mass. 1979), 634 F.2d 650 (1st Cir.1980)

Rogers, C. R. (1951). *Client-centered therapy.* Boston: Houghton Mifflin.

Rogers, C. R. (1959). A theory of therapy, personality, and interpersonal relationships, as developed in client-centered framework. In S. Koch (Ed.), *Psychology: A study of science* (Vol. 3, pp. 123–148). New York: McGraw-Hill.

Rogers, C. R. (1961). *On becoming a person.* Boston: Houghton Mifflin.

Rogers, C. R. (1987). The underlying theory: Drawn from experiences with individuals and groups. *Counseling and Values, 32,* 38–45.

Rogers, J. R. (1992). Suicide and alcohol: Conceptualizing the relationship from a cognitive-social paradigm. *Journal of Counseling and Development, 70,* 540–543.

Rogers, R. L., & Petrie, T. A. (2001). Psychological correlates of anorexic and bulimic symptomatology. *Journal of Counseling and Development, 79,* 178–187.

Rogers, S. J. (2009). What are infant siblings teaching us about autism in infancy? *Autism Research, 2,* 125–137.

Rohrmann, S., Hopp, H., & Quirin, M. (2008). Gender differences in psychophysiological responses to disgust. *Journal of Psychophysiology, 22,* 65–75.

Rohsenow, D. J., Monti, P. M., Hutchinson, K. E., Swift, R. M., Colby, S. M., & Kaplan, G. B. (2000). Naltrexone's effects on reactivity to alcohol cues among alcoholic men. *Journal of Abnormal Psychology, 109,* 738–742.

Rohsenow, D. J., Monti, P. M., Martin, R. A., Michalec, E., & Abrams, D. B. (2000). Brief coping skills treatment for cocaine abuse: 12-month substance use outcomes. *Journal of Consulting and Clinical Psychology, 68,* 515–520.

Rohter, L. (2006, December 30). Burst of high-profile anorexia deaths unsettles Brazil.

The New York Times. Retrieved from http://query.nytimes.com/gst/fullpage.html?res=9905E1 DF1630F9

Rokem, A., & Silver, M. A. (2010). Cholinergic enhancement augments magnitude and specificity of visual perceptual learning in healthy humans. *Current Biology, 20*(19), 1723–1728. doi: 10.1016/j.cub.2010.08.027. Retrieved from http://www.cell.com/current-biology/retrieve/pii/S0960982210010171

Rolland, Y., van Kan, G. A., & Vellas, B. (2010). Healthy brain aging: Role of exercise and physical activity. *Clinics in Geriatric Medicine, 26,* 75–87.

Rollnick, S., Miller, W. R., & Butler, C. C. (2008). *Motivational interviewing in health care: Helping patients change behavior.* New York: The Guilford Press.

Rommelse, N. N., Franke, B., Geurts, H. M., Hartman, C. A., & Buitelaar, J. K. (2010). Shared heritability of attention-deficit/hyperactivity disorder and autism spectrum disorder. *European Child and Adolescent Psychiatry, 19,* 281–295.

Rommelse, N. N., Peters, C. T., Oosterling, I. J, Visser, J. C., Bons, D., . . . Buitelaar, J. K. (2011). A pilot study of abnormal growth in autism spectrum disorders and other childhood psychiatric disorders. *Journal of Autism and Developmental Disorders, 41,* 44–54.

Rood, L., Roelofs, J., Bogels, S. M., & Alloy, L. B. (2010). Dimensions of negative thinking and the relations with symptoms of depression and anxiety in children and adolescents. *Cognitive Therapy and Research, 34,* 333–342.

Roos, R. A. (2010). Huntington's disease: A clinical review. *Orphanet Journal of Rare Disorder, 5,* 40. Retrieved from: http://www.ojrd.com/content/5/1/40.

Root, M. P. (1996). *The multiracial experience.* Thousand Oaks, CA: Sage.

Root, R. W., & Resnick, R. J. (2003). An update on the diagnosis and treatment of attention-deficit/hyperactivity disorder. *Professional Psychology: Research and Practice, 34,* 34–41.

Rose, D., Stuart, B., Hardy, K., & Loewy, R. (2010). Re-envisioning psychosis: A new language for clinical practice. *Current Psychiatry, 9,* 23–29.

Rosen, H. J., & Levenson, R. W. (2009). The emotional brain: Combining insights from patients and basic science. *Neurocase, 15,* 173–181.

Rosen, H. R., & Rich, B. A. (2010). Neurocognitive correlates of emotional stimulus processing in pediatric bipolar disorder: A review. *Postgraduate Medicine, 122,* 94–104.

Rosen, J. C., Reiter, J., & Orosan, P. (1995). Assessment of body image in eating disorders with the body dysmorphic disorder examination. *Behaviour Research and Therapy, 33,* 77–84.

Rosen, R. C., & Leiblum, S. R. (1987). Current approaches to the evaluation of sexual desire disorders. *Journal of Sex Research, 23,* 141–162.

Rosen, R. C., & Leiblum, S. R. (1995). Hypoactive sexual desire. *Psychiatric Clinics of North America, 13,* 107–121.

Rosenberg, J., & Rosenberg, S. (2006). *Community mental health: Challenges for the 21st century.* New York: Routledge.

Rosenfarb, I. S., Bellack, A. S., & Aziz, N. (2006). Family interactions and the course of schizophrenia in African American and White patients. *Journal of Abnormal Psychology, 115,* 112–120.

Rosenfarb, I. S., Goldstein, M. J., Mintz, J., & Nuechterlein, K. H. (1995). Expressed emotion and subclinical psychopathology observable within the transactions between schizophrenic patients and their family members. *Journal of Abnormal Psychology, 104,* 259–267.

Rosenfeld, B. (2004). *Assisted suicide and the right to die.* New York: Guilford Press.

Rosenfield, A. H. (1985). Discovering and dealing with deviant sex. *Psychology Today, 19,* 8–10.

Rosenhan, D. (1973). On being sane in insane places. *Science, 179,* 250–258.

Rosenstreich, D. L., Eggleston, P., & Kattan, M. (1997). The role of cockroach allergy and exposure to cockroach allergen in causing morbidity among inner-city children with asthma. *New England Journal of Medicine, 336,* 1356–1363.

Rosenthal, D. (1970). *Genetic theory and abnormal behavior.* New York: McGraw-Hill.

Rosenthal, J., & Jacobson, L. (1968). *Pygmalion in the classroom.* New York: Holt, Rinehart & Winston.

Rosenthal, N. E. (2009). Issues for DSM-V: Seasonal affective disorder and seasonality. *American Journal of Psychiatry, 166,* 852–853.

Ross, C. A. (2009). Ethics of gender identity disorder. *Ethical Human Psychology and Psychiatry, 11,* 165–170.

Ross, C. A., Anderson, G., Fleisher, W. P., & Norton, G. R. (1991). The frequency of multiple personality disorder among psychiatric inpatients. *American Journal of Psychiatry, 148,* 1717–1720.

Ross, K., Freeman, D., Dunn, G., & Garety, P. (2011). Can jumping to conclusion be reduced in people with delusions? An experimental investigation of a brief reasoning training module. *Schizophrenia Bulletin, 37,* 324–333.

Rossignol, D. A. (2009). Novel and emerging treatments for autism spectrum disorders: A systematic review. *Annals of Clinical Psychiatry, 21,* 213–236.

Rossignol, D. A., & Frye, R. E. (2011). Mitochondrial dysfunction in autism spectrum disorders: A systematic review and meta-analysis. *Molecular Psychiatry.* doi: 10.1038/mp.2010.136

Rossler, W., Riecher-Rossler, A. R., Angst, J., Murray, R., Gamma, A., . . . Gross, V. A. (2007). Psychotic experiences in the general population: A twenty-year prospective study. *Schizophrenia Research, 92,* 1–14.

Rossow, I., & Amundsen, A. (1995). Alcohol abuse and suicide: A forty-year prospective study of Norwegian conscripts. *Addiction, 90,* 685–691.

Roth, M. E., Cosgrov, K. P., & Carroll, M. E. (2004). Sex differences in the vulnerability to drug abuse: A review of preclinical studies. *Neuroscientific Biobehavioral Review, 28,* 533–546.

Roth, R. M., Flashman, L. A., Saykin, A. J., McAllister, T. W., & Vidaver, R. (2004). Apathy in schizophrenia: Reduced frontal lobe volume and neuropsychological deficits. *American Journal of Psychiatry, 161,* 157–159.

Rothbaum, B. O., Hodges, L., Watson, B. A., & Kessler, G. S. (1996). Virtual reality exposure treatment of fear of flying: A case report. *Behaviour Research and Therapy, 34,* 477–481.

Rothman, B. M., Ahn, W. K., Sanislow, C. A., & Kim, N. S. (2009). Can clinicians recognize DSM-IV personality disorders from five-factor model descriptions of patient cases? *American Journal of Psychiatry, 166,* 427–433.

Rothschild, L., Cleland, C., Haslam, N., & Zimmerman, M. (2003). A taxometric study of borderline personality disorder. *Journal of Abnormal Psychology, 112,* 657–666.

Rouse v. Cameron, 373 F. 2d 451 (D.C. Cir. 1966).

Rowland, D. L., Tai, W., & Brummett, K. (2007). Interactive processes in ejaculatory disorders. Psychophysiological considerations. In E. Janssen (Ed.), *The psychophysiology of sex* (pp. 227–243). Bloomington: Indiana University Press.

Roy, A. (1992). Suicide in schizophrenia. *International Review of Psychiatry, 4,* 205–209.

Roy, A. (1994). Recent biologic studies on suicide. *Suicide and Life-Threatening Behavior, 24,* 10–24.

Roy-Byrne, P. P., Craske, M. G., & Stein, M. B. (2006). Panic disorder. *Lancet, 368,* 1023–1032.

Rozen, T. D. (2010). Cluster headache with aura. *Current Pain and Headache Reports, 15*(2), 98–100. doi: 10.1007/s11916-010-0168-9

Rucker, J. H., & McGuffin, P. (2010). Polygenic heterogeneity: A complex model of genetic inheritance in psychiatric disorders. *Biological Psychiatry, 68,* 312–313.

Rudaz, M., Craske, M. G., Becker, E. S., Ledermann, T., & Margraf, J. (2010). Health anxiety and fear of fear in panic disorder and agoraphobia vs. social phobia: A prospective longitudinal study. *Depression and Anxiety, 27,* 404–411.

Rudd, M. D., Joiner, T., & Rajab, M. H. (2004). *Treating suicidal behavior.* New York: Guilford Press.

Rudolph, K. D., Flynn, M., Abaied, J. L., Groot, A., & Thompson, R. (2009). Why is past depression the best predictor of future depression? Stress generation as a mechanism of depression continuity in girls. *Journal of Clinical Child and Adolescent Psychology, 38,* 473–485.

Rueger, D., & Liberman, R. (1984). Behavioral family therapy for delinquent and substance-abusing adolescents. *Journal of Drug Issues, 14,* 403–417.

Rusanen, M., Kivipelto, M., Quesenberry, C. P., Zhou, J., & Whitmer, R. A. (2010). Heavy smoking in midlife and long-term risk of Alzheimer disease and vascular dementia. *Archives of Internal Medicine, 170*(14), 1191–1201. doi: 10.1001/archinternmed.2010.393

Ruscio, J., & Ruscio, A. M. (2000). Informing the continuity controversy: A taxometric analysis of depression. *Journal of Abnormal Psychology, 109,* 473–487.

Rush, A. J., Trivedi, M. H., Wisniewski, S. R., Stewart, J. W., Nierenberg, A. A., STAR*D Study Team. (2006). Bupropion-SR, sertraline, or venlafaxine-XR after failure of SSRIs for depression. *New England Journal of Medicine, 354,* 1231–1242.

Rushton, J. P., & Jensen, A. R. (2005). Thirty years of research on race differences in cognitive ability. *Psychology, Public Policy, and Law, 11,* 235–294.

Russell, J. J., Moskowitz, D. S., Zuroff, D. C., Bleau, Z. P., & Young, S. N. (2010). Anxiety, emotional security and the interpersonal behavior of individuals with social anxiety disorder. *Psychological Medicine, 41*(3), 545–554. doi: 10.1017/S0033291710000863

Rutter, M., MacDonald, H., LeCouteur, A., Harrington, R., Bolton, P., & Bailey, A. (1990). Genetic factors in child psychiatric disorders: II. Empirical findings. *Journal of Child Psychology and Psychiatry, 31,* 39–83.

Rutter, M. L. (1997). Nature-nurture integration: The example of antisocial behavior. *Journal of the American Psychological Association, 52,* 390–398.

Ryder, A. G., Yang, J., Zhu, X., Yao, S., Yi, J., . . . Bagby, R. M. (2008). The cultural shaping of depression: Somatic symptoms in China, psychological symptoms in North America? *Journal of Abnormal Psychology, 117,* 300–313.

Rynn, M., Puliafico, A., Heleniak, C., Rikhi, P., Ghalib, K., & Vidair, H. (2011). Advances in psychopharmacology for pediatric anxiety disorders. *Depression and Anxiety, 28,* 76–87.

Sable, P. (1997). Attachment, detachment, and borderline personality disorder. *Journal of Psychotherapy, 34,* 171–181.

Sacynski, J. S., Beiser, A., Seshadri, S., Auerbach, S., Wolf, P. A., & Au, R. (2010). Depressive symptoms and risk of dementia: The Framingham Heart Study. *Neurology, 75,* 35–41.

Sadovsky, R. (1998). Evaluation of patients with transient global amnesia. *American Family Physician, 57,* 2237–2238.

Safarinejad, M. R. (2006). Female sexual dysfunction in a population-based study in Iran: Prevalence and associated risk factors. *International Journal of Impotence Research, 18,* 382–395.

Saha, S., Chant, D., Welham, J., & McGrath, M. (2005). *A systematic review of the prevalence of schizophrenia.* Retrieved from http://medicine.plosjournals.org/perlserv/?request=getdocument&doi=10.1371/journal.pmed.0020141

Sajatovic, M., Ignacio, R. V., West, J. A., Cassidy, K. A., Safavi, R., Kilbourne, A. M., & Blow, F. C. (2009). Predictors of nonadherence among individuals with bipolar disorder receiving treatment in a community mental health clinic. *Comprehensive Psychiatry, 50,* 100–107.

Sakauragi, S., Sugiyama, Y., & Takeuchi, K. (2010). Effect of laughing and weeping on mood and heart rate variability. *Journal of Physiological Anthropology and Applied Human Science, 21,* 159–165.

Saklofske, D. H., Hildebrand, D. K., & Gorsuch, R. L. (2000). Replication of the factor structure of the Wechsler Adult Intelligence Scale—Third Edition with a Canadian sample. *Psychological Assessment, 12,* 436–439.

Sakolsky, D., & Birmaher, B. (2008). Pediatric anxiety disorders: Management in primary care. *Current Opinion in Pediatric Care, 20*(5), 538–543.

Saks, E. R. (2007). *The center cannot hold: My journey through madness.* New York: Hyperion.

Saks, E. R. (2009). Some thoughts on denial of mental illness. *American Journal of Psychiatry, 166,* 972–973.

Saldano, D. D., Chaviano, A. H., Maizelsk, M., Yerkes, E. B., Cheng, E. Y., . . . Kaplan, W. E. (2007). Office management of pediatric primary nocturnal enuresis: A comparison of physician advised and parent chosen alternative treatment outcomes. *Journal of Urology, 178,* 1758–1762.

Salgado-Pineda, P., Caclin, A., Baeza, I., Junque, C., Bernardo, M., Blin, O., & Funlupt, P. (2007). Schizophrenia and the frontal cortex: Where does it fail? *Schizophrenia Research, 91,* 73–81.

Salthouse, T. A. (2004). What and when of cognitive aging. *Current Directions in Psychological Science, 13,* 140–144.

Salvadore, G., Quiroz, J. A., Machado-Vieira, R., Henter, I. D., Manji, H. K., Zarate, C. A., Jr. (2010). The neurobiology of the switch process in bipolar disorder: A review. *Journal of Clinical Psychiatry, 71,* 1488–1501.

Sammons, M. T. (2004). Healthcare trends. *Register Report, 30,* 16–18.

Samuels, J., Shugart, Y. Y., Grados, M. A., Willour, V. L., Bienvenu, O. J., . . . Nestadt, G. (2007). Significant linkage to compulsive hoarding on chromosome 14 in families with obsessive-compulsive disorder: Results from the OCD Collaborative Genetics Study. *American Journal of Psychiatry, 164,* 493–499.

Samuels, J. F., Bienvenu, O. J., Grados, M. A., Cullen, B., Riddle, M. A., . . . Nestadt, G. (2008). Prevalence and correlates of hoarding behavior in a community-based sample. *Behaviour Research and Therapy, 46,* 836–844.

Sanchez, H. G. (2001). Risk factor model for suicide assessment and intervention. *Professional Psychology: Research and Practice, 32,* 351–355.

Sanchez-Meca, J., Rosa-Alcazar, A. I., Marin-Martinez, F., & Gomez-Conesa, A. (2010). Psychological treatment of panic disorder with and without agoraphobia: A meta-analysis. *Clinical Psychology Review, 30,* 37–50.

Sanders, A. R., & Gejman, P. V. (2001). Influential ideas and experimental progress in schizophrenia genetics research. *Journal of the American Medical Association, 285,* 2831–2833.

Sanders, J., Diamond, S. S., & Vidmar, N. (2002). Legal perception of science and expert knowledge. *Psychology, Public Policy, and Law, 8,* 139–153.

Sands, S. H. (2003). The subjugation of the body in eating disorders: A particularly female solution. *Psychoanalytic Psychology, 20,* 103–116.

Sands, T. (1998). Feminist counseling and female adolescents: Treatment strategies for depression. *Journal of Mental Health Counseling, 20,* 42–54.

Santiago-Rivera, A. L., Arredondo, P., & Gallardo-Cooper, M. (2002). *Counseling Latinos and la familia.* Thousand Oaks, CA: Sage.

Santisteban, D. A., Muir, J. A., Mena, M. P., & Mitrani, V. B. (2003). Integrative borderline adolescent family therapy: Meeting the challenges of treating adolescents with borderline personality disorders. *Psychotherapy: Theory, Research, Practice, Training, 40,* 251–264.

Sarbin, T. R. (1997). On the futility of psychiatric diagnostic manuals (DSMs) and the return of personal agency. *Journal of Applied and Preventative Psychology, 6,* 233–244.

Sarter, M., Bruno, J. P., & Parikh, V. (2007). Abnormal neurotransmitter release underlying behavior and cognitive disorders: Toward concepts of dynamic and function-specific dysregulation. *Neuropsychopharmocology, 32,* 1452–1461.

Satir, V. (1967). A family of angels. In J. Haley & L. Hoffman (Eds.), *Techniques of family therapy.* New York: Basic Books.

Satir, V. (1983). *Conjoint family therapy* (3rd ed.). Palo Alto, CA: Science and Behavior Books.

Satir, V. M., & Bitter, J. R. (1991). The therapist and family therapy: Satir's human validation process model. In A. M. Horne & J. L. Passmore (Eds.), *Family counseling and therapy* (2nd ed., pp. 13–45). Itasca, IL: Peacock.

Satow, R. (1979). Where has all the hysteria gone? *Psychoanalytic Review, 66,* 463–477.

Satre, D. D., Campbell, C. I., Gordon, N. S., & Weisner, C. (2010). Ethnic disparities in accessing treatment for depression and substance use disorders in an integrated health plan. *International Journal of Psychiatry in Medicine, 40,* 57–76.

Satz, P. (2001). Mild head injury in children and adolescents. *Current Directions in Psychological Science, 10,* 106–109.

Saudino, K. J. (1997). Moving beyond the heritability question: New directions in behavioral genetic studies of personality. *Current Directions in Psychological Science, 6,* 86–90.

Sauer, S. E., Burris, J. L., & Carlson, C. R. (2010). New directions in the management of chronic pain: Self-regulation theory as a model for integrative clinical psychology practice. *Clinical Psychology Review, 30,* 805–814.

Saulny, S. (2006, June 21). Suicide rate soars in devastated New Orleans. *Seattle Post Intelligencer,* p. A1.

Saunders, S. M., Miller, M., & Bright, M. M. (2010). Spiritually conscious psychological care. *Professional Psychology: Research and Practice, 41,* 355–362.

Savely, V. R., Leitao, M. M., & Stricker, R. B. (2006). The mystery of Morgellons disease: Infection or delusion? *American Journal of Clinical Dermatology, 7,* 1–5.

Saxena, S. (2007). Is compulsive hoarding a genetically and neurobiologically discrete syndrome? Implications for diagnostic classification. *American Journal of Psychiatry, 164,* 380–384.

Saxena, S., Brody, A. L., Maidment, K. M., Smith, E. C., Zohrabi, N., . . . Baxter, L. R., Jr. (2004). Cerebral glucose metabolism in obsessive-compulsive hoarding. *American Journal of Psychiatry, 161,* 1038–1048.

Saxena, S., Brody, A. L., Schwartz, J. M., & Baxter, L. R. (1998). Neuroimaging and frontal-subcortical circuitry in obsessive-compulsive disorder. *British Journal of Psychiatry, 35,* 26–37.

Schacht, T. E. (1985). DSM-III and the politics of truth. *American Psychologist, 40,* 513–521.

Schacht, T. E., & Nathan, P. E. (1977). But is it good for the psychologists? Appraisal and status of DSM-III. *American Psychologist, 32,* 1017–1025.

Schachter, S. (1977). Nicotine regulation in heavy and light smokers. *Journal of Experimental Psychology (General), 106,* 5–12.

Schachter, S., & Latané, B. (1964). Crime, cognition, and the autonomic nervous system. *Nebraska Symposium on Motivation, 12,* 221–274.

Schafer, J., & Brown, S. A. (1991). Marijuana and cocaine effect expectancies and drug use patterns. *Journal of Consulting and Clinical Psychology, 59,* 558–565.

Schauer, M., & Elbert, T. (2010). Dissociation following traumatic stress: Etiology and treatment. *Journal of Psychology, 218,* 109–127.

Schempf, A. H., & Strobino, D. M. (2008). Illicit drug use and adverse birth outcomes: Is it drugs or context? *Journal of Urban Health, 85,* 858–873.

Schiavi, R. C., & Segraves, R. T. (1995). The biology of sexual dysfunction. *Psychiatric Clinics of North America, 18,* 7–23.

Schienle, A., Schafer, A., & Naumann, E. (2008). Event-related brain potentials of spider phobics to disorder-relevant, generally disgust- and fear-inducing pictures. *Journal of Psychophysiology, 22,* 5–13.

Schindler, A., Thomasius, R., Petersen, K., & Sack, P. M. (2009). Heroin as an attachment substitute? Differences in attachment representations between opioid, ecstasy and cannabis abusers. *Attachment & Human Development, 11*(3), 307–330.

Schlesinger, L. (1989). *Sex murder and sex aggression.* New York: Wiley.

Schmauk, F. J. (1970). Punishment, arousal, and avoidance learning. *Journal of Abnormal Psychology, 76,* 325–335.

Schmidt, N. B., & Harrington, P. (1995). Cognitive-behavioral treatment of body dysmorphic disorder: A case report. *Journal of Behavior Therapy and Experimental Psychiatry, 26,* 161–167.

Schmidt, N. B., Keough, M. E., Mitchell, M. A., Reynolds, E. K., MacPherson, L., . . . Lejuez, C. W. (2010). Anxiety sensitivity: Prospective prediction of anxiety among early adolescents. *Journal of Anxiety Disorders, 24,* 503–508.

Schmidt, N. B., Kotov, R., Bernstein, A., Zvolensky, M. J., Joiner, T. E., & Lewinsohn, P. M. (2007). Mixed anxiety depression: Taxometric exploration of the validity of a diagnostic category in youth. *Journal of Affective Disorders, 98,* 83–89.

Schmidt, N. B., Lerew, D. R., & Jackson, R. J. (1997). The role of anxiety sensitivity in the pathogenesis of panic: Prospective evaluations of spontaneous panic attacks during acute stress. *Journal of Abnormal Psychology, 106,* 355–364.

Schmidt, N. B., Lerew, D. R., & Trakowski, J. H. (1997). Body vigilance in panic disorder: Evaluating attention to bodily perturbations. *Journal of Consulting and Clinical Psychology, 65,* 214–220.

Schmidt, N. B., Richey, J., Buckner, J. D., & Timpano, K. R. (2009). Attention training for generalized social anxiety disorder. *Journal of Abnormal Psychology, 118,* 5–14.

Schneider, M. S., Brown, L. S., & Glassgold, J. M. (2002). Implementing the resolution on appropriate therapeutic responses to sexual orientation: A guide for the perplexed. *Professional Psychology: Research and Practice, 33,* 265–276.

Schneier, F. R. (2006). Social anxiety disorder. *New England Journal of Medicine, 355,* 1029–1037.

Schnittker, J. (2010). Gene-environment correlations in the stress-depression relationship. *Journal of Health and Social Behavior, 51,* 229–243.

Schnurr, P. P., Friedman, M. J., & Rosenberg, S. D. (1993). Premilitary MMPI scores as predictors of combat-related PTSD symptoms. *American Journal of Psychiatry, 150,* 479–483.

Schoeneman, T. J. (1984). The mentally ill witch in textbooks of abnormal psychology: Current status and implications of a fallacy. *Professional Psychology, 15,* 299–314.

Schonfeldt-Lecuona, C., Connemann, B. J., Spitzer, M., & Herwig, U. (2003). Transcranial magnetic stimulation in the reversal of motor conversion disorder. *Psychotherapy and Psychosomatics, 72,* 286–290.

Schreiber, F. R. (1973). *Sybil.* Chicago: Regnery.

Schreiber, J. L., Breier, A., & Pickar, D. (1995). Expressed emotion: Trait or state? *British Journal of Psychiatry, 166,* 647–649.

Schreier, A., Wittchen, H.-U., Hofler, M., & Lieb, R. (2008). Anxiety disorders in mothers and their children: Prospective longitudinal community study. *British Journal of Psychiatry, 192,* 308–309.

Schreier, A., Wolke, D., Thomas, K., Horwood, J., Hollis, C., Gunnell, D., . . . Harrison, G. (2009). Prospective study of peer victimization in childhood and psychotic symptoms in a nonclinical population at age 12 years. *Archives of General Psychiatry, 66,* 527–536.

Schrut, A. (2005). A psychodynamic (nonOedipal) and brain function hypothesis regarding a type of male sexual masochism. *Journal of the American Academy of Psychoanalysis and Dynamic Psychiatry, 33,* 333–349.

Schuckit, M. A. (1990). A prospective study of children of alcoholics. In C. R. Cloninger & H. Begleiter (Eds.), *Genetics and biology of alcoholism* (pp. 183–194). Cold Spring Harbor, NY: Cold Spring Harbor Laboratory Press.

Schuckit, M. A. (1994). A clinical model of genetic influences in alcohol dependence. *Journal of Studies on Alcohol, 55,* 5–17.

Schulman, S. L., Collish, Y., von Zuben, F. C., & Kodman-Jones, C. (2000). Effectiveness of treatments for nocturnal enuresis in a heterogeneous population. *Clinical Pediatrics, 39,* 359–364.

Schulz, A. J., Gravlee, C. C., Williams, D. R., Israel, B. A., Mentz, G., & Rowe, Z. (2006). Discrimination, symptoms of depression, and self-rated health among African American women in Detroit: Results from a longitudinal analysis. *American Journal of Public Health, 96,* 1265–1270.

Schumann, C. M., Bloss, C. S., Barnes, C. C., Wideman, G. M., Carper, R. A., . . . Courchesne, E. (2010). Longitudinal magnetic resonance imaging study of cortical development through early childhood in autism. *Journal of Neuroscience, 30,* 4419–4427.

Schur, E., Noonan, C., Polivy, J., Goldberg, J., & Buchwald, D. (2009). Genetic and environmental influences on restrained eating behavior. *International Journal of Eating Disorders, 42,* 765–772.

Schwartz, A. (2010, September 13). Suicide reveals signs of a disease seen in N.F.L. *The New York Times.* Retrieved from http://www.nytimes.com/2010/09/14/sports/14football.html

Schwartz, A. J. (2006). Four eras of study of college student suicide in the United States: 1920–2004. *Journal of American College Health, 54,* 353–366.

Schwartz, A. J., & Whittaker, I. C. (1990). Suicide among college students: Assessment, treatment, and intervention. In S. J. Blumenthal and D. J. Kupfer (Eds.). *Suicide over the life cycle: Risk factors, assessment, and treatment of suicidal patients.* Washington, DC: American Psychiatric Press.

Schwartz, B. S., Stewart, W. F., Simon, D., & Lipton, R. B. (1998). Epidemiology of tension-type headache. *Journal of the American Medical Association, 279,* 381–383.

Schwartz, L., Slater, M. A., & Birchler, G. R. (1994). Interpersonal stress and pain behaviors in patients with chronic pain. *Journal of Consulting and Clinical Psychology, 62,* 861–864.

Schwartz, L. M., & Woloshin, S. (1999). Changing disease definitions: Implications for disease prevalence. *Effective Clinical Practice, 2,* 76–85.

Schwartz, M. S., & Andraski, F. (2003). *Biofeedback: A practitioner's guide.* New York: Guilford Press.

Schwartz, R. P., Kelly, S. M., O'Grady, K. E., Mitchell, S. G., & Brown, B. S. (2010). Antecedents and correlates of methadone treatment entry: A comparison of out-of-treatment and in-treatment cohorts. *Drug and Alcohol Dependence, 115*(1–2), 23–29.

Schwartzman, J. B., & Glaus, K. D. (2000). Depression and coronary heart disease in women: Implications for clinical practice and research. *Professional Psychology: Research and Practice, 31,* 48–57.

Schweinsburg, A. D., Brown, S. A., & Tapert, S. F., (2008). The influence of marijuana use on neurocognitive functioning in adolescents. *Current Drug Abuse Reviews, 1*(1), 99–111.

Schwitzer, A. M., Rodriguez, L. E., Thomas, C., & Salimi, L. (2001). The eating disorders NOS diagnostic profile among college women. *Journal of American College Health, 49,* 157–166.

Science Daily (2010, October 12). New way to classify personality disorders proposed. *Science Daily.* Retrieved from http://www.sciencedaily.com/releases/2010/10/101012141927.htm

Scott, C., & Resnick, P. J. (2009). Assessing potential for harm: Would your patient injure himself or others? *Current Psychiatry, 24,* 26–33.

Scott, J., Martin, G., Welham, J., Bor, W., Najman, J., . . . McGrath, J. (2009). Psychopathology during childhood and adolescence predicts delusion-like experiences in adults: A 21 year birth cohort study. *American Journal of Psychiatry, 166,* 567–574.

Scott, M. J., & Stradling, S. G. (1994). Posttraumatic stress disorder without the trauma. *British Journal of Clinical Psychology, 33,* 71–74.

Scribner, C. M. (2001). Rosenhan revisited. *Professional Psychology: Research and Practice, 32*(2), 215–216.

Scroppo, J. C., Drob, S. L., Weinberger, J. L., & Eagle, P. (1998). Identifying dissociative identity disorder: A self-report and projective study. *Journal of Abnormal Psychology, 107,* 272–284.

Seagraves, R. T. (2010). Considerations for diagnostic criteria for erectile dysfunction in DSMV. *Journal of Sexual Medicine, 7,* 654–660.

Seal, K. H., Bertenthal, D., Miner, C. R., Sen, S., & Marmar, C. (2007). Bringing the war back home. *Archives of Internal Medicine, 167,* 476–482.

Seale, C., & Addington-Hall, J. (1995). Dying at the best time. *Social Science Medicine, 40,* 589–595.

Searight, H. R., Rottnek, F., & Abby, S. L. (2001). Conduct disorder: Diagnosis and treatment in primary care. *American Family Physician, 63,* 1579–1588.

Seemüller, F., Riedel, M., Obermeier, M., Bauer, M., Adli, M., . . . Möller, H. J. (2009). The controversial link between antidepressants and suicidality risks in adults: Data from a naturalistic study on a large sample of in-patients with a major depressive episode. *International Journal of Neuropsychpharmacology, 12,* 181–189.

Seethalakshmi, R., Dhavale, S., Suggu, K., & Dewan, M. (2008). Catatonic syndrome: Importance of detection and treatment with lorazepam. *Annals of Clinical Psychiatry, 20,* 5–8.

Segall, R. (2001). Never too skinny. *Psychology Today, 34,* 2–3.

Segerstrom, S. C., & Miller, G. E. (2004). Psychological stress and the human immune system: A meta-analytic study of 30 years of inquiry. *Psychological Bulletin, 30,* 601–630.

Segerstrom, S. C., & Sephton, S. E. (2010). Optimistic expectancies and cell-mediated immunity: The role of positive affect. *Psychological Science, 21,* 448–455.

Segrin, C., Powell, H. L., Givertz, M., & Brackin, A. (2003). Symptoms of depression, relational quality, and loneliness in dating relationships. *Personal Relationships, 10,* 25–36.

Sehlmeyer, C., Dannlowski, U., Schoning, S., Kugel, H., Pyka, M., . . . Konrad, C. (2011). Neural correlates of trait anxiety in fear extinction. *Psychological Medicine, 41*(4), 789–798. doi: 10.1017/S0033291710001248

Seidel, L., & Walkup, J. T. (2006). Selective serotonin reuptake inhibitor use in the treatment of non-obsessive compulsive anxiety disorders. *Journal of Child and Adolescent Psychopharmacology, 16,* 171–179.

Seitz, V. (2007). The impact of media spokeswomen on teen girls' body image: An empirical assessment. *Business Review, 7,* 228–236.

Selby, E. A., & Joiner, T. E., Jr. (2009). Cascades of emotion: The emergence of borderline personality disorder from emotional and behavioral dysregulation. *Review of General Psychology, 13,* 219–229.

Seligman, M. E. P. (1971). Phobias and preparedness. *Behavior Therapy, 2,* 307–320.

Seligman, M. E. P. (1975). *Helplessness.* San Francisco: Freeman.

Seligman, M. E. P. (1996). Science as an ally of practice. *American Psychologist, 51,* 1072–1079.

Seligman, M. E. P. (2007). Coaching and positive psychology. *Australian Psychologist, 42,* 266–287.

Seligman, M. E. P., & Csikszentmahalyi, M. (2000). Positive psychology: An introduction. *American Psychologist, 55,* 5–14.

Seligman, M. E. P., & Levant, R. F. (1998). Managed care policies rely on inadequate science. *Professional Psychology: Research and Practice, 29,* 211–212.

Seligman, M. E. P., Reivich, K., Jaycox, L., & Gillham, J. (1995). *The optimistic child.* Boston: Houghton Mifflin.

Selten, J. P., Cantor-Graee, E., & Kahn, R. S. (2007). Migration and schizophrenia. *Current Opinions in Psychiatry, 20,* 111–115.

Selvin, I. P. (1993). The incidence and prevalence of sexual dysfunctions. *Archives of Sexual Behavior, 19,* 389–408.

Selye, H. (1956). *The stress of life.* New York: McGraw-Hill.

Selye, H. (1982). Stress: Eustress, distress, and human perspectives. In S. B. Day (Ed.), *Life stress* (pp. 3–13). New York: Van Nostrand Reinhold.

Senate Committee on the Judiciary. (1991). Violence against women: The increase of rape in America 1990. *Response to the Victimization of Women and Children, 14* (79, No. 2), 20–23.

Serpe, G. (2009). Tyra's alleged stalker goes on trial. Retrieved from http://www.eonline.com/uberglog/b119280_tyras-alleged_stalker_goes_on_trial.html

Severeijns, R., Vlaeyen, J. W. S., van den Hout, M. A., & Picavet, H. S. J. (2004). Pain catastrophizing is associated with health indices in musculoskeletal pain. *Health Psychology, 23,* 49–57.

Sexton, T. L., Alexander, J. F., & Mease, A. L. (2004). Levels of evidence for the models and mechanisms of therapeutic change in family and couple therapy. In M. J. Lambert (Ed.), *Bergin and Garfield's handbook of psychotherapy and behavior change* (pp. 590–646). New York: Wiley.

Shadlen, M. N., & Kiani, R. (2007). Neurology: An awakening. *Nature, 448,* 539–540.

Shaffer, A., Huston, L., & Egeland, B. (2008). Identification of child maltreatment using prospective and self-report methodologies: A comparison of maltreatment incidence and relation to later psychopathology. *Child Abuse & Neglect, 32*(7), 682–692.

Shafran, R., Booth, R., & Rachman, S. (1993). The reduction of claustrophobia: II. Cognitive analysis. *Behaviour Research and Therapy, 31,* 75–85.

Shahidi, S., & Salmon, P. (1992). Contingent and non-contingent biofeedback training for type A

and B health adults: Can type A's relax by competing? *Journal of Psychosomatic Research, 36,* 477–483.

Shalev, A. Y., Freedman, S., Peri, T., & Brandes, D. (1998). Prospective study of posttraumatic stress disorder and depression following trauma. *American Journal of Psychiatry, 155,* 630–637.

Shan, Y. (2010). Malicious use of pharmaceuticals in children *The Journal of Pediatrics, 157,* 832–836.

Shandera, A. L., Berry, D. T. R., Clark, J. A., Schipper, L. J., Graue, L. O., & Harpe, J. P. (2010). Detection of malingered mental retardation. *Psychological Assessment, 22,* 50–56.

Shapiro, D. L. (1984). *Psychological evaluation and expert testimony.* New York: Van Nostrand Reinhold.

Sharma, A., Chaturvedi, R., Sharma, A., & Sorrell, J. H. (2009). Electroconvulsive therapy in patients with vagus nerve stimulation. *Journal of Extra Corporeal Technology, 25,* 141–143.

Sharma, V., Khan, M., Corpse, C., & Sharma, P. (2008). Missed bipolarity and psychiatric comorbidity in women with postpartum depression. *Bipolar Disorders, 10,* 742–747.

Sharp, S. I., Aarsland, D., Day, S., Sonnesyn, H., & Ballard, C. (2010). Hypertension is a potential risk factor for vascular dementia: Systematic review. *International Journal of Geriatric Psychiatry.* Retrieved from http://www.ncbi.nlm.nih.gov/pubmed/21192013

Shaw, P., Eckstrand, K., Sharp, W., Blumenthal, J., Lerch, J. P., . . . Rapoport, J. L. (2007). Attention-deficit/hyperactivity disorder is characterized by a delay in cortical maturation. *Proceedings of the National Academy of Sciences, 104,* 19649–19654.

Shea, S. C. (2002). *The practical art of suicide assessment.* Hoboken, NJ: Wiley.

Shedler, J., & Block, J. (1990). Adolescent drug use and psychological health: A longitudinal inquiry. *American Psychologist, 45,* 612–630.

Sheehan, W., Sewall, B., & Thurber, S. (2005). *Dissociative identity disorder and temporal lobe involvement: Replication and a cautionary note.* Retrieved from www.priory.com/psych/did.htm

Sheline, Y. I., Morris, J. C., Snyder, A. Z.,. Price, J. L., Yan, Z., . . . Mintun, M. A. (2010). APOE4 allele disrupts resting state fMRI connectivity in the absence of amyloid plaques or decreased CSF Aβ42. *Journal of Neuroscience, 30,* 17035–17040.

Shelley-Ummenhofer, J., & MacMillan, P. D. (2007). Cognitive-behavioural treatment for women who binge eat. *Canadian Journal of Dietetic Practice and Research, 68,* 139–142.

Shelton, R. C., Osuntokun, O., Heinloth, A. N., & Corya, S. A. (2010). Therapeutic options for treatment-resistant depression. *CNS Drugs, 24,* 131–161.

Sher, K. J., Bartholow, B. D., & Wood, M. D. (2000). Personality and substance use disorders: A prospective study. *Journal of Consulting and Clinical Psychology, 68,* 818–829.

Sher, K. J., Dick, D. M., Crabbe, J. C., Hutchison, K. E., O'Malley, S. S., & Heath, A. C. (2010).

Consilient research approaches in studying gene x environment interactions in alcohol research. *Addiction Biology, 15,* 200–216.

Sher, K. J., & Trull, T. J. (1994). Personality and disinhibitory psychopathology: Alcoholism and antisocial personality disorder. *Journal of Abnormal Psychology, 103,* 92–102.

Sher, L. (2008). The concept of post-traumatic mood disorder and its implications for adolescent suicidal behavior. *Minerva Pediatrics, 60,* 1393–1399.

Sherry, A., & Whilde, M. R. (2008). Borderline personality disorder. In M. Hersen & J. Rosqvist (Eds.), *Handbook of psychological assessment, case conceptualization, and treatment, Vol. I: Adults* (pp. 403–437). Hoboken, NJ: Wiley.

Sherwood, N. E., Harnack, L., & Story, M. (2000). Weight-loss practices, nutrition beliefs, and weight-loss program preferences of urban American Indian women. *Journal of the American Dietetic Association, 100,* 442–446.

Shi, J., Wittke-Thompson, J. K., Badner, J. A., Hattori, E., Potash, J. B., . . . Liu C. (2008). Clock genes may influence bipolar disorder susceptibility and dysfunctional circadian rhythm. *American Journal of Medical Genetics: Part B: Neuropsychiatric Genetics, 147B,* 1047–1055.

Shibasaki, M., & Kawai, N. (2009). Rapid detection of snakes by Japanese monkeys (Macaca fuscata): An evolutionarily predisposed visual system. *Journal of Comparative Psychology, 123,* 131–135.

Shiffman, S., Hickcox, M., Paty, J. A., Gnys, M., Kassel, J. D., & Richards, T. J. (1996). Progression from a smoking lapse to relapse: Prediction from abstinence violation effects, nicotine dependence, and lapse characteristics. *Journal of Consulting and Clinical Psychology, 64,* 993–1002.

Shiffman, S., Scharf, D. M., Shadel, W. G., Gwaltney, C. J., Dang, Q., Paton, S. M., & Clark, D. B. (2006). Analyzing milestones in smoking cessation: Illustration in a nicotine patch trial in adult smokers. *Journal of Clinical and Consulting Psychology, 74,* 276–285.

Shiffman, S., & Waters, A. J. (2004). Negative affect and smoking lapses: A prospective analysis. *Journal of Consulting and Clinical Psychology, 72,* 192–201.

Shih, R. A., Miles, J., Tucker, J. S., Zhou, A. J., & D'Amico, E. J. (2010). Racial/ethnic differences in adolescent substance use: Mediation by individual, family, and school factors. *Journal of the Study of Alcohol and Other Drugs, 71,* 640–651.

Shin, L. M., Lasko, N. B., Macklin, M. L., Karpf, R. D., Milad, M. R., . . . Pitman, R. K. (2009). Resting metabolic activity in the cingulate cortex and vulnerability to posttraumatic stress disorder. *Archives of General Psychiatry, 66,* 1099–1107.

Shin, L. M., Rauch, S. L., & Pitman, R. K. (2006). Amygdala, medial prefrontal cortex, and hippocampal function in PTSD. *Annals of the New York Academy of Sciences, 1071,* 67–79.

Shin, M., Besser, L. M., Kucik, J. E., Lu, C., & Siffel, C., Correa, A., & CSABA (2009).

Prevalence of Down syndrome among children and adolescents in 10 regions of the United States. *Pediatrics, 124,* 1565–1571.

Shinohara, M., Mizushima, H., Hirano, M., Shioe, K., Nakazawa, M., . . . Kanba, S. (2004). Eating disorders with binge-eating behaviour are associated with the s allele of the 3'UTR VNTR polymorphism of the dopamine transporter gene. *Journal of Psychiatry and Neuroscience, 29,* 134–137.

Shirani, A., & St. Louis, E. K. (2009). Illuminating rationale and uses for light therapy. *Journal of Clinical Sleep Medicine, 15,* 155–163.

Shisslak, C. M., Pazda, S. L., & Crago, M. (1990). Body weight and bulimia as discriminators of psychological characteristics among anorexic, bulimic, and obese women. *Journal of Abnormal Psychology, 99,* 380–384.

Shmueli, D., Prochaska, J. J., & Glantz, S. A. (2010). Effect of smoking scenes in films on immediate smoking: A randomized controlled study. *American Journal of Preventive Medicine, 38,* 351–358.

Shneidman, E. S. (1968). *Classification of suicide phenomena: Bulletin of suicidology.* Washington, DC: U.S. Government Printing Office.

Shneidman, E. S. (1992). What do suicides have in common? Summary of the psychological approach. In B. Bongar (Ed.), *Suicide: Guidelines for assessment, management, and treatment.* New York: Oxford University Press.

Shneidman, E. S. (1993). *Suicide as psychache: A clinical approach to self-destructive behavior.* Northvale, NJ: Aronson.

Shore, M. F. (2006). The new manual is outstanding contribution. *National Psychologist, 15,* 20–21.

Shore, S. (2003). Life on and slightly to the right of the autism spectrum: A personal account. *Exceptional Parent, 33,* 85–89.

Shorter, E. (2010). Disease versus dimension in diagnosis: Response to Dr. van Praag. *Canadian Journal of Psychiatry, 55,* 63.

Shreve, B. W., & Kunkel, M. A. (1991). Self-psychology, shame, and adolescent suicide: Theoretical and practical considerations. *Journal of Counseling and Development, 69,* 305–311.

Shrivastava, A., Shah, N., Johnston, M., Stitt, L., & Thakar, M. (2010). Predictors of long-term outcome of first-episode schizophrenia: A ten-year follow-up study. *Indian Journal of Psychiatry, 52,* 320–326.

Shulman, C., Yirmiya, N., & Greenbaum, C. W. (1995). From categorization to classification: A comparison among individuals with autism, mental retardation, and normal development. *Journal of Abnormal Psychology, 104,* 601–609.

Shuman, D. W., Cunningham, M. D., Connell, M. A., & Reid, W. H. (2003). Interstate forensic psychology consultations: A call for reform and proposal of a model rule. *Professional Psychology: Research and Practice, 34,* 233–239.

Shuman, D. W., & Greenberg, S. A. (2003). The expert witness, the adversary system, and the voice of reason: Reconciling impartiality and advocacy. *Professional Psychology: Research and Practice, 34,* 219–224.

Schweckendiek, J., Klucken, T., Merz, C. J., Tabbert, K., Walter, B., . . . Stark, R. (2011). Weaving the (neuronal) web: Fear learning in spider phobia. *NeuroImage, 54,* 681–688.

Shweder, R. A., Goodnow, J., Hatano, G., LeVine, R. A., Markus, H., & Miller, P. (2006). The cultural psychology of development: One mind, many mentalities. In W. Damon (Ed.), *Handbook of child development* (pp. 716–792). Chicago: University of Chicago Press.

Sibitz, I., Unger, A., Woppmann, A., Zidek, T., & Amering, M. (2011). Stigma resistance in patients with schizophrenia. *Schizophrenia Bulletin, 37,* 316–323.

Sidhu, K. A. S., & Dickey, T. O. (2010). Hallucinations in children: Diagnostic and treatment strategies. *Current Psychiatry, 9,* 53–61.

Siebert, D. C., & Wilke, D. J. (2007). High-risk drinking among young adults: The influence of race and college enrollment. *American Journal of Drug & Alcohol Abuse, 33,* 843–850.

Siegel, D. M. (2009). Munchausen syndrome by proxy: a pediatrician's observations. *Families, Systems & Health, 27,* 113–115.

Siegel, M. (1979). Privacy, ethics, and confidentiality. *Professional Psychology, 10,* 249–258.

Siegel, R. A. (1978). Probability of punishment and suppression of behavior in psychopathic and nonpsychopathic offenders. *Journal of Abnormal Psychology, 87,* 514–522.

Siegel, S. (1990). Drug anticipation and drug tolerance. In M. Lader (Ed.), *The psychopharmacology of addiction.* New York: Wiley.

Siegle, G. J., Carter, C. S., & Thase, M. E. (2006). Pretreatment neuronal activity predicts response to CBT for depression. *American Journal of Psychiatry, 163,* 735–738.

Sierra, M. (2009). *Depersonalization: A new look at a neglected syndrome.* New York: Cambridge University Press.

Sieswerda, S., & Arntz, A. (2007). Successful psychotherapy reduces hypervigilance in borderline personality disorder. *Behavioral and Cognitive Psychotherapy, 35,* 387–402.

Sigstrom, R., Ostling, S., Karlsson, B., Waern, M., Gustafson, D., & Skoog, G. I. (2011). A population-based study on phobic fears and DSM-IV specific phobia in 70-year-olds. *Journal of Anxiety Disorders, 25,* 148–153.

Silagy, C., Lancaster, T., Stead, L., Mant, D., & Fowler, G. (2003). Nicotine replacement therapy for smoking cessation (Cochrane Review). *The Cochrane Library, 1.* Oxford, UK: Update Software.

Silberg, J., Picles, A., Rutter, M., Hewitt, J., & Simonoff, E. (1999). The influence of genetic factors and life stress on depression among adolescent girls. *Archives of General Psychiatry, 56,* 225–232.

Silberg, J. L., Maes, H., & Eaves, L. J. (2010). Genetic and environmental influences on the transmission of parental depression to children's depression and conduct disturbance: An extended children of twins study. *Journal of Child Psychology and Psychiatry, 51,* 734–744.

Silberstein, S. D. (1998). *Migraine and other headaches: A patient's guide to treatment.* Chicago: American Medical Association.

Silver, E., Cirincione, C., & Steadman, H. J. (1994). Demythologizing inaccurate perceptions of the insanity defense. *Law and Human Behavior, 18,* 63–70.

Silverman, J. M., Mohs, R. C., Davidson, M., Losonczy, M. F., Keefe, R. S. E., . . . Davis, K. L. (1987). Familial schizophrenia and treatment response. *American Journal of Psychiatry, 144,* 1271–1276.

Silverman, W. K., & La Greca, A. M. (2002). Children experiencing disasters: Definitions, reactions, and predictors of outcomes. In A. M. La Greca, W. K. Silverman, E. M. Vernberg, & M. C. Roberts (Eds.), *Helping children cope with disasters* (pp. 11–33). Washington, DC: American Psychological Association.

Silverman, W. K., Ortiz, C. D., Viswesvaran, C., Burns, B. J., Kolko, D. J., Putnam, F. W., & Amaya-Jackson, L. (2008). Evidence-based psychosocial treatments for child and adolescent exposed to traumatic events: A review and meta-analysis. *Journal of Clinical Child & Adolescent Psychology, 37,* 156–183.

Silverman, W. K., Pina, A. A., & Viswesvaran, C. (2008). Evidence-based psychosocial treatments for phobic and anxiety disorders in children and adolescents: A review and meta-analyses. *Journal of Clinical Child & Adolescent Psychology, 37,* 105–130.

Silverstein, L. B., Auerbach, C. F., & Levant, R. F. (2006). Using qualitative research to strengthen clinical practice. *Professional Psychology: Research and Practice, 37,* 351–358.

Sim, K., DeWitt, I., Ditman, T., Zalesak, M., Greenhouse, I., . . . Heckers, S. (2006). Hippocampal and parahippocampal volumes in schizophrenia: A structural MRI study. *Schizophrenia Bulletin, 32,* 332–340.

Sim, L. A., Sadowski, C. M., Whiteside, S. P., & Wells, L. A. (2004). Family-based therapy for adolescents with anorexia nervosa. *Mayo Clinic Proceedings, 79,* 1305–1308.

Simeon, D., Gross, S., Guralnik, O., Stein, D. J., Schmeidler, J., & Hollander, E. (1997). Feeling unreal: Thirty cases of DSM-III-R depersonalization disorder. *American Journal of Psychiatry, 154,* 1107–1113.

Simeon, D., Guralnik, O., Hazlett, E. A., Spiegel-Cohen, J., Hollander, E., & Buchsbaum, M. S. (2000). Feeling unreal: A PET study of depersonalization disorder. *American Journal of Psychiatry, 157,* 1782–1788.

Simeon, D., Guralnik, O., Schmeidler, J., Sirof, B., & Knutelska, M. (2001). The role of childhood interpersonal trauma in depersonalization disorder. *American Journal of Psychiatry, 158,* 1027–1033.

Simmons, A. M. (2002, January 13). Eating disorders on rise for South African blacks. *The Los Angeles Times,* p. A3.

Simon, G. E., & Gureje, O. (1999). Stability of somatization disorder and somatization symptoms among primary care patients. *Archives of General Psychiatry, 56,* 90–95.

Simon, G. E., & Savarino, J. (2007). Suicide attempts among patients starting depression treatment with medications or psychotherapy. *American Journal of Psychiatry, 164,* 1029–1034.

Simon, G. E., Savarino, J., Operskalski, B., & Wang, P. S. (2006). Suicide risk during antidepressant treatment. *American Journal of Psychiatry, 163,* 41–47.

Simon, G. E., & VonKorff, M. (1991). Somatization and psychiatric disorder in the NIMH Epidemiologic Catchment Area study. *American Journal of Psychiatry, 148,* 1494–1500.

Simon, L. M. J. (1998). Does criminal offender treatment work? *Journal of Applied and Preventative Psychology, 7,* 137–159.

Simon, R. I., & Gold, L. H. (Eds.). (2004). *The American Psychiatric Publishing textbook of forensic psychiatry.* Washington, DC: American Psychiatric Association.

Simons, J., Correia, C. J., Carey, K. B., & Borsari, B. E. (1998). Validating a five-factor marijuana motives measure: Relations with use, problems, and alcohol motives. *Journal of Counseling Psychology, 45,* 265–273.

Singh, B. S. (2007). *Managing somatoform disorders.* Retrieved from www.mja.com.au/public/mental-health/articles/singh/singh.html

Singh, S. P., & Lee, A. S. (1997). Conversion disorders in Nottingham: Alive but not kicking. *Journal of Psychosomatic Research, 43,* 425–430.

Singhal, V., Schwenk, F., & Kumar, S. (2007). Evaluation and management of childhood and adolescent obesity. *Mayo Clinic Proceedings, 82,* 1258–1264.

Sjöholm, L. K., Backlund, L., Cheteh, E. H., Ek, I. R., Frisén, L., . . . Nikamo, P. (2010). CRY2 is associated with rapid cycling in bipolar disorder patients. *PLoS One, 5,* e12632.

Skinner, B. F. (1990). Can psychology be a science of mind? *American Psychologist, 45,* 1206–1210.

Skodol, A. E., & Bender, D. S. (2009). The future of personality disorders in DSM-V? *American Journal of Psychiatry, 166,* 388–390.

Skokauskas, N., & Gallagher, L. (2010). Psychosis, affective disorders and anxiety in autistic spectrum disorder: Prevalence and nosological considerations. *Psychopathology, 43,* 8–16.

Slavich, G. M., Thornton, T., Torres, L. D., Monroe, S. M., & Gotlib, I. H. (2009). Targeted rejection predicts hastened onset of major depression. *Journal of Social and Clinical Psychology, 28,* 223–243.

Slavich, G. M., Way, B. M., Eisenberger, N. I., & Taylor, S. E. (2010). Neural sensitivity to social rejection is associated with inflammatory responses to social stress. *Proceedings of the National Academy of Science U S A, 107,* 14817–14822.

Sleegers, K., Lambert, J. C., Bertram, L., Cruts, M., Amouyel, P., & Van Broeckhoven, C. (2010). The pursuit of susceptibility genes for Alzheimer's disease: Progress and prospects. *Trends in Genetics, 26,* 84–93.

Sloane, C., Burke, S. C., Cremeens, J., Vail-Smith, K., & Woolsey, C. (2010). Drunkorexia: Calorie restriction prior to alcohol consumption among college freshman. *Journal of Alcohol & Drug Education.* Retrieved from http://findarticles.com/p/articles/mi_go2545/is_2_54/ai_n55140635/

Sloane, R. B., Staples, F. R., Cristol, A. H., Yorkston, N. J., & Whipple, K. (1975). *Psychotherapy versus behavior therapy.* Cambridge, MA: Harvard University Press.

Slotema, C. W., Blom, J. D., Hoek, H. W., & Sommer, I. E. (2010). Should we expand the toolbox of psychiatric treatment methods to include repetitive transcranial magnetic Stimulation (rTMS)? A meta-analysis of the efficacy of rTMS in psychiatric disorders. *Journal of Clinical Psychiatry, 71,* 873–884.

Slovenko, R. (1995). *Psychiatry and criminal culpability.* New York: Wiley.

Slutske, W. S., Heath, A. C., Dinwiddie, S. H., Madden, P. A. F., Bucholz, K. K., . . . Martin, N. G. (1997). Modeling genetic and environmental influences in the etiology of conduct disorder: A study of 2,682 adult twin pairs. *Journal of Abnormal Psychology, 106,* 266–279.

Smeets, T., Jelicic, M., & Merckelbach, H. (2006). Reduced hippocampal and amygdalar volume in dissociative identity disorder: Not such clear evidence. *American Journal of Psychiatry, 163,* 1643.

Smith, B., Fowler, D. G., Freeman, D., Bebbington, P., Bashforth, H., . . . Kuipers, E. (2006). Emotion and psychosis: Links between depression, self-esteem, negative schematic beliefs and delusions and hallucinations. *Schizophrenia Research, 86,* 181–188.

Smith, C. (2002, August 7). Persecuted parents or protected children. *Seattle Post Intelligencer,* pp. A1, A10.

Smith, C. S. (2003, September 27). Son's wish to die, and mother's help, stir French debate. *The New York Times,* pp. A1, A4.

Smith, D. A., Smith, S. M., de Jager, C. A., Whitbread, P., Johnston, C., . . . Bush, A. I. (2010). Homocysteine-lowering by B vitamins slows the rate of accelerated brain atrophy in mild cognitive impairment: A randomized controlled trial. *PLoS ONE, 5*(9), e12244. Retrieved from http://www.ncbi.nlm.nih.gov/pmc/articles/PMC2935890/

Smith, G. C., Clarke, D. M., Handrinos, D., Dunsis, A., & McKenzie, D. P. (2000). Consultation-liaison psychiatrists' management of somatoform disorders. *Psychosomatics, 41,* 481–489.

Smith, G. T., Goldman, M. S., Greenbaum, P. E., & Christiansen, B. A. (1995). Expectancy for social facilitation from drinking: The divergent paths of high-expectancy and low-expectancy adolescents. *Journal of Abnormal Psychology, 104,* 32–40.

Smith, G. T., & Oltmanns, T. F. (2009). Scientific advances in the diagnosis of psychopathology: Introduction to the specific section. *Psychological Assessment, 21,* 241–242.

Smith, J. E., Meyers, R. J., & Delaney, H. D. (1998). The community reinforcement approach with homeless alcohol-dependent individuals. *Journal of Consulting and Clinical Psychology, 66,* 541–548.

Smith, K. (1988, May). Loving him was easy. *Reader's Digest*, pp. 115–119.

Smith, L. (2006). Addressing classism, extending multicultural competence, and serving the poor. *American Psychologist, 61,* 338–339.

Smith, L. (2010). *Psychology, poverty, and the end of social exclusion.* New York: Teachers College Press.

Smith, L., & Redington, R. M. (2010). Class dismissed: Making the case for the study of classist microaggressions. In D. W. Sue (Ed.), *Microaggressions and marginality: Manifestation, dynamics and impact* (pp. 269–285). Hoboken, NJ: Wiley.

Smith, P. N., Cukrowicz, K. C., Poindexter, E. K., Hobson, V., & Cohen, L. M. (2010). The acquired capability for suicide: A comparison of suicide attempters, suicide ideators, and non-suicidal controls. *Depression and Anxiety, 27,* 871–877.

Smith, S. L., & Choueiti, M. (2010). Gender disparity on screen and behind the camera in family films. Retrieved from http://www.thegeenadavisinstitute.org/downloads/fullstudy-genderdisparityfamilyfilms/

Smith, T. W., Ruiz, J. M., & Uchino, B. N. (2000). Vigilance, active coping, and cardiovascular reactivity during social interaction in young men. *Health Psychology, 19,* 382–393.

Smoller, J. W., Pollack, M. H., Wassertheil-Smoller, Barton, B., Hendrix, S. L., . . . Sheps, D. S. (2003). Prevalence and correlates of panic attacks in postmenstrual women. *Archives of Internal Medicine, 163,* 2041–2050.

Smoller, J., Sheidly, B., & Tsuang, M. T. (Eds.). (2008). *Psychiatric genetics: Applications in clinical practice.* Washington, D.C.: American Psychiatric Publishing.

Smyke, A. T., Koga, S. F., Johnson, D. E., Fox, N. A., Marshall, P. J., Nelson, C. A., . . . BEIP Core Group (2007). The caregiving context in institution-reared and family-reared infants and toddlers in Romania. *Journal of Child Psychology and Psychiatry, 48,* 210–218.

Snyder, S. (1986). *Drugs and the brain.* New York: Scientific American Library.

So, J. K. (2008). Somatization as a cultural idiom of distress: Rethinking mind and body in a multicultural society. *Counselling Psychology Quarterly, 21,* 167–174.

Soares, S. C., Esteves, F., Lundqvist, D., & Ohman, A. (2009). Some animal specific fears are more specific than others: Evidence from attention and emotion measures. *Behaviour Research and Therapy, 47,* 1032–1042.

Sobell, M. B., & Sobell, L. C. (2007). Substance use, health, and mental health. *Clinical Psychology: Science and Practice, 14,* 1–5.

Society for Personality Assessment. (2005). The status of the Rorschach in clinical and forensic practice: An official statement by the Board of Trustees of the Society for Personality Assessment. *Journal of Personality Assessment, 85,* 219–237.

Sola, C. L., Chopra, A., & Rastogi, A. (2010). Sedative, hypnotic, anxiolytic use disorders. Retrieved from http://emedicine.medscape.com/article/290585-overview

Solano, J., Jr., & De Chavez, G. M. (2000). Premorbid personality disorders in schizophrenia. *Schizophrenia Research, 44,* 137–144.

Solem, S., Haland, A. T., Vogel, P. A., Hansen, B., & Wells, A. (2009). Change in metacognitions predicts outcome in obsessive-compulsive disorder patients undergoing treatment with exposure and response prevention. *Behaviour Research and Therapy, 47,* 301–307.

Sollman, M. J., Ranseen, J. D., & Berry, D. T. R. (2010). Detection of feigned ADHD in college students. *Psychological Assessment, 22,* 325–335.

Solomon, A. (2010). An authority on airbrushing: Government and body image. Retrieved from http://www.nourishing-the-soul.com/2010/07/an-authority-on-airbrushing-government-and-body-image/

Solomon, D. A., Leon, A. C., Endicott, J., Coryell, W. H., Li, C., . . . Keller, M. B. (2009). Empirical typology of bipolar I mood episodes. *British Journal of Psychiatry, 195,* 525–530.

Sommers-Flanagan, J., & Sommers-Flanagan, R. (2004). *Counseling and psychotherapy theories in context and practice.* Hoboken, NJ: Wiley.

Song, A. V., Ling, P. M., Neilands, T. B., & Glantz, S. A. (2007). Smoking in movies and increased smoking among young adults. *American Journal of Preventive Medicine, 33,* 396–403.

Sontag, D. (2002, April 28). Who was responsible for Elizabeth Shin? *New York Times Magazine,* 1–17.

Sørensen, H. J., Mortensen, E. L., Schiffman, J., Reinisch, J. M., Maeda J., & Mednick, S. A. (2010). Early developmental milestones and risk of schizophrenia: A 45-year follow-up of the Copenhagen Perinatal Cohort. *Schizophrenia Research, 118,* 41–47.

Sorensen, P., Birket-Smith, M., Wattar, U., Buemann, I., & Salkovskis (2011). A randomized clinical trial of cognitive behavioural therapy versus no intervention for patients with hypochondriasis. *Psychological Medicine, 41,* 431–441.

Sorenson, S. B., & Siegel, J. M. (1992). Gender, ethnicity, and sexual assault: Findings from a Los Angeles study. *Journal of Social Issues, 48,* 93–104.

Soria, V., Martínez-Amorós, E., Escaramís, G., Valero, J., Pérez–Egea, R., . . . Urretavizcaya, M. (2010). Differential association of circadian genes with mood disorders: CRY1 and NPAS2 are associated with unipolar major depression and CLOCK and VIP with bipolar disorder. *Neuropsychopharmacology, 35,* 1279–1289.

Sorkin, A., Weinshall, D., & Peled, A. (2008). The distortion of reality perception in schizophrenia patients, as measured in Virtual Reality. *Proceedings of the 16th Annual Medicine Meets Virtual Reality Conference (MMVR),* Long Beach, CA.

Sotres-Bayon, F., Bush, D. E., & LeDoux, J. E. (2004). Emotional perseveration: An update on the prefrontal-amygdala interactions in fear extinction. *Learning and Memory, 11,* 525–535.

Southwick, S. M., Morgan, C. A., III, Nicolaou, A. L., & Charney, D. S. (1997). Consistency of memory for combat-related traumatic events in veterans of Operation Desert Storm. *American Journal of Psychiatry, 154,* 173–177.

Sowell, E. S., Leow, A. D., Bookheimer, S. Y., Smith, L. M., O'Connor, M. J., . . . Thompson, P. M. (2010). Differentiating prenatal exposure to methamphetamine and alcohol versus alcohol and not methamphetamine using tensor-based brain morphometry and discriminant analysis. *The Journal of Neuroscience, 30,* 3876–3885.

Spanos, N. P. (1978). Witchcraft in histories of psychiatry: A critical analysis and an alternative conceptualization. *Psychological Bulletin, 85,* 417–439.

Spanos, N. P. (1994). Multiple identity enactments and multiple personality disorder: A sociocognitive perspective. *Psychological Bulletin, 116,* 143–165.

Sparrevohn, R. M., & Rapee, R. M. (2009). Self-disclosure, emotional expression and intimacy within relationships of people with social phobia. *Behaviour Research and Therapy, 47,* 1074–1078.

Spector, I. P., & Carey, M. P. (1990). Incidence and prevalence of sexual dysfunctions: A critical review of the empirical literature. *Archives of Sexual Behavior, 19,* 389–408.

Speer, D. C. (1971). Rate of caller re-use of a telephone crisis service. *Crisis Intervention, 3,* 83–86.

Speer, D. C. (1972). *An evaluation of a telephone crisis service.* Paper presented at the meeting of the Midwestern Psychological Association, Cleveland, Ohio.

Spence, S. H., Donovan, C. L., March, S., Gamble, A., Anderson, R., . . . Kenardy, J. (2008). Online CBT in the treatment of child and adolescent anxiety disorders: Issues in the development of BRAVE–ONLINE and two case illustrations. *Behavioural and Cognitive Psychotherapy, 36,* 411–430.

Spencer, S. L., & Zeiss, A. M. (1987). Sex roles and sexual dysfunction in college students. *Journal of Sex Research, 23,* 338–347.

Spencer, T. J., Biederman, J., & Mick, E. (2007). Attention-deficit/hyperactivity disorder: Diagnosis, lifespan, comorbidities, and neurobiology. *Journal of Pediatric Psychology, 32,* 631–642.

Spiegel, D. (2006). Recognizing traumatic dissociation. *American Journal of Psychiatry, 163,* 566–568.

Spitzer, R. L., Gibbon, M., Skodol, A. E., Williams, J. B., & First, M. B. (Eds.). (1994). *DSMIV: Casebook.* Washington, DC: American Psychiatric Press.

Spodak, C. (2010, March 18). College on edge after recent wave of student suicides. Retrieved from http://articles.cnn.com/2010–03–18/us/cornell.suicides

Spradlin, L. K., & Parsons, R. D. (2008). *Diversity matters.* Belmont, CA: Thomson Wadsworth.

Springen, K. (2006, December 7). *Study looks at pro-anorexia web sites.* Retrieved from www.msnbc.msn.com/id/16098915/site/newsweek/print

Staal, W. G., Pol, H. E. H., Schnack, H. G., van Haren, N. E. M., Seifert, M., & Kahn, R. S. (2001). Structural abnormalities in chronic schizophrenia at the extremes of the outcome spectrum. *American Journal of Psychiatry, 158,* 1140–1142.

Staats, A. W., & Heiby, E. M. (1985). Paradigmatic behaviorism's theory of depression: Unified, explanatory, and heuristic. In S. Reiss & R. R. Bootzin (Eds.), *Theoretical issues in behavioral therapy* (pp. 279–330). Orlando, FL: Academic Press.

Stack, S. (1987). Celebrities and suicide: A taxonomy and analysis, 1948–1983. *American Sociological Review, 52*, 401–412.

Stacy, A. W., Newcomb, M. D., & Bentler, P. M. (1991). Cognitive motivation and drug use: A 9-year longitudinal study. *Journal of Abnormal Psychology, 100*, 502–515.

Stader, S. R., & Hokanson, J. E. (1998). Psychosocial antecedents of depressive symptoms: An evaluation using daily experiences methodology. *Journal of Abnormal Psychology, 107*, 17–26.

Stafford, K. P., & Wygant, D. B. (2005). The role of competency to stand trial in mental health courts. *Behavioral Sciences and the Law, 23*, 245–258.

Stahl, S. M. (2007). The genetics of schizophrenia converge upon the NMDA glutamate receptor. *CNS Spectrums, 12*, 583–588.

Stalberg, G., Ekerwald, H., & Hultman, C. M. (2004). At issue: Siblings of patients with schizophrenia: Sibling bond, coping patterns, and fear of possible schizophrenia heredity. *Schizophrenia Bulletin, 30*, 445–451.

Stambor, Z. (2006). Stressed out nation. *Monitor on Psychology, 37*, 28–29.

Stamova, B., Green, P. G., Tian, Y., Hertz-Picciotto, I., Pessah, I. N., . . . Sharp, F. R. (2011). Correlations between gene expression and mercury levels in blood of boys with and without autism. *Neurotoxicity Research, 19*, 31–48.

Staniloiu, A., & Markowitsch, H. J. (2010). Searching for the anatomy of dissociative amnesia. *Journal of Psychology, 218*, 96–108.

Stanley, M. A., Beck, J. G., Novy, D. M., Averill, P. M., Swann, A. C., Diefenbach, G. J., & Hopko, D. R. (2003). Cognitive-behavioral treatment of late-life generalized anxiety disorder. *Journal of Consulting and Clinical Psychology, 71*, 309–319.

Stanley, M. A., & Turner, S. M. (1995). Current status of pharmacological and behavioral treatment of obsessive-compulsive disorder. *Behavior Therapy, 26*, 163–186.

Stapinski, L. A., Abbott, M. J., & Rapee, R. M. (2010). Evaluating the cognitive avoidance model of generalized anxiety disorder: Impact of worry on threat appraisal, perceived control and anxious arousal. *Behavior Research and Therapy, 48*, 1032–1040.

Starcevic, V. (2005). Fear of death in hypochondriasis: Bodily threat and its treatment implications. *Journal of Contemporary Psychotherapy, 35*, 227–237.

Starcevic, V. (2006). Somatoform disorders and DSM-V: Conceptual and political issues in the debate. *Psychosomatics, 47*, 277–281.

Starcevic, V., & Janca, A. (2011). Obsessive-compulsive spectrum disorders: Still in search of the concept-affirming boundaries. *Current Opinion in Psychiatry, 24*, 55–60.

Stark, E. (1984). The unspeakable family secret. *Psychology Today, 18*, 38–46.

Stark, J. (2004, July 25). Twin sisters, a singular affliction. *Bellingham Herald*, p. A1.

Stark, M. J. (1992). Dropping out of substance abuse treatment: A clinically oriented review. *Clinical Psychology Review, 12*, 93–116.

Startup, H., Freeman, D., & Garety, P. A. (2006). Persecutory delusions and catastrophic worry in psychosis: Developing the understanding of delusion distress and persistence. *Behaviour Research and Therapy, 45*, 523–537.

Stathopoulou, G., Powers, M. B., Berry, A. C., Smits, J. A. J., & Otto, M. W. (2006). Exercise interventions for mental health: A quantitative and qualitative review. *Clinical Psychology: Science and Practice, 13*, 179–193.

Stead, L. F., Perera, R., & Lancaster, T. (2006). Telephone counseling for smoking cessation. (2006). *Cochrane Database of Systematic Reviews, 3*, CD002850.

Steadman, H. J., Monahan, J., Robbins, P. C., Appelbaum, P., Grisso, T., Klassen, D., et al. (1993). From dangerousness to risk assessment: Implications for appropriate research strategies. In S. Hodgins (Ed.), *Mental disorder and crime*. New York: Sage.

Steege, J. F., Stout, A. L., & Carson, C. C. (1986). Patient satisfaction in Scott and Small-Carrion penile implant recipients: A study of 52 patients. *Archives of Sexual Behavior, 15*, 171–177.

Steel, Z., Silove, D., Giao, N. M., Phan, T. T. B., Chey, T., Whelan, A., . . . Bryant, R. A. (2009). International and indigenous diagnoses of mental disorder among Vietnamese living in Vietnam and Australia. *British Journal of Psychiatry, 194*, 326–334.

Steele, C. M., & Josephs, R. A. (1988). Drinking your troubles away: II. An attention-allocation model of alcohol's effect on psychological stress. *Journal of Abnormal Psychology, 97*, 196–205.

Steele, C. M., & Josephs, R. A. (1990). Alcohol myopia: Its prized and dangerous effects. *American Psychologist, 45*, 921–933.

Steele, M. S., & McGarvey, S. T. (1997). Anger expression, age, and blood pressure in modernizing Samoan adults. *Psychosomatic Medicine, 59*, 632–637.

Stefanidis, E. (2006). Being rational. *Schizophrenia Bulletin, 32*, 422–423.

Steffen, J. J., Nathan, P. E., & Taylor, H. A. (1974). Tension-reducing effects of alcohol: Further evidence and methodological considerations. *Journal of Abnormal Psychology, 83*, 542–547.

Steiger, H., & Bruce, K. R. (2007). Phenotypes, endophenotypes, and genotypes in bulimia spectrum eating disorders. *Canadian Journal of Psychiatry, 52*, 220–227.

Steiger, H., Richardson, J., Schmitz, N., Israel, M., Bruce, M. I., & Gauvin, L. (2010). Trait-defined eating-disorder subtypes and history of childhood abuse. *International Journal of Eating Disorders, 43*, 428–432.

Stein, D. J. (2001). Comorbidity in generalized anxiety disorder: Impact and implications. *Journal of Clinical Psychiatry, 62*, 29–34.

Stein, D. J., Ruscio, A. M., Lee, S., Petukhova, M., Alonso, J., . . . Kessler, R. C. (2010). Subtyping social anxiety disorder in developed and developing countries. *Depression and Anxiety, 27*, 390–403.

Stein, D. J., Scott, K., Haro Abad, J. M., Aguilar-Gaxiola S., Alonso, J., . . . Van Korff, M. (2010). Early childhood adversity and later hypertension: Data from the World Mental Health Survey. *Annals of Clinical Psychiatry, 22*(1), 19–28.

Stein, M. B., Simmons, A. N., Feinstein, J. S., & Paulus, M. P. (2007). Increased amygdala and insula activation during emotional processing in anxiety-prone subjects. *American Journal of Psychiatry, 164*, 318–327.

Steinberg, J. S., Arshad, A., Kowalski, M., Kukar, A., Suma, V., . . . Rozanski, A. (2004). Increased incidence of life-threatening ventricular arrhythmias in implantable defibrillator patients after the World Trade Center attack. *Journal of the American College of Cardiology, 44*, 1261–1264.

Steinhausen, H. C., & Weber, S. (2009). The outcome of bulimia nervosa: Findings from one-quarter century of research. *American Journal of Psychiatry, 166*, 1331–1341.

Steketee, G., & Barlow, D. H. (2002). Obsessive-compulsive disorder. In D. H. Barlow (Ed.), *Anxiety and its disorders: The nature and treatment of anxiety and panic* (2nd ed.). New York: Guilford Press.

Steketee, G., Frost, R. O., Tolin, D. F., Rasmussen, J., & Brown, T. A. (2010). Waitlist-controlled trial of cognitive behavior therapy for hoarding disorder. *Depression and Anxiety, 27*, 476–484.

Stergiakouli, E., & Thapar, A. (2010). Fitting the pieces together: Current research on the genetic basis of attention-deficit/hyperactivity disorder (ADHD). *Journal of Neuropsychiatric Disease and Treatment, 6*, 551–560.

Stern, J., Murphy, M., & Bass, C. (1993). Personality disorders in patients with somatisation disorder: A controlled study. *British Journal of Psychiatry, 163*, 785–789.

Sternberg, R. J. (2004). Culture and intelligence. *American Psychologist, 59*, 325–338.

Sternberg, R. J. (2005). The theory of successful intelligence. *Interamerican Journal of Psychology, 39*, 189–202.

Sterzer, P. (2010). Born to be criminal? What to make of early biological risk factors for criminal behavior. *American Journal of Psychiatry, 167*, 1–3.

Sterzer, P., & Stadler C. (2009). Neuroimaging of aggressive and violent behaviour in children and adolescents. *Frontiers in Behavioral Neuroscience, 3*, 35.

Stewart, W. F., Lipton, R. B., Celentano, D. D., & Reed, M. L. (1992). Prevalence of migraine headache in the United States. *Journal of the American Medical Association, 267*, 64–69.

Stice, E. (2001). A prospective test of the dual-pathway model of bulimic pathology: Mediating effects of dieting and negative affect. *Journal of Abnormal Psychology, 110*, 124–135.

Stice, E., & Bearman, S. K. (2001). Body-image and eating disturbances prospectively predict increases in depressive symptoms in adolescent girls: A growth curve analysis. *Developmental Psychology, 37,* 597–607.

Stice, E., Marti, C. N., Shaw, H., & Jaconis, M. (2009). A 8-year longitudinal study of the natural history of threshold, subthreshold, and partial eating disorders from a community sample of adolescents. *Journal of Abnormal Psychology, 118,* 587–597.

Stice, E., & Shaw, H. (2004). Eating disorder prevention programs: A meta-analytic review. *Psychological Bulletin, 130,* 206–227.

Stice, E., Shaw, H., & Nemeroff, C. (1998). Dual pathway model of bulimia nervosa: Longitudinal support for dietary restraint and affect-regulation mechanisms. *Journal of Social and Clinical Psychology, 17,* 129–149.

Stillion, M. J., McDowell, E. E., & May, J. H. (1989). *Suicide across the life span: Premature exits.* Washington, DC: Hemisphere.

Stip, E. (2009). Psychosis: A category or dimension. *Canadian Journal of Psychiatry, 54,* 137–139.

Stitzer, M., & Petry N. (2006). Contingency management for treatment of substance abuse. *Annual Review of Clinical Psychology, 2,* 411–434.

Stitzer, M. L, Petry, N. M., & Peirce, J. (2010). Motivational incentives research in the National Drug Abuse Treatment Clinical Trials Network. *Journal of Substance Abuse Treatment, 38*(Suppl 1), S61–69.

Stober, G. (2006). Genetic correlates of the nosology of catatonia. *Psychiatric Annals, 37,* 37–44.

Stone, A. A., Smyth, J. M., Kaell, A., & Hurewitz, A. (2000). Structured writing about stressful events: Exploring potential psychological mediators of positive health effects. *Health Psychology, 19,* 619–624.

Stone, L. B., Uhrlass, D. J., & Gibb, B. E. (2010). Co-rumination and lifetime history of depressive disorders in children. *Journal of Clinical Child and Adolescent Psychology, 39*(4), 597–602.

Stone, M., Laughren, T., Jones, M. L., Levenson, M., Holland, P. C., . . . Rochester, G. (2009). Risk of suicidality in clinical trials of antidepressants in adults: analysis of proprietary data submitted to US Food and Drug Administration. *British Medical Journal, 339.* doi: 10.1136/bmj. b2880

Stone, M. H. (2001). Schizoid and schizotypal personality disorders. In G. O. Gabbard (Ed.), *Treatment of psychiatric disorders* (pp. 2237–2250). Washington, DC: American Psychiatric Press.

Stoolmiller, M., Eddy, J. M., & Reid, J. B. (2000). Detecting and describing preventative intervention effects in a universal school-based randomizing trial: Targeting delinquent and violent behavior. *Journal of Consulting and Clinical Psychology, 68,* 296–306.

Storch, E. A., Larson, M. J., Muroff, J., Caporino, N., Geller, D., . . . Murphy, T. K. (2010). Predictors of functional impairment in pediatric obsessive-compulsive disorder. *Journal of Anxiety Disorders, 24,* 275–283.

Story, M., Neumark-Sztainer, D., Sherwood, N., Stang, J., & Murray, D. (1998). Dieting status and its relationship to eating and physical activity behaviors in a representative sample of U.S. adolescents. *Journal of the American Dietetic Association, 98,* 1127–1135.

Stout, C., Kotses, H., & Creer, T. L. (1997). Improving perception of air flow obstruction in asthma patients. *Psychosomatic Medicine, 59,* 201–206.

Strakowski, S. M., Fleck, D. E, DelBello, M. P., Adler, C. M., Shear, P. K., Kotwal, R., & Arndt, S. (2010). Impulsivity across the course of bipolar disorder. *Bipolar Disorder, 12,* 285–297.

Street, A. E., Vogt, D., & Dutra, L. (2009). A new generation of women veterans: Stressors faced by women deployed to Iraq and Afghanistan. *Clinical Psychology Review, 29,* 685–694.

Striegel-Moore, R. H., & Bulik, C. M. (2007). Risk factors in eating disorders. *American Psychologist, 62,* 181–198.

Stringaris, A., Baroni, A., Haimm, C., Brotman, M., Lowe, C. H., . . . Leibenluft E. (2010). Pediatric bipolar disorder versus severe mood dysregulation: Risk for manic episodes on follow-up. *Journal of the American Academy of Child and Adolescent Psychiatry, 49*(4), 397–405.

Streissguth, A. P. (1994). A long-term perspective of FAS. *Alcohol Health and Research World, 18,* 74–81.

Strenziok, M., Krueger, F., Despande, G., Lenrook, R. K., van der Meer, E., & Grafman, J. (2010). Frontal-parietal regulation of media violence exposure in adolescents: A multi-method study. *Social Cognitive and Affective Neuroscience.* doi: 10.1093/scan/nsq079

Strickland, B. R. (1992). Women and depression. *Current Directions in Psychological Science, 1*(4), 132–135.

Striegel-Moore, R. H., Dohm, F. A., Kraemer, H. C., Taylor, C. B., Daniels, S., Crawford, P. B., & Schreiber, G. B. (2003). Eating disorders in white and black women. *American Journal of Psychiatry, 160,* 1326–1331.

Streiner, D. L. (2008). When what is ethical may not be right: A reply to Dr Glass. *La Revue Canadienne de Psychiatrie, 53,* 434.

Strobeck, C. (2002, August). What it feels like to have an obsessive compulsive disorder. *Esquire, 138,* 76–77.

Strober, M., Freeman, R., Diamond, C. L. J., & Kaye, W. (2000). Controlled family study of anorexia nervosa and bulimia nervosa: Evidence of shared liability and transmission of partial syndromes. *American Journal of Psychiatry, 157,* 393–401.

Stroebe, M., & Stroebe, W. (1991). Does "grief work" work? *Journal of Consulting and Clinical Psychology, 59,* 479–482.

Stoessl, A. J. (2011). Movement disorders: New insights into Parkinson's disease. *The Lancet Neurology, 10,* 5–7.

Ströhle, A. (2009). Physical activity, exercise, depression and anxiety disorders. *Journal of Neural Transmission, 116,* 777–784.

Strohman, R. (2001, April). Beyond genetic determinism. *California Monthly, 111*(5), 24–27.

Strom, L., Pettersson, R., & Andersson, G. (2000). A controlled trial of self-help treatment of recurrent headache conducted via the Internet. *Journal of Consulting and Clinical Psychology, 68,* 722–727.

Strong, B., & DeVault, C. (1994). *Human sexuality.* Mountain View, CA: Mayfield.

Strong, J. E., & Farrell, A. D. (2003). Evaluation of the computerized assessment system for psychotherapy evaluation and research (CASPER) interview with a psychiatric inpatient population. *Journal of Clinical Psychology, 59,* 967–984.

Strong, R. E., Marchant, B. K., Reimherr, F. W., Williams, E., Soni, P., & Mestas, R. (2009). Narrow-band blue-light treatment of seasonal affective disorder in adults and the influence of additional nonseasonal symptoms. *Depression and Anxiety, 26,* 273–278.

Strong, S. M., Williamson, D. A., Netemeyer, R. G., & Geer, J. H. (2000). Eating disorder symptoms and concerns about body differ as a function of gender and sexual orientation. *Journal of Social and Clinical Psychology, 19,* 240–255.

Strous, R. D., Alvir, J. M., Robinson, D., Gal, G., Sheitman, B., Chakos, M., & Lieberman, J. A. (2004). Premorbid functioning in schizophrenia, treatment response, and medication side effects. *Schizophrenia Bulletin, 30,* 265–272.

Stuart, F. M., Hammond, D. C., & Pett, M. A. (1987). Inhibited sexual desire in women. *Archives of Sexual Behavior, 16,* 91–106.

Stuart, S., & Noyes, R., Jr. (2005). Treating hypochondriasis with interpersonal psychotherapy. *Journal of Contemporary Psychotherapy, 35,* 269–283.

Study confirms importance of sexual fantasies in experience of sexual desire. (2007, June 28). *Science Daily.* Retrieved from www.sciencedaily.com/releases/2007/06/070627223851.html

Study suggests difference between female and male sexuality. (2003, June 13). *Science Daily.* Retrieved from www.sciencedaily.com/releases/2003/06/030613075252.htm

Stunkard, A. J., Allison, K. C., Geliebter, A., Lundgren, J. D., Gluck, M. E., & O'Reardon, J. P. (2009). Development of criteria for a diagnosis: Lessons from the night eating syndrome. *Comprehensive Psychiatry, 50,* 391–399.

Su, S., Miller, A. H., Snieder, H., Bremner, J. D., Ritchie, J., . . . Vaccarino, V. (2009). Common genetic contributions to depressive symptoms and inflammatory markers in middle-aged men: The Twins Heart Study. *Psychosomic Medicine, 71,* 152–158.

Substance Abuse and Mental Health Services Administration. (2002). At any age, it does matter. *Center for Substance Abuse Prevention online course.* Retrieved from http://pathwayscourses.samhsa.gov/index.htm

Substance Abuse and Mental Health Services Administration. (2003). *Children's mental health facts: Children and adolescents with conduct disorder.* Retrieved from mentalhealth.samhsa.gov/publications/allpubs/CA-0010/default.asp

Substance Abuse and Mental Health Services Administration. (2007). *Results from the 2006 National Survey on Drug Use and Health: National findings* (Office of Applied Studies, NSDUH

Series H-32, DHHS Publication No. SMA 07-4293). Rockville, MD.

Substance Abuse and Mental Health Services Administration (SAMHSA). (2008). 12:>*Caravan® Survey for SAMHSA on Addictions and Recovery: Summary Report.* Rockville, MD: Substance Abuse and Mental Health Services Administration. Retrieved from http://www.samhsa.gov/attitudes/CARAVAN_LongReport.pdf

Substance Abuse and Mental Health Services Administration (SAMHSA). (2009). *Results from the 2008 National Survey on Drug Use and Health: National findings* (DHHS Publication No. SMA 09–4434, NSDUH Series H–36). Rockville, MD: Substance Abuse and Mental Health Services Administration. Retrieved from http://oas.samhsa.gov/nsduh/2k8nsduh/2k8Results.cfm

Substance Abuse and Mental Health Services Administration (SAMHSA). (2010a). *Results from the 2009 National Survey on Drug Use and Health: National findings* (DHHS Publication No. SMA 09–4434, NSDUH Series H–36). Rockville, MD: Substance Abuse and Mental Health Services Administration. Retrieved from http://www.oas.samhsa.gov/NSDUH/2k9NSDUH/2k9Results.htm

Substance Abuse and Mental Health Services Administration (SAMHSA). (2010b). *The DAWN Report: Trends in emergency department visits involving nonmedical use of narcotic pain relievers.* Retrieved from http://www.oas.samhsa.gov/2k10/dawn016/opioided.htm

Substance Abuse and Mental Health Services Administration (SAMHSA). (2010c). *Substance Abuse Treatment Admissions Involving Abuse of Pain Relievers: 1998–2008.* Retrieved from http://oas.samhsa.gov/2k10/230/230PainRelvr2k10.cfm

Substance Abuse and Mental Health Services Administration. (2010d). *Results from the 2009 National Survey on Drug Use and Health: Mental Health Findings* (Office of Applied Studies, NSDUH Series H–39, HHS Publication No. SMA 10–4609). Rockville, MD.

Sue, D. W. (2010). *Microaggressions in everyday life: Race, gender and sexual orientation.* Hoboken, NJ: Wiley.

Sue, D. W., & Constantine, M. G. (2003). Optimal human functioning in people of color in the United States. In W. B. Walsh (Ed.), *Counseling psychology and optimal human functioning* (pp. 151–169). Mahwah, NJ: Lawrence Erlbaum Associates.

Sue, D. W., & Sue, D. (2003). *Counseling the culturally diverse: Theory and practice.* Hoboken, NJ: Wiley.

Sue, D. W., & Sue, D. (2008a). *Counseling the culturally diverse: Theory and practice* (5th ed.). Hoboken, NJ: Wiley.

Sue, D., & Sue, D. M. (2008b). *Foundations of counseling and psychotherapy: Evidence-based practices in a diverse society.* Hoboken, NJ: Wiley.

Sue, S., & Abe, J. (1988). *Predictors of academic achievement among Asian American and white students.* New York: College Board.

Sue, S., & Nakamura, C. Y. (1984). An integrative model of physiological and social/psychological factors in alcohol consumption among Chinese and Japanese Americans. *Journal of Drug Issues, 14,* 349–364.

Sugar, M. (1995). A clinical approach to childhood gender identity disorder. *American Journal of Psychotherapy, 49,* 260–281.

Sugawara, J., Tarumi, T., & Tanaka, H. (2010). Effect of mirthful laughter on vascular function. *American Journal of Cardiology, 15,* 856–859.

Sugiura, T., Sakamoto, S., Tanaka, E., Tomada, A., & Kitamura, T. (2001). Labeling effects of Seishin-Bunretsu-Byou, the Japanese translation for schizophrenia: An argument for relabeling. *International Journal of Social Psychiatry, 47,* 43–51.

Sui, X., LaMonte, M. J., Laditka, J. N., Hardin, J. W., Chase, N., Hooker, S. P., & Blair, S. N. (2007). Cardiorespiratory fitness and adiposity as mortality predictors in older adults. *Journal of the American Medical Association, 298,* 2507–2516.

Suicide belt. (1986, February 24). Time, 116, 56.

Suicide rate climbing for Black teens. (1998, March 20). *San Francisco Chronicle,* p. A17.

Sullivan, E. V., Harris, R. A., & Pfefferbaum, A. (2010). Alcohol's effects on brain and behavior. *Alcohol Research & Health.* Retrieved from http://findarticles.com/p/articles/mi_m0CXH/is_1-2_33/ai_n55302111/

Sullivan, B., & Payne, T. W. (2007). Affective disorders and cognitive failures: A comparison of seasonal and nonseasonal depression. *American Journal of Psychiatry, 164,* 1663–1667.

Sulser, F. (1979). Pharmacology: New cellular mechanisms of antidepressant drugs. In S. Fielding & R. C. Effland (Eds.), *New frontiers in psychotropic drug research.* Mount Kisco, NY: Futura.

Sundberg, N. D., Taplin, J. R., & Tyler, L. E. (1983). *Introduction to clinical psychology.* Englewood Cliffs, NJ: Prentice-Hall.

Sundel, M., & Sundel, S. S. (1998). Psychopharmacological treatment of panic disorder. *Research of Social Work Practice, 8,* 426–451.

Sundstrom, E. (2004). First person account: The clogs. *Schizophrenia Bulletin, 30,* 191–192.

Suokas, J., & Lonnqvist, J. (1995). Suicide attempts in which alcohol is involved: A special group in general hospital emergency rooms. *Acta Psychiatrica Scandinavia, 91,* 36–40.

Suominen, K., Mantere, O., Valtonen, H., Arvilommi, P., Leppämäki, S., & Isometsä, E. (2009). Gender differences in bipolar disorder type I and II. *Acta Psychiatrica Scandanavica, 120,* 464–473.

Sureshkumar, P., Jones, M., Caldwell, P. H., & Craig, J. C. (2009). Risk factors for nocturnal enuresis in school-age children. *Journal of Urology, 182,* 2893–2899.

Surtees, P. B., Wainwright, N. W. J., Luben, R., Wareham, N. J., Bingham, S. A., & Khaw, K.-T. (2010). Mastery is associated with cardiovascular disease mortality in men and women at apparently low risk. *Health Psychology, 29,* 412–420.

Sussman, S., Dent, C. W., McAdams, L. A., Stacy, A. W., Burton, D., & Flay, B. R. (1994). Group self-identification and adolescent cigarette smoking: A one-year prospective study. *Journal of Abnormal Psychology, 103,* 576–580.

Sussman, S., Sun, P., & Dent, C. W. (2006). A meta-analysis of teen cigarette smoking cessation. *Health Psychology, 25,* 549–557.

Sutherland, S. M. (2001). Avoidant personality disorder. In G. O. Gabbard (Ed.), *Treatment of psychiatric disorders* (pp. 2327–2340). Washington, DC: American Psychiatric Press.

Suzuki, K., Takei, N., Kawai, M., Minabe, Y., & Mori, N. (2003). Is Taijin Kyofusho a culture-bound syndrome? *American Journal of Psychiatry, 160,* 1358.

Suzuki, L., & Aronson, J. (2005). The cultural malleability of intelligence and its impact on the racial/ethnic hierarchy. *Psychology, Public Policy, and Law, 11,* 320–327.

Svaldi, J., Caffier, D., Blechert, J., & Tuschen-Caffier, B. (2009). Body-related film clip triggers desire to binge in women with binge eating disorder. *Behaviour Research and Therapy, 47,* 790–795.

Swaab, D. F. (2005). The role of hypothalamus and endocrine system in sexuality. In J. S. Hyde (Ed.), *Biological substrates of human sexuality.* Washington, DC: American Psychological Association.

Swann, A. C., Dougherty, D. M., Pazzaglia, P. J., Pham, M., Steinberg, J. L., Moeller, F. G. (2005). Increased impulsivity associated with severity of suicide attempt history in patients with bipolar disorder. *American Journal of Psychiatry, 162,* 1680–1687.

Swann, A. C., Moeller, F. G., Steinberg, J. L., Schneider, L., Barratt, E.S., & Dougherty, D. M. (2007). Manic symptoms and impulsivity during bipolar depressive episodes. *Bipolar Disorders, 9,* 206–212.

Swann, A. C., Steinberg, J. L., Lijffijt, M., Moeller, G. F. (2009). Continuum of depressive and manic mixed states in patients with bipolar disorder: quantitative measurement and clinical features. *World Psychiatry, 8,* 166–172.

Swanson, J., Holzer, C., Ganju, V., & Jono, R. (1990). Violence and psychiatric disorder in the community: Evidence from the Epidemiological Catchment Area Surveys. *Hospital Community Psychiatry, 41,* 761–770.

Swanson, J. W. (1994). Mental disorder, substance abuse, and community violence: An epidemiological approach. In J. Monahan & H. J. Steadman (Eds.), *Violence and mental disorder: Developments in risk assessment* (pp. 101–136). Chicago: University of Chicago Press.

Swartz, M., Landerman, R., George, L. K., Blazer, D. G., & Escobar, J. (1991). Somatization disorder. In L. N. Robins and D. A. Regier (Eds.). *Psychiatric disorders in America* (pp. 220–255). New York: Free Press.

Swedo, S. E., Rapoport, J. L., Leonard, H., Lenane, M., & Cheslow, D. (1989). Obsessive-compulsive disorder in children and adolescents. *Archives of General Psychiatry, 46,* 335–341.

Swindler, J. (2004, September 10). Latest death at NYU tests new mental health program. *Columbia Spectator,* p. A1.

Syed, Z., Imam, S. Z., Zhou, Q., Yamamoto, A., Valente, A. J., . . . Senlin, L. (2011). Novel regulation of parkin function through c-Abl-mediated tyrosine phosphorylation: Implications for Parkinson's disease. *The Journal of Neuroscience, 31,* 157–163.

Sykes, R. (2007). Somatoform disorders in DSM-IV: Mental or physical disorders. *Journal of Psychosomatic Research, 60,* 341–344.

Syzdek, M. R., & Addis, M. E. (2010). Adherence to masculine norms and attributional processes predict depressive symptoms in recently unemployed men. *Cognitive Therapy and Research, 34,* 533–543.

Szasz, T. (1986). The case against suicide prevention. *American Psychologist, 41,* 806–812. Szasz, T. (2007). *Coercion as cure: A critical history of psychiatry.* Edison, NJ: Transaction.

Szasz, T. S. (1970). *The manufacture of madness: A comparative study of the inquisition and the mental health movement.* New York: Harper & Row.

Szasz, T. S. (1987). Justifying coercion through theology and therapy. In J. K. Zeig (Ed.), *The evolution of psychotherapy.* New York: Brunner/Mazel.

Tabakoff, B., Whelan, J. P., & Hoffman, P. L. (1990). Two biological markers of alcoholism. In C. R. Cloninger & H. Begleiter (Eds.), *Genetics and biology of alcoholism* (pp. 195–204). Cold Spring Harbor, NY: Cold Spring Harbor Laboratory Press.

Taber, K. H., Warden, D. L., & Hurley, R. A. (2006). Blast-related traumatic brain injury: What is known? *Journal of Neuropsychiatry and Clinical Neuroscience, 18,* 141–145.

Tabert, M. H., Manly, J. J., Liu, X., Pelton, G. H., Rosenblum, S., Jacobs, M., . . . Devanand, D. P. (2006). Neuropsychological prediction of conversion to Alzheimer's disease in patients with mild cognitive impairment. *Archives of General Psychiatry, 63,* 916–924.

Takahashi, T., Tsunoda, M., Miyashita, M., Ogihara, T., Okada, Y., . . . Amano, N. (2011). Comparison of diagnostic names of mental illnesses in medical documents before and after the adoption of a new Japanese translation of 'schizophrenia.' *Psychiatry and Clinical Neurosciences, 65,* 89–94.

Takahashi, T., Wood, S. J., Yung, A. R., Soulsby, B., McGorry, P. D., . . . Pantelis, C. (2009). Progressive gray matter reduction of the superior temporal gyrus during transition to psychosis. *Archives of General Psychiatry, 66,* 366–376.

Takeuchi, J. (2000). Treatment of a biracial child with schizophreniform disorder: Cultural formulation. *Cultural Diversity and Ethnic Minority Psychology, 6,* 93–101.

Talavage, T. M. Nauman, E., Breedlove, E. L., Yoruk, U., Dye, A. E., . . . Leverenz, L. J. (2010). Functionally-detected cognitive impairment in high school football players without clinically-diagnosed concussion. *Journal of Neurotrauma.* Retrieved from http://www.liebertonline.com/doi/pdfplus/10.1089/neu.2010.1512

Talleyrand, R. M. (2006). Potential stressors contributing to eating disorder symptoms in African American women: Implications for mental health counselors. *Journal of Mental Health Counseling, 28,* 338–352.

Talleyrand, R. M. (2010). Eating disorders in African American girls: Implications for counselors. *Journal of Counseling and Development, 88,* 319–325.

Tan, E. K., Ho, P., Tan, L., Prakash, K. M., & Zhao, Y. (2010). PLA2G6 mutations and Parkinson's disease. *Annals of Neurology, 67,* 147–148.

Tan, H.-Y., Chen, Q., Sust, S., Buckholtz, J. W., Meyers, J. D., . . . Callicott, J. H. (2007). Epistasis between catechol-*O*-methyltransferase and type II metabotropic glutamate receptor 3 genes on working memory brain function. *Proceedings of the National Academy of Sciences of the USA, 104,* 12536–12541.

Tang, T. Z., DeRubeis, R. J., Hollon, S. D., Amsterdam, J., Shelton, R., & Schalet, B. (2009). Personality changes during depression treatment: A placebo-controlled trial. *Archives of General Psychiatry, 66,* 1322–1330.

Taniai, H., Nishiyama, T., Miyachi, T., Imaeda, M., & Sumi, S. (2008). Genetic influences on the broad spectrum of autism: Study of proband-ascertained twins. *American Journal of Medical Genetics. Part B, Neuropsychiatric Genetics, 147B,* 844–849.

Tarasoff v. the Board of Regents of the University of California, 17 Cal. 3d 435, 551 P.2d, 334, 131 Cal. Rptr. 14, 83 Ad. L. 3d 1166 (1976).

Tardiff, K. (1984). Characteristics of assaultive patients in private psychiatric hospitals. *American Journal of Psychiatry, 141,* 1232–1235.

Tardiff, K., & Koenigsberg, H. W. (1985). Assaultive behavior among psychiatric outpatients. *American Journal of Psychiatry, 142,* 960–963.

Tardiff, K., & Sweillam, A. (1982). Assaultive behavior among chronic inpatients. *American Journal of Psychiatry, 139,* 212–215.

Tarkan, C. L. (1998). Diary of an eating disorder. *Joe Weider's Shape, 18,* 116–119.

Tárraga, L., Boada, M., Modinos, G., Espinosa, A., Diego, S., . . . Becker, J. T. (2006). A randomised pilot study to assess the efficacy of an interactive, multimedia tool of cognitive stimulation in Alzheimer's disease. *Journal of Neurology, Neurosurgery, and Psychiatry, 77,* 1116–1121.

Task Force on Promotion and Dissemination of Psychological Procedures. (1995). Training in and dissemination of empirically validated psychological treatments: Report and recommendations. *Clinical Psychologist, 48*(1), 3–23.

Tatman, S. M., Peters, D. B., Greene, A. L., & Bongar, B. (1997). Graduate student attitudes toward prescription privilege training. *Professional Psychology: Research and Practice, 28,* 515–517.

Taylor, C. T., & Alden, L. E. (2010). Safety behaviors and judgmental biases in social anxiety disorder. *Behaviour Research and Therapy, 48,* 226–237.

Taylor, E. H. (1990). The assessment of social intelligence. *Psychotherapy, 27,* 445–457.

Taylor, J. L., & Seltzer M. M. (2010a). Employment and post-secondary educational activities for young adults with autism spectrum disorders during the transition to adulthood. *Journal of Autism and Developmental Disorders, 41*(5), 566–574. doi: 10.1007/s10803-010-1070-3

Taylor, J. L., & Seltzer, M. M. (2010b). Changes in the autism behavioral phenotype during the transition to adulthood. *Journal of Autism and Developmental Disorders, 41,* 566–574.

Taylor, K. N., Harper, S., & Chadwick, P. (2009). Impact of mindfulness on cognition and affect in voice hearing: Evidence from two case studies. *Behavioural and Cognitive Psychotherapy, 37,* 397–402.

Taylor, S., Asmundson, G. J. G., & Coons, M. J. (2005). Current directions in the treatment of hypochondriasis. *Journal of Cognitive Psychotherapy: An International Quarterly, 19,* 285–304.

Taylor, S., Jang, K. L., Stein, M. B., & Asmundson, G. J. G. (2008). A behavioral-genetic analysis of cognitive-behavioral model of hypochondriasis. *Journal of Cognitive Psychotherapy: An International Quarterly, 22,* 143–154.

Taylor, S., Thordarson, D. S., Maxfield, L., Fedoroff, I. C., Lovell, K., & Ogrodniczuk, J. (2003). Comparative efficacy, speed, and adverse effects of three PTSD treatments: Exposure therapy, EMDR, and relaxation training. *Journal of Consulting and Clinical Psychology, 71,* 330–338.

Taylor, S., Woody, S., Koch, W. J., McLean, P. D., & Anderson, K. W. (1996). Suffocation fear alarms and efficacy of cognitive behavioral therapy for panic disorder. *Behavior Therapy, 27,* 115–126.

Taylor, S. E., Kemeny, M. E., Bower, J. E., Gruenewald, T. L., & Reed, G. M. (2000). Psychological resources, positive illusions, and health. *American Psychologist, 55,* 99–109.

Teachman, B. A., Marker, C. D., & Clerkin, E. M. (2010). Catastrophic misinterpretations as a predictor of symptom change during treatment for panic disorder. *Journal of Consulting and Clinical Psychology, 24,* 300–308.

Teicher, M., Andersen, S. L., Polcari, A., Anderson, C. M., & Navalta, C. P. (2002). Developmental neurobiology of childhood stress and trauma. *Psychiatric Clinics of North America, 25,* 397–426.

Teicher, M. H., Samson, J. A., Polcari, A., & McGreenery, C. E. (2006). Sticks, stones, and hurtful words: Relative effects of various forms of childhood maltreatment. *American Journal of Psychiatry, 163,* 993–1000.

Telch, M. J., Lucas, J. A., & Nelson, P. (1989). Nonclinical panic in college students: An investigation of prevalence and symptomatology. *Journal of Abnormal Psychology, 98,* 300–306.

Terman, L. M., & Merrill, M. A. (1960). *Stanford-Binet intelligence scale.* Boston: Houghton Mifflin.

Terr, L. C. (1991). Childhood traumas: An outline and overview. *American Journal of Psychiatry, 148,* 10–20.

Thanos, P. K., Michaelides, M., Piyis, Y. K., Wang, G. J., & Volkow, N. D. (2008). Food restriction markedly increases dopamine D2 receptor (D2R) in a rat model of obesity as assessed with in-vivo muPET imaging ([(11)C] raclopride) and in-vitro ([(3)H] spiperone) autoradiography. *Synapse, 62,* 50–61.

Tharp, B. R. (2003). Contributions of neurology. In S. Ozonoff, S. J. Rogers, & R. L. Hendren (Eds.), *Autism spectrum disorders: A research review for practitioners* (pp. 111–132). Arlington, VA: American Psychiatric.

Thase, M. E. (2001). Depression-focused psychotherapies. In G. O. Gabbard (Ed.), *Treatment of psychiatric disorders* (pp. 1181–1226). Washington, DC: American Psychiatric Press.

Thiedke, C. C. (2003). Nocturnal enuresis. *American Family Physician, 67,* 1499–1506.

Thigpen, C. H., & Cleckley, H. M. (1984). On the incidence of multiple personality disorder: A brief communication. *International Journal of Clinical and Experimental Hypnosis, 32,* 63–66.

Thirthalli, J., & Benegal, V. (2006). Psychosis among substance users. *Current Opinion in Psychiatry, 19,* 239–245.

Thom, A., Sartory, G., & Johren, P. (2000). Comparison between one-session psychological treatment and benzodiazepine in dental phobia. *Journal of Consulting and Clinical Psychology, 68,* 378–387.

Thomas, A., Chess, S., & Birch, H. G. (1968). *Temperament and behavior disorders in children.* New York: New York University Press.

Thomas, C. P., Conrad, P., Casler, R., & Goodman, E. (2006). Trends in the use of psychotropic medications among adolescents, 1994 to 2001. *Psychiatric Services, 57,* 63–69.

Thomas, J. D., Warren, K. R., & Hewitt, B. G. (2010). Fetal alcohol spectrum disorders: From research to policy. *Alcohol Research & Health.* Retrieved from http://findarticles.com/p/articles/mi_m0CXH/is_1–2_33/ai_n55302110/

Thomas, J. J., Vartanian, L. R., & Brownell, K. D. (2009). The relationship between eating disorder not otherwise specified (EDNOS) and officially recognized eating disorders: Meta-analysis and implications for DSM. *Psychological Bulletin, 135,* 407–433.

Thomas, K. (2010, October 12). Transgender woman sues L.P.G.A. over policy. *The New York Times,* B13.

Thomas, P. (1995). Thought disorder or communication disorder: Linguistic science provides a new approach. *British Journal of Psychiatry, 166,* 287–290.

Thomas, T., Stansifer, L., & Findling, R. L. (2011). Psychopharmacology of pediatric bipolar disorders in children and adolescents. *Pediatric Clinics of North America, 58,* 173–187.

Thompson, J. K., & Stice, E. (2004). Thin-ideal internalization: Mounting evidence for a new risk factor for body-image disturbance and eating pathology. In T. F. Oltmanns & R. E. Emery (Eds.), *Current directions in abnormal psychology* (pp. 97–101). Upper Saddle River, NJ: Prentice Hall.

Thompson, P. M., Vidal, C., Giedd, J. N., Gochman, P., Blumenthal, J., . . . Rapoport, J. L. (2001). Mapping adolescent brain change reveals dynamic wave of accelerated gray matter loss in very early-onset schizophrenia. *Proceedings of the National Academy of Sciences, 98,* 11650–11655.

Thoresen, C. E. (1998). Spirituality, health and science: The coming revival? In S. R. Roemer, S. R. Kurpius, & C. Carmin (Eds.), *The emerging role of counseling psychology in health care* (pp. 409–431). New York: Norton.

Thorn, L., Evans, P., Cannon, A., Hucklebridge, F., Evans, P., & Clow, A. (2010). Seasonal differences in the diurnal pattern of cortisol secretion in healthy participants and those with self–assessed seasonal affective disorder. *Psychoneuroendocrinology.* In press.

Thorndike, R. L., Hagen, E. P., & Sattler, J. M. (1986). *The Stanford-Binet intelligence scale: Guide for administration and scoring* (3rd ed.). Chicago: Riverside.

Thornton, D. (2009). Evidence regarding the need for a diagnostic category for a coercive paraphilia. *Archives of Sexual Behavior, 39*(2), 411–418. doi: 10.1007/s10508-009-9583-6

Thorpe, K. E. (2009). *The future costs of obesity.* Retrieved from http://www.fightchronicdisease.org/pdfs/CostofObesityReport-FINAL.pdf

Thorpe, S. J., Barnett, J., Friend, K., & Nottingham, K. (2011). The mediating roles of disgust sensitivity and danger expectancy in relation to hand washing behaviour. *Behavioural and Cognitive Psychotherapy, 39,* 175–190.

Thorpe, S. J., & Salkovskis, P. M. (1998). Studies on the role of disgust in the acquisition and maintenance of specific phobias. *Behaviour Research and Therapy, 36,* 877–893.

Thorup, A., Waltoft, B. L., Pedersen, C. B., Mortensen, P. B., & Nordentoft, M. (2007). Young males have a higher risk of developing schizophrenia: A Danish register study. *Psychological Medicine, 37,* 479–484.

Thurston, R. C., & Kubzansky, L. D. (2009). Women, loneliness, and incident coronary heart disease. *Psychosomatic Medicine, 71,* 836–842.

Tian, Y., Green, P. G., Stamova, B., Hertz-Picciotto, I., Pessah, I. N., . . . Sharp, F. R. (2011). Correlations of gene expression with blood lead levels in children with autism compared to typically developing controls. *Neurotoxicity Research, 19,* 1–13.

Tienari, P., Wynne, L. C., Moring, J., Lahti, I., Naarala, M., . . . Kaleva, M. (1994). The Finnish adoptive family study of schizophrenia: Implications for family research. *British Journal of Psychiatry, 164,* 20–26.

Tienari, P., Wynne, L. C., Sorri, A., Lahti, I., Laksy, K., . . . Wahlberg, K. E. (2004). Genotype-environment interaction in schizophrenia-spectrum disorder. Long-term follow-up study of Finnish adoptees. *British Journal of Psychiatry, 184,* 216–222.

Tierney, J. (1988, July 3). Research finds lower-level workers bear brunt of workplace stress. *Seattle Post Intelligencer,* pp. K1–K3.

Tietjen, G. E., Brandes, J. L., Peterlin, B. L., Eloff, A., Dafer, R. M., . . . Khuder, S. A. (2010). Childhood maltreatment and migraine (part III). Association with comorbid pain conditions. *Headache, 50*(1), 42–51.

Tiggemann, M., & Kuring, J. K. (2004). The role of body objectification in disordered eating and depressed mood. *British Journal of Clinical Psychology, 43,* 299–311.

Tikhonova, I. V., Gnezditskii, V. V., Stakhovskaya, L. V., & Skvortsova, V. I. (2003). Neurophysiological characterization of transitory global amnesia syndrome. *Neuroscience and Behavioral Physiology, 33,* 171–175.

TimeSocket (2008). Morgellon's disease pictures and story. Retrieved from http://www.timesocket.com/disease/morgellons-disease-pictures-and-story/

Tindle, H. A., Chang, Y.-F., Kuller, L. H., Manson, J. E., Robinson, J. G., . . . Matthews, K. A. (2009). Optimism, cynical hostility, and incident coronary heart disease and mortality in the Women's Health Initiative. *Circulation, 120,* 656–662.

Titone, D., Levy, D. L., & Holzman, P. S. (2000). Contextual insensitivity in schizophrenic language processing: Evidence from lexical ambiguity. *Journal of Abnormal Psychology, 109,* 761–767.

Tobin, J. J., & Friedman, J. (1983). Spirits, shamans, and nightmare death: Survivor stress in a Hmong refugee. *American Journal of Orthopsychiatry, 53,* 439–448.

Tolan, P. H., Gorman-Smith, D., Huesmann, L. R., & Zelli, A. (1997). Assessment of family relationship characteristics: A measure to explain risk for antisocial behavior and depression among urban youth. *Psychological Assessment, 9,* 212–223.

Tolin, D. F., & Foa, E. B. (2006). Sex differences in trauma and posttraumatic stress disorder: A quantitative review of 25 years of research. *Psychological Bulletin, 132,* 959–992.

Tolin, D. F., Lohr, J. M., Sawchuk, C. N., & Lee, T. C. (1997). Disgust and disgust sensitivity in blood-injection-injury and spider phobia. *Behaviour Research and Therapy, 35,* 949–953.

Tolin, D. F., Meunier, S. A., Frost, R. O., & Steketee, G. (2010). Course of compulsive hoarding and its relationship to life events. *Depression and Anxiety, 27,* 829–838.

Tolin, D. F., Meunier, S. A., Frost, R. O., & Steketee, G. (2011). Hoarding among patients seeking treatment for anxiety disorders. *Journal of Anxiety Disorders, 25,* 43–48.

Tolin, D. F., Steenkamp, M. M., Marx, B. P., & Litz, B. T. (2010). Detecting symptom exaggeration in combat veterans using the MMPI-2 symptom validity scales: A mixed group validation. *Psychological Assessment, 22,* 729–736.

Tolin, D. F., & Villavicencio, A. (2011). Inattention, but not OCD, predicts the core features of hoarding behavior. *Behaviour Research and Therapy, 49,* 120–125.

Tollefson, G. D., Rampey, A. H., Potvin, J. H., Jenike, M. A., Rush, A. J., . . . Genduso, L. A. (1994). A multicenter investigation of fixed-dose fluoxetine in the treatment of obsessive-compulsive disorder. *Archives of General Psychiatry, 51,* 559–567.

Tolman, A. O., & Mullendore, K. B. (2003). Risk evaluations for the courts: Is service quality a function of specialization? *Professional Psychology: Research and Practice, 34,* 225–232.

Tolmunen, T., Joensuu, M., Saarinen, P. I., Mussalo, H., Ahola, P., . . . Lehtonen, J. (2004). Elevated midbrain serotonin transporter availability in mixed mania: A case report. *BMC Psychiatry, 4,* 27.

Torgersen, S. (1986). Genetics of somatoform disorders. *Archives of General Psychiatry, 43,* 502–505.

Torgersen, S., Kringlen, E., & Cramer, V. (2001). The prevalence of personality disorders in a community sample. *Archives of General Psychiatry, 58,* 590–596.

Toro, P. A., & Wall, D. D. (1991). Research on homeless persons: Diagnostic comparisons and practice implications. *Professional Psychology: Research and Practice, 22,* 479–488.

Torpey, D. C., & Klein, D. N. (2008). Chronic depression: Update on classification and treatment. *Current Psychiatry Reports, 10,* 458–464.

Townsend, M., & Weisler, R. (2007). *Post-disaster psychiatry: Lesson from Katrina.* Retrieved from www.medscape.com/viewprogram/7466_pnt

Trampe, D., Stapel, D. A., & Siero, F. W. (2010). On models and vases: Body dissatisfaction and proneness to social comparison effects. *Journal of Personality and Social Psychology, 92,* 106–118.

Trautmann, E., & Kroner-Herwig, B. (2008). Internet-based self-help training for children and adolescents with recurrent headache: A pilot study. *Behavioural and Cognitive Psychotherapy, 36,* 241–245.

Trautmann, E., & Kroner-Herwig, B. (2010). A randomized controlled trial of internet-based self-help training for recurrent headache in children and adolescents. *Behaviour Research and Therapy, 48,* 28–37.

Treasure, J. L. (2007). Getting beneath the phenotype of anorexia nervosa: The search for viable endophenotypes and genotypes. *Canadian Journal of Psychiatry, 52,* 212–219.

Tregellas, J. R., Shatti, S., Tanabe, J. L., Martin, L. F., Gibson, L., Wylie, K., & Rojas, D. C. (2007). Gray matter volume differences and the effects of smoking on gray matter in schizophrenia. *Schizophrenia Research, 97,* 242–249.

Treloar, A., Crugel, M., Prasanna, A., Solomons, L., Fox, J., Paton. C., & Katona, C. (2010). Ethical dilemmas: Should antipsychotics ever be prescribed for people with dementia? *The British Journal of Psychiatry, 197,* 88–90.

Triffleman, E. G., & Pole, N. (2010). Future directions in studies of trauma among ethnoracial and sexual minority samples. *Journal of Consulting and Clinical Psychology, 78,* 490–497.

Tripp, M. M., & Petrie, T. A. (2001). Sexual abuse and eating disorders: A test of a conceptual model. *Sex Roles, 44,* 17–32.

Trivedi, M. H., Hollander, E., Nutt, D., & Blier, P. (2008). Clinical evidence and potential neurobiological underpinnings of unresolved symptoms of depression. *Journal of Clinical Psychiatry, 69,* 246–258.

Trottier, K., Polivy, J., & Herman, C. P. (2007). Effects of exposure to thin and overweight peers: Evidence of social comparison in restrained and unrestrained eaters. *Journal of Social and Clinical Psychology, 26,* 155–172.

Troxel, W. M., Matthews, K. A., Bromberger, J. T., & Tyrrell, K. S. (2003). Chronic stress burden, discrimination, and subclinical carotid artery disease in African American and Caucasian women. *Health Psychology, 22,* 300–309.

Trull, T. J., Solhan, M. B., Tragesser, S. L., Jahng, S., Wood, P. K., Piasecki, T. M., & Watson, D. (2008). Affective instability: Measuring a core feature of borderline personality disorder with ecological momentary assessment. *Journal of Abnormal Psychology, 117,* 647–661.

Trull, T. J., Useda, J. D., Conforti, K., & Doan, B.-T. (1997). Borderline personality disorder features in nonclinical young adults: Part 2. Two-year outcome. *Journal of Abnormal Psychology, 106,* 307–314.

Tsai, G., & Gray, J. (2000). The Eating Disorders Inventory among Asian American college women. *Journal of Social Psychology, 140,* 527–529.

Tsai, G. E., Condie, D., Wu, M.-T., & Chang, I.-W. (1999). Functional magnetic resonance imaging of personality switches in a woman with dissociative identity disorder. *Harvard Review of Psychiatry, 7,* 119–122.

Tsang, H. W., Leung, A. Y., Chung, R. C., Bell, M., & Cheung W. M. (2010). Review on vocational predictors: A systematic review of predictors of vocational outcomes among individuals with schizophrenia: An update since 1998. *Australia and New Zealand Journal of Psychiatry, 44,* 495–504.

Tsoi, W. F. (1993). Male and female transsexuals: A comparison. *Singapore Medical Journal, 33,* 182–185.

Tucker, B. T. P., Woods, D. W., Flessner, C. A., Franklin, S. A., & Franklin, M. E. (2011). The skin picking impact project: Phenomenology, interference, and treatment utilization of pathological skin picking in a population-based sample. *Journal of Anxiety Disorders, 25,* 88–95.

Tucker, E. (2002, August 28). 2 men missing since 9/11 found alive in hospitals. *Houston Chronicle,* p. 15.

Tucker-Drob, E. M., Rhemtulla, M., Harden, K. P., Turkheimer, E., & Fask, D. (2011). Emergence of a gene x socioeconomic status interaction on infant mental ability between 10 months and 2 years. *Psychological Science, 22,* 125–133.

Tuller, D. (2004, June 21). Gentlemen, start your engines? *New York Times,* pp. F1, F11.

Tully, E. C., Iacono, W. G., & McGue, M. (2010). Changes in genetic and environmental influences on the development of nicotine dependence and major depressive disorder from middle adolescence to early adulthood. *Developmental Psychopathology, 22,* 831–848.

Tunks, E. R., Weir, R., & Crook, J. (2008). Epidemiologic perspective on chronic pain treatment. *Canadian Journal of Psychiatry, 53,* 235–242.

Tuomisto, M. T. (1997). Intra-arterial blood pressure and heart rate reactivity to behavioral stress in normotensive, borderline, and mild hypertensive men. *Health Psychology, 16,* 554–565.

Turetsky, B. I., Calkins, M. E., Light, G. A., Olincy, A., Radant, A. D., & Swerdlow, N. R. (2007). Neurophysiological endophenotypes of schizophrenia: The viability of selected candidate measures. *Schizophrenia Bulletin, 33,* 69–78.

Turk, D. C., Swanson, K. S., & Tunks, E. R. (2008). Psychological approaches in the treatment of chronic pain patients—When pills, scalpels, and needles are not enough. *Canadian Journal of Psychiatry, 53,* 213–223.

Turkheimer, E., & Parry, C. D. H. (1992). Why the gap? *American Psychologist, 47,* 646–655.

Turner, E. H., Matthews, A. M., Linardatos, E., Tell, R. A., & Rosenthal, R. (2008). Selective publication of antidepressant trials and its influence on apparent efficacy. *New England Journal of Medicine, 358,* 252–257.

Turner, H. A., Finkelhor, D., Ormrod, R., & Hamby, S. L. (2010). Infant victimization in a nationally representative sample. *Pediatrics, 126,* 44–52.

Turner, W. J. (1995). Homosexuality, Type 1: An Xq28 phenomenon. *Archives of Sexual Behavior, 24,* 109–134.

Turtle, L., & Robertson, M. M. (2008). Tics, twitches, tales: The experiences of Gilles de la Tourette's syndrome. *American Journal of Orthopsychiatry, 78,* 449–455.

Tutkun, H., Sar, V., Yargic, L. I., & Ozpulat, T. (1998). Frequency of dissociative disorders among psychiatric inpatients in a Turkish university clinic. *American Journal of Psychiatry, 155,* 800–805.

Tuttle, J. P., Scheurich, N. E., & Ranseen, J. (2010). Prevalence of ADHD diagnosis and nonmedical prescription stimulant use in medical students. *Academic Psychiatry, 34,* 220–223.

Tylka, T. L., & Subich, L. M. (2004). Examining a multidimensional model of eating disorder symptomatology among college women. *Journal of Counseling Psychology, 51,* 314–328.

Tynan, W. D. (2008). Oppositional defiant disorder. Retrieved from http://emedicine. medscape.com/article/918095-print

Tynan, W. D. (2010). Conduct disorder. Retrieved from http://emedicine.medscape.com/ article/918213-print

Tyre, P. (2004, September 27). Combination therapy. *Newsweek,* 66–67.

Udal, A. H., Malt, U. F., Lövdahl, H., Gjaerum, B., Pripp, A. H., & Groholt, B. (2009). Motor function may differentiate attention deficit hyperactivity disorder from early onset bipolar disorder. *Behavior and Brain Function, 5,* 47.

Ungvari, G. S., Caroff, S. N., & Gerevich, J. (2009). The catatonia conundrum: Evidence of psychomotor phenomena as a symptom dimension in psychotic disorders. *Schizophrenia Bulletin, 36,* 231–238.

United Nations Office on Drugs and Crime. (2010). World drug report. Retrieved from http://www.

unodc.org/unodc/en/data-and-analysis/WDR-2010.html

University of Michigan. (2010, October 28). Friends with cognitive benefits: Mental function improves after certain kinds of socializing. *Science Daily*. Retrieved from http://www.sciencedaily.com/releases/2010/10/101028113817.htm

U.S. Court of Federal Claims. (2010). The autism proceedings. Retrieved from http://www.uscfc.uscourts.gov/node/5026

U.S. Department of Education, National Center for Education Statistics. (2010). Digest of Education Statistics, 2009 (NCES 2010-013). Retrieved from http://nces.ed.gov/fastfacts/display.asp?id=64

U.S. Department of Health and Human Services. (1995). Update: Trends in fetal alcohol syndrome. *Morbidity and Mortality Weekly Report, 44*, 249–251.

U.S. Department of Health and Human Services. (2003). *Ending chronic homelessness*. Washington, DC: Author.

U.S. Department of Health and Human Services. (2006). *The health consequences of involuntary exposure to tobacco smoke: A report of the Surgeon General*. Rockville, MD: U.S. Department of Health and Human Services, Centers for Disease Control and Prevention, Coordinating Center for Health Promotion, National Center for Chronic Disease Prevention and Health Promotion, Office on Smoking and Health.

U.S. Department of Health and Human Services. (2007). *Child maltreatment 2005*. Washington, DC: U.S. Government Printing Office.

U.S. Department of Health and Human Services. (2009). Child maltreatment. Retrieved from http://www.acf.hhs.gov/programs/cb/pubs/cm09/cm09.pdf#page=66

U.S. Food and Drug Administration. (2007). Antidepressant use in children, adolescents, and adults. Retrieved from http://www.fda.gov/drugs/drugsafety/informationbydrugclass/ucm096273.htm

U.S. Food and Drug Administration. (2010a). FDA warning letters issued to four makers of caffeinated alcoholic beverages. Retrieved from http://www.fda.gov/NewsEvents/Newsroom/PressAnnouncements/ucm234109.htm

U.S. Food and Drug Administration. (2010b). FDA approves injectable drug to treat opioid-dependent patients. Retrieved from http://www.fda.gov/NewsEvents/Newsroom/PressAnnouncements/ucm229109.htm

U.S. Food and Drug Administration (FDA). (2011). FDA drug safety communication: Antipsychotic drug labels updated on use during pregnancy and risk of abnormal muscle movements and withdrawal symptoms in newborns. Retrieved from http://www.fda.gov/DrugsSafety/ucm243903.htm

U.S. Surgeon General. (1999). *Mental health: A report of the Surgeon General*. Washington, DC: U.S. Government Printing Office.

Ucok, A. (2007). Other people stigmatize.... But, what about us? Attitudes of mental health professionals towards patients with schizophrenia. *Archives of Neuropsychiatry, 44,* 108–116.

Ullmann, L. P., & Krasner, L. (1965). Introduction. In L. P. Ullmann & L. Krasner (Eds.), *Case studies in behavior modification*. New York: Holt, Rinehart & Winston.

Ullmann, L. P., & Krasner, L. (1975). *A psychological approach to abnormal behavior* (2nd ed.). Englewood Cliffs, NJ: Prentice-Hall.

Ulloa, R.-E., Nicolini, H., Avila, M., & Fernandez-Guasti, A. (2007). Age onset subtypes of obsessive-compulsive disorder: Differences in clinical response to treatment with clomipramine. *Journal of Child and Adolescent Psychopharmacology, 17,* 85–96.

Underwood, A. (2005, October 3). The good heart. *Newsweek,* 49–55.

Underwood, A. (2007, June 11). It's called "sexsomnia." *Newsweek,* 53.

United Nations Development Programme. (2006). *Human development report. 2006*. New York: Author.

Utsey, S. O., Stanard, P., & Hook, J. N. (2008). Understanding the role of cultural factors in relation to suicide among African Americans: Implications for research and practice. In F. Leong & M. M. Leach (Eds.), *Ethnic suicides* (pp. 57–80). New York: Routledge.

Uthman, O. A., & Abdulmalik, J. O. (2008). Adjunctive therapies for AIDS dementia complex. *Cochrane Database of Systematic Reviews, 3,* CD006496. doi:10.1002/14651858.CD006496.pub2

Vaillant, G. E. (1994). Ego mechanisms of defense and personality psychopathology. *Journal of Abnormal Psychology, 103,* 44–50.

Valderhaug, R., Larsson, G., & Gotestam, K. G. (2007). An open clinical trial of cognitive-behavioral therapy in children and adolescents with obsessive-compulsive disorder administered in regular outpatient clinics. *Behaviour Research and Therapy, 45,* 577–585.

Valenstein, M., Blow, F. C., Copeland, L. A., McCarthy, J. F., Zeber, J. E., . . . Stavenger, T. (2004). Poor antipsychotic adherence among patients with schizophrenia: Medication and patient factors. *Schizophrenia Bulletin, 30,* 255–264.

Valentiner, D. P., Foa, E. B., Riggs, D. S., & Gershuny, B. S. (1996). Coping strategies and posttraumatic stress disorder in female victims of sexual and nonsexual assault. *Journal of Abnormal Psychology, 105,* 455–458.

Valsiner, J. (2007). *Culture in mind and societies*. New Delhi, India: Sage.

Van Amsterdam, J., & van den Brink, W. (2010). Ranking of drugs: A more balanced risk-assessment. *The Lancet, 376,* 1524–1525.

van der Gaag, M. (2006). A neuropsychiatric model of biological and psychological processes in the remission of delusions and auditory hallucinations. *Schizophrenia Bulletin, 32,* 113–122.

van der Gaag, M., Stant, A. D., Wolters, K. J. K., Burkens, E., & Wiersma, D. (2011). Cognitive-behavioral therapy for persistent and recurrent psychosis in people with schizophrenia-spectrum disorder: Cost-effectiveness analysis. *British Journal of Psychiatry, 198,* 59–65.

Vanderlinden, J., Norre, J., & Vandereycken, W. (1992). *A practical guide to the treatment of bulimia nervosa*. New York: Brunner/Mazel.

van der Werf, M., Thewissen, V., Dominguez, M. D., Lieb, R., Wittchen, H., & van Os, J. (2011). Adolescent development of psychosis as an outcome of hearing impairment: A 10–year longitudinal study. *Psychological Medicine, 41,* 477–485.

Van Lankveld, J. (2008). Problems with sexual interest and desire in women. In D. Rowland & L. Incrocci (Eds.), *Handbook of sexual and gender identity disorders* (pp. 154–187). Hoboken, NJ: Wiley.

van Winkel, R. (2011). Evidence that familial liability for psychosis is expressed as differential sensitivity for cannabis. *Archives of General Psychiatry, 68,* 138–147.

van der Zwaluw, C. S., Engels, R. C., Vermulst, A. A., Franke, B., Buitelaar, J., Verkes, R. J., & Scholte, R. H. (2010). Interaction between dopamine D2 receptor genotype and parental rule-setting in adolescent alcohol use: evidence for a gene-parenting interaction. *Molecular Psychiatry, 15,* 727–735.

van der Zwaluw, C. S., Kuntsche, E., & Engels R. C. (2011). Risky alcohol use in adolescence: The role of genetics (DRD2, SLC6A4) and coping motives. *Alcoholism: Clinical and Experimental Research, 35*(4), 756–764. doi:10.1111/j.1530–0277.2010.01393.x

Vandrey, R., Bigelow, G. E., & Stitzer, M. L. (2007). Contingency management in cocaine abusers: A dose-effect comparison of goods-based versus cash-based incentives. *Experimental and Clinical Psychopharmacology, 15,* 338–343.

Vandrey, R., & Haney, M. (2009). Pharmacotherapy for cannabis dependence: How close are we? *CNS Drugs, 23,* 543–553.

Vandrey, R. G., Budney, A. J., Kamon, J. L., & Stanger, C. (2005). Cannabis withdrawal in adolescent treatment seekers. *Drug and Alcohol Dependence, 78,* 205–210.

Van Evra, J. P. (1983). *Psychological disorders of children and adolescents*. Boston: Little, Brown.

Van Gestel, S., Forsgren, T., Claes, S., Del-Favero, J., van Duijn, C. M., . . . Van Broeckhoven, C. (2002). Epistatic effects of genes from the dopamine and serotonin systems on the temperament traits of novelty seeking and harm avoidance. *Molecular Psychiatry, 7,* 448–450.

van Goozen, S. H., Fairchild, G., Snoek, H., & Harold, G. T. (2007). The evidence for a neurobiological model of childhood antisocial behavior. *Psychological Bulletin, 133,* 149–182.

Van Gundy, K., Cesar, J., & Rebellon, C. (2010). A life-course perspective on the "gateway hypothesis." *Journal of Health and Social Behavior, 51,* 244–259.

Van Hoeken, D., Seidell, J., & Hoek, H. W. (2003). Epidemiology. In J. Treasure, U. Schmidt, & E. Van Furth (Eds.), *Handbook of eating disorders* (pp. 11–34). Chichester, UK: Wiley.

Vahid, B., & Marik, P. E. (2007). Severe emphysema associated with cocaine smoking: A case study. *Journal of Respiratory Diseases.* Retrieved from http://goliath.ecnext.com/coms2/gi_0199-7248880/Severe-emphysema-associated-with-cocaine.html

Van Hulle, C. A., Waldman, I. D., D'Onofrio, B. M., Rodgers, J. L., Rathouz, P. J., & Lahey, B. B. (2009). Developmental structure of genetic influences on antisocial behavior across childhood and adolescence. *Journal of Abnormal Psychology, 118,* 711–721.

Van Noppen, B., & Steketee, G. (2009). Testing a conceptual model of patient and family predictors of obsessive compulsive disorder (OCD) symptoms. *Behaviour Research and Therapy, 47,* 18–25.

van Praag, H. M. (1983). CSF 5-H1AA and suicide in non-depressed schizophrenics. *Lancet, 2,* 977–978.

van Praag, H. M. (2010a). Functionalization of psychiatric diagnosis. *Canadian Journal of Psychiatry, 55,* 61–63.

van Praag, H. M. (2010b). Does psychiatry really know "solid disease diagnoses?" *Canadian Journal of Psychiatry, 55,* 64.

Van Vlierberghe, L., Braet, C., Bosmans, G., Rosseel, Y., & Bogels, S. (2010). Maladaptive schemas and psychopathology in adolescence: On the utility of Young's schema theory in youth. *Cognitive Therapy and Research, 34,* 316–332.

Vassilopoulos, S. P. (2009). Interpretations for safety behaviours in high and low socially anxious individuals. *Behavioural and Cognitive-Psychotherapy, 37,* 167–178.

Vassilopoulos, S. P., Banerjee, R., & Prantzalou, C. (2009). Experimental modification of interpretation bias in socially anxious children: Changes in interpretation, anticipated interpersonal anxiety, and social anxiety symptoms. *Behaviour Research and Therapy, 47,* 1085–1089.

Vaughan, S., & Fowler, D. (2004). The distress experienced by voice hearers is associated with the perceived relationship between the voice hearer and the voice. *British Journal of Clinical Psychology, 43,* 143–147.

Vazquez-Nuttall, E., Li, C., Dynda, A. M., Ortiz, S. O., Armengol, C. G., Walton, J. W., et al. (2007). Cultural assessment of culturally and linguistically diverse students. In G. Esquivel, E. C. Lopez, & S. G. Nahari (Eds.), *Handbook of multicultural school psychology: An interdisciplinary perspective* (pp. 265–288). Mahwah, NJ: Erlbaum.

Vega, W., & Rumbaut, R. G. (1991). Ethnic minorities and mental health. *Annual Review of Sociology, 17,* 351–383.

Veling, W., Selten, J.-P., Mackenbach, J. P., & Hoek, H. W. (2007). Symptoms at first contact for psychotic disorder: Comparison between native Dutch and ethnic minorities. *Schizophrenia Research, 95,* 30–38.

Velligan, D. I., Weiden, P. J., Sajatovic, M., Scott, J., Carpenter, D., Ross, R., Docherty, J. P. (2009). The expert consensus guideline series: Adherence problems in patients with serious and persistent mental illness. *Journal of Clinical Psychiatry, 70*(Suppl 4), 1–46.

Verboom, C. E., Sentse, M., Sijtsema, J. J., Nolen, W. A., Ormel, J., & Penninx, B. W. (2011). Explaining heterogeneity in disability with major depressive disorder: Effects of personal and environmental characteristics. *Journal of Affective Disorders, 132,* 71–81.

Vermetten, E., Schmahl, C., Lindner, S., Loewenstein, R. J., & Bremner, J. D. (2006). Hippocampal and amygdalar volumes in dissociative identity disorder. *American Journal of Psychiatry, 163,* 630–636.

Viding, E., & Blakemore, S. (2007). Endophenotype approach to developmental psychopathology: Implications for autism research. *Behavior Genetics, 37,* 51–60.

Vigezzi, P., Guglielmino, L., Marzorati, P., Silenzio, R., De Chiara, M., . . . Cozzolino, E. (2006). Multimodal drug addiction treatment: A field comparison of methadone and buprenorphine among heroin- and cocaine-dependent patients. *Journal of Substance Abuse Treatment, 31,* 3–7.

Vigod, S. N. (2009). Understanding and treating premenstrual dysphoric disorder: An update for the women's health practitioner. *Obstetric and Gynecological Clinics of North America, 36,* 907–924.

Vigod, S. N., & Stewart, D. (2009). Emergent research in the cause of mental illness in women across the lifespan. *Current Opinion in Psychiatry, 22,* 396–400.

Villagonzalo, K. A., Dodd, S., Ng, F., Mihaly, S., Langbein, A., & Berk, M. (2010). The relationship between substance use and posttraumatic stress disorder in a methadone maintenance treatment program. *Comprehensive Psychiatry.* Retrieved from http://www.ncbi.nlm.nih.gov/pubmed/21109242Adi

Vincent, M. A., & McCabe, M. P. (2000). Gender differences among adolescents in family, and peer influences on body dissatisfaction, weight loss, and binge eating disorders. *Journal of Youth and Adolescence, 29,* 205–221.

Virués-Ortega, J. (2010). Applied behavior analytic intervention for autism in early childhood: Meta-analysis, meta-regression and dose-response meta-analysis of multiple outcomes. *Clinical Psychology Review, 30,* 387–399.

Visek, A. J., Olson, E. A., & DiPietro, L. (2011). Factors predicting adherence to 9 months of supervised exercise in healthy older women. *Journal of Physical Activity and Health, 8,* 104–110.

Visser, B. A., Bay, D., Cook, G. L., & Myburgh, J. (2010). Psychopathic and antisocial, but not emotionally intelligent. *Personality and Individual Differences, 48,* 644–648.

Vita, A., De Peri, L., & Sacchetti, E. (2009). Gray matter, white matter, brain, and intracranial volumes in first-episode bipolar disorder: A meta-analysis of magnetic resonance imaging studies. *Bipolar Disorders, 11,* 807–814.

Vitiello, B. (2009). Treatment of adolescent depression: What we have come to know. *Depression and Anxiety, 26,* 393–395.

Vocks, S., Tuschen-Caffier, B., Pietrowsky, R., Rustenbach, S. J., Kersting, A., & Herpertz, S. (2010). Meta-analysis of the effectiveness of psychological and pharmacological treatments for binge eating disorder. *International Journal of Eating Disorders, 43,* 205–217.

Vobrecht, M. M., & Goldsmith, H. H. (2010). Early temperamental and family predictors of shyness and anxiety. *Developmental Psychology, 46,* 1192–1205.

Vogel, G., Vogel, F., McAbee, R., & Thurmond, A. (1980). Improvement of depression by REM sleep deprivation. *Archives of General Psychiatry, 37,* 247–253.

Vogele, C., Ehlers, A., Meyer, A. H., Frank, M., Hahlweg, K., & Margraf, J. (2010). Cognitive mediation of clinical improvement after intensive exposure of agoraphobia and social phobia. *Depression and Anxiety, 27,* 294–301.

Volavka, J. (1995). *Neurobiology of violence.* Washington, DC: American Psychiatric Press.

Volkmar, F., Charwarska, K., & Klin, A. (2005). Autism in infancy and early childhood. *Annual Review of Psychology, 56,* 315–336.

Volkow, N. D., & O'Brien, C. P. (2007). Issues for DSM-V: Should obesity be included as a brain disorder? *American Journal of Psychiatry, 174,* 708–710.

von Gontard, A. (2011). Elimination disorders: a critical comment on DSM-5 proposals. *European Child and Adolescent Psychiatry, 20*(2), 83–88.

Vossekuil, G., Reddy, M., Fein, R., Borum, R., & Modzeleski, W. (2000). *U.S. Secret Service Schools Initiative: An interim report on the prevention of targeted violence in schools.* Washington, DC: U.S. Secret Service, National Threat Assessment Center.

Wade, N. (2007, September 10). Study finds evidence of genetic response to diet. *The New York Times.* Retrieved from http://www.nytimes.com/2007/09/10/science/10starch.html?ref+todayspaper

Wade, T., George, W. M., & Atkinson, M. (2009). A randomized controlled trial of brief interventions of body dissatisfaction. *Journal of Consulting and Clinical Psychology, 77,* 845–854.

Wade, T. D. (2007). A retrospective comparison of purging type disorders: Eating disorder not otherwise specified and bulimia nervosa. *International Journal of Eating Disorders, 40,* 1–5.

Wade, T. D., Bulik, C. M., Sullivan, P. F., Neale, M. C., & Kendler, K. S. (2000). The relationship between risk factors for binge eating and bulimia nervosa: A population-based female twin study. *Health Psychology, 19,* 115–123.

Wadia, R. S., Pujari, S. N., Kothari, S., Udhar, M., Kulkarni, S., Bhagat, S., & Nanivadekar, A. (2001). Neurological manifestations of HIV disease. *Journal of the Association of Physicians in India, 49,* 343–348.

Wagner, A. K., Zhang, F., Soumerai, S. B., Walker, A. M., Gurwitz, J. H., Glynn, R. J., & Ross-Degnan, D. (2004). Benzodiazepine use and hip fractures in the elderly: Who is at greatest risk? *Archives of Internal Medicine, 164,* 1567–1572.

Wagner, D. (2007, June 26). Injured man's awakening called "miracle." *USA Today*. Retrieved from www.usatoday.com/news/nation/2007-06-26-comatose_N.htm

Wagner, D. D., DalCin, S., Sargent, J. D., Kelley, W. M., & Heatherton, T. F. (2011). Spontaneous action representation in smokers when watching movie characters smoke. *Journal of Neuroscience, 31*, 894–898.

Wagner, J., & Abbott, G. (2007). Depression and depression care in diabetes: Relationship to perceived discrimination in African Americans. *Diabetes Care, 30*, 364–366.

Wagner, K. D., Ritt-Olson, A., Chou, C. P., Pokhrel, P., Duan, L., . . . Unger, J. B. (2010). Associations between parental family structure, family functioning, and substance use among Hispanic/Latino adolescents. *Psychology of Addictive Behaviors, 24*, 98–108.

Wakefield, H., & Underwager, R. (1993). Misuse of psychological tests in forensic settings: Some horrible examples. *American Journal of Forensic Psychology, 11*, 55–57.

Waldrop, D., Lightsey, O. R., Ethington, C. A., Woemmel, C. A., & Coke, A. L. (2001). Self-efficacy, optimism, health competence, and recovery from orthopedic surgery. *Journal of Counseling Psychology, 48*, 233–238.

Walfish, S., Barnett, J. E., Marlyere, K., & Zielke, R. (2010). "Doc, there's something I have to tell you": Patient disclosure to their psychotherapist of unprosecuted murder and other violence. *Ethics and Behavior, 20*, 311–323.

Walker, E., & Tessner, K. (2008). Schizophrenia. *Perspectives on Psychological Science, 3*, 30–37.

Walker, J. R., & Furer, P. (2008). Interoceptive exposure in the treatment of health anxiety and hypochondriasis. *Journal of Cognitive Psychotherapy, 22*, 367–380.

Walkup, J. (1995). A clinically based rule of thumb for classifying delusions. *Schizophrenia Bulletin, 21*, 323–331.

Wall, T. L., Shea, S. H., Luczak, S. E., Cook, T. A. R., & Carr, L. G. (2005). Genetic associations of alcohol dehydrogenase with alcohol use disorders and endophenotypes in White college students. *Journal of Abnormal Psychology, 114*(3), 456–465.

Waller, G., Babbs, M., Milligan, R., Meyer, C., Ohanian, V., & Leung, N. (2003). Anger and core beliefs in the eating disorders. *International Journal of Eating Disorders, 34*(1), 118–124.

Waller, R., & Gilbody, S. (2009). Barriers to the uptake of computerized cognitive behavioural therapy: A systematic review of the quantitative and qualitative evidence. *Psychological Medicine, 39*, 705–712.

Walling, A. D. (2007). Potential new treatment for premature ejaculation. *American Family Physician, 75*, 555–556.

Wallis, C. (2007, September 24). Hyper kid? Check their diet. *Time Magazine, 170*, 68.

Wallis, D., Russell, H. F., & Muenke, M. J. (2008). Review: Genetics of attention deficit/hyperactivity disorder. *Pediatric Psychology, 33*, 1085–1099.

Walsh, B. T., & Devlin, M. J. (1998). Eating disorders: Progress and problems. *Science, 280*, 1387–1390.

Walsh, B. T., Kaplan, A. S., Attia, E., Olmsted, M., Parides, M., . . . Rockert, W. (2006). Fluoxetine after weight restoration in anorexia nervosa: A randomized controlled trial. *Journal of the American Medical Association, 295*, 2605–2612.

Walter, H. J. (2001). Substance abuse and substance use disorders. In G. O. Gabbard (Ed.), *Treatment of psychiatric disorders* (pp. 325–338). Washington, DC: American Psychiatric Press.

Walter, K. H., Gunstadt, J., & Hobfoll, S. E. (2010). Self-control predicts later symptoms of posttraumatic stress disorder. *Psychological Trauma: Theory, Research, Practice, and Policy, 2*, 97–101.

Walters, A. M., Henry, J., & Neumann, D. L. (2009). Aversive Pavlovian conditioning in childhood anxiety disorders: Impaired response inhibition and resistance to extinction. *Journal of Abnormal Psychology, 118*, 311–321.

Walters, J. T. R., & Owen, M. J. (2007). Endophenotypes in psychiatric genetics. *Molecular Psychiatry, 12*, 886–890.

Wampold, B. E., Lichtenberg, J. W., & Waehler, C. A. (2002). Principles of empirically supported interventions in counseling psychology. *Counseling Psychologist, 30*, 197–217.

Wang, G. J., Volkow, N. D., Logan, J., Pappas, N. R., Wong, C. T., . . . Fowler, J. S. (2001). Brain dopamine and obesity. *Lancet, 357*, 354–357.

Wang, S.-J. & Fu, J.-L. (2010). The "other" headaches: Primary cough, exertion, stress and primary stabbing headaches. *Current Pain and Headache Reports, 14*, 41–46.

Wang, Y., & Beydoun, M. A. (2007). The obesity epidemic in the United States—gender, age, socioeconomic, racial/ethnic, and geographic characteristics: A systematic review and metaregression analysis. *Epidemiologic Reviews, 29*, 6–28.

Wang, X. P., & Ding, H. L. (2008). Alzheimer's disease: Epidemiology, genetics, and beyond. *Neuroscience Bulletin, 24*, 105–109.

Ward, M. J. (1946). *The snake pit.* London: Cassell.

Ward, M. P., & Irazoqui, P. P. (2010). Evolving refractory major depressive disorder diagnostic and treatment paradigms: Toward closed-loop therapeutics. *Frontiers in Neuroengineering, 3*, 7.

Ward, T., & Stewart, C. A. (2003). The treatment of sex offenders: Risk management and good lives. *Professional Psychology: Research and Practice, 34*, 353–360.

Wardle, J., Robb, K. A., Johnson, F., Griffith, J., Brunner, E., Power, C., & Tovee, M. (2004). Socioeconomic variation in attitudes to eating and weight in female adolescents. *Health Psychology, 23*, 275–282.

Warman, D. M., Lysaker, P. H., Martin, J. M., Davis, L., & Haudenschield, S. L. (2007). Jumping to conclusions and the continuum of delusional beliefs. *Behaviour Research and Therapy, 45*, 1255–1269.

Warmerdam, L., van Straten, A., Twisk, J., Riper, H., & Cuijpers, P. (2008). Internet-based treatment for adults with depressive symptoms: Randomized controlled trial. *Journal of Medical Internet Research, 10*, e44.

Warner, R. (2009). Recovery from schizophrenia and the recovery model. *Current Opinions in Psychiatry, 22*, 374–380.

Warner, T. D., & Roberts, L. W. (2004). Scientific integrity, fidelity, and conflicts of interest. *Current Opinion in Psychiatry, 17*, 381–385.

Wartik, N. (1994, February). Fatal attention. *Redbook*, pp. 62–69.

Warren, Z. E., Sanders, K. B., & Veenstra-VanderWeele, J. (2010). Identity crisis involving body image in a young man with autism. *American Journal of Psychiatry, 167*, 1299–1303.

Wash, R., & Shapiro, S. L. (2006). The meeting of meditative disciplines and Western psychologies. *American Psychologist, 61*, 227–239.

Washington, C. S., Norton, P. J., & Temple, S. (2008). Obsessive-compulsive symptoms and obsessive compulsive disorder: A multiracial/ethnic analysis of a student population. *Journal of Nervous & Mental Disease, 196*, 456–461.

Watson, D. (2005). Rethinking the mood and anxiety disorders: A quantitative hierarchical model for DSM-V. *Journal of Abnormal Psychology, 114*, 522–536.

Watson, D., Weber, K., Assenheimer, J. S., Clark, L. A., Strauss, M. E., & McCormick, R. A. (1995). Testing a tripartite model: I. Evaluating the convergent and discriminant validity of anxiety and depression symptom scales. *Journal of Abnormal Psychology, 104*, 3–14.

Watson, J. B., & Rayner, R. (1920). Conditioned emotional reactions. *Journal of Experimental Psychology, 3*, 1–14.

Watson, J. B., & Rayner, R. (2000). Conditioned emotional reactions [Reprint]. *American Psychologist, 55*, 313–317. (Original work published 1920)

Watt, M. C., O'Connor, R. M., Stewart, S. H., Moon, E. C., & Terry, L. (2008). Specificity of childhood learning experiences in relation to anxiety sensitivity and illness/injury sensitivity: Implications for health anxiety and pain. *Journal of Cognitive Psychotherapy: An International Quarterly, 22*, 128–143.

Wax, E. (2000, March 6). Immigrant girls are starving to be American, studies find. *Washington Post*, p. B1.

Webb, T. L., Joseph, J., Yardley, L., & Michie, S. J. (2010). Using the internet to promote health behavior change: a systematic review and meta-analysis of the impact of theoretical basis, use of behavior change techniques, and mode of delivery on efficacy. *Journal of Medical Internet Research, 12*, e4.

WebMD. (2011). Bipolar disorder guide. Retrieved from http://www.webmd.com/bipolar-disorder/guide/hypomania-mania-symptoms

Wechsler, D. (1981). *Wechsler Adult Intelligence Scale.* New York: Harcourt, Brace, Jovanovich.

Wedding, D. (1995). Current issues in psychotherapy. In R. J. Corsini & D. Wedding (Eds.), *Current psychotherapies* (pp. 419–437). Itasca, IL: Peacock.

Weems, C. F., Hayward, C., Killen, J., & Taylor, C. B. (2002). A longitudinal investigation of anxiety sensitivity in adolescence. *Journal of Abnormal Psychology, 111*, 471–477.

Weems, C. F., Pina, A. A., Costa, N. M., Watts, S. E., Taylor, L. K., & Cannon, M. F. (2007). Predisaster trait anxiety and negative affect predict posttraumatic stress in youth after Hurricane Katrina. *Journal of Counseling and Clinical Psychology, 75*, 154–159.

Wehmeier, P. M., Barth, N., & Remschmidt, H. (2003). Induced delusional disorder. *Psychopathology, 36*, 37–45.

Weich, S., Patterson, J., Shaw, R., & Stewart-Brown, S. (2009). Family relationships in childhood and common psychiatric disorders in later life: Systematic review of prospective studies. *British Journal of Psychiatry, 194*, 392–398.

Weiden, P. J., Mann, J. J., Haas, G., Mattson, M., & Frances, A. (1987). Clinical nonrecognition of neuroleptic-induced movement disorders: A cautionary study. *American Journal of Psychiatry, 144*, 1148–1153.

Weijerman, M. E., & de Winter, J. P. (2010). The care of children with Down syndrome. *European Journal of Pediatrics, 169*, 1445–1452.

Weihold, B. (2006). Epigenetics: The science of change. *Environmental Health Perspective, 114*, 160–167.

Weinberger, A. H., Desai, R. A., & McKee, S. A. (2010). Nicotine withdrawal in U.S. smokers with current mood, anxiety, alcohol use, and substance use disorders. *Drug and Alcohol Dependence, 108*, 7–12.

Weiner, I. B. (1995). How to anticipate ethical and legal challenges in personality assessments. In J. N. Butcher (Ed.), *Clinical personality assessment: Practical approaches* (pp. 95–106). New York: Oxford University Press.

Weiner, I. B., & Greene, R. L. (2008). *Handbook of personality assessment*. Hoboken, NJ: John Wiley & Sons.

Weiner, I. B., Spielberger, C. D., & Abeles, N. (2002). Scientific psychology and the Rorschach Inkblot Method. *Clinical Psychologist, 55*, 7–12.

Weiner, I. B., Spielberger, C. D., & Abeles, N. (2003). Once more around the park: Correcting misinformation about the Rorschach assessment. *Clinical Psychologist, 56*, 8–9.

Weiner, I. W. (1969). The effectiveness of suicide prevention programs. *Mental Hygiene, 53*, 357–373.

Weiner, R. D., & Krystal, A. D. (2001). Electroconvulsive therapy. In G. O. Gabbard (Ed.), *Treatment of psychiatric disorders* (pp. 1267–1293). Washington, DC: American Psychiatric Press.

Weinman, J., & Petrie, K. J. (1997). Illness perceptions: A new paradigm for psychosomatics. *Journal of Psychosomatic Research, 42*, 113–116.

Weintraub, D., Comella, C. L., & Horn, S. (2008). Parkinson's disease—Part 3: Neuropsychiatric symptoms. *American Journal of Managed Care, 14*(2 Suppl), S59–S69.

Weintraub, D., & Hurtig, H. (2007). Presentation and management of psychosis in Parkinson's disease and dementia with Lewy bodies. *American Journal of Psychiatry, 164*, 1491–1498.

Weiser, B. (2000, December 16). Judge rules defendant's amnesia is feigned in terror case. *New York Times*, p. B2.

Weishaar, M. E., & Beck, A. T. (1992). Clinical and cognitive predictors of suicide. In R. W. Maris, A. L. Berman, J. T. Maltsberger, & R. I. Yufit (Eds.), *Assessment and prediction of suicide*. New York: Guilford Press.

Weisman, A. G., Nuechterlein, K. H., Goldstein, M. J., & Snyder, K. S. (2000). Controllability perceptions and reactions to symptoms of schizophrenia: A within-family comparison of relatives with high and low expressed emotions. *Journal of Abnormal Psychology, 109*, 167–171.

Weiss, D. S. (1988). Personality assessment. In H. H. Goldman (Ed.), *Review of general psychiatry* (pp. 221–232). Norwalk, CT: Appleton & Lange.

Weiss, H., Rastan, V., Mullges, W., Wagner, R. F., & Toyka, K. V. (2002). Psychotic symptoms and emotional distress in patients with Guillain-Barre syndrome. *European Neurology, 47*, 74–78.

Weissberg, M. (1993). Multiple personality disorder and iatrogenesis: The cautionary tale of Anna O. *International Journal of Clinical and Experimental Hypnosis, 41*, 15–34.

Weissman, M. M. (1993). The epidemiology of personality disorders: A 1990 update. *Journal of Personality Disorders* (Suppl. 1), 44–62.

Weitzman, E. R., Nelson, T. F., & Wechsler, H. (2003). Taking up binge drinking in college: The influences of person, social group, and environment. *Journal of Adolescent Health, 32*, 26–35.

Weisz, J. R., Weiss, B., Suwanlert, S., & Chaiyasit, W. (2006). Culture and youth psychopathology: Testing the syndromal sensitivity model in Thai and American adolescents. *Journal of Consulting and Clinical Psychology, 74*, 1098–1107.

Welch, S. S., & Linehan, M. M. (2002). High-risk situations associated with parasuicide and drug use in borderline personality disorder. *Journal of Personality Disorders, 16*, 561–569.

Welham, J., Isohanni, M., Jones, P., & McGrath, J. (2009). The antecedents of schizophrenia: A review of birth cohort studies. *Schizophrenia Bulletin, 35*, 603–623.

Wells, A. (2005). The metacognitive model of GAD: Assessment of meta-worry and relationship with DSM-IV generalized anxiety disorder. *Cognitive Therapy and Research, 29*, 107–121.

Wells, A. (2009). *Metacognitive therapy for anxiety and depression*. New York: Guilford Press.

Wells, A., & Carter, K. (2001). Further tests of a cognitive model of generalized anxiety disorder: Metacognitions and worry in GAD, panic disorder, social phobia, depression, and non-patients. *Behavior Therapy, 32*, 85–102.

Wells, A., & Papageorgiou, C. (1999). The observer perspective: Biased imagery in social phobia, agoraphobia, and blood/injury phobia. *Behaviour Research and Therapy, 37*, 653–658.

Wells, K. B., Sturm, R., Sherbourne, C. D., & Meredith, L. S. (1996). *Caring for depression*. Cambridge, MA: Harvard University Press.

Werner, S., Malaspina, D., & Rabinowitz, J. (2007). Socioeconomic status at birth is associated with risk of schizophrenia: Population-based multilevel study. *Schizophrenia Bulletin, 33*, 1373–1378.

Werth, J. L. (1996). *Rational suicide? Implications for mental health professionals*. New York: Taylor & Francis.

Werth, J. L., Weifel, R., & Benjamin, G. A. H. (2009). *The duty to protect: Ethical, legal, and professional considerations for mental health professionals*. Washington, DC: American Psychological Association.

Wertheim, E. H., Paxton, S. J., Schutz, H. K., & Muir, S. L. (1997). Why do adolescent girls watch their weight? An interview study examining sociocultural pressures to be thin. *Journal of Psychosomatic Research, 42*, 345–355.

West, A. E., & Newman, D. (2007). Childhood behavioral inhibition and the experience of social anxiety in American Indian adolescents. *Cultural Diversity and Ethnic Minority Psychology, 13*, 197–206.

West, K. (2007). *Biofeedback*. New York: Infobase Publishing.

Westberg, J. (2011). Abilify commercials: There's something missing–and it might make you even more depressed. Retrieved from http://www.examiner.com/mental-health-in-portland/abilify-commercials-there-is-something-missing-and-it-might-make-you-even-more-depressed

Westen, D., & Harnden-Fischer, J. (2001). Personality profiles in eating disorders: Rethinking the distinction between axis I and axis II. *American Journal of Psychiatry, 158*, 547–562.

Westermeyer, J. (1987). Public health and chronic mental illness. *American Journal of Public Health, 77*, 667–668.

Westheimer, R. K., & Lopater, S. (2005). Human sexuality: A psychosocial perspective. Baltimore: Lippincott Williams & Wilkins.

Westin, D., DeFife, J. A., Bradley, B., & Hilsenroth, M. J. (2010). Prototype personality diagnosis in clinical practice: A viable alternative for DSM-5 and ICD-11. *Professional Psychology: Research and Practice, 41*, 482–487.

Weston, C. G., & Riolo, S. A. (2007). Childhood and adolescent precursors to adult personality disorders. *Psychiatric Annals, 37*(2), 114–120.

Westrin, A., & Lam, R. W. (2007a). Seasonal affective disorder: A clinical update. *Annals of Clinical Psychiatry, 19*, 239–246.

Westrin, A., & Lam, R. W. (2007b). Long-term and preventative treatment for seasonal affective disorder. *CNS Drugs, 21*, 901–909.

Wetherell, J. L., Gatz, M., & Craske, M. G. (2003). Treatment of generalized anxiety disorder in older adults. *Journal of Consulting and Clinical Psychology, 71*, 31–40.

Wexler, B. E., Zhu, H., Bell, M. D., Nicholls, S. S., Fulbright, R. K., . . . Peterson, B. S. (2009). Neuropsychological near normality and brain structure abnormality in schizophrenia. *American Journal of Psychiatry, 166,* 189–195.

Wheaton, M. G., Abramowitz, J. S., Berman, N. C., Riemann, B. C., & Hale, L. R. (2010). The relationship between obsessive beliefs and symptom dimensions in obsessive-compulsive disorder. *Behaviour Research and Therapy, 48,* 949–954.

Whitaker, A. H., Feldman, J. F., Lorenz, J. M., Shen, S., McNicholas, F., Nieto, M., . . . Paneth, N. (2006). Motor and cognitive outcomes in nondisabled low-birth-weight adolescents: Early determinants. *Archives of Pediatrics and Adolescent Medicine, 160,* 1040–1046.

White, G. M. (1982). The role of cultural explanations in "somatization" and "psychologization." *Social Science Medicine, 16,* 1519–1530.

White, K. S., Craft, J. M., & Gervino, E. V. (2010). Anxiety and hypervigilance to cardiopulmonary sensations in non-cardiac chest pain patients with and with psychiatric disorders. *Behaviour Research and Therapy, 48,* 394–401.

White, P. D., & Moorey, S. (1997). Psychosomatic illnesses are not "all in the mind." *Journal of Psychosomatic Research, 42,* 329–333.

Whitehouse, A. J., Durkin, K., Jaquet, E., & Ziatas, K. (2009). Friendship, loneliness and depression in adolescents with Asperger's Syndrome. *Journal of Adolescence, 32,* 309–322.

Whiteside, S. P., & Abramowitz, J. S. (2004). Obsessive-compulsive symptoms and the expression of anger. *Cognitive Therapy and Research, 28,* 259–268.

Whitfield, C. L., Dube, S. R., Felitti, V. J., & Anda, R. F. (2005). Adverse childhood experiences and hallucinations. *Child Abuse and Neglect, 29,* 797–810.

Whittal, M. L., & Goetsch, V. L. (1995). Physiological, subjective, and behavioral responses to hyperventilation in clinical and infrequent panic. *Behaviour Research and Therapy, 33,* 415–422.

Whittal, M. L., Suchday, S., & Goetsch, V. L. (1994). The panic attack questionnaire: Factor analysis of symptom profiles and characteristics of undergraduates who panic. *Journal of Anxiety Disorders, 8,* 237–245.

Whittal, M. L., Woody, S. R., McLean, P. D., Rachman, S. J., & Robichaud, M. (2010). Treatment of obsessions: A randomized controlled trial. *Behaviour Research and Therapy, 48,* 295–303.

Whitten, L. (2009). Ethnic groups have contrasting genetic risks for nicotine addiction. *National Institute on Drug Abuse Notes, 22,* 1–8.

Wickramasekera, I. (1976). Aversive behavior rehearsal for sexual exhibitionism. *Behavioral Therapy, 1,* 167–176.

Wicks, S., Hjern, A., & Dalman, C. (2010). Social risk or genetic liability for psychosis? A study of children born in Sweden and reared by adoptive parents. *American Journal of Psychiatry, 167,* 1240–1246.

Wicks, S., Hjern, A., Gunnell, D., Lewis, G., & Dalman, C. (2005). Social adversity in childhood and the risk of developing psychosis: A national cohort study. *American Journal of Psychiatry, 162,* 1652–1657.

Widiger, T. A. (2007). Current controversies in nosology and diagnosis of personality disorders. *Psychiatric Annals, 37*(2), 93–99.

Widiger, T. A., & Coker, L. A. (2002). Assessing personality disorders. In J. N. Butcher (Ed.), *Clinical personality assessment: Practical approaches* (pp. 407–434). New York: Oxford University Press.

Widiger, T. A., & Mullins-Sweatt, S. N. (2005). Categorical and dimensional models of personality disorders. In J. M. Oldham, A. E. Skodol, & D. S. Bender (Eds.), *American Psychiatric Publishing textbook of personality disorders* (pp. 35–53). Washington, DC: American Psychiatric.

Widiger, T. A., & Samuel, D. B. (2005). Diagnostic categories or dimensions? A question for the *Diagnostic and Statistical Manual of Mental Disorders,* 5th ed. *Journal of Abnormal Psychology, 114,* 494–504.

Widiger, T. A., & Shea, T. (1991). Differentiation of Axis I and Axis II disorders. *Journal of Abnormal Psychology, 100,* 399–406.

Widiger, T. A., & Spitzer, R. L. (1991). Sex bias in the diagnosis of personality disorders: Conceptual and methodological issues. *Clinical Psychology Review, 11,* 1–22.

Widiger, T. A., & Trull, T. J. (2007). Plate tectonics in the classification of personality disorder. Shifting to a dimensional model. *American Psychologist, 62,* 71–83.

Widom, C. S. (1977). A methodology for studying noninstitutionalized psychopaths. *Journal of Consulting and Clinical Psychology, 45,* 674–683.

Wiens, A. N. (1983). The assessment interview. In I. B. Weiner (Ed.), *Clinical methods in psychology.* New York: Wiley.

Wiersma, D., Nienhuis, F. J., Sloof, C. J., & Giel, R. (1998). Natural course of schizophrenic disorders: A fifteen-year follow-up of a Dutch incidence cohort. *Schizophrenia Bulletin, 24,* 75–85.

Wiesel, F.-A. (1994). The treatment of schizophrenia (Part 2). *British Journal of Psychiatry, 164,* 65–70.

Wightman, D. S., Foster, V. J., Krishen, A., Richard, N. E., & Modell, J. G. (2010). Meta-analysis of suicidality in placebo-controlled clinical trials of adults taking bupropion. *Journal of Clinical Psychiatry, 12*(5), ii.

Wilens, T. E., Adler, L. A., Adams, J., Sgambati, S., Rotrosen, J., Sawtelle, R., Utzinger, L., Fusillo, S. (2008). Misuse and diversion of stimulants prescribed for ADHD: A systematic review of the literature. *Journal of the American Academy of Child and Adolescent Psychiatry, 47,* 21–31.

Wilfley, D. E., Dounchis, J. Z., Stein, R. I., Welch, R. R., Friedman, M. A., & Ball, S. A. (2000). Comorbid psychopathology in binge eating disorder: Relationship to eating disorder severity at baseline and following treatment. *Journal of Consulting and Clinical Psychology, 68,* 641–649.

Wilfley, D. E., Pike, K. M., Dohm, F.-A., Striegel-Moore, R. H., & Fairburn, C. G. (2001). Bias in binge eating disorder: How representative are recruited clinic samples? *Journal of Consulting and Clinical Psychology, 69,* 383–388.

Wilfley, D. E., Wilson, G. T., & Agras, W. S. (2003). The clinical significance of binge eating disorder. *International Journal of Eating Disorders, 34,* 96–106.

Willenbring, M. L. (2010). The past and future of research on treatment of alcohol dependence. *Alcohol Research & Health.* Retrieved from http://findarticles.com/p/articles/mi_m0CXH/is_1-2_33/ai_n55302104/

Williams, D. R., González, H. M., Neighbors, H., Nesse, R., Abelson, J. M., Sweetman, J., & Jackson, J. S. (2007). Prevalence and distribution of major depressive disorder in African Americans, Caribbean blacks, and non-Hispanic whites: Results from the National Survey of American Life. *Archives of General Psychiatry, 64,* 305–315.

Williams, J. B. (1999). Psychiatric classification. In R. E. Hales, S. C. Yudofsky, & J. A. Talbott (Eds.), *Textbook of psychiatry* (pp. 227–252). Washington, DC: American Psychiatric Press.

Williams, K., Wheeler, D. M., Silove, N., & Hazell, P. (2010). Selective serotonin reuptake inhibitors (SSRIs) for autism spectrum disorders (ASD). *Cochrane Database Systematic Review, 4*(8), CD004677.

Williams, K. E., Chambless, D. L., & Steketee, G. (1998). Behavioral treatment of obsessive-compulsive disorder in African Americans: Clinical issues. *Journal of Behavior Therapy and Experimental Psychiatry, 29,* 163–170.

Williams, L. M., & Finkelhor, D. (1990). The characteristics of incestuous fathers: A review of recent studies. In W. L. Marshall, D. R. Laws, & H. E. Barbaree (Eds.), *Handbook of sexual assault: Issues, theories, and treatment of the offender* (pp. 231–256). New York: Plenum Press.

Williams, M., Powers, M., Yun, Y. G., & Foa, E. (2010). Minority participation in randomized controlled trials for obsessive–compulsive disorder. *Journal of Anxiety Disorders, 24,* 171–177.

Williams, N. M., Zaharieva, I., Martin, A., Langley, K., Mantripragada, K., . . . Thapar, A. (2010). Rare chromosomal deletions and duplications in attention-deficit hyperactivity disorder: A genome-wide analysis. *Lancet, 376,* 1401–1408.

Williams, R. J., & Chang, S. Y. (2000). A comprehensive and comparative review of adolescent substance abuse treatment outcome. *Clinical Psychology: Science and Practice, 7,* 138–166.

Williams, R. J., Taylor, J., & Ricciardelli, L. A. (2000). Brief report: Sex-role traits and self-monitoring as dimensions in control: Women with bulimia nervosa versus controls. *British Journal of Clinical Psychology, 39,* 317–320.

Williamson, D., Robinson, M. E., & Melamed, B. (1997). Patient behavior, spouse responsiveness, and marital satisfaction in patients with rheumatoid arthritis. *Behavior Modification, 21,* 97–106.

Williamson, P. (2007). The final common pathway of schizophrenia. *Schizophrenia Bulletin, 33,* 953–954.

Williamson, S. (2009). The relationship between severity of childhood sexual abuse and adult perceptions of intimacy with internalized shame as a mediator. (Unpublished masters thesis). Brigham Young University: Provo, UT.

Willis, A. W., Bradley, A., Evanoff, M. L., Criswell, S. R., & Racette, B. A. (2010). Geographic and ethnic variation in Parkinson disease: A population-based study of US Medicare beneficiaries. *Neuroepidemiology, 34,* 143–151.

Willis, S. L., Tennstedt, S. L., Marsiske, M., Ball, K., Elias, J., . . . ACTIVE Study Group. (2006). Long-term effects of cognitive training on everyday functional outcomes in older adults. *Journal of the American Medical Association, 296,* 2805–2814.

Wilson, G. T., & Shafran, R. (2005). *Eating disorders guidelines from NICE. Lancet, 365,* 79–81.

Wilson, J. L., Peebles, R., Hardy, K. K., & Litt, I. F. (2006). Surfing for thinness: A pilot study of pro-eating disorder web site usage in adolescents with eating disorders. *Pediatrics, 118,* 1635–1643.

Wilson, P., Minnis, H., Puckering, C., & Gillberg, C. (2009). Should we aspire to screen preschool children for conduct disorder? *Archives of Disorders of Childhood, 94,* 812–816.

Wilson, R. S., & Bennett, D. A. (2003). Cognitive activity and risk of Alzheimer's disease. *Current Directions in Psychological Science, 12,* 87–91.

Wilson, R. S., Krueger, K. R., Arnold, S. E., Schneider, J. A., Kelly, J. F., . . . Bennett, D. A. (2007). Loneliness and risk of Alzheimer disease. *Archives of General Psychiatry, 64,* 234–240.

Wilson, R. S., Scherr, P. A., Schneider, J. A., Tang, Y., & Bennett, D. A. (2007). Relation of cognitive activity to risk of developing Alzheimer disease. *Neurology, 69,* 1911–1920.

Wilson, R. S., Schneider, J. A., Arnold, S. E., Tang, Y., Boyle, P. A., & Bennett, D. A. (2007). Olfactory identification and incidence of mild cognitive impairment in older age. *Archives of General Psychiatry, 64,* 802–808.

Wincze, J. P., Bansal, S., & Malamud, M. (1986). Effects of medrox progesterone acetate on subjective arousal, arousal to erotic stimulation, and nocturnal penile tumescence in male sex offenders. *Archives of Sexual Behavior, 15,* 293–305.

Wincze, J. P., Hoon, E. F., & Hoon, P. W. (1978). Multiple measure analysis of women experiencing low sexual arousal. *Behaviour Research and Therapy, 16,* 43–49.

Windle, M., & Windle, R. C. (2001). Depressive symptoms and cigarette smoking among middle adolescents: Prospective associations and intrapersonal and interpersonal influences. *Journal of Consulting and Clinical Psychology, 69,* 215–226.

Wingo, A. P., Wingo, T. S., Harvey, P. D., & Baldessarini, R. J. (2009). Effects of lithium on cognitive performance: A meta-analysis. *Journal of Clinical Psychiatry, 70,* 1588–1597.

Winter, K. (2007, September 30). Issues of GID diagnosis for transsexual women and men. *GID Reform Advocates.* Retrieved from http://www.gidreform.org/GID30285a.pdf

Winton, E. C., Clark, D. M., & Edelmann, R. J. (1995). Social anxiety, fear of negative evaluation, and the detection of negative emotion in others. *Behaviour Research and Therapy, 33,* 193–196.

Wise, M. G., Gray, K. F., & Seltzer, B. (1999). Delirium, dementia, and amnestic disorders. In R. E. Hales, S. C. Yudofsky & J. A. Talbott (Eds.), *Textbook of psychiatry* (pp. 317–362). Washington, DC: American Psychiatric Press.

Wise, M. G., Hilty, D. M., & Cerda, G. M. (2001). Delirium due to a general medical condition, delirium due to multiple etiologies, and delirium not otherwise specified. In G. O. Gabbard (Ed.), *Treatment of psychiatric disorders* (pp. 387–412). Washington, DC: American Psychiatric Press.

Wise, R. A. (1988). The neurobiology of craving: Implications for understanding and treatment of addiction. *Journal of Abnormal Psychology, 97,* 118–132.

Wise, T. N., Fagan, P. J., Schmidt, C. W., & Ponticas, Y. (1991). Personality and sexual functioning of transvestitic fetishists and other paraphilics. *Journal of Nervous and Mental Disorders, 179,* 694–698.

Wiseman, F. (Director). (1967) *Titicut follies* [Motion picture]. United States: Zipporah Films.

Witek-Janusek, L., Albuquerque, K., Chroniak, K. R., Croniak, C., Durazo-Arvizu, R., & Mathews, H. L. (2008). Effect of mindfulness based stress reduction on immune function, quality of life and coping in women newly diagnosed with early stage breast cancer. *Brain and Behavioral Immunology, 22,* 969–981.

Witkiewitz, K., & Marlatt, G. A. (2004). Relapse prevention for alcohol and drug problems: That was zen, this is tao. *American Psychologist, 59,* 224–235.

Wittchen, H. U., & Hoyer, J. (2001). Generalized anxiety disorder: Nature and course. *Journal of Clinical Psychiatry, 62,* 15–21.

Wittchen, H.-U., Zhao, S., Kessler, R. C., & Eaton, W. W. (1994). DSM-III-R generalized anxiety disorder in the National Comorbidity Survey. *Archives of General Psychiatry, 51,* 355–364.

Witte, T. K., Timmons, K. A., Fink, E., Smith, A. R., & Joiner, T. E. (2009). Do major depressive disorder and dysthymic disorder confer differential risk for suicide? *Journal of Affective Disorders, 115,* 69–78.

Wittstein, I. S., Thiemann, D. R., Lima, J. A. C., Baughman, K. L., Schulman, S. P., . . . Champion, H. C. (2005). Neurohumoral features of myocardial stunning due to sudden emotional stress. *New England Journal of Medicine, 352,* 539–548.

Woike, B. A., & McAdams, D. P. (2001). TAT-based personality measures have considerable validity. *APS Observer, 14,* 10.

Wolanczyk, S. R., Wolanczyk, T., Gawrys, A., Swirszcz, K., Stefanoff, E., . . . Brynska, A. (2008). Prevalence of tic disorder among school children in Warsaw, Poland. *European Child and Adolescent Psychiatry, 17,* 171–178.

Woliver, R. (2000, March 26). 44 personalities, but artist shines. *New York Times,* pp. 6–9.

Wollschlaeger, B. (2007). The science of addiction: From neurobiology to treatment. *Journal of the American Medical Association, 298,* 809–810.

Wolpe, J. (1958). *Psychotherapy by reciprocal inhibition.* Stanford, CA: Stanford University Press.

Wolpe, J. (1973). *The practice of behavior therapy.* New York: Pergamon.

Wolpe, J., & Rachman, S. (1960). Psychoanalytic "evidence": A critique based on Freud's case of Little Hans. *Journal of Nervous and Mental Disease, 130,* 135–148.

Wolraich, M. L., Wilson, D. B., & White, J. W. (1995). The effect of sugar on behavior or cognition in children. *Journal of the American Medical Association, 274,* 1617–1621.

Wonderlich, S. A., Crosby, R. D., Engel, S. G., Mitchell, J. E., Smyth, J., & Miltenberger, R. (2007). Personality-based clusters in bulimia nervosa: Differences in clinical variable and ecological momentary assessment. *Journal of Personality Disorders, 21,* 340–357.

Wonderlich, S. A., deZwaan, M., Mitchell, J. E., Peterson, C., & Crow, S. (2003). Psychological and dietary treatments of binge eating disorder: Conceptual implications. *International Journal of Eating Disorders, 34,* 58–73.

Wong, Q. J. J., & Moulds, M. L. (2009). Impact of rumination versus distraction on anxiety and maladaptive self-beliefs in socially anxious individuals. *Behaviour Research and Therapy, 47,* 861–867.

Wood, J. M., Lilienfeld, S. O., Nezworski, M. T., Garb, H. N., Allen, K. H., & Wildermuth, J. L. (2010). Validity of Rorschach inkblot scores for discriminating psychopaths from nonpsychopaths in forensic populations: A meta-analysis. *Psychological Assessment, 22,* 336–349.

Wood, M. D., Capone, C., Laforge, R., Erickson, D. J., & Brand, N. H. (2007). Brief motivational intervention and alcohol expectancy challenge with heavy drinking college students: A randomized factorial study. *Addictive Behaviors, 32,* 2509–2528.

Woods, N. F., Mitchell, E. S., Percival, D. B., & Smith-DiJulio, K. (2009). Is the menopausal transition stressful? Observations of perceived stress from the Seattle Midlife Women's Health Study. *Menopause, 16,* 90–97.

Woody, S. R., Chambless, D. L., & Glass, C. R. (1997). Self-focused attention in the treatment of social phobia. *Behavior Research and Therapy, 35,* 117–129.

Woolgar, M., & Tranah, T. (2010). Cognitive vulnerability to depression in young people in secure accommodation: The influence of ethnicity and current suicidal ideation. *Journal of Adolescence, 33,* 653–661.

Wootton, J. M., Frick, P. J., Shelton, K. K., & Silverthorn, P. (1997). Ineffective parenting and childhood conduct problems: The moderating role of callous-unemotional traits. *Journal of Consulting and Clinical Psychology, 65,* 301–308.

Wootton, J., & Norfolk, S. (2010). Nocturnal enuresis: Assessing and treating children and young people. *Community Practice, 83,* 37–39.

Work Group on Obsessive-Compulsive Disorder. (2007). Practice guidelines for the treatment of patients with obsessive-compulsive disorder. *American Journal of Psychiatry, 164,* 1–56.

World Health Organization. (1987). The Dexamethasone Suppression Test in depression. *British Journal of Psychiatry, 150,* 459–462.

World Health Organization. (2010). Obesity and overweight. Retrieved from http://www.who.int/dietphysicalactivity/publications/facts/obesity/en/

World Health Organization. (2011). What causes mental retardation? Retrieved from http://www.searo.who.int/en/Section1174/Section1199/Section1567/Section1825_8090.htm

Worley, C. B., Feldman, M. D., & Hamilton, J. C. (2009). The case of factitious disorder versus malingering. Psychiatric Times, 26, 1–4.

Wright, E. J. (2009). Neurological disease: The effects of HIV and antiretroviral therapy and the implications for early antiretroviral therapy initiation. Current Opinions on HIV and AIDS, 4, 447–452.

Wright, M. O., Crawford E., & Del Castillo, D. (2009). Childhood emotional maltreatment and later psychological distress among college students: The mediating role of maladaptive schemas. Child Abuse and Neglect, 33, 59–68.

Wrosch, C., Schulz, R., Miller, G. E., Lupien, S., & Dunne, E. (2007). Physical health problems, depressive mood, and cortisol secretions in old age: Buffer effects of health engagement control strategies. Health Psychology, 26, 341–349.

Wu, E. Q., Birnbaum, H. G., Shi, L., Ball, D. E., Kessler, R. C., Moulism, M., & Aggarwal, J. (2005). The economic burden of schizophrenia in the United States in 2002. Journal of Clinical Psychology, 66, 1122–1129.

Wu, L., Ringwalt, C., Mannelli, P., & Patkar, A. (2008). Hallucinogen use disorders among adult users of MDMA and other hallucinogens. The American Journal on Addictions, 17, 354–363.

Wu, L. T., Parrott, A. C., Ringwalt, C. L. Yang, C. M., & Blazer, D. G. (2009). The variety of ecstasy/MDMA users: Results from the National Epidemiologic Survey on Alcohol and Related Conditions. American Journal on Addictions, 18, 452–461.

Wu, L. T., Pilowsky, D. J, Schlenger, W. E., & Galvin, D. M. (2007). Misuse of methamphetamine and prescription stimulants among youths and young adults in the community. Drug and Alcohol Dependence, 89, 195–205.

Wu, L. T., Ringwalt, C. L., Weiss, R. D., & Blazer, D. G. (2009). Hallucinogen-related disorders in a national sample of adolescents: The influence of ecstasy/MDMA use. Drug and Alcohol Dependence, 104, 156–166.

Wu, N. S., Schairer, L. C., Dellor, E., & Grella, C. (2010). Childhood trauma and health outcomes in adults with comorbid substance abuse and mental health disorders. Addictive Behavior, 35, 68–71.

Wyatt v. Stickney, 344 F. Supp. 373 (Ala. 1972).

Wyatt, S. (2006, May). Positive influence of religion and spirituality on blood pressure in the Jackson Heart Study. Paper presented at the annual Scientific Meeting of American Society of Hypertension, New York.

Wyatt, W. J. (2001). What does it mean that addiction is a brain disease? Behavior Analysis Digest, 13. Retrieved from http://www.behavior.org/journals_BAD/V13n3/digest_V13n3_addiction.cfm

Xiang, B., Li, A., Valentin, D., Nowak, N. J., Zhao, H., & Li, P. (2008). Analytical and clinical validity of whole-genome oligonucleotide array comparative genomic hybridization for pediatric patients with mental retardation and developmental delay. America Journal of Medical Genetics, 146, 1942–1954.

Xie, P., Kranzler, H. R., Poling, J., Stein, M. B., Anton, R. F., Brady, K., . . . Gelernter, J. (2009). Interactive effect of stressful life events and the serotonin transporter 5–HTTLPR genotype on posttraumatic stress disorder diagnosis in 2 independent populations. Archives of General Psychiatry, 66, 1201–1209.

Yadin, E., & Foa, E. B. (2009). How to reduce distress and repetitive behaviors in patients with OCD. Current Psychiatry, 8, 19–23.

Yalom, I. D. (1970). The theory and practice of group psychotherapy. New York: Basic Books.

Yalom, I. D. (2005). The theory and practice of group psychotherapy. New York: Basic Books.

Yang, L. H., & WonPat-Borja, A. J. (2007). Psychopathology among Asian Americans. In F. T. L. Leong, A. Ebreo, L. Kinoshita, A. G. Inman, Fu, M. & Yang, L. H., (Eds.), Handbook of Asian American psychology (pp. 379–405). Thousand Oaks, CA: Sage.

Yanovski, S. Z. (2003). Binge eating disorder and obesity in 2003: Could treating an eating disorder have a positive effect on the obesity epidemic? International Journal of Eating Disorders, 34, S117–S120.

Yassa, R., & Jeste, D. V. (1992). Gender differences in tardive dyskinesia: A critical review of the literature. Schizophrenia Bulletin, 18, 701–715.

Yates, W. R. (2010). Somatoform disorders. Retrieved from http://emedicine.medscape.com/article/294908-print

Yeh, P. H., Gazdzinski, S., Durazzo, T. C., Sjöstrand, K., & Meyerhoff, D. J. (2007). Hierarchical linear modeling (HLM) of longitudinal brain structural and cognitive changes in alcohol-dependent individuals during sobriety. Drug and Alcohol Dependence, 91, 195–204.

Yehuda, R. (2000). Biology of posttraumatic stress disorder. Journal of Clinical Psychiatry, 61, 14–21.

Yehuda, R., Cai, G., Golier, J. A., Sarapas, C., Galea, S., . . . Buxbaum, J. D. (2009). Gene expression patterns associated with posttraumatic stress disorder follow exposure to the World Trade Center attacks. Biological Psychiatry, 66, 708–711.

Yehuda, R., & McFarlane, A. C. (1995). Conflict between current knowledge about posttraumatic stress disorder and its original conceptual basis. American Journal of Psychiatry, 152, 1705–1713.

Yen, S., Shea, M. T., Sanislow, C. A., Grilo, C. M., McGlashan, T. H., . . . Morey, L. C. (2003). Axis I and Axis II disorders as predictors of prospective suicide attempts: Findings from the Collaborative Longitudinal Personality Disorders Study. Journal of Abnormal Psychology, 112, 375–381.

Yerys, B. E., Wallace, G. L., Sokoloff, J. L., Shook, D. A., James, J. D., & Kenworthy, L. (2009). Attention deficit/hyperactivity disorder symptoms moderate cognition and behavior in children with autism spectrum disorders. Autism Research, 2, 322–333.

Yeung, A., & Deguang, H. (2002). Somatoform disorders. Western Journal of Medicine, 176, 253–256.

Yoo, J. P., Brown, P. J., & Luthar, S. S. (2009). Children with co-occurring anxiety and externalizing disorders: Family risks and implications for competence. American Journal of Orthopsychiatry, 79, 532–540.

Young, J. A., & Tolentino, M. (2011). Neuroplasticity and its applications for rehabilitation. American Journal of Therapeutics, 18, 70–80.

Young, K. A., Bonkale, W. L., Holcomb, L. A., Hicks, P. B., & German, D. C. (2008). Major depression, 5HTTLPR genotype, suicide and antidepressant influences on thalamic volume. British Journal of Psychiatry, 192, 285–289.

Young, M. A., Meaden, P. M., Fogg, L. F., Cherin, E. A., & Eastman, C. I. (1997). Which environmental variables are related to the onset of seasonal affective disorder? Journal of Abnormal Psychology, 106, 554–562.

Youngberg v. Romeo, 457 U. S. 307 (1982).

Youngren, M. A., & Lewinsohn, P. M. (1980). The functional relation between depression and problematic interpersonal behavior. Journal of Abnormal Psychology, 89, 333–341.

Youngstrom, N. (1991). Spotting serial killer difficult, experts note. APA Monitor, 22, 32.

Yu, K., Cheung, C., Leung, M., Li, Q., Chua, S., & McAlonan, G. (2010). Are bipolar disorder and schizophrenia neuroanatomically distinct? An anatomical likelihood meta-analysis. Frontiers in Human Neuroscience, 4, 189.

Yu-Fen, H., & Neng, T. (1981). Transcultural investigation of recent symptomatology of schizophrenia in China. American Journal of Psychiatry, 138, 1484–1486.

Zamichow, N. (1993, February 15). The dark corner of psychology. Los Angeles Times, p. A1.

Zanarini, M. C., Parachini, E. A., Frankenburg, F. R., & Holman, J. B. (2003). Sexual relationship difficulties among borderline patients and Axis II comparison subjects. Journal of Nervous and Mental Disease, 191, 479–482.

Zanetti, M. V., Cordeiro, Q., & Busatto, G. F. (2007). Late onset bipolar disorder associated with white matter hyperintensities: a pathophysiological hypothesis. Progress in Neuropsychopharmacology and Biological Psychiatry, 31, 551–556.

Zapf, P. A., & Roesch, R. (2006). Competency to stand trial: A guide for evaluators. In A.K. Hess & J. B. Weiner (Eds.), Handbook of forensic psychology (pp. 305–331). Hoboken, NJ: Wiley.

Zayas, E. M., & Grossberg, G. T. (1998). The treatment of psychosis in later life. Journal of Clinical Psychiatry, 59, 5–9.

Zeanah, C. H., Egger, H. L., Smyke, A. T., Nelson, C. A., Fox, N. A., Marshall, P. J., & Guthrie, D. (2009). Institutional rearing and psychiatric disorders in Romanian preschool children. *American Journal of Psychiatry, 166*, 777–785.

Zeanah, C. H., & Gleason, M. M. (2010). Reactive attachment disorder: A review for DSM-V. Retrieved from http://www.dsm5.org/Proposed%20Revision%20Attachments/APA%20DSM-5%20Reactive%20Attachment%20Disorder%20Review.pdf

Zeidan, F., Johnson, S. K., Nakia, S., Gordon, N. S., & Goolkasian, P. (2010). Effects of brief and sham mindfulness meditation on mood and cardiovascular variables. *Journal of Alternative and Complementary Medicine, 16*, 867–873.

Zeldow, P. B. (2009). In defence of clinical judgment, credentialed clinicians, and reflective practice. *Psychotherapy Theory, Research, Practice, Training, 46*, 1–10.

Zerdzinski, M. (2008). Olfactory obsessions—individual cases or one of the symptoms of obsessive-compulsive disorder? An analysis of 2 clinical cases. *Archives of Psychiatry and Psychotherapy, 3*, 23–27.

Zetzsche, T., Rujescu, D., Hardy, J., & Hampel, H. (2010). Advances and perspectives from genetic research: Development of biological markers in Alzheimer's disease. *Expert Review of Molecular Diagnostics, 10*, 667–690.

Zhang, A. Y., & Snowden, L. R. (1999). Ethnic characteristics of mental disorders in five U.S. communities. *Cultural Diversity and Ethnic Minority Psychology, 5*, 134–146.

Zhang, T.-Y., & Meaney, M. J. (2010). Epigenetics and the environmental regulation of the genome and its function. *Annual Review of Psychology, 61*, 439–466.

Zhang, Y., Young, D., Lee, S., Zhang, H., Xiao, Z., . . . Chang, D. (2002). Chinese Taoist cognitive therapy in the treatment of generalized anxiety disorder in contemporary China. *Transcultural Psychiatry, 39*, 115–129.

Zhou, J. N., Hofman, M. A., Gooren, L. J. G., & Swaab, D. F. (1995). A sex difference in the human brain and its relation to transsexuality. *Nature, 378*, 68–70.

Zigler, E. (1967). Familial mental retardation: A continuing dilemma. *Science, 155*, 292–298.

Zilboorg, G., & Henry, G. W. (1941). *A history of medical psychology.* New York: Norton.

Zimmermann, G., Favrod, J., Trieu, V. H., & Pomini, V. (2005). The effect of cognitive behavioral treatment on the positive symptoms of schizophrenia spectrum disorders: A metaanalysis. *Schizophrenia Research, 77*, 1–9.

Zimmerman, M., Rothchild, L., & Chelminski, I. (2005). The prevalence of DSM-IV personality disorders in psychiatric outpatients. *American Journal of Psychiatry, 162*, 1911–1918.

Zinzow, H. M., Resnick, H. S., McCauley, J. L., Amstadter, A. B., Ruggiero, K., & Kilpatrick, D. G. (2010). The role of rape tactics in risk for posttraumatic stress disorder and major depression: Results from a national sample of college women. *Depression and Anxiety, 27*, 708–715.

Zito, J. M., Safer, D. J., dos Reis, S., Gardner, J. F., Boles, M., & Lynch, F. (2000). Trends in the prescribing of psychotropic medications to preschoolers. *Journal of the American Medical Association, 283*, 1025–1030.

Zohar, J., Hollander, E., Stein, D. J., Westenberg, H. G. M., & the Cape Town Consensus Group. (2007). Consensus statement. *CNS Spectrums, 12*, 59–63.

Zoons, E., Weisfelt, M., de Gans, J., Spanjaard, L., Koelman, J. H., Reitsma, J. B., & van de Beek, D. (2007). Seizures in adults with bacterial meningitis. *Neurology, 70*, 2109–2115.

Zoroya, G. (2007, November 23). 20,000 vets' brain injuries not listed in Pentagon tally. *USA Today.* Retrieved from http://www.usatoday.com/news/military/200711-22-braininjuries_N.htm

Zotova, E., Nicoll, J., Kalaria, R., Holmes, C., & Boche, D. (2010). Inflammation in Alzheimer's disease: Relevance to pathogenesis and therapy. *Alzheimer's Research and Therapy, 2*, 1. Retrieved from http://alzres.com/content/2/1/1

Zucker, K. J. (1990). Gender identity disorders in children: Clinical descriptions and natural history. In R. Blanchard & B. W. Steiner (Eds.), *Clinical management of gender identity disorders in children and adults* (pp. 1–24). Washington, DC: American Psychiatric Press.

Zucker, K. J. (2009). The DSM diagnostic criteria for gender identity disorder in children. *Archives of Sexual Behavior, 39*(2), 477–498. doi: 10.1007/s10508-009-9540-4

Zucker, K. J., & Cohen-Ketteris, P. T. (2008). Gender identity disorder in children and adolescents. In D. Rowland & L. Incrocci (Eds.), *Handbook of sexual and gender identity disorders* (pp. 376–422). Hoboken, NJ: Wiley.

Zuckerman, M. (1996). Sensation seeking. In C. G. Costello (Ed.), *Personality characteristics of the personality disordered* (pp. 317–330). New York: Wiley.

Zwaigenbaum, L. (2010). Advances in the early detection of autism. *Current Opinions in Neurology, 23*, 97–102.

Name Index

Subject Index